AMERICAN THEATRE

AMERICAN THEATRE

A CHRONICLE OF COMEDY AND DRAMA
1969–2000

Thomas S. Hischak

OXFORD
UNIVERSITY PRESS

2001

OXFORD
UNIVERSITY PRESS

Oxford   New York
Athens   Auckland   Bangkok   Bogotá   Buenos Aires   Calcutta
Cape Town   Chennai   Dar es Salaam   Delhi   Florence   Hong Kong   Istanbul
Karachi   Kuala Lumpur   Madrid   Melbourne   Mexico City   Mumbai
Nairobi   Paris   São Paulo   Shanghai   Singapore   Taipei   Tokyo   Toronto   Warsaw

and associated companies in
Berlin   Ibadan

Published by Oxford University Press, Inc.
198 Madison Avenue, New York, New York 10016

Oxford is a registered trademark of Oxford University Press

Library of Congress Cataloging-in-Publication Data
Hischak, Thomas S.
American theatre : a chronicle of comedy and drama, 1969–2000 /
Thomas S. Hischak.
p. cm.
Continues: G. Bordman's American theatre.
Includes index.
ISBN 0-19-512347-6
1. Theater—New York (State)—New York—History—20th century.
I. Bordman, Gerald Martin. American theatre.   II. Title.
PN2277.N5 H57   2000
792'.09747'1—dc21   00-028287

1 3 5 7 9 8 6 4 2

Printed in the United States of America
on acid-free paper

PREFACE

While the intent has been to continue Oxford University Press's *American Theatre: A Chronicle of Comedy and Drama* in the same manner and format as Gerald Bordman's previous three volumes, the New York theatre during the last three decades of the twentieth century has posed unique problems and gone through unusual changes that rarely troubled previous decades. As the number of Broadway productions in the 1960s dropped, Off Broadway provided the majority of theatrical offerings in New York. But even Off Broadway was eclipsed in the mid-1970s by Off Off Broadway, which was producing hundreds of plays each season that played to small audiences in very limited engagements, were loosely recorded and seldom reviewed, and often disappeared without a trace. While Off Broadway was housed in small, intimate (and sometimes shabby) theatres, Off Off Broadway was more likely to be found in church basements, storefronts, community centers, even warehouses. Where Off-Broadway audiences were adventurous playgoers who looked beyond Broadway, Off-Off-Broadway audiences were often special interest groups, patrons of specific racial or sexual preferences, multilingual New Yorkers, and others unlikely to frequent conventional theatres.

Off Off Broadway quickly established itself as a vital and exciting part of the city's theatre scene, providing the training ground and experimental environment for countless actors, playwrights, directors, and designers. Off Off Broadway remained hard to pinpoint, but it was even more difficult to ignore. So theatre became a three-ring circus, each venue vying for attention in its own particular way. In other words, theatre in New York during much of this period could be summarized as Neil Simon on Broadway, Sam Shepard Off Broadway, and the Ridiculous Theatrical Company Off Off Broadway. A chronicle that could not capture this threefold identity would not be a truly accurate record of theatre as it existed at this time.

So *American Theatre: A Chronicle of Comedy and Drama, 1969–2000* aims for a slightly wider scope than the previous volumes. All Broadway non-musical productions are included, as well as virtually all Off-Broadway entries and a representative selection of Off-Off-Broadway offerings. Each season (June 1 to May 31) is covered chronologically, jumping back and forth between the three venues as the shows opened. As in the previous volumes, puppet presentations, magic shows, multi-media performance pieces, and musicals are not included. This last genre became more difficult to distinguish as more plays added songs and called themselves a "play with music." For our purposes, a production with enough songs for "musical numbers" to be listed in the program is considered a musical. An entry such as *The Song of Jacob Zulu*, which used live choral music to heighten the action, is termed a play.

Also problematic, especially during the 1990s, was the proliferation of one-person shows, usually written and performed by a lone actor. Many of these solo entries were autobiographical musings in which no fictional characters nor structured plot was involved. Yet many of these programs were essential to the theatre scene, and several were very popular, some later produced as plays by others. We have included a good number of these monologue pieces to give a fair representation of what theatre audiences were embracing each season.

As in the previous volumes, facts about the plays, plot summaries, critical reaction, and biographies of notable individuals are included. While the number of performances is given for all Broadway productions, the length of the run of Off-Broadway and Off-Off-Broadway entries is provided if the play ran an unusually short or long time. Both new plays and revivals, commercial and non-profit, American and foreign productions are included. More important, I have tried to convey the *feel* of each show: the kind of play it was, the mood or tenor of the piece, and some indication of what it was like visually. Covering nearly three thousand plays, one is limited in space. But the hope is that each entry is specific and vivid enough to represent this *feel*.

I would like to thank Maribeth Anderson Payne and Maureen Buja at Oxford University Press, the staffs at the Cortland State College Memorial Library and Cortland Free Library, and Gerald Bordman for his scholarship and insight in the previous volumes and for his time and dedication in helping me with this volume. Finally, I would like to once again acknowledge the continued support and devotion supplied by my wife, Cathy, who makes it all possible.

CONTENTS

Contents

AMERICAN THEATRE

ACT ONE, 1969–1975

GETTING THROUGH BY THE SKIN OF OUR TEETH

1969–1970

Theatregoers in 1969 seemed to be polarized into two extremes: those desperately trying to hold on to the old ways and those bored with the traditional and applauding anything different, irreverent, and outspoken. Of course, the same fragmentation could be seen in America in general as the war in Vietnam divided generations, neighbors, intellectuals, and, alas, theatre audiences. Established Broadway playgoers could support a traditional evening on Broadway if they could be assured of its entertainment value. And the avant-garde had Off Off Broadway, where they were guaranteed an experience that would not be conformist. This left Off Broadway as the only reasonable middle ground.

The problem was, Off Broadway was in deep trouble. While the number of new American plays produced off Broadway (fifty-three this season, though many of those were one-acts) held close to previous years, ticket prices were rising (tickets lower than $5 were scarce), production costs were soaring, and the small houses could not turn a profit. At the end of the 1969–1970 off-Broadway season, not one of the 119 plays, musicals, revues, imports, or revivals had earned back its initial investment, though many of these were non-profit productions never intended to do so. (Only *The Effect of Gamma Rays on Man-in-the-Moon Marigolds* would eventually become a hit by playing into the next season.) Seven off-Broadway plays closed on opening night. Another ten lasted less than a week. Only eight non-musicals ran 100 performances or more, the old milestone number, but not one that could guarantee a profit in the 1970 theatre market. Also, Off Broadway was facing an identity crisis. Conservative suburbanites coming to the city thought Off Broadway too risky; the young and adventurous playgoers were finding it too square. Off Broadway had been the savior of the New York theatre in the 1960s, but by 1969 it was struggling, and the struggle showed all season long.

As for Broadway itself, the shrinking number of productions had been so steadfastly predictable for so many seasons that few moaned about only twenty-one new American non-musicals on the Street this season. Ticket prices were rising there as well (an $8.50 top for plays), and a non-musical production as complex as *Indians* cost over $240,000 to mount. But that also was to be expected, and audiences accepted the prices, if not cheerfully, at least resignedly. After all, it was still possible in 1970 to make a killing on Broadway with a non-musical. Low-cost hits like *Butterflies Are Free* and *The Last of the Red Hot Lovers* were brought in under $100,000 each and were able to realize profits in the reasonably near future.

The line between Off Broadway and Off Off Broadway was still pretty firm, but a few shows crossed over it, moving from a church or a loft to a legitimate off-Broadway house. Non-profit theatre companies struggled, none more so than the ever-unprofitable Repertory Theatre at Lincoln Center. But these groups measured success in terms of outstanding new plays, not box-office receipts. Sad to say, they provided none this season. Of the ten *Best Plays*, only one came from a theatre company, *The Serpent* from the off-off-Broadway Open Theatre Ensemble, and it ran a total of three performances.

The 1969–1970 season saw the musical *Company* open new doors in musical theatre and lay the groundwork for *A Chorus Line* and many other conceptual musicals of the future. Nothing close to that happened in New York for the non-musical theatre. The best offerings were fairly traditional. Playwrights like Sam Shepard and Lanford Wilson were performed, but their best work was still ahead of them. All that audiences could do was decide which side of the fragmented American theatre they were on and then patronize it accordingly.

An off-Broadway evening of one-acts, **Tonight in Living Color** (6-10-69, Actors' Playhouse), featured two short comedies by a playwright who would dominate New York and regional theatre in the future. A. R. Gurney, Jr., still a literature professor at MIT, told two classic tales in modern terms. *The David Show*, which had been seen for one performance off Broadway in 1968, was the story of the biblical David (Anthony Call) ascending to the throne on a television show, much against the wishes of his father, Saul (Barney Martin), and battling the giant Goliath on the tube. The new Gurney script, *The Golden Fleece*, was a retelling of the Medea-Jason tragedy as witnessed by two friends of the unhappy couple. Bill (Tim O'Connor) had sailed with Jason when they captured the fleece, and Betty (Rue McClanahan) occasionally joined Medea for pottery class. These two modern messengers exit and reenter with the latest news, bringing a modern sensibility to the tale. Both pieces were anachronistic and playful, each ending on a bittersweet note. Edith Oliver of *The New Yorker* was one of the first to notice Gurney's distinctive voice, stating that "dramatic ingenuity is a rare quality, and irony is even rarer, and Mr. Gurney was able to keep his comic and tragic elements in balance, seldom showing his hand." The double bill only ran twenty-four performances, and Gurney would struggle with anonymity for another ten years.

On Broadway, the season could not have started worse than with **A Teaspoon Every Four Hours** (6-14-69, ANTA), a comedy by Jackie Mason and Mike Mortman that closed opening night. Actually, the actors had quite a run, for the play previewed a record-breaking ninety-seven performances while the playwrights tinkered with the hopeless comedy. Jewish widower Nat Weiss (Mason) finds out his son Bruce (Barry Pearl) is in love with Patty (Vera Moore), a gentile whom he has impregnated. Nat goes to the girl's mother, Trixie (Lee Meredith), to break up the liaison only to find that mother and daughter are black. It turns out Patty is not pregnant, Nat is drawn to Trixie, and the play ends with a double wedding. The comedy was unanimously panned ("an overdose of vulgarity"), critics arguing over whether it was more offensive to Jews or African-Americans. Author-performer Mason would not return to Broadway for twenty years, and then as a stand-up comic in a series of very popular one-man shows.

The political courtroom drama *In the Matter of J. Robert Oppenheimer* (3-6-69) by Heinar Kipphardt, one of the highlights of Lincoln Center's

---

JOSEPH [né Papirofsky] **PAPP** (1921–1991) was born in Brooklyn but studied theatre in California. From 1948 to 1950 he was managing director of Hollywood's Actors Laboratory. Working on a national tour of *Death of a Salesman* brought him back to New York, where he became a stage manager for CBS-TV. In 1953 Papp founded the Shakespeare Theatre Workshop, later the New York Shakespeare Festival, sometimes directing productions himself. Over the years he produced plays in Central Park, at the Public Theatre complex in the old Astor Library, off Broadway, and even on Broadway, most notably *Hair* (1967) and *No Place to Be Somebody* (1969)

1968–1969 season, returned to the Vivian Beaumont on June 26 for an additional 108 performances. Most of the original cast was reassembled, but Paul Sparer now played the title character. On September 10, the Grand Kabuki of Japan visited the City Center, performing four traditional Kabuki plays: *Chushingura* (The Treasury of Lord Retainers), *Kagami-Jishi* (The Mirror Lion Dance), *Kumagai Jinya* (General Kumagai's Battle Camp), and *Momiji-Gari* (The Maple Leaf-Viewing Picnic).

The open-air Delacorte Theatre in Central Park presented only one Shakespearean production this summer, *Twelfth Night* in August. Producer Joseph Papp opted to open the summer on July 8 with Ibsen's *Peer Gynt*, which proved again to be one of the most unproducible of great plays, but Gerald Freedman's adaptation and direction had some satisfying moments. Stacy Keach was the wanderlust-filled hero, and Estelle Parsons was his crusty mother, Ase. Pop singer Judy Collins played a lyrical Solvig, and Olympia Dukakis and John Heffernan were accomplished in a variety of supporting roles.

On July 20, Neil Armstrong walked on the surface of the moon, the first man to do so. Americans were momentarily glued to their television screens; then life continued on. What could have been an occasion for a surge in patriotism was dampened by the nation's escalating involvement in Vietnam. That war would have a considerable effect on theatre before long.

Of the four short plays by African-American playwrights that made up **A Black Quartet** (7-30-69, Tambellini's Gate), the two most effective were LeRoi Jones's *Great Goodness of Life*, about a man (Jimmy Hayeson) who hides a murderer (Sam Singleton) only to find out that he is his son, and Ed Bullins's *The Gentleman Caller*, a powerful piece about a maid (Minnie Gentry) who takes revenge on her vain white employer (Sylvia Soares) by shooting her and then taking her place and adopting her decadent ways. The later was a bit reminiscent of Jones's *Dutchman* (3-23-64), yet Bullins was developing a unique rage of his own. The other works in the program were Ben Caldwell's *Prayer Meeting or the First Militant Preacher* and Ronald Milner's *The Warning—A Theme for Linda*.

Twelfth Night, at the Delacorte on August 6, was directed by Papp himself with *Hair's* Galt MacDermot providing the music for Shakespeare's many songs. The cast included Barbara Barrie as Viola, Robert Ronan as Malvolio, Sasha von Scherler as Olivia, Stephen Elliott as Sir Toby, and (most impressive of the lot) Tom Aldredge as Andrew Aguecheek.

African-American playwright Douglas Turner Ward would provide two new plays this season. **The Reckoning** (9-4-69, St. Marks) was an acrid drama about a bigoted southern governor (Lester Rawlins) who is blackmailed by his favorite black whore, Baby (Jeannette DuBois), and her pimp Scar (Douglas Turner), who want him to turn over his graft money and provide safe conduct for a militant radical. The play was loud and swift, with plenty of oratory, long monologues and a razor-sharp battle of wits between the governor and the pimp. Some aisle-sitters found it "a hateful show . . . no doubt deliberately so," while others thought it a "simple but stunning allegory." The self-billed "surreal Southern fable" was held over for ninety-four performances.

Perhaps the oddest off-Broadway entry about racial affairs this season was **The Ofay Watcher** (9-15-69, Stage 73), a bizarre little play by Frank Cucci that started off as a hip comic book satire and then quickly turned into gory melodrama. Late one night in a public park, a black derelict named Rufus (Cleavon Little) is approached by a young scientist, Bruce Jennings (Terry Kiser), who has developed a solution that, taken over a period of time, will turn black skin to white. Rufus agrees to be a guinea pig for the drug and goes to Jennings's Greenwich Village apartment/laboratory. There we meet the scientist's girlfriend Daisy (Billie Allen), who is black (and taking treatments) but thinks like a white. After a time, Rufus starts to literally grow pale; we find out he is no derelict but someone who has heard of Jennings's experiments and wants to stop him. The play ends with a bloodbath as Rufus murders both Jennings and Daisy. *The Ofay Watcher* was

---

COLLEEN DEWHURST (1926–1991) was born in Montreal, Canada, and studied acting with Harold Clurman at the American Academy of Dramatic Arts in New York in the 1940s. She made her Broadway debut as a neighbor in the 1952 revival of *Desire Under the Elms* and later appeared in many New York Shakespeare Festival and off-Broadway productions, most memorably as Laetitia in *Children of Darkness* (1958). In 1960 she received recognition and a Tony Award for her steadfast Mary Follet in *All the Way Home*. Her husky-voiced, strong-faced persona made her ideal for tragic roles, particularly those by Eugene O'Neill, but she also excelled in comedy when given the rare opportunity.

---

an allegory of sorts, but some critics pointed out that Israel Horovitz's comic parable *Morning* (11-27-68) the previous season handled a similar premise much better. The genial Little was lauded as one of the freshest talents around, and before the season was out he was starring in the musical *Purlie*. As for *The Ofay Watcher* ("ofay" was pig Latin for "foe," a demeaning expression for whites already dated and replaced by "honkey'), it entertained the curious for forty performances.

Athol Fugard's **Hello and Goodbye** (9-18-69, Sheridan Square) was not about apartheid, as his previous *The Blood Knot* (3-1-64) was, but the racial segregation in South Africa was in the background at all times. In Port Elizabeth, the youth Johnny (Martin Sheen) has just buried his father when his estranged sister Hester (Colleen Dewhurst), whom he hasn't seen in fifteen years, shows up. Hester is a whore in Johannesburg and has come home to get some of the money she believes the father has hidden in the house. Johnny pretends that the father is alive and asleep in the next room, but that doesn't stop Hester from going through boxes and cupboards looking for the cash. Old objects bring on old memories, and the two antagonistic siblings are somewhat drawn together by the time Hester learns of her father's death. Fugard's dramaturgy was subtle: the lies and deceit of the family began to echo those of the nation itself. While critics found the play worthy, most complained about its talkiness. (The drama opened with a lengthy monologue showing Johnny trying to determine if he is going mad.) But there were no reservations about the acting. Newcomer Sheen was impressive, and Dewhurst braved new ground with Hester of whom Richard P. Cooke wrote in the *Wall Street*

Journal: "Stubborn, seemingly irreparably hardened by life, she lets slip small and sometimes touching evidences of a scanted warmth and a latent affection for the family she seems to scorn." Nevertheless, the quiet drama only lasted forty-five performances.

No other Broadway house saw as many different productions this season as the ANTA, to which producers Alfred de Liagre, Jr., and Jean Dalrymple brought a series of regional theatre productions for limited engagements as a way of illustrating the richness of professional theatre across the country. First up was San Francisco's American Conservatory Theatre, which brought its repertory of three revivals, beginning with a very stylized mounting of Edward Albee's *Tiny Alice* (12-29-64) on September 29. William Ball, ACT's artistic director, staged the enigmatic play, and some critics declared his version better than the original if no easier to understand. With Feydeau's *A Flea in Her Ear* on October 3, Gower Champion (in one of his rare non-musical efforts) staged the farce as a silent movie, complete with black-and-white sets and costumes and a flickering strobe light to start and end each act. Some reviewers found it refreshingly new, while others pronounced it "shockingly flat and deadly."

Producer David Merrick gave John Osborne's **A Patriot for Me** (10-5-69, Imperial) a superb production, but few could applaud the English play, first produced in London five years earlier. In pre–World War II Austria, intelligence officer Alfred Redl (Maximilian Schell) lives a life of not-so-latent homosexuality. Russian agents threaten to destroy his career unless he agrees to spy on Austria for them. Redl reluctantly agrees but, after a series of further incriminations and love affairs, is eventually found out by the Austrian government and given the chance to take his own life, which he does. Based on an actual case history, the tale was told in twenty bustling scenes requiring twenty lavish sets, but little could hide the fact that Redl was a rather selfish and ultimately uninteresting hero. A highlight of the evening was a drag ball in the second act in which Baron von Epp (Dennis King) and his officers paraded about in regal squalor. Critics admired Schell and director Peter Glenville's efforts, but the heartiest applause was for Freddy Wittop's outrageous costumes and Oliver Smith's grandiose sets. *A Patriot for Me* struggled on for forty-nine performances; alas, never again would a new Osborne play appear on Broadway.

Thomas Murphy's **A Whistle in the Dark** (10-8-69, Mercury), an Irish play previously produced

OLIVER (LEMUEL) SMITH (1918–1994) had been designing plays and musicals on Broadway since 1942 and during that time won seven Tony Awards, more than any other scenic designer. Smith was born in Waupaun, Wisconsin, and educated at the University of Pennsylvania. His style was widely eclectic, never in one characteristic mode, and his non-musical credits ranged from *The Perfect Marriage* (1944) and *Auntie Mame* (1956) to *Becket* (1960) and *The Odd Couple* (1965).

in London, arrived off Broadway from New Haven's Long Wharf Theatre. Michael Carney (Michael McGuire) has fled his family of street-brawling thugs in Ireland and emigrated to Coventry, England, where he has married a British girl and plans to settle down. But their home is soon invaded by members of the brutish family, including his cowardly braggart father (Stephen Elliott) and his warring brothers. Michael tries to rise above his family, but before long he is drawn into their violence and hatred. Arvin Brown directed the fine ensemble (which most critics thought deserved a better vehicle), who were kept employed for 100 performances.

ACT added *Three Sisters* (this version dropped the initial article from the title) to its ANTA repertory on October 9 and was greeted with mixed reactions. Some found William Ball's production "broad, sometimes coarse and always uneven," but others liked the playful interpretation and called it "a proud triumph for everybody concerned."

Like *A Patriot for Me*, Arthur Kopit's ambitious **Indians** (10-13-69, Brooks Atkinson) was a large and stunning production (complete with a mechanical horse for Buffalo Bill) of a problematic play. Previously produced by the Royal Shakespeare Company in England and at Washington's Arena Stage (which had originated last season's powerful *The Great White Hope*), *Indians* was a seething indictment of how America had treated native Americans in the past. Kopit, one of the best of the young absurdist playwrights to come out of the 1960s, chose to tell his story in the form of a Wild West Show with Buffalo Bill (Stacy Keach) as host, narrator, confessor, and sinner. In a series of non-linear vignettes occurring between 1846 and 1890, Kopit covered such weighty issues as the slaughter of buffalo, the starvation of the tribes, and the corruption of the West. The drama ended with the cast accusing the audience of genocide and walking off the stage without a curtain call. Sections of *Indians* were daring and adventurous; other parts, obvious and simpleminded. But the large cast was exemplary, and Gene Frankel's direction, while not able to overcome the play's many faults, was creative and ingenious. Keach was a fervent Bill; among the rest of the all-male cast, newcomer Raul Julia was particularly effective in three small roles. Reviews were mixed, most applauding the production but unsure of the script. Walter Kerr of the *New York Times* felt the work had noble sentiments but "the argument is unorganized, the conflict is undramatized [and] the irony is weighted to the point where it is indistinguishable from bad Burlesque." The drama managed to run ninety-six performances and later enjoyed mountings in regional and college theatres.

Two days later, a nationwide protest affected New York theatre. October 15 was declared Vietnam Moratorium Day, and several theatres canceled performances. When Woody Allen refused to perform in Broadway's *Play It Again, Sam*, producer David Merrick complained to Equity of "breach of contract." (Producer Harold Prince canceled the performance of *Fiddler on the Roof* but paid the cast anyway.)

Merrick celebrated Moratorium Day by opening his second offering of the month, Elliott Baker's **The Penny Wars** (10-15-69, Royale), a domestic drama set in Buffalo in 1939. Restless teenager Tyler Bishop (Kristoffer Tabori) wishes he could leave home and get involved in the upcoming war in Europe. He dreams of joining the Canadian Air Force but is too young to enlist. Tyler's father, Frank (Dolph Sweet), has his own dream: to appear on the local Major Bowes talent contest. But on the eve of Frank's big break, he drops dead. Soon a German dentist, Dr. Wolf Axelrod (George Voskovec), takes refuge in the Bishop household and fills the father role. The new family arrangement comes to an end when the encroaching war drives Dr. Axelrod to suicide by taking an overdose of his own laughing gas. Performer Barbara Harris directed, and most critics felt she and the cast did all that was possible with such a turgid script. Tabori was cited as promising, and there were kind words for Kim Hunter as Tyler's mother, but *The Penny Wars* was gone after five performances.

In some factions, the highlight of the season was the appearance of the Polish Laboratory Theatre in three plays presented at the Washington Square Methodist Church starting on October 16. *The Constant Prince*, *Acropolis*, and *Apocalypsis cum Figuris*, all directed by renowned Polish director

and theorist Jerzy Grotowski, were performed in Polish over the next two months, and patrons came to marvel at Grotowski's pioneering methods of "poor theatre." The presentations of actor-centered theatrics dazzled some and baffled others, yet by the end of the season similar approaches to text and performance would be seen in homegrown productions.

That same night one of the season's most entertaining revivals opened at the Lyceum: George Abbott's robust mounting of *Three Men on a Horse* (1-30-35), the comedy he had co-written with Cecil Holm. Sam Levene reprised his delightful gambler Patsy from the original cast and was joined by such deft comics as Jack Gilford as the mousy Erwin, Dorothy Loudon as ex-*Follies* gal Mabel, and Paul Ford playing the crusty Mr. Carver. Critics welcomed both the old play and the new production, and it ran a happy 100 performances. Two days later at the Ethel Barrymore, last season's popular revival of *The Front Page* (8-14-28) returned for another 158 performances. Robert Ryan and Bert Convy repeated their Walter and Hildy and were joined by a series of guest stars in some of the smaller roles. Molly Picon, Butterfly McQueen, Jules Munchin, Paul Ford, Maureen O'Sullivan, and Jan Sterling all made cameo appearances during the show's four-month run.

The success of *The Boys in the Band* (4-15-68), still running off Broadway, encouraged other mainstream plays about homosexuals, few of them worthwhile. David Gaard's **And Puppy Dog Tails** (10-19-69, Bouwerie Lane) concerned two lovers, John Hendrix (George Reede) and Tommy Spencer (Horton Willis), whose happy Upper East Side home is threatened by a love triangle with Bud (Ken Kliban). The play relied on a number of nude scenes to run three months.

The operative word for James Saunders's **A Scent of Flowers** (10-20-69, Martinique) was "sensitive," for the memory drama was deemed by critics to be sensitively written, staged, and acted. Few of them could work up any enthusiasm for the piece but, most agreed, it was no embarrassment. The young and radiant Zoe (Katharine Houghton) observes her own coffin as it travels from the funeral home to the church service to burial at the gravesite. Scenes from her past occur in scattered order throughout the proceedings, ending in her decision to commit suicide. The flashbacks, such as her ill-fated love affair with a married professor and her sexual assault by a kindly old uncle, were distant and, consequently, ineffective. Some critics even questioned such a luminous, self-reliant person committing suicide at all. Houghton had a striking stage presence, and Roderick Cook was quite amusing as the undertaker Scrivens.

By the end of October, Broadway was starved for a hit comedy, and it got one in Leonard Gershe's **Butterflies Are Free** (10-21-69, Booth). Twenty-year-old Don Baker (Keir Dullea) has left his home in Scarsdale and rented an East Village apartment, hoping to escape from his overprotective mother and make it on his own as a songwriter. His challenge lies in the fact that he was born blind and, because he has recently been dumped by a girl he loved, is feeling pretty vulnerable. When Don meets his next-door neighbor, the kookie actress Jill Tanner (Blythe Danner), they immediately hit it off; she does not realize Don is blind until much later in their conversation. She is not at all concerned about his handicap, and soon the two fall into bed together. Later Don's mother (Eileen Heckart) surprises them both by showing up while the lovers are still in their underwear. Her worst fears confirmed, Mrs. Baker tries to get Don to move back home. A showdown ensues; Jill leaves Don for a director she has just met, and Don caves in to his mother's wishes. But Mrs. Baker realizes she can no longer protect her son, so she retreats just as Jill returns, and all ends happily. The charming cast made *Butterflies Are Free* seem like gold when it was only an "unusual mixture of dashing wit and syrupy sentiment." Gershe knew how to write sassy dialogue (liberal Jill confesses to Don that she "joined the Young Republicans for Ronald Reagan. Another mistake. There's no such thing as a young Republican."), and his sentiment was in small enough doses to be palatable. Many of the reviews were valentines, and the comedy ran two and a half years.

John Herbert's prison drama *Fortune and Men's Eyes* (2-23-67) was revived off Broadway on October 22 at Stage 73. Sal Mineo directed the terse production in which homosexual acts only alluded to in the original were now rather explicitly portrayed onstage. The popular attraction ran out the season.

Two of the late Joe Orton's short (and lesser) works received their American premiere in the off-Broadway double bill **Crimes of Passion** (10-26-69, Astor Place). *The Ruffian on the Stair* was Orton's first work, performed as a radio play on the BBC in 1964; it foreshadowed his later works and his own death. Into the apartment of a moronic truck driver (Richard A. Dysart) and his sluttish wife (Sasha von Scherler) comes an effeminate hairdresser (David Birney) looking for a room to rent. The intruder, suicidal since his brother was run over by a truck, taunts the couple, accuses the husband of being the hit-and-run driver, and then is shot by him. *The Erpingham Camp* was a broad farce about a British holiday camp run by a fatuous headmaster (Dysart) and peopled by a bizarre staff and guests. When the entertainment director dies of poisoning, the ambitious Redcoat Riley (Birney) tries to take over, organizing a chaotic show that ends with the headmaster crashing through the floor and killing some dancers below. General consensus declared the plays worthy of interest but not nearly as inspired as Orton's later full-length works. The double bill closed in a week.

Sumner Arthur Long had come up with a gold mine of a comedy earlier in the decade with *Never Too Late* (11-27-62), but his **Angela** (10-30-69, Music Box) was a four-performance flop that even critics' favorite Geraldine Page could not save. Angela Palmer (Page), a housewife in suburban Boston, is bored and lonely because her naval officer husband, Brian (Simon Oakland), is always away at some military base where he has mistresses. So when the would-be inventor Jeff Dolan (Tom Ligon) comes to fix her television set, Angela is drawn to him. They make love, Angela hides his clothes so he can't leave, Brian returns, and, surprisingly, he and Jeff end up becoming friends. The comedy was greeted with an unbroken series of pans calling it "totally without humor, charm or anything in the way of dramatic interest."

An evening of British works entitled **The Local Stigmatic** (11-3-69, Actors' Playhouse) only managed to run a week despite the fact that the program opened with seven short plays by Harold Pinter not yet produced in New York. These were early playlets by Pinter, some mere fragments rather than one-act plays (one commentator described them as "shaggy dog skits"), and critical reaction was unenthusiastic. The major part of the evening was the longer one-act *The Local Stigmatic* by British playwright Heathcote Williams. Two violent thugs (Al Pacino and Michael Hadge), who live for greyhound racing, meet a movie actor (Joseph Maher) in a bar, befriend him, and, while walking him home, beat him and cut him up. The situation and the senseless violence reminded more than one critic of Israel Horovitz's superior *The Indian Wants the Bronx* (1-17-68), which also featured Pacino as a street punk bent on violence.

Lincoln Center opened its all-American season upstairs in the Vivian Beaumont with William Saroyan's *The Time of Your Life* (10-25-39) on November 6. John Hirsch directed a solid cast led by James Broderick as Joe, Biff McGuire as Tom, and Susan Tyrrell as Kitty. Often singled out in the reviews were Leonard Frey's Harry the Hoofer and Philip Bosco's bartender Nick. Saroyan's work was finding a new audience at this time, many detecting an individualistic, anti-establishment (i.e., hippie) quality in his plays. The critics generally applauded the production but differed greatly on the script; some claimed it had improved with time, while others found it dated and cloying. Another revival that severely divided the press was Michael Kahn's reworking of *Henry V* on November 10 at the ANTA, a production seen previously at Connecticut's American Shakespeare Festival. The setting was a contemporary playground, complete with swing sets and basketball hoops, where actors engaged in Frisbee and yo-yo antics. Lest anyone miss the point, Kahn's program notes explained that war is a game, and his actors, in modern athletic wear, "played" the history as if it were a sports competition. Some reviewers saw the production as boldly Brechtian (each scene was announced by a spoken placard), while others called it "witless Shakespeare."

Oliver Hailey's **Who's Happy Now?** (11-17-69, Village South) originated at Los Angeles's Mark Taper Forum and toured the country before opening off Broadway for a disappointing run of thirty-two performances. In an East Texas town, six-year-old Richard Hallen (Ken Kercheval) is brought to a local bar by his mother, Mary (Teresa Wright), so that he can get to know his father, Horse (Robert Darnell), who has left them for a waitress named Faye Precious (Rue McClanahan). The same people are gathered when Richard is sixteen years old and finally when he is twenty. A curious bond develops among the odd foursome, yet when Richard's career as a songwriter takes off, he tries to remove his mother from her unhappy past by taking her to live with him in another town. But the ties are too strong, and she refuses to go. Many critics liked the script and the production, McClanahan getting the best notices. But even the presence of Wright on the bill could not generate enough interest to allow the play to run.

The next regional theatre production to showcase at the ANTA was the Plumstead Playhouse's *Our Town* (2-4-38) on November 27, with Henry Fonda turning in an expert performance as the Stage Manager. Donald Driver directed the large cast, and many critics found Elizabeth Hartman's Emily particularly effective. With mainly favora-

ble reviews and Fonda's box-office draw, it could have stayed around much longer than its scheduled thirty-six performances.

Two plays by English playwright John Bowen, *The Coffee Lace* and *Trevor*, were produced off Broadway under the title **Little Boxes** (12-3-69, New Theatre) and ran only fifteen performances despite some encouraging reviews and first-rate writing. *The Coffee Lace* was a sad little playlet about a troupe of reclusive music hall performers kept alive by one of them going out and stealing and scavenging in the streets and Underground stations. When the grande dame of the troupe dies, the pathetic group is forced to face the reality of their situation. The tender drama was quite effective, but critics preferred *Trevor*, a spirited farce about a lesbian couple who hire an actor (Tony Tanner) to play the role of one girl's fictional fiancé, Trevor, when her parents arrive for a visit. The actor is pulling off the stunt pretty well when the other girl's parents unexpectedly arrive at the neighboring apartment and "Trevor" must rush back and forth, playing her fiancé as well. As outlandish as the plot was, there was a lot of charm in the piece. Bowen carefully shifts the tone in the final scene as one of the girls tries to tell her folks the truth and the parents ignore her, preferring not to know. Both plays were set in a musty Victorian mansion broken up into apartments, and the portmanteau title of *Little Boxes* referred to the closed world the characters created to escape a world that would not accept them.

The season of popular comedy revivals on Broadway continued on December 4 with Noel Coward's *Private Lives* (1-27-31) at the Billy Rose, a sterling production directed by Stephen Porter and featuring Brian Bedford and Tammy Grimes as the indefatigable Elyot and Amanda. Critics called the David Merrick production "gorgeous," "dazzling," and "faultless," and much adulation was heaped on Grimes, who won the season's Tony Award for her sparkling portrayal. The comedy played to crowded houses for the rest of the season.

Lincoln Center did not open its downstairs theatre season until December with the premiere of the Czech play **The Increased Difficulty of Concentration** (12-4-69, Forum) by Vaclav Havel. A womanizing scientist, Dr. Eduard Huml (Harold Gould), cannot seem to get any work done because of the demands of his wife, Vlasta (Jane Hoffman), his mistress, Renata (Jacqueline Brooks), and his secretary, Blanka (Alix Elias). When a social worker, Dr. Anna Balcar (Leona

Dana), comes to interview Eduard with a strange computer that has a mind of its own, he falls for her as well. Havel was known throughout Europe for his dangerous satire, but critics found this piece too heavy-handed to be effective, and the odd play could not last out the month.

At one time Ronald Ribman was considered quite a promising playwright, but his **Passing Through From Exotic Places** (12-7-69, Sheridan Square) was described as "false" and "synthetic" by most aisle-sitters. The program consisted of three unconnected short plays with jarringly different moods. *The Son Who Hunted Tigers in Jakarta* was a feeble character study about an encounter between a suburban couple (Vincent Gardenia and Tresa Hughes) and a burglar (Robert Loggia) in their bedroom one night. The satire *Sunstroke* concerned an overeager Bronx Jew, Arthur Goldblatt (Oliver Clark), who goes to a Pacific island as a Peace Corps volunteer only to find himself in an artificial antebellum South. *The Burial of Esposito* was a melodrama about an Italian barber, Nick Esposito (Gardenia), in mourning for his son killed in Vietnam; in his frenzy, the conjures up the boy and asks his forgiveness.

The Moon Dreamers (12-8-69, Ellen Stewart) was a noisy, frantic evening of theatrics by Julie Bovasso that opened a new theatre off Broadway. The concoction of murder mystery, satire, and camp, first presented at Café La Mama, was directed by the playwright as a tribute to La Mama founder Stewart. Three soldiers (dressed in uniforms of the Civil War, the Great War, and World War II) acted as a Greek chorus for the montage that included a husband and wife who watched their marriage break up over a mistress, a dwarf Chief of Police who dressed like Napoleon and went about whipping people with a stick, characters singing old favorites, a dog that barked out the tune of "Jingle Bells," and, at the end, an astronaut proclaiming a tongue-in-cheek tribute to America. One critic appropriately called it "a kind of mulligan stew of Americana."

Ron Cowen's domestic drama *Summertree* (3-3-68), which had successfully played in Lincoln Center's Forum Theatre the previous season, opened at the Players on December 9 with Lenny Baker as the youth, killed in Vietnam, whose life is examined in flashbacks. The popular attraction ran 184 performances.

At the American Place Theatre, Charlie L. Russell's **Five on the Black Hand Side** (12-10-69, St. Clements) was that rare thing in 1969: a freewheeling comedy about a black family with no racial agenda. The Brooks family in Harlem consists of a bossy, conservative barber (J. Errol Jaye) who lives by the *Wall Street Journal* and the doings of General Motors, his put-upon wife (Clarice Taylor) who has yet to be able to finish any sentence she ever started, an anthropology-major son (Matthew Bernard Johnson, Jr.) who stays on the roof in rebellion, and a daughter (Jonelle Allen) about to wed a man the father detests. Into this delightfully dysfunctional family comes their neighbor Stormy Monday (Judyann Elder), a liberated woman who wears striking black-and-white-checked outfits and urges the wife to stay and fight when she considers running off. At the daughter's wedding reception the daffy group of characters reach a bittersweet resolution. The actors were appropriately frantic, Oliver remarked that there was "more fun in it than in anything I've seen Off Broadway this season." The comedy was held over for sixty-two performances.

Irish playwright Brian Friel had proved a master at delicate characterization in *Lovers* (6-25-68) and *Philadelphia, Here I Come!* (2-16-66), so audiences were not ready for the cartoonish political satire of his **The Mundy Scheme** (12-11-69, Royale). An Irish-American philanthropist named Mundy (unseen in the play) has come up with a plan which the Irish prime minister, F. X. Ryan (Godfrey Quigley), and the minister of foreign affairs, Mick Moloney (Jack Cassidy), are considering to save Ireland's economy: to sell the western islands as idyllic gravesites for wealthy Irish Americans. The two ministers plan to work the scheme to their own economic advantage, but they are overheard by the wily secretary Roger Nash (Patrick Bedford), who wants to be part of the deal and blackmails the two into including him. After a lot of skulduggery, Ryan concedes, and the play ends with him babbling as a child in the arms of his kindly Irish mother (Dorothy Stickney). While the cast was roundly applauded, critics disdained the one-joke play, and it was gone after four performances.

Billed as a "fable," Seymour Simckes's **Seven Days of Mourning** (12-16-69, Circle in the Square) turned out to be a pretty unpleasant tale. In the 1930s, in the slum apartment of the Shimansky family on the Lower East Side, all are in silent confusion because six days ago the daughter committed suicide by jumping out the window. Suicide being against the Jewish law, they are not allowed to mourn her, but a mystical character called "the doctor" enters and forces the family to own up to its grief and begin a formal mourning. The characters were overbearing and overwritten (the mother was a ruthless tyrant, the father a slob, the son a vindictive cripple, the surviving daughter a conniving crook), and the acting was criticized as too broad to be effective. Yet the drama was kept on the boards for six weeks.

Veteran playwright John Patrick found no success with **Love Is a Time of Day** (12-22-69, Music Box), a dreary two-character comedy about college lovers. Although it was set in the present, there was something antiquated about this tale of co-ed April MacGregor (Sandy Duncan) fighting off the awkward advances of graduate student Skipper Allen (Tom Ligon). There was much talk, some compromises were made, then a hollow happy ending was reached. At one point, Skipper pretends to seduce a store mannequin in order to make April jealous. It convinces April, but playgoers were aghast, one critic calling the scene "one of the theatrical low points of the decade." The two likable actors struggled in vain. After a universal drubbing, the little comedy closed in a week.

Broadway had come to depend on Neil Simon for reliable and satisfying comedies, and **Last of the Red Hot Lovers** (12-28-69, Eugene O'Neill) delivered the goods, even though there was some disappointment in the predictability of the script. Barney Cashman (James Coco), the owner of a fish restaurant, has hit middle age and, despite a faithful wife and a thriving business, has started to have regrets about his "nice" life. Hoping to put a little color in his waning years, he attempts an extramarital fling with three different women in his mother's studio apartment. His first amour is Elaine Navazio (Linda Lavin), a hardboiled, chain-smoking cynic he met at his restaurant. The second is the cheerfully psychotic actress Bobbi Michele (Marcia Rodd), whom Barney loaned some money to in the park. The final would-be lover is Jeanette Fisher (Doris Roberts), a severely depressed Montauk housewife who is actually a close friend of Barney's wife, Thelma. Of course, each rendezvous is a disaster. Elaine wants quick, impersonal sex, and when she doesn't get it she calls Barney "either sexually retarded or a latent idiot." Bobbi sees Barney as a kindly uncle and proceeds to get him high on marijuana. Jeanette ends up depressing Barney and sending him back to Thelma. While Simon kept each of Barney's attempts fresh by building on the information learned from the previous escapade, there was a weariness about the triple program that caused one aisle-sitter to comment, "By the end of the third act I felt as frustrated as Coco." Robert Moore directed, and all three actresses turned in deft performances. As for Coco, the role made the polished character actor a marketable star. The "squirrel look of damp desperation in his eyes" and his sincere panic at his own normalcy made Barney much more than the foolish straight man for three funny women. Critics, for the most, applauded the comedy, and audiences kept *Last of the Red Hot Lovers* on the boards for nearly three years.

On December 30, Charles Gordone's Pulitzer winner *No Place to Be Somebody* (5-4-69) came to Broadway's ANTA Theatre. It stayed for a limited engagement of sixteen showings before reopening at the Promenade Theatre off Broadway on January 20 for an additional 252 performances.

The Negro Ensemble Company began its season late with Joseph A. Walker's **The Harangues** (12-30-69, St. Marks), a play with songs. After a prologue about an African couple who drown their baby rather than see it captured and taken into slavery, there followed two one-act plays about men who crack under the pressure of their anger and hate, set out to commit murder but, in turn, are murdered. There was some forceful acting to be found, but the evening was considered overwrought and the playwright confused but promising.

Lincoln Center offered the first New York revival of Tennessee Williams's *Camino Real* (3-19-53) on January 8 in the Vivian Beaumont, though this production had been seen earlier in Los Angeles. There was mixed reaction to Williams's surrealistic drama, some reviewers finding it dated, others declaring it had improved with time. Milton Katselas directed a superior cast that included Jessica Tandy as the former beauty Marguerite, Philip Bosco as the Baron de Charlus, Clifford David as Lord Byron, Sylvia Syms as the crafty Gypsy, and Al Pacino as the bewildered GI Kilroy (though some critics felt he was badly miscast).

The National Theatre of the Deaf was the next guest at the ANTA, opening on January 12 for a week with a signed and spoken program that consisted of Molière's one-act *Sganarelle* and a collage of Dylan Thomas material called *Songs from Milk Wood*.

One of the most discussed theatre events of the season was LeRoi Jones's powerful indictment called **Slave Ship** (1-13-70, Theatre-in-the-Church), which was vividly remembered by all who saw it. Designer Eugene Lee turned the theatre space into a slave ship (with the audience looking down onto the prisoners in the hold), and director Gilbert Moses moved the violent action all around the space. More a docudrama about conditions on the ships than a play, *Slave Ship* graphically showed the cramped quarters, the passengers living in filth, and the slaves being beaten and raped by the sailors, punctuated by flashbacks to the tribal Africa of their past and visions of their tap-dancing future in the New World. The fiery drama ended with a Masai warrior stepping forward and entreating the African-American members of the audience to stand and join in song and learn to hate all whites, including those seated with them in the theatre. Few other plays have ended as uncomfortably for both black and white patrons as this one, intent on polarizing its audience. The production itself had a nightmarish history. The play was first performed at the Brooklyn Academy of Music on November 18 and ran an impressive fifty-six performances. When it transferred to off Broadway's Theatre-in-the-Church, it was halted after three performances by a strike. A week later it reopened, but after one performance a fire damaged the theatre, and it closed for good on January 20.

Richard Seff's **Paris Is Out!** (1-19-70, Brooks Atkinson) was a good example of an "audience show," for all the critics hated it but admitted the public would feel otherwise. In fact, the producers tried to avoid reviews by asking the newspapers to wait a few weeks until the comedy had established itself before sending the critics. Surprisingly, many papers did wait, which helped the show run its still unprofitable 104 performances. A middle-aged couple, Daniel (Sam Levene) and Hortense Brand (Molly Picon), are making preparations for a trip to Europe, something he has been promising her for twenty-five years. Even so, he is still fighting the idea. Some predictable complications occur when their stockbroker son, Roger (Terry Kiser), falls for their pretty travel agent, Arlene Kander (Zina Jasper); otherwise, not much of anything happens while Daniel makes jokes about European plumbing and the sewage problem in Venice. Audiences enjoyed the cast, though Martin Gottfried of *Women's Wear Daily* pointed out that "Miss Picon and Mr. Levene have long since become caricatures of themselves and look like puppets in a screaming match."

The Playwrights Unit, a theatre workshop group founded in 1961 to develop new plays, was Broadway's next guest with its double bill **Watercolor & Criss-Crossing** (1-21-70, ANTA) by Philip Magdalany. *Watercolor* consisted of a series of conversations on a beach at night, including some sexual activity and an old lady dying. *Criss-Crossing* was set in three rooms of a motel where a dowdy couple on vacation, a hired assassin and his pimp son, and three reform school escapees planning a career as prostitutes are all staying. An unseen monster attacks the town, and the motel inhabitants go crazy, some shooting others in the confusion. Critics found the pieces absurdist and satiric but lacking any focus. Five performances were more than enough to satisfy the curious.

Herman Shumlin, the distinguished director-producer who had not been active in theatre for a few years, presented and staged the triple bill **Transfers** (1-22-70, Village South), three forgettable plays by Conrad Bromberg. Only the last playlet, entitled *Dr. Galley*, was considered worthwhile because of a tour-de-force performance by Ron Leibman. Dr. Galley, a psychiatrist substituting for a university psychology professor, launches into a self-revealing tirade about his futile life and how he destroyed his wife and his career. *Transfers* and *The Rooming House* were the other playlets in the program, which managed to stay afloat only for a month.

Veteran playwright Dore Schary had even less success when his pretentious drama **Brightower** (1-28-70, John Golden) closed on opening night. In the mountains of Vermont, a Hemingway-like author named Brightower (Robert Lansing) believes he is losing his mind, so he kills himself by jumping off a cliff. When a would-be biographer, Clay Benson (Arlen Dean Snyder), comes to do research, Brightower's widow, Sara (Geraldine Brooks) tries to hide the suicide from him, then confesses the truth but refuses to cooperate on the biography. (Veteran theatregoers may have recalled a very similar plot from 1954's *The Starcross Story*, which also closed on opening night.) Aisle-sitters complimented the cast but uniformly agreed that the play was a disaster.

Lincoln Center's only American offering downstairs this season was Jeff Wanshel's nightmarish comedy **The Disintegration of James Cherry** (1-29-70, Forum). James Cherry (Stephen Strimpell) tells the audience that awful things have always happened to those close to him. In a series of vaudeville-like blackout scenes, we see eight-year-old James as his grandparents fall down the stairs to their deaths, his father stumbles into the crocodile tank at the zoo, and his sister leaps off the roof. Once he moves to New York City, James's misfortunes continue: his roommate is eaten by his pet pig, and James accidentally shoots his agent while auditioning for a cowboy role. The flashbacks end with twenty-year-old James being shot to death, his disintegration complete. Although the writing was surely scattershot, several critics found "a fresh, inventive wit and whimsical sagacity" in the script.

Popular newspaper columnist Art Buchwald made his playwriting debut with **Sheep on the Runway** (1-31-70, Helen Hayes), a satire on American imperialism that provided more thought-provoking laughs than anything else seen on Broadway all season. In the mythical Himalayan country of Nonomura, everything is peaceful as the wistful Prince Gow (Richard Castellano) rules over the hidden kingdom. But U.S. Ambassador Raymond Wilkins (David Burns) feels Washington has forgotten him, so when the Prince suggests they stir up some subversive activities in order to get American aid, Wilkins willingly goes along with the idea. Journalist Joseph Mayflower (Martin Gabel) arrives in Nonomura, and his paranoia convinces him that Reds are everywhere, so he cries wolf and chaos breaks out. Unfortunately Buchwald could come up with no satisfactory conclusion to the daffy premise, and the comedy seemed to stop dead before the final curtain. Gene Saks directed with great flair, and the skillful cast also included Elizabeth Wilson, Will Mackenzie, Barnard Hughes, and Remak Ramsay. Critics loved the performers and Buchwald's trenchant sense of humor but had to admit the comedy was structurally a mess. The satire only lasted 105 performances, and Buchwald never returned to the stage, much to Broadway's loss.

Paris's renowned Comédie Française arrived at the City Center on February 3 for a month-long repertory engagement of five Molière plays performed in French: *La Troupe du Roi, Amphitryon, Dom Juan, Les Femmes Savantes,* and *Le Malade Imaginaire.*

Off Off Broadway came to Broadway with a two-week engagement of Julie Bovasso's **Gloria and Esperanza** (2-4-70, ANTA), which originated at the La Mama Experimental Theatre Club. The poet Julius Esperanza (Kevin O'Connor) seeks fulfillment in life with his girlfriend Gloria B. Gilbert (Bovasso), a kinky writer who is being blackmailed by her mailman. Esperanza's Candide-like adventures take him to a psychiatrist, a mental asylum, a television studio, and, finally, Hollywood, where he races through a chorus line of girls in a movie spectacular. Bovasso directed the carnival-like production (a circus parade down the theatre aisles opened and closed the play), which managed to be as noisy as her *The Moon Dreamers* earlier this season, adding songs, bird calls, and gunshots. Critical reaction was mixed and best summarized by Clive Barnes of the *Times,* who wrote, "It represents La Mama both at its most adventurous and at its most self-indulgent."

The most successful Broadway drama of the season was Robert Marasco's **Child's Play** (2-17-70, Royale), a spine-tingling thriller without a murder or a murderer. Strange and unexplainable things have been going on at St. Charles's Roman Catholic boarding school for boys. Fights have broken out for no reason, a student has been tortured by his classmates, and someone is sending obscene photographs to Latin teacher Jerome Malley (Fritz Weaver) and his dying mother. Paul Reese (Ken Howard), a young gym teacher who was once a student at St. Charles's, seeks to find the answer, and the popular teacher Joseph Dobbs (Pat Hingle) promises to use his friendly demeanor to help. Reese soon discovers the problem is not the boys but a deadly evil that is emanating from the hatred Dobbs has long felt for his colleague Malley. The pressure is so great it drives Malley to suicide. In the last scene the boys, his evil now transferred to them, menacingly surround Dobbs. A few critics balked at the obvious melodramatics, but most marveled at the engrossing power of the piece. And there was no grousing about the production, from Jo Mielziner's atmospheric setting and lighting (dusty shafts of light making shadows on worn wooden staircases) to Joseph Hardy's taut direction to the fine all-male cast. Weaver, Howard, Hardy, and Mielziner all won Tony Awards at season's end, and the David Merrick-produced drama ran ten months.

Cartoonist Jules Feiffer had taken violence in America to task in his *Little Murders* (4-25-67). He widened his scope to include international politics in **The White House Murder Case** (2-18-70, Circle in the Square), a "grim farce" that met with favorable reviews. In a future "several Presidential elections hence," America has declared war on Brazil, and an incompetent general has approved the use of nerve gas on the battlefield. Unfortunately the wind shifted, and 700 American soldiers have been poisoned. At the White House, President Hale (Peter Bonerz) and his chiefs of staff are trying to come up with a story that will appease the American people before the upcoming election. The First Lady (Cynthia Harris), a longtime radical sympathizer, catches on to the cover-up and attempts to phone the *New York Times* but is murdered in the Oval Office, a peace protester's sign embedded in her chest. The murder investigation is a sham, another cover-up is planned, and the play ends with Postmaster General Stiles (Paul Benedict) confessing to the crime but blackmailing the President into making him Secretary of State after the next election. Although critics agreed that the Brazil battlefield scenes scattered throughout the evening did not work, they applauded Feiffer's script for its "devastating Swiftian clout." Alan Arkin directed a cast of fine farceurs that also included Paul Dooley, Bob Balaban, and Richard Libertini. The comedy ran 119 performances.

An "audience show" that failed to find an audience, Ron Clark and Sam Bobrick's comedy **Norman, Is That You?** (2-19-70, Lyceum) lasted less than two weeks. Ohio dry-cleaning mogul Ben Chambers (Lou Jacobi) finds out that his wife has run off with his own brother. So Ben goes to New York City to commiserate with his son Norman (Martin Huston), only to find that the boy is living with a boyfriend, Garson (Walter Willison), in a homosexual love nest. After the usual comic reactions and jokes, Ben tries to straighten his son out by hiring a pretty prostitute (Dorothy Emmerson), but the tryst is a disaster. By the final curtain, Ben's wife, Beatrice (Maureen Stapleton), has returned to him, Norman is drafted into the army, and the Chamberses decide to take the limp-wristed Garson home with them. George Abbott directed the talented cast, but there was no hiding the offensive nature of the piece, especially in light of the slow acceptance of homosexuality as a legitimate subject for drama. One critic lamented, "More plays like this could make me regret the entirely justified success of *The Boys in the Band.*"

Director Stephen Porter scored his second triumph of the season with his estimable revival of *Harvey* (11-1-44) on February 24 at the ANTA featuring James Stewart as Elwood P. Dowd and Helen Hayes as his bewildered sister Veta. Surprisingly, it was the first New York revival on record, and critics, for the most part, welcomed the vintage comedy with pleasure. The two stars also received plaudits, some reviewers commenting that Stewart was better suited for the role now than when he did it on film in 1950. The popular attraction could run only seventy-nine performances because the busy ANTA was booked for a May arrival.

There was a lot of fun to be had at Ted Shine's triple bill **Contributions** (3-9-70, Tambellini's Gate). Each play was about the generation gap in black society. *Shoes* portrayed an ambitious youth who is working his way through school but decides to spend his hard-earned wages on expensive alligator shoes. *Plantation* presented a racist southern millionaire who is shocked to find that his first-born son happens to be black. Best of all

was the title playlet, in which a subservient black cook for the local sheriff confronts her militant grandson who has returned home to take part in a civil rights sit-in. It seems she has been protesting in her own quiet way all these years, poisoning her bigoted employers. The critics were responsive, but the triple play only lasted two weeks, despite the presence of the respected Claudia McNeil as the cook.

A Douglas Turner Ward double bill by the Negro Ensemble revived his vivacious 1965 satire *A Day of Absence* and premiered a new work, **Brotherhood** (3-10-70, St. Marks Playhouse). A wealthy white couple, Tom (Tom Rosqui) and Ruth Jason (Tiffany Hendry), welcome their new African-American neighbors, James (William Jay) and Luann Johnson (Frances Foster), into their sheet-shrouded living room. Both couples put on false cordiality, the whites filled with hypocrisy and the blacks barely disguising their contempt. Once the guests leave, the sheets are removed, revealing a collection of plaster "pickaninnies" and other racist artifacts. Most agreed that the new work could not compete with the older one, but the double bill played successfully for two months.

Murray Schisgal had scored two Broadway hits in a row with *Luv* (11-11-64) and *Jimmy Shine* (12-5-68), but his double bill **The Chinese and Dr. Fish** (3-10-70, Ethel Barrymore) was a two-week disappointment. *Dr. Fish* (Marvin Lichterman) is a young sex therapist (his doctorate is in American history) whose dotty grandmother (Paula Trueman) supplies him with unwanted advice and homemade lentil soup. When a middle-aged couple (Vincent Gardenia and Charlotte Rae) come to Dr. Fish to make their sex life more "meaningful," the doctor tries to get them to rid themselves of their inhibitions. The trio meets with cockeyed success: the husband goes off with Grandma and her soup, and the wife takes a shine to the young therapist. *The Chinese* presented the Lee family, who run a Chinese laundry. Their son Chester (William Devane) is inexplicably Caucasian. In fact, he pretends to be Jewish in order to impress his Hebrew girlfriend Gladys Hoffman (Louise Lasser). The parents want Chester to marry a girl fresh off the boat from Hong Kong, and comic complications arise when both brides-to-be converge on the laundry one day. Commentators felt that Schigal's comic talents were still potent but that the plays were more "amusing and oddly charming" than satisfying.

Lincoln Center's only new work in the Vivian Beaumont Theatre this season was the six-week engagement of **Operation Sidewinder** (3-12-70), a

SAM[UEL] SHEPARD [Rogers, Jr.] (1943–) was born in rural Illinois but raised in California, and his plays often reflect the struggle between the America of the open frontier and the sophistication of the two coasts. Shepard arrived in New York in 1963 where his one-act plays were first produced in off-off-Broadway theatres such as the Theatre Genesis. *Icarus's Mother* (1965), *Red Cross* (1967), and *La Turista* (1967) attracted attention and won him some off-Broadway awards, but *Operation Sidewinder* was his first mainstream production.

surreal drama that was originally to be produced at Yale University until African-American students on campus protested the way black militants were portrayed in the work and the play was canceled. The author was Sam Shepard, a playwright to be reckoned with.

In an American desert, a giant mechanical rattlesnake (which is also a computer) has escaped from a nearby air force base. Honey (Barbara Eda-Young) and a young rebel (Andy Robinson) are in the desert to try to poison the water supply of the military. Some Hopi Indians arrive to vanquish the CIA agents in the area, and a carload of Black Panthers pulls up looking for a revolution. The snake, which according to the Hopi is a symbol of the end of the world, seizes Honey. Some Hopi rituals are staged, a rock group plays throughout, and the Indians are victorious in the end. The early work contained many of Shepard's characteristic themes (American materialism, the decaying of the American West, the power of myth, the use of rock-and-roll music) as well as a beguiling monologue by the rebel, describing a double murder he committed, which foreshadowed Shepard's later use of the hypnotic soliloquy. Critics were at a loss for what to say; Gottfried captured the play best when he wrote, "It is conceived and written in the pop style, a sort of cross between pop art and McLuhanism." Shepard was quoted as calling Lincoln Center a "totally bourgeois scene," and many subscribers returned the compliment by threatening to cancel their membership. Over the succeeding decades Shepard's work would be consistently produced in New York, but not until 1996 would a production of his land on Broadway again.

A double bill consisting of **Grin and Bare It!** and **Postcards** (3-16-70, Belasco) was a Broadway embarrassment for two weeks and for many represented the depths to which New York theatre had sunk. Tom Prideaux's *Postcards* was a sad little drama about two people (Kate Wilkinson and

Ray Stewart) who for thirty years have written postcards to celebrities, never getting any responses back. *Grin and Bear It!* was actually a 1929 play written by nudist advocate Tom Cushing. Diana Smith (Joleen Fodor) brings her straitlaced, Boston-bred fiancé, Derek Leet (David Christmas), home to meet her parents (Barbara Lester and James Burge), who, unknown to him, are nudists. The unconventional family shocks and then befriends Derek, and the liberated snob eventually joins in their philosophy. Cushing titled his script *The Unplayable Play*, and it was, understandably, never produced. But times being more permissive, Ken McGuire adapted the script, keeping it in the 1929 setting and giving it the sophomoric new title. The play was the first extended use of nudity on a Broadway stage, and critics all agreed on how boring the play (and the nudity) was after the initial shock had worn off. The musical revue *Oh! Calcutta!*, which had opened off Broadway the previous June, also used extensive nudity, and its notoriety turned the piece into a success. But *Grin and Bare It!* was one skin show too many and warned producers that nudity in itself was not a guaranteed moneymaker.

The ambitious playwright of the ambitious drama **Nobody Hears a Broken Drum** (3-19-70, Fortune) was Jason Miller, who was considered promising by some critics even though this first effort didn't quite work. In a Pennsylvania mining town in 1862, a handful of ignorant Irish immigrants are falsely accused of being Molly McGuires (radical unionists). The men are not members but get so caught up in the spirit of unionism and are so dazzled by the way people worship them that they confess to being Molly Maguires. Miller's play included a strike by the workers, a cave-in at the mine, a riot with the militia called in, and an ending with everybody burning down everything. The play only lasted a week, but Miller would return with a more successful Pennsylvania play in the near future.

An off-Broadway revival of Giraudoux's *The Madwoman of Chaillot* (12-27-48) opened on March 22 at the Sokol. It only lasted a week but did boast an unusual cast. Blanche Yurka was the pleasantly demented Aurelia, notorious novelist Jacqueline Susann was her loony friend Josephine, and the company also included veteran actors Lois Wilson and Staats Cotsworth, producer Leonard Sillman, and operetta diva Peggy Wood.

Dublin's Abbey Theatre sent Broadway one of the most acclaimed dramas of the season, **Borstal Boy** (3-31-70, Lyceum), a play fashioned by Frank McMahon from Irish poet Brendan Behan's autobiography. In 1939, young Behan (Frank Grimes) is caught smuggling dynamite for the IRA and is convicted and sent to a British reformatory (called a borstal in Ireland). There he is subjected to three years of cruelty and abuse, emerging with no political ideals left but with the soul of a poet. The large cast of characters included the grown-up Behan (Niall Toibin), who acted as narrator and commentator and provided doses of humor that made the play less grim. (Behan tells the audience that the Irish are "very popular . . . among ourselves" and that he and the borstal lads were "all the kids our mothers warned us against.") Tomas MacAnna designed the suggested scenery and directed the sparse production filled with vivid images, such as a young inmate trying to wipe his friend's blood off his own hands by scraping them against a stone wall. The acting was uniformly excellent, and critical response was enthusiastic. *Borstal Boy* ran four months and won the season's Tony and New York Drama Critics Circle awards.

While Sam Shepard's *Operation Sidewinder* was still running at Lincoln Center, two of his one-acts premiered off Broadway on a double bill, **The Unseen Hand** and **Forensic and the Navigators** (4-1-70, Astor Place). The Old West was conjured up in the Kafka-esque *The Unseen Hand* as three nineteenth-century desperados materialized near a California freeway and waged a revolution against modern technology. *Forensic and the Navigators* showed two revolutionaries hoping to blow up a prison but confronted by two "exterminators" who fill the stage with smoke and confusion. Both pieces were very absurd, very funny, and very mystifying.

Harold Pinter seemed to be moving into Beckett territory with his double bill **Landscape** and **Silence** (4-2-70, Forum), two very subliminal pieces that were described as "staged readings of introspective moments." In *Landscape* a married couple recall memories, each on his or her own wavelength, never connecting. In *Silence* three people recite individual thoughts contrapuntally, their musings flowing together gracefully. Barnes and other reviewers thought the program contained the playwright's best work, yet some noted the lack of tension or sense of evil usually found in Pinter. Several also complained about the length of the evening. Each play was only twenty-some minutes long, so *Silence* was repeated at the end of the double bill for those who wanted to stay and get their money's worth. The Lincoln Center premiere featured an American cast (Robert Symonds, Mildred Natwick, James

Patterson, and Barbara Tarbuck) directed by Peter Gill. It held the boards for fifty-three performances, nearly twice as long as any other work at the Forum that season.

The popular folk-tale thriller *Dark of the Moon* (3-14-45) by Howard Richardson and William Berney was revived off Broadway at the Mercer-Shaw Arena on April 3. With nude witches, not possible in the original production, it was able to run ten weeks.

Two fine performances by promising young actors was all that **Dear Janet Rosenberg, Dear Mr. Kooning** (4-5-70, Gramercy Arts) had to recommend it. The evening of two British plays by Stanley Eveling opened with the title piece, in which a fifty-year-old author of some fame corresponds with a nineteen-year-old girl who worships him. In *Jakey Fat Boy*, a long-haired, false-bearded man in dark glasses has an encounter with a young hippie girl, relating his sexual dreams and idolizing the British critic Kenneth Tynan. Kevin O'Connor was outstanding as both men, and a young Catherine Burns was hailed for her starstruck Janet Rosenberg.

A lackluster production of Shaw's *Candida* came to the Longacre on April 6 from the Great Lakes Shakespeare Festival and lasted less than a week. Celeste Holm, as the title character, received mixed notices, and some critics even found fault with the play itself. The next night Marcel Marceau opened at the City Center for twenty-three performances of Bip and other assorted characters in his repertoire.

The most honored off-Broadway play of the season was Paul Zindel's drama **The Effect of Gamma Rays on Man-in-the-Moon Marigolds** (4-7-70, Mercer-O'Casey) which had been produced previously at Houston's Alley Theatre and at the Cleveland Playhouse. In a garbage-ridden house that had once been a vegetable store live the abrasive Beatrice Hunsdorfer (Sada Thompson) and her two teenage daughters: tartish Ruth (Amy Levitt), who is prone to convulsions, and quiet, withdrawn Tillie (Pamela Payton-Wright), who is fascinated by science. Also in the household is the senile old Nanny (Judith Lowry), who is no relation but is tolerated as a boarder for the extra money. Beatrice, feeling persecuted by the entire world, has belligerently withdrawn from it, spending her days looking through the want ads and dreaming of owning a tea shop. The household is thrown into excitement when Tillie's botany project (the play's lengthy title) is a finalist at the school science fair, and even Beatrice considers leaving the house and attending. But the vindictive Ruth, upset because she has to stay home and watch Nanny, tells her mother that the whole school is waiting for Beatrice to come to the fair so they can laugh at "Betty the loon." Beatrice refuses to go, instead staying home, killing the family's pet rabbit, throwing out Nanny along with boxes of garbage, and making plans to turn the dilapidated house into a tea shop. Tillie wins the science award, and her summary, about how outside forces (such as gamma rays) can change life forms, ends the play. Zindel's plotting was a bit sluggish, but his precise characterizations and crackling dialogue more than made up for it. There were also moments of poetry in the piece, as in Beatrice's relating her dream of a white circus horse pulling her father's vegetable wagon, or Tillie's mystical fascination with the nature of the atom. Melvin Bernhardt directed with great sensitivity, and the whole cast was exceptional, even Swoozie Kurtz in a brief role as Tillie's obnoxious rival at the science fair. Thompson's wisecracking, wounded Beatrice made her a recognized star, and the reliable character actress saw her career soar. The reviews were all laudatory, Jerry Tallmer of the *New York Post* going so far as to claim, "I do not know of a better play of its genre since *The Glass Menagerie*." *Marigolds* won the Obie Award, the New York Drama Critics Circle Award for best American play, and, the following season, the Pulitzer Prize. The off-Broadway run of two years was followed by hundreds of productions in regional, community, and educational theatres.

A dreadful "character play" called **The Nest** (4-9-70, Mercury) was an unpromising debut for playwright Tina Howe, who would eventually contribute some worthwhile works. Five housemates, three girls and two boys, share a duplex apartment, their lives all intertwined and complicated by their many personal problems. The whole project would have been easily forgettable except for a scene in which one of the men licked cake frosting from the bare breasts of one of the women. Fortunately audiences were subjected to this odd spectacle for only one performance.

Aeschylus's seldom-performed *The Persians* was mounted by the Phoenix Theatre on April 15 at St. George's Church for twenty-one performances. John Lewin adapted the original text, and Gordon Duffey directed it as a commentary on the current situation in Vietnam, the imperialist Greeks/Americans ravaging the Persians/Vietnamese in Salamis/Southeast Asia. Critics found the parallels forced (after all, the Greeks were victorious at Salamis while the U.S. was clearing losing in Vietnam), but some approved of the inventive staging, defined as a "ceremony for our time" in the playbill.

The Broadway season's final one-night stand was Lonnie Coleman's comedy **A Place for Polly** (4-18-70, Ethel Barrymore), which came from summer stock. Cheerful housewife Polly (Marian Mercer) is content living in a modern-day doll's house with her publisher husband, Otis (Konrad Matthaei), until her older sister, Angela (Cathryn Damon), arrives for a visit and Otis is smitten with her. Angela is a famous foreign correspondent and has just completed a book about growing up black in South Africa. Polly is upset enough about Otis and Angela's affair, but when she finds out Angela's manuscript is plagiarized from a young South African's work, she leaves the doll's house and takes a job, for some unknown reason, as a secretary to a Broadway producer. Critics felt the actors struggled in vain to bring life to such a "tepid," "obvious," and "hokey" play. Most mentioned Clark Dunham's unusual set, an apartment with floor-to-ceiling glass windows that seemed illogical anywhere but certainly in Greenwich Village, where the comedy supposedly took place.

Peter Keveson's **How Much, How Much?** (4-20-70, Provincetown Playhouse) was a morality play about money and how we are obsessed with it. Teenager Charley Gordon (Kristoffer Tabori) has a scheme for making a lot of money: go into the sale of aspirin and pornography, two essential items with low overhead and high profits. He interests his new girlfriend, Joyce Monash (Neva Small), and her slovenly parents, Peggy and Carl (Nancy Andrews and Hy Anzell), in his plan, hoping to impress his own father (Hugh Franklin), a lawyer for the Mafia. To the surprise of everyone but the audience, money doesn't bring happiness, and Charley is left sadder but wiser at the end. The strong cast made the show almost bearable, but in four weeks it was gone.

A dynamic cast was also the only reason to see **Inquest** (4-23-70, Music Box), a self-billed "tale of political terror" about convicted spies Julius and Ethel Rosenberg. Donald Freed adapted the play from a book by Walter and Miriam Schneir that argued for the Rosenbergs' innocence. Such an important subject deserved better than Freed's melodrama, which played up the emotional aspects of the story and was so blatantly sympathetic to its heroes that they became inconsequential. The scene is the courtroom where Julius (George Grizzard) and Ethel (Anne Jackson) are being tried, but a large screen behind them projects slides about past events. Actual documents were used for the testimony, and more than one critic complained about the flatness of the dialogue. Most reviewers agreed it was "often tiresome theatre . . . guilty of non-objective reporting of its serious subject," but everyone considered the performances accomplished, particularly James Whitmore as the gentle defense attorney Emanuel Bloch. Regardless, the drama closed after a month.

The American Place finished its season with a loose, plotless slice-of-life play by Ed Bullins called **The Pig Pen** (4-29-70, St. Clements). A wealthy black couple is throwing a party in their country house in the California hills. As jazz musicians play, a poet is honored, the wife sleeps with various male guests, a bigoted white policeman makes a few ineffectual appearances, and the guests prattle on and on about diverse topics. Then another guest arrives and announces that Malcom X has been murdered. The party continues in a more somber vein, and the cop laughs uproariously as the play ends. Only open to subscribers, the drama ran out its scheduled forty-six performances, then was rarely heard from again.

What the Butler Saw (5-4-70, McAlpin Rooftop), British playwright Joe Orton's last and possibly finest comedy, was given its American premiere with an American director (Joseph Hardy) and American cast. While not as violent as Orton's previous dark comedies, *What the Butler Saw* utilized all of his satirical tricks, outrageous characters, outlandish sexuality, and farcical plotting. At a private psychiatric clinic, Dr. Prentice (Laurence Luckinbill) tries to seduce the pretty Geraldine Barclay (Diana Davila) when she comes to apply for a secretarial job. But the nymphomaniacal Mrs. Prentice (Jan Farrand) shows up, followed by bellhop Nicholas (Charles Murphy), who had attempted to rape her in a linen closet. The arrival of state inspector Rance (Lucian Scott) and the obliging Sergeant Match (Tom Rosqui) sets off a series of mistaken identities, with people hiding in closets and behind curtains, and plenty of cross-dressing. (Geraldine spends much of the play in Nick's bellhop uniform while he wears her dress.) Orton ties it all together in a mock–Oscar Wilde ending with long-lost siblings and parents reunited. While the cast got mixed reviews, critics were very supportive of the script, calling it "hilariously bitter" and "disarming to the point of charming." The comedy ran six merry months and soon became the most-produced Orton play across the country.

The next regional company to be featured at ANTA was the Meadow Brook Theatre of Rochester, Michigan, but its revival of Chekhov's *The Cherry Orchard* on May 6 received mediocre to negative reviews and lasted less than a week. Although the group was from the American heartland, the cast, gathered by director John Ferland, was mostly British, many of the actors being recent graduates of the Royal Academy of Dramatic Arts in London. Talmer spoke for several when he called the production "over-fussy, over-detailed, over-mannered, and certainly, as tongues go, over-Britished."

Zoe Caldwell gave one of the finest performances of her career in **Colette** (5-6-70, Ellen Stewart), a biographical drama by Elinor Jones about the famed French authoress. The first act was a chronicle of Colette's life, from her youth in Burgundy to her marriage to M. Willy and her arrival in Paris to her subsequent marriages and appearances in music halls. Most of the second act took the form of an interview as newspaper reporters gathered around Madame and listened to her *bons mots*. The press thought the play "tedious" and a "mere recitation," but all marveled at Caldwell's brilliant characterization. *Colette* ran 101 performances; when it reopened next season with a different cast without Caldwell, it only lasted a week.

Success eluded two off-Broadway revivals in May. *Room Service* (5-19-37) on May 12 only managed to run at the Edison for two months despite an inspired comic performance by Ron Leibman as the shyster producer Gordon Miller. Opening the next night at the Sheridan Square, William Hanley's drama *Slow Dance on the Killing Ground* (11-3-64) survived only half as long, even though its skillful cast consisted of George Voskovec, Madeline Miller, and Billy Dee Williams.

Lincoln Center concluded its upstairs season with a revival of Kaufman and Hart's expressionistic comedy *Beggar on Horseback* (2-12-24) on May 14 and gave it what John Chapman of the *New York Daily News* called the "most elaborate production I have ever seen at the Vivian Beaumont." John Hirsch directed the large cast, which featured Leonard Frey as the dreamy artist Neil McRae, and Michael Annals provided the bizarre sets and costumes, including enormous cogwheels that rotated and a jury contained inside an oversized piano. Critics agreed that it was overproduced (one described it as a "gigantic, monstrous curio"), and most felt the play had dated badly. The expensive entry ran through the end of June, and Lincoln Center was left in greater debt than usual.

The renowned French actor-director Jean-Louis Barrault brought his biographical play **Rabelais** (5-16-70, City Center) to Broadway for two weeks. The evening was a cornucopia of Rabelaisian ideas with scenes from his life scattered throughout, all accompanied by rock music. Barrault directed the large company (who performed in French) as well as appearing in the cast himself.

As with his *The Gingham Dog* (4-23-69) last season, Lanford Wilson would collect several encouraging reviews for his domestic drama **Lemon Sky** (5-17-70, Playhouse) which opened a new theatre off Broadway, but success would elude him for a few more seasons. Teenager Alan (Christopher Walken) visits the California home of his estranged father, Douglas (Charles Durning), who abandoned Alan and his mother years ago. Douglas has a new wife and family now, and Alan feels accepted by them at first, even considering staying and going to the local college. But old wounds resurface, and eventually Alan must leave, reconciled to the realization that he must live without his father. Walken impressed critics, as did Wilson's tender script. Gottfried was not alone in claiming Wilson as "one of the very most talented writers in all the American theatre." But *Lemon Sky* was too small an achievement, and it only lasted two weeks.

Cries of "stupid and offensive" greeted an embarrassing dark comedy called **The Engagement Baby** (5-21-70, Helen Hayes) by screenwriter Stanley Shapiro. Ad writer Walter Whitney (Barry Nelson) has a lousy marriage with his frigid wife, Vivian (Constance Towers), and fondly recalls an affair he had many years ago with an African-American woman. One day an eighteen-year-old black militant named Roger (Clifton Davis) shows up, claiming to be Walter's "engagement baby," a euphemism for a bastard. When Vivian finds out, she leaves Walter, who loses his job and is reduced to cleaning stables in Bedford-Stuyvesant. (What horses were doing in that urban location was not explained.) In the end, Vivian returns, Walter gets his old Madison Avenue job back, and Roger gives up his radical ways and enters medical school. One sequence considered particularly offensive showed Walter, disguised as a burglar, breaking into his former home and raping Vivian, the wife enjoying the experience because she thought Walter a stranger. Shapiro wrote his odd comedy in screenplay format, and Robin Wagner designed several musical comedy–like sets that seemed to be moving all the time. But all the scenery went to the warehouse after four performances.

Broadway's final offering of the season was the Trinity Square Repertory Theatre's production of Roland van Zandt's historical drama **Wilson in the Promised Land** (5-26-70, ANTA) for a week. Adrian Hall, the theatre's artistic director, staged the imaginative piece with a flourish, and it was a proficient showcase for this outstanding regional theatre. But the script was a shambles. Ten hippies awaken the spirit of Woodrow Wilson (William Cain) and in a series of flashbacks illustrate how U.S. presidents have always acted out of personal vanity. Washington, Jefferson, Jackson, Lincoln, and both Roosevelts made jarring appearances as the life of Wilson was examined. Van Zandt was a historian but, the critics conceded, no playwright.

There was much talk about the Open Theatre Ensemble's brief repertory of three plays off Broadway, two of them actor-generated rather than formally written down by a playwright. **Terminal** (5-26-70, Washington Square Methodist Church) was a collage of music, sketches, dance, and movement about various aspects of death, developed by the company and given a "text by Susan Yankowitz." In various sequences a body was embalmed, an actress went on and on about funeral parlor cosmetics, and a dead soldier marched back and forth, getting angrier with each "yes, sir!" Popular off-Broadway playwright Jean-Claude van Itallie was the credited author of **The Serpent: A Ceremony** (5-29-70, Washington Square Methodist Church), but it too had been developed by the actors in workshop. Using familiar Garden of Eden sequences from Genesis, the loosely structured piece brought up the issues of violence and authority in short scenes filled with repetition and choral echoes. Both programs were so visual, relying on dynamic ensemble movement, that the printed play text was only a shadow of the actual production. The third Open Theatre offering was a revival of Beckett's *Endgame* (1-28-58) on May 30 with Peter Maloney as Clov and Open Theatre artistic director Joseph Chaikin as Hamm. Critics were baffled, impressed, or bored by the three offerings. (Oddly, *Best Plays* editor Otis L. Guernsey, Jr., chose *The Serpent* as one of the season's ten best scripts.)

Clifford Odets's *Awake and Sing!* (2-19-35) had its first major New York revival in thirty years when a production opened at the Bijou on May 27 and ran two months. Joan Lorring played Bessie Berger, and Robert Salvio was her son Ralph. Lincoln Center's season in the Forum ended with yet another stage version of *Amphitryon* on May 28, this time by German playwright Peter Hacks and translated by Ralph Manheim. The familiar tale was given a breezy adaptation, but most critics felt it became too heavy-handed near the end when pompous moralizing set in. All the same, the ever-reliable Philip Bosco made a dandy Jupiter, and Harold Gould stole the show with his wily servant Sosias.

1970–1971

The 1970–1971 season might be described as one of compromise. Theatre owners, producers, and actors, threatened by the falling number of productions and ever-decreasing audiences, made compromises with their audiences and with each other in order to stay alive. A new and earlier curtain time was established to attract commuters to stay in town and attend plays; unions agreed to a "Limited Broadway" plan that would help reduce expenses if seating in certain houses were reduced; actors off Broadway went on strike over wages and a month later compromised with the League of Off-Broadway Theatres and Producers; and the mayor established Broadway as a "special district" with increased police protection and a zoning agreement that allowed skyscrapers to be built in the neighborhood if they included a new theatre in the structure. Everyone seemed to be bending over backward. But few of these plans were very successful in the long run, and it would be many a season before the theatre environment in New York would improve.

One group that would not compromise was the *New York Times*. There had long been complaints about the power the *Times* held now that there were so few daily newspapers in New York. It seemed to have a monopoly on both advertising and reviews. *Times* critic Clive Barnes was British and had more background in dance than theatre, but his ability to close a show was unmistakable. True, the admired Walter Kerr also wrote for the *Times*, but he was the Sunday columnist, and too often the damage had already been done by the time his reviews came out. Producers and playwrights offered various solutions to the problem, from occasional guest reviewers to running a box score of other critics' opinions next to Barnes's copy. But the *Times* would not budge, and Barnes continued to be the most powerful critical force in New York theatre.

Only fourteen new American plays opened on Broadway this season (as compared to twenty-one the previous season), and Off Broadway offered thirty-nine to last season's fifty-three. While the top ticket for a Broadway non-musical held at about $9.00, the off-Broadway top was now up to a not-unusual $7.50. Off Broadway continued to be Broadwayized as production costs continued to rise (the "average" off-Broadway play cost $41,400, according to *Variety*) and audiences decreased. Artistically, though, Off Broadway did provide most of the best new American plays this season, so the struggling venue was deemed more important than ever.

The season began with a drama that was a bit too close to reality for most. Rick Cluchey's **The Cage** (6-18-70, Playhouse) was a brutally honest look at prison life and how a raw newcomer (Cluchey) tries to adjust to a world of horror and helplessness. Cluchey and the five other actors were all ex-convicts from San Quentin, so they knew what they were talking about. But life experience didn't necessarily make for good playwriting skills, and there was an amateur quality to the whole enterprise. Edith Oliver, writing in *The New Yorker*, noted that "the situation depicted is indeed dreadful, but the play could be a lot better." Yet the drama intrigued audiences for 126 performances before setting out on tour.

The promise glimpsed in Athol Fugard's *The Blood Knot* (3-1-64) was, for some, fulfilled with his **Boesman and Lena** (6-22-70, Circle in the Square), a plotless examination of two Hottentot drifters who live off the white man's trash and are, in turn, the cast-off trash of South Africa. On the mud flats of the river Swartkops, the black couple Boesman (James Earl Jones) and Lena (Ruby Dee) carry all their worldly possessions on their backs as they move across the land and scavenge what they can. The two have been kicked out of the shack they inhabited the night before, and as they travel they gently argue about which places they have and have not been. Soon an ancient old African (Zakes Mokae), who only speaks the Xhosa language, enters, and they communicate enough for Lena to invite the old man to sit by their fire and have a drink. Boesman begrudges the old man's presence, especially when Lena offers to shelter him in their makeshift hut. When Boesman refuses to share the primitive lodgings with the old man, the couple are forced to look at each other in a new light. The old African dies during the night; Boesman and Lena move on, sure of nothing but their identity and their existence at the lowest level of society. Some critics complained of the play's length and lack of action but found the performances quite vibrant. Publicity regarding the production was generated when Fugard, because of his political writings, was denied a passport from South Africa to come to New York for the rehearsals or performances. There was enough interest on the part of theatregoers to keep *Boesman and Lena* on the boards for seven months.

At the Delacorte in Central Park, the New York Shakespeare Festival's summer was devoted to *The War of the Roses*, a three-play repertory of Shakespeare's *Henry VI, Parts 1 and 2*, and *Richard III*. The three histories were performed in chronological order beginning on June 23 and closing on August 22. Stuart Vaughan directed all three plays with Nicholas Kepros as Henry and Donald Madden as Richard. On June 27, the audience had an opportunity to view the entire history in a twelve-hour dusk-to-dawn performance.

From Off Off Broadway's La Mama came the season's most blatantly titled play, Tom Eyen's **The Dirtiest Show in Town** (6-27-70, Astor Place), which purported to be about pollution in the contemporary world but was really a series of skits and blackout scenes filled with homosexual and Jewish jokes and a good deal of nudity. Most critics read the title and stayed away from such an obvious ploy (*The New Yorker* announced the title was an inflated claim: " 'most predictable' might be closer"), but audiences were more susceptible, and the embarrassment ran 509 performances.

Magazine humorist Bruce Jay Friedman had amused and outraged many with his long-running comedy *Scuba Duba* (10-10-67), but his more worthy **Steambath** (6-30-70, Truck and Warehouse) only lasted 128 performances despite a lot of publicity. Director Anthony Perkins and the producers kept recasting the male lead and postponing the opening. When the comedy did open, Perkins himself played the frustrated writer Tandy who awakens in a steambath and soon realizes he is dead and the misty room is Purgatory. The steambath is populated with bizarre comic types, such as the crusty Old Timer (Conrad Bain) who hopes Tandy's son is an alcoholic because it'll "keep him off drugs," two gay dancers (Jere Admire and Teno Pollick) who committed suicide because they both loved the same chorus boy, the uninhibited Meredith (Annie Rachel) who is through with love "until Labor Day," and the disgusting Bieberman (Marvin Lichterman) who spits on the floor and does exercises in his underwear. Tandy soon realizes that the

Puerto Rican Attendant (Hector Elizondo), who sweeps up and gives orders to a television monitor, is actually God, and he pleads in vain with the foul-mouthed deity to let him return to life. Friedman's premise was not original (Sutton Vane offered a similar conceit nearly fifty years earlier in *Outward Bound*), but his bold caricatures, irreverent humor, and facile dialogue were uniquely his own. Critics felt the problem lay in his plotting, which was aimless and undramatic, and a forced ending: Tandy launches into a monologue about how much he has to live for, defeating his arguments with his own contradictions. Otis L. Guernsey, Jr., who chose *Steambath* as one of the *Best Plays*, and others thought the comedy exceptional, but most had mixed feelings about the production itself, except for David Mitchell's ingenious set design with jets of steam emanating from the floor and ceiling.

The Broadway season opened on July 4 with a lackluster revival at the Brooks Atkinson of Brandon Thomas's nineteenth-century farce *Charley's Aunt*, which was generally dismissed except for television comedian Louis Nye's inspired comic performance as the cross-dressing Babberley. Critics concurred that Nye was no actor but raved about his vaudeville-like bits that relieved the dull evening. The revival lasted only a week. Two weeks was all that was scheduled for *Othello* on September 14 at the ANTA, and the poor reviews did not encourage any extension. Moses Gunn received mixed notices for his Moor, and Lee Richardson's Iago was deemed too transparent, but many were taken with Roberta Maxwell's childlike Desdemona. The Michael Kahn production was a successful summer entry at the American Shakespeare Festival in Stratford, Connecticut, but New York critics and audiences were nonplused.

Broadway's first "new" entry, **Bob and Ray the Two and Only** (9-24-70, John Golden), was a comic revue made up of old radio sketches and characters created over the years by comedians Bob Elliott and Ray Goulding. Comic character favorites such as the dense Wally Ballou and the Komodo Dragon Expert seemed quite at home onstage, but even those who enjoyed the two veteran performers—and there were several who endorsed the evening—had to question what such a non-show was doing on Broadway. But Bob and Ray were indeed funny, and their loyal fans kept the show on the boards for five months.

Joseph Papp opened his season and his new theatre, the 300-seat Newman, with Dennis J. Reardon's mysterious drama **The Happiness**

Cage (10-4-70, Public: Newman). The restless Reese (Lewis J. Stadlen) is discharged from the army with a broken arm and transferred, inexplicably, to a terminal cancer ward run by an authoritative General (Paul Sparer) and a mystical Dr. Freytag (Henderson Forsythe). Reese soon realizes that the doomed patients are being used as guinea pigs for the doctor's experiments in mental illness and that he is the next subject. The authority figures in the play took on mythic proportions, and the military's attempt to create artificial happiness pushed the play into agitprop science fiction. Critical reaction was mixed; several reviewers pointed out that the play was too long, too excessive, and tried to touch on too many topics, but others found value in the writing.

The Public always favored new American works, so the choice of Arthur Wing Pinero's nineteenth-century British comedy *Trelawny of the "Wells"* on October 11 in the Anspacher was an unusual one. But the 1898 work, about a theatre company and how times change the styles of acting and playwriting, got surprisingly good reviews. Critics complimented the Public on the lush production, fine acting, and stylish direction by Robert Ronan (who also played the struggling playwright Tom Wrench). Nancy Dussault was a charming Rose Trelawny, but the highest praise was given to Sasha von Scherler as the witty actress Avonia Bunn. The lovely production ran its scheduled forty-eight performances with full houses.

A curiosity that most felt belonged off Broadway if, indeed, in any theatre at all was **Opium** (10-5-70, Edison). Roc Brynner (son of Yul Brynner) adapted the one-man show, devised from Jean Cocteau's notebooks about overcoming his drug addition in 1928, and performed it as a patient giving up his opium like a man forsaking a destructive but beloved mistress. Critics applauded Brynner but found the material stagnant and untheatrical. It closed in a week.

Pop novelist Kurt Vonnegut, Jr., made his playwriting debut with the surreal comedy **Happy Birthday, Wanda June** (10-7-70, Theatre de Lys). Because of the writer's popularity, it received a good deal of attention. The play was a modern take-off on the Homeric tale of Odysseus's homecoming. Penelope Ryan (Marsha Mason) and her son Paul (Steven Paul) believe her husband, the macho explorer Harold, has died deep in the Amazon jungle, and she is trying to decide between two suitors: a doctor (Keith Charles) and a vacuum cleaner salesman (William Hickey). But

Harold (Kevin McCarthy), to everyone's surprise, returns, and on his birthday no less. (The play's title comes from the wording on the cake that is hurriedly purchased; it was made for a little girl, but she died before her birthday party.) Harold is a bragging, crude, mock-heroic fool who tries unsuccessfully to get his own son to shoot him to prove his masculinity. Harold even attempts a Hemingway-like suicide but cannot go through with it, leaving him a shallow and shattered man. Vonnegut's unique way with offbeat characters and ripe dialogue (Penelope tells the audience: "This is tragedy. When it's done my face will be as white as the snows of Kilimanjaro.") carried onto the stage, but his storytelling techniques were unsuccessful. Reviews ranged from "aimless, plotless play" to "a loving, charming and intelligent experience, a special time with an imagination that could only be Vonnegut's." Despite the mixed reviews, Vonnegut's popularity helped the comedy run for forty-seven performances before an Actors' Equity strike off Broadway closed it. But it reopened with the same cast at the Edison on December 22 and ran an additional 143 performances.

The next night off-off Broadway, the Manhattan Project had such success with their modern take on *Alice in Wonderland* that they moved it to the off-Broadway Extension Theatre for 119 bewitching performances. The cast of six and director André Gregory developed the script, which turned Lewis Carroll's tale into an actual nightmare filled with Freudian implications and many references to drugs. This "manic-depressive" version was not for everyone, but most critics had to admit it had the maddest Mad Hatter's tea party ever seen.

The British melodrama **Conduct Unbecoming** (10-12-70, Ethel Barrymore) by Barry England had been a successful venture in London; on Broadway it managed a respectable but unprofitable 144 performances. In Queen Victoria's India, a proud army regiment must investigate a question of assault on an English woman by an unknown officer of the corps. (The lady's bare backside has been struck by the flat of a ceremonial sword.) The informal inquiry reveals the hypocrisy of the spit-and-polish gentlemanly group as their mistreatment of animals and Indian locals leads to desecrating even their own class. The resolution involves justified murder and honorable suicide on the part of the guilty parties, but the double standard continues on. While the British cast was cited as thoroughly competent and the large, handsome production was endorsed, critics felt the melodrama was too staid and old-fashioned to be taken seriously.

The American Place Theatre had been encouraging noted American authors to try their hand at playwriting, but when Joyce Carol Oates, recent winner of the National Book Award for fiction, offered her **Sunday Dinner** (10-16-70, St. Clements Church), the critics pounced on it, one calling the drama "pretentious, studiously obscure, and ponderous in what I suppose is intended to be an allegory." Three brothers and their two sisters visit the gravesite of their departed mother every Sunday, then return home for dinner. All five siblings feel guilty about the mother, the father who deserted them all, and each other. Then a shabby, blind old man enters, claiming to be a census taker, but asking personal questions that allow the siblings to spill their secrets and regrets. Eventually they weary of the omniscient old man, and the youngest son pokes out his blind eyes with a spoon and sends him on his way.

New York saw three professional revivals of *Hamlet* this season, each a bit unusual and each short-lived. The Roundabout Theatre's all-male production of the tragedy on October 18 directed by Gene Feist featured Art Burns as the prince. Little approval of his performance, the rest of the cast, and the production itself could be found.

The new Limited Gross Broadway Theatre Agreement, whereby producers in smaller Broadway houses limited the weekly gross to $25,000 and kept the top ticket price at $5 in order to get reduced union costs, was first attempted with the biographical flop **Gandhi** (10-20-70, Playhouse), which closed on opening night. The purpose of the agreement was to foster new and experimental work on Broadway, but *Gandhi* proved that no compromise with unions and theatregoers could make a bad play run. Gurney Campbell's drama was less a play than a series of disjointed episodes and Gandhi quotations, and neither a capable performance by Jack MacGowran nor the direction by the capable José Quintero could save it. The "moribund pageant" did boast a superb setting by Ming Cho Lee that consisted of a complex series of wooden structures that burst forth into ramps, bridges, and stairways.

Although most enjoyed themselves, critics were not quite sure how to categorize **Story Theater** (10-26-70, Ambassador), Paul Sills's loose dramatization of tales by the Brothers Grimm and Aesop's fables. Clearly intended for children, the highly theatrical, improvisational production seemed ritualistic at times with quirky storytell-

> **MING CHO LEE** (1930–   ) was born in Shanghai, the son of an insurance representative. He received his B.A. at Occidental College, studied art and design at UCLA in the early 1950s, and after graduation worked as an assistant to Jo Mielziner for five years. Lee's scenic designs were seen in regional theatres and off Broadway, and by 1962 his work was occasionally seen on Broadway. He gained widespread recognition for his striking designs for the Public Theatre and the New York Shakespeare Festival, in particular his settings for the outdoor Delacorte Theatre. Unlike most top designers, he would usually eschew musical productions throughout his career.

ing techniques that had actors shifting from character to narrator in midsentence. The stories were mostly familiar (Henny Penny, the Bremen Town Musicians, and so on), and the writing was bluntly unliterary, but the style intrigued everyone. (In fact, such an approach to children's theatre production would be known as "Story Theatre style" for years afterwards.) Except for those reviewers who professed to be bored sitting through a children's show, most commended the simple staging (lighting, sound, and movement instead of scenery and costumes created the locale and atmosphere for each tale the agile cast, and the unpretentious fun the evening had to offer. The program ran in the large theatre for eight months and spawned a sequel of sorts later in the season.

Ray Cooney and John Chapman's sex farce **Not Now, Darling** (10-29-70, Brooks Atkinson) ran nearly two years in London but could barely muster three weeks on Broadway. The posh London furriers Arnold Crouch (Norman Wisdom) and Gilbert Bodley (Rex Garner) endure a day of furious misunderstandings in their salon when a husband is sold a fur for his wife that was intended for his mistress. Suspicious wives enter, scantily clad girls are hidden in closets, and everyone is doubled over with double entendres until the final curtain mercifully falls. Critics lowered their guns, calling it "infantile," "singularly flat, [and] lugubrious" and warning patrons to "check your mind at the door." British comic Wisdom was cited as both the best and the worst of the frantic cast.

On November 3, the one-man show *Emlyn Williams as Charles Dickens* returned to New York for five performances at Lincoln Center's Alice Tully Hall.

Unlike *Not Now, Darling*, a foreign import with a particularly foreign sense of humor fared much better with the critics. **Orlando Furioso**, (11-4-70, Bryant Park) a lively stage adaptation of the epic Renaissance poem by Ludovico Ariosto, performed in a specially constructed bubble theatre in Bryant Park for thirty-four rollicking performances. The picaresque plot followed the exploits of Charlemagne's paladin Orlando in his battle to win the bewitching Angelica from the enchanted Ruggiero. The production, performed in Italian with a European cast of sixty, had previously played at the Spoleto and Edinburgh festivals, and this theatre-in-the-round engagement in the lighter-than-air structure was deemed quite enjoyable by the critics who covered it. Brendan Gill in *The New Yorker* described it best as "a manic, perhaps even demonic, Wild West show in a Renaissance setting . . . incomprehensible and enlightening and well worth a visit."

A polished if lifeless revival of Brecht's *The Good Woman of Setzuan* opened Lincoln Center's sixth season in the Vivian Beaumont on November 5. Ralph Manheim's translation (or was it the play itself?) was cited as simplistic and outdated by many, and even Colleen Dewhurst's multi-faceted Shen Teh was only mildly approved of. A common complaint concerned the discrepancy between the realistic acting style of parts of the production and the awkward histrionics of the fantasy aspects. David Birney, as the suicidal aviator Yang Sun, seemed to carry off the double feat best.

Irv Bauer's domestic drama **A Dream Out of Time** (11-8-70, Promenade) reminded some of an Arthur Miller drama with its powerful conflict between father and son. Mike Gordon (James J. Sloyan) was raised in a Jewish family with the importance of a solid business career instilled in him. But once he proved himself a bright and successful businessman, he quit, moved to a Paris cold-water flat, and tried to become a writer. He now returns to his family home on the upper West Side of Manhattan, where he must deal with his disapproving father, Aaron (Sam Levene), and his disillusionment about the American work ethic. In a series of flashbacks and dream sequences we see how Aaron stopped a gentile girl from marrying Mike, and how Aaron himself was once a radical dreamer (as a young man he wanted to go to Spain and fight the Fascists) but relented to the American standard of success. Father and son are not reconciled at the end, and the struggle for self-fulfillment continues. Sloyan was generally applauded, and critics saluted Lev-

ene for taking on a serious role, but reactions to the play were mixed, from "overblown and pretentious" to "strong, honest and serious." The intriguing drama ran six weeks, but the actors' strike off Broadway interrupted its run, and it never found an audience after the strike was resolved.

A Broadway revival of Noel Coward's *Hay Fever* (10-5-25) at the Helen Hayes on November 9 was berated as a sluggish production by all, and critics were in agreement that Shirley Booth was hopelessly miscast as the flamboyant English actress Judith Bliss. Only Carole Shelley, as the dim flapper Jackie, was generally approved of. In three weeks the enterprise was gone.

A British import that caught fire on Broadway was Anthony Shaffer's witty thriller **Sleuth** (11-12-70, Music Box). Barnes called it the best melodrama since *Dial "M" for Murder* (10-29-52), and John Chapman of the *New York Daily News* went all the way back to *Angel Street* (12-5-41) to find its equal. Into the posh Wiltshire home of mystery writer Andrew Wyke (Anthony Quayle) comes a young local, Milo Tindle (Keith Baxter), invited by Wyke for a drink and some civilized talk. After a bit of cordial banter about writing detective novels, Wyke casually says, "I understand you want to marry my wife." It seems that Tindle has been having an affair with Marguerite Wyke for some time, and Wkye, who is weary of her and has a Finnish mistress of his own named Tea, believes that his wife would leave him and marry Tindle if the young man could afford to keep her "in the style to which she wasn't accustomed before she met me, but now is." Tindle admits he is not financially secure, so Wkye proposes the younger man steal some heavily insured jewelry from the house. Tindle will sell the jewels (Wyke even has contacts with fences) and get Marguerite; Wyke will collect the insurance money and live happily ever after with Tea. Tindle reluctantly agrees, and Wkye has a field day dressing Tindle up in a clown outfit, blowing up the safe, and leaving obvious clues all about. But then, as Tindle believes the charade is over, Wkye pulls out a gun, confesses he still loves his wife, and says he will now kill Tindle, claiming a break-in to the police. Tindle pleads for his life, but Wyke pulls the trigger as the first-act curtain falls. Two days later, Wyke is enjoying caviar and listening to Beethoven when rumpled old Inspector Doppler arrives and questions Wyke about the disappearance of Tindle. Wkye tells the inspector everything that happened—then adds that the gun had blanks in it, and the trick gave Tindle a good scare and Wyke a good laugh. But when Doppler starts investigating, he discovers real bloodstains on the stairs and a bullet hole in the wall. Wyke panics and begs the inspector to believe him, that it was all a game and that Tindle left the house alive. When Wyke is reduced to frantic pleading, Doppler removes his disguise and reveals himself as Tindle, getting even with the mystery writer. Wyke is shaken but admits it was quite a good performance; Tindle in turn admits that he has gone too far in his revenge. He has murdered Tea and planted three incriminating objects in the house that tie Wyke to the killing. Waiting for the police to arrive, Tindle gives Wyke oblique hints as to where the clues are hidden. Wkye solves the riddles and obtains the objects at the last moment, then Tindle laughs and admits it was another joke and that Tea is alive. Humiliated and insulted, Wyke shoots Tindle (with real bullets this time) as the sirens of the approaching police cars are heard. Even the most demanding critics had to admit that *Sleuth* was very ingenious (the playbill even listed Doppler and other imaginary people in its cast of characters) and actually witty at times. Audiences were in agreement, and *Sleuth* ran for 1,222 performances, twice as long as *Dial "M" for Murder* and only two months shy of *Angel Street's* record for a thriller.

Everyone had heard about Edward Bond's **Saved** (11-13-70, Cherry Lane) before it opened because of its notorious history. A scene in the play where a group of thugs stone a baby to death in its carriage got the play banned from production in England in 1965, and it was produced only after the official censor's job was dissolved. Twice the play had been booked for New York, but both times it was canceled. *Saved* received its U.S. premiere at Yale, then the Chelsea Theatre Center of Brooklyn presented it in October at the Brooklyn Academy of Music, moving the production to Off Broadway for twenty-nine disturbing performances. In South London, the unhappy loner Len (James Woods) falls in love with the tartish Pam (Dorrie Kavanaugh) and moves into her family home, where Pam's mother (Margaret Braidwood) starts making passes at him. But Pam loves the brutish Fred (Kevin Conway) and has a child by him, which Len cares for as if it were his own. When Fred and his gang kill the baby, he is sent to prison. Len sticks around, his guilt over the death giving him the feeling he has been "saved." Alan Schneider directed the difficult play well (he staged the stoning of the baby in a surrealistic, choreographed fashion), but it had no

firm resolution, and several complained about its three-hour length. Yet many of the reviews were positive, pointing out the play's flaws but excited about the powerful theatrics of the young Bond.

A play that took quite a while to open on Broadway was Lorraine Hansberry's **Les Blancs** (11-15-70, Longacre). Hansberry had died in 1965, and her husband, Robert Nemiroff, finished the ambitious drama from her early drafts. After postponing three times, the play finally opened to mostly negative reviews and closed in a month. The English-educated Tshembe Matoseh (James Earl Jones) returns to an African village to bury his father, who was the chief. There he is confronted by his teenage brother (Harold Scott) on the verge of alcoholism, an older brother (Earle Hyman) who is preparing to betray his people, and a seething tension between blacks and whites that is about to erupt into a civil war. Tshembe only wishes to return to London and his white wife, but he gets entangled in local affairs. While the play boasted some interesting characters (such as a cynical American journalist played by Cameron Mitchell) and thought-provoking ideas, much of *Les Blancs* was full of didactic talk and obvious imagery.

On November 16, negotiations between Actors' Equity and the League of Off-Broadway Theatres and Producers broke down, and a strike began over actors' and stage managers' salaries for off-Broadway productions. Seventeen shows (involving some 200 actors) struck for thirty-one days before a new minimum was agreed on. Thirteen of those productions reopened eventually, but the momentum was lost and few were able to run very long after the strike.

British playwright David Storey didn't get as much attention as he deserved when his quiet drama **Home** (11-17-70, Morosco) opened on Broadway because all the focus was on its stars, John Gielgud and Ralph Richardson, in a rare New York appearance. Into Jocelyn Herbert's stark garden setting (one critic compared it to an Edward Hopper painting) come two old gentlemen of the Empire, reserved and meticulous Harry (Gielgud) and chatty, personable Jack (Richardson), who discuss the weather, items in the newspaper, school days, the war, and other people in this seemingly upper-class retirement estate. But when they go off for a pre-luncheon stroll, two slovenly, lower-class women (Mona Washbourne and Dandy Nichols) enter complaining and joking, and we realize that this is some sort of state-run home. The foursome meet, resulting in hilarious class discrepancies, and go off together. But in the second act an obviously retarded adult (Graham Weston) enters, and the locale now defines itself as a mental institution. The foursome reenter, and soon we see that the genteel and chummy exteriors of the quartet disguise deep emotional scars. The performances, under Lindsay Anderson's direction, were remarkable all around. The women were callously funny, Richardson was a delicious dandy, and Gielgud's restrained and tormented Harry was a brilliant piece of subtlety. At one point, as Washbourne derides him and exposes his grimy past, Gielgud with perfect manners hides his grief, and only a lone tear streaking down his cheek gives his tormented soul away. As expected, critics concentrated on the actors and heaped superlatives on all five. Some praised the play ("the most extraordinary piece of theatre in years"), but others were not impressed ("like Beckett without the anguished poetry, like Pinter without the tension"). The play did receive the Drama Critics Circle Award, and Guernsey begrudgingly named it one of the *Best Plays*. The limited eight-week engagement was a highlight of the season and sold very well.

A German ensemble from Munich called Die Brücke (The Bridge) opened a two-play repertory in German at the Barbizon Plaza on November 17. The Molière-von Kleist *Amphitryon* led the one-week engagement, followed by a program consisting of Tankred Dorst's *The Curve* and Brecht's *The Wedding Feast*.

A harmless little comedy by Mel Arrighi called **The Castro Complex** (11-18-70, Stairway) opened the next night in the basement space of the Paramount Hotel that had gone by various names over the years, now called the Stairway. New Yorker Betsy Kress (Marian Hailey) has this thing about Fidel Castro, so much so that she cannot make love to her straitlaced Republican fiancé, Hadley (Terry Kiser), unless he dresses up like the revolutionary, complete with false beard and cigar. Hadley argues, "I don't think this makes for a very healthy relationship," and suggests Betsy consider therapy. Then a true revolutionary, Paco Montoya (Raul Julia), bursts into the attic apartment and seeks asylum from the CIA. Of course Betsy is immediately drawn to Paco, and Hadley gives up on her until the genial Paco, who knows Castro personally, disillusions her about the Cuban hero. The mild sex farce received mostly pans and closed in a week.

A limited engagement at the Public, with the self-descriptive title **Jack MacGowran in the Works of Samuel Beckett**, (11-19-70, Newman),

was a critical hit for sixty-seven performances. The Irish actor, long considered the definitive interpreter of Beckett, performed selections from the absurdist author's novels, poems, and plays. Alan Schneider directed the one-man show. Ming Cho Lee's stark setting, consisting of a rock and a mesmerizing floor pattern (one critic called it a "swirling limbo"), was also commended.

Broadway's first one-night disaster of the season was John Grissmer's **The Candyapple** (11-23-70, Edison), a lame comedy dismissed as "pathetic," "witless," and "incredibly clumsy and tiresome." On the night before Frank McGrath (Ray Edelstein) is to marry, his brother Larry (Arlen Dean Snyder), a Roman Catholic priest who will perform the ceremony, arrives on a motorcycle with his mistress, Connie Antonelli (Pat Garrett). Larry has cast off his religion and gone secular, and everyone fears how the strong-willed father (John Beals) will react to the news. But it turns out Father has always disliked the Catholic faith ("the candyapple of all regions") and is happy for Larry.

Playwright Steven Tesich, who would be called promising for many years and never quite fulfill the hopes critics held for him, made his debut at the American Place with **The Carpenters** (12-10-70, St. Clements Church), a family drama that was "inescapably a parable, that most annoying of all literary forms." An inept father (Vincent Gardenia) tries to keep his literally crumbling household together by listening to tape recordings of past times when the family was happy. But his wife (Alice Drummond) has stopped caring about anything but preparing dinner, while their son Mark (Glenn Walken) toys with ways of killing off his father. The dim-witted younger son Waldo (John Korkes), who describes himself as a "hard-core retard," dreams of escaping to Oregon where he can frolic with nature, and the college-dropout daughter (Laura Esterman) drifts into a pseudo-erotic affair with her father and brothers. The symbolic drama caused little excitement, but several were anxious to see what would become of Tesich.

Presented under the Limited Broadway Agreement, Robert M. Lane's **Foreplay** (12-11-70, Bijou) was an inept drama that inspired gossip. According to the word on the Street, an actor had refused to accept a leading role in it because of its tasteless nude homosexual love scene. The plot concerned a married man who admits his homosexuality, leaves his wife, and faces a challenging new lifestyle. Aisle-sitters called it "shoddy stuff . . . badly written and much given to moralizing." Limited or not, the play was gone in a month.

For the past several seasons Neil Simon had brought a comic gift to Broadway each December. This season, for the first time, Broadway looked askance at the gift, for **The Gingerbread Lady** (12-13-70, Plymouth) was "his first determinedly serious play." The Simon laughs were still there in abundance, but the pain was closer to the surface than holiday theatregoers really wanted. Evy Meara (Maureen Stapleton), an over-the-hill singer and chronic alcoholic, returns to her apartment after ten weeks of drying out at a sanitarium and tries to get a new start in life with the help of her friends Toby (Betsy von Furstenberg), a vain fashion plate posing as a housewife, and Jimmy (Michael Lombard), a middle-aged homosexual actor. Evy's seventeen-year-old daughter, Polly (Ayn Ruyman), arrives with the news that she is going to try living with her mother instead of her father, Evy's ex-husband, and the singer reluctantly agrees. Then Evy's ex-lover Lou (Charles Siebert), a musician who dumped Evy for a younger woman, arrives and wants to pick up where they left off, but Evy, gaining strength from her friends, sends him packing with "what I need now is a relative, not a relationship." Her new life with Polly seems to be working out, but when Jimmy is fired from his first Broadway job and Toby's husband leaves her, Evy gets so upset she starts drinking again. She goes back to Lou ("he plays requests, I was lonesome"), who gives her a black eye for insulting him and breaking his guitar. Returning the next day, friends and daughter rally around Evy, and together they face their uncertain future with comic courage, Evy telling Polly, "When I grow up, I want to be just like you." Structurally and in terms of character development, *The Gingerbread Lady* was vintage playwriting (Jimmy's account of how he got fired was both hysterical and humiliating), but audiences and some critics were uncomfortable with the issues of alcoholism and physical abuse in a Neil Simon play. Critics were mixed in their reaction, one stating that Simon's "characteristic wit and humor are at their brilliant best, and his serious story of lost misfits can often be genuinely and deeply touching," but another noting that "what is written is not serious but earnest." Yet they all lauded Stapleton's penetrating performance; one commentator wrote, "The spectacle of Miss Stapleton tossing a steady stream of Simon witticisms as if she were making each one up as it comes along is too marvelous to be missed." Stapleton won the Tony

Award, but the play ran a disappointing five months, the shortest run yet for a Simon play.

Many troupes off-off Broadway continued to explore the "tribal ritual" aspects of theatre. One of the most recognized of them, Richard Schechner's Performance Group, brought their **Commune** (12-17-70, Performance Garage) to an off-Broadway venue for a four-month run. Patrons were asked to remove their shoes upon entering the space, and all the footwear was collected in a giant heap representing the communal utopia. (Gathering the shoes afterwards was somewhat less an experience in harmony.) The show itself was a series of improvisations on a wide variety of themes, some topical (such as the Tate–LaBianca murders) and others more universal. But such tribal doings were losing their uniqueness. One critic remarked, *"Commune* was a not-even-more-communal rehash of *Dionysus in '69."*

French playwright Marguerite Duras saw her play **A Place Without Doors** (12-22-70, Stairway) produced in both French and English in New York this season. A Barbara Bray translation was presented for a month under the Limited Broadway Agreement. Pierre Lannes (Richard A. Dysart) and his wife, Claire (Mildred Dunnock), have murdered their housekeeper and are being questioned by an authority figure (Alvin Epstein). Although based on an actual murder in France four years earlier, the drama concentrated on lengthy stream-of-consciousness soliloquies by the two prisoners. While some critics admired the acting (Dysart in particular), the play was dismissed as "shallow and pretentious." A French version, produced by Le Tréteau de Paris under its original title *L'Amante anglaise*, opened at the Barbizon Plaza on April 14 and ran two weeks.

The season's second *Hamlet*, a touring import from England that played eight performances beginning on December 26 at Hunter College, was directed by Jonathan Miller with a cast of Oxford and Cambridge students. Unlike the Roundabout's all-male version, actresses were used for the female roles. Hugh Thomas played Hamlet.

Actress Shelley Winters turned playwright with a program of three playlets called **One Night Stands of a Noisy Passenger** (12-30-70, Actors' Playhouse), which barely managed not to become a one-night stand itself. The "foolish and vulgar affair," commentators decided, was more like "an evening of audition material," but some excellent young actors were seen, especially Sally Kirkland as a nutty actress and Robert De Niro as a drugged-out kid. In less than a week the talented cast was available for other projects.

On January 4, Broadway theatres officially changed the evening curtain time from 8:30 to 7:30. Richard Barr, representing the League of New York Theatres, explained to the media that the earlier time was agreed on "to reduce the time span between the end of the business day and the start of performances, to allow our audiences to get home an hour earlier." Some restaurants and group sales agents balked that the early curtain time hurt their business, but most went along with the change without complaint. Implied in the decision was the fact that the Broadway district was not a very safe place late at night, and the sooner patrons got out of there the better.

January was filled with classic revivals both on and off the Street. Dino DeFilippi's "reconceived" production of *Macbeth* on January 4 at the Mercer-O'Casey presented the tragedy as a fantasy all taking place in Macbeth's brain. The Scottish thane viewed scenes he was not in, and sometimes a double portrayed him in other scenes so that he could continue his observations. The gimmicky show was criticized for its lack of real characters and for its poor acting, but it found an audience for 132 performances. Lincoln Center celebrated John Millington Synge's centennial by presenting his *The Playboy of the Western World* on January 7 in the Vivian Beaumont, and just as many endorsed the revival as dismissed it. David Birney was merely competent as Christy, but Martha Henry was a poignant Pegeen, and Frances Sternhagen pleased many with her Widow Quin.

As was too often the case at the Negro Ensemble Company, the acting far outshone the playwriting in a pair of one-acts called **Perry's Mission** and **Rosalee Pritchertt** (1-12-71, St. Marks). Clarence Young III's *Perry's Mission* illustrated racial tensions that erupt in a bar frequented by white and black patrons. Carlton and Barbara Molette's *Rosalee Pritchett* showed an affluent black family in a southern city trying to ignore the race riots going on outside their house. What mattered were the accomplished performances by such talents as Adolph Caesar, Esther Rolle, Arthur French, Clarice Taylor, and Frances Foster.

One of the surprises of the season was the popularity of two Ibsen revivals in repertory starring Claire Bloom that producer Hillard Elkins brought to Broadway. *A Doll's House*, opening on January 13 at the Playhouse, was greeted with raves, not only for Bloom but for the production (directed by Patrick Garland), the lively new translation by Christopher Hampton, and the play itself, which had not been seen on Broadway

since 1937. Donald Madden was applauded for his exacting Torvald. The expert scenery, lighting, and costumes by John Bury were also extolled. The limited run of 111 performances quickly sold out. Critics were less pleased with Bloom's *Hedda Gabler* when it was added to the Ibsen repertory on February 17. Where her transformation in *A Doll's House* was luminous, she was considered too detached and mannered as Hedda Tesman. Again Garland directed, and again Bloom got strong support from Madden as the self-destructive Lovborg. The revival was given fifty-six showings before the two-play repertory closed on June 19.

Shakespeare enthusiasts who found the Roundabout's all-male *Hamlet* unsatisfying had two chances to see the seventy-two-year-old actress Judith Anderson play the melancholy Dane at Carnegie Hall on January 14 and 15. Anderson's was the only gender switch in the William Ball production; Ophelia and Gertrude were still played by women. There was some reminiscing about Sarah Bernhardt's famous tour as Hamlet, but this revival, stopping in New York on its cross-country tour, was a curiosity at best.

On January 20, the finest revival of the season (for several, the most adventurous Shakespeare production seen in New York in many a year) was the Royal Shakespeare Company's *A Midsummer Night's Dream* directed by Peter Brook at the Billy Rose. Breaking with every known tradition, this production of the pastoral comedy was performed in a stark white box without a tree or bush in sight. Sally Jacobs's scenery and costumes consisted of splashes of color that blazed against the white canvas; actors tumbled from above on trapezes or rose from the ground on feathery nests. Even the costumes were white with streaks of tie-dyed color filtering throughout. Some critics found the circus-like production a little thick with gimmicks, but most were thrilled with Brook's expansive take on the classic. Jack Kroll in *Newsweek* summed up the experience accurately when he noted, "The upshot of all this is a production that obliterates all categories of traditional and avant-garde to reach the radical conservatism of sheer life." The David Merrick–sponsored event played a merry sixty-two performances on Broadway, added sixteen more at the Brooklyn Academy of Music, and then set off on a cross-country tour.

The Roundabout's revival of Chekhov's *Uncle Vanya* on January 24 was deemed successful enough that the company moved it to the Cherry Lane for an additional week after its scheduled run. Gene Feist adapted and directed, Sterling

Jensen essayed Vanya, and Winston May was Dr. Astrov. The production tallied fifty performances, the longest Roundabout run of the season.

Ed Bullins offered another entry in his proposed twenty-play cycle about black Americans with **In New England Winter** (1-26-71, Henry Street Playhouse). This angry and mysterious play shifted locales back and forth from a city apartment in 1960 to a house in a snowbound New England town in 1955. In the city a gang of frustrated black youths plan a robbery, while in the country one of the gang is seen struggling with a half-mad wife and his forbidding in-laws. As usual Bullins found humor in the most dire situations, but the play was too murky for most and was shown for only a week.

Abe Burrows had enjoyed so much success with his previous adaptations of French farces that the utter failure of his **Four on a Garden** (1-30-71, Broadhurst) left audiences aghast. The program's four short plays were based on some one-acts by Pierre Barillet and Jean-Pierre Gredy, who had provided Burrows with fodder for his *Cactus Flower* (12-8-65) and *Forty Carats* (12-26-68). But the production experienced so much trouble on the road that Renee Taylor and Joseph Bologna were brought in for rewrites. After several delays, the comedy opened—so altered that the French authors insisted their names be removed from the new work. Sid Caesar and Carol Channing (in a rare non-musical performance) were the designated stars who tried to save the playlets, each one with a surprise ending that surprised no one. In one, Caesar played a man who preys on young girls and discovers at the last moment that his latest intended is his own daughter. In another, Channing was a society lady who decides to bed down with the man painting her lover's apartment. In the third, they played former lovers who had killed her husband and are now, years later, getting together again. The evening ended with the stars as a couple of seventy-year-olds who meet at the Roseland dance hall and come back to his apartment for a night of whoopee, finding only the energy to discuss their many ailments. A Manhattan apartment looking out onto a garden was the unifying element of the quartet, but no one was fooled into thinking this was another *Plaza Suite*. The unanimous pans ranged from "slender entertainment" to "a vacancy" to "a bomb," and while the critics appreciated the clowning efforts of the two stars, they found the task hopeless. The comedy struggled on for nearly two months.

Another of the season's highly respected revivals was the successful off-Broadway return of Beckett's *Waiting for Godot* (4-19-56) at the Sheridan Square on February 3 directed by the busy Alan Schneider. Critics thought it faithful but not slavish to the original New York production and found Henderson Forsythe's Vladimir powerful enough to rise above the memory of Bert Lahr in the role. They were less impressed with Paul B. Price's Estragon, but the solid production caught on and ran eight months. Lincoln Center's off-Broadway season began late with a revival of Harold Pinter's *The Birthday Party* (10-3-67) on February 5 in the Forum. It was roundly rejected. Jules Irving directed the American cast, in which only Betty Field as the slovenly landlady Meg shone. On February 9, last season's Pinter double bill of *Landscape* and *Silence* was added to the Forum schedule and played in repertory with *The Birthday Party* for six more performances.

An entry that found success off Broadway but fared less well when it later transferred to Broadway was **The Trial of the Catonsville Nine** (2-7-71, Good Shepherd Faith Church). *Time's* T. E. Kalem called it "a play in name only . . . [that] falls within the area of theatre of fact." Indeed, the script was an edited transcript of the trial of Revs. Philip and Daniel Berrigan, who, with seven others, entered the Selective Service office in Catonsville, Maryland, in 1968, removed draft records, and burned them in the parking lot to protest the war in Vietnam. Much of the text was by Daniel, a published poet, and it was given some dramatic shape by playwright Saul Levitt, who had written *The Andersonville Trial* (12-29-59). While there was no suspense or surprises to be found (everyone recalled that the nine had been found guilty), the play had a rational elegance that many found quite moving. Each defendant reads his prepared statement to the jury, and each is persuasive without being oppressive. Ed Flanders was a riveting Daniel, and Sam Waterston was quite affecting as Thomas Lewis, an artist who teaches in the Baltimore ghetto. Critics admired the docudrama more than they recommended it, but the subject was of great concern, and the piece ran for 130 performances before the producers closed it, recast some of the roles, and reopened it at the Lyceum on June 2. Either the momentum must have gone or summer audiences were not as susceptible to the piece, for it closed after twenty-nine performances.

Rochelle Owens, a distinctive voice in radical 1960s theatre, was already becoming somewhat passé, and her **Istanbul** (2-8-71, Actors' Playhouse) only ran a week. The ritualistic play was ostensibly about the escapades, mostly sexual, of European knights in Constantinople during the

Crusades, but modern viewpoints and overt crudities were presented for those who didn't care much for history.

Arguably the best American comedy of the season was John Guare's **The House of Blue Leaves** (2-10-71, Truck and Warehouse), a dark farce that managed to be outrageously scatterbrained and still structurally compact. It is October 4, 1965, and Pope Paul is arriving in New York to say mass in Yankee Stadium. Into the Queens apartment of zookeeper and frustrated songwriter Artie Shaughnessy (Harold Gould) comes his mistress, Bunny Flingus (Anne Meara), excited about the Pope's visit and trying to get Artie to come and watch as his motorcade passes through Queens on its way from J F K Airport. Artie is not interested in seeing the Pope and only complains about his poor showing at the El Dorado Bar Amateur Night the previous evening, where no one liked his songs. Bunny wants the Pope's blessing, hoping Artie will leave his sickly, demented wife, Bananas (Katherine Helmond), and run off with her to Hollywood, where his old chum Billy Einhorn, a big-time producer, will hire Artie to write songs for the movies. Bunny convinces Artie to call Billy on the phone, and the producer seems encouraging, but then events go haywire. Artie's son, Ronny (William Atherton), AWOL from the army, breaks into the apartment with plans to blow up the Pope, a trio of frustrated nuns who lost their spot on the curb come in looking for a television set, and Billy's hard-of-hearing starlet girlfriend, Corrina Stroller (Margaret Linn), stops by on her way to an ear operation in Australia. The MPs come looking for Ronny, who explodes the bomb, killing Corrina and two of the nuns. Billy (Frank Converse) arrives to collect Corrina's body, tells Artie he must stay in Queens, where he serves as inspiration for Billy's films, and the producer goes back to Hollywood with Bunny. Artie, left alone with the childlike Bananas, strangles her to death and is

last seen plugging his songs at another amateur night. The play's odd mixture of comedy and tragedy should not have worked, but Guare found the right level of farcical writing that made the pathetic and frustrated characters very endearing. He also wrote some of the sharpest comic dialogue and funny character situations witnessed in New York all season. Bunny, who admits, "I'm a rotten lay and I know it," will sleep with Artie anytime he wants, but she refuses to cook for him until after they are married. The surviving nun proclaims she used to be a bride of Christ but has now decided to become a "young divorcee." And Ronny's monologue about how he hoped to play Huckleberry Finn in Hollywood was top-notch writing. Yet critics were mixed in their reaction, many labeling Guare more promising than accomplished. The production itself was not very strong, and it would not be until the acclaimed 1986 revival that the play would get the recognition it deserved. All the same, the original ran off Broadway for 337 performances, won an Obie and a New York Drama Critics Award, and soon became a popular choice in regional and educational theatres.

The Public had a surprise hit with Robert Montgomery's **Subject to Fits** (2-14-71, Anspacher), an imaginative adaptation that was not so much a dramatization of Dostoevsky's novel *The Idiot* but a "response" to it. The epileptic Prince Myshkin (Andy Robinson) declares that he is "subject to fits . . . whereas the rest of you are subject to life." The "rest" includes the murderous Rogozhin (Jason Miller), who loves and hates the idiot, the stammering Ganya Ivoglin (James DeMarse), and the beautiful Natasha (Sharon Laughlin), whose affections are torn among the three men. Several reviews were enthusiastic, and the A. J. Antoon production ran an admirable 127 performances.

Israel Horovitz, who had grabbed everyone's interest with his one-act *The Indian Wants the Bronx* (1-17-68), managed to draw all the major critics to Off Broadway to see his two-play program **Acrobats** and **Line** (2-15-71, Theatre de Lys). *Acrobats* was a slight curtain raiser about a husband-and-wife acrobatic team who have a marital squabble during a performance. *Line* was much more intriguing and garnered some encouraging notices. Five people wait on line for an unspecified event. In their manipulating, cheating, and physical maneuvers to be the first in line, they become an allegory for the American obsession with success. Horovitz was aided by James Hammerstein's tight direction and five gifted players: John Randolph, John Cazale, Richard Dreyfuss, Ann Wedgeworth, and Barnard Hughes. The double bill ran only a month, but *Line* would become something of a cult favorite, being repeated off-off Broadway on an irregular basis for the rest of the century.

Another surprisingly popular revival was Molière's *The School for Wives* in a pungent new verse translation by Richard Wilbur that opened at the Lyceum on February 16. Except for Bronson Howard's adaptation entitled *Wives* in 1879, this was the play's first English version on Broadway. Stephen Porter directed an expert cast headed by Brian Bedford, who won a Tony Award for his scheming Arnolphe, and reviews were uniformly enthusiastic. The sprightly comedy ran for 120 performances, spurred new interest in the neglected script, and encouraged Wilbur to do further translations of Molière's plays.

Slag (2-21-71, Public: Anspacher) was an allegorical play that introduced New Yorkers to David Hare, a young British playwright who would become very well known in future decades. In a dying private school for girls, three militant and feminist teachers (Roberta Maxwell, Margo Ann Berdeshevsky, and Kathryn Walker) hold on to their ideals and remain in the empty school, a symbol of Britain's decay and stubbornness. The production ran its scheduled thirty-two showings but created little excitement. It was followed at the Public by one of the most acclaimed attractions of the season, Siobhan McKenna's one-woman show called **Here Are Ladies** (2-22-71, Newman). McKenna performed women from the works of twentieth-century Irish writers, from Yeats to Shaw to Beckett, ending the evening with her sterling interpretation of Molly Bloom's stream-of-consciousness soliloquy that concludes James Joyce's *Ulysses*. Critics and awards committees handed McKenna bouquets of adulation, and the program was presented sixty-seven times. There were also compliments for Sean Kenny, who directed her and designed the Stonehenge-like setting, which included a clothes tree filled with props and costume pieces.

The American Place's disappointing season continued to disappoint with George Tabori's anti-war drama **Pinkville** (2-22-71, St. Clements Church). The angry and simple-minded play showed how the U.S. Army took pink-cheeked boys and systematically turned them into savage fighting machines let loose in the jungles of Vietnam. Critics could find little to endorse in the enterprise, despite such fine actors as James Tolkan, Raul Julia, and Michael Douglas in the cast.

A much better play on a similar theme would arrive at the Public at the end of the season, and *Pinkville* would be quickly forgotten.

Heathcote Williams's **AC/DC** (2-23-71, BAM) had been highly esteemed at the Royal Court in London, but New York critics were not so impressed with the American-Canadian mounting that the Chelsea Theatre Center sponsored for twenty-eight performances. The frenetic production used five actors and twenty television screens to tell the story of Maurice (Edward Zang), a repairman in a pinball arcade, and his roommate/lover Perowne (Stefan Gierasch), who meet up with three Americans for a night of electronics and sex. The anti-McLuhan piece ended with Sadie (Susan Batson) destroying Maurice's apartment and seemingly drilling a hole in Perowne's head to enable him to assimilate information in the modern way.

Paul Zindel could not capture the off-Broadway success of his *The Effect of Gamma Rays on Man-in-the-Moon Marigolds* of last season when his dark comedy **And Miss Reardon Drinks a Little** (2-25-71, Morosco) opened on Broadway, but he certainly knew how to write juicy roles for women, and the actresses had a field day with the script. Deserted by their father when they were children, the three Reardon sisters have been raised in a strong female environment lorded over by a domineering mother (not unlike the one in *Marigolds*) who has recently died. The frail and mentally unstable Anna (Julie Harris) teaches high school but has been accused of sexually assaulting a student and is on a leave of absence. The wisecracking Catherine (Estelle Parsons) teaches at the same school and blames the deteriorating New York public education system for everything. Ceil (Nancy Marchand) is the only sister to wed (she stole Catherine's boyfriend) and is now a superintendent in the school system and must consider having Anna committed. Into this pack of sibling wolves comes daffy Fleur ("just think of flower") Stein (Rae Allen) who is trying to climb the administrative ladder and offers to clear up the scandal if Anna is committed. After some wild accusations on the part of all three sisters, Ceil acts as cruelly as her mother would have and announces that Anna will be sent away. Aside from a few gunshots (which turn out to be blanks), there was little action in the play, but Zindel kept the evening lively with Catherine's sarcasm, Ceil's icy triumphs, and Anna's pathetic ravings. While critics called it "an oddly unrealized piece of work" and a "serious disappointment," the actresses were handed bouquets. Allen won a Tony Award, but Harris's waif-like trembling, Marchand's steel demeanor, and Parsons's boozy bluntness were all exceptional. The play ran only three months but was popular with regional and educational theatres for several years.

The Negro Ensemble's finest offering of the season was Trinidad poet Derek Walcott's fascinating fantasy **The Dream on Monkey Mountain** (3-9-71, St. Marks), which had previously been seen in Trinidad, in Los Angeles, and at the O'Neill Playwrights Conference. On a West Indies isle, the poor charcoal peddler Makak (Roscoe Lee Browne) has been thrown into jail for disturbing the peace (he tore up a bar while yelling that God is black). There, he has a strange and beguiling dream that utilizes the jailer and the felons surrounding him. In his dream, Makak travels to Africa, where he has many wives and, at every full moon, a beautiful white woman as his mistress. But he learns that she is just a symbol of his people's obsession to become white, so he beheads her and frees his race from slavery. Walcott's storytelling was rich with imagery and ritual; the Don Quixote–like Makak even had his Sancho Panza in the form of the crippled Moustique (Antonio Fargas). Critical response was very positive, but the play ran only forty-eight performances; it became somewhat popular later, after Walcott won the 1992 Nobel Prize.

The British import **Abelard & Heloise** (3-10-71, Brooks Atkinson) was deemed a classy production of a classic love story but, despite a rather graphic nude scene, it never really caught fire. Ronald Millar dramatized the tale of the young Heloise (Diana Rigg), who falls in love with her celibate tutor, Abelard (Keith Michell), has a child by him, and secretly marries him. Found out by a jealous uncle, Abelard is emasculated, and Heloise is sent to a nunnery. The touching coda showed the aged Abelard handing over the religious community he founded to Heloise, now an abbess. Critics were cautious in their acceptance, several of them comparing it to the contemporary novella *Love Story* that was on the best-seller list. Rigg and Michell got several nods, and many felt their softly lit, lyrical nude scene was the most tasteful yet seen on a stage. But the play was no *Love Story* at the box office, and it struggled on for fifty-three performances.

Ibsen was represented for a third time on Broadway this season with the Lincoln Center revival of *An Enemy of the People* on March 11 in the Vivian Beaumont, using Arthur Miller's 1950 adaptation. Jules Irving directed, and the solid production was greeted with respectful if unenthusiastic reviews. Stephen Elliott's Dr. Stockmann was commended, and Philip Bosco, as was often the case, shone in a supporting role, this time as the mayor, Peter Stockmann. While most acknowledged the power of the play, some felt Miller's version was a bit dated and too preachy in spots.

While his Ibsen translations were being presented on Broadway, the young English playwright Christopher Hampton saw his London comedy **The Philanthropist** (3-15-71, Ethel Barrymore) open on the Street as well. But, aside from Alec McCowen's mesmerizing performance, critics were not overwhelmed with the play. Two university professors, Philip (McCowen) and Donald (Ed Zimmermann), listen to a student read his play aloud and question the validity of the suicidal ending. So the student takes out a gun and demonstrates, accidentally killing himself. A few days later Philip is having a dinner party where Braham (Victor Spinetti), an obnoxious author, is holding court and flirting with Philip's fiancée, Celia (Jane Asher). When the party breaks up, Philip is left with the sluttish Armaminta (Penelope Wilton), who offers to sleep with him; he agrees because he "didn't want to hurt her feelings." The next day Celia arrives, finds Armaminta in the apartment, and tells Philip she has decided to break off their engagement. It is not because of Philip's infidelity (she has spent the night with Braham and tells Philip so) but because he is too polite and too willing to please; he is an emotional philanthropist. She leaves him; the lonely Philip considers suicide, then decides to have a cigarette instead. Hampton's dialogue was ripe with wit and pithy observations, sometimes painfully so, and he created a fascinating character in Philip: a reticent philologist who is content to hear people say anything because he loves the mystery of words. McCowen played Philip as a fine-tuned instrument; Kalem noted, "At one moment he is the bemused absent-minded professor, at another the twinkling champion of verbal pingpong, and at still another, an anguished human with a parched heart." Audiences got to see the cunning performance seventy-two times.

Oliver Hailey's brittle comedy **Father's Day** (3-16-71, John Golden) was cited by many as an example of the monopolist power of the *New York Times*. Clive Barnes's review of the show was so negative that producers Joseph Kipness and Lawrence Kasha closed the play immediately after the first performance. Some of the other papers were kinder, but the die seemed to be cast.

After the closing, reviews from the weeklies came in, and some were outright raves. The producers admitted they had been too hasty in their decision, but most commentators blamed the *Times*. In an affluent Upper East Side apartment building three divorcées (Brenda Vaccaro, Jennifer Salt, and Marian Seldes) gather to dish about men, sex, and their bitter memories. On Father's Day the ex-husbands (Ken Kercheval, Donald Moffat, and Biff McGuire) arrive. A dignified demeanor is maintained for a while, but the encounter soon dissolves into emotional revelations and saddened resignation. The plot was negligible, but Hailey's dialogue crackled with life, and there was some top-notch acting to be found; Seldes was most often cited by the critics. There were compliments also for Jo Mielziner's set, three terraces of an ugly, forbidding high-rise.

Al Fann's **King Heroin** (3-17-71, St. Philip's Community Theatre), an off-off Broadway entry that attracted some attention, ran a month in Harlem. The drama about drug abuse was inspired by recent headlines, specifically the death of Walter Vandermeer, a twelve-year-old student who died from an overdose.

The most successful off-Broadway revival of the season was *One Flew Over the Cuckoo's Nest* (11-13-63) on March 23 at the Mercer-Hansberry. Dale Wasserman's dramatization of the popular Ken Kesey novel had only managed eighty-two performances in 1963 despite the presence of Kirk Douglas as the vivacious McMurphy. Wasserman did a few rewrites, Lee D. Sankowich directed, and, with William Devane as McMurphy, the production ran an astounding 1,025 performances. It was a competent production, but much of the revival's success could be attributed to the change in attitude in America over the past eight years. The character of McMurphy had risen from unconventional curiosity to cult hero. It was the popularity of this revival that prompted the 1975 award-winning film version.

The next night, Off Broadway had another huge hit, although no one could call **The Proposition** (3-24-71, Gramercy Arts) a true play. Six actors improvised comic situations entirely from suggestions from the audience each night. It was nothing new for nightclubs and comedy clubs, but off-Broadway audiences embraced it for 1,109 performances.

The same evening, the National Theatre of Japan gave its first of three performances of various Noh and Kyogen plays in Carnegie Hall. On the bill were *Kirokuda, Boshibari, Shidohogaku, Funa-Benkei, Aoi-No-Ue*, and *Sumidagawa*.

Scenes From American Life (3-25-71, Forum), A. R. Gurney, Jr.'s first full-length comedy, was as promising as his previous one-acts, though still somewhat unsatisfying. The evening was comprised of eight actors playing a multitude of characters in thirty-six sketches that covered various aspects of Americana over the decades, even going into the future to show an authoritarian 1980s. The show was loosely structured with no chronological logic to it, the result being a panorama of hypocritical adults and frustrated youths that was quite potent at times. A mother calling her son at college to ask where he keeps his marijuana, a WASP blackballing his Jewish friend from a country club, eager teens praying to God for sex, and other sequences offered glimpses into the Gurney that would later emerge. Critics applauded Lincoln Center for presenting a new American play (all of the other offerings in the Forum were foreign revivals) and found Gurney's comedy admirable, if flawed.

Edward Albee's new play, **All Over** (3-28-71, Martin Beck), was greeted with a wide range of opinions, from "his quietest drama" to "a bore." A famous man lies dying in his enormous house, the press is stationed outside for the latest developments, and in an anteroom the family is gathered to wait for the end. The man's wife of fifty years (Jessica Tandy) is there with her adulterous daughter (Madeleine Sherwood) and pathetic son (James Ray), both of whom she despises. The wife feels much more kinship with the man's mistress of the past twenty years (Colleen Dewhurst) and the man's best friend (George Voskovec). While they wait the group reminisces, argues, and laments until the doctor comes out to tell them that it is "all over." (The nurse who stays with them was played by Betty Field in her last stage performance.) With such a powerhouse cast sparks were expected to fly, but Albee's approach was understated, and John Gielgud directed in a quiet, stagnant style that recalled his own vehicle *Home*. The drama lasted barely a month.

The next night English playwright Alan Ayckbourn made his Broadway debut with **How the Other Half Loves** (3-29-71, Royale), but it was a miscalculated venture. Ayckbourn, who would later be dubbed the British Neil Simon, wrote contemporary comedies of manners. But it was felt the manners he chronicled were too British for American audiences, so he was persuaded by New York producers to rewrite his comedy, setting it in suburban America. Unfortunately, the satire on the different classes made no sense in the U.S.A., with characters played by Phil Silvers and Sandy Dennis reading the *New York Times*. The farce deals with three couples, the husbands all working for the same firm. One husband is having an affair with another's wife. When they are both caught coming home late, they use a visit to the third couple as an excuse. The farce proceeds in customary fashion, except Ayckbourn complicates the complications by having all the action of two households take place in one living room. It was an obvious gimmick, but one with myriad possibilities, and Ayckbourn developed them all. A highlight of the evening was a hilarious scene with two different households dining at the same table. The American cast, which also included Richard Mulligan, Bernice Massi, Jeanne Hepple, and Tom Aldredge, was applauded for its farceur abilities, but the play was greeted with mixed to negative reviews. All the same, it ran three months and would often be produced in this country, usually in the correct English setting.

William Wellington MacKey's **Behold! Cometh the Vanderkellans** (3-31-71, Theatre de Lys) sounded like a comedy, but audiences were subjected to a rather messy treatise on Truth. Dr. Vanderkellan (Graham Brown), the president of a southern black college, is dealing with revolt on two fronts: the students are rioting on campus, and at home, his college-age children (Roxie Roker and Carl Byrd) return for Easter break and rebel against the respectable "Negro" role the father has raised them to conform to. To make matters worse, he has been fired by the governor and is trying to keep the news from his wife (Frances Foster). But the children insist on the truth coming out, and come out it did for twenty-three performances.

A curiosity at the Public was the two-week visit by Chicago's Organic Theatre Company in an improvisational version of Voltaire's *Candide* beginning on April 14 in the South Hall. While some enjoyed the six-actor approach that updated Candide's adventures into a modern context, others found it a "sophomoric romp" and pointed out that Voltaire's original contained much stronger satire. The next attraction at the Public, a pair of one-acts under the title **Underground** (4-18-71, Other Stage), was not much of an improvement. Both plays, Edgar White's *The Life and Times of J. Walter Smintheus* and Walter Jones's *Jazznite*, were about an educated and sophisticated African American (Dennis Tate) confronted by his lowly past. Jones's piece was the more intriguing, a plotless, free-flowing cantata about an art professor (Sam Singleton) who returns to the ghetto of

his youth and, facing his deserted, drugged sister and her six children, must face himself.

The season of revivals continued on April 21 at the Promenade with O'Neill's *Long Day's Journey into Night* (11-7-56), which stayed for 121 showings. The press marveled at how the drama's power had not diminished over the years and sanctioned the new production with few criticisms. Of those who recalled the original José Quintero production, many felt Geraldine Fitzgerald's Mary Tyrone was even more moving than Florence Eldridge's had been; but most also agreed that Robert Ryan, while quite capable as James Tyrone, did not have the presence and faded-matinee-idol persona that Fredric March had exhibited. Stacy Keach and James Naughton played the Tyrone sons, Jamie and Edmund, and Arvin Brown directed with precision and care.

Paul Sills and his company of agile *Story Theatre* players added **Ovid's Metamorphoses** (4-22-71, Ambassador) to their repertory, and critics, on the whole, found it entertaining but not as charming as the earlier fairy tale program. Ten magical stories from mythology were presented in the unique "Story Theatre style" for thirty-five performances, but the first show was the one that kept drawing the crowds until the repertory closed on July 3.

Three more revivals opened within the week. The Roundabout's *She Stoops to Conquer* on April 25 was greeted with some interest; Strindberg's *Dance of Death* at the Ritz on April 28, with Rip Torn and Viveca Lindfors, was criticized for its huffing and puffing performances and survived on Broadway for only five performances; and Paul Shyre's adaptation of Sean O'Casey's multivolume autobiography entitled *Pictures in the Hallway* on April 29 closed the Lincoln Center season downstairs in the Forum. The last was part drama, part reading, with the actors confined to stools as they related the young O'Casey's development from a child to a radical activist. The adaptation had first been produced off Broadway in 1956.

The American Place ended its season with Sam Shepard's **Back Bog Beast Bait** (4-29-71, St. Clements Church), a drama set in a bayou about two hired men who must battle a mythical beast in the swamp. The "work-in-progress" was performed for subscribers only and not submitted for review.

The last opening-night closer of the season was Rod Parker's "sleazy satire" **And Whose Little Boy Are You?** (5-3-71, McAlpin Rooftop). A Vietnam vet (Richard Dreyfuss) returns home to find his common-law wife is pregnant. She says God is the father, so the vet marries her, then goes crazy, turning on wife and family. Seeing Dreyfuss for the second time this season, critics found him interesting but agreed that he overacted and needed the firm reins of a strong director. Dreyfuss's theatre appearances would rarely find success but, ironically, his film career would take off because of the very same excessive kind of performance.

Acclaimed poet Archibald MacLeish turned Stephen Vincent Benét's simple short story *The Devil and Daniel Webster* into the complex, multi-set play **Scratch** (5-6-71, St. James), which producer Stuart Ostrow booked into the large musical house. While a few aisle-sitters thought it had "moments of brilliance," and one cited Will Gere as the "most amusing Devil I have encountered," most denounced the talky, laborious work. Will MacKenzie played the New Hampshire farmer who makes a pact with Scratch, and Patrick Magee was Daniel Webster, who defends him in the didactic trial. Peter H. Hunt directed the large cast, John Conklin designed the elaborate sets, and Patricia Zipprodt did the regional costumes, none of which were needed after four performances.

Lincoln Center closed its season with Sophocles' *Antigone* on May 13 in a translation by Dudley Fitts and Robert Fitzgerald at the Vivian Beaumont. Reviews ranged from politely respectful to exemplary, most agreeing that Martha Henry was a skillful Antigone and Philip Bosco an inspiring Creon. If the revival of *Long Day's Journey into Night* had to contend with the ghost of the original, the off-Broadway revival of Harold Pinter's *The Homecoming* (1-5-67) on May 18 at the Bijou had to overcome very recent history, the acclaimed Royal Shakespeare Company production still fresh in everyone's mind from four years earlier. Comparisons were unavoidable, and the American cast was kindly saluted for its efforts but deemed inferior to the London ensemble.

The Public's most impressive offering of the season, David Rabe's **The Basic Training of Pavlo Hummel** (5-20-71, Newman), was called by the press "the first play to deal successfully with the Vietnam war and the contemporary U.S. Army." Hapless Pavlo Hummel (William Atherton) is one of life's losers. When he gets drunk, he tries to outrace a cop. He has few brains, no prospects, and a fate that can only be tragic. In basic training he is the slacker, the least likely to succeed and most likely to get beat up. He is

even a failure at suicide, trying to kill himself by taking 100 aspirins. The play follows Pavlo through his training to his assignment in Vietnam as a medic to his death in a fragging incident in Saigon. Rabe, a veteran of the Southeast Asian conflict, employed a large cast of characters in a telling series of episodes that contained humor as well as anger. Critical reaction was positive, even though many found the work "somewhat incoherent". The play ran 363 performances, and Rabe was considered the most promising of Papp's playwright discoveries.

The Negro Ensemble's weakest entry, John Scott's **Ride a Black Horse** (5-25-71, St. Marks), closed out their season. Douglas Turner Ward directed the drama about a progressive black professor of sociology, Carl Blanks (Graham Brown), who acts as a mediator between some militants and the city hall administration; when he fails, his family deserts him, he loses his job, and the militants take revenge by killing him. The drama had "a hollow, second-hand ring" to it with false dialogue and a pretentiousness seen even in the playwright's program note, "Place: In the mind of the city and in the city of the mind."

The Broadway season ended not with a whimper but with a loud, in-your-face bang of a production called **Lenny** (5-26-71, Brooks Atkinson), an expressionistic, surrealistic play "based on the life and words of Lenny Bruce." Not everyone liked the bang, but it was loud enough that everyone took notice, and they continued to take notice for 453 performances. Julian Barry fashioned his script as a nightmare in which events from the controversial comedian's life were played out amidst his nightclub routines and hallucinations about American history and ideals. Tom O'Horgan directed the hyperactive production, and Robin Wagner designed the white-tiled setting (a giant bathroom to represent Bruce's toilet humor?) populated with characters dressed in Randy Barcelo's exaggerated costumes and giant puppets from the radical Bread and Puppet Theatre. The plot covered events such as Bruce's early performing days, his relationship with his mother (Erica Yohn), his association with drug-oriented musicians, his marriage with a stripper (Jane House), and his death from an overdose in 1966. But Barry also tried to make Bruce's tragic story the great American tragedy, and there wasn't enough noise to convince critics of that. The centerpiece of the festivities was Cliff Gorman's spellbinding performance as Lenny, handling both the multi-charactered monologues and the plot scenes with dynamic frenzy. Douglas Auchincloss wrote in *Time*, "Gorman dominates every scene—belting out the bitter monologues, batting back the foul-mouthed wisecracks, delivering dialects, imitations, sound effects—including a tour de force impersonation of a tape recorder on fast rewind." It was the role of Gorman's career, and he won a Tony Award for it.

The recession deepened across America, and it was noticeable on Broadway as the season ended. A year earlier, eighteen productions were playing on Broadway, and only two of them were giving away "twofer" discount coupons; as this season ended, twenty-four houses were lit, but thirteen of them were offering twofers.

1971–1972

Although the new Broadway season managed to match the previous one in total number of productions—fifty-six plays, musicals, and revivals—the continuing trend of fewer successful productions was unmistakable. At the season's end, the only new non-musical to be enjoying sellout crowds was Neil Simon's *The Prisoner of Second Avenue*. Three Broadway plays closed on opening night, and seven lasted less than a week. Much of the activity on Broadway came in the form of holdovers and musicals. This was the season that saw *Fiddler on the Roof* break the long-run record and also saw the advent of the eventual record-breaker *Grease*. Much of what Broadway had to boast of in the new-play line plays came from either London or Off Broadway. In fact, for the first time in its fifty-three-year history, half of the ten *Best Plays* choices came from Off Broadway.

Yet there was much excitement both on and off the Street, even if such excitement did not translate into box-office profits. Controversial plays abounded, and disturbing new playwrights were discussed. Producers and audience advocates argued about the role of the media in promoting plays, especially the use of "false and misleading" quotations in newspaper ads. Theatre owners quibbled over the starting times of shows. And nearly everybody had an opinion about what to do with the financially disastrous Theatre at Lincoln Center. But eventually the smoke cleared, and the luxury of hindsight has shown us there was indeed more smoke than fire. The much-discussed controversial plays, such as *Sticks and Bones* and *Where Has Tommy Flowers Gone?*, have fallen out of the repertory of American drama. Promising new playwrights, such as

Jason Miller, Romulus Linney, Michael Weller, and Richard Wesley, have failed to fulfill the promise accorded them. Producers cited the First and Fourteenth Amendments and continued to use quotes "creatively." David Merrick settled the curtain-time question by starting his shows at 8:00 P.M., and everyone else soon followed suit. An Ad Hoc Committee to Save Theatre at Lincoln Center was formed, but despite its impressive roster of names, no accord was reached, and Lincoln Center would not become a consistently productive theatre center for two more decades.

The 1971–1972 season off Broadway was one of transition. While the number of productions held from previous years, attendance dropped, prices rose (a $10 top was now usual), production costs rose (about $40,000 for a non-musical, according to *Variety*), and, many felt, the venue was losing its experimental identity. The casual audiences who had supported Off Broadway as a looser, more adventurous form of theatregoing were finding it difficult to distinguish the intimate little theatres from Broadway. And if a show of quality did appear, it seemed to pick up and go uptown before you had a chance to check it out.

None of the above speaks to the quality of the theatre off Broadway this season, and the quality was notable. Several new playwrights provided memorable offerings, and there were new works by such established authors as Tom Stoppard, Athol Fugard, Jean Genet, and Tennessee Williams. Joseph Papp's Public Theatre and New York Shakespeare Festival each had outstanding seasons, both venues sending works to Broadway and winning all the major awards. And while there were few lasting works by black playwrights, they were writing more and better offerings. Add to this a handful of distinguished holdovers that ran far into the season, and things off Broadway were not so bleak.

Lincoln Center experienced a shaky season both upstairs in the Vivian Beaumont and downstairs at the Forum. Just after the 1970–1971 season closed, it presented the American premiere of Dürrenmatt's **Play Strindberg** (6-3-71, Forum). This heavy-handed parody of Strindberg's *The Dance of Death* with Conrad Bain and Robert Symonds camping it up as two men battling over a notalent actress (Priscilla Pointer) amused some critics ("bright and dazzling") and confused others. The evening was broken up into twelve "rounds," each punctuated by a bell ringing, to illustrate the combative nature of the piece. Strindberg's tragedy-turned-into-farce overcame its mixed reviews and ran through the summer and into October before setting out on a tour to regional theatres.

An early impressive play of the off-Broadway season was J. E. Franklin's **Black Girl** (6-16-71, Theatre de Lys) which was produced by the Henry Street Settlement's New Federal Theatre. In a small Texas town, young Billie Jean (Kishasha) has dropped out of high school and, unbeknownst to her family, works as a dancer in a local bar. She dreams of escaping her present life and becoming a ballet dancer, but the reality of her situation, the jealousy of her two sisters stuck in early and futile marriages, and her own mother's rejection stand in her way. Finally, with the help of her grandmother, Billie Jean makes the first step toward her goals and reconciles herself to her family. In some ways a rural variation of *A Raisin in the Sun* (3-11-59), *Black Girl* was rich and compelling because the complex forces working against the heroine—race, class, family, sex— kept the play from simply being about issues. Critics particularly praised the piece's hopefulness and positive approach to character. The performances by Kishasha and Louise Stubbs as Mama were also cited by many and awarded at the end of the season. *Black Girl* ran out the year, racking up 234 performances before going on tour.

The Circle in the Square Uptown presented only two non-musicals this season. A June 23 revival of Saul Bellow's *The Last Analysis* (10-1-64) featured Joseph Wiseman as Bummidge, the man who tries to conduct his own psychoanalysis. This revised version ran forty-six performances, nearly twice as long as the original.

Three of the Bard's rarely done works were presented by the New York Shakespeare Festival at the outdoor Delacorte Theatre in Central Park. The summer season opened on June 25 with *Timon of Athens*, directed by Gerald Freedman and featuring Shepperd Strudwick as the bankrupt hero. It was the first professional New York production of the Shakespeare work on record since 1894. But the big hit at the Delacorte that summer was the musical version of *Two Gentlemen of Verona*, which opened on July 22 and transferred to Broadway in December.

The ever-growing audience for gay theatre had to content itself with **Georgie Porgie** (8-10-71, Village Arena), a play by George Birimisa about a homosexual (Claude Barbazon) and his dealings with his wife, mother, lovers, and even a statue. The entry received mixed notices, but audiences kept it alive for two months.

The third offering at the Delacorte was *Cymbeline* on August 12, directed by A. J. Antoon and billed here as *The Tale of Cymbeline*. Tom Aldredge, who would have a busy season in the park, off Broadway, and then on Broadway, played the title character. The cast also featured Sam Waterston, Jane White, Christopher Walken, William Devane, and Karen Grassle. *Cymbeline* had not been seen in New York since E. H. Sothern played it in 1923. Broadway had to settle for holdovers all summer long until Charles Gordone's Pulitzer winner *No Place to Be Somebody* (5-4-69) was revived at the Morosco on September 9. Gordone directed the competent revival, and, with fine performances by Terry Alexander and Mary Alice, the drama proved to be durable if not marketable; a month later it closed.

The Broadway season's first new play was by established playwright Robert Anderson, but **Solitaire/Double Solitaire** (9-30-71, John Golden) yearned, some said awkwardly so, to be the youthful and adventurous work of a young writer. The first half of the double bill was set in a future society where world-weary Sam Bradley (Richard Venture) goes to an illegal service that provides him with an artificial family for his fantasies. Sam basks in the glow of a traditional family and even starts to believe that the son is really his own, but soon the masquerade is ended by a police raid; in despair, Sam elects to commit state-encouraged suicide. The second play, *Double Solitaire*, was set in more familiar Anderson territory: a middle-aged couple, Charley (Venture) and Barbara (Joyce Ebert), reexamining their marriage in the wake of the husband's parents' fiftieth wedding anniversary. The drama was a series of monologues and two-character confrontational scenes; the final encounter between Charley and Barbara, in which compromises are reached and the couple discover the importance of fellowship in marriage, was the longest and most involving. Anderson's potent sense of humor, so enjoyable in his *You Know I Can't Hear You When the Water's Running* (3-13-67), was evident here as well, especially in the blunt observations of the worldly-wise friend Sylvia (Martha Schlamme) who cannot understand why her many lovers object to her dog watching their lovemaking. While a handful of critics felt the double bill to be Anderson's finest achievement, too many others found it only mildly interesting and intermittently touching. The play, which originated at the Long Wharf Theatre and had played successfully at the Edinburgh Festival, probably belonged off Broadway. Its limited engagement of thirty-five performances in a Broadway house was the season's only venture into the Limited Broadway ar-

TERRENCE MCNALLY (1939–) was born in St. Petersburg, Florida, and raised in Corpus Christi, Texas. He received a degree in English from Columbia University, where he started writing plays and adaptations and contributed to the varsity shows. His adaptation of Dumas's *The Lady of the Camellias* was seen briefly on Broadway (1963), as was his original *And Things That Go Bump in the Night* (1965). Various McNally one-acts were produced off Broadway in the later 1960s, most memorably the farce *Next*, which, paired with Elaine May's *Adaptation*, ran 707 performances. McNally would move from unconventional comedy to more mature comedies of character, usually displaying his talent for comic dialogue but rarely developing a plot with a satisfactory conclusion.

rangement in which producers reduce ticket prices while unions agree to reduced wages.

One of the liveliest offerings of the Off-Broadway season was Terrence McNally's **Where Has Tommy Flowers Gone?** (10-7-71, Eastside), a breezy, frustrating, joyous ode to aimlessness by a playwright who was coming into his own.

Where Has Tommy Flowers Gone? takes the form of a random series of skits, flashbacks, encounters, and monologues. Tommy Flowers (Robert Drivas) is a child of the 1950s set adrift in the New York City of the 1970s. Tommy starts by listing some hundred names of people (from Mom and Dad to the Man from Glad) and cultural icons (from the Little Engine That Could to Cream of Wheat) that have made him what he is today. A rebel against society but also a carefree soul with no set purpose, he befriends the old actor Ben (Wallace Rooney) and an oversize sheep dog named Arnold, floats in and out of love with a music student (Kathleen Dabney), and generally lives by his wits, stealing from the world around him and collecting things in his bright red shopping bag. The reasons for Tommy's alienation are provided with glimpses of his unhappy home in Florida and failed relationships with his family and former girlfriend. After further rejection, Tommy resolves to blow up himself and a little bit of the world, using a bomb he has manufactured from the items in his shopping bag. What made McNally's play unique was his refusal to make Tommy endearing. He was funny, infuriating, and never uninteresting, even if the thin narrative went on a bit too long. Several critics saw a lot of J. D. Salinger's fictional hero Holden Caulfield in Tommy (so did Tommy

himself) as well as touches of Saroyan's free-wheeling sense of storytelling. At times the piece was rather sloppy, but then McNally's nimble way with a brief scene and the vitality of the characters seemed to win out. When Tommy is shoplifting in Bloomingdale's, he hides from the police in the ladies' room, only to emerge from a stall dressed as an Ursuline nun. The play was cited as one of the ten best of the season by *Time*, the *Best Plays*, and others, and it ran seventy-eight performances. Perhaps the most telling words about the work and its author were written by Richard Watts, Jr., of the *New York Post*, who described McNally as "a young playwright with a talent for going short distances but . . . serious difficulties in filling out an entire evening." Similar observations would be made about McNally's work for decades to come.

An audience participation event billed as the **James Joyce Memorial Liquid Theatre** had nothing to do with the Irish writer, and there was no water or other liquids to be seen. Critics found it difficult to describe the "experience," which first took place at the Guggenheim Museum on October 11. The large cast of performers sang songs, played games (many of which involved the audience), went through some sensitivity exercises (also with the audience), and ended up with some dancing. There was no formal text, but Steven Kent was credited with direction (if such a free-flowing "happening" could be directed). It was oddly popular and was repeated 189 times before it closed on March 15.

The Roundabout Theatre Company opened its season off Broadway on October 17 with its first Ibsen attempt, *The Master Builder*. Paul Sparer's Halvard Solness was applauded, but there were very mixed opinions about Jill O'Hara's Hilde.

Two established playwrights, Jerome Lawrence and Robert E. Lee, faced disappointment this season with **The Incomparable Max** (10-19-71, Royale), two Max Beerbohm stories, *Enoch Soames* and *A. V. Laider*, dramatized with Beerbohm (Clive Revill) himself as narrator and commentator. Richard Kiley gave a crisp performance as the arrogant Enoch, a poet who gets a glimpse of a posterity that has rudely forgotten him. Kiley then played A. V. Laider, a weak-willed student of palmistry who also sees briefly into the future. The tentative Laider has knowledge of an impending railroad wreck but lacks the stamina to warn his friends not to board the fateful train. Some aisle-sitters called the evening "civilized," "literate," and "sophisticated," while most dismissed it as "musty," "tepid," and "boring." Audiences, not even sure who Max was, stayed away, closing the play after only twenty-three showings.

Yet another established author, though a newcomer to the theatre, found Broadway unresponsive with **Unlikely Heroes: 3 Philip Roth Stories** (10-26-71, Plymouth). Larry Arrick dramatized Roth's *Defender of the Faith, Epstein,* and *Eli the Fanatic,* short stories that had been widely read when published with the popular novella *Goodbye, Columbus* twelve years earlier. The theme of modern Jewish culture in mainstream America tied the three disparate tales together, but the stageworthiness of Roth's fiction was suspect. Despite solid performances by Lou Jacobi as the unlucky Epstein, Michael Tolan as a lawyer battling anti-Semitic zoning laws, and David Ackroyd as a Jewish army sergeant trying not to favor a sluggish Jewish recruit, *Unlikely Heroes* was poorly received and lasted no longer than *The Incomparable Max* did. The adage that evenings of one-act plays always fail on Broadway seemed to be supported this season by *Solitaire/Double Solitaire* and these two offerings.

The most talked-about play of the season, first at the Public and then later on Broadway, was David Rabe's **Sticks and Bones** (11-7-71, Anspacher). Rabe's *The Basic Training of Pavlo Hummel* (5-20-71) was still running off Broadway and raising disturbing questions about Vietnam when *Sticks and Bones* opened and created such an uncomfortable stir that it made Pavlo Hummel's death in Saigon seem a positive release. For *Sticks and Bones* was about a survivor, David (David Selby), who returns to his American apple-pie family consisting of a commanding father, Ozzie (Tom Aldredge), a religious mother, Harriet (Elizabeth Wilson), and a dense younger brother, Rick (Cliff DeYoung). The homecoming is strained, for David is now blind, and the family knows no other way to react than with foolish optimism and archaic principles. David is also haunted by memories of the war and the Vietnamese girl (Asa Gim) he left behind, who appears to him throughout the inane family conversations. When Harriet calls in a priest (Charles Siebert) to help David, the meeting erupts into a fight. The family members start to detach themselves from the blind son, even suggesting that David's suicide might be the tidiest solution to all their problems. The play ends with a surreal sequence in which Rick helps David slit his wrists and the family members make pleasant comments while David bleeds to death. Innocent Pavlo Hummel dying in Vietnam was one thing, but *Sticks and Bones* was seen by some as a direct assault on everything Pavlo had died for. Naming the characters after those on the popular sitcom *Adventures of Ozzie and Harriet* was an unsubtle reference to idealistic television families and perhaps a lame joke at first, but Rabe's Ozzie and Harriet were filled with prejudices and stubborn convictions, and the joke became oppressive to audiences, especially in a Broadway house. Reviews, for the most part, praised the drama. Douglas Watt of the *New York Daily News* echoed several others when he called it "a searing and original anti-war play, a powerful human document of the sort commercial theatre has not had much use for during the many troubled years behind us." It would seem that a play with such a determined agenda would result in one-dimensional acting, but in fact Aldredge and Wilson gave two of the most dynamic performances of the season. Ozzie's internal rage and Harriet's painful complacency were exciting feats of theatrics and saved what might have become dreary bombast in the hands of lesser actors. The drama moved to Broadway's John Golden Theatre on March 3 and stayed for 366 performances, thanks to its Tony Award for best play and controversy that, in this case, translated into ticket sales.

One contributor to *Sticks and Bones* who was not much noticed at first but would become more evident later in the year with *That Championship Season* was the designer of the bold setting, which depicted a stark and imposing version of an American middle-class home. The young designer was Santo Loquasto in his Broadway debut.

A few days later the Public offered **The Black Terror** (11-10-71, Other Stage), the first of two

---

SANTO LOQUASTO (1944–) was born in Wilkes-Barre, Pennsylvania (the Lackawanna Valley setting of *That Championship Season*), where his father sold cooking utensils and his mother ran a cocktail lounge. He attended the local King's College and then studied design at Yale, graduating in 1969. While still a student he started designing sets for the Williamstown Festival, the Hartford Stage Company, and the Long Wharf Theatre, eventually arriving in New York in 1970. After designing several one-acts at the Astor Place Theatre he was hired by Joseph Papp at the Public, where he would make his reputation. Loquasto also designed costumes and, later in his career, did a good deal of film work.

plays by newcomer Richard Wesley that Papp would present this season. In the "near future" when black guerrilla groups are terrorizing the country, Keusi (Kain), the assigned executioner for one of these militant units, has killed a police commissioner with no regrets. But when the group orders him to assassinate a black civic leader he respects, Keusi starts to doubt his role in such radical social change. Some critics found the piece too contrived and melodramatic, but most endorsed Nathan George's expert direction and Kain's riveting performance. The explosive drama ran at the Public for four months.

Once again it fell to Neil Simon to save the season, and his **The Prisoner of Second Avenue** (11-11-71, Eugene O'Neill) provided Broadway with its first and only non-musical hit. Mel Edison (Peter Falk) is a middle-aged ad man who resides with his wife, Edna (Lee Grant), in one of those faceless high-rises on the Upper East Side. As a prisoner of their "luxury" apartment with broken air-conditioning, paper-thin walls, noisy neighbors, and a toilet that must be "jiggled" into working, Mel is starting to overreact to the pressures of modern urban living. When he loses his job because of downsizing and then their apartment is robbed, Mel heads for a nervous breakdown. Edna rejoins the workforce to keep them in the inconvenient conveniences they are used to, and Mel goes through a series of fruitless job inquiries, realizing he is too old for a miracle to happen. (Miracles, he decides, only happen to the young; when Moses "saw that burning bush, he must have been twenty-three, twenty-four, the most . . . never forty-seven.") Edna even appeals to Mel's family for a loan to help him realize his dream: to run a camp for kids in the country. But when Edna loses her job and starts to crack as well, the couple learn to gain strength from each other and face life in Manhattan with a determined stubbornness. The situation for the comedy seemed at first an extended series of "I hate New York" jokes, but Simon soon went beyond the stand-up comic's one-liners; a gritty, taut subtext underlay Mel and Edna's misadventures. Mel's idleness leads him into paranoia (he suspects a worldwide conspiracy to keep him out of work), and the effect was alternately hysterical and sobering. Like last season's *The Gingerbread Lady* (12-13-70), this was uncomfortable Simon comedy, but this time audiences responded favorably. Perhaps the most telling scene in the play was the gathering of Mel's brother (Vincent Gardenia) and sisters (Florence Stanley, Tresa Hughes, and Dena Dietrich) as they discuss contributing "*x* number of dollars" to Mel, trying to balance family responsibility with greedy practicality. Otis Guernsey, writing in *Best Plays*, deemed the scene "worthy of Molière in its cartoons of avarice, role-playing, hypocrisy, sibling rivalry." Reviews were exemplary; Barnes and others called it Simon's best script to date. The comedy stayed on the boards for 780 performances.

Schiller's *Mary Stuart*, in a freely translated adaptation by poet Stephen Spender, had its American premiere at Lincoln Center's Vivian Beaumont for a month beginning November 11. Jules Irving directed a cast featuring Salome Jens as the title monarch, but many critics felt there was finer acting to be found in Nancy Marchand's conscientious Elizabeth and Philip Bosco's fervent Dudley.

Sada Thompson first attracted wide attention as the blisteringly bitter mother in Off Broadway's *The Effect of Gamma Rays on Man-in-the-Moon Marigolds* (4-7-70), so there was no question she could carry a Broadway vehicle such as **Twigs** (11-14-71, Broadhurst). And a vehicle it was, in the traditional sense of the word. Thompson played three sisters in three different kitchens during the same day, ending the evening with a farcical coda in which she played their crotchety mother. George Furth's four playlets were well crafted and occasionally involving, but it was Thompson's vibrant characterizations that made the evening exceptional. In addition to the expected changes in hair, makeup, and costumes (which were done before the audience at the side of the stage while the kitchen sets were changed), Thompson found quirky, vulnerable qualities for each woman, at the same time holding on to family similarities. Her Emily was a brusque, independent divorcée who attacked a new romance as confidently as she moved kitchen appliances across the room. Her fragile Celia lived in a world of daydreams of Hollywood while being bullied by her vulgar ex-army husband. (Celia's warm, but pathetic song-and-dance number for a visiting friend was considered by many the play's most poignant moment.) Thompson's Dorothy was hysterically proper and stiff with an awkward gait in contrast to her delicate demeanor. In some ways the crusty old mother in the last playlet was the least original character in Furth's script. But the comedy came to a satisfactory climax as Ma and Pa (Robert Donley), who have never been officially married, call in a young priest (Mac-

Intyre Dixon) to perform a ludicrous marriage ceremony. Critics and audiences (as well as the Tony voters) thought it the performance of the season even if some had reservations about Furth's script. *Newsweek's* Jack Kroll spoke for many of his colleagues when he wrote, "There can't be a better actress in America than Miss Thompson, and it is fun to see her ride to the top, even if *Twigs* is no Rolls Royce." The comedy ran through July before going on tour.

One of Harold Pinter's most accomplished plays, **Old Times** (11-16-71, Billy Rose), did not enjoy the box-office success some of his earlier works had on Broadway, but critics were enthralled, and discerning audiences got caught up in the usual discussions regarding the meaning of a Pinter play. At a dinner party, Deeley (Robert Shaw), his wife, Kate (Mary Ure), and her visiting old schoolmate Anna (Rosemary Harris) recall times past with increasing contradictions. Deeley and Anna have supposedly never met before, yet halfway through the play they start recalling episodes together that Kate was unaware of. Perhaps, some observed, Deeley and Anna were once lovers. Or maybe the two women are really the same woman, bisected in the husband's mind. What *was* clear was Peter Hall's cunning direction, the tantalizing performances by all three actors, and John Bury's white-on-white scenery and furniture, which seemed to comment on the very murkiness of the situation. The London import from the Royal Shakespeare Company only managed 119 performances but was roundly hailed as "steadily interesting while still disturbingly puzzling."

The Negro Ensemble Company's season off Broadway offered its best production first and introduced a promising new playwright with Philip Hayes Dean's **The Sty of the Blind Pig** (11-16-71, St. Marks), which was given for sixty-four performances. The setting is Chicago in the 1950s, the days before the civil rights movement and a time of confusion for young blacks, such as Alberta (Frances Foster), who feels change coming but cannot quite determine what form it will take. The older generation is represented by her mother, Weedy (Clarice Taylor), who relies on religion to ease her confusion, and Uncle Doc (Adolph Caesar), a wandering gambler who asks no questions of life. Into this arrangement comes Blind Jordan (Moses Gunn), a street singer looking for a long-lost woman he once knew, and his presence electrifies Alberta's awareness of herself and brings a sort of reconciliation between

mother and daughter. While some commentators found the quasi-symbolic piece dull and undramatic, others thought it superior theatre. The performers were roundly commended, all four cited for nominations or awards at the end of the season. The play enjoyed subsequent productions regionally.

Two days later Lincoln Center presented the American premiere of Athol Fugard's **People Are Living There** (11-18-71, Forum), a compassionate portrayal of four South Africans living on the edge of despair. Kind-hearted Milly (Estelle Parsons) operates a run-down boardinghouse in Johannesburg. Although she has just been jilted by a German lodger whom she has lived with for the past ten years, she decides to gather some of her boarders, a slovenly group of outcasts, to celebrate her fiftieth birthday. Fugard's talent for realistic conversation that penetrates the characters' exterior bluster was evident, and critics found the talky drama quite forceful.

The Chelsea Theatre Center at the Brooklyn Academy of Music continued to offer bold and unusual fare for discerning New Yorkers. Its season opened with the American premiere of Jean Genet's **The Screens** (11-30-71, BAM), an epic work about the waning of colonialism in Algeria in the 1950s that was symbolic of mankind's inhuman behavior and doomed future. Genet wrote the play back in 1959, but because of its politically inflammatory subject, it did not receive its first production until 1966 in Paris. This translation by Minos Volanakis, who also directed, featured forty-three actors portraying eighty-eight characters in seventeen episodes that took four and a half hours to perform. Reviewers were more impressed by the ambitious bravado of the Chelsea company than by the play itself (one called it "grandiose pretentiousness"), but the New York Drama Critics Circle gave it their "best foreign play" award.

Off Broadway's often-interesting American Place Theatre moved into a new theatre in the lower level of a skyscraper on West 46th Street near Sixth Avenue, opening its new home with a pair of lackluster one-acters: Ron Ribman's **Fingernails Blue as Flowers** (12-6-71, American Place), about a high-strung American tourist (Albert Paulsen) in Jamaica who is cursed by his inability to adapt to contemporary life, and Steve Tesich's **Lake of the Woods,** about the frustrated camper Winnebago (Hal Holbrook) whose attempt to survive in the Great Outdoors symbolizes man's losing efforts in making a place for himself in society today. It was an inauspicious start for the new space and disappointing work from two highly thought-of young playwrights.

"Lee Barton" was a pseudonym for a writer not wishing to be identified as the author of **Nightride** (12-9-71, Vandam). Since the play was about a famous playwright who had been hiding his homosexuality for years, patrons were curious. Lester Rawlins played Jon Bristow, a distinguished man of letters who must confront his closeted sexuality when a new age of open-mindedness arrives. Rawlins was cited by critics and awards committees for his piquant portrayal, and the dark comedy ran ten weeks.

Conor Cruise O'Brien, the author of **Murderous Angels** (12-20-71, Playhouse), was a special representative to U.N. Secretary-General Dag Hammarskjöld in Africa during the events of 1961 that brought on the deaths of both Hammarskjöld and Congo leader Patrice Lumumba. O'Brien's play was an awkward mixture of history and personalized fiction about the tragic events (one aisle-sitter complained it was "more a staged treatise than an actual play"), and soon after the play opened, friends and colleagues of both leaders complained about it's misrepresentation of both people and facts. The controversy did little for business; *Murderous Angels* only lasted two weeks. There were compliments for Gordon Davidson's production, which came from his Mark Taper Forum in Los Angeles before being presented by the Phoenix Theatre on Broadway, and for Jean-Pierre Aumont (Hammarskjöld), Lou Gossett (Lumumba), and Richard Venture as the Belgian industrialist Baron d'Auge.

Fun City (1-2-72, Morosco), a jokey comedy about the travails of living in New York City, paled in comparison with Simon's similar but superior *The Prisoner of Second Avenue*. The script, by Lester Colodny, Joan Rivers, and Edgar Rosenberg, concerned the attempts of one Jill Fairchild (Rivers) to liberate Gotham and have it become the fifty-first state. Her busy political agenda keeps frustrating Paul Martino (Gabriel Dell), a musician who loves Jill but cannot sidetrack her from her quest. Both performers gave likable performances, and audience favorites Rose Marie and Paul Ford (in his last Broadway appearance) were wasted in minor roles as Jill's musician-hating mother and a weary postman who arrives late with a registered letter. The comedy was roasted by the critics and closed after nine showings.

David Merrick brought a new (to New York) Feydeau farce down from the Stratford National Theatre of Canada, and it was received with enthusiastic critical approval. *Le Dindon*, freely translated here as **There's One in Every Marriage** (1-3-72, Royale), was set in a traditional Feydeau hotel where bumbling Major Pinchard (Tony Van Bridge) arrives with his deaf wife to celebrate their twenty-fifth anniversary, only to find his room booked by several other parties. The usual confusions followed, and the result was approved as hilarious by nearly all the critics. But Broadway audiences have always been wary of the French master of bedroom comedy, and the hotel was shuttered after sixteen performances. Suzanne Grossmann and Paxton Whitehead did the lively adaptation and, Jean Gascon directed a cast of Stratford regulars including Peter Donat, Roberta Maxwell, Jack Creley, and Patricia Gage, as well as the blusteringly funny Van Bridge.

There was much advance word on **Rosebloom** (1-5-72, Eastside), a dark comedy by Harvey Perr that had won prestigious awards when previously produced at Los Angeles's Mark Taper Forum. Perr had been proclaimed the new Edward Albee by many; his poor reception by New York was perhaps a case of East Coast snobbery. The play got mixed reviews (Barnes and others did compare Perr favorably to Albee), but *Rosebloom* only survived twenty-three performances. A neurotic mother (Sylvia Miles), her crippled son (Ron Rifkin), and his oversexed wife (Regina Baff) await the homecoming of the father, Harry Rosebloom (Harold Gary), who has been in prison for twenty-six years. The fantasy-like atmosphere allows each character to launch into monologues about the past, and when Harry does arrive the quartet bursts into verbal abuse and violence. The stinging dialogue and the oblique sense of reality were awkward at times and occasionally amateurish. (Did the daughter-in-law have to be named Enola Gay?)

Lincoln Center gave controversial British playwright Edward Bond's **Narrow Road to the Deep North** (1-6-72, Vivian Beaumont) an American premiere with an American cast directed by Daniel Sullivan, but once again Bond's work refused to catch fire in New York. While there was nothing so disturbing as the stoning of a baby, as in Bond's *Saved* (11-13-70), the new work was still challenging fare. The Candide-like poet Basho (Robert Symonds) travels through a violent Japan of some vague past century in order to study solitude in the deep north. He discovers an abandoned baby as he begins his quest but takes time only to feed it and move on. After thirty years of traveling and a series of misadventures along the way, including encounters with the dictator Shogo (Cleavon Little), Basho encounters the disciple Kiro (Andy Robinson), the neglected baby now grown to a man, who teaches him that true enlightenment can only come from where you are. Themes ranging from destructive colonialism to Buddhist-like philosophy filled the allegorical piece, and audiences were intrigued if not passionate about it. Critical response was quite negative, many questioning why Lincoln Center was presenting such a work. Despite future efforts, Bond would never appeal to Americans as so many of his British colleagues did. A week later Lincoln Center, in its downstairs theatre, presented yet another foreign work in an American premiere: Austrian playwright Peter Handke's **Ride Across Lake Constance** (1-13-72, Forum) in which the actors used their own names for the characters, as stated in the playwright's directions, and the plotless text consisted of words and phrases tossed about in an unstructured format.

Vivat! Vivat! Regina! (1-20-72, Broadhurst) was the second of Broadway's three plays about Elizabeth I this season (the Virgin Queen was a major character in the earlier *Mary Stuart*). Veteran playwright Robert Bolt told a familiar tale with taste, lively dialogue, and even humor. The conflict between the political Elizabeth (Eileen Atkins) and the compassionate Mary Queen of Scots (Claire Bloom) wages on for decades, and each queen's stubbornness and reliance on ill-advised advisers keep it a hotbed of political and religious controversy. Bolt took the approach that both queens were victims of the time and of attractive men who used romance for power. The result was a skillful historical piece without cobwebs. While everyone in the large cast was commendable, Atkins's performance as a woman of quick instincts and slow-burning regret shone most brightly. With Carl Toms's lavish costumes and suggestive sets and the large production fluidly staged by Peter Dews, *Vivat! Vivat! Regina!* was a true spectacle. But despite appreciative reviews, the play never caught on like Bolt's earlier *A Man for All Seasons* (11-22-61), and by May it was gone.

Some original songs were added to the late Lorraine Hansberry's *The Sign in Sidney Brustein's Window* (10-15-64) for an unsuccessful revival at the Longacre on January 29. Robert Nemiroff and Charlotte Zaltzburg tinkered with the problematic text, and Gary Williams and Ray Errol Fox wrote the songs, but this production lasted less than a week despite Alan Schneider's proficient direction and the amiable Hal Linden as the idealistic publisher Sidney.

Simon Gray's **Wise Child** (1-29-72, Helen Hayes) was the British playwright's first New York production, but he would have to wait until the next season before Broadway would enjoy his kind of humor. Alec Guinness, Gordon Jackson, and Simon Ward had made Gray's dark sex farce sparkle in London, and most critics in New York agreed that Donald Pleasance, George Rose, and Bud Cort were quite adept at handling the quirky characters in the American production. Pleasance spent the evening in drag as a crook hiding out in a hotel and passing himself off as Mother to the younger Jerry (Cort). When the nosy hotel manager, Mr. Booker, discovers Mother's identity and unmasks him, Jerry kills the manager to prove his masculinity. Most accomplished was Rose's perverted Booker, a brilliant and disarming turn that kept the baffled audience intrigued. Critics were unsure whether the play was supposed to be comic or melodramatic, so after four performances this *"Charley's Aunt* of the criminal classes"* was gone.

Off Broadway, the Roundabout continued its series of classic revivals with *The Taming of the Shrew* on January 30. Joan Bassie and Michael Wager were the battling Kate and Petruchio, and Gene Feist directed.

The Chelsea went from the epic spectacle of *The Screens* to a more intimate, multi-media approach for **Kaddish** (2-1-72, BAM), a theatre piece based on Allen Ginsberg's poem. This experiment in live theatre and televised sequences was popular enough that it moved from Brooklyn to the Circle in the Square on March 7, where it tallied a total of 100 performances.

Sidney Michaels's biographical *Dylan* (1-18-64) was revived at the Mercer-O'Casey on February 7 for forty-eight showings. Will Hare's Dylan Thomas was competent, if overshadowed by the recent memory of Alec Guinness's portrayal, but Rue McClanahan was hailed for her forceful Caitlin Thomas.

A new American playwright, Romulus Linney, made his debut with **The Love Suicide at Schofield Barracks** (2-9-72, ANTA), a military courtroom drama about a double suicide. During a Halloween gathering of military personnel at a Hawaiian army base, the commanding officer and his wife performed a Japanese-style playlet in which they committed actual suicide before the spectators. At the subsequent investigation, various witnesses and acquaintances testify, and it is eventually revealed that the couple's tragic act was a plea for responsibility and a condemnation of the Vietnam War. Some commentators declared the play powerful and thought-provoking, while most critics called the writing stiff and its political agenda too obvious. But there was no disagreement about Mercedes McCambridge's engrossing performance as Lucy Lake, who, wearing an incongruous pink jumpsuit in the drab courtroom, testifies about the late couple's friendship with a poet. Critics also applauded William Redfield's supporting performance as Colonel Moore, the chief of staff who disliked the late commander and all officers who succumb to the weakness of familiarity. Such qualities were not enough, and before the week was out the drama closed.

Jack Gelber's **Sleep** (2-10-72, American Place), a slight little comedy about dreams, was featured for twenty-four performances. Gil (David Spielberg) has volunteered to be used in a scientific experiment studying the nature of sleep, and while he dreams four actors act out his fantasies.

Another promising playwright was Michael Weller, whose first Broadway effort was **Moonchildren** (2-21-72, Royale), discovered at Washington's Arena Stage. David Merrick and others brought it to Broadway; in retrospect, it probably belonged off Broadway. Weller's episodic tale takes place in a student apartment in a college town in the mid-1960s. While the war is being waged in Vietnam and student protests are raging outside the apartment, *Moonchildren* concentrates on the various inhabitants and visitors inside and their personal problems and imaginative fantasies. Mike (Kevin Conway) and his girlfriend, Kathy (Jill Eikenberry), are drifting apart, although she cannot tell if it is due to personal or political reasons. They are surrounded by wacky, drugged-out, and sometimes endearing roommates played by such later notable talents as Edward Herrmann, Maureen Anderman, Stephen Collins, Christopher Guest, James Woods, and Cara Duff-MacCormick. Robert Prosky and Louis Zorich portrayed some of the adults who invade the students' lair, often with hilarious results, as when the landlord, Willis (Prosky), goes off into a steamy description of a dream in which he is the king of the jungle and a sexual athlete. Some critics described the loose plotting as Chekhovian, while others pointed out its faults of repetition and aimlessness. It only lasted sixteen performances but soon enjoyed many productions regionally and in college theatres.

Night Watch (2-28-72, Morosco), the season's only thriller to have a considerable run, was a tidy domestic cat-and-mouse piece by Lucille Fletcher, whose radio play *Sorry, Wrong Number* thirty years earlier had remained popular in various media. One night the insomniac Elaine Wheeler (Joan Hackett) sees a dead body in the vacant tenement across the courtyard of her Manhattan town house. Her domineering husband, John (Len Cariou), tries to be understanding about it, even after the police investigate and find nothing there. When Elaine sees a woman's body in the same place the next day, the police ignore her, and John makes plans to have his wife committed to a Swiss sanitarium. Of course audiences familiar with Fletcher's earlier hit and with memories going back to *Angel Street* (12-5-41) suspected the husband right away and were not surprised to find that John and his mistress (Elaine Kerr) have set the whole thing up in order to put Elaine away and live off her considerable wealth. But Fletcher came up with a chilling twist at the end: Elaine shoots the lovers in the empty tenement, then calmly calls the police to report seeing two bodies, knowing that they will not believe her. The tight little mystery and the appealing cast pleased several critics, and audiences kept *Night Watch* on the boards until June.

An off-Broadway revival of Sean O'Casey's *The Shadow of a Gunman* (10-0-32) on February 29 at the Sheridan Square found an audience for two months. Both critics and audiences were struck with how timely the play was. (Only a month before, on January 31, the "Bloody Sunday" uprising occurred in Northern Ireland.) The Manhattan Project's take on Lewis Carroll's *Alice in Wonderland*, first seen in 1970, was revived at the Performance Garage on March 1 and stayed for fifty performances. Lincoln Center presented a competent if unmemorable *Twelfth Night* on March 2 for a scheduled run of forty-four performances. Ellis Rabb directed a worthy cast that included Blythe Danner as Viola, Martha Henry as Olivia, and René Auberjonois as Malvolio.

The winter's second thriller was Jack Horrigan's **Children! Children!** (3-7-72, Ritz). On New Year's Eve in a wealthy Gramercy Park duplex apartment, a fashionable couple leave their three children in the care of a new babysitter, Helen Giles (Gwen Verdon in a rare non-musical appearance), who conscientiously admits that she is recovering from a nervous breakdown. The children then proceed to torment her with tales of the previous babysitter's heart attack (which they happily witnessed) and then make sadistic and even amorous advances to the frightened Helen. When the parents return home, not only do they not believe any of Helen's narrative, but it is suggested that the children's diabolism comes from the parents themselves. Garnering unanimous pans, the play closed on opening night.

Lincoln Center's off-Broadway venue finally got around to an American play with Ed Bullins's **The Duplex** (3-9-72, Forum), an angry slice-of-life drama about an all-night drunken party of California blacks that was so derogatory and bitter toward its characters that it seemed to many to have been written by a white racist. Critics gave the play mixed notices, and Bullins himself caused a bit of controversy by publicly stating that he objected to the Lincoln Center production of his own play. Nine days into the run Bullins and some supporters marched into the theatre and stopped the performance, proclaiming that director Gilbert Moses had cheapened his tragedy with "show material." *The Duplex* continued the next night and ran out its scheduled twenty-eight performances without further incident.

A revival of Clifford Odets's *The Country Girl* (11-10-50) that had originated at the Kennedy Center in Washington arrived at the Billy Rose on March 15 and stayed for sixty-four performances. John Houseman directed, and Jason Robards shone as the down-on-his-luck actor Frank Elgin, ably assisted by Maureen Stapleton as his wife and by George Grizzard as Bernie Dodd, the director who enters their lives and creates an emotional triangle. In addition to commending the acting, many critics pointed out how well the Odets drama, perhaps his least political, held up after twenty-two years.

Vinnie Burrows's one-woman show, **Walk Together Children** (3-16-72, Mercer-Brecht), was self-billed as "the black journey from auction block to new nation time" and included selections written by various African-American personages over the years. The popular attraction ran eighty-nine times.

Two other off-Broadway revivals arrived in March. The feverish *Rain* (11-7-22), John Colton and Clemence Randolph's dramatization of a Somerset Maugham story, opened on March 23 at the Astor Place and only lasted for a week. Antonia Rey played the sultry Sadie Thompson, and a young John Travolta was featured in the cast. Shaw's *Misalliance* was revived by the Roundabout on March 28 for a month. Hugh Franklin and Ruth Warrick played the wealthy Mr. and Mrs. Tarleton, and again Gene Feist directed.

The fact that a new Tennessee Williams play premiered off Broadway rather than on was seen as either a sign of the playwright's declining fortune or an indication of the "Broadwayization" of the alternative venue. Most likely it was a matter of economics. But **Small Craft Warnings** (4-2-72, Truck and Warehouse) was a worthy if flawed play that deserved to be produced regardless of the location. Williams's latest was an O'Neill/Saroyan-like slice-of-life drama, set in a dingy Southern California saloon, peopled with various low-life characters revealing secrets in a drunken, chatty manner. Similarities with *The Time of Your Life* were pointed out both by critics who liked the play and by those who dismissed it. *Small Craft Warnings* may have been "warmed-over Williams," but there was plenty of evidence that the master still knew how to create fragile, poetic, and individual characters deserving of our attention. The plotless drama, involving a weepy hooker (Cherry Davis), an alcoholic doctor (David Hooks), a professional stud (Brad Sullivan), a sister in mourning for her kid brother (Helena Carroll), and others, was held together by the homosexual porno-film writer Quentin (Alan Mixon), who seemed the strongest of the group, still fighting when most of the others were defeated and resigned to it. Notices were mixed, and business was marginal, so Williams himself played the doctor for two performances in June to revive interest. It must have worked, for the play ran through the summer and racked up 200 performances.

A ghost story set in an abandoned house during a snowstorm sounded ripe for parody, but Richard Lortz's **Voices** (4-3-72, Ethel Barrymore) played it straight. Robert (Richard Kiley), a middle-aged teacher, and his suicidal wife, Claire (Julie Harris), are still lamenting the loss of their young son who drowned the previous summer. Traveling through a Maine blizzard, the couple takes refuge in the proverbial deserted mansion, where Claire starts to hear the voices of children. Soon she glimpses a young girl, then a boy as well, but Robert sees and hears nothing, causing him to question her sanity. Eventually even he is aware of the ghosts, and the question is raised about how much is really happening and how much is only in their minds. Jo Mielziner, in one of his last Broadway assignments, designed the atmospheric setting featuring a massive window and a seemingly endless staircase. While some reviewers admitted that the second act was fairly intriguing, all agreed that the trite tale was spread too thin, and in a week it was gone.

The season's second Richard Wesley play was a one-act called *Gettin' It Together*, the best of the four short works that made up **Black Visions** (4-

4-72, Annex) at the Public. Nate (Morgan Freeman) and Coretta (Beverly Todd) are lovers with a child, but the relationship is suffering from his need to make something of himself before committing to marriage. Wesley described the tragicomic playlet as a "steady rap," and the script's honesty came to life with Freeman and Todd's musical performances. The program, which also included short works by Sonia Sanchez and Neil Harris, stayed on the boards for sixty-four performances.

Paul Foster's **Elizabeth I** (4-5-72, Lyceum), the season's third offering that featured the Virgin Queen, took the form of a group of Elizabethan strolling players who try to perform a piece about their monarch but are run out of London and stage their little drama elsewhere. A cast of eleven actors portrayed the various characters in a lively and impressionistic manner, staged by John-Michael Tebelak, who had created similar theatrics for the musical *Godspell* (5-17-71). While some critics found the script and production too busy and the actors, save Penelope Windust, amateurish, others admired the inventiveness of the piece. But after *Mary Stuart, Vivat! Vivat! Regina!*, the recent television *Elizabeth R*, and the 1971 film *Mary, Queen of Scots*, this must have been one Elizabeth work too many. It was forced to close after five performances.

Promenade, All! (4-16-72, Alvin) by David V. Robison was a playful experiment in extended plotting and role-playing, asking its cast of four to portray six generations of an American family from 1895 to "Approximately Now." Because the comedy featured stars (Eli Wallach, Anne Jackson, Hume Cronyn) it might be mistaken for a mere vehicle, but the writing was quite succinct, and the many characters, though quickly sketched, were enjoyable. Jackson played all the mothers and grandmothers of the Huntziger (later Hunt) tribe, and Wallach and Cronyn portrayed various fathers and grandfathers as the family business grows from a small button-manufacturing firm to an international perfume corporation. (The company's product "Belle Nuit" is wisely called "Enchanted Evening" when sold in Paris.) Playing all the Hunt boys and young men was newcomer Richard Backus, who held his own with the stellar cast and was favorably cited by the critics. Robison knew how to create a potent vignette, and some of the comic sequences, such as a puritanical mother reading biblical passages to her son and missing all the sexual innuendoes, or the nonagenarian Cronyn eager to be the subject for a sex experiment, were

splendid. Most reviews were quite favorable, though more than one critic confessed to being confused by all the doubling. The bright comedy only lasted six weeks.

The most eagerly awaited revival of the season was Shaw's *Captain Brassbound's Conversion* with Ingrid Bergman repeating her Lady Cecily from a London production. The engagement at the Ethel Barrymore beginning on April 17 was limited to a two-week stop as part of an American tour. Several aisle-sitters pointed out how miscast the exotic, Scandinavian Bergman seemed as the no-nonsense aristocratic Englishwoman, but all agreed she was radiant in the part, the grandest star appearance of the season.

While the subject of homosexuality was finally being treated with some seriousness elsewhere, Broadway's **All the Girls Came Out to Play** (4-20-72, Cort) seemed a throwback to the days when the mere suspicion of a character being gay was played for laughs. Agent Angel Rodriguez (Jay Barney) moves into a suburban house with his client, theatre composer Ronnie Ames (Dennis Cole), so that Ronnie will settle down to work and stop chasing females. But the neighbors suspect the newcomers are gay, and when the wives go to investigate, Ronnie takes advantage of the situation and seduces three of them. The comedy was offensive on more levels than audiences thought possible, and it was gone in three days.

Perhaps the most brutal play of the season was Fernando Arrabal's prison drama **And They Put Handcuffs on Flowers** (4-21-72, O'Casey). Arrabal had been a political prisoner in Spain during the Franco regime, so he wrote (and directed) from experience: humiliation, abuse, torture, even a lifelike garroting and disembowelment. In true "theatre of cruelty" fashion, audience members were forced to find their seats in the dark and were confined to the space for the duration. To say this was a powerful play was understatement, but, as more than one critic pointed out, the horror was so disorienting and the disgusting situation so devoid of characters to pity that the experience was more numbing than anything else. Surprisingly, the play managed to run 172 performances and was the source of much discussion.

The cleverest comedy of the season was to be found off Broadway with **The Real Inspector Hound** (4-23-72, Theatre Four) and its curtain raiser *After Magritte* by that cleverest of playwrights, Tom Stoppard. The shorter of the two pieces was an odd mixture of comedy and mystery about a bumbling Scotland Yard inspector

(Edmond Genest) and his constable (Remak Ramsay) who enter the flat of a bizarre family and accuse them of robbing the box office of a minstrel show. Absurdism takes over as talk turns to a Magritte exhibit, the mother-in-law's obsession with her tuba, and the discovery that there was no minstrel show. Much more satisfying was *The Real Inspector Hound*, a delightful parody of Agatha Christie plays, drama critics, Pirandellian paradoxes, and the nature of the theatre itself. Two theatre critics sit in their seats waiting for a West End thriller to begin. Birdboot (Tom Lacy), an established aisle-sitter who has been having an affair with one of the show's actresses, gives advice to another paper's second-string critic, Moon (David Rounds), who is paranoid about his second-class status and fantasizes about murdering his superior. The play-within-the-play, an absurdist version of a drawing room mystery, begins, and the amorous Birdboot is attracted to a different actress, eventually getting on the stage and becoming part of the story. Soon there is a murder and Moon joins the action, mistaken for the long-awaited Inspector Hound from Scotland Yard. By the end of the comedy, the different levels of reality have come full circle with some of the play's actors sitting in the critics' seats and reviewing the actions of the desperate Moon as he discovers who the inspector really is. While not nearly as complex or profound as the author's earlier *Rosencrantz and Guildenstern Are Dead* (10-16-67), this was a delicious piece of comic writing and imaginative plotting. Moon, for example, delivers an extended speech in which he calls to arms all of the secondary personages in England, urging the "stand-ins of the world to stand up!" Reviews were propitious, audiences responded to the British satire, and the double bill ran well over a year.

Lincoln Center's final entry, a revival of Arthur Miller's *The Crucible* (1-22-53) on April 27 in the Vivian Beaumont, was its best offering of the season. Newcomer Robert Foxworth was a proficient Proctor, and he got strong support from Martha Henry as his wife, Elizabeth, and Pamela Payton-Wright as the provocative Abigail. Many critics, in their commendatory reviews, pointed out that this was what Lincoln Center should be doing: revivals of American classics, ideally in repertory. The popular attraction ran six weeks.

The Broadway season concluded with four quick flops that totaled only twenty-five performances all together. **The Little Black Book** (4-29-72, Helen Hayes) was Jerome Kilty's Americanized version of Jean-Claude Carrière's *L'Aide-Memoire*. An amorous lawyer (Richard Benjamin) is bedazzled and conquered by a beautiful stranger (Delphine Seyrig) who makes him give up both his wanderlust and his profession in order to stay home and make love to her for the rest of his days. Besides being unfunny, critics complained, the translation made no sense (why him? why her?) and proved more irritating than bearable. (Guernsey called Seyrig's character "the most repellent nuisance to appear on a stage this season.") Oddly, international film director Milos Forman directed the short-lived comedy.

The Little Black Book lasted less than a week, but Jane Trahey's **Ring Round the Bathtub** (4-29-72, Martin Beck) never saw a second performance. This sentimental comedy about an Irish-American family in Chicago struggling through the Depression came from Houston's Alley Theatre. Perhaps scenes such as the unemployed father trudging through the snow to spend his last pennies on a Christmas tree for the impoverished family played better in Texas, but the play was roundly panned in New York as "inept" and "tiresome."

Broadway had reasonable expectations for Gore Vidal's **An Evening With Richard Nixon And . . .** (4-30-72, Shubert), for the author had not been represented on Broadway since *Weekend* (3-13-68), and his satiric wit was much needed. But this unwieldy comedy struck the critics as more ponderous than funny. Vidal used many authentic Nixon quotes and, to attempt a somewhat balanced slate, offered characters named Pro (Gene Rupert) and Con (Humbert Allen Astredo) as well as throwing in stinging portrayals of J F K, Truman, LBJ, Eisenhower, FDR, and even George Washington to show that American leaders have always been imperialistic. George S. Irving played Nixon so bravely that one started to admire the actor and feel sorry for the character. Edwin Sherin directed the large production, which played in a musical house that was empty after sixteen performances.

The Public's next offering, Jason Miller's drama **That Championship Season** (5-2-72, Newman), was arguably the finest new play of the season. Although rather traditional in its structure (a three-act drama with the unities of time, place, and action) and familiar in its style (post-war American realism reminiscent of Inge and Miller), *That Championship Season* excited audiences with an enthusiasm usually accorded innovative or groundbreaking works. The play was neither, but it was so well written, with such vital characters and captivating ideas, that it seemed to breathe fresh air into the theatre season. All the action takes place in a rambling and nostalgic house that suggests an America of the past (beautifully realized in Santo Loquasto's superb design) in a mid-sized city in the Lackawanna Valley of Pennsylvania. It is the home of the Coach (Richard A. Dysart) and the setting for a reunion of four members of his high school basketball team that won the state championship twenty years ago. Gathered are George (Charles Durning), a smiling, foolish man who is now the mayor; Phil (Paul Sorvino), an insatiable man who has made a fortune by strip-mining coal; James (Michael McGuire), a frustrated junior high school principal; and Tom (Walter McGinn), James's younger brother and an alcoholic drifter recently returned to the area. The Coach himself is a stubborn, inspiring racist with a sentimental streak, and he still treats his "boys" with bullying affection. Martin, the fifth member of the winning team, has moved away and never attends these annual reunions. What starts out with jovial, locker room–like socializing dissolves into bitter feuding and disillusionment as various issues come up during the evening: George is in a tough reelection fight and is losing the support of his friends, Phil has been sleeping with George's wife, and James insists on getting the recognition he has earned saving George's face all these years. It is even discovered that the championship itself might have been a fraud: Martin was ordered by the Coach to surreptitiously injure a black player on the opposing team in order to win the all-important game. But even as the men are being torn apart, the memory of their past glory ties them together; with the Coach's help, the desperate quartet end up clinging to each other because winning that championship together was the only meaningful moment in their frustrated lives. A. J. Antoon directed the play like a maestro, and the mounting drama was profoundly affecting. While the acting by all five men was superior, two actors, neither of them newcomers to the profession, saw their careers take off because of the play. Sorvino would go on to a lucrative career in films, occasionally returning to the musical stage. The blue-collar-looking Durning would also become a familiar character actor on film but would continue a memorable stage career as well. *That Championship Season* received the most glowing reviews of the season. Martin Gottfried of *Women's Wear Daily* captured the theme of the play best when he wrote, "It is about the emptiness of the American success ethic, its demand of inhumanity and hatred for the sake of winning

something essentially worthless." The drama won all the major awards, including the Pulitzer Prize, and ran through the summer at the Public before reopening on Broadway in September, eventually tallying 844 performances.

Lincoln Center concluded its off-Broadway season with David Wiltse's **Suggs** (5-4-72, Forum), an engaging drama about an idealistic country boy (William Atherton) who comes to the big city to become a sportscaster but grows disillusioned about love and his job, ending up as one of the city's human flotsam. Several critics found the writing perceptive and honest, and newcomer Atherton was applauded.

The final entry on Broadway was Steve Gordon's dark comedy **Tough to Get Help** (5-4-72, Royale). Clifford Grant (Dick O'Neill), a liberal ad man who lives in Larchmont, has problems with his domestic servants, a black couple (John Amos and Lillian Hayman), when their radical son Leroy (John Danelle) comes on the scene. The subservient parents end up turning militant themselves, helping Leroy escape to Algeria after he bombs a courthouse. Carl Reiner directed, and Abe Vigoda got to play Abraham Lincoln in a dream scene, but the whole enterprise closed on opening night.

Critics were enthusiastic about **Anna K** (5-7-72, Actors' Playhouse), Eugenie Leontovich's loose adaptation of Tolstoy's *Anna Karenina* that was far from a musty period piece. On a bare stage a group of modern actors are rehearsing a play version of the Tolstoy classic. In between scenes the actors discuss the material and bring their own contemporary lives into the rehearsal, resulting in two parallels stories being dramatized. Leontovich directed the stimulating program and played a few old Russian dowagers along the way. (Catherine Ellis was the play-within-the-play Anna.) The admirable venture ran a successful seven months.

Polish playwright Stanislaw Witkiewicz's 1921 fable **The Water Hen** (5-9-72, BAM) closed the Chelsea's season. It was the American premiere for the "spherical tragedy" about a family bewitched by a femme fatale. Since Witkiewicz was a forerunner of the absurdist movement, the piece played more like a dark comedy for its twenty-one performances.

The season's second Clifford Odets play, **The Silent Partner** (5-11-72, Actors Studio), was written in 1937 but had never been produced before this two-week showcase. The drama, about labor relations in a factory town, was no lost masterpiece, but the four-member cast (Viveca Lindfors,

William Prince, Sally Kirkland, Peter Masterson) was thought engaging by the press.

The Public's season continued with **Older People** (5-14-72, Anspacher), a series of comic vignettes about the aged written by twenty-eight-year-old John Ford Noonan. The sixteen brief sketches often came down to jokes about sex among senior citizens, but there were two capable scenes. In one, two aging rock idols try to sing their past hit "Penny Arcade" but cannot remember the second stanza until an aging groupie shows up and supplied the missing lyrics. In the other, a touching monologue, a famous scientist's wife (Madeleine Sherwood) attempts to honor her late husband in a lecture but ends up revealing her frustrated love life. Most critics found the script lacking (one termed it "sub-Saroyan cuteness"), but it was gratifying to see veterans such as Sherwood, Barnard Hughes, Polly Rowles, Will Hare, and Stefan Schnabel still giving animated performances.

The American Place's final offering, Frank Chin's **The Chickencoop Chinaman** (5-27-72, American Place), was no more successful than the rest of its season, but it was an important, if flawed, work. Tam Lum (Randy Kim), a Chinese-American filmmaker, flies from Los Angeles to Pittsburgh to interview the elderly Charley Popcorn (Leonard Jackson), the black manager of a porno house, about his once-famous boxer son. Lum stays at the house of a Japanese friend, Kenji (Sab Shimono), with his white mistress (Sally Kirkland) and hanger-on Tom (Calvin Jung), a Chinese intellectual writing a book about the culture of his homeland. What follows is a series of conversations and commentary on Asian stereotypes in America with Lum cracking jokes in a variety of international dialects. Most critics thought the play incoherent and felt it reinforced racial stereotypes; others saw what the playwright was attempting and thought it unique and impressive. The only Asian critic to review it, William Wong writing for the *Wall Street Journal*, declared the play "historic . . . the first American play fashioned out of unromanticized Asian-American sensibilities by an Asian-American writer." But it would be another decade before a play by an Asian American would be fully recognized by critics and audiences, and *The Chickencoop Chinaman* would become a footnote in the history of Asian theatre in America.

This was, perhaps, the last season in which Off Broadway was the only major alternative to Broadway. Theatre companies such as the Manhattan Theatre Club, Circle Theatre Company, Equity Library Theatre, La Mama Experimental Theatre Club, and other groups, usually relegated to a category somewhere below Off Broadway, were now being considered more professional. And dozens of storefronts, churches, and found spaces were being used to present theatre that provided escape from the growing formality of the traditional Greenwich Village off-Broadway house. Back in February the Off-Off-Broadway Alliance had been formed, and these scattered groups now took on a unified identity. Off Off Broadway was growing, and it would slowly change Off Broadway and Broadway with it.

1972–1973

Walking around the Theatre District during the 1972–1973 season, one was accosted by symbols of Broadway's darkest hour. Several theatre marquees advertised shows long closed. Porn movie houses were proliferating beyond 42nd Street and Eighth Avenue, some opening next door to legitimate theatres. Additional policemen on duty at curtain time only emphasized New York's rising crime rate, something that was affecting box-office figures. Not visible, but well known, was the dwindling number of new plays, especially off Broadway. More plays were coming from London and regional theatres. Box-office receipts were down, and *Playbill* was losing so much money it announced that it might have to start charging for its theatre programs.

Yet there were signs of hope if one looked closely enough. A makeshift trailer booth in Times Square, sponsored by the Theatre Development Fund, started selling half-price tickets for shows that were far from capacity for that day. Many theatregoers were suspicious of such discounts, questioning the quality of a show that had to resort to such measures. But the TKTS Booth, as it would soon be called, held its own and would eventually turn into a major ticket-buying source in New York and later be copied by other major cities across the country. Also visible were three new theatres, the first to be built in the Theatre District in nearly fifty years. Many found the Uris (on Broadway at 50th Street) and the Minskoff (Broadway at 45th Street) too cold and too large, but the fact that anyone would build a new theatre when half a dozen existing houses were usually vacant was a sign of stubborn optimism. The third new venue, the Circle in the Square Joseph E. Levine Theatre, was housed in the same skyscraper as the Uris but was in an arena format, Broadway's only such house. The Street's oldest existing legitimate theatre, the Lyceum, built in 1902, was designated a landmark by the State of New York at the end of the season. The fact was not widely noticed, nor was it of much interest to most, but such a designation's importance would become major news in future seasons when area theatres were faced with demolition.

Less visible but influential all the same was the rise of Off Off Broadway. Over one hundred theatre companies were listed by the Theatre Development Fund as off-off-Broadway theatres, and many were starting to make waves felt in the mainstream of theatregoing. Several of these groups, especially those emphasizing new works, would reach their full potential in future seasons, but this was the first season in which their strong presence could not be ignored.

While Broadway had to content itself with holdovers all summer long, Joseph Papp and his various venues provided enough excitement off Broadway to keep theatregoers satisfied. His New York Shakespeare Festival initiated the season outdoors on June 20 at the Delacorte with a lopsided *Hamlet*, directed by Gerald Freedman, in which the audience got more caught up in James Earl Jones's masterful Claudius than in Stacy Keach's unexciting Prince. Established and promising actors such as Colleen Dewhurst, Sam Waterston, Raul Julia, Barnard Hughes, and Linda Hunt kept the production somewhat interesting, and Tom Aldredge and Charles Durning, recent stars due to Papp productions the previous season, showed up as the Gravediggers.

Frank D. Gilroy, whose *Who'll Save the Plowboy?* (1-9-62) and *The Subject Was Roses* (5-25-64) were so satisfying, floundered with his bill of one-acts called **Present Tense** (7-19-72, Sheridan Square). The title playlet was a Beckett-like exercise about a husband and wife refusing to let an elusive stranger into their house, *'Twas Brillig* concerned a Hollywood screenwriter who is tormented by a studio boss with nonsense games, *Come Next Tuesday* revealed the death of trust in a couple married eighteen years, and *So Please Be Kind* was set in a hotel room where two lovers argue about the forgotten name of a movie actor. Despite a fine cast that included Lois Smith and Biff McGuire, the quartet was a hollow experience, and it closed after a week.

The Delacorte's widely admired *Much Ado About Nothing* on August 10 was the highlight of the summer and, for many, the best revival of the season. Director A. J. Antoon set the Italianate piece in small-town America during the era of innocence before the First World War. Don Pedro (Douglas Watson) and his comrades returned from the Spanish-American War to an America of straw-hatted men in striped coats and parasoled ladies who motored in vintage automobiles or played their Victrolas while they spoke of love. The approach seemed the least forced resetting of Shakespeare within memory, even when Dogberry (Barnard Hughes) and his officials resembled Keystone Kops. With an onstage band playing Peter Link's original music and some traditional rags, this *Much Ado* had a musical comedy feel to it that managed to enhance the play rather than sidetrack it. The cast was mostly laudable. Kathleen Widdoes was a graceful but authoritative Beatrice. Sam Waterston's Benedick was the evening's grandest portrayal, moving from a stiff-mustached soldier in the early scenes to a smooth-shaven and expansive lover later on.

The Roundabout Theatre Company continued its interest in foreign plays with Pirandello's *Right You Are* on September 12. Eric Bentley's English-language version of the illusionary play about truth and madness was used. Dorothy Sands played Signora Frola, and John LaGioia was her son-in-law Signor Ponza.

Off-Broadway's finest play of the previous season, *That Championship Season* (5-2-72), reopened at the Booth on September 14 with the same cast and played to healthy houses for nearly two years. With his transferred *Sticks and Bones* also still running on Broadway and his *Much Ado About Nothing* preparing to open in a Broadway house in November, producer Papp clearly dominated the New York theatre scene both on and off the Street.

Papp's indoor season opened with Alice Childress's evocative slice-of-life drama **Wedding Band** (9-26-72, Public: Newman), set in a small South Carolina city in the summer of 1918. A black seamstress, Julia (Ruby Dee), and a white baker, Herman (James Broderick), have been involved in a secret love affair for ten years. As he visits her neighborhood, they are surrounded by such vivid characters as Fanny (Clarice Taylor), the pesky landlady, and the illiterate waif Mattie (Juanita Clark) who needs Julia to read to her the letters from her common-law husband in the navy. One night Herman has an influenza attack in Julia's bedroom, and the neighbors prevent her from calling a doctor for fear of the police discovering their relationship. Herman is smuggled out of the apartment after dark, but he returns the next day to confront Julia, both realizing that the forces keeping them apart are stronger than their love. Like Childress's other work, the play was unhurried, atmospheric, and highly lyrical. Yet critics' opinions were mixed. Many felt that the characters were likable but far from riveting, one aisle-sitter going so far as to call the play "like a story from the pages of what used to be known as a magazine for women." Several reviews mentioned Ming Cho Lee's scenic design, a ramshackle backyard of three houses and Julia's apartment, all crumbling with age and despair. Word of mouth (and the high level of admiration for Papp) made it the Public's most popular attraction of the season, running 175 times.

The City Center Acting Company, a new group made up of recent graduates of Juilliard who wished to continue to work together, presented a season of six revivals at the Good Shepherd Faith Church under the direction of John Houseman. Its first offering, Sheridan's *The School for Scandal* on September 27, was perhaps the most interesting. Commentators agreed that there was talent here but that it was unquestionably new and sometimes a bit raw. David Ogden Stiers's stuffy Joseph Surface got most of the plaudits, but there was a definite future for company members Kevin Kline, Patti LuPone, David Schramm, and Mary Lou Rosato.

Bob Randall's **6 Rms Riv Vu** (10-17-72, Helen Hayes) was that increasingly rare Broadway product: a romantic comedy with few pretensions except to entertain on a modest scale. A popular staple before television replaced it, this kind of escapist situation comedy had trouble holding its own on Broadway unless Neil Simon's name was attached to the title. But this slight yet charming comedy pleased audiences and even some critics and managed to run out the season. Ad writer Paul Friedman (Jerry Orbach), who wanted to be a penetrating novelist of modern Jewish themes until Philip Roth came along and stole his thunder, inspects an empty Riverside Drive apartment on the same day that the bored housewife Anne Miller (Jane Alexander) is checking it out. In one of those contrivances acceptable in boulevard comedy, they are accidentally locked inside when the door handle comes apart. After the usual futile efforts to be rescued, the two find much in common, mostly their dissatisfaction with their spouses, professions, and life in general. Too old to comfortably jump into the sexual revolution, Paul and Anne have a one-night love affair filled more with reticence than passion. Rescued by the super, Paul and Anne part, but the next day the two accidentally meet again when they return

JANE ALEXANDER (née Quigley) (1939–) was born in Boston and educated at Sarah Lawrence College and the University of Edinburgh. After appearing in various regional theatres, she made her Broadway debut (and won a Tony Award) as Ellie, the white mistress of African-American boxer Jack Jefferson, in *The Great White Hope* (1968), which originated at the Arena Stage in Washington. Alexander's critically acclaimed Lavinia in *Mourning Becomes Electra* was seen at the American Shakespeare Theatre Festival, at the Kennedy Center, and at the Huntington Theatre in Los Angeles in 1971 and 1972. Throughout her Broadway career she would often return to regional theatres. Her second husband, Edwin Sherin, directed her in *The Great White Hope* and several other productions. A tall and sharply sculptured actress, Alexander rarely played conventional heroines but usually proper and intelligent women with a vulnerable side to them.

with their spouses to inspect the apartment. Left alone momentarily, they are yet again locked in by the same faulty doorknob and come to the conclusion that an extended affair is not possible. Randall's characters were agreeable enough, especially as played by the appealingly unromantic Orbach and Alexander, and his perky dialogue made up for his clumsy plotting. While a few critics complained ("has nthg mch to offr," one of them wagged), the majority thought the comedy was, like its classified-ad title, concise, to the point, and tantalizing enough to please.

Reviewers were in agreement about **The Lincoln Mask** (10-30-72, Plymouth), though, and roundly slammed every aspect of the preachy V. J. Longhi drama, which closed in a week. Using the performance of *Our American Cousin* at Ford's Theatre as its leitmotif, the play explored Lincoln's career from his days as a senator until that fated night of his assassination. Lincoln (Fred Gwynne) was portrayed as a moody, righteous, and even clairvoyant man obsessed with emancipation though the price was a war and the destruction of his own family. The effect was irritatingly melodramatic, and more than one critic declared it unintentionally funny in spots. Longhi's dialogue was so banal and anachronistic that aisle-sitters had only to quote from the play to make their point. (Abe's comment on theatregoing as a pleasant experience gathered the most chuckles.) Brendan Gill of *The New Yorker* even pointed out that Mary Todd Lincoln (Eva Marie Saint) recited lines from Browning fifteen years before the poet had written them. The cast was also dismissed; Gwynne got the worst of the knocks, and even Saint was gently scolded. The first of three beloved actresses to play Mrs. Lincoln this season, she certainly had the weakest of the three vehicles.

The next night, Alan Bates received the acting raves of the season and secured the career of the British playwright Simon Gray on Broadway. **Butley** (10-31-72, Morosco) was a tour-de-force comedy about a manic London University professor whose life is collapsing all around him. When Ben Butley (Bates) cuts his chin shaving one morning, little does he know it will be the least unpleasant thing to happen to him all day. Arriving at his office, Butley finds that the reason his officemate and lover, Joey (Hayward Morse), stood him up the previous evening is that Joey has decided to leave him and move in with a man named Reg. Butley's wit and sense of sarcasm goes into high gear when there is a crisis, and he bombards Joey with insults, accusations, and nursery rhymes. He is intermittently interrupted by a co-ed (Geraldine Sherman) wishing to read her paper on *A Winter's Tale* and by a colleague, Edna (Barbara Lester), complaining about the vulgarity of her students. Soon Butley's wife, Anne (Holland Taylor), enters and tells him she is going to marry their mutual friend Tom. Before the day is out, the beleaguered professor has an altercation with the muscular Reg (Roger Newman) that leaves Butley with a cut lip. Joey moves out, and the play ends with Butley hoping to make Joey jealous by trying to seduce one of Edna's radical male students (Christopher Hastings). What could have been a soap-operaish situation was made gloriously funny by Butley's dazzling wit and, of course, Bates's zestful performance. While some of the critics felt the play was "thin" and "actionless," all proclaimed Bates's as the performance of the season. *Time*'s T. E. Kalem declared, "Bates makes the evening blazingly his as a man slouching toward bedlam—hair bedraggled, trousers rumpled, eyes aglaze, and an adder's tongue in his cheek." But even the critics forgot that a playwright wrote the words for that adder's tongue, and few acknowledged Gray's superior dialogue and stinging observations. Also, many ignored James Hammerstein's taut direction (based, no doubt, on Harold Pinter's staging of *Butley* in London). *Butley* ran through February, and Bates won the Tony Award at the end of the season.

The season at Lincoln Center began on an awkward note. Artistic director Jules Irving turned in his resignation before the first performance, and the company struggled through without him until a successor was chosen in the spring. The opener was the first professional production in America of Gorky's little-seen 1907 drama **Enemies** (11-9-72, Vivian Beaumont). Ellis Rabb directed the large production based on a translation by Jeremy Brooks and Kitt Hunter-Blair that had been done by the Royal Shakespeare Company in London the year before. Gorky's naturalistic piece explored the stirrings of revolution in the Bardin household on a provincial estate in 1905 Russia. The large cast was uneven, but critics favorably singled out Nancy Marchand as the actress Tatiana, Josef Sommer as the prosecutor Skobofov, and Susan Sharkey as the rebellious Nadya. They were also impressed with Douglas W. Schmidt's stunning set, a revolving stage that allowed the garden and house to be viewed at different angles at different times. Like too many Lincoln Center offerings, it was a production more respected than cherished.

The summer's popular outdoor production of *Much Ado About Nothing* reopened on Broadway on November 11 in the Winter Garden Theatre with few changes, and it garnered another set of adoring notices. It played in the large house until mid-February and was nominated for several Tony Awards, some rarely afforded to a Shakespeare revival, such as Best Score and Best Choreography. (Director A. J. Antoon was also nominated but won instead for his staging of the other Public Theatre transfer, *That Championship Season*.)

No Broadway revival was greeted with such vehemence this season as *Lysistrata*, Aristophanes's comedy adapted and directed by Michael Cacoyannis, which opened at the Brooks Atkinson on November 13. This misconceived production set the play in an inconsistent modern setting with many allusions to the Vietnam War. (One commentator called the style "cockamamie Cacoyannis.") Some critics gave Melina Mercouri, as the feminist Lysistrata, the benefit of the doubt by wishing her a better production, but most disdained the entire venture, and in a week it was gone.

Playwright Paul Zindel turned from the tart comedy-drama of his *The Effects of Gamma Rays on Man-in-the-Moon Marigolds* (4-7-70) and *And Miss Reardon Drinks a Little* (2-25-71) to a Walter Mitty–like fantasy called **The Secret Affairs of Mildred Wild** (11-14-72, Ambassador). In a cluttered apartment behind a Greenwich Village candy store live frowzy Mildred Wild (Maureen

Stapleton) and her diabetic husband, Roy (Lew Wallace), who is addicted to Clark bars. Mildred is an avid fan of old movies and has a forty-year-old collection of film magazines, many pictures from them plastered on her walls. She is hassled by a meddling sister-in-law (Elizabeth Wilson), a demanding landlady (Florence Stanley), and a wrecking crew trying to tear down the building, so she retreats into a fantasy world in which she appears in such film classics as *King Kong* and *Gone With the Wind*. This dream existence is given new impetus one day when Mildred is phoney, by a TV contest to answer three movie questions and win a trip to Hollywood to take a screen test. Of course Mildred knows the answers, but it turns out the contest is phony, and she slips back to reality and her husband. Zindel's dialogue was crisp and irreverent, but the comedy's most enjoyable sequences were Mildred's flights of fancy and watching Stapleton tap-dancing like Shirley Temple or being grabbed by a giant ape's hand. Also memorable were Santo Loquasto's sets, which moved from Mildred's movieland apartment decor to the glitzy Hollywood scenes. Critics admired Stapleton for her no-holds-barred performance (and her many rapid costume changes) but found the whole venture disappointing. The play closed in three weeks, and Zindel's playwriting career never recovered.

Since the Circle in the Square and the whole off-Broadway movement had first gained recognition with the 1956 revival of O'Neill's *The Iceman Cometh*, it was appropriate that an O'Neill work open the new Circle in the Square Theatre uptown. The trilogy *Mourning Becomes Electra* (10-26-31) was edited and condensed into a three-and-a-half-hour version, which inaugurated the new 650-seat, U-shaped theatre on November 15. Reaction to both the production and the theatre was mixed, some finding the play dated and others finding the space an awkward compromise between a Broadway and an off-Broadway house. Theodore Mann directed a cast headed by Colleen Dewhurst as the matriarch Christine and Pamela Payton-Wright as Lavinia/Electra; both received plaudits even from those who disliked the play. The drama played to healthy business during its scheduled fifty-five performances and proved an admirable start for the new theatre.

Some found Paul Ableman's British comedy-drama **Green Julia** (11-16-72, Sheridan Square) quite engaging (Otis L. Guernsey, Jr., editing the *Best Plays*, chose it as one of the season's ten best) while others thought it just a clever exercise in role-playing. Robert Lacey (Fred Grandy) and Ja-

cob Perew (James Woods) are flatmates just graduated from the university and have invited Jacob's sluttish girlfriend, Julia, to join them during their last evening together. Jacob is leaving the country, so he offers Julia to his friend, a gift at which Robert takes offense. While waiting for Julia, the two friends thrash out their feelings for each other by assuming different characters and play-acting various comic situations. The subtext for all this is really their uncertainty about the future, and by the time Jacob has departed, Robert can only stand immobile as Julia keeps ringing the doorbell. After the swift and deadly wit of *Butley* the collegiate antics of *Green Julia* paled, but the tight little production managed to run four months.

Lincoln Center's season downstairs in the Forum opened and closed with a Beckett festival presenting revivals of *Happy Days* and *Act Without Words 1* on November 20. Hume Cronyn, Jessica Tandy, and Henderson Forsythe performed the pieces under the direction of Beckett expert Alan Schneider. Two days later two plays were added, *Krapp's Last Tape* and **Not I** (11-22-72, Forum), the last a world premiere. Announced as Beckett's first play written in English (his usual practice was to write in French and later translate it into his native language), *Not I* was a fifteen-minute monologue by Mouth (Tandy), an old woman incoherently recalling sad memories supposedly about another woman but actually about herself. The playlet began in darkness, then gradually only her mouth was lit and then a listening figure with his back to the audience, the Auditor (Forsythe), was revealed. The Mouth eventually faded away, but her nonsensical words echoed long after the image was gone. Critics, always cautious when dealing with Beckett, delicately approved of the plays but were more comfortable praising the actors. But when the Mouth faded away, so did the Forum. Soon after the repertory closed on December 17, Lincoln Center announced that there were no more funds to produce plays in the space, and it was dark the rest of the season.

At the Public, Michael McGuire's fantasy **The Children** (11-28-72, Other Stage) ran out its scheduled eight weeks without much excitement. On a midwestern farm, Kathleen (Fern Sloan) is dying. Gathered around her to share painful memories are her husband, Dan (Kevin McCarthy), her lover, Christopher (Bob Balaban), and her son (Terry Kiser). The eerie piece sought to be symbolic but turned out merely vague and rambling.

The Creation of the World and Other Business (11-30-72, Shubert) was an important event of the season, for it marked Arthur Miller's first new play on Broadway in four years. In the Garden of Eden, Adam (Bob Dishy) and God (Stephen Elliott) are pals, naming the animals and enjoying the always perfect weather. When Adam longs for a mate, God creates Eve (Zoe Caldwell), and the traditional series of events follows: Lucifer (George Grizzard), taking the form of a snake, tempts Eve with the apple; Adam joins her, and they are expelled from the garden; Eve suffers the pains of childbirth; Cain (Barry Primus) kills Abel (Mark Lamos), and the survivors set out to seek answers in a brutal new world. Miller's play wavered between comedy and didactic drama, spending more time on philosophical discussions than on dramaturgy. The dialogue ranged from the lofty ("his simple praise for surfaces made me impatient to show him the physics of my art, which would raise him to a god") to the anachronistic ("the middle of a perfect, moonlit night and they're playing handball") to the farcical ("as for you, schmuck, cursed is the ground for thy sake"). Reaction to the play was radically diverse. Some critics, surprised to find so much humor in a Miller play, hailed it as an inventive comedy. Others thought it the most pretentious of works, coy without being clever. The fine actors were generally applauded with Grizzard getting most of the compliments. Guernsey, who choose it as one of the *Best Plays*, thought the script a "muscular comedy which will undoubtedly live on in future productions around the globe and even in New York." Such was not to be. The odd play closed after twenty performances and has rarely been heard of since.

The finest play by an African-American playwright this season was Joseph A. Walker's **The River Niger** (12-5-72, St. Marks), a family drama rich with penetrating characters and plot situations. Johnny Williams (Douglas Turner Ward) is a poet at heart (the play's title is the name of a poem he has been working on) but a house painter by profession. He lives in Harlem with his no-nonsense wife, Mattie (Roxie Roker), and his inebriated mother (Frances Foster), but the pride of his life is his son Jeff (Les Roberts) who is in the air force and has just made lieutenant. Johnny's boozy doctor friend Dudley (Graham Brown) sees no glory in being honored by the white man's military, but Johnny waits for Jeff's upcoming leave with enthusiasm. Before the son returns, though, Jeff's current girlfriend Ann (Grenna Whitaker), a nurse from South Africa, arrives and befriends the parents but not the grandmother. Also, members of a black militant

DOUGLAS TURNER WARD (1930–) was born in Burnside, Louisiana, but educated in the north at Wilberforce University and the University of Michigan. In New York he trained at the Paul Mann Theatre Workshop and appeared in roles off Broadway before making his Broadway debut in the small role of a moving man in *A Raisin in the Sun* (1959). Ward made his professional playwriting debut with the one-acts *A Day of Absence* and *Happy Ending* (1965), which ran over a year off Broadway. In 1968, Ward, Robert Hooks, and Gerald Krone founded the Negro Ensemble Company, and was its artistic director, staging such memorable plays as *Ceremonies in Dark Old Men* (1969) and this season's *The River Niger*. Ward was not the most radical of black authors and producers, but through the satire in his writing and an eloquent form of realism in his acting he served as a powerful voice for African-Americans.

group that Jeff once belonged to come looking for him, wanting him to lead the gang once again. When Jeff arrives, both family and gang are surprised and disappointed that Jeff has changed. He has given up the idea of a military career and also dismisses the militant group, saying he wants to become a lawyer and fight the system from within. Johnny goes off on a drunken binge, and the gang involves Jeff in a plan to blow up a police station. But there is an informant in the gang; the plan backfires, and a policeman is shot. The gang converges on the Williams household just as the disheveled Johnny returns and recites his finally completed poem. Violence breaks out at the discovery of the informer, and Johnny is shot. The police surround the house, so the dying Johnny says he will admit to the murder of the cop, thereby saving his son and giving him a chance for a better life than he himself had. Walker's writing was rich with humor, compassion, and exciting storytelling that rarely slipped into melodrama. Each character was vividly drawn, from the expansive and life-filled Johnny to the jokingly cynical Dudley to each individual gang member. The Negro Ensemble Company cast was solid throughout, and critical reception was enthusiastic. The Obie-winning drama ran 120 performances off Broadway, then transferred on March 27 to the Brooks Atkinson, where it ran an additional 280 performances and won the next season's Tony Award. The production was also a high point in the career of its director and leading actor, Douglas Turner Ward.

The announcement of an all-black production of *The Cherry Orchard* at the Public seemed like a gimmick to many, especially since the play's Russian locale was retained and the cast still portrayed European characters. But there was a different feel to this Chekhov production, which opened on December 7 in the Anspacher. Hellbent on not duplicating the stiff, British approach to the play, director Michael Schultz (using a concept proposed by James Earl Jones) opened the characters up, making them passionate in their emotions and overt in their intentions. Gloria Foster was an extroverted Ranyevskaya, her Chekhovian tête-à-têtes becoming all-out fights. Jones, as the upstart merchant Lopahin, was clumsy and self-conscious but also very aware of his destiny. His announcement that he has acquired the cherry orchard was filled with such joy that no words could escape his lips, and he mouthed "I bought it" in a harsh silence that was unforgettable. *The Cherry Orchard* ran eighty-six performances, yet another triumph for the Public.

The New Phoenix Repertory Company ran two difficult revivals in true rep in the Lyceum Theatre for two months and was greeted with appreciative nods. O'Neill's problematic *The Great God Brown* (1-23-26) opened on December 10. While the play itself caused a wide range of opinions, there was little question about the superior production it received. Harold Prince, in one of his rare non-musical efforts, staged the inventive piece, and designer Boris Aronson came up with a series of revolving units of furniture that created the different locales over the play's twenty-year time span. John Glover was a solid Brown, but John McMartin's tormented artist Dion was the focal point of the evening, and the musical comedy player was greeted with laudatory reviews. The next night Molière's infrequently done comedy *Don Juan* opened at the Lyceum, and the New Phoenix was praised for the production and its true repertory nature. Paul Hecht, who had played a minor role in the O'Neill drama, attacked Don Juan with gusto. But again McMartin, as the wily servant Pierrot, got most of the laughs. Stephen Porter adapted and directed the Molière comedy in a straightforward manner on a sparse set, and the play surprised and pleased many.

As had been true for her most recent vehicles, Julie Harris was the main reason to see **The Last of Mrs. Lincoln** (12-12-72, ANTA), a biographical drama by James Prideaux about the eighteen years following Lincoln's assassination. The drama took an episodic form, starting with a senator on Capitol Hill proposing that pension funds for the president's widow be cut. Succeeding scenes dealt with Mary's forced travels, the suspicion by many that she had been a southern sympathizer, the death of her young son Tad (Tobias Haller), her son Robert (David Rounds) committing her to a mental asylum, her release, and finally her death. Prideaux presented Mary as courageous and impulsive, and Harris brought to the character a fragile kind of dignity that rose above the mediocre writing. Critics carped about the melodramatic nature of the play, but Harris, with her desperate and wistful voice speaking lovingly of "Mr. Lincoln," was one of the highlights of the season. She won the Tony Award, but the play only survived sixty-three performances.

Neil Simon continued his string of hits with the season's best comedy, **The Sunshine Boys** (12-20-72, Broadhurst), a play that managed to be more gentle and delicate than many thought the laugh master capable of. In a shabby New York apartment hotel, ex-vaudevillian Willie Clark (Jack Albertson) is living out his days auditioning for TV commercials he doesn't get hired for and reading obituaries in *Variety* of old friends and enemies His nephew Ben Silverman (Lewis J. Stadlen) is his agent and caretaker, but he seems to be failing on both accounts. Ben can't get him work because Willie can no longer memorize lines and his hands shake too much, especially for the razor blade commercial the agent had lined up. Willie's health and living habits are just as precarious, but he is too stubborn to change his ways. Ben arrives for his weekly visit to check on Willie and announces that CBS-TV is doing a special on the history of comedy and wants Willie and his old partner Al Lewis to perform their famous doctor sketch. Willie is thrilled to perform again but refuses to work with Lewis, his partner for forty-three years and, for the past eleven years, retired and living with his family in New Jersey. The team of Lewis and Clark was quite popular on the vaudeville circuit but, Willie admits, the two comics never liked each other. Ben tells Willie that Lewis is willing to give it a try, so a rehearsal is set up. Lewis (Sam Levene) is more mellow than Willie, but at the rehearsal each explodes at the other's slight alteration of the lines or gestures. (Willie hates it when Al pokes him in the chest to make a point.) The two veterans actually get before the cameras for the CBS taping, but an argument breaks out, Al walks off the set, and Willie flies into a rage that brings on a heart attack. Two weeks later Willie is convalescing in his apartment with a nurse (Minnie Gentry) to care for him when Al comes to visit his old partner. Ben has convinced Willie to retire, and it turns out both vaudevillians are going to the same actors' home in New Jersey, where they will live out their days fighting with each other. Because of the vaudeville sketches in the play and Willie's rapid burlesque patter, *The Sunshine Boys* had more one-liners than usual even for a Neil Simon play. But the quiet and intimate scenes were perhaps the most heartfelt he'd yet written, and the comedy pleased in ways not previously experienced. Simon also showed great insight into the workings of show business in this, his first play about entertainers. Willie's instructions to Ben about the nature of comedy (words with a *k* in them are funny: "chicken is funny, roast beef is not funny") and the conjuring up of old vaudevillian humor made the play as informative as it was enjoyable. Audiences had seen Levene do this sort of banter before, but Albertson was a revelation, and the two pros played off each other beautifully. The reviews were valentines, the audiences agreed, and *The Sunshine Boys* ran 538 performances.

Geraldine Page was the season's third Mary Todd Lincoln, but not for long. **Look Away** (1-7-73, Playhouse) closed on opening night. Jerome Kilty's talky two-character drama was set in an insane asylum where Mary's son has committed her. It is the day before her release, and Mrs. Lincoln reminisces, reads old letters, dresses in old costumes, and complains to her companion Elizabeth Keckley (Maya Angelou), the black seamstress who served the First Lady in the White House. The play treated Mary sympathetically, but most found Page's mannered rantings and neurotic ravings more irritating than effective. Angelou brought a quiet dignity to the role of the servant (who actually wrote a book about her days serving the Lincolns), and audiences felt Elizabeth was a far more likable character. Also more intriguing than Mary was Ben Edwards's gloomy set filled with trunks and memorabilia.

Off Broadway, absurdist playwright Jean-Claude van Itallie turned his satirical pen to the mystery genre in the bluntly titled **Mystery Play** (1-3-73, Cherry Lane), but the result was no *America Hurrah* (11-6-66). In the posh drawing room of a senator are gathered his wife, his bisexual son (whose schizophrenia was signaled by having two actors play the role), the son's fiancée, who is a Harvard professor, and a subdued butler. A mystery writer from next door acts as narrator for this bizarre piece, telling both actors and audi-

ence what events are to occur and how the murders are to be committed. While spoofing the *And Then There Were None* mode of thriller, van Itallie also took potshots at social hypocrisy and made each victim more disgusting than the last. Michael Feingold of the *Village Voice*, and others sympathetic to one of Off Broadway's favorite sons, found the piece "continuously amusing and provoking," while most described it as unfunny and tedious, a farce that "remains firmly clamped to the ground." It was gone in two weeks.

Sean O'Casey's *The Plough and the Stars* (11-28-27) at the Vivian Beaumont on January 4 was another ambitious production of a foreign classic at Lincoln Center that was greeted with respect rather than enthusiasm. Director Dan Sullivan and the repertory company tackled the difficult piece with intelligence and care, but everyone agreed that non-company actor Jack MacGowran (the only Irishman in the cast) as the cowardly carpenter Fluther Good was the best thing about the show. The most successful production at the Roundabout Theatre this season was the Molnár/Wodehouse comedy *The Play's the Thing* (11-3-26) on January 9, which received exemplary reviews. Hugh Franklin played the rascally playwright Sandor, David Dukes was the adlebrained composer Albert, and Elizabeth Owens was the jealous prima donna Ilona. Gene Feist directed the charming comedy, which moved to Broadway after sixty-four performances, the first such transfer in the company's seven-year history.

Having originated at the University of Michigan and tried out by the Actors Studio the previous summer, Dennis J. Reardon's anti-war drama **Siamese Connections** (1-9-73, Annex) received a mainstream production at the Public. The farm boy James (James Staley) has always envied the family favorite, his brother, Franklin (David Selby). When Franklin dies in battle and is enshrined forever in the family's mind, James goes on a killing spree, murdering his grandmother, a hired hand, and even a pregnant sow. What kept the play intriguing was the presence of the ghosts of all the murdered characters, who stay on the farm and haunt James. This was potent if faulty playwriting, and there were memorable scenes, such as the grief-stricken father (Roberts Blossom) taking his belt and lashing Franklin's tombstone while his ghost cried out in pain.

Another one of the Broadway season's opening-night closers was the self-billed "serious comedy" **The Enemy Is Dead** (1-14-73, Bijou) by Don Peterson, which reopened the intimate old theatre after years as a movie house. Emmett (Arthur Storch), a schoolteacher who aspires to be a novelist, his neurotic health-nut wife, Leah (Linda Lavin), their infant, and the family cat arrive at an upstate New York summer rental and immediately encounter harassing phone calls from the locals because Leah is Jewish. Then the bigoted Mr. Wolfe (Addison Powell) arrives and threatens the family, but Emmett humiliates the local fool, thereby realizing his ideals and saving his marriage. Before nightfall the family flees back to the city, and the audience is left wondering how such talented actors got involved in so inferior a play.

The all-star revival of Shaw's *Don Juan in Hell* on January 15 at the Palace hoped to recreate the magic of Charles Laughton's concert staging twenty years before. Paul Henreid, Edward Mulhare, Ricardo Montalban, and Agnes Moorehead (who had been in the Laughton version) tried to fill the large empty stage of the Palace, but the evening was only a curiosity, appealing to few. Most critics felt Montalban's Don Juan was excellent, but after twenty-four performances the concert drama picked up and went on tour.

The second Broadway one-night disaster of the week was the lame comedy **Let Me Hear You Smile** (1-16-73, Biltmore) by Leonora Thuna and Harry Cauley. On the eve of her fortieth birthday, Hannah Heywood (Sandy Dennis) is depressed and considers leaving her husband, Neil (James Broderick). Before any decision can be reached, we are back in time thirty-four years, and the kindergartner Hannah (also played by Dennis) is trying to get a kiss from schoolmate Neil (also Broderick). By the third act Hannah is sixty-nine years old and is talking her retired husband out of selling his business and running off to New Zealand. Audiences found the play as pointless and meaningless as the title, and even critics' darling Dennis was roundly scolded.

Uptown's Circle in the Square took a feminist approach to Euripides' *Medea* on January 17, arguing that all of Medea's troubles were heaped on her because she was a woman. The overproduced presentation, complete with a massive set, heavy masks, and costumes that were more sculpted than sewn, was adapted and directed by Minos Volanakis. Irene Papas was the revengeful queen, and the Greek actress got mixed reviews, many complaining about her limited grasp of the English language. All the same, the revival managed to run two months.

A British hit that had played two years in the West End, **The Jockey Club Stakes** (1-24-73, Cort), was a comedy that overflowed with En-

glishness. When the racehorse Jabberwock suspiciously wins the Windsor race after showing poorly in the trials, an investigation is called and justice and truth are sought out. But the three men leading the investigation, the Marquis of Candover (Wilfred Hyde-White), Lord Coverly de Beaumont (Geoffrey Sumner), and Col. Sir Robert Richardson (Robert Coote), are a bunch of aristocratic rogues who, the moment suspicion starts to fall on one of the members of their honored Jockey Club, arrange a genteel cover-up. The plotting was thin, but all the characters, with such Congreve-like names as Coverly, Candover, and Ursula Itchin, were enjoyable company, especially when played by such adroit veterans as Hyde-White, Sumner, and Coote. If *The Jockey Club Stakes* seemed like an old play, it was understandable. The author was William Douglas Home, who had written twenty-six such comedies since 1937, all in the same upper-crust mode. Commendatory reviews, particularly for the old gentlemen, were not enough to ward off audiences' fears of the extreme Britishness of the piece, and the comedy ran only sixty-nine performances.

The finest play presented in the American Place season was Philip Hayes Dean's **Freeman** (1-25-73, American Place), a complex drama with no simple issues and no easy solutions. In an industrial city in Michigan, a black youth, Freeman Aquila (Bill Cobbs), strives for success first in politics and then in real estate, but fails because of outside forces. These forces are not simply the white establishment but Freeman's own family and friends. His conservative parents, a foundry-worker father (Dotts Johnson) and practical-nurse mother (Estelle Evans), see Freeman's ambitions as disrespectful, and his boyhood friend Rex (J. A. Preston), a successful doctor, views Freeman's radical ways as a threat to the respected black community. Dean's dramaturgy, as in his *The Sty of the Blind Pig* (11-16-71), was potent, but *Freeman* was even more compassionate. John Lahr, writing for the *Village Voice*, said Dean "has captured the brittle soul of a man and conveyed a kind of suffering that is undeniable and illuminating."

Tom Eyen's **The White Whore and the Bit Player** (2-5-73, St. Clements) received its first professional production this season although the tragicomedy had been kicking around Off Off Broadway for eight years and had become something of a cult favorite. A washed-up sex symbol (Candy Darling), supposedly based on Marilyn Monroe, is sent to a sanitarium run by Franciscan nuns where she develops two personalities: herself as a nun and as a whore. Eyen's play had often been performed in Spanish, and for this production's eighteen showings, English and Spanish-language performances were alternated.

One of the most talked-about productions of the off-Broadway season was the Chelsea Theatre Center's **Kaspar** (2-6-73, BAM) by Europe's hottest avant-garde playwright, Peter Handke. In 1828 a sixteen-year-old youth, Kaspar Houser, was discovered in Nuremburg, unable to talk or walk and with the IQ of a toddler. The boy was educated, wrote his autobiography, and died (either by suicide or murder) when he was twenty-one. Handke turned this piece of historical trivia into a vindictive diatribe on how words destroy mankind, making his point in unsubtle and repetitive ways. The Chelsea production, directed by Carl Weber and designed by Wolfgang Roth, was a high-powered multi-media circus and exactly the bold kind of theatrics that one had come to expect at its Brooklyn Academy of Music home. Kaspar (Christopher Lloyd) is portrayed as a hyperactive clown destroying furniture and bellowing the same phrase dozens of times while four other masked Kaspars, called Prompters, echo his words. Adding to the kinetic effect were sixteen television monitors onstage that broadcast live coverage of the play and even used instant replay to repeat the many repetitions. As disturbing and exciting as all this may have seemed, the Chelsea had taken similar roads before (the previous season's *Kaddish* also used multi-media in a like manner), and the shock value was diminishing. But the notices were generous, Lloyd was praised for his virtuoso solo turn, and *Kaspar* ran forty-eight high-voltage performances.

Those searching for a sunny comedy about mid-life crisis need look no further than Jean Kerr's **Finishing Touches** (2-8-73, Plymouth). College teacher Jeff Cooper (Robert Lansing), his chipper wife, Katy (Barbara Bel Geddes), and their three sons live a suburban life filled with everyday crises cured by everyday common sense. But lately Jeff is attracted to a young co-ed in one of his classes, and Katy is drawn to the appealing professor who rents the room over their garage. When the eldest son, Steve (James Woods), returns from Harvard with his mistress, Felicia Andrayson (Pamela Bellwood), and she starts showing affection for Jeff, the lid on the conventional Cooper family starts rattling, and only conventional wisdom on the part of all brings everything to a satisfactory compromise. Kerr's old-fashioned dramaturgy was greeted with both affection and derision; one critic's descrip-

tion of it as "a solid trifle" was probably closest to the truth. Bel Geddes' Katy seemed a slightly more mature version of her Mary McKellaway from Kerr's *Mary, Mary* (3-8-61) and was all the more welcome during a season overflowing with psychotics onstage. The comedy worked its gentle magic for five months.

There was some favorable press for Ron Whyte's drama **Welcome to Andromeda** (2-12-73, Cherry Lane), but not enough to allow it to run more than three weeks. A paralytic boy (David Clennon) in his book-filled bedroom is celebrating his twenty-first birthday. While his domineering mother is out shopping for his present, he tries in vain to convince his live-in nurse (Bella Jarrett) to give him a fatal injection, using humor and threats and getting her drunk in the process. Tom Moore directed the taut drama, which had a curtain raiser titled *Variety Obit,* a musical sketch about the death of a vaudevillian.

A trilogy of science-fiction comic-book extravaganzas called **Warp** (2-14-73, Ambassador) had become a cult fascination in Chicago, but when Part One (titled *Warp I: My Battlefield, My Body*) opened on Broadway there were few takers. The opening night audience was filled with teenagers who cheered the epic adventures of David Carson (John Heard), who, in the midst of psychiatric treatment, is whisked off to outer space, where he becomes Lord Cumulus and battles his archenemy, the Prince of Chaos (Tom Towles). There were plenty of special effects, agile gymnastics, and flashy battle scenes, but the whole enterprise left most critics cold. The evening ended in true serial format: with the hero cornered by a fire-breathing monster, the audience was promised "To Be Continued." Part One closed after a week, and Broadway was never invaded by any subsequent *Warps*.

There was unquestionably some ambitious playwriting going on in **Status Quo Vadis** (2-18-73, Brooks Atkinson), Donald Driver's epic satire about the American class system, organized religion, racial bigotry, literary censorship, and just about everything else. The Candide-like hero, Horace Elgin (Bruce Boxleitner), a sort of modern Horatio Alger as his name implied, is born on the wrong side of the tracks but aspires to be a poet and rise to the top. He spurns his lower-class girlfriend Joyce Grishaw (Rebecca Taylor) and seduces a rich heiress, Irene Phillips (Gail Strickland), who volunteers at night school, soon impregnating her. But Horace is in turn cast off by Irene, and he returns to Joyce, who, pregnant by a Dartmouth man, takes him back, class winning out once again. Driver directed the production, in which all the characters wore numbers to signify their class (Horace was a 5, the debutante a 1), and Edward Burbridge designed the set that resembled a game board complete with panels and arrows. The unwieldy affair got some favorable reviews, but most found the satire too scattered to be effective. Although it had been produced successfully in Chicago and Washington, D.C., it went on record as yet another one-night casualty on Broadway.

Hardly more successful (only sixteen performances) was the British import **No Sex Please, We're British** (2-20-73, Ritz) by Anthony Marriott and Alistair Foot, which failed in New York but would go on to become one of the longest-running plays on record in the West End where it originated. The very British Peter Hunter (Stephen Collins) and his very proper wife, Frances (J. J. Lewis), live above the bank where Peter works. She orders some Swedish glassware for her very proper home, but through a mistake of some bureaucratic kind, the Hunter home is inundated with Swedish pornography: magazines, books, films, even two nubile young girls who arrive as some sort of bonus gift. The sex farce, complete with a series of doors and misunderstandings, is propelled by the Hunters' and the bank clerk Runicles's efforts to keep the porn from Peter's boss, his mother, and a police superintendent. The acting was vigorous and expectedly frantic, critics finding Tony Tanner's mousy Runicles either the funniest or most obnoxious performance. (Maureen O'Sullivan was wasted in the supporting role of the mother.) But it was the play itself that got the worse drubbing, nearly all the reviews registering disapproval.

Off Broadway's **Penthouse Legend** (2-22-73, McAlpin Rooftop) was Ayn Rand's courtroom melodrama *Night of January 16* (9-16-35) given a new title. Kay Gillian played the accused murderer Karen Andre, and, as in the original, a jury was selected from the audience to determine which of the two endings would be performed. The disguised revival ran just less than a month.

If audiences were disappointed in Tennessee Williams's *Small Craft Warnings* (4-2-72) last season, they were downright dismayed with this season's **Out Cry** (3-1-73, Lyceum). Under the title *The Two-Character Play*, the enigmatic drama had been previously produced in London and Chicago. Felice (Michael York) and his sister, Clare (Cara Duff-MacCormick), who are touring some cold foreign country, are abandoned by the rest of their acting troupe, who believe the siblings to

be insane. In a dark theatre the two insist on acting out "The Two-Character Play," a gothic drama set in a southern mansion where they recall the murder of a mother by her husband and his subsequent suicide. Neither the play-within-the-play nor the story of the two siblings is resolved. (The two actors have always "suspected that theatres are prisons for players," so they continue on, in Beckett-like fashion, with no end in sight.) Producer David Merrick gave the play a top-notch production, designed by Jo Mielziner and directed by Peter Glenville, but there was no disguising the pall the drama cast on even the most willing patron. Some critics saw Williams boldly experimenting with new forms, but most found the occasion a sad and puzzling shadow of a great playwright's torment. After twelve performances it was gone.

Radically mixed reviews greeted the March 1 revival of *The Merchant of Venice* at Lincoln Center's Vivian Beaumont, which director Ellis Rabb set in a 1960s Italianate setting with a modern look that reminded many of a garish Fellini film. Miniskirts, bikini-clad bathers, and lots of Italian leather filled the stage, but in the midst of it all Sydney Walker and Rosemary Harris gave intelligent performances as Shylock and Portia. Notices ranged from "Lincoln Center's most intriguing Shakespeare ever" to a "ridiculous and irrelevant production."

No American production on Broadway got better reviews than David Storey's **The Changing Room** (3-6-73, Morosco), a British play produced at New Haven's Long Wharf Theatre and brought to Broadway with its American cast intact. Like Storey's previous *Home* (11-17-70), this was a plotless and atmospheric piece. But nothing could be further from the genteel old folks' home of that play than the rugged and teeming-with-life locker room of this one. The first act of the slice-of-life drama depicts the gathering of a North England rugby team before a game. As the working-class players arrive, undress, suit up, and prepare themselves, the coach, owner, and various helpers scurry about. Few particular characters stand out, but we get a sense of the group as a whole as they leave the room and take to the field. Act II shows the activities during the first-half break as wounds are attended to and comments on the game (the score is tied) fly fiercely and freely. Soon the team returns to the field, one of the players, "Kenny" Kendal (John Lithgow), is severely hurt and brought back to the changing room, examined, and sent to the hospital. The last act covers the post-game elation (the team has won the match), undressing, showering, redressing, and eventual departure of the players and staff. The naturalistic play was very specific in its details, and the stunning production, under the direction of Michael Rudman, was never less than fascinating. Many felt the twenty-two-member cast gave one of the finest ensemble performances seen on Broadway in years, and even the extensive nudity onstage was commended for its unerotic realism. The play won the New York Drama Critics Circle Award and ran 192 performances.

Off Off Broadway's Performance Group presented the season's most original avant-garde play, Sam Shepard's **The Tooth of Crime** (3-7-73, Performing Garage), and brought further recognition to the unique American playwright. The established rock star Hoss (Spalding Gray) has come up through the ranks in the traditional manner but is now threatened by the upstart Crow (Timothy Shelton), an icy young performer who uses shock techniques to destroy establishment music. Their confrontation takes the form of a science fiction allegory with short scenes with songs. The play climaxes with a duel to the death, the two musicians competing in a barrage of words, music, and sounds. Richard Schechner's environmental staging had the audience twisting and shifting in their seats to view the action on staircases, ladders, and wooden scaffolding. Although chaotic in spirit, the production was finetuned and polished, having been developed and previously produced in London and at the McCarter Theatre at Princeton. Audiences and critics sensed they were in the presence of something bold, hip, and original, so the play ran a successful 123 performances.

Louis Del Grande's comedy **42 Seconds From Broadway** (3-11-73, Playhouse) probably belonged on television rather than Broadway, but it deserved more than the one-night run it was afforded. It is 1957, and would-be actors John (Henry Winkler) from Hoboken and Robin (Regina Baff) meet working for Western Union and decide to share an apartment in Manhattan. The platonic couple, posing as brother and sister, rent a cheap place on West 47th Street (if you lean out the bathroom window you can actually see a Broadway theatre) and pursue their careers. It was a pleasant enough start for a play, but little that followed worked. John, who feels he ought to be more sexually attracted to Robin than he is, fears he is a homosexual, so he attends a bizarre therapy group that proved as unfunny as tiresome. Critics dismissed the play, but there

> **LANFORD WILSON** (1937–) was born in Lebanon, Missouri (the rural setting for many of his later plays), and attended the University of Chicago, where he studied playwriting. Arriving in New York in 1963, his short works were seen at the Café Cino, the Circle, and other off-off-Broadway venues. His full-length plays *The Gingham Dog* (1969) and *Lemon Sky* (1970) received mainstream productions and were favorably reviewed, but both had short runs. Unlike the work of many of the young playwrights coming from the 1960s, Wilson's tended to be naturalistic and subtle with emphasis on character and atmosphere.

were several kind comments for Winkler, who would go on to do a similar kind of comedy on television.

Beatrice Straight was cited for her fine portrayal of Mrs. Alving in a serviceable revival of Ibsen's *Ghosts* on March 13, the Roundabout's final offering of the season and, at eighty-nine performances, its longest running. Newcomer Victor Garber as Osvald also was noticed by the press, who were positive if unenthusiastic about the production.

Lanford Wilson's **The Hot l Baltimore** (3-22-73, Circle in the Square Downtown) was considered by many the best American play of the season. With it Wilson moved to the forefront of American playwrights, just as his favorite director, Marshall W. Mason, gained recognition. *The Hot l Baltimore* was first produced by the off-off Broadway Circle Theatre Company in February, then transferred to the larger Circle in the Square Downtown in March, where it received unanimously laudatory reviews. Mel Gussow in the

> **MARSHALL W. MASON** (1940–) was born in Amarillo, Texas, and educated at Northwestern University. He studied at the Actors Studio and in 1962 started directing at Café Cino and other off-off-Broadway spaces. In 1969 he co-founded (with Lanford Wilson, Robert Thirkield, and Tanya Berezin) the Circle Repertory Theatre, which concentrated on the work of new American playwrights. He served as artistic director of the innovative company until 1986 but always kept his ties to the theatre, especially the plays by Wilson. His directorial style was characterized by his realistic use of details, overlapping dialogue, and a loose rein on his actors, many of whom worked in the method style.

New York Times compared Wilson's writing to that of Saroyan and Wilder, calling him a "very American playwright with a nostalgic longing for a lost sensibility." Wilson was not an angry playwright but a vocal one all the same, in effect orchestrating the sounds of his characters. In fact, this script identifies characters as "having a mellow alto laugh," "a mezzo," "a baritone," or "thin-voiced." The play's title refers to the marquee of a crumbling downtown Baltimore hotel (the *e* has been missing for some time) that had flourished when the railroads, Baltimore, downtowns, and America did. All the action takes place in the faded lobby of the hotel, characters coming and going as if in a *Grand Hotel* on the skids. The reticent switchboard operator Bill (Judd Hirsch) has long been attracted to a perky young prostitute (Trish Hawkins), called the Girl because she still hasn't decided on her name, but can never bring himself to pursue her. Jackie (Mari Gorman), a butch health food addict, and her dim-witted brother, Jamie (Zane Lasky), are always planning to make it big out west, while the naive hooker Suzy (Stephanie Gordon) romanticizes that something wonderful will happen to her. April (Conchata Ferrell), a hardboiled streetwalker, makes everybody's business her own, commenting freely in her foul-mouthed manner, while Millie (Helen Stenborg), a mild, retired waitress, brings a calming spiritualism to the lobby gatherings. This tragic-comic *Lower Depths* is filled out by a suspicious old man, a college student searching for his grandfather, a whining mother removing her retarded son's belongings, and various unfeeling employees of the hotel who keep their distance from the troublesome residents. Holding together the slice-of-life piece is the news that the hotel is to be torn down. But this is no aristocratic cherry orchard being destroyed, and these characters are not going to fade away quietly like a dying aristocracy. Mason directed the masterful ensemble with seemingly casual precision (the use of overlapping dialogue was particularly effective), and a first-class playwright was given a first-class production. The play won the New York Drama Critics Circle Award and ran 1,166 performances, one of the longest off-Broadway runs on record.

There was no shortage of schizophrenic characters this season, and nowhere were they more tiresome than in **Echoes** (3-26-73, Bijou), a drama by N. Richard Nash, whom everybody remembered fondly for *The Rainmaker* (10-28-54) and other plays. Sam (David Selby) and Tilda (Lynn Milgrim), two inmates in a bare asylum cell who are perhaps lovers as well, keep decorating invisible Christmas trees in February and speak in a cryptic manner that made the two actors in *Out Cry* seem positively lucid. A third character (Paul Tripp) is silent, going over to Sam on occasion and whispering in his ear. The play ends when the mute informs him that Sam has a wife and child and Sam exits. Few plays this season took such a critical beating, the unhappy enterprise closing on opening night.

Rex Harrison's performance in the limited engagement (thirty-seven showings) of Pirandello's *Emperor Henry IV* at the Ethel Barrymore beginning on March 28 was the star turn of the season, and while there may have been finer portrayals elsewhere, none commanded the awe of Harrison's demented emperor, alternately wild-eyed and sedated. The Clifford Williams production, the first seen on Broadway since the premiere fifty years ago when Pirandello's psychodrama was translated as *The Living Mask* (1-21-24), featured a strong supporting cast including Eileen Herlie, Paul Hecht, and David Hurst.

Expectations were perhaps too high for David Rabe's **The Orphan** (3-30-73, Public: Anspacher), an ambitious retelling of Aeschylus's *Oresteia* that also sought to cover such murderous activities as the Vietnam War and the Tate–LaBianca killings. Rabe retained the Greek names, but this Orestes (Cliff DeYoung) had more than the curse of the House of Atreus to deal with. Various horrors from different times occurred simultaneously onstage, and audiences lost interest long before the cluttered production wore itself out. The critics, realizing that Rabe could not mine the same lode and strike gold three times running, were politely negative. The noisy production was kept on the boards for the curious for fifty-three performances.

The National Puppet Theatre of Japan presented two Bunraku plays, *The Priest in Exile* and *The Double Suicide at Sonezaki*, for sixteen performances at the City Center beginning on April 3.

Expectations were also high for a new American farce featuring Eddie Albert and Nanette Fabray and directed by veteran funnyman Abe Burrows, but Sam Bobrick and Ron Clark's **No Hard Feelings** (4-8-73, Martin Beck) was the Broadway season's fifth one-night closer. George Bartlett (Albert), a successful lighting-fixture manufacturer, has married off his daughter and is looking forward to old age when his wife (Fabray) announces that she is leaving him for a Greek waiter (Conrad Janis) she has been sleeping with and is pregnant by. George goes off the deep end, tries to shoot the waiter (only injuring him in the foot), and then runs about town with a rifle. The town being Manhattan, no one on the street seems to pay him much attention. (That was the biggest laugh of the evening.) Arrested and subdued, George must submit to psychiatric care and learn to live with reality. It was an energetic production, especially for the mature stars, and some critics admitted to having a good time. More pointed out the amateur summer-stock nature of the script, and several were impressed by a young actress named Stockard Channing in a minor role.

The City Center went from highly stylized puppet theatre to highly stylized mime when Marcel Marceau performed his popular one-man pantomime show for twenty-four performances beginning on April 18.

Crystal and Fox (4-23-73, McAlpin Rooftop) was perhaps Irish playwright Brian Friel's darkest play yet, and its very foreign milieu (touring Irish vaudeville) made the drama too remote for even off-Broadway audiences. Theatre manager Fox Melarkey (Will Hare) is systematically driving off all his vaudeville acts (he even poisons the dog in an animal act) and proceeds to destroy his own family when his estranged son arrives, hiding from the police. The play appealed to few, but Rue McClanahan got good notices (as usual) for her portrayal of Fox's adored wife, Crystal. The play, previously done in Dublin and Los Angeles, lasted less than a month.

While some felt the play was dated, there was much fun to be had at the revival of *The Women* (12-26-36), the Clare Boothe Luce comedy that opened on April 25 at the 46th Street Theatre featuring a stellar cast: Kim Hunter, Alexis Smith, Rhonda Fleming, Dorothy Loudon, Myrna Loy, Jan Miner, Mary Louise Wilson, Polly Rowles, and on and on. Morton Da Costa staged the huge production like a whirling musical comedy, even adding an overture with credits on a projection screen while the stars stepped forward and took a bow. Oliver Smith designed the parade of lavish sets, and Ann Roth came up with racks of 1930s ladies garb, all witty and dazzling. (Even the Countess De Lage's ludicrous cowboy outfit was Park Avenue chic.) Reviews were mixed, but even the naysayers made the show sound too delicious to be missed. The original production had also received weak reviews but ran two seasons; this revival had to settle for sixty-three performances.

Lincoln Center ended its season on a high note: a beautifully realized revival of *A Streetcar Named Desire* (12-3-47) on April 26 in the Vivian Beaumont, directed by Ellis Rabb and featuring Rosemary Harris as Blanche and James Farentino as Stanley. Critics saluted the twenty-five-year-old play as more stageworthy than ever and compared the production favorably with the original. Patricia Connolly and Philip Bosco were also first-rate as Stella and Mitch. The revival ran a profitable 110 performances before reopening at the St. James Theatre in October for another fifty-three showings.

The title character of Terrence McNally's **Whiskey** (4-29-73, St. Clements) was a horse (unseen) who stars in a popular television series and performs with the Lush Thrushes, a cowboy singing group. After the troupe bombs in an appearance at the Houston Astrodome for the President of the United States, they retreat to a motel room for a night of boozing and reminiscing. (The horse spends the night in the shower.) When the hotel catches on fire, the cowboys are too drunk to notice, and all end up in heaven dressed in white western garb, looking down on Whiskey and his new TV series. Most critics found the proceedings tedious, and the piece was gone before the week was out.

The American Place concluded its season with Steve Tesich's **Baba Goya** (5-9-73, American Place), a scattershot farce that took aim at just about everything, only scoring intermittently. Wisecracking Goya (Olympia Dukakis) lives in Queens with her fourth husband, Mario (John Randolph), and an Old Man (Lou Gilbert) who once wooed Goya and gets furious every time he's called "grandpa." Mario thinks he is dying, so, with Goya's help, he advertises in the newspaper for a replacement for himself for after he's gone. Also on the scene are Bruno (R. A. Dow), Goya's depressed policeman son who has arrested a Japanese youth (Randy Kim) for stealing a camera and chains him to the radiator, and her bawling, divorced daughter, Sylvia (Peggy Whitton), who admits she voted for Nixon and cannot overcome the guilt. The press was not enthralled but thought Dukakis was nothing short of hilarious. After twenty-five performances, the comedy shut down for rewrites, reopening the next season.

The two-performance flop **Owners** (5-14-73, Mercer-Shaw) was notable only because it was the first New York production of a Caryl Churchill play. A cutthroat North London real estate developer pursues romance in the same way she buys up speculative land, and before the comedy is over, Churchill has covered everything from baby selling to murder. It was an inauspicious start, and a decade would go by before Churchill was a familiar name in America.

As the season was concluding, an announcement was made that gave even the most cynical observers reason for cautious optimism: Joseph Papp and his New York Shakespeare Festival would take over the problematic Repertory Theatre at Lincoln Center. Bringing his own board of directors and new money (Mrs. Samuel I. Newhouse alone contributed $1 million, and Papp renamed the downstairs Forum the Mitzi E. Newhouse Theatre), Papp presented ambitious plans for both new works and classic revivals at Lincoln Center, while still continuing his operations on Lafayette Street and in Central Park. It sounded too good to be true, but desperate times called for desperate optimism.

1973–1974

"The worst season in memory" was a catchphrase that had been employed regularly by theatre commentators since the turn of the century, so few were distraught when it was used to describe 1973–1974. But the description was probably true even for those with very long memories. Only ten new American plays opened on Broadway and twenty-seven (several of them one-acts) off Broadway. More disturbing, there was not one work of any major significance (not to mention excellence) to be found among them. The season for musicals was just as bad, and the quality British plays that were seen in New York were secondary works by major talents such as David Storey, Noel Coward, and Tom Stoppard. For the most part, the mediocre was considered the best at hand and the worst was far worse than many could recall. Many reliable and established American playwrights, from Tennessee Williams to Edward Albee to Arthur Miller, had no new offerings, and those who did, such as Terrence McNally, Murray Schisgal, David Rabe, Arthur Laurents, and Neil Simon, came up short. The season's few new and promising playwrights, such as Edward J. Moore and Miguel Piñero, failed to deliver in future seasons. It was indeed an unmemorable season.

What made theatregoing bearable (and often much more than that) was the number of satisfying revivals (a record nineteen on Broadway and twenty-two off) and a spate of truly memorable performances, particularly by men. Four different Chekhov plays were seen this season (five if you include Neil Simon's redaction The

Good Doctor), practically the Russian playwright's complete full-length oeuvre. There was plenty of Shakespeare, some of it estimable, and even three Strindberg works. The biggest non-musical hit of the season, in terms of box-office demand and critical acclaim, was the Broadway revival of O'Neill's A Moon for the Misbegotten. As far as actors go, James Earl Jones, Jason Robards, Henry Fonda, Zero Mostel, George C. Scott, and some other established American actors were giving performances that were, if not the finest of their careers, pretty darn close.

While ticket prices rose slightly, the curtain time receded from 8:30 to 8:00 P.M. for plays (most musicals stayed at 7:30 P.M.). Production expenses jumped perceptibly, Lincoln Center's Boom Boom Room set it back a record $250,000, the season's most expensive non-musical failure. Off Broadway saw the most dramatic rise: Mart Crowley's three-character A Breeze from the Gulf cost $70,000, seven times what it cost to bring in his nine-character The Boys in the Band five years earlier. On a more optimistic note, the TKTS booth in Times Square was growing in popularity and helped many struggling and established shows run longer. Few non-musicals on and off the Street realized a profit, but they were playing to more patrons. That, at least, was memorable.

The new season started early and successfully with the uptown Circle in the Square's unlikely hit Uncle Vanya on June 4. Director Mike Nichols

MIKE NICHOLS (né Michael Igor Peschkowsky) (1931–) was born in Berlin to a Russian émigré father and German mother and came to America when he was seven. He entered the University of Chicago to study medicine but discovered theatre and trained with Lee Strasberg in New York. Working in improv clubs, he and his partner Elaine May soon gained recognition and became one of America's most innovative and popular comedy acts. His first directing attempt was the Broadway production of Barefoot in the Park (1963) which launched his new career, and he branched out into film directing with Who's Afraid of Virginia Woolf? in 1966. Although he would concentrate on movies and return to theatre directing intermittently, Nichols usually found success on Broadway. An often temperamental and excitable director, Nichols emphasized truth of character, which made his staging of Neil Simon's comedies and others' dramas quite human and engaging.

GEORGE C[ampbell] SCOTT (1927–1999) was born in rural Virginia and educated at the University of Missouri. After serving in the marines, he acted in summer stock, on college campuses, and on television before making his New York debut in the title role in *Richard III* (1957) for the New York Shakespeare Festival. He also played Shylock and Antony for the festival and appeared in such dramas as the 1958 revival of *Children of Darkness*, *The Andersonville Trial* (1959), and the 1967 revival of *The Little Foxes* (also directed by Nichols). Too often thought of as only a dramatic actor, Scott was also a fine farceur, as seen in *Plaza Suite* (1968). The growly-voiced character actor was once married to Colleen Dewhurst.

showed he could handle a period piece as well as contemporary plays. George C. Scott's Dr. Astrov was a marvel of method acting used in a classic context, and Nicol Williamson was a penetrating Vanya. There were also splendid performances by Julie Christie, Elizabeth Wilson, Barnard Hughes, Conrad Bain, Cathleen Nesbitt, and Lillian Gish. Laudatory reviews and potent word of mouth packed the small house for eight weeks.

The off-Broadway season started inauspiciously with the one-performance flop **The Boy Who Came to Leave** (6-6-73, Astor Place), a drama by Lee Kalcheim about a poet (Jordan Charney) and a composer (Fred Grandy) who try to share a Greenwich Village apartment despite their conflicting personalities.

The busy producer Joseph Papp, now running Lincoln Center, the Public Theatre, and the outdoor Delacorte Theatre in Central Park, presented fifteen shows this season, beginning with *As You Like It* in the outdoor venue on June 21. Kathleen Widdoes (Rosalind), Raul Julia (Orlando), Mary Beth Hurt (Celia), and John Harkins (Touchstone) headed the cast, and Papp himself directed. What the revival lacked in style, the critics felt it made up for in energy. The Roundabout Theatre opened their season early with a revival of Harold Pinter's *The Caretaker* (10-4-61) on June 23 with William Prince as the decrepit old Davies, Philip Campanella as Mick, and W. T. Martin as the brain-damaged Aston.

Papp had been applying multi-racial casting to his productions of the classics in recent seasons, using African-American, Hispanic, and Asian actors in traditionally white roles. Nowhere was the mix more noticeable and more effective than in his Delacorte revival of *King Lear* on July 26. It boasted an exceptional cast with Paul Sorvino as Gloucester, Douglas Watson as Kent, Raul Julia as Edmond, René Auberjonois as Edgar, and Tom Aldredge as the Fool, all dominated by James Earl Jones as the legendary king. Some critics objected to the unevenness in the casting of the smaller roles, but the Edwin Sherin production was applauded as the liveliest and most dynamic *King Lear* in many years. For the forty-two-year-old Jones, the role was a triumph of classical acting too rarely offered to black Americans. Charles Michener in *Newsweek* described Jones thoroughly, citing how he "begins with an expansive petulance that is genuinely stunning, becomes a caged animal of frightening confusion, and declares 'I shall go mad!' with all the mournful anger of a wolf howling at the moon."

It seemed Nicol Williamson had some energy left over each evening after playing the title role in *Uncle Vanya*, so he developed a ninety-minute one-man show, titled it **Nicol Williamson's Late Show** (6-26-73, Eastside Playhouse), and ran it at 10:45 P.M. for thirty performances. The informal program included poetry, speeches from plays, and even a few songs. The critics were approving, patrons were pleased, and Williamson was in two simultaneous hits.

The pairing of Strindberg's *Miss Julie* with a new French farce, **The Death of Lord Chatterly** (7-31-73, Roundabout), was an odd but interesting study in contrasts. Henry Pillsbury translated Christopher Frank's two-character comedy about a wealthy Madam (Linda Carlson) who is amorously involved with her butler (Philip Campanella) for twenty years while her husband lies dying (very slowly) in the next room. Pillsbury also adapted *Miss Julie*, setting it in the American South with Jean (Albert Hall) and Christine (Mary Alice) as plantation servants to a southern-belle Julie (Carlson). The unusual double bill ran two weeks. A month later the Roundabout offered another Strindberg, *The Father*, on September 11. Critics felt only Robert Lansing's Captain rose above the mediocre, but the revival found an audience for nearly three months.

Jean Anouilh's bombastic comedy *The Waltz of the Toreadors* (1-17-57) returned to Broadway on September 13 at the Circle in the Square using the reliable Lucienne Hill translation. Brian Murray provided the lively direction, but Anne Jackson and Eli Wallach, as the battling Madam and General St. Pe, got mixed notices, most critics feeling the duo captured none of the French flavor of the play but were entertaining in their own right.

The love letters between Elizabeth Barrett (Janet Kapral) and Robert Browning (Gregory Abels) were turned into **I Love Thee Freely** (9-17-73, Astor Place) by Benjamin Bernard Zavin. The epistolary piece ran twenty-three performances.

The season's first thriller, Peter Keveson's **Nellie Toole & Co.** (9-24-73, Theatre Four), was only able to run a week longer. The unemployed and desperate Paul (Lou Tiano) answers a mysterious want ad that calls him to a Second Avenue bar at two o'clock in the morning. There, the tormented Nellie Tool (Sylvia Miles) and her two henchmen force Paul to reenact scenes from her tortured past. Paul finally revolts and tells off the loony Nellie, who breaks down emotionally, her heart purged of her past. The critics dismissed the sinister piece, and the whole enterprise would have been quietly forgotten except that John Simon's scathing review so riled the leading lady that when she found herself a few days later at a gathering with Simon she dumped a plate of food over his head. The brief moment of notoriety in the press helped the play limp along a few extra weeks.

The abdication of King Edward VIII for "the woman I love" seemed to have the makings of a strong romantic and historical drama, but Royce Ryton's London hit **Crown Matrimonial** (10-2-73, Helen Hayes) did not appeal to American audiences despite a lavish production and some fine acting. This being a behind-the-scenes look at the political shift in power, Edward's beloved Wallis Simpson is not even in the play. Instead we are made privy to the inner workings of the royal family as Queen Mary (Eileen Herlie) tries to reason with her son Edward (George Grizzard) and then, in turn, must encourage her other son Bertie (Patrick Horgan) to succeed him. Critics felt that the shy, stammering Bertie was the most intriguing character in the play and that the scene in which Mary convinces the young Duke of York to take the throne, building his confidence and then bowing graciously and calling him King George VI, was the most moving. But too much of the rest was stuffy and reserved, so seventy-nine performances was enough to satisfy the diehard Anglophiles in New York.

Nourish the Beast (10-3-73, Cherry Lane) was a revised and retitled version of Steve Tesich's *Baba Goya* (5-9-73), which the American Place had offered the previous season. Critics felt the comedy's many problems had not been solved, one naysayer claiming the play was now "no longer promising." Despite this, Tesich was still considered someone to keep an eye on, and the off-Broadway entry ran seven weeks.

The popular revival of Williams's *A Streetcar Named Desire* (12-3-47), which had played to much acclaim at Lincoln Center the previous spring, reopened at the St. James on October 4 but with a new director and a different cast. Jules Irving staged the revised production with Lois Nettleton as Blanche, Alan Feinstein as Stanley, Barbara Eda-Young as Stella, and John Newton as Mitch. Some critics thought the new group stronger; others felt they were lacking. Either way, the revival managed to run an additional fifty-three performances in the large house.

Critics were also divided on Mart Crowley's autobiographical drama **A Breeze From the Gulf** (10-15-73, Eastside Playhouse); some found it exhilarating, but others were disappointed in the author of *The Boys in the Band* (4-15-68). Fifteen-year-old asthmatic Michael Connelly (Robert Drivas) moves into a new house on the Gulf of Mexico with his loutish father, Teddy (Scott McKay), a volatile man torn between the Church, the bottle, and his family, and his sickly mother, Loraine (Ruth Ford), who uses drugs to smother her disappointments in life. Teddy is repulsed by Loraine sexually, so she is drawn to her son with overriding affection. The drama followed the next fifteen years in Michael's life as each parent drifts away; the mother ends up in an asylum, and the father, before he dies, encourages Michael to be his own person and pursue his dreams of writing in New York City. All three actors were exemplary but the Williams-esque drama ran only forty-eight performances.

African-American playwright Ed Bullins called his **House Party** (10-16-73, American Place) "a soulful happening," and it was indeed loose and plotless. In a garish nightclub that represents some sort of hell for black Americans, characters bare their souls, listen to jazz, and dance to the flashing lights all about them. In two of the most effective vignettes, the exasperated Emcee (Jimmy Pelham) vainly urges the partying patrons toward revolution, and a Harlem politician (Earle Hyman) stopps the party and the play to complain of the author's trivial portrayal of blacks.

Although David Storey's **The Contractor** (10-17-73, BAM) was the third of his major works to reach New York, it had been written and produced in London before *Home* (11-17-70) and *The Changing Room* (3-6-73) were written. Ewbank (John Wardwell), a self-made successful Yorkshire contractor, is having one of his company's marquee tents set up on his front lawn for his daughter's wedding. In Act I the workmen, a colorful bunch of misfits supervised by the close-mouthed Mr. Kay (Reid Shelton), assemble the tent, in Act II they decorate and furnish it for the wedding reception, and in Act III they take it all down on the day after the festivities. While there were few overt confrontations or scenes of theatrics, the play was quietly fascinating, filled with engaging characters such as the gruff but soft-hearted Ewbanks, the halfwit youth Glendenning (Kevin O'Connor) who tries to please the very men who make fun of him, the talkative Irishman Fitzpatrick (Joseph Maher), Ewbank's aimless son (John Roddick), and the senile grandfather (Neil Fitzgerald) who wanders the grounds with a piece of rope, longing for the days of the true craftsman. The American production, directed by Barry Davis, came from New Haven's Long Wharf Theatre, and it was a beautifully sustained ensemble piece. Reviews were laudatory and the gentle drama ran two months and won the New York Drama Critics Circle Award.

The off-Broadway season had its second one-night flop with **The Indian Experience** (10-23-73, Playhouse 2), a two-character play that came down to a one-man show, John Kauffman acting out stories and relating historical accounts about Native American culture over the past three centuries. Kauffman and Wayne Johnson devised the "revue," and John Aylward assisted Kauffman by playing minor roles.

The Broadway season's shortest run went to Jerry Devine's sentimental show biz drama **Children of the Wind** (10-24-73, Belasco), which lasted only six performances. Veteran stock actor Daniel A. Brophy (James Callahan) finally has a shot at the big time: a role in a Broadway production. He moves into a theatrical rooming house, run by the soft-hearted May Walker (Ann Thomas), and awaits the arrival of his wife, Kitty (Sarah Hardy), and young son, John (Barry Goss), promising himself to cut back on the drinking and finally give his family a decent lifestyle. But once the family joins him and opening night approaches, Daniel is back to the bottle, and only a last-minute surge of love from his family gets him on the stage. Critics found little to be harsh about, but neither could they find much worth in the melodrama. A subsequent production in Los Angeles fared somewhat better.

There was much to recommend in Ira Levin's thriller **Veronica's Room** (10-25-73, Music Box), although the ending left some audiences (and critics) baffled and others quite grossed out. A young Girl (Regina Baff) arrives at an aristocratic home outside of Boston that belongs to a Man

(Arthur Kennedy) and Woman (Eileen Heckart). They seem very friendly and cordial at first, even if the Young Man (Kipp Osborne) of the household seems a bit strange. It turns out the Girl resembles the long-deceased Veronica, whose room has been faithfully maintained over the years. But soon the couple turn nasty, the Girl is imprisoned in Veronica's room, and the truth comes out: the Man and Woman are brother and sister, and the result of their incestuous union is the necrophiliac Young Man. The heroine tries unsuccessfully to escape but is murdered, and the curtain falls as the Young Man exits to Veronica's room, where the body lies. Notices were mixed, although most agreed the acting was uncomfortably splendid. The creepy drama ran two months.

A group called the Greek Art Theatre of New York revived Euripides' *Medea* on October 30 at the Players for a month, with George Arkas adapting the original and directing a cast led by Yula Gavala as the tragic mother. The most popular revival of the off-Broadway season was Michael Weller's *Moonchildren* (2-21-72) on November 4 at the Theatre de Lys. While the original production shuttered after only sixteen performances, this John Pasquin–directed revival ran nearly a year. Not that this production was better (the original cast was superb), but, as Otis L. Guernsey in the *Best Plays* argued, audiences were now more susceptible to the rebellious and youthful characters than they were two seasons ago.

The late novelist Erich Maria Remarque's only play, **Full Circle** (11-7-73, ANTA), had been seen in Germany, but Peter Stone was hired to doctor it up for American audiences, and Otto Preminger was selected to direct it, all to no avail; it closed in less than three weeks. Erich Rohde (Leonard Nimoy) has escaped from a German concentration camp where he has been kept for seven years and arrives in Berlin just as the Gestapo is leaving and the Russians are arriving. He falls into the hands of the victorious Russians and is treated just as he was by the Germans seven years earlier. In case the audience missed the point, the same actors played both his German and Russian tormentors. The press was harsh, one critic calling it "melodramatic claptrap, actually a bloodless exercise in dialectics dressed up to look like theatre." The only performer who was saluted was film star Bibi Andersson, in her Broadway debut, as a young widow haunted by the memory of her husband.

Perhaps the biggest disappointment of the season was David Rabe's **Boom Boom Room** (11-8-73, Vivian Beaumont), the play that began Papp's tenure at Lincoln Center and promised to illustrate the new direction that troubled organization would take. Young and passionate Chrissy (Madeline Kahn) works as a half-naked go-go dancer in a sleazy club. Because her mother tried unsuccessfully to abort Chrissy before birth and her father tried to rape her as a teenager, the heroine is vulnerable and confused but knows there must be more to life than her current job. Her search for fulfillment brings her into contact with Eric (Michael Kell), a suitor who thinks he wants to take care of her; Guy (Peter Bartlett), a homosexual who donates to sperm banks and tries to pass Chrissy off as a man; Susan (Mary Woronov), a lesbian co-worker who wants Chrissy to experience a new kind of love; and Al (Robert Loggia), a criminal who marries Chrissy and eventually beats her to death. The production was plagued with problems from the start (Papp himself had to replace Julie Bovasso as director a few days before opening), and critics let Papp and Rabe down gently with mixed reviews that went from "theatrically thrilling" to "somewhat obscure" to "long and tedious." There was general commendation for Kahn, but in one month she was at liberty.

After being dark for over a year because of lack of funds, Lincoln Center's downstairs performance space, now called the Mitzi E. Newhouse Theatre, reopened with a production by the New York Shakespeare Festival. On November 10 Papp presented the rarely produced *Troilus and Cressida*, directed as high camp by David Schweizer. John Christopher Jones and Madeleine Le Roux were the title lovers, Leonard Frey essayed Ulysses, Christopher Walken was Achilles, and Charles Kimbrough was the foul-mouthed Thersites.

Audiences and critics tried to figure out why E. A. Whitehead's **The Foursome** (11-12-73, Astor Place) had been such a success at the Royal Court in London when most agreed with Richard Watts of the *New York Post* when he called it "boring and meaningless" and declared that "its only virtue was brevity." The explanation may have had something to do with the New York production changing the play's locale from rural England to Texas. On a beach outside of Galveston, two dense teenage boys (Matthew Coles and Timothy Myers) bring two inarticulate girls (Lindsay Crouse and Carole Monferdini) to a deserted location for the purpose of sex but instead engage in arguments, verbal taunts, and, eventually, physical abuse (the boys resort to hitting the girls on the head with beach balls). The play climaxed with one boy's monologue describing with ferocious detail and disgust how he once had to paint the inside of a women's public toilet. Although it was clear that the vicious play sought to speak about violence in society, it only got to do so for three weeks.

The Broadway season's biggest hit was not a play at all but a British comic revue written and performed by Peter Cook and Dudley Moore, **Good Evening** (11-4-73, Plymouth). Both men were veterans of the popular *Beyond the Fringe* (10-27-62), and the new program contained some sketches from that beloved revue (in London the new show was called *Behind the Fringe*), including the one-legged actor trying out for the role of Tarzan and the coal miner who wanted to be a judge. The new material included a nonplused shepherd at the Nativity and a French singer who misunderstands English vulgarities and puts them into song. The reviews were all raves, and the two Brits packed the house for a little over a year.

Arthur Laurents, who had written about anti-Semitism so potently years ago in *Home of the Brave* (12-27-45), turned to the subject of homosexual prejudice in **The Enclave** (11-15-73, Theatre Four). A group of liberal-minded friends are restoring some adjoining New York townhouses with the idea of moving in and creating an enclave of people living in communal harmony. But one of the group, Ben (Barton Heyman), upsets the noble plan by revealing that he is gay and that he would like his young lover added to the group. Although the friends have always prided themselves on their open-mindedness, the news causes outrage and some self-disclosure before all admit to their hidden prejudices and finally accept the two homosexuals. The play was greeted with mixed notices, and audiences saw the moralizing palatable for only twenty-two performances.

The New Phoenix Repertory Company, true to its name, came up out of the ashes and presented three worthy revivals in repertory at the Ethel Barrymore. Dürrenmatt's *The Visit* (5-5-58) opened the series on November 25. While some reviews complained that the drama was dated and that the leads were miscast, the Harold Prince production was generally welcomed. Rachel Roberts played the wealthy Clare Zachanassian, and John McMartin was her former lover, Schill, whom she seeks to destroy. The next night Feydeau's *Chemin de Fer* was added to the repertory in a new adaptation by Suzanne Grossman and Paxton Whitehead. Stephen Porter directed a strong cast that included David Dukes, John Glover, Richard Venture, and Merwin Goldsmith, as well as McMartin and Roberts. The French farce got

[ARTHUR] **CHRISTOPHER** [Orme] **PLUMMER** (1929–) was born in Toronto and appeared in dozens of Canadian productions before making his New York debut in 1954. He was featured in such Broadway dramas as *The Lark* (1955), *J. B.* (1958), and *The Royal Hunt of the Sun* (1965). Yet Plummer is mostly known for his handful of film roles, Captain von Trapp in *The Sound of Music* (1965) in particular. A superb Shakespearean actor, Plummer played major roles for Shakespeare festivals in Ontario and Connecticut, as well as in London and on British television. This season he won the Tony Award for playing the title role in the musical *Cyrano*. Byronically handsome and distinguished-looking, Plummer could play villains and menacing characters as well as noble heroes. He was once married to actress Tammy Grimes, and their daughter is actress Amanda Plummer.

even better notices and was performed in the repertory forty-two times.

There was definitely something charming about Neil Simon's **The Good Doctor** (11-27-73, Eugene O'Neill), his dramatization of a handful of short stories by Anton Chekhov, but Broadway wanted more from Simon than charm. The Writer (Christopher Plummer) was the evening's emcee, introducing the tales, commenting on the woes and joys of being a writer, and taking roles in the vignettes. The more satisfying of the nine playlets were *The Audition*, in which a shy actress (Marsha Mason) awkwardly promotes herself at a tryout then shatters the Writer with her reading from *The Three Sisters; The Seduction*, in which Peter (Plummer), a seducer of other men's wives, eventually gets his comeuppance and marries, only to suspect other men of trying to seduce his spouse; and *The Arrangement*, about a father (Plummer) who tries to introduce his son (René Auberjonois) to manhood by bringing him to a brothel. Critics had high praise for the cast, which also included Frances Sternhagen (who won a Tony Award) and Barnard Hughes, but were divided on how well the Simon-Chekhov marriage worked. (Ted Kalem in *Time* questioned why Chekhov himself hadn't turned these short stories into plays if they were so stageworthy.) Also, the play's nineteenth-century Russian setting was disappointing to audiences who expected Simon's usual contemporary comedy of manners. The play ran a respectable but unprofitable 208 performances.

A drama about cerebral palsy that was successfully presented in Canada, **Creeps** (12-4-73, Play-

house 2) was written by Canadian author David E. Freeman, himself a "spastic," who provided some humor but much bitterness in his portrayal of a group of people with CP who work at a rehabilitation center weaving rugs and folding boxes. The play is set in the dirty men's toilet where the workers escape to smoke, complain, and joke, away from the eyes and ears of their irritating supervisor, Miss Saunders (Robin Nolan). The plot centers on two of the workers, Jim (Richard DeFabees), who wants to be a writer, and Tom (Mark Metcalf), whose paintings have been well received, and the drama ends with the two of them quitting the rehab center and striking out to try to make it on their own. Critics found the play deserving but lacking in dramatic forcefulness and complimented the players. But the little drama never found an audience and closed in two weeks.

A much noisier little drama was Mark Medoff's **When You Comin' Back, Red Ryder?** (12-6-73, Eastside Playhouse), which many critics compared (unfavorably) to *The Petrified Forest* (1-7-35). Reviews ranged from "very skillful and very effective" to "a pointless thriller, a cheat." Into a remote New Mexico diner come a drug runner named Teddy (Kevin Conway) and his girl, Cheryl (Kristen Van Buren), needing repairs to their van. Teddy starts off humorously taunting the diner's occupants—the overweight waitress, the restless cook, the limping gas attendant, a wealthy couple traveling to New Orleans—but soon pulls a gun, verbally abuses them, and forces them to sing, dance, and play the violin, eventually wounding the rich businessman and ripping the blouse off the wife. The van is repaired, Teddy leaves without Cheryl, the cook heads east with the couple, and the others try to go back to their normal lives. The play, first seen off-off Broadway at the Circle Rep, transferred to off Broadway, where it won some awards and ran through the summer.

Having essayed King Lear earlier in the season, James Earl Jones next attacked one of modern drama's most demanding roles, the cajoling salesman Hickey in O'Neill's *The Iceman Cometh* (10-9-46) on December 13 at the Circle in the Square Uptown. Some critics felt Jones lacked "the hint of menace" in the character, but most cheered his performance, even if the production was deemed slow and sluggish and director Theodore Mann couldn't make the difficult play cohesive. Also featured in the cast were Stefan Gierasch, Michael Higgins, Tom Aldredge, and Lois Smith.

Avant-gardist Robert Wilson's **The Life and Times of Joseph Stalin** (12-15-73, BAM) was a theatrical event for the adventurous playgoer, the performance beginning at 7:00 P.M. and continuing through the night until 7:00 A.M. The leisurely mosaic of scenes, songs, dance, and images (both visual and aural) was very abstract and often eccentric, but most felt there were some startlingly beautiful moments in the event, which employed a cast of 144 people, mostly amateurs. A parade of characters appeared, including Stalin and his family, Freud and his daughter Anna, and even Wilson's eighty-eight-year-old grandmother, who showed up as herself. The collage was given two performances on successive weekends.

Jack Gelber's **Barbary Shore** (12-18-73, Public: Anspacher), adapted from Norman Mailer's novel, took place during the McCarthy era in a Brooklyn boardinghouse where a struggling young writer, Mike Lovett (Lenny Baker), befriends the faded old revolutionary William McLeod (Rip Torn), who now works as a window dresser at Abraham and Strauss. Also at the house is the aging but still sensuous landlady, Guinevere (Estelle Parsons), and the talkative Leroy Hollingsworth (Lane Smith), who claims to work for an important "organization." Hollingsworth questions McLeod about his past activities, which gives the old radical a chance to rant Marxist ideas. But it soon develops that the inquisitive Hollingsworth works for the government, and McLeod is exposed and incriminated. Despite some fine acting, critics felt the play started out promisingly and then went nowhere.

Four revivals opened in the next week. The Roundabout's *The Seagull* on December 18 marked seventy-five years and one day since the original Moscow Art Theatre production of the Chekhov "comedy." The cast included Linda De Coff (Nina), Christopher Lloyd (Konstantin), Dolores Sutton (Madame Arkadina), and Tom Klunis (Trigorin), and it was kept on the boards for three months, the longest Roundabout run of the season. The next night Chekhov's *Three Sisters* opened at the Billy Rose, the first of four revivals by the City Center Acting Company on Broadway this season. The young cast, which included Kevin Kline, Patti Lupone, David Ogden Stiers, Mary-Joan Negro, and Mary Lou Rosato, was deemed too inexperienced for the difficult drama, but the 1971 Juilliard graduates were thought very promising. A week later the same company presented Shakespeare's *Measure for Measure*, and reviews were a bit more favorable. John Houseman directed, and Stiers was cited for his Duke and David Schramm for his Angelo. Also on December 26, Philip Barry's *Holiday* (11-26-28) was revived at the Ethel Barrymore, the third and final

> **CHARLES DURNING** [Durnham] (1933–) was born in Highland Falls, New York, and educated at Columbia and New York University. After serving in the army and then working as a cab driver, boxer, and construction worker, he started to appear in supporting roles in various New York Shakespeare Festival productions in 1962. Durning first gained recognition, and made his Broadway debut, as the clownish mayor George in *That Championship Season* (1972). The beefy character actor was often cast as inept, foolish characters but later graduated to more complex roles.

entry in the New Phoenix's repertory. Critics welcomed the old play (this was its first professional New York revival) but felt the production values were skimpy and the cast, aside from David Dukes and John Glover, was uneven.

Irish playwright Hugh Leonard's comedy **The Au Pair Man** (12-27-73, Vivian Beaumont) was an unusual entry for Lincoln Center in that it was essentially a star vehicle. Into the cluttered London townhouse of the aristocratic Elizabeth Rogers (Julie Harris) comes the rough Irish workman Eugene Hartigan (Charles Durning) to do some odd chores. But soon the crusty fellow becomes Elizabeth's love slave and companion as she teaches him the genteel ways of the British upper crust. The seriocomic squabbling between the two was supposed to illustrate the conflicting British and Irish temperaments, but audiences simply enjoyed the two charming stars as lovable characters. While critics were not overjoyed with the script, they were pleased to see Harris in a comic role again, and there were plaudits for Durning's clowning, his drunken rendition of "Flying Down to Rio" being one of the comedy's highlights. There was also much praise for John Conklin's set, a crumbling Victorian living room full of rococo design details and shelves of bric-a-brac that resembled a British museum of the past, complete with dust and plaster that fell from the ceiling on occasion. The two-character play ran only a month, but Leonard would return to Broadway with greater success in the future.

Just as the José Quintero revival of O'Neill's *The Iceman Cometh* with Jason Robards in 1956 made that once-neglected play a modern classic, so too it took Quintero's revival of O'Neill's *A Moon for the Misbegotten* (5-2-57) on December 29 at the Morosco (again with Robards) to give this drama the respect it had long deserved. Colleen Dewhurst portrayed Josie, and Ed Flanders was her father (both won Tony Awards, as did Quintero), and the sterling production was greeted with rave reviews. Jack Kroll in *Newsweek* described the two leads well when he wrote of Robards's "definitive portrayal of a man walking the weaving line that is the track of the mortally alienated creature, the drunk who is really intoxicated by his own guilt," and Dewhurst as "a radiant animal who looks as if she bites off chunks of the sun for breakfast." The popular attraction ran into July, recessed for the rest of the summer, then reopened in September for another ten weeks.

Although John Hopkins's **Find Your Way Home** (1-2-74, Brooks Atkinson) was a British play, it had its world premiere on Broadway, an unlikely home (at the time) for this very explicit view of a homosexual romance. The young hustler Julian Weston (Michael Moriarty) is finally getting over his lover, the married businessman Alan (Lee Richardson), who walked out on him a year ago. Then Alan returns one night to announce that he is leaving his wife and children to be with Julian again. After many incriminations about the past, they make love and begin to reconcile themselves to each other. But Alan's wife, Jackie (Jane Alexander), shows up, having followed Alan because she suspected that he was having an affair with a woman. Husband and wife thrash out their problems with anger and bitterness, Jackie leaves, and Alan and Julian start the difficult task of building a trusting relationship. Critics had mixed reactions to the script (though Guernsey named it a *Best Play*), but the acting was highly thought of (Moriarty won that season's Tony Award). It ran 135 performances but rarely has been heard of since.

The City Center Acting Company closed their stint at the Billy Rose on January 2 with two performances of James Saunders's allegorical drama *Next Time I'll Sing to You* (11-27-63). Three distinguished theatre companies from England would visit the Brooklyn Academy of Music this season. On January 9 the Royal Shakespeare Company arrived in Brooklyn with *Richard II* directed by John Barton. Ian Richardson and Richard Pasco alternated as Bolingbroke and the deposed king. While the critics applauded the actors' crisp and lucid delivery, they found the dry and formal production too "static" and "stilted."

Only subscribers were admitted to David Scott Milton's **Bread** (1-12-74, American Place), a "banal and obvious" political allegory set in a Pittsburgh bakery. A used cigar, a dead rat found in a loaf of bread, and the remains of a cat discovered in the oven were among the symbolic images used to illustrate a declining civilization.

No author was credited with the RSC's **Sylvia Plath** (1-15-74, BAM), which ran in repertory with its *Richard II*. Three actresses performed a staged reading of the poet's work, leading up to her suicide at the age of thirty-one. Critics were interested but not excited by the program.

Papp's second Shakespeare entry at Lincoln Center's Newhouse, *The Tempest* on January 26, was much more successful than his earlier *Troilus and Cressida*. The energetic production was led by Sam Waterston as a youthful and hyperactive Prospero instead of the grandfatherly sage usually expected. The rest of the cast may have been uneven, but critics cheered Christopher Walken's oily Antonio and Randy Kim's hilarious Trinculo.

The recently formed Actors Company, another British visitor at BAM, presented another Chekhov play, *The Wood Demon*, on January 29. The little-known comedy was the playwright's earlier draft of *Uncle Vanya*, translated by Ronald Hingley. Aside from serving as an interesting companion piece to the recent *Vanya* revival at the Circle in the Square, *The Wood Demon* was quite entertaining in itself, staged as a knockabout farce by David Giles. The company offered a new work the next night, **Knots** (1-30-74, BAM), a dramatization by Edward Petherbridge of ideas from the book by R. D. Laing, an author-psychiatrist who was quite popular at the time. Using sketches, songs, mime, jokes, and plenty of repetition, the piece explored human hangups and the "knots" people make for themselves. Critics dismissed the "psychological *Sesame Street*" as a waste of fine actors. The costumes and scenery for the Actors Company's entry on February 2, *King Lear* directed by David William, were lost in transit from London, so audiences and critics on opening night viewed the production on a bare stage with the actors in jeans and T-shirts. The company's superior talent was evident all the same, and the reviews were auspicious. Robert Eddison (Lear), Ronald Radd (Gloucester), John Woodvine (Kent), and Edward Petherbridge (Fool) were all excellent, but perhaps the actor who most dazzled the spectators was Ian McKellen as Edgar. Playgoers only had ten opportunities to see *King Lear* before the company closed its visit with five showings of Congreve's *The Way of the World* beginning on February 13. The Restoration comedy was updated to modern times with characters using telephones and gramophones and ladies smoking cigarettes. Much farce was added to the high verbal wit (John

Woodvine's Sir Willful had a merry old time beating a tiger rug to death with his golf club), and critics deemed the production quite accessible and fun.

Terrence McNally, who often seemed to have trouble filling out a full evening, returned to the one-act form with his **Bad Habits** (2-4-74, Astor Place), a program of two farces set in nursing homes. In *Ravenswood*, rich and famous couples who have become "unglued" come to an exclusive sanatorium where the wheelchair-ridden Dr. Pepper (Paul Benedict) treats his patients by letting them indulge in their worst habits, from smoking to sexual promiscuity. In *Dunelawn*, the saintly but inaudible Dr. Toynbee (J. Frank Lucas) treats his patients' bad habits with a magical drug that tranquilizes all their urges. There was little in the way of plot, but the play was propelled by its outlandish characters, such as Nurse Benson (Cynthia Harris), who has undergone years of dieting and makeovers in order to win the heart of Hugh Gump (Benedict), who now rejects her because she is too perfect, or the quarreling Hiram Spane (Emory Bass) of the Newport "Old Bingo money" Spanes and Francis Tears (Lucas) of the Baltimore "plumbing dynasty" Tears, who associate with each other because "no one else in the world would put up with us." Critics found the evening slight but enjoyable; audiences liked it enough that after ninety-six performances off Broadway it transferred to the Booth on May 5 and ran into October.

One of the most consistently zany theatre groups off-off Broadway was the Ridiculous Theatrical Company, which had been providing outrageous spoofs since 1966. This season they brought two of their better efforts to Off Broadway, beginning with Charles Ludlam's **Hot Ice** (2-7-74, Evergreen), a take-off on the James Cagney gangster movie *White Heat*. When the millionaire Markus P. Malone dies and asks to be frozen, the Euthanasia Police suspect his widow, Ramona (Black-Eyed Susan), and radio reporter Buck Armstrong (Ludlam) senses a story. What follows is a descontructionist view of theatre as performers (and audience members) interrupt the play for questions and actors converse with each other using their real names. In keeping with the spirit of the ridiculous, the play had multiple endings with the actors throwing away their scripts in frustration.

The Negro Ensemble Company opened its season with Paul Carter Harrison's **The Great MacDaddy** (2-12-74, St. Marks), a "musical odyssey" about a bewildered con artist, MacDaddy

(David Downing), from his bootlegging days in Los Angeles during Prohibition to the present, when he finds his long-lost friend Wine (Graham Brown) in South Carolina. The story was told in scenes that flashed back and forth through time, and the African-American actor Al Freeman, Jr., played all the white characters (all nicknamed Scag) that MacDaddy and his girlfriend Leionah (Hattie Winston) encounter along the way. It was a messy script (critics termed it "undramatic" and "difficult to follow"), but Douglas Turner Ward's direction was zesty, and the use of some songs and dance throughout gave the piece a celebratory feel. The most memorable scene took place in a St. Louis boardinghouse where some restless card players and their girls burst out singing "Amazing Grace."

Two nights later, critics saw a black drama that they could more easily understand, Ron Milner's morality play **What the Wine-Sellers Buy** (2-14-74, Vivian Beaumont), but several rejected it as "too trite" and "spread out too long." High schooler Steve Carlton (Glynn Turman) hopes, with the support of his hard-working mother (Marilyn B. Coleman) and his sweetheart, Mae Harris (Loretta Green), to escape the Detroit ghetto by becoming a basketball pro. But when his mother gets sick and his basketball dreams dry up, Steve grows anxious to make money fast and falls under the influence of the sinister neighbor Rico (Dick A. Williams), who starts Steve out as a pimp. Soon the two of them develop a scheme to blackmail a middle-aged lecher using Mae as a prostitute. She reluctantly agrees, but at the last minute Steve grabs Mae in his arms and they flee the opportunist Rico. The drama was shuttered after a month.

Irish playwright Brian Friel's latest play to reach America, **The Freedom of the City** (2-17-74, Alvin), was political in nature but contained the warm and rich characterizations he was known for. A Catholic civil rights march in Londonderry gets dispersed by the police, and three fleeing demonstrators find themselves taking refuge in the mayor's empty office in Town Hall. The three unlikely radicals—the youths Skinner (Lenny Baker) and Michael (Allen Carlsen) and a middle-aged mother of eleven, Lily (Kate Reid)—start to enjoy their predicament, singing and dancing in the swank office, but the police outside are told that forty armed rebels are inside the building and surround the area. When the three Catholics willingly surrender, they are gunned down by the police. William Woodman directed the American production (which had originated at the Goodman Theatre in Chicago), but critical opinion was mixed and the subject had too limited appeal, so the tragicomedy closed after only nine performances.

An unlikely one-woman show that found an audience for seventy-one showings was **Dear Nobody** (2-19-74, Cherry Lane), a dramatization of the diaries of Fanny Burney, a lady in the court of George III and a unique eighteenth-century novelist. Terry Belanger and Jane Marla Robbins adapted the material, and Robbins played Burney and all her associates. Critics found the evening spirited and anything but a musty historical chronicle, as Burney's comments on London society and her thoughts as a teenager, a young woman, and later a mother were both revealing and enjoyable.

Another disjointed celebration of black America that used songs throughout was Edgar White's **Les Femmes Noires** (2-21-74, Public: Other Stage), an oral collage of scenes and voices, mostly of women, that Novella Nelson directed in a highly rhythmic style. Critics said it went nowhere, but it was enjoyable all the same and stayed at the Public for seven weeks.

Scott Mansfield's **Once I Saw a Boy Laughing** (2-21-74, Westside) could not last even one week, though it, too, had a half dozen songs dispersed throughout. On a surrealistic battlefield, six U.S. infantrymen die one by one, killed by unseen forces that the audience was asked to ponder.

The Chelsea offered its second contemporary British play of the season with Christopher Hampton's **Total Eclipse** (2-23-74, BAM), a drama about the tempestuous relationship between nineteenth-century poets Paul Verlaine (Christopher Lloyd) and Arthur Rimbaud (Michael Finn). The documentary-like drama began with the two men meeting in Paris in 1871 and chronicled their violent homosexual love affair until they parted in Stuttgart four years later. An epilogue showed Verlaine learning of Rimbaud's death seventeen years later and the beginning of Verlaine's decline. Critics were sharply divided on the play's merits and the use of so much male nudity onstage, some finding *Total Eclipse* the most honest view yet of homosexual love, others finding the two main characters unlikable bores. The controversial play, seen in London six years earlier, ran four weeks.

The last Noel Coward play to reach Broadway during his lifetime was titled **Noel Coward in Two Keys** (2-28-74, Ethel Barrymore), an evening of two one-acts that had been seen in London eight years earlier in a different format that included a third playlet. In *Come Into the Garden Maud*, a rich American cornhusker, Vernon Conklin (Hume Cronyn), and his social-climbing wife, Anna-Mary (Jessica Tandy), are in a lavish Swiss hotel suite. She is trying to make connections, and he longs to go back home and make money. The honest, straight-talking Countess Maud Caragnami (Anne Baxter) is the only European Vernon likes, and when life with his self-absorbed wife gets unbearable, he decides to run off with Maud. *A Song at Twilight* is set in the same suite, where the famous, curmudgeonly author Hugo Latymer (Cronyn) has dinner with actress Carlotta Gray (Baxter), whom he had an affair with many years ago. When Hugo refuses to let Carlotta publish some of his old love letters to her in her autobiography, she blackmails him with letters the once wrote to a male lover. Hugo, desperate to retain his heterosexual public persona, agrees to Carlotta's demands. She gives him the old letters, and Hugo is left tearfully reading them as his German wife, Hilde (Tandy) accepts him for what she always knew he was. Many playgoers read Somerset Maugham for Hugo, although there was more than just a trace of Hugo in Coward himself, whose own autobiographies were painfully secretive about his sexuality. Reviews were divided on the script's merits but extolled the cast. The double bill ran to the end of June, but Coward had died in March in Jamaica.

For some the best American play of the season was Miguel Piñero's **Short Eyes** (2-28-74, Public: Anspacher), a prison drama that won the New York Drama Critics Award. The playwright was a paroled convict who was active in drama workshops while at Sing Sing. He and a group called the Family had first presented *Short Eyes* in January off-off Broadway, where it came to the attention of Papp, who brought it to the Public for fifty-four performances and then to Lincoln Center on May 23 for an additional 102 performances. Into a detention center populated mostly by blacks and Puerto Ricans comes the white convict Clark Davis (William Carden). When they learn that Clark is a child molester (a "short eyes"), both the convicts and the ruthless guard Mr. Nett (Robert Maroff) taunt and abuse him. While the others are at lunch, Clark confides to the sympathetic Juan (Bimbo) that he has had sex with young girls but has no recollection of raping the child he is accused of molesting. The day passes and tension in the room grows until the white convict Longshoe (Joseph Carberry) slits Clark's throat, despite Juan's efforts to stop him. When Captain Allard (H. Richard Young) investigates the murder, all the convicts say they weren't there and saw nothing. Then Allard tells them that Clark was not guilty, for the hysterical victim was unable to identify Clark in a lineup. Reviews were all laudatory for the devastating script and the potent acting, one aisle-sitter calling it "an authentic, powerful theatrical piece that tells you more about prison life than any play outside the work of Genet."

The Young Vic, yet another British company to visit BAM this season, had made its reputation in Europe as a group of young actors doing lively productions at low prices for young audiences. Its first entry, *The Taming of the Shrew* on March 6, was a vibrant example of the company's strengths. The production, directed with panache by Frank Dunlop, opened with the Induction played in modern dress and Christopher Sly (Richard Gere, the only American in the cast) portrayed as a Manhattan drifter. Once the play proper began, period costumes were used, but the production was loose in its historical look and carefree with Shakespeare's text. Jim Dale (Petruchio) and Jane Lapotaire (Katharina) led the fiery cast, which also included Ian Charleson, Gavin Reed, Denise Coffey, and Hugh Hastings. The comedy received propitious notices all around, and before the season was out, Dale would be a bona fide star on the Street.

Broadway's most expensive non-musical revival was *Ulysses in Nighttown*, Marjorie Barkentin's 1959 dramatization of sections of James Joyce's *Ulysses*, which opened on March 10 in the Winter Garden. Zero Mostel reprised his Leopold Bloom, and the large cast included Tommy Lee Jones as Stephen Daedalus, David Ogden Stiers as Buck Mulligan, W. B. Brydon as a Narrator, and Fionnuala Flanagan, who, as Molly Bloom, spent most of the evening stark naked on her bed except when she got up to use a chamber pot. Critics liked Ed Wittstein's set of ramps and platforms and Pearl Somner's imaginative costumes but considered the revival less satisfying than the original (despite Mostel's towering performance). Two months was all the expensive show could afford to run.

Jay Broad's drama **The Killdeer** (3-12-74, Public: Newman) was described by Martin Gottfried of *Women's Wear Daily* as "a surrealist *Death of a Salesman* . . . imaginative but undisciplined," and other critics were equally unfavorable in their opinions. Salesman Ted Snyder (Ralph Waite) comes home from making the sale of a lifetime only to find his wife, Sparky (Barbara Barrie), suicidal and his children in revolt. Arguments about

the American work ethic and the importance of success clumsily followed. The stress drives Ted to drink; Sparky walks out, then returns for an ending that left audiences puzzled: Sparky comforts her husband optimistically then goes resolutely into the bedroom to either commit suicide, pack her clothes to leave him, or take a nap. (The curtain fell before the audience was told which.) Playgoers had forty-eight opportunities to ponder the question.

The Young Vic's second offering at BAM, *Scapino* on March 12, was their most accomplished entry and one of the most popular comedies of the season. Authors Frank Dunlop and Jim Dale took Molière's *Les Fourberies de Scapin* and roughed it up, set it in Naples, and filled it with delightful anachronisms (including references to Baskin-Robbins ice cream and Hollywood gangster films) and some of the most inventive slapstick seen in many a season. Dunlop directed, and Dale starred as the wily servant Scapino, who plots, plans, disguises himself, and juggles the plot's many threads. Dale also got to swing on ropes, toss plates of spaghetti in the air, and limp along comically as a one-legged pirate with an imaginary parrot on his shoulder. Notices unanimously cheered the "inspired floppy-hatted foolery." After its scheduled ten performances at BAM, *Scapino* was remounted at the Circle in the Square Uptown on May 18. After the fireworks of *Scapino*, the Young Vic's third offering, a revival of Terence Rattigan's *French Without Tears* (9-28-37) on March 15, was a bit of a letdown. But critics marveled how well the clowning actors of *Scapino* handled Rattigan's light comedy, especially Gavin Reed as the naval commander Rogers and Ian Charleson as the young Scot, Brian Curtis.

The Negro Ensemble's month-long "season-within-a-season" program of four new plays, each running one week, opened with A. I. Davis's **Black Sunlight** (3-19-74, St. Marks), a drama about the struggles of a newly independent African nation. The small country's leader, the ambitious MHandi (Richard Jackson), oversteps his power in order to gain control, but he is at odds with his old friend NKundi (Robert Christian), who strives for democracy. Critics found the cast very proficient (especially Mary Alice as MHandi's wife) but thought the writing stiff and hollow. Herman Johnson's episodic melodrama **Nowhere to Run, Nowhere to Hide** (3-26-74, St. Marks), was better received, though one critic suggested it might make a better film than a play. Two corrupt cops (Frankie Faison and Leon Morenzie) have been supplying dope to Harlem high schoolers but must get rid of their contact in the school, a student named Jesse (Roland Sanchez). One of the cops kills Jesse and then both try to frame the troublesome youth Willie (Todd Davis) for the murder. But the cops' scheme fails, and Willie is found to be innocent.

The Roundabout closed its season with a revival of Somerset Maugham's *The Circle* (9-12-21) on March 26. Commentators thought it an adequate production of "a dated but not entirely lifeless play." Some felt the piece needed stars in order to sparkle, but they thought Christopher Hewitt's choleric Lord Porteus came close to the mark. In any case, audiences enjoyed the old comedy, and it ran ninety-six performances.

While some considered **Clarence Darrow** (3-26-74, Helen Hayes) a "slightly musty one-man show," most saw it as the vehicle in which Henry Fonda gave the stage performance of his career. Clive Barnes of the *New York Times* led the raves, marveling at "the way he visibly ages as the evening wears on, the way he snakes out with Darrow's sly and country humor, the way he never shrinks from sentiment and yet never stresses it." David W. Rintels wrote the script (using a biography by Irving Wallace) in which the noted defense lawyer addresses invisible witnesses, judges, opponents, and juries as if they were sitting in H. R. Poindexter's realistic courtroom set. The drama only ran twenty-two performances because of Fonda's physical collapse, but he would return the next season and repeat it on tour over the next few years.

Charles Laurence's **My Fat Friend** (3-31-74, Brooks Atkinson) was a thin British comedy about a girl with a weight problem. Vicky (Lynn Redgrave), a London bookstore manager, has always been kidded about her weight problem, particularly by her Scottish neighbor James (John Lithgow) and her aging homosexual lodger Henry (George Rose). But when she meets the handsome Tom (James Ray Weeks), who seems attracted to her, she goes on a crash diet and, with the help of James and Henry, exercises herself into a new and slimmer Vicky. The kicker is, Tom was drawn to her rotundity and rejects the new woman, and Vicky is left being consoled by Henry. (A similar tale was seen earlier this season as a subplot in *Bad Habits*.) Critics dismissed the play altogether but thought Redgrave, Lithgow, and Rose gave expert comic performances, and the three stars kept the box office healthy for 288 performances.

The Negro Ensemble's new play series continued with Steve Carter's **Terraces** (4-2-74, St.

Marks), four short plays that each took place in a ritzy terrace apartment in Harlem. The untitled playlets were mostly satiric. In one, a couple using sophisticated movie-like banter discuss the fact that the husband caught the wife in bed with another man the night before. In another scene, an engaged couple come to inspect the apartment, have a fight, and call off the wedding before they leave. As was often the case at the Negro Ensemble, the performances far outshone the writing.

Viveca Lindfors's **I Am a Woman** (4-2-74, Theatre in Space) was a one-woman show filled with characters from history and fiction, ranging from Portia to Anaïs Nin. Lindfors and Paul Austin compiled the program, and it ran a month.

Lincoln Center offered a valiant revival of Strindberg's *The Dance of Death* on April 4 in the Vivian Beaumont. Director A. J. Antoon trimmed the long and difficult drama about marriage as a battleground (much of Strindberg's Part 2 was cut), and there were commendable performances by Robert Shaw as the drunken husband, Zoe Caldwell as the venomous wife, and Hector Elizondo as her cousin Kurt.

Herb Gardner's comedy **Thieves** (4-7-74, Broadhurst) managed to overcome mainly negative reviews and run 312 performances on the strength of its cast and positive word of mouth. The Cramers have recently moved into an expensive high-rise on Manhattan's Upper East Side. Martin Cramer (Richard Mulligan) has grown a bit daffy, playing his flute on the terrace at one A.M., while his distracted wife, Sally (Marlo Thomas), has misplaced all their antique furniture. They are surrounded by various levels of New York life, from bums on the street to discontented neighbors, as they go through a mid-life crisis of their own. The slice-of-life comedy took place all during one warm June night, and while there was no plot progression as such, Gardner orchestrated the various stories and characters into a satisfying ending: the old doorman, Devlin (Sammy Smith), quietly dies on the job, and the busy New Yorkers must stop their harried lives for a moment and acknowledge each other as human beings. In addition to some fine-tuned performances, *Thieves* boasted an ingenious set by Peter Larkin that revealed several floors of the apartment house, balconies of other buildings seemingly floating about them, and the street below.

J. E. Gaines's **Heaven and Hell's Agreement** (4-9-74, St. Marks) closed the Negro Ensemble's new plays series and was considered the best of the lot. Buddy (Gary Bolling) has been missing in action for ten years, and his wife (Michele Shay) has fallen in love with another man. But Buddy's mother (Mary Alice) still believes he is alive and is not surprised when he walks in one day, having survived in the mountain caves of Vietnam all this time. The drama centered on the shifting relationship of husband and wife, for she has been haunted by his presence all these years and he has had visions of her in the cave each night. Critics again found the acting superior to the script but were supportive of Gaines's talents.

The French Institute / Alliance Française arrived in New York on April 15 to give nine performances of Ionesco's *Exit the King* (1-9-68) at the American Place. The absurdist drama, billed under its native title *Le Roi Se Meurt*, was performed in French.

If Edward J. Moore's tender **The Sea Horse** (4-15-74, Westside) seemed at times more like an acting-class exercise than a play, it may have been because he first wrote parts of it as an audition duologue. But the piece grew: it was first staged off-off Broadway at the Circle Rep, then was moved to Off Broadway (the third Circle Rep production to transfer within the past year). The Sea Horse is a weatherbeaten old bar on the California waterfront run by Gertrude (Conchata Ferrell), an overweight, tough-as-nails woman who can handle the rough clientele and is not above sleeping with one of them if she feels like it. The brash sailor Harry (Moore) returns from sea one night after the bar is closed and, instead of simply taking the night of sex that Gertrude usually gives him, proposes marriage and talks of starting his own business and having a son to leave it to. Gertrude's reaction is one of disgust and fear, not believing that anyone could truly love her. Their confrontation throughout the night consists of insults, physical fights, revelations about the past, and eventually some kind of understanding. Most of the reviews were favorable, so the two-character play ran into August.

The Royal Shakespeare Company had two more productions up its sleeve before the season ended. On April 18 the troupe revived John Barton's anthology program about British royalty, *The Hollow Crown* (1-29-63), and then presented a new but similar entertainment called **Pleasure and Repentance** (4-21-74, BAM). Terry Hands devised the new program that provided a "light-hearted look at love" in a variety of literary and historical selections. What mattered in each case was the sterling cast led by Michael Redgrave.

A cast of skillful American comic actors was assembled for Murray Schisgal's dark farce **An American Millionaire** (4-20-74, Circle in the Square), but most felt that Bob Dishy, Paul Sor-vino, Joseph Bova, Austin Pendleton, and others were either miscast or misused in the frantic comedy. Reviewers felt "there was very little play to like or dislike," and it was withdrawn after two weeks. Textile millionaire Nathaniel Schwab (Sorvino) is watching his world fall apart around him. His wife, Jennifer (Lee Lawson), has left him, his partner, Arnold Brody (Dishy), has lost his faith in him, and someone disguised as a hockey player (Joshua Mostel) is trying to kill him. Schwab's law student daughter, Debbie (Linda Eskenas), and her lover, Professor Bobby Rudetsky (Pendleton), come on the scene to help, but only chaos results, ending in a bomb explosion that no one pays much attention to. Rumor on the Street had it that in the original script the character of the millionaire's daughter was kidnapped and then joined the criminals, but after the sensational Patty Hearst kidnapping case, that subplot was altered.

Tom Stoppard was at his most brilliant in **Jumpers** (4-22-74, Billy Rose)—perhaps too brilliant, for many critics found his new work, seen in London two years earlier, so complex and its allusions so obscure that they gave it faint praise, and audiences stayed away. Some of the fault may have been with the American production, which originated at Washington's Kennedy Center, for Brian Bedford was considered the only cast member up to the difficult play. George (Bedford) is a London professor of moral philosophy who argues life's most ponderous questions, in particular the existence of God. As he tosses ethical questions about, the stage is filled with acrobats (jumpers, in British English) who are being tossed about as well. George's wife, Dotty (Jill Clayburgh), a former musical comedy star, has a wild party one night in their Mayfair home at which George's secretary (Joan Bryon) does a striptease while swinging from a chandelier and one of the performing jumpers is shot dead. When Inspector Bones (Ronald Drake) comes to investigate, he is at first too smitten with Dotty to notice the body hanging in her closet. It turns out the dead jumper was another moral philosopher whom George was planning to debate. Dotty's lover-psychiatrist-lawyer, Archie (Remak Ramsay), is called in, an astronaut and the Archbishop of Canterbury make appearances, the crime is hushed up, and the comedy concludes with George still pondering life's unponderable questions. The characters were often thinly drawn, but Stoppard's verbal wit was at full throttle. For instance, Dottie, contemplating astronauts living on the lunar surface, states that "to somebody *on* it, the moon is always full, so the local idea of a sane action may well differ from ours." The comedy struggled on for forty-eight performances.

Ray Aranha's **My Sister, My Sister** (4-30-74, Little) was an ambitious black drama that switched back and forth through time to explore the maturing of a young African American in the 1950s American South. Sue Belle (Seret Scott) lives in a lower-class neighborhood with her evangelist mother and amiably alcoholic father. Her sister, Evalina (Jessie Saunders), has already turned to prostitution and decides to initiate Sue Belle into womanhood by bringing a white man home for her to have sex with while their parents are out of town. When the mother returns home unexpectedly and discovers what Evalina has done, the furious Evalina leaves home and never returns. Sue Belle spends the years afterward searching for Evalina and falls into prostitution herself. The play ends as the pregnant Sue Belle looks optimistically to the future while a parade of specters from her past fill the stage. Reviews ranged from polite encouragement to "steadily foolish and tedious," but audiences connected with the play, and it ran nearly four months.

Many people who had never heard of Off Off Broadway were confronted with its existence on May 4 when the Off-Off-Broadway Alliance presented a parade, festival, and day of celebration in Lincoln Center Plaza. Mayor Abe Beame officially renamed the street Broadway "Off Off Broadway" for the day, and there was a lot of press coverage.

James Whitmore's one-man show **Will Rogers' U.S.A.** (5-6-74, Helen Hayes) stopped in New York for four weeks as part of its cross-country tour. Critics gave it unenthusiastic notices, applauding Whiteman's performance and Rogers's wit but finding Paul Shyre's script lacking in variety and cohesiveness.

The Ridiculous Theatrical Company's outrageous version of Dumas's *Camille* opened at the Evergreen on May 13 and entertained audiences for 113 performances. Charles Ludlam did the adaptation, directed the revival, and played the heroine, Marguerite Gautier, with an unrealistic but sincere style of camp that actually brought audiences from tears of laughter to tears of pathos. *Camille* would become the company's most famous piece, and Ludlam would play Marguerite over 500 times in various venues over the next few years.

Considering that the Circle in the Square Uptown had started its season with the popular *Uncle Vanya*, many were surprised to hear that the company was broke at the end of the season and had to cancel its last production. Instead a benefit

was held to pay off debts, and the popular *Scapino* was brought in on May 18. The slapstick hit ran 121 performances and helped save the troubled organization.

Frank Chin, the era's sole Asian playwright to get a hearing in mainstream New York theatre, followed up his flawed but interesting *The Chickencoop Chinaman* (5-27-72) with the more satisfactory **The Year of the Dragon** (5-22-74, American Place). In San Francisco's Chinatown, Fred Eng (Randall Kim, formerly Randy Kim), a forty-year-old tourist guide, is celebrating the Chinese New Year with his puritanical Pa (Conrad Yama), who is mayor of the community, his bemused Ma (Pat Suzuki), who avoids confrontations by hiding in the bathroom and reading her favorite books, and his sister, Sissy (Tina Chen), who owns a string of Chinese restaurants in the Boston area and is visiting for the holiday with her white husband, Ross (Doug Higgins). Pa knows he is dying and wants the family to continue on traditionally after he is gone. But Fred wants to quit his job, leave San Francisco, and pursue a writing career. The battle between father and son wages on until the story ends with the old ways dying as the family disperses. Chin's writing was passionate but also very funny, bashing stereotypes by having characters exaggerate them.

1974–1975

After a dismal season, the most mediocre of succeeding seasons might look appealing in comparison. But 1974–1975 was much better than mediocre, and optimism ran high on Broadway. The total number of entries rose perceptibly (sixty-two offerings, forty-seven of them non-musicals and eighteen of those new American plays), ticket prices held steady, and a few more plays showed a profit than in several previous seasons. Even troubled Off Broadway offered thirty new American plays, thanks to the various non-profit theatre companies; the commercial entries numbered only ten, none of which paid back its investors.

In both venues revivals were popular (thirty-seven on and off the Street) but, unlike last season, there were excellent new works to help balance the theatregoers' bill of fare. Granted, the British invasion of new works and revivals was making some New Yorkers uncomfortable. But the imports didn't seem to be getting in the way of a productive season of American offerings. During the last weeks of the season, the musical *A Chorus Line* opened at Joseph Papp's Public

Theatre and gave the theatre scene a marked glow of accomplishment that everyone seemed to enjoy. It seemed the worst was behind us.

The season's first entry was actually the Negro Ensemble Company's final offering from the 1973–1974 season, Charles Fuller's **In the Deepest Part of Sleep** (6-4-74, St. Marks). A black household in 1956 Philadelphia is being tormented by Maybelle (Mary Alice), a middle-aged mother who has returned home after two years in a mental hospital. It looks like Maybelle is heading for another nervous breakdown, staying in her room, ranting and complaining. Her ineffectual husband, Ashe (Charles Weldon), is quite repulsed by Maybelle but hasn't the courage to leave her. His confused seventeen-year-old stepson, Reuben (Todd Davis), studies his textbooks to get ahead while vainly trying to seduce his mother's live-in nurse, Lyla (Michele Shay), who happens to be pregnant by Ashe. Although the drama went nowhere, Fuller skillfully created an atmosphere of sexual and emotional tension. His promising talents would produce a fine play five seasons down the road.

Off Broadway's first commercial venture was the sixteen-performance flop **Some People, Some Other People, and What They Finally Do** (6-5-74, Stage 73), a comic revue by Jordan Crittenden in which the author and three others performed satiric sketches about contemporary life, mostly dealing with urban angst and failed relationships.

More successful was Frank Speiser's one-man show **The World of Lenny Bruce** (6-11-74, Players) in which he performed some of the late stand-up comic's nightclub patter as well as his courtroom defense when charged with obscenity. This attraction was able to run four months.

Shakespeare's rarely done *Pericles, Prince of Tyre* was the New York Shakespeare Festival's first summer offering on June 20 in Central Park's outdoor Delacorte, and the preposterous tale was found to be quite entertaining in Edward Berkeley's production. A group of strolling players presented the epic piece on Santo Loquasto's skeletal set that featured a ship's mast (complete with crow's nest) and myriad clotheslines from which costumes were hung. Randall Kim, who had been stealing the show playing supporting roles in previous Delacorte productions, was the wandering hero, but critics were most impressed with Lenny Baker's salacious Boult in the brothel scene.

Off Off Broadway had seen earlier versions of Tom Eyen's tragicomedy **Why Hanna's Skirt Won't Stay Down** (7-1-74, Village Gate), so when it arrived off Broadway it immediately became a cult favorite, playing 137 performances and returning off and on over the years. In a Coney Island funhouse, Hanna (Helen Hanft), a half-Irish, half-Jewish movie ticket taker, is reunited after twenty-five years with her bald sister, Sophie (Mary Carter), an Avon lady. Also on hand are Arizona (Steven Davis), a self-absorbed bodybuilder who is captivated by the distorted mirrors, and the midway Barker (William Duff-Griffin) whose patter holds the whole freak show together. (The title is easily explained: Hanna stands over the fun-house breeze hole to keep cool.)

The Roundabout Theatre opened its second performance space with Ugo Betti's **The Burnt Flowerbed** (7-2-74, Stage Two), an Italian drama written twenty-two years earlier but given its New York premiere in a translation by Henry Reed. Betti's plays often took the form of an inquest, and this was no exception, with a European politician defending his actions to his followers who have turned against him. The suspense drama ran six weeks.

Another Shakespeare Festival favorite in supporting roles took on a lead when Barnard Hughes essayed Falstaff in *The Merry Wives of Windsor* on July 25 at the Delacorte. Marcia Rodd and Cynthia Harris were Mistresses Page and Ford, George Hearn and Joseph Bova their husbands. Also of interest were the very tall Lenny Baker as Slender and the very short Danny DeVito as Rugby.

Theatres received a different kind of competition from television on August 9 as Richard M. Nixon went on the air and resigned as the nation's president. The producers of *Good Evening* (11-14-73) handled the problem by setting up a large television screen onstage and showing the live broadcast before the comic revue began.

Off Off Broadway's Manhattan Theatre Club moved Michael Sawyer's **Naomi Court** (9-10-74, Stage 73) to Off Broadway, where it ran seventy-three performances before returning to its home for further showings. The soon-to-be-demolished apartment building of the title is the setting for two separate plays about the Court's desperate residents and, in the second play, the violent end that comes to an aging homosexual. Critics found the evening's contrasts startling, with a first play that "breaks your heart" and a second that "skewers it with an ice pick."

Broadway's initial non-musical of the season was the first professional New York revival of Tennessee Williams's *Cat on a Hot Tin Roof* (3-24-55), a summer production from the American Shakespeare Theatre in Connecticut that opened at the ANTA on September 24. Director Michael Kahn utilized parts of Williams's original script, such as the bittersweet ending that Elia Kazan had jettisoned in the first production, and he got riveting performances from his cast: Elizabeth Ashley (Maggie), Keir Dullea (Brick), Fred Gwynne (Big Daddy), and Kate Reid (Big Mama). Critics approved of the play, production, and cast (especially Ashley's restless, cat-like performance), and the revival ran nearly five months. Williams's colleague Arthur Miller fared less well when the Roundabout revived his *All My Sons* (1-29-47) on September 27. Critics found the whole enterprise amateurish, questioned the quality of the play, and felt even the gifted Beatrice Straight was sorely miscast as the forlorn mother. The revival ran its scheduled seven and a half weeks. On the other hand, critics and audiences welcomed back the previous season's *Scapino* on September 27 (its third New York showing) at the Ambassador, where it ran into March.

Classic Greek tragedy had always been a risky commercial enterprise on Broadway, and the one-performance flop **Medea and Jason** (10-2-74, Little) did nothing to help matters. Eugenie Leontovich directed and freely adapted Robinson Jeffers's adaptation of Euripides' original, and the Finnish actress Aria Oho and Richmond F. Johnson played the title roles. It was greeted with vitriolic reviews, from "shatteringly boring" and "bad beyond the bounds of necessity" to "like a pilot for a proposed Greek TV series."

Joseph Papp opened his Public Theatre season with a guest production of Brecht's **The Measures Taken** (10-4-74, Little); the 1930 courtroom drama had never received a professional production in New York before. There was some question as to how professional this production was, being presented by the Shaliko Company, a troupe made up of recent NYU drama graduates. Four agitators return to Moscow from an assignment in China, where they had to kill one of their collaborators who was endangering the mission. The four Soviets appear before the Control Commission and act out the events of their story, arguing that the end justifies the means in the political world. Critics found the drama worthy but the company lacking, one calling their efforts a "drab audience-participation production." But ambitious theatregoers were drawn to the new Brecht work, and it ran eighty-nine performances before recessing and returning for thirteen more showings in April.

The next night the Public offered John Ford Noonan's farce **Where Do We Go From Here?**

(10-5-74, Newman), the first of many plays this season about transvestites. Johann Sebastian Fabiani (Jake Dangel) was a successful ad executive, but he threw it off to become a drag queen. In his Boston apartment he is dressing for an important annual drag ball and has even convinced his straight roommate, Remo Weinberger (Gabriel Dell), to accompany him wearing a purple satin gown. Then the apartment becomes a madhouse with a delirious woman seeking revenge for her brother's death, a cop who wears a dress under his uniform, and a stranger calling himself Zorro who hates homosexuals and wants to rid the world of them. Except for the cross-dressing and abrasive language, it was a pretty traditional farce but, critics felt, not a very accomplished one.

Later that week theatregoers got to see a British variation on transvestism with **Flowers** (10-7-74, Biltmore), a ninety-minute pantomime that had no dialogue except for one character ordering tea near the end of the program. The London import was devised, directed, and designed by Lindsay Kemp who played a drag queen dressed in silver who seeks revenge after being spurned at his/her wedding because he/she is bald. The episodic piece explored every aspect of decadence and the cast of eight played all sorts of lowlifes and deviates. Critics were curious and gave it mixed reviews; audiences were not as curious, and *Flowers* closed after three weeks.

Alan Ayckbourn, who was starting to be called the "British Neil Simon," had his first Broadway success with **Absurd Person Singular** (10-8-74, Music Box), a drawing room comedy set in a kitchen (three different kitchens, in fact). On Christmas Eve, the up-and-coming Sidney (Larry Blyden) and Jane Hopcroft (Carole Shelley) are throwing a party to impress his boss, Ronald Brewster-Wright (Richard Kiley), the architect Geoffrey Jackson (Tony Roberts), and their wives. Sidney is proud of all the new gadgets in his state-of-the-art kitchen, and Jane is happiest when cleaning the oven. The guests frown on the Hopcrofts but put up with the "lower-class" couple because they are necessary to the company. The next Christmas Eve, the Jacksons are entertaining the same crowd, but the depressed Eva Jackson (Sandy Dennis) is more interested in trying to commit suicide. (The series of misinterpreted suicide attempts climaxes when she puts her head in the gas oven; Jane assumes she wants to clean it, so she grabs a sponge and helps.) The last act takes place in the kitchen of the Brewster-Wrights while they entertain on the succeeding Christmas

Eve. It is clear now that the Hopcrofts are pretty much in control of the social and business set, and the play ends with the begrudging upper classes playing one of Sidney's idiotic games. Most critics fell in line with Clive Barnes of the *New York Times*, who felt it was "the best comedy Britain has sent us in years and years," endorsing the script and the American cast (especially Dennis) and helping the play run a year and a half.

Another British play with an American cast sharply divided the critics. Some found it "obnoxious," while others saw "a flawed work of pure genius." But audiences found its subject too British and too uncomfortable, and it struggled through its scheduled fifty-three performances. The drama was Peter Nichols's **The National Health** (10-10-74, Circle in the Square Uptown), about medical care in contemporary Britain. In a men's ward of a British hospital, some patients are admitted; others are released; some linger in limbo while others die and are quickly and quietly removed. The slice-of-life drama was almost documentary in its feel except for sequences scattered throughout in which staff members became characters in a satirical hospital soap opera on TV. The production, which originated at the Long Wharf Theatre in New Haven, was highly thought of, especially Richard Venture as Mervyn Ash, a former teacher reduced to making baskets to pass the time, and Leonard Frey as the frank orderly Barnet. But the real star of the show was the director, Arvin Brown, who created an ensemble that moved in and out of the various situations with documentary-like truth.

French-Canadian playwright Michel Tremblay provided Broadway with its next transvestite show with the three-week failure **Hosanna** (10-14-74, Bijou), a drama previously produced in English and in French in Canada. Hairdresser Claude (Richard Monette), who goes by the

name of Hosanna, has just endured supreme humiliation at a drag ball. It seems Claude opted to go as his idol Elizabeth Taylor in *Cleopatra*, but the other participants stole his thunder by all dressing as the Egyptian queen as well. Claude's lover and roommate, Cuirette (Richard Donat), was in on the joke, and the two fight, make up, strip to the buff, and embrace, Cuirette explaining to Claude that he will never be Cleopatra and that one cannot disguise what one really is. In Canada, critics saw this resolution as a powerful statement on French Canadian separatism. New York notices ranged from "monotonous and depressing" to "truthful and ultimately noble."

The Chelsea Theatre Center opened its season in Brooklyn with Megan Terry's domestic drama **The Hothouse** (10-15-74, BAM). Three generations of Sweetlove women have always shared an insatiable appetite for men, liquor, and life. The men in their lives, on the other hand, are weak and disappointing, all survivors of major wars but emotionally crippled by them. The plotless drama was filled with earthy talk and coarse humor, and Helen Gallagher was particularly effective as the lusty Roz.

Roy Dotrice returned to Broadway as the seventeenth-century gossip John Aubrey in Patrick Garland's one-man play *Brief Lives* (12-18-67) on October 16 at the Booth. Dotrice gathered complimentary reviews, and he stayed for over six weeks this time.

Jean-Claude Grumberg's Paris hit **Dreyfus in Rehearsal** (10-17-74, Ethel Barrymore) must have lost something in Garson Kanin's adaptation, because critics found the play's serious subject matter (anti-Semitism and European pogroms) handled carelessly with Jewish stereotypes and mindless humor. In a Jewish ghetto in Poland in 1931, the high-strung director Morris (Allan Arbus) rehearses a troupe of actors in a play he has written about the courageous Alfred Dreyfus and Emile Zola's defense of his military persecution. The ham actor Arnold (Sam Levene) is to play Zola but complains that he'd much rather act the role of Dreyfus. His mistress, Zina (Ruth Gordon), and the other actors feel the story has no relevance to today's world, there being no anti-Semitism in Poland. Then two drunken thugs who hate the Jews break into the rehearsal hall and attack the company. The production is canceled, and the actors flee to various foreign lands with the cold realization that the Dreyfus affair continues on. The powerhouse cast also included Avery Schreiber, Peter Kastner, and Tovah Feldshuh, who was lauded for her tender portrayal of

ARVIN BROWN (1940–) was born in Los Angeles and educated at Stanford, Harvard, the University of Bristol (England), and the Yale School of Drama. After directing a powerful *Long Day's Journey Into Night* at the Long Wharf Theatre in 1966, he was made artistic director there the next year and remained until 1996, during which time he sent more productions to Broadway than any other regional theatre in America. One of the finest directors outside of New York, he has directed for several major theatres across the country and lectured at schools worldwide.

Dreyfus's wife. But they were all out of work after twelve performances.

Few Shakespeare revivals caused such contrasting feelings as Lincoln Center's *Richard III* on October 20 in the Newhouse. Michael Moriarty's villain was quiet, subtle, and understated; he had no visible handicaps but was instead an emotional cripple. Some thought it the most daring of interpretations; others found Moriarty fey and laughable. (Neil Simon later used this production as the source for his film *The Goodbye Girl* in which Richard Dreyfuss had to play an outrageously effeminate Richard III.) The curiosity piece kept tongues wagging for two months.

No less divided was the reaction to Mark Medoff's **The Wager** (10-21-74, Eastside Playhouse). Some critics thought it was farcical, but others found it deadly serious, with reviews ranging from "a dandy new comedy" to "a two-and-a-half-hour exercise in collegiate cleverness" to "utter nonsense." Last season Medoff's *When You Comin' Back, Red Ryder?* (12-6-73) showed how a coarse redneck tormented the occupants of a rural diner. In *The Wager*, a graduate student badgers fellow academics with much the same vehemence. The acid-tongued Leeds (Kristoffer Tabori) bets his womanizing roommate, Ward (Kenneth Gilman), that the jock cannot seduce Honor (Linda Cook), the wife of a young professor, within forty-eight hours. He also wagers that if Ward should succeed, the husband will make some attempt to kill him. Ward agrees and has no trouble bedding the discontented Honor right away. But when her husband, Ron (John Heard), finds out, his first reaction is to kill Leeds for making such a bet. After many accusations and revelations, the marriage breaks up, Ron flies off to Israel to fight Arabs, Honor dumps Ward, and she and Leeds are left in a battle of love and hate. The well-acted comedy-drama ran three months.

The American Place Theatre presented one of its infrequent revivals when it offered subscribers S. J. Perelman's failed comedy *The Beauty Part* (12-26-62) on October 23. Many had considered this *Candide*-like satire a lost gem, the victim of a newspaper strike during its original production. The James Hammerstein-directed revival was quite competent, with accomplished performances by Peter Kingsley as the hapless hero and Joseph Bova as a multitude of characters he encounters. But it soon became evident that *The Beauty Part* was much funnier on the page than on the stage.

The season's finest play was Peter Shaffer's London hit **Equus** (10-24-74, Plymouth), which se-

cured the New York reputation of the British playwright, as well as the director and leading actors. In rural England, a seventeen-year-old stable boy, Alan Strang (Peter Firth), has, for no apparent reason, blinded six horses with a metal spike. When brought to the overworked child psychiatrist Martin Dysart (Anthony Hopkins), Alan only sings commercial jingles and ignores the doctor's questions. After interviewing Alan's overly religious mother (Frances Sternhagen) and atheistic father (Michael Higgins), Dysart begins to realize that Alan has made horses his gods for the modern age, and his worship of them is so intense that the doctor envies the boy his passion and unfaltering belief. But as a doctor he must "cure" him, so, convincing Alan that he has been administered a truth drug, Dysart probes into what really happened the night of the blinding. It turns out that Alan had tried to make love to Jill (Roberta Maxwell), a girl who works at the stables; their futile lovemaking took place within sight of the god-like horses, so the sexually and emotionally frustrated Alan stabbed the horses, seeking to kill his gods. Revealing the truth cures Alan but leaves Dysart saddened by the absence of passion in his life. John Dexter staged the psychological thriller using both ritual and realism on John Napier's stark set. The horses were played by actors in steel headpieces that suggested god-like icons. Hopkins was considered, by those who saw the original London production, a much more human and tormented Dysart than Alec McCowen's crisp portrayal overseas. Firth, repeating his London performance, was deemed no less superb. But it was the play itself that critics cheered, led by T. E. Kalem's proclamation in *Time* that "Broadway desperately needed an *Equus* . . . about as desperately as did Richard III." The drama won the New York Drama Critics Circle and Tony awards (so did Dexter) and ran 1,209 performances, one of the longest-running nonmusical imports on record.

A British importation that Americans did not embrace was **Bullshot Crummond** (10-29-74, Theatre Four), a satire on the very English "Bulldog Drummond" kind of thriller. The cast of five wrote the comedy that New York audiences could barely follow, and it closed in a week.

For many the most repugnant play of the season was Ann Burr's **Mert & Phil** (10-30-74, Vivian Beaumont), Papp's season opener in the upstairs Lincoln Center space. Slovenly Mert (Estelle Parsons) has had one breast removed because of cancer and has taken to drink while her oversexed truck driver husband Phil (Michael Lombard) cheats on her. Also in the household is Mert's senile and incontinent mother (Marilyn Roberts), who wears roller skates so she can get to the bathroom quickly. Phil eventually leaves, and Mert, in disgust, throws her mother and all the furniture out of the house, dresses in a white robe, and spends all her time daydreaming. When Phil returns, Mert faints onto the floor, and Phil lies down next to her as the curtain falls. The abrasive mix of realism and absurdism was literally booed and hissed by the opening-night audience. (On WNEW-TV later that night critic Stewart Klein declared he wanted to burn down Lincoln Center as well as director/producer Papp.) The next day's reviews were not as severe but more in the line of Barnes's "both repulsive and honest . . . I have rarely disliked a play more or could, in general terms, recommend a play less."

The next night the amateurish **Tubstrip** (10-31-74, Mayfair), A. J. Kronengold's comedy about a men's steambath frequented by homosexuals, opened, and critics, having used up all their venom on *Mert & Phil*, just dismissed it. The comedy lasted twenty-two performances, but the same subject would serve for a much better work later in the season.

The flops kept coming with the one-night stand of **Mourning Pictures** (11-10-74, Lyceum), an autobiographical drama by the poet Honor Moore. Fifty-year-old Maggie (Leora Dana) is dying of liver cancer, and the play chronicles how her minister husband, family, and friends cope with the news, their forced hopes, and her eventual death. There were few surprises along the way, but the events were seen through the eyes of Maggie's daughter, the twenty-seven-year-old poet Margaret (Kathryn Walker), who records her feelings with sincerity and honesty. The play was so personal that audiences actually felt uncomfortable seeing it done in public. Reviews were respectful but unencouraging.

The New Phoenix Repertory Company brought three revivals to Broadway this season, beginning with Congreve's comedy of manners *Love for Love* on November 11 at the Helen Hayes. The difficult Restoration piece received a competent production and introduced Glenn Close, who took over the principal role of Angelica when Mary Ure had to be dropped just before opening. Harold Prince directed, and critics felt his musical staging techniques worked well for the rhythmical period comedy.

The most spectacular revival of the season opened the next evening: the Royal Shakespeare Company's mounting of the old Arthur Conan Doyle–William Gillette *Sherlock Holmes* (11-6-1899) on November 12 at the Broadhurst. The popular melodrama had not been seen on Broadway since 1929, when Gillette himself essayed the British sleuth. Frank Dunlop directed the script in a swift and musical style but didn't camp it up. John Wood was a splendid Holmes, and he was ably assisted by Tim Pigott-Smith (Watson), Philip Locke (Moriarty), and a stage full of RSC actors who made each character, from society lady to messenger boy, vivid and entertaining. In many ways the real stars of the show were Carl Toms's sets and costumes and Neil Peter Jampolis's lighting (they both won Tony Awards). The many interiors revolved on and off amidst fog-filled London streets peopled with all sorts of riffraff peering out of the shadows. The notices were all raves, and the popular attraction remained for 471 performances.

Two other imports, this time from South Africa, would also thrill the critics and win several awards at season's end. Athol Fugard worked so closely with the two actors, John Kani and Winston Ntshona, on **Sizwe Banzi Is Dead** (11-13-74, Edison) that all three were listed as authors. The black laborer Sizwe Banzi (Ntshona) cannot get work in South Africa because his identity papers are incorrect. But he must somehow find a job in order to support his wife and four children. Coming home one night from a bar where he has been drinking with his friend Buntu (Kani) to forget their troubles, they come across the body of a dead man who has an official passbook on him. Sizwe steals the papers and gets a photographer to take his picture, replacing the dead man's photo with his own. Sizwe is glad to become an official worker but regrets that he must "kill" his true identity and become someone else in order to live. The second offering, **The Island** (11-24-74, Edison), was greeted with similarly laudable reviews. Two political prisoners on the maximum security prison island of Robben rehearse in their small cell a crude version of *Antigone* for an upcoming prison entertainment. The implications of Sophocles' tale take on new meaning under their circumstances, especially after one prisoner hears that he is soon to be released while his friend is condemned for life. Even more so than in *Sizwe Banzi Is Dead*, the acting by Kani and Ntshona was like a beautifully played duet with all sorts of subtle and unspoken variations. The Tony Award committee considered their duo performance so compelling they honored the two South Africans together as Best Actor. Ironically, the two men could not get working papers to leave South Africa (the category of "actor" or "artist" did not exist there for "coloreds") until Fugard listed them on the visas as his personal house servants. The two plays ran in repertory until May 18, *Sizwe Banzi Is Dead* playing 159 times and *The Island* giving fifty-two performances.

After extolling two Broadway plays in a row, critics had to search for invectives to describe their feelings about **Fame** (11-18-74, John Golden). Douglas Watt of the *Daily News* felt "watching a cow chew cud for two hours on end would prove more rewarding," and Barnes admitted he counted the number of embossed bumps and diamonds in the proscenium to pass the time. The Anthony J. Ingrassia drama was a thinly disguised retelling of the Marilyn Monroe story. Diane Cook (Ellen Barber) is born out of wedlock, struggles to become a model, marries three times (including once to an famous athlete and another time to a renowned writer), becomes a star, endures loneliness and depression, and eventually commits suicide. There were arguments over which was worse: the script, the production, or the performances. The dreary play closed on opening night.

A revised version of David Rabe's disappointing *Boom Boom Room* (11-8-73) opened at the Public's Anspacher on November 20 with the revised title *In the Boom Boom Room*, a new cast, and new realistic sets and costumes. Critics felt the play had not improved and, if anything, seemed longer and less effective than in its earlier version. Ellen Greene as the go-go girl Chrissy was commended, but little else was, so the play was taken off the boards in less than a month. On the same day, the San Francisco Mime Troupe brought the first of two programs to the Westside Theatre in Brooklyn. Gorki's *The Mother*, in a dramatization by Bertolt Brecht, ran twenty-one performances, and, opening on November 24, the cast-created comic revue *The Great Air Robbery* played fourteen times.

Eduardo de Filippo, Italy's leading contemporary dramatist, rarely got a Broadway showing. Unfortunately, his **Saturday Sunday Monday** (11-21-74, Martin Beck) closed after twelve performances. Using a translation by Keith Waterhouse and Willis Hall that was a hit in London, the piece struck New Yorkers as a very thin boulevard comedy that, like bad pasta, was all bulk but no flavor. The wealthy Priore family of Naples started as hatters under grandfather Antonio (Walter Abel), then became fashionable outfitters

under his son-in-law Peppino (Eli Wallach). His wife, Rosa (Sada Thompson), is having an affair with the handsome neighbor Luigi Ianniello (Ron Holgate), and Peppino knows it. He holds his tongue until tempers flare at Sunday dinner and he accuses the two lovers right at the table in front of all the family and friends. After much yelling and much eating of food, everything settles down by Monday morning. Aisle-sitters enjoyed the performances, particularly Jan Miner as the widowed Aunt Meme, who was always on the make for the family doctor (Sam Gray), but found the comedy noisy and stereotypic.

London's other renowned theatre company, the National Theatre of Great Britain, also to came to Broadway this season, but its all-male production of *As You Like It* on December 3 at the Mark Hellinger got mixed reviews instead of the raves the RSC had received for its *Sherlock Holmes*. Clifford Williams staged the pastoral comedy in a modern setting (Ralph Kotai's scenery was all white with panels of Plexiglas, and his costumes utilized white and black leather and vinyl), and the actors playing Rosalind, Celia, and Phoebe avoided camp and brought wonderfully new aspects to the characters. (Rosalind's epilogue was particularly beautiful.) But it sounded like another drag show to New Yorkers, and its one-week engagement on Broadway (as part of an international tour) was not well attended.

Off Broadway, the Roundabout revived two classics on December 3 in their two performance spaces. Sheridan's *The Rivals* seemed to lose much of its wit when played very broadly in the larger Stage One, but Christopher Hewitt was an admirable Sir Anthony, and Jane Connell's Mrs. Malaprop was a farcical joy. Ibsen's difficult and rarely produced *Rosmersholm* at Stage Two was considered too weak in production and performance to be effective. The former was kept on for seventy-nine showings, the latter for only thirty-two.

If the RSC's triumph with the 1899 *Sherlock Holmes* surprised some, its successful mounting of the 1841 Dion Boucicault comedy *London Assurance* was a downright phenomenon. The British import opened on December 5 at the Palace for a six-week visit, with critics lauding the company and the handsome production even if a few felt the play was a bit too antique. Donald Sinden shone as Sir Harcourt Courtly, the elderly fop bent on remarriage, and no less enjoyable were Roger Rees as the man-about-town Charles, Polly Adams as the ingenue Grace Harkaway, and Elizabeth Spriggs in the role most often featured in the nineteenth century, Lady Gay Spanker, the lusty horsewoman whom Harcourt pursues.

Off Off Broadway's Ridiculous Theatrical Company edged a bit closer to the mainstream by bringing two more of their past productions to Off Broadway. Charles Ludlam's travesty **Stage Blood** (12-8-74, Evergreen) was about a theatrical family that has been touring *Hamlet* for too many years. The dissolute patriarch Carlton Stone (Jack Mallory) is now too old to enact the hero (he's stuck playing the Ghost), so he tries to encourage his reluctant son (Ludlam) to play the Prince as he once did. Soon there is a play within the play, a murder within the play's murder, and even a happy ending to boot. Critics were warming up to Ludlam's kind of comedy, calling *Stage Blood* "literary and terribly funny . . . the very essence of clownmanship" and defining it as "Hamlet and Freud on wry."

Peter Ustinov's **Who's Who in Hell** (12-9-74, Lunt-Fontanne) was a British play that had its world premiere in New York with an American director and (except for the author in a leading role) an American cast. In a purgatory-like anteroom where the recently deceased wait until they take an elevator to either the "penthouse" or the "basement," the English judge Sir Augustus Ludbourne (Joseph Maher), a century dead, interviews the new arrivals and determines where their future lies. On this day the president of the United States (George S. Irving) and the Russian premier (Ustinov) arrive, both having been assassinated by the young radical Arlo Forrest Buffy (Beau Bridges), who was in turn killed by the FBI and has joined them in the anteroom. This intriguing premise gave way to a three-hour Shavian drama of debate that touched on politics, philosophy, and religion. The play concludes when the black elevator operator (Bob Lawrence), who was lynched by a mob in 1932, goes on strike and the elevator temporarily stops working. Director Ellis Rabb got some worthy performances from the cast, but critics found the play endlessly talky and rarely dramatic. When audiences did not disagree, the comedy closed in a week.

Everyone had much more fun at Terence Rattigan's tearjerker **In Praise of Love** (12-10-74, Morosco), for it was an old-fashioned well-made play with likable characters performed by beloved stars. The former Marxist author Sebastian Cruttwell (Rex Harrison) is now a critic who is jealous of younger writers, especially his best friend, Mark Walters (Martin Gabel), and his own son, Joey (Peter Burnell), who is writing for television. The difficult Sebastian has been married to the Estonian refugee Lydia (Julie Harris) for twenty-eight years, but not until he learns that she is dying does he realize how much he loves her and eventually tell her so. Critics found nothing special in the script, but Harrison and Harris were luminous together, and they filled the house for the five-month engagement.

Neil Simon had been taking steps toward serious issues in his last three efforts, but he stumbled awkwardly with **God's Favorite** (12-11-74, Eugene O'Neill), a modern version of the story of Job that moved into schtick the closer it edged toward genuine grief. (The play was written, Simon later said, as a reaction to his wife's untimely death from cancer.) The Long Island home of prosperous businessman Joe Benjamin (Vincent Gardenia) is broken into one night by Sidney Lipton (Charles Nelson Reilly), a zany movie buff from Queens who claims he is a messenger from God ("Important documents only; no packages"). He warns Joe that God and the Devil have a bet on to see whether or not Joe breaks under a run of bad luck. Joe doesn't believe Sidney, but immediately the phone rings with news that Joe's factory has burned down. "I didn't believe in insurance. God was my insurance," he tells Sidney, who admits that "even God uses John Hancock." Joe's troubles escalate from chapped lips to burning skin and lumbago to boils all over his body, but still he will not renounce God, even though he is financially bankrupt and losing the love and support of his family. Sidney returns to taunt Joe, listing the even worse calamities awaiting him, but Joe is steadfast, and when his estranged son David (Terry Kiser) returns, Joe feels the important things in life have not been taken away from him. There were plenty of laughs in *God's Favorite* (the comic exchange between Sidney and Joe in the first act was perhaps, line for line, the funniest scene Simon had ever written), but many had trouble laughing at what was put before them onstage. The reviews were mixed, ranging from "awesomely funny . . . and rather sweet" to "a most abysmally empty-headed play," and the comedy struggled on for an unprofitable 119 performances. With three commercial failures in a row, America's most successful playwright left New York and settled in California, where he concentrated on movies for a while. He promised to return to the theatre, but it would be many years before he enjoyed the Broadway success of his earlier days.

The Phoenix's second offering of the season was Pirandello's *The Rules of the Game* on December 12 at the Helen Hayes. The 1918 play was remembered (if at all) as the comedy the actors are rehearsing at the beginning of his *Six Characters in Search of an Author*, and it had been seen off Broadway in 1961. Critics thought it an intellectual exercise more than an engrossing theatre piece and felt the acting was weak except for John McMartin as an estranged husband who is bored with life.

The Chelsea's **Yentl the Yeshiva Boy** (12-17-74, BAM) was based on an Isaac Bashevis Singer short story and dramatized by Singer and Leah Napolin. In 1873 Poland, the rabbi's daughter Yentl (Tovah Feldshuh) longs to be educated and study the Torah, rather than just marry and keep a home. When her father dies, she disguises herself as a boy and travels to another village, where she enrolls as a yeshiva student. She befriends fellow student Avigdor (John V. Shea) and soon finds herself wed to his fiancée, Hadass (Neva Small), when her family rejects Avigdor. Yentl's identity is eventually discovered, and she sets out for new lands where she believes a woman has a better future. The scheduled forty-eight performances were so popular that the Chelsea moved the play to Broadway the following season.

On the same night, a new Tom Stoppard play, **Enter a Free Man** (12-17-74, St. Clements), made its New York debut, but instead of a flashy Broadway production it was afforded a small one off-off Broadway for a limited engagement of twenty-five performances. It was Stoppard's most realistic effort yet seen, about a dreamy inventor (David Rounds) who has come up with a double-gummed envelope that can be used twice. On the strength of his prospects, he leaves his weak-willed wife (Alice Drummond) and restless daughter (Swoosie Kurtz) but ends up returning home when someone at the local pub points out how an envelope, whether double-gummed or not, is torn apart by the first person to use it. Stoppard's wit was in low gear but unmistakable all the same. According to the notices, the production, directed by Brian Murray, suffered from actors too young for the roles.

Another American classic that had not yet seen a Broadway revival was John Steinbeck's *Of Mice and Men* (11-23-37), which Elliott Martin brought to the Brooks Atkinson on December 18. Kevin Conway played the ever-complaining George, and James Earl Jones was his half-witted partner, Lenny. While most critics applauded both men, some felt that an African-American Lenny clouded the issues of the play. The rest of the production was thought unimpressive, and the revival ran less than two months.

After a handful of misfires, Murray Schisgal came back with a moderate hit, **All Over Town** (12-29-74, Booth), which ran seven months. The recognized psychiatrist Dr. Lionel Morris (Barnard Hughes) has started to despair at the state of the world around him and plans to become a Buddhist monk. But his daughter, Sybil (Jill Eikenberry), and her social worker fiancée, Charles (Jim Jansen), convince Morris to take on the unusual case of Louie Lucas, a young man who has fathered nine children by five different women, all out of wedlock and now all on welfare. When a hip black delivery boy named Lewis (Cleavon Little) arrives at the doctor's home, everyone mistakes him for the notorious womanizer, and Lewis goes along with it, moving into the plush town house, ordering expensive clothes, and hustling the doctor and his friends into investing in his Harlem tap-dancing school. When the real Louie (Zane Lasky) shows up, a shy and unassuming white man whose gentle smile and line "as soon as I get a little bread together, we'll get married" make him such a ladies' man, Lewis hides him in the guest room. While Morris tries to rehabilitate Lewis on his womanizing, Louie seduces the Swedish maid Millie (Pamela Payton-Wright) and the frustrated singer Philomena (Polly Holliday), the wife of Dr. Morris's best friend (who's having an affair with the doctor's wife). A bogus French cook and maid, who try to steal some jewels using a nearsighted thief, bring on the police, and matters are finally resolved: Dr. Morris gives up his Buddhist plans, Philomena goes back to her husband, Lewis gets his dance school, and Louie returns to his many women, one of whom has just given birth. Film star Dustin Hoffman, in his professional directorial debut, staged the farce at breakneck speed but couldn't keep the disjointed plot together. Critics enjoyed the performers, especially Little, and many felt it was Schisgal's best script since *Luv* (11-11-64).

Treading a fine line between a play and a musical, Richard Foreman's **Hotel for Criminals** (12-30-74, Westbeth) sought to both satirize and pay tribute to the French filmmakers who turned out lurid serials at the turn of the century. The cast reenacted old melodramas by portraying exaggerated villains, heroes, and vampire characters. The attraction by the Performance Group ran fifteen performances and was thought to be more fun than usual for a Foreman production.

The Phoenix's last revival was a competent but uneven version of Carson McCullers's *A Member of the Wedding* (1-5-50) on January 2 at the Helen Hayes. Mary Beth Hurt (Frankie), Marge Eliot (Berenice), and Eamon MacKenzie (John Henry) made valiant efforts to dispel memories of the original cast (which even younger playgoers remembered from the film version), and some critics felt they managed to hold their own.

Lance Larsen's **The Hashish Club** (1-3-75, Bijou) came from Los Angeles but was welcomed on Broadway for only eleven performances. Five friends from college, who in their younger days belonged to a secret society mainly concerned with drugs, reunite years later and plan to reenact old rituals by indulging in a high-dose drug orgy. Much of the play was about their hallucinations while "tripping," with the gathering turning violent. Reviewers agreed that for anyone not on drugs, it was a very dull evening.

Two more classic revivals opened on January 8. At the Public, André Gregory's Americanization of Chekhov's *The Sea Gull* was considered a mess. By adding all kinds of contemporary references to make the work more accessible, the play fell apart. That same night, Lindsay Kemp, the drag queen seen earlier on Broadway in *Flowers*, led an all-male production of Oscar Wilde's *Salome* at the 62 East 4th Street Theatre. It seemed this transvestite season would never end, but *Salome* was gone after three and a half weeks.

The next night André Gregory was back with a new work, Wallace Shawn's **Our Late Nite** (1-9-75, Public: Martinson), an hour-long play about lewd talk, impulsive lovemaking, and periodic vomiting at a party in a Manhattan high-rise. Partygoers told strangers their most intimate secrets, then the gathering broke up. The production, presented by Gregory's Manhattan Project, was featured at the Public for thirty-eight performances.

Paul Shyre's one-man show **Blasts and Bravos: An Evening With H. L. Mencken** (1-16-75, Cherry Lane) was considered by the press to be interesting enough, notices decreeing that Shyre and the curmudgeonly Baltimore journalist he portrayed were both stageworthy. Some commented that Mencken's outspoken prejudices came across as pure bigotry today, but there was audience enough to let the piece run forty-six times.

Lincoln Center's second Shakespeare in the downstairs Newhouse was *A Midsummer Night's Dream* on January 19. Edward Berkeley staged the

comedy as a rip-roaring farce along the lines of a Marx Brothers movie, with all the play's characters performed as broadly as the mechanicals. The costumes were traditionally Elizabethan, but the sensibility was definitely modern, with Puck (Larry Marshall) as a hip street arab who gave Oberon (George Hearn) plenty of sass.

Adela Holzer had a triumphant season coproducing *Sherlock Holmes* and *All Over Town* but found herself sole producer of an even bigger hit when she gambled on Terrence McNally's **The Ritz** (1-20-75, Longacre), bringing it into a Broadway house and seeing it run a year. Gaetano Proclo (Jack Weston), a rotund garbage contractor from Cleveland, finds out his Mafia brother-in-law has put out a contract on his life, so he flees Ohio and hides in a Manhattan Turkish bath, not knowing it is a notorious homosexual trysting place. There he is pursued by the flamboyant Chris (F. Murray Abraham), the nerdy Claude (Paul B. Price), who likes them fat, the falsetto-voiced detective Brick (Stephen Collins), and the Puerto Rican songstress Googie Gomez (Rita Moreno), who misunderstands and thinks Proclo is Joe Papp (he, on the other hand, thinks she's a transvestite). All the towel-clad characters get involved in mistaken identity and sexual confusion, with Proclo ending up in drag as part of an Andrews Sisters act. Carmine Vespucci (Jerry Stiller), the Mafia brother-in-law, arrives, but Proclo is saved by his wife, Vivian (Ruth Jaroslow), who pleads with Carmine. It was McNally's most sustained and accomplished effort yet, and the critics were able to recommend it without reservation as "a very funny play, Puerto Rican funny, homosexual funny, Mafia funny and show business funny." The cast was in fine form (Moreno won a Tony Award) under the expert direction of Robert Drivas, and the setting by Lawrence King and Michael H. Yeargan was a farce extravaganza with no less than thirty-five doors leading to cubicles, baths, and steam rooms.

A small and potent little play from the La Mama Experimental Theatre Club called *Dance wi' Me* by Greg Antonacci was seen at the Public in 1971 and was liked well enough to be revised and retitled **Dance With Me** (1-23-75, Mayfair). In a grimy and realistic subway station, born loser Honey Boy (Antonacci), while waiting for his train, jumps into Walter Mitty–like fantasies and flashbacks to his past, such as imagining himself as a 1950s bobby-soxer making the girls swoon. The original production had been deemed quite enjoyable, but many of the critics felt it lost

EDWARD [Franklin] **ALBEE** [III] (1928–), the adopted grandson of vaudeville magnate E. F. Albee, was born in Washington, D.C., and attended several prestigious schools, rarely staying at any very long. He turned to playwriting in the 1950s but found no success until his *The Zoo Story* was first produced in Germany in 1959. In 1960 his one-acts, such as *The Sandbox* and *The American Dream,* were seen in New York. Two years later his first full-length play, *Who's Afraid of Virginia Woolf?,* was produced on Broadway. Albee's subsequent plays all received mixed reviews and were known more for their controversy than financial success: *Tiny Alice* (1964); *A Delicate Balance* (1966), which won a Pulitzer Prize; *Everything in the Garden* (1967); and *All Over* (1971). Albee's plays are marked by a mysterious and abstract atmosphere, characters fighting against conceptual foes, and often sparkling dialogue that mixes absurdism and realism.

something in its more lavish reincarnation. Also, some of the nostalgia that seemed so entertaining in 1971 was now a bit cloying after the popularity of *Grease.* But audiences felt differently, and word of mouth let the "comedy with music" run nearly a year in the small theatre.

Edward Albee's new play **Seascape** (1-26-75, Shubert) might have succeeded by word of mouth if it hadn't closed before it was awarded the Pulitzer Prize. But even though the play was a financial failure, it proved that Albee was still a playwright to be watched.

On a deserted stretch of beach, a late-middle-aged couple, Charlie (Barry Nelson) and Nancy (Deborah Kerr in her first Broadway role in twenty-two years), talk about their "pleasant" marriage and what lies in store now that they are well off and their children are grown up and gone. Out of the sea come two human-size lizards, Leslie (Frank Langella) and Sarah (Maureen Anderman), who have taken a giant step in the evolutionary process and are considering becoming land creatures. The humans are startled at first but soon engage the lizard couple, who speak perfect English, in conversation and discuss the important changes each is about to undertake. Leslie and Sarah ultimately decide that they will return to the sea, but Nancy warns them, "You'll have to come back . . . sooner or later." The play received every kind of reaction possible, from "bland and innocuous" and "fake sensitivity" to "provocative and tantalizing rather than

profound" to "of all Mr. Albee's plays, *Seascape* is the most exquisitely written." Critics agreed that the actors, especially Langella, were laudable and that James Tilton's amphibious costumes were excellent. But audiences were confused and put off by the conflicting reports, and the play closed after two months.

Thomas Babe's first effort, **Kid Champion** (1-28-75, Public: Anspacher), was considered effective enough by some that the young playwright would enter the growing ranks of promising talents who would strive vainly for decades to fulfill that promise. The rock star Kid Champion (Christopher Walken) is at the peak of his career with sold-out concert engagements, ridiculous wealth, and crowds of groupies, members of the press, and would-be biographers following him about. But Kid isn't happy, has taken to drugs, liquor, and impersonal sex, and keeps wondering how a nice boy from Kansas has gotten so off the track. So he dies of an overdose and becomes a symbol of the brief, remarkable 1960s. The B-movie, cliché-ridden vehicle used slides, soliloquies, movie clips, and rock music to tell its story, and Walken's powerful performance impressed many. The drama ran six weeks, as did the Public's next entry, **Fishing** (2-1-75, Newman) by Michael Weller, which was a sequel of sorts to his college-setting comedy *Moonchildren* (2-21-72). Bill (Tommy Lee Jones) and Shelly (Lindsay Crouse) have been out of college for some time but are still trying to get started in life. Living in a cabin in the Pacific Northwest, they have (unsuccessfully) tried farming and are looking to buy a boat to go into commercial fishing. Robbie (Guy Boyd), their drifter friend from college, is staying with them, and when another couple from the past comes up for the weekend, the five try to recreate the old days, indulging in drugs and memories. Robbie is in love with Shelly, but she

FRANK LANGELLA (1940–) was born in Bayonne, New Jersey, and educated at Syracuse University. After graduating in 1959, he studied acting and dance in New York and in 1963 became a member of Lincoln Center's first repertory training program. Langella played classical and contemporary roles off Broadway and in regional theatre from 1963 until his Broadway debut as the young Will Shakespeare in *A Cry of Players* (1968). The youthful-looking actor was ideal for classical heroes, and only later in his career did he get to portray villains and comic roles.

does not return his affection, so he tries (unsuccessfully) to commit suicide. He then gives all his money to Bill to buy the boat; Robbie himself will just stay and love Shelly from afar. Some critics thought the play and the characters likable and enthralling; others found both obnoxious. The work did foreshadow a whole breed of plays and films that looked back at the 1960s with bittersweet nostalgia.

Lanford Wilson's **The Mound Builders** (2-2-75, Circle), presented off-off Broadway in a limited engagement of twenty-nine performances, did not move to Off Broadway but was one of his better works all the same. On an archaeological dig in rural Illinois, Dr. Howe (Rob Thirkield) and his family and associates are exploring the remains of an ancient culture that has left behind curious burial mounds. A local boy, Chad (John Strasberg), joins the group, getting socially and even romantically involved with the work party. In the end, spurned by the wife of one of the archaeologists, Chad destroys the dig and the mysterious culture is buried once again. The most interesting character in the play was Howe's sister, D. K. Eriksen (Tanya Berezin), a Dorothy Parker–like writer drying out from alcoholism treatments and flinging bitter barbs all over the place. Most critics found it artificial in some spots, "original and brilliant" in others.

Having dazzled Broadway with their *Sherlock Holmes* and *London Assurance*, the Royal Shakespeare Company presented four productions in repertory for a month in Brooklyn, beginning with Maxim Gorky's 1904 **Summerfolk** (2-5-75, BAM), never seen in New York before. The English version by Jeremy Brooks and Kitty Hunter Blair had a very Chekhovian feel to it; in fact, the play was viewed as a sequel of sorts to Chekhov's *The Cherry Orchard*. At the beginning of the new century, the recently prosperous Russian bourgeoisie find leisure time to spend at the summer villa of the lawyer Bassov (Norman Rodway) with his wife, Varvara (Estelle Kohler), and their family and neighbors. One of the visitors is the cynical writer Shalimov (Ian Richardson), who prods the twenty-six characters into discussions about life and philosophy. Many little situations develop, but there is no main plot to speak of. Near the end of the play the unhappy Varvara prophetically comments: "Tomorrow some bold people will come and sweep us away like so much litter." Critics praised the newly discovered script and the company, yet the play has rarely been heard of since.

The next night on Broadway, Maggie Smith led a British invasion of her own, garnering rave reviews for her Amanda Prynne in a revival of Noel Coward's *Private Lives* (1-27-31) at the 46th Street Theatre. John Gielgud directed the British-American cast that featured John Standing as Elyot and Remak Ramsay and Niki Flacks as their unhappy spouses. While all of them were cheered, the evening was Smith's; according to Jack Kroll in *Newsweek*, she "turns [her voice] into a bewitchingly adenoidal purr that insinuates every utterance into an almost sensual facetiousness." There was one disturbing aspect to the evening: the players were miked for the large house. The revival, a touring production from London, did excellent business for its two-and-a-half-month stay.

An evening that consisted of a revival of Eugene O'Neill's *Hughie* (12-22-64) and a new play, David Scott Milton's **Duet** (2-11-75, John Golden), turned into a showcase for the considerable talents of Ben Gazzara. As the rambling Erie Smith who tells a night clerk all about his predecessor Hughie, Gazzara was appropriately blustering but with a tormented subtext. In the new work, a one-man play that was seen in an earlier draft off Broadway in 1970, Gazzara played a paranoid ex-novelist, Leonard Pelican, who is convinced that the Mafia has sent a Russian agent to kill him. This, strangely enough, was a farce, and Gazzara was applauded for his fine comic antics, which contrasted nicely with *Hughie*'s sobering character study. The touring production, coming out of Chicago, stayed for four weeks.

The RSC's masterful production of Shakespeare's tricky early work *Love's Labours Lost* on February 13 was their second offering at BAM. David Jones, who had also directed the earlier *Summerfolk*, staged the talky comedy under an expansive green cloth that hung over the actors like a forest umbrella. Ian Richardson, as the inflated lover Berowne, led the sparkling company in a production cited as "impeccable by any standard" and "a graceful and joyous thing indeed."

A one-performance flop about four Yale roommates and their love affairs after graduation, **Four Friends** (2-17-75, Theatre de Lys), is worth noting as the first professional production by Larry Kramer, a playwright who would become a controversial force to reckon with a decade down the road.

The RSC's third offering at BAM, *King Lear* on February 25, was a distinct disappointment. This "abbreviated" version ("gutted" was how one critic described it) concentrating on the few central characters was intended for school groups. Adult audiences found it empty and passionless, despite a fine Edgar by Mike Gwilym and a heartfelt Cordelia by Louise Jameson.

There had been consistent complaints about the Roundabout's new space as too big and impersonal for most plays, and the intimate **James Joyce's Dubliners** (2-25-75, Roundabout: Stage One) surely suffered from being seen there. J. W. Riordan adapted Joyce's brother Stanislaus's *My Brother's Keeper* and some of Joyce's short stories to create a series of vignettes about the Joyce household, the father (Stan Watt) taking center stage for much of the evening. The reviews for the "long, uneventful, and generally meaningless evening" were all negative, though several critics liked Martin Cassidy as the young Jimmy. Nevertheless, the drama was kept on at the Roundabout for eighty performances, the longest run of its season.

The Chelsea received little applause for Allan Knee's **Santa Anita '42** (2-27-75, BAM), but reviewers criticized the play gently because of its delicate subject matter. In 1942, the Japanese-American mother Tamako (Lani Gerrie Miyazaki) and her family, along with hundreds of other Asian Americans, are interred in a camp on the grounds of the Santa Anita racetrack outside of Los Angeles. When Teacher (Henry Kaimu Bal), who acts as a Chorus throughout the play, tries to soothe the distraught Tamako, her story is told: her arrival in America twenty years before as a mail-order bride, her unhappy marriage, her love affair with the white man Paul (Stephen D. Newman) she met, ironically, at the same racetrack in better days, and the murder of her grown son (Sab Shimono) by the camp guards when he went wild with grief and anger. Teacher tries to console Tamako by telling her to arrange her life as an orderly Japanese garden, and she vows to return to Japan after the war and begin anew.

The Negro Ensemble Company had a hit with Leslie Lee's **The First Breeze of Summer** (3-2-75, St. Marks), a domestic drama that ran two months off Broadway, then reopened on Broadway in June for an additional six weeks. Milton Edwards (Moses Gunn), a plasterer in a northeastern city, receives a weekend visit from his mother (Frances Foster), called Gremmar by the family, which includes the sensitive high schooler Lou (Reyno), who wants to be a doctor or a scientist. Two stories are then told: the grandmother's recollecting her past as the young Lucretia (Janet League) with her three lovers and

two pregnancies, and Lou's problems with his sexuality and race identity. The play concludes with Gremmar being reconciled to Lucretia without regret and, on her deathbed, helping Lou accept who he is. Though considered "overlong and confusing" by some critics and filled with too many incidents, the drama boasted powerful writing and vigorous characters throughout, and the NEC gave it a superior mounting. It was, unfortunately, the only major work by the then-promising playwright.

More revivals appeared on and off the Street. Henry Fonda returned in his one-man drama *Clarence Darrow* on March 3 at the Minskoff but, as had happened the season before, his engagement was cut short (eighteen performances) due to the star's illness. But the acclaimed European film actress Liv Ullman was in fine health for her Broadway debut in Ibsen's *A Doll's House* at the Vivian Beaumont on March 5, gathering rave reviews for her effervescent Nora. The notices weren't much needed, since the seven-week engagement was sold out before opening night. Critics declared the rest of the cast less thrilling but felt Ullman was show enough for their money. They were not at all enthusiastic about another Ibsen revival (the third of the season) that opened the next night: the Shaliko Company's environmental production of *Ghosts* at the Public. Jerry Rojo's setting placed the action all over the Little Theatre for reasons no one could quite figure out. On Broadway, Molière's *The Misanthrope* was also tinkered with (a modern-dress production set in 1966), but with Diana Rigg as the aloof beauty Célimène and Alec McCowen as the morose Alceste, theatregoers didn't seemed to mind. The National Theatre of Great Britain production, seen two years earlier in London, opened on March 12 at the St. James and stayed for twelve weeks. Critics were disappointed, not in the two leads, but in the rest of the cast and in John Dexter's staging, which seemed more gimmicky than ingenious.

With the British invasion in full force on Broadway, off Broadway, and even in Brooklyn, everyone was ready for an all-American hit, and they got it (sort of) with Canadian Bernard Slade's **Same Time, Next Year** (3-13-75, Brooks Atkinson). It is 1951 and the accountant George (Charles Grodin) wakes up in a northern California guest cottage with a married woman, Doris (Ellen Burstyn), whom he has had a one-night fling with. The two virtual strangers get to know each other, talk about their spouses and lives at home, and agree to try to meet again. So they do on the first weekend of every February after that, George telling his wife it's a business trip and Doris saying she's going on a religious retreat. The next six scenes cover every five years in the couple's ongoing affair, often catching each other at opposing points in their lives. When Doris is in a flower child phase, for example, George is in a stuffy, conservative, money-making frame of mind. Slade kept the episodes from being repetitive by throwing new complications in the way. (For one of the trysts Doris is very pregnant and goes into labor when George embraces her.) The chronicle ends in 1975 as the two of them, now middle-aged and spouseless, realize that they have always been friends as much as lovers and promise to continue their yearly ritual into old age. While some reviews carped about the implausibility of the play, calling it "slight and facile" and describing it as an unmarried version of *The Fourposter* (10-24-51), most critics admitted to having a great time. Audiences agreed with them for 1,453 performances. (Interestingly, no reviews mentioned the 1968 comedy *Avanti!* in which an unmarried couple meet yearly in Italy; when they die, their two children decide to continue the tradition.)

Russell O'Neil's **Don't Call Back** (3-18-75, Helen Hayes), the first of two hostage thrillers, both failures, that threatened Broadway this spring, opens with a famous actress, Miriam Croydon (Arlene Francis), returning home to her plush Park Avenue duplex to find her spoiled son (Richard Niles) and three ghetto friends (a black, a Puerto Rican, and a psychotic white) wanted for murder and hiding from the police. Holding Miriam and her secretary hostage, they phone the mayor and ask for money and safe passage, then watch the TV news to see if they are getting any coverage. Disappointed in the results, the gang members leave and are shot by the police. As the curtain falls the son is seen on the phone plotting his mother's murder while she is listening in on the extension. Len Cariou, joining the ever-increasing ranks of actors who turned to directing this season, staged the melodrama with embarrassing results. Critics called it "unbearable," so the "play for the bigots" closed on opening night.

Reviving O'Neill's *All God's Chillun Got Wings* (5-15-24) was a risky proposition at best, but all the same the Circle in the Square brought it back on March 20. The tale of a white girl (Trish Van Devere) who weds a black man (Robert Christian) and then goes insane due to social pressures was found to be hopelessly dated, and the reviewers had few good things to say about the

actors or the production directed by yet another actor, George C. Scott.

Robert Wilson's strangely beautiful non-plays certainly had their place somewhere in the American theatre but, most agreed, Broadway was not that place. His three-hour "opera" **A Letter for Queen Victoria** (3-22-75, ANTA) was but a flash of an eyelid compared to his twelve-hour *The Life and Times of Joseph Stalin* (12-15-73), but most critics found it endless all the same. The plotless attraction consisted of brief scenes from nonexistent operas and plays and used a lot of verbal repetition and phrases echoed by the twelve-member cast as a way of making the passage of time into some sort of an art form. Wilson's eighty-eight-year-old grandmother (Alma Hamilton) appeared as Queen Victoria, but the character was inconsequential to the action. Even fans of Wilson's work bemoaned the lack of interesting visuals and the humorlessness of the program. Such extravaganzas off-off Broadway were usually one or two-night stands, but *A Letter for Queen Victoria* was slated for a four-week run and managed to find an audience for the month.

Beginning on March 25, French mime Marcel Marceau, who had been wowing New Yorkers with his visits since 1955, appeared at the City Center for three weeks.

The Hollow Crown, an anthology program about English kings, had successfully visited New York twice, so its sequel, **He That Plays the King** (3-29-75, BAM), was highly anticipated. Ian Richardson compiled the program of selections about Shakespearean royalty, and three fellow actors (Susan Fleetwood, Tony Church, and Mike Gwilym) from the RSC performed the accomplished anthology piece until the RSC repertory ended on April 6.

Producer Alexander H. Cohen came a cropper with the season's second hostage thriller, Norman Krasna's **We Interrupt This Program** (4-1-75, Ambassador). The curtain rose on a fashionable apartment setting and the beginning of a domestic comedy. Then a gang of black thugs with submachine guns, led by Al Seaver (Dick Anthony Williams), took over the stage, hustled the "actors" off, and took the whole theatre audience as hostages. The gang must have been present for *Don't Call Back*'s one performance, because they used the stage manager's phone to call the mayor and demand money and safe passage for themselves and a brother of a gang member who was in jail for shooting a cop. While "killing time" waiting for their demands to be met, the gang pulled a priest and some others out of the audience and hassled them and even sang a few songs. Finally, one hardened member of the gang called his mother on the phone, and in a moment of weakness, the gang was overpowered by the police. First-nighters reported that the audience could not believe in any of the proceedings and that the evening was filled with unintentional laughs. All the reviews were scathing, and the Ambassador was kidnapped only seven times— losing $285,000, the most expensive non-musical flop of the season.

Audiences for Sam Shepard's work had been growing, but two short, abstract, and absurd plays, **Killer's Head** and **Action** (4-4-75, American Place), seemed to be a throwback to his early and awkward works. In *Action*, two bald men who are subject to fits and two domestic homemakers celebrate Christmas on a bleak landscape; one of the women is so hungry for the turkey in the oven that she eats her own arm while waiting. *Killer's Head* was an eight-minute stream-of-consciousness monologue by a horse dealer strapped to an electric chair. He rapidly talks of horses, his job, and his future until the switch is pulled and he dies smiling. The month-long engagement was for subscribers only.

James Kirkwood's "three-hour sleeping pill" **P.S. Your Cat Is Dead!** (4-7-75, John Golden) was roasted by the critics, but the playwright and the play would eventually have the last laugh after the sixteen-performance comedy closed. New York actor and "flaming heterosexual" Jimmy (Keir Dullea) is having a string of bad luck: his girlfriend has left him, he lost his role in a Broadway show, and his character in a long-running TV soap opera is going to be killed off. To top things off, on New Year's Eve a cat burglar named Vito (Tony Musante) breaks into Jimmy's Greenwich Village apartment. Using all his built-up anger, Jimmy knocks out the burglar and ties him up, the two of them getting into conversation when Vito comes to. It turns out that Vito is bisexual (his wife has lost interest in him ever since their daughter was born), and he tries to convince Jimmy to explore new areas of sexuality. As the curtain falls, he gets Jimmy to let him stay the night. As one of the authors of *A Chorus Line* that opened a month later, Kirkwood soon found himself a successful playwright, and even *P.S. Your Cat Is Dead* would later return in a popular revival.

The National Theatre of the Deaf stopped in Brooklyn for a week with its tour of S. Ansky's *The Dybbuk* paired with a new work, **Priscilla, Princess of Power** (4-13-75, BAM) by James Ste-

venson. The short comic book–like comedy was used as an afterpiece to the Ansky drama and concerned a girl (Linda Bove) who works in a jelly bean factory and rises to the heights of business and romance.

The most commercially successful revival of the season was Somerset Maugham's *The Constant Wife* (11-29-26) on April 14 at the Shubert. The reason for all the fuss was Ingrid Bergman as Constance Middleton, the wife who accepts her husband, John (Jack Gwillim), and his infidelity with great poise. While some critics had reservations about the play, John Gielgud's direction, and the rest of the company, all agreed in their high esteem for Bergman. Martin Gottfried (now writing for the *New York Post* since the retirement of Richard Watts) said: "She projects brains, charm, and devastating sexuality. That she projects them while playing light comedy is the least of things." The comedy stayed only for four weeks while on its tour from London, but during that time it broke the Shubert house record for a weekly gross.

The Manhattan Project brought two of its works back to the Public for return engagements: the company-devised *Alice in Wonderland* on April 15 for twenty showings and Beckett's *Endgame* on the 29th for twelve performances.

The Ridiculous Theatrical Company brought back its first off-off-Broadway hit, Charles Ludlam's **Bluebeard** (4-18-75, Evergreen), a riotous take-off on H. G. Wells's *Island of Dr. Moreau*. On an isle off the coast of Maine, the insane Baron Khanazar von Bluebeard (Ludlam) searches for a third sex, experimenting on various women and hoping for "some new and gentle genital." The spoof, described by one commentator as a "grotesque right out of Bela Lugosi with Noel Coward thrown in for good measure," stayed for seven weeks.

The **Augusta** (4-20-75, Theatre de Lys) of the title of Larry Ketron's drama was not a woman but the Georgia town near the play's setting, a house in the woods. The sluttish Betty (Faith Catlin), who years before as a teenager seduced the older Champion (Kenneth Harvey), has graduated from college and, with her fiancé Boyd in tow, finds Champion's home and tries to cause trouble for him and his wife (Elizabeth Franz). Instead both men turn on Betty and the little vixen is put in her place. *Augusta*, which originated off-off Broadway at Playwrights Horizons, was deemed uninteresting in character, plot, and performance, and the commercial offering closed after nine showings.

The Negro Ensemble's annual Spring "Season-Within-a-Season" featured four programs that ran a week each, beginning with Burial Clay's **Liberty Call** (4-29-75, St. Marks). The black seaman John Wilheart (Samm Williams) is on trial for sodomy and manslaughter, and in a series of flashbacks, we see how he got there from the navy flagship where he trained and befriended the white Yale graduate H.O.B. Rothschild II (Michael Jameson). John, so caught up in his pride and illusions about the power of the U.S. Navy he didn't notice that Rothschild had fallen in love with him, is aghast when the boy propositioned him. John agrees to have sex for money, but the affair goes sour, and he ends up killing the young sailor.

Tom Eyen's **Women Behind Bars** (5-1-75, Astor Place), a travesty of Hollywood B movies of the 1950s, was so much fun off-off Broadway that it moved on to an off-Broadway run of fifty-four performances. Into the Greenwich Village Woman's House of Detention, ruled by the sadistic giant Matron (Pat Ast), comes the innocent but duped ingenue Mary-Eleanor (Mary-Jennifer Mitchell), who must deal with the tough women around her, such as the wisecracking lesbian-on-the-make Gloria (Helen Hanft) and the wizened old Granny (Mary Boylan), who shouts "croaaak!" as she drops dead of natural causes. When confronted with rape, the befuddled Mary-Eleanor can only say, "I have a headache," but eventually she ends up as hard and cynical as the others. Mixed reviews ran from "junk theatre" to "grade A tomfoolery."

The New Federal Theatre and Joseph Papp got together to co-produce the outstanding black play of the season, Ed Bullins's **The Taking of Miss Janie** (5-4-75, Lincoln Center: Mitzi E. Newhouse), which won the New York Drama Critics Circle citation for best American play. The drama started at the end of the story, with the white California beach girl Janie (Hilary Jean Beane) in shock because her friend of many years, the black student Monty (Adeyemi Lythcott), has just raped her. She cannot understand it, telling him, "I thought of you as my special friend," but he says she always knew their relationship would come to this. The scene switches back to the 1950s, and in a series of episodes we see how Miss Janie, who represents all patronizing white liberals and their attitudes to blacks, and Monty and his friends, who stand for the misguided hopes of his race, have been drawn to each other in a mission of failure. Both supporters and critics of Bullins's work thought it his most accomplished play, filled

with vivid characters and building in intensity rather than taking his usual scattershot approach. The good reviews encouraged Papp to keep the drama on the boards for five weeks.

A double bill of plays by Don Evans, **Sugar Mouth Sam Don't Dance No More** and **Orrin** (5-6-75, St. Marks), was the next Negro Ensemble offering off Broadway. The charming drifter "Sugar Mouth" Sammy (Carl Gordon) has had an on-and-off affair with Verda Mae (Lea Scott) for so long that, when he returns to her after a long absence, Verda Mae accepts him back. But at the same time, the growing independence within her foreshadows an end to the relationship. In the second playlet, Orrin (Taurean Blacque), a junkie and drug pusher, returns to his middle-class family, who threw him out eight months earlier. He taunts his "uptight" parents and studious brother, but underneath the bravado we see a lonely and desperate "prodigal son."

Papp's uneven season in Lincoln Center's upstairs venue concluded with Anthony Scully's anti-Catholic farce **Little Black Sheep** (5-7-75, Vivian Beaumont), which Barnes called "a religious play in need of extreme unction." In fact, the hateful reviews rivaled those for the Beaumont's opener Mert & Phil, which was no easy task. In a Jesuit house of study on the morning that Robert Kennedy died, a group of dysfunctional priests, ruled over by the fierce German housekeeper Willie (Stefan Schnabel), have their infighting and bickering disturbed by a fugitive nun, Sister Mary Charles (Diane Kagan), who is running away from her convent because she has fallen in love with a priest. Before the first act was over she had stripped to the waist, and before the final curtain descended the deviate Father Caputo (Gatone Rossilli) came out in drag and sang "Heat Wave," making sure the season contained just one more transvestite act. The farce ended with the Jesuits as rebellious as ever and the nun giving up sex and heading to Peru to do missionary work.

The Negro Ensemble's **Welcome to Black River** (5-20-75, St. Marks) by Samm Williams completed the new-plays series. Williams's drama, about sharecroppers in North Carolina in the 1950s, is worth noting because it contained the seeds for a later and more important play he would write under the name of Samm-Art Williams.

The American Place ended its season with a hit. In fact, reviews were so encouraging and demand for tickets so great that the company dropped its subscribers-only policy for the first time and opened the Jonathan Reynolds double bill **Rubbers** and **Yanks 3 Detroit o Top of the Seventh** (5-16-75, American Place) to the public for 145 performances. *Rubbers* took place in the Assembly Chamber of the State Legislature, where Democratic representative Mrs. Brimmins (Laura Esterman) is arguing for a bill that would require druggists to display condoms and other contraceptives in plain view, much to the shock and political sidestepping of the other representatives. The more substantial playlet was the baseball fantasy, in which aging big-league pitcher "Duke" Bronkowski (Tony Lo Bianco) goes through a series of self-doubts and memories of his past mistakes while on the mound during the seventh inning. Although some critics complained that both pieces were a bit overextended, they all hailed the comic writing (it was Reynolds's first play) and the splendid cast (staged by yet another actor turned director, Alan Arkin).

The Negro Ensemble closed its season with Silas Jones's "nightmare comedy" **Waiting for Mongo** (5-18-75, St. Marks), which was kept on the boards for four weeks. In rural Mississippi in the recent past, the black teenager Virgil (Reyno), orphaned when his parents were killed by local whites, cowers in the basement of a church, terrified because he has been accused of attacking a white girl. A preacher (Bill Cobbs) has found the boy and hides him from the lynch mob that has set out to find him. In his frightened sleep, Virgil's imagination turns the preacher into Mongo, the head of a black army coming to invade the South and free him. Much of the play was about these fantasies, with Cobbs playing the virtuous and all-powerful Mongo, and about tragicomic memories of different people in the church community. But the play ends in the real world with the mob finding Virgil and putting a noose around his neck.

The Roundabout's revival of James M. Barrie's 1908 play *What Every Woman Knows* on May 28 was admired for trusting the script and not trying to give it a modern interpretation. Fran Brill shone as Maggie Wylie, the sly wife who molds her husband's career in politics without his ever knowing it. The solid production pleased audiences for two months.

The season ended on a sour note when Papp announced that Off Broadway was "dead . . . D E A D." (He spelled it out for the *New York Times*.) His efforts at the Public to present new works had been so discouraging, he said, that he was abandoning full productions in the place and would move to Broadway's Booth Theatre for premieres. The Public, he announced, would be turned over to workshops and limited engagements, the Beaumont would house safe revivals, and the Newhouse would become the home to children's theatre. Papp did not make good on many of these promises (threats?), but the fact that the most productive producer in New York was turning his back on Off Broadway was not encouraging. (What Papp could not foresee was how his hit musical *A Chorus Line*, already scheduled to move to Broadway, would help finance all of his theatre activities over the next dozen years.) Because of the critical acclaim for *The Taking of Miss Janie*, Papp made an agreement with the New Federal Theatre to work with them in promoting some of their productions in his more marketable venues. So perhaps Off Broadway wasn't dead after all. It just needed, according to Papp, to go to Broadway whenever possible.

ACT TWO, 1975–1984

EVERYTHING OLD IS NEW AGAIN

1975–1976

With the approaching Bicentennial celebration, it was not surprising to find several revivals of American classics in New York. But there must have been more than patriotism behind all the theatrical looking back this season. One half of all the entries on and off the Street were revivals, and a good number of new works were nostalgic (or anti-nostalgic) pieces. There were plays looking back at the Old West with a cockeyed pessimism and others examining the follies of youth and more innocent eras; plays about the recent Vietnam nightmare continued to be presented, and there were already works trying to figure out the crazy 1960s. Reminiscing seems to have been the theme for the season.

Without a steep rise in ticket prices, box-office figures rose 20 percent over the previous season because more theatres were open and running. During the week of January 4, Broadway brought in a record $2 million. By the end of May the TKTS Booth in Times Square was responsible for over $600,000 worth of ticket sales for Broadway and off Broadway shows. But the profit margin was still hazardous, and several critical and even popular hits lost money. While there were no megahits like last season's *Equus* or *Same Time, Next Year* (not to mention the musical *A Chorus Line*, which moved to Broadway in July), it was still possible for a play to break even before the end of May.

But nostalgia and box-office records couldn't hide the fact that, after the revivals and British imports, Broadway presented only ten new American plays, and most of those were transfers from Off Broadway or originated in regional theatres. Off Broadway did better with twenty-six new American scripts, a good number of them worthwhile. (Six of the eight non-musical *Best Plays* came from Off Broadway this season; the other two were London imports.) So maybe

downtown theatre wasn't dead after all. Certainly Off Off Broadway was alive as the Circle Repertory Company, the Manhattan Theatre Club, and other groups edged closer and closer to Off Broadway. The hazy line between the two venues was getting hazier.

The Broadway season started with the transfer of last season's drama *The First Breeze of Summer* (3-2-75) on June 10. It only ran forty-eight additional performances, but its venue was, inexplicably, the huge Palace Theatre. Central Park's Delacorte began this season of revivals with a *Hamlet* on June 18 that divided audiences and critics right down the middle. Sam Waterston played the prince in a modern production complete with European uniforms and goose-stepping guards. The twenty-eight showings were so well attended that producer Joseph Papp had the production revised and moved to Lincoln Center in December.

The first American classic revival was, appropriately enough, Arthur Miller's *Death of a Salesman* (2-10-49) on June 26 at the Circle in the Square Uptown. George C. Scott directed and played Willie Loman, and he was showered with adulation for both efforts. Scott played Loman like a feisty King Lear, fighting and hissing with life, rather than the more fatalistic approach usually seen. James Farentino and Harvey Keitel were deemed a competent Biff and Happy, but most critics were disappointed in Teresa Wright's Linda Loman. The drama played in the small house for eight weeks.

The New York Shakespeare Festival's second Central Park entry was *The Comedy of Errors* on July 24. It was enjoyable enough but caused no fireworks as *Hamlet* had. Neither was there much excitement over the Broadway revival of Thornton Wilder's *The Skin of Our Teeth* (11-18-42) on September 9 at the Mark Hellinger. The first of five American Bicentennial revivals sponsored by the Kennedy Center in Washington and the Xerox Corporation, this lackluster production directed by José Quintero was scheduled for six weeks but called it quits after seven performances. The critics thought Elizabeth Ashley's Sabina was the best thing about the evening despite a cast that included Alfred Drake and Martha Scott as the Antrobuses.

September saw five more revivals in a row. The Roundabout Theatre opened its season with Tennessee Williams's *Summer and Smoke* (10-6-48) on September 16 with Debra Mooney and Michael Storm as the ill-matched lovers. Eugene O'Neill's *Ah, Wilderness!* (10-2-33), on September 18 at the Circle in the Square Uptown, was much better. The Arvin Brown production came from his Long Wharf Theatre in New Haven, and it was a beautifully realized depiction of a simpler and more innocent America, probably the ideal Bicentennial show. William Swetland and Geraldine Fitzgerald were the understanding parents, Teresa Wright the spinster Lily, and Richard Backus and Swoozie Kurtz the youngsters in love. Critics welcomed the play and the production, and the nearly ten-week engagement was well attended.

The Classic Stage Company, another one of those off-off-Broadway groups that was edging toward Off Broadway, presented Shakespeare's *Measure for Measure* on September 18 at the Abbey, adding Ibsen's *Hedda Gabler* to the repertory on September 20 and Chekhov's *A Country Scandal* (5-5-60) on September 25. The last had only had an off-Broadway showing in New York before.

It wasn't until the end of September that a new play opened, and one had to go to Off Off Broadway to find the limited engagement of David Mamet's **Sexual Perversity in Chicago** (9-29-75, St. Clements). The hustling, macho Bernie (Robert Townsend) is always coaching Danny (Robert Picardo) about women and sex, but when Danny meets Deborah (Jane Anderson) he forgets all of Bernie's advice and asks her to live with him. Deborah's roommate, Joan (Gina Rogers), says it won't last, and it doesn't. Soon Danny is back with Bernie, eying girls on the beach and once again reducing women to sexual objects. What made everyone sit up and take notice was Mamet's foul-mouthed poetic dialogue that was funny and revealing. The companion piece for the comedy was a short duologue called **Duck Variations** about two old men (Paul Sparer and Michael Egan) in a park overlooking Lake Michigan who are discussing life in silly pseudophilosophical terms. Edith Oliver in *The New Yorker*, one of the few major critics to seek out the double bill, wrote, "Mr. Mamet is a true and original writer who cherishes words and, on ev-

idence at hand, cherishes character even more." Within a year Mamet's name would no longer be unknown.

Two quick failures off Broadway contained two of the season's favorite themes: bittersweet nostalgia for the Kennedys and for the Old West. Frank Hogan's **Finn MacKool, the Grand Distraction** (9-29-75, Theatre de Lys) was about a wealthy Irish-American family who dabbled in politics. Michael Ondaatje's **The Collected Works of Billy the Kid** (10-13-75, BAM) looked at the western hero poetically with short vignettes and folk songs. Hogan's play closed on opening night, and the western piece only lasted ten performances.

Papp opened his Lincoln Center season with Pinero's nineteenth-century parable about the theatre, *Trelawney of the "Wells,"* on October 15 in the Vivian Beaumont. The play had been done there five years before to great acclaim, and critics compared this production unfavorably to it. Director A. J. Antoon moved the locale from London to New York and featured such promising new talents as Mary Beth Hurt (as Rose Trelawney), Meryl Streep, and Mandy Patinkin, but the expensive production never took flight.

Broadway's first new work of the season, Louis LaRusso II's **Lamppost Reunion** (10-16-75, Little), was a thinly disguised tale about Frank Sinatra with the names changed to avoid legal tangles. Superstar Fred Santora (Gabriel Dell) left his humble roots in Hoboken, New Jersey, twenty-five years ago and has never looked back. But after a singing engagement at Madison Square Garden, Fred crosses the river late at night and visits his old hangout, the Lamppost Bar, with his right-hand man Jobby (George Pollock). (Everyone knew that Sinatra's sidekick was nicknamed Jilly.) Some of his foul-mouthed friends from the past are still there—the happy bookie Tommy (Frank Bongiorno); Mac (Frank Quinn), a cynical Irish tough; and the bartender Biggie (Danny Aiello)—and the reunion is joyous at first but soon turns sour as we learn that Fred had treated these and others cruelly when he started on his climb to success. Changed names or not, Sinatra was not pleased (his lawyers tried to stop the production); neither were the critics, who described the obvious melodrama as "derivative" and "crude." Despite a vigorous ad campaign to help the play catch on, it only lasted seventy-seven performances.

Critics were mixed about the next night's offering, David Freeman's **Jesse and the Bandit Queen** (10-17-75, Public: Other Stage). In a fantasy limbo, Jesse James (Kevin O'Connor) reads about his exploits in the *Police Gazette* and Belle Starr (Pamela Payton-Wright) plays the piano as both recall and argue over the events of their lives, including their outlawing together and their deaths. We see Jesse as a young renegade terrorizing the Missouri countryside with Captain Quantrill, holding up banks with his brother Frank ("Hell, woman, I invented the American bank robbery," he boasts), and later robbing trains with Belle. Her memories are more painful: sexual abuse by a teacher at the age of eleven, her various love affairs and children with Indian men, selling her story to the *Gazette*, even being raped by her own son Ed. The two actors played all the roles, Jesse even acting the part of Belle's beloved horse Venus at times. Reviews ranged from "sparkles with intelligence and sly humor" to "out-takes from a 30's western" to "doesn't add up to a hill of beans." But most complimented the two busy actors and felt that Freeman was a playwright worth watching.

Papp's promise to use Broadway's Booth for five new works this season was given its first test with Dennis J. Reardon's ambitious but embarrassing **The Leaf People** (10-20-75, Booth). Anthropologist Dr. Shaughnessy (Tom Aldredge) has been tramping through the Amazon jungle for four years seeking the mysterious "leaf people" who have a vocabulary of 400 funny-sounding words and believe that they have sprung from trees. When the expedition does find them, the tribe attacks the whites (whom they call Fishbellies) but in turn are either killed, die of whiteman diseases, or end up begging coins from tourists. Two interpreters, inside glass booths suspended from above, translated for the audience but, aside from a lot of acrobatics and swinging from vines in the background, the leaf people struck critics as a fairly dull group. Besides dismissing the silly script, reviewers found Tom O'Horgan's frantic staging extravagant and vulgar. The experiment closed in a week, losing $400,000, and Papp brought no more untried works to the Booth, returning instead to the Public for any risky ventures.

Broadway had never seen Christopher Marlowe's history play *Edward II*, so critics were curious to see what the young Acting Company would make of it on October 21 at the Harkness. It was a stark and uncompromising production of a brutal play, and reviews were mostly approving. The homosexual element of the drama was quite clear but handled well by director Ellis Rabb. The touring production was scheduled for only a week. On October 23, the Chelsea Theatre's off-Broadway hit *Yentl* from last season moved into the Eugene O'Neill and stayed for the rest of the season. (The play had been called *Yentl the Yeshiva Boy* in the Brooklyn production.) Tovah Feldshuh recreated her poignant performance and became Broadway's newest star.

Another play experienced a title change but did not fare as well. William Inge had always felt that his *Picnic* (2-19-53) was too romanticized and rewrote it a few years after its original run. The new version, now called **Summer Brave** (10-26-75, ANTA), caused critics to question the validity of the original since they found the reincarnation so corny. The only significant change in the new script was in the third act when Madge (Jill Eikenberry) decides not to run off with the drifter Hal (Ernest Thompson) but to stay in town, where she deteriorates into the local sexpot. Alexis Smith was cited for her feisty schoolteacher, Rosemary, but little else was applauded, and the revival closed after two weeks.

Critics also questioned the staying power of William Saroyan's *The Time of Your Life* (10-25-39) on October 28 at the Harkness, but most blamed the dismal evening on the Acting Company's sluggish and miscast production.

A theatre season would not be complete without a handful of one-man shows. The first one to come along this season was **Conversations with an Irish Rascal** (10-29-75, Top of the Gate), which lasted only nineteen performances. Kathleen Kennedy and David O. Frazier adapted Irish author Brendan Behan's writings, and Frazier performed them, with a guitarist named Gusti intermittently providing some Irish songs.

The first British import of the season, Tom Stoppard's **Travesties** (10-30-75, Barrymore), was arguably the best. Stoppard built his comedy on a historical footnote: in Zurich, Switzerland, in 1917, James Joyce (James Booth) was in exile writing *Ulysses* while the Dadaist poet Tristan Tzara (Tim Curry) was promoting anti-art in the cafes and Lenin (Harry Taub) was biding his time, waiting for revolution to break out in Russia. A British Consular Service employee, Henry Carr (John Wood), was also there and performed in an amateur production of *The Importance of Being Earnest* with Joyce. *Travesties* is about the aged Carr looking back and trying to write his memoirs, but in his semi-senility, the story comes out in disjointed fragments, some parodying Wilde's comedy, other sections as absurdist Dadaism, and still others as Leninist political diatribes. The wordplay (one scene is written entirely in limericks and another in a vaudevillian "Mr. Gallagher and Mr. Shean" patter) was perhaps Stoppard's most dazzling yet, and his power of pastiche (the use of Wilde's conversational wit was very cunning) amazed even the most devout fans of Wilde and Stoppard. The reviews were all raves, but the complex comedy was a tricky thing to sell, so it only managed 155 performances, closing before it won the Drama Critics Circle and Tony awards for best play. (Wood also won the Best Actor Tony.)

Robert Patrick was a playwright who had been produced up and down Off Off Broadway for years. He made the jump to Broadway with his **Kennedy's Children** (11-3-75, John Golden), a drama previously seen downtown and in London. In a quiet Lower Manhattan bar on Valentine's Day 1974, five patrons speak to the audience in alternating monologues. The spokesperson for the sixties generation is Wanda (Barbara Montgomery), a schoolteacher who idolized J F K and will not believe anything negative about him. The homosexual actor Sparger (Don Parker) comically recounts the bizarre underground theatre happenings he has been in (one company gathered and telepathically tried "to draw Clive Barnes to us with the power of prayer") but despairs that it has all gone commercial. The Vietnam vet Mark (Michael Sacks) relates in a series of letters to his mother how he became a drug addict, while the political activist Rona (Kaiulani Lee) tells how she lost her husband and all her ideals during the anti-war movement. Most disillusioned of the group is the blond aspiring actress Carla (Shirley Knight), who emulates Marilyn Monroe and, seeing her image commercialized, takes an overdose as her heroine did and dies as the play ends. Critics called it a non-play and complained of its lack of dramatic action, but most admitted to being moved by it. The cast of unknowns was quite gifted, especially Knight, who won a Tony Award, but nine weeks was all the play could survive. The little drama went on to become very popular with college and regional theatre groups.

After knocking much of the Acting Company's repertoire all fall, critics came down strongly on its side for the final offering, Chekhov's *Three Sisters* on November 4 at the Harkness. Some had seen the production in 1973 before it went on tour, but all agreed that it had now settled into a striking ensemble production. The cast featured Patti LuPone (Irina), Mary-Joan Negro (Masha), Mary Lou Rosato (Olga), and Peter Dvorsky (Vershinin). J. B. Fagan's *And So to Bed* (11-9-27), a comedy about the famous chronicler Samuel Pepys, received its first New York revival on November 5 at Stage 73 but was gone in a week. Harold Pinter's *The Homecoming* (1-5-67) lasted no longer when revived on November 6 at the Wonderhorse.

The Chelsea Theatre crossed the Harlem River for three productions in Manhattan this season. The Dutch playwright Lodewijk de Boer's domestic epic **The Family, Parts 1 and 2** (11-12-75, Westside) was translated by Albert Maurits, and the two full-length works (out of a four-play cycle) were presented with a dinner break for twenty-three showings. A prizewinner in Holland, the peculiar play concentrated on Doc (David Selby), his kid brother, Kil (Brent Spiner), and their mute sister, Gina (Dale Soules), who collect damaged furniture from empty lots, pile them in a wheelbarrow, and bring it back to their basement home in a condemned building outside of Amsterdam. There they are visited by some strangers and friends, and soon chaos commences, resulting in rape, incest, and mayhem. The drama was supposedly an allegory for the German occupation of Holland, but Americans saw only a confusing and tedious soap opera. Another foreign play about the German occupation could be found in Brooklyn a week later. Norwegian playwright Tankred Dorst's **Ice Age** (11-18-75, BAM) was about a Scandinavian author who cooperated with the Nazis during World War II and is tried and committed to an old people's home after the war.

Habeas Corpus (11-25-75, Martin Beck), a British import that was roundly panned for its low humor and juvenile obsession with breasts, was by Alan Bennett, a playwright who would do much better in the future. At a seaside resort near Brighton, the lecherous Dr. Arthur Wicksteed (Donald Sinden) pursues the pretty young Felicity (Constance Forslund) when not in view of his overly busty wife (Rachel Roberts). Wicksteed's spinster sister, Constance (Jean Marsh), on the other hand, is so flat-chested that her beau, Canon Throbbing (Paxton Whitehead), thinks of her as one of the choirboys he is so unnaturally fond of. Constance has ordered for herself a pair of falsies ("Rubens made of sensitized fablon as used on Apollo space missions"), but she is out with the Girl Scouts when the salesman-fitter (Richard Gere) arrives, so he mistakenly tries to fit the portable breasts on various other women in the house, including Felicity's "pillar of the Empire" mother (Celeste Holm). From there the usual complications and confusions take over until, after enough doors have been slammed and a few ladies are left running about in their underwear, all is sorted out. Frank Dunlop directed the British-American cast with great aplomb, and the comedy managed to stay on the boards for ninety-five performances on the strength of its cast. (Marsh was particularly popular because her British television series *Upstairs, Downstairs* was still running in this country.)

Two important playwrights had inferior products presented on the same night in the Manhattan Theatre Club's different performance spaces. David Storey was known for his truthful slice-of-life plays, but **Life Class** (12-4-75, Manhattan Theatre Club) struck critics as cynical, bleak, and not very credible. At a British art school, the instructor Allott (Kevin Conway), who is upset about his wife leaving him, tells his class that art is dead and that the transitory moment is all. He encourages the students to free themselves from the rigid world, so soon the whole class are taking off their clothes with wild abandon. But things get out of hand, one ruthless student (Lenny Baker) rapes the nude model, and, in the end, Allott is fired. In the same building, Sam Shepard came a cropper with **Geography of a Horse Dreamer** (12-4-75, Manhattan Theatre Club). Cody (Rick Warner), a young man from Wyoming, recently had the ability to determine racehorse winners in his sleep. Although he has lost the gift, some gangsters hold him prisoner in a shoddy hotel in case his powers should return. When the head racketeer, Fingers (John Mitchell), decides to put his money into greyhound racing, Cody senses a kinship with the dogs and soon is correctly guessing winners again. The plot was very similar to the farce favorite *Three Men on a Horse* (1-30-35) but Shepard found no humor in the situation. Each play was presented for a two-week engagement.

Alan Ayckbourn, the British playwright who built plays like intricate puzzles, topped himself with three full-length comedies presented under the portmanteau title **The Norman Conquests** (12-7-75, Morosco). The action of all three plays takes place over a weekend at the home of unmarried Annie (Paula Prentiss) and her sickly mother (who is never seen). Annie has asked her brother, the affable Reg (Barry Nelson), and his uptight wife, Sarah (Estelle Parsons), to watch Mother for the weekend while Annie gets a holiday away. The getaway was to be an illicit tryst with her brother-in-law Norman (Richard Benjamin), but Norman's wife, Ruth (Carole Shelley), and the others find out, so instead the group

spends the weekend together. With Annie's dense beau, the neighbor Tom (Ken Howard), joining them, they struggle through not-so-polite graciousness and domestic squabbling. *Table Manners* recounted the activities that occurred in the dining room over the three days, Norman trying to appease Annie and his wife between meals. *Living Together* showed the goings-on in the living room, including Norman's drunken binge and attempts by the group to play board games. *Round and Round the Garden* took place in the backyard where the trilogy's events began and ended, Norman even trying to seduce the icy Sarah but ultimately being scorned by all three women. The critics proclaimed the comedies first-rate and recommended that audiences see them in any order they wished because each stood up hilariously on its own. Some Anglophiles quibbled about the American cast and its lack of style, but audiences found the trilogy inventive and engaging. The repertory ran into June—but at a loss of $235,000.

Two very un-Bicentennial revivals followed. Racine's *Phèdre* was performed in French by Le Tréteau de Paris on December 8 at the American Place, and the Classic Stage Company presented the Anouilh version of *Antigone* (in English) on December 9 at the Abbey. The former played a week, the latter five weeks.

A three-week run was sufficient for Andrew Colmar's drama **Dancing for the Kaiser** (12-14-75, Circle), about a fanatical Englishman who, during World War I is determined to smash a spy ring made up, he believes, of homosexuals and lesbians, in particular an Isadora Duncan–like American dancer.

The summer's much talked-about outdoor production of *Hamlet*, redesigned and redirected with a partially different cast, reopened on December 17 in the Vivian Beaumont. The production was now more traditional, staged by Michael Rudman on a giant tilted wooden disc, but again was met with sharply divided reviews. Some declared it the finest American *Hamlet* in memory; others found it lacking and called Sam Waterston's Prince "peevish, sniveling," and "thoroughly unsympathetic and unlikable." Audiences had forty-seven chances to see for themselves.

Reviews were also mixed for Circle in the Square Uptown's revival of *The Glass Menagerie* (3-31-45) on December 18. While most thought that Maureen Stapleton was a heartfelt Amanda, several aisle-sitters stated the production was too obvious and blunt with no poetry. Rip Torn (Tom), Pamela Payton-Wright (Laura), and Paul Rudd (Jim) completed the cast. The revival ran a little over two months. A far less famous play, Booth Tarkington's *Clarence* (9-20-19) on December 23 at the Roundabout, also suffered from a misguided production, but critics were grateful to see the old comedy again and let it down lightly. They had more trouble hiding their disappointment over the Broadway revival of Patrick Hamilton's *Angel Street* (12-5-41) on December 26 at the Lyceum. The thriller's original producer and director, Shepard Traube, repeated the same tasks for the revival, but critics uniformly dismissed the "creaky suspense play" and the cast, which included Dina Merrill and Michael Allinson. It struggled on for fifty-two performances.

Commentators were just as unimpressed with a new thriller, Bob Barry's **Murder Among Friends** (12-28-75, Biltmore). The vain and impossible Broadway star Palmer Forrester (Jack Cassidy) lives in a plush Manhattan town house with his put-upon wife, Angela (Janet Leigh in her Broadway debut). Palmer is so difficult that one can understand why Angela and Palmer's agent, Ted Cotton (Lewis Arlt), who have fallen in love, plan to have the star murdered on New Year's Eve as part of a false break-in. But we soon learn that Palmer and Ted are also lovers and together are plotting to kill off the interfering Angela. Comic confusion occurs when friend Larry (Michael Durrell), posing as the hit man, enters the scene. Neither Palmer nor Angela is murdered in the anti-climatic conclusion that includes a gun with blanks and the revelation that Ted is a double agent spy. Negative notices, unlikable characters, and a disappointing performance by Leigh contributed to the play's closing after two weeks.

With the opening of *Sweet Bird of Youth* (3-10-59) on December 29 in the Harkness, there were three Tennessee Williams plays running in New York. This revival, another Bicentennial offering from the Kennedy Center and Xerox, was seen regionally and in Brooklyn earlier in the season, so word was out that this was no ordinary tour. Edwin Sherin directed the problematic piece with a tough-as-nails approach (one critic commented it was "more in the style of Bertolt Brecht than Tennessee Williams"). Irene Worth, as the fading film star Princess Kosmonopolis, and Christopher Walken, as her gigolo lover Chance Wayne, were electric together. (She won the season's Tony Award.) A set of rave reviews helped fill the house for the six-week engagement.

Word was also out about another Kennedy Center–Xerox revival that stopped in Brooklyn first, but no one anticipated the hit that Kaufman and Ferber's *The Royal Family* (12-28-27) would

ROSEMARY [Ann] HARRIS (1930–), a British-born actress who lived and raised a family in America, studied at the Royal Academy of Dramatic Arts in 1951 and 1952 and then acted with the finest English-language theatre companies on both sides of the Atlantic, from the Old Vic, Chichester Festival, and National Theatre in Britain to the APA, Lincoln Center, and the American Shakespeare Festival in the United States. Because she also appeared in many regional theatres, her Broadway appearances were sporadic but memorable. Harris won a Tony Award for her Eleanor of Aquitaine in *The Lion in Winter* (1966) and much acclaim for her Blanche in the 1973 Lincoln Center revival of *A Streetcar Named Desire*. A classically beautiful actress, Harris is particularly adept at playing elegant and slyly comic women. She is the mother of actress Jennifer Ehle.

turn into. The finest revival in this season of revivals, the comedy about the theatrical Cavendish family opened on December 30 at the Helen Hayes and thrilled audiences for seven months. "Positively adorable" and "vintage comedy" were typical of the accolades that greeted the play, the production, and the finest cast seen all season: Rosemary Harris as the actress Julie; Eva Le Gallienne as her mother, Fanny; Sam Levene as the theatrical producer Wolfe; George Grizzard as the womanizing movie star Tony; Joseph Maher as the ham actor Herbert Dean; Mary Louise Wilson as his ham actress wife, Kitty; Rosetta LeNoire as their housekeeper, Della; and on and on. For the seventy-seven-year-old Le Gallienne, it was a triumphal return to the limelight. Fanny's speech in the second act, in which she tries to

EVA LE GALLIENNE (1899–1991), the London-born actress who was also a pioneer in American repertory and the staging of classic revivals, was the daughter of poet-novelist Richard Le Gallienne and studied acting at the Royal Academy of Dramatic Arts. She made her American debut in 1915 and came to fame as Julie in *Liliom* (1921). As a co-founder of the Civic Repertory Theatre in 1926 and the American Repertory Theatre in 1946, she directed many Ibsen and Chekhov revivals, while giving renowned performances in *Peter Pan* (1928), *Alison's House* (1930), *Uncle Harry* (1942), and many other productions. Le Gallienne was a small, thin woman with sharp-edged features who approached her roles intellectually rather than emotionally.

ELLIS RABB (1930–1998), an actor, director, and producer who spent his life working to establish true repertory in America, was born in Memphis, Tennessee, and educated at the University of Arizona and Carnegie Institute of Technology. In the 1950s, he directed and produced at the Antioch Arena Theatre in Ohio and the American Shakespeare Festival in Connecticut. In 1960, he founded the Association of Producing Artists (APA), which in 1964 joined with the Phoenix Theatre and presented some of the most beloved revivals of the era, often featuring his then-wife Rosemary Harris. When the APA dissolved in 1970, he became a freelance director. His most accomplished productions were usually revivals, such as *The Royal Family*, which earned him a Best Director Tony.

describe what goes through her mind each evening as she prepares to go onstage, was met with a hushed silence and then applause from the audience. The revival also gave the tireless Levene a long-awaited hit, placed Harris at the top of her profession, and demonstrated that Ellis Rabb was still one of the finest directors of American plays.

A one-man show titled **From Sholom Aleichem with Love** (1-7-76, Marymount Manhattan) ran four weeks off Broadway. Elliot Levine adapted the Jewish writer's works and performed the material.

Ronald Ribman, a playwright who had come close to writing a success several times in the past, came close again with his prison drama **The Poison Tree** (1-8-76, Ambassador) but once more missed the mark. In a western prison, a deranged inmate strangles a guard and is in turn killed by the other guards. One of them is so vengeful he forces an aging homosexual stoolie prisoner to plant a knife in the cot of a young black convict who is about to be released on parole. Unable to prove his innocence, the youth hangs himself. Critics felt the drama wavered between old-fashioned melodrama and a sociological morality play. But there was no question about the fine performances by Moses Gunn, Cleavon Little, Northern J. Calloway, Dick Anthony Williams, and others. The drama folded after five performances.

At the Public, John Guare tried to follow his *The House of Blue Leaves* (2-10-71) with another hit but had a rough time with **Rich & Famous** (1-13-76, Newman), which postponed its opening three times while he and director Mel Shapiro tried to pull the unwieldy fantasy into shape. Bing Ring-ling (William Atherton), "the world's oldest living promising young playwright," is finally about to have one of his plays (his 844th effort) produced off-off Broadway. Unfortunately his lady producer has had nothing but hits and feels she ought to produce a flop in order to provide for a big comeback. Bing's old friend Tybalt Dunleavy, now a Hollywood star, is to play the leading role, but his identity crisis makes him a neurotic mess as opening night approaches. Bing himself is caught in his own nightmare in which his overbearing, anal-retentive parents and depressed old girlfriend appear and haunt him, showing him the high cost of being rich and famous. The farce climaxes with Bing's decision to end it all. He climbs a Times Square marquee (which happens to be advertising Tybalt's new film) only to find the distraught Tybalt on top with his own suicide plans. Telling Bing that he has already sold the TV and film rights to his life for a tidy amount, Tybalt jumps, and the downcast Bing leaves New York and returns to the home of his parents. Anita Gillette and Ron Leibman played all the characters Bing encountered, and their quicksilver portrayals were the highlight of the show. Reviews were mixed on Guare's script, yet it ran ten weeks.

Several aisle-sitters could not help but call Phillip Hayes Dean's **Every Night When the Sun Goes Down** (1-16-76, American Place) a black version of *The Iceman Cometh* (10-9-46). In the barroom of a seedy Michigan hotel in a black neighborhood gather a group of escapists and dropouts from society: the pimp (Roscoe Orman), whose girl (Marge Eliot) earns him enough to keep him on drugs; the black cop (Norman Matlock) who has learned to turn a blind eye whenever possible; the would-be dancer (Markie Bey), whose husband once owned the hotel but is now in jail; the cynical but ambitious Clean Sam (Richard Ward), who has taken over the hotel; the tattered old Cockeyed Rose (Billie Allen), who still insists she's a lady and expects to be treated like one; and so on. Into this group comes the long-absent racketeer Blood (Frank Adu), just returned from prison, who stirs up the lowlifes by prompting them to make society know that they count. Blood gives them bottles of kerosene, and they set fire to the old hotel. Reviewers pronounced the drama aimless and tedious at times, riveting and affecting at other times.

The small but ambitious Circle Repertory Company found themselves with a big hit on their hands: Jules Feiffer's surrealistic comedy **Knock Knock** (1-18-76, Circle). In a seedy cabin in the woods, two bickering recluses, both aging

Jews, live together and argue over philosophy and food. Abe (Neil Flanagan), a former stockbroker and would-be writer (every once in a while he hits one key on the dusty typewriter), is a realist but believes anything is possible. Cohn (Daniel Seltzer), an ex-musician who does all the cooking, is more rigid and, in a fit of anger, wishes Abe was gone. A flash and puff of smoke make Abe disappear, and he is replaced by Wiseman (Judd Hirsch), the play's cockeyed jack of all trades who returns throughout the evening in various disguises. Soon a knock at the door brings Joan of Arc (Nancy Snyder) and all of her Voices. She converts Cohn when she is able to bring Abe back and tells them she has a mission: to bring two of every species, including Abe and Cohn, to heaven in a spaceship. Cohn is willing, but Abe refuses, so Joan stays and sets up housekeeping, even though she is not very good at it. A few months later the clumsy Joan accidentally cuts her finger in the kitchen. She faints and dies, getting to heaven without the spaceship, and Abe and Cohn are left arguing with her spiritual Voices. While several critics applauded the play, it was the expert production, directed with wacky precision by Marshall W. Mason, that they found so satisfying. After forty-one performances, the Circle Rep moved it on February 24 to Broadway, where it played at the Biltmore until June. Then a curious thing happened: the producers closed the show, recast it, brought in a new director, and reopened it. The revised production received negative reviews and soon closed at a loss of $250,000.

The author for **Jinxs Bridge** (1-21-76, Public: Newman) was listed as Michael Moran, but, as was usually the case with productions by André Gregory's Manhattan Project, the cast helped conceive, write, and direct, the work. In an empty office building located under an old bridge across the Harlem River, a painter, an actor, and a writer live in sweet Bohemian peace. But the city wants to tear down the bridge and sell it for scrap to a rich Arab in exchange for fuel. When the city employee Maria comes to inform the three free spirits that they will be displaced, she is charmed by the men and is soon rallying them to fight City Hall. Together they campaign to have the bridge declared a historic landmark and win the day.

Lincoln Center's downstairs theatre, which Papp had said would present children's plays, instead offered two very adult works. The first was Michael Dorn Moody's dark melodrama **The Shortchanged Review** (1-22-76, Mitzi E. New-

house). Nicky Shannigan (Mason Adams), a middle-aged radio disc jockey, has long held on to his liberal ideals: he refuses to accept advertising even though his listener-sponsored station is in a financial crisis, and he prefers to promote new talent instead of playing the Top Forty. But Nicky's friends and family are bringing him down. He has used his son Darrell's inheritance (from his first wife) to bail out a young rock singer (William Russ) arrested on a drug charge. When the wounded and unbalanced Darrell (T. Miratti) returns from Vietnam, he is bitter toward his father and his stepmother (Virginia Vestoff), as is Nicky's rebellious stepdaughter (Tricia Boyer). Family tensions are combined with legal ones when Nicky refuses to give up a subpoenaed tape made by a young protégé (Herbert Braha). Darrell explodes and commits murder and rape, and Nicky is abandoned by family and friends.

Two short works by major American playwrights were revived by the Phoenix Theatre on January 26 at the Playhouse: Tennessee Williams's *27 Wagons Full of Cotton* (4-19-55) and Arthur Miller's *A Memory of Two Mondays* (9-29-55). Arvin Brown directed the double bill, and there were some splendid performances, particularly John Lithgow as the self-destructive poet in the Miller piece and Meryl Streep as the sluttish Flora in the Williams one-act. Critical response was mildly approving. The next night the Phoenix added Sidney Howard's *They Knew What They Wanted* (11-24-24) to its repertory, and the critics were pretty much in agreement that the melodramatic comedy was hopelessly dated. Stephen Porter directed, and again the cast was estimable: Louis Zorich (Tony), Lois Nettleton (Amy), and Barry Bostwick (Joe).

Katharine Hepburn returned to Broadway this season and proved that a popular star could overcome the risky economics of theatre: her ten-week engagement managed to turn a profit of $350,000. Her vehicle, Enid Bagnold's **A Matter of Gravity** (2-3-76, Broadhurst), was less of a success story. The wealthy and slightly eccentric old Mrs. Basil (Hepburn) lives on an English country estate surrounded by kooky and sexually convoluted people such as Dubois (Charlotte Jones), her lesbian cook from the asylum who drinks too much and defies gravity with her power to levitate. Mrs. Basil's grandson Nicky (Christopher Reeve) comes down from Oxford for a visit and brings a selection of oddball friends: a left-wing lesbian, Shatov (Elizabeth Lawrence); her Jamaican girlfriend, Elizabeth (Wanda Bimson); Herbert (Paul Harding), a homosexual don; and his suicidal lover, Tom (Daniel Tamm). Nicky is in love with Elizabeth, and when he proposes marriage she accepts because she wants to inherit the estate. Mrs. Basil eventually gets rid of her guests and banishes the new couple to Jamaica. Eight years later Nicky and Elizabeth return to the house and Mrs. Basil, weary of them all and their crazy problems, agrees to join her cook in the local asylum. All the reviewers found the comedy lacking, but even those who proclaimed that Hepburn was playing Hepburn extolled her performance. Howard Kissell wrote in *Women's Wear Daily* that her presence onstage was "commanding, arch when necessary, always vital, and, in the play's few genuinely magical moments, radiant."

A Kennedy Center–Xerox revival tour that didn't get as far as Broadway but played eleven performances at BAM in Brooklyn was O'Neill's *Long Day's Journey Into Night* (11-7-56) on February 8. Jason Robards, who had played Jamie in the original production, directed the revival and this time essayed the father, James Tyrone. It was his directorial debut, and all the reviews commented on how sluggish and colorless the production was. Even his Tyrone was lacking the energy and fire that the demanding role required. But there was high enthusiasm for Zoe Caldwell's Mary Tyrone, played not as a fragile pathetic creature but a woman alert and still fighting. Kevin Conway (Jamie) and Michael Moriarty (Edmund) were also saluted.

Martin Sherman's **Cracks** (2-10-76, Theatre de Lys), one of the few off-Broadway commercial entries this season, was an attempt to turn a stranded group of discontented 1960s leftovers into the pawns in an Agatha Christie–like murder mystery, a sort of *Kennedy's Children* meets *Ten Little Indians*. When a rock star is murdered, all his friends and hangers-on become suspects. The play closed on opening night.

Another commercial effort, Israel Horovitz's **The Primary English Class** (2-16-76, Circle in the Square Downtown), fared somewhat better, running 120 performances but still ending up in the red. Debbie Wastba (Diane Keaton), an ambitious English-language teacher, has a night class comprised of new citizens, none of whom speak English or understand any of the others' languages. The class includes the excitable Italian Patumiera (Robert Libertini), the over-eager Frenchman LaPoubelle (Jean-Pierre Stewart), the nearsighted German Mulleimer (Sol Frieder), the elderly Chinese Mrs. Pong (Lori Tan Chinn), and the young Japanese Yoko Kuzukago (Atsumi Sakato), all speaking at once and creating an academic Tower

of Babel. The voice of a translator tells the audience what the students are saying, but Debbie has no idea what is being said. With such frustration, combined with her fear that a mugger is lurking outside their classroom door, Debbie loses her temper and scares all the students away. It was a one-joke play with nowhere to go, but Horovitz knew how to write farcical characters, and Keaton was quite expert as the teacher.

The press was in agreement about Papp's handsome revival of Shaw's *Mrs. Warren's Profession* on February 18 in the Vivian Beaumont. Lynn Redgrave was deemed a vibrant and inspiring Vivie Warren, but Ruth Gordon was hopelessly miscast and lost as the worldly Mrs. Warren. The cast also featured Milo O'Shea (Rev. Gardner), Philip Bosco (Crofts), Ron Randell (Praed), and Edward Herrmann (Frank Gardner), who won a Tony Award.

On February 23, the Polish Mime Theatre arrived at the Beacon for five performances of Wedekind's fairy-tale drama *Die Kaiserin von Neu Funland*, which was translated as *The Menagerie of the Empress*. The next night, another American play from way back, Edward Sheldon's Ibsen-like "problem play" *The Boss* (1-30-11), was revived at BAM for three weeks. The drama, about a self-made business tycoon who blackmails a society woman into marrying him, was directed by Edward Gilbert without a hint of camp, and except for its length, critics felt the melodrama held up well. Andrew Jarkowsky played the "boss," and Louise Shaffer was his determined wife.

The Negro Ensemble Company had a hit with its first production of the season: Steve Carter's **Eden** (3-3-76, St. Marks), a domestic drama with more than a passing nod to *Romeo and Juliet*. Two opposing families reside in the same apartment house in 1927 Manhattan. The youth Eustace (Samm-Art Williams) lives with his Aunt Lizzie (Barbara Montgomery), while across the hall is a West Indies family led by the proud Joseph Barton (Graham Brown), who believes in black nationalism and the eventual return of his race to Africa. When Eustace falls in love with Barton's daughter Annetta (Shirley Brown), her mother, Florie (Ethel Ayer), is in favor of the match, but Joseph rails against it. In fact, he has a stroke after a confrontational scene with Annetta in which she tells Joseph that she is pregnant. At the wedding, Annetta meets some of Eustace's layabout pool-hall buddies and has her doubts, so after the reception she rushes home to her wheelchair-ridden father and promises to raise her son in his beliefs. While the script was uneven and hackneyed in spots, it was a superior production, and audiences applauded it. Word of mouth encouraged the Ensemble to move the melodrama to the Theatre de Lys after its scheduled run, and it ended up tallying 181 performances.

A. R. Gurney, Jr., kept writing and getting produced, but he had not yet written the play to set his career flying. Certainly his **Who Killed Richard Cory?** (3-10-76, Circle) was not going to do it. Inspired by Edward Arlington Robinson's famous poem, the play is a series of vignettes showing the hero's growing dissatisfaction with life and his eventual suicide. Richard (Bruce Gray) is born of good family, and all his life he seeks to keep the Cory name high on a pedestal. He is a successful lawyer and idealized father and husband who is well respected in the community but dismayed at how progress has changed his town and how easily his friends and colleagues have lowered their standards and ideals. He takes a mistress to find the fulfillment he does not get at home or at his job and also initiates good works in the community to give his life meaning. But all his efforts turn hollow, and, weary of upholding his "good name," Richard (in the words of Robinson's poem) "one calm night went home and put a bullet through his head." The drama ran four weeks but received little attention.

Acclaimed author Elie Wiesel tried his hand at playwriting with **Zalem or The Madness of God** (3-17-76, Lyceum). The Rabbi (Joseph Wiseman) of a synagogue in an isolated Russian village in the late 1950s is incited by the words of his buffoonish, idealist sexton, Zalem (Richard Bauer). At the service on the eve of Yom Kippur, the Rabbi rails at his congregation, urging them to stand up for their beliefs and to go out into the world and demand justice. The Synagogue Council is baffled by the outburst, and soon the State Inspector (Lee Wallace) is called in to find out who is responsible for such an offense against the Establishment. In the hearing that follows, disagreement among the congregation members convinces the Inspector that the Jews will remain silent about the outburst, and he dismisses the charges, proclaiming "the event did not take place." The play ends with the Rabbi's twelve-year-old grandson gazing at his defeated grandfather and suggesting that he will not be silent. The drama received mixed notices; some commentators found it "tedious" and "torturously heavy," while others saw a "moving play to be seen and even pondered upon." It only lasted twenty-two performances.

A second Redgrave came to Broadway in the Circle in the Square's revival of Ibsen's rarely-produced *The Lady from the Sea* on March 18. Vanessa Redgrave made her New York debut as the mysterious Ellida and was met with complimentary reviews, even if the strong-featured actress was more "radiant" than mysterious. Aisle-sitters uniformly disliked the script and the production (directed by Tony Richardson) and felt Pat Hingle was wasted as Ellida's older husband, Dr. Wangel. But Redgrave's popularity kept the small house filled for its two-month run.

Nostalgia for the recent past helped Jack Heifner's **Vanities** (3-22-76, Westside) overcome disparaging reviews and become one of the longest-running off-Broadway plays on record. The bittersweet comedy followed three Texas cheerleaders from their senior year of high school into their disillusioned thirties. In 1963, Joanne (Kathy Bates), Kathy (Jane Galloway), and Mary (Susan Merson), the most popular girls in school, prepare cheers for the prep rally, dish about the other students, and talk excitedly about their boyfriends and all three going to college together. In 1969, the college seniors are all members of the same sorority but have started drifting apart as their love affairs overlap or die out. In Kathy's Manhattan apartment six years later, the three reunite but the old camaraderie is gone. Joanne has wed her long-time boyfriend, and they live in the suburbs with their children, but she has taken to drink. Mary runs a gallery of erotic art and, it turns out, has been sleeping with Joanne's husband. Most lost of all is Kathy, who broods on how her life has no direction, admitting to the others that the apartment belongs to a man she is living with but hardly knows. Critics considered the "lemon meringue of a play" nothing but "lightweight and obvious" and "not much more than aimless prattle," but audiences felt differently, and *Vanities* ran 1,785 performances.

The only thing to recommend in the Shaliko Company revival of Georg Büchner's *Woyzeck* on March 24 at the Public was a powerful performance by Joseph Chaikin as the murderous title character.

There were two piercing performances to recommend in Tom Cole's drama **Medal of Honor Rag** (3-28-76, Theatre de Lys). In an office of the Valley Forge Army Hospital, the black Vietnam hero Dale Jackson (Howard E. Rollins, Jr.), who was awarded the Congressional Medal of Honor, talks with a psychiatrist (David Clennon) and tries to overcome his feelings of guilt. It seems D. J., as he likes to be called, found his heroism in the hate he had for the enemy when they killed his GI buddies. But further probing reveals that the doctor, also a Vietnam vet, is similarly haunted, and D. J. sees no help in sight. So he goes AWOL and is gunned down in a grocery-store robbery attempt. Notices were mixed with Cole acclaimed for "his gift for creating deep, humanly credible fiction" or derided because "his heart is in the right place but his writing isn't." All agreed that Rollins and Clennon were excellent, but the commercial venture closed after forty-one performances.

A more recent American classic than all the O'Neill, Williams, and Miller revivals this season was the return of Edward Albee's *Who's Afraid of Virginia Woolf?* (10-13-62) on April 1 at the Music Box. The author directed the revival, and there were raves all around for the play and the cast: Ben Gazzara as the low-key George, Colleen Dewhurst as the fiery Martha, and Richard Kelton and Maureen Anderman as their unfortunate guests. The drama ran into August. On the other hand, the Roundabout's revival of Chekhov's *The Cherry Orchard* on April 2 was generally slammed.

The most interesting offering in the Negro Ensemble's "Season-Within-a-Season" this year was Reginald Vel Johnson's **The Trap Play** (4-6-76, St. Marks). A college football team gathers after a game to discuss what can be done about their star quarterback, who is failing an English course and may not be allowed to play in an important upcoming game. The ruthless coach and members of the mostly black team plan to frame the English professor as a homosexual, using an innocent white student, and get him fired. The plan doesn't work, and racial tensions on campus escalate.

Three American revivals followed each other during the next week. The American Place presented Robert Lowell's *The Old Glory* (11-1-64) on April 9. The triple bill dramatized Hawthorne's *Endecott and the Red Cross* and *My Kinsman, Major Molineux*, which critics pronounced dull and poorly produced, and Melville's *Benito Cereno*, which found gentle approval. Alan Mixon was quite moving as Cereno, the slave ship's captain who becomes the slave of his charges. The Phoenix offered a second repertory program on April 12 that consisted of William Gillette's Civil War spy drama *Secret Service* (10-5-1896) and, added the next night, Bella and Sam Spewack's Hollywood satire *Boy Meets Girl* (11-27-35). The Gillette melodrama, not seen in New York since 1915, seemed to hold up well despite the complaint from some critics that certain performers tended to camp it up a bit. John Lithgow and Meryl Streep shone in the leading roles. The Spewack comedy received mixed reactions: some critics found it timeless, others extremely dated. Lithgow directed, and most commented on the funny physical bits he worked into the farce.

The British comedy troupe called Monty Python's Flying Circus, widely known from their television shows broadcast in America, invaded Manhattan in a revue called **Monty Python Live!** (4-14-76, City Center), and their fans filled the large house for the three-week engagement. As on the tube, the merry troupe presented sketches that wove together classical literature, absurdism, and low music-hall comedy.

Another cult favorite, though with a much smaller audience, was the Ridiculous Theatrical Company, which moved **Caprice** (4-15-76, Provincetown Playhouse), their satire on the world of fashion, from the Performing Garage to Off Broadway. As was usually the case, Charles Ludlam wrote, directed, and starred, but this time he played a male character, the eccentric designer Claude Caprice, who battles his fashion-house rival Twyfford Adament (Bill Vehr). The farce tallied forty-five showings in the two spaces.

While Richard Kiley and Jane Alexander were hailed as a battling father and daughter, most critics felt that Ruth and Augustus Goetz's *The Heiress* (9-29-47), revived on April 20 at the Broadhurst, was a bland and dated play, and it closed in three weeks. Granted, it was not the most admirable of productions. Reviewers would all be proved wrong about the script in 1995 when the period drama returned to Broadway with a vengeance.

The best American play of the season, according to the New York Drama Critics Circle and many others, was David Rabe's **Streamers** (4-21-76, Lincoln Center: Mitzi E. Newhouse). The drama was the final play of Rabe's Vietnam trilogy, the first two parts being *The Basic Training of Pavlo Hummel* (5-20-71) and *Sticks and Bones* (11-1-71). Clive Barnes in the *New York Times* spoke for most of his colleagues when he remarked, "In some ways this is the best of the trio—although, surprisingly perhaps, it is the most conventional and least adventurous." In an army barracks in 1965, three young soldiers ponder their future as the war escalates in Vietnam, a place they were barely aware of when they enlisted. The midwesterner Billy (Paul Rudd) and the black, streetwise Roger (Terry Alexander) are heterosexual friends, but Richie (Peter Evans), who is struggling with his sexuality, tags along and keeps teasing Billy with "faggot" jokes. Two career sergeants (Kenneth McMillan and Dolph Sweet) appear periodically, drunk and singing a cockeyed parody of "Beautiful Dreamer" about parachute jumpers falling to their death when their ripcords fail them. When the newly arrived pathological black soldier Carlyle (Dorian Harewood) comes looking for a fellow "brother," he disrupts the trio's relationship, taunting the white soldiers but eventually coming on to Richie for sex. Billy tries to stop the two; Carlyle stabs Billy, and when Sergeant Cokes comes in to investigate, Carlyle kills him as well. The MPs take Carlyle and the bodies away, and Richie and Roger are left to mop up the blood and argue if Billy was ever sexually attracted to them. Mike Nichols directed expertly, handling the graphic violence well and sustaining the sexual and racial tension throughout. The drama ran 478 performances, another hit for Rabe and Papp.

The Royal Shakespeare Company returned to BAM on April 22 with a rousing two- and-a-half-week run of *Henry V* with Alan Howard as the fiery king. Terry Hands directed the period piece with a Chorus (Emrys James) dressed in contemporary clothes who moved in and out of the action, commenting and confiding in the audience. The company also offered two performances of their often-revived anthology program *The Hollow Crown* on May 1. Also returning was last season's hilarious spoof *Women Behind Bars* (5-1-75), which opened on April 25 and ran at the Truck and Warehouse for another 311 showings. The cultist transvestite Divine played the prison matron this time.

For the first time in a long while, Julie Harris found a vehicle worthy of her when she got to play poet Emily Dickinson in William Luce's one-character play **The Belle of Amherst** (4-28-76, Longacre). Emily welcomes the audience to her Amherst, Massachusetts, home with baked goods fresh from her oven and introduces the various (unseen) people in her life, including family and friends who influenced her over the years. Emily reads some of her poems, but most of the play is conversational, and director Charles Nelson Reilly kept the piece from turning into a recitation. While some critics vetoed the script, Harris's performance was esteemed by all. Edwin Wilson, writing in the *Wall Street Journal*, stated, "With her technical ability and her emotional range, Miss Harris can convey profound inner

turmoil at the same time that she displays an irrepressible gaiety of spirit." It was Luce's first play, and he would, over the years, pen a handful of other one-person dramas based on famous people, none as beloved as *The Belle of Amherst*, which ran 116 performances.

Critical reaction for Lanford Wilson's **Serenading Louie** (5-2-76, Circle) was generally disdainful (although Otis L. Guernsey, Jr., did select it as one of the *Best Plays*) and it did not move on after its thirty-three performances off-off Broadway. Two suburban Chicago couples have reached a crisis point in their lives and have "lost their way" (as in "The Whiffenpoof Song"). The former college football star Carl (Edward J. Moore) bemoans the lack of true "events" in his life and knows that his wife, Mary (Tanya Berezin), is having an affair with his firm's accountant. Gabby (Trish Hawkins) tries to use sex to keep her husband, Alex (Michael Storm), close to her, but he is platonically obsessed with a teenage girl who has the life-affirming energy he so misses. Three of them were friends in college, and the couples gather occasionally for reminiscing and telling each other (and sometimes directly the audience) about their dashed hopes. Eventually Gabby confronts Alex about his teenager and Carl tells Mary he knows about her love affair. They seem to reach an understanding, but in the play's final moments Carl takes a rifle and murders Mary and their sleeping daughter. Like *Kennedy's Children*, it was another in a developing line of plays and films about disillusioned "baby boomers." The genre would eventually become known as *The Big Chill*, named after the popular 1983 film.

Neil Harris's **So Nice, They Named It Twice** (5-5-76, Public: Other Stage) was about New York City (as indicated in the sloganized title), Harlem in particular, and how it destroys its residents. A respectable black couple (he's a prosperous businessman, she's a college-educated worker for the NAACP) find that their nineteen-year-old daughter has hooked up with a local drug pusher, and soon the whole family is involved with a gang of addicts and sellers. The next night, also at the Public, Thomas Babe's drama **Rebel Women** (5-6-76, Newman) opened to mixed reviews. During the last days of the Civil War, Mrs. Law (Leora Dana) and a group of women wait in her Georgia plantation as Sherman's "march to the sea" approaches. They expect the Union soldiers to loot and burn their home, but when Sherman (David Dukes) himself arrives and uses the house as his temporary quarters, they find him a gruff but complex man. Mary Robarts (Kathryn Walker), the pregnant wife of a minister who has been captured by the Union and accused of spying, tells Sherman what she thinks of him to his face. But soon an understanding develops between them, and Mary ends up sleeping with the general (and not just to save her husband). A subplot dealt with the young belle Kate (Deborah Offner), who falls in love with the mercenary Yankee provisions officer, Dr. Sutler (John Glover), and after spending the night with him vows to join him up north when the war is over.

Le Tréteau de Paris returned to Broadway for eleven showings with a new work performed in French. Although it had been a hit in Paris, New Yorkers (those who understood French, that is) thought Marguerite Duras's **Des Journées entieres dans les abres** (*Days in the Trees*) (5-6-76, Ambassador) a muddled family drama. But they extolled the performance by the acclaimed European actress Madeleine Renaud, whose husband, Jean-Louis Barrault, directed. A wealthy Mother (Renaud) comes to Paris after an absence of five years to see her son Jacques (Jean-Pierre Aumont), a host at a nightclub who lives in a cheap apartment with his lover, Marcelle (Francoise Dorner). The Mother is dying and wants to see him once again, admitting that he was always her favorite child even though she has always been a success and he has always been a failure. Jacques has no love for her, and Mother leaves, announcing that she will take her pride in him with her to the grave.

A new American playwright, Christopher Durang, would always struggle with coming up with a fully satisfactory full-length comedy but could always be counted on for laughs. His **Titanic** (5-10-76, Van Dam) was a farce dealing with the sexual confusions and frustrations of an American family aboard the fated ocean liner. The mother tells the father that their son is not really his (to which the father tells the mother that the daughter is not really hers) while an aunt tries to seduce her nephew and her own sister. Meanwhile, both father and son are after a handsome young sailor on board. During all this, the *Titanic* is desperately searching for an iceberg so that all the wacky ensemble can be silenced by drowning. Oliver, always one to spot an interesting new writer, called Durang "a spirited, original fellow . . . who brings back to the theatre a welcome impudence and irreverence." The one-act was performed with a musical nightclub spoof called *Das Lusitania Songspiel*. The double bill only ran a week, but the young Durang was here to stay.

A much older and established playwright, Samuel Taylor, came a cropper with **Legend** (5-13-76, Ethel Barrymore), another dreamlike approach to the American Old West. The overly romantic Betsey-No-Name (Elizabeth Ashley) arrives in a dusty mining town looking for legendary heroes and is soon captivated by three men in the all-male burg: the outlaw Virgil Biggers (Stephen Clarke), the banker F. P. Morgan (George Dzundza), and the sheriff/doctor Jesse Lymburner (F. Murray Abraham). With the outlaw she participates in a bank robbery, with the banker she considers running off to Chicago, and, when taken into custody by the sheriff, she experiences unaccustomed domesticity. The outlaw is eventually shot but does not die, because "nobody ever dies in a legend." The critics all castigated the play, Gottfried leading the assault with "it is not merely bad or pretty bad. It is very very bad and with all the gunfire it involves someone might have put it out of its pain." *Legend* was put out of pain after five performances.

Perhaps the season's most unlikely hit was African-American poet Ntozake Shange's **for colored girls who have considered suicide/when the rainbow is enuf** (5-17-76, Public: Anspacher). The "choreopoem" consisted of seven actresses delivering poems and monologues about being a black woman in America today, mostly about how they are treated by black men. Although each piece was a solo, the cast stayed onstage and listened to, commented on, and even danced to each other's words. Two of the most memorable sequences: a woman (Paula Moss) whose boyfriend steals all her possessions realizes no one can rob her of her spirit and soul and tells him she wants her stuff back because "I'm the only person who can handle it"; and the desperate Crystal (Trazana Beverley) pleads with her deranged boyfriend who is holding her two children over a high ledge and threatens to throw them off if she won't marry him. The critics praised the unusual program for its surprisingly hopeful and triumphant spirit, and it ran 120 performances before Papp moved it in the fall to Broadway, where it ran nearly two years.

Milton Stitt's **The Runner Stumbles** (5-18-76, Little) took a long time to get to Broadway, having been done as a workshop, then at the Manhattan Theatre Club, and later rewritten and staged at Stamford's Hartman Theatre. The melodrama, based on an actual case in 1911 in which a Catholic priest was tried for the murder of a nun, alternates between the courtroom and past events as they are related at the trial. Father Rivard (Stephen Joyce), a radical priest sent to a rural Michigan parish by the bishop as punishment for his newfangled ideas, meets the lively and free-spirited Sister Rita (Nancy Donohue). When sickness at the convent forces the nun to move into the rectory, under the suspicious eye of the housekeeper Mrs. Shandig (Sloan Shelton), Rivard and Rita fall in love. He tries to resist her (he even writes to the bishop to have Sister Rita transferred to another parish school), but they cannot deny their love and plan to tell the world. The next day the nun's body is found in a ditch. Rivard is charged by the police, and only at the last minute does the fervent and overrighteous Mrs. Shandig admit she murdered Sister Rita and spared the community a disgrace worse than death. Critical response was mixed, some seeing a "substantial, impressive and challenging work" and others called "a whodunit that exhausts a listener's interest in the outcome long before it arrives." The drama ran five months and was later popular in college and regional theatre.

The season concluded in Brooklyn when Joseph Szajna's Studio Theatre from Poland presented two pantomime dramas: **Dante** (5-25-76, BAM), based on the poet's *The Divine Comedy*, and **Replika** (6-1-76, BAM), a fantasy about the Holocaust. Szajna wrote and directed both plays, which ran a week each.

1976–1977

Although the Bicentennial celebration continued across the country, climaxing on July 4, there were far fewer revivals of American classics in New York as new plays and new playwrights dominated the theatre scene this season. Broadway saw seventeen new American plays (nearly double the number from the previous season), and Off Broadway, still emphasizing revivals (thirty-four this season) over new works, offered twenty-two, most of them full-length entries. New American playwrights included Preston Jones, Michael Cristofer, Albert Innaurato, and David Mamet, but, alas, only the last would have a substantial career in future seasons.

Box-office figures continued to rise, almost a 32 percent increase over the last season's record-breaking total. Musicals and musical revivals accounted for much of the money, as well as a rise in ticket prices (the top for non-musicals edging over the $15 mark), but again the number of patrons was encouraging, especially when so many entries this season, both on and off the Street,

were dramas about such serious issues as suicide, infertility, alienation, and death. All in all, a good season for the adventurous playgoer and enough to keep the "tired businessman" happy.

The season began off Broadway with that too rarely seen genre: a comedy by and about African Americans. Judi Ann Mason called her **Livin' Fat** (6-1-76, St. Marks) a "soul farce," and it was one of the Negro Ensemble Company's most delightful entries, running eight weeks. A poor black family in the South has always struggled to get by and be respectable. Daddy (Wayne Elbert) holds two jobs, Mama (Frances Foster) is a revivalist, and together they managed to send their son David Lee (Dean Irby) to college. But after graduation the only job David Lee can get is as a janitor in a bank, which is held up one day by two white men wearing Batman masks. In their getaway the robbers drop a bag of money containing $50,000, which David Lee picks up and uses to make a new start for himself and his family. When the family later learns where he got the money, the parents insist he return it to the bank. It takes the foxy grandmother (Minnie Gentry), who observes that the Lord works in mysterious ways, to convince everyone to keep the cash.

Neil Simon returned to Broadway with a throwback to his earlier days (i.e., less serious works) with **California Suite** (6-10-76, Eugene O'Neill), obviously patterned after his popular *Plaza Suite* (2-14-68). While any review comparing the two comedies had to admit that the new entry was less accomplished, most critics were pleased with the lightweight evening of four playlets, each set in the Beverly Hills Hotel. In *Visitor from New York,* an ambitious career woman, Hannah Warren (Tammy Grimes), is anxious to get back to Manhattan but must first confront her laid-back ex-husband, William (George Grizzard), a confirmed California health nut, about getting her teenage daughter Jenny back. Once she realizes that Jenny is happier with her father, she relents. Marvin Michaels (Jack Weston), the *Visitor from Philadelphia,* has just spent a night with a high-class hooker who, because she drank a whole bottle of vodka, is out cold on the bed when Marvin's wife (Barbara Barrie) arrives. After plenty of accusations ("Millie, I deny nothing." "Interesting, because I accuse you of EVERYTHING!") the couple make up and agree to forget the incident ever happened. The finest playlet concerned two *Visitors from London,* a famous British actress, Diana Nichols (Grimes), and her bisexual antique dealer husband, Sidney

(Grizzard), both in town for the Academy Awards ceremony. When Diana doesn't win the Oscar, she takes her frustration out on Sidney and throws his sometime homosexuality in his face. But the couple admit they still love one another because "we are each a refuge for our disappointments out there." The last playlet was a farce about two couples, *Visitors from Chicago,* vacationing together and getting on each other's nerves, particularly after a mishap on the tennis court that leaves some of the characters limping. By the final curtain the four are doubled over in pain, pratfalls, and insults. The comedy entertained audiences for thirteen months, Simon's first hit since *The Sunshine Boys* (12-20-72).

An evening of four comic playlets could also be found the next night off Broadway when the Roundabout Theatre closed its 1975–1976 season with an eight-week summer revival of Arnold Perl's *The World of Sholom Aleichem* (5-1-53) on June 11. Mark Blum, Carol Teitel, Dick Shawn, and Rita Karin were among the players to enact the folk tales suggested by works by Aleichem, the "Jewish Mark Twain."

Allen Swift's **Checking Out** (9-14-76, Longacre) was also a Jewish comedy but, in the opinion of most critics, a very poor one. The lively octogenarian Morris Applebaum (Swift), former star of the Yiddish stage and lifelong dandy with the ladies, observes: "Why is it that a man can live a happy life and ruin it all by dying?" Determined to go out with a bang, he calls together his three children—the haywire California shrink Theodore (Mason Adams), the overemotional accountant Bernard (Hy Anzell), and the often-married divorcée Florence (Joan Copeland)—for a true "going away" party. Also joining the odd celebration are Gilbert (Tazwell Thompson), a black male nurse who wishes he were Jewish; Schmuel (Michael Gorrin), a feeble old family friend; and hippie psychiatrist Sheldon Henning (Larry Bryggman). The two shrinks argue with Morris (and each other) about his proposed suicide, Florence pegs the hippie as husband number four, and many jokes about death and psychiatrists unfold before all ends happily. The comedy lasted two weeks.

Off Broadway saw one of its shortest and longest runs open that same week. Sandra Jennings's **Beware the Jubjub Bird** (6-14-76, Theatre Four), a drama about the neuroses of four actors in rehearsal for Chekhov's *The Sea Gull,* lasted two performances. Like many entries this season, it was "a play with songs." On the 16th at the Cherry Lane, David Mamet's double bill from Off

Off Broadway last season, *Sexual Perversity in Chicago* and *Duck Variations,* was recast and restaged and became the most talked-about hit of the off-Broadway season, running ten months. Peter Riegert and F. Murray Abraham were the immature males, and Jane Anderson and Gina Rogers were their brief amours, while Mike Kellin and Michael Egan played the two old men discussing ducks and life.

George M. Cohan's melodrama spoof *The Tavern* (9-27-20) was revived by the Actors' Alliance on June 24 as the first of three summer revivals at the Provincetown Playhouse. The subsequent offerings were Don Appell's little-remembered *Lullaby* (2-3-54), a domestic comedy about newlyweds with mother-in-law problems, on July 14 and Noel Coward's screwball farce *Hay Fever* (10-5-25) on the 30th.

Producer Joseph Papp directed the summer's first Shakespeare in Central Park, *Henry V* on June 24, with Paul Rudd playing the heroic king. Most critics said he lacked the humanity and maturity the role required, but they praised the brisk and clear production. The second offering at the Delacorte was *Measure for Measure* on July 29, and it was thought less satisfactory, described as "rather disorganized and most perplexing" or "wretched." Even popular favorites Sam Waterston (Duke Vincentio), Meryl Streep (Isabella), John Cazale (Angelo), and Lenny Baker (Lucio) were deemed disappointing.

The Roundabout opened its new season with a revival of Shaw's early effort *The Philanderer* (12-30-13) on September 8. While Donald Madden was quite expert as the roving Leonard Charteris, the production was called more farce than high comedy. On September 15 Ntozake Shange's "choreopoem" *for colored girls who have considered suicide/when the rainbow is enuf* transferred from the Public to the Booth, where it stayed on Broadway, next door to Papp's other transfer, *A Chorus Line,* for 742 performances.

The season's second "play with songs" was Josh Greenfeld's **I Have a Dream** (9-20-76, Ambassador), an evening about Martin Luther King, Jr., that included speeches, gospel numbers, and autobiographical writings, described by critics as more a "theatrical tribute" than a play. Billy Dee Williams was commended for his solid portrayal of Dr. King, and the program was repeated eighty times.

In many ways the major disappointment of the Broadway season was Preston Jones's ambitious **A Texas Trilogy** (9-21-76, Broadhurst). Not that the plays themselves were so disappointing (many reviews were quite laudatory), but the hype from Dallas, where they originated, and from Washington's Kennedy Center, where they were a big hit, forced New Yorkers to expect a masterpiece from the forty-year-old Jones in his first playwriting effort. No doubt there was a bit of snobbery in the cool Broadway reception the trilogy received, and the mixed reviews could not sustain such an expensive undertaking. The three full-length plays, each standing on its own with some overlapping of characters and events, took place in the same Texas town. **Lu Ann Hampton Laverty Oberlander** chronicles twenty years in the life of the title heroine (Diane Ladd) as she adds to her name with each marriage. We first see her as an ambitious high school cheerleader looking forward to leaving the "little old dried-up West Texas town" of Bradleyville. After marrying the dull Korean War vet Dale Laverty (Everett McGill), she meets the lively Corky Oberlander (Baxter Harris) who works for the Highway Department, and they wed. But Corky dies in a road accident, and we later see the middle-aged Lu Ann cheerfully resigned to a quiet life looking after her senile mother (Avril Gentles) and keeping her dissipated brother Skip (Graham Beckel) out of trouble. **The Last Meeting of the Knights of the White Magnolia** takes place in a dusty meeting room in the Cattleman's Hotel where the remnants of a once-flourishing Ku Klux Klan offshoot meet to play dominoes and go through an antiquated ritual that has lost its meaning over the years. This particular meeting is different because, for the first time since anyone can remember, a new member is to be initiated into the group. But the inductee, the nerdy mamma's boy Milo Crawford (Josh Mostel), ends up running away, and the oldest member, the wheelchair-ridden Colonel Kinkaid (Fred Gwynne), suffers a stroke. The group disbands, unlikely ever to meet again. **The Oldest Living Graduate** centers on Colonel Kinkaid, a World War I vet who still suffers from shellshock and is a burden to his social-climbing family. When the colonel's alma mater, a military academy in Galveston, sends representatives to honor the old man because he is the oldest grad on record, the colonel goes into a fit as he recalls the war and the young men blown to bits all around him. This last play received the best notices, but the acting throughout the trilogy and Alan Schneider's masterful direction could not be faulted. The repertory only survived a month, but the individual plays were produced across the country for several years following.

Some New Yorkers had already seen Marguerite Duras's *Days in the Trees* when it was presented in French for eleven performances the previous season. Beginning September 26, the Circle in the Square Uptown offered the drama, in a translation by Sonia Orwell, for two months. Stephen Porter directed a fine cast that included Mildred Dunnock as the affluent Mother and Joseph Maher as her estranged son. Reaction to the script was mixed, but the performances were applauded.

Despite some effective moments here and there, critics could not recommend **Jack Gelber's New Play: Rehearsal** (9-28-76, American Place), an "uneasy comedy" about the theatre. During a rehearsal of a new prison drama, the actors wrangle with the director (Sam Schacht) over their interpretation of the characters while the producer (Grayson Hall) frets over the news that another prison drama will be coming to town soon. As opening night approaches, the director decides to change the climactic rape scene from offstage to onstage. The actors are getting quite caught up in the action when the producer enters and announces that the backers have withdrawn their money and the production is canceled. All the personnel pack up and depart, leaving the dejected playwright (Robert Burgos) alone on the dark stage. Gelber's script was deemed too long and drawn out for what little it had to say.

The Circle Repertory Company continued to find exciting new American scripts (and sending one to Broadway) this season, but they opened with a British play, David Storey's **The Farm** (10-10-76, Circle). On a Yorkshire farm, the hard-drinking, hard-working Slattery (Jack Gwillim) dominates his gentle wife (Ruby Holbrook) and his three beautiful daughters (Debra Mooney, Trish Hawkins, and Nancy Snyder). When his poet son Arthur (Jeff Daniels) returns home and announces he is going to wed a divorced woman (and an actress, no less), the family reaction is volatile with harsh words exchanged. But Arthur stands up to his father (and the old man actually admires him for doing so), and that encourages the youngest daughter (Snyder) to bring her shy beau to the house and pursue her own happiness. While reviews ran the gamut, ranging from "uneventful and inconsequential" to "funny, stormy, tender, and compassionate," most approved of Marshall W. Mason's graceful direction and the admirable ensemble cast.

The Classic Stage Company, usually home to revivals, premiered British playwright Edward Bond's **Bingo** (10-12-76, Abbey), about the last days of William Shakespeare (Tom Donaldson) as he sits in his garden in Stratford and ponders the futility of a life in the theatre when he could have done some social or moral good. After Bond's shocking earlier efforts, such as *Saved* (11-13-70), this work was thought rather tame, even a little dull.

The same night, Emlyn Williams brought his one-man show *Dylan Thomas Growing Up* (10-7-57) back to New York for a two-week engagement at Theatre Four; bolstered by rave reviews, he returned on November 26 for an additional twenty performances. The Roundabout found that their revival of Anouilh's tragicomedy *The Rehearsal* (9-23-63) on October 14 was popular enough to keep it on the boards for twelve weeks.

Louis LaRusso II's *Lamppost Reunion* (10-16-75) last season was declared by the press to be crude and vulgar but somewhat promising. This season they omitted to say La Russo was promising but felt **Wheelbarrow Closers** (10-16-76, Bijou) was equally crass. Chester Grant (Danny Aiello) is a salesman who worked his way to the top of one of America's biggest corporations. Approaching retirement, he invites two top salesmen, the middle-aged loudmouth John Morgan (Ray Serra) and the young, aggressive Larry Freede (Harvey Siegel), to his gaudy and expensive house to award them gold watches. But when they arrive Chester says that he wants one of them to take over the company instead of someone from his executive board. Wilfred Dee (Tom Degidon), an old friend of Chester's also getting ready to retire, joins them. A night of drinking, blue stories, and jockeying for control commences, with Chester's emotionally damaged family taking part. Larry makes a play for Chester's daughter (Norah Foster), Wilfred has a heart attack, everyone blames everyone else, and the play ends with Chester drinking alone in the dark and facing his retirement with fear. The drama closed in a week.

While critics were a bit harsh with *Wheelbarrow Chasers*, they got downright hostile with Michael Sawyer's **Best Friend** (10-19-76, Lyceum); veteran aisle-sitter Brendan Gill of *The New Yorker* led the assault, calling it "among the worst plays I have ever seen." When the seemingly-well adjusted Carolyn Parsky (Barbara Baxley) returns from her vacation, she is anxious to share her experiences with her neighbor and close friend Anita (Mary Dyle). But while she was gone Anita has gotten engaged, and the neurotic Carolyn sets out to destroy the match by telling Anita's fiancé, John (Michael M. Ryan), that she and Anita are lesbian lovers. He runs off, and Anita believes she has

been jilted until John returns and Carolyn's underhanded ways are revealed. The drama lasted one less performance than *Wheelbarrow Closers*.

Heinrich Von Kleist wrote *The Prince of Homburg* in 1811, the same year the thirty-four-year-old playwright committed suicide, yet it had never received a professional New York production until the Chelsea Theatre Center presented James Kirkup's translation on October 19 at BAM. The story concerned a courageous Prussian soldier, Prince Freidrich (Frank Langella), who disobeys orders, leads an attack, and wins a decisive battle against the Swedish army. Despite the victory, he is court-martialed and sentenced to death. The Prince searches his soul and, being a noble hero, agrees that the verdict is a just one and submits, only to have the order rescinded at the last moment. Critics thought the period piece quite stageworthy and Langella a fine romantic hero. Like all the Chelsea's productions this season, it played in Brooklyn briefly, then moved to Theatre Four in Manhattan for a limited engagement.

One of Broadway's most challenging offerings of the season was Czech playwright Pavel Kohout's popular European drama **Poor Murderer** (10-20-76, Barrymore), adapted by Herbert Berghof (who directed) and Laurence Luckinbill (who starred). In the St. Elizabeth Institute for Nervous Disorders, the actor Anton (Luckinbill) is suffering from guilt because, while playing Hamlet onstage, he actually killed the actor who was playing Polonius. In order to determine whether Anton is insane or is using insanity to hide his intentional murder, the head of the asylum (Larry Gates) agrees to let Anton act out his life, from childhood to the accident. The experiment fails and Anton is declared insane, but one of the actresses (Maria Schell) decides to stay and help him recover his senses, throwing off her lover Alexey (Kevin McCarthy), who played Polonius in the mock drama. The play ends with the distraught Alexey telling Anton, "So you really did kill me!" While notices were in agreement about the solid acting, particularly Schell's, they were mixed as to the quality of the script; some described a "strange, dazzling and intellectual play," while others found only a "shallow, pseudo-Pirandellian, boring play." Adventurous playgoers kept the drama open for eighty-seven performances.

The same night Off Off Broadway, A. R. Gurney, Jr., was still struggling to find his own voice, adapting a John Cheever short story, giving it a Chekhov flavor, and calling it **Children** (10-20-76,

Manhattan Theatre Club). A widowed Mother (Nancy Marchand) calls her grown children to her summer cottage on an island off the New England coast to tell them she is remarrying but wants to leave the old house to them. Her spoiled son Randy (Dennis Howard) and his immature wife, Jane (Swoozie Kurtz), want to keep the house in the family but fear that his absent brother, Pokey, and his sister, Barbara (Holland Taylor), a divorcée who is running around with a local contractor building tacky houses on the island, might want to sell it. When Pokey (Gary Smith) arrives, putting his Jewish wife and three wild kids in a nearby motel, tensions mount. Recriminations are voiced, and because Pokey wants his share, the house will be sold. Commentators agreed that this Wasp *Cherry Orchard* was lacking in theatricality but approved of the cast and Melvin Bernhardt's seamless direction.

A Broadway revival of William Archibald's ghostly *The Innocents* (2-1-50), which opened on October 21 at the Morosco, faltered and closed after twelve performances. Commentators were in agreement that the play had dated badly and that Harold Pinter's eerie direction was all atmosphere and no substance. Claire Bloom was an engaging governess, and the two young children were well played by Sarah Jessica Parker and Michael MacKay.

The Phoenix Theatre, always a reliable source of fine revivals, presented a season of new works, none of which caught fire. In Kevin O'Morrison's **Ladyhouse Blues** (10-28-76, Marymount Manhattan), the women in a St. Louis family await the return of the men during the last days of World War I. The mother, Liz (Jo Henderson), a strong-hearted widow who has sold the family farm to pay debts, waits with her four daughters (Christine Estabrook, Cara Duff-MacCormick, Gale Garnett, and Mary-Joan Negro), all on the brink of change as America seems poised to move on to greatness. But the women feel left out of the new era and fall into despair when a telegram arrives informing them that the lone surviving brother has died in battle. Reviews were along the lines of "a bland and aimless evening" and "diffuse and uneventful," yet the drama would find an audience when revived three years later.

With Ralph Richardson and John Gielgud starring in Harold Pinter's London import, reviews mattered little for **No Man's Land** (11-9-76, Longacre). While few critics sought to explain the piece, most spoke of its high entertainment value and the virtuoso playing of its stars. In a comfortable London sitting room, renowned poet Hirst (Richardson) invites failed writer Spooner (Gielgud) in for a nightcap. It is not clear whether the two men are acquainted with each other or not. Two sinister servants (Michael Kitchen and Terence Rigby) come and take Hirst to bed, and Spooner is left in solitude until the next morning, when Hirst reappears and treats Spooner as an old school chum. Spooner plays along until both, shutting out the cold outside world, learn to inhabit the no man's land where they await death. Peter Hall directed, John Bury provided the homey but chilling scenery, and the six-week engagement was very popular.

William Hauptman's **Comanche Cafe** and **Domino Courts** (11-11-76, American Place) was a double bill in which the two one-acts shared a common character. The Comanche Cafe is a seedy diner outside of Oklahoma City where in the mid-1930s two waitresses talk of dashed dreams. The overweight Mattie (Sasha von Scherler) once had a passionate fling that came to nought, while the virginal Ronnie (Jane Galloway) longs for marriage before her chances are gone. Four years later, in a tourist cabin at Domino Courts, two former bank robbers meet with their wives. Floyd (Guy Boyd) has gone straight and married the waitress Ronnie. Roy (Conrad Fowkes), who has joined a mob from the North, arrives with his mousy wife, Flo (Regina Baff), but the happy reunion soon grows sour as Roy's blustering is deflated by Floyd and Ronnie's comments. The American Place, no longer operating on a subscribers-only policy, could only keep the plays on the boards for twenty-eight showings.

On November 12, the National Theatre of Greece, as a gift from the government of Greece for the Bicentennial, arrived at the City Center for a brief repertory of Sophocles' *Oedipus at Colonus* and Aristophanes' *Knights* performed in Greek. Another acclaimed European troupe, the Abbey Theatre of Dublin, celebrated the fiftieth anniversary of O'Casey's *The Plough and the Stars* (11-28-27) with a tour that arrived on November 16 at BAM. While the cast included such Irish luminaries as Cyril Cusack and Siobhan McKenna, and the revival was greeted with some positive notices, many were disappointed in the ragtag scenery, ponderous direction, and brogues so thick that the play sometimes slipped into parody.

Broadway saw two "new" Tennessee Williams plays this season, the first being a revision of *Summer and Smoke* (10-6-48) now called **The Eccentricities of a Nightingale** (11-23-76, Morosco). The tender drama still told the story of the frail Alma

Winemiller (Betsy Palmer), whose repressive family causes her to reach out to the dashing young doctor John Buchanan (David Selby) in order to avoid a life of spinsterhood. The new version concentrated more on Alma's family and acquaintances who are suffocating her: her stern minister father (Shepperd Strudwick), her mentally unbalanced mother (Grace Carney), and the town misfits who gather at the Winemiller home to pursue culture in order to fill the void in their empty lives. Notices varied in their estimation of the new version, some preferring it over the original, others finding both lacking. Howard Kissell in *Women's Wear Daily* probably best summed up the morning-after reaction, noting, "If the new version is less extravagant, less haunting, it is probably more cogent for contemporary audiences." Palmer was extolled for her affecting, Alma but the rest of the cast and production were less successful. The play closed after three weeks.

The same night, Le Tréteau de Paris opened its one week engagement of Corneille's *Rodogune*, performed in French at the American Place.

It took courage—or blind optimism—for producer Alexander Cohen to bring Trevor Griffiths's abrasive London play **Comedians** (11-29-76, Music Box) to Broadway. Six budding comedians who have been taking night classes from an old comic, Eddie Waters (Milo O'Shea), in a school near Manchester gather for some last-minute advice before performing at a workingman's pub, where the talent agent Bert Challenor (Rex Robbins) will give them a tryout. Waters has taught them to look for truth in comedy, but Challenor tells them he's looking for superficial, escapist humor. The comics perform their acts at the pub to half-hearted applause, some quickly adjusting to please Challenor, others sticking to what Waters rehearsed with them. The last to perform is the quirky Gethin Price (Jonathan Pryce), whose strange and hypnotic act consists of savagely insulting the audience and physically and verbally attacking a pair of life-size dummies. Back at the classroom, Challenor critiques each act, offers a contract to two of the men, then leaves Price and Waters alone, the old man admitting that the young comedian's act was repulsive and terrifying but quite brilliant. Because of Pryce's mesmerizing performance (he won the Tony Award), everything Waters said was quite true. Audiences found it hard to like the cold and off-putting play, even though several critics acclaimed it the season's finest. Mike Nichols directed the American-British cast, which also included John Lithgow, Armand Assante, and Jeffrey DeMunn. Although

the "serious comedy" ran 145 performances, it still lost $350,000.

The next night's entry, Dore Schary and Amos Elon's **Herzl** (11-30-76, Palace), lost the same amount even though it only lasted a week. This bio-drama about Theodor Herzl (Paul Hecht), the father of Zionism, chronicled the life of the "modern Moses" from his youth as a playwright in Vienna to his travels as a journalist to Paris, where the Dreyfus case rouses him to fight and raise money to create an Israeli state, to the First Zionist Conference in 1897. While critics admired the man, this episodic view of his life was deemed "dramatically static" and "ponderous theatre" that "plays like a paid political announcement." (More than one review mentioned that it would have made an ideal 1930s bio-pic starring Paul Muni.) The failure marked a sad end to Schary's illustrious career in theatre and film.

Two one-man shows premiered on the same night in two of BAM's many performance spaces. Saul Levitt's **Lincoln** (11-30-76, BAM) featured Fritz Weaver as the sixteenth president, and he was backed up with a multi-media presentation that captured the sights and sounds of the era. Abbey Theatre actor Eamon Kelly put together an evening of Irish stories and fictional characters and titled it **In My Father's Time** (11-30-76, BAM). The Levitt play ran a month; the Eamon show had a one-week engagement.

In a mid-season report, *Variety* noted that all of the Shubert Organization's theatres were occupied or booked and nineteen of the twenty independent Broadway houses were similarly engaged.

The Negro Ensemble Company had a critical and box-office hit with Charles Fuller's **The Brownsville Raid** (12-5-76, Theatre de Lys), which ran 112 performances. In 1906, a company of black soldiers is stationed in the all-white border town of Brownsville, Texas. One night the community is raided by some horsemen who shoot up the town, kill one white resident and wound a policeman, then disappear into the night. Some discarded cartridge shells are used to blame the raid on the black soldiers, and, without a hearing or trial, President Teddy Roosevelt orders a dishonorable discharge for all of them. Only years later is it learned that the soldiers were innocent and the whole raid was probably the work of the locals. Fuller's play concentrated on two of the soldiers: Sergeant Major Mingo Saunders (Douglas Turner Ward), a career man and veteran of two wars who is reduced to working menial jobs in Washington after the discharge, and Private Dorsey Willis (Reyno), who in 1973 is an eighty-seven-year-old shoeshine boy. Both were finally given an honorable discharge from the army. The writing was vivid and truthful, and the production and acting were both cheered.

It was encouraging news on Broadway that an expensive multi-set, period-costume new play could open in December and show a profit by season's end, for that is what Larry Gelbart's comedy **Sly Fox** (12-14-76, Broadhurst) managed to do. The fact that the plot was derived from Jonson's classic comedy *Volpone* and that George C. Scott was starred certainly helped. In late nineteenth-century San Francisco, the miserly Foxwell J. Sly (Scott) has his right-hand man, Simon Able (Hector Elizondo), whom he rescued from debtors' prison and who must pay off Sly for his freedom, send word about town that the old man is dying without an heir. The greedy lawyer Craven (John Hefferman), the ancient skinflint Jethro Crouch (Jack Gilford), and the possessive Abner Truckle (Bob Dishy) all make overtures to win the favor of the dying Sly. Crouch goes so far as disinheriting his son, Captain Crouch (John Ramsey), and leaving his estate to Sly, and Truckle offers his wife (Trish Van Devere) to the old lecher, hoping the sexual strain will kill him. But the Captain stops the seduction just in time, and Sly and Able are pulled into court. A pompous Judge (Scott again) tries the case, but it is the word of all the greedy fortune hunters against the Captain, so Sly is free to go. But before he skips town, Sly has Able send out word that he is dead. When all the vultures gather to hear the will, it reads that Able is the inheritor. It looks like Able will double-cross them all (including Sly), but he takes enough money to pay off his debt, repays the others what they gave in wooing Sly, and goes off happy to be his own man again. Gelbart's funny, vaudeville-like one-liners and a cast overflowing with expert comedians kept the show popular long after Scott left the cast, but in many ways he was the show, "his broken body and wheezing tones all betokening a very cemetery smell" when needed and then, when not observed by his dupes, "a friendly monster, grinning like a vacationing shark." The comedy ran fourteen months.

Many still considered *The Night of the Iguana* (12-28-61) Tennessee Williams's last great play, and the revival (its first in New York) on December 16 at the Circle in the Square Uptown gave them a chance to evaluate that opinion. Television stars Richard Chamberlain (Shannon) and Dorothy McGuire (Hannah) joined Sylvia Miles (Maxine) in a production that garnered modest approval and ran ten weeks. The Roundabout's revival of Ibsen's *John Gabriel Borkman* on December 30 was described as slow and sluggish by some critics, although most complimented the group for producing the too rarely seen drama.

Broadway's lone one-night flop this season was Henry Denker's archaic Jewish family comedy **Something Old, Something New** (1-1-77, Morosco). Widower Samuel Jonas (Hans Conreid) and widow Laura Curtis (Molly Picon), both in their seventies, find comfort in each other's company and decide to go on a honeymoon cruise together—but not to get married, because it would reduce their Social Security benefits. When they gather their children—Sam's daughter, Cynthia (Holland Taylor), and her psychiatrist husband (Matthew Tobin); Laura's hyperactive son, Mike (Dick Patterson), and his sex-starved wife (Lois Markle)—the younger generation is shocked (which surprised the audience more than the aging couple) and encourage marriage. After many jokes about psychiatrists and sex among senior citizens, it is revealed that the widowed pair haven't slept together yet and will get married after all. Unanimous pans pointed out that Conreid and Picon kept some sort of dignity onstage while all the other actors were directed to act like adolescents in a bad cartoon.

John Bishop's **The Trip Back Down** (1-4-77, Longacre) was seen briefly last season off-off Broadway and received enough encouragement that it was brought to Broadway. It was another in a long line of "retrospective dramas" that were appearing all over the place. Professional racecar driver Bobby Horvath (John Cullum) returns from the racing circuit and comes back to his blue-collar hometown of Mansfield, Ohio, to be reunited with family and friends after being away eight years. A series of flashbacks show how Bobby once dreamed of being the best racer in the world, but too many lost races, accidents, drunken brawls, and whores have made him a has-been before his time. He finds no comfort in the depressing town and its inhabitants, so Bobby sets off again to race, knowing he will always lose. While none of the reviews were enthusiastic, they ranged from "a talented new playwright with a voice that rings true" to "a soapy, sentimental bore." But Cullum's performance was proclaimed quite effective, and the play held on for two months.

Tom Stoppard's **Dirty Linen & New-Found-Land** (1-11-77, John Golden) was not a typical double bill, because Stoppard, never one to do things simply, had the playlet *New-Found-Land* take place in the middle of the longer *Dirty Linen*. In a claustrophobic meeting room in London's Parliament building, a select committee gathers to look into exposing illicit behavior among certain members of both Houses. It turns out that the stenographer assigned to the committee, Maddie Gotobed (Cecilia Hart), is the mysterious woman who has slept with several high-ranking officials and is working her way through the committee members as well. While the group adjourns for lunch, two Civil Servants enter. One is an ancient semi-senile man (Humphrey Davis) who recalls the day Lloyd George had an affair with his mother, the other a brash young man (Jacob Brooke) who launches into an extended monologue about America filled with travel-agent platitudes and hitting all the tourist high points from one coast to another. The play ends with the committee reconvening and reaching the conclusion that there is no scandal and that the sensation-seeking press made the whole thing up. As usual, Stoppard's wordplay was the highlight of the comedy (the opening exchange between two members was done entirely in foreign-phrase clichés). *Dirty Linen* was much more accessible than his recent intellectual ventures, so it ran 159 times and made a profit in doing so.

Papp opened his belated season at the Public with John Guare's fantasy-farce **Marco Polo Sings a Solo** (1-12-77, Newman). The play was set not in the past but in the future (A.D. 1999) on an island off the coast of Norway, where the young movie director Stony McBride (Joel Grey) is writing a film about Marco Polo that will star his over-the-hill actor-father, Lusty McBride (Chev Rodgers). Surrounding Stony are a flock of odd characters, including his transsexual mother (Anne Jackson), his concert pianist wife (Madeline Kahn), who is having an affair with a politician (Chris Sarandon) who is selfishly sitting on the cure for cancer, and an astronaut friend, Frank (Larry Bryggman), who has astrally impregnated a maid (Sigourney Weaver). The absurdity climaxes with a destructive earthquake, the discovery of a new planet, and the birth of a new hero (who may be Stony himself). Guare had his supporters, but most reviews were along the lines of "glib and strident comedy" and "extravagantly self-indulgent."

Three foreign works appeared off Broadway during the next week, each demanding much of its audience. Peter Handke's monodrama **A Sorrow Beyond Dreams** (1-13-77, Marymount Manhattan), in a translation from the German by Ralph Manheim and adapted by Daniel Freuden-

berger, was an hour-long soliloquy in which a Writer (Len Cariou), using slides and film footage projected behind him, recounts the history of his mother, who recently committed suicide: her life of poverty in Austria, a love affair that left her pregnant, her marriage to a Nazi soldier who accepted the child as his own, her struggles to raise a family, and her decision to take a hundred sleeping pills at the age of fifty-one when she learned of her terminal illness. Surprisingly, the piece was far from depressing or self-pitying, and all the critics praised its power and theatricality, as well as Cariou's performance. Polish playwright Stanislaw Ignacy Witkiewicz's 1923 "comedy" *The Crazy Locomotive* had not been seen in this country until January 18 when the Chelsea Theatre presented it at BAM. Two criminal lunatics take over a train filled with passengers and hurl along the tracks at 130 mph as they discuss Einstein's theories and the people they have murdered. The locomotive runs headlong into an approaching train on the same track (shown on film footage), then the lights rise to reveal mangled bodies and metal wreckage. The expressionistic play was a metaphor of some sort, but most reviewers thought it too didactic and pretentious to care and dismissed it. The Manhattan Theatre Club mounted a fine revival of Fugard's *Boesman and Lena* (6-22-70) on January 19; with Robert Christian and Frances Foster as the "coloreds," the production gathered commendatory reviews.

Another retrospective evening of theatre was Corinne Jacker's **My Life** (1-23-77, Circle). San Francisco physicist Edward Howe (William Hurt) is suffering from emotional burnout and wants to explore his past scientifically to see how he arrived at his doleful present. In his fantasy, young Eddie (Jeff Daniels) and people from the past, such as his parents and girlfriend, start to intermingle with themselves in the present. But Howe eventually learns that past wrongs cannot be righted and the future has already been firmly set in motion.

No play this season was more difficult to watch or, for many, brought such satisfaction as David Rudkin's **Ashes** (1-25-77, Public: Anspacher). The British drama was about a married couple in their thirties who go through the rigors of trying to have a baby, a metaphor for Northern Ireland's struggle to continue its own bloodline. Irish-born teacher Colin (Brian Murray) and his wife, Anne (Roberta Maxwell), live in England and have been trying to have a child for two years without success, so they submit themselves to a battery of tests and brutal clinical treatments in order for her to conceive. After several different demeaning methods are tried, Anne is pregnant, but later her body rejects the fetus and she must have a hysterectomy. The couple then pursues adoption through the cold bureaucratic channels available to them, only to be rejected by the official agency. Together they face a future with no more hope of being parents, Colin poetically musing, "Laughter of children in our house, not for us." Although it was very graphic in its details and uncomfortably private in its characterizations, the play was beautifully staged by Lynne Meadow and acted by Murray and Maxwell, receiving propitious reviews along the lines of "steely, uncompromising and honest." After playing at the Manhattan Theatre Club, it transferred to the Public, where it ran 167 performances.

The American Place continued its faltering season with Jeff Wanshel's provocatively titled **Isadora Duncan Sleeps With the Russian Navy** (1-25-77, American Place). A down-on-his-luck author (David Ackroyd) agrees to write a film biography of the pioneering dancer, and as he creates scenes for the film in his mind, they are enacted by historical figures such as Isadora herself (Marian Seldes), Stanislavsky (Christopher Curry), Walt Whitman (Anita Dangler), Gordon Craig (Dennis Jay Higgins), and Anna Pavlova (Annette Kurek). The author gets caught up in the tales and is determined to make a film about the "first modern woman," but his crass producer (Robert Lesser) agues for the popular demands of the box office, and they end up with a movie on the level of the play's title.

Simon Gray scored a second Broadway hit in a row with his London import **Otherwise Engaged** (2-2-77, Plymouth), which ran nine months. Whereas Gray's *Butley* (10-31-72) was about a man who interferes with everyone else's lives, the hero in *Otherwise Engaged* seeks to remove himself from all the people around him. Prosperous London publisher Simon Hench (Tom Courtenay) is looking forward to a quiet day, with his wife out of town and his answering machine saying he is "otherwise engaged," so that he can listen to his new recording of Wagner's *Parsifal*. But the day is filled with interruptions and crises dealing with his boorish tenant (John Christopher Jones), a beautiful young woman (Lynn Milgrim) who bares her breasts in order to interest Simon in a book, his brother Stephen (John Horton) in anxiety over a headmaster's job he wants, and an old schoolmate, Wood (Michael Lombard), searching for revenge for Simon's seducing his fiancée. When Simon's wife, Beth (Carolyn Lagerfelt), returns early, she

DAVID MAMET (1947–) was born in Flossmore, Illinois, and educated at Goddard College in Vermont. In 1974 he co-founded the St. Nicholas Theatre Company in Chicago, where his early one-acts, such as *Sexual Perversity in Chicago*, were first produced. He made his New York debut in 1975 off-off Broadway with that play and *Duck Variations*, both of which moved to Off Broadway this season. Mamet's work is characterized by his profane but poetic language and his quirky, on-the-edge characters.

tells him that she is pregnant and the father is either Simon or her lover, Stephen. Wood calls and leaves a message on the phone as he commits suicide, another writer named Jeff (Nicolas Coster) and Simon have words, then settle their disagreement, and the play ends as they sit down to listen to *Parsifal*. The reviews were approving of the play, Harold Pinter's sly direction, and the expert cast.

Another play with the author's name in the title, **Jules Feiffer's Hold Me!** (2-14-77, American Place), fared better than Jack Gelber's earlier effort. Five actors performed a series of sketches, scenes, and duologues illustrating Feiffer's satirical view of man in the modern urban environment, many dealing with romantic and sexual neuroses. While some critics felt Feiffer's comic strips were best enjoyed in small doses, several enjoyed the comic revue, helping it run an even 100 performances.

David Mamet's **American Buffalo** (2-16-77, Ethel Barrymore) ran a bit longer (135 showings) yet still lost $100,000. But that in no way diminished the young playwright's first Broadway venture, garnering laudatory reviews and wide recognition.

In a cluttered junk shop, proprietor Donny Dubrow (Kenneth McMillan) gives advice to a dense young thug, Bobbie (John Savage), about a job he wants the youth to undertake: stealing some rare coins from a collector who they believe is out of town. The hyper but seasoned crook Walter Cole (Robert Duvall), called "Teach," enters as a partner in the crime. He soon convinces Donny that Bobbie is too inexperienced for the heist. Donny sends Bobby away and calls up the reliable Fletcher to be the second man even though Teach wants to do the job alone. That night Fletcher doesn't show up because, we find out later, he was mugged outside a local diner. Bobby returns, still wanting in on the job, then confesses that the coin collector is not out of town. The job is called off, and an angry Teach lashes out at both men, then lamely begs for Donny's forgiveness. All three performances were razor sharp, and Santo Loquasto's set—piles of appliances, furniture, and equipment in a dusty Aladdin's cave of wonders—was one of the season's most memorable.

The most controversial revival of the season was Lincoln Center's startling version of Chekhov's *The Cherry Orchard* on February 17 in the Vivian Beaumont. Working with a loose new English version by Jean-Claude van Itallie, director Andrei Serban turned the quiet comedy-drama into a bold and outrageous farce with Russian characters dashing across the stage in hot pursuit of love and land, a striptease maid, and somersaulting servants. Santo Loquasto's Tony Award–winning set and costumes utilized white on white with no walls or doors; instead, stranded pieces of furniture floated in space, and white cherry blossoms surrounded the interior and exterior action. Some found the experience a "celebration of genius, like the cleaning of a great painting," while others saw "distortion by design." Most agreed that it had a superb cast, including Irene Worth (Madame Ranevskaya), George Voskovec (Gayev), Raul Julia (Lopakhin), Michael Cristofer (Trofimov), Meryl Streep (Dunyasha), Cathryn Damon (Charlotta), and Mary Beth Hurt (Anya). For sixty-two performances audiences got to look and decide for themselves.

There was little controversy over the Broadway revival of Shaw's *Caesar and Cleopatra* (10-20-06) at the Palace on February 24, but plenty of disappointment. Rex Harrison and Elizabeth Ashley seemed ideal choices for the title roles, but the production was marred by many miscalculations, including the large house chosen for the revival. Director Ellis Rabb cut the play down to less than two hours; the cast and settings were stripped down to a mere handful of actors on the sparse stage; Harrison played the Roman general as a tired businessman, and Ashley's pert performance came across as histrionic in comparison. The engagement was to be limited, but with damaging reviews and poor attendance, the producers called it quits after twelve performances.

One had to go off-off Broadway to see British playwright Christopher Hampton's latest offering, **Savages** (2-24-77, Hudson Guild). The action alternated from 1963, when an Amazon tribe is systematically murdered by a white army, to 1971, when an English diplomat, Alan West (Joseph Maher), is kidnapped by Brazilian guerrillas led

by Carlos Esquerdo (Mandy Patinkin). The tale then went back to 1970, when West and his wife (Alice Drummond) visit the anthropologist Mark Crawford (Stephen Joyce), who had studied the massacred tribe. Gordon Davidson directed the tricky script with vivid action scenes and strong performances, but there was no hiding the fact that there was very little drama in Hampton's thesis.

Six performances was all that Jerome Crittenden's embarrassing comedy **Unexpected Guests** (3-2-77, Little) could last. Like Simon Gray's solitude-seeking hero in *Otherwise Engaged*, Harry Mullin (Jerry Stiller) anticipates quiet and even loneliness when he returns home from work one day to find a note from his wife saying she has run off with a cello salesman. But within minutes Harry is visited by his parents, a voyeur disguised as a policeman, his ex-scoutmaster, his collegiate son's girlfriend, and others. Before long his wife, Melissa (Zohra Lampert), returns (the cello salesman decided to become a priest), but instead of reconciling with Harry, she then runs off with the voyeur. Harry decides to go back to college and live with his son's girl.

London playwright Edna O'Brien found little success with the American production of her family drama **The Gathering** (3-2-77, Manhattan Theatre Club), which might be seen as an Irish version of the earlier *Children*. When the grown-up O'Shea children gather for their parents' fiftieth wedding anniversary, a series of arguments break out, especially concerning the daughter Emer (Maria Tucci), an author in England who has written plays depicting her family as barbarians. In truth, each of the family members is suspicious and resentful of the others, but they return to the unhappy homestead hoping to get a piece of the tawdry estate. The drama was criticized for being dreary and unrelentless.

There were fights of a different sort in Ernest Joselovitz's **Hagar's Children** (3-8-77, Public: Martinson). On Christmas Eve at Bridgehaven Farm, a home for emotionally disturbed teens, tensions are running high as two staff members, a young black man, Oliver (Lloyd Davis, Jr.), and a Jewish woman, Esther (Carmen Vickers), notice minor confrontations and restless behavior. But soon there is an emotional explosion and a pet lamb is brutally killed. The teenagers themselves, led by a longtime resident, Diana (Dorothy Hayden), decide to hold their own investigation. The culprit is found, and some painful memories are unleashed. But soon all the teenagers are put to bed, and Diana is left sorting out her bitterness and taking a step toward rehabilitation. Joselovitz was himself a former staff member at a similar kind of shelter, and his melodrama rang true at times. The play ran at the Public for ten weeks.

A double bill titled **Monsters** (3-10-77, Astor Place) was another difficult evening for the casual playgoer, but it introduced one promising playwright and some unforgettable performances. The opening playlet was William Dew's grotesque one-act **Side Show,** in which a pair of Siamese twins (Robert Drivas and Richard De Fabees) celebrate their birthday with cake, balloons, and party hats while the bodies of their parents, whom they have just murdered, lie bleeding under a sheet. The second half of the bill, Albert Innaurato's **The Transfiguration of Benno Blimpie,** was even more disturbing. Overweight and unloved Benno Blimpie (James Coco) is the "monster" of the family and, in a desperate attempt to earn their love, is literally eating himself to death. While Benno sits atop a platform gorging himself with ice cream, his abusive father (Roger Serbagi), uptight mother (Rosemary De Angelis), and perverted grandfather (Peter Carew) recreate scenes from the past, with the present-day Benno providing the voice for the invisible young Benno. The scenes are graphic and crude, as when the old man tries to rape a thirteen-year-old girl, or when Benno is sexually assaulted in a playground. At the close Benno is covered with a white sheet while the grandfather marks him up like a butcher's chart ready for the slaughter. Coco's performance was devastating, and there were plaudits also for De Angelis as the foul-mouthed, resilient mother. The reviews called the evening "ghastly, unforgettable, riveting" and "strong stuff, but good stuff," so it ran out the season.

Those interested in new playwright Innaurato didn't have to wait long to see more of his work, because three days later the Circle Repertory presented his full-length comedy **Gemini** (3-13-77, Circle). On the twenty-first birthday of Francis Geminiani (Robert Picardo), two classmates from Harvard, the blond Wasp Randy Hastings (Reed Birney) and his attractive sister, Judith (Carol Potter), visit him in his South Philadelphia Italian neighborhood. Francis is embarrassed about his crude father (Danny Aiello): his dad's finicky girlfriend, Lucille (Anne DeSalvo), who picks at other people's plates; their brazen, foul-mouthed neighbor, Bunny (Jessica James), who is always about to fall out of her tight clothes; and her asthmatic, overweight son Herschel (Jonathan Hadary), who collects subway tokens. But even

worse is Francis's own sexual confusion: Judith is supposedly Francis's girlfriend, but he finds he is physically attracted to Randy. During a birthday celebration Francis loses his cool, turns on the oddball gathering, and destroys the cake. But by the end he and the family have made up, and the three youths head back to Harvard to try and work things out. Critics and audiences were much more comfortable with the Geminianis than they were with Benno Blimpie's family, and the reviews were salutatory, calling *Gemini* "a grand comic soap opera." It played for sixty-three performances at the Circle, then moved to Broadway's Little Theatre on May 21, where it delighted audiences for 1,778 performances.

On March 14 Hal Holbrook brought back to Broadway his one-man show *Mark Twain Tonight!*, a beloved performance he had been doing on and off since 1959. The twelve-performance engagement played to healthy box office in the large Imperial Theatre. The Circle in the Square Uptown presented a competent but unexceptional *Romeo and Juliet* on March 17. The cast included Pamela Payton-Wright (Juliet), Paul Rudd (Romeo), Jan Miner (Nurse), and David Rounds (Mercutio). Much more enthusiastic reviews were written about the newly formed BAM Theatre Company's revival of Langdon Mitchell's *The New York Idea* (11-19-06) on March 18. Blythe Danner played the wealthy Cynthia Karslake, who sets her cap for the stuffy judge Philip Phillimore (Stephen Collins) while her ex-husband John (René Auberjonois) is chased by Philip's ex-wife, Vida (Rosemary Harris). Yet the show was stolen by Denholm Elliot as Sir Wilfred, the Englishman who loves both women. Frank Dunlop directed smashingly, and critics rejoiced in the production and how well the old comedy held up. The scheduled twenty-eight performances quickly sold out, and the new company was on its way.

Lily Tomlin in "Appearing Nitely" (3-24-77, Biltmore), a one-woman show by Jane Wagner and Tomlin, also sold out its limited engagement of eighty-four performances. Tomlin and the various characters she portrayed—five-and-a-half-year-old moppet Edith Ann, switchboard impresario Ernestine, bag woman Tess who talks to space aliens, and others—were well known from her television appearances, but critics and audiences cheered her virtuosity and stage presence, making the attraction one of the hottest tickets of the season.

Two plays whose main characters are dying opened within the week, and both were well received. Ronald Ribman's **Cold Storage** (3-27-77,

American Place) concerned two terminal patients who clash and reveal themselves as they await death. On a hospital roof garden, the tempestuous Joseph Parmigian (Martin Balsam) complains about the hospital, the doctors, the food, and life in general. The secretive, withdrawn art dealer Richard Landau (Michael Lipton) arrives at the hospital for "an exploratory," and despite his icy reserve, the belligerent Parmigian badgers Landau into revealing his secret: as a youth, Landau saw his parents and younger sisters taken by the Nazis while he escaped. Although most critics felt the play was unbalanced—a cynical comedy in the first act, a sentimental melodrama in the second—they approved of the evening, remarking that they never thought of Ribman as a comic playwright before. The scheduled forty-eight performances sold well enough that the play moved to Broadway the next season.

The season's second long run, the Swiss pantomime attraction **Mummenschanz** (3-30-77, Bijou), stayed almost as long as *Gemini*. Andrés Bossard, Floriana Frassatoetto, and Bernie Schürch devised and performed the wordless entertainment, featuring some traditional mime and some very nontraditional uses of props and masks that were more entertaining than arty. The unusual program ran in the small theatre for 1,326 performances.

The second play about dying, Michael Cristofer's **The Shadow Box** (3-31-77, Morosco), did even better than *Cold Storage*, winning a Tony Award and a Pulitzer Prize. In three rustic cottages on the grounds of a California hospital, three terminally ill patients are joined by their loved ones. Middle-aged Joe (Simon Oakland), who has worked hard all his life, tries to reconcile with his wife (Joyce Ebert) and teenage son (Vincent Stewart) for the years he wasted on the wrong goals. The prolific writer Brian (Laurence Luckinbill) finds comfort with his lover, Mark (Mandy Patinkin in his Broadway debut), until his promiscuous ex-wife, Beverly (Patricia Elliott), comes on the scene and a three-way battle commences. In the third cottage is the aged, difficult Felicity (Geraldine Fitzgerald), who sings bawdy songs and berates her slavish daughter Agnes (Rose Gregorio), who cares for her despite the abuse. Felicity claims that her other daughter, Claire, is coming, and she will not die until she arrives. But Claire is dead, and Agnes has been lying to please her mother by faking postcards from the favored sibling. With the help of a psychiatrist (Josef Sommer), Agnes tells her the truth, and Felicity, like Joe and Brian, accepts the

---

GORDON DAVIDSON (1933–) was born in Brooklyn, the son of a theatre professor at Brooklyn College, but he studied electrical engineering at Cornell University before turning to the stage and receiving a master's in theatre at Case Western University. Davidson was a protégé of John Houseman and directed for his Theatre Group at UCLA, later becoming artistic director of the company. In 1967 it became the Center Theatre Group and took over Los Angeles's Mark Taper Forum, eventually becoming one of the outstanding regional theatres in the nation. A handful of Davidson's California productions had already transferred to Broadway, most memorably the two docudramas *In the Matter of J. Robert Oppenheimer* (3-6-69) and *The Trial of the Catonsville Nine* (2-7-71), but *The Shadow Box* was his first major hit, winning him the Tony Award. Davidson is known as a playwright's director, working closely with writers on new scripts and helping develop new ways to tell a story.

---

reality of death. While some critics pointed out flaws in the script, all agreed that it was a sterling production with exemplary acting throughout. Ming Cho Lee's scenery was especially effective: one wall-less cottage (each story took place in different parts of the same house) that sat on short stilts while towering redwoods loomed heavenward as Ronald Wallace's lighting broke through in fragments as if in a large cathedral. The drama went through several cast changes during its 315 performances, but the production remained superior, in no small part due to Gordon Davidson's direction.

At one point in Paul Zindel's **Ladies at the Alamo** (4-7-77, Martin Beck) one character stops the others to admonish, "You're all giving one-woman shows!" Zindel was known for writing gutsy women's roles, and this play, though overlong and overwritten, was no exception. In a reception room of a multimillion-dollar theatre complex in Texas City, Texas, a power struggle is going on prior to a meeting of the board of directors while a performance of *The Sea Gull* is taking place in the Alamo Theatre downstairs. Dede Cooper (Estelle Parsons), founder and artistic director of the theatre that started in a converted church and is now one of Texas's cultural beacons, is threatened by attractive spinster Joanne Remington (Rosemary Murphy), the chairman of the board, who wants to oust Dede and replace her with a fading movie star, Shirley Fuller (Jan Farrand), who still has a lot of public visibility. Dede is supported by her longtime friend, the promiscuous drunkard Bella Gardner (Eileen Heckart), even though Bella has recently slept with Dede's husband. Although Dede has buried her own mother that same day, she is ready for a fight, verbal and physical, and what results is "the bitchiest, most hilarious female free-for-all since *The Women*." In the end, the *Sea Gull* curtain comes down and Dede keeps her job, but the damage done during the battle has left the theatre changed forever. Insiders saw the in-house struggles at Nina Vance's famed Alley Theatre in Houston as the inspiration for the script, but critics saw a "weak and artificial" play that served as a vehicle for some no-holds-barred acting. But it wasn't enough, and the ferocious comedy closed after twenty performances.

Plays about Vietnam were still being presented in 1977, and the most notable effort this season was David Berry's **G. R. Point** (4-7-77, Marymount Manhattan), which the Phoenix offered for twelve showings. The title referred to a Graves Registration checkpoint in Vietnam where the bodies of American soldiers are brought and paperwork is processed before burial. The outfit consists of a handful of unintelligent enlistees who deal with their gruesome job with drugs and a bizarre sense of humor. When the Ivy Leaguer Micah Broadstreet (John Heard) is assigned to the unit, he is considered a freakish outsider. But soon Micah is smoking pot and verbally and physically sparring with the others, sinking to their level. His letters to his mother back in New England chronicle his downfall so graphically that the woman has a heart attack, and Micah, in one fight that goes overboard, kills a man for the first time, deriving, he later says, a sexual pleasure from the act. His disintegration is now complete.

José Quintero, the definitive director of O'Neill's works, scored another triumph with *Anna Christie* (11-2-21) on April 14 at the Imperial. The star was Liv Ullmann, who brought a tender realism to the melodramatic heroine. Douglas Watt in the *New York Daily News* praised "her husky, expressive voice and that strange mix of innocence and sensuality that keeps crossing and recrossing her individually somewhat plain but collectively beautiful features." Robert Donley played her father, John Lithgow her beau, and Mary McCarty the crafty Marthy Owen. Critics felt what might be termed a clunky play was turned into thrilling theatre. It was producer Alexander Cohen's second valiant offering this season, but unlike *Comedians*, it turned a profit.

ALEXANDER H. COHEN (1920–2000) was born in New York and educated at NYU and Columbia University. His first producing effort on Broadway was the unsuccessful *Ghost for Sale* in 1941, but later that year he had a major hit co-presenting *Angel Street*. A commercial producer who also presented many classic revivals and English imports, Cohen was known for his good taste and integrity, as when he produced *King Lear* in 1950 with a cast of blacklisted actors, or when he brought the Royal Shakespeare Company production of *The Homecoming* (1967) from London. From 1967 to 1986 he produced the televised Tony Awards.

The Public revived a pair of Strindberg one-acts, *Creditors* and *The Stronger*, on April 15 in the Newman with actor Rip Torn directing his wife, Geraldine Page, and himself in the featured roles. The mostly negative notices found the direction and the acting overblown and uneven. At the City Center, Le Tréteau de Paris presented thirteen performances of Giraudoux's *La Guerre de Troie n'aura pas lieu* (The Trojan War Will Not Take Place) in French starting on April 20. Americans playgoers remembered the play from Christopher Fry's adaptation *Tiger at the Gates* (10-3-55).

Another Broadway revival that turned a profit (in only 107 performances, no less) was David Rabe's *The Basic Training of Pavlo Hummel* (5-20-71) at the Longacre on April 24 with film star Al Pacino as the hapless hero. Some critics felt the script paled in comparison to Rabe's later, more satisfying Vietnam plays, but they gave Pacino raves all around.

AL [berto] **PACINO** (1940–) was born and raised in the South Bronx and briefly attended the Manhattan High School for the Performing Arts. He later studied with Herbert Berghof and Lee Strasberg and started appearing as street toughs and delinquents in such plays as *The Indian Wants the Bronx* (1968) and *Does a Tiger Wear a Necktie?* (1969); the latter, his Broadway debut, won him a Tony Award. By 1969 Pacino was consistently making films but, more than almost any other major movie star, often returned to Broadway in challenging roles, such as Kilroy in the Lincoln Center revival of *Camino Real* (1970). Usually cast as intense, anti-heroic characters, Pacino won another Tony for playing Pavlo Hummel.

The new BAM Theatre Company received decidedly mixed reviews for its second revival offering, Chekhov's *The Three Sisters* on April 26. Reactions ranged from "muted, accurate, honest" to "a disaster," but again the cast was first-rate: Ellen Burstyn (Masha), Rosemary Harris (Olga), and Tovah Feldshuh (Irina), as well as Denholm Elliott, Barnard Hughes, Margaret Hamilton, Stephen Collins, Austin Pendleton, René Auberjonois, and Rex Robbins. The Roundabout revived Jerome Kilty's correspondence play *Dear Liar* (3-17-60) on April 28 with the author as Bernard Shaw and Deann Mears as Mrs. Patrick Campbell. Like the earlier *The New York Idea*, J. Hartley Manners's *Peg o' My Heart* (12-20-12) was cited for holding up so well after all these years. It was revived on May 4 at Theatre Four for fifteen performances with Sofia Landon as the irrepressible Peg.

Tennessee Williams's second new offering of the season was his atmospheric **Vieux Carré** (5-11-77, St. James). The title is the name of a rooming house in New Orleans's French Quarter in the 1930s where a young Writer (Richard Alfieri), recently arrived from St. Louis, lives and interacts with various tenants, in particular an elderly painter (Tom Aldredge) who seduces him. Also in the building are two "ladies" (Iris Whitney and Olive Deering) getting too old for their trade and a young girl (Diane Kagan) dying of leukemia and in love with a stud (John William Reilly) who is torn between staying with her and and seeking fresh pastures. There was no plot as such, and the only unifying element was the characters of the Writer and the loony harridan of a landlady (Sylvia Sidney). Critics were pleased to see Williams abandon the surreal-absurdist mode of his last few efforts, but they couldn't fully endorse the new work either. The production suffered from "inept direction," uneven acting, and being presented in such a large house. Many felt it was not a terrible play, but it closed after seven performances all the same.

Andrei Serban's reworking of Aeschylus's *Agamemnon* on May 18 in the Vivian Beaumont received reviews as mixed as had his earlier *The Cherry Orchard*, but the arguments were less passionate this time. Serban and composer Elizabeth Swados turned the Greek tragedy into an oratorio with a lively masked chorus backing up three actors who played all the roles. David W. Schmidt's setting was extraordinary, turning the Beaumont into a theatre-in-the-round with the actors emerging from a wire cage where the orchestra pit used to be. It was a very theatrical

production, far from formal or stuffy, and Papp thought well enough of it to move it to Central Park in the summer.

Critics were running out of things to say about Robert Wilson's avant-garde theatre pieces except for how long they lasted and how many were in the cast. His new work, **I Was Sitting on My Patio This Guy Appeared I Thought I Was Hallucinating** (5-22-77, Cherry Lane), was only ninety minutes long and employed two characters, Wilson and Lucinda Childs. The audience heard a telephone ring throughout the program, as well as unexplained gunshots and monologues on tape echoed by live recitation, and even saw a film of penguins walking on the ice. Years later such programs would be termed "performance art," but at the time it was just another Wilson fantasy.

The season ended with two notable exits. Clive Barnes, the *New York Times* critic for the past ten years and the city's most powerful aisle-sitter, stepped down as drama critic and announced that he would concentrate on dance in the future. (In reality, he left the *Times* and became drama critic at the *New York Post*. His replacement, Richard Eder, would not last long and would rarely have the impact, good or bad, that Barnes had.) Also, Joseph Papp gave up on Lincoln Center, relinquishing all control over the troublesome theatre organization, and returned to Off Broadway (although three of his productions were still playing on Broadway as the season closed).

1977–1978

While the season did not have the quality of the previous one, it was an American season, with fifteen of the twenty-two new plays on Broadway penned by native playwrights and thirty-seven of Off Broadway's fifty new works by Americans as well. More encouraging, the better plays seen in both venues were native, only one foreign play, the Irish import *'Da'*, making the *Best Plays* list. The total number of productions was down a bit, but there were fewer revivals and fewer musicals, so it seemed like a season of new American comedies and dramas.

Broadway broke the $100 million mark in box-office revenue, but as usual, numbers were deceiving. Ticket prices rose considerably: Broadway musicals now demanded a $25.00 top, plays a typical $17.50 on Saturday night, and Off Broadway $10.00. Only four Broadway plays turned a profit by season's end. Happily there was quality to be found. Even though they met with varying levels of success, most of the reputable young playwrights (Lanford Wilson, John Guare, Thomas Babe, Steve Tesich, David Mamet, Albert Innaurato, and Sam Shepard) were represented, along with old-timers Neil Simon, William Gibson, and Ira Levin and newcomers Tina Howe, Harvey Fierstein, and Wendy Wasserstein.

Both *Variety* and the *New York Times* gave up trying to distinguish between Off Broadway and Off Off Broadway in their season summaries. The Manhattan Theatre Club and the Circle Repertory Theatre, which had sent so many hits to Off Broadway and even Broadway, were now firmly entrenched off Broadway, while a newer off-off-Broadway group, the Hudson Guild Theatre, made a splash providing one of Broadway's most popular transfers, '*Da*'. To further confuse matters, less than a fourth of all off-Broadway productions this season were commercial enterprises. Off Broadway now meant non-profit theatre companies. And even they jumped to Broadway whenever prospects looked good. The New York theatre was indeed complicated.

The season would provide more than the usual number of one-man shows (ten on and off the Street), featuring both historical and fictional characters. The entries started right away with Dick Shawn's **The 2nd Greatest Entertainer in the Whole Wide World** (6-2-77, Promenade). In a cluttered dressing room, a middle-aged comic (Shawn) prepares to go onstage to perform for the first time in five years. He practices some of his routines in front of the mirror, going off on tangents and ranting about politics, show business, and his hostility toward all young people, young comics in particular. In the second act we see his Las Vegas act, complete with a noxious "I Gotta Be Me" kind of song opener, impressions of celebrities, and some juggling and dancing—all done poorly. This schizoid kind of comedy (so vividly portrayed last season in *Comedians*) allowed for some dazzling acting on the part of Shawn, but the critics felt he needed a strong playwright to structure his fascinating material. All the same, the show ran two months on the strength of the comic's kinetic performance.

Later in June, Adolph Caesar took to the stage alone in the anthology program **The Square Root of Soul** (6-14-77, Theatre de Lys). The veteran African-American actor performed prose and poetry by various black writers under the guise of an old actor making his farewell appearance. While parts of the evening were very moving,

reviewers decreed it ultimately unsatisfying. The Negro Ensemble Company presentation ran through July in two different engagements.

The season's first revival, Wilde's *The Importance of Being Earnest* at the Circle in the Square Uptown on June 16, was one of its best. Stephen Porter directed a first-rate cast that included James Valentine (Jack), John Glover (Algernon), and Elizabeth Wilson (Lady Bracknell). Commentators called it "deliciously satisfying" and "close to perfection." The comedy ran through the summer. At Lincoln Center, Joseph Papp closed his tenure there with a return engagement of last winter's controversial *The Cherry Orchard* on June 29 in the Vivian Beaumont for forty-eight showings. Off Broadway, the Ridiculous Theatrical Company brought back one of its audience favorites, Charles Ludlam's *Stage Blood*, on July 1 at the Truck and Warehouse for two weeks.

The next new play was another solo piece. Brazilian playwright Roberto Athayde's blistering satire on dictatorship, **Miss Margarida's Way** (7-31-77, Public: Newman), used an eighth-grade biology class as metaphor. An engaging but monstrous teacher, Miss Margarida (Estelle Parsons), warns her students (the audience) that she wields considerable power, telling them that pupils she sends to the principal never return. She encourages the students to ask questions but usually bulldozes her way through the lesson, occasionally touching on biology ("Do you think Miss Margarida is here to exalt the human body? You're very mistaken.") but often sidetracking herself into different subjects. Asking them how to divide twelve bananas among a class of thirty-five students, she answers herself with "the strongest will get eight or nine bananas, the second strongest will get three or four, and the remaining students will be left perfectly without bananas. That is division." In the end, Miss Margarida explodes in a tirade of frustration, then falls silent and collapses on her desk. A mute student (Colin Garrey) from the class goes to her and takes her in his arms, and the monster is reduced to a mere human. Parsons's performance was a tour de force, allowing her to improvise at times and work the audience like a stand-up comic. Critics cheered her unequivocally, but some felt the premise for this "provocative, metaphysical monodrama" was a bit "feeble" at times. Nonetheless, the show was so popular at the Public that after thirty performances it reopened on Broadway on September 27 at the Ambassador and stayed for ninety-eight more showings.

At the outdoor Delacorte in Central Park, Papp revived last season's *Agamemnon* on August 2 for three weeks. (The Delacorte's other entry was the musical *The Threepenny Opera*, also a holdover from Lincoln Center, which meant that for the first time since 1962, when the Delacorte was built, there was no summer Shakespeare in the park.) All the marquee lights on Broadway were dimmed on August 5 to honor Alfred Lunt, who had died two days earlier. It was only the third time the Street had seen such a gesture, previously made for Gertrude Lawrence in 1952 and for Oscar Hammerstein II in 1960. On August 31, the Grand Kabuki National Theatre of Japan arrived at the Beacon with the Kabuki play *Yoshitsune Senbonzakura* and the Noh play *Kurozuka*. The double bill ran through September 18 in two separate engagements.

The fall season began with a superb revival of Molière's *Tartuffe* on September 6 at the Circle in the Square Uptown. British actor John Wood earned raves for his sly Tartuffe, but the supporting cast of American actors was also applauded: Stefan Gierasch (Orgon), Tammy Grimes (Elmire), Patricia Elliott (Dorine), Victor Garber (Valere), Mildred Dunnock (Mme. Pernelle), and Swoozie Kurtz (Mariane). Although it was a very traditional production (the Richard Wilbur translation was used), the masterful direction by Stephen Porter made the comedy seem sparklingly new.

The same night, two revivals appeared off Broadway. Elmer Rice's legal drama *Counsellor-at-Law* (11-6-31) opened at the Quaigh with George Guidall as the Jewish lawyer George Simon heading the large cast. Some reviews criticized the production for being too slow and drawn out, but the old melodrama was appealing enough to audiences to run eight weeks. On the other hand, critics felt that the Roundabout's revival of Pirandello's *Naked* (11-8-26) was too fast paced, staged more like a French farce than an introspective comedy. Aisle-sitters were also quite divided on the quality of the acting. But again the fascinating play held audiences, and the company kept the revival on the boards for sixteen weeks.

John Guare's newest effort, **Landscape of the Body** (9-27-77, Public: Newman), met with particularly hostile reviews, described as "often banal and sometimes grisly" and "flatulent afflatus." Betty (Shirley Knight) arrives in New York with her fourteen-year-old son, Bert (Paul McCrane), in order to convince her porn-actress sister, Rosalie (Peg Murray), to return home to Maine with her. But Rosalie dies in a freak accident (run over by a racing bicycle), so Betty stays in Manhattan and soon is taking over her sister's job and lifestyle. Then Bert's body is found decapitated and dumped in the Hudson River. Betty is suspected, but the investigation by Police Captain Holohan (F. Murray Abraham) reveals in flashbacks how Bert lost his rural innocence and got involved in down-and-dirty Greenwich Village street life. He and his friend Donny (Anthony Maricona) lure homosexuals into an apartment and then beat them with a wrench. One of the escapades goes awry, Bert is killed, and Donny and his gang cut off the head and roll it down to the river. John Pasquin directed in a fluid, cinematic style that was reminiscent of an old movie melodrama.

Three Dracula plays were planned for this season (one didn't open), the first a "smart and stylish" new version by Bob Hall and David Richmond called **The Passion of Dracula** (9-28-77, Cherry Lane), which originated at the George Street Playhouse in New Jersey. Billed as "a gothic entertainment," the play followed the Bram Stoker novel closely, keeping all the action in the study of Dr. Cedric Seward (K. Lype O'Dell), emphasizing the romantic and sensual aspects of Count Dracula (Christopher Bernau), and allowing for humor in the supporting characters without slipping into camp. It was greeted with mostly enthusiastic reviews and played to full houses even after a bigger and more spectacular *Dracula* opened on Broadway a week later. By the time the playful thriller closed, it had run 714 performances.

The first of a handful of Shaw plays this season was the Roundabout's *You Never Can Tell* (1-9-05) on October 4. Tony Tanner directed a strong ensemble that was favorably reviewed, Rachel Gurney as the progressive Mrs. Clandon and Richard

STEPHEN [Winthrop] PORTER (1925–) was born in Ogdensburg, New York, and educated at Yale University and the Yale School of Drama. After teaching at McGill University in Montreal and directing at various theatres in Canada, Porter made his New York directing debut with *The Misanthrope* at Theatre East in 1956. He staged classics and modern revivals at all the major Shakespeare festivals and regional theatres across the United States, as well as in New York, where he was artistic director of the New Phoenix Repertory Company from 1972 to 1975. Porter excels at style pieces, in particular works by Molière and Shaw.

Niles as her son Philip being cited as particularly accomplished.

For the second season in a row, British playwright Christopher Hampton premiered a new play off-off Broadway. But **Treats** (10-5-77, Hudson Guild) was a small and minor effort and probably belonged there, for the three-week engagement attracted little attention. Free-spirit Londoner Ann (Suzanne Lederer) has taken a new lover, the conventional businessman Patrick (John Glover), when her journalist boyfriend, Dave (Kenneth Welsh), is out of the country on an extended assignment. Dave returns and the usual complications arise, both men threatening to leave her. But Ann is too weak to do without one of them, so she reinstates Dave and sends Patrick packing, hinting to him that she will very likely be changing her mind again soon.

Newcomer D. L. Coburn scored a hit his first time at bat with **The Gin Game** (10-6-77, Golden), a vehicle for two veteran actors. In the Bentley Nursing and Convalescent Home for the Aged, disgruntled Weller Martin (Hume Cronyn) does not socialize with the other residents until he meets the prim "Old Time Methodist" Fonsia Dorsey (Jessica Tandy) and teaches her how to play gin rummy. They embark on a series of card games together, each of them revealing incidents from their past as they play. Fonsia always wins the hand, which irritates Weller and makes him obsessive about gaining a victory in order to counteract his lifetime of defeats. (Fonsia suggests that they try a different card game, but he refuses.) Unable to beat her, Weller finally explodes, pounds the card table violently with his cane, and walks away. Fonsia realizes that her self-righteous behavior has caused her a future filled with loneliness. Reviews for Cronyn and Tandy were valentines (Tandy won a Tony Award), but the play itself received a very mixed reaction, from "a dark, sharp, clever, two-actor play" to "workable and accomplishes most of what it is trying to do" to "if *The Gin Game* were any slighter, it would be solitaire." Regardless, it won a Pulitzer Prize and ran a profitable 517 performances.

The American Place Theatre had a very disappointing season, none of its four entries finding critical or popular favor. Elaine Jackson's **Cockfight** (10-7-77, American Place) was a black drama with a feminist outlook. Schoolteacher Reba (Mary Alice) has moved from New York to a farmhouse outside of San Francisco because her husband, Jesse (Gylan Kain), is always changing careers. He used to be a country-western singer but now makes original jewelry and hangs out

with his freeloader friend Carl (Charles Brown). The two men put on a macho front, and Jesse tries to boss his wife into submission, but she grows into a feminist as the marriage disintegrates.

The Negro Ensemble co-produced a commercial offering before its season at the St. Marks began. **Survival** (10-9-77, Astor Place) was a play of protest about South African apartheid using sketches, songs, and dance, the action moving from a Johannesburg prison to the black ghetto of Soweto. The cast of four and the director, Mshengu, wrote the revue, which was originally seen in South Africa. The most interesting of the sketches concerned a released prisoner who returns home to his miserable neighborhood and realizes it is more dangerous than the jail where he was beaten and humiliated, so he makes an effort to get arrested and sent back there.

A major Broadway disappointment was Swedish author Per Olov Enquist's drama **The Night of the Tribades** (10-13-77, Helen Hayes). The fictional piece about playwright August Strindberg had been performed all over Europe but found little favor in New York and lasted only twelve performances. On the stage of Copenhagen's Dagmar Theatre, Strindberg (Max Von Sydow) and his estranged wife, Siri (Bibi Andersson), are preparing for the premiere of *The Stronger*, the play about two women fighting over an unseen man. The other actress in the playlet is the alcoholic Marie Caroline David (Eileen Atkins), who Strindberg suspects is having a lesbian love affair with his ex-wife. (The word "tribade" was a synonym for lesbian.) The lines of the play being rehearsed take on new meaning in light of the triangle. After Marie delivers a haunting soliloquy about a night of lesbian love, the two women perform the scene saying what they want to say (neither of them needs any man) rather than what Strindberg had written. Critics admired the players, though some thought them miscast, but most agreed the script, direction, and production were stilted and awkward.

The Circle Repertory Company opened its season with Patrick Meyers's drama **Feedlot** (10-13-77, Circle). In the control room of a feedlot where food is electronically dispensed to the cattle below, the night shift keeps watch on the many dials and gauges that operate the facility. The crew consists of three macho cowboys and the sensitive college student Gene (Mark J. Soper). Left alone with the swaggering Vietnam vet Billy Fred (Joseph Ragno), Gene is taunted by the cowboy for being a "faggot." The tension between the two builds until Gene surprisingly pulls out a gun and ridicules the stupid cowboy, suggesting Billy Fred's overzealous masculinity is probably hiding his own sexual uncertainty. Billy Fred is strangely cowed by the accusations, as if Gene has hit on the truth, so when the others return and work continues there is an odd but unmistakable bond between the two men.

Trinidad playwright Mustapha Matura's **Rum an Coca Cola** (10-18-77, BAM) was seen briefly first in Brooklyn and then at the Westside in Manhattan. (All three Chelsea Theatre Center productions followed the same pattern this season.) On a beach in the West Indies, an aging calypso singer called Creator (Leon Morenzie) works on a new song with his apprentice, Bird (Lou Ferguson), the two of them jumping into songs (such as the title) and acting like smiling natives every time some tourists walk by. But Creator hates the foreigners, especially since one of them, a young girl with money, has fallen in love with Bird. Eventually Bird leaves both the girl and the old man to promote his own singing career, and the bitter Creator is left with no one to help introduce his new song at the upcoming competition. The acting was judged to be more impressive than the script, but the three-piece steel band onstage gave the production a nice atmospheric touch.

Another import, this time from Australia, was the one-person comedy **Housewife! Superstar!** (10-19-77, Theatre Four), an outrageous piece written and performed by "down under" comedian Barry Humphries. He portrayed the middle-aged, jowly lady Dame Edna Everage, who comments on sex, men, and marriage, often in a ribald but good-natured way. Humphries's humor was definitely an acquired taste, and while he could only find an audience for one month, "Dame Edna" later became very popular on British (and even later American) television. The Australian would return to the New York stage twenty-two years later with much more success.

The season's most popular revival was the Hamilton Deane and John L. Balderston *Dracula* (10-5-27) at the Martin Beck on October 20. Frank Langella turned the Count into a matinee idol and offered audiences the sexiest vampire imaginable. Dennis Rosa directed a capable cast, but the evening's co-star was Edward Gorey's playful scenery and costumes. The locations were all sketched with busy ink strokes (often with bats drawn into the architectural details and drapery design), and each black-and-white setting was set off with a splash of bright red on a costume or

a prop. Reviews were all laudatory, Howard Kissell in *Women's Wear Daily* comparing the two concurrent vampire productions: "You can go downtown for deeper philosophy and emotions, uptown for visual frissons and Langella's performance. Surely New York is big enough to be a two-Dracula town." It was, and the Broadway version ran 925 performances.

Nothing could have been further from David Mamet's brutal *American Buffalo* last season than his affectionate **A Life in the Theatre** (10-20-77, Theatre de Lys). Two actors, the veteran Robert (Ellis Rabb), who is eloquent and poetic about his profession, and the younger John (Peter Evans), who politely listens to Robert's opinions and suggestions, go through the routines of a repertory company actor: rehearsals, putting on makeup, performing in various genre plays (from World War I battle melodramas to drawing room comedies to medical soap operas), and the ritual after-performance banter. The relationship is an odd one; Robert is at times a father figure, at other times a rival, and at still other moments has the protective jealousy of a lover. The comedy won unanimous plaudits for the script ("overflows with good feeling and humanism . . . surely the warmest and often the funniest play in town") and the cast. Some even pointed out the expert direction by the young and promising Gerald Gutierrez. The intimate comedy ran into July.

Richard Eder, the new drama critic for the *New York Times*, led the assault of pans for Stanley Hart's seven-performance flop **Some of My Best Friends** (10-26-77, Longacre), calling the comedy "lacking in density, characters, conflict or one single line that is either witty or graceful." When the autocratic tycoon Andrew Mumford (television star Ted Knight) had a mental breakdown, he was put in a sanatorium, where the shock treatments gave him the power to converse with animals and plant life. Once released, he abandons his family and former lifestyle and moves into a Manhattan apartment where he talks with his Afghan hound, Albert (Gavin Reed), who talks back, converses with a tree named Irving Buxbaum (Lee Wallace), who is just as communicative, and has intricate conversations with an articulate baby (Ralph Williams), the child of a neighbor girl, Sari (Trish Hawkins). Andrew is content in his multi-lingual fantasy until his wife, Dorothy (Alice Drummond), and pompous son, Lawrence (Bob Balaban), arrive and convince him to return to his former life. The innovative Harold Prince directed (though most couldn't believe it).

Prince was not the only talent to stumble that night. Peter Nichols, author of such penetrating comedy-dramas as *A Day in the Death of Joe Egg* (2-1-68) and *The National Health* (10-10-74), came a cropper with his artificial play **Chez Nous** (10-26-77, Manhattan Theatre Club). Successful London pediatrician Dick (John Tillinger), who has written a best-selling book on adolescent sexual behavior, and his wife, Liz (Barbara Caruso), have left England and moved to the South of France. They are visited by their oldest and dearest friends, the semi-successful architect Phil (Sam Waterston) and his wife, Diana (Christina Pickles). The marriages are far from perfect, and, all four being sexually unhappy, they contemplate swapping partners. But the foursome's friendship is nearly destroyed when Dick and Liz learn that Phil slept with their thirteen-year-old daughter and that he is the father of the girl's illegitimate infant son. The embarrassment lingered for twenty-eight performances.

After an unsuccessful attempt to turn the Belasco into a cabaret with tables replacing the orchestra seats, the venerable old theatre was remodeled back to its original design and reopened with Judith Ross's slight comedy **An Almost Perfect Person** (10-27-77, Belasco). When widowed and liberated Irene Porter (Colleen Dewhurst) loses her bid for a congressional seat to an elderly male Republican incumbent ("I am the only woman and the only Democrat who lost!"), her despair makes her vulnerable and she succumbs to the charms of her campaign manager, Dan Connally (George Hearn), and sleeps with him. The very next day her campaign treasurer, Jerry Leeds (Rex Robbins), gives Irene the news that she is $75,000 in debt and that he loves her. He's even willing to leave his newly liberated wife and run off with Irene, informing her that he is free now because it's not the tax season. Irene refuses to run off, but they spend the night together, and fireworks explode the next morning when Dan returns. Both men are shocked at Irene's sudden sexual activity because they always thought of her as a perfect human being. Finally off her pedestal, Irene scolds both men, chooses Dan, sends Jerry back to his wife and kids, and announces that she is going to run for mayor. The plot was uncomfortably close to the earlier *Treats*, but at least the actors were charming and there were some enjoyable lines. Actress Zoe Caldwell directed with style, but it was not enough. The critics neither condoned nor damned the play, calling it "a small comedy but not an unappealing one" and "a slick old-fashioned women's play."

The three-character piece ran an unprofitable 108 performances.

Having essayed Harry Truman and Will Rogers, James Whitmore took on Teddy Roosevelt in the one-man show **Bully** (11-1-77, 46th Street). Jerome Alden's script covered such personal memories as TR's sickly childhood, his devotion to his family, and his grief at his son's death in battle, as well as public causes such as his fight against powerful business trusts and his instigation of conservation legislation. While Teddy was theatrical enough, his writings and speeches were not, and despite Whitmore's blustering, critics found the evening "disjointed and distant" and "a noisy bore."

Off-off Broadway, A. R. Gurney, Jr.'s **The Wayside Motor Inn** (11-2-77, Manhattan Theatre Club) failed to catch fire. In a motel outside of Boston, five different plays are being enacted in the same depersonalized, antiseptic room that stands for five different rooms in the motel, all the actors occupying the same space as their divergent stories overlap in space and theme. The point of the stories had to do with the impersonality of modern American life, but the effect was very unsatisfactory. Gurney would have much better success a few years later when he tried a similar premise using a dining room.

Veteran playwright William Gibson did not fare any better with his large-scale biography **Golda** (11-14-77, Morosco). During the ten days of the 1973 Yom Kippur War, Israeli prime minister Golda Meir (Anne Bancroft) leads her nation from a disastrous start to a decisive victory, interrupted by memories of her past: her childhood in Russia with the ever-threatening pogroms, growing up in Milwaukee and her marriage to the shy Morris Meyerson (Gerald Hiken), their emigration to Palestine and struggle to create a strong Israeli nation, and her regrets over the suffering her family has endured because of her political life. Golda's character was well written and well acted, but the other characters in the epic tale were reduced to trivial caricatures. The "relentlessly episodic" drama received all negative reviews, T. E. Kalem in *Time* going so far as to call it "a conscientious, reverential, monumental bore. The real Golda should sue." The expensive production struggled on for 108 performances.

When Zero Mostel died suddenly while in rehearsals for Arnold Wesker's **The Merchant** (11-16-77, Plymouth), the producers decided to continue with Mostel's understudy, Joseph Leon, rather than postpone the opening and secure a new star. The ambitious drama was *The Merchant*

WENDY WASSERSTEIN (1950–) was born in Brooklyn, the daughter of a textile manufacturer, and educated at the Calhoun School in Manhattan, Mount Holyoke College, CCNY, and the Yale School of Drama. Before her graduation from Yale in 1976, her early plays were read or staged there and off-off Broadway. *Uncommon Women and Others* went through various readings and workshops before appearing off Broadway this season. One of the most successful women playwrights of her era, Wasserstein concentrates on characters and themes that she experienced firsthand: intelligent, wealthy women dealing with their role in the modern world and, sometimes, coming to terms with their Jewish heritage.

of Venice retold without the strain of anti-Semitism found in Shakespeare's work. Shylock (Leon) is a man of ideas and a philosopher at heart, Portia (Roberta Maxwell) is a liberated woman, and Antonio (John Clements) is a burnt-out merchant who jokingly suggests the "pound of flesh" pact as a mockery of Venetian law. While the writing was intelligent and the acting quite capable, critics found the "wordy" piece "bloodless" and lacking in theatrical suspense. *The Merchant* closed after five performances; general consensus was that it probably would not have run much longer even with Mostel in it.

The most interesting new American playwright introduced this season was Wendy Wasserstein, whose **Uncommon Women and Others** (11-17-77, Marymount Manhattan) attracted a lot of comment during its twenty-two performances.

Six years after graduation, five classmates from the all-women Mount Holyoke College gather to compare notes on how they have fared since going out into the world. This leads to a series of flashbacks showing how the different women reacted to the sheltered and sometimes archaic atmosphere of the all-female environment. The residents include the saccharine Susie (Cynthia Herman), who upholds all the school traditions such as folding napkins in floral designs or acting as one of the Elves who leave chocolate kisses in the freshmen's mailboxes so they feel loved; the arty and morose Carter (Anna Levine), who types to the tempo of the "Hallelujah Chorus"; the smart, practical Kate (Jill Eikenberry), who is destined for a brilliant law career and is petrified at the prospect of it; the sexually liberated Rita (Swoozie Kurtz); the warm, overweight, and wealthy Holly (Alma Cuervo); and the plucky

Muffet (Ellen Parker), who is torn between being a feminist and finding a Prince Charming. Although lacking in plot development, Wasserstein's dialogue crackled with humor and truth, and the characters, as Edith Oliver in *The New Yorker* observed, "are never allowed to be types and, for all their funny talk and behavior, they are sympathetically drawn."

The American Place continued to support playwright Steve Tesich season after season, and just as consistently, he provided promising but unsatisfying plays. His latest, **Passing Game** (11-18-77, American Place), once again met with mostly negative reviews. In a seedy resort with few guests, two once-promising actors—one white, Richard (William Atherton), and one black, Henry (Howard Rollins, Jr.),—play basketball with violent frustration because their careers now consist of doing voice-overs and commercials, something their irritating wives keep reminding them of. A series of unexplained killings in the area prompt the two men to discuss how fortunate it would be if the mysterious sniper should pick off one of their wives. Henry has already tried to murder his wife, Rachel (Novella Nelson), by running her down with his car, but it only left her crippled. The gun-toting caretaker Andrew (Pat McNamara), his nasty nephew Randy (Paul C. O'Keefe), and the nephew's ex-girlfriend Debbie (Susan MacDonald) are also on the scene, and soon the two actors have designs on Debbie. Henry and Richard then make a pact: each will murder and bury the other one's wife. But before they can do so, the two actors are gunned down, supposedly by the offstage sniper.

At the Public, Paul Sill's **Tales of the Hasidim** (11-18-77, Martinson), a sort of Jewish *Story Theatre* (10-26-70), was performed in a cabaret setting for three weeks. Sills adapted Martin Buber's Hasidic tales, and six actors (including *Story Theatre* alumnus Paul Sand) acted them out in an improvisational style.

The Negro Ensemble Company opened its season with a strong selection, Gus Edwards's **The Offering** (11-26-77, St. Marks). The layabout Bob Tyrone (Douglas Turner Ward) sits in his shabby West Side apartment all day watching television with his young wife, Princess (Olivia Williams). One day, Martin (Charles Weldon), a flashy dresser from Las Vegas, and Ginny (Katherine Knowles), his white girlfriend who is a showgirl at the casino, arrive unexpectedly, mysteriously offering Tyrone three thousand dollars. Tyrone senses that Martin is a hitman sent by one of his old enemies from Tyrone's former mob days, so he refuses the money and invites the young couple to stay the night. As a young boy, Martin knew and idolized Tyrone, who had become his mentor. But now a struggle for sexual dominance has evolved between the two men, with Tyrone seducing Ginny and Martin being temporarily deflated by the old man. The drama ran until January 1, then reopened in February for a total of fifty-nine performances.

Even though Lynn Redgrave had portrayed Joan of Arc in last season's comedy *Knock Knock*, having her play the lead in Shaw's *Saint Joan* was a bold choice because the British actress was known mainly for her lightweight comic roles. But she garnered highly favorable notices in the November 29 revival at the Circle in the Square Uptown. Clive Barnes, now writing for the *New York Post*, said the casting of Redgrave was "initially interesting and ultimately so rewarding," but reviews for the production itself were decidedly mixed, ranging from "a decided triumph" to "disappointingly earthbound." The play ran for twelve weeks.

Ntozake Shange's "poemplay" **A Photograph** (12-1-77, LuEsther) did not meet with the same success as her runaway hit *for colored girls . . .* (5-17-76), yet it received respectful reviews and ran sixty-two performances at the Public. It was another poetic piece on contemporary life, this time held together by a plot: a young black man, Sean David (Avery Brooks), struggles to become a professional photographer, but except for his liberated and life-affirming girlfriend (Michele Shay), all the black people he sees around him seem to be caricatures of the failures of his race. Sean is also haunted by the memory of some dead soldiers he photographed on a hillside in Vietnam. His last ounce of confidence is shattered when he is turned down for a grant that he was counting on.

Neil Simon combined his talent for comedy and his penchant for serious drama and came up with **Chapter Two** (12-4-77, Imperial), an autobiographical play that everyone knew was about his deceased wife, Joan Simon, and his new wife, Marsha Mason. While some critics thought the comedy-drama combination was awkward and unbalanced, most applauded the new work as "affectionate and compelling." When writer George Schneider's (Judd Hirsch) wife died, he took off on a long trip to Europe to help him get over it, but he returns home to New York more miserable than ever. Since his return, he tells his sympathetic brother, Leo (Cliff Gorman), women are

calling him on the phone all the time trying to start a new relationship: divorcées, widows, "one woman, I swear to God, I think her husband was just on vacation." In another Manhattan apartment, Jennie Malone (Anita Gillette) returns from a trip to Mexico to get over her divorce and tells her friend Faye (Ann Wedgeworth) that she is finished with romantic relationships; "if one more man greets me at the door with his silk shirt unbuttoned to his tanned navel . . . and wearing more jewelry around his neck than me, I am turning celibate." But when George accidentally calls Jennie on the phone, they are so amused by each other's sense of humor that they cautiously make arrangements to meet. As the tentative pair carefully fall into a romance, both Leo's and Faye's marriages are on the rocks and the two of them, having met through George and Jennie, have an unsatisfying one-night stand together. George and Jennie wed, but when they return from a honeymoon filled with mishaps, the strain starts to show because George cannot completely let go of his deceased wife. The couple nearly breaks up, but George returns to Jennie with the realization that what he has most feared in this second marriage is happiness. With Jennie he plans to start fresh with the second chapter of his life. Herbert Ross directed, the players handled the bittersweet humor well (Wedgeworth won a Tony Award), and the play ran 857 performances.

The Public had success with two revivals the next week. S. Ansky's drama about demonic possession, *The Dybbuk*, opened on December 6 with a new adaptation by Mira Rafalowicz and Joseph Chaikin, who directed. In this production filled with bravado acting, singing, choral chants, and ritualistic movement, most reviewers found the old play very theatrical and absorbing. Machiavelli's *The Mandrake*, in a new version by Wallace Shawn, arrived on December 7, and Wilford Leach's staging was called "racy and robust." The Ansky piece ran two months, the Machiavelli a little over five months.

After two hits last season, playwright Albert Innaurato began a gradual but definite decline into obscurity with his **Ulysses in Traction** (12-8-77, Circle). It is 1970, and while the cast of a college play rehearses inside a Detroit arts complex, a student riot rages outside the building. The play in rehearsal is a parody of a Vietnam War play written by an impotent graduate student (William Hurt), and the company consists of a cross-section of colorful academic types: the pompous head of the department and the tart-tongued student he is sleeping with, an alcoholic director, a flaming homosexual on the faculty, an over-intense student actor, and so on. The petty arguments at the rehearsal give way to the larger understanding that the artificial world of the theatre inside pales in comparison to the more dangerous demands of the real world outside.

Two Samuel Beckett plays were introduced to New York in the triple bill **Play and Other Plays** (12-14-77, Manhattan Theatre Club). Alan Schneider, the American Beckett expert, directed the three short works that included the previously seen *Play* (1-4-64). **Footfalls** showed a middle-aged woman, May (Suzanne Costallos), wandering the stage bent over and speaking to her invisible mother (Sloane Shelton), whose faint voice is heard over a microphone. May keeps asking that the carpet be taken up so that she can hear the sound of her own footsteps. **That Time** spotlighted an old, gray-bearded man (Donald Davis) who is half-asleep, dreaming and listening to three voices in his head: a child, a young man on the beach with his girlfriend, and an old man seeking shelter in the rain. The voices are his own, of course, and in the end the old man gives in to despair.

David Mamet's second new play this season, the "American fable" **The Water Engine** (12-20-77, Public: Martinson), was greeted with mixed reviews, from "a vivid theatrical experience reverberating in the mind like an echo mike" to "fitfully atmospheric but basically false." The long one-act was a play-within-a-play. The cast of a radio program gathers in a studio in 1934 and "reads" the tale of Charles Lang (Dwight Schultz), a factory worker who has invented an engine that runs on distilled water. He hopes to sell his invention and secure the future for his sister (Penelope Allen) and himself. But Lang is no match for the sinister forces of big business. Crooked lawyers try to buy his invention from him, and when he refuses to sell they threaten him. So Charles seeks out a journalist to print his story, but he and his sister are murdered first and the engine is destroyed. Fortunately, Charles has left blueprints with a science-minded boy (Michael Miller, Jr.) who may someday bring the invention to light. Audiences responded to the play, and after sixty-three performances Papp moved it to Broadway.

Papp's next entry, Thomas Babe's drama **A Prayer for My Daughter** (12-27-77, Public: Anspacher), also received mixed notices, although they leaned toward the negative ("preposterous case study" and "mired in gluey moral, ethical, and philosophical considerations"), but again audiences were responsive, and it was held over for sixteen weeks. In an urban police station late one night, two cops—the middle-aged boozer Francis Kelly (George Dzundza) and the younger, drugged-up Jack Delasante (Jeffrey DeMunn)—bring in two suspects in the murder of an old lady. The intellectual homosexual Simon Cohen (Laurence Luckinbill) and the drug addict Jimmy (Alan Rosenberg), who clings to him pathetically, are bullied, beaten, and ridiculed by the two cops as a series of desperate phone calls from Kelly's suicidal daughter interrupt the interrogation. In the end, the daughter shoots herself in the head before the police reach the house, Jimmy manages to get Kelly's gun but doesn't have the courage to use it, and the two suspects are sent off to the jail.

A series of revivals and transfers followed, the best being a well-acted, beautifully directed production of Eugene O'Neill's late play *A Touch of the Poet* (10-2-58) on December 28 at the Helen Hayes. Jason Robards was the boastful Irishman Con Melody, Geraldine Fitzgerald was his quietly suffering wife, and Kathryn Walker was his outspoken daughter. Also in the José Quintero–directed drama were Milo O'Shea and Betty Miller. Robards received the lion's share of the compliments, but most commentators agreed with Eder that O'Neill's script "was not one of his greatest but it has greatness in it." The revival ran 141 performances, long enough to show a profit. Last season's off-Broadway entry, Ron Ribman's *Cold Storage* (3-27-77), reopened at the Lyceum on December 29 with Len Cariou now co-starring with Martin Balsam as two mismatched terminal patients. The critics felt the play improved with Cariou's deft playing of the taciturn Richard Landau matching Balsam's colorful portrayal of Parmigian, though many still found the script's ending weak. The Broadway version ran 180 performances.

It was said that African-American actor Earle Hyman had played Othello more than any other living actor (including many performances in Norwegian while he lived in Scandinavia for eight years), and the Roundabout was wise to get him to do their January 3 revival, because aisle-sitters felt Hyman was the only saving grace in the lackluster production. Notices praised Hyman's keen, steady, and military-like Moor and, at the same time, noted his passion as well. Veteran critic Oliver commented, "He is the only

Othello in my experience who appears to love Desdemona more than himself." The revival was kept on the boards for ten weeks.

The American Place's only intriguing entry this season was Maria Irene Fornes's **Fefu and Her Friends** (1-6-78, American Place), though that was because of a gimmick rather than the writing. In the New England house of Fefu (Rebecca Schull) in 1935, eight women gather one spring day. Because of unspoken bonds and intricate relationships, the group soon splits up, and in twos and threes the women retreat to various parts of the house and garden. The audience also breaks up into small groups and follows certain characters to certain parts of the theatre to see specific plots develop. By the end of the play all are gathered back together. It made for an unusual evening of theatre (a forerunner of the participatory plays that would become popular a decade hence), but several critics pointed out that the gimmick wore out long before the play ended.

Because it marked Mary Martin's return to Broadway after a ten-year absence, Aleksei Arbuzov's **Do You Turn Somersaults?** (1-9-78, 46th Street) was particularly disappointing. (The Russian comedy-drama was more appropriately titled *Old Country* in London, where it starred Peggy Ashcroft and Anthony Quayle.) In a sanatorium on the Baltic coast, the lonely surgeon Dr. Rodion (Quayle) treats the spirited widow Lidya (Martin), who has a heart ailment. Lidya is a cheerful soul who recites poetry all night and is not above breaking into a song or dance on occasion. She has had a fulfilling life as an actress but also several hardships, such as a failed marriage and a lost son. After much coaxing, Lidya gets Rodion to open up, and he tells how his wife died as an army surgeon during the war. The two fall into an autumnal romance, with the sprightly Lydia teaching the doctor about optimism in the world. While the critics were politely complimentary to the two stars, they uniformly dismissed the play as "tedious," "trivial," and "saccharinely obvious." The engagement was announced for ten weeks but closed after two, losing its entire $400,000 investment.

Simon Gray's British play **Molly** (1-11-78, Hudson Guild) was based on an actual murder case in England in 1936. The lonely Molly (Tammy Grimes) has married a Canadian (Michael Higgins) thirty years older, only to feel more discontented than she was before. When she takes up with the gardener, Oliver (Josh Clark), she is only looking for sexual and emotional comfort. But Oliver is obsessive about Molly and, in a moment of passion, murders her old husband with gardening shears. Molly tries to take the blame for the crime, but the court finds out the truth, and Molly is alone once more.

Another import, this one from Canada, was David French's **One Crack Out** (1-12-78, Marymount Manhattan), a slice-of-life look at small-time grifters in a Toronto pool hall. A has-been pool hustler, Charlie Evans (Kenneth Welsh), is deep in debt, so he and his pals hustle unsuspecting players while the sadistic collector Bulldog (Al Freeman, Jr.) is out looking for him. When Bulldog (who has had a fling with Charlie's wife) catches up with him, Charlie challenges him to a billiards game; if he wins the debt is erased, but if he loses Bulldog will break his hands. The curtain falls just as the decisive game begins.

The first of the Broadway season's two one-night flops was Gus Weill's misguided melodrama **The November People** (1-14-78, Billy Rose). Mitch (Cameron Mitchell), the Chief Finance Officer for the state, has been in prison for eighteen months for taking kickbacks. (He was up for twenty years but bribed the judge.) When he is released, Mitch expects a grand homecoming party, but no one shows up except his family: his long-suffering wife, Mary (Jan Sterling); his elder son, Brian (James Sutorius), who is a press secretary for the governor; his younger pill-popping brother, Donny (John Uecker), who believes himself a poet; and Brian's estranged wife, Kathleen (Pamela Reed), who left him because she hates all the low-grade political graft the family is involved in. Among the disappointments, accusations, and revelations that follow, it is learned that Brian has been having an affair with the governor's wife, and Mary has to tell Brian that the governor is his real father.

There was plenty of Shaw this season on and off the Street, and the man himself stopped in town for three weeks as part of a tour of Michael Voysey's one-man show **My Astonishing Self** (1-18-78, Astor Place). Irish actor Donal Donnelly portrayed GBS as he spoke on various matters, the text taken not from his plays but from his essays, letters, prefaces, and radio and television interviews. Critics approved of the portrayal and the show. Curiously, few remembered that Voysey had presented a very similar piece called *By George* (10-12-67), in which Max Adrian played Shaw, on Broadway and had been rejected by the press.

Another historical figure was featured in Romulus Linney's **Old Man Joseph and His Family**

(1-18-78, BAM), a folk-tale version of the story from the New Testament. When longtime widower Joseph (Lou Gilbert) is forced by the law to take a new wife, he weds the much younger Mary (Jacqueline Cassel), and soon after she gives birth. Joseph accepts the son (Peter Scolari) and puts up with his rebellious teenage ways; later the even advocates the boy's unusual "tricks." Chelsea Theatre Center's artistic director, Robert Kalfin, staged the tale in a freewheeling *Godspell* style. The folk play ran three weeks in engagements in Brooklyn and at the Westside in Manhattan.

Still another historical figure arrived on Broadway the next night with Phillip Hayes Dean's **Paul Robeson** (1-19-78, Booth). James Earl Jones played the famous African-American actor-singer, and Lawrence Brown was Robeson's longtime accompanist Burt Wallace. The play's setting was a seventy-fifth birthday tribute at Carnegie Hall, where Robeson tells stories, has imaginary conversations with family and friends, chats with Wallace, and sings a few songs. Robeson's life, from his days as an All-American at Rutgers to his final years as a recluse in Philadelphia, was touched on in bits and pieces, but little of it was acted out. Just as the subject (Robeson had died the previous January) had been so controversial, so too the play stirred up some controversy: some black groups protested the production for what they considered factual inaccuracies, and several prominent African Americans took out a two-page ad in *Variety* claiming that Robeson was diminished "from Revolutionary heroic dimensions to manageable sentimentalized size." Critics applauded Jones, though most felt his singing was not near the quality of Robeson's. The drama ran forty-five performances before joining *for colored girls . . .* in repertory for an additional thirty-two showings.

The same night, the Negro Ensemble added Gus Edwards's **Black Body Blues** (1-19-78, St. Marks) to a repertory with his earlier *The Offering*. The ex-boxer Arthur (Samm-Art Williams) now works as a butler for a wealthy white man and lives quietly in his Times Square–area apartment with his girlfriend, Joyce (Catherine E. Slade), who is both a drug addict and a prostitute. Into their relatively peaceful lives come Arthur's brother Andy (Norman Bush) running from the police, Joyce's demanding drug supplier Louis (Frankie R. Faison), and the blind old Fletcher (Douglas Turner Ward) from upstairs. The results include predictable family friction as well as violence and mayhem. Critics thought the play

"thin" and "patchy" but, as was usually the case at the Ensemble, the acting and directing (Ward staged both plays) expert.

Michael Jacobs's sex farce **Cheaters** (1-15-78, Biltmore) was considered old-fashioned by all the reviewers, some meaning it as a compliment, others as a criticism. (Brendan Gill in *The New Yorker* called the twenty-two-year-old Jacobs "the most uninteresting playwright of the year.") Although Michelle (Roxanne Hart) and Allen (Jim Staskel) have been living together for over a year, Allen is very hesitant about getting married. Michelle confides in her father, Howard (Lou Jacobi). Both of them are unaware that Monica (Rosemary Murphy), the woman he is cheating with, is Allen's mother. Allen's father, Sam (Jack Weston), says he spends his Friday nights playing poker; Monica claims her Fridays are canasta nights. In reality, they are having a tryst on Fridays. Howard suggests the two sets of parents have dinner with the young couple and share the wisdom of their experiences. But when they do all is exposed. Everyone accuses everyone else of loose morals, and Allen's mother, Grace (Doris Roberts), ends up singing "Bali Ha'i" as the young couple agree to make a better marriage than their elders have. Some fine comic acting couldn't keep the comedy on the boards any longer than four weeks.

A double bill of dramas from South Africa, previously seen in London, opened off Broadway. Steve Wilmer's **Scenes From Soweto** (2-1-78, Manhattan Theatre Club) told of a South African mathematics professor (Robert Christian) at Oxford who has avoided politics all his life. But when he returns to Johannesburg he is sucked into a race riot in the ghetto of Soweto and is strangled by a white policeman. Athol Fugard's **Statements After an Arrest Under the Immorality Act** was the focus of the evening. Although it is forbidden by South Africa's Immorality Act, the "colored" school principal Errol Philander (Robert Christian) and the white librarian Frieda Joubert (Veronica Castang) have fallen in love and have slept together. When a white woman who has been spying on them calls the police, the couple is visited by Detective-Sergeant DuPreez (John C. Vennema). During the interrogation they lose their dignity and self-respect, and their love for each other is crippled beyond repair. The critics felt the Wilmer piece was preachy and obvious, but the Fugard play was proclaimed quite powerful and moving.

Tina Howe's ambitious **Museum** (2-7-78, Public: LuEsther), an entertaining attack on art snobs and artists, was a slice-of-life play about the last day of a museum exhibit in a major art gallery. The works of three contemporary American artists are on display as forty-four characters come and go, including art lovers, skeptics, students, strays, foreign tourists, artists, and so on. The visitors reveal some part of their own vision and a little of their own dreams as they enter, comment on the art, and then move on. The play ended with the museum guard (Larry Bryggman) stepping out for a few moments and some visitors destroying the soft human sculptures that are hanging from a clothesline. Critical reaction was mixed, from "a sharply comic theatrical essay" to "overextended and shapeless," but Howe was a playwright worth watching, and audiences did so for ten weeks.

The BAM Theatre Company's revival of *The Devil's Disciple* on February 8 also received mixed reviews, but Shaw's Revolutionary War comedy of ideas was also worth watching. Frank Dunlop directed the piece as a farce, and there were complaints about the broad acting, but everyone agreed that George Rose made a dandy General Burgoyne. The fine cast also included Chris Sarandon, Carole Shelley, Barnard Hughes, and Margaret Hamilton. The Circle Repertory's revival of *Lulu* the next night was an odd choice for the company, which usually emphasized new American works. The German play, like Alban Berg's opera, was actually Wedekind's plays *Earth Spirit* and *Pandora's Box* combined. Rob Thirkield staged it as a circus with a ringmaster introducing characters and scenes. The critics found both the script and the production rather trying.

Sam Shepard was moving away from absurdism and into a heightened kind of realism with **Curse of the Starving Class** (2-14-78, Public: Newman), but the effect was nonetheless puzzling and disturbing. A family on a western farm has enough food to eat, but they are starving all the same, longing for something which is unknown or unattainable. The ragged father, Weston (James Gammon), who owes money to the mob since he was cheated on a land deal, drinks a lot and disappears often, while his slatternly wife, Ella (Olympia Dukakis), dreams of selling off the farm and going to Europe. The precocious thirteen-year-old daughter, Emma (Pamela Reed), is restless for life to start, and the son, Wesley (Ebbe Roe Smith), is emotionally numb but tries to keep the family intact. Emma is killed when some of Weston's creditors blow up the family car, and then father and son exchange personalities. Eventually Weston sobers up and tries to

take control of his world while his wife falls asleep on the kitchen table. Wesley, on the other hand, goes berserk, gorging himself on all the food in the refrigerator, from raw meat to whole heads of lettuce, and goes so far as to butcher the pet lamb and smear his own body with its blood in some kind of ritual cleansing. Reviews were a very mixed bag, with Barnes summing up the general feeling when he called the play "ornate, opaque, at times almost tauntingly ineluctable, gory, explicit, but it had the quality of statement about it."

The season's longest run (in fact, the longest-running thriller in Broadway history) was Ira Levin's **Deathtrap** (2-26-78, Music Box), a five-character, one-set, tight little thriller with both chills and laughs. It is exactly the kind of play author Sidney Bruhl (John Wood) wishes he could write, because he hasn't had a hit in seventeen years and is weary of living off the considerable wealth of his wife, Myra (Marian Seldes). Then one day he gets a script in the mail from a student at a seminar he taught; it is called *Deathtrap*, and it has success written all over it. Sidney invites the youth to the house that night and tells him to bring the original of the script (the only other copy) and they will collaborate on it. But Sidney confesses to Myra that he will murder the young writer if that's the only way to make *Deathtrap* his. When the writer arrives, a personable young man named Clifford Anderson (Victor Garber), the three get along well. Sidney shows off his collection of weapons, and Myra toasts the new collaboration with drinks. But Clifford feels the play is in pretty good shape as it is and decides to show it to some producers before rewriting any of it. Once he has confirmed that Clifford told no one where he was going tonight, Sidney strangles the boy and drags the body out into the garden and buries it. Myra, who has a weak heart, survives the ordeal, and she and Sidney are about to commence lovemaking when Clifford reenters, covered with dirt, and attacks Sidney. The strain is too much and Myra drops dead, which is exactly what Sidney and Clifford have planned, having been lovers for some time and needing to get their hands on Myra's wealth. Of course there is no money-maker script, but Clifford, who has moved in, begins to write a thriller based on Sidney's plan. The older writer finds out and is aghast, and the two engage in a deadly cat-and-mouse game, resulting in Sidney shooting Clifford with a medieval crossbow and the wounded Clifford stabbing the older writer to death as he tries to call the police for help. A brief coda scene showed the local clairvoyant, Helga Ten Dorp (Marian Winters), who had made a few appearances forecasting danger earlier in the play, and Sidney's attorney, Porter Milgrim (Richard Woods), both suspecting how the double murder occurred and fighting over Clifford's *Deathtrap* manuscript. Considering the subsequent success of the play, it is interesting how many negative reviews it received: "a series of endings that keep taking over each other" and "a trashy play"; as Edwin Wilson in the *Wall Street Journal* pointed out, "there is so much emphasis on reversals that there is little time to get to know the characters well enough to care about them." But audiences agreed with the notices proclaiming "a literate, amusing" play and "an ingenious comedy-thriller." Wood's diabolical performance certainly helped, but *Deathtrap* was just as popular with his many replacements.

The same evening, Ferenc Molnár's *The Play's the Thing* (11-3-26) was revived at BAM, and once again George Rose, as the actor Almady, walked off with the best notices. The critics liked Dunlop's frantic staging this time, and although the rest of the cast was thought by some to be uneven, the old comedy was heartily approved of.

David Mamet's *The Water Engine* transferred to Broadway, and to fill out the evening the playwright wrote a short curtain raiser called **Mr. Happiness** (3-6-78, Plymouth). On a 1930s radio show, Mr. Happiness (Charles Kimbrough) reads sob letters from "lonely hearts" and gives moralistic and sometimes dangerous words of wisdom to his troubled listeners. The move from Off Broadway was perhaps too precipitous; the double bill received mixed notices and closed in two weeks.

There had always been complaints about the limitations of the uptown Circle in the Square stage in regard to proscenium shows, and they were voiced once again when Feydeau's *13 Rue de l'Amour* opened there on March 8 and critics asked how one could do a bedroom farce without walls and doors. Written in 1892 as *Monsieur Chasse*, the comedy had been produced as *The Sportsman* (2-14-1893) with the characters' names changed. Louis Jourdan was quite appealing as the roving husband, and Patricia Elliott was applauded as his wife. The comedy overcame its mixed reviews and ran ninety-eight performances.

Two of the Circle Repertory's favorite playwrights were featured in a double bill called **Two from the Late Show** (3-9-78, Circle); each had been briefly shown the previous fall at the Circle's off-off-Broadway "Late Show" series. Lanford Wilson's **Brontosaurus** was about a cynical, sophisticated antiques dealer (Tanya Berezin) and her taciturn, theologian nephew (Jeff Daniels), who attempts to explain a mystical experience he has had. John Bishop's **Cabin 12** was thought to be the better script. When a young truck driver, a former high school football star, dies in a road accident in Virginia, his father (Edward Seamon) and brother (Jonathan Hogan) come to make funeral arrangements and put up at a small motel. The situation forces the father and son to reevaluate their strained relationship, and they arrive at the realization that the death was not an accident but an escape from a life of disappointment.

Richard Nelson, an American playwright who would always be more appreciated in England than in his homeland, met with negative reviews for his **Conjuring an Event** (3-10-78, American Place). The overwrought reporter Charlie (Michael Cristofer) wants to break the bounds of ordinary journalism: he not only wants to cover an event, he wants to create it as well. His girlfriend, Annabella (Sigourney Weaver), and his brother, Smitty (Dan Hedaya), try to get Charlie to ease off, but he brushes them aside and sets out to make news. What results is a fantasy-like riot in which Annabella and Smitty are killed and Charlie, bloody and bruised, stands victoriously successful in his goal.

It was perhaps too soon for a revival of Paul Zindel's prizewinning drama *The Effect of Gamma Rays on Man-in-the-Moon Marigolds* (4-7-70), for the Broadway production starring Shelley Winters on March 14 at the Biltmore only lasted two weeks. While reviews were not disapproving, neither were they "money" notices. Winters found all the humor in the monstrous Beatrice but little of the pathos and none of the subtlety. On the other hand, Carol Kane was lauded as the shy Tillie.

No other Broadway entry received such hostile reviews as Stuart Ostrow's **Stages** (3-19-78, Belasco), and none closed more quickly. The surreal play was divided into five separate playlets, each named after one of the five steps of reaction that the dying go through: Denial, Anger, Bargaining, Depression, and Acceptance. Jack Warden played the central character in each segment: a man testifying before an Un-American Activities Committee, a playwright in his press agent's office listening to terrible reviews of his play, a Greek tycoon on his yacht having trouble seducing his new young wife, a guest in a hotel assaulted by doctors and various hotel staff members, and a haberdasher who dies and leaves his partner to watch the store. Avant-garde director Richard Foreman didn't help matters with bizarre touches such as amplified heavy breathing throughout, and Douglas W. Schmidt's expensive set of gleaming white vinyl panels that moved into different configurations only enhanced the waste of money and talent. The only noteworthy remnant of the "lugubrious vaudeville" was Maurice Sendak's logo design (a lion in eighteenth-century garb) that was the finest poster art of the season and became a collector's item.

A commercial venture off Broadway that eventually turned a profit was the revival of James Kirkwood's comedy *P.S. Your Cat Is Dead* (4-7-75) on March 22 at the Promenade. The original production had only lasted two weeks, but Kirkwood revised the script and cut it from a seven-character play to a quartet. The reviewers still found the piece wanting, but this time audiences enjoyed it, and the comedy ran 301 performances.

Papp had so many shows running at the Public this spring that he presented Istvan Orkeny's gentle Hungarian drama **Catsplay** (4-5-78, Manhattan Theatre Club) at another company's theatre. The high-strung widow Ersi Orban (Helen Burns) lives in her untidy Budapest apartment and still feels like a child, writing her wheelchair-bound sister, Giza (Katherine Squire), in Germany and idolizing an egocentric opera singer, Victor Vivelli (Robert Gerringer). When Ersi's neighbor and best friend, Paula (Jane Cronin), a dentist's widow, steals Victor away from her, Ersi fantasizes about committing suicide and even views her own funeral; but in the end decides to continue on with life. The critics felt the play was too long and too slight but admitted to its particular charm and cited Burns's performance as one of the season's best. After thirty-five performances at the Manhattan Theatre Club, *Catsplay* transferred to the Promenade, where it played an additional fifty-three times.

A new group calling themselves the New York Actors' Theatre debuted with Brecht's *Life of Galileo* on April 5 in a lecture room in Havemeyer Hall at Columbia University. The academic milieu was intentional; the didactic drama was presented as a scientific debate with blackboards covered with notes behind the action. The quality of the acting varied, but most commentators agreed that Laurence Luckinbill was a commanding Galileo. On the same night, the similarly named Acting Company presented another Brecht script, *Mother Courage and Her Children,* at the American

Place. (Both productions used Ralph Manheim translations.) The no-longer-novice troupe had matured in its acting, but several thought Alan Schneider's direction was static and humorless. Mary Lou Rosato was an accomplished Mother, and her children were played by Kevin Conroy, Jeffrey Hayenga, and Frances Conroy.

The most talked-about (and for many the most ridiculous) Shakespearean production of the season was BAM's *Julius Caesar* on April 7. Purposely casting against type, director Frank Dunlop turned the play upside down and presented a pathologically insane Caesar (George Rose), a chubby "Borscht Belt" Cassius (Richard Dreyfuss), a pipsqueak Marc Antony (Austin Pendleton), and a neurotic pawn of a Brutus (René Auberjonois). Some critics found it different and challenging but most thought it lacked heroism, political logic, and common sense. The Acting Company added *King Lear* to its repertory on April 9, and it was unconventionally cast as well, the thirty-year-old David Schramm playing the old king. Artistic director John Houseman directed, and Schramm offered a fiery, intellectual approach to the character.

Yet another one-man show about a historical figure was John Gay's **Diversions and Delight** (4-12-78, Eugene O'Neill), in which an aging Oscar Wilde (Vincent Price) lectures before a Paris audience in 1899, the year before his death. He entertains the crowd with his famous *bons mots*, often digressing into introspective monologues about his anguished life. While the notices took kindly to Price, they felt the premise was forced and the evening lacked theatricality. The program, part of a national tour, remained only thirteen performances.

There was much talk of money in Dick Goldberg's melodrama **Family Business** (4-12-78, Astor Place), and audiences found the subject satisfying enough to keep the play on the boards for a year. The Stein's family business is retail toy stores, and the patriarch of the family and the business is the widower Isaiah (Harold Gary), who lives in a big house in Beverly, Massachusetts. Of his four sons, Isaiah trusts his oldest, Bobby (Richard Greene), who works hard, and Phil (David Rosenbaum), a psychiatrist who is married with children. The youngest son, Jerry (Joel Polis), is the baby of the family and resolutely immature. Isaiah dislikes Norman (David Garfield) because he was driving the car in the accident that killed the mother. When Isaiah announces that he is very ill and wants to change his will and rearrange how the money will be distributed, Phil panics because he is deep in debt. Tempers flare up, Isaiah has a heart attack, and Phil delays in calling the doctor so that his father will die before any financial changes can be made. After the funeral the internal squabbling for money is complicated by Bobby's finding out that Jerry is gay, Phil's need to sell his own house to pay off debts and move back to the family home, and Norman's desperate need for acceptance by his brothers. Phil eventually confesses that he let his own father die, and the brothers agree to attempt to live together in peace for the sake of their mother's memory.

While Jack Heifner's *Vanities* (3-22-76) was approaching its third year off Broadway, his Broadway double bill **Patio/Porch** (4-13-78, Century) could not make it through its third week. On the backyard patio of a middle-class Texas home, Pearl (Fannie Flagg) is preparing a going-away party for her older sister, Jewel (Ronnie Claire Edwards), a beautician who is bored in the small town and wants to try her luck in the big city. As they set out the food and decorations, the two sisters reveal how different they are in their aspirations about life and realize how deep the emptiness that lies between them has become. In the second play, sickly old Dot (Flagg) sits on her ramshackle porch with her restless, spinster daughter, Lucille (Edwards), and complains about the heat. But the lack of warmth between the mean-spirited mother and frustrated daughter is what is really making them so discontent. Generally negative notices said the people were caricatures and the talk was tedious.

Two black dramas opened in succession, both intriguing in spots, both failing to hit the mark. The Negro Ensemble presented Lennox Brown's intimate drama **The Twilight Dinner** (4-14-78, St. Marks) about the loss of the revolutionary spirit of the 1960s, in many ways a black version of *Kennedy's Children*. Seventeen years after they participated in student riots at Columbia University, two former students meet in the back dining room of a swank Manhattan restaurant. Jimmy (Leon Morenzie) vowed to go south after graduation and fight the Jim Crow laws against his people. Instead he stayed in New York and is now an overpaid city employee working on civic housing projects that demoralize the inner-city tenants. Islander Ray (Reuben Green) had planned to go back to his native West Indies home after school and help the locals, but his political power on the island has been secured by promoting tourism and letting social reforms fall by the wayside. The two talk of their failed lives and failed

marriages, and as they long for their past dreams, it becomes clear they are really mourning for their lost youth. Both actors were riveting, but critics complained that the drama was all talk and no action, and several pointed out the cheap production values of the financially strapped company.

Richard Wesley's **The Mighty Gents** (4-16-78, Ambassador) had originated off-off Broadway but was substantially rewritten and retitled and brought to Broadway by the Shubert Organization. Perhaps more suited for Off Broadway, it only survived nine performances in the big house. The street gang of the title had once been a force to be reckoned with in the Newark black ghetto. But now the gang members are all in their thirties and scattered, each a failure of some kind. The remnants of the Gents include the alcoholic Zeke (Morgan Freeman), the flashy small-time racketeer Braxton (Howard Rollins, Jr.), and the ex-leader Frankie (Dorian Harewood), who believes the gang will rise again. In a desperate attempt to do this, Frankie gets together some members and plans a robbery of Braxton's mob-earned cash. But the raid goes awry, Braxton is killed, and Zeke destroys their brief moment of victory with a searing monologue about dissipated street bums like himself who are going nowhere and can be ignored but not dismissed because they are reflections of what the Mighty Gents have become. Notices ran the gamut, but Freeman received raves.

The Roundabout's revival of George Kelly's *The Show-Off* (2-5-24) on April 25 received mixed notices, but most agreed that veteran Polly Rowles made a fine Mrs. Fisher and that Paul Rudd displayed the necessary jauntiness as the title character. The comedy was held over for eighty-nine performances.

Lanford Wilson's best play since *The Hot l Baltimore* (3-22-73) and the first work in his planned *Talley Trilogy* was the Chekhovian drama **The Fifth of July** (4-27-78, Circle). The legless Vietnam vet Ken Talley (William Hurt) lives on his ancestors' Missouri farm with his lover, Jud (Jeff Daniels), a quiet horticulturist. For the Fourth of July weekend they are joined by Ken's sister, Ruth (Joyce Reehling), a former activist with a teenage daughter, Shirley (Amy Wright); their elderly Aunt Sally (Helen Stenborg), who has come to the farm to spread the ashes of her late husband; an old friend, John (Jonathan Hogan), who is in the record business with his wife, Gwen (Nancy Snyder), a pill-popping heiress trying to become a rock singer; and drugged-out guitarist Weston

(Danton Stone), who believes in UFOs and any other strange aspect of life. Gwen loves the farm and wants to buy it and turn it into a recording studio. Ken is willing to sell because he fears going back to teaching at the local high school since his legs were amputated and wants to move away. But Jed, who is planting an elaborate English garden on the grounds, and June want Ken to keep the house and give teaching a chance. Over the weekend some old accusations arise, such as the reasons John abandoned Ken and how he was drafted, and by the fifth of July, Ken decides to keep the farm and try teaching again. Marshall W. Mason directed the flawless ensemble, and with appreciative reviews, the play ran five months.

The Broadway season's final non-musical entry, Hugh Leonard's Irish family comedy-drama **'Da'** (5-1-78, Morosco), was the most acclaimed new play of the season, winning the New York Drama Critics Circle and Tony awards. Charlie (Brian Murray), a successful London playwright, returns to Dublin for the funeral of his foster father (Barnard Hughes), hoping to bury many irritating memories along with the body. But after the ceremony he returns to the family kitchen only to see (and hear) the ghost of Da stubbornly sitting in his favorite chair, cracking jokes, and handing out his usual blarney. Together they recall (and argue about) events from the past, the teenager Young Charlie (Richard Seer) appearing for flashbacks with Mother (Sylvia O'Brien), his old friend Oliver (Ralph Williams), and his ex-boss Mr. Drumm (Lester Rawlins). Among the recreated incidents are Charlie's embarrassment about being an orphan and foisted off on others, his feeble old employer's feeble advice ("in a public-house lavatory, incoming traffic has the right of way"), and his futile attempt to seduce the "Yellow Peril" (Mia Dillon), the town's most voluptuous girl. But all of his memories and regrets seem to come back to Da, and Charlie realizes "love turned upside down is love for all of that" as he escapes the house and the ghostly figure promises to follow him. Previously seen in Dublin and then regionally, this Hudson Theatre Guild production was presented briefly off-off Broadway in March and rushed to Broadway. Hughes, Rawlins, and director Melvin Bernhardt all won Tonys, and the lovable play ran a year and a half.

On May 16 the Lyceum Theatre was officially designated a New York City landmark. The oldest operating legit house in the city, the Lyceum was the first to be so designated, which meant it could not be destroyed or altered without authorization.

Norman Fenton and Jon Blair's **The Biko Inquest** (5-17-78, Theatre Four) was a docudrama about the investigation into the death from brain damage of Stephen Biko while in a South African prison for distributing subversive literature. The lawyer Sidney Kentridge (Fritz Weaver) represents Biko's widow at the inquest, which had made headlines around the world the previous September, and shows that Biko had been beaten and purposely left unattended by the prison authorities. Using actual court transcripts, the play was noticeably lacking in drama (Douglas Watt in the *New York Daily News* called it "the dullest courtroom drama I have ever sat before"), and most critics felt that the epilogue, with Weaver reading the names of recent South Africans who had died mysteriously in custody, was more effective than anything that came before it.

At the season's end a notable playwright, Harvey Fierstein, was introduced with his long one-act **International Stud** (5-22-78, Players). The drag queen Arnold (Fierstein) has engaged in casual sex and brief flings for so long that he yearns for true affection and a long-term relationship. He seems to find it in Ed (Richard Dow), a bisexual he meets at a club called The International Stud. The romance grows, but Ed is afraid to commit and goes off to try women again. When he returns, Arnold tells him he cannot play his game of pretending, commenting, "I have never done time in the closet and I sure as hell ain't gettin' in one for you." Ed leaves and marries the woman he's been dating, and Arnold continues looking for true love. The simple boy-meets-boy tale was distinguished by a wry sense of humor (Arnold's intermittent commentary to the audience was hilariously truthful) and the compelling presence of Fierstein himself as the hero. The play ran two months and would reappear four years later in a popular Fierstein trilogy.

British playwright Stephen Poliakoff's melodrama **Strawberry Fields** (5-24-78, Manhattan Theatre Club) had been a moderate success at London's National Theatre but could not attract much attention here. The well-born Charlotte (Susan Sharkey) and the lower-class Kevin (Nicholas Woodeson) are both right-wing extremists who travel Britain's motorways collecting arms and ammunition at various stops. When they pick up a hitchhiker, the schoolmaster Nick (Brad O'Hare), the radicals' horrendous ideas about race and government are challenged.

The Ridiculous Theatrical Company opened an ambitious repertory of old favorites, including *Stage Blood* and *Camille*, on April 24. The one new entry in the rep, **The Ventriloquist's Wife** (5-25-78, One Sheridan Square), was a comic thriller about a ventriloquist (Ludlam), his wife (Black-Eyed Susan), and a wooden dummy named Walter Ego that starts to take on a life of its own. Adding other plays in the next season, the repertory ran through December.

The season ended with BAM's revival of *Waiting for Godot* on May 31 featuring Sam Waterston (Vladimir), Austin Pendleton (Estragon), Michael Egan (Pozzo), and Milo O'Shea (Lucky). The absurdist classic was directed by Walter D. Asmus, the playwright's assistant when he staged the play in Berlin, and was announced as the authorized version. Some critics saw a "straightforward and instructive production," while others thought it "lifeless."

1978–1979

Fifteen new American plays opened on Broadway (the same number as last season), and while none was a runaway hit, a certain level of quality was maintained. Off Broadway saw an increase in native drama: thirty-eight entries, with its best offerings moving on to Broadway. Unlike the previous season, British imports stole much of the limelight; even the American-born playwright Bernard Pomerance's *The Elephant Man* was completely English in subject and origin. The most adventurous drama of the season was the musical thriller *Sweeney Todd, the Demon Barber of Fleet Street*. It also was very British in subject, and librettist Hugh Wheeler was a transplanted Englishman (composer/lyricist Stephen Sondheim was American). That there was more "drama" in a musical than in the non-musical entries spoke candidly of the season.

There were fewer revivals both on and off the Street (only five on Broadway and eighteen off Broadway), and only a few of them were noteworthy. Both Lincoln Center theatre spaces remained dark all season while that troubled organization once again was being reinvented in the boardroom. More encouraging, a section of 42nd Street west of Times Square was renovated, and a string of small off-off Broadway theatres there became known as Theatre Row. Despite much optimistic talk and plans, it would be another twenty years before the Broadway section of 42nd Street would be revitalized.

While more plays managed to run longer than usual, few showed a profit. The Broadway box-office gross rose another 20 percent, but the reason were long-running plays and musicals held over from previous seasons and the increase in ticket prices. *The First Monday in October* was the first to break the $20 top for a non-musical ticket, and most other Broadway offerings were not far behind. Off Broadway, no commercial ventures managed to break even by season's end (and only two ran long enough into the next season to show a profit), and many of the various theatre companies either cut back their seasons or found little reason to keep shows on the boards very long.

The season started promisingly with a solid commercial hit, Bernard Slade's comic and sentimental vehicle for film star Jack Lemmon entitled **Tribute** (6-1-78, Brooks Atkinson). (Otis L. Guernsey, Jr., included *Tribute* as one of the *Best Plays* of the previous season even though it officially opened in June.) The charming Scottie Templeton (Lemmon) has spent fifty years making friends, telling jokes, and having a good time. But the sometime PR man, sometime screenwriter now finds out that he has leukemia, and he wants to be on good terms with the only person who is not his friend: his grown son, Jud (Robert Picardo). The two meet to try to make amends, but the uptight Jud still blames his father for the ruined marriage that left him fatherless. Scottie's ex-wife, Maggie (Rosemary Prinz), hears of Scottie's illness and goes to him, and the two happily spend the night together. When Jud returns to his father's home to try to patch things up and sees his mother there in a slip, he is furious. But she tells him that Scottie is dying, and Jud agrees to "stick around to see if there's anything about the son of a bitch I can admire." Father and son eventually reconcile; Jud even gets Scottie to go back to the hospital and take his medical treatments seriously. The play ends, as it had started, at a tribute to Scottie in a theatre with all his friends gathered to tell funny stories about this perennial Peter Pan, the last and most important guest being Jud. Lemmon had not been seen on Broadway since the short-lived *Face of a Hero* (10-20-60) and was welcomed back with rave reviews. Holly Hill in the *Wall Street Journal* noted, "It is difficult to believe that Jack Lemmon has been away from Broadway so long. His performance is so measured to theatrical size that he seems more a product of repertory than of film experience." But all the critics thought Slade's "sticky morass" of a play wanting, so the producers wisely closed it when Lemmon's contract ran out, managing a six-month run.

The Phoenix closed its 1977–78 season with Stephen Poliakoff's dark comedy **City Sugar** (6-1-78, Marymount Manhattan), which had attracted some attention in Britain. The Leicester disc jockey Leonard Brazil (Jeff Goldblum) is full of bitterness and hate, and it shows in his on-the-air spiel and in his private monologues. When Leonard runs a quiz contest on the air, a supermarket clerk, Nicola (Christine Estabrook), is a finalist, and though she answers the final question correctly, the cruel DJ cheats her out of the prize.

Gathering some encouraging reviews during its month-long run was the comedy **Bleacher Bums** (6-6-78, American Place) by Chicago's Organic Theatre. The script was "conceived" by Joe Mantegna but, in true Organic fashion, actually developed and written by the company. The bleachers are those of Chicago's Wrigley Field, and the "bums" are a group of hard-core Cubs fans who are rooting their team to victory over the St. Louis Cardinals. They include an optimistic cheerleader, a blind old man who follows the game by transistor radio, a bathing beauty called Melody King, a baseball nerd, and a deceitful cad named Marvin who always bets against the Cubs, figuring he can't lose. The fans watch the game but are just as interested in a little betting among themselves, eating and drinking, and trying to score with Melody. The Cubs lose the game in a ninth-inning flub, Marvin makes out like a bandit, and the disgruntled fans depart, agreeing to meet at the next home game.

The Yale Repertory Theatre brought two productions to the Public this season, both garnering excellent reviews. The first, an evening of four Molière one-acts under the umbrella title *Sganarelle*, opened on June 7 and offered *The Flying Doctor, The Forced Marriage*, the title comedy, and a clever version of *The Doctor in Spite of Himself*, here called *A Dumb Show* and performed as a pantomime with the actors speaking gibberish and placards held up for crucial pieces of information. Director Andrei Serban took "a gymnastic approach to the material," but the cartoonish fun pleased audiences and critics for its two-week engagement. On Broadway, an American farce brought the uptown Circle in the Square 1977–78 season to a close with a hit. Kaufman and Hart's Hollywood spoof *Once in a Lifetime* (9-24-30) was revived on June 15. John Lithgow, Treat Williams, and Deborah May were in fine form as the three New Yorkers who pose as voice experts during the early days of the talkies. The well-received comedy was held over for a total of eighty-five performances.

The Yale Repertory's second summer offering was Arthur Kopit's acclaimed drama **Wings** (6-21-78, Public: Newman), the unsentimental record of a stroke victim and her gradual recovery, told from the patient's point of view. The silver-haired Emily Stilson (Constance Cummings), an intelligent and independent woman in her seventies who was once an aviatrix and aerial stunt performer, sits reading in her room when the lamp flickers, furniture disappears, the ticking of the clock goes awry, and she is plunged into a world of strange noises and incomprehensible voices. The rest of the play chronicles the next two years as Emily attempts to understand the gibberish of her doctors and they try to translate hers. Emily learns to use language again through the help of the therapist Amy (Marianne Owen), leading to her breakthrough in both communication and self-discovery. While plunged into her nether world, Emily experiences vivid flashbacks of her flying days, and the metaphor of flight serves as a background to the struggle to recover. Some critics found the script limited, but most proclaimed Kopit (heretofore known mainly as an absurdist playwright) and his work "compelling" and "extraordinarily luminous," and Cummings received unanimously enthusiastic reviews, winning a Tony Award at season's end. *Wings* sold out its two-week engagement at the Public, then reopened on January 28 on Broadway, where it ran out the season at the Lyceum. A faithful musical version, also called *Wings*, ran off Broadway in 1993.

An off-Broadway curiosity that found an audience all summer long was **Crimes Against Nature** (6-22-78, Actors' Playhouse), a montage of scenes, statements, and movement about the difficulty of being gay and living in an anti-gay world. Like the earlier *Bleacher Bums*, it was written by its cast. It was presented by the Gay Men's Theatre Collective.

Joseph Papp brought Shakespeare back to the outdoor Delacorte in Central Park on June 29 with a satisfying production of *All's Well That Ends Well*. Wilfred Leach directed a gifted cast that included Mark Linn-Baker (Bertram), Elizabeth Wilson (Countess of Rousillon), Remak Ramsay (King of France), Larry Pine (Parolles), and Frances Conroy as both Isabel and Diana. A week later Papp sponsored a Juilliard production of Frank Wedekind's expressionistic fable *Spring Awakening* at the Public on July 7. The 1891 play was adapted from the German by British playwright Edward Bond, and Romanian avant-gardist Liviu Ciulei directed and designed the theatrical piece about youth and its sexual and political awakening.

Playwright Louis LaRusso II, who had been providing flop melodramas annually, came up with two this season, each still receiving a critical drubbing but each running over the 100-performance mark. The first was the domestic drama **Momma's Little Angels** (7-20-78, Quaigh). The Mastice family gathers in their home after the funeral of their mother and exchange fond memories with Aunt Tillie (Mimi Cecchini) and the family doctor, Carillo (Raymond Serra), who attended Momma during her final illness. But after the doctor leaves, the daughter, Patsie (Janet Sarno), tells her brothers, Larry (David Proval) and Tony (Matt Landers), that she is convinced that the mother died through the doctor's deliberate neglect. The brothers and aunt are disbelieving at first, but Patsie convinces them that the doctor's actions have been dictated by their estranged father, now a powerful underworld figure. The brothers wring the truth from the doctor and then set out to revenge themselves upon the real culprit: the absent father who abandoned them years ago.

The second Shakespeare Festival entry outdoors was the popular *The Taming of the Shrew* on August 3. Again Wilford Leach directed, and Papp-created stars Raul Julia and Meryl Streep played the battling lovers with great gusto.

On August 9 the major New York newspapers went on strike, and publication was not resumed until November. In the past such an event would have been crippling to the New York theatre, but because of television, the impact was not as strongly felt. *Variety* reported that box-office grosses did not fall drastically, and the new shows that opened during the next three months contained the usual percentage of hits and misses.

But the newspaper strike certainly did not help **Players** (9-6-78, Lyceum), a drama by the popular Australian playwright David Williamson, which lasted only twenty-two performances despite favorable, if not rave, reviews. In the boardroom of a professional football team in Australia, politics rather than sports is the source of dramatic fireworks. The main confrontation is between the coach, Laurie Holden (Rex Robbins), once a champion manager but now quickly waning, and the ruthless business manager, Gerry Cooper (Gene Rupert), a cold Machiavellian who cares nothing for the game and sees only the market value of teams and players. Also caught up in the

broil are the president, Ted Parker (Thomas A. Carlin), an arrogant new player, Geoff Hayward (Michael O'Hare), who was purchased at a high price and has turned out to be less than satisfactory, and the touchy vice-president, Jock Riley (Fred Gwynne), who was once a star player and head coach and is jealous of any upstart who might eclipse his former glory. The issue at hand is Gerry's plan to oust Laurie and bring in a new high-priced coach. Riley is for the plan and is even prepared to reveal a squalid sexual misadventure in Parker's past to gain favor. But the lovers of the game eventually win out, and the club survives the meeting until next time.

British actor Alec McCowen brought a successful one-man show from London to Off Broadway, presenting what Walter Kerr in the *Times* called "the unlikeliest evening in town this fall and one of the most provocative and most riveting." His colleagues agreed, and **St. Mark's Gospel** (9-7-78, Marymount Manhattan) became the surprise critical hit of the season. On a bare stage with only a table and three chairs, McCowen delivered the full text of the King James version not as a preacher or reciter but as an enthusiastic storyteller. The two-hour program was not read but memorized and acted out, never settling for theatrics beyond the power of the words themselves. The two-week engagement quickly sold out, and McCowen repeated it for eighteen more performances starting on October 24 at the Playhouse on Broadway.

Although it would not enjoy the same level of success it had with last season's '*Da*' (5-1-78), the little off-off-Broadway Hudson Guild Theatre (now classified as Off Broadway) premiered another highly satisfying comedy-drama, Ernest Thompson's **On Golden Pond** (9-13-78, Hudson Guild). Norman (Tom Aldredge) and Ethel Thayer (Frances Sternhagen) have been coming to their summer cottage on Golden Pond in Maine for many years, but curmudgeonly old Norman feels this summer is his last. He complains about old age, reads the classified ads as if he were searching for a job, and thinks a lot about death. "Nothing else quite as interesting," he tells his cheerful wife, who still has a childlike streak in her whenever she comes back to the pond. Norman's eightieth birthday is approaching, and the couple gets a surprise visit from their daughter, Chelsea (Zina Jasper), whom they haven't seen in several years. She brings along her new husband, middle-aged dentist Billy Ray (Stan Lachow), and his sassy young California son, Billy (Mark Bendo). Norman and Chelsea never got along very well (she calls him Norman but calls Ethel Mommy), and she is hoping to heal old wounds but has little success. Chelsea and Billy Ray go off on a late honeymoon, leaving young Billy at the cottage, and as a few weeks pass, Norman and the sprightly Billy hit it off. By the end of the summer, Norman's temperament has improved, but while packing to return home, he has a slight attack. He recovers quickly, but it scares the old man enough to knock some of the superiority and cynicism right out of him. The play ends with the old couple going out to say their annual good-bye to the pond until they return next year. Edith Oliver in *The New Yorker* wrote, "What courage it must have taken for Mr. Thompson, in the 1970s, to write a play with so much affection in it," and other critics applauded the gentle comedy as "an endearing hymn to old age" and "a work of rare simplicity and beauty." Both Aldredge and Sternhagen, decades younger than the characters they played, were also cheered. After thirty performances off Broadway, the play transferred to the New Apollo on February 28 and ran 126 more performances, returning yet again next season.

Dan Lauria's "clumsy" melodrama **Game Plan** (9-14-78, Theatre Four), one of the few commercial enterprises off Broadway this season, only lasted two weeks. Fred Ryan (Fred J. Scollay) of "Bakersville, U.S.A." has always planned on his athletic son John (Lauria) becoming the football coach at the local Catholic school. But when John, a U.S. Marine vet, returns from Vietnam bitter and disillusioned, he refuses, thereby shattering his father's dreams. The press declared the performances as weak as the script.

The Circle in the Square Uptown was turned into a true circle with Liviu Ciulei's theatre-in-the-round staging of Nikolai Gogol's *The Inspector General* on September 21. Max Wright played the hapless Khlestakov, Bob Balaban was his funny sidekick, and Theodore Bikel was the Mayor in this broadly played farce. Some critics thought it "more labored and frantic than humorously diverting," while others found it "performed with love and spirit." The ambitious off-Broadway Classic Stage Company offered Shakespeare's "Hollow Crown" trilogy in repertory at the Abbey during the fall. *Richard II* opened on September 24 and was joined by *Henry IV, Part 1* on October 8 and *Part 2* on October 22. On two occasions, all three plays were performed in sequence on one day. Stephen Joyce played Richard, and Christopher Martin (who also directed) was Falstaff.

Sherlock Homes returned to Broadway in a new thriller by Paul Giovanni entitled **The Crucifer of Blood** (9-28-78, Helen Hayes). In Agra, India, two British officers—Neville St. Claire (Nicolas Surovy) and Alistair Ross (Dwight Schultz)—steal a casket of priceless jewels, committing three murders in doing so and having a curse put on them. They sign a pact in blood not to reveal the circumstances of their wealth. Thirty years later in London, Irene St. Claire (Glenn Close), Neville's daughter, goes to Holmes (Paxton Whitehead) and Dr. Watson (Timothy Landfield) to find her missing father, now an opium addict and recently ranting about a curse. Their adventures take them to a gloomy Maidenhead country house where the decrepit Ross is murdered; a paper with a crucifer (an ancient cross design) is found on his body. Then the locale shifts to a Limehouse opium den where Holmes disguises himself as a Chinese drug lord and finds the murdered Neville. The melodrama climaxed with a boat chase on the Thames, where they catch up with the villainous Jonathan Small (Christopher Curry), who was duped by the two officers in India and has carried out his revenge. A subplot concerned a possible romance between Irene and Watson. Critical response wavered on the script, from "campy and confusing" to "captivating entertainment," but all concurred that Whitehead made an admirable Holmes. There was also agreement about John Wulp's atmospheric sets and Roger Morgan's dramatic lighting, in particular the exciting chase on the river with two Victorian yachts pushing through the dense fog. Audiences responded to the melodrama, and it ran six months, unfortunately not long enough for the expensive production to break even.

Jerome Lawrence and Robert E. Lee's **First Monday in October** (10-3-78, Majestic) ran only a third as long but did show a profit because Henry Fonda and Jane Alexander filled the large house for many of its seventy-nine performances. When one of the Justices of the Supreme Court passes away, there is much speculation as to whom the President will appoint to fill his place. There is consternation when the conservative, squeaky-clean Court of Appeals Judge Ruth Loomis (Alexander) is selected and, after some harsh interrogation, approved by the Senate. Her primary rival on the bench is the liberal free-speech advocate Judge Dan Snow (Fonda). The two butt heads immediately on a case about pornography and the First Amendment's right to protect acts, according to Dan, "which revolt us, repel us, disgust us, make us vomit." He loses that battle, and soon the two are embroiled in a patent case. The two antagonists develop a healthy respect for each other, despite the fact that they have opposite opinions on everything. In one heated argument, Dan suffers a heart attack and is rushed to the hospital. But on the day of the voting he shows up at the Supreme Court, ready and happy to fight Ruth on this and many other cases in the future. While many critics called the script "shallow" and nothing more than a vehicle, the acting was roundly commended. John Beaufort of the *Christian Science Monitor* summed up Fonda's unique appeal when he described how he "plays the venerable Snow with the kind of concentration and vitality that makes acting look easy." More than one critic complained about the miking of the play, seemingly unneccesary in a house that once presented unmiked musicals.

Eric Bentley, the respected critic and translator, scored an unlikely success with his **Are You Now or Have You Ever Been?** (10-15-78, Promenade), a docudrama about the infamous HUAC hearings in the 1950s in which show business figures were subpoenaed to testify as to their loyalty as Americans and asked to name Communists in their industry. The script was fashioned from the transcript testimonies of Abe Burrows (Frank Gero), Ring Lardner, Jr. (Benjamin Bettenbender), Elia Kazan (Tom Fuccello), Paul Robeson (Avery Brooks), Lillian Hellman (Colleen Dewhurst), and others. The dramatic highlight of the evening was the reading of Hellman's famous letter refusing to testify or tailor her political convictions to the fashion of the times. (Throughout the run such diverse guest stars such as Dina Merrill, Tammy Grimes, Peggy Cass, Louise Lasser, and Liza Minnelli made cameo appearances to play Hellman.) An unusual aspect of the low-budget production was Joseph J. Miklojcik's set design, which utilized white plaster dummies that sat among the real-life committee members at the hearing tables. The drama ran 129 performances off Broadway, then transferred on February 6 to the Century, where it had thirty-two more showings.

Jay Broad's **White Pelicans** (10-18-78, Theatre de Lys) was an attempt to tell the story of the Klondike gold rush through a conversation between two failed prospectors, strangers who converse while waiting for a boat to take them back to the States. The ragged Winston (Morgan Freeman) talks about how he cannot get the stench of dead mules out of his nostrils; the dapper, gentlemanly Harry (José Ferrer) recalls the Klondike loneliness that will haunt him all his life. While the acting could not have been finer, the talk was not dramatic enough to sustain a whole play, and the two-character piece lasted only fourteen performances.

The same night, a new off-Broadway theatre opened, the Harold Clurman on Theatre Row, with a revival of Eugene Ionesco's *The Lesson* (1-9-58). Critics liked the small, tidy new performance space but thought the entry a "boring, depressing production" with a miscast Joseph Wiseman as the sadistic Professor. On the other hand, Didi Conn, in her professional debut, was applauded for her portrayal of the unfortunate Young Pupil. Harsh reviews aside, the revival ran seven weeks.

The previous year, the American Theatre Critics Association initiated a new program whereby they voted for the best new play to come out of the regional theatres. The first winner was Marsha Norman's **Getting Out** (10-19-78, Marymount Manhattan), which had premiered at the Actors Theatre of Louisville in 1977. So when the Phoenix Theatre presented the New York production, expectations were high. For once, audiences and local critics were not disappointed. Richard Eder of the *Times* led the praise, calling the drama "a blaze of theatrical energy that lights up the Off-Broadway scene as nothing else has this season." It was Norman's first play and a sensational debut for the former social worker. When Arlene Holsclaw (Susan Kingsley) is paroled from prison (she was jailed for shooting a cab driver several years ago), she gets help moving into a dingy Louisville apartment from Bennie (Barry Corbin), a guard at the prison who has befriended her. Arlene wants to start fresh, but the image of her younger self, Arlie (Pamela Reed), a rebellious teenage prostitute always in trouble for her violent behavior, keeps appearing and taunts the older Arlene. A visit from her mother (Madeline Thornton-Sherwood) makes Arlene recall when Arlie was raped by her father. Her former lover/pimp, Carl (Leo Burmester), who is also the father of her son, Joey, now in a foster home, arrives and talks about the two of them going to New York and continuing where they left off. Bennie brings Arlene dinner and then gets amorous, treating her like the teenage slut she used to be. Arlene fights him, and only when she calls him a rapist does he stop. Arlene befriends a neighbor, Ruby (Joan Pape), who gets her a job cooking in a restaurant. Soon Arlene realizes that she doesn't need Carl or Bennie and that she has finally killed off the haunting Arlie. After the Phoenix's scheduled forty-one performances, *Get-*

ting Out was slightly recast and reopened on May 15 at the Theatre de Lys, where it ran an additional 237 times.

The prestigious Circle Repertory Company, which had a disappointing season until its last entry in May, opened with Patrick Meyers's domestic melodrama **Glorious Morning** (10-22-78, Circle). In a Catskill cottage, Sally (Tanya Berezin) is dying of cancer, attended by her weak-willed husband, Frank (Douglass Watson), a professor of philosophy. Their estranged son, Robbie (Jonathan Hogan), arrives on his motorcycle with his silent girlfriend, Alicia (Nancy Snyder), whose head is always buried in a book. Robbie says he is a pimp and a dangerous character, and he threatens to kill Frank to prove it. But his bluster eventually fades, and Robbie admits he is only a lowly worker at a hospital. After much bearing of souls (Sally even admits that she once slept with her own son), Robbie leaves and Frank crawls into bed with the dying Sally. The drama was roundly dismissed as "dismal" and "pretentious guff."

Broadway would see four one-night flops this season, the first being the curiously unsatisfying **Gorey Stories** (10-30-78, Booth), an assortment of weird characters from the dark Edwardian world of Edward Gorey's illustrated books. The tales were often humorous and horrid at the same time, sometimes taking the form of drawing room fables with inexplicably odd endings. Perhaps the most satisfying story was "The Unstrung Harp," a quasi-autobiographical tale about C. F. Earbrass (Leon Shaw), a writer of bizarre fiction, and the various stages of ennui and disappointment he goes through in writing and revising his new book, examining the proofs, and seeing the final published copies. While everyone enjoyed Gorey's designs (just as they had for the still-running *Dracula*), Gorey the writer was an acquired taste. Stephen Currens's adaptation and David Aldrich's psuedo-Edwardian songs could not manage to make the odd material palatable for Broadway audiences.

The Manhattan Theatre Club opened its season with British playwright Simon Gray's historical drama **The Rear Column** (11-7-78, Manhattan Theatre Club). In 1886, explorer H. M. Stanley, on his last African expedition, leaves some officers, under the leadership of Major E. M. Barttelot (Remak Ramsay), camped on the banks of the Arruimi River in the Congo while he heads into the Sudan to rescue what remains of General Gordon's command. The men are left there for a year and, under the sadistic reign of the paranoid Barttelot, the whole "column" is destroyed by malaria, starvation, snakebite, and even cannibalism. When Stanley (Edward Seamon) returns, only the sly medical orderly W. Bonny (Josh Clark) is still alive to greet him. Although critics felt it was a "literate, authoritative play" and that it received a "faultless production," most also found it "grim, sometimes gruesome, and generally oppressive."

The rewarding season at the Hudson Guild continued with a new 1930s-style farce, the kind director George Abbott used to excel at. In fact, they got the ninety-one-year-old Abbott to direct Lee Kalcheim's **Winning Isn't Everything** (11-8-78, Hudson Guild), the veteran's 119th New York production. In the hotel-room campaign headquarters for a senatorial candidate (who is never seen), campaign manager Sam Duffy (Byran E. Clark) and his cronies must try to get an endorsement from the racist, corrupt Congressman Jack Davis (Richard Kuss) before the election three days hence in order to carry the district. It does not help that the candidate's wife (Bobo Lewis) wants him to lose and is publicly asking for a divorce. Also damaging the campaign is Sam's assistant, P. J. Whittlesie (Marshall Purdy), who is always on the phone to his analyst in Boston. The crass Davis is interested in taking the young and pretty research assistant Kathy (Forbesy Russell) to Puerto Rico, but he eventually wheels and deals with Sam, and the endorsement comes on the eve of the election. While none of the reviews claimed that the new work held up to the vintage comedies of old, most found it agreeable enough, enjoyed the cast, and marveled at the still-evident "Abbott touch." The "admirable but undistinguished" comedy ran out its thirty scheduled performances and was rarely heard of again.

Papp's discovery Thomas Babe had two new offerings this season. The three-week "experimental" production of **Fathers and Sons** (11-10-78, Public: Other Stage) was about the final days of the legendary Wild Bill Hickok. In a Deadwood saloon, old and weak Bill (Richard Chamberlain) still holds a fascination for the locals until the arrival of Jack McCall (Tom McKitterick), a hot-tempered young desperado who claims to be Bill's illegitimate son and has come to kill him. Calamity Jane (Dixie Carter) prods Jack to vent his anger and talk about his bitterness toward Bill (in particular, the way Hickok abandoned Jack's mother). The old gunslinger does not resist Jack, who guns him down, desperately trying to connect with the man he both loves and hates.

Emlyn Williams took a break from portraying Charles Dickens and instead offered a one-man show called **The Playboy of the Weekend World**

(11-16-78, Playhouse), which he devised from the short stories of H. H. Munro (who wrote under the pen name of Saki). Williams told some dozen tales in a low-key and offhand manner that some commentators felt lacked dramatic interest. But other reviews thought it "mildly diverting entertainment," and a few even saw a "dazzling one-man multi-voiced entertainment." The engagement was limited to twenty-nine performances.

Celebrated novelist E. L. Doctorow tried his hand at playwriting with the talky drama **Drinks Before Dinner** (11-22-78, Public: Newman), which ran a controversial fifteen performances. Gathered in a chic Manhattan living room overlooking Central Park are three married couples and a single woman, all having cocktails while they await the guest of honor, the Secretary of State. The philosophical and talkative Edgar (Christopher Plummer) seems in an unusually gloomy mood as he talks about the end of the world. He then pulls out a gun, which he bought from a street punk when he was stalled in traffic on the way to the dinner party. Taunting the other guests with the weapon, Edgar "hijacks the living room" as the celebrated Secretary, Alan (Josef Sommer), arrives, having left his bodyguards down in the car. Alan, a winner of the Nobel Peace Prize, is in just as gloomy a mood, and Edgar sees him as a symbol of all the institutional horrors of civilized man. He ties Alan to a chair, and the two of them exchange philosophy, threats, and views on the futility of life. Then Edgar frees Alan, the guests relax, and the hosts' two young children enter to kiss everyone goodnight before going off to bed. The negative reviews declared the "talk . . . pretentious and basically dull" and the play "more like a Platonic dialogue." It must be noted that the critics were not in a very receptive mood; producer Papp, in a tiff over theatrical criticism in New York, scheduled the opening on Thanksgiving Day in order to inconvenience the aisle-sitters.

Playwright Leonard Melfi, a holdover from the brazen 1960s, came back with two new plays this season. The author's characteristic "affection for spiritual vagabonds" was in full force in the comedy **Porno Stars at Home** (11-28-78, Courtyard). For the birthday party of blue-movie star Georgia Lloyd Bernhardt (Tata Tyson), some of her porno film colleagues gather, and in the course of the celebration, each reveals his or her own fantasies: Uta Bergman-Hayes (Meg Wittner) wants to be a serious actress (so do they all), Norma Jean Brando (Jody Catlin) wishes she had a child, and the gay porno star Montgomery McQueen (Alan Brooks), who is really heterosexual, longs to be

able to play out that persona someday. The provocative title and some favorable reviews helped the play run eight weeks.

The Circle Rep garnered mixed notices, from "stale and unamusing" to "unusually witty," for James Farrell's **In the Recovery Lounge** (12-3-78, Circle), a slice-of-life drama that Marshall W. Mason directed with his usual talent for effortless movement and quiet character development. Six patients in a private Manhattan hospital are gathered together by the staff to talk about their ills, romances, and dreams. The lounge is dominated by the elderly John Zachs (Burke Pearson), a demanding man of indeterminate foreign nationality, who seems a charity case but turns out to be rather wealthy and prefers hospitals to luxury hotels. The wisecracking Ruth McGinn (Helen Stenborg) is the mother figure of the group with her orange-dyed hair and off-color jokes. The tough-talking Stanley Hauch (Jack Davidson) suffers from hemorrhoids, while the gentle, cultured Bill Colby (Nick Smith) is subjected to a life with his mean-spirited wife. The plumb and plain Alice Williams (Sharon Madden) is outwardly cheerful but painfully loves the loud and theatrical Jack Gerabauldi (Danton Stone), a cab driver who longs to be a professional actor and uses the lounge as his personal stage. Little happened plot-wise (except for the blossoming romance between Alice and Jack), but the talk was lively and the ensemble was admirable.

Sam Shepard's latest offering, **Buried Child** (12-5-78, Theatre de Lys), was similar to last season's *Curse of the Starving Class* (2-14-78) in subject and theme but was so much more vivid and satisfying that it was seen by most as an important step for this ever-emerging playwright. On a remote and squalid farm lives a family under a shadow of sin: the ranting, alcoholic grandfather, Dodge (Richard Hamilton); the innocent and simple-minded grandmother, Halie (Jacqueline Brooks), who goes on drinking bouts with the local minister (Bill Wiley); Dodge and Halie's son Tilden (Tom Noonan), a football star now disintegrating into a half-wit; and the other son, Bradley (Jay O. Sanders), who lost one of his legs in a chainsaw accident. The long-lost grandson, Vince (Christopher McCann), whom no one seems to remember, returns to the farmhouse with his girlfriend, Shelly (Mary McDonnell), who finds the odd ensemble bewildering and hypnotic. The family secret turns out to be a newborn baby that Dodge buried in a hidden spot on the farm many years ago. When Tilden eventually unearths the child's mummified remains and brings the body up to his mother, the family curse is exorcised, and the untainted Vince becomes the hope for the future. Notices ranged from "a haunting, wounded beauty, strong, sweet, sad, and totally dramatized" to a "dismal, unstructured exploitation of both our malaise and our patience." (Despite the Pulitzer Prize given to the play, Guernsey refused to include it as one of the ten *Best Plays* of the season.) The drama ran 152 performances and soon received many productions in college and regional theatres.

Three accomplished actors allowed a comedy that the critics called "paper thin," "wan and feeble," and "only rarely amusing" to run 182 performances and show a handsome profit. The play was William Douglas Home's London comedy **The Kingfisher** (12-6-78, Biltmore), and the three rescuing stars were Rex Harrison, Claudette Colbert, and George Rose. Fifty years ago Cecil (Harrison) proposed to Evelyn (Colbert), but she turned him down and married Reginald. Now Cecil is a famous novelist living comfortably with his fussy butler, Hawkins (Rose), who oversees every aspect of Cecil's ordered life. But when Reginald dies on the seventeenth hole of the golf course and is buried nearby, Evelyn stops by after the funeral to see Cecil and the old romantic flame is rekindled. Cecil proposes to Evelyn, Hawkins is miffed and gives notice, and Evelyn wavers back and forth in the moonlight. The morning comes, she accepts, and Hawkins swallows his pride.

The Negro Ensemble Company opened its season with its best offering, Steve Carter's enthralling drama **Nevis Mountain Dew** (12-7-78, St. Marks). In the Manhattan home of a proud West Indies family in 1954, Jared Philibert (Graham Brown) is crippled with infantile paralysis and is confined to an iron lung. He is tended to by his wife, Billie (Barbara Montgomery), and his sisters, the overprotective Everalda (Frances Foster) and the flirty Zepora (Ethel Ayer). Everalda, separated from her husband, Bushie, maintains the family superiority by bad-mouthing both Billie and Zepora's lover, Ayton (Arthur French), outsiders she considers beneath them. When Billie and two co-workers bring home a television set as a birthday present for the quarrelsome Jared, Everalda suspects that Billie is sleeping with one of them, the handsome Boise (Samm-Art Williams). At the troublesome birthday celebration tempers run high, and Billie admits that she and Boise are lovers but assures Jared that she will never leave him. Jared insists that all the lights be turned off and says that if anyone truly loves him, he or she will disconnect his respirator and

let him die. In the dark silence footsteps are heard, Jared recognizes who it is but the audience cannot, and the machine is turned off. After Jared's funeral, Zepora goes off with Ayton, Billie leaves with Boise, and the bitter Everalda, the house now to herself, calls out Bushie's name in frustration. Notices were commendatory (Guernsey included it as one of the ten *Best Plays*), and the Ensemble held the engagement over for sixty-one performances.

The American Place Theatre continued to showcase playwright Steve Tesich with his evening of three one-acts called **Touching Bottom** (12-10-78, American Place). *Road* was about two hitchhikers of opposing temperaments going in opposite directions. He is cynical and leaves the city with disgust; she is life-affirming and heads toward the city with high hopes. In *A Life*, a lonely old man recalls images of his past, mostly about his mother, and rails at the wretchedness of old age to his faithful dog, who, he does not yet realize, is dead. *Baptismal* concerns a widow and widower listening to an elegy in a country graveyard and, in flashbacks, reliving their past mistakes in marriage. Harold Gould and Lois Smith played all the roles, and their polished performances were much more appreciated than the scripts.

Artistic and administrative differences at the Chelsea Theatre Center in Brooklyn resulted in a new theatre organization, Dodger Theatre, which premiered with London's Royal Court hit **Gimme Shelter** (12-10-78, BAM), three interrelated plays by Barrie Keeffe about the compromises of rebellious youth in modern Britain. In *Gem*, four young renegades who work for a large corporation sit on the sidelines during the company's annual cricket match and sneer at the complaisant employees who play the bosses' game. But at the same time they wish they could be part of it, and one of them ends up joining the cricket game and scores the winning goal for the company. In *Gotcha*, an overlooked, bitter young man, called Kid (Keith Gordon) because no one can recall his name, takes two teachers and the headmaster (Kensyn Crouch) hostage in a supply room at the school holding a cigarette near the open fuel tank of his motorcycle and threatening to blow them all up. The female teacher (Judith Calder) slowly gains his confidence, but the gym teacher (Maury Chaykin) takes advantage of a momentary weakness to wrestle the Kid to the ground, beat him up, and send him off to a mental institution. The final play, *Getaway*, ties the two plots together. At the next year's annual cricket outing, the restless employees have all conformed and are playing the game. The Kid, released from the institution, works as a groundskeeper and has lost his rebellious spirit. When the disgruntled Kev (Richard Backus) finds out that the Kid is the student who made the news last year with his act of defiance, he praises him, calling him an inspiration for all his generation. But the Kid only wants to be left alone and forget the past. All the characters are now "playing the game," and the company wins the cricket match once again. Clive Barnes in the *New York Post* summed up the critical reaction with his announcement that "it is an evening of oddity but also an evening of power."

The Circle in the Square revived Shaw's *Man and Superman* on December 14 and included an abridged version of the *Don Juan in Hell* sequence that brought the evening to a three-and-a-half-hour running time. (A similar cutting had been used in an off-Broadway APA revival in 1964.) Stephen Porter directed a superior cast that included George Grizzard (Tanner), Ann Sachs (Ann), and Philip Bosco (Mendoza). The next night the Roundabout revived Shaw's *Candida* as part of its abbreviated season of two plays. The former comedy was greeted with mostly favorable comments and ran ten weeks; the latter received less favorable ones but was kept on the boards for fourteen weeks.

Perhaps the most unconventional one-man show all season was **An Evening with Quentin Crisp; or, The Naked Civil Servant** (12-20-78, Players), an extended monologue in which the homosexual celebrity Crisp spoke about his life over the past sixty years. Much of the material came from Crisp's autobiography, the source of the program's subtitle. Questions from the audience were encouraged, and they were forthcoming for eighty-one performances.

After the accomplished *Nevis Mountain Dew*, the rest of the Negro Ensemble season was rather lackluster. Judi Ann Mason's **The Daughters of the Mock** (12-20-78, St. Marks) was "a hollow gothic drama" about voodoo in rural Louisiana, where the malignant old Maumau (Frances Foster) practices the pagan rites with her daughter (Barbara Montgomery) and her granddaughters.

No more satisfying was Eduardo de Filippo's **Grand Magic** (12-26-78, Manhattan Theatre Club), a Pirandello-like comedy about illusions, reality, and cuckoldry. The down-on-his-luck magician Professor Otto Marvuglia (Fred Gwynne) helps the married Matilde (Vera Lockwood) escape from her rich husband, Calogero (Tony Mu-

sante), so she can run off with her lover. But then Otto is left with the sobbing Calogero for four years, their roles getting confused in a battle between what they recall and what really happened. The "skimpy play" was not well received.

A commercial revival off Broadway that struggled on for seventy-eight performances but still lost $46,000 was Frances Goodrich and Albert Hackett's *The Diary of Anne Frank* (10-5-55) on December 28 at Theatre Four. The production was a family affair with Eli Wallach as Mr. Frank, his wife, Anne Jackson, as Mrs. Frank, and their daughters, Katherine and Roberta Wallach, as sisters Margot and Anne. While notices were mostly affirming, Douglas Watt in the *New York Daily News* was not alone in his disappointment in the younger Wallach daughter in the pivotal role, calling the production "a generally engaging one even without a spark at its center."

Leonard Melfi's second offering was **Taxi Tales** (12-28-78, Century), five short plays that take place in or around five Manhattan taxicabs. The characters included the music-loving Toddy (Ken Olin), who listens to Stravinsky as he drives two hookers and their john to the airport; the lesbian cabby Taffy (Julie DeLaurier), who deals with curious tourists, sexually adventurous couples, and an aggressive lesbian fare who's out for action; the druggie Tripper (Al Corley), who finds incest going on in his back seat; the terminally ill Mr. Tucker (Michael Strong), whose wife accompanies him as he drives and whose cab is hijacked by a bank robber; and the innocent Teaser (Corley), who dreams of being a pop singer and helping all the hard-luck cases in Manhattan. The unanimously negative reviews called the evening "infantile" and spoke of its "strained humor," one commentator writing that Melfi was "suffering from a case of arrested development." The bill ran only six times.

The comedy team of John Monteith and Suzanne Rand, who had been honing their skills in comedy clubs and, earlier this season, during a trial run off Broadway, brought their improvisational program **Monteith and Rand** (1-2-79, Booth) to Broadway, where they received critical endorsement and ran ten weeks. Some of the sketches were prepared and set, but the most intriguing parts of the evening were those characters and situations suggested by the audience and improvised on the spot.

The Negro Ensemble's program of one-acts by Nigerian Obotunde Ijimere called **Plays From Africa** (1-10-79, St. Marks) featured two short allegorical plays about the interaction between men and gods. *Everyman*, like its European counterpart, was about a wealthy man who is deserted by his fair-weather friends when Death comes to call. *The Imprisonment of Obatala* concerned the battle between creativity and destruction waging inside a king who is ultimately crushed through the machinations of an old colleague. Both parables used dancing and drumbeats to accent their tales, but reviewers found the evening "monotonous and disappointing."

Like the Negro Ensemble, the Phoenix Theatre suffered a lackluster season after its vibrant opener, *Getting Out*. Corinne Jacker's domestic drama **Later** (1-11-79, Marymount Manhattan) dealt with the power men hold over the women in their lives even after they are dead. The recently widowed Molly (Pauline Flanagan) spends the Labor Day weekend with her grown daughters at a Rhode Island beach house where they discuss the mother's future. The older daughter, Kate (Louise Sorel), a frustrated secretary in Manhattan, wants her mother to sell the family house and move into the city to be close to her. The younger, Laurie (Dorothy Lyman), seems secure in life, married with children and living in St. Louis. But all three recall the oppressive father and realize they are still crippled by him: the bright and promising Kate letting male supervisors play the father role, and Laurie slipping into being a woman who exists only as a wife and mother.

The season's hit drama was Bernard Pomerance's **The Elephant Man** (1-14-79, St. Peter's Church), which, although based on historical facts, was contemplative, theatrical, and mystifying rather than in the documentary style that might be expected. In Victorian London, Dr. Frederick Treves (Kevin Conway) discovers the misshapen, seemingly retarded John Merrick (Philip Anglim) in a freak show and finds him a home in London Hospital, where he can be protected and studied. Merrick turns out to be unusually bright (he is seen intermittently working on his architecturally accurate model of St. Philip's Church) and also a great romantic (he discusses poetry fervently and intelligently). Treves opens up Merrick's social life, and with the help of the renowned actress Mrs. Kendal (Carole Shelley) who befriends him, the freakish man becomes a pet of Victorian high society. But his deformed exterior and his isolated heart are too much for him to bear; in despair he quietly commits suicide. Director Jack Hofsiss staged the twenty-one scenes fluidly on David Jenkins's stark Industrial Revolution setting, and an onstage cellist accompanied the action with haunting underscoring. Anglim played the deformed Merrick without any special makeup, suggesting the physically tormented body though evocative contorted poses and gestures. The critics were all adulatory, calling the dreamy work "enthralling," "sensitive, never sentimental," and "dangerously entertaining." The London play (Pomerance was an American residing permanently in England) ran seventy-three times off Broadway, then transferred on April 19 to the Booth, where it stayed for 916 performances. In addition to making a handsome profit, the play won the New York Drama Critics Circle Award, a Tony, and several other honors, and Hofsiss and Shelley also won Tonys for their efforts.

The Circle Rep rarely offered revivals but presented Milan Stitt's drama *The Runner Stumbles* (5-18-76) beginning on January 14 for a month. William Hurt was the parish priest; Joyce Reehling, the nun who falls in love with him.

Once again a new Tennessee Williams drama opened to mixed reviews and failed to find an audience. Critics thought **A Lovely Sunday for Creve Coeur** (1-17-79, Hudson Guild) was everything from "an exceptional excursion" to "rather ordinary" to "second-hand Tennessee Williams." In 1935, high school teacher Dorothea (Shirley Knight) lives in St. Louis with the plain but kindhearted spinster Bodey (Peg Murray) and romanticizes about marrying the school's principal, with whom she has an "understanding." Bodey, seeing in the morning paper that the principal is engaged to someone else, hides the news from Dorothea and tries to interest her in Bodey's overweight brother, suggesting they both join him that afternoon at Creve Coeur, the local amusement park. But Helena (Charlotte Moore), an overbearing art teacher from the school, enters and wants Dorothea to move into an apartment with her in a better neighborhood. A triangle develops, with the unworldly Dorothea caught in the middle until she is shocked into reality with the news of her supposed beau's engagement.

Papp, who had always been interested in colorblind casting, presented two Shakespeare dramas with a company of black and Hispanic actors in repertory at the Public starting with *Julius Caesar* on January 25. While some saw the move as a fund-raising gimmick, most critics approved of the production, citing uneven acting but thrilling moments. The revival featured some of New York's finest ethnic actors—Arthur French, Morgan Freeman, Mary Alice, Earle Hyman, Sonny Jim Gaines, Roscoe Orman—but the performance most often singled out was Jaime Sanchez's thrilling Marc Antony. *Coriolanus* was added to the repertory on March 16. Morgan Freeman as the title hero received varied comments, but most critics agreed that Robert Christian stole the show as Tullus Aufidius, the emperor's enemy-turned-friend. The repertory closed on April 1.

Larry Cohen's **Trick** (2-1-79, Playhouse), a Broadway comedy thriller that lasted only nine performances, met with vitriolic reviews that declared it "excessively far-fetched" and "a satire on a thriller [that] works neither in the first place nor even in the second." Particularly irritating to the critics and playgoers were the play's efforts to keep tricking the audience, for every new deception was a blind alley with no satisfactory conclusion. In the opening scene Paula Cramer (Tammy Grimes) is seen struggling with someone behind a sofa. The struggle ends with a dead body; Paula goes upstairs, changes clothes, then exits the London flat. The BBC newscaster Wallace Barrows (Donald Madden) enters, discovers his wife's body, and calls in the odd detective investigator Andrew Creed (Lee Richardson) who offers Wallace flowers and proposes they go off to the South of France together. Paula reenters, claims she was a friend of the wife (though Wallace has never seen her), and ends up in Andrew's arms. A series of red herrings follows before it is suggested that Paula is a professional killer hired by either Wallace or Andrew to kill off the wife.

The most interesting play presented at the American Place this season was Sam Shepard's second offering, **Seduced** (2-2-79, American Place), which contained the author's characteristic view of a disintegrating America, this time as seen through a mythic Howard Hughes–like figure. Henry Hackamore (Rip Torn), an aviation pioneer and shrewd businessman, is reputed to be the richest man in the world. But now he is old, weak, bearded, and paranoid, residing in the top floor of a Caribbean luxury hotel as a recluse attended by his bodyguard, Raul (Ed Setrakian). Living off of pills and blood transfusions, Henry, dressed in the flying gear of his youth, seeks one last taste of life, so he has two women from his past flown in. Luna (Pamela Reed) and Miami (Carla Borelli) are still attractive and spirited, but they only remind Henry of his futile life, and he sinks into a seductive boredom that will sustain him until his inevitable death. Notices were mostly dismissive; the play was considered "provocative and amusing rather than profound." It was kept on the boards for forty-four perform-

ances, the longest run of the dismal American Place season.

The Grand Kabuki National Theatre of Japan brought two Kabuki plays to the Beacon on February 6. Chikamatsu Monzaemon's *Shunkan* and Kawatake Mokuami's *Renjishi* were performed as a double bill for two weeks.

A limited engagement of Hugh Whitmore's London play **Stevie** (2-6-79, Manhattan Theatre Club) garnered some attention and praise, Oliver noting that it "presents and then shatters the stereotype of the English spinster." While much of the play was a one-woman show about British poetess Stevie Smith (Roberta Maxwell), it often developed into touching and funny scenes with her aged aunt (Margaret Hilton), whom she lived with, and a onetime beau (James Higgins). The suicidal Stevie was far from depressing; instead she was full of vivid commentary and delicious tales from her tragicomic life.

Like the previous *Later*, Gus Edwards's **Old Phantoms** (2-7-79, St. Marks) was another drama about a family trying to escape from the powerful bonds of a dead father, this time a prosperous African American. When property owner Jack Hamilton (Douglas Turner Ward) dies in his small southern town, his two sons and daughter gather and, in flashback sequences, recall the man who so dominated their lives. The Willy Loman–like Hamilton forced his sense of pride and ambition onto his children, rejecting the suitor to his daughter, Ruth (L. Scott Caldwell), because he was poor and not promising enough and setting impossibly high standards for his sons, Nick (Chuck Patterson) and James (Samm-Art Williams). When his wife died in childbirth, Hamilton replaced her with the submissive Mavis (Barbara Montgomery) and ruled the household with an iron hand. But all of Hamilton's plans come to nought: the bright James slips into a life of crime, Nick settles for routine and meaningless jobs; and the defeated Ruth spends her life caring for the demanding old man. After the funeral the three children squabble over the money, then part company, still trying to escape the father's influence on them.

The Manhattan Theatre Club continued its season of non-American plays with Canadian Joanna McClelland Glass's **Artichoke** (2-13-78, Manhattan Theatre Club). On the Saskatchewan farm of the Morely family, Margaret (Patricia Elliott) lives in the large farmhouse while her husband, Walter (Rex Robbins), is banished to the smokehouse because years ago he had an affair with a "water witch." Margaret is now raising the illegitimate child from that brief union, Lily Agnes (Amanda Plummer). Also on the farm is Margaret's father, Gramps (Michael Higgins), whose adopted son, Gibson McFarland (Nicholas Hormann), is coming for a visit after many years' absence. Gibson, who knew Margaret as a child, is a college professor who is recovering from a nervous breakdown. His love of poetry appeals to the culture-starved Margaret, and they have a love affair. After he leaves, Walter moves back into the house, feeling the score is now even and harmony in the family can be restored. The title was a metaphor, one of the characters describing the artichoke as "an eccentric vegetable . . . it takes a long time to get to the heart."

The Phoenix Theatre mounted a splendid production of Ron Hutchinson's "talky" Irish play **Says I, Says He** (2-19-79, Marymount Manhattan). In a Belfast pub, two blue-collar workers—the alert and challenging Mick Phelan (Joe Grifasi) and the elephantine punchdrunk oaf Pete Hannafin (Brian Dennehy)—return home from England, where they were employed as construction workers by day and stole building materials from the company at night. They now hope to start a demolition business in Belfast, but two terrorists (Jeanne Ruskin and Andrew Davis) take over the pub, gun down some of the patrons, and kidnap Mick and Pete and force them to help them in their destructive activities. The acting throughout was exemplary, especially Christine Baranski as Mick's girlfriend, Maeve.

Again, the acting far outshone the script when the Public offered Thomas Babe's **Taken in Marriage** (2-22-79, Newman), which one critic described as "less a play than an opportunity for players." In the basement of a New Hampshire church, bride-to-be Annie Chandler (Kathleen Quinlan) waits with her genteel mother, Ruth (Colleen Dewhurst), her cynical, oft-married sister, Andrea (Meryl Streep), and her quirky Aunt Helen (Elizabeth Wilson) for the men to arrive for the wedding rehearsal. It seems the groom's side of the family are all at the local hostelry getting drunk, which shocks the patrician New Yorkers who have come for the festivities. One of the men has hired the earthy, outspoken Dixie Avalon (Dixie Carter) to sing at the wedding, and she shows up at the rehearsal, her outgoing personality rubbing against the other ladies' cool demeanor. Eventually the group loosens up, we discover the frustrations and anxieties that the well-bred women have so carefully hidden, and the plays ends with the wedding being called off.

The National Theatre of Prague brought an unusual theatre-circus-film event called **Coquel-**ico** (2-22-79, 22 Steps) to Broadway for forty-five performances. The multi-media entertainment was written, designed, and directed by the acclaimed scenic designer Josef Svoboda, and the startling visuals of the piece, including projections behind actors and screen images distorted on curtains, were the highlight of the program. Also included were masks, dolls, a ringmaster, ballerinas, gypsies, and animal acts, all telling the tale of two clowns who pursue the goddess Venus. The 22 Steps Theatre was the old Latin Quarter nightclub, reached by taking twenty-two steps below the Times Square pavement.

Sherman Yellen's **Strangers** (3-4-79, John Golden), a biographical drama about the relationship between the author Sinclair Lewis (Bruce Dern) and his wife, the journalist Dorothy Thompson (Lois Nettleton), only lasted nine performances. The drama chronicled the couple's courtship and marriage, his fading career as a novelist, her ambitious rise as a publicist, lecturer, and radio personality, their quarrels, his alcoholism and breakdown, and their eventual divorce. Reviews were mostly uncomplimentary, calling the drama "an interminable dramatized program note" and "sheer rhetoric."

The Circle Rep continued to support and produce John Bishop, but his **Winter Signs** (3-4-79, Circle) was considered too contrived and the characters too stereotypic. The Minnesota drama professor Leslie Finley (Jack Davidson) and his wife, Judith (Stephanie Gordon), who teaches dance, seem to be happily settled in a small midwestern college town until an old friend, the Broadway director Ken Timmons (Bruce Gray), comes for a visit and destroys their serenity. The old-fashioned drama, filled with ghostly and homosexual undertones, ran four weeks.

The Hudson Guild fared no better with David Mercer's London drama **Ride a Cock Horse** (3-7-79, Hudson Guild). The play dealt with successful novelist Peter (Kenneth Welsh), a coal miner's son obsessed with his lowly Yorkshire background, and the three women in his life: his wife, Nan (Megan Cole), who is a doctor; Myra (Barbara Caruso), an aging actress who is his mistress; and his new fling, the young computer programmer Fanny (Veronica Castang), who became pregnant to please him. Peter is a childish, funny, spoiled man who plays the women off each other and eventually has a nervous breakdown. The play was considered "thin," but there were some compliments for the actors.

A program of two short Joe Orton plays off Broadway offered a revival of *Ruffian on the Stair* (10-26-69) and the New York premiere of **Funeral**

Games (3-8-79, South Street), an outrageous satire on religious hypocrisy originally written for British television. Two defrocked Church of England priests—Caulfeld (Kenneth Meseroll) and Pringle (Louis Turenne)—have hidden the body of Caulfeld's murdered wife in the basement, but her severed hand keeps showing up to complicate matters. The production was declared uneven, and the curious only had twenty-seven opportunities to see it.

Ralph Pape's **Say Goodnight, Gracie** (3-12-79, 78th Street) was another in the long line of plays about survivors of the 1960s at sea in the 1970s, though there was more humor in Pape's version than in most. The characters are all products of the "Golden Age of Television" (the title comes from the sign-off expression of the George Burns and Gracie Allen radio and TV sitcom) who are now in their thirties and facing some sobering truths about themselves. Gathered in the Greenwich Village apartment of the still-aspiring actor Jerry (Willard Morgan) and his supportive live-in girlfriend, Ginny (Molly Regan), are the rock musician Bobby (Danton Stone), who is forever struggling and performing gigs in suburban New Jersey, the would-be writer Steve (Mark Blum), trying to break into big-time television, and his girlfriend, Catherine (Carolyn Groves), a spacy airline stewardess. It is the night of Jerry and Steve's high school reunion, but they delay going to it, instead smoking pot and drinking and recalling old and better times. Jerry finally decides he cannot face seeing the old crowd and accepts the failure he has become. While the critics only mildly approved of the comedy-turned-drama, audiences latched on to it, and the play ran out the season and returned the following one.

Stewart Parker's Irish play **Spokesong; or, The Common Wheel** (3-15-79, Circle in the Square) was one of the season's most difficult entries to categorize. A fantasy that utilized a handful of original songs, it was almost a musical, yet it used the songs in a very Brechtian manner. Frank (John Lithgow) runs a Belfast bicycle shop that was begun by his grandfather. The grandson believes that all of mankind's problems are connected to the automobile and that if everyone went back to cycling for transportation, the world would be a better place. Frank's adopted brother, Julian (John Horton), a left-wing journalist who lives in London, returns to Ireland and complicates matters when the local schoolteacher, Daisy (Virginia Vestoff), who is Frank's girl, falls for Julian as well. While Frank and the other characters are living in the 1970s, the play covers events of the past eighty years, all the

scenes using the bicycle as a metaphor for the innocence of times past (with many references to war-torn Northern Ireland) and tied together by a character called the Trick Cyclist (Joseph Maher), who rides about the stage, plays various minor characters, and comments on the events. The unusual play received decidedly mixed reactions; Beaufort wrote, "It touches the heart, stirs the mind, and delights the imagination," but others called it "downright tiring." Difficult to describe and sell to audiences, the freewheeling piece only managed to run ten weeks.

A one-man show by Steve J. Spears titled **The Elocution of Benjamin** (3-20-79, Theatre Four) allowed Gordon Chater to perform a tour de force, playing many different characters. The Australian play concerned an elocution professor with multiple personalities, each given vent in his vivid imagination.

A major disappointment was Luis Valdez's **Zoot Suit** (3-25-79, Winter Garden), a hit at Los Angeles's Mark Taper Forum and the first major Hispanic play to appear on Broadway. The epic drama dealt with the plight of Chicano youths in Los Angeles in the early 1940s, specifically the notorious 1942 "Sleepy Lagoon" murder case and the Zoot Suit Riots that resulted from it. The youth Henry Reyna (Danial Valdez), his girl, Della Barrios (Rose Portillo), and a gang of zoot-suited Chicano teens are accused of a murder at the Sleepy Lagoon reservoir, a popular trysting place in the area. They are tried and convicted but, after there is rioting in the streets of Los Angeles, are released on appeal. The episodic play was held together by El Pachuco (Edward James Olmos), a red-shirted zoot-suiter who slithered in and out of the action cynically commenting on it. The mostly derogatory reviews complained that the "flat and boring child's play" was "poorly written and atrociously directed," and more than one commentator compared it to 1930s agitprop theatre. Peter J. Hall's vibrant costumes were noteworthy, though, causing one critic to note that *Zoot Suit* "makes a better fashion show than a play." Despite some controversy and a promotion of the zoot-suit look in department stores, the drama lasted only forty-one performances.

The National Youth Theatre of Great Britain, a company whose actors were all under twenty-two years old, brought Peter Terson's drama **Good Lads at Heart** (3-27-79, BAM) for two weeks to Brooklyn, where it was played at the Opera House with no scenery and the audience sitting on the bare stage. At a British reform school "for boys that can be helped," the students put on a modern version of Hogarth's *Rake's Pro-*

gress set in London with drug dealers instead of gamblers and a contemporary mental hospital in lieu of Bedlam. The production gets out of hand, and as in the similar *Marat/Sade* (12-27-65), the dramatics lead to a real-life uprising and riot. Much of the action was improvisational, and the acting by the young company was energetic and engaging.

That same night, the Phoenix offered the American premiere of an expressionistic German play, Botho Strauss's **Big and Little** (3-27-79, Marymount Manhattan), in which the lonely Lotte (Barbara Barrie) is rejected by her husband and sets off to find another human being to connect with. Her episodic wanderings come to nought, for all she meets in the outside world is indifference. While notices felt the play was weak, the performances by Barrie, Peter Maloney, Peter Friedman, Carol Teitel, and others were lauded.

A one-night Broadway fiasco called **A Meeting by the River** (3-28-79, Palace), adapted from Christopher Isherwood's 1967 novel by Don Bachardy and the novelist himself, met with some of the most scabrous reviews of the season, from "laborious" to "high twaddle" and "almost a travesty of the novel." Oliver (Simon Ward), the son of an English country gentleman, has forsaken his family and class and has opted for a life of self-sacrifice as a Hindu monk in a monastery on the banks of the Ganges. Oliver's brother, Patrick (Keith Baxter), who has made a fortune in book publicity and moviemaking, is in Singapore for filming and decides to visit Oliver just as he is about to be ordained a swami. The two brothers engage in rhetorical discussions and arguments while, back in England, Oliver's mother, Margaret (Siobhan McKenna), and Patrick's wife, Penelope (Meg Wynn-Owen), write (and read) letters to the brothers. (Penelope has always been in love with Oliver.) Also in England, the spirited youth Tom (Keith McDermott), who is in love with Patrick, tries to telephone him in India but ends up talking with Oliver. The play climaxes with the Hindu ordination, a naked and shaved Oliver in a lot of smoke while Patrick stands at the side and gapes. Only the superb cast made the evening bearable, including Sam Jaffe in a cameo role as a friend of the guru. The expensive production lost $250,000, the season's biggest non-musical flop.

Producer Roger Stevens had his name on six productions this season (including the successful *First Monday in October* and *Wings*), but none ran longer than the British import **Bedroom Farce** (3-29-79, Brooks Atkinson), Alan Ayckbourn's clever comedy that, despite its title, was not about sex. True to its title, though, the setting is three bedrooms side-by-side on the stage. In the first is the well-adjusted couple of Malcolm (Derek Newark) and Kate (Susan Littler), who are having a party downstairs and using the bedroom for the guests' coats. They have a healthy, if sometimes silly, marriage (each likes to hide shoes and kitchen utensils in their bed to surprise the other), as opposed to Delia (Joan Hickson) and Ernest (Michael Gough), the elderly couple who occupy the second bedroom. They are extremely conservative (she is shocked the way girls today allow the label on their clothes to be seen) and yet remarkably frank; we see them before and after they go out for the evening to celebrate their wedding anniversary. In the third bedroom lies the upwardly mobile executive Nick (Michael Stroud), flat on his bed because of a sprained back. His wife, Jan (Polly Adams), goes off to the party at Malcolm and Kate's, leaving Nick to perform all sorts of contortions to get comfortable or get himself a drink. During one Saturday evening, all three bedrooms are invaded by Delia and Ernest's son, Trevor (Stephen Moore), who is having martial problems with wife, Susannah (Delia Lindsay); their problems overflow into everybody else's lives and sleep. But late that night the couple come to a reconciliation and snuggle into Malcolm and Kate's bed, pushing aside a saucepan and a pair of boots to get comfortable. Notices were unqualified raves for the script, Ayckbourn and Peter Hall's co-direction, and the masterful British cast (Gough and Hickson won Tony Awards). The comedy ran 278 happy performances.

The Manhattan Theatre Club ended its foreign-play season with Odon Von Horvath's Austrian allegory **Don Juan Comes Back from the War** (4-3-79, Manhattan Theatre Club), about the legendary Juan (Peter Evans) seeking true love in war-torn Europe after World War II. The cast included twelve actresses who portrayed thirty-five women in Juan's love life.

Another foreign play, Brian Friel's **Faith Healer** (4-5-79, Longacre), had its world premiere on Broadway but met with conflicting reviews and a run of only twenty performances. The "strangely enthralling play" consisted of four lengthy monologues by three characters at the end of their lives looking back. The traveling faith healer Frank (James Mason) wandered across Scotland and Wales with his wife, Grace (Clarissa Kaye), and his agent, Teddy (Donal Donnelly), for many years, laying hands on the ill and sometimes healing them. Part con man, part artist, Frank sees himself as a creator and a destroyer of life. Grace recalls running away from a law career to join the mountebank Frank and the time she gave birth to a stillborn child. The cockney Teddy, who travels with them in their beat-up van, has a vivid memory of a wedding in Donegal. The evening ended with a monologue by Frank in which he tries to reconcile himself to the life he has led. The acting was magnetic, particularly Mason's; he had not been seen on Broadway in thirty-two years.

Yet another foreign play, this time from Switzerland, was offered by the newly organized Chelsea Theatre Center, now located in Manhattan. Max Frisch's **Biography: A Game** (4-5-79, Westside) concerned old Kurmann (George Morfogen), a professor of behavioral psychology, who is given a chance to relive important and determining segments of his past in order to test his belief that different decisions would have affected the last seven years of his life. This "game" is presided over by the Recorder (Paul Sparer), who oversees all the action, Kurmann's dossier in his hand for reference. Old love affairs and political decisions are examined, resulting in a sometimes theatrical if not very profound drama.

David Berry's Vietnam drama *G.R. Point* (4-12-77) was given a Broadway revival on April 16 at the Playhouse with a production that originated at Baltimore's Center Stage. Some commentators still felt the "old-style war melodrama" was weak and stilted, but the acting by Michael Moriarty, Michael Jeter, Howard Rollins, and others was considered first rate. The revival survived thirty-two performances.

As in the earlier *Nevis Mountain Dew*, the hero of Brian Clark's **Whose Life Is It Anyway?** (4-17-79, Trafalgar) was also a patient asking to die. The sculptor Ken Harrison (Tom Conti) has been paralyzed from the neck down in a car accident. He is quite lucid and rational about his situation (he also is adept at making jokes about it) and, rather than spend the rest of his life in a hospital this way, seeks a way to legally end his life. Ken hires a lawyer to fight to have him released from the hospital, removing him from the life support system and allowing him to quietly expire. The supervising physician, Dr. Emerson (Philip Bosco), fights the action on legal and moral grounds, but the understanding Dr. Scott (Jean Marsh) sympathizes with Ken and comes around to his way of thinking. A judge is brought in for a hearing, Ken wins his case, and Emerson reluctantly agrees to disconnect the patient and let nature

take its course. Reviews for the script were cautious (one aisle-sitter called it "didactic and padded with anemic subplots"), but Conti, in his New York debut, was proclaimed "an actor of immeasurable charm and strength" and "simply devastating." He had originated the role in London and won a Tony Award for his Broadway performance. Despite its touchy subject matter, the dark comedy ran 223 performances.

Raymond Serra, who possessed an uncanny resemblance to the late Edward G. Robinson, wrote and performed in **Manny** (4-18-79, Century), a bio-drama about the famous screen gangster who was really a very cultured gentleman and astute art collector. The play dramatized Robinson (born Emmanuel Goldenberg) in his personal life rather than his screen career, showing arguments with his wife, his son's alcoholic troubles, and his battle with the House Un-American Activities Committee. For those who missed the real Sam Jaffe in *A Meeting by the River*, the Hollywood actor was portrayed by Pierre Epstein as a smiling hanger-on. Notices were not favorable, calling the play "a domestic soap opera" and the writing "amateurish and obvious" but admitting that Serra made a believable Robinson. The drama struggled on in the small house for thirty-one performances.

Two revivals of American plays opened the next night. Clifford Odets's *Awake and Sing* (2-19-35) was mounted by the Roundabout, and critics found the acting, direction, and even the play itself lacking. But Arthur Miller's *The Price* (2-7-68) at the Harold Clurman was roundly praised, some reviewers stating it was superior to the original production. The cast included Mitchell Ryan and Fritz Weaver as the quarreling brothers and Joseph Buloff as the ancient furniture dealer. The Miller play ran thirty-four performances before transferring to Broadway the next season.

Two new works at the Public featured lesser efforts by major writers. Trinidad poet and playwright Derek Walcott's **Remembrance** (4-24-79, Other Stage) explored the past life of Albert (Roscoe Lee Brown), a retired teacher and author who mourns the killing of his son by the British police and is interviewed by a local newspaper about his past. David Mamet's **The Woods** (4-25-79, Newman) was a two-character play that takes place one night in a cabin in the woods where Ruth (Christine Lahti) and Nick (Chris Sarandon) are in the midst of an end-of-summer romance. During the night their relationship shifts by the hour. She sees their love as expansive and encompassing, but he wants only quiet and private fulfillment. After the couple make love, their perspectives change. Nick feels threatened and insecure; she tries to give him strength. After a violent quarrel they start to part, then desperately cling to each other, afraid of any other alternative.

The surprise one-night failure of the Broadway season was Ira Levin's comedy **Break a Leg** (4-29-79, Palace). In the Middle European theatre world of long ago, the theatrical producer Dietrich Merkenschrift (Jack Weston) is so furious with drama critic Johann Schiml (René Auberjonois) for condemning his last production that he sets out on a series of vendettas. He commissions the hack playwright Imre Laszlo (David Margulies) to write a play that will infuriate the critic, and then he convinces his leading lady, Gertie Kessel (Julie Harris), to seduce Schiml and get him into a compromising position. But Gertie falls for the critic, and all of Dietrich's plans to drive Schiml out of town fail. The production was plagued with problems in rehearsals (director Charles Nelson Reilly quit and Frank Dunlop was brought in), and critics were aghast that so many proven talents could come up with such a "jerrybuilt backstage comedy" that suffered a "terminal case of mediocrity."

Broadway's next entry also closed on opening night. Herb Gardner's offbeat comedy *The Goodbye People* (12-3-68) was revived on April 30 at the Belasco with Herschel Bernardi as the retired Coney Island hot dog vendor who tries to reopen his boardwalk stand in the middle of winter. Gardner had revised the script, but critics still found it "sentimental," "schmaltzy," and "sticky."

The Circle Rep came up with one of its greatest hits at the season's end: Lanford Wilson's romantic two-character comedy-drama **Talley's Folly** (5-1-79, Circle). The German-Jewish St. Louis businessman Matt Friedman (Judd Hirsch) tells the audience that the play will run "ninety-seven minutes here tonight," during which time he will woo and win the hand of Sally Talley (Trish Hawkins). It is the moonlit evening of July 4, 1944, and Matt has driven down from the city to the rural town of Lebanon, Missouri, where Sally works in a hospital for wounded GIs. He has called for her at her family farmhouse, but Sally's brother (who sees Matt as a foreigner and a Communist) runs him off. So Matt goes down to the river and waits for Sally in a crumbling Victorian boathouse, a folly built by an eccentric member of the Talley family years before. Sally arrives, tells him he is crazy to keep courting her, and tries to get him to leave. But Matt has charm

JUDD HIRSCH (1935–) was born in New York City and studied physics at CCNY and architecture at the Cooper Union before turning to acting. He attended the American Academy of Dramatic Arts and other acting studios, then made his Broadway debut as the Telephone Repairman in *Barefoot in the Park* (1966). Long associated with the Circle Repertory Company, he played the night clerk, Bill, in Lanford Wilson's *The Hot l Baltimore* (1973) before gaining popularity on television and in films for his comic character roles. Hirsch often returned to the stage, as in *Knock Knock* (1976) and *Chapter Two* (1977). The Jewish character actor has been described as having a "street face, a face of interchangeable ethnicities and professions."

and a seductive sense of humor, and she remains to reminisce, argue, and dream about a future after the war. But still Sally resists Matt's marriage proposals, and when Matt lets slip that he doesn't want to bring children into this prejudiced world, Sally breaks down into tears and anger. She reveals that she was once engaged to marry the son of the most prosperous family in the county but contracted a case of TB that left her unable to bear children. Her secret exposed, Matt understands her past fear of marriage, and Sally finally accepts his proposal. Some playgoers recalled the character of the aged Sally Talley, who returns to the river to scatter Matt's ashes many years later, from Wilson's *Fifth of July* (4-27-78). *Talley's Folly* met with unanimous raves for the script, Marshall W. Mason's sensitive direction, John Lee Beatty's atmospheric boathouse setting filled with rustic remnants from the past, Dennis Parichy's delicate lighting with the moon unobtrusively rising over the landscape, and the performers, particularly Hirsch for his "quintessen-

JOHN LEE BEATTY (1948–) was born in Palo Alto, California, and educated at Brown University, graduating in 1970 with an English literature degree, and at Yale University, where he worked closely with scenic designer Ming Cho Lee, his greatest influence. After designing several seasons for the Circle Repertory Company and Manhattan Theatre Club, he made his Broadway debut with the 1976 revival of *The Innocents*. By the late 1970s, he would become one of the most prolific New York scenic designers, rarely doing musicals, but concentrating on lyrical settings using naturalism and suggested realism.

tial portrait of an outsider," according to Mel Gussow in the *Times*. "He is part bookkeeper, part clown, an irrepressible romantic who dramatizes himself with jokes, games and imitations." The play ran its forty-four performances at the Circle, then transferred to Broadway the next season.

The Comédie Française was also greeted with raves when it brought Molière's *Le Misanthrope* to BAM on May 1 for ten performances and Feydeau's *La Puce a l'oreille* (better known here as *A Flea in Her Ear*) on May 10 for six showings.

The Hudson Guild closed its admirable season with Abe Polsky's **Devour the Snow** (5-2-79, Hudson Guild), which received largely appreciative notices, ran thirty performances, and transferred to Broadway the next season. The play was a courtroom drama based on a historical event (the ill-fated Donner Party expedition) but, unlike the earlier *Are You Now or Have You Ever Been?*, there were no transcripts to quote from and the playwright imagined what the follow-up trial must have been like. At Sutter's Fort in northern California, the German immigrant Lewis Keseberg (Jon De Vries), a survivor of the Donner expedition, is suing some other survivors for libel because they have said Lewis murdered members of the party and robbed their graves. The court proceeding recreates the historic events that occurred in the Sierra Nevada mountains in 1847: the oppressive snows that stranded the party, the death by starvation of women and children, and the desperation by those alive to cannibalize the corpses of the dead in order to survive the winter. Keseberg wins his case and clears his name, but the horrors of the situation haunt all the survivors and those who witnessed the telling of the facts.

Off-Broadway playwright John Guare made one of his rare forays onto Broadway with **Bosoms and Neglect** (5-3-79, Longacre), a three-character dark comedy about the insecure bachelor Scooper (Paul Rudd) and his relationship with his mother and girlfriend. When Scooper finds out that his blind, wacky mother, Henny (Kate Reid), has been hiding her breast cancer from him, he pulls himself together and convinces her, with great difficulty, to go into the hospital for an operation. Meanwhile, he meets the neurotic Deirdre (Marian Mercer) in the waiting room of his shrink, and their common fear of how they will survive when their doctor goes on vacation brings them together. During an emotional and physical mishap, Deirdre accidentally stabs Scooper in the spleen and he unwit-

tingly injures her foot, so they both end up in the hospital with the recovering Henny and listening to her cockeyed philosophy. Scooter eventually give his mother pills and encourages her to commit suicide, but Henny throws them away and, thinking her son is still in the room, delivers a soliloquy telling him that, despite everything, life is still worth living. The critics were mixed in their reactions; some saw "a piercing intelligence and chilling comedic style," while most found "a static play" and "a grotesque farce." Without enough "money" reviews, the odd play closed after four performances.

Another three-character play, Mario Fratti's **Victim** (5-3-79, Quaigh), opened the same night off Broadway but managed a run of seven weeks. The play was a philosophical thriller about the desirable Diana (Greta Thyssen), who is visited by the gasman Kirk (Dan Grimaldi), who turns out to have murdered someone on her doorstep. Diana is more intrigued by Kirk than afraid of him, and she initiates a contest of wills that also involves her sinister husband, Warren (Michael Dorkin).

Louis LaRusso II's second melodrama this season was **Knockout** (5-6-79, Helen Hayes), about the world of small-time boxing in Hoboken, New Jersey, in 1948. The kindhearted former champion Damie Ruffino (Danny Aiello) is now past his prime and works as a trainer. But a young, upstart contender, the sadistic Paddy Klonski (Edward O'Neill), comes on the scene, and Damie falls for Klonski's British wife, Kay (Margaret Warncke), who is bullied by her brutish husband. The two men literally fight over Kay, the play climaxing with an extended boxing match that ends with Damie victorious. Reviews said the drama resembled a B movie in its obvious characters and thick sentiment, but audiences liked it enough to allow the melodrama to run 154 performances.

The off-Broadway season ended with a series of short runs. Robin Swicord's **Last Days at the Dixie Girl Cafe** (5-16-79, Theatre Four) was a comedy about a family of southern eccentrics. The religious fanatic Wayne Blossom, Sr. (Ronald Johnson), a widower, runs a sheet-metal business and has a profitable sideline building bomb shelters in the small Georgia town where he lives. His son, Wayne Jr. (Robert Schenkkan), runs the filling station and philanders with all the women in town, much to the bewilderment of his tomboy wife, Joy (Julie Nesbitt). The Blossom family's daughter, Lanette (Lisa Brown), is off to college on a baton-twirling scholarship. The action all takes place in the title cafe, run by the sweet if rather dotty Jeri Lee (Lorna Johnson), who believes she is destined to bear the next Messiah and wants to marry Wayne Sr.

At the Public, Carson Kievman wrote a modern version of the Orpheus legend, added some songs and many sound effects, and called it **Wake Up, It's Time to Go to Bed** (5-16-79, LuEsther). Keith Carradine played Orpheus, and Ellen Greene was his Eurydice.

Broadway's last non-musical of the season was Ron Clark and Sam Bobrick's **Murder at the Howard Johnson's** (5-17-79, John Golden), an "empty-headed, vacant hearted" suspense comedy set in a motor inn. The self-deluded dentist Mitchell (Tony Roberts) sees himself as a dashing Don Juan, and the middle-aged Arlene (Joyce Van Patten) sees herself as a notorious femme fatale, so in a moment of romanticism they plan and attempt to murder Arlene's husband, the blundering used-car salesman Paul (Bob Dishy). When Arlene discovers that Mitchell has been unfaithful to her, she schemes with her husband to do in Mitchell. Then both men, seeing that they are being strung along by Arlene, plot to murder her. All three murder attempts fail, and so did the play, closing after four performances.

The Phoenix closed its reputable season with a disappointing bio-drama from Scotland called **Chinchilla** (5-31-79, Marymount Manhattan) about the dancer Nijinsky (Joseph Pugliese) and his tyrannical mentor Diaghilev (Michael Cristofer), who was referred to throughout by the play's title. Playwright Robert David MacDonald subtitled his drama "Figures in a Classical Landscape with Ruins." Laura Esterman, Merwin Goldsmith, June Gable, Wallace Shawn, and Philip Casnoff were among those who peopled the landscape for twenty-two performances.

Yet another play with songs was Mark Razovsky's **Strider: The Story of a Horse** (5-31-79, Westside), a dramatization of the Tolstoy short story that looked at life through the eyes of a piebald horse. Strider (Gerald Hiken) looks slovenly but, as he tells his story to the other horses in the stable, was once a thoroughbred and a champion. But his fortunes, like those of his rider, Prince Serpuhofsky (Gordon Gould), fell on bad times, and only their indomitable spirit allowed them to survive and triumph. The Chelsea Theatre Center production, directed by Robert Kalfin, who also helped write the English-language version, was played on a stark white stage with eighteen actors who asked the audience to use

their imagination. Some critics found the evening "perfectly magical," while others thought it "a trifle silly" and "wearing." But audiences responded to the lively and unique piece, and it ran into November and then transferred to Broadway the next season.

1979–1980

The appellation "worst season in years" was heard often as the decade came to a close, and it was difficult to dispute such naysayers when faced with the record. Not only were the best plays not all that good, but the dreadful plays were unusually awful. One third of all the new plays that opened on Broadway in 1979–1980 closed in a week or less. More disturbing, they (with the exception of one or two) deserved to close that quickly. In a season of such dismal offerings, the claim of "worst new play of the season" became the only contest of interest.

Broadway saw twenty-nine new non-musicals, eighteen of which were American. (That was three more than the previous season.) Off Broadway was healthier with forty-nine new works, thirty-seven of them American. The number of Broadway revivals stayed at five, but off Broadway there were twenty-nine (as opposed to only eighteen revivals last season). With more specialty entries than usual, "plays with songs" defying categorization, and the uneven boundaries of off-off Broadway, the counting of non-musicals was an inaccurate venture to say the least. But the pattern was clear: quality and quantity on Broadway was shrinking, and Off Broadway was holding its own.

Variety reported that attendance was up 6 percent this season, but again holdovers and musicals accounted for the slight rise. The "show business Bible" also reported that ticket prices had nearly doubled in the past five years, a fact no one had any trouble believing. The top for a Broadway non-musical was $22.50 at the beginning of the season and $25.00 at the end. A half million dollars to open a play on Broadway was now a reality, and this season several non-musicals lost investments large enough to equal those of a major musical a few seasons back. There were still the small-cast hits like *I Ought to Be in Pictures* and *Romantic Comedy* to encourage producers, but the plight of the British import *Betrayal* illustrated how precarious Broadway economics had become. The three-character Harold

Pinter drama cost $300,000 to mount, received enthusiastic reviews, won some awards, played 170 performance, and still lost $100,000.

While the Morosco, Bijou, and Helen Hayes theatres were being threatened with demolition and Lincoln Center remained dark, the New Apollo and Rialto became legitimate houses once again, and the recent Theatre Row development off Broadway was growing. Some theatre companies, such as the American Place and the Chelsea Theatre Center, offered fewer works as they struggled to survive, but on the whole Off Broadway was doing well. (Only four commercial ventures out of forty-nine new plays closed within a week there.)

Another portent of the future: the Shuberts fully computerized their box office at the Royale in June; within two years every Shubert house across the nation would be similarly computerized and linked up.

The season's first entry was actually the final production of the 1978–1979 season at Joseph Papp's Public Theatre: a skillful mounting of Samuel Beckett's *Happy Days* (9-14-65), which opened on June 1 and ran through the summer. Irene Worth was the semi-buried Winnie, and her portrayal was cited as "pure gold" and an "incandescent performance." There were also raves for Andrei Serban's "illuminating production," and even those who sneered at his handling of the classics in the past felt he was very adept with the Beckett work.

On Broadway, Michael Weller's **Loose Ends** (6-6-79, Circle in the Square) was something of a follow-up to his comedy *Moonchildren* (2-21-72) about college students in the late 1960s. The disillusioned Peace Corps worker Paul (Kevin Kline) meets the photographer Susan (Roxanne Hart) on a beach in Bali in 1970, and the play chronicles their relationship over the next decade. Both afraid of commitment, they live together in Boston and try not to discuss anything that might threaten their arrangement. Paul's career as a film editor and Susan's as a photographer both blossom, so they wed and live in New York though their work often keeps them apart. He wants a child, but she sees it as another form of commitment and secretly has an abortion when she gets pregnant. Paul finds out a few years later and they separate. The two finally meet in a cabin in New Hampshire in 1979 as lovers, cheating on their new partners and enjoying a relationship without permanent attachment. Reviews were mixed regarding Weller's script, some aisle-

KEVIN [Delaney] KLINE (1947–) was born in St. Louis, the son of a toy and record store owner and a singer. He studied speech and theatre at Indiana University and trained in performance at the Juilliard School. After graduating in 1972, he became a founding member of the Acting Company (a professional troupe made up of recent Juilliard grads) and toured the country in such roles as Charles Surface in *The School for Scandal* and Vershinin in *The Three Sisters*. He also appeared in musicals, playing Macheath in *The Beggar's Opera* and Jamie Lockhart in *The Robber Bridegroom*. While most of the Acting Company productions played in New York, Kline did not make his Broadway debut until the musical *On the Twentieth Century*, winning a Tony Award for his farcical lover Bruce Granit. Although his movie career would take off with his film debut in *Sophie's Choice* (1982), Kline would return to the New York stage frequently. Equally adept at farce, musicals, contemporary works, and classics, his work is usually characterized by its high level of energy and very physical manifestations of character.

sitters finding it "full of talent, laughs and smart-sweet awareness," while others felt "the play comes to share the flatness that is its theme." As with *Moonchildren*, the characters either intrigued one or irritated one into declaring, "Grow up!" Alan Schneider's production, which originated at the Arena Stage in Washington, where it was cited by the American Theatre Critics as the best new script to come from 1978–1979 regional theatre, was roundly commended. *Loose Ends* ran 284 performances, thanks somewhat to the strength of Kline, who received critical plaudits from all.

Veteran playwright Robert Anderson's **The Days Between** (6-6-79, Park Royal) was written back in 1965 and had been produced regionally over the years, but New York did not see it until two engagements this season. The family drama about a writer (Dan Hamilton) and his shaky home life with his wife (Kathleen Nolan) and young son (Jansen Lambie) played twenty-three performances, then reopened for a week in November.

James McLure's double bill **Lone Star** and **Pvt. Wars** (6-7-79, Century) had premiered with success at the Actors Theatre of Louisville, but Broadway only kept it on the boards for two months. The first play was set in Maynard, Texas, where returning Vietnam vet Roy (Powers

Boothe) is on a drinking binge with his younger brother, Ray (Leo Burmester), bragging about his wartime exploits and how proud he is of his sexy young wife and his pink 1959 Thunderbird. When the local wimp, Cletis (Clifford Fetters), joins them, he is bullied and teased by the macho Roy until it comes out that Ray has slept with Roy's wife while he was away and has also crashed his prized Thunderbird. *Pvt. Wars* is a character study consisting of a series of short scenes set in a veterans' hospital. The Georgia country boy Gately (Gregory Grove), the shrewd operator Silvio (Tony Camisi), and the rich kid Natwick (Clifford Fetters) from Great Neck are wounded Vietnam vets who while away the time arguing, bragging, and sometimes solacing each other as all their frustration about the future comes to the surface. While many critics thought McLure promising, reaction to the script ranged from modest approval to "as funny as an outhouse in a dust storm." Most preferred *Lone Star* over the hospital black comedy, but both plays were later produced at colleges and community theatres with some frequency.

There was not much Shakespeare this season, but what was there was notable and was mostly to be found in the summer months. The Broadway revival of *Richard III* at the Cort on June 14 was greeted with largely negative reviews, the production often cited as unfocused and inconsistent. But aisle-sitters were, as usual, in disagreement about the revival's star, Al Pacino. While the leaden production was very conventional (some said it was even nineteenth century–like in its stagnant staging), Pacino's approach to the role was very modern with a lot of sarcasm and flippancy. Critics argued, yet audiences filled the theatre for its scheduled thirty-three performances.

A Norwegian feminist drama by Bjørg Vik titled **Wine Untouched** (6-18-79, Harold Clurman) had been seen briefly off-off Broadway three years earlier in a translation by Erle Bjørnstad and arrived off Broadway with a superior cast that consisted of Donna McKechnie, Patricia Elliott, Swoozie Kurtz, Susan Slavin, and Glenn Close. Five old school chums gather in the flat of one of them and, during a long and drunken evening, pour out their woes and frustrations. One despises her role as mother, another cheats on her husband to gain strength, another has lesbian tendencies, all hated their mothers, and each has a bounder for a husband. While the critics found the cast enthralling, they all dismissed the play, which, according to Christopher Sharp of

Women's Wear Daily, "not only ignores action, it also makes movement superfluous." Despite such pans, audiences were interested enough to extend the play's one-week engagement for a second week.

Three American revivals opened in the next three days. Arthur Miller's *The Price* (2-7-68) had sold out its off-Broadway engagement last season, so it transferred to the Playhouse on June 19 and stayed for 144 performances. The same cast was featured, and critics again applauded both the play and the production, several preferring it to the original. Sam Shepard's *Buried Child* (12-5-78) returned to Off Broadway after winning the Pulitzer Prize, opening on June 20 at the Circle and staying for ninety more performances. A less likely revival was Oliver Hailey's dark comedy *Father's Day* (3-16-71) on June 21 at the American Place. The original production had survived only one performance on Broadway despite some encouraging reviews. Critical response was still mixed; some commentators felt it was still a "limp and stilted play," while others found it a "witty, perceptive and penetrating social satire." Most admired the new production, directed by Rae Allen and featuring Susan Tyrrell, Mary Beth Hurt, and Tammy Grimes as the three divorcées, and the revival played for 101 performances.

The Public's multi-racial *Coriolanus* from the previous spring was remounted and presented at the outdoor Delacorte on June 22 for twenty-seven performances. Morgan Freeman (Caius Martius), Earle Hyman (Cominius), Gloria Foster (Volumnia), and Robert Christian (Tullus Aufidius) were again featured under the direction of Wilfred Leach.

One of the longest-running one-person shows of the decade was Marty Martin's **Gertrude Stein Gertrude Stein Gertrude Stein** (6-24-79, Circle), which featured Pat Carroll as the famous expatriate. In her Paris studio in 1938, on the rainy afternoon before she is to leave what has been her home for the past forty years, Stein packs her things and reminiscences about her youth in California, studying psychology with William James at Radcliffe and medicine at Johns Hopkins, emigrating to Paris in the 1920s, and meeting Matisse, Isadora Duncan, Picasso, Apollinaire, Hemingway, and other celebrities of the era. Some of her most touching memories dealt with her lifelong companion, Alice B. Toklas, who was supposedly napping in the other room. Critics found the evening "intelligently drawn" and "poignant," and comedienne Carroll (who had commissioned the work and polished it while on tour) received the best reviews of her career, capturing both the exuberant humor and the unsentimental pathos of the character. The bio-drama had been seen for a week in early June at the Circle Rep as a special event, and the reaction was so positive it reopened on June 24 and played seventy times in alternating repertory with *Buried Child*. The show then transferred on October 23 to the Provincetown Playhouse, where it stayed for an impressive 373 performances.

The only new production of the summer in Central Park was Wilfred Leach's simple, straightforward, and traditional production of *Othello* that opened on June 27 to mostly laudatory reviews and played to full houses for its twenty-five performances. Raul Julia essayed the Moor; in an unlikely bit of casting, Richard Dreyfuss played the conniving Iago. As was usual with the movie star's performance, one either praised his Iago highly or was repulsed by it. The capable supporting cast featured Frances Conroy (Desdemona), John Heard (Cassio), Kaiulani Lee (Emilia), and James Rebhorn (Roderigo).

The Roundabout would present a series of rarely revived classics this season, beginning with Ibsen's *Little Eyolf* on June 28. Ross Petty and Concetta Tomei played the troubled parents, and Jacob Tanenbaum was their young son, Eyolf. The problematic tragedy was only retained for thirteen performances. On July 6, last season's contemporary comedy of manners *Say Goodnight, Gracie* (3-12-79) returned to the Actors Playhouse and chalked up a total of 417 performances before it closed in March.

Ntozake Shange's third "choreopoem" presented by the Public was entitled **Spell #7** (7-15-79, Anspacher). Like its predecessors *for colored girls . . .* (5-17-76) and *A Photograph* (12-1-77), it explored the black experience through soliloquies and dance. This piece was set in a St. Louis bar that is the favorite haunt of local artists and musicians. Although there were some men in the cast, the point of view was still primarily that of the female African American. The evening's narrator (Larry Marshall), the son of a magician, told the audience how, as a little boy, he once requested that his father use his magic to make him white. But the parent said he performed only "black magic." So the evening, the narrator explained, would celebrate being African-American. Again Oz Scott directed, and the adroit cast included Mary Alice, Avery Brooks, Reyno, and La Tanya Richardson, who delivered a poignant monologue about a woman who loved her unborn child within her but killed it after birth because it became part of a painful world. Several aisle-sitters agreed that it was a "lovely and powerful work," and the Public kept it on the boards for 175 performances.

British playwright Tom Stoppard would be represented by three new plays in New York this season, but none of them would enter the repertory of his often-produced works. The first and the most unusual was **Every Good Boy Deserves Favor** (7-30-79, Metropolitan Opera House), which was aptly described by the author as "a play for actors and orchestra." (The title comes from the mnemonic device taught to British children to learn the notes on the lines of the musical scale, similar to the American phrase "Every Good Boy Does Fine.") A full orchestra was onstage with the cast, and music composed by André Previn accompanied much of the dialogue. Alexander (Eli Wallach) is a political dissident who has written about the silencing of writers against the state. Ivanov (René Auberjonois) is a mental patient who believes he has a full orchestra that he must always rehearse. Both men are put in a state insane asylum where they share a cell, or rather a ward, as the Doctor (Remak Ramsay) insists it be called. Alexander's son, Sasha (Bobby Scott), tries to study geometry at school while waiting for his father to be released, but Alexander is stubborn and will not lie and say he has been cured by the state, even though it means his freedom. Scenes between the Doctor and the patients crisscross back and forth as the orchestra plays and geometric theories are entangled with political and musical ones. The play concludes with a military colonel (Carl Low), who has been promoted to doctor, releasing the two men when he gets them mixed up and asks each one the wrong questions. Notices ranged from "extraordinary piece of theatre, it is trenchant and funny at the same time" to "unwieldy." The limited one-week engagement in the large venue was well attended, but there was no call for an extension.

A summertime diversion that filled another large house for fifty-one performances was the self-explanatory **Gilda Radner: Live From New York** (8-2-79, Winter Garden) which boasted ten authors and a cast of eight, but all that mattered was the versatile television comedienne, who portrayed her gallery of familiar and beloved characters. The critics, not expecting to find a play, cheered the evening for what it was and, along with the crowds, enjoyed themselves.

The first of Off Broadway's short-lived commercial ventures was Gerhard Borris's **After the**

Rise (9-10-79, Astor Place), subtitled "An Illustrated Interview" and employing both live action and film footage. The play's title, an arch reference to Arthur Miller's autobiographical *After the Fall*, hints at the subject matter: a marriage not unlike Miller's to Marilyn Monroe during the turbulent 1950s witch hunt. The drama lasted a week.

The Manhattan Theatre Club opened its varied season with John Hopkins's **Losing Time** (9-11-79, Manhattan Theatre Club Downstage), a "shallow melodrama" about sexually frustrated women that pleased few critics, despite a talented cast. Late one night the over-the-edge New Yorker Ruth (Shirley Knight) bursts into the apartment of her friend Joanne (Jane Alexander) and rants about being sexually assaulted by a young man on the street. But as her hysterics dwindle Kate admits that the man was someone she picked up in a coffee shop because she has been so upset since her divorce. Soon Joanne opens up and confesses that Kate's ex-husband was among her many sexual conquests over the past few years, and the two women launch into a tirade about their attraction to and repulsion of men.

Ernest Thompson's sentimental comedy *On Golden Pond* (9-13-78) returned to Broadway on September 12 with the original cast and happily racked up another 252 performances at the Century.

True to its title, Martin Fox's thriller **The Office Murders** (9-18-79, Quaigh) concerned several homicides, and the bodies piled up for the final curtain, quite a feat considering there were only four actors in the cast. In the grimy headquarters of a small and dying magazine, a strong sexual and professional triangle develops between a married publisher, his seemingly heterosexual editor, and the overtly homosexual assistant editor. Passion soon turned to murder, and the deaths were both violent and graphic in the intimate theatre-in-the-round space. Austin Pendleton, Bob McDonald, and Joel Crothers played the dangerous trio for twenty-four performances, then the melodrama reopened for a week on November 30 with porno film star Harry Reems in Pendleton's role.

Eric Chappell's "agreeably foolish" British play **The Banana Box** (9-19-79, Hudson Guild) gained some attention during its month-long run off Broadway. Undergraduate roommates Phillip Smith (Howard Rollins, Jr.), a rugby champ who keeps his African tribal roots a secret, and Noel Parker (Brad O'Hare), a sex-obsessed virgin who

is studying science hoping to prove the existence of God, try to entertain two co-eds (Janet League and Veronica Castang) in their digs but are continually interrupted by their nosy and eccentric landlord, Rooksby (Edward Zang). Both play and production were favorably reviewed.

Tom Stoppard had played fast and loose with *Hamlet* in his *Rosencrantz and Guildenstern Are Dead* (10-16-67), and he returned to Shakespeare for the comic double bill **Dogg's Hamlet, Cahoot's Macbeth** (10-3-79, 22 Steps). At a boys' boarding school, Headmaster Dogg (Louis Haslar) has devised a new language for his students, giving already existing English words new meanings. ("Testing, testing, one, two, three" translates as "Breakfast, breakfast, sun, dock, trog.") As the boys (all played by adults) prepare for their shortened version of *Hamlet* to be presented at the awards assembly, they communicate freely in this riotously incongruous language but speak Shakespeare's words exactly when rehearsing the play. A lorry driver named Easy (John Challis) enters with supplies for the production; he speaks normal English and, consequently, is misunderstood by everyone. The one-act farce ends with a fifteen-minute version of *Hamlet* using a greatly abridged text, and then, as an encore, the students perform a two-minute version, turning the tragedy into a farcical dance of words. The second play shows a private theatrical performance played in the living room of an actor-director (Stephen D. Newman) because public performances have been outlawed. (The play was dedicated to Czech dramatist Pavel Kohout, who did such performances in his home during a similar ban in Prague.) The play performed is an abridged version of *Macbeth*, which is interrupted by a comic Inspector (Peter Woodthorpe) who breaks into the living room and into the action of the tragedy, hilariously checking on the actors' credentials and giving a running commentary about art and politics. At the end of *Cahoot's Macbeth* the lorry driver Easy from the first play enters speaking Dogg's language, and soon the actors are delivering famous speeches from *Macbeth* in the nonsense tongue. Aisle-sitters were mixed in their opinions, several calling it a "curiosity" but having difficulty endorsing the double bill. Mel Gussow in the *New York Times* perhaps summed up the reaction best, calling it "marginal, more a double-jointed exercise than a full Stoppard spree, but with, as usual, imagination and cleverness to spare."

Mary O'Malley's comedy **Once a Catholic** (10-10-79, Helen Hayes) had somehow tickled the funny bone of audiences at London's Royal Court Theatre, but on Broadway the humor failed to translate, and it lasted only six performances. Set in a convent school in London in the 1950s where all the girls are called Mary and all the nuns have masculine names, the autobiographical play concerned the sexual oppression Mother Peter (Rachel Roberts) and her staff exert over the girls, who are, consequently, all the more fascinated by the subject. (In one scene a group of the Marys are caught in the lavatory reading "dirty" passages from the Bible.) The central character, Mary Mooney (Mia Dillon), who is a newcomer and the victim of the girls' vicious frustration, actually comes close to a sexual encounter with a visiting teenage boy, but the venture is so unsuccessful that Mary decides to become a nun. The reviews were largely negative, most critics feeling the jokes ran out long before the play did, and Walter Kerr in the *New York Times* dismissed the comedy with "*Once a Catholic* is twice a bore."

The American Place Theatre opened its abbreviated season with Rose Leiman Goldenberg's dramatization of the late poet Sylvia Plath's **Letters Home** (10-12-79, American Place), a correspondence between Plath (Mary McDonnell) and her mother (Doris Belack). The evening was more literary than dramatic, but the play garnered some positive reviews and played to subscribers and interested parties for thirty-six performances. Also very literary but more satisfying was a two-week engagement of **Letters of Love and Affection** (10-16-79, Roundabout: Stage One), a one-person show compiled and performed by Irene Worth. Using letters in the Pierpont Morgan Library, Worth read correspondence from such varied personages as Mozart, Lincoln, Browning, Twain, Voltaire, Elizabeth I, Flaubert, and others. The response was healthy enough that the program was repeated for another week starting on November 6.

Kevin Morrison's *Ladyhouse Blues* (10-28-76) had only been seen in a brief engagement at the Phoenix in 1976. On October 17 ANTA revived the World War I homefront drama off Broadway at St. Peter's Church. Laurie Kennedy, Christine Estabrook, Jobeth Williams, Wendy Fulton, and Jo Henderson played the waiting women, and the well-received production ran two months.

The Circle Repertory Theatre presented a season with some classic revivals sandwiched in between its usual offerings of new American plays. It opened with three new one-acts by David Mamet under the umbrella title **Reunion** (10-18-79, Circle). Each of the duologues was sparse and, as

some critics pointed out, in a Pinteresque mode. In **Dark Pony** a father told a familiar bedtime story to his daughter as they drove through the night; **The Sanctity of Marriage** explored a couple whose marriage was falling apart even as they recalled a past vacation to Europe together; and *Reunion* concerned an alcoholic father and his daughter meeting after a twenty-five-year estrangement. Reviewers preferred the last playlet and complimented Lindsay Crouse and Michael Higgins, who played all three couples.

The season off Broadway at the Phoenix Theatre began with David Lan's **The Winter Dancers** (10-18-79, Marymount Manhattan), a leaden exposé on the plight of a tribe of Native Americans in late nineteenth-century Canada. The play illustrated with great detail the daily life of a primitive tribe on Vancouver Island, then how their way of life was forever changed by the coming of the white man. Lan had impressive archaeological and anthropological credentials, but the press found his playwriting skills hopeless. It also did not help that the cast was comprised of blond-haired Wasp types bearing such character names as One Foot and Mouse, Blood Lip, Well Washed Stone, and Life Owner.

The American Humorists Series at the American Place had one of its most popular entries with **Smart Aleck: Alexander Woolcott at 8:40** (10-19-79, American Place). Howard Teichmann wrote the script from his Woolcott biography, and Peter Boyden impersonated the colorful critic and radio personality with great aplomb. Instead of running a week as most entries in the series did, it played seventy-one times.

Two foreign plays were introduced in October with little excitement. At the Public, Frederick Neumann adapted Samuel Beckett's novel **Mercier & Camier** (10-25-79, LuEsther) for the stage; Philip Glass provided background music. Neumann and Bill Raymond played the two itinerant title characters who search for order in a fantastical world. In Brooklyn, the Dodger Theatre's lackluster season opened with Slawomir Mrozek's **Emigrés** (10-28-79, BAM) with Jon Polito and Brent Spiner as refugees with opposing backgrounds who are forced by circumstances to room together in a foreign land. The Beckett work ran a month, and the Slawomir duet ran seventeen performances.

David Edgar's adaptation **The Jail Diary of Albie Sachs** (11-6-79, Manhattan Theatre Club) was a British play making its world premiere off Broadway with an American cast. Brian Murray played Sachs, a lawyer imprisoned in South Africa in the early 1960s for his political beliefs who kept an accurate account of his ordeal there. The docudrama, staged by Lynne Meadow, ran forty-eight times.

Devour the Snow (5-2-79), Abe Polsky's powerful drama about the Donner expedition, had done well enough off Broadway that it transferred to the John Golden on November 7. The play was not greeted with the kind of "money" reviews needed to sell its dark subject matter to the public and closed after five performances. Michel Tremblay's transsexual comedy-drama *Hosanna* (10-14-74) was revived by the Production Company on November 7 at Playhouse 46 and ran forty-two performances. Kenneth Norris and Kevin Wade played the quarreling lovers.

The Broadway season's first commercial hit was Bernard Slade's **Romantic Comedy** (11-8-79, Ethel Barrymore), a play as straightforward and unsurprising as its title. Successful playwright Jason Carmichael (Anthony Perkins) considers himself the American Noel Coward, although all he shares with the British master is a sharp tongue and a lot of arrogance. On the day of his wedding to socialite Allison St. James (Holly Palance), Jason meets his new collaborator, Phoebe Craddock (Mia Farrow), under very awkward conditions: she walks in on him while he is stark naked waiting for a massage. The next ten years bring the odd couple a variety of hits and flops, Jason's marriage falls apart, and Phoebe plans to marry the journalist Leo (Greg Mullavey) until the ending the audience expects is arrived at. The comedy was rather forced (even by Slade standards), and critical reaction was mixed, ranging from "a darling of a play . . . a zesty entertainment of cool wit and warm sentiment" to "one long credibility gap." Most felt the performers were better than the limp *bons mots* they were provided with, and Perkins's brief but bold nude scene was just racy enough to spark comment without discouraging conservative audiences. The comedy ran a year and enjoyed some success in stock, but Slade, who had squeaked by on three questionable hits, was rarely heard from again.

A commercial off-Broadway entry that actually proved profitable was Dennis McIntyre's stormy bio-drama **Modigliani** (11-11-79, Astor Place) about the Italian artist's last year. In 1916 Montparnasse, the impoverished Amedeo Modigliani (Jeffrey DeMunn) tries to scrounge up enough money to leave Paris, even attempting a robbery with his fellow artists Soutine (George Gerdes) and Utrillo (Ethan Phillips) that fails. When his agent (Michael Tucker) sets up a meeting with a renowned art dealer (Richard Seff), the encounter turns into an explosive tirade and Modigliani destroys several of his paintings. Only his British mistress, Beatrice (Mary-Joan Negro), is able to convince the tormented artist of the value of his work, and the plays ends with Modigliani beginning a self-portrait. Most of the critics approved of the play and the hyperactive production, calling it "wonderfully exciting" and "wildly funny and moodily provocative," which helped it to run 119 performances.

A short-lived off-Broadway curiosity was Ken Eulo's **The Frankenstein Affair** (11-13-79, Courtyard Playhouse), a play about the stormy marriage of Percy (Charles Regan) and Mary Shelley (Liza Vann). The drama chronicled the unhappy couple from 1814 to 1820, and the action was interspersed with Mary's creations, Dr. Frankenstein (Dana Mills) and his monster (Alan Bruun), in similar scenes of conflict. The two couples quarreled for twenty-eight performances.

Like David Mamet, Sam Shepard presented an evening of new one-acts this season and came up with minor-league offerings. If the Mamet plays were considered Pinteresque, Shepard's **Tongues** (11-15-79, Public: Other Stage) was in the style of Beckett. Joseph Chaikin, billed as collaborator, performed the monodramas, one titled **Savage/Love** and the other *Tongues*. Each was a stream-of-consciousness rambling of a patient under analysis, and all the big themes, from love to death, were touched upon. The plays aroused little interest, but there were enough endorsements for Chaikin's performance to help the double bill run forty-four times.

A London import from the Royal Court that managed to find an audience off Broadway for 184 performances and gather some respectable reviews was Nigel Williams's **Class Enemy** (11-19-79, Players). Ballsache High is a state comprehensive school in impoverished South London, and the students, who have nicknames such as Nipper, Snatch, and Racks, are a pretty volatile bunch. But when the belligerent ringleader Iron (Maxwell Caulfield) stirs the teens up, violence erupts, and the classroom becomes a metaphor for social warfare in Britain. The climactic fistfight between Iron and the philosophical Sky-Light (Bruce Wall) leaves the ringleader victorious but shunned by the other students, so he destroys the classroom and ends up a sobbing shadow, impotent in his own anger. Comparisons with John Osborne's *Look Back in Anger* (10-1-57) were inevitable, but as one critic pointed out, these boys "looked to the future with anger." The play also had a Beckett-like tone: the six students lost in an empty classroom without a teacher for them to torment. Tony Tanner directed the young and promising cast, which featured stand-out performances by Caulfield and Lonny Price as the complex student Racks.

Frank D. Gilroy had not enjoyed any success on Broadway since his three-character drama *The Subject Was Roses* (5-25-64), and his latest three-handed piece, a seventy-minute comedy-drama titled **Last Licks** (11-20-79, Longacre), continued the trend by closing after fifteen performances. The ailing widower Matt Quinlan (Ed Flanders) has not left his Brooklyn house since his wife died eight months before, so his son, Dennis (J. T. Walsh), wants him to go into a home or get a full-time housekeeper. But the old man is stubborn and fights with his son until the doorbell rings and the prospective housekeeper arranged by Dennis arrives. Fiona Raymond (Susan Kellermann) is a tough and determined ex-nun and, unknown to Dennis, was Matt's mistress for many years. When alone together Fiona derides Matt for breaking off with her when his wife died, takes the job as housekeeper, and insists that their sex life will flourish once again, his poor health notwithstanding. But when Dennis returns and discovers that the two are sleeping with each other, he is shocked (even though he overheard some of their conversation earlier and learned of their relationship), and the comedy dissolves into a "turgid" family argument about the past, Dennis proclaiming, "Every son competes with his father for his mother—and I won!" The mostly negative reviews were gentle in their dismissal.

An off-Broadway transfer that did survive on Broadway was the Chelsea's *Strider: The Story of a Horse* (5-31-79), which opened on November 21 and remained at the Helen Hayes into May, racking up a total of 214 performances.

Tom Stoppard's third offering of the season was the London success **Night and Day** (11-27-79, ANTA), which was brought to Broadway with a mostly American cast surrounding its British star, Maggie Smith. Stoppard, never one to narrow his subject matter to a single idea, this time covered British imperialism, contemporary journalism, Third World politics, unionism, and the battle of the sexes—a true Shavian feast, but one that offered satisfying morsels rather than a complete meal. In the fictional African republic of Kambawe, ruled over by the Idi Amin–like President Mageeba (Clarence Williams III), a Soviet-backed political uprising draws journalists from around the world, including the tough-as-nails Australian

veteran Dick Wagner (Paul Hecht), the "objective" photographer George Guthrie (Dwight Schultz), and the attractive novice Jacob Milne (Peter Evans), all of whom gather at the home of British industrialist Geoffrey Carson (Joseph Maher), who owns Kambawe's largest copper mine. Carson's wife, Ruth (Smith), has little use for journalists and takes the opportunity to offer her acid-tongued opinions of the press ("We play Monopoly . . . as far as I remember, Fleet Street was yellow and rather cheap") and of Wagner, with whom she had a brief affair when last in London. But when the attractive Milne manages to get an interview with the rebel leader, the restless Ruth is drawn to him, and the two fall into a tropical romance. After each major character, including the President, gets to express himself on the question of a free press and other issues, Milne is killed in the fighting. Ruth argues that no news story was worth his death; she gets drunk, and the play ends with her singing old songs such as the play's title. Smith received unanimous adulation from the critics, but several had misgivings about the play, finding more to admire in Stoppard's writing than to actually enjoy. The male characters were thought to be the weakest aspect of the play, Kerr calling them "attitudes." *Night and Day* hung on for an unprofitable ninety-five performances.

William Inge's *The Dark at the Top of the Stairs* (12-5-57) received its first New York revival on November 29. The Roundabout production featured Earl Hindman as the moody salesman Rubin Flood, Dorothy Tristan as his wife, and Patricia Sales as her interfering sister.

At mid-season, *Variety* reported that four times as many Broadway houses were dark as were open. Yet business was up: the trend of fewer but more expensive productions on the Street was becoming very obvious.

Martin Sherman's melodrama **Bent** (12-2-79, New Apollo), about the Nazi persecution of homosexuals, was first produced in London, but the author was an American who had tested the work at the Eugene O'Neill Theatre Center in Connecticut. In 1934 Berlin, lovers Max (Richard Gere) and Rudy (David Marshall Grant) awaken from a night of alcohol and sex with an SS guard to have storm troopers burst into their apartment and slit the throat of the gay soldier. What follows is a series of scenes in which the two lovers try to survive Hitler's purge of homosexuals in Germany. Later captured and put in a boxcar to Dachau, Rudy is beaten to death, and Max is forced to rape a dead thirteen-year-old girl to convince the Nazis that he is not a homosexual but a Jew. At the camp Max finds love with Horst (David Dukes); in the play's most memorable scene, the two men, standing apart and at attention during a rest period in the prison yard, bring each other to a sexual climax by verbally describing images of their imagined lovemaking. Eventually the sickly Horst attacks a German guard and is shot, and Max commits suicide by walking into the electrified fence surrounding the camp. Reviews were mostly positive, calling *Bent* everything from "an explosive, overpowering experience" to "audacious theatre." The drama was stern stuff for Broadway, but Robert Allan Ackerman's taut direction, Santo Loquasto's simple but evocative scenery, and the fine acting throughout kept it on the boards for 240 performances. (Movie star Gere's presence certainly helped; the play survived only a month after he was replaced by Michael York.)

Papp continued to support playwright Tina Howe by presenting her comedy of contemporary manners **The Art of Dining** (12-6-79, Public; Newman), but he only kept it around for six performances despite some encouraging reviews. Ellen (Suzanne Collins), a chef, and her husband, Cal (Ron Rifkin), own and operate a small but classy restaurant on the New Jersey shore, and the magnificent dishes she prepares for her customers reveal not only different people's dining habits but also their sensual behavior. As in her earlier *Museum* (2-7-78), Howe presented a series of short scenes that quickly sketch individuals' private dramas in a public place. The diners include a couple who find sensuality in just reading the menu, career girls who are numb to any kind of delicacy in life, and a neurotic authoress who falls apart over a meal with a prospective publisher. Kathy Bates and Dianne Wiest were among the strong actors who played the dining customers. Less than a week later Papp presented Peter Parnell's first play, **Sorrows of Stephen** (12-11-79, Public: Cabaret), which was considered by some a less satisfying work than Howe's but ran 167 performances. When the hopeless romantic Stephen Hurt (John Shea) is dumped by his girlfriend (Sherry Steiner), he sets out to find true love in modern Manhattan, using Goethe's tragic novel *The Sorrows of Young Werther* as his guidebook. He attempts to woo a hardened female cab driver (Kathy McKenna), foolishly makes a stranger (Barbara Williams) at the opera his secret love, falls for a too-willing waitress (Anne De-Salvo), and even attempts to win his best friend's fiancée (Pamela Reed) away from him. But all of

Stephen's overtures turn to rejection, so he plans to commit suicide like his literary hero, only to end up shooting his ficus plant. Parnell's writing was breezy and literary (there were references to Tolstoy, Stendahl, and Balzac scattered throughout), and reviewers thought him very promising.

The Roundabout's finest revival of the season was Turgenev's rural tragicomedy *A Month in the Country*, which opened on December 11 and was held over into April. Michael Kahn directed the worthy ensemble that featured Tammy Grimes (Natalya), Philip Bosco (Shpigelsky), Farley Granger (Ratikin), Jerome Kilty (Islayev), Boyd Gaines (Aleksei), and Amanda Plummer (Vera). The critics saluted both the play and the "superlative new production." They also admired the repertory of two classics that the Circle Rep initiated on December 12, even if the productions were not as strong as one could hope for. *Hamlet* featured William Hurt as the Prince with support from Douglass Watson (Claudius), Beatrice Straight (Gertrude), Lindsay Crouse (Ophelia), and Michael Ayr (Laertes). Schiller's *Mary Stuart* joined the repertory the next night with Stephanie Gordon in the title role and Tanya Berezin as her rival, Elizabeth. Marshall W. Mason directed both productions, and more than one commentator felt that such classics were not the ideal vehicles for this director and his Circle players. But the two-month repertory was well attended.

Harvey Fierstein's comedy **Fugue in a Nursery** (12-12-79, Orpheum) was a sequel to his earlier *The International Stud* (5-22-78) and part of a planned trilogy concerning the drag queen Arnold and his up-and-down romantic adventures. *Fugue in a Nursery* explored the comic and awkward ramifications when Arnold (Fierstein) and his new young lover Alan (Christopher Marcantel), spend a weekend with Arnold's ex-lover Ed (Will Jeffries) and his new girlfriend Laurel (Maria Cellario) at their upstate New York farm. Ed resents the presence of the handsome model Alan (Laurel insisted that he be invited) and tries to come on to Arnold again but, instead, ends up being seduced by Alan. When Ed confesses the liaison to Laurel, she admires his honesty but separates from him and consoles herself with Arnold (who had not heard about Ed and Alan's fling until she told him). Ed and Laurel get back together and become engaged, and Alan buys Arnold a dog, a symbol of his willingness to make his relationship with Arnold permanent. The entire play was presented in a giant bed that filled the stage, the couples moving to different sections of it for brief scenes and then tumbling about in new combinations, sometimes with three-way conversations on the phone or two simultaneous conversations crisscrossing. Fierstein's dialogue was as crackling and quick as in the first play, and the effect was that of a playful fugue moving in new and surprising directions all the time. The sharp little comedy ran fifty-three times.

The Negro Ensemble Company's best offering in years was the irresistible comedy **Home** (12-14-79, St. Marks) by Samm-Art Williams, an actor who had appeared in several Ensemble productions. *Home* was refreshingly different for the black theatre group in that it was a boisterous folk comedy and advocated a simple and old-fashioned life on the farm rather than success in the big city. Cephus Miles (Charles Brown) sits on a rocking chair on his North Carolina farmhouse porch and spins tales about himself, with the actresses L. Scott Caldwell and Michele Shay enacting all the characters he encounters in his adventures. Cephus is a lively raconteur, and he often gets sidetracked by relating tall tales and colorful rural legends in a Mark Twain manner. Young Cephus is in love with the pretty and smart Pattie Mae Wells (Caldwell), and the two plan to wed and settle on his uncle's farm. But Patti Mae goes off to college, learns there is more to life than fish frys and a house full of hungry kids, and marries a Boston-born lawyer. Cephus inherits the farm but is soon called up for the draft and, refusing to fight in Vietnam, goes to jail for five years. Losing the farm to back taxes, he decides to head north, where the big city swallows him up. Cephus becomes an alcoholic and has a seesaw love affair with Myrna (Shay). Eventually she leaves him. "Where there is no money," she says, "there can be no love. I think the Bible says that." Cephus, hearing from relatives that the farm has been bought by a mysterious Mr. Harper and given back to him, returns south on a Greyhound bus with all the other southerners going home for the Christmas holidays. "Mr. Harper" turns out to be Patti Mae, who has divorced her husband and returned home to live with Cephus on the farm as they had always meant to do. The press applauded Williams's vigorous style of storytelling, calling it "a joyous Whitmanesque song" and "one of the most joyous and amusing plays of several seasons." The company kept the comedy on the boards for eighty-two performances (three times its scheduled run), then transferred it on May 7 to Broadway's Cort Theatre, where it totaled 279

performances. Unfortunately, *Home* was Williams's only play of note.

An Isaac Bashevis Singer fable set in nineteenth-century Poland, **Teibele and Her Demon** (12-16-79, Brooks Atkinson) was adapted for the stage by the author and Eve Friedman but only managed to survive twenty-five performances. In the Polish city of Frampol in the 1880s, the passionate young wife Teibele (Laura Esterman) has been deserted by her husband but cannot remarry until he is officially declared dead. The penniless scholar Alchonon (F. Murray Abraham) has long worshipped Teibele, and her open hostility to him has not dampened his admiration. Knowing of her interest in demons and their mystical (and sexual) powers, Alchonon disguises himself as a demon, comes to her in the night, woos her, and wins her affection. Because marriage to a demon is impossible, Alchonon forges a letter saying that the husband is dead and then, as the demon, tells Teibele the devil needs his services elsewhere but she should marry Alchonon. After protesting, she agrees to the marriage but will not sleep with her new husband, longing instead for the return of her demon. When Teibele is dying, the rabbi convinces Alchonon to tell her the truth so that she can die in peace. What started as a childlike fable turned too dark for some critics, but others called it "unusual theatre, funny, moving, and full of wonder."

The one-person show **Paris Was Yesterday** (12-19-79, Harold Clurman) had limited appeal but was thoroughly enjoyed by those who had been reading the reports from Genêt in *The New Yorker* over the past fifty years. Janet Flanner, who had died the previous year, was the woman behind the pen name, and she had collected her articles into a book that Paul Shyre adapted into a monodrama. Celeste Holm played Genêt and shared her opinions and observations about Paris and its inhabitants (including Gertrude Stein and many of the folk discussed in that other one-woman show).

The Phoenix's odd season continued with **Shout Across the River** (12-27-79, Marymount Manhattan), a domestic drama by prolific British playwright Stephen Poliakoff, who never found as many admirers here as in England. Scatterbrained city dweller Mrs. Forsythe (Barbara Eda-Young) and her daughter, Christine (Ellen Barkin), do not get along. The troubled daughter has been expelled from school once again and, in frustrated fury, kidnaps her own mother and abuses her physically and verbally. But when Christine has a nervous breakdown, the mother pulls her few wits together and saves her daughter. Critics rejected the "incoherent little play."

The new year began with three interesting revivals. Beckett's *Endgame* (1-28-58) on January 1 at the Manhattan Theatre Club was staged by Joseph Chaikin as a vaudeville, and several reviews thought it worked quite well. Daniel Seltzer and Michael Gross were Hamm and Clov; James Barbosa and Joan McIntosh, the geriatric couple in trash cans. Molnár's *The Guardsman* (10-13-24) cried out for stars and high style, neither of which was in evidence in the Production Company's revival on January 2 at Playhouse 46. On Broadway, New Haven's Long Wharf Theatre brought its acclaimed revival of Lillian Hellman's *Watch on the Rhine* (4-1-41) to the John Golden on January 3, and there was quite a difference of opinion as to whether the anti-Fascist drama was still relevant today. Arvin Brown directed the propaganda piece, and George Hearn and Harris Yulin played the two Germans with opposing agendas. Also featured in the cast were Jan Miner, Jill Eikenberry, and Joyce Ebert. The regional production stayed for a month.

Harold Pinter's **Betrayal** (1-5-80, Trafalgar), perhaps his least obscure and most conventional play, told the tale of an extramarital affair in reverse. Two years after literary agent Jerry (Raul Julia) and his best friend's wife, Emma (Blythe Danner), have ended their dalliance, they meet in a pub once again. Emma and her publisher husband, Robert (Roy Scheider), are getting a divorce, and she seeks an understanding ear. It seems Robert has been unfaithful. In an ironic twist, Jerry feels betrayed by the news. She also realizes that Robert was aware of her and Jerry's romance but regarded it as insignificant. The play then moves backwards, showing various stages of the triangle, ending nine years earlier with the beginning of the affair and the start of all the little betrayals to come. The intricate and chilly drama received propitious reviews all around (the New York Drama Critics Circle named it Best Foreign Play); although some complained about the American actors using a stiff mid-Atlantic accent in place of a British one, the cast was also lauded. The "mesmerizing" drama ran five months.

James Lapine had stirred up some interest with his surreal play *Twelve Dreams* off-off Broadway in 1978 but made a much bigger noise with **Table Settings** (1-14-80, Playwrights Horizons), a Jewish comedy using the dining room table as the family battlefield. The stereotypic Jewish Mother (Frances Chaney) is an old-fashioned immigrant from Minsk who frets over her life ("Do you think I like being the topic of conversation at psychiatrists' offices?" she asks) and her family: the lawyer son (Brent Spiner) who drinks too much and wishes his *shiksa* wife and kids would leave him alone, the younger son (Mark Blum) who hasn't found himself yet but is stoned most of the time he is looking, a granddaughter (Marta Kober) whose curiosity about sex is unnerving, and a grandson (Eric Gurry) who finds life so overwhelming that he spends much of the time hiding under the table. There was no through-plot, and some of the scenes were only brief monologues, but the comedy bounced along, and the critics approved, calling it "hilarious and endearing" and an "original, swift-paced, and unfailingly likable comedy." *Table Settings* ran 264 performances, but it would be Lapine's only non-musical play of note; his career shifted, and he became better known as a director and the author of musical librettos.

Yves Jamiaque, a popular French playwright who was rarely produced in America, was represented this season with **Monsieur Amilcar** (1-15-80, Chelsea), a boulevard comedy that played a limited engagement of forty performances off Broadway. The prosperous Parisian businessman Alexander Amilcar (Larry Keith) has been deceived by his wife and sets out to see that it never happens again. He hires "a family in good working order," and they perform for him each evening, playing the perfect family but not, he insists, getting personally involved. His wife, Eleanor (Judith Barcroft), is an actress well suited for the role, his daughter, Virginia (Sheila K. Adams), is a tough street urchin, and his best friend, Machou (K. Lype O'Dell), is a man Alexander found in the unemployment line. Of course the charade does not work, the three impostors beginning to quarrel and carry on like a real family. Then Eleanor starts to fall in love with Alexander, or is it still part of the act? (The author leaves the question unresolved.) So Alexander, who had hoped never to be deceived or hurt again, is once again caught up in the painful complications of the heart. George Gonneau and Norman Rose adapted the French text, and the Chelsea Theatre Center's producing director, Robert Kalfin, directed the unusual comedy. While some critics were not amused (one called it "uninspired Neil Simon overdosed on Pirandello"), most thought it an "enticing exercise with comic overtones."

The Public and Thomas Babe continued their mutual admiration for each other with **Salt Lake City Skyline** (1-23-80, Anspacher), a courtroom drama set in 1915 about labor organizer and songwriter Joe Hill. Accused on the flimsiest of evidence of murdering a grocery store owner and his son, Swedish-born Hill (John Lithgow) takes on his own defense and uses the Salt Lake City courtroom as a platform for his ideas on labor and radical politics. During his defense he launches into songs and fantasy sequences that ridicule his accusers. In the end, refusing to use his alibi because it would compromise the woman he loves, Hill is found guilty, is executed by firing squad, and becomes a martyr and a folk hero. John Beaufort of the *Christian Science Monitor* called it "an erratic piece of work. The treatment ends up diminishing Joe Hill, vulgarizing his situation, trivializing his plight," and most aisle-sitters agreed. But there was general approval for Lithgow's fiery Hill and for Fred Gwynne's touching portrayal of the terminally ill judge who tries the case. Hellbent on stirring up controversy, the melodrama ran out its month-long engagement with minimal agitation.

A wild and allegorical comedy by Paul D'Andrea called **The Trouble with Europe** (1-24-80, Marymount Manhattan) continued the Phoenix's disappointing season. When the presidents of both the United States and France decide that the world is in a mess, they send the arrogant Inspector Jogot (Kristoffer Tabori) and the dewy-eyed cowboy Wilbur Tilbury (Perry King) to ascertain the problem and fix it in six days. The two men's journey, which occurrs more in their heads than on any map, takes them to the underworld before they return to the surface with knowledge and friendship and, indeed, fix up the century's problems in twelve hours. The conceit was reminiscent of Giraudoux's similar fable *The Madwoman of Chaillot* (12-27-48), but D'Andrea's fantasy was more heavy-handed and not nearly as whimsical as the earlier work.

Edward Albee's **The Lady from Dubuque** (1-31-80, Morosco) only lasted twelve performances, but several felt this play, unlike most of the season's other short runs, deserved better. Jo (Frances Conroy) is dying of some unnamed but painful disease, and her husband, Sam (Tony Musante), tries to bring her comfort by inviting four of their friends to the house to play Twenty Questions and other diverting games. But the two other couples only cause Jo to lash out, insulting them and exposing their shortcomings and failures. Late at night the elegant and mysterious Elizabeth (Irene Worth), dressed in black and claiming to be Jo's mother, arrives with a distinguished African-American gentleman called Oscar (Earle Hyman) to comfort the ailing Jo.

IRENE WORTH [Hattie Abrams] (1916–) was born in rural Nebraska, the daughter of a school superintendent, and was educated at the University of California at Los Angeles where she received a degree in education in 1937. After graduation she became a schoolteacher before turning to the stage in 1942. Worth made her Broadway debut in a supporting role in *The Two Mrs. Carrolls* (1943) but before long left New York to study classical theatre in London. While there she gained attention for her Celia in the Edinburgh world premiere of T. S. Eliot's *The Cocktail Party* (1949) and several roles at the Old Vic. She helped Tyrone Guthrie found the Stratford Festival in Ontario, Canada, and played many classical roles there in the 1950s before joining the Royal Shakespeare Company in England in the 1960s. Occasionally returning to Broadway, she scored a triumph as the wealthy title character in Albee's difficult *Tiny Alice* (1964) and as Madame Arkadina in the controversial 1977 Lincoln Center production of *The Cherry Orchard*. Often mistaken for a British actress because of her classical training and many roles in England, Worth possessed a rich and musical voice and a striking stage presence that made her among the most distinguished of American stage actresses.

Sam insists they are frauds and has a minor nervous breakdown trying to convince the others that they are lying, but Jo finds great comfort in the two strangers and willingly lets them put her to bed. The deathlike couple soon emerge from the bedroom, tell Sam not to worry about Jo any longer, and start to depart. When Sam insists on knowing who Elizabeth really is, she tells him, "Why, I'm the lady from Dubuque. I thought you knew." Then she turns to the audience and states, "I thought he knew," as the curtain falls. (The title came from Harold Ross's famous edict that his *New Yorker* magazine was *not* for the little old lady in Dubuque.) Critical opinion was varied, and much discussion was generated about the puzzling play. Some commentators agreed it was a "somewhat strained, oddly bifurcated, and finally compelling two-act play," but Kerr felt that Albee "failed to give his on-stage mannequins any actual identities to uncover . . . we're shooting at zeros." Editor Otis L. Guernsey, Jr., included *The Lady from Dubuque* as one of the season's ten *Best Plays*, and he was not alone in the opinion, but even the favorable notices were not "money" reviews, so the producers closed it on February 9. What was not questioned was Alan Schneider's

ALAN SCHNEIDER [Abram Leopoldovich] (1917–1984) was born in Krakov, Russia, to parents who were both doctors. The family moved to the United States and settled in Maryland in 1923. Schneider studied medicine briefly at Johns Hopkins University but turned to theatre and received degrees from the University of Wisconsin and Cornell. During World War II he taught theatre and directed plays at Catholic University before working professionally in summer stock and off Broadway. Schneider's Broadway directing debut was *A Long Way from Home* (1948), and he quickly established himself as a superb interpreter of serious drama. In addition to many outstanding productions at the Arena Stage in Washington, he directed such memorable Broadway shows as *Who's Afraid of Virginia Woolf?* (1962), *Tiny Alice* (1964), *Entertaining Mr. Sloane* (1965), *A Delicate Balance* (1966), *The Birthday Party* (1967), *Moonchildren* (1972), and *A Texas Trilogy* (1976). Considered one of the finest directors of Samuel Beckett's works, Schneider staged the American premiere of *Waiting for Godot* (1956). Although he studied with Lee Strasberg at the Actors Studio, Schneider was an eclectic director who went far beyond the method, giving a great deal of attention to the text and approaching both realism and absurdism with a meticulous sense of study and discovery.

taut direction and Worth's beguiling performance as "the most elegant and commanding of supernatural creatures imaginable." It was her third stunning turn of the season and reestablished Worth as one of our premiere stage actresses.

Wallace Shawn began a series of plays that always seemed to arouse passionate praise or denial with **Marie and Bruce** (2-3-80, Public: Newman), a tragicomic view of a failed marriage. Foul-mouthed Marie (Louise Lasser) continually demeans her weak-willed husband, Bruce (Bob Balaban), who manages to fall asleep in the middle of their arguments. Seen in various situations with their bizarre friends (some of whom were played by mannequins), the couple ride a roller coaster of emotions, she often threatening to leave him and he barely able to grasp what she is saying. In the end, Marie realizes that it is Bruce's weakness and vulnerability that makes him so attractive and decides to maintain their tormented marriage. The critics felt television star Lasser gave a strong and funny performance, but only a handful could tolerate the script and its scatological dialogue. Lasser's appeal helped

fill the house for the forty-seven scheduled performances.

No Broadway offering this season closed more quickly than **Harold and Maude** (2-7-80, Martin Beck), a stage adaptation of the popular cult film. Colin Higgins, who had written the screenplay for the 1971 black comedy, did the stage adaptation, which was a resounding success in Paris but was greeted with unanimously vilifying reviews in New York, folding after four performances. The wealthy but morbid teenager Harold (Keith McDermott) is fascinated by suicide and often stages killing himself to upset his mother. But when he meets the life-affirming octogenarian Countess Maude (Janet Gaynor) at a funeral (attending the funerals of strangers is a hobby they share), they fall in love and are constant companions during the old lady's final days. The odd twosome learn to share life as it comes and even make love together. But Maude's inevitable death comes sooner than expected, and her loss brings a sense of salvation to the youth. What had been quirky and captivating on film was embarrassing and considered in poor taste when presented onstage. Notices declared it "downright grisly whenever it decides to make a joke" and a "mawkish little piece about the milder shores of love." Film legend Janet Gaynor (in her Broadway debut) was ingratiatingly saluted and not blamed for the "truly dopey play."

The Negro Ensemble's season after the success of *Home* brought nothing of interest until its last offering, a double bill that consisted of Ali Wadud's two-character **Companions of the Fire** and Roy R. Kuljian's **Big City Blues** (2-7-80, St. Marks). When an overweight Harlem woman (Barbara Montgomery) picks up a young man (Charles Brown) in the park and brings him home to celebrate her birthday with a passionate fling, little does she realize that he is a fervent orator who speaks long and hard about saving the black race. But in her efforts at first, to seduce him and then to get rid of him, she begins to see herself in a new light. The big city of the second play is Los Angeles, where three citizens each deliver a monologue describing his or her life. The writing may have been suspect, but Samm-Art Williams, Chuck Patterson, and Frances Foster as the three monologists were riveting.

Eduardo de Filippo's **Filumena** (2-10-80, St. James) was a new version of his *The Best House in Naples* (10-26-56), which had survived only three performances in an earlier translation by F. Hugh Herbert. Keith Waterhouse and Willis Hall wrote the new English version, which was a hit in London for two years, and it was brought to Broadway with some of the British cast for a limited engagement. The elderly Naples businessman Domenico Soriano (Frank Finlay) considers marrying a much younger woman, but his mistress of twenty-five years, the determined Filumena (Joan Plowright), pretends to be dying and insists that Domenico wed her and give his name to her three illegitimate sons, one of whom is his. She will not say which son is the true Soriano, and Domenico tries in vain to find out, so he marries her to learn the truth. But Filumena refuses to divulge the information even after the wedding, claiming that Domenico would favor the one over the other two men. In the end Domenico accepts all three as his offspring, and Filumena "recovers" to spend many more years with her new family. Laurence Olivier directed the familiar story (the popular 1964 Italian film *Marriage, Italian Style* had been based on the play) and the exemplary cast, which aisle-sitters enjoyed more than the script. While they questioned the need for all the exaggerated (and inconsistent) Neapolitan accents, most critics thought it "a thoroughly delightful confection" and an "unabashedly old-fashioned comedy."

A new and promising theatre company was launched in Brooklyn when *The Winter's Tale* opened on February 12. It was the first of five revivals to be presented in rotating repertory by David Jones's BAM Theatre Company, and both audiences and critics welcomed the new group and its ambitious season. Jones directed, and David Gropman provided a simple setting filled with toy soldiers, a rocking horse, and large building blocks. The company included Brian Murray (Leontes), Sheila Allen (Paulina), Marti Maraden (Hermione), Joe Morton (Autoclycus), and Christine Estabrook (Perdita). Newcomers in the cast who would later find recognition included Boyd Gaines and Cherry Jones. The difficult play was presented twenty-seven times during the next two months.

Mayo Simon's **These Men** (2-14-80, Harold Clurman) seemed to be the umpteenth two-character play this season about frustrated women; it certainly was among the worst. In a cabin in California's Laurel Canyon, the vulgar and promiscuous Shelly (Alix Elias) and the repressed, easily shocked Cloris (Jill Larson) thrash out their difficulties with men, sex, and each other. There was much talk about an unseen psychiatrist who was obviously (except to the two

women) some kind of charlatan, and the dialogue was peppered with the kind of scatological seasoning so prominent in such plays. The press thought Zoe Caldwell did a fine job directing the two talented actresses but that the venture was hopeless. It remained hopeless for thirty-seven performances.

Lanford Wilson's *Talley's Folly* (5-1-79) transferred from Off Broadway to the Brooks Atkinson on February 20 with the same cast (Judd Hirsch and Trish Hawkins) and a larger but still pristine setting by John Lee Beatty, and the production was greeted with another round of cheers. Aided by winning the Pulitzer Prize in the spring, the romantic comedy-drama ran for 277 performances and became a favorite in regional and stock companies for several seasons thereafter.

BAM added Charles MacArthur's short-lived comedy *Johnny on a Spot* (1-8-42) to its repertory on February 21, and several thought it a lost gem rediscovered. Brendan Gill in *The New Yorker* called it "a sensationally attractive new production" of a "noisy, outrageous and sentimental piece of work, every moment of which gave me pleasure." Edward Cornell directed the proficient BAM company in the political comedy. Singled out by the notices were Gary Bayer as the campaign manager, Nicky Allen, and Roxanne Hart as the governor's secretary, Julie. There was also applause for John Lee Beatty's set filled with doors, elevators, a sprinkler system, and a giant iron lung, all of which were cunningly used. The shenanigans were on view twenty-seven times during the four-month repertory season.

The Colonnades Theatre Lab's short season presented a new and an old Irish play together for a three-month run. Wolf Mankowitz's **The Irish Hebrew Lesson** (2-22-80, Colonnades) concerned a fiery young Irish revolutionary (Curtis Armstrong) who, fleeing from British soldiers in the turbulent Ireland of 1921, breaks into the home of an old Jew (Nicholas Kepros) to hide. He threatens to kill the elderly man, but soon the two are deep into discussion about Judaism, Christianity, and God. When the soldiers bang on the door looking for the youth, the old man tries to conceal the boy, but his efforts are in vain. The second half of the double bill, *Guests of the Nation*, was based on Frank O'Connor's short story and had been seen off Broadway in 1958. It also was set in Ireland during the troubles and told the story of two British soldiers (Charlie Stavola and Nesbitt Blaisdell) held hostage by Irish revolutionaries in a remote cottage in the countryside.

(The story was more familiar to audiences as the source of Brendan Behan's *The Hostage*.)

Brian Clark's popular tragicomedy *Whose Life Is It Anyway?* (4-17-79) returned to Broadway on February 24 but with a few twists. The locale was changed from England to America, the paralyzed sculptor Ken Harrison was now named Claire Harrison and played by Mary Tyler Moore (in her Broadway debut), and her doctor and some other characters experienced a sex change as well. Most commentators agreed that the changes did not diminish the thought-provoking play, and all agreed that Moore was sharp and lucid in the role. (The American Theatre Wing presented her with a special Tony Award at the end of the season.) Supportive reviews and Moore's strong appeal kept the Royale crowded for its ninety-six performance engagement.

Another limited engagement (two weeks) was Herbert Mitgang's **Mister Lincoln** (2-25-80, Morosco), a one-man drama with British actor Roy Dotrice as the sixteenth president. At Ford's Theatre, Lincoln is shot, and in the split second after the bullet hits him and before he loses consciousness, his whole life flashes before him. It was a contrived premise, but there were impressive moments to be found along the way, and Dotrice, who was far too English and too short to recall the man accurately, was applauded for his deft handling of the material. Notices offered faint praise, much along the lines of "an interesting, carefully-detailed, but less than inspiring monodrama."

Circle in the Square revived Shaw's *Major Barbara* on February 26 as its season opener (the financially strapped theatre had kept its money-making summer production of *Loose Ends* on the boards and started the winter season late) and received appreciative notices all around, particularly for Philip Bosco's Andrew Undershaft. Stephen Porter directed the social comedy, which also featured Laurie Kennedy (Barbara), Nicolas Surovy (Cusins), and Rachel Gurney (Lady Britomart). The circular theatre space was filled for many of the scheduled forty performances. Less accomplished but still worthwhile was the Manhattan Theatre Club's revival of S. N. Behrman's comedy *Biography* (12-12-32) on February 26. Piper Laurie was the enticing artist Marion Froude, and the men in her life were played by Alan Rosenberg and P. L. Carling. Most reviews were along the lines of Gill's "conscientious if not very inspired production."

Peter Hacks's **Charlotte** (2-27-80, Belasco) was a monodrama from Germany that brought Uta Hagen back to the New York stage after an absence of twelve years, and she garnered laudatory reviews for her acting even if the play, translated by herself and Herbert Berghof, was unanimously panned. Charlotte von Stein (Hagen) has been Goethe's mistress for the past ten years, but one day in 1786 he leaves both his home in Weimar and Charlotte behind. The bitter woman rants and raves about Goethe to her silent husband Josias (Charles Nelson Reilly), who spends the evening nodding, smoking his pipe, eating pie, and listening to her. At first Charlotte insists that she and Goethe were only friends, but soon she admits that they were lovers and that it was she who inspired him and made him what he is. The play ends with Josias finally mumbling the word "Charlotte" in consolation. While the critics dismissed the script as "hopelessly boring" and felt that "the play as well as the character is a tease," Hagen and Reilly were both praised. Gussow noted that Hagen "takes command of the play and of the stage, exuding an aura of confidence and magnetism," but even he could not wholly recommend the enterprise, which shuttered after five performances.

The most interesting of the Hudson Guild Theatre's offerings this season was Ed Graczk's **Come Back to the Five & Dime, Jimmy Dean, Jimmy Dean** (2-27-80, Hudson Guild) about a handful of devoted fans of the late movie star. In 1975 in a five-and-dime store in McCarthy, Texas, a reunion of the local James Dean Fan Club is taking place, and its members recall that their idol was in nearby Marfa in 1955 making the movie *Giant*. Reminiscences soon turn to revelations, the most interesting ones being a woman claiming Dean fathered her child when she played an extra in the film and the return of a male fan who has had a sex-change operation. Although this intriguing play gathered little notice during its month-long run, the script would arrive on Broadway two years later with great notoriety.

After saving the world with *The Trouble with Europe* earlier in the season, the Phoenix tried to do the same with a renowned landmark in **Save Grand Central** (2-28-80, Marymount Manhattan). *New Yorker* cartoonist William Hamilton's comedy of manners dealt with the Manhattan cocktail party set (also the subject of his cartoons). Idealistic architect Roger Maynard (Remak Ramsay) has opened a gourmet restaurant in a historic building, but the ambitious lawyer Charles Malcolm (Michael Ayr), who owns the building, wants to turn the space into a Burger King. Maynard's bored wife, Lucy (Linda Atkinson), and

Malcolm's aggressive wife, Cristina (Jill Eiken-berry), join in the fight, which turns into both a business and romantic competition. Some of the brightest lines came from the Maynards' Puerto Rican maid, Maria (Evelyn Mercado), and her Filipino boyfriend, Luis (Luis Avalos), who claims to be Puerto Rican so that he can climb to success in New York using his strong "work ethnic." Audiences and critics were amused, if not enthused, for the scheduled twenty-two performances.

Censored Scenes from King Kong (3-6-80, Princess) was a British import billed as "a comic extravaganza," but it did not take audiences long to realize they were facing one of the most tedious of the season's short-lived disasters. Howard Schumann's comedy was set in a tacky 1930s-style nightclub in present-day London, where investigative journalist Stephen (Stephen Collins) has come from Tokyo because he is searching for the truth regarding classified information. It seems that the old film *King Kong* contained information for secret agents but the pertinent scenes were cut before the movie was distributed in Europe. At the club Stephen encounters the tough proprietor Benchgelter (Chris Sarandon) and his piano player Walter Wilma (Edward Love), who echo Bogey and Sam in *Casablanca*, the singing and dancing Fantucci sisters (Carrie Fisher and Alma Cuervo), who perform some ludicrous songs, and a variety of shady characters all played by Peter Riegert. The reviews were vehemently negative ("a lousy evening . . . the worst!"), and the annoying venture closed after five showings. (The Princess was the new name given to the former 22 Steps Theatre, a later reincarnation of the famous Latin Quarter nightclub.)

Two stories unfolded side by side in John Huer's drama **Innocent Thoughts, Harmless Intentions** (3-6-80, Circle). In the attic of a Minnesota country house during the winter of 1931, a young pregnant girl (Patricia Wettig) hides from her disapproving family as time draws close for her to give birth to her illegitimate baby. The remaining action takes place during the Korean War in an Alaskan army barracks, where the outfit's misfit and scapegoat, Paul Johnson (Zane Lasky), is teased and later tormented by his fellow soldiers. By the end the girl is revealed as Paul's mother, and the parallels between their sufferings are made clear.

Although Argentina, Paris, and London had cheered the animal fantasy **Heartaches of a Pussycat** (3-19-80, ANTA), it only survived on Broad-way for five performances, gathering some of the most derisive reviews in a season filled with critical derision. Lower-class feline Beauty (Marilu Marini) is nonetheless raised to appreciate the finer things in life. She weds a fat cat of London society who snores a lot, is courted by a French diplomat, has a tragic affair with a dashing scoundrel, then retires to write her best-selling memoirs. The Balzac tale was adapted for the stage by Genevieve Serrau and James Lord, and the international theatre troupe called Group TSE presented it in English, dressed in elaborate costumes that dazzled the eye but rendered the actors expressionless and difficult to hear. This odd fantasy was roundly denounced as an "anthropomorphic abomination" even though Rostislav Doboujinsky's creative costumes and masks were cited as some of the most accomplished of the season.

On March 23 the Roundabout revived Athol Fugard's *The Blood Knot* (3-1-64), but it was considered miscast by some critics. Danny Glover was too young for the "dark" brother, Zachariah, and Cotter Smith was too old and too white for Morris. It was the first New York revival of the powerful Fugard drama but was kept on the boards for only twenty-five performances. The Classic Theatre's revival of R. C. Sherriff's World War I drama *Journey's End* (3-22-29) opened on the same day but only managed fifteen performances in a commercial run off Broadway.

Tennessee Williams's last new play to arrive on Broadway during his lifetime was **Clothes for a Summer Hotel** (3-26-80, Cort), a dramatization of the last meeting of F. Scott Fitzgerald (Kenneth Haigh) and his wife, Zelda (Geraldine Page). Zelda has been sent for treatment of her mental illness to an Asheville, North Carolina, asylum, and Scott, now an alcoholic making a living writing forgettable movie scripts, comes to visit her. (Scott's inappropriate vacation clothes that Scott wears when he comes to the asylum to visit provided the title.) Williams treated the subject matter as "a ghost play," filled with flashbacks that chronicle the long descent they both have endured. The play was poetic without being as surreal or expressionistic as his later works often were, and Page, who had brought memorable Williams characters to life in the past, was applauded for her tormented Zelda. But critics concurred in their genuine disappointment in the script, calling it "a blur" and a "bleak play, a play of defeat and dejection." The ghosts haunted the Cort for only fifteen performances, and Williams's career came to a sad and quiet close.

The season's most acclaimed new American play was Mark Medoff's **Children of a Lesser God** (3-30-80, Longacre), which originated at the Mark Taper Forum in Los Angeles. When James Leeds (John Rubinstein) gets out of the Peace Corps he obtains a job at a school for the deaf, teaching students to read lips. He is fascinated by the deaf dropout Sarah Norman (Phyllis Frelich), who works there as a cleaning woman and is unwilling to communicate with either hearing or deaf people. James takes a special interest in her, speaking to her in sign language and eventually discovering the radical and frustrated woman inside. They fall in love and marry, but soon Sarah's militant efforts for the deaf and her denial that the hearing world is superior to her own silent one start to tear the marriage apart. The two part, knowing that to be together demands that they change who and what they are. Frelich, a deaf actress and founding member of the National Theatre of the Deaf whose own marriage inspired the play, was both irritating and endearing as Sarah, and Rubinstein, who not only spoke and signed most of his lines but also translated her words as well, gave the performance of his career. (Both won Tony Awards at seasons's end, as did the play.) While the notices were laudatory ("the find of the season," "a play you will never forget," "joyous, witty and touching"), most of the critics found fault with some aspects of the play: its clumsy storytelling, its messages that could not be debated, and its unanswered questions. Howard Kissell in *Woman's Wear Daily* endorsed the drama but summed up its shortcomings, noting it "has the weakness of many polemic works—it is too patently an argument, and too many of its characters simply represent points of view." Regardless, *Children of a Lesser God* remained on Broadway for two years.

Henry Denker's "shamelessly sentimental comedy" **Horowitz and Mrs. Washington** (4-2-80, John Golden) gave audiences one more chance to see Sam Levene grace a Broadway stage, but the critics could find nothing good to say about his vehicle, "the sort of junk play that used to give Broadway a bad name." After retired Manhattan businessman Samuel Horowitz (Levene) is mugged by some black thugs and suffers a stroke, he returns home from the hospital to find Harriet Washington (Esther Rolle), a brittle African-American physical therapist, assigned to nurse him, and the expected sparks fly about the apartment. Horowitz's sharp racial insults ("There is nothing worse than an educated Negro!") are matched by Mrs. Washington's tyrannical methods; at one point the old Jew asks her, "Did you ever have an ambition to run a concentration camp?" and states he's willing to open a chain of them for her. Despite such tactless mudslinging the two eventually soften, and when Horowitz's daughter, Mona (Patricia Roe), tries to put her father in a home, the two senior citizens band together and win the day. Sadly, the lame comedy, which survived only six performances, was Joshua Logan's last directorial effort on Broadway.

Neil Simon returned to Broadway and found success once again with his **I Ought to Be in Pictures** (4-3-80, Eugene O'Neill), an economical three-character piece that quickly showed a profit. Spunky nineteen-year-old Libby Tucker (Dinah Manoff) has backpacked her way from Brooklyn to Hollywood to break into the movies (relatives have told her that she is "kind of a female Dustin Hoffman"), but her real mission is to meet her father, who left his family sixteen years ago. When she arrives at the run-down bungalow of screenwriter Herb Tucker (Ron Leibman) she finds a hungover slob with writer's block and a mature girlfriend, Steffy (Joyce Van Patten), whom he has kept on the string for two years. The initial meeting is awkward, but Herb invites Libby to stay with him while she pursues an acting career. Gradually the father and daughter get to know each other, and although Libby gets no closer to stardom than parking cars for celebrities at a posh Hollywood party, she decides to return to Brooklyn having found her father and herself. Leibman and Van Patten did journeyman's work, but Manoff was a delightfully fresh talent and won a Tony Award for her matter-of-fact Libby. Critical reaction ranged from "empty and labored evening" to "finely tuned blend of hilarity, honesty and deeply felt emotion." Although it was one of Simon's thinnest plays, audiences enjoyed it for nearly a year. For producer Emanuel Azenberg, it was another Simon success and one of five plays he presented this season.

No other Broadway revival was so unexpected, as enthusiastically acclaimed, and successful as Paul Osborn's forgotten comedy *Morning's at Seven* (11-30-39), which opened on April 10 at the Lyceum and stayed for 564 heartwarming performances. Vivian Matalon directed the all-star cast with sure-handed delicacy, never allowing the small-town comedy to slip into camp. He reset the 1939 play back in 1922 and, with scenic designer William Ritman, created an idealized American neighborhood as nostalgic as it was de-

EMANUEL AZENBERG (1934–) was born and raised in New York City and studied at New York University before beginning to produce Broadway plays in the 1960s. One of the few sole producers to survive into the 1990s, Azenberg gained distinction (if not financial success) with *The Lion in Winter* (1966) and went on to present dozens of plays and musicals of wide variety. In 1972 he produced his first Neil Simon play, *The Sunshine Boys*, and the partnership was repeated with every Simon play and musical after that. This season Azenberg was also represented by *Whose Life Is It Anyway?*, *Children of a Lesser God*, *Devour the Snow*, and *Last Licks*.

tailed. Teresa Wright, Elizabeth Wilson, Nancy Marchand, and Maureen O'Sullivan played the four Gibbs sisters, Richard Hamilton, Maurice Copeland, and Gary Merrill played three of their husbands, and the younger generation was represented by David Rounds as the homebody Homer and Lois de Banzie as his cheerful and determined fiancée, Myrtle. Reviews for both the old play and the new production were valentines, capped by Kerr, who called it "a perfect production of a uniquely shaped play, merry and mellow and possibly a bit mad." Matalon and Rounds won Tony Awards, and *Morning's at Seven* was deemed the Best Reproduction of a Play or Musical by the Tony Committee. The success of the revival put Osborn's comedy back in circulation, and there were dozens of regional, stock, and community theatre productions during the next decade.

BAM's season of unusual entries continued with a first-rate production of Maxim Gorky's 1905 social comedy **Barbarians** (4-10-80, BAM), which had never been produced in New York before. The lively translation was by Kitty Hunter Blair, Jeremy Brooks, and Michael Weller. The barbarians in question are two engineers, Cherkoon (Jon Polito) and Tsyganov (John Seitz), who arrive at a small provincial Russian town to prepare for the railroad line that will be coming through. Not only will this coming of modern technology cause upheaval in the community, the two visitors also wreck havoc with the locals' private lives, causing bourgeois political types to scamper, stalled romances to smolder, and bored marriages to catch fire. While all the aisle-sitters agreed that this was a lesser work of Gorky's, they disagreed as to its playability, some finding it "dispiriting," "harsh," and a "clumsy play lacking in design, focus, and purpose," but others de-

claring it "steadily engrossing." But few faulted the spirited production, which ran twenty-seven times in the repertory.

An off-Broadway commercial enterprise that played only twenty-four performances was Alan Gross's Chicago import **The Man in 605** (4-15-80, Theatre de Lys). The aging and failing poet Eldon Schweig (Byrne Piven) lives in a grimy Greenwich Village boarding hotel, where he battles with writer's block and the contrary desk clerk (Dick Cusak) and drinks at the local White Horse Tavern as his idol Dylan Thomas once did. In 1966 the college freshman Jerry Green (W. H. Macy) searches out the old poet he so admires and even gets a job as a bellhop in the hotel in order to meet him. But their meeting becomes a confrontation between youthful idealism and bitter disillusionment, both men diminished by the experience.

The indefatigable Louis LaRusso II, who often aped older dramatic styles in his plays, provided an O'Neill-esque waterfront drama with **Marlon Brando Sat Right Here** (4-16-80, Boltax) and populated it with such colorful (and familiar) types as Fat the Miser (Hy Anzell), Nick the Cripple (Dan Lauria), Sonny Swag (Michael J. Aronin), and Nunzie Clark Gable (Leonard D'John). The main plot dealt with tough-hearted Gracie (Janet Sarno), who owns a Hoboken restaurant, and her suitor Beep-ity-Beep (Paul Sorvino), a down-and-out singer who loved and lost her eighteen years ago. The title refers to the movie *On the Waterfront*, which had been filmed locally the year before the play's action; the longshoremen often speak wistfully of it as the one shining moment in their frustrated lives. The melodrama ran forty-six performances in the off-Broadway house.

The long-lasting grip that Puritanism has on American mores was the subject of Milan Stitt's philosophical drama **Back in the Race** (4-17-80, Circle). Jonathan Edwards VII (William Carden) returns to the crumbling country house of his ancestors (he is a direct descendant of the renowned Calvinist preacher of that name) where he had spent many summers as a boy. His father had willed the old house to the caretaker, Cliff (John Randolph), and a half-Indian girl, Zabrina (Joyce Reehling), who everyone assumes is Cliff's daughter. Loaded with questions about the relationship between Cliff and his father, Jonathan tries to get the old man to speak but is met with stubborn silence or outright antagonism. But he and Zabrina (who is very possibly his half sister) dig through the past together, discover the hypocrisy of their puritanical forefathers, and symbolically free themselves from the past by burning the Edwards family album.

A two-character comedy-drama that found favor for 104 performances first off then on Broadway was Bill C. Davis's **Mass Appeal** (4-22-80, Manhattan Theatre Club). The aged and congenial Fr. Tim Farley (Milo O'Shea) has long been pastor of St. Francis Catholic Church and has learned to keep his generous parishioners happy by never preaching anything too disturbing or threatening. When the young seminarian Mark Dolson (Eric Roberts) is assigned to the parish, sparks immediately fly because the youth is afire with alarming questions and challenging rhetoric. The two men clash at first (Mark calls Tim "a song and dance theologian, a phony, and a drunkard"), but soon the older priest starts to doubt his own spiritual life. He even begins to understand the youth when Mark confesses to him that he is bisexual. After Mark delivers a tirade of a sermon and upsets the congregation, the diocese recalls the seminarian and he is expelled. Things return to normal at St. Francis Church, but the pastor breaks down during a sermon, admits that he is "your little wind-up priest doll," and urges the congregation to write to the diocesan office and support Mark. While some critics thought the piece contrived and pat, others saw "a luminous parable about the indivisibility of love."

One of the Broadway season's most ambitious offerings was Howard Sackler's epic drama **Goodbye, Fidel** (4-23-80, Ambassador), which used twenty actors and half a dozen set changes to tell the four-year saga of a group of upper-class Cuban exiles searching for an identity in a new life. In 1958 Havana, a party takes place in which some of Cuba's intellectual set are trying to ignore the imminent political change in the air. The independent widow Natalia (Jane Alexander) is in love with the younger British diplomat James Sinclair (Christopher Cazenove), but she is concerned over her aging mother (Gale Sondergaard) as well as the homosexual painter Miguelito (David Schramm). Also on hand are the sugar mill entrepreneur Alvaro (Lee Richardson) and Natalia's friend Isabel (Kathy Bates), who has turned militant. The play follows their exploits as they try to adapt to the New Cuba, but end up leaving the country. A good many of them are seen gathered in 1962 in Madrid for another party, all of them now filled with despair and aimlessness. Critics unanimously dismissed the "banal domestic drama" and complained about the "hollowness of the writing." Even the fine cast was

faulted, few of the seventeen Hispanic characters being played by Hispanic actors. In fact, on opening night the play was picketed by minority actors who complained about the casting. The controversy put the production on all the front pages, but the issue died when the play closed after six performances, losing all of its hefty $770,000 investment.

The next night Broadway experienced a much smaller drama, Jack Zeman's two-character piece about marriage called **Past Tense** (4-24-80, Circle in the Square). When advertising executive Ralph Michaelson (Laurence Luckinbill) comes home from work to announce that he has landed a big account, he finds Emily (Barbara Feldon), his wife of twenty-one years, packing up and leaving him. He asks why, and neither he nor the audience gets much of an answer as the two commence to argue, reminisce, make love, weep, and wallow. Their children are grown and out of the house, but the recollection of a four-year-old son crushed by a truck brings on a lot of pathos, if little revelation about Emily's dissatisfaction with the marriage. Throughout the evening the two characters addressed the audience, commanded light and sound cues, and made wry jokes amid their pain. By the end it is not clear whether or not Emily will leave. The mostly negative reviews found the play too arch and the flip style "wears thin disastrously fast," so it struggled through its scheduled forty-five performances.

An involving courtroom drama that entertained Broadway for ninety-six performances was Tom Topor's **Nuts** (4-28-80, Biltmore). High-class call girl Claudia Faith Draper (Anne Twomey) has stabbed an abusive customer to death, and she is arrested for manslaughter. But a psychiatrist at Bellevue hospital has examined her and determined she is not mentally fit to stand trial. Claudia appeals the decision, and a trial is held to determine her sanity. Claudia comes from a middle-class home and was very intelligent and promising. (She is financing her law school education at NYU through prostitution.) But under the testimony of her mother (Lenka Peterson) and stepfather (Hansford Rowe), an unhappy home life and instances of sexual abuse are revealed, and Claudia wins her plea and will stand trial as a sane woman. Topor's dialogue was brittle and cliche-free, and Claudia's quick-witted comebacks and sensual powers of persuasion (at one point she verbally seduces the court to prove her qualifications as a first-class hooker) made her the centerpiece of the melodrama. While all the reviews esteemed Twomey (who remained silent for the first two-thirds of the drama), reaction to the script was divided—from "a slashing courtroom drama" to "very foolish."

John Ford Noonan came up with an economic little off-Broadway comedy that quickly showed a profit: his two-character **A Coupla of White Chicks Sitting Around Talking** (4-28-80, Astor Place). In a Westchester County kitchen, straightlaced Maude Mix (Susan Sarandon) tries to face the day, knowing her husband is off for the weekend with his secretary. She has little patience for her new neighbor, Hannah Mae Bindler (Eileen Brennan), who barges in and wants them to become close friends. Where Maude is reserved and a bit oppressed, Hannah is a talkative, demonstrative former cheerleader from Texas who lives life to the fullest. The first encounter does not go well, but Hannah is not deterred, and over a series of visits the two do become friends, have a wild weekend together in New York City, and help each other survive their worthless husbands. The reviews concentrated on the rich performances by the two actresses but differed on the play itself, calling it everything from "a lighter-than-air comedy on female bonding" to "forgettable." Audiences were not so torn and kept the two-hander on the boards for 432 performances.

The Roundabout season concluded with Shaw's *Heartbreak House* on April 29. British actresses Louise Troy and Rachel Gurney played the Shotover sisters and were the best things in the sluggish production. That same night the Acting Company came to town to present two plays at the American Place. The first was Paul Foster's *Elizabeth I* (4-5-72) featuring Janet DeMay and Lisa Banes as the real and pretend monarchs. Liviu Ciulei directed and designed the lively production, which stayed for a week. On May 4 the company gave one performance of John Webster's *The White Devil*, directed by Michael Kahn.

For some the "most exciting and provocative event of the theatre season" was neither on or off Broadway but at the off-off-Broadway venue La Mama Experimental Theatre Club, where Peter Brook presented three programs from his International Center for Theatrical Creations starting on April 30. While all three presentations in the repertory were in French, there were English translations and explanations to help, though the events were so visually oriented that they hardly seemed necessary. The first program featured Alfred Jarry's early absurdist farce *Ubu Roi* (here just billed as *Ubu*) coupled with a new work, **L'Os** (4-30-80, La Mama), adapted by Malick Bowens and Jean-Claude Carrière from a fable by Birago Diop. The Jarry piece was played as uproarious comedy, but the new play took a very disturbing turn as it showed a primitive man (Bowens) so concerned about his life's possessions (symbolized by a single bone) that he fights to the death to keep it for himself. Even more tragic was **The Ik** (5-1-80, La Mama), a modern tragedy based on a story by Colin Turnbull. The African tribe of the title are hunters, but the Uganda government takes away their land, relocates them, and makes them farmers. The concept is so foreign to the tribe that they are bereft of their humanity and eventually decay into nothingness. Dennis Cannan, Colin Higgins, and Turnbull adapted the tale for the stage; it was first produced in Europe in 1976. The final (and by consensus, the best) of the programs was **The Conference of the Birds** (5-2-80, La Mama), an epic parable that Carrière and Brook adapted from a twelfth-century poem by Farid Uddin Attar. A nation of birds is in crisis and needs leadership, so, under the guidance of Hoopoe (Bob Lloyd), the flock sets out on a journey to find their king, telling stories along the way like the pilgrims in *Canterbury Tales*. Many of the birds perish on the long and perilous journey, and when they do find the king they realize that the answers they sought were within them all along. Brook staged the fantasy on a giant flying carpet and presented a theatrical cornucopia of bird costumes, masks, and hand puppets that critics cited as "astonishing" and "utterly serious and utterly whimsical." The three stimulating programs ran in repertory through June 15.

Broadway's only thriller this season was Lezley Havard's short-lived **Hide and Seek** (5-4-80, Belasco). City dwellers Richard (David Ackroyd) and Jennifer Crawford (Elizabeth Ashley) are expecting their first child after eighteen years of marriage, so they buy a long-abandoned farmhouse in the country and plan to restore it and raise their child there. But the mysterious old house appears to resist their efforts (the lights and plumbing seem to have a mind of their own), and odd neighbors hint at destruction and offer them a prayer book for the burial of the dead as a housewarming present. While Richard commutes to the city for work, Jennifer is left alone in the house and sometimes sees a silent little girl swinging in the backyard. The ghostly image seems to be another ominous threat, this time against their unborn child (whose biological father is Richard's ne'er-do-well brother), and there is much local talk about a missing twin long thought murdered. It turns out the ghostly figure is the deceased offspring of two neighbors who see the restoration of the house as a sacrilege and a desecration of their memory of the little girl. Critics as a whole looked askance at the play with its barren red herrings and disappointing ending. But they complimented Ashley on her skillful performance and John Lee Beatty for his foreboding interior setting that provided old wooden cupboards large enough for cast members to hide in. One week and the thriller was gone.

The Broadway season's parade of short-lived, unanimously panned new plays continued with **The Roast** (5-8-80, Winter Garden), an exposé about the seamier side of show business penned by television writers Jerry Belson and Garry Marshall and directed by television comedian Carl Reiner. The action occurs before, during, and after a private Hollywood roast in which Phil Alexander (Peter Boyle), a renowned comic and spokesman for children's diseases, is honored and kidded before an audience of "two thousand horny Jews." But unlike the staged, jovial roasts seen on television, this is a vicious affair with plenty of backbiting, bitterness, and regrets about a seedy past. Alexander's former protégé the comic Danny (Rob Reiner), who is recovering from drug addiction and a nervous breakdown, wants to expose the popular comedian by revealing how he raped a stoned sixteen-year old girl and made Danny take the blame. But Danny's outburst at the roast is considered the ranting of an unsuccessful comic, so he is scolded for interrupting the jokes and insults and removed from the room. Despite the appearance of such gifted actors and stand-up comics as Bill Macy, Joe Silver, Arny Freeman, David Huddleston, and Antonio Fargas, the humor could not carry this "undramatized sledgehammer of a comedy." Reviews were hostile, so the "witless, shapeless, pointless, offensively vulgar" proceedings ended after four showings.

Lavonne Mueller's ridiculous thriller **Crimes and Dreams** (5-15-80, Theatre Four) managed two more performances than *The Roast* but was equally disliked. On an Illinois farm where the annual meeting of Mothers and Fathers of Murdered Children is to take place, a collection of odd suspects gather: the host parents of a murdered girl, a television reporter back from covering wars abroad, a guitar-strumming vendor selling balloons and other souvenirs, an ex-convict, a drunk, a crazed Vietnam vet, and a little boy. Not only is there a murder, but the culprit is lynched and the party is called off.

Just as the Public's season opened with an Ntozake Shange work, it closed with her new and loose adaptation of Brecht's *Mother Courage and Her Children*, which premiered on May 13 in the Newman. In this version, set in the American South during Reconstruction, Mother Courage (Gloria Foster) was a black opportunist who lived off the wars between U.S. troops and the Indians. The action was interrupted by some Old West songs that had a curiously Kurt Weill-like flavor to them, and Wilfred Leach staged the epic drama on a spare turntable set that he also designed. Critical reaction was very mixed about the adaptation, the acting, and the production. Some found the evening true to Brecht's ideas of historification and thought the new approach refreshing and potent; others saw an unfocused and forced concept that reduced the original to a series of American stereotypes. Audiences loved or loathed the venture for forty performances.

Rachel Crothers's insightful look at the sexes, *He and She* (2-12-20), was ripe for revival, but the script deserved better than the BAM production that was added to its repertory on May 22. Director Emily Mann kept the time period in 1911 but gave the play a 1970s mentality that struck some as false and annoying. Laurie Kennedy's freethinking Ann was endorsed by the critics, but little else was. The same night, in another space at BAM, a double bill consisting of Brecht's *The Wedding* and Feydeau's *The Purging* was offered under the umbrella title *The Marriage Dance, an Evening of Farce*. Like the Crothers play, it was repeated twenty-seven times.

Broadway's non-musical season closed with Canadian playwright David French's domestic drama **Of the Fields, Lately** (5-27-80, Century) which only lasted a week. When the stern patriarch Jacob Mercer (William Cain) suffers a heart attack and can no longer work, his son, Ben (Christopher W. Cooper), returns home to Toronto to help his mother (Mary Fogarty) and family friend Wiff Roach (John Leighton) care for the difficult old man. What follows is a series of incriminations and revelations (Jacob beat his son, Ben left two years ago, and so on) bringing the two to a brief understanding, then another quarrel, and finally Ben leaves for good. The four-character drama, which had been previously seen off-off Broadway at the Theatre Off Park, met with tepid notices, most aisle-sitters agreeing with Frank Rich, the newest critic for the *New York Times*, who found it "worthy but never exciting, convincing but rarely gripping." Rich, whose reviews had been appearing in the *Times* sporadically throughout the season, would become the new decade's most powerful (and, hence, the most reviled) theatre critic in New York. He certainly had quite a season to sharpen his teeth on.

1980–1981

Following such a lackluster season, the 1980–1981 offerings could only seem like an improvement, and, in truth, they were. In addition to a handful of memorable plays, attendance increased and (because of inflation) the box-office grosses jumped up to nearly $200 million on Broadway alone. But it was a season in which British, Irish, and other foreign plays dominated both on and off the Street and promising new American playwrights were far and few between. Such dependable veterans as Arthur Miller, Edward Albee, and Jean Kerr were all represented on Broadway, but only the last found success there. Meanwhile, from overseas Peter Shaffer, Brian Friel, Hugh Leonard, Athol Fugard, and others came up with exemplary plays, and some of them were financial hits as well.

The number of entries dropped slightly both on and off Broadway, even though Lincoln Center reopened and both of its houses were quite active. Seventeen new American plays opened on Broadway (down just one from the previous season), but six foreign works got most of the attention. Of forty new off-Broadway works, all but six were American. The season's finest native entry came from Off Off Broadway: *Crimes of the Heart* at the Manhattan Theatre Club. Off Off Broadway had been introducing exciting new works for the past half decade, but this season the scattered venue made a lot of noise. Much of it had to do with the new Showcase Code that Actors' Equity was demanding, to guarantee that actors in showcase productions could retain their roles in any subsequent transfer to Off Broadway or Broadway. Some playwrights promised to avoid Off Off Broadway, claiming the experimental nature of the venue would be threatened when such commitments were placed on showcase productions. The arguments continued throughout the season with no clear resolution. As for *Crimes of the Heart*, it ran out its scheduled thirty-five-performance showcase engagement, collected an armful of awards (including the Pulitzer Prize), and would eventually transfer to a long run on Broadway with, it must be noted, the original showcase cast.

The top ticket for a Broadway play rose to $30.00 (for *Amadeus*), and Off Broadway was asking a top of $18.50 for *Cloud 9*, which cost $175,000 to open but was a hit. On Broadway, *Frankenstein* cost $2 million to open (a new high) and closed on opening night. The numbers were worrying everyone, yet optimism was high. Plans were unveiled for turning some of the movie houses on 42nd Street back into legit theatres. It would not happen for another sixteen years, but it was bold thinking at the time. Also, the makeup of the Broadway audience was changing. A study showed that 11 percent of the patrons were foreigners (which surprised few) and that 10 percent were African-Americans (which pleasantly surprised many). So the climate was encouraging; if only there were more notable American plays to take advantage of it.

William Mastrosimone's two-character drama **The Woolgatherer** (6-5-80, Circle) marked the debut of a playwright whom several critics thought promising. They greeted the play with such accolades as "an auspicious beginning" and "absorbing, arresting, moving." Five-and-dime salesgirl Rose (Patricia Wettig) is practically a recluse, spending all her non-working hours in her bleak Philadelphia apartment either daydreaming or reliving old nightmares. When the bold and hard-drinking truck driver Cliff (Peter Weller) comes into her life and tries to bed her, the confrontation exposes each character as tormented and desperate. Much of the play was taken up with lengthy monologues, such as Cliff telling about his futile life on the road filled with one-night stands and Rose recalling the time she watched four rare birds brutally murdered at the zoo. The intimate drama was actually the Circle Repertory Theatre's final entry of the 1979–1980 season, but it was the best new script to be seen at the little theatre this season as well.

Also continuing its 1979–1980 season, the Roundabout Theatre had a winner with its revival of John Osborne's *Look Back in Anger* (10-1-57) on June 6. Acclamations of "spine-tingling," "splendid," and "conceivably the best thing the Roundabout Theatre has ever done" welcomed the British drama's first New York revival, and Malcolm McDowell, as the mocking Jimmy Porter, was roundly approved. Lisa Banes was his put-upon wife Alison, and Raymond Hardie was his rival-friend, Cliff. The popular attraction was held over into October.

A playwright making a notable debut (and launching a substantial career) was David Henry Hwang with his **FOB** (6-8-80, Public: Martinson). Dale (Calvin Jung) is a second-generation Chinese-American college student in California

DAVID HENRY HWANG (1957–) was born in Los Angeles to Chinese immigrants, a banker father and a mother who was a professor of piano. He graduated from Stanford University in 1979 and attended Yale University briefly before teaching creative writing at a high school in Menlo Park, California. His first play, *FOB*, was written while at Stanford, and he directed a production of it there. After being chosen to participate in the O'Neill National Playwrights Conference (where *FOB* was presented), Hwang relocated to the East Coast and pursued his playwriting career. His works vary in style and tone but always deal with Asian subjects (usually Asian Americans) and utilize some aspects of Asian performance techniques in the telling of the story.

who meets at his favorite Chinese restaurant with his cousin Grace (Ginny Yang), a first-generation immigrant who still holds on to some of the customs of the old country. When the FOB ("fresh off the boat") exchange student Steve (John Lone) joins their party, Dale mocks Steve's poor English and his old-world manner. But Grace defends Steve and is drawn to the provocative and defiant newcomer. The trio eventually reach a kind of truce, one that parallels the compromises Chinese Americans make in adopting their new culture. Hwang used some Chinese theatre conventions in telling his story (onstage musicians, visible stagehands, the use of ritual in the staging), yet the play was very American in its headlong attack on the issues. The reviews were supportive, the play won an OBIE Award, and its run of forty-two performances at the Public created a great deal of interest. Hwang would soon develop into New York's premiere Asian-American playwright.

For one week this summer, Lincoln Center's downstairs space was active again with avant-gardist Robert Wilson's latest theatre piece, **Dialog/Curious George** (6-24-80, Mitzi E. Newhouse), though it was a matter of contention just how active the venture was. Given that he had previously tackled Stalin, Einstein, Freud, and Queen Victoria, Wilson's choice of the popular *Curious George* children's stories was, well, curious. Christopher Knowles wrote the text and performed it with Wilson, the two of them playing "worrisome adults behaving like children in an outsize playpen," as Douglas Watt in the *New York Daily News* described it. Most reviews were equally dismissive, although David Sterritt in the *Christian Science Monitor* was not alone is finding the program "fascinating, disorientating, bewil-

dering, and cheerfully entertaining at the same time."

To Bury a Cousin (5-16-67), Gus Weill's drama about a writer returning to his southern roots for a funeral, only lasted five performances in its original production, but when revived on June 25 at the Cherry Lane, it found enough playgoers to run ten times that number. Robert Bloodworth played the writer, and the cast also featured Harry Goz and Diane Tarlton. The Circle in the Square revived Kaufman and Hart's perennial favorite *The Man Who Came to Dinner* (10-16-39) on June 26, and it stayed for eighty-five happy performances. Some aisle-sitters found Stephen Porter's direction routine and rather lifeless, but most applauded Ellis Rabb as the curmudgeonly Sheridan Whiteside. He was ably assisted by Maureen Anderman (Maggie Cutler), Carrie Nye (Lorraine Sheldon), Roderick Cook (Beverly Carlton), and Leonard Frey (Banjo). The Roundabout was less successful with its revival of Noel Coward's *Fallen Angels* (1-12-27), which opened on July 10 but was only retained for thirteen showings. Carol Teitel and Valerie French played the love-starved housewives.

The Circle Rep added a guest production, Frank Barrie's **Macready!** (7-29-80, Circle), to run in repertory with its *The Woolgatherer* for thirty-four showings, just as it had successfully done the previous summer with *Gertrude Stein Gertrude Stein Gertrude Stein* (6-24-79). But Barrie's one-man show, about the famous nineteenth-century actor-director William Charles Macready, was less popular and, according to the notices, less engaging. Barrie also played Macready (as he had done in England), using material from the actor's published diaries, commenting on the theatre of his day, and recreating some of his most famous roles.

Irish playwright Hugh Leonard would see two of his plays make their New York debut this season. His 1974 work **Summer** (9-17-80, Hudson Guild) was a poignant character study showing three middle-aged couples and two of their children on a picnic in the Irish countryside during a summer day in 1968. In the second act the same ensemble was seen picnicking together in the same place six summers later. Little happens plotwise (the young folk tend to talk and dream about the future, while the older generation always gets back to reminiscing about the past) but, as one critic wrote, "the evening slowly but surely enchants us and fills us with a rush of goodwill as the lights finally dim on these Dubliners." His colleagues were just as enchanted with the direction by Brian Murray (who had played the grown son in Leonard's *'Da'* three seasons back) and the American cast that included Swoozie Kurtz, Pauline Flanagan, Charlotte Moore, Mia Dillon, David Canary, and Thomas A. Carlin. The Hudson Guild production was limited to thirty-five performances, and, oddly, the work has rarely been produced since.

With Albert Innaurato's *Gemini* (3-13-77) still running after three years, everyone was more than curious to see what his new **Passione** (9-23-80, Morosco) had to offer. The answer was: more of the same thing but bigger, louder, and less effective. Like *Gemini*, it was set is an Italian neighborhood in South Philadelphia. Berto (Jerry Stiller) is throwing a family party for his aged father, Oreste (Daniel Keyes), who is let out of the nursing home once a month to visit the ramshackle homestead. Gathered are Berto's suicidal son, Little Tom (Richard Zavaglia), Tom's obese and vulgar wife, Francine (Laurel Cronin), and her horny father, Renzo (Dick Latessa). The festivities are interrupted by Aggy (Angela Paton), Berto's estranged wife who took off ten years ago, and her loudmouth sister, Sarah (Sloane Shelton), who runs a farm in North Carolina. Aggy has come to serve Berto divorce papers, but she really hopes for a reconciliation with Little Tom, who will have none of it. In the emotional chaos that follows, Renzo pursues Sarah, the women fight over who "saved" Little Tom, and Berto and Aggy come to an understanding. Critics still spoke of Innaurato as a talented and promising playwright, but few could endorse the noisy and empty theatrics at the Morosco. The comedy departed in two weeks, and, sadly, Innaurato was rarely heard from again.

David Rimmer's comic look at youth, **Album** (10-1-80, Cherry Lane), began off-off Broadway at a WPA workshop, then successfully transferred to Off Broadway, where it stayed for 254 performances. The episodic comedy follows four teenagers starting high school in 1963 through to graduation. Billy (Kevin Bacon) is the "cool" one, a jock who hides his insecurities behind a lot of bluster, while his friend Boo (Keith Gordon) is a sensitive, self-described "freak." Peggy (Jenny Wright) is an attractive and popular high schooler, whereas her friend Trish (Jan Leslie Harding) is the "ugly duckling" who transfers all her fantasies of love and sex to unattainable rock stars. The foursome grappled with sex, love, and growing up to the tunes of 1960s popular music (the play was divided into Side 1 and Side 2 rather than acts) in a series of scattered vignettes that

were not unique but enjoyable all the same. Notices were mostly complimentary, calling the play a "keenly observed chronicle" and Rimmer's writing "as delicate and firm as [the characters'] behavior is fumbling and tentative." Newcomer Bacon was cited as the most interesting of the foursome.

The Circle in the Square Uptown opened its season on October 2 with Euripides' battle of wills between a vengeful god and his unfaithful subjects, *The Bacchae*, translated and directed by Michael Cacoyannis. Although the critics were mixed in their feelings about the production (a stark and traditional presentation free of the modern gimmicks that were foisted on the play throughout the 1960s), all praised Philip Bosco as Cadmus and Irene Pappas in the brief role of Agave, just as most found Christopher Rich's Dionysus rather silly and lacking authority.

The Negro Ensemble Theatre would have an uneven season, starting with Samm-Art Williams's **The Sixteenth Round** (10-7-80, Theatre Four), a three-character piece that was as "slack and lifeless" as his three-character *Home* (12-14-79) was vibrant and spirited. The punchdrunk boxer Jesse Taft (Paul Benjamin) has accidentally killed his opponent in the ring, so he hides from the mob in a North Philadelphia apartment with his girlfriend, Marsha (Rosalind Cash). They are joined by Jesse's old friend and sparring partner Lemar Jefferson (Roscoe Orman), and the three are soon embroiled in a deadly triangle, complicated by the suggestion that Lemar is now working for the mob.

Steve Tesich, an off-Broadway playwright whose work was usually seen at the American Place Theatre, made a brief appearance on Broadway with his farce **Division Street** (10-8-80, Ambassador). Although it was another piece about 1960s radicals trying to find themselves a decade later, Tesich's approach was broad and comic. (He dictated that the farce's tempo should be "allegro con sentimento.") Burnt-out political radical Chris (John Lithgow) has given up the fight and lives in an apartment in Chicago, where he works as an insurance underwriter. Hoping for quiet obscurity, Chris is bombarded by people from his past and present who expect more from him: Betty (Justin Lord), a black militant who has had a sex change and is now a female cop; Yovan (Keene Curtis), a Mafia-like Serbian who fervently runs his restaurant like a guerrilla stronghold; Chris's wife, Dianah (Christine Lahti), who still speaks in 1960s jive; Roger (Joe Regalbuto), his radical partner of yesteryear who is threat-

JOHN LITHGOW (1945–) was born in Rochester, New York, the son of a producer and a teacher. He studied at Harvard, graduating in 1967, then trained at the London Academy of Dramatic Arts. Lithgow was on the stage as a boy, playing youths in summer Shakespeare productions in Antioch, Ohio, and in the 1960s appearing in musicals and Shakespeare productions regionally. He made his Broadway debut in 1973 when *The Changing Room* transferred, and he won a Tony Award for his performance as the rugby player Kendall. He would begin a successful film career with *Obsession* in 1976 (and later score on television as well) but would return to the stage frequently. The tall and sometimes awkward Lithgow specializes in Everyman character types with a vulnerable and often comic persona.

ened by the women's movement; Mrs. Bruchinski (Theresa Merritt), an interfering black-Polish landlady; and others. Chris and Dianah's marriage falls apart, she ends up with the Serb, the militant turns out be the long-lost child of the landlady, and the shenanigans conclude with the characters dreaming of a new movement for the new decade and all singing "America the Beautiful." The production, directed by Tom Moore, hailed from the Mark Taper Forum in Los Angeles, where it had caused quite a stir, but it folded inside of three weeks on Broadway. Some New York critics found it a "life-embracing, funny, funny farce about America," but most agreed it was "ultimately more frantic than funny." For its leading actor, though, there was another round of applause. He was proving to be one of the theatre's most consistently masterful performers.

Nikolai Erdman's satire **The Suicide** (10-9-80, ANTA) had an unusual history. Written in the 1920s, the social comedy was promoted by Brecht, Meyerhold, Stanislavsky, and Gorky, the last pleading with Stalin that it be produced. Permission was given, but the production was halted after rehearsals began, and it was never seen in Russia until the 1970s. This version, translated by George Genereux, Jr., and Jacob Volkov for the Royal Shakespeare Company, was adapted by the Trinity Square Rep in Providence and featured RSC actor Derek Jacobi (in his New York debut) with an American cast. When the out-of-work nonentity Senya Podsekalnikov (Jacobi) despairs and mentions he might commit suicide, everyone takes notice of him for the first time. Various groups, from the butchers' union to the intellectual class, want his suicide to become a meaning-

ful gesture on their behalf, and the timid Senya becomes a celebrity. But his newfound sense of worth teaches Senya how precious life and freedom are, and, far from committing suicide, he finds the strength to speak out, calling Moscow on the phone and telling them he doesn't much care for Marx. Despite some laudatory reviews for the play, Jacobi's mesmerizing metamorphosis of a performance, and the striking production directed by Soviet dissident Jonas Jurasas, *The Suicide* struggled along for its two-month run.

A series of five new works was presented by the Phoenix Theatre, beginning with French Canadian playwright Michel Tremblay's **Bonjour, La Bonjour** (10-9-80, Marymount Manhattan), a domestic drama about family incest through the generations. Serge (William Katt) returns from a trip abroad to his Montreal home, where he continues to pursue his sexual attraction to one of his three sisters. Ironically, the other two sisters are pursuing Serge. Ultimately their old father (Fred Stuthman) admits that he had incestuous relations in the past and explains that practically the whole family is inbred. Some commentators declared the play "fascinating"; most others thought it preposterous.

The Circle Rep had an uneven season of new and old plays, but its first entry, Jim Leonard's **The Diviners** (10-16-80, Circle), was the most intriguing of the lot. In the mythical small Indiana town of Zion in the 1930s, a disturbed youth, Buddy Layman (Robert MacNaughton), has been petrified of water ever since he nearly drowned in an accident that killed his mother. The colorful C. C. Showers (Timothy Shelton), who comes from a long line of Kentucky preachers, moves to town but is content to be a mere car mechanic. Showers befriends the grime-covered Buddy, trying to get him to wash. When the town is in need of a preacher, the local women try to convince Showers to answer his family calling, but he refuses. But he does get the boy to wade in the river with him, and the townsfolk, thinking Showers is baptizing Buddy, rally to the water's edge. In the confusion that follows, Buddy drowns. The script, which had come from the American College Theatre Festival in Washington, D.C., was commended for the way it "renders the humor and horror of the hinterlands with staggering accuracy." The drama was played forty-one times, then was brought back the following season.

An uneven season was also the case at the Manhattan Theatre Club, as witnessed by its opener. Steve Metcalfe's **Vikings** (10-21-80, Manhattan Theatre Club) was a domestic drama about a contemporary household of Danish descent who are proud of their Scandinavian roots, their strength of character, and the family carpentry business. Yens Larsen (William Swetland) founded the company, and it has been the occupation of his son Peter (Tom Atkins) and grandson Gunnar (Boyd Gaines). But new methods of concrete construction are hurting the craft, and when Peter's wife dies, he loses interest in the company and in life. Father and son try to help Peter, even going so far as to try to match him up with the lonely divorcee Betsy Simmons (Sheila Allen), whom Peter knew back in his school days. Their efforts are successful, so Gunnar quits the business and goes off to college.

The Roundabout opened its new season of five revivals of foreign works on October 28 with an unlikely choice, Terence Rattigan's problem play *The Winslow Boy* (10-29-47), and found itself with a surprise hit. The critics were quite taken with the drama (this was its first New York revival) and the masterful performances, especially that by Remak Ramsey as the lordly barrister who defends the wrongly accused Winslow youth. The Roundabout extended the scheduled run to 104 performances.

A true curiosity for Broadway (or anywhere outside vaudeville) was **Quick Change** (10-30-80, Bijou), a one-man program by Michael McGiveney illustrating the lost art of the quick-change artist. McGiveney's father, Owen, had made a career doing this sort of thing, his mini-version of *Oliver Twist*, in which he played all the characters, being his calling card. The son recreated the famous sketch, along with several others, for this engagement, but critics were unimpressed and audiences were not interested, so it left after five showings.

Hugh Leonard's second offering of the season, **A Life** (11-2-80, Morosco), was an engrossing character study about two Irish couples in a small town near Dublin. Drumm (Roy Dotrice), a meticulous and high-prinicpled civil servant, has been married to the docile and worshiping Dolly (Helen Stenborg) for forty years. But when he learns that he has only six months to live, he attempts to reconcile with Mary (Aideen O'Kelly), the woman he truly loved but lost when she refused him only to marry the village idler Kearns (Pat Hingle). When Drumm confronts Kearns and Mary with his true feelings, old wounds are opened up, and Drumm is forced to look accurately at his own life as he has always insisted others do themselves. Just as in the au-

thor's *'Da'* (5-1-78), scenes from the past are woven into the tale, showing the young Drumm (Adam Redfield) and young Kearns (David Ferry) vying for the love of young Mary (Lauren Thompson). Many theatregoers recalled the older Drumm as the hero's humorless employer in *'Da'* (Lester Rawlins had won a Tony Award for playing the minor role), but here he was a fully realized character, a man of unwavering principles who must find the courage to face death with the same kind of reserve he has lived with. Aisle-sitters generally approved of the script and the production but with a low-key kind of enthusiasm echoing the play itself. All the same, the drama hung on for seventy-two performances.

Lanford Wilson's Off-Broadway success *The Fifth of July* (4-27-78) was revived on Broadway on November 5 at the New Apollo, but the title's *The* was dropped along with half of the original cast. Again Marshall W. Mason directed, but film star Christopher Reeve played the crippled vet Kenneth Talley, and most commentators felt he did not compare favorably to the original William Hurt. Swoozie Kurtz, on the other hand, was warmly welcomed to the new cast, her hyperactive Gwen garnering the best reviews. Critical response was all over the ballpark: some preferred the original production, others thought this was an improvement; some felt it inferior to Wilson's recent *Talley's Folly* (5-1-79), others deemed *Fifth of July* his masterwork. Audiences seemed less divided and kept the comedy-drama on the boards for 511 performances.

An early but strong candidate for the worst play of the Broadway season was Sidney Michaels's **Tricks of the Trade** (11-6-80, Brooks Atkinson), which mercifully closed on opening night. Psychologist Dr. August Browning (George C. Scott) uses all the emotional tricks of his profession on his beautiful new patient Diana Woods (Trish Van Devere). He then pulls a few more tricks as we find out he is an agent for the CIA and has a piece of microfilm that three of his associates have been murdered for. An unknown KGB agent named Nadia seems to be responsible for the deaths, and long after the audience has considered it, the possibility that Diana may be Nadia arises. The play was self-described as "a romantic mystery," and a liaison did develop between doctor and patient over a series of sessions, but playgoers found the love story as tedious and unbelievable as the cat-and-mouse intrigue going on. The conclusion, a triple twist revolving around everybody being a triple agent, brought the lovers together, but even though Scott and

Van Devere were married in real life, the lack of chemistry between them was cited by all the critics.

Luba Kadison and Joseph Buloff adapted three short stories by Anton Chekhov and presented them under the umbrella title **The Chekhov Sketchbook** (11-9-80, Harold Clurman), which ran 104 times. In *The Vagabond*, a chained prisoner (John Heard) on his way to Siberia tells his two guards a fanciful tale about growing up as the son of a housemaid in a baronial estate, and he temporarily charms the guards before reverting back to the role of captive. *The Witch* concerns an unhappily married couple (Penelope Allen and Heard) and how their marriage is further shaken by a visit from a postman (Stephen D. Newman) one dark night. The farce *In a Music Shop* concluded the evening; a customer (Joseph Buloff) tries to purchase the sheet music for a song his wife has requested, but he cannot recall the title, composer, or melody of the song.

More Chekhov followed when the Public's revival of *The Sea Gull* opened on November 11. Andrei Serban directed the new Jean-Claude Van Itallie adaptation; compared to their controversial *The Cherry Orchard* in 1977, this production was more conventional and, according to a majority of the critics, more satisfying. There were still the odd Serban touches (stark Japanese-style scenery by Michael Yeargan, Liz Swados's Hare Krishna–like score, too many characters played for farce rather than comedy), but the effect did not seem so jarring this time around, and the reviews were supportive. The expert cast certainly helped: Rosemary Harris (Arkadina), Christopher Walken (Trigorin), Kathryn Dowling (Nina), Brent Spiner (Treplev), Pamela Payton-Wright (Masha), George Hall (Sorin), Joyce Van Patten (Paulina), and F. Murray Abraham (Dorn).

Theatregoers had flocked to see television comedienne Gilda Radner onstage the previous season in an evening of her familiar comic characters, and they willingly returned this season to see how she managed in **Lunch Hour** (11-12-80, Ethel Barrymore), a new comedy by veteran playwright Jean Kerr. Neither lady disappointed her public. Radner was as bright and daffy in a sustained character as she was in sketches, and Kerr demonstrated that she still knew how to write that rapidly vanishing staple, the Broadway romantic comedy. Psychiatrist Oliver DeVreck (Sam Waterston) is so caught up in his new book and his demanding patients that he hardly notices how frustrated his wife, Nora (Susan Kellerman), has become. But when the desperate and determined Carrie Sachs (Radner) bursts into his house in the Hamptons and informs Oliver that Nora is having an affair with her husband, Peter (David Rasche), the doctor realizes that his marriage is far from perfect. To get her husband back, Carrie suggests that she and Oliver pretend to be having trysts during his lunch hour, and the two are drawn to each other as they work out the details of the plot. When Nora and Peter enter and are told of the fabricated romance, both couples are forced to discuss their faltering marriages. Soon everyone returns to the proper mate, but Carrie decides to become Oliver's patient and some future lunch hour encounters are hinted at. Kerr's plotting was a bit contrived, but her dialogue shone as sparkling as ever. (Carrie describes herself to Oliver as "a beautiful person," which means "I am not beautiful . . . I'm quick and reliable and I have a good disposition. Exactly the qualities you'd look for if you were buying a Labrador retriever.") The amiable cast, under Mike Nichols's tight direction, got the most out of the script, and audiences were delighted. The press response was a mixed bag, ranging from "a dreary piece of coyness" to "a very slight, very warm and most amusing diversion." *Lunch Hour* was Radner's only Broadway play, television and her busy movie career keeping her occupied until her premature death at forty-three. It was also Kerr's last play but, at 262 performances, a good old-fashioned hit.

Dark for three years, Lincoln Center's Vivian Beaumont reopened on November 14 with a sprightly mounting of Philip Barry's comedy of manners *The Philadelphia Story* (3-28-39), this durable classic's first major New York revival. Ellis Rabb directed, and while there were the usual complaints about the house's odd configuration for doing proscenium plays, the critics were highly appreciative. Blythe Danner managed to make audiences forget Katharine Hepburn's stage and film Tracy Lord long enough to enjoy her own radiant approach to the role, and she was capably supported by Frank Converse as her ex-husband, C. K. Dexter Haven, and Edward Herrmann as the journalist who charms and is charmed by her. The high-style comedy did brisk business for its scheduled sixty performances.

Athol Fugard's new drama from South Africa, **A Lesson From Aloes** (11-17-80, Playhouse), was cited as his most accomplished work yet by several critics, and the propitious notices helped the "grim and powerful" work stay on the boards for ninety-six showings. Piet Bezuidenhout (Harris Yulin), a middle-aged Afrikaner once very active in protesting apartheid, is content in 1963 to stay in his Port Elizabeth home and tend his collection of aloe plants. His wife, Gladys (Maria Tucci), has recently returned from the sanitarium where she was recovering from a nervous breakdown that was brought on when the police raided their home looking for evidence of Piet's radical activities and connections. Piet's good friend Steve Daniels (James Earl Jones), a black South African recently released from jail, is coming with his family that night to bid farewell before leaving for England. While they prepare for their guest, Piet confesses to Gladys that there is talk in certain circles that it was Piet who informed on Steve and sent him to jail. Piet is convinced that Steve does not believe this, but when Steve arrives without the family (it turns out his wife does believe the story) the two old friends have a strained reunion. Gladys, on the verge of another breakdown, bluntly announces to Steve that it was Piet who turned him in. She then derides the man for believing her and not trusting his old friend, telling him how the police ransacked their home looking for information against Steve. The two friends part amicably, and Gladys prepares to return to the sanitarium in the morning.

JoAnne Akalaitis and her Mabou Mines troupe brought a program entitled **Dead End Kids** (11-18-80, Other Stage) to the Public and preached about the dangers of radiation, the cast quoting everyone from Madame Curie to government studies on nuclear power. The next night an even more grim theatrical was offered: Barry Collins's one-man drama **Judgment** (11-19-80, St. Peter's Church), which had been seen at the Stratford Festival in Canada and elsewhere. Philip Anglim played a German soldier who describes how his outfit, trapped in a church basement, turned to cannibalism to survive.

Considerable interest was generated off-off Broadway with John Byrne's British drama **The Slab Boys** (11-19-80, Hudson Guild). In the slab room of a carpet factory in Scotland in 1957, a group of young men toil as they mix and match paints for the company's designers. Phil McCann (Daniel Gerroll) hides his concern over his suicidal mother by joking with the others and dreaming of attending art school. Cynical Sparky Farrell (Gene O'Neill) leads the group in impromptu clowning and picking on nerdy Hector McKenzie (John Pankow), who seems to enjoy the attention. The boys toss off jokes as easily as they toss about buckets of paint. What little plot there was concerned how each of the boys tries

to woo the company's design artist, Lucille Bentley (Noreen Tobin), a symbol of escape from the slab room. The one-month engagement drew enough compliments that the play appeared on Broadway a few seasons down the road.

Arthur Miller's return to Broadway with **The American Clock** (11-20-80, Biltmore) was greeted with mixed reviews and a run of only twelve performances. Described by the author as "a mural for the theatre," the epic-scale drama offered a panorama about the American Depression through dozens of vignettes featuring fifty-two characters. The centerpiece of the mural is the Baums, a family of means who are wiped out in the stock market crash: the businessman Moe (John Randolph), his warm and life-fulfilling wife, Rose (Joan Copeland), and their son, Lee (William Atherton), who acts as a narrator of sorts for the scattered collage. Surrounding the Baums are a variety of characters illustrating the effects of the Depression on different levels of society. (Most of the episodes were drawn from Studs Terkel's book *Hard Times*, which "inspired" the new play.) While a handful of critics thought the drama Miller's finest in years and recommended it, most registered disappointment. Frank Rich of the *New York Times* thought the play very promising when he saw it at the Spoleto Festival in South Carolina the previous spring but declared the rewritten version "smashed beyond recognition."

Ted Tally found some success with his **Coming Attractions** (12-3-80, Playwrights Horizons), a broad satire on America's fascination with celebrity. Petty crook Manny Alter (Larry Block) has the heart of a notorious criminal but not the flair needed to get noticed in this sensation-craving world. So he embarks on a series of outrageous stunts to gain attention, from dressing as a skeleton and going door to door killing people to disguising himself as Miss Wyoming and trying to murder Miss America (Christine Baranski) on the television broadcast. Instead he falls for Miss America and ends up being executed in the electric chair during a prime-time broadcast. Some aisle-sitters thought the farce "fizzles with pixilated laughter," but most were in agreement with Edith Oliver of *The New Yorker* when she described it as "too gleeful and too scattershot for satire, and not shrewd enough in its choice of targets." Audiences thought differently and kept *Coming Attractions* on the boards for 145 performances.

The Negro Ensemble's best new work of the season was Charles Fuller's **Zooman and the**

Sign (12-7-80, Theatre Four). Lester Howard, called Zooman (Giancarlo Esposito) on the street, is a restless black teen so full of aimless rage that he can hardly stand still. He shows off his gun and "Magic," his switchblade, to the audience before blurting out that he has just killed someone, a "little girl, I think." The victim was Jinny Tate, the young daughter of a black working-class Philadelphia family, who was accidentally shot when Zooman opened fire on some rival teens. Jinny's parents, Reuben (Ray Aranha) and Rachel (Mary Alice), believe that several neighbors saw the shooting but are all too afraid to speak to the police. So Reuben hangs a large sign on his porch accusing the neighbors of cowardice. The neighbors then harass the Tates for giving the neighborhood a bad name. But Reuben, despite even some death threats, insists on keeping the disturbing sign posted. Zooman, on the run from the police when one of his buddies squeals on him, is also upset by the sign. When he goes to the Tates' house to remove it, Jinny's uncle Emmett (Carl Gordon), thinking the neighbors have come to burn the house down, shoots and kills Zooman. The next day Reuben hangs a new sign on the porch: "Here, Lester Howard was killed. He will be missed by family and friends. He was known as Zooman." The OBIE-winning drama received highly favorable reviews, Walter Kerr in the *New York Times* calling it "rich in contradiction" and Rich noting that "there are no real villains, only victims." Its month-long engagement was well attended, and the drama returned the next season.

Beth Henley made a sensational New York debut with her wacky and touching comedy **Crimes of the Heart** (12-9-80, Manhattan Theatre Club). The McGrath family of Hazelhurst, Mississippi, has always been notorious for their eccentricity, such as the time Momma hung both herself and the family cat and made national news. Her three daughters, now grown up but still viewed with suspicion by the locals, are brought together when the youngest sister, the flaky but effervescent Babe (Mia Dillon), shoots her lawyer husband, Zachary, because she "didn't like his looks." When she hears the news, her sister Meg (Mary Beth Hurt), who was the local flirt in bygone days, returns to town from California, where she has been pursuing a fruitless singing career. But once home, Meg seems more interested in seeing an old boyfriend, Doc (Stephen Burleigh), who has married a "Yankee" woman. Lenny (Lizbeth Mackay), the eldest sister, trying to hold the family together while vis-

iting their ailing "grandaddy" in the hospital, attempts to maintain the crumbling family home and appease ruffled relatives. Since Zachary was the best lawyer in town, the sisters hire young and inexperienced Barnette Lloyd (Peter MacNicol), who has an "unrelenting personal vendetta against" the wounded husband, and he plans a plea of self-defense. Over the next twenty-four hours, the sisters engage in fights, play the card game of Hearts, reminisce about their estranged father and screwy mother, and end with a better understanding of each other as they eat Lenny's day-old birthday cake for breakfast. Rich led the cheers for Henley's sparkling script, describing the writing as "a pure vein of Southern Gothic humor worthy of Eudora Welty and Flannery O'Connor." The thirty-five scheduled performances were enough to get noticed, and the comedy was awarded the Pulitzer Prize while plans were being made to bring it to Broadway the next season.

The Circle Rep abandoned new works for its next two offerings. Playwright David Mamet directed a raucous *Twelfth Night* on December 12 that was criticized for its uneven acting. Circle director Marshall W. Mason essayed Malvolio and was roundly scolded for his dull and ponderous portrayal. But Lindsay Crouse's Viola was deemed luminous by all. (Oliver, who had seen all the major Violas going back to Jane Cowl, declared Crouse's the finest in her theatregoing career.) On December 16, the Roundabout offered a reader's theatre production of Shaw's *Don Juan in Hell* for forty-eight showings. Arlene Francis as Dona Ana may have been the draw, but it was Paul Sparer (Don Juan), Ronald Drake (Commandant), and Philip Bosco (Devil) who made the evening fly.

Prolific British playwright Stephen Poliakoff was presented to Stateside audiences once again with his **American Days** (12-16-80, Manhattan Theatre Club), but, once again, Americans were not interested. This harsh drama about a struggling rock group trying to break into the London record business was performed forty-eight times then, like other Poliakoff scripts, disappeared from American consciousness.

New Yorkers showed more curiosity for another foreign author, Italy's controversial farceur Dario Fo. His **We Won't Pay! We Won't Pay!** (12-16-80, Chelsea Theatre Center) was a Marxist farce set in motion when the Italian housewife Antonia (Karen Shallo) comes home from the market with a bag full of groceries she has stolen, something she and three hundred other Milan housewives have done in protest against the high cost of living. Trying to keep the theft a secret from her husband, Antonia hides the bag of groceries under the raincoat of her friend Margherita (Bonnie Braelow), thereby instigating rumors that Margherita is pregnant. The various confusions are cleared up when all the neighbors unite to resist their eviction from their housing project. While the wild play was thought invigorating, some critics carped about the "miserable performances" in the production. But audiences were amused and kept it on the boards for 120 performances. Sadly, it was the last hurrah for the struggling Chelsea Theatre Center, which folded after this production.

Peter Shaffer's much talked-about London hit **Amadeus** (12-17-80, Broadhurst) arrived on Broadway to a bouquet of raves and proved the most engrossing (and successful) drama of the season. As the aged composer Antonio Salieri (Ian McKellen) lies dying in 1823, rumors are circulating throughout Vienna that the old man is raving about having poisoned Mozart decades ago. Salieri confesses to the audience that he started the rumors himself and then proceeds to narrate the action, which begins in 1781 when he was a respected court composer for Emperor Joseph II and Wolfgang Amadeus Mozart (Tim Curry) was an overgrown child prodigy and foul-mouthed upstart trying to break into court. Salieri sees no threat in the childish cad until he hears one of the youth's compositions performed and he realizes that this is the work of genius, "the voice of God." Finding it grossly unfair that God should choose this "obscene child" to create brilliant music when Salieri's own compositions are merely routine, the passionate Italian defies his God and swears to destroy Mozart. Over the next ten years he keeps Mozart from getting court assignments, arranges for him to be thrown out of the secret society of Masons, and even contributes to the disintegration of Mozart's stormy marriage to Constanze (Jane Seymour) by trying to seduce her. But it is the self-destructive Mozart, not Salieri, who really destroys the young genius with his uncontrollably decadent lifestyle. The drama ends years after Mozart's death with Salieri slitting his own throat and wallowing in his own "mediocrity." Peter Hall's direction was very elegant but had a shrewd eye for the comic and ironic twists in the tale, and McKellen's sly performance kept the piece from ever approaching stodgy historical drama. Tony Awards were won by the play, McKellen, Hall, and John Bury for his ingenious scenery and lighting (he had also done the costumes). *Amadeus* ran just short of three years and was a favorite in theatres across the nation.

A professional production of Ibsen's late drama *John Gabriel Borkman* had not been seen in New York since 1946, so the Circle in the Square revival that opened on December 18 had most critics and patrons discussing the merits of the play itself. Austin Pendleton's sparse production received mixed notices, but everyone found the acting praiseworthy: E. G. Marshall as the disgraced banker Borkman, Rosemary Murphy as the woman he married for business reasons, and Irene Worth as her sister, the woman Borkman really loved.

One of the first mainstream plays about lesbians was Jane Chambers's **Last Summer at Bluefish Cove** (12-22-80, Actors Playhouse), a quiet but affecting drama that ran eighty performances and enjoyed several subsequent productions in regional theatres. A group of lesbian friends have always summered together in a handful of cottages by the sea, but this year Lil (Jean Smart) is dying of cancer and, not telling the others of her condition, seems more moody and secretive than usual. When an unhappy housewife, Eva (Susan Slavin), needs time alone to think, she rents a place on the same cove, and when she meets Lil one day on the beach, the two are emotionally drawn together. They become lovers and are accepted by the rest of the group. By the fall Lil has died, and Eva mourns her with the others. The drama was unusual for its lack of bitterness or political agenda in its subject matter. There was also nothing sensational about the writing or the presentation, recalling more a traditional "women's story" than a shocking lesbian diatribe.

A lot of unplanned publicity centered on Sam Shepard's **True West** (12-23-80, Public: Martinson) before it opened. Producer Joseph Papp feuded with director Robert Woodruff, who quit and disavowed the production. Then Shepard, far away in California and never having seen any rehearsals, sided with Woodruff and swore he'd never let Papp do one of his plays again; whereupon Papp finished the direction himself and declared he would never present a Shepard play again. It sounded like a mess, and what was shown onstage was indeed a shambles with vague blocking, actors stumbling over lines, and a confusing ending. But underneath all the name-calling was quite a script. While his mother is vacationing, Austin (Tommy Lee Jones) housesits her immaculate California home and works on his screenplay, which has caught the interest of film producer Saul Kimmer (Louis Zorich). But soon Austin's slob of a brother, Lee (Peter Boyle), comes to visit, and the two brothers, as opposite as can be, continue their lifelong animosity and rivalry with each other. Ironically, Lee has an idea for a movie (a "true-to-life Western") and Saul's interest in it encourages the two brothers to collaborate on the script. Over time the petty thief and layabout Lee becomes driven and ambitious while Austin slips into a slovenly and derelict manner, trashing his mother's house and, in effect, becoming the old Lee. When Mom (Georgine Hall) returns, the sibling rivalry for her attention turns into a bloody fight to the death, though it was not clear in this production if anyone actually died. (The script and subsequent mountings reveal that both brothers live.) Some critics rejected the troubled production and the play as a lesser Shepard effort, but others saw a missed opportunity and reserved judgment for a better production. As Rich pointed out, "it's impossible to evaluate a play definitively when it hasn't been brought to life on stage." *True West* ran its scheduled twenty-four performances for the curious but would later emerge as one of Shepard's finest (and most produced) works.

The old year went out with James Prideaux's lame comedy **Mixed Couples** (12-28-80, Brooks Atkinson), unanimously disdained as "thin-blooded and unappealing" and "a crashing bore." Soon after the turn of the century, Clarice (Julie Harris) and her husband, Alden (Michael Higgins), switched partners with another couple, Elberta (Geraldine Page) and Don (Rip Torn), and haven't see each other since. In 1927 the foursome meet up accidentally in an airplane hangar in New Jersey as they wait for the fog to lift before taking off in their respective planes. The awkward situation allowed for some forced wit at first, then comic bitchiness, and finally heartwrung revelations proving that none of the four had gained much by the switch twenty-five years ago. No one questioned the ability of the superior cast (the two women received the lion's share of the praise), but audiences and critics alike found the evening "lifeless." After nine performances it was announced that Harris was suffering from an undisclosed illness and the show closed.

The new year came in with a more satisfying comedy, Christopher Durang's **Beyond Therapy** (1-1-81, Marymount Manhattan). Prudence (Sigourney Weaver) has been encouraged by her macho psychiatrist, Dr. Stuart Framingham (Jim Borrelli), to be more assertive, so she takes out a personal ad and meets up with Bruce (Stephen Collins). Although Bruce is gay and lives with Bob (Jack Gilpin), his flighty therapist, Mrs. Charlotte Wallace (Kate McGregor-Stewart), pushes Bruce to try the opposite sex, something which greatly displeases Bob. Bruce and Prudence make an unstable couple, both being so dependent on a professional to make their decisions for them, but eventually both move "beyond therapy" and start to put their lives in order. While all the reviews still insisted Durang was a talent to be reckoned with and admitted he knew how to write a funny line or a hilarious situation, few could wholly recommend the shapeless, meandering script as a satisfying play. One commentator stated, "At most, it is clever and amiable." The Phoenix production, directed with furious ingenuity by newcomer Jerry Zaks, only ran for a month, but *Beyond Therapy* would be heard from again.

The most expensive non-musical flop of the season (indeed, of all previous seasons) was Victor Gialanella's adaptation of **Frankenstein** (1-4-81, Palace), and it was easy to see where the money went. Douglas Schmidt's mammoth and evocative sets, ranging from a haunting graveyard to a gothic boudoir to a giant laboratory filled with gadgets, were the talk of the theatre district. Just as accomplished were Carrie Robbins's costumes, Jules Fisher and Robby Monk's lighting, and the many special effects by Bran Ferren. But the press was in agreement that the script was a shambles and that the actors were swallowed up in all the pyrotechnics. David Dukes was the scientist Victor Frankenstein, Keith Jochim was his Creature, and such notable actors as John Glover, Dianne Wiest, and John Carradine (in his last stage role) were to be glimpsed through all the smoke. The venture closed on opening night, and it took days to carry out all the paraphernalia.

The BAM Theatre Company was another adventurous group that was struggling, and it showed in its very spotty season of five classics in repertory. The opening production of *A Midsummer Night's Dream* on January 4 was not favorably reviewed, only Brian Murray as Oberon receiving complimentary notices. Like all the offerings in the repertory, it played twenty-six times. Reaction to the Circle Rep's revival of Gerhart Hauptmann's *The Beaver Coat* on January 11 was not much better. The nineteenth-century comedy about thieves and rogues in the German government was performed "with maximum hokum," but few found it funny. Another return engagement of *Emlyn Williams as Charles Dickens* opened on January 14 at the Century, gathered a bouquet of critical raves, and stayed for twenty-two performances. Williams had first essayed the role on Broadway in 1952, and this was his fourth and final visit.

Superb acting almost saved Joanna M. Glass's domestic comedy-drama **To Grandmother's House We Go** (1-15-81, Biltmore) but not quite; sixty-one performances was as long as the fine cast could keep it alive. The children and grandchildren of Connecticut matriarch Grandie (Eva Le Gallienne) gather at her Victorian home for Thanksgiving. Times are hard, and each family member has a request, emotional and/or financial, to make of the old lady. Because the group consists of various divorced, separated, and aimless offspring, there was plenty of fodder for mildly interesting drama. Rich led the generally unfavorable reviews by describing some of the characters as "stereotypes who have been plugged into a mechanical story built around a preordained message." But what mattered was the superb cast made up of revered veterans such as Shepperd Strudwick, Ruth Nelson, Kim Hunter, and (best of all) Le Gallienne. Clive Barnes in the *New York Post* observed: "Some actresses are content merely to get older; others insist on getting better. Eva Le Gallienne is one of the latter persuasion." With her elegant but unmistakable authority, splendid poise, and, as Rich described it, a "diaphanous smile that has no equal on Broadway," Le Gallienne was at the peak of her powers. Sadly, it was her last Broadway appearance.

BAM added George Farquhar's Restoration comedy *The Recruiting Officer* to its repertory on January 15, and critics had their doubts about both the play and the production. But certain BAM company members continued to shine, and there was admiration for Laurie Kennedy as the wily, cross-dressing Sylvia, Brian Murray as lusty Captain Plume (the officer of the title), Richard Jamieson as his rival, Captain Brazen, and Laura Esterman as the neurotic Melinda. The second offering at Lincoln Center's Vivian Beaumont was an elaborate and grandiose *Macbeth* on January 22 that was staged by opera director Sarah Caldwell, and met with decidedly mixed reviews. Some found her version "spectacular" and "stately,"; others thought it "pointless" and a piece of "operatic woodenness." But all were in agreement that Philip Anglim's Macbeth was severely lacking and that Maureen Anderman made a youthful and sexy queen.

Most of the critics commended the first act of Gus Edwards's **Weep Not for Me** (1-27-81, Theatre Four), as he found humor and truth in a bleak situation; but the Negro Ensemble presentation turned to lurid melodrama in the second act and left aisle-sitters cold. In the crumbling, nightmarish South Bronx of today, "or in the very near future," Zake Hendricks (Bill Cobbs), a retired army sergeant, keeps his cockeyed family together through sheer determination and devotion. He has forgiven his wife, Lillian (Ethel Ayler), her extramarital affair and showers her with love and presents. Similarly he has lavished affection on his four grown children: the neurotic divorcée Crissie (Seret Scott), the near-comotose rape victim Janet (Phylicia Ayers-Allen), the sex-starved would-be model Deanie (Elain Graham), and the drug addict Wilbur (Chuck Patterson), who lusts after his own sisters. Edwards managed to find the right comic touch in portraying this daffy family, but the piece degenerated into a preachy tirade with multiple killings by the end, and an interesting play was wiped out along with the Hendricks family. As was often the case at the Ensemble, the performances shone and were applauded for forty-eight performances.

Two off-Broadway theatre companies presented new works by Romulus Linney a month apart, the first his dreamy **The Captivity of Pixie Shedman** (1-29-81, Marymount Manhattan) by the Phoenix. Sensitive southern writer Bertram Shedman (William Carden) hopes to write a novel based on his grandmother's diary, but as he attempts it the ghost of Pixie Shedman (Penelope Allen) appears and scenes from the past are reenacted to prove to the young man that these events were real, not the mere stuff of romantic fiction. Pixie was seen being taken by her U.S. senator father (Ron Randell) to Washington, where she was wooed and won by Doc Bertram Shedman (Jon DeVries), who then neglected her for his waitress-mistress. Bertram's own father (Leon Russom) also appeared, another captive of stronger people and the victim of cancer at a young age. All the ghosts dissolve, and Bertram puts his own life in order and attacks his novel. While not exactly panned, the drama was not applauded either. One commentator's label of "a minor disaster" was probably closest to the mark.

Richard Foreman and his Ontological-Hysteric Theatre brought their self-described "sort of intellectual *Hellzapoppin*" called **Penguin Touquet** (2-1-81, Newman) to the Public for twenty-six puzzling performances. Despite a lavish production filled with all sorts of lighting effects, masks, oversized penguins, loud recorded sounds, and unintelligible ranting, it was considered a rather uninteresting affair by all but the most die-hard Foreman fans. Agatha (Kate Manheim) is being treated by her psychiatrist (David Warrilow), and once her subconscious takes over, all hell breaks loose. Heidi Landesman's surreal sets were noted, but little else seemed to stick in the mind of the audience.

Disparaging notices for Pam Gems's bio-drama **Piaf** (2-5-81, Plymouth) didn't stop it from running nearly five months and providing one of the season's most electrifying performances. Jane Lapotaire had played the "Little Sparrow" in England to great acclaim, and the British production, with some American actors added, was brought to Broadway where the actress triumphed. The play itself was a series of scenes that chronicled Edith Piaf's tragic life from her teenage years as a prostitute in the 1920s to her early death from drugs, alcohol, sex, and heartbreak. Gems was more interested in the shocking details (Piaf was seen urinating onstage in one scene) and scatological aspects of the famous singer's persona than in what made Piaf such a unique talent. But when Lapotaire took the stage all the Hollywood biography clichés seemed less annoying and the character, as irritating and pathetic as she was, became a vibrant and engaging star. John Beaufort in the *Christian Science Monitor* wrote that Lapotaire's "portrayal exults in a shrewd toughness, raucous humor, and an indomitability that grows with adversity. It is this indomitability that sustains Piaf's tremendous determination to perform." His colleagues were in enthusiastic agreement, and Lapotaire won the season's Tony Award. *Piaf* was far from a one-woman show, though. A large cast played the dozens of characters that drifted in and out of Piaf's life, and there were memorable appearances by Judith Ivey, Zoe Wanamaker, David Leary, Peter Friedman, Jean Smart, Robert Christian, and others, all under Howard Davies's tight direction.

Simon Gray's plays usually have a main character (often a literary or educational type) who is bombarded by a group of troubled individuals (family, colleagues, lovers), and the result is wicked satire or, at least, pointed comedy. His new work, **Close of Play** (2-10-81, Manhattan Theatre Club), was in a similar vein but with a major difference: the central character is dead (or symbolically dead). A family patriarch, Professor Jasper Spencer (William Roerick), sits in his easy chair at home, and his mixed-up family and friends parade in and spill out their problems. But Jasper says only a few words in the entire play,

and his ghostly presence and unemotional disregard make the other characters all the more ludicrous. The play's title is a cricket term, referring to the score of a game when it is interrupted until the next day; most critics thought Gray's comedy was equally suspended and unfinished. The comedy had been produced at the National Theatre in London, and comparisons with this American cast under Lynn Meadow's direction were inevitable. Some critics actually preferred the American production, but no one could heartily recommend the piece.

D. B. Gilles's **The Legendary Stardust Boys** (2-12-81, South Street) was among the few commercial ventures off Broadway this season, and it only lasted twelve performances. The "Stardust Boys" of the title is a polka band made up of Ohio working-class men who have been performing on weekends for years without much recognition. Tension is created when one member announces he is getting married and will quit the group, thus destroying the pipe dream they have had of making the big time.

It was not Schiller's masterpiece but a new, absurdist **Mary Stuart** (2-15-81, Public: LuEsther) by German playwright Wolfgang Hildesheimer (translated by Christopher Hampton) that was a guest at the Public for forty-one performances. While the imprisoned Mary (Roberta Maxwell) awaits her execution, a circus of sorts erupts in her dungeon cell. Old friends come to call, Mary's beloved pet dogs (now dead and stuffed) are brought in, she makes sexual advances to the assistant executioner, an apothecary gets everyone high on his potions, farcical last rites are performed like a Marx Brothers skit, and Mary rants and carries on so that she loses her head figuratively before she gets a chance to lose it literally. Des McAnuff staged the chaos with panache, and the cast ran with the show with no holds barred. Some critics were amused, some bored, others confused.

Nicol Williamson recreated his tormented lawyer Bill Maitland in the Roundabout's revival of John Osborne's *Inadmissible Evidence* (11-30-65) on February 23 for forty-nine performances, and most felt he was even better than he was fifteen years ago, though just as many felt the play itself had not aged well. Anthony Page directed (as he had the original production), and the expert supporting cast included Philip Bosco, Anthony Heald, and Christine Estabrook.

Three weeks was the longest Kevin Heelan's melodrama **Heartland** (2-23-81, Century) could survive in Broadway's smallest house. The quiet repose of a small midwestern town is destroyed one day in late spring when a homicidal psychopath murders several prominent citizens in a rampage downtown. That night Earl (Larry Nicks), the town loser and continual joke, decides to seek out the murderer and thereby raise himself in the eyes of the community. But Earl's venture is a suicidal one; discovering the local teen James (Sean Penn) is the deranged culprit, he is added to the maniac's victims. A few reviewers thought it a "mayhem suspense drama with a touch of class," but most described it as "a shoddy little shocker" and a "hackneyed melodrama." (More than one notice pointed out the electric quality of the youthful Penn.)

The Circle Rep presented the second Linney play this winter, the biographical drama **Childe Byron** (2-26-81, Circle) about Lord Byron (William Hurt) and his sole legitimate daughter, Ada (Lindsay Crouse). When Ada is dying of cancer at the age of thirty-six (the same age her illustrious father was when he died), the drugs she is taking help her conjure up visions of Byron and various people in his life. Six actors played several characters as they presented Byron's wild youth, abnormal sexual interest in his sister, homosexual encounters, brief marriage, and sensational career. Using pretty much the same theatrical device as he did in *The Captivity of Pixie Shedman*, Linney was a bit more successful this time (also, Byron's life was much more interesting than Pixie's), although critics, finding the flashback chronicle awkward and unfocused, spent much of their reviews cheering Hurt's performance.

The notices for Susan Nanus's Holocaust drama **The Survivor** (3-3-81, Morosco) were gently (but unanimously) dismissive, the consensus being that the drama was no match for its difficult subject matter. Based on a memoir by Jack Eisner, the play centered on a Polish teenager, Jacek (David Marshall Grant), who led a gang of Jewish youths in the Warsaw ghetto who stole food and goods from the Aryan section of town for the starving inhabitants of the Jewish sector. Soon the deportation begins, then the resistance rises, and the Germans retaliate. Only Jacek survives to tells his story so that the world will know what his comrades did for humanity. But the characters were mostly stereotypes, the plotting was clumsy, and the imposing topic was trivialized to mere melodrama. The drama closed in a week.

Lincoln Center continued to experiment with what to do in its downstairs space and presented a *One-Act Play Festival* (3-5-81, Mitzi E. Newhouse)

for thirty-seven performances, but the program generated little excitement. Percy Granger's *Vivian* was generally considered the "most substantial of three insubstantial one-act plays." Paul (James Woods), a highstrung theatre director for a production of *The Sea Gull*, drives to a sanitarium to pick up his father, Vivian (Michael Egan), whom he has not seen in over twenty years, and brings him to a matinee of his show. Vivian is as sedate and calm as Paul is hyperactive, so the conversation going to the theatre and at a restaurant after the performance is strained, comic, and sobering. John Guare's *In Fireworks Lie Secret Codes* was also an extended conversation, this time conducted by a group of characters as they watch the Macy's fireworks display on the Fourth of July from the penthouse terrace of a homosexual couple. Jeffrey Sweet's *Stops Along the Way* was deemed the "flimsiest of the lot," a series of episodes in which an Ohio teacher (Graham Beckel) drives a student (Kathleen Widdoes), who is also his former lover, back to her husband in Baltimore. The two stopped at a gas station, a diner, a drugstore, and a motel during their trip, but the play went nowhere.

BAM's revival of Ibsen's *The Wild Duck* on March 5 met with mixed reviews, from mild approval to the designation of "thin and silly." The new adaptation by Thomas Babe (from Erik J. Friis's translation) and Arthur Penn's direction were cited as the production's weaknesses. A revival of Ira Levin's thriller *Veronica's Room* (12-29-73) on March 8 at the Provincetown Playhouse managed to find an audience and run ninety-seven performances (twenty more than the original could muster on Broadway).

Black Elk Lives (3-12-81, Entermedia) originated at the Folger Theatre in Washington, D.C. Christopher Sergel adapted John Neihardt's book *Black Elk Speaks*, a history of the American Plains Indians from 1492 to the massacre at Wounded Knee in 1890, as seen by the spiritual leader Black Elk (Manu Tupou) and his cousin Crazy Horse (Carl Battaglia). Although the epic-style piece only lasted six performances off Broadway, the play would become popular with regional and educational theatres, usually under the title *Black Elk Speaks*.

Producing Eugene O'Neill's *Long Day's Journey Into Night* (11-7-56) with an all-black cast sounded like a gimmick, but there was nothing gimmicky about Geraldine Fitzgerald's solid production, which played a brief engagement off-off Broadway and was then brought to the Public on March 18 for a successful run of eighty-seven performances. Jack Kroll in *Newsweek* observed, "The cast plays it straight, with no attempt to assume Irish-Catholic mannerisms. They play it for the universal rhythms and passions that override the play's social specifics, and it works." Most of his colleagues agreed, saluting the performances of Gloria Foster (Mary Tyrone), Earle Hyman (James), Al Freeman, Jr., (Jamie), and Peter Francis-James (Edmund).

Edward Albee's adaptation of Vladimir Nabokov's celebrated novel **Lolita** (3-19-81, Brooks Atkinson) postponed its opening several times while the playwright wrestled with how to bring the difficult work to the stage. When it finally opened, the press was dismayed to find that he had, unintentionally or not, turned the piece into a farce. Donald Sutherland played the academic Humbert Humbert who weds the frumpy Charlotte (Shirley Stoler) but is obsessed by his stepdaughter, the "nymphet" Lolita (Blanche Baker). Clive Revill was the lively nemesis Clare Quilty (Otis L. Guernsey, Jr., in the *Best Plays*, described him as "weirdly colorful"), and Ian Richardson played the "Certain Gentleman" who was Nabokov himself as a narrator. Frank Dunlop, a master of farce, directed and was held somewhat accountable for the misshapen result, but it was Albee's "vulgarized and trivialized" adaptation that received the brunt of unanimously negative reviews. Despite all the publicity over the delays and the controversy that arose when the Nabokov estate complained about the script, *Lolita* closed on opening night and was quickly forgotten.

Just as Jane Lapotaire made it worth transporting the poorly written *Piaf* from London to New York, so too Glenda Jackson justified New York audiences sitting through Andrew Davies's **Rose** (3-26-81, Cort). The play concerns an English elementary school teacher who battles petty people all day at school and then comes home to a husband (John Cunningham) who seems bored and uninterested in her. When Rose has a fling with a freethinking school administrator (J. T. Walsh), she considers divorcing her husband until her lover points out that the general dissatisfaction she has with her life may be rooted in herself. Jackson's fine performance was matched by that of Jessica Tandy as her wry and opinionated mother, and the few scenes the two had together were the best moments in the play. As with *Piaf*, the reviews hailed the British star and lamented her weak vehicle. *Rose* remained on Broadway for two months.

Mustapha Matura, a Trinidadian playwright living in London, gave his new drama **Meetings** (3-26-81, Marymount Manhattan) to the Phoenix for its world premiere, and his cautionary parable about consumerism ran a month off Broadway. In the state-of-the-art kitchen of Trinidad engineer Hugh (Carl Lumbly) there is everything but food. His upwardly mobile wife, Jean (Michele Shay), is too busy marketing cigarettes to cook anything, so when he longs for a home-cooked meal, Hugh hires a native girl (Seret Scott) who knows all the regional dishes. During a series of breakfasts, we see the glossy facade of their marriage explode while in the background looms the plight of the island's working folk, who are being destroyed by the entrepenurial success of Hugh and Jean. Critical response ranged from "an amazing piece of theatre" to "thin" and "monotonous." The play would soon be forgotten, but Matura's name would be seen again.

The Circle in the Square continued its ambitious season of neglected classics with Strindberg's *The Father* on April 2. Ralph Waite played the tormented Captain, and a majority of the reviewers thought he was either miscast or not up to the demands of the role. Frances Sternhagen played his cruel wife, Laura, very matter-of-factly, which some found effective, others lackluster. The drama was repeated twenty-nine times, the shortest engagement at the Circle this season.

The bumpy season at the Negro Ensemble continued with Larry Neal's **In an Upstate Motel** (4-4-81, Theatre Four). Professional hitman Duke (Charles Henry Patterson) and his lethal girlfriend, Queenie (Donna Bailey), have bungled a job and hide out from their bosses in a motel high in the mountains. As a blizzard rages outside, the two self-destructive lovers indulge in cocaine, sex, reminiscences, and tearing each other apart. The depressing little drama seemed incomplete, which it was, the playwright having died in January before rewrites and revisions could be made.

Neil Simon backed off from his recent trend of writing tragicomic pieces and came up with an all-out comedy with **Fools** (4-6-81, Eugene O'Neill), but it only managed forty performances, the shortest run of his career to date. The merry folk tale is set in the Russian peasant town of Kulyenchikov, where the inhabitants have been cursed with chronic stupidity for over two hundred years. (The housewives, for example, sweep dirt into their houses each morning, and a dog is considered housebroken if he relieves himself inside the home.) When the young schoolmaster Leon Tolchinsky (John Rubinstein) arrives to take up his first teaching job, the villagers hope he can cure them of the curse, not telling him that after twenty-four hours in the town he will be as stupid as they. But Leon is immediately enamored of the doctor's daughter Sophia (Pamela Reed), a girl so dim she has only recently discovered how to sit down to rest, that he sets up a plan to save the village and win his love. After the twenty-four hours he only pretends to be stupid, adopts a local name to put a hoax on the curse, saves the town, and then weds Sophia. Reviews ranged from disappointment to curt dismissal, everyone agreeing that the one-joke comedy outlasted its one joke. Mike Nichols directed the quaint production (John Lee Beatty's setting was described by Rich as "jolly and elaborate . . . [it] looks like the cross between the shtetl of *Fiddler on the Roof* and an idyllic Alpine village in a Swiss tourism brochure"), and the cast was strong all around: Gerald Hiken, Joseph Leon, Mary Louise Wilson, Harold Gould, and Florence Stanley. But the largely negative reviews were insurmountable and Simon had his first true flop. Ironically, *Fools* would become very popular in community theatres and would remain on the Top Ten list of the most-produced high school plays for many years.

Brian Friel's arresting drama **Translations** (4-7-81, Manhattan Theatre Club) would have had its American premiere on Broadway in better days; nonetheless, the off-Broadway production it was afforded was first class, and the difficult piece about language was well served by director Joe Dowling and a gifted cast. The aging schoolmaster Hugh (Barnard Hughes) teaches at a "hedge-school" in a rural Irish-speaking community in 1833 with the help of his son Manus (Jarlath Conroy), who is in love with a local girl, Maire (Ellen Parker). When Hugh's elder son, Owen (Stephen Burleigh), arrives from Dublin with British soldiers assigned to survey and rename the area towns with English names, the locals are curious at first. Maire falls in love with the handsome British Lieutenant Yolland (Daniel Gerroll), who is charmed by Ireland and hopes to settle there. But after a dance one night Yolland disappears (it is suggested by the locals that radical twin brothers have murdered him and hidden the body), and the British threaten to kill livestock and tear down homes if the inhabitants do not produce the missing lieutenant. The drama ends with a foreshadowing of the upcoming tragedy of Ire-

land: the British interference and the dreaded potato blight. Both the Irish and English speakers dialogue was performed in English, so the audience could "understand" both languages, while most of the characters could only understand one or the other without translation; the device made for some effective moments, such as a tender love scene between Yolland and Maire as each tentatively tries to communicate with the other, or a wry sequence in which Owen alters and expurgates the British soldiers' instructions as he translates them aloud for the locals. Mixed reaction in the press called *Translations* everything from "an astonishingly turgid and quite literally tongue-tied comedy-drama" to a "sweet and subtle play which deals tenderly with the rape of a culture."

Although Brecht's **Jungle of Cities** (4-9-81, BAM) dated back to 1923, it did not receive its first professional production in New York until this season. Richard Nelson's version of the gangster piece was directed by David Jones and featured Don Scardino and Seth Allen as the two Chicago underworld figures drawn together in a homosexual and sadomasochistic battle to the death. Nelson also adapted Goldoni's *Il Campiello*, the first of three classic revivals the Acting Company brought to the Public's Newman starting on April 15. It was followed by Beckett's *Waiting for Godot* and *A Midsummer Night's Dream*. The first generation of this young touring company had all moved on, and few of their replacements captured much attention.

BAM ended its season with an impressive *Oedipus the King* on April 16 with Emily Mann directing Joe Morton as the cursed monarch and Sheila Allen as his queen. Ming Cho Lee designed the stark but evocative set, and there was much about the production that was encouraging for the troubled company. But it was not to be. The Brooklyn-based group's expenses, according to *Variety*, far exceeded their $1 million in income this season, and the company closed up shop for good.

Another one-night flop on Broadway (there were seven this season, four of them nonmusicals) was Eddie Lawrence's triple bill **Animals** (4-22-81, Princess), which was roundly panned as "inept," "grotesque," and "a void." In *The Beautiful Mariposa*, a Spanish torero (Lazaro Perez) comes to America to kill a bull in each state; but in Kansas he gores a cow instead and gets in trouble with the state police. *Louie and the Elephant* concerned a San Francisco restaurant owner (Joel Kramer) with the head of an elephant who rejects an offer to become fully human when he realizes a 110-year-old human is not sexually attractive to women. The final playlet was called *Sort of an Adventure* and dealt with a half-human, half-duck female (Cara Duff-MacCormick) who is fed roast duck by a jealous wife; surprisingly, the dinner turns the ugly fowl into a human beauty.

Woody Allen the playwright returned to Broadway after twelve years with **The Floating Light Bulb** (4-27-80, Vivian Beaumont) and surprised everyone by coming up with a very conventional domestic drama unlike his previous theatre or film work. Enid Pollack (Beatrice Arthur) dominates her family in their 1945 Brooklyn apartment while her husband, Max (Danny Aiello), spends his hard-earned waiter's pay on the numbers and his young mistress. Their two sons have found similar escapes: thirteen-year-old Steve (Eric Gurry) makes cynical Woody Allen–like wisecracks for self-protection, and sixteen-year-old Paul (Brian Backer) has immersed himself in magic tricks that he gets through mail order. (The play's title is the name of one of the illusions he has purchased.) Enid gets a theatrical agent, Jerry Wexler (Jack Weston), to come to the apartment, then orders Paul to give a performance that will launch his magician career. But Paul's stuttering and hapless act is a disaster, and it is then learned that Wexler is a loser himself, his most profitable client being a singing dog. As several critics pointed out, the play was similar to *The Glass Menagerie* in many ways (Depression-era crippled family with a forceful mother and a shy offspring who pin all their hopes on a stranger with crushing results) but Allen's sense of deadpan humor, even as restrained as it was here, remained evident. Reviewers admired the skillful production, especially the performances of Backer (who won a Tony Award) and Weston, but the play itself was called everything from "invigorating, illuminating, highly original" to something that "could easily be mistaken for a journeyman effort by a much younger and less experienced writer." The scheduled sixty-five performances at Lincoln Center were well attended but, curiously, the play has rarely resurfaced anywhere else.

The very successful season at the Roundabout continued with the first New York revival of Shelagh Delaney's *A Taste of Honey* (10-4-60) on April 28, and most reviewers felt the working-class drama held up very well. There were many compliments for Valerie French as the tart-like mother, but the most enthusiastic praise was reserved for Amanda Plummer (in her first major role) as the resilient teenager Jo. Audiences also took to the new actress, and the production filled the theatre for its scheduled fifty-five performances, transferring to Broadway the next season.

The Circle Rep had another fumble with Roy London's **In Connecticut** (4-30-81, Circle), a play that it had tried out earlier in a workshop under the title *In Vienna*. The name change did little to help the wan piece about suburbanites adjusting to Manhattan life.

Veteran West Coast performer Barbara Perry wrote and performed **Passionate Ladies** (5-5-81, Bijou), a one-woman program about five women in the arts. But all the notices agreed that Perry was a better performer than a writer. She played a grandmother stripper, a hard-nosed English lady teaching Shakespeare, the acting coach Josephine Dillon, who married Clark Gable, a dance teacher no longer able to perform, and an aging hoofer who can still dance and does a terrific tap routine that was the sole redeeming scene of the evening. Aside from Perry's versatility, there was little to hold one's interest as each of the five ladies outwore her welcome long before she was finished. The odd program lasted one week.

A. Marcus Hemphill's comic fable **Inacent Black** (5-6-81, Biltmore), subtitled "A Heaven-sent Comedy," was about a messenger (Melba Moore) from God who enters the life of an affluent black family, fixes up all their squabbles, and sets everyone on the right path. It was easygoing fun that was likable in spite of itself, and more than one critic admitted to having a good time at the simple-minded proceedings. Barbara Montgomery shone as the matriarch of the family, and her children were played by Bruce Strickland, Gregory Miller, Reginald Vel Johnson, and Count Stovall. But it was Moore, known for musicals and recordings, who was most appreciated as her no-nonsense angel confronted a pimp, consulted with God, and went head-to-head with the strong-willed family members. Despite a set of reviews that made the evening sound highly entertaining, *Inacent Black* only lasted two weeks on Broadway.

A sterling cast graced the Roundabout's *Hedda Gabler* on May 5. Michael Kahn directed Christopher Hampton's translation in a mounting that was considered adequate, but the actors were applauded: Susannah York (Hedda), Harris Yulin (Tesman), Philip Bosco (Brack), Paul Shenar (Lovborg), and Roxanne Hart (Mrs. Elvsted). The revival ran fifty-one times, a decent run to end the Roundabout's most successful season yet.

In certain circles (and they were wide circles indeed), the most anticipated theatre event of the season was Elizabeth Taylor's Broadway debut in a revival of Lillian Hellman's *The Little Foxes* (2-15-39) on May 7 at the Martin Beck. The film star was insured by Lloyd's of London for $27,000 per performance (with a three-day deductible), which made the revival sound like a heavily financed Hollywood project. (Taylor ended up missing sixteen of the 126 performances due to illness.) But *The Little Foxes* was a play, and seeing the famous star onstage and holding her own in a major role was what all the excitement was about. Even the critics were not immune: nearly every review mentioned how well Taylor looked at her age (forty-nine years) and how flattering Florence Klotz's period costumes were on the great lady. As for her acting, most felt she was in fine form, and others felt her very presence carried the part of the conniving, seductive Regina Giddens. The critics found Austin Pendleton's direction spotty and some of the cast members lacking, though Maureen Stapleton as the put-upon Birdie was unanimously praised.

After some less than satisfying new offerings, the Negro Ensemble brought back Samm-Art Williams's *Home* (12-14-79) on May 8 to Theatre Four for forty-five showings. Samuel L. Jackson played the hero of the tall tale, and Michele Shay and L. Scott Caldwell returned as the women in his life.

Producer David Merrick, who had been absent from Broadway for a few years while he toyed with Hollywood, returned and scored a triumph with the musical hit *42nd Street* at the top of the season but finished with the one-night fiasco **I Won't Dance** (5-10-81, Helen Hayes) near the season's end. (Technically, it was not a one-night run since it opened and closed during a Sunday matinee.) Oliver Hailey's dark comedy, which shifted unsteadily from fantasy to reality, centered on Dom (David Selby), a wheelchair-bound paraplegic whose movie star brother has been murdered. Dom's sister-in-law's sister Lil (Gail Strickland) from New Mexico, who specializes in seducing Pueblo men, and the kookie starlet-insurance underwriter Kay (Arlene Golonka), who lusts after Dom, fill out the three-character play, which reaches its climax, in a surrealistic sequence, when two wheelchairs get to fornicate. Dom confesses to the police that he murdered his own brother, but they don't believe him. (It turns out the Hollywood celebrity was killed in an act of random violence, but several audience members had left before then.) Tom O'Horgan's excessive direction (he even provided his own incidental music) only complicated matters, and the single matinee engagement was declared "overwrought," "stupid," and a "dreary, pointless little enterprise." Although no one was aware of it at the time, *I Won't Dance* was the last production presented in the revered Helen Hayes Theatre; it would remain dark for months while its fate was debated and decided in courtrooms before being torn down in 1982.

Broadway's final new offering of the season was the romantic comedy **It Had to Be You** (5-10-81, John Golden), a two-hander written and performed by Renée Taylor and Joseph Bologna. Failed actress and frustrated playwright Theda Blau has not found the answer to her problems in health food nor analysis, so in desperation she lures TV commercial director Vito Pignoli to her New York apartment on Christmas Eve and holds him hostage. During her long harangue the two fall in love and end up matrimonial and professional partners. While all the aisle-sitters pronounced the play "drippy," "silly, vulgar, brash," and "as flawed as the San Andreas Fault in California," some admitted they enjoyed it and the two performers. Audiences agreed for only forty-eight performances.

Alec McCowen brought his acclaimed one-man performance of *St. Mark's Gospel* (9-7-78) to the Playhouse on May 13 for twenty performances and collected another set of rave reviews.

The British playwright Caryl Churchill finally captured the attention of New York with a splashy and delectable American production of her satiric comedy **Cloud 9** (5-18-81, Theatre de Lys). In a British colony in Africa during the height of nineteenth-century imperialism, Clive (Jeffrey Jones) and his wife, Betty (Zeljko Ivanek), try to keep a stiff upper lip while the natives, represented by the houseboy Joshua (played by the white actor Dom Amendolia), get restless and sexual frustrations throughout the household get out of control. The family's stalwart friend, explorer Harry Bagley (Nicholas Surovy), arrives and promptly seduces everyone: Betty, Joshua, the nine-year-old son, Edward (Concetta Tomei), and even the lesbian governess, Ellen (E. Katherine Kerr). At the peak of all the amatory goings-on, the natives rise in revolt and Joshua supposedly kills all the white people. But one hundred years later, in modern London, some of the same characters are still dealing with their sexual confusion. Grown-up Edward (now played by Jones) is quarreling with his male lover Gerry (Ivanek) yet is sexually drawn to his own sister Victoria (Tomei), who has strong feelings for the divorcée Lin (Veronica Castang). Meanwhile Gerry is somehow attracted to the middle-aged Betty (Kerr), who is only now abandoning her Victorian ideas of sex. The round robin of relationships concludes with both Bettys embracing, finally finding sexual and emotional satisfaction in each other. Director Tommy Tune requested a few changes in the script for the off-Broadway production, and some felt the result was superior to the London version. Tune, known mainly as a choreographer and director of musicals, made the wacky play dance: Lawrence Miller's simple but effective scenery slid back and forth like revolving boudoir doors, characters entered and exited as if in a raucous ballet, and scenes moved like an old George Abbott farce. Yet the performances were still sharp and, especially in the second act, penetrating. While the reviews were supportive, few expressed the kind of enthusiasm that the audiences experienced, an enthusiasm that kept the comedy on the boards for three and a half years.

Wendy Wasserstein continued to strike a comic nerve with **Isn't It Romantic** (5-28-81, Marymount Manhattan), a comedy of manners about women balancing personal independence with romantic fulfillment. Recent college graduate Janie Blumberg (Alma Cuervo) is short and overweight and has ambitions of being a writer. Her classmate Harriet Cornwall (Laurie Kennedy) is a drop-dead gorgeous Wasp, but the two friends share a thirst for independence, especially from overprotective parents. In a series of brief scenes, the two explore the ups and downs of their dilemma; Janie gets involved with the Jewish doctor Marty Sterling (Peter Riegert), with unsatisfying results, and Harriet climbs the corporate ladder and has an affair with her married boss, the accountant-on-the-make Paul Stuart (Bob Gunton). Throughout their trials the two young women are hounded by their mothers: Janie's mom (Jane Hoffman) sings "Sunrise, Sunset" to her over the phone, while the feminist Mrs. Cornwall (Barbara Baxley) dismisses Harriet's questions about life with a curt "What is this, *Youth Wants to Know?*" As in previous Wasserstein works, both woman are smart, sharp, and observant, and their commentary on their various situations keeps the episodes lively and brittle. The

comedy ran its scheduled thirty-seven performances but would return later in a much longer run.

1981–1982

While a British import (*Nicholas Nickleby*) was the centerpiece of the theatre season, there were some American plays of quality to be found this year on and off the Street. Fifteen new native works (plus three transfers from Off Broadway) opened on Broadway, and forty-one appeared off Broadway, as compared to eighteen and thirty-seven the season before. And when one considers Off Off Broadway, where ninety-four theatre groups were members of the Off-Off-Broadway Alliance, the amount of American theatre in New York was substantial. Yet attendance on Broadway declined slightly, and more shows than ever were depending on twofers (coupons offering two tickets for the price of one) and the TKTS booth. (*Variety* calculated that 10 percent of Broadway's box-office revenue came by way of TKTS this season.)

The number of revivals also fell both on and off Broadway, with only six on the Street and twenty-two off. But if older plays were not in abundance, older stars certainly were. Claudette Colbert, Katharine Hepburn, and Judith Anderson led the parade of actresses that dominated the season, and Hollywood provided Faye Dunaway, Anne Bancroft, Joanne Woodward, Cher, Karen Black, and others. Add to this such dependable stage stars as Zoe Caldwell, Geraldine Page, Sandy Dennis, Elizabeth Ashley, and Dorothy Loudon, and you had a season of ladies' night out. The fact that many of these women had substandard vehicles was not lost on the critics and public alike, but the presence of so many stars at least gave Broadway the illusion of glamour.

The most successful off-Broadway revival of the season was the first, New Haven's Long Wharf Theatre's production of David Mamet's *American Buffalo* (2-16-77), which opened on June 3 at the Circle in the Square Downtown and stayed for 262 showings. The critics were more accepting of Mamet's play this time around, and the performance by Al Pacino, the revival's selling point, as the volatile burglar Teach was considered one of the best of the season. "Pacino makes it all fall into place, with his richly expressive, funny, only slightly scary picture of Teach, slouching about the shop in deep thought and with a mind as cunning as, but no more so than, a wharf's rat," Douglas Watt wrote in the *Daily News*. "He is simply marvelous, at times hilarious, in a perfectly coordinated performance." Arvin Brown directed, and Clifton James and Thomas Waites played Pacino's partners in crime.

One of Off Broadway's few commercial entries this season was Walter and Peter Marks's **The Butler Did It** (6-3-81, Players), a comic thriller about a theatre troupe rehearsing a comic thriller. On-the-skids playwright-director Anthony J. Lefcourt (Alan Mixon) has withheld the final scene of his play from the actors in order to stimulate their creativity. But the cast's insecurity (compounded by the fact that all the characters in the piece are named Butler) only makes the internal rivalries and romantic entanglements worse, and when the staged murder of an actress turns out to be real, Detective Mumford (John Hallow) is brought in to discover which Butler is the culprit. While most commentators pronounced the pseudo-Pirandellian thriller a complicated mess, some thought it "lightheaded, lighthearted, and funny."

The Broadway season started early and on the worst possible footing with Sam Bobrick and Ron Clark's comedy **Wally's Cafe** (6-12-81, Brooks Atkinson), which only lasted twelve performances. In 1940, a New Jersey couple, Louise (Rita Moreno) and Wally (James Coco), open a hamburger stand in the desert sixty miles outside of Las Vegas and are dismayed to find business is negligible. Their only customer is the footsore would-be actress Janet (Sally Struthers), who is hitchhiking her way to Hollywood. Eighteen years later the business is still there and struggling, and Janet returns, fresh from a disastrous non-career in the movies, takes a job at the hamburger stand, and has a brief fling with Wally behind her friend Louise's back. The final scene takes place in the present as Wally and Louise are planning to close the business and retire to an old folks' home. But out of the desert comes Janet, now the wealthy widow of a mob boss, who bails out her old friends. Called everything from a "plastic farce" to "a bore," *Wally's Cafe* was unfavorably compared to television, and while some complimented Struthers on her proficient sitcom performance, the only aspect of the production that was endorsed was Stuart Wurtzel's hamburger-shaped cafe that changed in its details over the years.

Irish actor Shay Duffin brought his one-man show *Shay Duffin as Brendan Behan* (1-2-73) back to New York on June 9 at the Astor Place. The program, drawn from the words and songs of the Irish author, stayed for two weeks.

The Circle Repertory Theatre's last new work of the 1980–1981 season was Lanford Wilson's **A Tale Told** (6-11-81, Circle), the third part of his Talley trilogy. The action takes place in the Talley house on July 4, 1944, while the events of his earlier *Talley's Folly* (5-1-79) are being played out that same night down by the river. Three generations of Talleys in the house are arguing about whether the family garment business ought to be sold to a big corporation, and in the heated discussion, old wounds are opened, sordid business dealings are revealed, and some sexual affairs are unearthed. The talk was somewhat interesting but hardly gripping even if the characters were sharply defined: the stubborn patriarch (Fritz Weaver), his grasping children, in-laws, and grandchildren (Michael Higgins, Helen Stenborg, Timothy Shelton, Patricia Wettig), Sally's conniving fiancé (Jimmie Ray Weeks), and even Sally (played again by Trish Hawkins), who made a brief appearance near the end to get her suitcase and run off with Matt. Critical reaction was mixed and rather tepid, none either strongly liking or disliking the drama, and the month-long engagement passed uneventfully. Wilson would later revise and retitle the work as *Talley & Son*.

A commercial revival of Joe Orton's *Entertaining Mr. Sloane* (10-12-65) on June 12 at the Cherry Lane seemed like a risky venture, but with a strong cast and supportive reviews, the dark comedy ran 269 performances. Barbara Byrne was the naive Kath, Joseph Maher her avid brother Ed, Gwyllum Evans played the senile old Kemp, and the dynamic newcomer Maxwell Caulfield essayed the handsome and dangerous Sloane. John Tillinger directed the revival, one of the longest-running of all Orton productions in New York.

The young Dodger Theatre Company and its director Des McAnuff, who had shown such inventive theatrics in last season's *Mary Stuart*, returned as guests to the Public and offered the political docudrama **How It All Began** (6-18-81, Other Stage). Based on an autobiography by the notorious German terrorist Michael "Bommi" Baumann, the piece was written by McAnuff and the thirteen Juilliard theatre students who comprised the cast. While the drama had some potent scenes, in particular those illustrating how Baumann (Val Kilmer) grew from a restless kid to a dangerous anarchist, most of the critics felt it was still at the classroom workshop level.

The Negro Ensemble Company brought back Charles Fuller's *Zooman and the Sign* (12-7-80) on

June 20 at Theatre Four, and the acclaimed drama ran an additional forty-four performances. The Roundabout Theatre concluded its 1980–1981 season with another successful revival, Shaw's *Misalliance* on June 23. The reliable Stephen Porter directed the production, which some deemed "creditable though no better than that," but there was general commendation for Philip Bosco and Patricia O'Connell as Mr. and Mrs. Tarleton and Anthony Heald as Gunner. The comedy ran a healthy 192 performances.

Another one-man show about a famous Irishman, **Oscar Remembered** (6-23-81, Provincetown Playhouse), took a different approach in telling the Oscar Wilde story. Maxim Mazumdar wrote and performed the piece as Lord Alfred Douglas, recalling his tragic association with the famous writer.

Last season's Roundabout revival of Shelagh Delaney's *A Taste of Honey* (10-4-60) moved to Broadway on June 24 and stayed for a gratifying 157 performances at the Century. Notices paralleled the glowing approval the show had received earlier, especially for newcomer Amanda Plummer as the troubled youth Jo.

The Circle in the Square concluded its 1980–1981 season with, atypically for the company, a new American play: Elan Garonzik's family drama **Scenes and Revelations** (6-25-81, Circle in the Square). In 1894 Lancaster, Pennsylvania, four sisters (Valerie Mahaffey, Christine Lahti, Marilyn McIntyre, and Mary-Joan Negro) have just buried their last parent and must decide whether they should sell the farm and move on. This quandary leads to several flashbacks that show how each sister lost the man in her life and how all of them have been subjugated by parents, society, and the world. In the end they finally decide to move to the big city; not Moscow like Chekhov's sisters had hoped, but Manchester, England, where a rich uncle has invited them to stay. While a few critics found the drama palatable and the characters moving, most agreed with Frank Rich in the *New York Times* that these women were "at best skin-deep, and their predicaments ready-made."

Joseph Papp presented *The Tempest* on June 25 at the outdoor Delacorte and garnered the worst set of reviews afforded the New York Shakespeare Festival in many a season. Mabou Mines director Lee Breuer staged the fantasy with a mishmash of styles, and the audience members disappearing at intermission was the evening's neatest magic trick. Raul Julia's Prospero was judged passable,

if a little bored and distracted, but nothing of value was to be said for the ninny Miranda of Jessica Nelson, the W. C. Fields–like Stephano of Louis Zorich, the street punk Caliban of Barry Miller, and an Ariel played by a dozen actors of various sexes, races, and sizes, including a Sumo wrestler. A second commercial Joe Orton revival this season did not fare as well as *Entertaining Mr. Sloane*. Porno film star Harry Reems was featured as the lewd Dr. Prentice in *What the Butler Saw* (5-4-70) on July 3 at the Westside Arts, but it met with little approval and closed after twelve showings.

Kevin Wade's agreeable comedy **Key Exchange** (7-14-81, Orpheum) was so successful in its off-off-Broadway engagement at the WPA that it was moved to Off Broadway, where it ran out the season. Three Manhattan singles "from the same general gene pool" meet each Sunday in Central Park to bicycle together. Michael (Mark Blum) is recently married, but his young wife seems to be spending more time with her music teacher than with him. Philip (Ben Masters), an aspiring novelist, has been dating and sleeping with the bright photographer Lisa (Brooke Adams), but when she suggests they exchange keys to each other's apartment as a form of some sort of "commitment," Philip panics and the relationship gets rocky. In a series of scenes in the park over the course of a summer, these engaging people try to work out their feelings about each other. The play does not end with tidy resolutions: Philip and Lisa do exchange keys, but the seriousness of their relationship is still questioned, and Michael accepts his unfaithful wife with relief and dread. Yet the characters were so fully realized that the audience felt they grew with them during the performance. Aisle-sitters found the comedy inviting, and Wade was declared very promising. Unfortunately, it was his only play of note.

The Public Theatre presented two new David Henry Hwang works this season. **The Dance and the Railroad** (7-16-81, Anspacher) was a one-act character study about two Chinese laborers in 1867 building the transcontinental railroad and how they survive the drudgery of their "slavery" by escaping into the wondrous beauty of theatre. Lone (John Lone) was training at the opera school in China when his family sent him overseas to work on the railroad and send his money back home. He is distant from his fellow laborers (he calls them "dead men") and goes to a nearby mountaintop at the end of the workday and practices the dance and performance techniques of the Chinese opera. The recent arrival Ma (Tzi Ma) joins him and convinces Lone to teach him the noble arts of the stage, the two of them bonding in a teacher-pupil relationship. (Hwang named the two characters after the actors who helped him develop the piece.) The workmen have gone on strike for an eight-hour day (which the white workers have) and more pay, but settle for less as Ma returns to work and Lone retreats deeper into the ancient art form to hide his misery. Lone directed and choreographed the well-received little play; Otis L. Guernsey, Jr., in the *Best Plays* called it "a unique combination of dance movement, sound, and dramatic insight, a very large entertainment in a small package."

Across town, Papp also presented *Henry IV, Part 1* on July 31 at the outdoor Delacorte for thirty-one performances, and it met with a better response than *The Tempest* did. Des McAnuff directed a cast that included Kenneth McMillan (Falstaff), John Vickery (Prince Hal), Mandy Patinkin (Hotspur), and Stephen Markle (King Henry). On August 4 the Circle brought back Jim Leonard, Jr.'s *The Diviners* (10-16-80) and kept it on the boards for forty performances.

George Furth's lightweight comedy **The Supporting Cast** (8-6-81, Biltmore) struck audiences and critics alike as the sort of summer tent comedy that would never dream of going to Broadway. But it did, and the reviews, more dismissive than scolding, told the public enough to warn them of the kind of evening they were in for. Malibu resident Ellen (Hope Lange) has just finished a tell-all book about her famous author husband, so she invites four of her friends, all related to celebrities, to her home to warn them that they are also in the book, warts and all. Gathered are Mae (Betty Garrett), the pushy mother of a celebrated (and secretly gay) conductor; Arnold (Jack Gilford), the nervous husband of a popular playwright; Florrie (Joyce Van Patten), the vulgar wife of a movie star; and Sally (Sandy Dennis), the neurotic pill-popping wife of a congressman who has left her for another woman. Although the foursome react with hysterics at having their dirty laundry exposed, feelings change when Ellen tells them there is a movie of her book planned, and the four friends happily argue about which film star should portray them and which talk show engagements they should accept. As much as the notices admired the winning cast (Dennis was considered the funniest or the most grotesque, depending on the reviewer), none

could fully recommend the play, and it closed after a month.

The Phoenix Theatre would have a lukewarm season, beginning with Linda Griffiths and Paul Thompson's topical comedy **Maggie & Pierre** (9-17-81, Marymount Manhattan), which had been a hit in Toronto. Its title characters are the famous Trudeaus in Canadian government, and both husband and wife were played by Griffiths. A *New York Times* reporter (Eric Peterson) interviews the celebrated couple and covers their courtship, marriage, and rise to power, with a lot of bitter Canadian jokes about the United States thrown in for spice. Critics were not sure what to make of the odd little show, and it ran out its twenty-two performances without much fanfare.

The new season at the Roundabout began on September 22 with two Strindberg plays presented in repertory: *Miss Julie* and *Playing with Fire*. Michael Meyer translated both, and the dramas ran into 1982. On the same night, yet another one-man show about a famous author was revived. Elihu Winer's *Chekhov on the Lawn* (11-22-72) was presented for eight weeks at the Theatre East with William Shust playing the Russian writer.

Gardner McKay's two-character drama **Sea Marks** (9-24-81, Players) came to Off Broadway by way of several regional theatres and a brief appearance off-off Broadway. Its run of sixty-two performances was surprising considering the press pronounced it "dull," and "utterly lifeless" and said that "it seems to have a cash register where its heart should be." Irish fisherman Colm Primrose (John Getz), who likes to dabble in poetry, briefly met Timothea Stiles (Leslie Lyles), a publishing house employee from Liverpool, at a rural wedding, and he plummets into poetic love with her from a distance. Finally working up enough nerve to write her, Colm arranges a rendezvous, where she falls for him and his poetry. But when Timothea brings him back with her to the big city, the poor simple fellow is out of his league. He gets drunk before an important promotional appearance, then returns to a life on the sea. Regional and community theatres looking for an economical little drama with plenty of heart gave it several subsequent productions.

Claudette Colbert made another classy return to Broadway with **A Talent for Murder** (10-1-81, Biltmore), a thriller by veteran writers Jerome Chodorov and Norman Panama. Anne Royce McClain (Colbert), a wheelchair-bound mystery writer, lives in her Berkshires mansion Twelve

Oaks with her $15 million art collection, her trusty Indian manservant, Rashi (Shelly Desai), and her doctor, Paul Marchand (Jean-Pierre Aumont), who was once her lover in Paris. For Anne's birthday her family gathers at the house, any one of them is willing to murder her or the others for Anne's art and money. But Anne has rigged her home with hidden microphones and other gadgets (including a suffocating vault) that detect the plans of her cruel offspring. By the end, after all these gadgets have been used, Anne triumphs. Critics commented on how well the seventy-eight-year-old actress looked and acted, but her vehicle was unanimously declared "several cuts below claptrap" and "the cadaver of a comic suspense thriller, and not even a warm one." Still, Colbert managed to enchant audiences for two months.

For most, the theatre season in New York began (and for many, also ended) with the Royal Shakespeare Company's three-month engagement of **The Life & Adventures of Nicholas Nickleby** (10-4-81, Plymouth), an epic presentation of Dickens's tale employing forty-two RSC actors playing 138 speaking roles. The adaptation was developed over a series of workshops before David Edgar solidified the script. Trevor Nunn and John Caird directed the eight-and-a-half hour melodrama, which was presented in two parts shown on succeeding days or in a combination of a matinee and an evening show on the same day. Something this big did not sneak into New York by surprise, especially when the group of American producers (the Shuberts and the Nederlanders, in a rare joint venture, among them) announced that tickets would cost $100, three times the going rate for a play. (Of course, one saw two plays, and two long plays at that, so, minute-for-minute, it was the typical Broadway price.) Word had traveled about the hysteria over *Nicholas Nickleby* back in London, and once the show opened, a similar excitement sprang up in New York, where every ticket for the ninety-eight performances (forty-nine of each part) quickly sold out. Reportedly scalpers were easily getting $2,000 a ticket, and judging by the lines at the box office each day for returns, it was not hard to believe. So what was all the fuss about? A rousing good show, for one thing. Here was passion, humor, pathos, thrills, intrigue, villainy, redeeming values, and a story with something for everyone. The actors served as both narrators and characters, sometimes switching roles mid-sentence, sometimes becoming characters who narrate. Similar techniques had been used before (Robert Breen had outlined the idea years before and called it Chamber Theatre) but never in such thrilling ways as presented here. Then there were those RSC actors, not one a well-known name upon arrival and all of them beloved favorites by the time they left. Roger Rees as the earnest hero of the title, John Woodvine as his grasping uncle Ralph, Emily Richard as his noble and valiant sister Kate, Edward Petherbridge as the knowing clerk Newman Noggs, Alun Armstrong as the vicious schoolmaster Mr. Squeers, David Threlfall as the deformed and feeble-minded Smike, and others created vivid characterizations that were branded into one's memory. Just as enthralling were those actors that made such startling transformations during the course of the melodrama that audience members were poring through their *Playbills* to discover if it was possible two such opposing characters were really played by the same actor. Most astonishing of those performing this feat were Suzanne Bertish, who played the disgustingly predatory Fanny Squeers, the very grande dame actress Miss Snevellicci, and the grimy old hag Peg Sliderskew, and Bob Peck, who essayed the deadly villainous Sir Mulberry Hawk and the simple and jovial Yorkshireman John Browdie. *Nicholas Nickleby* opened to the most enthusiastic round of rave reviews experienced in decades, and the phrase "theatrical experience of a lifetime" was used unabashedly by several critics. The production won both the Drama Critics Circle and Tony awards, and there were also Tonys for Rees, Nunn, Caird, and scenic designers John Napier and Dermot Hayes. But the show was long gone by awards time, and in the *Dramatists Guild Quarterly* Guernsey described the theatre season after *Nicholas Nickleby* had returned to England as very much like a small rural village after the circus had left town; all that remained were memories and the glow on the face of everyone who saw it.

A rare revival of Heinrich von Kleist's *The Broken Pitcher*, which was more familiarly known as *The Broken Jug* (4-1-58), opened on October 7 at the Martinique and was labeled "a tedious farce" by most aisle-sitters. Only Larry Pine as the corrupt judge's sneaky clerk was generally applauded.

The title character in Jane Stanton Hitchcock's **Grace** (10-13-81, American Place) may have been the most detestable character theatre audiences met this season. Grace (Scotty Bloch) runs a laundromat in rural Oklahoma and loves to insult and mock her simpleminded, innocent patrons, be they white or Native American. She takes greatest pleasure in berating their idea of religion, be it Christian or tribal. Yet in the second act outspoken Grace has found a gold mine of a job: as the paid companion to the rich invalid Mrs. Meers (Hope Cameron). Ironically, Grace treats the poor Mrs. Meers as dreadfully as she does everyone else. The dark comedy ("hardly a play at all; it's an oral portrait in two acts") opened the American Place's dismal season.

Another "oral portrait" of sorts was Marilyn Campbell's **My Own Stranger** (10-13-81, Provincetown Playhouse), an evening of readings from the works of the poet Anne Sexton. Campbell performed the selections with Pat Lysinger and Nancy-Elizabeth Kammer.

A program of one-acts entitled **2 by South** (10-14-81, St. Clements) came to New York from Los Angeles and brought along a new director, the independent filmmaker Robert Altman in his stage debut. Although the two short plays, consisting mainly of monologues, were by Frank South, Altman was clearly the draw and the star of the evening, creating on the stage a dreamy yet harsh picture of Americana gone wrong. In the first play, **Precious Blood**, a registered nurse (Alfre Woodard) wanders from room to room talking of her past, her dreams, her fears. She pays no attention to a kitchen furnishings salesman (Guy Boyd) who also moves about the space. Soon the two monologues start to overlap, the characters meet, and a violent rape takes place. In **Rattlesnakes in a Cooler**, a young, successful doctor (Leo Burmester) leaves his practice and his wife and family in Kentucky and goes out west to become a cowboy. In his long monologue he relates how disappointed he was to find cowboys driving Buicks rather than riding horses, but he is so ambitious to connect to the Old West that he turns outlaw, and this play, too, ends in violence. While the critics thought South a promising writer, neither playlet sustained itself very well. But Altman's staging so enthralled them that many aisle-sitters recommended the play.

The most successful entry by the Circle in the Square this season was its first one, a revival of Shaw's *Candida* on October 15 with Joanne Woodward in the title role. Playwright-turned-director Michael Cristofer staged the "limp enterprise," and the "imbalanced cast" also included Ron Parady (Morell), Tait Ruppert (Marchbanks), and Jane Curtin (Prossy). While some critics enjoyed Woodward, most found the revival one that could "kill the public's taste for Shaw." But the public wanted to see Woodward, who had not been on Broadway in decades, so the revival was held over for ninety performances.

With his *The Dance and the Railroad* still playing across the lobby of the Public, David Henry Hwang's **Family Devotions** (10-18-81, Newman) opened to reveal another side of this remarkable young playwright. His new work took the form of a situation comedy, although there was still an unmistakable mystical quality about it that recalled the earlier play. Two aging Chinese sisters, Ama (Tina Chen) and Popo (June Kim), left China before the Communist takeover and still adhere to the Christian beliefs taught to them by a beloved missionary. They now live in a gleaming Bel Air home furnished in an expensive contemporary style. Their fully Americanized daughters, the girls' prosperous husbands, and their rebellious offspring, who want to break away from the tight family structure and go away to school or careers of their own, gather one afternoon to greet Uncle DiGou (Victor Wong) from China, who has not seen his sisters in thirty years. DiGou has forsaken Christian ways and, having suffered under Mao, is now an atheist. The clash of two cultures and three generations is mostly satiric at first, but when the two old aunts pull out the family shrine and attempt to perform the ritual "devotions," DiGou destroys the family's illusions about the missionary who saved them (she was a tramp with an illegitimate child, he informs them), and in the shock Popo and Ama die of heart failure. The family question the gods of Bel Air and the Western world and embrace the family bloodline as the youngest generation escapes to a new life. While most of the reviews praised Hwang's handling of the difficult themes in the play, they all thought it less effective than his more stylized *The Dance and the Railroad*. Some of the play's sitcom aspects were indeed forced, but as Rich wrote, *Family Devotions* was another "invigorating early step in what increasingly promises to be an important theatrical career." The play was performed seventy-six times, less than half the run of Hwang's earlier entry at the Public.

After some impressive seasons, the Manhattan Theatre Club's offerings this time around were disappointing even though the production quality remained high. Alonso Alegría's **Crossing Niagara** (10-20-81, Manhattan Theatre Club) was the opening entry and a good example. The play was not awful, but neither was it worthy of the splen-

CHRISTOPHER [Ferdinand] **DURANG** (1949–) was born in Montclair, New Jersey, the son of an architect and a secretary. He received degrees from Harvard University in 1971 and Yale University in 1974, his first scripts being produced as a student at Yale. While pursuing a career in acting and writing he taught briefly at Southern Connecticut State College and Yale. His first New York productions were off-off Broadway: *Titanic* (1976), the musical *A History of the American Film* (1978), and *The Nature and Purpose of the Universe* (1979). *Beyond Therapy* (1981) gave Durang his first recognition and established his talent for irreverent, broad satire with an intellectual bent.

did production the off-Broadway company afforded it. The nineteenth-century French daredevil Blondin (Alvin Epstein), who has walked across Niagara Falls on a tightrope twenty-one times, is looking for a new challenge, and he finds it in the talkative youth Carlo (Paul McCrane), who barges into his hotel room and suggests Blondin carry him on his back for the next crossing. After much discussion (a lot of it philosophical and hardly germane to the situation) the two of them do exactly that. The stunt is performed on August 18, 1859, and we see, through the magic of Santo Loquasto's scenic cleverness and Jennifer Tipton's evocative lighting, Blondin stop and panic halfway across, then how Carlo gives him the strength to continue by discussing even more philosophy. André Ernotte staged the production faultlessly, and the critics extolled Epstein, Loquasto, and Tipton without reservation. But the drama, which had seen productions in Latin America and across this country, was deemed by most "a static play."

Christopher Durang came up with his first hit this season with **Sister Mary Ignatius Explains It All for You** and **The Actor's Nightmare** (10-21-81, Playwrights Horizons), a double bill that ran 247 wacked-out performances and made many new converts to Durang's sense of humor.

The curtain raiser *The Actor's Nightmare* is a surreal farce about an accountant (Jeff Brooks), with the *Playbill* name of George Spelvin, who finds himself on a bare stage dressed as Hamlet and is told he must go on for Eddie, who has been in a car accident. The unwilling George soon finds himself in scenes from *Private Lives*, *A Man for All Seasons*, and the absurdist *Endgame* as fellow actors, going by the names of Sarah Siddons, Henry Irving, and Ellen Terry, come and go. But soon

George gets caught up in the drama and attacks his role(s) with relish, only to be executed like Thomas More and denied a final curtain call. The nun of the second play's title is a long-in-the-tooth teacher at Our Lady of Perpetual Sorrows Catholic School, where she lectures to a group of adults about church dogma and answers questions written out by them on index cards. Sister Ignatius (Elizabeth Franz) is self-righteous, combative, and harsh, yet smiles a lot and carries the glow of an anointed one. For demonstration purposes, she has grade-schooler Thomas (Mark Stefan) recite catechism statements, and she rewards each correct recitation with a cookie. But when a handful of her former students (all miserable failures in love and life) arrive and confront her, proceedings darken, and in a blaze of gallows humor, the holy woman guns them down. While Durang was declared "the jolliest maverick of the younger American playwrights," most reviews felt that the plays went on too long for what they had to say and that Durang "seems incapable of writing a fully-sustained play." Although the longer work had been workshopped off-off Broadway two years earlier at the Ensemble Studio Theatre, this production shone because of the expert work of its rising new director, Jerry Zaks.

Jonathan Bolt's domestic drama **Threads** (10-25-81, Circle) was written in the kind of lyrical realism that Circle playwrights excelled at, but the plot and even much of the characterization were so familiar that it almost looked like a parody of a typical Circle drama. In a small mill town in the hills of North Carolina in 1965, the matriarch of the Owens family is dying. Sally Owens (Jo Henderson) is a refined, gentle soul, and all her dreams hang on her son Clyde (Jonathan Hogan) who has gone off to Hollywood to become an actor. Her coarse husband, Abner

JERRY ZAKS (1946–) was born in Germany, the son of a butcher, but grew up in America, where he was educated at Dartmouth College and Smith College. He began acting in regional theatre productions but was soon seen in such Broadway musicals as *Grease*, *The 1940s Radio Hour*, and *Tintypes*. Zaks had directed regionally before getting to stage Durang's *Beyond Therapy* off Broadway in 1981. Although he would be pegged as a director of wacky farce and broad comedy in the early part of his career, within a few seasons Zaks was staging dramas and musicals as well. He quickly became one of the most sought-after directors in the business.

(William Andrews), and younger son, David (Ben Siegler), try to comfort the ailing Sally, but it is when Clyde comes home to see her that she perks up. The family and Clyde's old friends now working in the mill see the actor as some sort of celebrity, so all are crushed when he announces that his Hollywood career is washed up and that he is staying in town and hopes to get a job at the mill. As Sally passes on, father and son come to grips with each other and are reconciled. Edith Oliver of *The New Yorker* felt that "the audience [was] three giant steps ahead of the characters at every turn of the plot," and most of her colleagues also found the play clumsily plotted.

Tom Griffin, a young playwright who would move on to better things, made an ill-advised Broadway debut with his comedy **Einstein and the Polar Bear** (10-29-81, Cort), which transferred from the Hartford Stage. Bill Allenson (Peter Strauss), a reclusive J. D. Salinger–like novelist, lives quietly in a small New England town with his semi-senile father, Andrew (John Wardwell), hiding from the world and unknown by the locals as the author who wrote two books that transformed a whole generation. During a blizzard, Manhattan advertising artist Diane Ashe (Maureen Anderman) knocks on the door, saying her car had broken down. The reticent Bill greets the stranger with some literary allusions, then finally invites her in, the two gradually moving into a romantic relationship punctuated by wily barbs from old Andrew. Of course Bill eventually finds out that Diane's arrival was no accident, and revelations about the past (such as his wife's suicide) come spilling forth, but in the end true love helps the recluse to finally open up. What most annoyed the press was Griffin's achingly artificial dialogue, as though a famous author would speak such contrived drivel as "a beautiful bibliophile in a blizzard is better than a dour dietitian in a desert." The reviews were generally abusive, and the play closed after four performances.

Beth Henley's *Crimes of the Heart* (12-21-80), which had won the Pulitzer Prize since its brief off-off-Broadway engagement last season, arrived on Broadway on November 4 with the same cast and director and stayed at the John Golden for 535 performances. Off Broadway, another return was less successful. Thomas Babe's *Taken in Marriage* (2-22-79) was given another chance on November 1 at the Harold Clurman, but without the riveting kind of cast that the original had boasted, it only survived twenty-five performances.

It took a long time for Sheldon Rosen's **Ned and Jack** (11-8-81, Little) to arrive on Broadway (it was first produced at the Stratford Festival three years earlier and off-off Broadway at the Hudson Guild the previous spring), so its closing on opening night was sad, especially since the drama seemed so promising. Late on the evening of November 17, 1922, actress Ethel Barrymore (Barbara Sohmers) has come to the penthouse apartment of ailing playwright Edward Sheldon (John Vickery) to give him the details of her brother John's opening night as *Hamlet*. Presently the drunken Jack Barrymore himself (Peter Michael Goetz) bursts into the apartment and gives his own boozy account of the proceedings. Soon the two men, old friends going way back, are left alone, and the talk gets loose and then sobering, Jack telling Ned that he will leave the stage for the movies, knowing it will be the ruin of him, and Ned informing his friend that his rare arthritic disease will soon leave him blind and invalid. Although the meeting portrayed was fictional, most of the details were true and ripe for dramatization. But Rosen's play was "essentially static," and several aisle-sitters also registered disappointment in some of the performances.

On the other hand, a British import opened the next night and found a critical and financial welcome: Ronald Harwood's **The Dresser** (11-9-81, Brooks Atkinson). (The play was scheduled to open on November 8, but a fire alarm the night before set off the sprinkler system, and the scenery and house suffered water damage.) The backstage comedy-drama featured Tom Courtenay in one of his finest portrayals. Based on the legendary British actor Sir Donald Wolfit, who stubbornly toured England with his classic repertory deep into his old age, *The Dresser* viewed a similar old tragedian, simply called Sir (Paul Rogers), through the eyes of his faithful dresser, Norman (Courtenay). Reliable to a fault, Norman is a gay, opinionated alcoholic who whines and bitches about everything but is a slave to the theatre and, in particular, to the ailing Sir. Unfortunately the old man is getting so senile he starts putting on his Othello blackface when he's supposed to be getting ready to play King Lear. After a night of mishaps both onstage and off, climaxed by a bombing raid that ends the performance early, Sir drops dead in his dressing room. Norman begins to go into deep grieving until he reads the old man's last will and testament, in which he thanks everybody except Norman; the shattered dresser takes to the bottle once again. Although most of the play consisted of scenes between Sir and Norman, the supporting cast was exceptional in sometimes mere cameo roles. Rachel Gurney as

Sir's younger, impatient wife, Douglas Seale as a dreadfully inadequate understudy, Lisabeth Bartlett as an ambitious ingenue, and Marge Redmond as the no-nonsense stage manager all shone in brief appearances. With favorable critical reaction to the script and the production (some preferred it to the London version), the play ran a healthy 200 performances.

Bill C. Davis's off-Broadway two-hander *Mass Appeal* (4-22-80) was brought to Broadway's Booth on November 12 and stayed for a profitable run of 214 performances. Again Milo O'Shea played the comfortable older priest, Father Tim Farley, but the radical young cleric was portrayed this time by Michael O'Keefe, and several aisle-sitters found him less effective than Eric Roberts had been in the earlier Manhattan Theatre Club production.

A seemingly untiring Katharine Hepburn returned to the stage again this season, but like her last few vehicles, Ernest Thompson's **The West Side Waltz** (11-19-81, Ethel Barrymore) was as creaky and outdated as the seventy-two-year-old actress was spry and game. Retired concert pianist Margaret Mary Elderdice (Hepburn) lives in a grand but fading apartment building on Manhattan's West Side and spends her time playing duets with the spinster violinist Cara Varnum (Dorothy Loudon) from down the hall. Margaret Mary's health is failing, and Cara suggests her friend move in with her so she can better be taken care of. But Margaret Mary is too independent to become the subject of Cara's priggish ways, so she advertises and hires a kookie young actress named Robin Bird (Regina Baff) to be her live-in companion. Cara is quite miffed, and a comic triangle develops among the threesome. While Margaret Mary's physical conditions weakens, she remains resilient and, after helping along the romance between Robin and a young lawyer (Don Howard), accepts Cara as a housemate on her own terms. One commentator remarked that Thompson's script "may be the thinnest play I have ever seen," and most of his colleagues agreed with him, but the attraction was Hepburn, and she received raves, not just for her very commanding presence but for her performance as well. Edwin Wilson in the *Wall Street Journal* explained: "Everything we expect from Ms. Hepburn is there: the famous face . . . the voice, firmer than it was in her Broadway show five years ago . . . and, most of all, the intelligence; the actress's no-nonsense attitude has never been more firmly in place." Hepburn agreed to play the role 126 times in New York, then continued

to tour in the comedy. It was her last Broadway appearance and one that could be remembered with warmth.

British feminist author Fay Weldon's **After the Prize** (11-19-81, Marymount Manhattan) was the next offering at the Phoenix. Edwin (John Horton) and Wasp (Veronica Castang) are physicists married to each other, but when she wins the Nobel Prize he becomes (temporarily) impotent. So the vindictive Wasp has an affair with Brian (David McCallum) while she encourages her twin sister (Lois Markle) to try to bed Edwin. Most notices were derisive for the "thin-lipped play" and found the characters "so shallow they verge on the unplayable."

The Negro Ensemble Company scored a hit with its fifteenth season's first entry, Charles Fuller's powerful World War II–era drama **A Soldier's Play** (11-20-81, Theatre Four). When a tyrannical black sergeant, Vernon Waters (Adolph Caesar), is murdered one night returning to his barracks in a Louisiana army camp, the local Ku Klux Klan is suspected. But it seems Waters was strongly disliked by his own troops, so a black investigator, Captain Richard Davenport (Clarence Brown), is assigned to the case. In a series of interviews and flashbacks, we see the vicious Waters raving against whites and, even more strongly, against ignorant southern blacks who give his race a bad name. His most frequent victim in these tirades is the simple, blues-singing C. J. Memphis (Larry Reilly), who takes the sergeant's abuse in stride. Davenport uncovers many layers of racism in his investigation and, just as the black troops are finally called to action in Europe, finds out that the cool renegade Melvin Peterson (Denzel Washington) murdered the drunken Waters in cold blood, hoping that the white folks would be blamed. Peterson is arrested and taken away, but the whole incident is brushed aside by the white Captain Charles Taylor (Peter Friedman) as "the usual, common violence any commander faces in Negro military units." Reviews were laudatory for Fuller's script and for Douglas Turner Ward's superlative production, which never let any of the characters become stereotypes or symbols. Jack Kroll in *Newsweek* spoke for several of his colleagues when he wrote, "Fuller takes the supposedly outmoded form of 'realism' and finds the inner dynamics that revitalize it, freshening our vision of reality." Helped by winning the Pulitzer Prize, the taut melodrama ran 468 performances, one of the Ensemble's greatest commercial and critical accomplishments.

The parade of one-man shows continued with Lawrence and Maggie Williams's **Whistler** (12-6-81, Provincetown Playhouse). John Cullum gave a vivid performance as the artist James McNeill Whistler and some two dozen of his friends and relations.

Jules Feiffer came back to Broadway with his most vicious and searing play yet, a seriocomic dissection of the American family called **Grown Ups** (12-10-81, Lyceum). New York journalist Jake (Bob Dishy) is a resounding success, a reporter at the top of his profession (he is just about to interview Henry Kissinger) with a lovely wife (Cheryl Giannini), a little girl (Jennifer Dundas), and two parents (Harold Gould and Frances Sternhagen) who dote on him even as they expect nothing less from a son of theirs. But amid all the success, Jake is unsatisfied. He is not looking for the meaning of life or a higher plane of existence; he just wants to grow up and be free of the restraints he still feels from his parents. His dissatisfaction soon turns to bitterness and then rage as all members of the family turn against one another and destroy each other with resentment and humiliation. Although the reviewers found Feiffer's blistering view of family "moving and provocative" and endorsed the incisive performances and the sharp direction by John Madden, *Grown Ups* was a difficult play to love (Rich thought it Feiffer's best work and yet wrote that the evening became "one long piercing cry of rage"), and its favorable notices were off-putting to some potential playgoers. All the same, the satire ran eighty-three performances and would return in the future in a revised version.

Edward Sheehan's **Kingdoms** (12-13-81, Cort) was an intelligently written and proficiently produced historical costume drama, but intelligence and proficiency were no longer enough on Broadway. Called everything from "a fascinating evening of theatre" to "a chunk of bombast," the play closed after seventeen performances. In 1804, Napoleon Bonaparte (Armand Assante) meets Pope Pius VII (Roy Dotrice), and the two develop a warm father-son relationship. But years later, when the Pope stands in the way of one of his many conquests, the Emperor has the pontiff kidnapped and brought to France for four years. There the two old friends are reunited and lock horns in a philosophical battle of wits, each promoting his idea of a kingdom, until the Pope is released.

The Manhattan Theatre Club presented British playwright Howard Baker's satirical **No End of Blame** (12-15-81, Manhattan Theatre Club) for forty-eight performances but inspired no fireworks. Hungarian political cartoonist Bela Veracek (Michael Cristofer) gets in hot water in Budapest and is expelled from the Institute of Fine Arts, so he goes to Moscow, where he finds more trouble when he upsets the artists' union. Bela then heads for the Free World and settles in England, where, working on a left-wing newspaper, he comes across just as many restrictions as back behind the Iron Curtain; so he goes mad and ends up in a mental institution. While some approved of the cast, few could condone the preachy comedy.

Like Robert Altman, William Friedkin was another Hollywood director making his theatre directing debut this season. Although his project was no better than the one Altman was saddled with, not many complimentary things were said about Friedkin's staging of the two-character weeper **Duet for One** (12-17-81, Royale), and it only lasted twenty performances. Tom Kempinski's play, about a famous cellist, Stephanie Abrahams (Anne Bancroft), who is stricken with multiple sclerosis and can no longer perform, was a hit in London, but the American production fell short. In a series of scenes between Stephanie (inspired, no doubt, by the cello virtuoso Jacqueline du Pré, who suffered from MS) and Dr. Alfred Feldman (Max von Sydow), a psychiatrist her husband has sent her to, Stephanie reveals her past demons, comes to terms with her predicament, and discovers new reasons to live. The press was divided about Bancroft; some thought her "first-rate" and "superb," and others found her "steely" and "always conscious that she is working hard, acting with a capital A."

James Lapine's **Twelve Dreams** (12-22-81, Public: Martinson) was another play drawn from a real story, a case history recorded by Carl Jung in which a young girl's dreams foretold her own death. In a New England college town in 1936, psychiatrist Charles Hatrick (James Olson) is grieving the death of his wife when his ten-year-old daughter, Emma (Olivia Laurel Mates), gives him a disturbing Christmas present: a booklet illustrating her dreams. Confused by their possible meaning, Hatrick shows the pictures to a visiting Professor (Stefan Schnabel), who sees them as the work of an elderly person contemplating death. Emma's dreams are enacted with various characters in her life (governess, best friend, neurotic patient of her father's, a handsome young student), and the effect was quite stunning at times, if unclear and unfocused. It turns out Emma is suffering from a fatal disease, so her dreams were far from morbid girlish fancies. Lapine directed the elaborately conceived production designed by the up-and-coming Heidi Landesman. Carole Shelley, Marcell Rosenblatt, Thomas Hulce, and Valerie Mahaffrey were among the strong supporting cast.

Kaufman at Large (12-25-81, Marymount Manhattan) was more than just another one-man program about a celebrated author, since John Lithgow adapted the writings of George S. Kaufman, directed the production, and played the acerbic Kaufman himself. Fleeing Hollywood after the scandal about his affair with movie star Mary Astor has become public knowledge, Kaufman arrives in New York in 1936 and tells the audience about the troubles he's seen. Mixed notices for the Phoenix production felt that Lithgow was a much better performer than author and that the evening's highlights occurred when he portrayed various characters in Kaufman's plays.

Israel Horovitz turned his hand to farce (an unlikely genre for this author of character dramas) with **The Good Parts** (1-7-82, Astor Place) but met with little success. Having hit a midlife crisis, New York lawyers "Sonny" Levine (Tony Roberts) and Eugene Jacoby (Stephen Strimpell) react by leaving their jobs and families and taking an impromptu vacation to Greece, where they hope to find romance and adventure. They definitely find the latter when the two sneak into the Acropolis late at night. (Sonny once flubbed his role in a school production of *Electra*, and it has long been his dream to recite the lines of the drama in the Athens theatre in moonlight.) Mistakenly believing they have killed a security guard, the two go on the run in underground Athens, where they don't even know the language, and further complications arise until their wives arrive from America to drag them back home.

The Circle Rep presented three of its best playwrights in a triple bill called **Confluence** (1-10-82, Circle). The title playlet by John Bishop concerned a retired football star (Jimmie Ray Weeks) who encounters his greatest role model, an aging basketball Hall of Famer (Edward Seamon), in Pittsburgh at the confluence of three rivers. Lanford Wilson's comedy **Thymus Vulgaris** dealt with a slovenly mother (Pearl Shear) living in a trailer surrounded by the herbal plant of the title. Her opportunistic daughter (Katherine Cortez) arrives to say she is going to marry the wealthy "Grapefruit King," and they anticipate a life of luxury. Beth Henley's sensitive character study **Am I Blue** brought together a kookie teenager

(June Stein) and a shy fraternity brother (Jeff McCraken) on his eighteenth birthday, the two social outcasts sharing a moment of understanding on a rainy night. All three plays met with favorable, if not enthusiastic, reviews.

For the third time Harvey Fierstein wrote about his drag queen hero Arnold Becker and, with the earlier *The International Stud* (5-22-78) and *Fugue in a Nursery* (12-12-79), created a long evening program called **Torch Song Trilogy** (1-15-82, Actors' Playhouse), the most successful gay play yet seen in New York. Arnold's affair with Ed was chronicled in the first play, and a hectic weekend in the country with Ed, Ed's fiancé, and Arnold's new boyfriend was recounted in the second. The new work was titled **Widows and Children First,** and it brought a sense of closure to Arnold's world. Living in an apartment near Central Park, Arnold (Fierstein) has taken in a troubled youth, the gay fifteen-year-old David (Matthew Broderick), whom he plans to adopt. But soon Ed (Joel Crothers), whose marriage has broken up, wants to return. When Arnold's mother (Estelle Getty) comes on the scene, Arnold has his hands full. Although he has turned into a nurturing and demanding parent like his own mother, the two have several unresolved differences to settle before they can accept each other for what they are. The triple bill was greeted with such encouraging reviews and brisk business that after its run of 117 performances off Broadway, it transferred to Broadway the next season and ran over a thousand times.

Director Andrei Serban continued to intrigue and anger critics with his theatrically inventive staging, this time with **Zastrozzi** (1-17-82, Other Stage), an allegory by George F. Walker that played the Public for forty-nine performances. The arch criminal Zastrozzi (Jan Triska) sets out to get revenge against a virtuous painter, and soon all of nineteenth-century Europe is caught up in the conflict. Czech actor Triska was applauded for his deft performance, but much of the press found the "odd and baffling play" as unsatisfying as it was nonsensical.

Harold Pinter's *The Caretaker* (10-4-61) was given a passable revival by the Roundabout on January 21. Considering its powerful cast—Daniel Gerroll (Mick), Anthony Heald (Aston) and F. Murray Abraham (Davies)—the critics complained that it should have been much more than that.

Faye Dunaway first received attention in William Alfred's *Hogan's Goat* (11-11-65), so it seemed fitting that her return to Broadway be in another

Alfred work. Unfortunately, Dunaway's loyalty to Alfred was not justified, since his melodrama **The Curse of an Aching Heart** (1-25-82, Little) was severely lacking. In a poor Irish Catholic neighborhood in Brooklyn in 1923, the fourteen-year-old orphan Frances Walsh (Dunaway) is being raised by relatives until her Uncle Jo Jo (Bernie McInerney) starts to lust after her. She runs away to make it on her own, and over the next twenty years we see Frances struggle as a secretary, marry a man who becomes an alcoholic, and try to raise her son alone. In 1942 she returns to her old neighborhood and is reconciled with Jo Jo, now a wheelchair-bound recluse.While the play was written off as "overcooked and sketchy, at once obvious and elusive," Dunaway was declared luminous in a demanding role that required rollerskating, romance, heartbreak, and an endless succession of costume changes. The production, capably directed by the young newcomer Gerald Gutierrez and beautifully designed by John Lee Beatty (a period streetcar moved back and forth across the stage with great effect), boasted a large supporting cast (Audrie Neenan as France's streetwise chum Lulu was especially fine). Alas, none of it survived the script, and the play closed in a month.

A double bill of early Sam Shepard plays opened at the Provincetown Playhouse on January 27, and only half of it ran out the season. *The Unseen Hand* (4-1-70) was directed by Tony Barsha with *Killer's Head* (4-4-75) as a curtain raiser. After opening night the prologue piece was dropped, and the surreal drama *The Unseen Hand* played by itself for the rest of its 127 performances.

The second Broadway revival of *Macbeth* in as many seasons opened on January 28 at the Circle in the Square and, like its predecessor, failed miserably. Nicol Williamson, as the title thane, was thought to be up to the task. But he also directed the production, and reviewers found the swift, intermissionless production "incomplete" and a "farrago." The supporting cast was also taken to task, especially Andrea Weber's "schoolgirl" queen. *Macbeth* ran only twenty-one performances, less than half that of the previous year's flop at Lincoln Center. Later in the week, a rare commercial Shakespeare production on Broadway, *Othello,* opened on February 3 at the Winter Garden. Its two acclaimed stars, James Earl Jones and Christopher Plummer in riveting performances, kept business healthy for its 123 performances. While Jones was deemed "impressive," "daring," "majestic and pitiful," Plummer's Iago stole his thunder and had the critics grasping for

superlatives. Charles Michener's reaction in *Newsweek* was typical, calling it "one of the wonderful Shakespearean performances of our time—a study in wickedness so richly detailed, so blazing with intelligence and energy, that you don't want it to end even if Iago *should* get his comeuppance." Dianne Wiest was generally considered miscast as Desdemona, the rest of the cast was thought sufficient, and the production values were deemed adequate; but what it all came down to was Jones and Plummer. Under Peter Coe's direction, the production had originated at Connecticut's American Theatre Festival (along the way it was touched up here and there by Zoe Caldwell) and won a Tony Award for Outstanding Revival of a Play. (*Othello* was the last play to perform in the Winter Garden before the musical *Cats* opened in the fall and occupied it until September of 2000.)

Bernard Slade's **Special Occasions** (2-7-82, Music Box) was roundly lambasted by the critics, Rich calling it "an attenuated television play that uneasily mixes the conventions of the situation comedy and soap opera." Amy (Suzanne Pleshette) and Michael Ruskin (Richard Mulligan) are celebrating their fifteenth wedding anniversary by working out the details of their upcoming divorce. Before you know it, flashbacks of weddings, funerals, anniversaries, birthdays, and other supposedly meaningful events fill the stage. Despite the presence of two marketable TV stars, the play closed on opening night.

Although it was very similar to *A Coupla White Chicks Sitting Around Talking* (4-28-80) in character, plot, and theme, Sybille Pearson's two-character comedy-drama **Sally and Marsha** (2-9-82, Manhattan Theatre Club) did not share the success of the long-running John Ford Noonan two-hander. Homespun South Dakota housewife Sally (Bernadette Peters) has been relocated to Manhattan by her husband's job, and she gets weary of staying in her West Side apartment with her two small children while he is off selling detergent. She ventures down the hall and strikes up an awkward friendship with Marsha (Christine Baranski), a cynical New Yorker whose husband, an orthopedist, is away on residency. Although the pair are as opposite as can be, a friendship develops over time. Sally grows more sophisticated, Marsha grows more neurotic, but by the end their close relationship helps them pull through their various difficulties. Reviews were largely supportive, calling the play "an engaging retelling of the tale of the town mouse and her country cousin."

With a popular revival of the musical *Fiddler on the Roof* on Broadway this season, it seemed a good time to revive Arnold Perl's non-musical version, *The World of Sholom Aleichem* (5-3-53), which opened on February 11 at the Rialto. Unfortunately, most commentators felt this evening of sketches had not stood the test of time very well, nor did its mediocre mounting and uneven casting help. But several thought Joe Silver as the pushcart narrator of the evening was effective, and all cheered character actor Jack Gilford (who had appeared in the original) in a variety of roles, agreeing that here was the real article. The comedy only lasted twenty-two performances.

A decade after the fact, plays about the Vietnam War were still being written, and Amlin Gray's **How I Got That Story** (2-17-82, Westside) was one of the liveliest entries in years. An American reporter (Don Scardino) goes to "Ambo Land" to cover the war, and there he meets The Historical Event (Bob Gunton), an allegorical figure who represents the twenty-one people the reporter interviews. Gunton played, among others, a teenage prostitute, a combat-hungry photographer, an evil woman high in government, a monk who immolates himself, foul-mouthed soldiers, peasants, and nuns. By the end the naive reporter goes mad, dresses as a native, and joins the ravaged throng. As expected, Gunton's wild, comic-strip portrayals were singled out as the highlight of the evening, and there were many compliments for Scardino as well. Notices for the script were mixed (some preferred an earlier and simpler production seen off-off Broadway in a workshop), but audiences took to the "bitterly funny and affecting piece," so it ran 111 performances.

A much-ballyhooed revival that suffered from its wide publicity was Ed Graczyk's *Come Back to the Five & Dime, Jimmy Dean, Jimmy Dean* (2-27-80), which opened on February 18 at the Martin Beck. After being acclaimed for his off-Broadway directing earlier this season, filmmaker Robert Altman tackled Broadway with a stellar cast, in particular Cher, whom everyone was anxious to see in a serious play after her comic turns on television. She played the wisecracking Sissy and most critics were not disappointed, but reaction to the play (few critics had seen it off-off Broadway), the plodding direction, and some of the other members of the cast (which included Sandy Dennis, Karen Black, and Kathy Bates) was largely negative. Yet audiences were curious enough to let the play run fifty-two performances.

With the Bijou Theatre already torn down, its neighbors, the Morosco and the Helen Hayes, were slated for demolition as well when the courts sided against a group called Save the Theatre, Inc. Joseph Papp and two hundred other demonstrators (including celebrities Tammy Grimes, Estelle Parsons, Richard Gere, Treat Williams, and Susan Sarandon) stood in the way of the bulldozers on March 22 and were arrested. Not present was the eighty-two-year-old Hayes. The corporation building the hotel and theatre on the site offered to name the new house after her, but she refused. As a result of the battle to save these theatres, a number of Broadway houses (including several grind movie houses on 42 Street) were declared landmarks and, consequently, protected from a similar fate.

A. R. Gurney, Jr., who had been writing intelligent and promising plays for a decade, finally had a hit with **The Dining Room** (2-24-82, Playwrights Horizons), a wry, entertaining commentary on the Wasp culture as witnessed though events that transpired in that last vestige of formality, the family dining room.

In a series of scenes that take place in a series of dining rooms from the 1940s to the present, characters from different families come and go, each adding a piece to the mosaic of social life for the vanishing upper classes. While each household and set of characters is different (no characters are repeated), they blend together to create a unified picture. Among the most memorable scenes: a stern father holds sway over the family at breakfast, two teenagers drink the family's liquor when the parents are away, an architect tries to redesign the old family dining room into something more modern, an old lady cannot

---

A[lbert]. R[amsdale]. **GURNEY, JR.** (1930–) was born in Buffalo, the son of a realtor, and educated at St. Paul's School and Williams College. After serving in the navy, he studied playwriting at Yale University, where his scripts were first produced. Pete Gurney, as he is familiarly known, joined the English faculty at MIT in 1960 and taught there while submitting scripts to various theatres. His first off-Broadway credit was the one-act *The David Show* in 1968, followed by many other short plays and the full-length *Scenes from American Life* (1971) and *Who Killed Richard Corey?* (1976). Gurney's plays usually explore the world of American Wasp society, finding both the ridiculous and the tender sides of these educated but fumbling people.

recognize her own sons at Thanksgiving dinner, an aging parent goes over his funeral plans with his distant son, and a children's birthday party is held while an illicit love affair falls apart. Each sketch was self-contained yet supported by the scenes surrounding it. As in the case of *How I Got That Story*, the piece was a tour de force for the six actors who played all the roles: Lois de Banzie, W. H. Macy, Ann McDonough, Pippa Pearthree, John Shea, and (especially effective) Remak Ramsay. But *The Dining Room* was much more than a gimmick or a clever acting exercise. The "clear-eyed, touching, and buoyantly funny" comedy was declared "a theatrical event of surpassing delights." After a brief workshop production upstairs at Playwrights Horizons, the play moved down into the larger space and stayed for a run of 583 performances. It then went on to become one of the works most produced by regional, community, and college theatres, with hundreds of productions each year over the next decade.

John Guare's new work **Lydie Breeze** (2-25-82, American Place) was less abrasive and surreal than his recent efforts; in fact, it was a period piece set on the island of Nantucket in 1895, but Guare's cockeyed, modern (or anachronistic) viewpoint was still evident. On the site of a failed Utopian community, once-idealistic Joshua Hickman (Josef Sommer) has just gotten out of jail for shooting his wife's lover. He returns to the crumbling old homestead to be reunited with members of the family and household: his daughters, the young Lydie (Cynthia Nixon) and her older sister, Gussie (Madeleine Potter), who is the secretary to a senator; an Irish maid, Beaty (Roberta Maxwell); a drunken Civil War veteran, Lucien Rock (James Cahill); and avid birdwatcher Jude Emerson (Robert Joy). We learn that Joshua's wife (also named Lydie) committed suicide when her lover was shot and that syphilis has run through the family for generations. When a dapper British stranger, Jeremiah Grady (Ben Cross), shows up, he is revealed to be the illegitimate son of the deceased wife and her lover. He now works as an actor in London (he recently played Frankenstein's monster onstage) and has come for emotional revenge. But the confrontation turns into a harrowing purge for all the family, prompting Jeremiah to commit suicide along with his old flame Beaty as the remaining members await death from the family's syphilitic curse. Very mixed reactions called the melodrama everything from a "lyrical, elegiac, melodramatic, funny, sorrowing and celebratory

play" to "pure hogwash." French filmmaker Louis Malle directed, the third major movie director working in New York this season.

The Phoenix closed its season with **Weekends Like Other People** (3-4-82, Marymount Manhattan), a two-character piece by David Blomquist that had originated at the Actors Theatre of Louisville. Warehouse worker Dan (Kenneth McMillan) and his restaurant employee wife, Laurie (Rose Gregorio), sit in their tacky home watching television and drinking beer as they talk about all the things they should be doing: reading the latest books, trying exotic foods and wines, getting ahead in the world. When Dan's glossy new boss hints at a promotion, the couple starts to pursue their pipe dreams. But after the new job falls through, they explode at each other in frustration before reverting to their past lifestyle. The small drama collected some appreciative reviews ("a beautiful piece of work" and "a play about stagnation yet [Blomquist] kept it always on the move") but was rarely heard of after its thirty showings.

The same night another A. R. Gurney, Jr., comedy opened off-off Broadway and, while it was overshadowed by the more popular *The Dining Room*, was a little comic gem of its own. **The Middle Ages** (3-4-82, Ark Theatre Company) was set in the trophy room of a men's club in a major city over the period of forty years, but the same four characters were examined rather than the cornucopia of types that passed through various dining rooms in Gurney's other work. In the mid-1940s, Charles (Steven Gilborn) is the conservative president of the club, but his teenage son Barney (Jack Gilpin) is a difficult youth who doesn't value the exclusive nature of the establishment and the "right" kind of people who belong to it. Yet Barney is drawn to the pretty teen Eleanor (Carolyn Mignini), who is being raised by her mother, Myra (Pat Lavelle), to marry well. Eleanor is attracted to Barney's wild and unconventional nature, but as they both grow older, she eventually plays it safe and weds Barney's dull but stable brother, Billy. As the years go by, Barney, still carrying a torch for Eleanor, turns to political activism, soldiering in the Korean War, graduate school, and other attempts at fulfillment. Forty years later, Charles has died, the club is suffering from a lack of support from the "right" kind of people, and Barney (who has made a fortune in the porno film industry) buys the faded institution as a sentimental tribute to his father and a way to endear himself to Eleanor. Favorable reviews noted that the play "often recalls Philip Barry" and that the playwright "has no current theatrical peer." The month-long engagement attracted some attention, and the play later found life off Broadway and in regional theatres.

Another two-hander, Leonard Melfi's *Birdbath* (4-11-66), was revived with a new work, Lewis Black's satire **Crossing the Crab Nebula** (3-7-82, Harold Clurman), the two odd plays making a quirky evening. Kevin O'Connor played Frankie in the former play, directed by Tom O'Horgan (both had done the same tasks in the original 1966 production), and Barbara Eda-Young was Velma Sparrow, the troubled waif he brings back from work, only to learn that she has murdered her mother with a kitchen knife. While the critics thought highly of O'Connor, they felt the drama was hopelessly dated. *Crossing the Crab Nebula* portrayed the talkative Booney (O'Connor) as he drives west, drinks beer, and tells his silent companion (Peter Crombie) the story of his life. Along the way they seem to meet up with the same carhop called Mirage (Eda-Young) wherever they stop to eat. Some notices thought the surreal piece "mystifying", others declared it just confusing.

Director Marshall W. Mason and other Circle Rep regulars presented a revival of *Richard II* on March 10 at the Entermedia and played sixteen times with no press night or reviews. William Hurt essayed the gentle monarch in a cast that also included Lindsay Crouse, Michael Higgins, Stephanie Gordon, Timothy Busfield, Edward Seamon, and Richard Cox.

The same night, the same company premiered a new work in its other space, Joe Pintauro's **Snow Orchid** (3-10-82, Circle). It was, like the Rep's season opener, another domestic drama sparked by the return of a family member: Rocco Lazarra (Peter Boyle) returns to his Brooklyn home after months in a rehab center recovering from drugs and a suicide attempt. His religious wife, Filumena (Olympia Dukakis), who has a fear of leaving her house, and their belligerent son Sebbie (Robert LuPone) await his homecoming with dread. But the younger son, Blaise (Ben Siegler), who is too young to remember the painful past, looks to befriend the father he hardly knows. The expected awkwardness soon turns into quarreling and family theatrics. (When Sebbie suggests that Rocco's improved behavior is the result of control drugs, the father dumps all his medication into the family rigatoni.) After revealing his homosexuality, Sebbie leaves for Texas with a boyfriend. Using his newfound hobby of orchid collecting, Rocco opens a new world for

his wife and, with Blaise's help, gets Filumena to venture outside her home. The four cast members (Siegler had played a very similar role in the earlier *Threads*) were thought to be more proficient than the script.

Paul Rudnick made an encouraging playwriting debut with **Poor Little Lambs** (3-14-82, St. Peter's Church), a comedy about contemporary Ivy League college life that ran two months. When the Whiffenpoofs, Yale's famous singing group, hold auditions, all eight men who try out are admitted to the glee club, but Claire Hazard (Blanche Baker), a determined feminist, is turned down. So Claire sets out to break down the sexual barrier, sleeping with member Davey Waldman (David Naughton) and blackmailing others. After a sly pregnancy scare, she gets to join the all-male group. Although several aisle-sitters thought the comedy was only "sporadically entertaining," all praised the glee club's deft handling of the nine old song favorites. Rudnick's offbeat sense of humor would find a wider audience later in the decade.

Moving away from realism, the Circle presented John Bishop's **The Great Grandson of Jedediah Kohler** (3-21-82, Entermedia), a free-floating farce that jumped through time with wild abandon. Working at his desk in an advertising agency, Jed Kohler (Michael Ayr) fantasizes about his ancestor Jedediah Kohler (Edward Seamon), a pistol-packing marshal of the Old West, and longs to become a legend like his great-grandfather. Scenes in the corporate world today mix with olden times on the frontier, the two worlds starting to resemble each other in the ways their respective heroes intrepidly manipulate their fates. Some critics saw a clumsy attempt at a Shavian comedy and "a notional comedy that doesn't come off," but others declared it an "extravagantly funny play."

A double-bill revival of Terence Rattigan's *The Browning Version* (10-12-49) and J. M. Barrie's *The Twelve-Pound Look* (2-13-11) opened at the Roundabout on March 23 and ran a surprising 200 performances. Ironically, many commentators found that Rattigan's more recent play had dated badly while Barrie's older piece sparkled with life. But both casts, under Stephen Porter's crisp and effective direction, were commended. Lee Richardson shone as the crumbling professor in the Rattigan drama, while Sheila Allen vividly portrayed the early feminist Kate (a role immortalized by Ethel Barrymore) in the Barrie comedy.

The Circle in the Square Uptown closed its abbreviated season with a new work also about a washed-up academic, Percy Granger's domestic drama **Eminent Domain** (3-28-82, Circle in the Square), a piece written in the old-fashioned well-made-play style. Holmes Bradford (Philip Bosco) teaches literature in a "cow college" somewhere in the Midwest even though he was an outstanding student at Harvard and almost got a job there. But Holmes's career is stalled, and his marriage to Katie (Betty Miller), a recently cured amphetamine addict, is dead. Their (unseen) son, Wendell, who ran away from home at sixteen and is now a cult-figure poet, has not communicated with them in years. When a Harvard grad student, Victor Salt (John Vickery), comes to the Bradford house to interview them about their son (he is hoping to spice up his dissertation on Wendell to interest publishers), the past is dredged up in a very neat and Ibsen-like way. Several reviewers found Granger very promising, and the play was considered "engaging" if "an agreeable evening rather than a compelling one." But Bosco's portrayal of a ruined academic was widely applauded.

Most of the reviews for John Pielmeier's **Agnes of God** (3-30-82, Music Box) could not help but mention the British play *Equus* (10-24-74), since there were too many similarities to ignore. A young nun, Agnes (Amanda Plummer), having been sexually molested by her mother as a child, has secretly given birth, strangled the newborn with its umbilical cord, and hidden it in a trash can. She is charged with manslaughter and turned over to the chain-smoking psychiatrist Martha Livingstone (Elizabeth Ashley), who has her own demons to battle, her sister having died in a convent years ago because of undetected appendicitis. The Mother Superior, Miriam Ruth (Geraldine Page), feels Agnes is a very special case, and when she suggests that the birth may have been a miracle, intense arguments arise between her and the doctor. Agnes is an angelic but neurotic creature who claims to have no knowledge of sex nor any memory of the conception or birth of her baby. So Livingstone hypnotizes the girl, and her theatrical exorcism reveals that some man raped her (the visiting priest? a local farm hand?) and that Mother Miriam knew of the pregnancy and hoped to give the baby away and avoid scandal, but the frightened Agnes killed it first. Agnes is freed from her inner torment, Mother Miriam confesses it is all true, and Livingstone gives up smoking. While the press agreed that the script "aspires to be a chilling thriller and a stirring reaffirmation of the power of faith [but] fails on both accounts," all of the critics endorsed the three actresses (Plummer won a Tony Award), who took dramatic hysterics to new heights, so most ended up recommending the torrid evening. The drama ran 486 performances. Because of its frugal requirements (three women, two chairs, one ashtray, and lots of cigarettes), *Agnes of God* was a favorite of financially strapped regional theatres for the next few seasons.

With the Negro Ensemble's production of *A Soldier's Play* doing such strong business at its home base at Theatre Four, the group occupied the Cherry Lane for Leslie Lee's historical panorama **Colored People's Time** (3-30-82, Cherry Lane). In a series of thirteen playlets illustrating important moments in African-American history, fictional characters at selected moments in time are swept up in the black experience, from the eve of the Civil War to the bus boycott in Montgomery, Alabama, in 1956. The history related was far from dry and factual, and the cast, which included Charles Cooper, L. Scott Caldwell, Charles H. Patterson, Curt Williams, and others, kept each vignette lively and accessible. (The title was a sly joke, as explained by the narrator, who said, "Us folks never get anywhere on time but we get there.")

The Roundabout closed its season with another unlikely revival that took off, Enid Bagnold's wry comedy-drama *The Chalk Garden* (10-26-55), which opened on March 30 and stayed for ninety-six performances. Most notices happily reported that the script held up well. Many compliments were paid to Constance Cummings as the aristocratic Mrs. St. Maugham, Sallyanne Tackus as her troublesome granddaughter, Laurel, and Irene Worth as the old woman's quiet but sharp-witted companion, Miss Madrigal.

Casey Kurtti's **Catholic School Girls** (4-1-82, Douglas Fairbanks) was yet another play this season that featured nuns, the comedy falling somewhere between the wicked satire of *Sister Ignatius* . . . and the dark mysticism of *Agnes of God*. Four girls at St. George's School in Yonkers go through the 1960s, from first to eighth grade, and experience all the expected joys and crushes of youth. The same four actresses also played four of their teachers during the decade, nuns at St. George's with various philosophies, demands, and hangups. Lynne Born, Maggie Low, Shelley Rogers, and Christine Von Dohln performed all eight roles, and they and the play were considered "fine, funny, loving" by some critics and "hardly gripping (but) unpretentious" by others. The comedy was probably one nun's story too many this season, and the play closed in a month.

Richard Foreman's puzzling production of **Three Acts of Recognition** (4-6-82, Anspacher) was grist for discussion for forty-eight perform-ances at the Public. The 1977 drama by German playwright Botho Strauss (translated by Sophie Wilkins) was set during the opening of an art exhibition entitled "Capitalist Realism." The cu-rator (Richard Jordan) tries to maintain decorum as several characters come and go, spilling out their woes and personal dramas rather than ap-preciating the art. The three-and-a-half-hour play was a series of short blackouts punctuated with pistol shots and other harsh noises, and the effect was purposely "eccentric and confusing."

If the exorcism in *Agnes of God* wasn't enough to satisfy your appetite for such things, a week later you could find a similar kind of deprogram-ming in Tom Dulack's **Solomon's Child** (4-8-82, Little), but you only had four performances to catch it. Research scientist Allan Solomon (John McMartin) has watched his son, Shelley (Evan Handler), a bright pre-med student, turn into a panhandler for a religious cult run by a wacked-out dentist, so he has the brainwashed boy kid-napped and brought to the family summer house in the Catskills. There, for a fee of $10,000 cash, Shelley is to be deprogrammed by the ex-evangelist Nicodemus Balthazar (Anthony Zerbe), an alcoholic anti-Semite who loves Shake-speare and uses outrageous methods to cure such wayward youths. Since much of the intense ses-sion takes place during intermission, we only hear about Balthazar's unconventional tech-niques. But soon the boy is spitting at his mother (Joanna Merlin), renouncing his father for his dis-tant ways and career obsession, and, after break-ing down (in yet another echo of *Equus*), rejoin-ing the human race. There were some compliments for selected cast members (Zerbe was considered the best or the worst, depending on how you liked your "hamming"), but not for the drama itself: "pointless," a "non-play," "none of it is particularly believable."

John Guare's **Gardenia** (4-13-82, Manhattan Theatre Club) was a prequel to *Lydie Breeze*, seen in February at the American Place. The setting is again Nantucket, but the year is 1875, when Joshua Hickman (Sam Waterston), a struggling author, and his associate Amos Mason (Edward Herrmann) have seen their New England utopia fall apart. Joshua's wife, Lydie (JoBeth Williams), returns from a nursing assignment on the main-land and is angry with her husband for letting her prized gardenia plant die. When a former member of the community, Dan Grady (James Woods), returns, a covert romance between him and Lydie blossoms, and Joshua, in a fit of jeal-ousy, kills his wife's lover. Amos acts as Joshua's lawyer and suggests that the author not have his book published, as its contents could only hurt him at the trial. Joshua eventually gives in to Amos's suggestion, watching his literary career and personal life dissolve before his eyes. Critical response was quite diverse ("a bold work of imag-ination," "inventive and flavorful," "more like a prologue in two acts"), yet the drama ran forty-eight performances, nearly twice as long as *Lydie Breeze*.

The touring Acting Company came to the American Place on April 15 and brought *Twelfth Night* for five showings and, on April 20, Wych-erley's *The Country Wife* for eight performances. Michael Langham directed the former; Garland Wright staged the latter. The young players were deemed proficient if not outstanding. The Circle Rep got together with the Dramatists Guild and promoted a different kind of talented youth with their *Young Playwrights Festival* on April 27. Ten one-act plays submitted by playwrights age eigh-teen or younger were produced in repertory over twenty-four performances; some were given a fully professional production, others a staged reading. The quality varied widely, and the critics applauded the inventive idea more than the plays themselves. While no notable scripts or play-wrights came from this first season, the project would become an annual event for several years, playing at various locations.

Two Greek tragedies were revived within a week, and both were successful. Joseph Chaikin staged *Antigone* on April 27 at the Public with Lisa Banes as the title heroine and F. Murray Abraham as Creon. Generally well received, it stayed for 109 performances. On Broadway, Robert White-head, who had produced Judith Anderson's ac-claimed *Medea* in 1947, presented the tragedy again this season on May 2 at the Cort, this time directing his wife, Zoe Caldwell, in the title role with Anderson as her old Nurse. Anderson was applauded (it was her last Broadway appearance), but the glowing reviews centered on Caldwell, who, according to one commentator, "makes our hair stand on end by the fierce animal vigor with which she embodies her needs and dire inten-tions." The revival ran a healthy sixty-five per-formances, and Caldwell won the Tony Award at season's end.

Athol Fugard's South African drama **"MAS-TER HAROLD" . . . and the boys** (5-4-82, Ly-ceum) gave the playwright the longest-running play of his American career. Fugard telescopes the complex race problem in his homeland into the character of a schoolboy and the turmoil he faces one afternoon in 1950. Seventeen-year-old Harold (Lonny Price), familiarly called Hally, considers the two black waiters in his family's public tearoom in Port Elizabeth his friends, having known them since he was a young child. One rainy afternoon, Sam (Zakes Mokae) and Willie (Danny Glover) are talking about the upcoming ballroom dance competition that Willie and his girl are entering when Hally returns from school. Usually friendly to the two men, Hally is preoccupied with his father, a cold, hard-drinking man who is in the hospital but will be returning home before long. But soon the three start speaking affectionately of other matters (such as Hally's studies and memories of when Hally was a child). Hally cannot understand why there is so much hatred in the world and lack of tolerance for all men. But when his mother calls to say that his father is coming home today, Hally gets angry and tense, calling his father names. Sam tries to tell Hally to calm down and be careful of what he says, only to have Hally pull rank, treat the two men as the servants they are, and demand they address him as Master Harold from now on. "If you make me say it once," Sam cautions Hally, "I'll never call you anything else again." Hally insists, so the dividing line between two friends and two races is permanently drawn. Notices were highly supportive, Mokae won a Tony Award, and the small but powerful drama ran 344 performances.

Actress Patrizia Norcia recreated ten of Ruth Draper's most memorable character monologues and titled them **Cast of Characters** (5-5-82, Cherry Lane). Although fewer and fewer spectators could recall the original artist, Norcia's versatility and the cleverness of the sketches themselves pleased audiences for fifty-five showings.

Those waiting for a new Harold Pinter play had to settle for his puzzling satire **The Hothouse** (5-6-82, Playhouse), a work he had written twenty years earlier that was being given its first New York production this season. The title is a nickname for a state-run mental institution managed by the pompous and partially psychotic Roote (George Martin) with the hopeless assistance of the silent but sinister Gibbs (Richard Kavanaugh), the appropriately named alcoholic Lush (Peter Gerety), and the willing sexpot Miss Cutts (Amy Van Nostrand), who is sleeping with the entire staff. Although a series of crises occur (including the discovery that one of the patients has gotten pregnant), Roote is more concerned about his speech at the staff Christmas party. Soon violence erupts, most of the characters are

killed, and the plays ends as mysteriously as it began. This Adrian Hall production came from his Trinity Square Repertory in Providence, Rhode Island, and it was thought to be an expert presentation of a difficult play. Reaction to the play itself was mixed; some commentators found it the chaotic work of a young playwright, where others declared it "blisteringly funny," "a bizarre horror comedy," and "Pinter's funniest play." *The Hothouse* only ran twenty-nine performances, Pinter's shortest Broadway run.

There was a lot of Pinter in David Rabe's new play, **Goose and Tomtom** (5-6-82, Public: Newman), but the tragicomedy struck most as a feeble imitation of that British playwright's classic two-hander *The Dumbwaiter* (11-26-62). The two characters of the title are small-time jewel thieves who are both friends and rivals, each one perpetually trying to convince the world of his criminal prowess. But the two inept crooks mysteriously find themselves involved in a kidnapping and murder they seem to have no control over. In an episode reminiscent of Papp's tiff with Sam Shepard last season, Rabe was so displeased with the Papp production that he disowned any involvement with it, and Papp similarly badmouthed the playwright.

A play from London called **Livingstone and Sechele** (5-11-82, Quaigh) by David Pownall managed to find an audience for 152 performances even though it was exceedingly long and, though "lucid and occasionally humorous," not able to sustain itself over three talky acts. The famous Scottish missionary-explorer Livingstone (Mike Champagne) discovers a tribe called the Crocodiles in the Kalahari Desert and sets out to convert them to Christianity. The tribe's chief, Sechele (Afemo), is curious but cautious, pretending to be a possible convert so that Livingstone and his men will stick around and help fend off the hostile Boers. Much of the play was about the clash of the two cultures, raising questions about which group was indeed more civilized.

Playwrights Horizons had its third hit in a row this season with Jonathan Reynolds's **Geniuses** (5-13-82, Playwrights Horizons), a satire on Hollywood moviemaking set in a Philippines jungle. Reynolds had worked with film director Francis Ford Coppola on the set of *Apocalypse Now*, so there was no mystery about where the play's premise came from. An egotistical director, Milo McGee McGarr (David Garrison), is making his war epic *Parabola of Death* in the rain forest two hundred miles south of Manila, but a monsoon has set in, and the crew has all left for the city except a cynical screenwriter, Jocko Pyle (Michael Gross), a sadistic scenic designer, Eugene Winter (David Rasche), makeup man Bart Keely (Kurt Knudson), who is obsessed with Ernest Hemingway to the point that he has made himself up to look like "Papa," and a sexy starlet, Skye (Joanne Camp), Milo's girlfriend, who has been flown onto the set to do a brief nude scene in the film. While wind and rain batter the little hut where this odd assortment waits it out, the talk is mostly Hollywood bashing, gossip about the business, and trading tales about the genius Milo. As tension mounts, the savage Eugene beats up Skye, and the others, in turn, help Skye get her revenge just as the storm abates and the godlike Milo makes a grand entrance in a helicopter. While the plotting was considered weak ("a very trying exercise in facetiousness"), most of the critics endorsed Reynolds's tangy dialogue, Mel Gussow in the *New York Times* noting, "Not since S. J. Perelman has anyone savaged Cloudland with such malice aforethought." Compliments were also handed to the able cast and to Gerald Gutierrez's detailed direction. *Geniuses* caught the public's fancy and ran a surprising 344 performances.

The American Place's only entry of note this season was a double bill entitled **The Regard of Flight** and **The Clown Bagatelles** (5-23-82, American Place) that stayed for eighty-three performances and would return to delight New York audiences on future occasions. The young clown and mime enthusiast Bill Irwin wrote, directed, and, with Michael O'Connor and Doug Skinner, performed the "comedy entertainment" *Regard of Flight,* which employed dialogue, songs, physical humor, parodies, and parodies of parodies. *The Clown Bagatelles* was a dumbshow epilogue that climaxed with plates of spaghetti being tossed about with hilarious dexterity. Reviews were not quite sure what to call the program or how to describe it, but most found it endlessly entertaining: "a funnier or, for that matter, a more imaginative evening cannot be imagined."

Christopher Durang's first Broadway venture was not a propitious one. A slightly revised version of his comedy of manners *Beyond Therapy* (1-1-81) opened at the Brooks Atkinson on May 26 with some cast changes (most notably, John Lithgow as the bewildered Bruce) but met with decidedly mixed notices and closed after eleven showings. Rarely would Durang stray onto Broadway in the future, finding more success in the more appropriate venue of Off Broadway.

The season ended with Granville Wyche Burgess's **The Freak** (5-27-82, Douglas Fairbanks), a

fictional dramatization about Edgar Cayce (Dann Florek), the famous psychic and faith healer at the turn of the century. Cayce was shown as a deeply religious man who does not want to possess the special powers that make him a freak in society but believes that they are gifts from God and that he can better mankind with them. His patient wife (Polly Draper), his stern father (James Greene), and various doctors who test Cayce's powers were also brought into the action, but most reviews complained that the play went nowhere. The drama had been seen briefly off-off Broadway at the WPA Theatre, but its transfer to Off Broadway only lasted twenty-two performances.

1982–1983

While the twelve new American plays on Broadway this season (plus two transfers from Off Broadway) were encouraging in their quality, the number was down from the previous season, and the eight British entries seemed to get most of the attention. Off Broadway also saw a decline in numbers, and, again, some of the most intriguing offerings were foreign. The number of Broadway revivals doubled, but the off-Broadway number shrank. So did audiences. *Variety* estimated a drop of 24 percent on the Street and, harder to estimate, declared a drop off Broadway as well. Indicative of the season, the Phoenix Theatre ceased operation after thirty years, and no new or growing theatre company took its place.

Ticket prices continued to climb (top price for the Elizabeth Taylor–Richard Burton *Private Lives* was set at $45), as did production costs. No new Broadway play showed a profit by season's end (the transfer *Plenty* was the only Broadway entry in the black by May 31), but hits still existed; it just took longer to reach that financial status. In fact, the season produced several long runs. *Torch Song Trilogy, Fool for Love,* and *Brighton Beach Memoirs* (all native works) each ran a thousand or more performances, and another half dozen productions (mostly off Broadway) hit the 500-performance mark.

Exciting new British playwrights dominated attention off and on the Street, but this was also a season in which Americans as diverse as Marsha Norman, Neil Simon, Lanford Wilson, Sam Shepard, and A. R. Gurney, Jr., introduced quality work as well and, for the most part, found audiences to support them. But it was disconcerting to see the Public Theatre and the Manhattan

Theatre Club, two of Off Broadway's bastions of native drama, presenting a record number of British works. Some were exchanges with London, but there was no question that the traffic across the Atlantic was predominantly westbound.

The season opener was a literary compilation called **With Love and Laughter** (6-2-82, Harold Clurman) in which Celeste Holm, Wesley Addy, and Gordon Connell read or performed selections dealing with male-female relationships over the ages. Quoted authors ranged from de la Rochefoucauld to Thurber to Saroyan to John Adams to Shakespeare to Margaret Mead. Though the performers were engaging, the nontheatrical nature of the program was unmistakable.

Broadway saw its longest-running gay play yet on June 10 when *Torch Song Trilogy* (1-15-82) transferred from Off Broadway to the Little, staying for 1,222 performances. Reviews were even more enthusiastic than they had been off Broadway, endorsing the long evening as an "unabashedly entertaining work that, so help me, is something for the whole family," as Jack Kroll wrote in *Newsweek*. Harvey Fierstein won Tony Awards for both his play and his performance as the philosophical drag queen Arnold Beckoff. (During the run, the Little would be rechristened the new Helen Hayes Theatre.)

Off Broadway's first commercial entry of the season was Robert A. Morse's **Booth** (6-10-82, South Street), an attempt to tell the story of the famous acting family through a series of brief, fragmented scenes. John Glover was an intriguing John Wilkes Booth, but, according to Edith Oliver in *The New Yorker*, "the script is in such disarray that it is all but impossible to have any opinion about it whatever." Other critics complained about many anachronisms in the writing. *Booth* only lasted twelve performances, which was eleven more than another bio-drama, **Looking-Glass** (6-14-82, Entermedia), was able to survive. The Michael Sutton and Cynthia Mandelberg play was about author and Oxford University don Charles Dodgson (aka Lewis Carroll) and the people in his life who became characters in the Alice books. John Vickery played the famous writer and, like Glover, was deemed better than the script.

The Manhattan Theatre Club concluded its 1981–1982 season with "a dramatic curiosity and a fascinating one," **The Singular Life of Albert Nobbs** (6-16-82, Manhattan Theatre Club). Abused as a child, a Victorian Englishwoman (Glenn Close) disguises herself as a man, takes on the name Albert Nobbs, and gets a job as a waiter

and, later, a gentleman's valet. Finding herself falling in love with her employer, "Albert" flees and considers throwing herself into the Thames. Instead she travels to Ireland, where she works for seventeen years as a waiter in a posh Dublin hotel. One day her identity is discovered by Hubert Page (Lucinda Childs), a hotel guest who is also a woman in disguise, and the two come up with an unlikely false relationship to survive. French playwright Simone Benmussa adapted a short story by George Moore, and it was translated by Barbara Wright and previously presented in London. Critics were bewildered but approving of the odd piece and found Benmussa's direction, the imaginative scenery, and Close's cunning performance worth applauding.

The month's third bio-drama lasted the longest (five weeks) and was the most interesting. Jane Marla Robbins's **Jane Avril** (6-22-82, Provincetown Playhouse) told the tale of the famous Parisian music hall singer (Robbins) and her devotion to Henri de Toulouse-Lautrec (Kevin O'Connor), whose paintings and posters immortalized the wispy songbird.

Two rarely performed Molière comedies opened off Broadway within the week. The Roundabout Theatre concluded its previous season with *The Learned Ladies* in a translation by Richard Wilbur that opened on June 22. Philip Bosco played Chrysale, and his family included Rosemary Murphy, Jennifer Harmon, Cynthia Dozier, and Carol Teitel. Surprisingly, it was New York's first English-language production of the play since 1911. The New York Shakespeare Festival featured *Don Juan* on June 25 at the Delacorte in Central Park in a translation by Donald A. Frame with John Seitz as the title character and Roy Brocksmith as Sganarelle. Richard Foreman directed, and Patricia Zipprodt provided the elegant costumes. The production (including the two main actors) had originated the year before at Minneapolis's Guthrie Theatre.

Jules Feiffer's latest satire on the American way of life, **A Think Piece** (6-26-82, Circle), was seen only nineteen times, then disappeared. On the surface, Betty (Debra Mooney) and Gordon (Andrew Duncan) have a rather dull and unimaginative family. But soon the stress and angst hidden beneath explode, and very troubled people are revealed. Feiffer's tone was more strident than usual, and only Mooney's expert performance drew any applause.

Allan Miller's stage adaptation of D. H. Lawrence's novella **The Fox** (7-8-82, Roundabout) garnered some favorable reviews, calling the three-character piece "a surprise and a distinct pleasure" and "the rare adaptation that honors its source, while having the guts to depart from it." Jenny O'Hara and Mary Layne played the repressed English spinsters trying to run a farm in 1918, and Anthony Heald was the World War I vet who arrives on the scene and becomes their hired hand. Just as a fox has been raiding the henhouse, so too the ex-soldier enters their lives, creating a passionate triangle. It was rare for the Roundabout to present a new work, yet the adaptation managed a run of eighty-five performances.

George C. Scott triumphed as both director and star of a riotous revival of Noel Coward's *Present Laughter* (10-29-46) that opened on July 15 at the Circle in the Square and ran for 180 performances. Eschewing all the traditional approaches to Coward in both performance and staging, Scott turned the drawing room comedy into a furious farce and played actor Garry Essendine (originally portrayed suavely by Coward) into a lively old ham who, with "bangs falling over his forehead and his rabbit's eyes popping, comes on like a burlesque Adolf Hitler." The rest of the cast performed similar highjinks, with Dana Ivey as brittle Monica the most subtle and newcomer Nathan Lane's bombastic playwright Roland Maule the most outrageous as he leapt over couches and endeared himself to audiences and critics alike in his Broadway debut.

The summer's second offering at the Delacorte in Central Park was *A Midsummer Night's Dream* on August 3, a production that met with mixed notices save general admiration for Heidi Landesman's bucolic scenery. The young designer turned the open-air stage, as described by John Beaufort in the *Christian Science Monitor*, "into an

undulant expanse of verdure—of grassy slopes and flowering shrubs, of grotto entrances, and a special tree-enclosed bower for Titania and her rollicking fairy brood." James Lapine staged the fantasy with "some odd directorial flourishes," and the uneven cast included William Hurt (Oberon), Christine Baranski (Helena), Jeffrey DeMunn (Bottom), and Michele Shay (Puck).

Dalton Trumbo's anti-war novel **Johnny Got His Gun** (8-10-82, Circle) was adapted into a stage monologue by Bradley Rand Smith with Jeff Daniels portraying the quadriplegic Joe Bonham, who recalls the events of World War I that led to his helpless condition. Trumbo had filmed the story in 1971, but most commentators felt this monodrama was more successful in capturing the book's morbid, if potent, sentiments.

Arthur Kopit provided a literate and stageworthy adaptation of Ibsen's *Ghosts* for a Broadway revival on August 30 at the Brooks Atkinson, but the production itself was disappointing. Liv Ullman was a younger but "strangely cold and unaffecting" Mrs. Alving, John Neville (who took over the play's direction from John Madden a week before opening) was a fussy but "persuasive" Pastor Manders, and newcomer Kevin Spacey gave an "unusually effective performance as the doomed Oswald." Even Kevin Rupnick's scenery fell short, offering a cheery and bright Scandinavian sitting room that several critics felt was at odds with the play. Theoni Aldridge, who would provide costume designs for six major productions this season, was better reviewed. The revival ran an unprofitable forty times.

John Byrum's **Inserts** (9-8-82, Actors & Directors) was based on his infamous cult film of 1976, which Larry Loonin adapted and directed for the stage. Boy Wonder (Kevin O'Connor) was one of the most promising film directors of the 1920s, but as the Depression sets in his career is in shambles, and he holes up in a decaying Hollywood mansion and makes porno movies. The cult following for the film was not repeated, so the commercial venture shuttered after fourteen performances.

More than the usual pre-production gossip surrounded the New York premiere of Jane Martin's **Talking With** (9-21-82, Manhattan Theatre Club). Selected by the American Theatre Critics Association as the best regional new play of 1982, the work came from the Actors Theatre of Louisville, which had recently introduced Beth Henley to the East Coast. Most of the talk involved the playwright. "Jane Martin" was a pseudonym for a person (or persons) who refused to come for-

NATHAN [né Joseph] **LANE** (1956–) was born in Jersey City, New Jersey, the son of a truck driver and a secretary. After graduating from St. Peter's Preparatory School in his hometown, he began acting in summer stock and regional theatre, changing his name to Nathan in 1977 after playing Nathan Detroit in a production of *Guys and Dolls*. He made his New York debut the next year off Broadway at an Equity Library revival of *A Midsummer Night's Dream* and was soon on Broadway at the Circle in the Square. The baby-faced Lane excelled in comedy, both in musicals and plays, and soon developed into one of the few marketable comics onstage as well as in film and television.

ward and identify herself/himself despite a handful of accomplished productions in the Kentucky city. *Talking With* is a series of eleven monologues delivered by different women on diverse topics. A bored housewife (Penelope Allen) imagines she is in Oz in order to escape her futile life, dressing up as "the Patchwork Girl" as she vacuums her house. A dying old lady (Anne Pitoniak) hides out in a loft surrounded by dozens of lamps, complaining how her sister has decided to live out her last days among strangers in a retirement community. A much-abused divorcee (Lynn Milgrim) charts her many disasters in life on the numerous scars and tattoos that cover her body. The two finest monologues (and the ones most often mentioned by the press) were more comic. A former rodeo performer (Margo Martindale) complains about the commercialism of all entertainment today, blaming cable television, the Dallas Cowgirls, and "astrodirt" for the worlds's ills; and an elderly black woman (Theresa Merritt), who sits all day in a brightly lit McDonald's "like some French fries they forgot," philosophizes on how no one dies in the famous fast-food restaurant chain "no matter how hard you try." The script and the eleven actresses (several of whom came from Louisville) were warmly welcomed by the critics. The fifty-six-performance run was well attended, and the play became a favorite in regional, community, and college theatres.

Wynyard Browne's domestic drama **The Holly and the Ivy** (9-21-82, Roundabout) was first produced in London in 1948 and filmed in 1952 but not seen on the New York stage until this season. Rev. Martin Gregory (Gwyllum Evans), an aging vicar near retirement in post-war Britain, is cared for by his daughter Jenny (Jennifer Harmon), who wishes to marry a local engineer (Gerald Walker) and go off with him to a long-term job in South America. When Jenny's brother and sister, black sheep Mick (Frank Grimes) and London fashion writer Margaret (Pamela Brook), return home for Christmas, Jenny hopes to convince either of them to stay and care for their father. But they will have nothing to do with the solemn old man until a night of drunkenness causes each to reveal dark secrets in their lives; by Christmas morning everything is settled to everyone's satisfaction. Some reviewers found the old play quaint and wholesome; others denounced it as "so mawkish and foolish it almost seems like a parody of British genteel domestic dramas." But the cast and production, delicately directed by Lindsay Anderson, were viewed with favor, and audiences found the evening comfortably satis-

fying enough to keep the early holiday attraction on the boards into March.

Two more unsuccessful bio-dramas followed, both commercial ventures off Broadway. In Maxim Mazumdar's **a/k/a Tennessee** (9-26-82, South Street), selections from Tennessee Williams's plays and other writings were read or performed by three actors (Carrie Nye, J. T. Walsh, Mazumdar) in order to explore "the facts and fictions" of the famous playwright. The venture closed on opening night. (Williams died five months later.) Betty Neustat's **The Price of Genius** (9-28-82, Lamb's) featured a less recognizable subject: Juana Ines de la Cruz (Patricia Norcia), a seventeenth-century playwright and poet who was also a nun. The finest Spanish-American writer of her time, Sor Juana was fascinating, but the drama was less so and closed after twenty-two performances.

A three-character play considered "rather aimless but rather amusing" was Grubb Graebner's **Baseball Wives** (9-29-82, Harold Clurman), a series of conversations between the wives of Astros players during the course of a season. Janelle (Marcella Lowery), the wife of the team's starring black player, Doris (Carol Teitel), the manager's wife, and Becky (Lynn Goodwin), married to a rookie, are seen together at various locations from the season opener to the playoffs, their commentary on the sport and their husbands carrying through all the scenes.

With *Present Laughter* doing boffo business in its usual home, Circle in the Square moved to Broadway's Plymouth on September 30 for its revival of Ugo Betti's *The Queen and the Rebels* (2-25-65). The little-known 1949 melodrama was rejected by the press as "all shopworn stage tricks in service of moral platitudes," so attendance during the scheduled forty-five performances was spotty. But Colleen Dewhurst shone as Argia, a soft-hearted prostitute who is mistaken by some revolutionary citizens for the war-torn Latin American country's queen. Notices called Dewhurst "grandly authoritative throughout" and "imbued with a kind of regal magnificence" and applauded others in the cast, notably Peter Michael Goetz and Betty Miller.

The fall's sixth biography play sounded the most promising, but it also failed. Bob Eaton's bio-documentary theatre piece **Lennon** (10-5-82, Entermedia), previously seen at theatres in England, caused little excitement with critics or audiences here, closing after three weeks. The chronicle attempted to explore the character of John Lennon, the most complex and fascinating of the Beatles, who had been murdered two years before. What enfolded onstage was far from the sensational but "always flavorless," "dull," and "rather tepid." Lennon was played by various actors at different stages of his life, and the large cast of characters included appearances by Pierre Trudeau, Timothy Leary, Dick Gregory, and Bertram Russell. Although some of the celebrated Lennon songs were heard, the lengthy drama was never very musical.

John Olive, a midwest playwright who would never quite catch on in New York, saw his drama **Standing on My Knees** (10-12-82, Manhattan Theatre Club) play off Broadway for forty performances, gathering such accolades as "a beautiful and hopeful play" by "a writer with a sharp eye for character and a strong sense of theatrical rhythm and shape." Young but promising poet Catherine (Pamela Reed) returns home from a hospital where doctors were battling her acute schizophrenia with doses of Thorazine. While the drug curtails her mental problems, it also numbs her ability to write. When Catherine meets and falls in love with Robert (Robert Neches), a stockbroker who admires her poetry, she tries to cut back on the Thorazine, only to see her erratic behavior drive Robert away and cause her to sink into complete madness. The taut drama was directed by Robert Falls, who had staged the work earlier in Chicago.

The first of the season's laudable British imports was C. P. Taylor's **Good** (10-13-82, Booth), a chilling and intellectual study of how a good man can, step by step, learn to accept evil. John Halder (Alan Howard), a literature professor living in Frankfurt in the 1930s, has written a novel (based on his own mother's frailty) about the pathetic plight of the ill and helpless in society and suggests a merciful relief for such unfortunates. Hitler reads the novel and has Halder approached by the Nazi party to oversee a euthanasia plan in the works. Halder, still in love with his slovenly wife, Helen (Meg Wynn-Owen), but having an affair with a student (Felicity Dean), feels he can make a difference in the New Germany even though he does not approve of the Nazis' anti-Semitic obsession. Even as he argues philosophically with his Jewish friend Maurice (Gary Waldhorn), Halder is steadily rising in the ranks, eventually becoming an SS officer. In the last scene, the idealistic hero arrives at his new post at Auschwitz, totally charmed by the sounds of a Schubert march being played by the inmates of the camp. Throughout the play, Halder's fascination with music (everything from Wagner to Bavarian folk songs to "Hold That Tiger" drifts in and out of his consciousness) parallels his quest for doing the right thing. Howard, Taylor (who had died the previous year), and the Royal Shakespeare Company mounting were all saluted. The "fascinating, grimly disturbing drama" ran 125 performances.

While audiences continued to find the eccentric southerners in Beth Henley's *Crimes of the Heart* (12-21-80) endearing, the grotesques in her new dark comedy **The Wake of Jamey Foster** (10-14-82, Eugene O'Neill) were less easy to love, and all the characters departed after twelve performances. Alcoholic poet Jamey Foster has died, kicked in the head by a cow while he cavorted in a pasture with his younger mistress. His family gathers at the house before the last rites and continue the quarrels and offbeat behavior that have long dominated their lives. Marshael Foster (Susan Kingsley), Jamey's estranged wife, has "mixed feelings" about the situation as she is romantically drawn to local pig farmer Brocker Slade (Brad Sullivan). Gathered with them are Jamey's brother, Wayne (Anthony Heald), an upwardly mobile banker with a matronly fussbudget of a wife (Belita Moreno), his sluttish sister, Collard (Patricia Richardson), and an oddball waif named Pixrose Wilson (Holly Hunter), who was burnt out of her home by her parents and now is displaying arson tendencies herself. Those assembled can agree on nothing except their dislike of the late Jamey, who somehow still has a hold on them all. Notices were polite but negative, still finding Henley a talent to reckon with even if they could not recommend her latest effort. Kingsley was generally admired, but newcomer Hunter was the one who caught everyone's attention. She would be associated with several other Henley works in the future.

Lanford Wilson was back off Broadway this season with his **Angels Fall** (10-17-82, Circle). In a remote New Mexico adobe church, six characters, waiting to continue with their lives, are detained because of a nuclear "accident" that has closed the highway. Niles Harris (Fritz Weaver), a burnt-out college professor, is traveling with his younger wife, Vita (Nancy Snyder), to a famous shrink in Phoenix, where the former art historian is to be admitted to a sanatorium. Gallery owner Marion Gray (Tanya Berezin), the widow of a famous artist, is en route to an important tennis tournament with her young paramour, the agile tennis champion Zappy (Brian Taratina). The little church's pastor, Fr. William Doherty (Barnard Hughes), is a whimsical and understanding priest who hails from Massachusetts but has stayed on in Navaho country trying to make a difference with the disheartened residents. He attempts to get Don Tabaha (Danton Stone), a brilliant Native American medical student, to return to the area after graduation, but the quiet youth has decided to accept a high-paying research job in California and is planning to leave on his motorcycle as soon as the highway reopens. As the six await the all-clear from the police, each opens up to the others, past demons are revealed, then they uncomfortably drift apart as they move on their way. While some aisle-sitters found the situation contrived and the characters only mildly interesting, Mel Gussow in the *New York Times* and others declared the piece "a compelling group portrait . . . from an artist creating at the peak of his form." Similar praise helped the two-month engagement sell out, prompting a transfer to Broadway on January 22 that became an eight-week stay at the Longacre.

Sam Shepard had two giant off-Broadway hits this season. The first was the neglected *True West* (12-23-80), given a sparklingly cohesive revival on October 17 at the Cherry Lane that received exemplary notices and ran 762 performances. Gary Sinise directed and played California screenwriter Austin, while John Malcovich essayed his drifter brother, Lee. Critics cited the explosive chemistry between the two as the production's glory and this time declared the script one of Shepard's finest.

Later in the week another off-Broadway hit arrived, **Greater Tuna** (10-21-82, Circle in the Square Downtown), which would run a successful 501 performances and go on to become one of the most-produced comedies across the country during the next decade. Jaston Williams, Joe Sears, and Ed Howard wrote the broad satire on small-town life in Texas (Tuna is a fictional locale that claims to be the "third smallest town" in the state), and Williams and Sears played all twenty male and female characters. The plotless spoof showed a typical day in Tuna, from a cockeyed broadcast on the local radio station to a wake in which two older ladies snicker over the body of a deceased judge. Among the most memorable citizens of Tuna were Petey Fisk, the veterinarian who tries to save animals in the hunting-crazy community; ammunitions dealer Didi Snavely, whose husband talks to UFOs; and the put-upon mother Bertha Bumiller, whose daughter is too fat to make the cheerleading squad and whose juvenile delinquent son murdered the judge for sending him to reform school. The quick changes

of character and costume were the highlight of the silly comedy, and Sears's and Williams's caricature portraits were precise and wickedly accurate.

British playwright David Hare's first New York appearance of note was **Plenty** (10-21-82, Public: Newman), a cinematic tale of a woman faced with a loss of purpose during the two decades following World War II. Seventeen-year-old Susan Traherne (Kate Nelligan) is a courier for the French Resistance during the war and thrives on the danger and close-knit camaraderie of dedicated people. But with peace, there seems to be plenty of wealth and good fortune for everyone, and Susan restlessly seeks fulfillment in her life. She tries (unsuccessfully) to have a child by Mick (Daniel Gerroll), a man far removed from her class, then weds the struggling diplomat Raymond Block (Edward Herrmann) and destroys his career with her meddling and tempestuous nature. In the last scene, Susan is seen bedding down with an aging Resistance fighter (Kelsey Grammer) she once had a brief encounter with in France. Susan was a fascinating and infuriating heroine, and Nelligan's performance was cheered. Many critics also found the play "relentlessly gripping" and "an explosive theatrical vision of a world that was won and lost," though Guernsey in the *Best Plays* was perhaps most accurate in describing it as "a play that was both arresting and repellent." Nevertheless, the New York Drama Critics Circle honored it with a Best Foreign Play citation. The American production, directed by its young author, sold out its six-week run at the Public, then transferred to the Plymouth on January 6 and remained for ninety-two more showings.

An unusual collage of scenes, period songs, and history called **Do Lord Remember Me** (10-24-82, American Place) provided one of the few successful runs at the American Place Theatre. James DeJongh compiled the program, using the firsthand accounts of former slaves that were recorded by the Federal Writers Project in the 1930s. Five actors performed the vignettes that ranged from horrifying to warmly humorous. The generally favorable reviews called the evening "an engrossing and informative tapestry" and "like a vivid etching come briefly to life." The program ran three months, then transferred to Town Hall, where it totaled up a run of 127 performances.

Chicago's Goodman Theatre brought its premiere production of David Mamet's **Edmond** (10-27-82, Provincetown Playhouse) to Manhattan, the setting of this stark allegory about a normal man who turns urban savage. Upper West Side resident Edmond Burke (Colin Stinton) decides he is bored with his wife and lifestyle, so he sets out into the New York underworld looking for sexual and personal satisfaction. Characters on the street treat him roughly (he is conned, mugged, thrown out of a fleabag hotel), but he returns the favors by ranting against blacks and homosexuals and murdering a waitress. Arrested and jailed, he is forced to have sex with a black inmate, the two become lovers, and Edmond finds a new spiritual satisfaction. Critics gave the short, multi-scened play a rather analytical hearing (several compared it to Buchner's *Woyzeck*, and the philosophy of conservative author Edmund Burke was often brought up) and Douglas Watt in the *Daily News* called it "an example of masterly control over a dizzying experience and it will knock your socks off." But Frank Rich in the *New York Times* and others complained of the play's "toothless ambiguity" and felt that "Mr. Mamet will toss off any fortune-cookie message to paper over the play's various narrative, philosophical, and psychological short circuits." Gregory Mosher's striking direction was viewed with favor. *Edmond* stayed in town for seventy-seven performances but never entered the repertory of frequently produced Mamet works.

John Ford Noonan had had a long-run success with *A Coupla White Chicks Sitting Around Talking* (4-28-80), in which two neighbors, strangers and quite opposite in temperament, become friends over a series of scenes in a kitchen. He tried to repeat the feat with **Some Men Need Help** (10-28-82, 47th Street), in which two male neighbors, also strangers totally at odds with each other, become friends over a series of kitchen scenes. Young Wasp business executive Hudley T. Singleton II (Treat Williams) is dead drunk on his suburban kitchen floor when his Italian-American neighbor, Gaetano Altobelli (Philip Bosco), enters, introduces himself, and proceeds to "save" Hudley from himself. The gruff, middle-aged Gaetano, a mob-connected owner of a moving van company, is insulted by the bitter Hudley (his wife's leaving him is the reason he has turned to drink), who makes fun of the older man's New York–ese way of talking, but this "guardian angel" is not easily put off. Soon a father-son relationship develops, Gaetano helps Hudley through a detox program, and the two weather emotional upheaval when Hudley finds out that his ex-wife has drowned. Noonan's script met with decidedly mixed reviews. Clive Barnes in the *New York Post*

found it "impossible to believe in what is happening, or even to care enough to worry about one's disbelief," while Watt described the comedy as "a cross between Pinter and Shepard with a little sweetening . . . a sorrowful little comedy-drama." The actors received consistently praiseworthy notices; Bosco was especially welcomed in his departure from the many classical roles he had been playing in the last decade. But Noonan was denied a second hit: *Some Men Need Help* struggled for fifty-three performances and, unlike *White Chicks*, has rarely been heard of again.

Both parts of Goethe's massive epic drama *Faust* were given a rare mounting on October 31 by the Classic Stage Company, a troupe dedicated to presenting seldom-seen classic works in spare but fluid productions. (This was cited as the first unabridged production of the play ever to be seen in America, a claim not easily refuted.) Philip Wayne's new translation shortened the poetic drama to five and a half hours (presented in two sittings), and Christopher Martin staged it simply but effectively. The doomed Faust was played by Martin, Gary Sloan, and Tom Spackman at various points in the character's adventures, and Noble Shropshire was noted for his chilling Mephisto. Notices were supportive and encouraging (though most critics noted that the problematic Part 2 offered "more for the ear than the eye"), and the little company kept *Faust* on the boards for 214 performances.

The two-week run of Michael Hastings's **Two Fish in the Sky** (10-31-82, St. Peter's Church) proved to be the swan song for the Phoenix Theatre. The British comedy tells of the plight of Meadowlark Rachel Warner (Cleavon Little), a stereotypic Jamaican who lives in the Brixton section of London but is going to be deported back to Kingston because of an error in his papers. At first Meadowlark hopes to wed a local whore (Laura Esterman) to secure his residency, but at the last moment he finds out she is an Irish citizen, so a marriage with her will not help him. At the last possible moment, Meadowlark finds a woman at the airport who marries him even as his plane to Jamaica takes off without him.

The husband-wife acting team of Eli Wallach and Anne Jackson, who might be considered the quintessential players for Murray Schisgal's comedies, had starred together in his *The Typists* and *The Tiger* (2-4-63) and *Luv* (11-11-64). Reunited for Schisgal's two-hander **Twice Around the Park** (11-4-82, Cort), the duo kept the double bill on the boards for 124 performances through their ability to rise above the material. In *A Need for*

Brussels Sprouts, out-of-work actor Leon Rose plays his opera records so loudly that his belligerent neighbor, a lady cop named Margaret Heinz, enters and threatens to arrest him for disturbing the peace. Soon the two lonely antagonists make peace, let loose their many hangups and insecurities, and discover a fondness for one another. *A Need for Less Expertise* concerns the crumbling marriage of Edie and Gus Frazier, who listen to tapes by Dr. Oliovski, a guru of mental, sexual, and physical health. The desperate couple dredge up the past as they engage in yoga exercises and spiritual meditation guaranteed to ease "selfness" and to "fight cellulite." Critical response was mildly dismissive of the script (most aisle-sitters preferred the second playlet) but approving of Wallach and Jackson, who were "delightful company even when running in place."

A Canadian farce by Allan Stratton called **Nurse Jane Goes to Hawaii** (11-4-82, New York State Pavilion) was presented by Off Off Broadway's Theatre in the Park for twenty performances in Flushing Meadow, and some critics found it "howlingly funny," "with characters whirling in and out of enough doors to make Feydeau dizzy." Romance novelist Vivian Bliss (Georgia Engel) comes to the Toronto home of schoolteacher Edgar Chisholm (Brandon Maggart) and his wife, Doris (Jennifer Bassey). Despite the arrival of an evil Russian physicist, a wacky advice columnist, a reporter with a nose for trouble, a long-lost orphan, and a doctor who likes to wear pantyhose, Vivian manages to finish her latest novel on time.

Another favorite acting couple, Hume Cronyn and Jessica Tandy, returned to Broadway in **Foxfire** (11-11-82, Ethel Barrymore), a rural memory play by Cronyn and Susan Cooper. The stars' luminous performances far outshone their ramshackle vehicle for 213 showings. Seventy-nine-year-old Appalachian mountain woman Annie Nations (Tandy) refuses to sell the land on which her weatherbeaten old house sits, despite offers from a real estate agent, Prince Carpenter (Trey Wilson), looking to develop the property. The reason for her stubbornness is her husband, Hector (Cronyn), who died five years earlier but still haunts the place and has daily conversations with Annie. Their grown son, Dillard (Keith Carradine), now a popular hillbilly singer, has a concert in the area, so he visits and tries again to convince his mother to give up the place and settle in Florida with his family. Flashbacks to times past (Annie first meeting Hector, her giving birth on the kitchen table, Dillard getting a whipping

from his stern father) were created simply by the mastery of the performers, and the proceedings were punctuated by a few country songs sung by Carradine. Annie finally decides to let her dead husband lie in peace and goes to help Dillard with his troubled marriage. The whole cast was adulated, but Tandy got the lion's share of the raves and won a Tony Award.

Jean-Claude van Itallie provided a new translation of Chekhov's *Three Sisters* for the Manhattan Theatre Club on November 30, and director Lynn Meadow assembled a masterful cast, but critics felt the humorless production was too bleak and the fine individual performances did not blend into an ensemble. Even veteran comic actor Jack Gilford, shrewdly cast as Dr. Chebutykin, was considered dry and somber, as were Lisa Banes (Olga), Dianne Wiest (Masha), and Mia Dillon (Irina). Also featured were Sam Waterston (Vershinin), Bob Balaban (Tuzenbach), Christine Ebersole (Natasha), and the ever-busy this season Jeff Daniels (Andrei). Mixed reviews also greeted the Public's revival of *Hamlet* on December 2 with Diane Venora as the melancholy prince. Notices declared Venora an estimable actress but "too girlish and tantrummy" to pull off the male role. Joseph Papp directed the "harmless curiosity," which featured strong performances by Kathleen Widdoes (Gertrude), Bob Gunton (Claudius), and George Hall (Polonius).

Helene Hanff's beloved 1970 chronicle **88 Charing Cross Road** (12-7-82, Nederlander), recreating her twenty-year correspondence with a London antiquarian bookseller, was faithfully adapted and lovingly directed by James Roose-Evans. However, the stageworthiness of the charming but undramatic material was questioned. Struggling television writer Hanff (Ellen Burstyn) first writes to Marks & Co. at the title address in 1949 looking for used copies of out-of-print classics. The bookseller Frank Doel (Joseph Maher), a mild and reticent businessman, replies, and the two discuss various topics as they correspond over the years. Even though the two central characters never meet face to face, the relationship is quite vivid and moving. (Doel died in 1969 before Hanff ever got to London.) Notices ranged from "a lovable piece of work" to "an evening of sedentary gentility" but pronounced the cast warm and engaging. Although the Roose-Evans version had been a hit in London, the intimate play only survived an unprofitable ninety-six performances on Broadway.

Another British success that failed to catch fire in New York was Nell Dunn's **Steaming** (12-12-

82, Brooks Atkinson), "a dull, sleazy sex farce," according to Beaufort, "masquerading as an expression of feminist and social concern." Six women of diverse ages, but all with plenty of man problems, meet regularly in a crumbling London Turkish bath to sweat off pounds, complain about males, and tell dirty jokes that they would never dream of uttering anywhere else. When the town council plans to tear down the bath house and replace it with a costly new library, the women protest, but the male-dominated board wins the battle. All the critics agreed that the most notable aspect of the show was the dazzling performance by Judith Ivey as the crass, honest cockney Josie. (Ivey won a Tony Award for her efforts.) Marjorie Kellogg's atmospheric setting, complete with vaulted scenery, stained titles, a pool of water for soaking in, and steam coming from all directions, was also praised. A considerable amount of nudity in *Steaming* (even the ancient character actress Polly Rowles stripped to the buff) may have helped the play hang on for two months.

Three Broadway flops arrived on three successive nights in December. The worthiest of the trio was William Gibson's **Monday After the Miracle** (12-14-82, Eugene O'Neill), a sequel to his memorable Helen Keller bio-drama *The Miracle Worker* (10-19-59). Blind and deaf Keller (Karen Allen) is now twenty-six years old, a student at Radcliffe living with her teacher Annie Sullivan (Jane Alexander), and together they are preparing to write Helen's autobiography. When Harvard instructor John Marcy (William Converse-Roberts) comes on the scene to help with the manuscript, he and Annie fall in love and marry. A complex triangle develops with Annie torn between her dedication to Helen and her romantic love for John. Matters are further complicated by Helen's sexual awakening, John's growing alcoholism, and Annie's deteriorating eyesight. The two women eventually reach an understanding as Helen takes on the role of teacher to Annie, who sets out on a difficult lecture tour. The mixed notices were supportive, Rich pointing out that the new work was "more ambitious than its predecessor—darker in mood, more mature in its themes, more troubling in its conclusions about human nature." Arthur Penn, who had directed *The Miracle Worker*, staged the sequel with exacting precision. General opinion on the Street felt the drama deserved to run longer than its mere seven performances.

Angela Lansbury made a rare non-musical return to Broadway with **A Little Family Business** (12-15-82, Martin Beck), a Gallic farce by Pierre Barillet and Jean-Pierre Gredy, the French playwriting team that had found success in America with *Cactus Flower* (12-8-65) and *Forty Carats* (12-26-68). Their latest work was Americanized by Jay Presson Allen and given a "coarse" production by musical comedy director-lyricist Martin Charnin. When the bigoted Boston manufacturer Ben (John McMartin) suffers a heart attack (presented onstage in a farcical manner), he is sent off to recover, and his addle-brained wife, Lillian (Lansbury), previously only interested in mail-order catalogs, takes over. Using her woman's intuition, Lillian averts a strike at the factory, increases production and profits, and is soon toying with the idea of a political career. The broadly played comedy found little favor in the press, though Lansbury's farceur talents were saluted. But even her presence could not keep the play running more than thirteen performances.

James Whitmore, who had previously essayed Harry Truman and Will Rogers onstage, put elements of the two portraits together to come up with the Colonel, a World War II vet and scoutmaster who leads the pack in Michael Kimberly's five-performance dud **Almost an Eagle** (12-16-82, Longacre). The aging Colonel assembles his four remaining Boy Scouts in the basement hall of a saloon in Table Rock, Iowa, to practice for the next day's annual Memorial Day cemetery ceremony. Taking swigs of vodka from his hip flask to fortify himself, the old trooper puts the unwilling boys through drills and delivers pep talks even as small-town animosities surface and resentment fills the air. The day after the ceremony (a miserable failure attended by only twenty people), the fellows regroup in the basement and provide support for the old man, who has been dismissed by the locals as incapable of leading Scouts any longer. The unanimously negative reviews could find little good to say even about Whitmore, the only professional aspect to the sorry enterprise.

Michael Cristofer's grim drama **Black Angel** (12-19-82, Circle) failed its somber subject matter (the conscience of a Nazi SS officer), which had been presented so effectively earlier this season with *Good*. Released from prison, Martin Engel (Josef Sommer) returns to the small French village that he commanded during the war hoping to retire in peace and serenity. But the memory of Engel's massacre of 247 Jews has not been forgotten by the local inhabitants, and Engel willingly submits to a group of them when they come hooded and seeking revenge. While a few commentators found the script moving, and others considered the cast worthy (especially Mary McDonnell and Tom Aldridge), the drama did not repeat the success it had enjoyed at the Mark Taper Forum in Los Angeles.

One of the season's greatest disappointments was the Broadway revival of the acclaimed Eva Le Gallienne–Florida Friebus adaptation of *Alice in Wonderland* (12-12-32) on December 23 at the Virginia. All the right elements were in place— John Lee Beatty's exquisite scenery and Patricia Zipprodt's delicious costumes all based on the original John Tenniel drawings, Jennifer Tipton's magical lighting, marvelous puppet work by the Puppet People, a sparkling performance by Kate Burton as Alice, a collection of proficient character actors such as Mary Louise Wilson, John Heffernan, and Curt Dawson, and even eighty-four-year-old Le Gallienne flying through the air as the White Queen—but the result was curiously lifeless and leaden. Some critics blamed the pacing (Le Gallienne directed, as she had in 1932 and again in 1946); others pointed to the outdated Victorian nature of the piece; still others said that audiences could not suffer that particular kind of whimsy anymore. Whatever the reason, the huge revival shuttered after twenty-one performances.

A British play that impressed some aisle-sitters was Catherine Hayes's domestic drama **Skirmishes** (12-21-82, Manhattan Theatre Club), which ran two months off Broadway. While stroke-ridden Mother (Hope Cameron) lies dying in her tiny bedroom in regional England, her two daughters air their long-withheld resentments for each other. Jean (Suzanne Bertish), the slovenly, childless wife of a traveling salesman, has tended to her mother during all her illness, while the younger Rita (Fran Brill), happily married with three children, left long ago and only returns now with a begrudging sense of duty. The two sisters quarrel, thinking the dying Mother cannot hear them, but she can, and, in the final moments, the old lady's scathing opinion of her daughters is made known.

Nicol Williamson dared to banish the ghost of Laurence Olivier and played the seedy music hall performer Archie Rice in the Roundabout's revival of John Osborne's *The Entertainer* (2-12-58) on December 21. Williamson's interpretation of the role was quieter, more cynical, and filled with more self-loathing than the famed Olivier performance. Critics were full of admiration, even if many felt the script had not held up well.

Few of this season's nail-bitingly tense dramas were more uncomfortable than William Mastro-simone's **Extremities** (12-22-82, Cheryl Crawford). In a remote New Jersey farmhouse shared by three single women, Marjorie (Susan Sarandon) is alone when a coarse intruder named Raul (James Russo) enters claiming to be looking for someone named Joe. Before Marjorie can escape, he pulls the telephone cord from the wall, locks the door, and, holding a pillow over her face to quiet her screams, tells Marjorie that he's had his eye on her for some time and is going to rape her and, when they return, her two housemates as well. But Marjorie manages to grab a can of insect repellent; spraying the deadly insecticide into his eyes and mouth, she overpowers Raul, then binds him with ropes and cords and imprisons him in the fireplace. The suffering Raul tells Marjorie that she will never be able to prove rape and swears to return one day and cut her face up. Marjorie, hardened to extremity, now becomes the tormentor and tells Raul that she plans to kill him and bury him in the backyard. When the housemates, Terry (Ellen Barkin) and Patricia (Deborah Hedwall), return, they barely recognize the vengeful Marjorie, question her story, and insist that the police be called. But under duress, Marjorie gets Raul to confess that he has raped several women, has been stalking this farmhouse for some time, and planned to have "a triple header" today. Knowing she has conquered and broken Raul, Marjorie finally allows Patricia to fetch the police. The mixed reviews ranged from "a good nasty, jolting evening of playgoing" to "a feeble play, feebly given, that never lives up to the modest pretensions of its theme." Audiences were not so divided, keeping the disturbing drama going for 325 showings.

With Caryl Churchill's *Cloud 9* (5-18-81) still running, New Yorkers were curious to see her **Top Girls** (12-29-82, Public: Newman), another of the playwright's time-bending comedies about women throughout history. Marlene (Gwen Taylor) has been made managing director of a powerful London employment agency, so she celebrates by having a surreal luncheon with both notable and obscure women from the past: Pope Joan, Lady Nijo, Isabelle Bird, and others. Lunchtime small talk reveals that all these women had to compromise or use vindictive methods to achieve their goals. In subsequent scenes, we see Marlene doing the same thing as she abandons her mentally disabled daughter and teaches her female employees to use aggressive and selfish tactics to succeed. Churchill's dialogue was a vivid mix of overlapping commentary and acute satire, yet the comedy turned very sobering at times. Critical feedback was mostly favorable (though few thought the play as effective as *Cloud 9*), so when the British cast had to return to London, an American ensemble (led by Lise Hilboldt as Marlene) replaced them, keeping the play on the boards for a total of sixteen weeks.

British playwright Anthony Shaffer had a new thriller on Broadway this season, but unlike his wry and literate long-run hit *Sleuth* (11-12-70), **Whodunnit** (12-30-82, Biltmore) was a broad spoof of the genre. Receiving mostly negative notices, it nevertheless hung on for 157 showings. Seven guests arrive at Orcus Champflower Manor on a stormy night, and before long the revolting Andreas Capodistriou (George Hearn) has had a private scene with each of the other guests, claiming to know enough to blackmail them for years. As the others go in to dinner, Andreas kneels to pray in the library. Each guest returns separately, grabs one of the seven swords conveniently hanging on the wall, then hides behind the curtains. When one sword pierces the back of the despicable Levantine (in London the play went by the unfortunate title *The Case of the Oily Levantine*), Scotland Yard is brought in, the suspects are all found to have second identities, and the audience stopped worrying about the plot long before it concluded. Because there was no mystery or chills in the piece, *Whodunnit* depended on comedy. Unfortunately, it was only sporadically funny, but the expert cast did their best to disguise the fact. Hearn was quite accomplished as the unsympathetic victim; Gordon Chater made a marvelous drunken butler, spilling drinks with great precision; Hermione Baddeley was a fine crusty anthropologist; Barbara Baxley was a delightfully stylized upper-class lady; and Fred Gwynne was enjoyable as a Yard inspector who kept reasoning that the stab in the back was obviously suicide.

The vibrant folk tale **Poppie Nongena** (1-12-83, St. Clements) took a long journey before it landed off Broadway, but once it got there it stayed for 131 performances. Based on a true story about a South African servant, the piece was first a popular book by Elsa Jobert, the white employer of Poppie. Sandra Kotze helped Jobert adapt the work into a play that was seen in two different off-off-Broadway mountings before this production directed by South African director Hilary Blecher. We first see Poppie (Thuli Dumakude) as a bright thirteen-year-old on the brink of life. But as the decades pass and she marries and has children, a life of toil and the restrictions of an apartheid state take their toll and nearly destroy Poppie's family and her will power. Presented simply on a bare stage with eight actors (most of them South Africans living in exile in America) playing the many people who move in and out of Poppie's life, the drama featured some spirited singing that gave the folk tale a mythic quality. Reviewers were approving, declaring the little drama "an arresting documentation of the personal effect of the policy of apartheid" and "beyond and above the ordinary experiences of playgoing."

Plays by British playwright Edward Bond continued to cross the Atlantic but refused to catch fire here; such was the case with his **Summer** (1-25-83, Manhattan Theatre Club). During World War II, Xenia (Frances Sternhagen) helped Marthe (Betty Miller) escape from Germany and got her a job as a servant in Xenia's home in England. Years later Xenia returns to the house to find Marthe living there with the servant's own family, and the old friendship crumbles as the past is examined.

When the Circle in the Square revived Molière's *The Misanthrope* on January 27, aisle-sitters unanimously lauded Brian Bedford's Alceste but were less in agreement about the Stephen Porter production. Also in the cast were Mary Beth Hurt (Célimène), David Schramm (Oronte), and Carole Shelley (Arsinoe).

The Negro Ensemble Company's lackluster season opened with Ray Aranha's **Sons and Fathers of Sons** (1-28-83, Theatre Four), an "unstable mixture of mysticism, fantasy, realistic drama, and comedy," according to Oliver, "that never combine into a play." Three generations of discontented African Americans are viewed, first in a Mississippi town in 1943, then ten years later in the same location, and finally in 1960 in a Florida college, where the grandson is still haunted by the family's past.

A "flawlessly cast and directed" revival of Arthur Miller's *A View from the Bridge* (9-29-55) opened on February 3 at the Ambassador and remained for 149 gripping performances. Arvin Brown staged the production, which originated at the Long Wharf Theatre in New Haven and featured Tony Lo Bianco as the tormented longshoreman Eddie Carbone. Just as powerful were Rose Gregorio as his wife, Beatrice, Saundra Santiago as his niece, Catherine, James Hayden as her sweetheart, Rodolpho, Alan Feinstein as the vengeful Marco, and Robert Prosky as the lawyer-narrator, Alfieri.

Though not as popular as some of his other works, A. R. Gurney's **What I Did Last Summer**

(2-6-83, Circle) was one of his most heartfelt efforts. (By this time, Gurney had dropped the Jr. from his name.) Charlie (Ben Siegler), an upper-class teenager, spends the summer of 1945 at a posh Canadian resort on Lake Erie with his mother and sister while his father is fighting in the Pacific. Charlie's Wasp ideals are shaken when he meets the art teacher and radical Anna Trumbull (Julie Bovasso), and soon the youth is rebelling against his family's plans to send him to an exclusive boarding school in the fall. As in his other plays, Gurney captured the white American upper echelon with accuracy, but there was a tenderness in *Summer* that was revealing. Despite reviews calling it "warm, touching and humorous" and a "most compelling sojourn into the discreet heart of America's leisure class," the play was kept on the boards for only thirty-seven performances and has rarely been produced since.

Arthur Bicknell's comedy melodrama **Moose Murders** (2-22-83, Eugene O'Neill) only lasted one performance but quickly became as famous as many a long-run hit. The family of rich and dying Sidney Holloway (Dennis Florzak) has bought Wild Moose Lodge in the Adirondack Mountains for the withered quadriplegic to live out his final days. When family members decide to play a game of "murder" to occupy their time at the lodge, the dull-witted Lauraine (Lillie Robertson) is murdered. Suspected is a legendary "Butcher Moose" that reputedly stalks the wilderness and haunts intruders. Other possible murderers include the Native American caretaker Joe Buffalo Dance (Jack Dabdoub), who talks with an Irish brogue, blind Howie Keene (Don Potter), who keeps tripping over the furniture, Sidney's mean-spirited wife, Hedda (Holland Taylor replacing Eve Arden, who abandoned the play in previews), her drug addict son, Stinky (Scott Evans), who wants to sleep with his mother, and her daughter, Gay (Mara Hobel), who breaks into irritating tap-dancing on occasion. As a thunderstorm rages outside, family members keep being bumped off, and the thriller turns (intentionally or not) into shrill farce. Two scenes in the play quickly became infamous: the comatose Sidney rises from his wheelchair to kick the Butcher Moose in the groin; and (the play's climax) Hedda poisons Gay's vodka martini, and the girl tap-dances herself to death while her mother laughs and applauds hysterically. The only person to emerge with any favorable comments was Marjorie Bradley Kellogg, whose sturdy-timbered lodge interior was filled with ominous stuffed moose heads. Critics had a field day lambasting

the play, and for several seasons after, the name *Moose Murders* was synonymous with a laughable Broadway turkey.

That same night Mabou Mines' production of **Cold Harbor** (2-22-83, Public: Martinson) opened off Broadway and was warmly received by the press, David Sterritt in the *Christian Science Monitor* calling it "a remarkably entertaining event, designed and executed with the mixed-media flourishes that have become a Mabou Mines hallmark." Other critics were equally impressed by the "sharply original piece of Americana" about Ulysses S. Grant. Bill Raymond and Dale Worsley collaborated on the text, using letters, diaries, and memoirs by Grant and his wife, Julia Dent. At first the future president was played by a large robotic puppet reciting excerpts from his memoirs, but then Raymond portrayed the elusive man. The production used creative tableaus, slides, and lively staging to cover his marriage, war years (the title refers to one of his disastrous Civil War battles), presidency, world travels, and lifelong battle with alcoholism.

After Simon Gray's London hit **Quartermaine's Terms** (2-24-83, Playhouse 91) had its American premiere in New Haven, the acclaimed Long Wharf Theatre production was brought to New York, where it beguiled audiences for 375 performances. St. John Quartermaine (Remak Ramsay), a mediocre British schoolteacher, ineffectively tries to teach the language to foreign students at Cambridge's Cull-Loomis School of English. Quartermaine is a likable nonentity, a welcome fixture in the staff room even though his colleagues spend much of their time forgetting that they promised to accompany him to the theatre or canceling dinner dates when something better turns up. As the academic terms come and go, the little school struggles to survive and Quartermaine continues to fumble in the classroom, resulting in the old teacher being politely but firmly dismissed when the school changes headmasters. The play's chief fascination was the enigmatic character of Quartermaine (beautifully captured by Ramsay), a fellow who was, as Gussow described him, "not merely absent-minded, he is absent." Other critics called Quartermaine everything from "alienated" to "a poignant victim" to "simply too good-hearted to suspect the infidelities, rivalries, and submerged relationships that swirl around him."

As he had with *The Goodbye People* (12-3-68), comic Milton Berle returned to the stage in a dramatic vehicle, Walter Landau's **Goodnight, Grandpa** (3-2-83, Entermedia) but, once again, found himself in a short-lived flop. As Isaac (Berle) approaches his one hundredth birthday, he is visited by Morris (Lee Wallace), his friend for over sixty years, and their reminiscences together lead to a series of flashbacks. The play concludes with Grandpa's birthday party, in which some not-so-startling revelations about the past are aired. Aisle-sitters did not blame Berle, who was judged quite capable in the underwritten role, but unanimously dismissed the "non-play" seen previously at some regional theatres. Like the earlier *Goodbye* play, this one only lasted a week.

John Byrne's working-class drama *Slab Boys* (11-19-80) returned to New York in a Broadway revival on March 7 at the Playhouse. Robert Allan Ackerman directed the American cast, which included Kevin Bacon, Sean Penn, Jackie Earle Haley, and Val Kilmer as the disgruntled "slab boys" mixing paints in a carpet factory. Despite a strong production and supportive reviews, the revival ran only six weeks.

Three young American playwrights were the focus of **Triple Feature** (3-8-83, Manhattan Theatre Club), a program of one-acts that ran forty times off Broadway. The most promising of the trio was Harry Kondoleon, whose "tabloid farce" **Slacks and Tops** was set in a motel room near Kennedy Airport where a philandering college professor and his wife are preparing to leave for Africa but are visited by their stoned daughter trying to stop them. The outrageous arguments that follow cover everything from organized religion to the "desiccation of European cities" until the madcap encounter ends in the murder of the parents. Mark Stein's **The Groves of Academe** was a series of short scenes, spread throughout a college semester, between an English professor and his precocious honors seminar student, the two of them questioning the very process of higher education. Stephen Metcalfe's **Half a Lifetime** concerned a group of contemporary teenagers dealing with the explosive problems of youth. While all three playwrights were considered worth watching, only Kondoleon would go on to an electric but tragically short writing career.

The next night New Yorkers were treated to *Marcel Marceau on Broadway*, the renowned French mime's first Manhattan appearance in nearly a decade. Marceau performed for six weeks at the Belasco.

Playwrights Horizons and the American Place joined forces to co-produce Ronald Ribman's five-performance flop **Buck** (3-10-83, American Place),

a play that recalled this season's earlier failure *Inserts*. Writer-director-producer Buck Halloran (Alan Rosenberg) has been reduced to making cheap cable-TV movies about crime and violence, spiced with plenty of sadistic and pornographic touches. In order to get at the "truth," he uses real whores, pimps, and street bums for his cast, but his professional career nosedives even as his personal life is also disintegrating. Such deserving actors as Morgan Freeman, Priscilla Lopez, Jimmy Smits, Joseph Leon, and Madeleine Le Roux played the supporting characters, but audiences and critics found the character of Buck as annoyingly repellent as the script and generally vetoed the whole tasteless venture.

Corrine Jacker's "unconvincing" **Domestic Issues** (3-13-83, Circle) was another in a line of plays about 1960s radicals floundering a few decades later. Activist Stephen Porter (Michael Ayr), who was pardoned for his violent acts through the manipulations of his well-connected older brother Larry (Robert Stattel), decides to write a book about his radical past but is haunted by the image of a fellow revolutionary who was killed when a bomb Stephen was constructing went off prematurely. When Stephen's estranged wife, Ellen (Caroline Kava), still on the run for her record of violence, shows up and tries to rekindle their love and Stephen's political ideology, the former activist is torn between family and a past that will not forsake him.

The Roundabout offered two European revivals in its two performance spaces in March. Tom Kempinski's *Duet for One* (12-17-81) opened on March 15 with Eva Marie Saint as the crippled cellist Stephanie, and although it did not receive much better notices than the play had the previous season with Anne Bancroft in the role, it managed a run of ninety-six showings. Brian Friel's *Winners* (7-25-68) and Shaw's *How He Lied to Her Husband* were teamed together on March 22, and the result was much more accomplished; the two charming one-acts ran for 193 performances.

Some lively dialogue helped to mask the plotting problems of Vaughn McBride's **Elba** (3-22-83, Manhattan Theatre Club) and provided juicy roles for its cast. Don (James Whitmore) and Flo (Audra Lindley) escape from a nursing home in their pajamas and head to their old farmstead in Elba, Idaho, where they break into the boarded-up house and make themselves at home. Soon their grown granddaughters (Ann Wedgeworth and Barbara Sohmers) and a neighbor (Frank

Hamilton) arrive on the scene and, noting their poor health and encroaching senility, talk the old couple into returning to the nursing home.

A. R. Gurney's comic chronicle *The Middle Ages* (3-4-82) opened on March 23 at St. Peter's Church for a commercial run and stayed for 110 showings. With a new director and some cast changes from the off-off-Broadway production, the comedy was declared even better by those critics who had caught its brief run the previous season.

Neil Simon's ailing career took on new life with **Brighton Beach Memoirs** (3-27-83, Alvin), the first of his trilogy of autobiographical plays. Fifteen-year-old Eugene Jerome (Matthew Broderick) lives with his family and assorted relatives in an overcrowded house in the seaside community of Brighton Beach, Brooklyn. "The tension in the air was so thick," Eugene tells the audience, recalling a particularly awful dinner, "that you could cut it with a knife. Which is more than you can say for the liver." He dreams of becoming a writer and narrates the events of the autumn of 1937 from the journal he has been keeping. His mother, Kate (Elizabeth Franz), is a sharp-tongued and unrelenting worker who counts every penny, so when Eugene's older brother, Stanley (Zeljko Ivanek), loses a week's pay gambling and then jeopardizes his job by standing up for a black employee, the household is thrown into a panic. Then Kate's sister, Blanche (Joyce Van Patten), a widow with two daughters, starts to date an Irishman from across the street, and hope springs eternal for all but Kate, who considers him a drunkard and gloats when he later abandons Blanche. This incident brings on the play's biggest confrontation, with years of repressed jealousy and resentment between the two sisters coming to the surface. But Simon's delicate touch and the caustic commentary coming from the mouth of Eugene kept *Brighton Beach Memoirs* from ever getting too grim or uncomfortable. Critics were delighted to see Simon in top form again, and for once they embraced the serious aspects of the show as well as its humor. T. E. Kalem in *Time* noted that "Simon looks back with fondly nourished compassion," and Watt called it his "richest play . . . the funniest and truest." Audiences agreed, and the autobiographical comedy ran 1,530 performances, tying with *Barefoot in the Park* (10-23-63) as the longest Simon run on Broadway. Ironically, the play was not even nominated for a Tony Award (although the committee awarded prizes to Broderick and director Gene Saks), and Guernsey refused to include it as one

MATTHEW BRODERICK (1962–), the son of stage and television actor James Broderick and writer-director Patricia Broderick, was born in New York, attended the Walden School, and studied acting with Uta Hagen before making his stage debut off-off Broadway in *Valentine's Day* (1980). He first gained attention as a troubled teen in the off-Broadway *Torch Song Trilogy* (1981) before making his Broadway debut in *Brighton Beach Memoirs*. Because of his youthful looks, Broderick played roles on stage, television, and film that were much younger than his actual age. Eventually he would graduate to more mature characters, becoming a much-demanded leading man in plays, musicals, and films.

of the ten *Best Plays* of the season, but it did win the New York Drama Critics Award. During the long run of *Brighton Beach Memoirs* the Alvin was renamed the Neil Simon Theatre.

Ming Cho Lee's Tony Award–winning scenery for Patrick Meyers's **K2** (3-30-83, Brooks Atkinson) outshone the two-character drama, yet the play managed a run of eighty-five performances and garnered some appreciative reviews. (Rich proclaimed it "Astounding! The tension is so strong we forget we're in the theatre.") Near the summit of K2, the world's second highest mountain, two climbers have been stranded on a ledge. Harold

GENE [Jean Michael] **SAKS** (1921–) was born in New York City and, after graduating from Cornell University in 1943, studied at the Actors Studio with Lee Strasberg and Sanford Meisner and at the Dramatic Workshop. Saks made his New York acting debut in an off-Broadway revival of *Juno and the Paycock* in 1947 and later that same year was on Broadway as a walk-on in *Topaze*. He turned to directing in the early 1960s, making his Broadway debut with *Enter Laughing* (1963), and went on to stage such successful comedies as *How the Other Half Loves* (1971) and *Same Time, Next Year* (1975), as well as such musical hits as *Mame* (1966) and *I Love My Wife* (1977). Although he directed the film versions of Neil Simon's *Barefoot in the Park* (1967), *The Odd Couple* (1968), and *The Last of the Red Hot Lovers* (1972), his first Broadway Simon assignment was *California Suite* (1976). Saks would go on to direct several subsequent Neil Simon plays, becoming the finest interpreter of the author's works.

(Jay Patterson) has broken his leg in an accident, and his companion, Taylor (Jeffrey DeMunn), attempts to retrieve some rope and other supplies from higher up the mountain so that he can lower his friend down to safety. The happily married Harold philosophizes about his roller-coaster life and the events that brought him here, while Taylor, a brunt district attorney, curses their situation. When all efforts to retrieve the missing equipment fail, Harold insists Taylor save himself and return to tell his wife about how grateful he was to have known her. Taylor at first refuses, but, faced with the reality of death, the two men come to an understanding, and Harold is left chanting words of encouragement to his friend and his family. Lee's set was a massive wall of ice rising up past the proscenium, which Taylor hammered ice nails into and scaled with frightening realism. The play also called for a small avalanche, which covered Harold and left Taylor swinging out over the abyss.

The next night a cliffhanger of a different sort opened. Marsha Norman's intense family drama **'night, Mother** (3-31-83, John Golden) was perhaps the nailbiter of the season as the audience watched the clock on the stage, awaiting the moment they were so dreadfully aware was coming. Middle-aged divorcée Jessie Cates (Kathy Bates) lives with her aging but spry mother, Thelma (Anne Pitoniak), in a small house on a remote country road. After dinner one Saturday night, Jessie calmly tells her mother that at nine o'clock she is going to shoot herself with her father's revolver. At first Thelma thinks it is some sort of joke, but as Jessie explains how she has done all the shopping and made other arrangements to ease the complications after her death, Thelma desperately tries to talk her daughter out of suicide. Jessie's reasons (her failed marriage, an estranged drug-addict son, and her chronic bouts with epilepsy) are clear, unemotional, and alarmingly rational, which only makes the prospect of her suicide more horrible. Thelma threatens to call Jessie's brother or the police to stop her, but Jessie simply states that she will shoot herself before they can get there. With all the preparations made, Jessie tells her mother to call the brother after she hears the shot, then to wash the dishes until he arrives. Jessie says goodnight, locks herself in the bedroom, and, at nine o'clock, pulls the trigger. Thelma numbly makes her phone call as the curtain falls. Notices were exemplary for the play, the cast, director Tom Moore, and his production, which had originated at the American Repertory Theatre in Cam-

bridge, Massachusetts. Brendan Gill in *The New Yorker* wrote, "What a feat of immaculate writing!" and John Simon in *New York* praised the "devastating psychological accuracy" that "gleams with wisdom." The drama ran 388 performances and won the Pulitzer Prize a few months after opening.

Perhaps the most delightful revival of the season was Ellis Rabb's buoyant staging of Kaufman and Hart's *You Can't Take It with You* (12-14-36) on April 4 at the Plymouth. The happy venture was well received critically and at the box office, playing for nine months. Among the many joys of the production was the chance to see two of America's finest tragedians, Jason Robards and Colleen Dewhurst, let loose in an all-American farce. Robards essayed the family patriarch Martin Vanderhof, Dewhurst was the transplanted Russian countess Olga, and they were surrounded by such gifted character actors as Elizabeth Wilson, James Coco, Bill McCutcheon, Alice Drummond, and Rosetta LeNoire.

Edward Albee's **The Man Who Had Three Arms** (4-5-83, Lyceum) was "a curiosity," according to Gill, "not so much a play as a literary exercise that happens to take place in a theatre." Other critics called the work everything from "condescending and smug, occasionally even coy" to "a temper tantrum in two acts." In a lecture hall, a speaker scheduled to talk as part of a series called "Man on Man" has died, so his replacement is introduced. Called Himself (Robert Drivas), the man was once a celebrity because a third arm grew from between his shoulder blades. When the arm withered away, so did his fleeting fame. Himself's talk is a scathing harangue about celebrity, how it corrupted him, how he lost popularity, and how that also corrupted him. The humorlessly numbing evening, directed by Albee, was only repeated sixteen times.

An uneven triple bill titled **About Heaven and Earth** (4-12-83, Theatre Four) was another case of a Negro Ensemble production with superlative acting but problematic writing. Douglas Turner Ward's **The Redeemer** is a mocking comedy about a group of black and white stereotypes that gather at a public picnic grounds on Easter Sunday, all awaiting some modern-day Messiah. Julie Jensen's **Nightline** also presented a multi-racial collection of stereotypes, this time traveling through Michigan on a Greyhound bus, as they deliver a series of monologues about themselves. The title character in Ali Wadad's **Tigus** is a blustering middle-aged African American who, in a long soliloquy delivered while he is dressing to go out dancing with a nineteen-year-old girl, talks about the many women he's had in his life. Although there was much humor to be found in all three pieces, it was performers such as Curt Williams, L. Scott Caldwell, and Ward that justified the evening's program.

William Shakespeare made a belated debut this season when the Royal Shakespeare Company brought its elegant revival of *All's Well That Ends Well* to the Martin Beck on April 13, the first time on record that the problematic work had been done in a Broadway house. Trevor Nunn directed the lavish mounting, set in the Belle Epoque with bejeweled Edwardian costumes and exquisite scenery that moved gracefully from country houses to palaces to the streets of European cities. While Margaret Tyzak (Countess of Rossillion) and Stephen Moore (Captain Parolles) were the most esteemed, the ensemble cast was distinguished down to the last footman. Notices were mostly rapturous, but audiences did not fill the large theatre and the engagement closed after thirty-eight performances.

On April 19, the Acting Company brought its repertory of three revivals to the American Place: a lively *Tartuffe* directed by Brian Murray, a less-than-satisfying *Pericles*, and an evening of Samuel Beckett short plays, again directed by Alan Schneider.

The oddest play to come from Britain (or from anywhere, for that matter) this season was the Americanized version of Claire Luckham's **Teaneck Tanzi: The Venus Flytrap** (4-20-83, Nederlander), a feminist play in the form of a wrestling match. Tanzi (Caitlin Clarke and Deborah Harry alternating in the role), a frustrated New Jersey housewife, has had enough of being subjugated by her brutish husband, Dean Rebel (Scott Renderer and Thomas G. Waites alternating), and confronts her spouse. In a match of ten rounds, the two verbally and physically attack each other in a ring as Tanzi's problematic life is reenacted. A referee (Andy Kaufman) called the count, and the audience was encouraged to shout and cheer by several actors planted in the house. "Grueling, excruciating, chaotic, and woefully amateurish" summed up the critical reaction to the play, which closed after two performances. The Nederlander was the new name for the Trafalgar Theatre, formerly the Billy Rose, but for most of its life known as the National.

An evening of two-character one-acts, also about women in confrontation, called **Win/Lose/Draw** (4-24-83, Provincetown Playhouse) managed to gather some positive reviews but only ran six weeks in a commercial off-Broadway venture. Mary Gallagher's **Chocolate Cake** (considered by the press the most satisfying of the trio) brought a naive country girl and a sophisticated city woman together at a women's conference. All they have in common is their secret lust for food, but soon each reveals layers of disappointment in their very different lives. Ara Watson's **Final Placement** is a desperate plea of a mother guilty of child abuse who tries to win back the custody of her son from a hardened social worker. Watson and Gallagher co-authored **Little Miss Fresno**, a comedy about two competitive mothers at a children's beauty pageant. Although their rivalry is soothed when both of their daughters are selected as winners, the thought of the upcoming finals sets them off again. Christine Estabrook and Lynn Milgrim, who played the three sets of women, were reviewed as favorably as the scripts.

The Manhattan Theatre Club's second triple bill of the season was **Early Warnings** (4-26-83, Manhattan Theatre Club), a program of new works by 1960s avant garde playwright Jean-Claude van Itallie. In **Bag Lady**, a Manhattan street person goes about stuffing her shopping bags with society's debris and commenting on a variety of subjects to passersby. **Sunset Freeway** depicts an actress stuck in traffic while on the way to an audition, oblivious to reports about the end of the world coming over the car radio. Two astronauts in **Final Orders** are told by Mission Control to detonate a nuclear device as their spaceship hurdles uncontrollably into oblivion. While naysayers found the playlets "hopelessly dated" and "dim," others thought them "vintage van Itallie" filled with "highly theatrical imagery and free-flowing dialogue."

A particularly dreary one-night failure on Broadway was Larry Atlas's **Total Abandon** (4-28-83, Booth), a drama about a father, Lenny Keller (Richard Dreyfuss), who, in a moment of irrational rage, brutally beats his two-year-old son, putting him in a coma. Lenny then spends the rest of the evening pleading not to have the child removed from the life support system that keeps him alive. The drama was labeled "preposterous," a "shabby little excuse for a play," and "cheap stuff masquerading as serious-minded drama."

Later in the week Broadway saw another one-performance flop, an inept revival of Terrence McNally's farce *The Ritz* (1-20-75) on May 2 at the Henry Miller. Taylor Reed and Holly Woodlawn headed the unfortunate cast.

Children's author Shel Silvestein came up with a decidedly adult program of three short plays and called it **Wild Life** (5-2-83, Vandam). The most interesting of the playlets was a modern reworking of the *Lady or the Tiger* tale, this time set as a large media event in the Astrodome. The triple bill ran ran six weeks.

Donal Donnelly returned as George Bernard Shaw in his one-man show *My Astonishing Self* (1-18-78) on May 3 at the Players and tossed about Shavian witticisms for five weeks.

Realistic dramatist Thomas Babe attempted a farce this season with **Buried Inside Extra** (5-4-83, Public: Martinson), a *Front Page*–like piece set in a small city newspaper office. The late-night shift has just put the morning edition "to bed" when the editor learns that this will be the last edition of the financially failing newspaper. Then the staff receives word that there is a bomb planted in the building. Chaos ensues, complicated by the return of the editor's ex-wife. In the end, the bomber is exposed, the bomb is defused, but the newspaper still goes under. Producer Papp assembled a proficient cast (Hal Holbrook, Sandy Dennis, Dixie Carter, Vincent Gardenia, William Converse-Roberts) and directed the play himself. Aisle-sitters generally thought little of the script, calling it "murky" and "senseless in almost every aspect." After its scheduled month at the Public, the production transferred to London's Royal Court for six weeks as part of an exchange that brought the British *Top Girls* to New York. Most commentators felt it was not a very equitable exchange.

Herman Wouk's *The Caine Mutiny Court-Martial* (1-20-54) received its first Broadway revival on May 5 at the Circle in the Square. Critics agreed that the script "remains a vigorous and agreeable feat of theatrical writing," and audiences enjoyed the theatrics for 213 performances. Michael Moriarty was a younger and more refined Queeg, while John Rubinstein's defense attorney Greenwald was sly in a more modern way, but both fulfilled the juicy roles. They received able support from William Atherton, Stephen Joyce, Jonathan Hogan, Brad Sullivan, and others. Less accomplished but just as juicy were Elizabeth Taylor and Richard Burton in a much talked-about revival of Noel Coward's *Private Lives* (1-27-31) on May 8 at the Lunt-Fontanne. To see the world's most famous divorced couple play the bantering ex-spouses Amanda and Elyot was something more akin to a sideshow attraction than a Broadway comedy of manners. As Rich noted, "nothing that happened at any time has

any bearing on Coward's classic comedy." Director Milton Katselas quit before opening and was not replaced. John Cullen and Katheryn Walker essayed the secondary couple of Sibyl and Victor bravely. Ticket sales were initially strong, but by late June the show was on twofers and it closed after sixty-three performances. Sadly, it was Burton's last New York appearance; he died a year later.

Peter Nichols's **Passion** (5-15-83, Longacre) was called *Passion Play* when it premiered at the Royal Shakespeare Company in England. A first-rate New York cast, directed by Marshall W. Mason, further Americanized this tale of adultery by the time it reached Broadway. James (Bob Gunton) is married to Eleanor (Cathryn Damon) but has fallen in love with the sensual and younger Kate (Roxanne Hart). What made the familiar triangular situation unique was the presence of Jim (Frank Langella) and Nell (E. Katherine Kerr), the married couple's alter egos, who revealed the characters' true feelings. The same device had been employed in Brian Friel's *Philadelphia, Here I Come!* (2-16-66), and Eugene O'Neill had used a similar technique in *Strange Interlude* (1-30-28), in which the characters spoke both their public and private thoughts. *Passion* received generally commendable reviews (especially for the cast), running ninety-seven performances.

Bertie Wooster, his valet Jeeves, and a handful of other wacky and delicious P. G. Wodehouse characters were all portrayed by Edward Duke in his compilation called **Jeeves Takes Charge** (5-17-83, City Center). The London import was highly British in temperament, but enough Americans were Wodehouse fans to let the happy show run eighty-three times.

Twice as loud and running half as long was **Egyptology: My Head Was a Sledgehammer** (5-17-83, Public: Other Stage), Richard Foreman's latest and, according to the press, most cluttered and abstract theatre piece yet. A 1920s aviatrix lands in the Egyptian desert and launches a series of tableaux, scattered dialogue, comic bits, and socio-political ideas, all accompanied by crashing sounds.

The Negro Ensemble closed its season with Gus Edwards's **Manhattan Made Me** (5-17-83, Theatre Four), a satiric and highly cynical piece about interracial relationships in the city. African-American Barry Anderson (Eugene Lee) is a close friend with the white couple Alan (David Davies) and Claire McKenzie (Kathleen Forbes), so much so that when Alan goes to California to make a TV pilot, Barry moves in with Claire and the two have a torrid affair. When Alan returns, they kick him out, Alan sinks in despair to the gutter, and Barry becomes the art director of a prestigious publishing house. But soon Claire tires of Barry and takes up with black derelict Duncan (Robert Gossett), an old buddy of Barry's, and the discarded Barry is soon on the street with Alan. Critics complained of the lack of style in the production, the uneven writing, and the miscasting of some of the roles.

Lee Kalcheim's **Breakfast With Les and Bess** (5-19-83, Lamb's) was a throwback to a simpler and more civilized time, both in its subject matter and in its temperament. Audiences responded to the "sweetly old-fashioned, wisecracking, almost screwball comedy" for 159 performances. Les Dischinger (Keith Charles) and his wife, Bess (Holland Taylor), have a genteel morning radio show in which civilized talk and behavior reign. But it is 1961, the world is changing, and such shows are becoming passé. Behind the congenial facade, the Dischinger family is coming apart at the seams. The radio show is about to be canceled and, in all probability, so is the marriage. Their son, David (John Leonard), is turning into a radical, and daughter Shelby (Kelle Kipp) is running around with a sailor. But amidst all these shenanigans, Les and Bess continue to display a sophisticated calm on the airwaves.

Caryl Churchill's second play at the Public this season, **Fen** (5-24-83, LuEsther), seemed a departure from her previous works, yet a feminist viewpoint was still evident. In England's fen country, a group of women take to the land and live in a community where one's ability to survive is more important than one's gender. As various women assert their independence (one leaves her husband and children, another finds religion, still another battles a willful farmer for her rights), a vivid portrait of the indomitability of women is created. The "wonderful and strange play" received some commendatory notices and, although only scheduled for two weeks at the Public, was extended to July.

The season's last offering was one of its most popular: Sam Shepard's **Fool for Love** (5-26-83, Circle), which had previously been presented at San Francisco's Magic Theatre. In a Spartan motel room on the edge of the Mojave Desert, short-order cook May (Kathy Baker) is visited by rodeo professional Eddie (Ed Harris), her off-and-on lover for some years. The two battle physically and verbally as their passion for one another turns them into deadly and revengeful animals. Outside on the porch, an Old Man (Will Mar-

chetti) sits in a rocker sipping whiskey and commenting on the action inside. When the hapless young Martin (Dennis Ludlow) arrives to take May on a date to the movies, Eddie verbally lashes out at him, humiliates the frighten suitor, and then reveals that May is Eddie's half sister. Martin runs off, and the two incestuous lovers continue their tempestuous love affair. Oliver wrote, "It is as mysterious and unsettling—now you see it, now you don't—as spare and, incidentally, as funny as anything [Shepard] has ever done," and most critics agreed with her, calling *Fool for Love* "furiously funny, unnerving, engaging" and "a very wise, courageous and sexy play." Shepard, who had often fought with producers and directors of his works, staged the play himself, and it ran an even 1,000 performances.

1983–1984

Those still maintaining the illusion that New York was the main source of new plays in the American theatre were sorely shaken this season. Not only did fewer works open on Broadway than in any season in the past century and a half, but those that did were mostly from Europe and regional theatres. Only eight new American plays appeared on Broadway (a drop by almost half from the previous season) and thirty off Broadway (a slightly lower drop from 1982–1983). But the seven revivals on Broadway and the twenty-five off were generally of higher quality than in previous seasons, and masterpieces by Eugene O'Neill, Tennessee Williams, and Arthur Miller were all present on the Street for decent runs.

As was often the case, British actors and playwrights dominated the season. Even the best American play of the season, David Mamet's *Glengarry Glen Ross*, had been seen in London first. Regionally, Chicago sent no fewer than eight works to New York, and even Louisville could claim three entries. Whereas in the past a sizable number of Broadway shows originated off Broadway, so now a considerable portion of off-Broadway productions came from off-off Broadway.

There were more musicals this season than usual, so the total of only twenty-one non-musicals on Broadway (a record low) looked puny indeed. And with the average top ticket price on the Street at $32.50 for non-musicals, theatre lovers started to worry that comedies and dramas on Broadway would disappear altogether. Ironically, the best of the fewer offerings were very good indeed, and while attendance numbers shrank somewhat, those who went to the theatre saw some exceptional works.

Seven short stories by *New Yorker* author Donald Barthelme provided the material for **Great Days** (6-7-83, American Place), which could not escape its literary roots but did provide a vehicle for some agile performers, including Paul Collins, Penelope Allen, Catherine Byers, Jeanne Ruskin, and James Greene. All the scenes were duets, the two most memorable being a jazz-accompanied scene in which two brothers list everything that their mother did not allow and a conversation in a train where two travelers confess to each other all the unusual things that frighten them.

The Roundabout Theatre's "pleasant" revival of Eugene O'Neill's *Ah, Wilderness!* (10-2-23) on June 14 was a diverting, if uninspired, summer attraction for six weeks. Cited for their fine performances were Philip Bosco as the family patriarch Nat Miller, Scott Burkholder as his son Richard, and Robert Nichols as Uncle Sid.

A program of one-acts with the self-explanatory title **Samuel Beckett's Ohio Impromptu, Catastrophe, What Where** (6-15-83, Harold Clurman) introduced to New York three short works by the celebrated absurdist, and the trio remained off Broadway for a surprising 350 performances. In *Ohio Impromptu*, a Reader (David Warrilow) and a Listener (Rand Mitchell) engage in reading and listening to a love story that ends prematurely with the visitation of death. (The title refers to the play's world premiere at Ohio State University in 1981.) *Catastrophe*, an homage to Czech playwright (and later president) Vaclav Havel, shows a tyrannical government official (Donald Davis) as he instructs his assistant (Margaret Reed) on how to prepare a symbolic victim (Warrilow) for public exhibition. Four figures in the shadows insisted throughout *What Where* that they had tortured a prisoner but got no confession out of him, even as a voice continues to command them to torture him further. Beckett master Alan Schneider directed, as he would another Beckett program later in the season.

The Pan Asian Repertory Theatre, an off-off-Broadway troupe dedicated to producing new plays about the Asian-American experience, had such a hit with R. A. Shimoi's **Yellow Fever** (16-16-83, 47th Street) last season that they brought it to Off Broadway, where it caught on and stayed for 138 performances. Sam Spade–like private eye Sam Shikaze (Donald Li) works in the Japanese section of Vancouver, where he investigates the kidnapping of Miss Cherry Blossom only to uncover an anti-Asian plot to stop the spread of emigrating Asians, or "yellow fever." While the play was a spoof of the detective genre, it also had its social digs, such as when Sam explains in a deadpan commentary how during World War II he was put on a train "to summer camp in winter."

The Broadway season started with a fumble, Howard Reifsnyder's **The Guys in the Truck** (6-19-83, New Apollo), which closed on opening night. Television director Al Klein (Harris Laskawy) sits in a truck parked outside the Cleveland football stadium and tries to run the broadcast of a game while his life is falling apart: his wife is threatening to leave him, the station's kid producer wants to fire him, a hitman is after him to collect his gambling debts, and his stripper girlfriend takes to the field and does her act. The farce had been seen briefly off-off Broadway the previous season; the revised version was judged bigger but less funny. Movie actor Elliot Gould had been cast as Klein but was fired during previews. His understudy, Laskawy (who had played the role originally), replaced him, gathering the only compliments in the sorry fiasco.

Ann Jellicoe's *The Knack* (5-27-64) received its first New York revival on June 21. The Roundabout production struck some critics as "tame and rather listless," and others thought the play about an early 1960s make-out artist had not dated well. Daniel Gerroll was the actor most often singled out for praise, and audiences kept him employed for ninety-six performances. In Central Park, Kevin Kline essayed *King Richard III* on June 30, at the outdoor Delacorte but it did not go down as one of his finest moments. Much more satisfying was Madeline Potter's vivid Lady Anne. The self-titled "Naked Civil Servant" revised and revived his *An Evening with Quentin Crisp* (12-20-78) on July 14 at the Actors Playhouse and entertained audiences (and their questions) for two months.

Estelle Parsons had shown how deftly she could hold an audience in a solo performance with *Miss Margarida's Way* (7-31-77). This season she went a step further, performing a solo turn in **Orgasmo Adulto Escapes from the Zoo** (8-2-83, Public: Newman), which took two nights to cover all its eight monodramas. An English version of an Italian play by Dario Fo and Franca Rame, this specialty program explored eight diverse women, ranging from mothers to whores, in a highly satirical manner that recalled Parsons's maniacal Margarida. The two parts were presented for a total of sixty performances.

Broadway's first revival of the season was a misconceived *The Corn Is Green* (11-26-40) on August 22 at the Lunt-Fontanne. Acclaimed African-American actress Cecily Tyson played Emlyn Williams's Welsh schoolteacher, Miss Moffat, and, as Brendan Gill in *The New Yorker* pointed out, "she [was] not so miscast as mistaken in her understanding of the role." To some, the drama's selfless champion became a "charmless busybody" in this version. When Tyson took off on a trip with her husband without telling the producers, missing a performance on September 8, they fired the actress, and her understudy completed the last two weeks of the run. (Interestingly, Tyson was later awarded $600,000 in damages when the dispute was brought to an arbitrator.) Off Off Broadway saw a controversial *Uncle Vanya* on August 30 at La Mama that reduced the play (in an adaptation by Jean-Claude van Itallie) into a ninety-minute one-act that Andrei Serban staged as a nightmare with hysterical characters running across Santo Loquasto's barren set filled with sunken pits. The only thing aisle-sitters agreed on was the expert performance by F. Murray Abraham as Dr. Astrov.

A product of the Actors Theatre of Louisville that did not catch fire in New York was Kathleen Tolan's **A Weekend Near Madison** (9-13-83, Astor Place), a tragicomedy lasting only two weeks. A group of college friends from the 1960s gather twenty years later to thrash out the past and to see Vanessa (Mary McDonnell), the feminist lesbian of the group, who has become a famous rock singer. It turns out the only reason "Nessa" has come to the reunion is because she and her waif-like lover, Samantha (Holly Hunter), are looking for a man to father their child. But the singer unwisely approaches her former lover Jim (Randle Mell), and recriminations over the past come spilling out. While some reviewers thought the piece "warm, vital, glowing" and the new playwright one of "sharp perceptions, humor, and tender sensibilities," others felt it "doesn't add up to much of a play."

Charles Ludlam's outrageous spoof **Galas** (9-13-83, One Sheridan Square) was one of the most notable offerings off-off Broadway this season, running 190 performances and joining the repertoire of favorites at the Ridiculous Theatrical Company. American opera diva Maria Magdalena Galas (Ludlam) tours Europe, falls for the wealthy shipowner Aristotle Plato Socrates Odysseus (John Heys), then lives passionately and tragically before committing suicide in Paris. The grand and satirical style of the company was find-

ing a wider audience, but there was still something subversively "off-off" about Ludlam and his works.

Several complaints surrounded the Roundabout's revival of Ibsen's *The Master Builder* on September 20, some concerning the "flat" new adaptation by Gene Feist, others regarding the "dim and lifeless" production itself. Two actresses, Laurie Kennedy (Hilda) and Joan Potter (Mrs. Solness), rose above the rest of the cast, and the Roundabout subscribers kept the drama on the boards for eleven weeks.

As if coming to New York in British plays and dazzling audiences wasn't enough, English actors Ben Kingsley and Ian McKellen each came this season without a play and still collected a trunkful of rave reviews. Kingsley's vehicle was **Edmund Kean** (9-27-83, Brooks Atkinson), a monodrama of sorts by Raymund Fitzsimons that only came to life when Kingsley performed pieces in the supposed style of the nineteenth-century star. At these moments the actor overcame his "unexpectedly ramshackle" vehicle and treated audiences to the sort of "flashes of lightning" that Kean was so famous for.

The tireless Roundabout had a winner with its third production of the young season on September 27. This first revival of Frank Marcus's *The Killing of Sister George* (10-5-66) boasted strong performances by Aideen O'Kelly as the title soap opera star and Tandy Cronyn as her sheepish lover, Childie. The comedy-drama played into March, the longest run of the Roundabout season. Just as skillful, though running only a third as long, was the Manhattan Theatre Club's mounting of Christopher Hampton's *The Philanthropist* (5-15-71) on the same night. The "stylish and spirited" production featured a cunning performance by David McCallum and expert support by Anthony Heald, Brent Spiner, Glenne Headly, Robin Bartlett, and Cherry Jones.

An Irish import by John B. Keane called **Big Maggie** (9-28-83, Douglas Fairbanks) claimed to be one of the most-produced works in its homeland, but forty-six showings off Broadway proved to be plenty in New York. Widowed Maggie Polpin (Robin Howard) looks upon the burial of her husband as her ticket to independence. She gets hold of the old man's money, puts her life, and the lives of her four grown children, in order, and, against their wishes, tries to keep the family together. But the headstrong mother only succeeds in alienating her children, all of whom abandon her by the end of the play. The "harsh comedy" met with either gentle approval ("oddly entertaining") or distaste ("soap opera"). Also, several aisle-sitters stated that the American cast struggled noticeably with the Irish dialect.

Eric Bogosian, who would make a name for himself in one-man shows that he wrote, directed, and performed, first came to the attention of New Yorkers with his **Fun House** (9-29-83, Actors' Playhouse), which ran nine weeks in a commercial offering off Broadway. Bogosian worked like a stand-up comic, yet he portrayed specific characters, which were sharply written and illustrated a theme running through the evening. This offering concentrated on society's odd or threatening figures, finding humor and scathing honesty in the portrayals.

The Public Theatre presented Len Jenkin's picaresque **My Uncle Sam** (10-11-83, Other Stage) for a run of only two weeks, but during that time it managed to attract some critical attention. In a series of short, abstract scenes, Young Sam (R. Hamilton Wright) goes in search of the true story of his novelties salesman uncle Sam (Mark Margolis), who died in a Pittsburgh hotel and left a past littered with clues and quixotic stories. Young Sam's journey, interrupted by appearances by landscape architect Capability Brown (Rocco Sisto), who discusses gardens, takes him everywhere from a solitary lighthouse to a menacing opium den to a cockeyed miniature golf course, and soon the young nephew develops into a second version of the larger-than-life salesman. Jenkins directed, and John Arnone provided the imaginatively lopsided scenery.

New Haven's Long Wharf Theatre's revival of David Mamet's *American Buffalo* (2-16-77), which was a hit off Broadway in 1981, reappeared on Broadway on October 27 at the Booth and chalked up another 102 performances. Once again Al Pacino starred.

David Henry Hwang continued to fascinate off-Broadway audiences even though his program of one-acts entitled **Sound and Beauty** (11-6-83, Public: LuEsther) was not up to his earlier efforts. **The House of Sleeping Beauties**, a fantasy based on a story by Yasunari Kawabata, told of a novelist (Victor Wong) who visits a famous brothel to research a story but is mesmerized by the unerotic practices going on there in which old men find comfort sleeping in the arms of beautiful drugged women. Soon the writer is facing his own mortality and asks the madam for a potion that will allow him to sleep indefinitely. **The Sound of a Voice** is a folk tale inspired by a Japanese legend about a samurai (John Lone) who seeks out a woman (Natsuko Ohama) suspected

of being a witch, hoping to kill her and bring glory to his name. But when the young soldier meets her, he is fascinated by her beauty and warm hospitality and becomes her lover. Later he decides to leave her in her cottage in the woods and spare her life, but destruction rains down on both of them. Hwang's use of Asian theatre techniques was again evident in the staging by Lone, and some critics found the ritualistic plays "gently mocking" and "significantly closer to perfect pitch."

When Christopher Durang, the era's favorite "bad boy" of playwrights, took aim at childrearing in **Baby With the Bathwater** (11-8-83, Playwrights Horizons), his scattered attack on parenthood elicited embarrassed laughter for eighty-four performances. After the frustrated romance writer Helen (Christine Estabrook) gives birth to a baby rather than a hit novel, she and her husband, John (W. H. Macy), are disappointed and name it Daisy without bothering to check the infant's true sex. Daisy (Keith Reddin) is raised by a Nanny (Dana Ivey) who engages in sex with John while she gives the baby lethal toys made of asbestos and Red Dye No. 2 to play with. Despite a bad habit of throwing himself in front of buses, Daisy miraculously reaches maturity. His analyst encourages him to stop wearing dresses and pursue the opposite sex, which he does with uncontained abandon. Finally he marries, has a child, and faces the task of trying not to destroy another newcomer to the human race. Highly stylized and comic-strip in tone (Loren Sherman's popout sets were very droll), the satire was so exaggerated that some critics found the play less potent than Durang's earlier efforts. Regardless, most commentators still saw the playwright as "one of the funniest dramatists alive," who "finds a way to turn rage into comedy that is redemptive as well as funny."

Broadway's second one-night dud of the young season was George Sibbald's family drama **Brothers** (11-9-83, Music Box), starring and directed by television favorite Carroll O'Connor in his Broadway debut. Tyrannical union boss Jim (O'Connor) has bullied his four sons over the years. When Tommy (Dennis Christopher) is smitten with a kidney disease and needs a blood-related donor, only his brother Harry (Frank Converse) is diagnosed as compatible. At first Harry agrees, but on the night before the transplant, he changes his mind. His decision grows from having been taught by his father to always look out for yourself and never jeopardize your own welfare. The "dreary play about a dreary family" was roundly dismissed by the press. Converse was well reviewed, but O'Connor's bluster was only appreciated by a few critics; Howard Kissell in *Women's Wear Daily* wrote that the drama "is too lame to be considered anything but a 'star vehicle,' but it really doesn't even provide much gas for the vehicle to go anyplace."

The Public hosted an evening of satiric one-acts by Czech dissident Vaclav Havel under the umbrella title **A Private View** (11-20-83, Public: Martinson), and off-Broadway audiences came for ninety-six performances. (The title was an inside joke: Havel's plays were outlawed in his native country and had to be performed in private homes.) The playlet **Interview** shows the brewery worker Vanek (Stephen Keep), an autobiographical character who appears in all three pieces, being bribed by his drunken boss to spy on his fellow workers. Vanek keeps refusing; the boss keeps passing out from drink, then recovering to start the interview all over again. In the title work, Vanek, now unemployed, visits a prosperous family who urge him to give up his dissident ways. In **Protest,** Vanek tries to convince a successful but wary television writer to sign a petition to free his own daughter's lover, who has been arrested for writing outspoken songs against the state. Don Nelson in the *Daily News* led the complimentary reviews, calling the evening "a salutary example of political theatre as fine entertainment."

Tina Howe's most successful effort to date was **Painting Churches** (11-22-83, Lamb's), which had been seen briefly off-off Broadway last season and was given a commercial run of 206 performances this season. Margaret Church (Elizabeth McGovern), a fledgling artist who returns to her family home in Boston, has always wanted to paint her parents' portrait. Her father, Gardner (George N. Martin), is a renowned poet who is gently slipping into senility and is begrudgingly cared for by Margaret's frustrated mother, Fanny (Marian Seldes). The old couple are preparing to move out of their expensive Boston residence to reside permanently in their summer home on Cape Cod because Gardner can no longer write poetry or give readings and funds are shrinking. But "Mags" seems oblivious to the reality of their situation and concentrates on the painting. Over the next few days the painting and the packing progress, but not without old wounds being opened and Mags coming to realize how fragile her parents' situation is. The generally laudatory reviews announced a "radiant, loving and zestfully humorous play" and called Howe "one of our most incisive and original dramatists." The performers were also endorsed, as was Heidi Landesman's clever setting in which paint-splattered drop cloths turned into walls and doorways.

The Negro Ensemble Theatre's abbreviated season began with Pearl Cleage's surreal **Puppetplay** (11-23-83, Theatre Four), set against jazz riffs played by Wendell Brooks on the saxophone. Two young and attractive women (Seret Scott and Phylicia Ayers-Allen) wait on a male puppet, feeding him, dressing him, and even sleeping with him to keep him company. Their slavery to the puppet has begun to affect their own puppetlike movements until they break away and free themselves, realizing that it is their own fears that held them in bondage. Edith Oliver in *The New Yorker* was among the play's supporters, commenting that the "writing is spare, lucid, occasionally witty and occasionally poetic."

The Circle Repertory Company's opener, a revival of Chekhov's *The Sea Gull* on November 25 at the American Place, met with mixed reviews. Only John Lee Beatty's evocative sets were unanimously approved of. Barbara Cason essayed Arkadina, Richard Thomas was Treplev, and Judd Hirsch was Trigorin.

C. P. Taylor, the British author of last season's *Good* (10-13-82), had died in 1981 but left a tender domestic drama called **And a Nightingale Sang . . .** (11-27-83, Mitzi E. Newhouse), which was a surprise hit at Lincoln Center. Helen Stott (Joan Allen), a plain and overlooked woman who is partially lame, narrates the events of the play about her Newcastle family during World War II. While her Granda (Robert Cornthwaite) rails against Hitler, her father, George (John Carpenter), starts to embrace Communism, and her mother, Peggy (Beverly May), tries to keep the household together through prayer. Helen embarks on a romance with a soldier named Norman (Peter Friedman), who turns out to be married but insists he loves Helen. Set against the troublesome marriage of her sister, Joyce (Moria McCanna Harris), and her new husband, Eric (Francis Guinan), Helen's affair ends just as victory is declared and Norman returns to his wife and child. Punctuated by period songs, which George played and sang at the family piano, the drama had a warm, nostalgic air about it. While the critics were divided in their opinions, from "a treasure of a play" to "a wasted effort," audiences were pleased with it for 177 performances.

As with all his other works, Michael Cristofer's **The Lady and the Clarinet** (11-28-83, Lucille Lortel) premiered at Los Angeles's Mark Taper Fo-

STOCKARD [née Susan Williams Antonia Stockard] CHANNING (1944–), the daughter of a shipping executive, was born in Manhattan to a wealthy and cultured family. After graduation from Radcliffe College in 1965, she went on the stage, making her professional debut as Stockard Channing (she took her stage name from her first husband, Walter Channing) the next year in *The Investigation* at the Theatre Company of Boston. Her New York debut was in *Adaptation/Next* in 1970, and she was on Broadway the next year as a member of the chorus in the musical *Two Gentlemen of Verona*. In 1973 Channing went to California, where she made a series of mostly unsuccessful films, briefly had her own network television show, and appeared in many plays in the Los Angeles area. She returned to the East Coast in 1981 and slowly became recognized as a formidable actress, equally adept at comedy, drama, and musical theatre. Channing excels at playing rich, smart, and articulate women.

rum, where it was directed by Gordon Davidson. Since Cristofer's *The Shadow Box* (3-31-77), none of his efforts had found success in New York, and this entry only managed to run five weeks off Broadway. Successful businesswoman Luba (Stockard Channing) has hired a clarinet player (Jay Dryer) to entertain her male guest during an intimate dinner in her apartment. While she waits for her new flame and as the clarinetist plays away, Luba recalls in flashback three men from her past: Paul (Kevin Geer), her father's employee who first introduced her to sex; TV producer Jack (Paul Rudd), who would not leave his wife for Luba; and George (Josef Sommer), an elderly widower who adored her but could not remain faithful. The play ends before Luba's latest beau arrives, but the sounds coming from the clarinet and the musician's gentle shrugs suggest another romantic dead end. The most notable aspect of *The Lady and the Clarinet* was the realization that movie starlet Channing was developing into one of the most accomplished actresses of the American theatre.

Two superlative revivals opened on Broadway in December. Tennessee Williams's *The Glass Menagerie* (3-31-45) on the first of the month brought Jessica Tandy as Amanda to the Eugene O'Neill, and she was cheered by the press and the public. Gill noted that she "brings to the role of Amanda Wingfield a vigor and sometimes an asperity that greatly adds to the robustness of the play." John Dexter staged the "exemplary production," which

featured Amanda Plummer (Laura), Bruce Davison (Tom), and John Heard (Jim) and ran ninety-two times. On December 7, Shaw's *Heartbreak House*, in a production that had originated in London, opened at the Circle in the Square with Rex Harrison joining an American cast for sixty-six performances. Harrison's Captain Shotover was the last great performance of his career, a sly, wistful, and intoxicating portrayal that filled the intimate space with warmth and intelligence. There was also a glowing performance by Amy Irving as the young Ellie, and the scenes between her and Harrison were considered by some commentators to be the finest moments of the season. Also in the distinguished cast were Rosemary Harris, Philip Bosco, Dana Ivey, Jan Miner, William Prince, and Stephen McHattie. The expert director was Anthony Page, and Marjorie Bradley Kellogg designed a wonderfully nautical drawing-room setting for the three-quarter space.

A new company, the Mirror Theatre, presented five revivals in repertory beginning with Clifford Odets's rarely seen *Paradise Lost* (12-9-35) on December 10 at the Real Stage. Geraldine Page and Madeline Sherwood were the "name" performers in the company, and both were featured in the Depression-era drama about a Jewish family torn apart by the outside world. The even rarer *The Inheritors* (3-21-21), Susan Glaspell's drama about compromise in the world of academia, joined the repertory on December 11. The Odets drama was performed ninety-two times, the Glaspell piece forty-seven times.

British bedroom farce had rarely transferred successfully from London to New York, so it was surprising that Michael Frayn's **Noises Off** (12-11-83, Brooks Atkinson), a backstage look at the kind of comedies Broadway had shunned, should become such a hit on the Street and run 553 performances. *Noises Off* works on two levels: it presents an addlebrained sex farce being performed by a second-rate company of actors, and it also illustrates the ridiculous (but accurate) trials of rehearsal and touring such a piece. During the final dress rehearsal of *Nothing On* (the farce within the farce), leading lady Dotty Otley (Dorothy Loudon) has trouble remembering her mindless blocking, and ancient actor Selsden Mowbray (Douglas Seale) takes to drink and keeps wandering off. Meanwhile, harried director Lloyd Dallas (Brian Murray) tries to soothe the high-strung tempers of Dotty's "toy boy," Garry Lejeune (Victor Garber), method actor Frederick Fellowes (Paxton Whitehead), and Lloyd's young mistress, Poppy (Amy Wright). The second act shows the same farce from backstage as it is being performed on tour, the company at odds with one another and dealing with a series of mishaps. In the third act, *Nothing On* (seen onstage once again) has disintegrated into an all-out battle with actors sabotaging each other, lines being rewritten, and multiple understudies trying to keep the show going. Michael Blakemore directed the American cast with precision and ingenuity (the second act, practically wordless, was a brilliantly sustained pantomime), and all involved garnered rave reviews, summed up by Jack Kroll in *Newsweek* as "the most complicated farce ever devised by the mind of man—and one of the funniest."

Lee Kalcheim's **Friends** (12-12-83, Manhattan Theatre Club) pitted two old Yale roommates against each other as they enter male menopause. Harold "Okie" Peterson (Craig T. Nelson), a respected diplomat with a wife, two kids, and a chance at an ambassadorial post, visits the Vermont cabin of society dropout Mel Simon (Ron Silver), who scratches out a living drawing occasional comic strips for the *Village Voice*. Okie starts by trying to buck up the lonely Mel, but soon the successful man breaks down and admits he suffers from depression and has even attempted suicide. Soon the two men have switched places and Mel is saving Okie.

After Wendy Wasserstein made some revisions to her comedy *Isn't It Romantic* (5-28-81), a sparkling new production directed by Gerald Gutierrez opened on December 15 at Playwrights Horizons, where it ran 733 performances. Cristine Rose and Lisa Banes played the wayward college grads, Betty Comden (in her non-musical debut) and Jo Henderson their mothers, and Chip Zien and Jerry Lanning the men in their up-and-down lives. Notices were mostly supportive, calling the new version "nouvelle cuisine comedy" and "bright, funny, sentimental and, throughout, inching toward wisdom." On December 20, two Americans (Marsha Mason and Jane Alexander) donned English accents and held their own with Brit Anthony Hopkins in the Roundabout's "commendable" production of Harold Pinter's *Old Times* (11-16-71). It was the first New York revival of the enigmatic comedy, and it played ninety times (nearly as long as the original).

Conrad Bishop and Elizabeth Fuller's drama **Full Hookup** (12-29-83, Circle) dealt with domestic violence in a gritty, sadly ironic way. Rosie (Jacqueline Brookes), a middle-aged bookkeeper, has escaped from her marriage to an abusive alcoholic with the help of her lover, Les (Edward Seamon), who refuses to leave his wife and

marry Rosie. So she seeks fulfillment in religion and numerology and takes in her daughter, Beth (Sharon Schlarth), when she flees from her jealous and abusive husband, Ric (Steve Bassett). Ric comes to Rosie's house to beg forgiveness from Beth but instead explodes with jealousy and kills her. Rosie finds the body but, instead of taking revenge on Ric, lies to the police and hires a lawyer to help Ric get off. He does, and the play ends with each of them starting a new life and forgetting the past.

The new year brought the finest new play of the season. Tom Stoppard's most conventional comedy (and, consequently, his most popular, at 566 performances) was **The Real Thing** (1-5-84, Plymouth), a look at love that was as lucid and dazzling as his previous forays into Marxism, Shakespeare, moral philosophy, and journalism. West End playwright Henry (Jeremy Irons in his Broadway debut) writes droll comedies of superficial brilliance (a scene from his most recent hit opens the play) and is married to actress Charlotte (Christine Baranski), who is starring in his play with Max (Kenneth Welsh). Henry is having an affair with Max's activist wife, Annie (Glenn Close), who is protesting the unjust jailing of a Scottish militant named Brodie (Vyto Ruginis). When their infidelity is discovered, Max and Charlotte obtain divorces, leaving Henry and Annie to wed, trying to discover a love more real than that they experienced in their previous marriages. When Henry and Annie quarrel over the Brodie issue (she wants Henry to help rewrite a dreadful play Brodie has penned), Annie has a brief affair with the young actor Billy (Peter Gal-

> **GLENN CLOSE** (1947–), the daughter of a surgeon, was born in Greenwich, Connecticut, and attended the College of William and Mary, graduating with a B.A. in drama in 1974. That same year she made her Broadway debut in a small role in a revival of *Love for Love* and appeared in several classic productions by the New Phoenix Repertory Company. Close had featured roles in such plays and musical as *Rex* (1976), *Barnum* (1980), and *The Crucifer of Blood* (1978) without attracting too much attention. But her film career, which began with a memorable performance in *The World According to Garp* (1982), brought her a reputation as a serious actress, and her stage roles became more challenging. The angular beauty would specialize in intelligent characters and refined older women, and she managed to maintain full careers both on the stage and in film.

lagher) before returning to Henry, the two of them dealing with the pain of "the real thing." The traditional plot was elevated to rare heights by the play's ingenious dialogue that recalled Noel Coward but had the searing honesty of the "kitchen sink" dramas. Scenes in which Henry compares writing to a cricket bat ("when we throw up an idea and give it a little knock, it might travel") or when Henry's promiscuous teenage daughter, Debbie (Cynthia Nixon), forces him to face true love by not intellectualizing it ("most people think not having it off is fidelity . . . sex or no sex . . . like an on/off switch") were as vivid and memorable as anything Stoppard had written. Mike Nichols directed the play fluidly, and Tony Walton's many sets flowed by cinematically. Critical response was propitious, such as Frank Rich in the *New York Times* stating that *The Real Thing* was "not only Mr. Stoppard's most moving play, but also the most bracing play that anyone has written about love and marriage in years." It won the New York Drama Critics Circle Award and the Tony Award, as well as Tonys for Nichols, Irons, Baranski, and, coming into her own, Close.

The Negro Ensemble's popular attraction *Do Lord Remember Me* (1-23-83) arrived at the American Place on January 14 for a return engagement and stayed for forty-two showings.

Absent from the New York theatre scene for a decade, the Living Theatre brought a new work by Julian Beck entitled **The Archeology of Sleep** (1-17-84, Joyce) to Off Broadway for ten performances as part of a repertory of four theatre pieces. A doctor (Beck) begins a discourse on the four phases of sleep, but soon the stage erupts into dreams enacted by the company in their usual physical and very visual style. Critics noted that the work was much more lighthearted and playful than Living Theatre presentations in the past, even if some found the latest offering a "pretentious mess masquerading as theatre." The other plays in the repertory were revivals of *The Antigone of Sophokles* on the 20th, *The Yellow Methuselah* on the 24th, and *The One and the Many* on the 28th.

The Second Stage, an off-off-Broadway company specializing in reviving recent works that they felt deserved a second look, presented Lanford Wilson's *Serenading Louie* (5-2-76) at the Public on January 17 in an "illuminating production" directed by John Tillinger. Jimmie Ray Weeks, Lindsay Crouse, Dianne Wiest, and Peter Weller played the two couples in turmoil, and all four were "enormously compelling." As for Wilson's

script, some commentators applauded "the wounding honesty of much of the writing" on second viewing; others still thought, "even in its revised state, this is a somewhat uneven work."

Ian McKellen Acting Shakespeare (1-19-84, Ritz) played a limited engagement of thirty-seven performances and further endeared the British actor (still fondly remembered for his Salieri in *Amadeus*) to New York audiences. Critics were also enthusiastic, calling the program "a learned, witty and highly informal disquisition on the Bard" and a "winningly intimate and highly accomplished solo entertainment."

Velina Houston, the author of **American Dreams** (1-28-84, Theatre Four), was part Japanese, part African American, and part Native American. Somehow she managed to get all three cultures into her family drama about veteran Creed Banks (Reuben Green), who returns to the States from Korea in 1955 with his Japanese bride, Setsuko (Nancy Hamada). When Creed brings her to the Lower East Side apartment of his low-life brother, Manfred (Count Stovall), the couple is greeted with icy prejudice by Manfred and his wife, who claim to have Indian blood, which makes them superior folk. When Creed finds out that Manfred bought a car with the money he sent him for a down payment on a house, family tensions explode. But Setsuko's cousin Fumiko (Ching Valdes) arrives on the scene and fixes everything up.

Shirley Lauro's off-off-Broadway drama **Open Admissions** (1-29-84, Music Box) was brought to Broadway, where it only lasted seventeen performances, despite a timely subject matter and some encouraging reviews. African-American Calvin Jefferson (Calvin Levels) has been admitted to a city college under its "open admissions" policy even though he can only read at the fifth-grade level. Now a sophomore, Calvin finds that all his instructors give him a B no matter the quality of his work and ignore him, preferring to work with the "real" students. His frustration climaxes in a confrontation with Ginny Carlsen (Marilyn Rockafellow), an underpaid speech teacher who has been as badly served by the system as Calvin, and the two realize they are both trapped. The drama had started as a one-act off-off Broadway, and some critics felt that, aside from a few potent scenes, the play was a padded version of, not an improvement over, the original.

Some talented ensemble acting brought Timothy Mason's autobiographical memory play **Levitation** (2-12-84, Circle) to life even if the play was lacking. Struggling New York playwright Joe (Ben Siegler) returns to his suburban Minneapolis home to find his parents, a sister, her child, a former lover, a former teacher, and a character named Orville Wright gathered there in a somewhat surreal manner, forcing the youth to contemplate death and the meaning of his own life. Trish Hawkins, Helen Stenborg, and other Circle Rep regulars shone with the kind of vital acting the little company was known for, but the "gentle, fanciful, sentimental, and somewhat droopy" play was rarely heard of after its scheduled forty-six performances.

Mark O'Donnell's **Fables for Friends** (2-16-84, Playwrights Horizons) was a series of nine playlets all dealing with growing up in America today, and some scenes were amusingly accurate. Highlights included a "secret society" run by young boys, a bride nervous about actually living in a new home with her new husband, college students boasting sophistication in their ideas but only fumbling in their sexual adventures, and a tragicomic sketch in which three girls at a pizza counter are flattered that a strange man keeps eying them, only to discover that he is looking at one girl's jacket: it once belonged to his son, but he gave it to the Salvation Army when the boy died. Notices pointed out the "deft characterization" and the author's "light touch and clever lines that ring true."

Alan Schneider's second Beckett program of the season introduced the absurdist's 1980 one-act **Rockaby** (2-16-84, Samuel Beckett) to New York. An old woman (Billie Whitelaw) sits dying in a rocking chair and performs a lyrical duet with her own recorded voice, the two drifting in and out of memories as death closes in. The piece was written for Whitelaw, and her performance was pronounced definitive. Rich noted, "You haven't really lived until you've watched Billie Whitelaw die." Also on the bill that ran for ten weeks were Beckett's previously seen *Enough* and *Footfalls*.

A Polish play that recalled *Marat/Sade* (12-27-65) was Janusz Glowacki's **Cinders** (2-20-84, LuEsther), translated by Christina Paul and presented at the Public for fifty-six performances. In a Warsaw reform school for girls, the inmates' school play of *Cinderella* is being filmed by a documentary director (Christopher Walken) to show how the state provides culture even for its most troubled citizens. But when Cinderella (Lucinda Jenney) refuses to cooperate, the full force of the totalitarian state comes down on both her and her disruptive Prince Charming (Dori Hartley), the little play becoming a symbol of repression

in Eastern Europe. The dark piece was applauded for its Kafkaesque quality.

South Africa's "spirited and heartfelt" **Woza Albert!** (2-23-84, Lucille Lortel) found humor in the most unlikely of places. Two actors (Percy Mtwa and Mbongeni Ngema) portrayed the population of their native land without the use of props or scenery but utilizing pantomime, donning bits of clothing, and adding pink plastic noses when they played white characters. In a series of brief sketches, we learn that the people of South Africa are waiting for the arrival of Moreno, a modern-day Messiah. He finally appears to a group of laborers in a brickyard, and soon the countryside is abuzz with the news. The play climaxes with the South Africans in a cemetery urging the dead hero Albert Luthuli to rise up as they shout the title phrase. Director Barney Simon co-wrote the script with the two actors; all of them pleased both critics and audiences for seventy-nine performances.

Caryl Churchill's *Fen* (5-24-83) returned to the Public on March 4, this time with an American cast, and chalked up another fifty-nine performances. Among the production's strengths was a memorable setting by Annie Smart: a dark and forbidding potato field with the crop sticking out of the rich soil. The Mirror Theatre added John Colton's *Rain* (11-7-22) to its repertory on March 6. Sabra Jones played the seductive Sadie Thompson, and David Cryer was the reverend who was tragically tempted by her. The second Odets revival of the season, *Awake and Sing!* (2-19-35) on March 8 at the Circle in the Square, was poorly received, notices pointing out the many weaknesses in both the script and the production. Nancy Marchand was miscast as the meddling Bessie Berger, and such reliable actors as Dick Latessa, Frances McDormand, Paul Sparer, and Michael Lombard were not shown in their best light.

Another transfer from Off Off Broadway to Off was Michael Brady's **To Gillian on Her 37th Birthday** (3-22-84, Circle in the Square Downtown), which only stayed a month but became a favorite with theatres around the country. Gillian has died in a boating accident, and two years later, on the eve of what would have been her thirty-seventh birthday, her husband, David (David Rasche), who is a schoolteacher, still mourns her. Unknown to his teenage daughter, Rachel (Sarah Jessica Parker), David continues to speak to his dead wife on the porch of their beachfront house in New England. When Rachel catches her father talking to thin air, she becomes more worried than ever and, together with a friend and an aunt, sets up a date for David with Esther (Jean DeBaer), a youthful divorcée and former student of his. The meeting is bumpy, but soon Gillian (Cheryl McFadden) actually appears to David and tells him the secret he has so often asked of her: "The secret is I'm dead. I'm very, very, very dead." Some aisle-sitters berated the play as too "precious" and "sweet," but others called it "tender, absorbing, slightly fantastic" and "touching, mystical, tantalizing theatre."

David Mamet's **Glengarry Glen Ross** (3-25-84, John Golden) arrived on Broadway after a successful premiere in London and a lauded production at Chicago's Goodman Theatre, so expectations were high. John Williamson (J. T. Walsh) runs a cutthroat real estate agency where his four salesmen will do anything for a sale. He promises a new Cadillac for the month's top salesman, a set of steak knives for the runner-up, and unemployment to the bottom two. The seasoned pro Shelly Levene (Robert Prosky) used to be top salesman but is having a losing streak, which he hopes to turn around. The hardened, up-and-coming Richard Roma (Joe Mantegna) beefs up his tactics, trying to sell some worthless Florida swamp land with exotic names like Glengarry and Glen Ross. When the real estate office is burglarized one night and the best "leads" are stolen, competition and suspicion increase and the play ends with the salesmen viciously continuing on, driven almost as if possessed. As with other Mamet works, the gritty, scatological dialogue gave the play its driving force. Critics extolled the script's "ferocious humor and drama," Gregory Mosher's brittle direction, and the ensemble performances (Mantegna won a Tony Award). *Glengarry Glen Ross* was awarded the Pulitzer Prize later that spring, and audiences were fascinated enough by the dog-eat-dog play to keep it on the boards for 378 performances.

That same night a drama about anti-British sentiments in Ireland opened that did not come from Britain or Ireland but was written by an American. Christopher Humble's **The Flight of the Earls** (2-25-84, Westside) chronicled the downfall of a County Tyrnne family in 1971 and how their fervent political beliefs came to destroy them. Brothers Ian (Guy Paul) and Michael Earl (Timothy Lanfield) are IRA members who finance their terrorist activities with money Michael's wife, Brigitte (Christine Estabrook), gives her husband, thinking it is for his imprisoned brother, Keith (Kenneth Meseroll). Despite efforts by the mother, Kate (Carol Teitel), to keep peace

in the family, Brigitte finds out the truth, confronts Michael, and in the argument is accidentally shot by her husband. The drama, which had won some playwriting competitions, was given a commercial mounting off Broadway but only lasted three weeks.

Frederick Lonsdale's comedy of manners *On Approval* (10-18-26) had never received a major New York revival, so the Roundabout production on March 27 introduced the play to more than one generation of theatregoers. While the mounting was considered less than perfect ("an acceptable summer-stock kind of revival"), critics cheered the still-timely script, and audiences joined in the enjoyment for 195 performances. Running nearly as long was the Broadway revival of Arthur Miller's *Death of a Salesman* (2-10-49) on March 29 at the Broadhurst. Dustin Hoffman essayed the archtypal character of Willie Loman (Hoffman's name on the bill netted the revival $1.8 million in advance sales) and was saluted as "very different from [Lee J.] Cobb and every bit as impressive." Hoffman's salesman was a smaller, more nasal wheeler-dealer whose nervous ticks betray the insecurities behind all his bluster. Kate Reid was his wife, Linda, and his sons were played by John Malkovich (Biff) and Stephen Lang (Happy).

John Bishop's detective whodunnit **The Harvesting** (4-1-84, Circle) was an engrossing "page-turner" set in Mansfield, Ohio, during the Bicentennial of 1976. When a double murder is discovered, chief detective John Torski (Jimmie Ray Weeks) is called in, only to find that the victims are Joyce Miller (Jane Fleiss), his former friend's wife, and her lover. Bim Miller (Edward Seamon), a ruthless businessman and the town's leading citizen, is suspected, but Torski's investigation does not get far before Bim is also murdered. After a series of revealing scenes about the Millers' difficult marriage, the culprit is discovered: a long-lost son who has exacted his revenge for the way he was treated as a youth by Bim and Joyce.

Three new Harold Pinter one-acts were given their American premiere under the umbrella title **Other Places** (4-10-84, Manhattan Theatre Club). *Victoria Station* is a humorously puzzling conversation on a car radio between a dispatcher (Henderson Forsythe) and a taxi driver (Kevin Conway). Because the cabbie has fallen in love with the passenger in the backseat (who is either asleep or dead), he cannot understand the directions given to him for a fare at the London train station of the title. In *A Kind of Alaska*, a woman

(Dianne Wiest) awakens from a coma after thirty years and believes she is still the sixteen-year-old she once was. *One for the Road* concerns a brutal interrogation of a subversive family by a government official (Conway) who humiliates his victims with excessive and mocking civility. Some reviewers proclaimed the short plays were "profoundly eloquent about the fragile joys of being alive" and "show[ed] Pinter's gift for pinning down the dream-like oddity of all waking existence," but only *A Kind of Alaska* was generally endorsed. The triple bill's busy director, Alan Schneider (he staged four productions this season), died three weeks after the play opened, killed by a motorcycle on a London street.

Young playwright Harry Kondoleon continued to intrigue critics and off-Broadway audiences with his cockeyed absurdism in **The Vampires** (4-11-84, Astor Place), a short-lived black comedy about eccentric theatre people. Ed (Graham Beckel) has given up carpentry to write plays. When his first production is panned by the critic Ian (John Vickery), who is also his own brother, Ed is livid and demands that Ian restage the work for an audience of VIPs. But Ian has lost his drama-critic job and decides he is a vampire, biting into his wife's neck and sending out to the butcher's for fresh blood. The chaos is further complicated by the return of Ed's long-lost junkie daughter (Elizabeth Berridge), who has fallen in love with her mother's guru and has gained supernatural powers. Reviewers continued to call Kondoleon a "promising young writer with a tart tongue and off-the-wall sensibility," but the play itself was heavily flawed and only lasted three weeks.

The next evening on Broadway, A. R. Gurney had one of his few failures (twenty-nine performances) with **The Golden Age** (4-12-84, Jack Lawrence), a retelling of Henry James's *The Aspern Papers*. Octogenarian Isabel Hastings Hoyt (Irene Worth) lives a reclusive life in her Manhattan town house with her granddaughter Virginia (Stockard Channing), a twice-divorced drinker who now serves as Mrs. Hoyt's companion. The old lady hopes to have Virginia settled before she "kicks the bucket," so she invites the young academic Tom (Jeff Daniels) to her home, tempting him with rare manuscripts and stories of her past. (In the 1920s, Isabel knew all the great writers, and rumors circulate she was the model for Daisy in Fitzgerald's *The Great Gatsby*.) Tom comes hoping to find a missing chapter of *Gatsby* but instead falls for Virginia. Suddenly the suspicious Isabel turns against Tom, pulls a gun on

him, and threatens to burn the prized manuscript. Virginia intercedes, Isabel dies, and the manuscript proves to be nothing but a bad melodrama written by someone else. Virginia and Tom leave the town house (and the past) behind them. The cast was given some wry and potent lines to speak, yet the script seemed to fall apart just when it should be gathering steam. Notices applauded the efforts of the actors (especially Worth) but admitted that the play was "irreparably flawed," "breathtakingly trivial, and insufferably cute." (The Jack Lawrence was a new name for the Playhouse Theatre. The owners had tried to name it the Tennessee Williams Theatre, but the playwright's estate blocked it, feeling it was just a way to cash in on Williams's name.)

In a move contrary to tradition, Marsha Norman's Pulitzer winner *'night, Mother* (3-31-83) transferred from Broadway to Off Broadway's Westside Arts on April 18 with the same cast and stayed for an additional fifty-four performances.

Peter Ustinov returned to Broadway as both author and star of **Beethoven's Tenth** (4-22-84, Nederlander) but found no success; the comedy closed in three weeks. London music critic Stephen Fauldgate (George Rose) takes time off from making acidic remarks about contemporary composers to write a book about what Beethoven's tenth symphony would have been like. Soon the great composer himself (Ustinov) appears to Stephen and, having learned English in heaven, engages in witty repartee with the critic. Stephen's wife, Jessica (Mary Jay), a former opera singer, wants to sing lieder with Beethoven accompanying her at the piano, and Pascal (Adam Redfield), Stephen's fledgling-composer son, petitions the master for his opinion of his work. (Beethoven hates it). Soon two aristocrats from Beethoven's day join the party, and there is much discussion over the true identity of his "immortal beloved." Beethoven sets the Fauldgates in order, and the family counsels the dead composer, cheering him up before he returns to the afterlife. Rich called it "an inert and sentimental domestic comedy," and most critics agreed, though there were some compliments for Ustinov's and Rose's performances.

Ted Tally's **Terra Nova** (4-25-84, American Place) had been performed with success at Yale and Los Angeles's Mark Taper Forum, but its engagement off Broadway was limited to two weeks. Famous British explorer Robert Falcon Scott (Robert Foxworth) and his men set out in 1911 to reach the South Pole, but, unlike his Norwegian rival Roald Amundsen (Anthony Zerbe) and his expedition, Scott refuses to use dogsleds, so he arrives at the pole a month after the Scandinavian team. On the journey back, Scott's group is stranded in a blizzard and one by one perish in the snow only eleven miles from their base camp. Tally based his play on the journals found on Scott's body and let the narrative shift from Antarctica to flashbacks with Scott's young wife (Christine Healy) and dream sequences illustrating the explorer's aristocratic pride and sense of destiny. Gerald Gutierrez directed the "unfailingly absorbing" play, which was favorably welcomed and enjoyed many subsequent productions elsewhere.

Canadian playwright Joanna M. Glass made an inauspicious Broadway debut with her family drama **Play Memory** (4-26-84, Longacre), which received a sterling production directed by Harold Prince (in one of his two non-musical assignments this season) yet closed after five showings. Saskatchewan salesman Cam MacMillan (Donald Moffat) prides himself on his rich ancestry (his forefathers came from Scotland and settled the area) and his powerhouse sales techniques. When World War II breaks out he gets involved with the black-market sale of gas-rationing coupons and, when discovered, loses his job but not his stubborn pride. As the years pass, Cam takes his frustration out on his family, turns to drink, and is last seen in 1968 still waiting for an apology from the world for his disenchanted life. Reviews ranged from "a drama of searing vitality and power" to "an untidy and increasingly gloomy work."

Beth Henley returned after last season's short-lived *The Wake of Jamey Foster* (10-14-82) with a delicious new comedy, **The Miss Firecracker Contest** (5-1-84, Manhattan Theatre Club). In the small Mississippi town of Brookhaven, Carnelle Scott (Holly Hunter) is known as "Miss Hot Tamale" because of her tarnished character. She plans to win the Fourth of July "Miss Firecracker" competition, then leave Brookhaven forever. (Her tap-dancing, baton-twirling routine is set to "The Star-Spangled Banner," complete with Roman candles and flags). But Carnelle's efforts are complicated by the return of her cousin Elain (Patricia Richardson), a former "Miss Firecracker" winner who has left her rich husband and coddled children in Natchez to return to the scene of her former glory, and the arrival of the screwy Delmount (Mark Linn-Baker), Elain's brother, who has just been let out of a mental institution. Helping Carnelle with her act is Popeye Jackson (Belita Moreno), an odd girl with bulging eyes

(when she was a little girl her brother accidentally put ear drops in her eyes, so now "I can hear voices through my eyes") who is sewing Carnelle's red, silver, and blue outfit and who falls for the wacky Delmount. At the competition Carnelle trips on her dress and falls, and some members of the crowd shout out, "Miss Hot Tamale!" Although she came in last, Carnelle takes a good look at herself and realizes she has spent too much time "tryin' so hard t'belong all my life." The play ends with her watching the holiday fireworks with Popeye and Delmount. Critics were enthusiastic, calling the piece "a comic volcano of a play, populated by offbeat, but vital, larger-than-life characters" and declaring Henley "a master at crafting 'kookie' characters" who "struggle against the inevitability of their lives with humor as well as pathos." The eccentrics entertained audiences for 131 performances, then returned the following season.

The superior 1973 Broadway revival of Eugene O'Neill's *A Moon for the Misbegotten* (5-2-57) haunted the production that opened on May 1 at the Cort, the new production falling short whenever the memory of Jason Robards or Colleen Dewhurst arose. Kate Nelligan was an admirable Josie Hogan, and Jerome Kilty shone as her father, but the James Tyrone of Ian Bannen was lacking ("his acting is about as stiff as a wooden fence post on the Hogan farm"), and the production itself met with conflicting reviews, ranging from "an urgent, vivid mounting" to a "vision quite cloudy."

Also disappointing was Harvey Fierstein's **Spookhouse** (5-2-84, Playhouse 91), his first non-musical work since the still-running *Torch Song Trilogy* (1-15-82). In a tacky apartment situated over a fun house at Coney Island, Connie Janik (Anne Meara) and her family are shattered when the eldest son, a drug addict, rapes an eight-year-old girl, sets her on fire, and throws her off a roof. A bad situation is made worse by a meddling social worker (Court Miller) who comes on the scene, asks Connie to accept her wayward son, and urges her to take him back into her home. The drama was impossible ("less a play than a cluster of monologues") and could not survive beyond one week.

A one-person show called **A Woman of Independent Means** (5-3-84, Biltmore) by Elizabeth Forsythe Hailey was based on her epistolary novel of the same name and cried out for some physical action onstage during its thirteen performances. Texas grande dame Bess Steed Garner (Barbara Rush) reads letters from her long lifetime (1899 to 1977), covering her two marriages, her many children, the acquisition of wealth, her various travels abroad, and the births, weddings, and deaths of loved ones. The action of the play was limited to the Dallas millionairess changing hats all evening long. The unanimously scathing reviews ("bizarre," "tasteless," "trash," and "a positively awful evening in the theatre") were kinder to Rush, who did her best "to conceal the painful thinness of her role."

Some years earlier, Arthur Kopit received a commission from a wealthy industrialist to write a play about the threat of a nuclear doomsday. Kopit struggled in vain to write it, then gave up, eventually writing **End of the World** (5-6-84, Music Box), a black comedy about a playwright commissioned to pen a play about impending doom. Sam Spade–like writer Michael Trent (John Shea) is surreptitiously approached by billionaire Philip Stone (Barnard Hughes) to write a drama that will awaken the population to nuclear threat and expose a conspiracy to blow up the world. Trent attacks the task like a private eye, interviewing both think-tank advisers and Pentagon officials, while his literary agent, Audrey Wood (Linda Hunt), tries to sell the project to show-business moguls at the Russian Tea Room. (Paramount is interested in the apocalyptic script as long as it has a happy ending.) Eventually the comedy turns into a didactic discussion, revealing paranoia and fatalism in both Stone and the forces he is so suspicious of. In the end Trent recalls an incident with his infant son (he had considered throwing him out of a window for some inexplicable reason) and realizes that evils rest inside even good people. While Benedict Nightingale in the *New York Times* declared the work "an exhilarating rush of oxygen to the brain," most critics condoned Kopit's ambitious attempt more than the end product. (Nightingale was a British critic who replaced Walter Kerr when the American writer retired from regular reviewing for the *Times*.) The dark piece only lasted a month on Broadway, but Kopit's subsequent revised version would enjoy some popularity regionally.

The Mirror Theatre's repertory added Ibsen's *Hedda Gabler* at a matinee on May 15 with Geraldine Page as Mrs. Alving and, that night, John Patrick's *The Hasty Heart* (1-3-45) with Victor Sle-

zak as the dying Scottish soldier, Lachlen. The repertory ended on July 1.

The last Broadway entry of the season, Bob and Ann Acosta's one-man bio-drama **The Babe** (5-17-84, Princess), lasted only five performances. Max Gail's portrayal of baseballer George Herman Ruth was "so totally lacking in personality" that the story of the sport's most colorful figure came out "dull, plodding," and a "peculiarly becalmed affair." Ruth spoke to the audience from 1923, when he was at the peak of his fame; from 1935, when he retired in a blaze of glory; and finally from 1948, when he was close to death and he donned a Yankee uniform for the last time. Some film footage helped break up the "seemingly interminable monologue," but commentators could find nothing to recommend in the enterprise.

A production of Sean O'Casey's *The Shadow of a Gunman* (10-30-32) off-off Broadway was so well received that it transferred to the Actors Playhouse on May 22 and, riding on strong word of mouth, stayed for six weeks.

The season ended with an old play by Lanford Wilson (it was actually his first full-length effort) given a long-belated major premiere by Chicago's Steppenwolf Theatre Company as guests at the Circle Rep. **Balm in Gilead** (5-31-84, Circle) had been done off-off Broadway at Café La Mama for a week in 1965 when Wilson was yet to be discovered, and critics rarely traveled so far off the Street. The large-cast drama is an American-style *Lower Depths* in which junkies, hookers, hustlers, pushers, and other lowlifes frequent an all-night cafe on upper Broadway. The twenty-two characters, all social outcasts sharing a similar sense of loneliness, come and go without benefit of plot, but the seemingly aimless play soon develops into a rich tapestry of sorts. John Malkovich directed the new production, and the cast included such notable (or soon to be notable) performers as Tanya Berezin, Laurie Metcalf, Gary Sinise, Danton Stone, Glenne Headley, Jonathan Hogan, and Giancarlo Esposito. While some notices dismissed the drama as an early and "ill-formed" work, others called it "a play that throbs with life" and "an explosive amalgam of realism and theatrical illusion." The 1960s slice-of-life drama immediately found an audience in the 1980s, and it played 253 times.

ACT THREE, 1984–1994

PLAYACTING DURING A PLAGUE

1984–1985

The radical drop in the number of Broadway non-musicals the previous season was only slightly corrected this season with a few more new entries and revivals to bring the total to a paltry twenty-three. Yet only four of those were British imports (two new and two revivals), so the number of new American plays climbed noticeably. Off Broadway the numbers remained about the same: thirty-nine new American works, nine foreign, and twenty-four revivals. Of course such definite numbers were arbitrary, since the line between Off Broadway and Off Off Broadway became hazier than ever. *Blue Window*, for example, opened as an off-off-Broadway entry but, after getting some encouraging notices, changed to off-Broadway not by moving but simply by rewriting all its contracts. *Man Enough* did the opposite, reverting from Off to Off Off when it needed to cut its overhead.

A similar experiment in cost cutting was tried by *Dancing in the End Zone*'s producer, Martin Gottlieb, who closed off the balcony and part of the orchestra seating at the Ritz in order to qualify for a "middle Broadway" contract. The show ran less than a month, so it was difficult to determine how well the experiment fared. When *Doubles* opened in the same theatre later in the season, the arrangement was tried again, and the result was more encouraging, although even at 277 performances *Doubles* failed to show a profit. In fact, only two Broadway entries were in the black by season's end: the one-person specialty program *Whoopi Goldberg* and the off-Broadway transfer *Hurlyburly*. With the average cost for a non-musical on Broadway now in the neighborhood of $600,000, realizing profits in a short term was no longer possible.

Two plays about the growing threat of Acquired Immune Deficiency Syndrome (AIDS) were prominent this season and would be fol-

lowed by dozens of others in the next few seasons. What was not evident during 1984–1985 was how AIDS would devastate the theatre community in the near future, silencing young artists in a wide variety of jobs and thereby altering the course of theatre history.

The season began with the debut of John Patrick Shanley, a playwright who would become a fixture off Broadway for several years. His two-character drama **Danny and the Deep Blue Sea** (6-6-84, Circle in the Square Downtown) explored the relationship between two volatile people who reach a warm understanding after a tempestuous long night together. Violence-prone Danny (John Turturro) strikes up a belligerent conversation with divorcée Roberta (June Stein) in a Bronx bar late one night. He is called "the animal" by his fellow truck drivers because of his uncontrollable temper. She is distrustful of men, having been sexually molested by her father and, years later, lost control (and custody) of her troubled teenage son. Danny and Roberta spend a night of sex, daydreaming, arguments, and then softening together, the two outcasts finding a more realistic view of each other by dawn. The little drama was generally saluted by the critics as flawed but promising, aptly described as "the equivalent of sitting at ringside watching a prize fight that concludes in a loving embrace." The play, which had originated at the Actors Theatre of Louisville, remained off Broadway for 117 performances.

Dennis McIntyre's **Split Second** (6-7-84, Theatre Four), which started as a gripping melodrama then moved into a tale of individual conscience, was a point of much discussion off Broadway and had audience members debating with each other for five months. African-American police officer Val Johnson (John Danelle), a young by-the-rules cop with an untarnished record, pursues a stolen Oldsmobile into a deserted street on the West Side of Manhattan and confronts William H. Wallis (Bill Cwikowski), a white petty thief who taunts the cop with a string of racial slurs. Val, who has been suppressing years of inner rage over prejudice, snaps inside and shoots Wallis down in cold blood. Finding a knife on the body, he plans to claim self-defense, but his conscience haunts him. He tells his wife, best friend, mother, and father (who is a retired policeman) the truth. They offer conflicting advice as to what action to take; in the end Val is seen testifying at the police hearing that Willis pulled a knife on him. Mel Gussow in the *New York Times* led the largely positive reviews, calling it "an explosive new play dealing with primal dramatic issues."

Playwright Craig Lucas and director Norman Rene began a long series of collaborations with **Blue Window** (6-12-84, Theatre Guinevere), a comedy about the impersonal plight of Manhattan residents. Seven New Yorkers (including a struggling songwriter, a lesbian couple, an egotistical actor, and a skydiving instructor) are seen before, during, and after a dinner party. At the gathering, played as a series of fragmented scenes and monologues, the characters fail to connect, and, seen leaving the party, they each continue on their disparate paths. Notices found the exercise more interesting than satisfying, but audiences latched on to the comedy for ninety-six performances.

Playwrights Horizons concluded its previous season with Mick Casale's **Elm Circle** (6-13-84, Playwrights Horizons) about the odyssey of a young teenager with celebrity delusions. Janet-Ann (Kelly Wolf) dreams of being a movie star, so she leaves her blue-collar family in Troy, New York, and seeks fame and fortune, gradually descending into self-destructive fantasy. The next night a bio-drama about Robert F. Kennedy (Christopher Curry) titled **Kennedy at Colonus** (6-14-84, 47th Street) opened to few compliments. The Laurence Carr script illustrated various Kennedys in scenes between 1936 and the fateful night in 1968 when Robert was gunned down in California. Neither entry lasted more than three weeks.

At the Public Theatre, Joseph Papp directed a contemporary Soviet comedy that was currently a hit at Moscow's Satire Theatre. Victor Rozov's **The Nest of the Wood Grouse** (6-14-84, Newman), in Susan Layton's translation, is a domestic comedy not unlike American family plays of the past (one critic referred to it as a Russian *Life with Father*) in which a blustering father figure holds a high position in society but cannot begin to control his own household. Fraudulent bureaucrat Stephen Sudakov (Eli Wallach) is a bit hard of hearing (in Russia, "wood grouse" is an ex-

pression for a semi-deaf person) but also is blind to the upheaval in his home. While his wife, Natalya (Anne Jackson), makes endless fish pies, his rebel teenage son, Prov (Ricky Paull), sneers at the establishment and lusts after the daughter of a fruit peddler. Sudakov's daughter, Iskra (Mary Beth Hurt), has married the conniving Georgy (Dennis Boutsikaris), one of her father's assistants, who is planning to take the old man's promotion away from him. When the troubled Iskra resorts to praying to icons, Sudakov is shocked that she would behave in such a way in a nice state-approved atheist household like theirs. Prov gets arrested for stealing a suitcase, and it is the fruit peddler (Rosemary de Angelis) who gets him sprung. Iskra finds out that Georgy is planning to divorce her to make a more lucrative match, so she kicks him out, foils his plan to displace her father, and saves the family. Notices found the play surprisingly delightful, though the production was judged uneven with performances that "were either first-rate or rock bottom, with no middle ground."

Donald Margulies made a noteworthy playwriting debut with his curiosity **Found a Peanut** (6-17-84, Public: Anspacher), declared by some critics "a thought-provoking play suffused with the poetry of reality," while others found "the performances far more interesting than the script." On the last day of summer, a group of eight children between the ages of five and fourteen (all portrayed by adults) play in a Brooklyn tenement backyard. When they find a dead bird, the kids go through an elaborate burial ritual that apes adult behavior. But when they dig a hole for the bird, the children discover some money buried long ago, and their squabbles and petty greediness become a potent foreshadowing of their future behavior. Peter MacNicol, Robert Joy, Robin Bartlett, and Kevin Geer were cited as the most accomplished of the cast, under the direction of Claudia Weill.

George C. Scott, who had directed Noel Coward's *Present Laughter* with robust playfulness last season at the Circle in the Square, staged the same playwright's *Design for Living* (1-24-33) on June 20 at the same theatre, and it also enjoyed a healthy run of 245 performances. Critics declared Frank Langella as the painter Otto the most adept at the Coward style. Jill Clayburgh and Raul Julia, as the other two members of the ménage à trois, received mixed notices. But most aisle-sitters agreed that the script was "as funny and nasty as ever" and that "this harsh and viperish comedy wears its years lightly."

After a long hiatus, David Rabe returned to the New York theatre with a play of note, the "grim, ribald and surprisingly compassionate comedy" **Hurlyburly** (6-21-84, Promenade). Mickey (Christopher Walken) and Eddie (William Hurt), two Hollywood casting agents, live in a swank house in the California hills, snorting cocaine all day, drifting in and out of relationships with women they feel nothing for, and speaking to each other in an inflated kind of dialogue that is half slang, half sales pitch. A frequent visitor is the volatile television actor Phil (Harvey Keitel), complaining about his messy private life, his wife (whom he has beaten up again), and his faltering career. Wheeler-dealer Artie (Jerry Stiller) brings the promiscuous teenager Donna (Cynthia Nixon), whom he found living in an elevator, to the house to amuse his friends, but Eddie is more interested in Darlene (Sigourney Weaver), a woman Mickey has tried out but returned to Eddie, who knew her first. When the men fix Phil up with stripper Bonnie (Judith Ivey), the encounter goes wrong and Phil, in a fit of unexplainable temper, pushes her out of a moving car. A year later, Phil's marriage has finally dissolved and he commits suicide, leaving his friends a note saying that his sad end was nothing but destiny. While the characters were far from likable, the drama crackled with a decadent fascination that audiences responded to, and after forty-five sold-out performances, the production transferred on August 7 to Broadway's Ethel Barrymore, where it ran another 343 performances. Christopher Walken was replaced by Ron Silver as Mickey for the transfer, and Judith Ivey won a Tony Award for her hardened stripper Bonnie. Some critics and audience members were dumbfounded and annoyed that certain actors were miked for the moderate-sized house, a rare but disturbing instance of a non-musical succumbing to electronic sound amplification.

Much of the rest of the summer was given over to revivals. The first New York Shakespeare Festival offering at the Delacorte in Central Park was *Henry V* on June 22 with Kevin Kline in robust form as the title monarch. Samuel Beckett's *Endgame* (1-28-58) was revived on June 28 at the Harold Clurman with Alvin Epstein directing and playing Hamm. Peter Evans was Clov, and the well-received mounting was retained for 123 performances. The Roundabout Theatre expanded its season by performing in two separate spaces: its old 150-seat Susan Bloch Theatre on 26th Street and a new 499-seat theatre called Roundabout One on 17th Street. Its first offering was

William Inge's *Come Back, Little Sheba* (2-15-50) on July 12, which boasted a superb cast: Philip Bosco (Doc), Shirley Knight (Lola), Mia Dillon (Marie), and Kevin Conroy (Turk). The drama ran out the summer.

Lincoln Center was home to guest productions this season, the first being the Greek National Theatre's *Oedipus Rex* on July 17 in the Vivian Beaumont. The tragedy was performed in Greek for one week. Papp's second offering in Central Park was quite a departure from the Shakespeare plays and musicals presented there over the past twenty-seven years. The Jewish legend *The Golem*, dramatized by H. Leivick, translated from the Yiddish by J. C. Augenlight, and directed and designed to within an inch of its life by avant-gardist Richard Foreman, opened on August 3. This early Frankenstein tale unfolded on a stage littered with beggars, devils, worshippers, and monks (even Christ on the cross made a brief appearance), and passing references to computers, global catastrophe, and nuclear war were sprinkled throughout the evening. F. Murray Abraham was the rabbi who created a monster (Randy Quaid) and then has to destroy him. Both actors were endorsed, though critical reaction to the production ranged from "endless, hateful" to "consistently thought-provoking."

The first of the season's countless one-man shows was **Viva Vittorio!** (9-19-84, Promenade), "a thin and amateurishly produced recital" that featured the Italian film actor Vittorio Gassman talking about himself and the theatre, performing (in English and Italian) favorite scenes from Sartre, Kafka, Pirandello, Shakespeare, and others. Three other actors were used briefly, but the show was essentially all Gassman, and critics, while decrying his floundering self-direction and uneven choice of material, saluted the star as "an actor of size and spirit, . . . a pleasure to watch and listen to even in this grab bag of an evening."

The second Samuel Beckett offering in this season of plenty of Beckett was *All Strange Away* (1-2-84), which opened on September 23 at the off-Broadway theatre named for the absurdist playwright. Robert Langdon-Lloyd played the drama's sole character, the last man on earth.

A comic "penny dreadful" titled **The Mystery of Irma Vep** (10-2-84, One Sheridan Square) would prove to be Charles Ludlam's most popular play, an Edwardian-style spoof that would be produced by theatres across the nation who had never heard of the Ridiculous Theatrical Company and its outrageous theatrics. Ludlam and Everett Quinton portrayed all the characters in this "quick-change act" about an Egyptian princess brought to life when her tomb is disturbed by a British archaeologist. The comedy came complete with landed gentry in England, strange intruders, and even a werewolf. Most of the major critics journeyed to the little off-off-Broadway theatre and agreed that it was "a lush and loving parody of every gaslight romance from *Jane Eyre* to *Rebecca* with glancing references [from] Shakespeare [and] Poe, to silent-movie serials [and] horror movies of the 30s." The spoof ran out the season.

The first New York revival of Arthur Miller's *After the Fall* (1-23-64) on October 4 at Playhouse 91 gave critics a chance to look at the play removed from the too-recent history and controversy that surrounded its initial production. Unfortunately, what they saw in this slightly revised mounting was still "alienating, unsatisfying," and "never as moving or profound as it wants to be." But all were in agreement that John Tillinger's mounting was "sleeked down, slicked up, and in altogether better shape" than the original. Frank Langella won kudos as the guilt-ridden lawyer Quinton, Edith Oliver in *The New Yorker* stating that his "efforts against terrible odds to make [Quinton] interesting and occasionally sympathetic are positively valiant." Compliments were also forthcoming for Dianne Wiest as the Marilyn Monroe–like Maggie, Laurie Kennedy as Quinton's Austrian wife, Holga, and Henderson Forsythe as his friend Lou, who collapses at the news that he must testify before a congressional committee. The presence of Langella and other cast members helped the revival run eight weeks. "Skillful and imaginative direction" by Daniel Gerroll distinguished the Roundabout's revival of Oliver Goldsmith's *She Stoops to Conquer* on October 9 at the Triplex. Nathan Lane's clowning as Tony Lumpkin further endeared the young performer to audiences and critics alike, and there were fine performances also by Tovah Feldshuh (Kate), E. G. Marshall (Mr. Hardcastle), and Kaye Ballard (Mrs. Hardcastle).

In the recent past Alec McCowen had found theatrical fire in performing the Bible, but try as he might, he could not breathe life into **Kipling** (10-10-84, Royale), a one-man play by Brian Clark in which the popular writer tells the story of his life as "seen through my books and only my books." Rudyard Kipling being a very private individual, the evening was rather static except when McCowen was acting out one of the more dramatic fiction passages or poems. While the press dismissed the play, they were enthusiastic

> **AUGUST WILSON** (1945–) was born in Pittsburgh, Pennsylvania (the setting for most of his plays), the son of a baker and a cleaning woman. Although he learned to read at a very early age, Wilson did not like school and dropped out before completing high school. He began writing poetry in 1965 and short plays a few years after that. His early drama *Jitney* was produced in 1978 by Pittsburgh's Black Horizons Theatre, a group Wilson helped found a decade before. Soon his scripts were being produced regionally and by the New Dramatists in New York. *Ma Rainey's Black Bottom* was workshopped in St. Paul and at the O'Neill Theatre Center in Connecticut before receiving its premiere production at the Yale Repertory, directed by Lloyd Richards, who would be associated with the playwright for many years.

about McCowen; Edwin Wilson in *The Wall Street Journal* wrote, "His command of dialects, his timing, his variety of delivery, his humor, his reinforcement of meaning are unmatched on the stage today." Nevertheless, audiences were not enticed, and the engagement was cut short after twelve showings.

With **Ma Rainey's Black Bottom** (10-11-84, Cort), Broadway was introduced to August Wilson who would go on to become the most produced, most successful, and most honored African-American playwright in the history of the American theatre.

A group of black musicians wait in a seedy recording studio in 1927 Chicago for the famous blues singer Ma Rainey to come and record some old favorites. The most restless of the side men is the young trumpet player Levee (Charles S. Dutton), who cockily frowns on the "jug music" they must play and dreams of making it big in show business with the new improvisational style of jazz, which allows for more individual freedom of expression. Ma (Theresa Merritt) finally arrives at the studio, having assaulted a cab driver who wouldn't let her in his taxi. With her is Ma's flirtatious female lover, Dussie Mae (Aleta Mitchell), and her stuttering nephew, Sylvester (Scott Davenport-Richards), who, Ma insists, must do the vocal introduction on the record. The singer complains and barks at her white manager, Irvin (Lou Criscuolo), and derides the studio head, Sturdyvant (John Carpenter), knowing that in the outside world she is a second-class citizen but in the studio she rules unchecked. During the course of the difficult recording session, tempers flare up (Ma refuses to use Levee's jazzy arrangements), but the record is finally completed and the group disbands. When Levee, who was hoping to interest Sturdyvant in recording his songs, is turned down, he takes his anger out on fellow musician Toledo (Robert Judd), stabbing him to death when the pianist accidentally steps on Levee's shiny new shoes. Powerful performances, under Lloyd Richards's astute direction, brought the potent play to life, and black and white audiences eagerly responded to it. Jack Kroll in *Newsweek* summed up the unanimously admiring reviews, describing the work as "a fierce and biting play, mixing the savage inevitability of black rage with the shrewd humor of jazz itself." The drama won the New York Drama Critics Circle Award and remained on Broadway for 275 performances.

As often happened when the Circle Repertory Company attempted period classics, its realistic style of acting did not work for several characters in *Love's Labors's Lost* on October 11. But Michael Higgins's daffy yet pedantic Holofernes was applauded by the press, who generally thought "the poetry goes for almost nothing" in this modern-dress production that was "cloudy when it should sparkle." On the other hand, the Bard was well served by the visiting Royal Shakespeare Company's *Much Ado About Nothing*, which opened on October 14 and ran in repertory with *Cyrano de Bergerac* for three months at the Gershwin. RSC stars Derek Jacobi and Sinead Cusack played the battling Benedick and Beatrice in a smart Restoration period treatment directed by Terry Hands. Ralph Koltai's simple scenic design featured stylized trees painted on Plexiglas and a wide apron that thrust deep into the huge auditorium, creating, as one critic noted, "a pleasingly humane theatrical environment" in the usually cavernous Gershwin. Notices were exemplary for the mounting and the cast (Jacobi won a Tony Award at season's end), and business was brisk in the large house. On the other hand, *Cyrano de Bergerac* met with some disappointment. Jacobi was a vibrant and accomplished Cyrano, but the production (again directed and designed by Hands and Koltai) was considered too busy, grandiose, and exaggerated even for the swashbuckling Rostand play. The dimly lit stage was filled with smoke, oversized chandeliers, and ear-piercing cannon fire, and Cyrano's first entrance on a high wire was just short of parody.

On October 15, the Manhattan Theatre Club brought back Beth Henley's *The Miss Firecracker Contest* (5-1-84) for a return engagement of 113 performances at the Westside Arts. A "laggard and

lackluster revival" of Clifford Odets's *The Country Girl* (11-10-50) opened on October 18 at the Chelsea Playhouse. Aside from several cheers for Hal Holbrook as down-and-out actor Frank Elgin, critics felt "the drama rarely lifts off." Christine Lahti (Georgie), Jeffrey DeMunn (Bernie), and other capable cast members were poorly directed, finding themselves out of work after forty-five showings.

Lawrence Roman, who had written the featherweight *Under the Yum Yum Tree* (11-16-60), came back to Broadway with **Alone Together** (10-21-84, Music Box), a comedy that seemed to ignore the passing of twenty-four years but brought mild satisfaction to theatregoers for three months. Having packed off their youngest son to college, George (Kevin McCarthy) and Helene Butler (Janis Paige) finally have an empty nest and look forward to a quiet middle age. But their eldest son, Michael (Don Howard), returns to live at home while he starts a new career in chemical engineering. Hot on his heels comes second son Elliot (Kevin O'Rourke), whose wife has kicked him out for his amatory indiscretions. He is followed by Janie Johnson (Alexandra Gersten), not one of the family but a homeless doomsday cultist who has been sent by the youngest son to occupy his old room. Before long Elliot is starting a mail order business out of his parents' home, Michael blows up part of the house during one of his chemistry experiments, the celibate Janie is sexually attracted to Michael while fighting off Elliot, and Helene takes to drink. But all is righted when George, with true sitcom logic, gives his sons a lecture and everyone moves out of the house. Critical opinion ranged from "an old-fashioned Broadway evening of good fun" to "a moderately amusing play" to "a one-joke comedy in triplicate."

Three one-woman shows followed. William Luce, who made a career out of writing solo pieces about famous people, dramatized the life of Mrs. F. Scott Fitzgerald and called it **Zelda** (10-23-84, American Place). Olga Bellin portrayed the fragile southern belle, reading from her letters and commenting on all the celebrities she encountered in her tragic life. Either because the play was weak or because it needed a star to carry it, *Zelda* only lasted twenty performances.

Mike Nichols, Emanuel Azenberg, and the Shuberts took a gamble bringing the unknown comic **Whoopi Goldberg** (10-24-84, Lyceum) to Broadway in a one-woman show, but word traveled quickly, and she stayed for a profitable 148 performances. Goldberg's gallery of six characters, deftly written by herself and directed with piercing effect by Nichols, went far beyond mere stand-up comedy. When a spaced-out junkie hops on a Pan Am jet to Europe because he liked the company's TV commercial, the expected laughs are forthcoming. But when he tours Anne Frank's hiding place in Amsterdam, the character unfolds (we find out he has a Ph.D. in literature) and the piece soars. Goldberg's other characters were just as fertile: a spacy California teen surfer whose sunny exterior hides a pathetic desperation, a deformed woman working in an old folks' home ("to make them feel better about dying"), a sly Jamaican immigrant who works for a rich white man, a young African-American girl imagining she is blond and white, and a former tap dancer now old and reduced to panhandling. Notices were almost all raves, calling the comic "an original" and "a new cult hero."

A very different one-person show for an African-American actress was Eric Hertz's **Between Rails** (10-26-84, South Street) in a commercial venture off Broadway for thirty-seven performances. Elderly Willie-mae (Thelma Louise Carter) sits in a train compartment, dressed in her Sunday best and holding on her lap a large bag with her cat inside. After working as a domestic for forty-six years in New York City, she is returning home to the South. Her thoughts as she rides through a snowstorm are filled with memories, and we learn all about her life from her childhood in the country to the reason she has left her most recent job. (Her employers' daughter had a run-in with Willie-mae's cat.) Without ever stirring from her seat, Carter held the audience with an extended monologue that found drama in the many details of the old woman's life.

David Storey's 1969 **In Celebration** (10-30-84, City Center), another play about returning sons, had been seen briefly off-off Broadway in 1977 but did not get a major mounting in New York until this masterful production directed by Lindsay Anderson. Yorkshire coal miner Mr. Shaw (Robert Symonds) and his wife (Pauline Flanagan) are about to celebrate their fortieth wedding anniversary, so their three sons return to the family home in North England for the festivities. Andrew (Malcolm McDowell), the eldest son, has forsaken the legal profession and wants to become an abstract painter. Colin (John C. Vennema) is a very prosperous automobile executive but a passionless bore. The youngest is Steven (Frank Grimes), a schoolteacher who is beginning to realize that he will never write the great novel

he has struggled with for seven years. Several past sins are hinted at (in particular the mother's infidelity and contemplated suicide), but the real issue comes down to class. All three sons were raised to "better themselves," but that goal now seems hollow and even hypocritical. Aisle-sitters found the production flawless but were less sure about the script. The Manhattan Theatre Club produced the drama in its new second space in the basement of the City Center, where it stayed for five weeks.

The most successful off-Broadway entry of the season was Larry Shue's comedy **The Foreigner** (11-1-84, Astor Place), which ran 686 performances and became a staple of regional and stock companies. British proofreader Charlie Baker (Anthony Heald), whose unfaithful wife is dying in a hospital, seeks refuge from the world in a rural Georgia fishing lodge run by Betty Meeks (Kathleen Claypool). His army friend "Froggy" LeSueur (Shue) tells Betty that Charlie is a foreigner who cannot speak a word of English and asks her to leave him in peace and quiet. Thinking the silent visitor cannot understand them, some of the locals reveal secrets and plots in Charlie's presence, such as a scheme by redneck Owen Musser (Christopher Curry) to cheat Betty out of the lodge and a plot by the conniving Rev. David Marshall Lee (Robert Schenkkan) to marry the wealthy Catherine Simms (Patricia Kalember) and use her money to fund Ku Klux Klan activities. Only Catherine's dim-witted brother, Ellard (Kevin Geer), treats Charlie like a human being, trying to teach him English words and happily accepting the foreigner's strange ways. With the help of Froggie, Charlie foils Owen's and David's plans and, hearing that his wife has recovered and run off with a proctologist, decides to stay in Georgia and woo the available Catherine. Jerry Zaks (who would stage three noteworthy plays this season) directed with whimsical panache. Many critics, while admitting the contrived, sometimes clumsy nature of the writing, confessed enjoying the comedy.

The Public Theatre opened its season late with Michael Weller's **The Ballad of Soapy Smith** (11-12-84, Newman), a large-cast historical epic about an actual con man in Alaska during the Gold Rush. In 1897, Colonel Jefferson Randolph Smith (Dennis Arndt), more familiarly known to his victims as "Soapy," arrives in Skagway, where he sets up a protection racket. Ironically, not only do his schemes take off but soon, because of him, law and order are brought to the disorderly town, and Soapy becomes a grand philanthropist building an infirmary and a church. But once he starts to believe his own con, Soapy slips; his best friend confronts him, and Soapy shoots the friend, only to be shot himself by an ex-vigilante. The sprawling three-hour epic, originally seen at the Seattle Repertory Theatre, met with lukewarm reviews and was only kept on for three weeks.

Playwrights Horizons also opened its season with a large-cast history piece set in the nineteenth century, but Peter Parnell's **Romance Language** (11-14-84, Playwrights Horizons) was a surrealistic comedy peopled with American literary giants. In 1876 Walt Whitman (Al Carmines) and runaway Huck Finn (Jon Matthews) take off on a dreamlike journey, encountering Thoreau (William Converse-Roberts), Alcott (Frances Conroy), Emerson (Philip Pleasants), Dickinson (Valerie Mahaffey), and others, ending at the battle of Little Big Horn, where they are massacred along with Custer (Converse-Roberts) and join the rest of the cast in literary heaven. Parnell employed the vocabulary and famous phrases of the American romantic writers, resulting in "a theatrical whirligig that sends sparks flying off in all directions." The "highly imaginative comedy" received mixed notices and ran more than six weeks but, curiously, has rarely been heard of since.

A very popular property in Europe, Dario Fo's political farce **Accidental Death of an Anarchist** (11-15-84, Belasco), arrived in New York courtesy of a production (with an English adaptation by Richard Nelson) that originated at Washington's Arena Stage. An anarchist has "accidentally fallen" from the window of police headquarters, and an inquiry has found no evidence of foul play. But when a Fool (Jonathan Pryce), a slick and absurd con man, enters the police station and, rapidly changing costumes, portrays a half dozen outrageous "witnesses," the authorities are so addled that they are forced to reopen the case and reveal the cover-up. Critics unanimously cheered Pryce, but reaction to the play ranged from "a majestically funny event about deadly serious matters" to "an evening of strained silliness" that was "Americanized out of all recognition." Audiences were not so torn, staying away in droves, so the comedy closed after twenty showings.

Patrick Tovatt's drama **Husbandry** (11-27-84, Manhattan Theatre Club), about the plight of small farms in America, collected such conflicting notices as "a literate exploration of family responsibilities in a mobile society" and "the play's only cash crop is corn." Les (Richard Hamilton)

is an aging tobacco farmer getting too weak to run his farm alone, so he appeals to his visiting son, Harry (James Rebhorn), to leave his big-city job and return to the homestead. But Harry's wife, Bev (Deborah Hedwall), is not about to leave her lucrative city job to become a farmer's wife, so Harry is torn between two loyalties. The issue is resolved (or at least put on hold) by a phone call informing Harry and Bev on the farm that one of their children has been rushed to the hospital, forcing the couple to leave immediately for the city. Jon Jory directed the drama, as he had at the Actors Theatre of Louisville, where the play originated.

Martin Sherman, the American author of *Bent* (12-2-79), who resided in London, was represented in New York this season with **Messiah** (12-11-84, Manhattan Theatre Club), a torrid melodrama about religious fanaticism set in the seventeenth century. When many of the Jews in Poland are massacred in a Cossack uprising in 1665, the survivors become obsessed with the idea of a Messiah coming to save them. Homely and dreamy Rachel (Diana Venora), who has married the grotesque fruit merchant Reb Ellis (David Warrilow), is particularly anxious for the second coming. Reb's nephew Asher (Mark Blum), a young scholar who has returned from the Middle East, tells Rachel that the Messiah has arrived in the form of a young rabbi named Sabbatai Sevi, who is preaching and working miracles in Gallipoli. Rachel sets off for Turkey with Asher, the two of them becoming lovers and finding new life in the teachings of Sevi. But the so-called Messiah, when under torture by the Sultan, admits that he is a fraud and becomes a Muslim. His idealism shattered, Asher rejects Rachel's love and commits suicide.

An off-off-Broadway entry that stirred up some interest was Stephen Metcalfe's **The Incredibly Famous Willy Rivers** (12-12-84, WPA), a caustic look at America's obsession with celebrity. Willy Rivers (Jay O. Sanders) is a talentless rock superstar whose popularity was starting to wane when a publicity miracle occurred: a crazed fan shot Willy while he was performing on a nationally televised concert. The singer survived the wound (the blazing red scar on his back has been photographed for all to see) and now is preparing for his comeback concert appearance. But Willy is so confused by his own image that he starts to search for his true identity, visiting other show business colleagues, old friends, his ex-wife, his senile father, and even the jailed gunman who tried to kill him. All Willy finds on his journey is fanatical devotion to his fame (one friend offers his celebrity-crazed wife for Willy to sleep with) or a bitter realization that it is all pretense (a reggae star confesses that he hates the white teens who worship him). Willy, finally discovering some answers in the incoherent ramblings of his feeble father, goes off to his concert with new vigor.

A commercial off-Broadway revival of Christopher Hampton's *Total Eclipse* (2-23-74) on December 12 at the Westside Arts folded in less than a week despite some very talented personnel. John Tillinger directed the biographical piece about poets and lovers Arthur Rimbaud (Michael Cerveris) and Paul Verlaine (Peter Evans), and all three were applauded for their efforts.

TV's popular Carroll O'Connor again came to Broadway in a family drama and again found himself "at liberty" after a two-week run. James Duff's **Home Front** (1-2-85, Royale) takes place during the Thanksgiving holiday of 1973 in the suburban Texas home of Bob (O'Connor) and Maurine (Frances Sternhagen). The couple and their daughter, Karen (Linda Cook), a graduate student who seems to be studying country-club living, appear very content with life but their son, Jeremy (Christopher Fields), recently returned from service in Vietnam, is silent and moody. During the course of the holiday, Jeremy's cutting remarks and sarcastic observations grow more confrontational as he begins to see his father as the begetter of Vietnam and all other wars as well. Eventually Jeremy explodes and pulls his army pistol on Bob, only to be subdued by his harridan of a mother, who insists everybody forget all about the outburst and enjoy the holiday. Notices ranged from "a stunning first play" to "pat and predictable." (Although it was an American play, *Home Front* premiered in London the previous season under the title *The War at Home*.)

Bill C. Davis's "sometimes merry, sometimes anguished" drama **Dancing in the End Zone** (1-3-85, Ritz) only lasted a week longer on Broadway. College quarterback James Bernard (Matt Salinger) is a soft touch, needing love from everyone and trying to please all around him. So James is torn between the urgings of his opinionated tutor, Jan Morrison (Dorothy Lyman), to pursue his education and the demands of his wheelchairbound mother (Pat Carroll) and his fanatical coach, Dick Biehn (Laurence Luckinbill), to go into professional football. In the end James realizes that all three people care less for him than they do about their own prejudiced beliefs and feels he can make the right decision on his own.

The most acclaimed American revival of the season was the Roundabout production of Peter Nichols's "matchless, bleak comedy" *Joe Egg* (2-1-68) on January 6. (The play had originally been billed as *A Day in the Death of Joe Egg*.) Arvin Brown directed, carefully balancing the script's pathos and savage humor, while Jim Dale and Stockard Channing gave sterling performances as the parents of a severely retarded child. Dale, in particular, surprised everyone. Known primarily as a very physical farceur, he showed "a depth and darkness of feeling that we have never seen before." Rave reviews and strong word of mouth encouraged the Roundabout to move the revival on March 27 to Broadway's Longacre, where it triumphed for 102 performances. It later won Tony Awards for Best Revival and for Channing's tragicomic performance.

One of the season's most uncompromising and disturbing entries was **Tracers** (1-21-85, Public: Shiva), a loosely constructed theatre piece written and performed by a group of Vietnam veterans who sought to tell those who had not been there what the war in Southeast Asia was like. Eight "grunts" are seen from their first day of boot camp to a reunion for the survivors years later, each scene a disjointed fragment that was all the more powerful for its unexpectedness. Whether they were facing death for the first time, engaging in a "beach-blanket party" (putting dismembered corpses together), or using drugs to escape from the reality of their situation, the authors/actors attacked each scene with poetic slang, chanting, and devastating jokes. Notices called it "a land mine of a play that blows complacency to shreds" and a "bleeding mural commemorating the war's legacy." Despite its grim subject matter, *Tracers* found an audience for 186 showings.

This month's second drama about a returning vet and the havoc he causes on the home front was Keith Reddin's **Life and Limb** (1-24-85, Playwrights Horizons), but this play took the form of a dark and fantastical comedy. When Franklin Roosevelt Clagg (Robert Joy) returns from Korea minus an arm, he finds the complaisant America of the 1950s too surreal to comprehend. His wife, Effie (Elizabeth Perkins), is always busy either having an affair or running off to the movies with the Rumanian refugee Doina (Robin Bartlett). Franklin's family is embarrassed by his presence, and the only job the vet can find is with the despicable Tod Cartmell (Patrick Breen), a manufacturer of artificial limbs. His life disintegrates further when Effie is killed by a collapsing moviepalace balcony, and the play ends in Hell with

Effie and Doira making potholders and the ever-confused Franklin still looking for a world that he can understand. Reddin was deemed very promising, and his "macabre journey through [the] American mainstream" was called a "broad, bitter, fantastic-satiric comedy."

The most notable new work of the Negro Ensemble season was Karen Jones-Meadows's **Henrietta** (1-25-85, Theatre Four), which stayed on the boards for nine weeks. Henrietta (Frances Foster) is a Harlem derelict woman who sits on a stoop and shouts incomprehensible comments to passersby. When the young accountant (and sometime prostitute) Sheleeah (Elain Graham) takes an interest in Henrietta, trying to rehabilitate her, we learn that the old lady is neither homeless nor a lunatic. Henrietta was once a teacher but, having buried her husband and three sons, has lost her grip on life. Sheleeah befriends the troubled woman, becoming the daughter she never had, until a rift occurs between them. Henrietta is last seen back on the stoop yelling at strangers.

The Roundabout's "dim, muffled revival" of Synge's *The Playboy of the Western World* on January 30 suffered from weak direction and garbled dialects. Ken Marshall was Christy Mahon, and Kate Burton was Pegeen. The Mirror Repertory Company, in its second season, offered three revivals beginning with Giraudoux's *The Madwoman of Chaillot* (12-27-48) on January 30 at St. Peter's Church. Stephen Porter directed the large cast, which featured Geraldine Page as the madwoman Aurelia; her portrayal was strongly endorsed. Also outstanding were Carrie Nye, Madeleine Sherwood, and Grayson Hall as her three loony friends.

Albert Innaurato's faltering career took a minor leap up with **Coming of Age in Soho** (2-3-85, Public: Martinson), a broad comedy that recalled moments from his earlier works. Curiously, while the play was floundering in previews, Innaurato rewrote the main character from a female to a male and thereby saved the show. Bartholomew Dante (John Procaccino), an author commonly called Beatrice, flees his wife of fourteen years and takes a loft apartment in Soho to deal with his writer's block and his late-blooming homosexuality. His solitude is soon broken by Dy (Scott DeFreitas), a rich teenager running away from prep school and his strict family, and then by Puer (Ward Saxton), a Teutonic-sounding youth who claims he is the child of Beatrice and a German terrorist he once had a passionate tryst with. In comes Beatrice's wife, Patricia (Mercedes Ruehl), who is running for Congress and needs a husband in tow to please her Mafia supporters and secure the Catholic vote. But Beatrice falls in love with Dy, who has happily gotten a job at McDonald's, so Patricia finally relinquishes her husband. Only after Dy returns to his family does Beatrice overcome his writer's block. Innaurato's "vitality and crazy sense of fantasy" were applauded by some of the critics, and the comedy was kept on the boards for eight weeks.

Papp arranged another exchange with London's Royal Court Theatre that brought Michael Hastings's bio-drama **Tom and Viv** (2-6-85, Lu-Esther) to the Public for a one-month run. American actor Edward Herrmann as T. S. Eliot headed the British company, and Julie Covington played his first wife, the well-situated aristocrat Vivienne Haigh-Wood. Hastings told the audience plenty of facts about the miserable, never-consummated marriage, but rarely was anything acted out. Vivienne eventually goes mad and is put in a sanitarium, but the "bloodless" play never satisfactorily explained why. Critics called the drama a "tedious impudent work—part fact, part speculation and invention" but lauded the cast (which also included Margaret Tyzak in a thankless role).

An "old-fashioned thriller/chiller" that failed to catch on was James Yaffe's **Cliffhanger** (2-17-85, Lamb's). Henry Lowenthal (Henderson Forsythe), an established philosophy professor in a small college, is about to be given an endowed chair that will ensure a comfortable completion to his academic career. But when disgruntled colleague Edith Wilshire (Natalia Nogulich) confronts Henry, telling him she is going to do all she can to block his promotion, the usually docile professor erupts and crowns her with his bust of Socrates, killing her. Henry's wife, Polly (Lenka Peterson), helps him get rid of the body, but soon a failing student (Keith Reddin) comes forth and, saying he saw the whole incident, bribes Henry for a passing grade. When the suspicious Lieutenant DeVito (Tom Mardirosian) comes on the scene, Henry panics, and eventually the truth is discovered.

Hugh Whitemore's drama **Pack of Lies** (2-11-85, Royale) was based on a true incident that occurred in the early 1960s. Bob (George N. Martin) and Barbara Jackson (Rosemary Harris) reside in an ordinary row house in a London suburb, where their best friends are Peter (Colin Fox) and Helen Kroger (Dana Ivey), who live directly across the street. Barbara has few friends but feels very close to Helen, who treats the Jacksons' teenager daughter, Julie (Tracy Pollan), like family. One day a British intelligence agent, Stewart (Patrick McGoohan), calls on the Jacksons, asking to use their home to stake out a KGB agent who visits the neighborhood weekly. Soon it becomes clear that the foreign spy is bringing information to the Krogers, and the Jacksons' lives are turned into inner turmoil. Eventually Stewart has both the spy and the Krogers arrested, and Barbara is left wondering if the only true friendship she ever had was a lie like all the others the Krogers told. The mostly favorable reviews thought it "a chilling and superbly written play" that "unfolds like a thriller but penetrates more deeply." The British import found an audience on Broadway for 120 performances.

The second offering in the Mirror's repertory was Booth Tarkington's *Clarence* (9-20-19) on February 13, which all the critics agreed held up beautifully even if the revival, directed by Arthur Storch, was considered by some "a disastrous production." Some of the cast clowned their way through the warm comedy, but Ivar Brogger was charming in the title role, and Laura Galusha shone as the spirited youth Cora. Reviewers were not in agreement about O'Neill's "epic soap opera" *Strange Interlude* (1-30-28) on February 21 at the Nederlander. Some judged the nine-act marathon to be a "stumbling, long-winded, intuitionless work," while others called it "an uncommonly absorbing evening of theatre." But all the critics mentioned the way British director Keith Hack found humor and liveliness in the drama (here cut down to five hours from the original two-part eight hours) and how beautifully Glenda Jackson, Edward Petherbridge, and other cast members kept the evening fresh and lucid. A London production with some American actors added, *Strange Interlude* did surprisingly healthy business during its limited eight-week engagement.

The second English bio-drama at the Public in as many months was Edna O'Brien's **Virginia** (3-4-85, Newman) which could only be recommended for Kate Nelligan's "glowing, versatile, commanding performance" as Virginia Woolf. The drama was essentially a monologue with Nelligan reading from Woolf's diary and letters, interrupted by fictional scenes with her father and husband (both played by Kenneth Welsh) or her sometime lover Vita Sackville-West (Patricia Elliott).

The steady stream of plays from the Actors Theatre of Louisville to Broadway continued with P. J. Barry's sentimental comedy **The Octette Bridge Club** (3-5-85, Music Box), but this time the reception was chilly, and the transfer folded in three weeks. Eight Irish-American (and very Catholic) sisters in Rhode Island meet every other Friday night to play bridge but spend much of the time in gossip, sisterly bantering, and eating fresh apple pie. We see the ladies first in 1934 and then a decade later on Halloween, when each dresses up and takes a turn acting out the persona of her costumed character. What little plot there was centered on the youngest sister (Gisela Caldwell), who is committed to a sanitarium, her illness brought on by the family's suffocatingly righteous atmosphere. Reviews ranged from "a Norman Rockwell illustration come to life" to "a veritable anodyne of a little play" to a "hollow period comedy," but there were compliments aplenty for the cast of splendid character actresses that included Nancy Marchand, Anne Pitoniak, Elizabeth Franz, Lois de Banzie, and Peggy Cass.

Nothing but pans greeted Circle in the Square's March 6 revival of Arthur Schnitzler's *Anatol*, here titled *The Loves of Anatol*, but previously seen in New York as *The Affairs of Anatol* (10-14-12) with John Barrymore and as *Anatol* (1-16-31) with Joseph Schildkraut. Ellis Rabb (who directed and did the adaptation with Nicholas Martin) seemed "to mutilate it willfully, with a thoroughness that could bring fans of the original text to tears even as the rest of the audience is put to sleep." Stephen Collins played Anatol "as a strenuous, distraught Boy Scout," and other usually reliable cast members (Philip Bosco, Mary-Joan Negro, Michael Learned) were swallowed up in the "sorry literary hash."

Another regional theatre transfer that failed this season was **Requiem for a Heavyweight** (3-7-85, Martin Beck), Rod Serling's classic 1956 television play that had been filmed in 1961 with success but was KO'd after four performances on Broadway. (Serling had originally conceived the piece as a play in the 1950s, but it was never produced.) John Lithgow played the punchdrunk boxer Harlan "Mountain" McClintock, who is too innocent to see how he is used and abused by conniving managers and promoters. Some critics were very enthusiastic, calling the drama "the most exciting thing to happen on Broadway in a long time," but most aisle-sitters disparaged the piece as too melodramatic for contemporary tastes. Lithgow was unanimously acclaimed for his "towering unforgettable performance" that found "terror, rather than cheap tears or laughs, in the boxer's pathetic, childlike stupidity." Arvin Brown directed the Long Wharf Theatre production with verve, and despite its short run on Broadway, the drama enjoyed subsequent productions elsewhere.

A "slight but frisky romantic comedy" that proved quite popular during its scheduled month-long engagement, Joseph Dougherty's **Digby** (3-8-85, Manhattan Theatre Club) concerned meek and overlooked copywriter Digby Merton (Anthony Heald), who is more than content to be left out of the sexual revolution, protecting himself from loveless sex. But then he is assigned to work with promiscuous Faye Greener (Roxanne Hart), an art gallery assistant who juggles many lovers at once and currently has in tow a beefcake actor (Tony Goldwyn), an avant-garde artist (John Glover), and a depressed policeman (Jon Polito). Against his better nature, Digby is attracted to the frivolous Faye and ends up spending a weekend with her in the country, only to have her three lovers all show up as well. The comic and romantic complications that ensue actually help bring Digby and Faye together for good.

The first of the season's notable AIDS plays was William M. Hoffman's **As Is** (3-10-85, Circle). Rich (Jonathan Hogan) is a promising poet who is leaving his long-time lover, Saul (Jonathan Hadary), for a young stud named Chet (Steven Gregan). While Rich and Saul are dividing up everything in their apartment, Rich lets it slip out that he has AIDS. Saul offers to stay with Rich, but the poet refuses, even later after Chet abandons him. Soon Rich has lost his job, his brother (Ken Kilban) is afraid to visit him, and his physical condition deteriorates. Only after he is hospitalized does Rich finally accept Saul's unselfish love, make peace with his brother, and start to deal with his bleak destiny. The free-flowing drama, carefully directed by Marshall W. Mason, included flashbacks to past events and commentary by hospice and hospital workers who spoke about the disease as it affects people emotionally rather than medically. The drama was neither clinical nor political but compassionate, and the press reacted accordingly, calling it "a wonderful and frightening play" and "tender entertainment, [filled with] terror and unexpected joy." After forty-nine performances, the drama transferred to Broadway's Lyceum on May 1, received further exemplary notices, and ran 285 more performances.

The Mirror added Robert Bolt's *Vivat! Vivat! Regina!* (1-20-72) to its repertory on March 14, and the "pokey revival" met with mixed notices. Geraldine Page made a very effective Queen Elizabeth, but Sabra Jones was miscast and inadequate as Mary of Scotland.

A blow to director Jerry Zaks, who seemed never to have anything but hits, came in the form of Michael Zettler's **Crossing the Bar** (3-21-85, Playhouse 91), which closed after only four performances. Six saloonkeepers drive through rural Pennsylvania in a hearse to bury their friend, also a bar owner, in a distant graveyard. They stop at a rural tavern, where they drink and talk; the driver passes out, and another of the men has a momentary fling with the proprietor's daughter. Once the soused group realize that they have missed the appointed funeral time, they bribe the owner to let them bury their friend under the new addition being built behind the bar. Although poorly reviewed, the play did boast an interesting set by Loren Sherman in which the walls were cluttered with deer antlers.

Aleksandr Borshchagovky's Soviet drama *A Ladies' Tailor* caused quite a stir in Moscow in 1980 when it argued that most of the Kiev citizens massacred by the Nazis near Babi Yar in 1941 were Jewish. But Joseph Stein's English adaptation entitled **Before the Dawn** (3-24-85, American Place) caused little interest; critics called the drama "a dull and colorless piece of theatre" and "a curiously remote and mechanical effort." While the Jewish Starkman family prepare to leave their Kiev home, as ordered by the Germans, the gentile family that is to inherit the dwelling arrives a day early, so the two families are forced to spend a night together. A gentle and even loving understanding develops between the two families, overshadowed by hints of the cruel destruction that awaits the Starkmans the next morning. The awkward direction, some stilted acting, and the problematic script contributed to the play's closing after one week.

Ibsen's *An Enemy of the People* was given a commendable mounting by the Roundabout on March 27 with a first-class performance by Roy Dotrice as the controversial doctor who is destroyed in trying to do the right thing. Oliver noted, "It would be hard to imagine a more exuberant, self-deluding, self-winding, or funnier Dr. Stockmann than Mr. Dotrice."

Neil Simon followed up his popular *Brighton Beach Memoirs* (3-27-83) with the profitable sequel **Biloxi Blues** (3-28-85, Neil Simon), which continued the story of the autobiographical Eugene Morris Jerome, again played by Matthew Broderick. In 1943 Eugene has been drafted and is on a train to boot camp in Biloxi, Mississippi. His goals for his army years: "to become a writer, not get killed, and lose my virginity." As in the first play, Eugene narrates the comedy, describing his five fellow recruits with comic flair and jotting down all the events in his writer's journal. When the men arrive at camp and are put through their paces, the Jewish intellectual Arnold Epstein (Barry Miller) is immediately singled out and becomes the butt of the group's jokes and the favorite whipping boy of Sergeant Merwin J. Toomey (Bill Sadler). After a few days Eugene is totally discouraged, confessing to his journal: "I thought of shooting off a part of my body I might not need in later life but couldn't find any." While being initiated into the cockeyed ways of the army, Eugene also has his first sexual encounter, with the wry southern prostitute Rowena (Randall Edwards), and his first case of true love, with Daisy Hannigan, a Catholic girl (Penelope Ann Miller) whom he meets at a dance. But it is his fellow Jew Epstein who teaches Eugene the most important lesson of his army years when he stands up to Toomey's bigotry, confronting him with brute courage, and wins. The comedy received even better reviews than the earlier play had, and Simon won his first Best Play Tony Award. Barry Miller and director Gene Saks also won, but, curiously, *Biloxi Blues* lasted only 524 performances, little more than half the run of *Brighton Beach Memoirs*.

Still one more British work at the Public was Louise Page's **Salonika** (4-2-85, Anspacher), an "elusive, moonstruck play" that was "made like a patchwork quilt of small conflicts between flesh and spirit." The aging British widow Charlotte (Jessica Tandy) visits a beach in Greece, the site of her husband's death in World War I, with her restless middle-aged daughter, Enid (Elizabeth Wilson). A naked young man (Maxwell Caulfield) lies sunbathing on the beach as the ghost of a doughboy David Strathairn) makes appearances throughout, speaking to Charlotte and Enid and eventually revealing himself as the deceased husband/father. English pensioner Leonard (Thomas Hill), who has long been in love with Charlotte, hitchhikes from Athens to find her and propose marriage, but in the end Charlotte refuses, saying she needs her old home and memories to sustain her. John Madden directed, eliciting mystical and entrancing performances from his gifted cast, especially Tandy.

The only comedy in the Negro Ensemble season was Trevor Rhone's **Two Can Play** (4-11-85, Theatre Four), a two-hander about a Jamaican husband, Jim Thomas (Sullivan H. Walker), who treats his wife, Gloria (Hazel J. Medina), like a servant; she responds by building up his chauvinistic ego. But when Gloria goes to Miami for a visit, she returns a changed woman and soon puts Jim in his place. The "rather beguiling if lightweight farce" met with some appreciative notices.

Jane Connell, a character actress who was always an audience favorite but never quite became a full-fledged star, was featured in the one-person show **The Singular Dorothy Parker** (4-14-85, Actors' Playhouse), which Rory Seeber compiled from the famous Algonquin wit's poems, essays, stories, and reviews. Notices pointed out that the highly quotable material did not necessarily make for satisfying theatre.

The same commentators felt that all the theatrics in Mark Lee's violent **California Dog Fight** (4-16-85, Manhattan Theatre Club) added up to less than a play as well. In a parched pear orchard in the Sacramento delta, illegal dog fights bring a collection of bloodthirsty characters together, the combative nature of the sport spilling over into the lives of the spectators. Despite some talented actors (Jimmy Ray Weeks, Mariel Hemingway, Darren McGavin, Sheree North), reviewers felt the drama was, "for all its strenuous activity and boiling emotion, as empty as a drum."

A trifle of a play about infidelity among the British upper classes, Frederick Lonsdale's *Aren't We All?* (5-21-23) was spiced up with a stellar cast for its revival on April 29 at the Brooks Atkinson after having conquered the West End. An ageless Claudette Colbert and a brittle Jeremy Brett, luminous Lynn Redgrave, scene-stealing George Rose, and mellow but still impish Rex Harrison breezed through the drawing-room comedy and delighted audiences for ninety-six showings.

The season's second major AIDS play, Larry Kramer's autobiographical **The Normal Heart** (4-21-85, Public: LuEsther), was a much more political and, consequently, angrier work than *As Is*. Ned Weeks (Brad Davis), a writer and gay activist, goes on a crusade to awaken the world to the spread of AIDS, founding the Gay Men's Health Crisis Center, getting funds for research, and badgering government officials to react. His campaign becomes more personal when he learns that his lover, Felix (D. W. Moffett), has contracted the disease. Most aisle-sitters supported the play, calling it "an angry, unremitting and gripping piece of political theatre." While Frank Rich in the *New York Times* decreed it "powerful," he criticized the drama's "pamphleteering tone."

(The critic was referring to the claim in the play that the *Times* tried to suppress early news about AIDS. The newspaper ran a denial with the review, stating its 1981 article was one of the first to bring the syndrome to the public's attention.) Producer Papp felt so strongly about the work that he kept it open for 294 performances, losing money after the initially strong attendance tapered off. *The Normal Heart* broke the record for the longest run at the Public.

A popular attraction off-off Broadway was E. Katherine Kerr's **Juno's Swans** (5-3-85, Second Stage), a three-character piece about a struggling bohemian of an actress, Cary Davis (Mary Kay Place), whose cluttered New York walkup is invaded by her straitlaced older sister, Cecilia (Betty Buckley), a well-groomed California housewife retreating from her husband and kids after a fight. The two sisters are opposite in everything, but soon they reach an understanding, helped by Cecilia's romance with Cary's songwriting friend Douglas Deering (Daniel Hugh-Kelly). While critics found it a "flat and formulaic, if sincere, New York comedy," audiences packed the small theatre for its thirty-nine scheduled performances.

Lyle Kessler's tragicomic **Orphans** (5-7-85, Westside) quickly developed a cult audience off Broadway that kept the play on the boards for 285 performances. Petty thief Treat (Terry Kinney) and his mildly retarded brother, Philip (Kevin Anderson), live in a North Philadelphia row house together, sometimes taking on child-like behavior and wallowing in their being orphans. Treat brings home Harold (John Mahoney), a rich businessman he hopes to get drunk and rob. It turns out Harold is indeed wealthy but has powerful enemies who are trying to kill him, so he shrewdly uses the brothers' house as a base for his underworld dealings. Soon the kidnap victim becomes the father Treat and Philip never had, and the trio find an odd but moving camaraderie together. In addition to advocating Kessler's "weird, wonderful thriller," critics cheered the three actors and director Gary Sinise, all of whom had done the play previously at Chicago's Steppenwolf Theatre.

Some of New York's most personable middle-aged actors helped bring David Wiltse's contrived comedy **Doubles** (5-8-85, Ritz) to life for 277 performances. Stockbroker George (Tony Roberts), philanderer Arnie (Austin Pendleton), Jewish businessman Lennie (Ron Leibman), and sportswriter Gus (John Cullum) engage in doubles tennis each week, and their pre-play and after-play locker room conversations over a period of months illustrate their competitive natures and the male bonding that helps them get through their midlife crises. Divorce, affairs, loss of job, a heart attack, and questionable business practices all come up between tennis games, the result moving between sitcom humor and sentimental melodrama. Critical feedback ranged from "a rowdy, appealing, and captivating comedy" to "a reasonably proficient, if overlong, exercise in innocuousness."

Another jokey sitcom of a play was Murphy Guyer's **Eden Court** (5-14-85, Promenade), an off-Broadway commercial entry that barely lasted two weeks. A married couple (Ben Masters and Ellen Barkin) living in a trailer park have their problems (he is in a panic about turning thirty, and she is an uncontrollable Elvis Presley fanatic), which are only exasperated by their two friends (Penny Marshall and Guy Boyd) who engage them in chatter, fights, and games, all heavily contrived but performed with panache.

One of the best plays ever discovered by the Negro Ensemble, Lonne Elder III's *Ceremonies in Dark Old Men* (2-4-69), was revived on May 15 at Theatre Four. Once again Douglas Turner Ward directed and played the central role of the aging hoofer Russell Parker. The drama was acclaimed again by the press, remaining on the boards for two months.

Depending on your point of view, Christopher Durang's satire was either getting sharper or going too far in **The Marriage of Bette and Boo** (5-16-85, Public: Newman), a scathing look at wedlock that was even more absurdist than his previous attacks on religion and parents. Soon after the vacuous Bette (Joan Allen) marries the dispassionate Boo (Graham Beckel), they have a son, Matt (Durang), who narrates the chronicle of this American family from hell. Bette wants to have lots of children, but the next four babies are stillborn, the doctor tossing them on the floor as a way of announcing the bad news. Boo takes to drink while interfering grandparents and relatives (as well as a dithering priest) help tear the couple further apart. After some failed counseling from the Church, Bette and Boo divorce, use their son as a weapon against each other, then are reunited as Bette is dying of cancer. The soap opera plot was made wickedly funny by the outlandish characters, whose stupidity and narrowmindedness kept events from approaching reality. Jerry Zaks directed with a flourish, and Loren Sherman (who had designed no fewer than six New York productions this season) provided the witty, cartoonish settings. Audiences laughed uncomfortably for eighty-six performances.

Patty Gideon Sloan's domestic drama **Man Enough** (5-19-85, Apple Corps) found an audience for only a month in a commercial offering off Broadway. After struggling for eighteen years, Brooklyn parents Jack (David S. Howard) and Josie Delaney (Marilyn Chris) have finally decided that they have to put their mentally retarded son, Joey (Bruce Roberts King), in a state institution. But before they do, their elder son, Donal (Will Jeffries), comes home for the weekend, finds out their plans, and is appalled at their decision. Ironically, it is Joey, in his quiet and reassuring manner, who explains the realities of life to Donel and teaches his brother to accept the inevitable.

A gentle two-character play by Andrew Johns called **The Return of Herbert Bracewell** (5-20-85, Chelsea) teamed up two favorite character actors, Milo O'Shea and Frances Sternhagen, for seven weeks in a reaffirming comedy about the theatre profession. In 1909, the has-been actor Herbert Bracewell climbs to the top floor of his New York town house in the middle of the night and rehearses a one-man show that will serve as his comeback vehicle. His wife, Florence, a younger and (in her day) more successful actress, comes up to call him to bed, but soon she is caught up in reliving past roles, pulling down old scripts and using faded props in putting together Herbert's show. As the playacting goes on, it becomes clear that Herbert's encroaching senility will keep him off the stage forever, and old wounds (such as Florence's past infidelity) are opened up in the impromptu performances the two actors work out. Their love for the theatre has sustained them over the years, but they must now rely solely on each other. Geraldine Fitzgerald directed the duet beautifully, and James Wolk provided the atmospheric attic setting overflowing with memorabilia of former glory.

The Public concluded its season with another guest production from London's Royal Court Theatre, Ron Hutchinson's **Rat in the Skull** (5-21-85, Martinson). In a London police station, Irishman Roche (Colum Convey) is being questioned by three cops, having been arrested for possession of guns and explosives in his apartment and suspected of being an IRA terrorist. One of the officers, Nelson (Brian Cox), is from Ulster and displays both camaraderie and contempt for his fellow Irishman. In the interrogation, Roche has been badly beaten (slides behind the action show close-up shots of his bruised and bloody face), and in the end he is released because authorities are fearful that his rough treatment will be made an issue. While the realistic and gritty play did not please all the critics, there was general admiration for the actors, especially Cox.

The Acting Company continued to bring an eclectic repertory of classics to New York as part of its national tour. Philip Massinger's *A New Way to Pay Old Debts* opened on May 21 at Marymount Manhattan and was joined by *As You Like It* on May 22 and Thornton Wilder's *The Skin of Our Teeth* (11-18-42) on May 24. The Roundabout revived a near-classic with a capable production of John van Druten's *The Voice of the Turtle* (12-8-43) on May 22. Chris Sarandon and J. Smith-Cameron were the wartime lovers, and Patricia Elliot was the interfering friend who almost breaks them up.

The memoirs of French writer Nathalia Sarraute were translated by Kate Mortley and Barbara Wright and dramatized by Simone Benmussa into **Childhood** (5-29-85, Samuel Beckett), a talky piece that would have been ignored if not for the presence of Glenn Close as the heroine. Sarraute's miserable youth (being shuffled back and forth between divorced parents in Russia and France) was considered too stagnant for the stage, though Close was applauded as "elegant" and "transfixing." Benmussa's curtain raiser, **For No Good Reason**, about two men who try to resolve the differences threatening their friendship, was hardly more stageworthy. (It had been written as a radio play originally.) Some commentators found the monodrama intriguing; others thought it "interminable." Oliver observed, "Whatever Nathalia Sarraute's contribution to French letters may be, her contribution to the theatre—as manifest in these two one-acters adapted from her work—is zero."

Critics enjoyed the "exaggerated, overly energetic production" of Shaw's *Arms and the Man* on May 30 at the Circle in the Square for Kevin Kline's very physical but lucid and intelligent Captain Bluntschli. Several aisle-sitters felt that the rest of the cast overacted and that the direction (by the unlikely John Malkovich) was gimmicky and annoying. But audiences had 109 performances to see Kline, and they gladly filled the little theatre.

Near the season's end, Lincoln Center, which had not produced any of its own shows this season but only housed guest productions, announced that Gregory Mosher, former artistic director of Chicago's Goodman Theatre, would run the troubled Center with the assistance of business manager Bernard Gersten, the Public Theatre's associate director, who had a falling-out with producer Papp. Once again Lincoln Center was poised to begin a new chapter in its seesaw history.

1985–1986

Despite the new Marquis Theatre, which opened this season in the high-rise Marriott Marquis Hotel, replacing the beloved Helen Hayes, Bijou, and Morosco theatres, Broadway was shrinking. In August, three Broadway theatres (the Neil Simon, Ambassador, and Virginia) were declared designated landmarks, and it seemed that the threat of similarly destructive ventures had passed. But no season can be measured by the number of playhouses. On Broadway, box-office grosses dropped 8 percent, and attendance nosedived an alarming 9 percent. Actors' Equity reported that, for the first time on record, there was more work this season for union actors in the non-profit regional theatres than in all the Broadway and touring shows combined.

The number of productions was not much different from the previous season: twenty-three non-musicals on Broadway, including nine new American plays, and roughly seventy off Broadway, about half of them native works. But fewer plays had lengthy runs and, more distressing, fewer were of high quality. For the first time since 1974, no Pulitzer Prize in drama was awarded. It was easy to see why: the American entries this season were lackluster, and few of the British offerings were much better. Of the fifty or so new plays introduced on and off the Street this season, only one—Sam Shepard's *A Lie of the Mind*—came close to becoming part of the regularly produced repertory.

Top ticket for a non-musical reached a record $37.50 on Broadway, yet only four plays (*Benefactors, I'm Not Rappaport, The Search for Signs of Intelligent Life in the Universe*, and the new version of *The Odd Couple*) broke even by season's end. But production costs also broke records. The Broadway revival of *Hay Fever* took $900,000 to open, ran for 124 performances, and ended up losing an even $1 million. The much-anticipated *A Lie of the Mind* broke the record for the highest advance sale for an off-Broadway play, yet when it closed after 186 performances, it still failed to show a profit. Box office and artistic quality have often been strangers to each other, but this season they kept each other company by both doing poorly.

The season started off disappointingly with Jonathan Reynolds's **Fighting International Fat** (6-5-85, Playwrights Horizons), a satire in which the playwright "never brings his script into focus or allows his points to register." Rosalind Gambol (Jessica Walter) runs the International Fat Fighters, a group that believes in losing weight through "obsessional self-denial." When television emcee Shep Bradley Diedricksen (John Gabriel) auditions members of the organization for his talk show, he falls in and out of love (and sex) first with Rosalind and then her rival, D. Raleigh Bell (Lisa Banes), who advocates weight loss through surgery. The wicked comedy plowed fertile ground but bore no fruit, disappearing after its two-week engagement.

Herb Gardner's **I'm Not Rappaport** (6-6-85, American Place), the only new American comedy hit of the season, originated at the Seattle Repertory Theatre, where it was directed by Daniel Sullivan. The play featured two seasoned character actors, Judd Hirsch and Cleavon Little, as crusty and determined octogenarians fighting the system just as the hero of Gardner's *A Thousand Clowns* (4-5-62) had done a quarter of a century ago. Nat (Hirsch), a diehard radical and former union organizer, spends most of his afternoons sitting on a bench in a quiet corner of Central Park, gabbing with Midge (Little), a nearly blind building super who is always hiding from his tenants. Just as Nat is being encouraged by his daughter Clara (Cheryl Giannini) to move in with her family in Great Neck (Nat calls it "Siberia"), so too is Midge being pushed by the dissatisfied residents in his building to retire. Various Central Park regulars (dope peddlers, muggers, exercise nuts) interrupt Nat's tall tales and sociopolitical debates with Midge. When a pusher named Cowboy (Ray Baker) threatens a young female user, Nat steps in and tries to convince the thug that Midge and he are government agents and are connected with the "Cuban Mafia." In the scuffle, Midge is wounded by Cowboy's knife but survives. The two old men bravely hang on. Reviews ranged from the *Daily News*'s Douglas Watt describing the play as "a synthetic but largely enjoyable wry comedy" to Frank Rich in the *New York Times* calling it "didactic and repetitive." But notices for the two polished actors were unanimously glowing, and audiences filled the small house for 181 performances before it moved to Broadway's Booth on November 19. It stayed 890 performances, winning Tony Awards for Best

Play, Hirsch's performance, and Pat Collins's evocative lighting.

The American Theatre Exchange, a showcase of new scripts introduced by regional theatres, featured three New York premieres throughout the summer. Heather McDonald's **Faulkner's Bicycle** (6-6-85, Joyce), a Canadian play mounted by the Yale Repertory Theatre, portrayed the famous author during his final days in Oxford, Mississippi. William Faulkner (Addison Powell) can no longer write, so he spends his time drunkenly riding around town on his bicycle, throwing apples at strangers, and irritating his neighbors. One of these fellow Oxfordians is the repressed wallflower Claire Pierce (Cara Duff-MacCormick), who cares for her ailing mother (Kim Hunter) and writes letters of admiration to her celebrated neighbor. Claire is also a writer who has temporarily lost her artistic passion, but her friendship with Faulkner restores her fire. When he dies, Claire is left with one of his old manuscripts, a recipe for apple bread, and the writer's rusted bicycle. Jeffrey Sweet, writing in the *Best Plays*, was among the commentators to point out the thinness of Claire's character, saying there was little "differentiating her from any other groupie who tries to build self-esteem by associating with the famous or talented."

The Broadway season started on June 11 with a profitable if unimaginative comic entry, Neil Simon's *The Odd Couple* (3-10-65) rewritten as a vehicle for two women. Oscar and Felix became slovenly divorcée Olive Madison (Rita Moreno) and neatnik TV news producer Florence Unger (Sally Struthers), the weekly poker games were turned into all-female sessions of Trivial Pursuit, and the English Pigeon sisters became (in the new version's best scene) two swanky but incomprehensible Spanish businessmen (Lewis Stradlen and Tony Shalhoub) trying to fit into the American way of life. Gene Saks directed with his customary verve, the laughs were in place, and the comedy entertained audiences at the Broadhurst through February. The "regenerated" script became extremely popular in stock and community theatres as well.

A little double bill by Charles Busch, **Vampire Lesbians of Sodom** and **Sleeping Beauty or Coma** (6-19-85, Provincetown Playhouse), was the biggest off-Broadway hit of the season, running 2,024 performances and establishing a record for the longest non-musical run off the Street for several years. *Vampire Lesbians of Sodom* was a campy spoof of vamps (and vampires) from the ancient days of Sodom to the Hollywood of the 1920s to Las Vegas today. The piece offered no lesbians, but the featured vamp, Madeleine Astarte, was played by the author in drag in a performance that was less exaggerated than Charles Ludlam's female portrayals but delightfully ludicrous all the same. The curtain raiser, *Sleeping Beauty or Coma*, concentrated on rival designers in the cutthroat fashion industry in the swinging mod London of the 1960s with Busch playing the heroine, Fauna Alexander, a Twiggy-like waif who rises to the top despite the efforts of her enemies. The critics who accepted the daffy pieces for what they were declared them "bizarre and wonderful," filled with "outrageous lines, awful puns, sinister innocence, [and] harmless depravity." Busch would write and perform in similar cross-dressing popular comedies (many of them better written than this) for his group Theatre in Limbo, but none would be as sensationally successful as this double bill.

The New York Shakespeare Festival's only nonmusical offering of the summer at the Delacorte was the problem play *Measure for Measure* on June 30, which director-producer Joseph Papp set in 1910 Vienna and presented as a comedy. Some commentators felt the conceit worked, calling the mounting a "bright, lively—almost coherent—staging of this less-than-coherent social comedy"; others felt it "lacks much in the way of creative spark or even attitude." Also mixed were opinions regarding the cast, led by Richard Jordan (Angelo), Mary Elizabeth Mastrantonio (Isabella), and John Getz (Vincentio). Generally approved were Lindsay W. Davis's lavish operetta-like costumes and Robin Wagner's setting of white lace dotted with red roses. Japan's renowned *The Grand Kabuki* arrived on July 8 and performed two programs of traditional works at the Metropolitan Opera for two weeks. Presented in Japanese were *Shibaraku* (Just a Moment), *Tachi-Nusu-bito* (The Sword Thief), *Kojo* (Name-Taking Ceremony), *Sakura-hime Azuma Bunsho* (The Scarlet Princess of Edo), *Tsuchi-gumo* (The Earth Spider), and *Kasane*. Ichikawa Danjuro XII, one of the principal actors in the troupe, was a direct descendant of the Danjuro who founded the company in 1697.

The first of the season's many father-son dramas was Neal Bell's **Raw Youth** (7-10-85, Playwrights Horizons). Sam (Ben Siegler), kicked off the police force for suspected corruption, is a bisexual who has long hoped for the approval of his father, Mel (John Seitz), a con man who now works for the FBI in an effort to have criminal charges against him dropped. So when Mel asks

Sam to act as a gay decoy to snare a closet-homosexual congressman, the son agrees. But the sexual liaison with Congressman Gary (James Ray) turns into true affection, the older man seeing Sam as the son he once lost and trusting him with his reputation even when he suspects the setup. In the end Sam throws the videotaped evidence into the sea as he and his own father reach an understanding and mutual respect.

Alan Ayckbourn's latest comedy, **Season's Greetings** (7-11-85, Joyce), came to New York by way of Houston's Alley Theatre and was presented for only twenty showings as part of the American Theatre Exchange. An extended British family gathers for Christmas and Boxing Day, and the various members find themselves alternately harassed and bored by each other. The one stranger in the assembly, the pompous writer Clive (Michael Alan Gregory), joins them to woo Rachel (Lawr Means), the family spinster, but instead falls for her married sister Belinda (Robin Moseley) with tragicomic results. The highlight of the evening was a rehearsal of a dreadful puppet show of "The Three Little Pigs" put on by incompetent Uncle Bernard (Dale Helward), his dashed dreams of being a father evident in his pathetic efforts to entertain the neighborhood kids. The comedy was greeted with approval, critics declaring it "superbly crafted" and "an enjoyable, efficient play."

Benn W. Levy's comedy *Springtime for Henry* (12-9-31), an old favorite not seen in New York since 1951, was revived on July 17 at the Roundabout for seven weeks. Peter Evans essayed the philandering playboy Mr. Dewlip and was supported by George N. Martin, Tovah Feldshuh, and Jodi Thelen. The Negro Ensemble Company offered a return engagement of Trevor Rhone's *Two Can Play* (4-11-85) on July 18 at Theatre Four, and audiences welcomed it for another eighty-six performances. Sam Shepard's *Curse of the Starving Class* (2-14-78) received its first revival on July 30 at the Promenade. Kathy Bates as the mother of a decaying family was considered the most impressive of the uneven cast. As with other Shepard revivals, the press found that they liked the "brilliant, humorous, passionate play" much more on second viewing. Audiences agreed, keeping the tragicomedy on the boards for 267 performances, more than four times the run of the original.

The third offering by the American Theatre Exchange was Jack Henry Abbott's **In the Belly of the Beast** (8-15-85, Joyce), presented by Los Angeles's Mark Taper Forum. Abbott, a con-victed murderer who put his letters from prison together with transcripts from his trial and interviews with the participants and came up with a best-selling book, adapted the work for the stage, creating a collage about life in prison. Another book, Edith Wharton's 1913 novel **The Custom of the Country** (9-22-85, Second Stage), was adapted for the stage by Jane Stanton Hitchcock. Valerie Mahaffney played the social-climbing Undine Spragg, who conquers first New York and then the French aristocracy. Those critics familiar with the complex and satirical novel found that the stage version made for a "slight, ironic, obliquely sympathetic play." The commercial venture closed in two weeks.

The Circle Rep presented Lanford Wilson's *Talley & Son*, a revised version of his *A Tale Told* (6-11-81), on September 24, and although critics felt it was an improvement over the original, few could heartily endorse it. The next night, the Roundabout revived Jean Anouilh's *The Waltz of the Toreadors* (1-17-57) with Carole Shelley stealing the show as the perennial virgin Mlle. de Ste.-Euverte. Critics felt that Lee Richardson was miscast as the amorous General St. Pé, but Tammy Grimes was saluted as his hypochondriac wife.

Comic actress Lily Tomlin had displayed a cornucopia of characters in a one-person show on Broadway seven years earlier, but this season's **The Search for Signs of Intelligent Life in the Universe** (9-26-85, Plymouth) was a revelation. Tomlin delved into much deeper characterization than previously, and the script, written and directed by Jane Wagner, turned into a true play. Trudy, a crazy Manhattan bag lady who has extended conversations with aliens, acts as the narrator of the piece; her mind waves turn her into different characters, such as the rebellious teenager Agnus, the physically fit but mentally confused Chrissy, and the bored matron Kate, who is bored discussing her boredom. Then in the second act the play gathers greater force as a history of the women's movement in the 1970s is portrayed through the diary of Lynn, a woman who moves through the era with a wry and nostalgic eye. By the end of the evening, the dozen or so characters are all connected by either coincidence or revealing Dickensian resolutions. Critics were mostly enthusiastic, calling the piece "an idiosyncratic, rude, blood-stained comedy" and describing Tomlin as "the incredible expanding woman," marveling how she "makes, unmakes, and remakes her various selves with a kind of ecstasy, a metamorphic bliss, that only great actors have." The program proved popular enough to run 398 performances, a new record for a one-person show on Broadway. For her 1977 appearance, the Tony committee gave Tomlin a special award; this time they rightly gave her a Tony for Best Actress in a Play.

Theatregoers got a chance to relive one of the great moments in off-Broadway history when director José Quintero and star Jason Robards presented O'Neill's *The Iceman Cometh* (10-9-46) on September 29 at the Lunt-Fontanne, just as they had in 1955 when they had set their careers in motion, kindled a renewed interest in O'Neill, and put Off Broadway on the cultural map. Robards was surrounded with a sterling cast that included Donald Moffat (Larry Slade), Barnard Hughes (Harry Hope), John Christopher Jones (Willie Oban), and John Pankow (Rocky). With three intermissions, the production ran nearly five hours, but rave reviews helped fill the large house for fifty-five showings.

British playwright David Hare's most ambitious effort yet, **A Map of the World** (10-1-85, Public: Newman), attempted to create a debate on world poverty on an epic scale, and the result, according to Rich, was an "extraordinarily clever, if erratic, comedy about the perilous intersection of literary esthetics, global politics, and private lives." Other critics chimed in, calling the puzzling work "provocative," "humane and infinitely beautiful," and "the most stimulating new play of the season." At a UNESCO conference on global poverty held at a plush Bombay hotel, people starve on the street while the intelligentsia inside are debating and a film crew is making a movie of a novel about such a conference. Victor Mehta (Roshan Seth), an Indian right-wing author who wittily scoffs at Third World politics from his Shropshire home, returns to his homeland for the conference and to see his novel filmed. He is pitted against young Stephen Andrews (Zeljko Ivanek), an idealistic English journalist covering the conference for a left-wing magazine. Their debate takes on a lustful quality when the American film actress Peggy Whitton (Elizabeth McGovern) promises to sleep with the man who wins the debate. The only voice of conscience on the scene is Elaine Le Fanu (Alfre Woodard), an American television correspondent who challenges both Mehta's and Andrews's arguments. Scenes from the movie being filmed overlap with the actual goings-on at the hotel, Mehta allows the filmmakers to change the "truth" for the screen version, and it all gets rather murky by the end. But the discussion was lively, articulate,

and even balanced. Audiences were engrossed for two months.

Paul Osborn's **Tomorrow's Monday** (10-4-85, Circle) had been written in 1936 and produced elsewhere but not in New York until the Circle Rep offered it in repertory with *Talley & Son*. New Yorker Richard Allen (Richard Backus) and his sophisticated wife, Lora (Diana Venora), return to his midwestern hometown when he hears that his mother (Helen Stenborg) is very ill. It turns out to be only indigestion, but the urban couple decide to stay for a while. Lora disrupts the simple inhabitants of the household, especially Richard's spinster sister, Esther (Trish Hawkins), by trying to convince young John Allen (Robert MacNaughton) to drop out of the local college and come back to New York with them. Although not nearly as splendid as Osborn's recently rediscovered *Morning's at Seven* (11-30-39), the "new" work had a similar kind of charm filled with "gentle laughter and a warm feeling for a time when life in America seemed more manageable."

"Gimmickry abounds" in the Circle in the Square revival of the rarely seen Beaumarchais masterwork *The Marriage of Figaro* on October 10, which Andrei Serban directed in a non-traditional manner that most critics felt was "more suggestive of the Three Stooges than Mozart." Scenery, props, lighting, and costumes were all white, and the actors cavorted, stripteased, rollerskated, bicycled, and swung on swings as the complex plot unfolded circus-style. Anthony Heald (Figaro), Mary Elizabeth Mastrantonio (Suzanne), and Dana Ivey (Countess) were the most often complimented of the cast. Richard Nelson's adaptation was staged for seventy-seven performances.

Another play about literary figures that originated elsewhere and arrived in New York this season was Stephen MacDonald's **Not About Heroes** (10-21-85, Lucille Lortel), a two-character drama about poets Wilfred Owen (Dylan Baker) and Siegfried Sassoon (Edward Herrmann). Using their letters and poetry, as well as MacDonald's imagination, the play chronicled the deep friendship that began when they met in a Scottish hospital in 1917, both victims of shell shock in the Great War. Seen previously at the Edinburgh Festival and the Williamstown Festival in Massachusetts, the play only survived three weeks in a commercial mounting off Broadway.

A sampling of Italian performing arts called *Italy on Stage* opened on October 21 at Lincoln Center with a series of plays, concerts, musicals, and puppet shows. Two comedies, *I Due Serpenti* (The Two Serpents) and *Il Campiello* (The Campiello), were performed in Italian with English subtitles in the Vivian Beaumont.

Samm-Art Williams continued to search for a hit like his earlier *Home* (12-14-79) but had to settle for a ten-week run of his **Eyes of the American** (10-25-85, Theatre Four) by the Negro Ensemble Company. Cheddy Boswell (Graham Brown), a CIA agent posing as a tourist to sniff out subversive activities in a West Indies island nation, comes across the leader of a revolution in the form of James Horsford Ottley III (Glynn Turman), a taxi driver who has dreams of being king of the island. In a series of short (and sometimes confusing) scenes, Cheddy gets involved with James's family and starts to empathize with the natives, but his very presence on the island soon leads to violence and bloodshed. Some critics applauded the play's willingness to "raise issues—especially such issues as power, dictatorship and colonialism," but most felt, as Edith Oliver in *The New Yorker* pointed out, that "the play has passion, humor and some urgency—everything, that is, except clarity and the spirit we expect from Mr. Williams."

Wallace Shawn's disturbing black comedy **Aunt Dan and Lemon** (10-28-85, Public: Martinson) was a source of much debate this season, starting with the mixed reviews that called it everything from "a quagmire of a play" to "the most stimulating, not to say demanding, American play to emerge this year." Reclusive young Lenora (Kathryn Pogson), a contemporary Londoner nicknamed Lemon, sits in her lonely flat and expresses her pro-Nazi philosophy to the audience, conjuring up people from her past who led her to her current viewpoint. Most effective of the influences on her was the Oxford don Danielle (Linda Hunt), affectionately recalled as Aunt Dan. The outspoken academic defends Henry Kissinger's policies in Vietnam and convinces Lemon that man's atrocities are part of his human nature, even part of his noble existence. Lemon is so attuned to this theory of self-preservation that she feels nothing when Dan dies. Much of the play consisted of monologues and short (sometimes graphic and shocking) scenes showing man's inhumanity to others, such as a police agent (Lynsey Baxter) strangling her naked victim (Mario Arrambide) in the act of lovemaking. Although it was an American work, the drama had premiered at London's Royal Court and some original cast members appeared at the Public for

ten weeks before being replaced by Americans for an additional fourteen weeks.

The second forgotten Paul Osborn play to be revived this season was *Oliver Oliver* (1-5-34) on November 12 at the Manhattan Theatre Club. The "dusty drawing room comedy" about homespun matchmaking was criticized for its outdated, languid manner, and the revival, directed by Vivian Matalon, needed "more energy, speed and, especially, sexual tension." The cast was led by shining performances by Frances Sternhagen as the wealthy Constance Oakshot and Nancy Marchand as her bored friend Judith Tiverton. The original 1934 mounting ran eleven performances; the revival lasted twenty-four. The next night, stately Dina Merrill was miscast as Lady Bracknell and floundered in a revival of Oscar Wilde's *The Importance of Being Earnest* at the Samuel Beckett. Commentators noted that the American cast effectively handled the British dialect and the Wilde witticisms. Most often cited with favor were Cynthia Dozier and Cherry Jones as Gwendolyn and Cecily.

Harry Kondoleon took on the idle rich in his satire **The Anteroom** (11-20-85, Playwrights Horizons), which recalled the screwball comedies of the 1930s even though it was very contemporary in its neuroses. The Southampton home of Fay Leland (Elizabeth Wilson) is overrun by a flock of characters, each with his own agenda. Fay's neighbor Craig (Colin Fox) has a flamboyant son, Parker (Albert Macklin), who wants to inherit Fay's fortune, so the youth tries to convince her that his father is in love with her, hoping the two will run off to Switzerland together. Parker's friend Wilson (Mitchell Lichtenstein) has been hired as Fay's butler and cook, although he knows nothing about either job, and so upsets the Polish maid Maya (Susan Cash) that she goes on strike. Parker then insults his father and his black mistress, Joy (Janet Hubert), by dressing up as Josephine Baker for the costume party on the estate. But the ditzy Fay survives unscathed by all the plotting going on around her, Parker is sent off to a mental institution, and the mindless rich carry on as before. Kondoleon's writing was described as "glib, witty, and outrageous," the comedy as a "horrific Felliniesque circus."

Off-Off-Broadway's Second Stage had revived Lanford Wilson's *Serenading Louis* (5-2-76) in 1983 and found new life in a neglected drama. This season it gave the same author's *Lemon Sky* (5-17-70) a fresh airing on November 25, and critics declared it an overlooked little gem of a play. Jeff

Daniels played the narrator-hero Alan, who looks back at his troubled teen years and his difficult relationship with his father (Wayne Tippet). Also outstanding in the acclaimed revival were Jill Eikenberry and Cynthia Nixon.

Uta Hagan returned to the New York stage as the title character in the Roundabout's revival of Shaw's *Mrs. Warren's Profession* on November 27. Praise for the actress was universal, even if the production received mixed notices. Pamela Reed as her daughter, Vivie, and Harris Yulin as the businessman Crofts also earned many compliments. John Madden's production lasted three months.

One week was all that John Pielmeier's **The Boys of Winter** (12-1-85, Biltmore) could survive even though it followed the same formula of his earlier popular melodrama *Agnes of God* (3-30-82). In the Quang Tri province of Vietnam, the virtuous and levelheaded marine lieutenant Bonney (D. W. Moffett) murders his Vietnamese mistress and six members of her family. An investigation is held, and in a series of flashbacks and monologues by fellow marines (all of whom are later killed in a suicide mission), we make the not-so-startling discovery that Bonney committed the atrocity because he had Native American blood and a Vietnamese scout teased him about it. Michael Lindsay-Hogg directed (after Herbert Ross quit) with grisly realism, and the cast, headed by movie actor Matt Dillon in his Broadway debut, was considered better than the trite pronouncements that they uttered all night long. Uniformly negative notices suggested that the play trivialized its important subject matter and noted that the "dialogue is utterly banal and boringly vulgar." But there were cheers for David Mitchell's ingenious setting, a great gnarled tree that broke through the floorboards of the stage and reached out into the house with draped military netting stretched out like spider webs.

With his **A Lie of the Mind** (12-5-85, Promenade), Sam Shepard moved from writing intimate and raw little dramas like *Fool for Love* (5-26-83) to a broader panorama of two families caught in a drama that extends across the miles and took nearly four hours (with two intermissions) to perform. When Jake (Harvey Keitel) beats up his wife, Beth (Amanda Plummer), one time too many, the brain-damaged woman leaves her California house and travels to her family homestead in Montana. Jake, worrying that Beth is dead, sends his brother Frankie (Aiden Quinn) to Montana to find out the truth, while he himself returns to his widowed mother, Lorraine (Geral-

dine Page), who imprisons her son in his boyhood bedroom by stealing his trousers. Frankie is greeted by Beth's brother Mike (Will Patton) with gunshots that wound him in the leg and keep him a captive of Beth's odd parents (Ann Wedgeworth and James Gannon). Jake sets out hitchhiking on the highway in his underwear and draped in an American flag, eventually arriving at the Montana farm, where he and Beth come to a bittersweet but romantic reunion. Sometimes as extreme as *Tobacco Road* (12-4-33), other times haunting and lyrical, *A Lie of the Mind* excited most critics with its "powerful blend of wild humor and tragic force," winning the New York Drama Critics Circle Award. Plummer was the most highly applauded of the strong cast, which Shepard himself directed. Audiences were puzzled and entertained by the "epic comedy" for six months.

The Yale Repertory production of Athol Fugard's *Blood Knot* (3-1-64) was brought to the John Golden on December 10 for a twelve-week engagement that was showered with adulation, mostly for the cast, Fugard and Zakes Mokae, who first performed the two-character drama twenty-five years ago in Johannesburg. A few critics commented that the play had dated, but the issues were still current, and the chemistry between the two actors gave "their performances a depth rarely seen in the theatre."

Charles Busch put his self-described "Hard Boiled Christmas Fantasy" called **Times Square Angel** (12-11-85, Provincetown Playhouse) into repertory with *Vampire Lesbians of Sodom* for twenty-three holiday performances. In the depths of the Depression, tough-talking (and stylishly costumed) Irish Flanagan (Busch) rises from Hell's Kitchen to become a noted nightclub singer. She soon falls into the decadence of celebrity and is saved by a guardian angel at the last possible moment. The spoof of heart-tugging "women's stories" was lauded for its wisecracking camp and faithful recreation of slick Hollywood pictures of the 1930s.

Critics welcomed the December 12 Broadway revival of Noel Coward's *Hay Fever* (10-5-25) with accolades of "stylish," "dashing," "sparkling," and "it's hard to imagine a more delightful production." Audiences agreed, filling the Music Box for 124 performances, though the venture still lost money. Rosemary Harris, as the dippy actress Judith Bliss, received the lion's share of the raves, but this "ideal production," directed by Brian Murray, was filled with other delicious performances as well: Roy Dotrice as David Bliss, Mia

Dillon and Robert Joy as his children, Barbara Bryne as their nonplused housekeeper, and Campbell Scott, Deborah Rush, Carolyn Seymour, and Charles Kimborough as their baffled guests.

Gerard Brown's tragicomedy **Joinin'** (12-17-85, Public: LuEsther) found little favor in the press, labeled as "shrill," "messy," and "neither pertinent nor particularly contemporary." In a fraternity house at a black university, the students crack jokes, trade insults, and play tricks on each other, all part of a verbal kind of hazing called "joinin'." But the jokes get nasty, the insults more explosive, and a student's suicide leaves all the fraternity brothers humbled and shaken.

The Mirror Repertory Theatre returned for its third season at St. Peter's Church, opening its repertory with William Saroyan's *The Time of Your Life* (10-25-39) on December 18. The large cast included Mason Adams (Joe), Charles Regan (Nick), and Tovah Feldshuh and Sabra Jones alternating in the role of Kitty.

Nancy Donohue's romantic comedy **The Beach House** (12-19-85, Circle) offered a lighter version of the season-endemic father-son conflict. John (George Grizzard), a bitter Yale immunologist who has retreated from life since his wife left him, moves with his teenage son, Chris (Robert Sean Leonard), into a Connecticut beach house, where they are constantly at odds. But one day Annie (Swoozie Kurtz), an ex-nun with a radical feminist turn of mind, misreads an address and enters their lives. Both men are charmed and soon come to depend on her, seeing her as the mother-wife-lover they have been missing. Word about the "funny, often insightful," "cheerful unpretentious play," and the gifted cast helped fill the off-Broadway space for its fifty-six showings.

Michael Frayn followed his popular farce *Noises Off* (12-11-83) with the very understated comedy-drama **Benefactors** (12-22-85, Brooks Atkinson), which had been a hit in London and found an audience on Broadway for 217 performances. David (Sam Waterston) and Jane (Glenn Close) are a liberal, well-meaning couple in the London of the late 1960s. He is an idealistic architect, she a bright anthropologist, and together they are always helping out their disheveled friends Colin (Simon Jones) and Sheila (Mary Beth Hurt) by providing meals, child care, and a sympathetic ear. But the foursome's friendship is shaken when David designs a high-rise housing project for a London slum and the cynical Colin joins the squatters who protest the plan by camping in the shabby neighborhood. Matters are further complicated by Sheila, who signs on as David's assistant and quietly falls in love with him. Colin's campaign fails, but the new project is never built, and the four friends never totally recover from the incident. The story was told by the four characters fifteen years after the events, each addressing the audience in turn and giving his or her private viewpoint to the public story. Michael Blakemore, who had also directed the play in London, handled the mostly American cast beautifully, letting the drama build slowly but surely. To some commentators "the whole thing adds up to less than its parts," but most found *Benefactors* an "extraordinarily rich play" and "one of the subtlest plays Broadway has seen in years."

Lincoln Center's new artistic director, Gregory Mosher, reopened the downstairs space with two David Mamet "ghost stories," **Prairie du Chien** and **The Shawl** (12-23-85, Mitzi E. Newhouse), which Mosher directed himself. In the curtain raiser, *Prairie du Chien*, two passengers (W. H. Macy and Tom Signorelli) on a night train from Chicago to Duluth play gin while a grisly old raconteur (Jerry Stiller) tells a gruesome tale about jealousy and murder. *The Shawl* shows a phony psychic (Mike Nussbaum) teaching the tricks of the trade to his young male lover (Calvin Levels) while trying to cheat a grieving woman (Lindsay Crouse) out of her inheritance. The six-week engagement met with mild disappointment, the press calling the evening "slim" and "atmospheric and puzzling, but more boring than stimulating."

Perhaps the most obscure revival of the season was Gorky's *Children of the Sun*, which the Mirror Rep offered on December 26. A 1905 domestic drama about the gulf that exists between the intellectual and the ordinary folk, it had been seen once in New York when Russian actress Vera Komisarzhevsky included it in her repertory during a 1908 visit. The Mirror cast featured Michael Moriarty, Tovah Feldshuh, Sabra Jones, Elizabeth Franz, and Katharine Houghton. Eight decades later, the play was perceived as more a "curiosity" than a lost treasure.

More laughs than chills were forthcoming in Gerald Moon's **Corpse!** (1-5-86, Helen Hayes), which had played in London and regionally in American before coming to Broadway. Evelyn Farrant (Keith Baxter), a destitute actor living in a cluttered Soho flat overseen by theatrical landlady Mrs. McGee (Pauline Flanagan), invites small-time hood Major Walter Powell (Milo O'Shea), a congenial Irishman who is on the lam from a Chinese gangster, to do a nasty job for him: kill Evelyn's twin brother (and mortal enemy) Rupert, who inherited all the family wealth. Powell agrees and, entering Rupert's swank Regent's Park home, murders the man, only to discover that the body is Evelyn's. He tries to explain to Rupert, who seems to have arranged the whole affair to kill his brother. Complications continue (aided by the fact that Baxter played both brothers) until Powell becomes the victim of Rupert's greed, stabbed and hidden in his revolving bar. Although it received better reviews in London and on the road than it did in New York, the thriller still managed to run 121 performances.

Jerry Sterner, a Wall Street broker hoping to be a playwright, struck out with **Be Happy for Me** (1-7-86, Douglas Fairbanks), a one-performance dud that boasted a superior cast. Middle-aged brothers Phil (David Groh) and Norman (Philip Bosco) have just buried their father and decide to deal with his death (and their own midlife crises) by vacationing in the Caribbean together and searching for new adventures. Bachelor Phil considers himself an experienced swinger and coaches Norman on how to pick up women. But Norman pines for his ex-wife, Elizabeth (Priscilla Lopez), so when she arrives on the island, he tries to woo her with Phil's surefire methods. Sterner showed some sense of comedy but had yet to find his own voice.

There were artists and writers aplenty in Win Wells's **Gertrude Stein and a Companion** (1-9-86, Lucille Lortel), which entertained audiences for fifty-four showings with two superb performers. After Gertrude Stein (Jan Miner) dies in 1967, she appears as a ghost to Alice B. Toklas (Marian Seldes), and the two reminisce together, portraying Picasso, Hemingway, and several other friends from the old days. Even if the same ground had already been thoroughly covered by *Gertrude Stein Gertrude Stein Gertrude Stein* (6-24-79) and other plays, some critics still rated the evening "imaginative and compelling" and "brisk, fun, and literate."

It was surprising that notices for Terrence McNally's **It's Only a Play** (1-12-86, Manhattan Theatre Club) did not mention Moss Hart's minor classic *Light Up the Sky* (11-18-48), for both comedies offered similar backstage views of the commercial theatre of their day. At the opening night party for the Broadway production of *The Golden Egg*, the creative staff gather at the town house of the show's desperately chic producer, Julia Budder (Christine Baranski), to wait for the reviews. The young playwright, Peter Austin

(Mark Blum), is the most nervous ("I don't want another OBIE, I want a hit!"), sending a mass card to Walter Kerr and dissolving into panic over the all-important *Times* review by Frank Rich. The drugged leading lady, Virginia Noyes (Joanna Gleason), a fading Hollywood starlet, is too high to care, while the demented wunderkind director, Frank Finger (David Garrison), is hoping for a flop because he is tired of critics drooling over his pretentious avant-garde theatrics. An outsider in the group is the insecure actor James Wicker (James Coco), a friend of the playwright who turned down the lead role in the play to do a TV series, hoping his decision is justified by a giant flop. It turns out most of the reviews are pans, James's series is canceled, and Julia is seen planning her next show and getting everyone excited about the new venture that is guaranteed to be a hit. The real critics agreed that McNally's lines were "hilariously, side-splittingly funny" (Julia, writing out a check, asks, "How many *p*'s are there in Papp?") even if the playwright had not solved his usual problem with satisfactory conclusions. Brendan Gill in *The New Yorker* noted: "To call the plot wafer-thin is probably to insult wafermakers from coast to coast." Interestingly, the real Rich reviewed the comedy in the *Times* and thought it filled with "genuine tributes to the theatrical calling." Despite some similarly favorable notices, the satire only ran seventeen performances. McNally later revised the play, and it enjoyed modest success in subsequent productions elsewhere.

The parade of literary figures onstage continued with William Luce's **Lillian** (1-16-86, Ethel Barrymore), in which Zoe Caldwell portrayed playwright Lillian Hellman. While her longtime lover Dashiell Hammett lies dying in a New York hospital, Hellman reviews her life, recalling events and people from her youth in New Orleans through her rise to fame as a writer and her liberal causes to the year 1961 when she is speaking. Because Hellman wrote several memoirs and autobiographical works, Luce was able to put her actual words and thoughts into his character's monologues. Yet the result was less than satisfying for many commentators. The only consistent praise the drama garnered was for the ever-versatile Caldwell, who was made up to look alarmingly like the real Hellman (who had died two years earlier) and could "impersonate George Washington and make us believe it."

Like Lily Tomlin, Eric Bogosian filled a one-person play with an exciting cavalcade of characters in his **Drinking in America** (1-19-86, Amer-

ZOE [née Ada] **CALDWELL** (1933–) was born in Hawthorn, Victoria, Australia, the daughter of a plumber and a singer-dancer, and educated at Methodist Ladies' College in Melbourne. By 1953 she was acting professionally in Melbourne and five years later was a member of the Royal Shakespeare Company in England. Her first Broadway appearance was as Sister Jean in *The Devils* (1965), but Caldwell came to prominence with her Tony Award–winning performance as gossip columnist Polly in *Slapstick Tragedy* (1966) and her portrayal of the liberal Scottish teacher in *The Prime of Miss Jean Brodie* (1968), for which she collected a second Tony. She won her third Tony for playing *Medea* in 1982, directed by her husband, Robert Whitehead, who staged *Lillian* as well. Also a director on Broadway and regionally, the weathered-faced actress excels in theatrical, powerful women but possesses a caustic sense of humor as well.

ican Place), twelve monologues by people from every stratum of society who share an obsession with alcohol. A Hollywood casting agent belts down Jack Daniels and snorts cocaine in order to get into the rhythm of dealmaking on the phone. A street wino imagines he is beleaguered with beautiful women and the possessor of wealth until he passes out from his cheap booze. A yuppie fails to satisfy his girlfriend in bed and lashes out at the world, drunkenly blaming a worldwide conspiracy. A Texas ceramics salesman plies a prostitute with champagne in his hotel room, desperate for affection rather than sex. The most harrowing monologue concerned a hyped-up youth who, nursing a hangover, recounts to a friend the previous night's adventures in drink and violence, filled with both disgust and admiration for his own lifestyle. Several critics thought Bogosian's performance "incandescently energetic" and his gallery of characters a "breakneck, hair-raising comic tour de force of the American psyche." Running ninety-four performances, the showcase established Bogosian as a writer-performer to be reckoned with.

Keith Reddin's mock documentary **Rum and Coke** (1-27-86, Public: Shiva) received many compliments, members of the press stating that his "inventiveness is original and acute and funny." Jake Seward (Peter MacNicol), a naive Yale graduate, is recruited by the CIA in 1959 to infiltrate Cuba because he once went there on a family vacation before Castro took over. Jake's mission is to stir up a revolution against the Communist

leader (the Americans are convinced that a Cuban underground is just waiting for the Yankees to arrive and lead them), but instead he becomes involved in the lives of several Cubans and ends up a pawn in the disastrous 1961 Bay of Pigs invasion. A handful of actors played the twenty characters Jake encountered in his adventure, from comic islanders to blockheaded bureaucrats.

The same Keith Reddin was hailed for his acting when the Roundabout revived John Murray and Allen Boretz's show business farce *Room Service* (5-19-37) two nights later. Ironically, Reddin, playing the befuddled playwright Leo Davis, was judged the shining spot in the uneven production. Alan Arkin directed a cast that also included Mark Hamill, Andrew Bloch, Ann McDonough, and Lonny Price. Chicago's Steppenwolf Theatre Company brought its revival of Harold Pinter's *The Caretaker* (10-4-61) to Broadway's Circle in the Square on January 30, and it also was disappointing, criticized for being a "wan" and "unendurably long, drawn out version" of the tight little drama. Gary Sinise, Jeff Perry, and Alan Wilder were misdirected by John Malkovich (also credited with designing the costumes!). The same night, Lanford Wilson's *The Mound Builders* (2-1-75) was given a second viewing by the Circle Rep, which had presented the original mounting. Three nights later the company offered a modern-dress version of Albert Camus's *Caligula* (2-16-60) in a second space. This experimental production had male and female actors alternating in the drama's pivotal roles while four television cameras onstage duplicated scenes as they occurred. Marshall W. Mason directed both Circle productions.

The finest offering this season at the Manhattan Theatre Club was the February 18 revival of Joe Orton's *Loot* (3-18-68), a dark farce about getting rid of an unwanted body. John Tillinger, who would stage four notable productions on and off the Street this season, directed the spirited revival that featured a zestful cast: Joseph Maher (Truscott), Zeljko Ivanek (Hal), Charles Keating (McLeavy), Zoe Wanamaker (Fay), and Kevin Bacon (Dennis). Because its month-long engagement quickly sold out, the comedy transferred to Broadway's Music Box on April 7 and stayed for ninety-six performances, the longest run of a Joe Orton play on the Street. A revival of William Somerset Maugham's *The Circle* (9-12-21) on February 20 by the Mirror Repertory at St. Peter's Church met with mixed notices. Veteran actors Geraldine Page (Lady Catherine), W. B. Brydon (Lord Porteous), and Bryan Clark (Clive) were applauded, but much of the rest of the cast, directed by Stephen Porter, seemed lost in the genteel drawing room comedy.

Nothing could have been further from Ted Tally's ice-cold drama *Terra Nova* (4-25-84) than his **Little Footsteps** (2-27-86, Playwrights Horizons), a caustic comedy about parenthood. Young New Yorkers Ben (Mark Blum) and Joanie (Anne Lange) are an open-minded yuppie couple. He is an enterprising Jew with a growing sports promotion career, and she is a Wasp who volunteers at the Metropolitan and dreams of becoming a recognized artist. But their eight-year marriage is jeopardized when Joanie becomes pregnant and never-discussed questions concerning religion and raising children come up. While Joanie paints butterflies on the nursery walls and Ben makes lists of Jewish names for the new arrival, her parents enter the troubled situation and expect the child to be raised in their own family tradition. Ben panics and deserts Joanie. But a year later, after the christening of the infant son at church, Ben sneaks into the nursery and intones some Jewish prayers over the child so that some of his Jewish heritage might rub off. Ben is discovered by the family, and the young couple are forced to look at themselves realistically, learning that they must grow up if they ever want their son to. Tally's dialogue was wry and knowing (one character describes parenting as "the Unprepared attempting the Impossible for the sake of the Ungrateful"), and the comedy had a very painful subtext. A number of critics agreed, calling it "civilized, literate, mind-stretching entertainment, its tomfoolery leavened by thoughtfulness and taste," though some dismissed it as "more an anthology of jokes than a play."

The Negro Ensemble contributed to the season's list of father-son dramas with Judi Ann Mason's two-character **Jonah and the Wonder Dog** (2-28-86, Theatre Four). Jonah Howard (Douglas Turner Ward) started as a street hoodlum but worked his way through academia and politics and now is preparing to run for the Senate. Nick (Kevin Hooks), Jonah's Harvard-grad son, visits his father in his plush Reno home to break the news that Jonah's wife of thirty years has left him. Nick has always feared his father, and Jonah has always been somewhat repelled by his bisexual son, so the exchange is fraught with tension. Jonah fluctuates between anger and despair as he recalls how his wife helped him in his career. Nick's repressed feelings come to the surface, and he fires a blank from his pistol; both men weep and then are reconciled. Despite the two strong performances, critics thought the evening "very trying" and the script "an inflated one-acter split in two."

Kevin Kline made a splendid *Hamlet* at the Public on March 9 (Oliver commented on how the usually hyperactive actor was "quiet, intense, eloquent in his silences and his listening"), but Liviu Ciulei's "foolish, intrusive production" was no help. Audiences had seventy showings to catch Kline's magnetic (and well-reviewed) performance.

The season's third courtroom drama, Emily Mann's documentary-like **Execution of Justice** (3-13-86, Virginia), explored why defendant Dan White (John Spencer) killed San Francisco mayor George Moscone and city supervisor Harvey Milk, a noted gay activist, and how the jury let White off with a verdict of only manslaughter. Mann drew her text from the 1978 trial transcripts as well as interviews and other sources. Some commentators thought it "a dynamite play . . . about the meaning of justice and politics in America," but just as many decreed it "practically unrelieved tedium." Criticism was just as mixed on Ming Cho Lee's scenery and Pat Collins's lighting. The grimy San Francisco courtroom set placed the audience in the position of the jury box, and other playgoers sat behind the actors while TV crew lights shone threateningly in the eyes of those sitting in the auditorium. Although it had been performed with success in regional theatres, the play shuttered after twelve showings on Broadway.

A Canadian play that showed off the Circle Rep's ensemble acting was Anne Chislett's **Quiet in the Land** (3-16-86, Circle). An Amish community in rural Ontario refuses to support the Canadian troops taking part in the Great War because of their pacifist beliefs, but young Jacob Bauman (Bruce McCarty) does not agree and enlists. Leaving behind his sweetheart, Katie Brubacher (Sharon Schlarth), and his stern father, Christy (Edward Seamon), one of the elders of the community, "Yock" travels to Europe, where he discovers the true meaning of pacifism as he looks upon the body of a slain German soldier. Although he is decorated by the army for his valor, Yock is scorned by the Amish when he returns. Katie has married another but still loves Yock. She offers to run off with him, but the disillusioned youth departs alone, and Christy, now a bishop in the community, weeps for the loss of his son.

The most awarded revival of the season (and the first hit at the "new" Lincoln Center) was John Guare's *The House of Blue Leaves* (2-10-71) which opened on March 19 downstairs in the Mitzi E. Newhouse but then on April 29 moved upstairs to the Vivian Beaumont. Jerry Zaks directed the odd comedy and was largely responsible for making the play "seem deeper, sadder, more passionate, and even funnier" than the original. John Mahoney (Artie), Swoozie Kurtz (Bananas), and Stockard Channing (Bunny) led a peerless cast, while Tony Walton's setting, with the city hovering over Artie and Bananas's little Queens apartment, was one of the most eye-catching of the season. The Beaumont gave the revival Broadway status, so it collected Tony Awards for Mahoney, Kurtz, Walton, and Zaks. The popular attraction filled the larger house through July.

Comedy writer-actor George Furth turned to family drama (yet another father-son conflict) with **Precious Sons** (3-20-86, Longacre), which provided two of the season's finest performances even if the play fell short. Fred Small (Ed Harris) has the opportunity to improve the life of his Chicago family by taking a promotion that would relocate them to another city. But his wife, Bea (Judith Ivey), a determined mother who will not risk the security of their present position, does not want Fred to accept the new job. Caught in between are their sons: athletic but dense Art (William O'Leary) and sensitive Freddy (Anthony Rapp), a high school student who wants to drop out and pursue his dream of becoming an actor or writer. Bea throws a crockery-smashing tantrum, Fred's ulcers act up, and Freddy goes off to take a small role in the touring company of *A Streetcar Named Desire*. The autobiographical drama (it was set in the late 1940s of Furth's teen years) received mixed reviews, from "ludicrously overloaded with major life crises" to "a play about real things [with] honest emotions." Harris and Ivey were enthusiastically acclaimed, but the drama could only survive two months.

Hollywood starlet Brooke Shields's New York stage debut in **The Eden Cinema** (3-23-86, Harold Clurman) did not cause enough interest to keep the drama open longer than nineteen performances. The 1977 play by Marguerite Duras (translated by Barbara Bray) concerned a French widow (Marylouise Burke) who sets out for Indochina in the early 1930s to make her fortune in plantation farming. The story of her vainglorious attempt and eventual failure was told through the memories of her children, in particular daughter Suzanne (Shields). Critics found Shields capable enough but the play and the production rather "limp."

Vaclav Havel's **Largo Desolato** (3-25-86, Public: LuEsther), in a translation by Marie Winn, was another much talked-of entry in the Public's season of controversial plays. The renowned Czech philosopher Dr. Leopold Kopriva (Josef Sommer) is hiding in his spacious Prague apartment, looking through the peephole in his door, and panicking every time he hears footsteps outside in the hall. He knows that at any moment the government might arrest him for his dissident writings. When Fellow I (Edward Zang) and Fellow II (Richard Russell Ramos) arrive, he is surprised to find them so affable as they happily suggest Leopold change his name and pretend he and his writings never existed. The professor seeks the advice of the three women in his life—his chilly mistress Zuzana (Sally Kirkland), his new, ever-complaining lover Lucy (Diana Venora), and the young philosophy student Marketa (Jodi Thelen), who dotes on him—but in the end he decides that he will refuse to sign away his life, only to learn that the two Fellows have already done it for him. Havel found humor in Leopold's dire situation, as in scenes where two factory workers both named Lada (Larry Block and Burke Pearson) enthusiastically express their support of the professor even though they cannot understand anything he has written. While approval of the script was heartfelt ("a play that makes bitter, funny, horrible, deadpan sense"), Richard Foreman's "woefully wrong-headed production of a good play" prompted critical disapproval. Certain actors were directed to move like puppets, and the amplified sound effects (doorbells, crashing noises, swelling music that drowned out dialogue) hammered the play's ideas mercilessly. (A much more literate translation of the satire by Tom Stoppard would later find life in regional theatres.)

Playgoers looking for more literary characters on stage had fifty-six opportunities to see David Allen's **Cheapside** (3-29-86, Roundabout), in which William Shakespeare (Robert Stanton) and Christopher Marlowe (Dennis Boutsikaris) engaged in political, theatrical and sexual discussions with poet Robert Greene (Daniel Gerroll) as they sat in a pub in the run-down London borough of the title. An Australian play, it had been previously mounted in England and regionally in the States.

A. R. Gurney continued to provide a new play each season, this time the comedy of manners **The Perfect Party** (4-2-86, Playwrights Horizons). Stuffy literature professor Tony (John Cunningham) has organized what he considers a "perfect party," one that contains a cross-section of America (Wasps, Jews, gays, old school friends, young swingers, a waiter from Buffalo, and even two registered Republicans) that will illustrate the way democracy works today. But he also has an ulterior motive: to leave teaching behind forever and become a nationally recognized "consultant" for perfect parties. To this end he has invited a New York newspaper critic, the sophisticated but deadly Lois (Charlotte Moore), to "review" the party and bring him glory. But when the event begins to falter (Lois believes it is because there is no sense of danger in the occasion), Tony dresses up as his fictitious no-good brother Tod (a notoriously oversexed Italian, no less) and seduces Lois in the master bedroom while his distraught wife, Sally (Debra Mooney), tries to handle the guests. Tod's sexual performance is as unsatisfying as the party, and Lois gives both bad reviews. So Tony has to settle for a more informal gathering with some old friends and his Jewish neighbors enjoying a bucket of Kentucky Fried Chicken together. Gurney's writing style shone with a Wilde-like flavor at times; when Tony explains that he inherited his collection of Oscar Wilde books from his grandmother, Lois warns, "The source is immaterial. I'd be careful of Wilde. He's not American, and tends to undermine everything that is." Reviews ranged from "surely Mr. Gurney's funniest, meanest, and most theatrical play yet" to "a sketch stretched into two acts and sometimes overburdened with metaphors." Audiences were less divided, keeping the "puzzle box of a play" on the boards for 238 performances. The comedy also brought further acclaim to director John Tillinger, who would stage many of Gurney's future works.

An entry from Atlanta's Alliance Theatre Company, Sandra Deer's **So Long on Lonely Street** (4-3-86, Jack Lawrence), drifted back and forth between comedy and melodrama for fifty-three performances. When crotchety old southerner Aunt Pearl dies, the family gathers at the deteriorating Vaughnum mansion for the reading of the will. Pearl's black companion, Annabel Lee (Lizan Mitchell), hopes to inherit the old house and the property it stands on, but first cousin King Vaughnum 3rd (Stephen Root), a boisterous businessman, and his wife, Clarice (Jane Murray), want to build a shopping center

> **JOHN** [né Joachim] **TILLINGER** (1939–) was born in Iran, the son of an American engineer stationed there. His only theatre training was at the Bristol Old Vic School in England, and his first acting roles were in London and British regional theatres in the early 1960s. Tillinger made his Broadway acting debut in *How's the World Treating You?* (1966), followed by appearances regionally before he turned to directing in 1980 at the Long Wharf Theatre in New Haven. While some of his Long Wharf productions continued on to Manhattan, such as *Solomon's Child* (1982), Tillinger became known as a New York director with Gurney's *The Golden Age* (1983). This season's acclaimed revival of *Loot* secured his reputation as a masterful director of contemporary plays who never imposed a personal stamp on his productions but served the playwright diligently.

on the site. Pearl's nephew Raymond Brown (Ray Dooley), a TV soap opera actor, arrives from New York to attend the funeral but primarily to see his poet sister, Ruth (Pat Nesbit), the two siblings having been fighting a sexual attraction for each other since they were children in the bathtub together. Reunited once more, Raymond and Ruth give in to their incestuous passions as the will is finally read: Annabel, who turns out to be the illegitimate daughter of one of the Vaughnum forefathers, gets the homestead. Notices ranged from "a funny and poignant human comedy" to "trash of a particularly old-fashioned and repellent sort."

Running the same number of performances was John Morgan Evans's **Daughters** (4-3-86, Westside) which also came from a regional theatre, the Philadelphia Drama Guild. Four generations of DiAngelo women are gathered in the kitchen of the Brooklyn family home while the dying patriarch sits in his bedroom and listens to old Caruso records. Grandma (Miriam Phillips) speaks no English and silently retreats to her room whenever she can. Her daughter Mom (Bette Henritze) and granddaughter Tessie (Marcia Rodd) quarrel a lot, but Tessie's seventeen-year-old daughter Cetta (Marisa Tomei) often acts as mediator. To add to all the tension, Tessie (who has had several nervous breakdowns in the past) finds out that her husband is having an affair with a waitress and rushes off, gun in hand, only to return deflated by her inability to follow through with her rage. Critical response ranged from "a warm, funny play" to "a stream of easy jokes and forced epiphanies," but there was general endorsement for Rodd and the young Tomei in her professional debut.

Richard Nelson's **Principia Scriptoriae** (4-10-86, Manhattan Theatre Club) found little favor off Broadway, only to be later greeted warmly in England, where Nelson would eventually emigrate and premiere most of his subsequent works. Two writers are imprisoned in a small jail cell in a Latin American country in 1970, both accused of subversive activities against its right-wing dictatorship. The American Bill Howell (Anthony Heald) was a draft dodger in the 1960s and is still full of idealism. Ernesto Pico (Joe Urla) is a native of the country but has been educated in the best European schools. The men find many common bonds as they discuss politics and writing. Fifteen years later the Communists have overthrown the fascist regime, and Ernesto is now an assistant to the Minister of Culture. Bill returns to the country for an international writers' conference and to protest the incarceration of a poet who expresses leftist ideas. The two friends now find themselves at odds, and their confrontation of ideas climaxes in a flashback to 1970 when the two writers were being tortured for their beliefs. While some aisle-sitters thought the piece "powerful and intelligent," many others called it "an imitation play, empty as a drum."

Hollywood screenwriter Andrew Bergman turned to the stage with his **Social Security** (4-17-86, Ethel Barrymore) and was rewarded with a profitable run of 385 performances. Barbara (Marlo Thomas) and David Kahn (Ron Silver), savvy New York art dealers, are about to wine and dine a celebrated artist, the ancient minimalist painter Maurice Koenig (Stefan Schnabel), when Barbara's nerdy sister, Trudy (Joanna Gleason), and her finicky husband, Martin (Kenneth Welsh), barge in to drop off the sisters' mother, the archtypal Jewish matron Sophie Greengrass (Olympia Dukakis). The suburbanites can no longer take the responsibility of caring for Sophie, since they have to fly to Buffalo to "save" their promiscuous college daughter, who is living only for sex. Just when it looks like the idiosyncratic Sophie (she keeps spitting candy on the floor and refuses to change out of her bathrobe) will ruin the Kahns' chances of wooing Koenig, the old man and Sophie hit it off and begin an autumnal romance. The comedy recalled the earlier *Barefoot in the Park* (10-23-63), in which a young urban couple was also upset by an interfering mother who has a romance with the old man upstairs. Notices ranged from "a sophisticated, even civilized hoot" to "a rather vulgar comedy," though most com-

plimented Mike Nichols on his spirited direction and the players for their affability.

The Acting Company, a touring troupe usually dedicated to period and modern classics, offered two original anthology programs this year during its New York stay. **Orchards** (4-22-86, Lucille Lortel) consisted of seven one-act plays based on Anton Chekhov short stories. Some of America's finest young playwrights provided the stage adaptations: Wendy Wasserstein, John Guare, David Mamet, Samm-Art Williams, Maria Irene Fornes, Michael Weller, and Spalding Gray. Ironically, critics noted that the most satisfying of the playlets (Wasserstein's *The Man in a Case* and Mamet's *Vint*) were those that strayed furthest from Chekhov. Clive Barnes of the *New York Post* thought it "an evening of numbing, trivializing boredom," and most of his colleagues were not much more encouraging.

Jessica Tandy and Hume Cronyn continued to search for a vehicle worthy of their considerable talents, but despite a strong production directed by Peter Hall, Brian Clark's British drama **The Petition** (4-24-86, John Golden) was not it. Retired army general Sir Edmund Milne has been married to the complacent Elizabeth for fifty years without ever engaging in any strife or major disagreement. But when she signs a petition against the use of nuclear weapons, the general is shocked. Years of repressed emotions and secrets come spilling out, the most disturbing revelation being Elizabeth's terminal illness. In the end the two reach a tentative reconciliation and Edmund goes off to his club as usual. Notices for Clark's contrived drama (having its premiere in New York before London) were decidedly mixed, but Cronyn and Tandy were extolled, helping the play run seventy-seven times. As Sweet wrote, "the effect was a bit like watching a pair of classical pianists dig into the subtleties of 'Chopsticks.'" Sadly, it would be the last Broadway appearance by the renowned acting couple.

A popular London production of O'Neill's *Long Day's Journey Into Night* (11-7-56) transferred to the Broadhurst on April 28 for fifty-four showings. Jack Lemmon essayed the patriarch James Tyrone, Bethel Leslie was an understated Mary, and Kevin Spacey (Jamie) and Peter Gallagher (Edmund) were added to Jonathan Miller's brisk but penetrating production. Some controversy revolved around Miller's decision to have the actors sometimes overlap each other in conversation, thereby eliminating some of the text. But the faster pace often added to the family tension and made the lengthy play considerably shorter. Critics, for the most part, liked what they saw and were in agreement with Ron Cohen of *Women's Wear Daily*, who wrote, "If this production dispels some of the darkness, even the spookiness, that often enshrouds the Tyrones, it also reveals the multiple dimensions O'Neill built for these haunted souls."

Broadway's final entry of the season was another case of two seasoned actors looking for an appropriate vehicle. Bernard Sabath's **The Boys in Autumn** (4-30-86, Circle in the Square) fantasized about what Tom Sawyer and Huck Finn were up to several decades after their adventures in the Mark Twain stories. In the 1920s, Huck is the middle-aged hardware store owner Henry Finnegan (George C. Scott), living in a farmhouse high on a bluff overlooking the Mississippi River near Hannibal, Missouri. In a beat-up Model T, Thomas Gray (John Cullum), who is Sawyer grown into a dapper, white-suited former vaudevillian, arrives for a visit. The reunion leads to unpleasant discoveries about each man's past: Huck murdered his wife, and Tom was a child molester. Reviews were all pans along the lines of a "terminally innocuous speculation" and "a grotesque . . . repellent little theatre piece." (More than one critic pointed out to the playwright that the two characters would be well into their eighties in the 1920s.) But there were few more talented performers than Scott and Cullum, and they helped the play survive two months.

Actor-writer Spalding Gray presented three solo programs at Lincoln Center throughout the summer, the first titled **Terrors of Pleasure** (5-15-86, Mitzi E Newhouse). Like all his works, it was very autobiographical. Gray explained how he bought an old house in the Catskill Mountains and then went into detail about how the structure proceeds to collapse all around him. So he abandons it and heads out to Hollywood, where he encounters obstacles of a different sort in the television industry. Gray was definitely an acquired taste; some critics were enthralled by his commentary, others bored or puzzled as to what such an aimless presentation was supposed to be.

The Negro Ensemble closed with its best (and most successful) entry, Gus Edwards's love story **Louie and Ophelia** (5-16-86, Theatre Four), which ran through the summer. Widower Louie (Douglas Turner Ward) is a short-order cook with little education, whereas Ophelia (Elain Graham) is an administrative assistant in an office with an estranged husband and two teenage kids she is raising alone. The two meet in a bar and begin a sometimes warm, often tempestuous relationship. Her radical, stubborn temperament is matched by his firm street sense; after separating briefly, both realize they need each other more than they ever thought they did. Favorable notices commended the fiery performances and noted how "free of clichés and full of surprising humanity" the script was.

Robert De Niro's return to the stage was the chief attraction of Reinaldo Povod's melodrama **Cuba and His Teddy Bear** (5-18-86, Public: Shiva). Small-time drug dealer Cuba (De Niro) is a macho blowhard, but he has real affection for his teenage son, Teddy (Ralph Macchio), who he hopes will make something of himself in the world. But the youth has fallen in with a down-and-out playwright (Michael Carmine) and is quickly becoming a heroin junkie. Regardless of mixed reviews for the play and even doubts about De Niro's high-volume performance, the three-week engagement quickly sold out, so producer Papp let the overflow crowds pay $7 to sit in an adjoining theatre at the Public and watch a live video transmission of the drama. The inevitable transfer to Broadway came next season.

The Acting Company's second anthology program was **Ten by Tennessee** (5-18-86, Lucille Lortel), which offered a series of Tennessee Williams one-acts over two nights. The short works, most of which had been previously seen either off Broadway or off-off Broadway, were *The Lady of Larkspur Lotion, Talk to Me Like the Rain and Let Me Listen, Portrait of a Madonna, The Unsatisfactory Supper, The Long Goodbye, Auto-da-Fe, The Strangest Kind of Romance, A Perfect Analysis Given by a Parrot, I Can't Imagine Tomorrow,* and *This Property Is Condemned*. While most Acting Company presentations only stayed a week, this one ran nearly seven weeks.

John Patrick Shanley's insightful **Women of Manhattan** (5-25-86, Manhattan Theatre Club) explored three women, all upscale yuppie New Yorkers who have prodigious careers, as they seek emotional satisfaction. Rhonda (J. Smith-Cameron) has finally found the courage to break up with her boyfriend, Duke, but is haunted by the pair of sneakers he left in her bedroom. Billie (Nancy Mette) is happily married but despairs because her relationship with her husband never progressed beyond the naive honeymoon stage. Judy (Jayne Haynes) has no trouble finding men she can love, but they all turn out to be gay. Yet each of the three women finds a happy ending of sorts. In a quarrel, Billie's husband gives her a black eye, and she is delighted that they have gone beyond the surface in their marriage.

Rhonda fixes Judy up with Duke (Tom Wright), a black executive who is extremely heterosexual, and then finds the courage to toss out Duke's sneakers and get on with her life.

Spalding Gray's continued autobiography **Sex and Death to the Age 14** (5-28-86, Lincoln Center: Mitzi E. Newhouse) closed the season. Talking about his youth in Rhode Island, the death of his favorite pets and his first exploration into his own sexuality, Gray either intrigued or bored one. It was an apt way to end a very unsettling season.

1986–1987

For the first time in five seasons, both Broadway attendance and box office increased. British musicals accounted for much of the rise, but eleven plays managed to last over 100 performances on the Street, and five of those ran over 300 times. Off Broadway, ten plays managed a run of over 100, and a handful were able to triple that. The number of productions both on and off Broadway rose slightly. Lincoln Center was back in business, but the Public Theatre's output decreased, affected by the ailing health of founder-producer Joseph Papp.

Ten new American plays reached Broadway (most of them seen somewhere else first), and thirty-two appeared Off Broadway. Of the eight revivals on the Street, most were either critically or financially successful; the eleven revivals off Broadway (the lowest figure in over a decade) were not as lucky. Putting it all together, the totals were mildly encouraging. Looking at the caliber of the new works was also encouraging. American entries such as *The Colored Museum, Broadway Bound, The Nerd, The Musical Comedy Murders of 1940, Sweet Sue, Fences,* and *Driving Miss Daisy* may have varied in their quality, but all entered the repertory of produced works and would enjoy future life in regional theatre, film and even television.

The new season started as the previous one had ended: with a Spalding Gray monologue. **Swimming to Cambodia** (6-4-86, Lincoln Center: Mitzi E. Newhouse) recounted his weeks on location as an actor in the 1984 film *The Killing Fields.* Whether he was explaining the history of genocide in Southeast Asia or his own neuroses about ocean travel, Gray's commentary was "deeply personal, squirmingly confessional." Reviewers continued to be divided as to the worth of such ruminations, but the program proved to be Gray's most successful, running fifty-one performances and returning later in the season for another three weeks.

Mark O'Donnell's broad satire **The Nice and the Nasty** (6-5-86, Playwrights Horizons) met with mixed comments during its two-week run. Cathexa Heitz (Marianne Owen), inheritor of the powerful Food Technology conglomerate, is taken with young scientist Junius Upsey (W. H. Macy), who has invented a plastic helmet that sucks up the sun's nutrients and supplies the body with the nourishment that conventional foods offer. Despite the threat this poses to Cathexa's empire, she and her father, the aged founder of the company, Hobart Heitz (Thomas Barbour), encourage Junius in his invention. But Food Technology's ruthless manager, Blade Crevvis (David O'Brien), sets out to steal Junius's contraption even as he and his oddball assistant, Smurgison (Kurt Beattie), plan to destroy Planet Earth itself. Their schemes go awry and all ends happily thanks to the curiosity of a ten-year-old TV reporter, who is popular on the airwaves because "everybody trusts a kid."

The Roundabout Theatre Company, which rarely presented new works, found a new British play by David Pownall titled **Master Class** (6-5-86, Roundabout) to offer its subscribers. At a 1948 musicians' conference in Moscow, Stalin (Len Cariou) and his arts monitor, Zhdanov (Philip Bosco), take composers Prokofiev (Werner Klemperer) and Shostakovich (Austin Pendleton) aside and enforce the Party line by demanding that the two composers stop writing dissonant music and stick to state-sanctioned melody. To bring home their point, the two officials sit down at the piano with the composers and hammer out an original folk song together. Despite a dark and disturbing subtext of totalitarianism at work, the play was often farcical with the two musical geniuses arguing about working methods as their bosses hum along, getting drunk as they nostalgically recall the Russia of old. Few critics thought the black comedy worked, one calling it "a play of ideas [with] a paucity of ideas." Cariou was highly effective, giving "a monstrous but human portrait of a dictator," but the other actors were scolded for their overacting and tendency to "chew the scenery as if they were starved Siberian rats."

The New York Shakespeare Festival's *Twelfth Night* on June 20 was the summer's first Shakespeare at Central Park's Delacorte. Wilfred Leach set the comedy in sixteenth-century Yugoslavia and filled it with lots of slapstick, camp, and pseudo-exotic music. F. Murray Abraham, as a very silly Malvolio, led the uneven cast. Aisle-sitters called the evening everything from "a marvelously comic and enchanting romp" to "a terminal case of the cutes." Reviews were equally mixed for the June 26 revival of Joseph Kesselring's summer-stock reliable *Arsenic and Old Lace* (1-10-41) at the 46th Street. Some thought the play dated and in poor taste, but others recommended the "improbable" hit. Television favorites Jean Stapleton and Polly Holliday played the murderous aunts; Tony Roberts was their theatre critic nephew, Mortimer; and Abe Vigoda was the Boris Karloff–like Jonathan. None seemed to be in top form, but audiences enjoyed them for a profitable 221 performances.

Israel Horovitz's trilogy about Jewish life in the 1940s (based on stories by Morley Torgov) had been seen on Canadian television and in various off-off-Broadway productions. His first installment, **Today I Am a Fountain Pen** (7-10-86, Theatre 890), moved to Off Broadway for a successful run of 117 performances and was declared "absolutely charming and delightful" and "sweet without being cloying, gentle, and even wise." Ten-year-old Irving Yanover (Danny Gerard), a bright Ontario youth who is also a prodigy at the piano, begins to question his strict kosher upbringing ("Being Jewish is bigger than a pork chop," he is told) when the family hires teenage Ukrainian Annie Ilchak (Barbara Garrick) as their housekeeper. Both Irving's and Annie's parents refuse to let her see her Italian boyfriend, hockey player Peter Lisanti (Grant Shaud), so she and Irving set out to expose the hypocrisy of the adults, pointing out to the Yanovers that the red bits in their Chinese food are bacon and to Annie's father that the operas he loves so much are written by Italians. When Annie finds out she is pregnant, a wedding is agreed upon, and the older generation begrudgingly accepts some of the ideas of the younger.

After its sold-out engagement off Broadway, Reinaldo Povod's *Cuba and His Teddy Bear* (5-18-86) transferred to the Longacre on July 16 and, thanks to Robert De Niro's star power, did brisk business for its seven-week booking. The rest of the summer was given over to revivals. The Roundabout's mounting (and first New York revival) of Lorraine Hansberry's *A Raisin in the Sun* (3-11-59) on July 23 was called everything from "a stirring production [that] was alive to the many levels of the text" to "somewhat lacking in urgency and fire." (The role of Karl Lindner, the white man who tries to buy off the black family to keep them from moving into a white neigh-

borhood, was played by John Fiedler, who originated the role twenty-eight years earlier.) The Royal Shakespeare Company's wondrous stage version of Charles Dickens's *The Life and Adventures of Nicholas Nickleby* (10-4-81) returned to Broadway on August 24 at the Broadhurst and, though it may have seemed "slightly tarnished" compared to the original cast, was still warmly received, each of the two parts playing twenty-nine times. Samuel Beckett's absurdist classic *Krapp's Last Tape* (1-14-60) was revived on August 27 in the off-Broadway theatre named after the absurdist playwright. Rick Cluchey, an ex-con who discovered Beckett's works while in prison and sought out the playwright for personal training, played the title role as a "very private, muted, at times all but inaudible old duffer." Since Beckett himself directed the production, most critics felt the interpretation was valid. So did audiences, who filled the little house 104 times. The second summer offering at the Delacorte was Japan's Toho Company, Ltd., version of *Medea* performed in Japanese by an all-male cast for a one-week engagement beginning September 3.

Another foreign visitor was the Woza Afrika Festival at Lincoln Center, consisting of seven works from South Africa that ran from September 10 to October 5. The most memorable presentations included Mbongeni Ngema's **Asinamali!** (9-10-86, Mitzi E. Newhouse) in which five actors portrayed political prisoners—their heads shaved, their bodies connected by invisible chains—telling each other about the so-called crimes that led them to prison. (The title means "We have no money!" and was shouted by the demonstrators at a rent strike.) Although it was difficult to follow at times, the play was very theatrical, filled with songs and celebrating. Some commentators thought it "as exhilarating as anything in town." The production returned on April 23 to Broadway's Jack Lawrence Theatre and stayed for three more weeks. Percy Mtwa's **Bopha!** (9-17-86, Mitzi E. Newhouse) dealt with a black police officer in South Africa who convinces his unemployed brother to join the force. But the brother, with the help of the officer's rebel son, soon sees the injustice in taking part in the subjugation of his people, so he throws down his gun and joins the demonstrators. The festival's final entry was considered the finest: the documentary drama **Born in the R.S.A.** (10-1-86, Mitzi E. Newhouse), written by Barney Simon and the cast. In 1985 South Africa, the genial white student Glen (Neil McCarthy) allows himself to become a spy for the government, reporting on the activities of a Marxist teacher at his Johannesburg college. He also betrays his wife, Nicky (Terry Norton), by having an affair with Susan (Vanessa Cooke), an art teacher who is a member of a leftist group. The apolitical Glen ends up betraying Susan as well, his information sending several members of the group to prison. Jeffrey Sweet in *Best Plays* (it was selected as one of the season's ten best) summarized the positive reviews when he stated it "seriously explored the psychology underlying the institutionalized moral corruption of the Republic of South Africa."

Ray Stricklyn played Tennessee Williams in the one-man drama **Confessions of a Nightingale** (9-23-86, Audrey Wood Playhouse), which Stricklyn and Charlotte Chandler fashioned from the late playwright's life. Because of Williams's tell-all autobiography, much of what Stricklyn spoke came directly from the playwright. The drama took the form of an interview, but the questions were unspoken and the playwright answered directly to the audience. Some acclamations of being "illuminating" and "ingratiatingly salty" helped the program run six weeks.

The Circle Repertory had a very uneven season, beginning with Bryan Williams's "frail" drama **In This Fallen City** (9-25-86, Circle). Elderly Abner Abelson (Michael Higgins) was been branded the "Bad Samaritan" by his neighbors since the night a Puerto Rican youth on the run sought refuge in Abner's house but was turned away, only to be murdered on his doorstep by a gang. Paul Forrest (Danton Stone), a high school teacher who taught the dead boy, comes to Abner's house seeking the truth. Did Abner really turn the boy out, or is he the victim of rumor and hearsay? For some reason Abner stalls and teases Paul (and the audience) before confessing that he tried to save the boy.

John Patrick Shanley's gift for pitting volatile characters against each other was shown once again in **The Dreamer Examines His Pillow** (10-5-86, 47th Street), his self-described "heterosexual homily" about the stormy relationship between a seemingly cold artist, Tommy (Scott Renderer), and his feisty lover, Donna (Anne O'Sullivan). Even though the two broke up a while ago, they still see each other on occasion to bicker and try to wrestle each other out of their hearts. When Donna finds out that Tommy is sleeping with her younger sister, sparks fly. Donna appeals to her Dad (Graham Beckel), a successful artist who gave up painting after the death of his much-abused wife, to force Tommy to marry her. Failing that, she'd like Dad to beat him up. But the men's meeting turns into a surging of emotions as the two discuss art and women and their need to be responsible to each.

A revival that was practically a whole new play was Lawrence Sacharow's 1968 drama *The Concept* about recovering drug addicts. A new version by Casey Kurtti opened on October 7 at the Circle in Square Downtown, featuring a cast of eight former addicts who spoke about their experiences at the Daytop Village treatment center. Kurtti created her revised text out of the material furnished by the participants (the original play had been fiction based on fact), and audiences were interested enough to keep the true-to-life program on the boards for six weeks.

In **Groucho: A Life in Revue** (10-8-86, Lucille Lortel) we first see the aged Groucho Marx (Frank Ferrante) performing his famous Carnegie Hall concert, then are soon plummeted back to a past where he is struggling with his brothers Chico and Harpo (both played by Les Marsden) to make it in show business. Groucho's son Arthur co-wrote the piece with Robert Fisher. Although it was not a musical, Groucho's singing of old favorites was considered by many the highlight of the "droll, affectionate portrait of one of our greatest clowns." The play found encouraging reviews and healthy box office for 254 performances. Also impressing the reviewers was newcomer Faith Prince playing Margaret Dumont and other women in the comic history.

Most of the critics applauded the Circle in the Square's October 9 revival of Shaw's *You Never Can Tell* as "a thoroughgoing delight" and a "polished and eminently pleasurable production." Audiences agreed for 125 performances. Uta Hagen led the cast as the liberated Mrs. Clandon, but Victor Garber as Valentine, Amanda Plummer as Dolly, and Philip Bosco as the worldly-wise Waiter garnered the bulk of the praise.

America was not yet ready for **Rowan Atkinson at the Atkinson** (10-14-86, Brooks Atkinson), a popular British TV personality whose vehicle closed in less than a week. Richard Curtis, Ben Elton, and Atkinson wrote the evening of sketches that the New York press considered either "silly, topical, witty" or "a puerile bore." It would be another decade before Atkinson became a favorite on this side of the ocean through his films and television shows.

But the West End did send New Yorkers something to cheer about with Simon Gray's **The Common Pursuit** (10-19-86, Promenade). The play repeated its London success off Broadway, albeit with an American cast, running 352 performances and gathering such accolades as "witty and poignant," "a real play of wit and irony and sadness," and "uncommonly good." Six bright and idealistic Cambridge seniors decide to start a literary magazine after graduation, but during the course of the next twenty years we see each individual compromise and change as youthful ideals give way to greed, fame, or disillusionment. The most dedicated of the lot is Stuart Thorne (Kristoffer Tabori), who edits the magazine with the help of Marigold Watson (Judy Geeson), his lover and later his wife. Even as Stuart's marriage dries up due to sexual impotence, so too Stuart lets his magazine die when he realizes it will never meet the high standards he has set for it. Womanizing Peter Whetworth (Dylan Baker) writes books that he is ashamed of, and eager Nick Finchling (Nathan Lane) sells out to *Vogue* and later television talk shows in order to achieve fame. Humphrey Taylor (Peter Friedman), a poet who maintains his ideals up to a point, becomes a morals professor but is eventually murdered by one of the boys he indiscriminately picks up in train-station restrooms. The play's last scene flashes back to the first with Stuart explaining to his fellow students how their literary magazine must maintain its integrity in an indifferent world.

October's last two entries both fared poorly. An off-Broadway commercial entry, Thomas Strelich's Sam Shepard–ish drama **Neon Psalms** (10-22-86, American Place), folded in two weeks. Luton Mears (Tom Aldredge), a retired operator of heavy equipment, lives with his born-again wife, Patina (Scotty Bloch), in a lone trailer in the California desert near the world's largest open-pit borax mine. Their uneasy marriage (he seems more interested in old episodes of *Bonanza* than in his wife) is further endangered by the arrival of Barbara (Cara Duff-MacCormick), their divorcée daughter, who brings out the worst in her parents when she decides to stay a while. Much talk of technology in the world (with some zesty commentary by a propane delivery man played by Kelly Connell) fills the time until the family reaches a tentative truce, realizing that they are all starved for love.

Caroline Kava's **The Early Girl** (10-30-86, Circle), an earthy look at mining-town brothel life, boasted better performances than writing. Lily (Demi Moore in her stage debut) has left her infant child with a friend and joins a house of ill repute, hoping to make enough money to escape her past debts. Her plan proceeds successfully,

GEORGE C. WOLFE (1955–) was born in Lexington and raised in Frankfort, Kentucky, then educated at Pomona College and New York University. He was twice cited as a winner in the American College Theatre Festival. After graduation he spent four years in Los Angeles writing and directing before his New York debut as the librettist and lyricist for the short-lived off-Broadway musical *Paradise!* (1985). Wolfe's *The Colored Museum* originated at the Crossroads Theatre in New Jersey before transferring to the Public in Manhattan. Although first recognized as a playwright of talent, Wolfe would soon be just as well known as a director and, later, one of his generation's most astute producers.

and it looks like she will become the winner in her brothel's monthly competition. When, strictly against the house rules, she accepts a phone call about her ailing baby daughter, a confrontation with the madam, Lana (Pamela Dunlap), ensues. Lily stands up to Lana then, departs with one of the other girls, the smart-aleck Jean (Robin Bartlett), only to be replaced by a new recruit as the play ends.

Newcomer George C. Wolfe made a startling debut with his satirical **The Colored Museum** (11-2-86, Public: Shiva), a revue consisting of eleven "exhibits" about African-American culture that critics cited for its "chilling dramatic points" and its "uncompromising wit." Among its memorable sequences: an airline stewardess (Danitra Vance) goes through her customary patter ("obey the FASTEN SHACKLES sign at all times") for a planeload of "celebrity" slaves traveling from Africa to Savannah; a Vietnam casualty (Tommy Hollis) laments the America that his surviving black brethren must return to; a prominent black executive (Hollis) deposits the relics of his past (FREE HUEY buttons, Sly Stone records, his first dashiki) in a trash can, only to be confronted by his youthful alter ego (Reggie Montgomery); and the evening's most talked-about scene: "The Last Mama-on-the-Couch Play," a wicked spoof of *A Raisin in the Sun* (3-11-59) in which the steadfast "mamma" character is lambasted. The comedy ran 198 performances and introduced one of the era's most potent theatre artists.

A much more serious work about African Americans, Leslie Lee's **The War Party** (11-5-86, Theatre Four), was the financially troubled Negro Ensemble Company's sole offering this season. Into the North Philadelphia ghetto headquarters of Marching on Poverty in 1978 comes the light-skinned Kathy Robbins (Carla Brothers), the daughter of a white mother and black father, who has decided to identify herself as African-American and join the movement. Because she is rich and appears to be white, the fellow workers at the headquarters do not welcome her at first. But Kathy manages to win some of them over, even having an affair with Stan Younger (Adam Wade), the overbearing clergyman who leads the movement, who has high ideals but treats his workers with scorn. While Stan is off on one of his business trips, Kathy falls in love with the more gentle Roosevelt Gwynne (Vondie Curtis-Hall), who runs the office and is always trying to soothe the abused helpers. When Stan returns, the rivalry between the two men over Kathy is echoed by the demonstrations occurring outside, and in the end Kathy dies violently. Lee was considered promising; Edith Oliver in *The New Yorker* described his work as "overloaded with plot, subplot and incidents, but . . . never tedious."

Even more complicated but far less satisfying was Keith Reddin's political satire **Highest Standard of Living** (11-13-86, Playwrights Horizons). Bob (Steven Culp), an American student of Russian literature, travels to Moscow to study with Mikhail Bulgakov but suffers from food poisoning so ends up in a Russian hospital, where his fellow patients are (or look like) his mother and other relatives. His nurse Ludmilla (Leslie Lyles) turns out to be a KGB agent, but Bob falls in love with her anyway. Before you know it, seven little boys enter his hospital room and start to beat Bob with little hammers. In the second act, Bob, having been kicked out of Russia, is back in America, bandaged and bruised. Yet he has Ludmilla with him and is glad to be back in New York. But soon CIA agents approach him and start harassing him in a very KGB-like manner. Eventually Bob and Ludmilla jump off the Staten Island Ferry together, either to freedom or to their deaths.

The Manhattan Theatre Club opened its season with Mark Medoff's Pirandellian drama **The Hands of Its Enemy** (11-18-86, City Center). Howard Bellman (Jeffrey DeMunn), a celebrated theatre director fresh from a stay in a drug and alcohol rehab center, returns to the southwestern university where he was once a faculty member to direct a play written by deaf student Marieta Yerby (Phyllis Frelich). Although her script is about an abused wife who shoots her alcoholic husband, Bellman believes that there is much more behind the story, so he has Marieta and the cast act out her past, bullying them into revealing

that Marieta was sexually molested by her father. Reviews, ranging from "a superbly crafted theatre piece" to "a profoundly trashy work," compared the drama unfavorably to *Six Characters in Search of an Author* (10-30-22) and Medoff's own *Children of a Lesser God* (3-30-80).

Veteran playwright Horton Foote saw two works from his ambitious nine-play *The Orphans' Home* cycle presented off Broadway this season, each running over 100 performances. The first was **Lily Dale** (11-20-86, Samuel Beckett), set at the turn of the century in Harrison, Texas, where nineteen-year-old Horace Robedaux (Don Bloomfield) works as a clerk in a dry-goods store. After his father died of alcoholism, Horace's mother, Corella (Julie Heberlein), moved to Houston and remarried. When she invites Horace to visit, he eagerly goes to be reunited with his teenage sister, Lily (Molly Ringwald). But his gruff stepfather, Pete (Greg Zittel), dislikes Horace even as he spoils Lily and, more upsetting, Horace learns that Lily and he disagree greatly in their views about their late father. When Horace is forced to prolong his stay because of a bout of malaria, he and Lily thrash matters out. Then he returns to Harrison, convinced that some of the family demons in his past have been exorcised. The reviews were appreciative, if not enthusiastic, calling the play "an affecting tapestry of family like" and a "fondly regarded family album."

An "attractively cast and appropriately slam-bang revival" of *The Front Page* (8-14-28) reopened the Vivian Beaumont on November 23, the first homegrown production in the Lincoln Center space in nearly two years. Jerry Zaks directed with his customary zeal; Richard Thomas (Hildy) and John Lithgow (Walter) led the large cast. Unanimously favorable notices allowed the popular comedy to run seven weeks.

Neil Simon's **Broadway Bound** (12-4-86, Broadhurst), the third in his trilogy of autobiographical plays (and the third "series" seen this season), returned to the Jerome household of *Brighton Beach Memoirs* (3-27-83) where Eugene (Jonathan Silverman) and his brother, Stan (Jason Alexander), are trying to break into show business by writing comedy sketches for that newfangled invention: television. While the brothers break each other up creating their comic routines, the Jerome family is in crisis. Parents Kate (Linda Lavin) and Jack (Philip Sterling) watch their thirty-three-year marriage fall apart even as Socialist grandfather Ben (John Randolph) resists the efforts of his daughter Blanche (Phyllis Newman) to send him to Florida to be reunited with his wife. The conflicts and tensions in the Brooklyn household are so interesting, Eugene notes, "maybe I don't have to be a writer; if I could just get people to pay for seats in the living room." The family pulls together at the news that one of Eugene and Stan's comedy sketches is to be broadcast over the radio. But when they listen to the show and realize that it is a comic version of their own lives, they feel betrayed. Eugene tells the audience in an epilogue that his parents eventually divorced, Ben "finally surrendered to Capitalism and Miami Beach," and he and his brother set off on lucrative careers as comedy writers. A particularly winning scene in the domestic piece was Kate's recalling the night she danced with George Raft and Jerome taking his mother in his arms and recreating the treasured moment. Gene Saks directed the superior cast, as he had done for the previous *Brighton Beach Memoirs* and *Biloxi Blues* (3-28-85), with a gentle touch. The "lovely, quiet, distinctive play" received the best reviews of the three works, helping it run 756 performances. In the spring Lavin and Randolph won Tony Awards.

The Roundabout had a disappointing season, both in quality and quantity. It presented only three plays, the first a revival of Robert Bolt's *A Man for All Seasons* (11-22-61) on December 11 that was nearly saved by Philip Bosco's solid and commanding performance as Thomas More. Charles Keating (Common Man), Robert Stattel (Cromwell), and J. Kenneth Campbell (King Henry VIII) were his colleagues in the revival.

Horton Foote's **The Widow Claire** (12-17-86, Circle in the Square Downtown) followed *Lily Dale* in the cycle, showing what happened to Horace Robedaux (Matthew Broderick) when he returned to Harrison, Texas. Taking lodgings in a rooming house while he pursues a six-week business course, Horace falls in love with the flirtatious widow Claire Ratliff (Hallie Foote), who has two young children and plenty of suitors. But Horace perseveres, even getting into a disastrous fistfight with one of his rivals, before concluding that Claire cares nothing for him. In truth, she does love him but accepts the proposal of a wealthier man to secure a stable future for her children. *The Widow Claire* received better reviews than *Lily Dale* (most commentators agreed it was a stronger production), remaining on the boards for nearly five months.

Chekhov's early rambling epic *Platonov* was given a shot in the arm by British playwright Michael Frayn, who retained the Russian setting and principal characters, calling it **Wild Honey** (12-18-86, Virginia). Rural schoolmaster Platonov (Ian

McKellen) is a disreputable fellow, always drinking, in debt, and unfaithful to his wife, Sasha (Kate Burton). But that doesn't keep local ladies Sofya (Kim Cattrell), Marya (J. Smith-Cameron), and Anna Petrovna (Kathryn Walker) from falling in love with him. Platonov enjoys the attention, but loving them back is a nuisance. His overlapping intrigues are eventually discovered, and rather than deal with all the fuss, he stands on the railroad tracks waiting for an oncoming train to end all his troubles. *Wild Honey* had been a hit in London, but despite encouraging New York reviews for Frayn's "ingenious" adaptation and "strange, wicked, funny play," audiences were not drawn to the dark comedy, and it closed after twenty-eight performances. A similar fate had befallen the previous Manhattan viewing of *Platonov*, which was set in modern-day Virginia and titled *Fireworks on the James* (5-14-40).

Yet another play about aimless youth trying to find satisfaction in life was Roger Hedden's **Bodies, Rest and Motion** (12-21-86, Mitzi E. Newhouse). Nick (W. H. Macy) and Beth (Laurie Metcalf) live in a rundown rental in Enfield, Connecticut. His selling TV sets provides the pair with the booze that they consume while they sit and watch television (a color set Nick stole from the store) and dream about moving to the Midwest and getting a fresh start. But one day Nick takes off for Ohio without Beth, and she slips into a love affair with Sid (Andrew McCarthy), the house painter who has come to repaint the place for the next tenants. Sid wants to marry her, but Beth is afraid of commitment, so she sells all the furniture (except for the precious TV) and takes off herself. When Nick returns to Beth, he finds only an empty house. Undeterred, he takes up with his old lover Carol (Christina Moore) and watches TV, while Sid quits his job and sets off to find Beth.

Jackie Mason's "The World According to Me!" (12-22-86, Brooks Atkinson) might have been nothing more than a Catskills' "borscht belt" show, yet the evening, written and delivered solely by Mason, was so polished (he had spent decades collecting the material) and hysterical that it became a Broadway hit, running 367 performances, winning a special Tony Award, and returning the following season. Mason's acidic commentary on the differences between Jews and goyim struck both groups as hilariously accurate. Even most of the critics lauded the one-man show.

The Manhattan Theatre Club continued to present new works from Great Britain, but Howard Benton's **Bloody Poetry** (1-6-87, City Center)

was not one of its finer efforts. Condemning the bourgeois ways of England and spending their summers in Switzerland, Percy Bysshe Shelley (Thomas Gibson), Lord Byron (Daniel Gerroll), Claire Clairmont (Jayne Atkinson), and Mary Shelley (Laila Robins) philosophize about art and radicalism. When Percy dies and his body is cremated on the beach at Viareggio, Byron delivers a wild-eyed oration and rants about the price of artistic freedom.

After years of notable off-Broadway entries, John Bishop finally had a hit with **The Musical Comedy Murders of 1940** (1-7-87, Circle), a farce that amused audiences for eighty-eight performances before transferring to Broadway's Longacre on April 6 for an additional 136 showings. Broadway investor Elsa von Grossenknueten (Ruby Holbrook) invites producer Marjorie Baverstock (Pamela Dunlap), California-tanned director Ken de la Maize (Michael Ayr), sarcastic composer Roger Hopewell (Richard Seff), and hard-drinking lyricist Bernice Roth (Bobo Lewis) to her Westchester County mansion on a snowy weekend ostensibly to audition their new musical *White House Merry Go Round*. But Elsa's true intent is to gather together the suspects in the Stage Door Slasher murders of a previous show in which three chorus girls were killed. Also gathered for the audition are comic Eddie McCuen (Kelly Connell), chorus girl Nikki Crandall (Dorothy Cantwell), and Patrick O'Reilly (Nicholas Wyman), an Irish tenor with a tendency to slip into German at times. Police officer Michael Kelly (Willie C. Carpenter), a black Irishman posing as a chauffeur, helps Elsa lure the murderer to the estate, but before anyone one knows it, a German spy murders the maid Helsa (Lily Knight) and, dressing in drag, takes her place. Next Marjorie is run through with a sword, a storm cuts off all the electricity, and characters are dashing through secret tunnels hidden behind revolving bookcases. In the end Nikki turns out to be an agent from naval intelligence, O'Reilly is the German spy, and Ken is discovered to be the Slasher. (His father had run off with a chorus girl, and it broke his mother's heart). Nikki falls in love with Eddie as Roger and Bernice decide to reset their musical in the Midwest and call it *Nebraska!* Reviewers differed sharply, some feeling it "lacks both satiric specificity and biting wit" but others calling it "daffy genre blending: a spoof within a parody within a whodunit."

A. R. Gurney went directly to Broadway with his latest comedy, **Sweet Sue** (1-8-87, Music Box), which was more a star vehicle than the ensemble pieces he usually wrote for Off Broadway. Susan (Mary Tyler Moore), a greeting card designer and artist, is a level-headed divorcée with three grown children who prides herself on her efficient suburban home, which she characterizes as "an oasis of decency in a world gone absolutely haywire on the subject of sex." But her inner self, Susan Too (Lynn Redgrave), is a romantic at heart, so as a result they are of "two minds" when it comes to many important subjects. When her son's Dartmouth roommate, Jake (John K. Linton), stays the summer, earning tuition money by house painting, both Sues are taken with him. His alter ego, Jake Too (Barry Tubb), is ripe for romance but was imagining someone closer to his own age. Sue asks Jake to pose in the nude for a life study and, after much discussion between the two Jakes, he agrees. Not surprisingly, the episode exposes all four characters' vulnerability, and Jake and Susan go their own ways but share a special understanding of each other. Unenthusiastic notices lamented the "sorry little waif of a play" but applauded the stars. The show cost $800,000 to mount, and its 164-performance run left its producers deep in the red.

With a title like **Stepping Out** (1-11-87, John Golden) and a director like Tommy Tune, audiences were expecting a musical. But Richard Harris's London hit was about a group of inhibited North Londoners who take dance lessons as a way to overcome their everyday inadequacies. In her rundown studio, Mavis (Pamela Sousa), an ex–professional dancer trying to make ends meet, teaches tap dancing to the ten women and one man, all of them handicapped with two left feet and personality quirks. Despite all their quarreling and last-minute fears, the group's recital comes off surprisingly well, and the oddballs take a big step in building their self-confidence. Tepid reviews mentioned how delightful the final production number was, so audiences came seventy-two times to see the showstopper when, as one critic put it, "there isn't a show to stop."

Colleen Dewhurst, perhaps the finest female interpreter of Eugene O'Neill's plays, portrayed the playwright's wife Carlotta in Barbara Gelb's one-woman drama **My Gene** (1-29-87, Public: Martinson). In New York's St. Luke's Hospital, where the anguished Carlotta has been confined for psychiatric help, the widow carries on one-sided conversations with her long-dead husband and others in her past. On a few (and most satisfying) occasions, Carlotta broke into some speeches from O'Neill's work, but rarely did *My Gene* turn into a play. Critics found the evening "surprisingly unaffecting" and a "well-intentioned, static monologue." But Dewhurst was "self-assured, radiant, and capable of self-mockery, scathing humor, and violent rages." Audiences were able to enjoy her performance for two months.

Arthur Miller, who was looked upon by many as O'Neill's successor, presented his first new work in seven years: **Danger: Memory!** (2-8-87, Mitzi E. Newhouse), a program of two short plays about the healing and destructive power of remembering the past. In *I Can't Remember Anything*, aged Leonora (Geraldine Fitzgerald) regularly visits with her late husband's old friend Leo (Mason Adams). While the two men held opposite political views (Leo was a devout Communist), the distance of time has softened these differences, and the dying Leo and the widow decide to forget the past's less savory chapters. In *Clara*, Albert Kroll (Kenneth McMillan), an elderly father whose daughter is the victim of a senseless murder, is being interrogated by Detective Lieutenant Fine (James Tolkan). The officer coldheartedly pushes Albert to recall events in his daughter's past that may point to a suspect. He remembers a Puerto Rican ex-con that Clara was seeing despite objections from her father. Only after Albert has a flashback, about a case of prejudice against some black soldiers in a southern town during World War II, does he recall the ex-con's name. Critics were politely dismissive of the two plays, Oliver noting that *Clara* was "about guilt, racism, racial hypocrisy, sexual hypocrisy, and other abstractions. It is certainly not about people."

A vulgar comedy about contemporary America, Steven Berkoff's British play **Kvetch** (2-18-87, Westside) explored the inner thoughts of a group of restless and dissatisfied Los Angeles Jews: Frank (Kurt Fuller), a bellyaching garment manufacturer, his ever-suffering wife, Donna (Laura Esterman), his abusive Mother-in-Law (Ruth Jaroslow), their put-upon dinner guest Hal (Mitch Kreindel), and Frank's repellent client George (Hy Anzell). Monologues and conversations filled with lengthy asides to the audience permitted the characters to rant in public and private about all their prejudices and hangups, slurring just about every known race, gender, and religion. Critics were mostly in agreement with Marilyn Stasio in the *New York Post*, who found "it conveys plenty of contempt but no compassion for its characters, depriving them of all vestiges of humanity," yet the editors chose it as one of the *Best Plays*.

William Gibson's *The Miracle Worker* (10-19-59) received its first New York revival on February 18 when the Roundabout offered Karen Allen as Annie Sullivan. Even though notices for her and Eevin Hartsough as her pupil Helen Keller were complimentary, the production failed to take off.

Richard Greenberg's "young and sharp and frisky" comedy **The Maderati** (2-19-87, Playwrights Horizons) poked fun at the Manhattan arts community filled with vapid yuppies or, as they call themselves, the "mad literati" (hence, the odd title). After the overweight poet Charlotte Ebbinger (Amanda Carlin) overcomes her periodic flirtation with suicide and decides to check into a mental hospital, her sudden disappearance convinces all of her colleagues that she has finally done herself in. Word filters through the artistic community, the details of the story growing more outrageous with each telling. Just as poets, artists, writers, and actors are all gathered at an impromptu party to memorialize the late Charlotte, she shows up as a surprise guest.

Having won the Nobel Prize for Literature the previous year, Nigerian playwright Wole Soyinka brought his **Death and the King's Horseman** (3-1-87, Vivian Beaumont) to Lincoln Center after notable productions in London, Chicago, and Washington. Based on a true incident that occurred in Nigeria in 1946, the story centered on Elesin (Earle Hyman), the tribal king's horseman and companion. The king has died, and tradition states that his horseman should commit suicide and follow his leader into the next world. Elesin plans to do exactly that until the British colonials hear of the barbaric plan and imprison him so that he cannot carry out his tragic fate. The incident serves to point out the wide gap in understanding between the two cultures; Elesin argues that the tribal ritual is no more barbaric than the "mass suicide" the British and others are engaged in during the current world war. By the final curtain Elesin has even convinced his English-educated son that his people's way is the only way, and Elesin commits suicide. Reviews wavered widely, though Clive Barnes's comment in the *New York Post* was probably nearest the truth: "this is both a play of wonder and a play worth wondering about; imperfect, difficult to Western ears, but poetically fascinating in its grasp of souls and their journeys."

On the Verge; or, The Geography of Yearning (3-2-87, John Houseman) by newcomer Eric Overmyer was as intriguing and fanciful as its title. Three nineteenth-century American lady explorers (Lisa Banes, Patricia Hodges, and Laura Hicks) set out in pith helmets and rucksacks to chart the future, traveling in 1888 to deepest, darkest Africa, then to the philosophical heights of the Himalayas, then finally to "terra incognita," the America of the 1950s. Faced with modern kitchen appliances, early TV sitcoms, and I LIKE IKE buttons, the three "sister sojourners" are dazzled and puzzled by what they see, one of them remarking, "I have seen the future and it is slang." Mel Gussow in the *New York Times* wrote, "Blending Tom Stoppard's limber linguistics with the historic overview of a Thornton Wilder, Mr. Overmyer takes his audience on a mirthful safari." Not all the reviews were as glowing, but audiences supported the Acting Company's production for seventy-two performances, and the script became popular in regional and college theatres.

Janusz Glowacki's "mordantly funny" **Hunting Cockroaches** (3-3-87, City Center) was thin on plot, but the Polish playwright cleverly portrayed the difficulties immigrants faced in contemporary New York. Jan (Ron Silver) is an author of note but, since coming to America, has been experiencing writer's block. His wife, Anka (Dianne Wiest), is an accomplished classical actress, but her thick Polish accent keeps her from getting acting jobs in Manhattan. To make matters worse, both are suffering from insomnia. As the two try to fall asleep in their Lower East Side firetrap of an apartment, people from their past literally crawl out from under the couple's bed and involve them in recollected incidents. Arthur Penn staged the odd comedy with a masterly touch, and Heidi Landesman designed an ingenious setting that allowed entrances from beneath the bed. But the highlight of the production was Wiest's thickly accented performance as a desperate, funny, and intelligent woman on the edge.

Tina Howe finally made it to Broadway with her romantic comedy **Coastal Disturbances** (3-4-87, Circle in the Square), a loose ensemble piece about vacationers of various generations spending the summer on a private New England beach. M. J. (Rosemary Murphy) and Hamilton Adams (Addison Powell) have been coming to this same spot for years, yet despite a long marriage and nine grown children, the site still recalls for both of them an affair Hamilton once had. Ariel Took (Jean De Baer), recuperating from a messy divorce, heads to the beach with her overactive ten-year-old son, Winston (Jonas Abry), and her old college roommate, Faith Bigelow (Heather MacRae) who has her adopted daughter, Miranda (Angela Goethals), in tow. Tying the various short scenes together is the blossoming romance between amiable lifeguard Leo Hart (Timothy Daly) and the very photogenic photographer

Holly Dancer (Annette Bening in her New York debut). Although some critics pointed out that Howe's script did "not seem a fully fleshed-out play," reviews were mostly favorable, and the slight comedy stayed for 350 showings. Bening was considered quite a find; unfortunately, she was immediately whisked off to the movies and would not return to the stage for twelve years. Also notable about the production was Bob Shaw's setting, filled with sand so deep that characters were able to bury themselves in it. Dennis Parichy's lighting "captured the entire spectrum of weather known to habitués of New England beaches in August." Frank Rich in the *New York Times* urther noted, "not merely the blinding sunniness of midday but also the frail pink cumulus clouds of dusk, the chilly mica silver of a lost rainy afternoon, and the pale smoky blue of a foggy dawn."

Larry Shue had died in a plane crash in 1985 but left behind **The Nerd** (3-24-87, Helen Hayes), a farce that would prove almost as durable as his earlier *The Foreigner* (11-1-84). Architect Willum Cubbert (Mark Hamill) and his hesitant fiancée Tansy McGuinnis (Patricia Kalember), are about to celebrate his thirty-fourth birthday when Rick Steadman (Robert Joy), a bespectacled, incorrigible nerd, comes to visit. Back in Vietnam, Rick saved Willum's life by dragging him to safety from an airstrip riddled with bullets. Willum has not encountered Rick since but owes his life to the goofy fellow, and at first he is pleased to see him show up at his Terre Haute, Indiana, home. But as Rick moves in to stay and has business cards printed with "Willum Cubbert and Rick Steadman, Architects and Best Friends," it becomes clear the nerd is going to destroy Willum's career, personal life, and sanity. After several weeks of Rick offending and disgusting Willum and his friends (especially the suave, cynical Axel Hamond, played by Peter Riegert), the tactless bore is lured away. The play ends with a forced twist: it turns out Rick is not a nerd at all but was acting the part with Axel to bring Tansy and Willum together. Commentators found the script "flimsy and preposterous" and the venture "well-acted junk," but audiences laughed for 441 performances.

The finest (and longest-running) American play of the Broadway season was August Wilson's **Fences** (3-26-87, 46th Street). Troy Maxson (James Earl Jones) was a major home-run hitter in the Negro baseball leagues, but by 1957 he is a sanitation worker in Philadelphia, proud to be the first black garbage-truck driver in the city. A larger-than-life fellow, Troy spins tales and jokes with the neighbors, but at home he is a strict taskmaster with his resilient wife, Rose (Mary Alice), and his teenage son, Cory (Courtney B. Vance). When the athletic Cory is scouted for a scholarship to attend college, Troy refuses to give his permission. Part of his reason is jealousy (Troy was too old by the time major league baseball was desegregated), but mainly Troy is bitter about the fences society has built for members of his race, and he doesn't want his son to suffer the frustration he has undergone. When one of Troy's infidelities results in a baby and the mother dies in childbirth, Rose throws him out of her bed and decides to raise the orphan herself, telling Troy, "From right now . . . this child got a mother. But you a womanless man." In 1965, Cory (now a marine corporal) returns to his Philadelphia home for Troy's funeral, befriends his eight-year-old half sister, Raynell (Karima Miller), and confers with his mother about the strange but powerful shadow that Troy still casts over their lives. Once again Lloyd Richards directed the Wilson script, and the cast was riveting, right down to Frankie R. Faison as Troy's brother Gabriel, half-witted since a war injury and hoping to open up the gates of heaven with his trumpet calls. Another novel aspect of the evening was the very vocal reactions the play elicited from audience members, many of the African-American spectators being more than willing to voice their opinion directly to the actors. Unanimous rave reviews helped the drama run 526 performances, as did winning every major award: the New York Drama Critics Circle, Outer Critics Circle, and Tony awards and the Pulitzer Prize. Tonys were also given to Richards, Jones, and Mary Alice.

Although glowing notices were not forthcoming, the star-studded revival of Noel Coward's *Blithe Spirit* (11-5-41) on March 31 at the Neil Simon managed to run 103 performances. Blythe Danner was a bewitching Elvira, Geraldine Page got the most out of scene-stealing Madame Arcati, Richard Chamberlain was a stiff but appealing Charles, and Judith Ivey was his stern wife, Ruth. Director Brian Murray was blamed for the production's inconsistent style and lagging moments. It was Page's last stage appearance; she died in June, and the revival closed a week later.

Safe Sex (4-5-87, Lyceum), Harvey Fierstein's triple bill about living with AIDS, returned to territory explored in his popular *Torch Song Trilogy* (1-15-82), but because the bittersweet playlets were "so soaked in sentimentality" and contained "little or no appeal for a general audience," the program closed in a week. *Manny and Jake* are two men (John Mulkeen and John Wesley Shipp) looking for sex in a gay bar, but one of them has AIDS and can only fantasize about kissing the other. The title play posed two former lovers, the motherly Ghee (Fierstein) and the virile stud Mead (Shipp), who meet after a long separation and try to use prophylactic protection as a way of avoiding emotional intimacy. Their seesaw-like confrontation was literally played on a seesaw, the two lovers (wearing nightshirts) rising and falling with the ups and downs of the conversation. *On Tidy Endings* was the most conventional of the trio, a realistic drama in which Arthur (Fierstein) is mourning the loss of his lover from AIDS when the dead man's ex-wife, Marion (Anne DeSalvo), and teenage son, Jimmy (Ricky Addison Reed), come to the apartment to collect some of his things. The animosity between wife and male lover soon develops into mutual understanding as they learn to share the love they have for the same man.

A much-ballyhooed play from the Actors Theatre of Louisville, **Tent Meeting** (4-7-87, Astor Place) by Rebecca Wackler, Larry Larson, and Levi Lee, only lasted two weeks in a commercial mounting off Broadway. In 1946, Ed Tarbox (Lee), an Arkansas redneck preacher, hears the word of God when his daughter, Becky (Wackler), gives birth to a misshapen baby (it is missing some vital organ, probably the result of an incestuous union between Ed and Becky) and announces that this new Messiah will be called Jesus O. Tarbox. Ed steals the baby from the laboratory where it is being studied and heads to the "promised land" with Becky and his dim son, Daniel (Larson), a World War II vet who claims his hernia operation scar is from a Nazi bayonet. They arrive in Moose Jaw, Saskatchewan, where Ed holds a tent revival and plans a ritual sacrifice of the infant. But a miracle occurs that saves the child: his bassinet lights up, and a typewriter mysteriously types by itself a message from God ordering that the new Messiah be spared.

Bill Irwin's comic twin bill, *Regard of Flight* and *The Clown Bagatelles* (5-23-82), returned to New York on April 12 for two weeks at the Vivian Beaumont, gathering a laudatory set of raves from critics both familiar and not familiar with his unique kind of performance art.

The sleeper of the season was Alfred Uhry's **Driving Miss Daisy** (4-15-87, Playwrights Horizons), a gentle character drama that maintained a following for 1,195 performances. When Daisy

Wertham (Dana Ivey), a Jewish widow in Atlanta, crashes her new 1948 Packard because her reflexes are going, her son, Boolie (Ray Gill), hires the soft-spoken black man Hoke Coleburn (Morgan Freeman) to be her chauffeur, much against the wishes of the stubborn, set-in-her-ways Daisy. But Hoke quietly perseveres, and over the next twenty-five years the two slowly becomes friends. The drama's special warmth emerged in touching episodes, such as Daisy's teaching the illiterate Hoke how to read or their drive to a banquet honoring Martin Luther King, Jr. As the social fabric of the country changed, so did Daisy and Hoke, and the final scene had Hoke visiting his ninety-seven-year-old ex-employer in a nursing home, the two still connected with an unlikely bond of understanding. Critics called the piece "utterly engaging," "sweet without being mawkish," and a "little gem [that] echoes decades of social change." Because of its late opening, *Driving Miss Daisy* won the Pulitzer Prize in 1988 and became the biggest hit in the history of Playwrights Horizons.

Another crotchety senior citizen was the focal point of Bob Larbey's **A Month of Sundays** (4-16-87, Ritz), but neither audiences nor critics could warm up to a play where "the people and events are so bland that the whole enterprise has the personality of a generic product," so it shuttered after four viewings. Rather than be a burden to his family, elderly Cooper (Jason Robards) goes into an exclusive Westchester retirement home, where he harasses the staff and other residents. The title came from the fact that Cooper's daughter and son-in-law always visit him on the first Sunday of every month, a time when the old man is more than usually impossible. Although this British play was Americanized by its author for Broadway, many lines and jokes retained a distinctly English ring.

While some aisle-sitters questioned some of the melodramatics in Arthur Miller's *All My Sons* (1-29-47), they all applauded the Long Wharf Theatre revival on April 22 at the John Golden. Richard Kiley was a powerful Joe Keller, Joyce Ebert was his wife, Kate, and newcomer James Sheridan was his son Chris. Arvin Brown's firm but sensitive directorial touch undeniably helped, for the Tony committee named it the season's best revival. Peter O'Toole made his belated Broadway debut on April 26 when he played Henry Higgins in a revival of Shaw's *Pygmalion* at the Plymouth. Amanda Plummer was his Eliza, and both met with decidedly mixed notices. Some commentators thought O'Toole appropriately physical and eccentric; others found him sloppy and self-indulgent. Similarly, Plummer was considered refreshingly unique by some, hopelessly miscast by others. Audiences had 113 performances to see for themselves. The same night, the Circle Rep revived William M. Hoffman's still-potent AIDS play *As Is* (3-10-85) for three weeks.

Beth Henley seemed to never run out of fresh southern eccentrics to populate her comedies, and **The Lucky Spot** (4-28-87, City Center) was no exception. In the depths of the Depression, gambler Reed Hooker (Ray Baker) wins a run-down dance hall in Pigeon, Louisiana, in a poker game; in the same game he also wins Cassidy Smith (Mary Stuart Masterson), a minor whom he dazzles and then impregnates. With the help of his faithful sidekick, Turnip Moss (Alan Ruck), Reed plans to turn the rural roadhouse into a citified dance hall complete with taxi dancers. The grand opening is set for Christmas Eve, but Reed's estranged wife Sue Jack Tiller (Amy Madigan) is let out of prison for the holidays (she was convicted for shooting one of Reed's girlfriends) and shows up at "The Lucky Spot," pistol in hand and drunk (literally and figuratively) with her first taste of freedom. The opening is a fiasco: Sue Jack makes a spectacle of herself, Reed's sinister creditor Whitt Carmichael (Lanny Flaherty) takes possession of the hall, Cassidy's hopes for marrying Reed are dashed, and Sue Jack and Reed find out they love each other even more passionately than they hate each other. Reviews varied from "touching comic theatre" to "self-parodistic effort which smothers the audience . . . under an avalanche of fortune cookie–sized truths." The Manhattan Theatre Club run was not extended beyond its scheduled three weeks, and the comedy was rarely heard of again.

As with its earlier entries this season, the Roundabout's "flatfooted revival" of Tom Stoppard's *Rosencrantz and Guildenstern Are Dead* (10-16-67) on April 29 was distinguished by a sole performance. In this case it was British actor John Wood, who had originated the role of Guildenstern twenty years earlier but had now grown comfortably into the crusty old Player. Stephen Lang and John Rubinstein played the title characters, and most critics thought them both lacking.

The most impressive British import of the season was Christopher Hampton's **Les Liaisons Dangereuses** (4-30-87, Music Box), an intelligent and thrilling adaptation of Choderlos de Laclos's amoral novel of sexual intrigue in late eighteenth-century France. The original book was composed solely of letters back and forth between the scheming characters, but Hampton turned their correspondence into funny and disturbing conversations and episodes. The seductive Vicomte de Valmont (Alan Rickman) and his accomplice, the Marquise de Merteuil (Lindsay Duncan), plot the rape of an innocent convent girl, Cecile (Beatie Edney), and the seduction of the virtuous Mme. de Tourvel (Suzanne Burden), succeeding on both accounts but ultimately destroying each other in the process. (Merteuil is shunned by society, and Valmont dies in a duel that he does not wish to win.) Howard Davies staged the multi-scened script on Bob Crowley's fascinating set, an expressionistic boudoir littered with rumpled linen, chiffoniers overflowing with lacy undergarments, and dried autumn leaves blown in from open windows and doors. Crowley also designed the costumes, all off-white and almost ghostly in appearance. Rave reviews declared the script, the Royal Shakespeare Company mounting, and the cast "spellbinding" and "an evening of high comedy, high drama, and surprising passion." The period piece was popular enough to stay for 148 performances and won that year's New York Drama Critics Circle Award for Best Foreign work.

Broadway's only thriller this season was a one-week dud, John Pielmeier's **Sleight of Hand** (5-3-87, Cort), which combined magic tricks with mystery and came up short on both accounts. Paul (Harry Groener) is a sadistic magician who, while drunk, decides to saw a woman named Alice in half. But, whether by accident or on purpose, the trick turns deadly; blood pours out of the magician's box, and Paul has to dispose of the mutilated body. On Christmas Eve, Dancer (Jeffrey DeMunn) enters, declares he is a police officer (although it seems quite obvious he is not), and says he is investigating the disappearance of Alice. Paul tries to sidetrack Dancer's probing with a series of magic tricks. Also, a rivalry develops between the two when Dancer shows an interest in Paul's girlfriend, Sharon (Priscilla Shanks), who happens to be a dancer in an upcoming Edgar Allan Poe musical called *Poe on Toe*. In the end Dancer wins and exposes Paul's treachery. The question of accident or premeditated murder was never addressed, and there was much Pirandellian musing about what is real and what is illusion that added an element of confusion. Generally negative reviews saluted magic consultant Charles Reynolds but had little good to say about anyone else.

Willy Russell's two-hander **Educating Rita** (5-7-87, Westside) had been a success in London, but it took the popularity of the 1983 film version to prompt a commercial run off Broadway. Disillusioned literature professor Frank (Austin Pendleton) has taken to drink to hide his unhappy marriage and dashed hopes of being a poet. But the arrival of his latest "open university" pupil, eager hairdresser Rita (Laurie Metcalf), puts some spark in his jaded life. Poorly educated but overflowing with unconventional enthusiasm for literature, Rita restores Frank's long-lost passion for his work. Although the twosome never pursue a romantic relationship, they do become close friends and together get her triumphantly through all her exams. Critics were mixed in their appraisal of the script; they generally liked Metcalf and disliked Pendleton. But the name value of the film helped the play run ninety-four performances.

The Acting Company's second offering this spring was *Much Ado About Nothing* on May 11 at the John Houseman for a week. The touring production, directed by Gerald Gutierrez, was set in a colorful Cuban marketplace with Beatrice (Alison Stair Neet) hiding in a cart of flowers to overhear her friends talk about Benedick (Philip Goodwin).

Murray Schisgal's string of failures continued with **Road Show** (5-21-87, Circle), a serious effort about the lost illusions of youth. Andy Broude (David Groh) has done so well in the competitive world of television producing in New York that he is offered a job as an executive in Hollywood. So he and his wife, Bianca (Anita Gillette), take off cross-country by car, stopping at every available phone booth to check on the negotiations Andy's agent is handling in California. When the couple stop for the night in a small midwestern town, Andy is reunited with Evelyn (Trish Hawkins), his long-lost first love. She is now married to Robert Lester (Jonathan Hadary), the local druggist, but the former lovers immediately drift back in time, recalling when she was a music student and he dreamed of being a serious writer. Despite their current spouses and the children each have, Andy and Evelyn consider running off together. But the agent calls to say that he has arranged for Andy's salary to exceed one million dollars, so Andy and Bianca take off with hardly a backward glance, leaving Robert (whose father has just died) and Evelyn to console each other. Negative reviews along the line of "a whimsical pain" helped *Road Show* disappear after its scheduled thirty-eight performances.

The Public concluded its season with a hit, Eric Bogosian's **Talk Radio** (5-28-87, Martinson), which ran 210 performances and was called "a compelling work that draws you straight into the heart of its fringe world," filled with "whiplash intensity and black, hard-edged cynicism." Barry Chamberlain (Bogosian) hosts a controversial late-night radio show in Cleveland on which he brutally insults the wounded listeners who call in to express their pathetic opinions. Even though he slurs every race and religion, Barry has become so popular that a national syndication company is listening in to decide whether or not to pick up the show. Although his producer, Dan Woodruf (Mark Metcalf), warns Barry not to say anything that might offend the sponsors, the outrageous DJ cannot help himself and is more insulting than ever. His harangue to one caller gets so abusive that Barry has a breakdown right in the studio, ending with the DJ spent and silent for forty seconds of dead air. Ted Savinar provided dozens of slides that were projected behind the actors; few commentators thought they added much to the proceedings.

The season ended on May 31 at Lincoln Center with the oddest of revivals: Shakespeare's *The Comedy of Errors* with jugglers rather than actors performing the two sets of twins. The acclaimed comedy-juggling act The Flying Karamazov Brothers adapted the text with director Robert Woodruff, working in flying objects at every opportunity and taking the play to its clownish extremes, including acrobatics, fire-eating, and tightrope walking. The unique clown Avner the Eccentric delivered a prologue, and drag queen Ethyl Eichelberger played both virtuous Emilia and the slutty Courtesan, while one of the Brothers (Timothy Daniel Furst) portrayed Shakespeare himself. Critical reaction varied from "fast, loose and lunatic" to "I was not sorry when it was over," but the juggling quintet definitely had its fans, so the shenanigans continued in the Vivian Beaumont for sixty-five showings.

1987–1988

Any season in which established American playwrights Terrence McNally, Christopher Durang, David Mamet, A. R. Gurney, Henry David Hwang, and the two Wilsons (August and Lanford) all provided worthwhile scripts cannot be *too* dismal. True, there were only eight new plays on Broadway (six of them American) and some forty-six off Broadway (thirty-six of them native works), but attendance climbed (as much as 17 percent on Broadway) and spirits were high. Musicals brought in all the money, but plays kept making news, so they were on people's minds as well.

Of course, fewer plays than ever originated on Broadway (or even off Broadway, for that matter), but some found a home there. Thirteen different regional theatres sent works to New York, and five entries originated in England. Yet both the Public Theatre and Lincoln Center Theatre, Manhattan's two primary resident theatres, had expanded and had notable seasons. Lincoln Center, for instance, not only kept both its upstairs and downstairs theatres busy but went directly to a Broadway house for *Speed-the-Plow*.

Once again no Broadway play recouped its investment by season's end, but *M. Butterfly* and *Speed-the-Plow* eventually showed a profit. Ticket prices on the Street soared as high as $40 for nonmusicals; $30 became the top off Broadway. (This does not include specialty programs such as the three-part *The Mahabharata* and the dinner/play *Tamara*.) Despite escalating prices, there were long runs, such as *Steel Magnolias, Perfect Crime, Frankie and Johnny in the Clair de Lune,* and other hits, to keep producers from giving up totally on the business side of theatre in New York.

During the season, the New York City Landmarks Preservation Committee designated twelve Broadway houses as landmarks: the Majestic, Ethel Barrymore, Brooks Atkinson, Eugene O'Neill, Plymouth, Lyceum, Martin Beck, Longacre, Lunt-Fontanne, Booth, Music Box, and (empty and unused) Henry Miller. Some theatre owners carped about the restrictions this designation put on them, but others saw it as a healthy sign that old theatres (and theatre itself) were here to stay.

The season opened with a thud. The Manhattan Theatre Club concluded its 1986–1987 schedule with Ken Friedman's "amateurish and lame" **Claptrap** (6-14-87, City Center), ostensibly a spoof of the popular *Deathtrap* (2-26-78) but really a farce without a thrill or chill in sight; "at heart it wasn't really *about* anything." Sam Krulik (Joel Polis) is a writer with no money but plenty of writer's block. Desperate for some cold cash, he convinces his girlfriend, Sally Littlefield (Cherry Jones), to let him arrange for the funeral of her departed father. Sam also hopes to ingratiate himself with the rich widow Cynthia (Tresa Hughes), Sally's mother. The funeral, set in a fast-food restaurant with the father's ashes displayed in a ludicrous art deco urn, degenerates into an idiotic disgrace, especially when unemployed actor Harvey Wheatcraft (Nathan Lane) stumbles into the proceedings thinking an audition is taking place. After some tedious confusions, Sam and Harvey find soulmates in each other and end up becoming roommates.

Four regional theatres were featured in this season's American Theatre Exchange, beginning with the Long Wharf Theatre which premiered Joe Cacaci's **Self Defense** (6-16-87, Joyce) for a two-week engagement. (The series had originated in 1985 but had been canceled last season because of funding problems.) Mickey Reisman (Michael Wikes), a burnt-out Bronx public defender, tries to keep the idealism he learned at Columbia as he strives for justice in a flawed system. His cohort and rival is Phil Lehman (Charles Cioffi), a foul-mouthed district attorney who tries to waken Mickey to the reality of their profession. Mickey fights to keep his clients (an accused child molester, a rapist, and a burglar) out of jail, but the legal machine devours them, and Mickey suffers a nervous collapse. Arvin Brown's expert mounting could not gloss over the "sprawling, untidy, rumpled" script "peopled with trite, TV-style stock characters."

The season's first long run began three days later: Robert Harling's **Steel Magnolias** (6-19-87, Lucille Lortel), a sentimental comedy that compiled 1,126 performances and became a popular staple in regional theatre and schools for several years thereafter. Ironically, critics only gave the play mild approval, most echoing Mel Gussow in the *New York Times* when he described it as "an amiable evening of sweet sympathies and small-town chatter." Truvy (Margo Martindale) has turned the garage of her Louisiana home into a beauty parlor, where her philosophy is "There is no such thing as natural beauty." Truvy's local clientele include former mayor's wife Clairee (Kate Wilkinson), who still roots for the local high school team ("I really do love football . . . but it's hard to parlay that into a reason to live."), cranky spinster Ouiser (Mary Fogarty), who only cares for her sickly-looking dog ("I'm not crazy, I've just been in a bad mood for forty years!"), and upper-class M'Lynn (Rosemary Prinz), who worries about her three children, especially the diabetic Shelby (Betsy Aidem), who is getting married that afternoon. Truvy and her new assistant, Annelle (Constance Shulman), get all the ladies ready for the big wedding as they gossip

about the townsfolk and complain about the men in their lives. A year later the married Shelby informs her mother that she is pregnant and, despite warnings from doctors about her frail health, wants M'Lynn to be happy for her. After much argument, a frightened M'Lynn decides to be supportive for her daughter. But after the baby is born, complications set in, and Shelby dies when a kidney transplant fails to take.

Joseph Papp's New York Shakespeare Festival (celebrating its twenty-fifth anniversary) offered *Richard II* on June 24 at the outdoor Delacorte, but to critics there was little cause for celebration. Peter MacNicol, a lightweight comic actor, proved ineffectual as a monarch, even one as weak-willed as Richard. Papp directed with madcap abandon, prompting one commentator to suggest the production "may be the only *Richard II* ever played for laughs." Another anniversary of sorts, George Abbott's one hundredth birthday, was celebrated by bringing his Great Lakes Shakespeare Festival mounting of *Broadway* (9-16-26), which he had co-written with Philip Dunning, to the Royale on June 25. While all the critics saluted Abbott and his seventy-four years in the theatre, few could endorse this revival of the old melodrama about bootlegging and show business. Some blamed the lackluster cast, others the dated script, others both. Whatever the case, the venture closed after four showings, thereby ending Abbott's long, illustrious Broadway career on a sad down note.

Next in the Theatre Exchange series was the Berkeley Repertory Theatre's **Hard Times** (7-7-87, Theatre 890), Stephen Jeffreys's dramatization of Charles Dickens's novel about the Industrial Revolution. Two men and two women played the wide array of Dickensian characters. One of the actresses, Kathleen Chalfant, displayed remarkable dexterity, ranging from the cold and scheming Mrs. Sparsit to the innocent and naive Sissy Jupe to the hilariously foolish Mrs. Gradgrind. It was a propitious start for a career filled with remarkable versatility.

For the third time, Bill Irwin's double bill *The Regard of Flight* and *The Clown Bagatelles* (5-23-82) returned to New York on July 10, this time at Lincoln Center's Mitzi E. Newhouse for a month.

Actor/author Charles Busch continued to spoof movies in his **Psycho Beach Party** (7-20-87, Players), and audiences enjoyed this one for 344 performances. In 1962, Malibu teenager Chicklet Forrest (Busch) hangs out with the surfing beach bums, idolizing the surfer king Kanaka (Ralph

Buckley) while having a crush on his protégé Star Cat (Arnie Kolodner). But Chicklet suffers from multiple personality disorder, sometimes thinking she is a black supermarket cashier, other times a radio talk show host, and still other times a power-hungry vamp. At a luau, Star Cat, who had been a psychology major in college, cures Chicklet's disorder through hypnosis. As in his past spoofs, Busch captured the silliness of the 1960s beach blanket movies, as well as *Three Faces of Eve* and the *Gidget* flicks.

Philadelphia's Wilma Theatre was the next featured troupe in the American Theatre Exchange, offering Czech playwright Pavel Kohout's stage version of George Orwell's **1984** (7-21-87, Joyce). The locale for the futuristic tale was changed from England to America with a large cast (some live, some on film) populating Phillip Graneto's setting: seven hexagonal screens on which slides, film clips, and laser beams were projected. The busy production, both directed and filmed by Jiri Zizka, struck some reviewers as powerful and potent, others as just plain silly.

Shakespeare fared much better in the second Delacorte offering, *Two Gentlemen of Verona* on July 24 with veteran Stuart Vaughan at the helm. While Valentine (James M. Goodwin) and Proteus (Thomas Gibson) were played in a straightforward manner, the rest of the cast clowned it up in psuedo-Restoration costumes and broad theatrics. Critics were mixed in their opinions of Julia (Elizabeth McGovern) and Silvia (Deborah Rush), but most admitted the comedy was "fine sport for a summer evening."

Screenwriter David Shaber employed events surrounding the Watergate scandal to fashion his barely disguised fiction fantasy **Bunker Reveries** (7-30-87, Roundabout). Jack Packard (Ralph Waite), a disgraced attorney general, is released from prison and joins his mistress, Margaret (Patricia Elliott), and his family. His wife, Annabelle (Sheila MacRae), whom he had mistreated during their stormy marriage, has died, but her ghost keeps appearing in Jack's swanky Washington hotel room. Also visiting Jack is the ex-president of the United States William Skinner (Robert Stattel), who has resigned in disgrace but is now hatching a political plan that includes Jack running for a New Jersey senatorial spot. Despite all the trouble Skinner has brought on him and his family, Jack is tempted by the offer, whereupon Margaret leaves him in disgust. The "competent but lackluster script" was considered less interesting than the actual historical events that inspired it, and the play was rarely heard of again after the Roundabout subscribers got to see it.

The Negro Ensemble Company opened its season with the second return engagement of Trevor Rhone's two-hander *Two Can Play* (4-11-85) on August 5 at Theatre Four. Hazel J. Medina and Sullivan H. Walker played the quarrelsome Jamaican couple for eighty showings.

The final entry in the American Theatre Exchange was considered the strongest: San Diego Repertory Theatre's mounting of Romulus Linney's 1971 rural drama **Holy Ghosts** (8-11-87, Theatre 890), which had previously been seen off-off Broadway. Nancy Shedman (Diana Castle) runs away from her hard-drinking, abusive husband, Coleman (Bradley Fisher), and finds shelter and comfort with a Pentecostal sect that engages in snake-handling rituals. She immediately falls for the oft-married Reverend Obediah Buckhorn (Dana Hart), a large and commanding personage who initiates Nancy into the ways of the snake cult. When Coleman comes to take Nancy back, he is no match for the overpowering reverend. During a lengthy and feverish ceremony, the believers carry the snakes about as they sing, dance, and worship, and even Coleman is converted to the sect's teachings.

Charles Marowitz's **Sherlock's Last Case** (8-20-87, Nederlander) was as much a parody of the great detective as a thriller, presenting a conceited, tightfisted, and even philandering Holmes (Frank Langella). Holmes is forever insulting and putting down Dr. Watson (Donel Donnelly), who is far from subservient, taking the detective's insults bitterly and seething inside with hurt. When the late Professor Moriarty's son Simeon plots to take revenge on Holmes for his father's death, Holmes is warned by the beautiful redheaded Liza (Melinda Mullins), Moriarty's daughter, and an attraction is sparked between the two. But soon Holmes is outwitted and trapped in a dark cellar, surprisingly not by Simeon but by Watson, who is out to exact his long-fermenting revenge on Holmes and come into his own as a mastermind. Although Watson supposedly kills Holmes with a suffocating gas, impostors claiming to be Holmes soon pop up, much to Watson's frustration. (One wily impostor, hammily played by Langella, turns out to be an Australian quick-change artist who is really Holmes in disguise.) When Watson returns to the cellar to inspect the bones of the famous detective, the real Holmes and Inspector Lestrade (Pat McNamara) appear and accuse Watson of attempted murder. Forced to return to his subservient role, Watson becomes Holmes's sidekick once again and is even knighted by Queen Victoria. But, after one further humiliation by Holmes (Liza returns disguised as Simeon and orders Holmes to execute the doctor), Watson crumbles and shoots himself in despair. Notices ranged from "entertainment pure and simple" to "resolutely unable to muster the characters, narrative, suspense, wit or even the fog-bound atmosphere of its prototype." This revisionist view of Holmes found an audience for an unprofitable 124 performances.

Papp directed the third Central Park Shakespeare, *Henry IV, Part 1*, which opened on August 27; he cut the text extensively and set the whole drama in the Boar's Head Tavern as a play-within-a-play. Donald Moffat's Falstaff, Tony Soper's Hal, and Michael Zaslow's King Henry were "competent" in an "adequate" production.

Sydney, London, Edinburgh, and Los Angeles had all raved about John Godber's **Bouncers** (9-17-87, Minetta Lane), but mixed notices in New York, ranging from "just another piece of camp, maybe even garbage" to "a grimly funny play," could not keep the commercial venture on the boards for more than a month. Four actors (Anthony La Paglia, Adrian Paul, Gerrit Graham, and Dan Gerrity) portrayed the many characters in a Yorkshire disco club on a Saturday night: disenchanted and crude working boys, vapid and desperate-for-fun girls, and the club's quartet of tough bouncers. There was much "toilet" humor, some ranting about Margaret Thatcher's England, and a lot of versatile acting onstage, but audiences did not buy it.

The Roundabout Theatre Company's season of four revivals started with John Steinbeck's *Of Mice and Men* (11-23-37) on October 7. Arthur Storch directed the "suitably dismal" production that featured Jay Patterson as the innocent giant Lenny and John Savage as his frustrated companion George.

The Circle Repertory Company began one of its weakest seasons in years with Rafael Lima's **El Salvador** (10-8-87, Circle). Six Western journalists cover ongoing hostilities and horrors occurring in the Central American country for an uninterested outside world. Most of the men have been hardened by experience and have no illusions left, yet their own confrontations and conflicts as they gather at an El Salvador hotel show a fighting spirit not quite dead. The fine ensemble acting was highly praised, and the Circle mounting was extended to fifty-two performances (the group's longest run of the season).

A festival of Italian theatre, opera, and puppet performances, called *Italy on Stage*, offered three plays by various theatre companies in Italian with English subtitles. Manilo Santanelli's *Pulcinella* opened the festival on October 9 in the Mark Hellinger, followed by Pirandello's *Il Berretto a Songali* (The Fool's Cap) on October 14 and Goldoni's *La Serva Amorosa* (The Loving Maid) on October 19.

Just as Jackie Mason, a comic from the 1950s and 1960s, had found a welcome spot on the Street, **Mort Sahl on Broadway** (10-11-87, Neil Simon) featured another stand-up commentator from the same period bringing his acute observations to contemporary audiences. Sahl was always known for his high-pitched, acerbic delivery, and critics noted that time had done little to soften the political comic's fire. Box office was healthy for the scheduled twenty-five performances but, unlike with Mason, there was no demand for more.

Terrence McNally's longest run to date (533 performances) and his first hit in years was **Frankie and Johnny in the Clair de Lune** (10-13-87, City Center), a two-character piece about ordinary yet unlikely lovers. Frankie (Kathy Bates) and Johnny (Kenneth Welsh) work in the same Manhattan restaurant (she is a waitress, he is a short-order cook) and, after knowing each other six weeks, go out on a first date. They end up in bed in Frankie's West Side walk-up apartment. Their lovemaking over, she hopes he will leave so she can be alone to watch television, eat ice cream, and continue with her bruised, disappointing life. But Johnny wants this to be more than a one-night stand and professes he loves Frankie, which terrifies her. They argue, joke, and confess through the night, ending up together back in bed watching TV and holding each other for security and affection. Reviews were along the lines of "romantic, ribald comedy" and "richly warm, humorous, clear-eyed," and both actors were commended for their unflattering portrayals of the two over-forty lovers. (A nude scene at the top of the play was memorable for its blunt and unerotic honesty.)

The same night, the renowned director Peter Brook returned to the New York stage with twenty-five showings of **The Mahabharata** (10-13-87, BAM), a nine-hour presentation based on the revered Sanskrit epic. (For $100 a ticket, audiences saw the program over three nights or in a marathon session in one day.) Jean-Claude Carrière's stage version (translated by Brook) followed the long and bloody rivalry of two families, the Pandavas and the Kauravas, which culminates in an apocalyptic war that determines the fate of the world. Along the way there are quieter moments of philosophical meditation and discussions of Hindu ideas. As with all Brook productions, some of the visuals were stunning (swirling ladders, billowing cloth, white arrows piercing dark space) as actors portrayed men, gods, and animals. Martial arts, acrobatics, and battles enacted ritualistically were among the production's most memorable theatrics. Yet there were criticisms as well: uneven and stilted acting by the international cast, an awkward translation that rendered the dialogue stiff, long sections of tedious talk, and the cloudy representation of Hindu thinking that reduced complex ideas to sermons or catch phrases. Most reviewers were in awe of Brook's achievement even if some called it "epic theatre in the extreme" and a "saga [that] impresses the mind, the eye, but seldom the heart."

Lanford Wilson seemed to be moving into David Mamet or David Rabe territory with his abrasive drama **Burn This** (10-14-87, Plymouth), which introduced one of the most hypnotic and fiery characters the seasoned playwright had yet created. Dancer-choreographer Anna (Joan Allen) lives with two gay men in a trendy Manhattan loft. One of her roommates, co-choreographer Robbie, has died in a freak boating accident, and Anna is distraught as she and Larry (Lou Liberatore), her other roommate, return from the funeral. In the middle of the night Robbie's brother, Pale (John Malkovich), bursts into the apartment to collect Robbie's things but stays to bewilder and torment the two inhabitants. The relationship between Anna and Pale is particularly vehement as she drifts from her well-mannered boyfriend, Burton (Jonathan Hogan), toward the explosive Pale, the two finding an odd sense of security in each other's uncertainty. Several critics thought it Wilson's finest play, agreeing with Howard Kissel in the *Daily News*, who called it a "powerful, dazzlingly comic play about love, art, and social disintegration in a SoHo loft." Although Allen won a Tony Award for her ever-growing and knowing Anna, it was Malkovich's scatological tirades, brawling macho pretense, and finally sensitive collapse that were the centerpiece of the drama. Strong word of mouth (and Malkovich's rising popularity) kept *Burn This* on the boards for 437 performances.

Warren Manzi's psychological thriller **Perfect Crime** (10-16-87, 47th Street) opened without much fanfare, gathering at best a few appreciative reviews that called it "a delightful blend of sus-

pense, sexuality and intellectual teasing." Without ever becoming a hot ticket, the play would run into the next century, establishing the longest non-musical run in Off-Broadway's history. Having achieved some fame as an author and psychiatrist, Margaret Thorne Brent (Cathy Russell) decides to move to an affluent Connecticut town with her husband, Harrison (Manzi), who is also a psychiatrist. A murder has already taken place in the community, so the local police, in the form of Inspector James Ascher (Perry Perkkanen), come on the scene. Ascher is soon obsessed with Margaret, her work, and her patients, believing the answer to his murder case lies in the Brents' sitting room. When Harrison is murdered, Ascher sets out to prove that Margaret has planned the "perfect crime," falling in love with her along the way but giving her up to the courts in the end. Russell would stay with the show for years, totaling over 4,000 performances in the role.

Barbara Lebow's "passionate, touching tale," **A Shayna Maidel** (10-29-87, Westside), edged over the 500-performance mark, audiences finding the "profound and startling exploration of family connections" to their liking. Mordechai Weiss (Paul Sparer) and his daughter Rose (Melissa Gilbert) got out of Poland in 1930, but his wife and elder daughter, Lusia, did not. Mrs. Weiss was murdered, but Lusia (Gordana Rashovich) survived Auschwitz and in 1946 is reunited with her family in New York City. Although Lusia is almost a stranger to her, the Americanized Rose agrees to share her West Side apartment with her sister. Mordechai feels guilt over the death of his wife, Rose is embarrassed by her foreign sister, and Lusia slips in and out of memories and fantasies, hoping to be reunited with her young husband, Duvid (Jon Tenney). A letter from the mother, written years before and kept by a Polish family, is discovered. Duvid is reunited with Lusia after six years' separation, so the family is drawn together and begins to understand each other. *The Shayna Maidel* (Yiddish for "a pretty girl") also enjoyed a healthy life in regional and community theatres.

An off-off-Broadway revival of Tennessee Williams's *The Milk Train Doesn't Stop Here Anymore* (1-16-63) on November 4 at the WPA may have contained some of the season's juiciest acting, but most critics still viewed the melodrama as "outrageous self-satire." Elizabeth Ashley was "lovably menacing" as the dying Flora Goforth, who dictates her memoirs to a young widow, Frances Black (Amanda Plummer), all the while she is pursuing the handsome young stud Christopher

Flanders (Stephen McHattie). In a cameo role, Marion Seldes shone as Flora's malicious neighbor Vera Ridgeway Condotti.

The Public began its schedule with Joe Cacaci's second play of the young season, **Old Business** (11-8-87, Shiva). Because of his poor health, Abe Fleischer (Joe Silver) has reluctantly turned over his prosperous real estate empire to his son, David (Michael Wikes), even though he does not approve of the younger generation's business practices. Soon Abe regrets his decision and tries (unsuccessfully) to oust David in a battle that turns very personal. Unlike the crackling confrontation scenes in Cacaci's earlier *Self Defense*, this play consisted entirely of monologues (on the phone, no less), thereby diminishing much of the potency of the piece.

More monologues were to be found in a minor effort by Christopher Durang called **Laughing Wild** (11-11-87, Playwrights Horizons), which provided a challenging vehicle for two players. In a long solo scene, a Woman (E. Katherine Kerr) rants about urban life, lashing out at such familiar targets as rude cab drivers, noisy street musicians, and mindless talk shows. But her most immediate gripe is a man who blocked her way in a supermarket and kept her from reaching a can of tuna fish. A Man (Durang) then delivers his solo lecture, complaining about nuclear waste, the inflexibility of the Catholic Church, and the crazy lady at the supermarket who attacked him in the tuna-fish section. The two characters then reenact various versions of the supermarket episode, each taking time for some wacky dream sequences. (The play's funniest moment was Kerr's interviewing Durang, who was dressed and responded as the Infant of Prague.) Reviews were largely along the lines of "odd, uncertain, clever, provoking, and infuriating," but, as Edith Oliver in *The New Yorker* noted, it was "non-vintage Durang—which, of course, is better than vintage a lot of other people."

A "truly astonishing" performance by Derek Jacobi overshadowed Hugh Whitemore's penetrating bio-drama **Breaking the Code** (11-15-87, Neil Simon) about Alan Turing, the British mathematician who cracked the German Enigma code during World War II. Shifting back and forth through time, we first see the youthful Alan (Jacobi) dazzling his teachers with his eccentric genius for numbers and falling in love with fellow classmate Christopher (Robert Sean Leonard). Because of the secret nature of his work in discovering the Nazi codes, Alan gets little acknowledgment after the war and lives a quiet and lonely

life developing the idea of a computer. When one of his male lovers robs his apartment, Alan calls the police, only to be arrested in turn for breaking a very different code: homosexuality. His mother, Sara (Rachel Gurney), sticks by Alan as he is convicted and given hormone treatments that debilitate him physically and mentally. Finally, Alan commits suicide by eating an apple sprinkled with arsenic, an idea he gets from watching the animated film *Snow White and the Seven Dwarfs*. Clifford Williams's fluid direction moved the players about Liz da Costa's encroaching set that suggested both a military barracks and the inside of a primitive computer. The fine supporting cast included Michael Gough as Alan's meticulous wartime superior Dillwyn Knox and Jenny Agutter as a colleague who is in love with Alan. But it was Jacobi's nail-biting, stammering, reticent portrayal that was unanimously acclaimed, Edwin Wilson in the *Wall Street Journal* calling it "a daring, explosive, yet controlled performance of the kind rarely seen these days." The drama ran five months but failed to show a profit.

The Negro Ensemble's finest offering of the season was Endesha Ida Mae Holland's **From the Mississippi Delta** (11-18-87, Theatre Four), which ran forty-eight performances in two separate engagements. The autobiographical play followed the journey of a young prostitute in the Deep South who, inspired by the civil rights movement, turns her life around and ends up an associate professor at a college. The episodes in her life were sometimes funny, often nostalgic, and usually pointed. Three actresses (Verneice Turner, Brenda Denmark, La Tanya Richardson) portrayed the main character at different ages, as well as the other characters she encounters. Few newspapers reviewed the play, and the work was not heard much of until four years when later it would return to Off Broadway with greater success.

Alonzo D. Lamont's **That Serious He-Man Ball** (11-19-87, American Place) was another case of a drama admired regionally (in this case, Los Angeles and Chicago) but scoffed at in Manhattan. Three African Americans, friends since high school, meet on a playground basketball court to throw a ball around and catch up on each other's news. Sky (Roger Guenveur Smith) works at a counseling center in the community but treats his friends with little patience or tact. Jello (Tom Wright) lives with his family while he tries to become a serious writer. Twin (Walter Allen Bennett, Jr.) works for Xerox and seems to be climbing the corporate ladder, although he is hesitant to take the next step. As the three play and talk, the frustrations of their lives come out on the court, and each loses some of his bluster as he confess his fears to the others.

One of the best American plays of the season, Tom Griffin's **The Boys Next Door** (11-23-87, Lamb's), managed to run 168 performances despite its difficult subject matter (mental retardation) and enjoyed some success in regional theatres thereafter. Social worker Jack (Dennis Boutsikaris) monitors several outpatients, in particular four men with various levels of genetic deficiencies who live together in an apartment in a New England city. The leader of the group is Arnold Wiggins (Joe Grifasi), a hyperactive worrier whose non-stop chatter orders the others about. Overweight Norman (Josh Mostel) works at a doughnut shop and gorges himself on the bakery's leftovers as he protects his oversize bundle of keys that gives him an identity. African-American Lucien P. Smith (William Jay) has the mind of a five-year-old, reading simple phrases aloud from huge library books. Schizophrenic Barry Klemper (Joe Urla) seems the most normal, a gentle but enterprising young man who thinks he is a golf expert and offers lessons to neighbors for $1.13 an hour. Various episodes, narrated by the "burned out" Jack, reveal both the comic and pathetic aspects of these men, from Norman's hilarious date with the retarded Sheila (Christine Estabrook) in which he offers her doughnuts but won't let her touch his keys to Lucien's appearance before a Senate committee in which he shows off his Spiderman tie and sings "The Alphabet Song" in order to impress them. But the final crushing blow for Jack is a visit by Barry's father (Ed Setrakian). His blunt dismissal of his son pushes Barry over the edge, precipitating the boy's institutionalization. Jack quits social work, takes a job in a travel agency, and bids farewell to the "boys" who have become "my closest associates." Reviews applauded the playwright's deft sense of humor, which did not demean or diminish his subjects, but rather "hit squarely on the truth of life with its constant interplays and shadings of triumphs and tears."

Reinaldo Povod's program of three short plays, **La Puta Vida** (This Bitch of a Life) **Trilogy** (11-24-87, Public: LuEsther), offered compassionate views of some of life's most miserable victims. *South of Tomorrow* dealt with drug addicts, including a young user (John Leguizamo) questioning a Vietnam vet (Michael Guess) about his missing eye and offering one of his own since he plans to kill himself soon. *Nijinsky Choked His Chicken* concerned a Hispanic youth (Miguel Correa) who naively seeks the help of a child molester (John Turturro). In *Poppa Dio!* a stripper (Rosana DeSoto) makes sexual advances toward her own son (Turturro) until he retaliates by beating her to death with a baseball bat. While some commentators found them "vivid" and "a raw-edged knockout," the three plays were too grim for most critics ("a truly miserable evening") and audiences. But both Turturro and Leguizamo would go on to memorable careers.

Louise Page's British drama **Real Estate** (12-1-87, St. Peter's Church) only managed a commercial run of fifty-five performances off Broadway despite the presence of Sada Thompson and Roberta Maxwell in the cast. Jenny (Maxwell) left her suburban London home twenty years ago but now returns, pregnant and seeking information about whether or not she had German measles as a child. Her mother, Gwen (Thompson), has become a successful real estate agent, and Gwen's husband, Dick (Charles Cioffi), who is Jenny's stepfather, has retired early to become a house husband. Eric (Lewis Arlt), the father of Jenny's baby, comes along with her, willing to marry her but refused by Jenny, who claims not to love him enough. When Jenny announces that she'd like to raise her child in her former home, Dick is thrilled but Gwen is not. Neither woman is the maternal type (while both men are), and when Jenny starts to work for Gwen they get on each other's nerves even more. But Gwen finally gives in and decides to quit the real estate business and try to love her grandchild. Reviews ranged from mild approval ("an absorbing little chamber drama") to dismissal ("smacks of old-time magazine fiction"), yet the editors of the *Best Plays* chose the script as one of the season's ten best.

A combination of dinner theatre and environmental theatre called **Tamara** (12-2-87, 7th Regiment Armory) was the most unusual offering of the off-Broadway season. John Krizanc wrote the thriller in which the aging poet and womanizer Gabriele d'Annunzio (Frederick Rolf) invites the Polish artist Tamara de Lempicka (Sara Botsford) to his Italian villa in 1927 to paint his portrait. Other suspicious characters include insidious chauffeur Mario (Jack Wetherall), scatterbrained ballerina Carlotta Barra (Cynthia Dale), and d'Annunzio's ex-mistress Luisa Baccara (Lally Cadeau). They wander through the house meeting and plotting, all of it culminating in a gunshot heard echoing throughout the rooms. Each patron is left to draw his own conclusion as to the culprit and the victim. What made the rather routine whodunit far from routine was the manner in which the audience of 160 viewed the play. Patrons arrived in the main hall of the villa, were greeted with canapés and drinks, stood and watched the opening scene, then followed the character of their choice as he/she took them to different scenes in the ten rooms of the villa recreated in the Armory. Intermission featured an elegant buffet dinner in the ballroom, and most critics complimented the chefs at Le Cirque (though ticket prices went as high as $135) on the evening's culinary quality. As for the play itself, it was generally dismissed as "camp and kitsch." Mel Gussow in the *New York Times* noted, "Whatever it is . . . it is unlike any other show currently in New York. It is a shot of adrenaline for sedentary theatregoers who are accustomed to sitting in the dark and watching actors do all the work." *Tamara* had been a hit in Toronto and Los Angeles; New Yorkers were curious enough to keep the attraction crowded though the holidays. The self-described "living movie" then reopened on February 2 and stayed for a total of 1,036 performances.

Caryl Churchill's broad satire **Serious Money** (12-3-87, Public: Newman) attempted to unveil the multi-leveled corruption of contemporary capitalism in a very Jonsonian manner. In fact, the play was written in rhymed couplets and included a scene from Thomas Shadwell's 1692 comedy *The Volunteers; or, The Stock Jobbers.* Eight actors played various traders, speculators, and wheeler-dealers from Wall Street and the London Exchange. What little plot there was centered on the mysterious death of a young corporate trader, Jake Todd (Scott Cherry), who seems to have been snuffed out as part of a conspiracy to take over a company. Jake's sister Scilla (Joanne Pearce) investigates the matter, not out of devotion to her brother but to find out where the money has gone. We never learn whether Jake was murdered, but Churchill's point about the lethal business of trading was made quite clear. A hit at London's Royal Court and then in the West End, the play received decidedly mixed reviews in New York. But prompted by a favorable notice by *New York Times* critic Frank Rich, producer Papp moved the comedy (now with an American cast) on February 9 to Broadway's Royale, where it only lasted two weeks.

Novelist Don DeLillo turned to the stage with the Pirandellian comedy **The Day Room** (12-8-87, City Center), which the Manhattan Theatre Club offered to its subscribers for six weeks. In a stark white hospital room, the health-conscious Budge (Mason Adams) does tai chi exercises while trying unsuccessfully to engage his roommate, Wyatt (John Christopher Jones), in talk. Doctors and nurses enter and exit, and it soon is revealed that they are not what they seem; in fact, most are patients from the adjacent Arno Klein Wing, the psychiatric section of the hospital. In the second act, set in Klein Wing, patients engage in a play-within-a-play while tourists traipse through looking for the renowned Arno Klein Theatre Company. It seems doctors and nurses are starting to play patients (one actor goes so far as to play a television set) when Arno Klein himself (Adams) enters and, echoing Budge's lines, the play ends where it began.

The plight of mismatched urban lovers was the subject of Timothy Mason's "glib comedy" **Only You** (12-10-87, Circle) which critics called everything from "a charming and disarming two hours of fun" to "a slightly pretentious and, at times, irritating play." Leo (Greg Germann), a tense and impatient young man, decides after a first date with Miriam (Julie Boyd) that he wants to spend his life with her. But she is put off by him and tells her troubles to Heather (Park Overall), a friend more in need of advice than Miriam. Leo pours his heart out to Eddie (Bruce McCarty), a worldly-wise cad who gives questionable advice on matters of love and sex, but mostly Leo listens to Big Voice (Richard Seff), a mysterious presence whose whispering comments try to lighten Leo up. After a disastrous party at Eddie's in which switched couples end up in bed, Big Voice takes the form of a *deus ex machina*, throws a costume ball, and gets all the right lovers together. As clever as some of Mason's writing was John Lee Beatty's set, which opened up in sections like a garage door to reveal new scenes.

The Roundabout's revival of Shaw's *Man and Superman* on December 16 eliminated the *Don Juan in Hell* third act, which helped director William Woodman propel the action along swiftly. David Birney as John Tanner and Frances Conroy as Ann Whitefield led the cast, but much of the praise was for secondary characters such as Michael Cumpsty's Octavius, Anthony Fusco's Henry Straker, and Kim Hunter's Mrs. Whitefield.

One of A. R. Gurney's most serious efforts, **Another Antigone** (1-11-88, Playwrights Horizons), offered a modern parallel to Sophocles' drama. Henry Harper (George Grizzard), a sedentary Greek drama professor at a small Boston college, is neither surprised nor amused when a Jewish student, the activist Judy Miller (Marissa Chibas), submits a modern version of *Antigone* (full of protest against nuclear weapons and corrupt authority) in place of a term paper in Henry's class. Henry brands the "juvenile" work "just another *Antigone*," refusing to pass the student. Judy and her radical boyfriend, David Appleton (Steven Flynn), decide to fight his decision. They produce the play on campus, thereby turning the issue into a community-wide debate. Henry is portrayed as a modern-day Creon with Judy as the wronged Antigone; yet when Judy goes to the campus grievance committee and (wrongfully) accuses Henry of anti-Semitism, the roles seem to be reversed as Henry must fight for his own integrity. He finally relents and gives Judy a passing grade, but she is not satisfied. In anger, Henry *does* make an anti-Semitic remark about an interfering Jewish professor, thereby sealing his doom. Gurney's sense of humor was still evident, but his subtext was deadly serious. The play met with mixed reviews and never entered the catalog of Gurney's more popular works.

Just when Papp's failing health seemed to be curtailing his operations about town, he announced his most ambitious project yet: a marathon of the complete Shakespeare canon to be presented over the next six years at a cost of $33 million. Subscriptions were sold to the whole series, and the marathon began with *A Midsummer Night's Dream* on January 12 in the Anspacher. A. J. Antoon set the fantasy in the Brazilian state of Bahia at the turn of the century with primitive rain-forest inhabitants as the fairies and the air filled with samba and bossa nova music. Outstanding in the merry cast were Elizabeth McGovern as Helena, Geoffrey Owens as Puck, and F. Murray Abraham as Bottom. Andrew Jackness created a splendid floral setting that had Titania (Lorraine Toussaint) swaying in a hammock high in the treetops. Positive reviews along the lines of "it brims with imagination and surprises" encouraged Papp to extend the run to eighty-one performances. (Papp would never live to see the end of the marathon that eventually took ten years to complete.)

Peter Brooks's much-anticipated revival of Chekhov's *The Cherry Orchard* on January 23 at BAM met with mixed notices; for many aisle-sitters and theatregoers it was "a major disappointment." The international cast was uneven and much of the action was considered too slow and ponderous. Brook set that action on a large bare stage with only a Persian carpet and scattered pieces of furniture to set the locales. While Natasha Parry's Lyubov was lifeless, Brian Dennehy made a powerful Lopakhin, Zeljko Ivanek a gleaming Trofimov, and Swedish film actor Erland Josephson a touching Gaev. The curious production remained for eleven weeks.

Like Gurney, comic playwright Alan Ayckbourn turned very serious with his **Woman in Mind** (2-2-88, City Center), "a witty . . . provocative black comedy with haunting overtones" about a vicar's wife, Susan (Stockard Channing, who received unanimous raves), who is losing her grip on reality. Ignored by her stuffy husband, Gerald (Remak Ramsay), nagged by her live-in sister-in-law, Muriel (Patricia Connolly), and out of touch with her morose son, Rick (John David Cullum), Susan finds herself suffocating in her English middle-class world. When she is knocked on the head by stepping on the end of a garden rake, Susan starts to hallucinate and sees herself as part of a fantasy family with a loving husband (Danny Gerroll), a warm and close daughter (Tracy Pollan), and a protective brother (Michael Countryman). The imagined family, dressed in white tennis garb and sipping champagne in their lush garden, intrude into Susan's real world until she realizes that she is steadily losing her sanity.

If *Tamara* was a bit too highbrow for some audiences, there was always **Tony 'n' Tina's Wedding** (2-6-88, Washington Square Church/Carmelita's), another dinner-play combination where the characters and the food were definitely not haute cuisine. Audience members were guests and participants in, as Gussow described it, "an intentionally tacky duplication of an Italian-American wedding ceremony" complete with church service and followed by a reception. The author listed was Artificial Intelligence, the name of the off-off-Broadway group presenting the bogus event that featured Nancy Cassaro and Mark Nassar as the title couple. Few reviewers would cover the "play" at first (in fact, the *Best Plays* refused to acknowledge it was a play until it had been running four years), but word of mouth made it the most popular show of the season, running into the millenium and sending dozens of Tonys and Tinas off into wedded bliss.

New Yorkers got to see a new Joe Orton play when his **The Good and Faithful Servant** (2-10-88, Actors' Playhouse), originally written for and shown on British television, enjoyed a run of 135 performances in a mounting off Broadway. George Buchanan (Michael Allinson) has retired after fifty sterile years working in a factory. But even in retirement he is badgered and abused by personnel officers and a bureaucracy that is supposed to help him in his old age. While tame by Orton standards, the play was still wicked in its social indictments.

Another "woman in mind" who hallucinates to escape her dreary marriage was Charleston (Robin Bartlett) in David Steven Rappoport's **Cave Life** (2-11-88, Circle). Married to Frank (Mark Blum), who has a mistress named Sophronia (Randy Danson) and a disturbed teenage son (Jeffrey Kearney) from a previous marriage, and tormented by her crazy mother (Jo Henderson), "Charly" imagines a Neanderthal caveman called Enki (Bruce McCarty) who gives her the love and attention so missing from her life. As in the Ayckbourn play, she is also losing her mind (Charly has a history of mental imbalance), but when she finds out that she is pregnant, Enki tells her she must choose between insanity or the baby. She wises up and decides on motherhood. Coming a week after the superior *Woman in Mind*, Rappoport's work suffered in comparison. But the play boasted a striking set by William Barclay in which a huge boulder upstage suggested a primitive cave dwelling even as it recalled the rock formations in Central Park.

More surrealism was afoot in Len Jenkin's **American Notes** (2-18-88, Public: Shiva), a collage of lowlifes not unlike the Public's earlier *La Puta Vida Trilogy*. The setting is a trashy motel, yet the various characters come and go in an avant-garde way. A mysterious drifter arrives at the motel, a carnival barker extols the qualities of his performing alligator Bonecrusher, the night clerk nervously waits for her unwanted suitor to arrive, a lunatic scientist communicates with aliens from outer space, an abandoned woman vainly hopes to be remembered by her lover, a mentally deficient handyman performs useless tasks, and inhabitants in a bar break out in song on occasion. JoAnne Akalaitis, who was building a reputation on her highly theatrical and puzzling stagings, directed the "haunting iconographic" work, and John Arnone provided the appropriately confusing scenery.

The closest Lee Blessing yet had to a hit was his two-character piece **A Walk in the Woods** (2-28-88, Booth), which ran 136 performances and garnered such endorsements as "a minor miracle on Broadway" and "a great treatise on the nature of mankind." Taking a break from the heated Geneva negotiations about nuclear disarmament, Russian diplomat Andrey Botvinnik (Robert Prosky) and American negotiator John Honeyman (Sam Waterston) take a quiet walk in a nearby wood to continue their discussion in a less formal manner. Botvinnik is a seasoned veteran of the bargaining table: crusty, sly, almost grandfatherly. Honeyman is younger, idealistic but a bit pedantic. While the American tries to stick to business ("We are not friends"), the Russian is casually cynical ("Even if we do agree, do you think it will matter?") and manages to break down the other's formality. A series of similar walks over the next year brings the two men into a friendship that ends when Botvinnik announces he is retiring and Honeyman knows he must return to a more formal battle with a new man. Blessing's script was limited to conversations, but he found wit and insight that kept the dialogue lively. Botvinnik observes that "without nuclear weapons we will be nothing more than a rich, powerful Canada and an enormous Poland" and wryly notes, "If mankind hated war there would be millions of us and only two soldiers." Des McAnuff, who had staged the play earlier in regional theatre, directed the duet with precision.

Howard Korder made a promising debut with **Boys' Life** (2-29-88, Mitzi E. Newhouse), a contemporary comedy of manners about how men refuse to grow up when it comes to the opposite sex. Three college buddies now in their thirties are working in the real world but are as immature as ever as they pursue various women who are wise to their delayed adolescence. Affable Don (Jordan Lage) is involved in a serious relationship with Lisa (Melissa Bruder), yet he sleeps with another woman to see if he "can get away with it." Aimless Phil (Steven Goldstein) meets up with Karen (Mary McCann), whom he dropped after a one-night stand, and attempts to resume where they left off. Married Jack (Clark Gregg), the most cynical of the threesome, tries to pick up Maggie (Felicity Huffman) in the park where his young son is playing. She sees right through his many lies but is attracted to him all the same. In the end, at Don and Lisa's wedding, the men are still trying to figure out when and if they will grow up. Complimentary reviews along the lines of "the most balanced and intelligent comment on the battle of the sexes" helped the play run 103 performances.

The late Larry Shue left behind his last and most serious play, **Wenceslas Square** (3-2-88, Public: Martinson), a "heartfelt and personal" work that little recalled his earlier farces. American college professor Vince Corey (Jonathan Hadary) has written a book about the vital arts movement in Czechoslovakia under the liberal Dubček regime in 1969. Five years later he returns to Prague with a young student, Bob Dooley (Bruce Norris), only to find a repressed cultural scene with brilliant authors reduced to writing propaganda films and radical artists shunned by society. According to Vince's contacts in Prague, publishing his book will only harm the careers of those who helped him in writing it. As the two Americans leave the country, Vince decides not to publish but asks the young Bob to remember all he has seen and to tell it to future generations. Victor Garber and Dana Ivey played all the Czech characters Vince and Bob encounter, and Jerry Zaks directed the play with exacting style.

Unlike the original Broadway production, the Roundabout's revival of *Rashomon* (1-27-59) on March 2 utilized a cast of Asian actors to tell three conflicting versions of a rape in medieval Japan. Robert Kalfin staged the Fay and Michael Kanin drama (based on an Akutagawa story and the renowned Kurosawa film) using traditional Asian theatre techniques such as Kabuki staging and Japanese stage music. Negative reviews for the Broadway revival of Tennessee Williams's *A Streetcar Named Desire* (12-3-47) on March 10 at the Circle in the Square expressed disappointment rather than hostility. Blythe Danner seemed a promising candidate for a first-class Blanche DuBois, but her performance was considered vague and unfocused, just as her scenes with Stanley (Aidan Quinn) lacked fire. Frances McDormand and Frank Converse were considered stronger as Stella and Mitch. Nikos Psacharopoulos's mounting won scant applause.

The first play by an Asian American to become a hit on Broadway was David Henry Hwang's **M. Butterfly** (3-20-88, Eugene O'Neill). French diplomat René Gallimard (John Lithgow) is bored with his wife, his friends, and his post in Bejing. So when he meets the quiet but intoxicating Song Liling (B. D. Wong), a Chinese opera star, he falls for her charms and has a twenty-year affair with her, passing on government secrets as she requests them. But it is finally revealed that Song is a man as well as a spy, although in a French court René claims he never knew his lover's true gender. Perhaps he did know but, as René tells the audience, she was every Western man's ideal of a woman. Confronting Song one last time as a man, René concludes, "I am a man who loved a woman created by a man. Everything else— simply falls short." A fan of Puccini's *Madame Butterfly*, the distraught René dresses in women's Oriental robes and kills himself. In addition to the salacious and bizarre story (which was based on a true incident from the 1960s), Hwang's play was filled with stimulating ideas about East-West cul-

ture differences and the role of the male and female in each world. (At one point Song notes: "Why, in the Peking Opera, are women's roles played by men? Because only a man knows how a woman is supposed to act.") Lithgow gave perhaps the finest performance of his career, and newcomer Wong was mystifying and sly as he shifted from male to female persona. John Dexter staged the drama with touches of Peking Opera techniques on Eiko Ishioka's set, a winding red ramp that curled off into the background like an ornamental snake. Enthusiastic reviews proclaimed the work "a brilliant play of ideas," "a richly layered script," and "a play once caught that will never be forgotten." The drama won the Tony Award, as did Wong and Dexter for their efforts. As a result *M. Butterfly* ran 777 performances.

Poor notices did not keep *Julius Caesar* from selling out its two-week engagement. The second entry in the Public's Shakespeare Marathon opened on March 22 in the Newman with a cast full of names: Martin Sheen as Brutus, Al Pacino as Marc Antony, Edward Herrmann as Cassius, and John McMartin as the title character. Complaints centered on miscasting, plodding direction, and a mishmash of acting styles. But Papp offered what he had promised his Marathon subscribers: American casts with guest stars.

Regarding marathons, August Wilson's planned saga of ten plays about American black life in the twentieth century, each play set in a different decade, continued with **Joe Turner's Come and Gone** (3-27-88, Ethel Barrymore), a drama set in 1911 in a Pittsburgh boardinghouse where all the characters seem to have a connection to past slavery. Seth (Mel Winkler) and Bertha Holly (L. Scott Caldwell) run the house, which attracts southern Negroes new to the North. The oldest resident, Bynum Walker (Ed Hall), conjures up rituals of the past even as he sees into the future. A young and fiery guitar player, Jeremy Furlow (Bo Rucker), is always getting drunk and fined for what little money he earns. Arriving at the house is Herald Loomis (Delroy Lindo), an intense man still scarred by his seven years' illegal bondage to a Mississippi bounty hunter called Joe Turner. Loomis travels with his young daughter, Zonia (Jamila Perry), the two of them looking for her mother, who ran off ten years ago. Herald pays a dollar to a local white man, Rutherford Selig (Raynor Scheine), who comes from a family of "people finders," to locate his wife, Martha. While Zonia befriends a neighbor boy, Reuben Mercer (Richard Habersham), who tells her haunting stories about Bynum, Herald is attracted to Mattie Campbell (Kimberleigh Aarn), waiting for her lover to return but currently living with Jeremy. Just as Herald and Zonia are leaving the boardinghouse to continue their search, Rutherford shows up with Martha (Angela Bassett). Having found the mother of his child, Herald plans to leave them both together. Martha, who works for a church, urges him to be saved in the blood of the Lord, whereupon Herald takes a knife and slashes his chest open, the blood making him "clean" and finally freeing him from Joe Turner. Most reviews were highly supportive, along the lines of Linda Winer's in *New York Newsday*: "It's a stunner . . . rich and engrossing, realistic yet mystical, and filled with strangeness and the wonders of the unpredictable." Even though it won the New York Drama Critics Circle Award and Caldwell won a Tony, the drama could only survive 105 performances on Broadway.

The Manhattan Theatre Club closed its season with Stephen Metcalfe's **Emily** (3-29-88, City Center), a comedy that took an anti-feminist tack. Emily (Lisa Banes) is a ruthless stockbroker who can outmaneuver men on the trading floor and in the bedroom. Yet she does not experience true love until she meets the penniless actor Jon (Brian Kerwin), who cares little for her power and exposes the fragile female deep inside her. Notices for the play, which originated at the Old Globe Theatre in San Diego, ran the gamut, from "a sparkling comedy with bite to it" to "dull and conventional in outlook." The press agreed on Banes's poignant performance, Gerald Gutierrez's insightful direction, and Heidi Landesman's set of blank walls on which a series of photographs of Manhattan were projected.

Joining stand-up comics Jackie Mason and Mort Sahl this season was Sandra Bernhard, whose one-woman show **Without You I'm Nothing** (3-31-88, Orpheum) found an audience off Broadway for 214 performances. Often going beyond comedy routines, the script by Bernhard and John Boskovich moved into autobiographical drama that was cited as "compelling and disturbing."

Two one-acts by John Bishop, under the umbrella title **Borderlines** (4-7-88, Circle), explored male hostility in contemporary America. *Borderline* concerns Charles Graham (Cotter Smith), a successful advertising executive with a wife and children, who becomes obsessed with violence when a double murder occurs next door. Soon he is off on extramarital affairs that end unhappily and even tragically. During Charles's downfall, a

Lecturer (Brenda Denmark) charts the Graham family history, showing that Charles's innate violence reaches back to medieval border wars in Scotland. *Keepin' an Eye on Louie* illustrated the pent-up emotions (some sexual, some vengeful) seething inside three police officers and an informant during a stakeout of a restaurant frequented by Mafia figures. Opinions in the press varied, calling it "absorbing theatregoing" and "two unpleasant and mildly exploitive one-act plays."

Athol Fugard abandoned his usual preoccupation with apartheid and instead explored the role of the artist as rebel in "one of his simplest, most beautiful plays," **The Road to Mecca** (4-12-88, Promenade), which won the New York Drama Critics Circle Award for Best Foreign Play and stayed on the boards for 172 performances. An old Boer woman, Miss Helen (Yvonne Bryceland), has upset her small South African town with her odd sculptures, which she displays in her garden and calls her "Mecca." Rev. Marius Byleveld (Fugard), a rigid Calvinist minister, feels that the troublesome widow belongs in a nursing home and tries to convince Helen to sign papers to commit herself. But the appearance of Elsa Barlow (Amy Irving), a Johannesburg schoolteacher who was once helped by Helen and has come hundreds of miles to see her, thwarts the minister's efforts. Marius relents, and after he leaves we learn that he has long loved Miss Helen, not as a pastor but as a man. Critics also endorsed the trio of actors, especially South African Bryceland, whose acting reputation in her homeland preceded her.

Pre-opening ballyhoo excited potential playgoers about the Broadway revival of *Macbeth* that opened on April 21 at the Mark Hellinger. This unlucky mounting had gone through a handful of Macduffs, three directors, two scenic designers, and two lighting designers, and star Christopher Plummer had incurred several injuries during its six-city tryout tour. What the critics saw on opening night was justifiably shaky. They pounced on Plummer, calling him everything from "surprisingly unpersuasive" to "unbearably actorish," but awarded Glenda Jackson favorable notices for her lively and sexy Lady Macbeth. The "tempest-tossed, star-crossed" revival remained on the boards for seventy-seven showings.

The renowned nineteenth-century actor Ira Aldridge was the subject of Lonne Elder III's one-man play **Splendid Mummer** (4-24-88, American Place). Charles S. Dutton played the internationally famous African American for two weeks as part of a "celebration of the black experience."

Quite a different solo show, *Jackie Mason's "The World According to Me!"* (12-22-86), returned on May 2 to the Brooks Atkinson and stayed for another 203 performances, making it one of the most successful one-man shows in Broadway history.

Madonna's star power and some "wonderful, dazzling, brilliant lines" kept David Mamet's Hollywood satire **Speed-the-Plow** (5-3-88, Vivian Beaumont) a hot ticket for 278 performances. Film producer Charlie Fox (Ron Silver) has interested a big box-office star in his trashy prison action film, so he goes to Bobby Gould (Joe Mantegna), head of production at a studio, and they salivate over all the money they are going to make. The two men also drool over the simple but alluring office temp Karen (Madonna) and make a bet that Bobby can sleep with her. As a come-on, Bobby gives Karen a novel by an East Coast "sissy writer" and asks her to read it before he rejects it. Karen ends up sleeping with Bobby but also getting him interested in the novel, which deals with the effects of radiation on mankind. Soon Bobby is planning to "greenlight" the book over Charlie's project. Charlie is furious with Bobby and gets even by making Karen confess she only slept with Bobby because she wanted him to film the book. When Bobby realizes this, he dumps Karen, and he and Charlie go off to hawk the action movie. Reviews concerning the merits of Mamet's script were secondary; everyone was more interested in hearing about superstar Madonna's stage debut. She received a very mixed press, but the box office didn't care. Silver, on the other hand, won a Tony at season's end.

Casey Kurtti's **Three Ways Home** (5-11-88, Astor Place) managed to run eighty-seven performances on the strength of young television star Malcolm-Jamal Warner. In a series of monologues, Dawn (S. Epatha Merkerson), a black welfare mom with three kids, is helped by social worker Sharon (Mary McDonnell) in saving her brilliant but misguided son, Frankie (Warner), from his too vivid imagination that sometimes makes him practically dysfunctional. The drama, previously seen at the McCarter Theatre in Princeton, was hailed as "contemporary, upbeat, and engaging" by some critics, but audiences came to see the likable youth, who, like Madonna, received mixed notices from the press.

The Roundabout dug deep into the past when it revived Arthur Wing Pinero's farce *Dandy Dick* (10-5-1887) on May 11. Jan Miner played the forthright Georgiana Tidman, who, in tandem with her staid minister brother, Rev. Augustin Judd (Gordon Chater), gets involved with the racehorse of the title. While the production was far from flawless, critics and audiences still got a charge out of the hundred-year-old comedy.

The Negro Ensemble's final season entry was perhaps its best: Martin Jones's **West Memphis Mojo** (5-21-88, Theatre Four). Teddy (Richard Grant) runs a barbershop in the small Arkansas town of West Memphis in the 1950s and, together with his younger partner, the shoeshine boy Elroi (Tico Wells), has written some rhythm-and-blues songs, which they hope their guitarist-singer friend Frank (Tucker Smallwood) will record. After some setbacks, Frank does record the song on a "race" label but, not trusting the white record producer, has asked for an outright selling of the songs rather than a royalty. Elroi, who realizes a fortune has slipped through their fingers, goes out on a drunken rampage. Maxine (Kate Redway), a white woman who gets her kicks hanging out with black musicians, brings Elroi home, but her public attentions to the youth are considered dangerous by Frank and Teddy, who know the KKK will attack Negroes seen with white women. So the men carefully get the oblivious Maxine to leave. They then reluctantly settle for the meager price paid for their songs.

The season ended with the third Shakespeare Marathon mounting, *Romeo and Juliet* on May 24 in the Anspacher. Reviewers thought Peter MacNicol a petulant Romeo, Cynthia Nixon a luminous (but woefully modern) Juliet, Courtney B. Vance a campy Mercutio, and Anne Meara a sly but incongruous Nurse. Subscribers could see they were in for a bumpy six years.

1988–1989

With only eleven new plays (three of them British), six musicals, and seven specialty items, the Broadway total of twenty-four productions hit a new low. Off Broadway, a total of thirty-five new plays included six foreign works. But revivals both on and off the Street turned New York into a museum of past theatre glories rather than a showcase for new plays. Eight Shakespearean plays were mounted (six as part of the continuing Shakespeare Marathon at the Public Theatre), joined by remountings of Eugene O'Neill, Tennessee Williams, Thornton Wilder, and other native playwrights' work. Samuel Beckett, Luigi Pirandello, Sean O'Casey, George Bernard Shaw, and Joe Orton were also represented. Although quality varied, so many offerings provided a rich selection for playgoers.

More encouraging, the Public, Manhattan Theatre Club, Lincoln Center, and Playwrights Horizons all had better than average seasons. Even the off-off-Broadway WPA Theatre offered a handful of exceptional programs. While few veteran dramatists came up with substantial contributions, several new playwrights made impressive debuts. Very few would go on to noteworthy careers, but they certainly helped theatregoers looking for something new this season.

The theatre district lost two theatres and gained two. The Biltmore was in such disrepair that it was boarded up. The Mark Hellinger was leased to a church for five years. (The group would eventually buy the building.) On Broadway on the site of the old Olympia, two new theatres, Criterion Right and Criterion Left, opened. Also, seven old theatres on 42nd Street were earmarked for restoration and use as legitimate houses. Another decade would past before this plan was partially realized.

Harry Kondoleon, who had proved very promising in his short, eccentric pieces, offered a full evening of his dark humor in **Zero Positive** (6-1-88, Public: LuEsther), a play about AIDS that forsook solemnity for wacky absurdism. Himmer Blank (David Pierce) hopes to console his father, Jacob (Edward Atienza), on the death of Jacob's estranged wife, even though the man seems more interested in his model trains, by staging a verse play that his mother had written in her youth. He gathers some of his gay, bisexual, and straight friends for the amateur production: his ex-lover Samantha (Frances Conroy), Prentice (Richard McMillan), who is recovering from an unsuccessful gay relationship, suicidal actor Patrick (Tony Shalhoub), and Debbie (Beth Austin), a wild young heiress who has a thing for older men, including Jacob. When both Himmer and Samantha test positive for HIV (the medical term is "seropositive," hence the odd title), the projected theatrical becomes a statement about the futility of life. The group performs the epic drama at an AIDS research center, Himmer substituting real poison for the prop hemlock that he will drink in the play. But Jacob drinks it first, and while waiting for a doctor to come, the old man welcomes release from such a senseless world. The "loony treatment of serious themes" was considered more interesting than satisfying and was only kept on the boards for a week.

Time's swift flight allowed Jason Robards, who had originated the role of Jamie in Eugene O'Neill's *Long Day's Journey Into Night* (11-7-56), to play the elder James Tyrone in a revival on June 14 at the Neil Simon. Colleen Dewhurst essayed the tormented mother, Mary. Seeing these two definitive O'Neill actors in his most demanding play was declared an opportunity not to be missed. The limited run, part of the First New York International Festival of the Arts, also featured Jamey Sheridan as Jamie and Campbell Scott as Edmund, all under the aegis of the original director, José Quintero.

In Ken Heelan's dark take on Americana, **Right Behind the Flag** (6-15-88, Playwrights Horizons), Bernie (Kevin Spacey), a Vietnam vet and blue-collar worker, recalls the days when American values meant something and there were leaders like his hero, General Robert E. Lee. Bernie's old Columbus Avenue neighborhood is being taken over by trendy shops catering to yuppies. A pharmaceutical conglomerate has offered to buy out his old friend Frankie (W. T. Martin), a third-generation owner of a barbershop, to use the space for something more profitable. Frankie is tempted even though it is clear to Bernie that the company is a front for highly sophisticated drug dealing. Together they try to battle the system (at one point Bernie takes out his penis and waves it at a yuppie gangster), turning down the offer and making the shop into an "Olde Time Barber Shoppe-Cafe." But the highly-polished drug dealers pop up elsewhere, and the forces of evil continue to grow unabated. Reactions in the press differed, from "an odd boneless little comedy" to a "furiously sad and funny play," but in two weeks it was gone.

Progress encroached on another neighborhood in Jim Leonard's **V & V Only** (6-16-88, Circle). Asian real estate firms are threatening Little Italy, in particular Vito (Dick Boccelli), the talkative but lonely proprietor of the V and V Coffee Shop, whose wife has recently left him. To add to his troubles, Vito must undergo heart surgery. He too falls victim to the system, losing his lease when the Asians buy his building. While some commentators thought it a "carefully observed, sensitive but unsentimental play," most found it "not dramatically engaging."

The annual American Theatre Exchange featuring three regional productions began with a numbing multi-media piece, **Green Card** (6-18-88, Joyce), written and directed by JoAnne Akalaitis, the first of her two entries this season that met with heated reaction. This collage on the plight of immigrants in America, first presented at the Mark Taper Forum in Los Angeles, recalled the confrontational kind of theatrics popular in the late 1960s. A bag lady, dressed as the Statue of Liberty, spouted off Emma Lazarus's poem as well as less illuminating comments about the new land. Actors flung racial slurs at the audience ("Where are the niggers sitting?"), and ethnic stereotypes were lampooned in a television quiz show. Audiences giggled uncomfortably, while critics expressed opposing opinions of the controversial piece.

Robards and Dewhurst turned to O'Neill's lighter side when they portrayed the well-adjusted parents in *Ah, Wilderness!* (10-2-33) which began running in repertory with *Long Day's Journey* on June 23 at the Neil Simon. The Yale Repertory mounting, directed by Arvin Brown, also featured George Hearn as the boozing Sid, Raphael Sbarge as the poetic youth Richard, and Kyra Sedgwick as the innocent Muriel. Notices were approving, encouraging audiences to experience O'Neill in two very different keys.

The Dublin Gate Theatre brought two highly acclaimed productions to New York as part of the same International Festival of the Arts. Sean O'Casey's *Juno and the Paycock* (3-15-26), directed by Joe Dowling, opened on June 21 at the John Golden. Reviews were propitious, one critic rejoicing, "It shatters Broadway's summer sky with unexpected lightning." A week later, Samuel Beckett's one-man play **I'll Go On** (6-22-88, Mitzi E. Newhouse) was fashioned by Gate director Gerry Dukes from three early novels (*Molloy, Malone Dies*, and *The Unnamable*) by the absurdist author and performed by Barry McGovern. The books' dense prose became lighter than air in McGovern's nimble portrayal, with critics lauding his "wonderfully expressive voice" and his "fascinating physical presence, clownish, shocking, abrasive, mocking, and very Godotish."

Tennessee Williams's *The Night of the Iguana* (12-28-61) received its first Broadway revival on June 26 at the Circle in the Square and met with severe reservations regarding both the script and the production. Nicolas Surovy was understated, even lifeless, as the defrocked minister Shannon. Maria Tucci played the gentle spinster Hannah who befriends him, and Jane Alexander the gutsy broad Maxine who runs the hotel. Most reviewers felt all three principals were miscast, but there were thumbs-up for Zack Brown's bungalow setting, which evoked the verdant locale with filmlike realism in the Circle's problematic space. Despite an "inadequate" mounting, it managed to run out the summer.

JON ROBIN BAITZ (1961–) was born in Los Angeles but at the age of seven moved to Brazil and then South Africa, where his family was relocated due to his father's position as an executive for Carnation Milk. Returning to California at the age of seventeen, Baitz attended high school for one year, got a diploma the next year, and ended his formal education. He started to write plays in the early 1980s and apprenticed at various California theatres. His first full-length play, *The Film Society*, was produced by the Los Angeles Theatre Center in 1987 and was cited by the American Theatre Critics Association. Baitz's plays usually have an international setting, concern themselves with global themes, and deal with the individual conscience.

A notable playwright made his debut off-off Broadway when Jon Robin Baitz's **The Film Society** (7-7-88, Second Stage) impressed critics and had a month-long run. A South African private school, modeled on the conventional British system, is thrown into a panic in 1970 when radical teacher Terry Sinclair (Daniel Gerroll) invites a black priest to speak at the school's centenary celebration. Terry is fired, so he tries to enlist the support of Jonathan Balton (Nathan Lane), a fellow teacher with high ideals but no courage to carry them out. Jonathan is more concerned about keeping his film club going, even though he is only allowed to show movies that do not threaten the status quo. When Jonathan's wealthy mother (Margaret Hilton) tries to buy her son the headmaster's job, he is more torn than ever between establishment and the freedom of the individual. But Jonathan sells out, accepts the headmaster position, refuses to take Terry back, and even dismisses Terry's wife, Nan (Laila Robins), a teacher known for her outspoken political views. Frank Rich of the *New York Times* spoke for several critics when he wrote: "What distinguishes Mr. Baitz's writing, aside from its wit and its manifest, if sometimes showy, literacy, is its ability to embrace the ambiguities of political and moral dilemmas that might easily be reduced to blacks and whites." Similar ambiguities would be found in Baitz's later and more polished plays.

The Theatre Exchange's *Green Card* was followed by Pirandello's *Six Characters in Search of an Author* (10-30-22) presented by the American Repertory Theatre on July 9 at the Joyce. Director Robert Brustein and his cast adapted the text. While considered "gimmicky" by some aisle-sitters, the powerful drama still played well. The Public's Shakespeare Marathon continued this season with *Much Ado About Nothing* on July 14 at the outdoor Delacorte in Central Park. Blythe Danner and Kevin Kline made a raucous but affecting Beatrice and Benedick in Gerald Freedman's "rollicking" production set in 1800. The entry was so popular that producer Joseph Papp talked of moving it to Broadway in the fall, but his plans never materialized.

Keith Reddin's **Big Time: Scenes From a Service Economy** (7-16-88, Joyce) was the third entry in the Theatre Exchange. The problematic satire about an overeager banker (William Converse-Roberts) who is destroyed by his corrupt ambition was not highly thought of by the critics. Little did they know the same plot would be seen again in a handful of entries this season.

Carlo Goldoni's eighteenth-century comedy *The Mistress of the Inn* was revived by the Roundabout on July 20, but the press thought little of the play or the production except for the lively presence of Tovah Feldshuh as the title mistress, Mirandolina.

Audiences were encouraged to move among the actors and scenes in Jim Cartwright's **Road** (8-28-88, LaMama Annex), which had been a hit at London's Royal Court but met with mixed reactions when Lincoln Center presented it off Broadway. The setting is a street in a slum section of a Lancashire town where, in one night, we witness a series of monologues and scenes delivered by the various inhabitants, all searching for a way to escape their dreary existence (mostly through drink, drugs, and sex). A middle-aged woman seduces a young drunk soldier, two guys pick up some girls at a bar and engage in frustrated taunts and sex, skinheads attack skinheads, old men wonder what became of the glory of Britain, and two desperate citizens lock themselves in a bedroom to starve themselves to death. The evening's guide is Scullery (Jack Wallace), a derelict and petty thief who caustically points out the many sights along the trash-laden road. Six actors (Kevin Bacon, Joan Cusack, Jayne Haynes, Gerry Bamman, Michael Wincott, and Betsy Aidem) played all the other roles, and their quicksilver portrayals were more appreciated than the script. But to many who caught the eight-week run, it was a unique theatre experience.

Critics had no use for Ronald Milner's African-American sitcom **Checkmates** (8-4-88, 46th Street), but audiences tittered away for 177 performances. Frank (Paul Winfield) and Mattie Cooper (Ruby Dee) have been married forty-six years and have four children, six grandchildren, and a large house in a Detroit suburb. Inexplicably, they have rented the top floor of their home to a young married couple, an enterprising liquor salesman, Sylvester Williams (Denzel Washington), and his career-minded wife, Laura (Marsha Jackson). While the older couple are products of the Depression and World War II (they have a series of flashbacks to show us this), the Williamses are selfish, small-minded (he hates homosexuals and women's magazines), and constantly arguing with each other in between sessions of lovemaking. The contrasts between the two couples filled out the weak-plotted play, aided by superb performances by a warmhearted Dee (her first Broadway appearance in twenty-six years), a solid Winfield, and, in particular, an exciting Washington. Clive Barnes in the *New York Post* was among the many admiring the young actor, noting his ability to be "smart without being wise, sexy without being passionate, and self-absorbed without being self-confident."

King John, so rarely produced, continued the Shakespeare Marathon on August 18 at the Delacorte; while it was a solid and conventional production, it did not win many new fans to the difficult play. But Kevin Conway's feeble yet manipulative monarch did not disappoint. The Negro Ensemble Company brought back Endesha Ida Mae Holland's autobiographical drama *From the Mississippi Delta* (11-18-87) on August 19 to Theatre Four, where it remained for ten weeks, nearly twice as long as its original engagement. The annual *Young Playwrights Festival* opened on September 22 at Playwrights Horizons and featured three original one-acts by teenage writers. One of the authors, Jonathan Marc Sherman, would actually go on to a playwriting career of minor note.

A handful of approving reviews helped Craig Lucas's bizarre fable **Reckless** (9-25-88, Circle) run 113 performances, the Circle Rep's only success this season. On Christmas Eve, scattered but likable Rachel (Robin Bartlett) chatters merrily to her husband, Tom (Michael Piontek), in their bedroom. Suddenly he blurts out that he has hired a hitman to kill her and that she had best run away before he arrives in a few minutes. Rachel escapes out a window in her nightgown into the snow to begin a series of picaresque adventures that cover several Christmases to come. She meets and takes up with Lloyd Bophtelophti (John Dossett), a fugitive from alimony payments, and his paraplegic girlfriend, Pootie

(Welker White), who pretends to be deaf in order to collect more benefits. When Rachel wins $100,000 on a television game show, Tom finds her and attempts a reconciliation, but he is accidentally poisoned by Lloyd. In time Rachel, after seeing a series of psychiatrists for her incipient insanity, ends up as a therapist herself, treating her own son one final Christmas Eve.

An off-off-Broadway revival of Philip Hayes Dean's *Paul Robeson* (1-19-78) in August received such laudatory reviews that it moved to the John Golden on September 28 for a limited run of eleven showings. Avery Brooks essayed the athlete-singer-actor and was acclaimed "absolutely riveting" and "a triple threat himself." Interestingly, the script was more highly thought of this time around. A tame revival of Ibsen's *Ghosts* at the Roundabout on October 5 offered an admirable Mrs. Alving by Fionnula Flanagan, but the rest of the cast and their creaky production failed to please.

Tom Mardirosian's **Saved from Obscurity** (10-13-88, Playwrights Horizons) was an extended monologue sprinkled with brief scenes with other actors to illustrate his story. That story was a familiar one—the saga of a would-be actor from his first school play through his minor career off Broadway and in films—but Mardirosian, as author and actor, delivered it "cheerfully, candidly, funnily" for fifty-four performances.

Richard Foreman was his usually enigmatic self with **What Did He See?** (10-18-88, Public: Shiva) but on a much smaller scale than usual. Three actors, occupying a Victorian parlor filled with bric-a-brac and human skulls, spoke about various unrelated topics for an hour. As if this were not uninvolving enough, Foreman placed a Plexiglas wall between the actors and the audience. Some critics frowned, others searched for meaning. All the same, Forman devotees came for five weeks.

No other American playwright captured the urbane wit of Philip Barry, S. N. Behrman, and similar dramatists of the past as well as A. R. Gurney, and his comedy of manners **The Cocktail Hour** (10-20-88, Promenade) was his finest effort yet in recreating that lost drawing room world. John (Bruce Davison), a reasonably successful publisher-playwright, visits his elderly, wealthy parents in their upstate New York home to show them a play he has written. Bradley (Keene Curtis) and Ann (Nancy Marchand) have rarely been to the theatre since the days of the Lunts so are not impressed by the prospect. When they hear that the play is about them, they are further put off. (Ann fears theatre critics will "think we're all

Republicans, and all trivial, and all alcoholics. . . . Only the latter is true.") Even John's sister, Nina (Holland Taylor), is not enthusiastic, although her real complaint is that her character, as John has written it, is such a secondary one. After a heated argument during the genteel ritual of the cocktail hour, John sees that this glossy veneer is really a cover to hide the truly frustrated lives his affluent Wasp family leads. John decides to put the play away, promising his parents not to produce it until after they are dead. Having won that promise, they generously offer suggestions for a title, and then everyone continues to enjoy civilized cocktail time together. Set in the 1970s, when his own playwriting career was beginning, the comedy was perhaps Gurney's most autobiographical and personal yet. Appreciative reviews all around called it "deliciously funny and touching" and "Gurney at the top of his form." Jack O'Brien directed the sterling quartet of actors for its premiere at San Diego's Old Globe Theatre; the same production came to New York, where it stayed for 351 performances.

That same night a much cruder comedy, **Just Say No** (10-20-88, WPA) by gay activist Larry Kramer, opened off-off Broadway and got considerable press, very little of it positive. Kramer's political satire, with more than a dash of sex farce thrown in, used barely disguised public figures (Ronald Reagan and family, in particular) to attack his many targets. (The title came from Nancy Reagan's anti-drug campaign in schools.) Foppy Schwartz (David Margulies) is a shining light in high society, throwing parties for the famous and getting the inside scoop on all the celebrities. When he comes across a videotape that shows the First Lady, Mrs. Potentate (Kathleen Chalfant), cavorting with married men (cabinet members, no less), she makes every effort to suppress the tape. Her son, Junior (Richard Topol), a ballet dancer who wants to come out of the closet, falls in love with Gilbert Perch (Keith Reddin), the ex-paramour of a loudmouth Mayor (Joseph Ragno). Also thrown into the scandalous ensemble is big-time business tycoon Herman Harrod (Richard Riehle), who suffers a stroke while making love to his mistress. The black maid Eustacia Vye (Tonya Pinkins) wants to use all this information to bring down the government, but in the end Foppy protects the First Lady, Junior goes back into the closet, and hypocrisy triumphs once again. Few critics endorsed the satire, most finding it noisy and empty, noting that the "discoveries Kramer's play makes . . . wouldn't shock a nun."

Cafe Crown (1-23-42), Hy Kraft's comedy about members of the Yiddish Theatre, may have seemed an unlikely choice for the Public, but its revival on October 25 at the Newman was greeted with affectionate approval even if one critic thought the script "a series of Jewish theatrical anecdotes in search of a play." The scintillating cast included Eli Wallach, Bob Dishy, Marilyn Cooper, Joseph Leon, Harry Goz, Anne Jackson, Walter Bobbie, and an actual veteran of the Yiddish theatre, Fyvush Finkel. Santo Loquasto's Tony Award–winning scenery created "a plush, sconce-lighted replica of an old Second Avenue cafe, with pickles at every table and autographed photographs on every wall." After fifty-six performances, *Cafe Crown* transferred to the Brooks Atkinson on February 18, but business was spotty, and it left after five weeks.

Richard Greenberg became a playwright to reckon with when his comedy **Eastern Standard** (10-27-88, City Center) opened to wan notices but became a much-discussed item. It was another play about yuppies but this time looking from the inside out. Stephen Wheeler (Dylan Baker), a prosperous Manhattan architect who makes his living gentrifying old neighborhoods, is lunching with his friend Drew Paley (Peter Frechette), a gay SoHo artist, when a disruptive bag lady, May Logan (Anne Meara), enters the restaurant shouting and throwing bottles. Ellen (Barbara Garrick), a waitress and aspiring actress, subdues the woman and restores some order to the place, allowing the patrons to start speaking to each other without their usual Manhattan reserve. Stephen is drawn to the attractive Wall Street banker Phoebe Kidde (Patricia Clarkson) at the next table while Drew is attracted to her brother, Peter (Kevin Conroy), a discontented TV producer with AIDS. The foursome hit it off and a month later are weekending in Stephen's beach house in the Hamptons. Stephen has also invited May and Ellen, hoping to deal with his guilt over the way the system mistreats some of its citizens. The weekend is a sociopolitical fiasco, but the two couples survive it, reaching an "accidental happiness" together. The Manhattan Theatre Club mounting ran forty-six performances off Broadway, then on January 5 transferred to Broadway's John Golden for another ninety-two showings.

Three days later, in its second space, the Manhattan Theatre Club opened John Patrick Shanley's least abusive and most warmhearted play yet, **Italian American Reconciliation** (10-30-88, City Center). Huey Maximilian Bonfigliano (John Pankow) may be divorced from the mean-spirited Janice (Jayne Haynes), but he still wants to win her back, hoping to regain his "manhood" and move on with his life. So he enlists the help of his friend Aldo Scalicki (John Turturro), a bachelor who cannot understand why Huey would want Janice back (after all, she even shot his dog) when he has the love of the gentle waitress Teresa (Laura San Giacomo). But a friend is a friend, so Aldo goes to the alley outside Janice's apartment and, in a silly but engaging balcony scene in the moonlight, convinces her to take Huey back. The comedy had a folk-tale quality to it, and Shanley's "wonderful Runyonesque dialogue" made his usually volatile characters very endearing. The "irresistible" play lasted seven weeks.

The hottest ticket of the season was Mike Nichols's mounting of Samuel Beckett's *Waiting for Godot* (4-19-56) with movie stars Robin Williams and Steve Martin as the two aimless tramps. The twenty-five-performance run was sold out long before it opened on November 6 at the intimate Mitzi E. Newhouse. (In fact, there were not enough seats for all subscribers, so tickets were distributed by lottery.) More than one critic assured readers that they were not missing much if they failed to get in. Neither star had much stage experience, so each relied on his comic tricks (Williams did his inevitable John Wayne impersonation and Martin his signature huffing and puffing), which were not out of keeping with Beckett's vaudeville characters. But very few aisle-sitters thought the two created characters, only personalities. F. Murray Abraham's Pozzo and mime favorite Bill Irwin's Lucky were more favorably reviewed. As Sylvianne Gold in the *Wall Street Journal* noted bitingly, "The most eagerly anticipated theatrical event of the season turns out—in true Beckett style—to be [an] anticlimax."

Kate Nelligan, who had found fame playing an irritating and fascinating heroine in *Plenty* (10-21-82), latched onto a similarly difficult character in Michael Weller's **Spoils of War** (11-10-88, Music Box). Before World War II, Elise (Nelligan) and her husband, Andrew (Jeffrey DeMunn), were leftist radicals. Times changed and they parted, but in the Red-baiting 1950s their teenage son, Martin (Christopher Collet), tries to get the couple together again. Andrew has succumbed to conservatism and works as a photographer. Elsie, on the other hand, is as feisty as ever, fighting the world, drinking too much, and maintaining her "gallant, wry, manipulative, self-destructive, and sexy" ways. Just as Martin fails to bring his parents together, most critics thought Weller failed in making the unwieldy play work. But he did create a fascinating character, and Nelligan played it for all it was worth. Even so, the drama closed after thirty-six showings.

Philip Bosco and Victor Garber were the main reasons to catch the "worthy but a little commonplace" revival of Shaw's The Devil's Disciple on November 13 at the Circle in the Square. Bosco, who was becoming New York's favorite Shavian interpreter, played General "Gentleman Johnny" Burgoyne with all the bluster of a cannon, and Garber was a sly and very sexy Dick Dudgeon. Stephen Porter directed the comedy, which was held over for 113 performances.

His serio-comic autobiographical trilogy completed, Neil Simon turned to broad and escapist farce with **Rumors** (11-17-88, Broadhurst), which entertained undemanding audiences for 531 performances. Deputy mayor Charley and his wife, Myra, have invited four couples to their town house for a party to celebrate their tenth anniversary. But Ken (Mark Nelson) and Chris Gorman (Christine Baranski), the first to arrive, find Charley in the bedroom wounded from a suicide attempt (he only managed to shoot himself in the earlobe) and Myra missing. In order to avoid scandal, they try to keep the hosts' predicament from the other couples when they arrive. But a second gunshot brings the police, and soon all four couples are manufacturing stories to continue the cover up. Critics were stingy in their approval ("old-hat humor not encountered in our time outside the world of dinner theatres") but applauded Gene Saks's razor-sharp direction and the farceur talents of the cast, which also included Ron Liebman, Joyce Van Patten, Jessica Walter, André Gregory, and Lisa Banes. Tony Straiges's elegant white setting, featuring several doors upstairs and down, garnered kudos. In time, the farce became a popular staple in community theatres.

No play yet in Papp's Shakespeare Marathon had received such glowing reviews as those for Coriolanus on November 22 at the Public, yet praise for the "updated and truncated, impertinent, overboard, but overwhelmingly beautiful production" was far from unanimous. British director Steven Berkoff cut the script radically, set it in modern times with black and gray costumes on a set of black slate, and punctuated it with an all-percussion score that added to the driving force of the brutal drama. Christopher Walken played the doomed Roman of the title.

David Williamson, an Australian playwright-screenwriter, set his **Emerald City** (11-30-88, Perry Street) in Sydney, but it had all the backstabbing and depersonalization of a Hollywood exposé. Writer Colin (Daniel Gerroll) and his editor wife, Kate (Gates McFadden), move from Melbourne to the bigger city, where his career is propelled upward by the fast-talking dealmaker Mike (Dan Butler). Before long Colin has abandoned serious projects, is considering television soap operas, and is infatuated with a public relations woman named Helen (Alice Haining). Mike takes one of Kate's favorite projects, a novel about aboriginal peoples, and hawks it as a film vehicle for Eddie Murphy reset in Tennessee. Forced to reevaluate themselves, Kate and Colin consider returning to Melbourne until they realize that Sydney is not the problem. "Don't blame the city. The demons are in us," Colin notes as they try to revive their marriage and artistic goals. The off-off-Broadway engagement was limited to seventeen performances, but the "insanely, cynical" comedy received many critical plaudits. The editors of the Best Plays included it as one of the season's ten best and, in an unprecedented move, published the entire text in that year's edition.

Romantic ideals of the Old West were celebrated and exploded in Mark Medoff's **The Majestic Kid** (12-1-88, St. Peter's Church), a fantasy that was not favored by the press but found life afterwards in regional theatres. Aaron Weiss (Stuart Zagnit), a New York activist lawyer, travels to the Southwest with his feminist assistant, Ava Jean Pollard (Kay Wallbye), to help the Apaches battle against eastern companies who hope to exploit their land and heritage. Ever since he was a child, Aaron has imagined himself as "The Majestic Kid," a gun-toting hero who fights for justice in the West. Aaron's primary rival is William S. Hart Finlay (Michael Cullen), a redneck judge who hopes to add to his fortune by the proposed land deals. Aaron's mentor is "The Laredo Kid" (Alex Wipf), a fantasy figure right out of B westerns, who guides the young lawyer in his fight but upbraids him when he starts to weaken and fall for the judge's ex-girlfriend Lisa Belmondo (Juliette Kurth). Finally Aaron finds his true inner self and no longer needs the Kid to help him win his battles.

The Lincoln Center revival of Thornton Wilder's Our Town (2-4-38) on December 4 at the Lyceum was well received, winning exemplary notices and a Tony Award for Best Revival. Much of the cheering was for the script itself, considered more powerful than ever, but Gregory Mosher's "robustly funny" mounting was also saluted. Monologuist Spalding Gray essayed the Stage Manager, Eric Stoltz and Penelope Ann Miller were George and Emily, and the parents were portrayed by Frances Conroy, James Rebhorn, Roberta Maxwell, and Peter Maloney. The revival ran 135 performances.

The most awarded new play of the season was Wendy Wasserstein's **The Heidi Chronicles** (12-11-88, Playwrights Horizons), an ambitious saga of the women's movement as seen through art historian Heidi Holland (Joan Allen). From her boarding school days in the mid-sixties through the anti-war campaigns of the early seventies to women's rights activism and its aftermath, Heidi discovers new pieces of herself as a woman and a person. Through the years she is entangled with two men who help and hinder her. Radical Scoop Rosenbaum (Peter Friedman) shifts from politics to nostalgic publishing and marries a wealthy southern belle (Anne Lange) because he cannot compete with Heidi's self-reliance. Her gay friend Peter Patrone (Boyd Gaines) becomes a pediatrician, but when the AIDS epidemic arises, he dedicates his career to helping others and cannot understand Heidi's self-centered concerns. In the end (which several critics and audience members found fault with), Heidi turns to motherhood and adopts a baby in order to continue her search for fulfillment. Reviews along the lines of "slickly written" and "not just a funny play but a wise one" helped sell out the eighty-one performances off Broadway, so the production transferred to the Plymouth on March 9 and stayed for another ninety-six showings. *The Heidi Chronicles* won the New York Drama Critics Circle and Tony awards (Gaines also won a Tony), and the next year it was awarded the Pulitzer Prize. Both the off-Broadway and Broadway mountings were directed by Daniel Sullivan, who was joining the front ranks of American directors.

Like his fellow African-American playwright August Wilson, Charles Fuller planned a cycle of plays about black Americans, which he titled **We** (12-18-88, Theatre Four). The first two parts, both full-length plays set during the Civil War, were **Sally** and **Prince,** which ran in repertory for forty-one performances each. The former chronicled a North Carolina woman (Michele Shay) who, recently freed from bondage, sets out with her sixteen-year-old son to start a new life after her husband is killed. In a subplot, Sergeant

> **DANIEL [J.] SULLIVAN** (1940–) was born in Wray, Colorado, and educated at San Francisco State University. After graduation he worked as an actor at San Francisco's Actors' Workshop in the early 1960s, then went to New York, where he directed school tours for Lincoln Center. He was assistant director for *Hair* (1968) and *An Enemy of the People* (1971) on Broadway before directing several off-Broadway shows at Lincoln Center, including A. R. Gurney's early work *Scenes from American Life* (1971). Through much of the 1970s Sullivan directed for various regional theatres, becoming a resident director at the Seattle Repertory Theatre in 1979 and its artistic director in 1981. His Seattle production of *I'm Not Rappaport* brought him back to Manhattan, and for the next decade he would divide his time between Seattle and New York. Sullivan would stage premiere mountings for several American playwrights, always letting the play dictate the style and keeping his direction unobtrusive but firm.

Prince (Samuel L. Jackson) struggles to get equal pay for black troops fighting for the North, but he meets up with federal bureaucracy that seems little better than the slavery his people have left behind. *Prince* was set on a Virginia farm where freed slaves are working for the North; not getting paid, they eventually rebel. (Sergeant Prince showed up in this play too.) The drama even had a Mother Courage–like character named Lu (Hattie Winston) who peddled her wares to the troops, living off the war and her own people's misery. Both plays were presented by the Negro Ensemble Theatre, which would continue the saga in future seasons.

The Roundabout's revival of Pirandello's *Enrico IV* (1-21-24) on December 21 was thought to be a solid and competent mounting of a difficult play. Paul Hecht, as the madman who thinks he is a German emperor, was roundly endorsed for "giving the role the strength and glittering lunacy it needs."

Perhaps the reason Garson Kanin's *Born Yesterday* (2-4-46) had never been revived on Broadway had something to do with finding a star to play the quintessential smart-dumb blonde Billie Dawn. Madeline Kahn's attempt on January 29 at the 46th Street pleased most critics, who considered her Billie "more tough, less ditzy, older, wiser, and a tad more cynical" than Judy Holliday's legendary stage and screen portrayal. Ed Asner was the gruff millionaire junk dealer Harry Brock, a role not dissimilar from his TV character

Lou Grant. Some commentators felt the script had dated, but most agreed with audiences who kept the comedy on the boards for 153 showings.

The Kathy and Mo Show: Parallel Lives (1-31-89, Westside) covered some of the same ground as *The Heidi Chronicles*, but Kathy Najimy and Mo Gaffney, who wrote and performed the piece, were more interested in satirizing aspects of the women's movement in this comic revue that quickly gathered a cult following and stayed for 466 performances. Playing a cornucopia of male and female characters, the duo jumped from broad farce (two goddesses in heaven arguing which sex should bear children) to incisive character comedy (a single mother is both appalled and amused by a Texas stud trying to pick her up in a bar).

The Circle Rep opened two productions in one week. Cindy Lou Johnson's outlandish **Brilliant Traces** (2-5-89, Cherry Lane) played in a leased space for five weeks. Rosannah DeLuce (Joan Cusack) flees her wedding ceremony in Arizona and hits the road still wearing her matrimonial regalia. In the middle of a snowstorm, she arrives at the Alaska cabin of reclusive Henry Harry (Kevin Anderson), pleads for sanctuary, and then falls asleep for two days. When she awakes, the feisty Rosannah and the reticent Henry find that they are both refugees from society and, after a series of arguments and the confessing of deep secrets, reach an understanding together. Although the exaggerated two-hander tried for an allegorical style, under all the bluster was "a slim and rather conventional one-act."

Also at the Circle Rep, Keith Curran's **Dalton's Back** (2-9-89, Circle) had a pair of plays occurring simultaneously on the same stage, neither one capturing the approval of the critics. Dalton Possil (John Dossett), a young schoolteacher, wants to marry Teresa MacIntyre (Colleen Davenport), the girl he has been living with, and have children together. But Teresa likes the less formal arrangement they have now and wants to pursue her career. On the other side of the stage, the boy Daltie (Matt McGrath) is being raised by his emotionally unstable Mom (Lisa Emery) while his alcoholic father is usually out of the picture. Fluctuating between strangling affection and outright abuse, the mother sows the seeds for all of Dalton's insecurities and anxiety. Before the play ends, Daltie and Dalton confront each other face to face and try to smother their fears in an embrace.

Ira Levin left the thriller genre of *Deathtrap* (2-26-78) and returned to comedy in **Cantorial** (2-14-89, Lamb's), though there was more than a little mystery in the piece. Yet another yuppie couple, Warren Ives (Anthony Fusco) and Lesley Rosen (Lesly Kahn), move into a Manhattan condominium and soon notice a haunting but beautiful voice whose song echoes through the apartment. Lesley is Jewish and recognizes the music as a cantor's chant. Warren becomes obsessed with the voice, investigates, and finds that a synagogue once stood on the spot. He is convinced that the ghostly cantor is praying for the site to be turned back into a shul. Warren even believes that his adopted parents lied to him and that his birth mother was Jewish. Feeling destined to search out his roots, he employs the help of neighborhood deli owner Morris Lipkind (Woody Romoff) to learn more about Judaism. But this obsession drives Lesley away, and when she returns at the end of the play a new synagogue sits on the site. The engaging play, which originated off-off Broadway at the Jewish Repertory Theatre, received some money reviews along the lines of "the most melodic non-musical in town" and "an easy, intriguing, and diverting page-turner" that helped it run four months.

British actress Pauline Collins was somewhat familiar to American PBS-TV viewers, but after appearing in Willy Russell's one-hander **Shirley Valentine** (2-16-89, Booth) she became a bona fide Broadway star, winning a Tony Award for her intoxicating performance and making the little play a profitable attraction for 324 performances. Shirley is a Liverpool housewife who spends the first act in her kitchen preparing breakfast and talking about her shallow husband, grown kids, and uneventful past. But a girlfriend has asked her to accompany her on a trip to Greece, so in the second act she brings us up to date on her adventures there. Having met and had a fling with a dashing Greek fisherman, she decides to forsake her dreary English life and remain in Greece. While there was little special about the script, Collins's "chatty intimacy, robust humor, and intense conviction" certainly were unique.

Wall Street broker-turned-playwright Jerry Sterner finally had a hit with **Other People's Money** (2-16-89, Minetta Lane), which was, not surprisingly, about stocks and bonds. Lawrence Garfinkle (Kevin Conway), known in the money world as Larry the Liquidator, is an obese, merciless trader who devours fragile companies as he does doughnuts, buying up stock, taking possession, stripping the company of its assets, and then destroying it forever. His latest victim is a Rhode Island company that manufactures steel cable. Its mild and principled president, Andrew Jorgenson (Arch Johnson), and his longtime assistant (and his mistress), Bea Sullivan (Scotty Bloch), seem powerless to stop Garfinkle, so they plead for the services of Kate (Mercedes Ruehl), an attractive and shrewd lawyer who is also Bea's daughter. She makes all the right moves: injunctions, deals, and hidden stock purchases. Of course Garfinkle counters, all the time attracted to his alluring opponent. When the future of the company comes down to a vote by the stockholders, Garfinkle wins, the company is dismembered, and even Kate gives in to his vulgar charm. Critics were enthusiastic, calling the play "funny, serious, suspenseful, involving, disturbing, and, above all, expertly crafted." The popular entry remained off Broadway for 990 performances. (A subsequent film version gave the story a happy ending.)

The Public's *Love's Labor's Lost* on February 22 boasted a capable cast directed by Gerald Freedman "with his customary light, precise touch" and set in the 1930s, James Scott costumed the young scholars as if they had strolled in from an Evelyn Waugh novel. William Converse-Williams was the academic cynic Berowne, Roma Downey his nemesis Rosaline, and Richard Libertini the pedantic Don Armado.

Even though the subject was the beloved New Yorker Fiorello La Guardia, Paul Shyre's one-man play **Hizzoner!** (2-24-89, Longacre) failed to find an audience and closed after twelve performances. Tony Lo Bianco essayed the colorful mayor by trying to ape the voice and phrasing of the politician. The result was described as everything from "an engaging and persuasive figure" to "he made the late mayor look like [the] fourth member of the Three Stooges."

Albert Innaurato was toying with autobiography again in his **Gus and Al** (2-27-89, Playwrights Horizons), in which a playwright, Al of the title, commiserates with famous composer Gustav Mahler, Gus of the title. After receiving another round of critical bashing for his latest play, Al (Mark Blum) travels back in a time machine invented by his talking-gorilla roommate named Kafka (Charles Janasz). Arriving in Vienna of 1901, Al befriends his idol Mahler (Sam Tsoutsouvas), who is also getting a lambasting by the critics. Al gets involved with Mahler's household, run by his lovesick housekeeper Natalie Bauer Lechner (Cara Duff-MacCormick), meets the beautiful Alma Schindler (Jennifer Van Dyck), who will later become the composer's wife, and even has a chat with a visitor named Sigmund Freud (Janasz). Before he returns to the present, Al gets a

> **PHILIP** [Michael] **BOSCO** (1930–) was born in Jersey City and educated at Catholic University of America in Washington. He made his professional stage debut in summer stock in 1954 and has rarely been unemployed since. Bosco spent many years in regional theatre as a resident actor at the Arena Stage in the late 1950s, the Shakespeare Festival in Connecticut in the early 1960s, and in the first company at Lincoln Center Repertory Theatre from 1969 to 1969. He made his Broadway debut as Heracles in *The Rape of the Belt* (1960) and received a Tony nomination for his efforts. Equally adept at the classics (in particular Shaw, Shakespeare, and Ibsen) and contemporary pieces, the tall and portly Bosco is a favorite "actor's actor" who, despite many featured roles in films, is mostly unknown outside of the theatre world.

glimpse of his own grandfather Camillo (Bradley White), who works as Mahler's gardener. While the fantasy met with some approval (the editors named it one of the ten *Best Plays*), it was not kept on beyond its scheduled three-week run.

The most successful American farce of the decade (although it was first a London hit) was Ken Ludwig's **Lend Me a Tenor** (3-2-89, Royale), an old-fashioned door-slammer that ran 481 performances and became a popular favorite in theatres across the nation. World-renowned Italian opera star Tito Merelli (Ron Holgate) has agreed to perform *Otello* for the Cleveland Grand Opera Company as their 1934 season gala opener. In the hotel suite waiting for Tito are Saunders (Philip Bosco), the high-strung general manager of the company, and his assistant, Max (Victor Garber), who is an aspiring opera singer himself. When Tito does arrive, late and half drunk, he is accidentally given tranquilizers and passes out cold on the bed. Reading a farewell letter written by Tito's jealous wife, Maria (Tovah Feldshuh), Saunders and Max think it is a suicide note from Tito. Desperate to provide his audience with a star, Saunders talks Max into disguising himself as Tito as Othello (blackface and all) and going on in his place. Max begrudgingly agrees, but when Tito comes to, he also gets into blackface and costume, so two Othellos are running in and out of the suite. Before the confusions are cleared up, there are some wonderfully daffy scenes, such as Max's starstruck girlfriend, Maggie (J. Smith-Cameron), being merrily seduced by Max but thinking he is the Italian tenor, and the Opera Guild chairwoman, Diana (Caroline Lagerfelt), complimenting Tito on his stage performance, the Italian thinking she is talking about their supposed lovemaking together. Jerry Zaks directed the animated cast, which also included Jane Connell as a ditzy opera patron and Jeff Brooks as a harried bellhop. Also cheered were Tony Walton's sleek art deco hotel suite and William Ivey Long's hysterical costumes (one dress being appropriately described by Saunders as the Chrysler Building). Tony Awards were won by Zaks and, after a long career with too few honors, Bosco.

Steven Berkoff's stage adaptation and direction of Kafka's **Metamorphosis** (3-6-89, Ethel Barrymore) was originally developed in the 1960s, and its mounting on Broadway definitely had a dated avant-garde feel to it. The attraction marked the stage acting debut of ballet star Mikhail Baryshnikov, who proved more than qualified to handle the very physical expressionistic style Berkoff favored. German worker Gregor Samsa (Baryshnikov) wakes up one morning as a beetle and soon discovers that his parents (René Auberjonois and Laura Esterman), sweetheart (Madeleine Potter), and co-worker (Mitch Kreindel) all are alienated from him. Generally negative reviews rejected Berkoff's "loud circus," but Baryshnikov was applauded for his athleticism, which was enough for his fans to keep the show alive for ninety-six showings.

Opening less than a week after *Lend Me a Tenor*, there was little hope for the less-original farce **Run for Your Wife** (3-7-89, Virginia), though it is questionable whether this very British brand of comedy would have played successfully on Broadway at any time. Ray Cooney's London hit (at well over 2,000 performances) concerned a taxi driver, John Smith (Cooney), who has two wives (Hilary Labow and Kay Walbye) in two houses in two separate areas of London. When John has a minor traffic accident and is taken to the hospital, both wives are notified and the confusion begins. Particularly funny was Paxton Whitehead as a hapless neighbor who gets embroiled in all the schemes to keep the cabbie's double life a secret. Reviewers declared the farce "vulgar, crass, and downright disgusting, and also about fifteen minutes too long." Since Cooney directed the play here as he had in England, it was a pretty accurate example of British sex farce. Some Americans enjoyed it, though only enough to let it run fifty-two times.

Two well-received revivals opened the next night. Carson McCullers's *A Member of the Wedding* (1-5-50) was judged to be as fine and moving a play as many remembered. Esther Rolle was the protective Berenice Sadie Brown, and Amelia Campbell was the sensitive teenager Frankie Addams. The one repeated complaint concerned the Roundabout's new large and acoustically poor home, the Christian C. Yegen Theatre, which hurt the intimate quality of the drama. Also on March 8, the Manhattan Theatre Club revived Joe Orton's *What the Butler Saw* (5-4-70), and more than one critic felt it was superior to the original American production. Charles Keating as the philandering Dr. Prentice and Carole Shelley as his wife led the merry cast, directed with precise abandon by John Tillinger. The dark farce kept playgoers laughing for ninety-nine showings. The next night Lincoln Center turned to Shakespeare, but its *Measure for Measure* in the Mitzi E. Newhouse was dismissed as dull, academic, and lifeless. Mark Lamos staged the difficult play, with Len Cariou (Duke), Campbell Scott (Angelo), and Kate Burton (Isabella) heading the cast.

A vulgar comedienne named Reno tried to do solo what *Kathy and Mo*'s stars had done as a team in **Reno in Rage and Rehab** (2-13-89, Actors' Playhouse), a brutal, funny program strictly for the performer's fans. Whether carping about living in New York City or discussing the various slang terms for the vagina, Reno rarely settled for subtlety or wit. But her in-your-face show caught on enough to last nearly twelve weeks.

Director James Lapine took a fairy-tale approach to *The Winter's Tale*, the Public's next Marathon offering on March 21. John Arnone created a psuedo-Elizabethan playhouse on the Anspacher stage, and William Finn and Michael Starobin provided lovely music for the dreamy piece. Sadly the poetry was lost, and the uneven, colorblind casting displeased several commentators. Yet others thought it the finest offering so far in the series. The cast included Christopher Reeve (Polixenes), Mandy Patinkin (Leontes), Diane Venora (Hermione), Alfre Woodard (Paulina), and Jennifer Dundas (Perdita).

Texan Larry L. King accurately captured small-town life in his home state in **The Night Hank Williams Died** (3-31-89, Orpheum), which ran eight weeks and collected some appreciative reviews for its "rich Texan vernacular—the rat-tat-tat of startling, bawdy similes and funny throwaway lines." During the summer of 1952, former high school football hero Thurmond Stottle (Matt Mulhern) works at a gas station in the remote West Texas town of Stanley and dreams of glory as a singer-songwriter in Nashville. When his ex-girlfriend Nellie Bess Powers Clark (Betsy Aidem) returns to town because her marriage is on the rocks, Thurmond decides to run off with her to the country-music capital. He tries to borrow money from his friend Gus Gilbert (Darren McGavin), who owns the bar that is Thurmond's favorite hangout, but Gus refuses. So Thurmond robs the gas station, fiercely beating up the owner. Thurmond is picked up the sheriff, and all his dreams of fame come to nothing but jail time. The comedy-drama was directed by the young and promising Christopher Ashley.

Paul Zindel, who liked long and intriguing titles, resurfaced with his **Amulets Against the Dragon Forces** (4-5-89, Circle), another drama set in the 1950s. Mrs. Boyd (Deborah Hedwall) is a live-in practical nurse for terminal patients, dragging her moody teenage son, Chris (Matt McGrath), wherever the job takes her. Arriving at the Staten Island home of Mrs. Dipardi, who is dying of cancer, Chris immediately clashes with Floyd (John Spencer), the dying woman's hard-drinking son. Floyd is the neighborhood disgrace, not because of his drinking and loud backyard parties but because he openly flaunts his homosexuality. Battling both his suffocating mother and the taunting Floyd, Chris is drawn to Harold (Loren Dean), a gay hustler who has moved in with Floyd. The triangle sets off a new round of emotional fireworks, but Chris survives, secure in his sexuality, determined to fight the "dragon forces" and make something of his life. The production received decidedly mixed reviews, from "gripping and disturbing" to "a numbing bore," most of the compliments going to the fine ensemble acting.

A similarly painful adolescence was explored in Bill Gunn's **The Forbidden City** (4-6-89, Public: LuEsther), a "work in progress" that never had much chance to progress, the playwright dying the day before opening. "Miss Molly" Hoffenburg (Gloria Foster), a bombastic black woman, hopes to rise above the restrictions put on her race in 1936 Philadelphia and mix with those on a higher cultural plane. Her efforts are dampened by her unsophisticated but good-hearted husband, Nick Sr. (Frankie R. Faison), and her sixteen-year-old son, Nick Jr. (Akili Prince), who still wets the bed and desperately clutches his teddy, both of whom she treats with scorn and humiliation. The play had little action, consisting mostly of monologues, but a scene in the second act when Molly confesses how her loneliness drove her to go to a hotel room with a rich white man revealed what the play might have become.

Later in the week, the Public presented the American premiere of **Temptation** (4-9-89, Mar-tinson) by Václav Havel who, at the time of this production, was in a Czech prison for his political writings. Scientist Dr. Henry Foustka (David Strathairn) is so obsessed with increasing his knowledge, he enlists the aid of the sinister Fistula (Billie Brown) and thereby brings on his own downfall. The modern Faust tale took on political overtones, but whether it was Marie Winn's translation or Jiří Zizka's cluttered and complicated staging, the three-hour drama was generally dismissed ("one of the most hateful, trying evenings in the history of the Public") and closed after a week.

Another foreign entry that failed was **Ghetto** (4-13-89, Circle in the Square), Joshua Sobol's grim, ironic drama with songs. Originally presented in Israel in 1984 and performed around the world since then, this new English version by David Lan opened to mixed reviews and closed in a month. In the Jewish ghetto of Vilna, Lithuania, the occupying Nazi forces encourage the community to form a theatre troupe to keep up morale, even as thousands of Jews are being eliminated every day. For two years the odd company, made up of singers, comics, and ventriloquists, perform their sorry shows until they also are killed as part of the Final Solution. Sobol's storytelling was haphazard, and many of the vignettes fell flat. But there were striking moments along the way, such as the German commander Kittel (Stephen McHattie) forcing the actors to don blackface and sing "Swanee," or the ventriloquist's dummy (Gordon Joseph Weiss) spouting anti-Nazi jibes at the audience and the German spectators laughing all the same.

A comedy about Jewish comedians that had real bite to it was Jim Geoghan's **Only Kidding** (4-14-89, Westside). In the first act, has-been Borscht Belt comic Jackie Dwayne (Larry Keith) employs the help of Sheldon Kelinski (Howard Spiegel), a young comic writer, to beef up his nightclub act. The two meet in Jackie's Catskills cottage and clash over their opposing ideas of what is funny. In a seemingly unrelated second act, two rising comics are on a high after a show in a sleazy comedy club. Hyped-up Jerry Goldstein (Paul Provenza) wants to sign a contract with the creepy owner, Sal D'Angelo (Sam Zap), a Mafia-backed agent, even though the mob will get a huge cut of future profits. Jerry's partner, Tom Kelly (Andrew Hill-Newman), is suspicious of the deal and refuses to sign; the two friends part in anger. The last act, set backstage of a popular TV talk show, brings all the characters together. Jackie has a chance of making a comeback with his appearance on the nationwide show. Also scheduled is the up-and-coming Jerry, getting more famous and more cutthroat every day. When the show starts to run overtime, Jerry gets Sal to have Jackie ousted from the program. But Tom, now working as a production assistant, and Sheldon, now a big-time writer, contrive to get Jerry out of the picture (they knock him out with an ice bucket) and let Jackie have his shot at a comeback. Positive reviews and strong word of mouth helped the perceptive comedy run an even 300 performances.

More than just a touch of Chekhov emerged in **Aristocrats** (4-25-89, Theatre Four), Brian Friel's understated drama about the end of a notable Irish family. In the mid-1970s, family and friends of the O'Donnell clan gather on the south lawn of a crumbling Georgian mansion that overlooks the town of Ballybeg in Ireland's County Donegal, brought together by the wedding of Claire (Haviland Morris), one of the family's four no-longer-young sisters, to a man everyone knows she doesn't love. But inside the house Judge O'Donnell (Joseph Warren), the stern family patriarch, is on his deathbed, and his demise postpones the wedding so that the funeral can be held first. The action of the play was minimal, but the various characters were quietly but assuredly lively. Eamon (John Pankow), the cynical working-class husband of one of the judge's daughters, expresses the Chekhovian theme that the O'Donnells are the last of a dying breed, and even Casimir (Niall Buggy), the judge's lone son, questions the stories and warm memories that have been foisted upon him. Senile old Uncle George (Thomas Barbour) wanders the estate, a symbol of the aimless O'Donnells, while Claire plays classical pieces on the piano and recalls the time the great tenor John McCormack visited the house and she accompanied him. (Gerard Manley Hopkins, William Butler Yeats, Hilaire Belloc, and G. K. Chesterton were among the other celebrated past visitors to the estate.) The critics applauded the script ("gently provocative and vastly entertaining") and the skillful Manhattan Theatre Club production, helping the run to extend to 186 performances.

There was a lot of discussion over whether **Largely New York** (5-1-89, St. James) was a play, since no words were spoken during the elaborate, ingenious mime program "written" by and featuring Bill Irwin. (Much of the argument arose when the Tony Award committee nominated it as Best Play.) A contemporary Everyman called Post-Modern Hoofer (Irwin) is confronted and beguiled by Manhattan's overwhelming technology. He fumbles through a series of vignettes involving street rappers with loud boomboxes, dancing penguins, pretentious performance artists, and even a cameraman who follows him about broadcasting a live video of the proceedings. Aisle-sitters were at a loss in describing the piece (the New York Drama Critics Circle gave the show a "Special Citation"), but most of them recommended it and audiences took their advice for 152 performances.

Lee Blessing's **Eleemosynary** (5-9-89, Manhattan Theatre Club) would enjoy many regional productions before and after its two-week run in New York. The play is a collage of thoughts, telephone conversations, and memories as three generations of women struggle to understand and accept each other. The eccentric grandmother, Dorothea (Eileen Heckart) so dominated her precocious daughter, Artemis (Joanna Gleason), that "Artie" fled as soon as she was old enough. When Artie's daughter, Echo (Jennie Moreau), an equally intelligent and sensitive girl who is a finalist in a national spelling contest, quarrels with her mother, she also leaves home and is brought up by Dorothea. Now that the old woman has suffered a stroke, the three women are brought together and, in a series of exchanges, gain the strength to let go of past estrangements.

The plight of Asian-American actors in the film business was the subject of Philip Kan Gotanda's **Yankee Dawg You Die** (5-14-89, Playwrights Horizons). Bradley Yamashita (Stan Egi) is a young and promising actor, having starred in an art film that made him a symbol of the bold and unstereotypic Asian actor. He arrives in Hollywood, where he meets the older, established character actor Vincent Chang (Sab Shimono), who has worked many years in the business, often playing roles not very complimentary to his race. Although Vincent has the respect of the film community (he was even nominated for an Oscar in the 1950s), the outspoken Bradley sees Vincent as a victim of the old school. But as Bradley finds good Asian roles difficult to come by, he begins to understand the dignified Vincent and the two learn to help each other survive their narrow-minded profession.

Shaw's *Arms and the Man* received a "satisfactory revival" on May 17 by the Roundabout that boasted a splendid Captain Bluntschli by Daniel Gerroll. Roma Downey was his beloved Raina; Christopher North, his rival Sergius Saranoff.

Lewis J. Stadlen was **S. J. Perelman in Person** (5-17-89, Cherry Lane), but he was done in by Bob

Shanks's script, which tried to turn the humorist's short pieces into two hours of theatre. Stadlen was a superb mimic (he had already played Groucho Marx on several occasions), and notices commended him, if not his vehicle.

The season ended with three revivals. The second *Love's Labor's Lost* of the year was the Acting Company's touring version on May 22 at the Marymount Manhattan. On May 30 the same troupe presented Bella and Sam Spewack's Hollywood satire *Boy Meets Girl* (11-27-35), directed by Brian Murray. The Public closed out the schedule with *Cymbeline* on May 31, a "relentlessly jokey" production that JoAnne Akalaitis staged with her usual "perverse" touches. Philip Glass provided the minimalistic music, Ann Hould-Ward dressed the cast in inexplicably Victorian costumes, and the whole enterprise was odd, much talked-about but generally disliked.

1989–1990

Say what you like about the quality of the plays, it certainly was an American season. Only four new British plays opened on Broadway, and only one of them (the star vehicle *Lettice & Lovage*) lasted very long. In contrast, the ten new American works on the Street provided five long runs. Nine of the ten *Best Plays* selections (including musicals) were native works, while American stars (a lot of them movie stars) dominated both new plays and revivals, even British revivals.

The total number of Broadway entries climbed slightly (twenty non-musicals this season), but off-Broadway numbers dropped somewhat: only forty-one new plays (again only four of them British) and eleven revivals. Established American playwrights Terrence McNally, August Wilson, Israel Horovitz, A. R. Gurney, Charles Busch, and others were represented alongside revivals of Arthur Miller and Tennessee Williams.

A heated debate in Congress about the National Endowment for the Arts supporting "obscene" art affected off-and off-off-Broadway companies when groups receiving funds were told that they must sign pledges agreeing to the new precepts of the NEA. Some producers refused to sign, such as Joseph Papp, who returned the $50,000 given to the New York Shakespeare Festival, while others agreed but added "signed under protest" to their signatures. Yet the season had no more or less "sadomasochism, homoeroticism, the sexual exploitation of children, or individuals engaged in sex acts" (the new NEA wording) than recent seasons.

The NEA would not be too thrilled with Terrence McNally's **The Lisbon Traviata** (6-6-89, City Center), a biting comedy that explored the world of "opera queens." Mendy (Nathan Lane) and Stephen (Anthony Heald) are homosexuals obsessed with opera and opera divas, the late Maria Callas in particular. When Mendy finds out that Stephen has a copy of a pirated recording of Callas's Portugal performance as Violetta in *La Traviata*, he asks, teases, begs, and even playfully threatens Stephen to convince him to go to his apartment and get it for him. But Stephen's long-time lover, Mike (Dan Butler), is entertaining his new paramour, Paul (John Slattery), there. Although Stephen jokes about the situation and seems to accept it with an open mind, underneath he is seething with jealousy. In the second act Stephen goes to the apartment, confronts the two men, sends Paul on his way, and then, in a jealous rage, threatens to kill Mike with a pair of scissors. But instead Stephen dissolves in despair and watches Mike move out for good. In an earlier version of the play off-off Broadway, Stephen stabbed Mike to death in grand-opera tradition, but most critics who saw both versions preferred the revised one. All the same, aisle-sitters still had their reservations about the script (though they were unanimous in their praise for Lane), but audiences were not so cautious. The Manhattan Theatre Club mounting ran 128 performances, then reopened on October 31 at the Promenade for another 104 showings.

The young season brought recognition to playwright Donald Margulies, who was considered a "genuinely talented, distinctive voice" and whose **The Loman Family Picnic** (6-20-89, City Center) was called "a bizarre and arresting family portrait" during its two-week run in the Manhattan Theatre Club's second space. Although always on the brink of bankruptcy, Herbie (Larry Block), an eruptive lighting fixture salesman, and his optimistic wife, Doris (Marcia Jean Kurtz), live in an upscale high-rise near Coney Island and put on the facade of a prosperous Jewish family. Their son Stewie (Judd Trichter) is anxiously looking forward to his bar mitzvah for the gifts and money it will bring, while his younger brother, Mitchell (Michael Miceli), is preoccupied with writing a musical version of *Death of a Salesman* for a class project. When the family's financial crisis gets too much for Herbie, he explodes in a tirade, takes Stewie's bar mitzvah money, and storms out. Mitchell reacts by writing a happy ending to his musical, and the play ends by showing four possible versions of what happens when and if Herbie returns.

It was hard to imagine why Alfred Jarry's *Ubu Roi* had caused such an uproar in 1895 judging by the "slipshod bore" of a revival Lincoln Center offered downstairs in the Mitzi E. Newhouse on June 25. Adapted by Larry Sloan and Doug Wright and simply titled *Ubu*, the early absurdist comedy featured Oliver Platt as the scatological king of Poland and Christopher Durang as "Ubu's Conscience." The only intriguing aspect of this misguided mounting was Douglas Stein's setting, a giant tiled bathroom with an oversized drain in the middle of the stage.

Joseph Papp had promised to present stars in his Shakespeare Marathon, so a handful of celebrities appeared on July 6 in *Twelfth Night,* the summer's first outdoor presentation at the Delacorte in Central Park. Michelle Pfeiffer was a tentative Olivia, Gregory Hines did his musical comedy best as Feste, and Jeff Goldblum ate up the scenery as Malvolio. Critics preferred Mary Elizabeth Mastrantonio's Viola and other performances by less stellar actors.

Charles Busch's latest film spoof, **The Lady in Question** (7-25-89, Orpheum), had a grand old time with 1940s B movies in which a damsel in distress manages to outwit the entire Nazi government. As usual, Busch played the heroine, the egocentric concert pianist Gertrude Garnet, who is really tough-talking Gertie from Brooklyn. When an international concert tour puts her in Bavaria as the Nazis are taking over Europe, Gertrude helps an American professor, Erik Maxwell (Arnie Kolodner), to get his wheelchair-bound old mother, the actress Raina Aldric (Meghan Robinson), who has insulted the Nazis, out of Germany even as Gertrude has love affairs with two dashing Aryans. With most critics recommending the stylized parody (several noting that this was the best structured and sustained of Busch's efforts), audiences flocked to it for five months.

The Delacorte's second Shakespeare entry was a "straightforward, if somewhat tame, production" of *Titus Andronicus* on August 17. Director Michael Maggio went easy on the gore and blood but sacrificed much of the play's power by having Donald Moffat play the title Roman in a very quiet and subdued manner. On the other hand, there were sharp and satisfying performances by Kate Mulgrew as evil queen Tamora and Keith David as an unusually strong Aaron.

A. R. Gurney came up with two intriguing characters for his hit attraction **Love Letters** (8-22-89, Promenade): the sober, cowardly politician Andrew Makepeace Ladd III and the free spirit and self-destructive artist Melissa Gardner. In a series of letters between the two, we follow their special friendship from when they were children in 1937 to her suicide nearly fifty years later. While everyone enjoyed *Love Letters*, it was producers nationwide that who fell in love with it. Here was a two-character romantic comedy-drama in which the actors read letters back and forth while sitting at two desks. With so little needed in terms of rehearsal, scenery, costumes, or props, the piece became a veritable gold mine. The original off-Broadway production featured Stockard Channing and John Rubinstein, but they were followed each week by other stars with limited availability but marketable talent. Unanimously favorable reviews and the series of star turns saw to it that *Love Letters* sold out its sixty-four performances off Broadway; it then transferred to the Edison on October 31 and stayed for another ninety-six showings. Dozens of regional productions followed.

On Broadway, Vanessa Redgrave made a rare New York appearance as the diva-like Lady Torrence in Tennessee Williams's *Orpheus Descending* (3-21-57), a revival by Peter Hall that had been a hit in London and (with American actors added to the cast) came to Manhattan's Neil Simon on September 24. The overwrought play was still considered second-rate Williams by most of the press, but there was little disagreement about Redgrave's "radiant performance, albeit a very nutty one," as Linda Winer in *New York Newsday* described it, "with a wild, fugitive kind of brilliance that seems to untame the stage as we watch." Kevin Anderson played the "Orpheus" who has a passionate and destructive affair with the loony lady. Tammy Grimes as a weird spiritualist and Anne Twomey as a wacked-out druggie provided additional color. Box office was brisk for the twelve-week engagement. (The Neil Simon was the old Alvin Theatre recently renamed for the popular playwright.)

Larry Gelbart attempted both political satire and verbal acrobatics in **Mastergate** (10-12-89, Criterion), succeeding somewhat only on the second account in this comedy about a congressional hearing similar to those held concerning the recent Iran-Contra scandal. The IRS has taken over a film studio, Master Pictures Incorporated, because of back taxes. All hell breaks loose when the media gets wind that the CIA used its financing for the movie *Tet, the Motion Picture* to aid rebels in San Elvador. The hearing is supposedly covered by TNN (Total News Network), so audience members could watch the proceedings live or on the the many monitors scattered through the theatre. Characters were stereotypic cartoons with such names as Wylie Slaughter, Major Manley Battle, Merry Chase, and congressmen Byers and Sellers. Gelbart's plot was just an excuse for political or military double talk, but some of the talk was dazzlingly playful. (One senator announced, "We are not looking for hides to skin or goats to scape," while a military commander noted, "Publicity is a small price to pay for secrecy.") The comedy's limited appeal kept it struggling for two months before the hearing was adjourned for good.

Movie star William Hurt came back to his roots off Broadway when the Circle Repertory Company opened its season with Joe Pintauro's **Beside Herself** (10-17-89, Circle). Yet Hurt's role was a supporting one at best, the focus of the play being Mary (Lois Smith), a retired schoolteacher and widow who is visited by three ghosts of her past: bright preteen Mary (Melissa Joan Hart), idealistic twenty-year old Mary (Calista Flockhart), and passionate mid-thirties Mary (Susan Bruce), who yearns to be a poet. The foursome piece together the past (Mary never became a poet; rejected by the man she loved, she married his awful brother and dedicated her life to teaching) and decide to give up on men. Then Augie-Jake (Hurt) enters, the new UPS delivery man. He is vulnerable, shy, and uncouth, and an unlikely romance develops. Aisle-sitters thought more highly of the cast than the script.

Cleavon Little gave one of the finest performances of the Off-Broadway season in **All God's Dangers** (10-22-89, Lamb's), a one-man drama in which he played the elderly African-American Nate Shaw (aka Ned Cobb). Historian Theodore Rosengarten taped a series of interviews with the real Cobb in the 1970s. Those tapes became a book, which was fashioned into a lengthy stage monologue by Rosengarten and Michael and Jennifer Hadley. Working on an Alabama cotton plantation as a boy in the 1920s, Cobb grows up to become a farmer, marries and has nine children, then during the Depression joins the Sharecroppers Union, an action that lands him in jail for twelve years because he would not name other members. Little conveyed Cobb's simple strength of character and wide-eyed wisdom, finding a sincerity in the old man that was missing when he "aged up" for *I'm Not Rappaport* (6-6-85) a few seasons earlier.

David Hare created quite a fuss after his melodrama **The Secret Rapture** (10-26-89, Ethel Barrymore) was dismissed by the critics and closed after twelve performances. He wrote a letter to the *New York Times* calling critic Frank Rich "dishonest" and "irresponsible" and proclaiming the death of serious theatre in New York. Rich had described the play as "pallid" and "an imitation of life," but few of the other notices were any kinder. Isobel Glass (Blair Brown) runs a small-time and very chummy graphics design studio with her obsessive boyfriend, Irwin Posner (Michael Wincott). But their modest happiness is upset when her Tory sister, Marion French (Frances Conroy), Marion's born-again husband, Tom (Stephen Vinovich), and their father's young and drunken widow, Katherine (Mary Beth Hurt), are taken into the business, expanding and depersonalizing it until Isobel walks away rather than be sucked into the soulless, self-absorbed world. But she doesn't walk far, being gunned down by a disappointed Irwin. The survivors, humbled by Isobel's death, become more human as they mourn her.

Another independent business was at risk in Richard Wesley's **The Talented Tenth** (10-29-89, City Center). The title refers to the 10 percent of African Americans who achieve a modicum of success in the U.S.A. Marvin (Richard Gant), educated at Howard University and now manager of a black radio station, feels threatened when the station is sold to white investors. He is also worried over whether they will allow him to use the airwaves to explore sociopolitical issues. The change in management forces Marvin to evaluate his own progress as compared to that of others of his race who never reached his level. The drama, presented by the Manhattan Theatre Club, tended to moralize rather than dramatize and found little approval in the press.

Israel Horovitz's **The Widow's Blind Date** (11-7-89, Circle in the Square Downtown) recalled some of the gripping tension that had brought this playwright to the public's attention with *The Indian Wants the Bronx* (1-17-68) two decades earlier. Margy Burke (Christine Estabrook), a recognized literary critic who has recently been widowed, returns to her hometown of Wakefield, Massachusetts, to see her blind brother, who is dying. But she makes a point of stopping at the local wastepaper baling plant where two of her high school classmates work. Archie Crisp (Paul O'Brien) and George Ferguson (Tom Bloom) are blue-collar workers who escape from their dead-end jobs by bragging to each other about their many sexual conquests. Margy is soon taunting the two men for their useless lives, enumerating her many accomplishments, then bringing up an ugly incident in their past: Margy was gang-raped by George, Archie, her own brother, and other guys during their senior class celebration. The two men try to explain their behavior ("nobody planned it...it just happened...everybody liked you"), but Margy grows more and more vindictive and ultimately violent, exacting her revenge on the two men. Some reviews were highly complimentary ("packs a wallop that few plays will be able to equal"), but the drama lasted only forty showings and was rarely produced thereafter.

Not to be put at a disadvantage by the Public's Shakespeare Marathon, the Roundabout Theatre opened its season on November 14 with *The Tempest*, which boasted a young and fiery Prospero in the person of Frank Langella. Also admirable was B. D. Wong, who played Ariel as a cautious, quiet, catlike presence rather than the usual whirlwind spirit. Little else in the revival, reset in the eighteenth century, found favor.

A "crackling good" courtroom drama, **A Few Good Men** (11-15-89, Music Box) by Aaron Sorkin, entertained audiences for 497 performances. At a U.S. military base on Guantánamo Bay in Cuba, a young marine dies when two fellow soldiers discipline him for his slovenly ways and poor attitude. The seemingly open-and-shut case is given to Navy Lieutenant Daniel Kaffee (Tom Hulce), a young lawyer known for his love of baseball and for plea-bargaining his way through his military tour of duty. Bound by a silent code of honor, the accused men refuse to speak. But with the help of astute Lieutenant Commander Joanne Galloway (Megan Gallagher), Kaffee discovers that the illegal reprimand (a marine tradition unofficially known as a "Code Red") was ordered by the base commander, Lieutenant Colonel Nathan Jessep (Stephen Lang), who has covered his tracks by fabricating orders that he tried to transfer the youth before he died. Testimony mounts in the courtroom until Jessep admits his guilt, and the two defendants are found innocent but receive dishonorable discharges. Don Scardino directed his large cast with an ear for the script's crisp dialogue and wry humor.

The three British stars of Broadway's revival of W. Somerset Maugham's *The Circle* (9-12-21) on November 20 at the Ambassador seemed older than the drawing room comedy itself, but Rex Harrison, Glynis Johns, and Stewart Granger (in his American stage debut) managed not only to keep breathing but to breathe life into the old-fashioned piece for 208 performances. Harrison (finally knighted the previous June at the age of eighty-one) had announced that this would be his valedictory performance, but many did not believe him. Alas, it was; he died the next year.

Moviemaking in the Golden Age was explored from a nightmarish point of view in Peter Par-nell's **Hyde in Hollywood** (11-29-89, American Place) which Playwrights Horizons offered for two weeks. Julian Hyde (Robert Joy) is an Orson Welles–like actor-director whose homosexuality is discovered by gossip columnist "Hollywood Confidential" (Keith Szarabajka). When the journalist promises not to reveal Hyde's secret if he supplies him with juicy gossip about his fellow filmmakers, Hyde agrees but gets even by making a *Citizen Kane*–like film with a thinly disguised gossip columnist as its central character. Parnell slammed Hollywood's hypocrisy in which Jews, gays, and leftists must be kept both from the public and out of the films they watch. Over the years the satire developed a small cult following despite its initial mixed reviews.

Tom Stoppard's newest offering, **Artist Descending a Staircase** (11-30-89, Helen Hayes), originally a radio play, was clever and complicated; so clever and complicated, in fact, that audiences stayed away despite generally favorable reviews that decreed it "a feast of tricky, eloquent charm" and "a play of shining wit, gleaming intelligence, and glintingly metallic heart." Like Marcel Duchamp's painting *Nude Descending a Staircase*, which shows many parts of one movement, the play's events are seen in various stages rather than in a complete whole. When Donner (John McMartin), an old artist, falls down a staircase in his studio in 1972 and dies, his fellow avant-garde artists Beauchamp (Harold Gould) and Martello (Paxton Whitehead) suspect each other of pushing him to his death. Eleven scenes follow, going backward to 1914 and then forward to 1972 again, each one giving more information about the trio of artists and their feuding over Sophie (Stephanie Roth), the love of their lives, who went blind and then committed suicide. (The artists as youths were played by Michael Winther, Michael Cumpsty, and Jim Fyfe.) A good deal of talk about art and love proved highly entertaining but not very involving. The unusual play lasted only a month in the small house.

Lucifer raised his satanic head in three different plays within a week, all at Lincoln Center. A double bill entitled **Oh, Hell** (12-3-89, Mitzi E. Newhouse) featured Shel Silverstein's **The Devil and Billy Markham** and David Mamet's **Bobby Gould in Hell** for a month. Silverstein's sixty-minute monologue is a ballad of rhymed couplets, sometimes sung, mostly spoken, about Nashville guitarist Billy Markham (rock singer Dennis Locorriere in his acting debut), who sells his soul to the devil for fame and fortune, then outwits Old Scratch by swapping souls with his wife, the girl the devil is planning on marrying. In the second play, Hollywood huckster Bobby Gould (Treat Williams), a character from Mamet's *Speed-the-Plow* (5-3-88), dies and must face Interrogator (W. H. Macy), a preoccupied Lucifer who would rather be fishing. Gould tries to defend himself, but his ex-girlfriend Glenna (Felicity Huffman) enters and testifies how shabbily Bobby treated her. Soon Glenna proves to be a young she-dragon and even turns on Interrogator, asking "Have you ever thought about counseling?" The men band together to dispose of Glenna, but still Gould is damned for being "cruel without being interesting." Gregory Mosher's direction elicited "fiendish fun" from the two works, though most critics preferred Mamet's piece. Upstairs in the Vivian Beaumont, Paddy Chayevsky's *The Tenth Man* (11-5-59), about members of a Long Island synagogue trying to exorcise a young girl (Phoebe Cates) possessed by the devil, was revived on December 10. Most commentators felt that talents such as Bob Dishy, Jack Weston, Joseph Wiseman, Ron Rifkin, and Peter Friedman were wasted in an overwrought drama.

An unlikely hit provided one of the season's most mesmerizing performances. Jay Presson Allen's one-man play **Tru** (12-14-Booth) gave musical comedy star Robert Morse a tour de force as the famous author-celebrity Truman Capote. Allen's script showed Capote in his sleek Manhattan apartment during the 1975 Christmas season, when many of his friends had abandoned him because of what he wrote about them in an *Esquire* article. Morse impishly captured Capote, "from the gurgling voice to the peremptory manner." But, as Rich noted, "he also manages to make him surprisingly poignant . . . makes us see, through the meanspiritedness and vanity, a Little Boy Lost." Whether dishing gossip on the phone or letting his guard down and confessing his insecurities, Morse created with *Tru* that rarity: "a celebrity profile/interview" that worked as theatre. The comic actor, who was recovering from a seventeen-year slump in his career, won a Tony Award and repeated his vivid performance 295 times before setting out on tour.

Athol Fugard attacked apartheid head-on in **My Children! My Africa!** (12-18-89, Perry Street) rather than letting it serve as the background as he had in most of his other works. Mr. Myalatya (John Kani), nicknamed "Mr. M," a humble but dedicated teacher in a small segregated South African town, tries to battle the system through the education of his people. He teams his prize student, Thami Mbikwana (Courtney B. Vance), with the liberal white girl Isobel Dyson (the play-

wright's daughter Lisa Fugard) to compete in an inter-school literature tournament. But Thami soon grows more revolutionary, rejects Mr. M's pacifist ideas, and joins a radical group of blacks boycotting the school system. Mr. M tries to help by cooperating with the police, but he is branded an informer by Thami's cohorts and is murdered in his classroom. Raves for the cast and notices calling the script "a play of the most magnificently marshaled passion" helped keep business healthy during the one-month engagement and secured future productions in regional theatres.

Peter Hall's second production of the season, his London revival of *The Merchant of Venice* with Dustin Hoffman as Shylock, opened on December 19 at the 46th Street and did boffo business for eighty-one performances. Unlike *Orpheus Descending*, the star did not dominate the production, since the role was not as large. Rather, Hoffman played the moneylender as "a character actor's polished gem rather than a tragedian's stab at the jugular." Aisle-sitters took kindly to Hoffman's Shakespearean debut, and the British cast was also applauded: Geraldine James's tart and intelligent Portia, Leigh Lawson's affecting Antonio, Nathaniel Parker's passionate Bassanio, and Michael Siberry's clownish but dangerous Gratiano.

Even though it was a British work, Nick Dear's **The Art of Success** (12-20-89, City Center) had parallels to the current National Endowment for the Arts controversy in America. Famous painter William Hogarth (Tim Curry) and celebrated author Henry Fielding (Nicholas Woodeson) are having their own trouble with state funding in 1730 London. Hogarth must put aside his artistic principles and appease government leader Robert Walpole (Daniel Benzali) in order to get his copyright legislation passed. Fielding, on the other hand, has ridiculed Walpole in his plays and is driven out of the theatre by the powerful statesman. The three leads received expert support from Mary-Louise Parker and Suzanne Bertish, but the play still deteriorated into smug sermonizing rather than engrossing drama. Ultz's setting was certainly one of the season's most unusual: an acting platform covered with white paper and surrounded by straw and excrement. Brit Adrian Noble staged the Manhattan Theatre Club mounting, which ran seven weeks.

Charles Fuller's saga of post–Civil War blacks continued with **We, Part III: Jonquil** (1-11-90, Theatre Four), which the Negro Ensemble Company presented for a month. The ex-slave Sally (Iris Little), who appeared in earlier portions of the cycle, is raped by three Ku Klux Klan members, but their identity is unknown until the blind woman Jonquil (Cynthia Bond) recognizes the voice of one of the men as that of Judge Bridges (William Mooney). Sally's politically active husband, Calvin (Charles Weldon), forms a black militia to bring the judge to justice, but the attack turns tragic on both sides. The "sometimes awkward, sometimes murky play" was more notable for its skillful performances than its writing.

Raul Julia essayed the lead in the Public's *Macbeth* on January 16 at the Anspacher, and his was the only performance approved of by the press. Richard Jordon's mounting languished "without the supernatural, without tragedy, without horror, without spirit." More lively was Shaw's *The Doctor's Dilemma*, which the Roundabout revived on January 25. The crucial role of Jennifer Dubedat, who must rationally appeal to the physicians to save her artist-husband, was miscast with an unconvincing Anne Newhall, but the doctors themselves (Charles Keating, Jerome Kilty, George Hall, and Victor Raider-Wexler) were right on target and brought the Shavian dialogue to life. That same night, the first of the season's two *King Lear* productions opened, this one an off-off-Broadway curiosity by Mabou Mines at the Triplex Performing Arts Center. Lee Breuer's free adaptation, simply called *Lear*, set in the American South of the 1950s, featured a female monarch (Ruth Maleczech) with three sons. Such odd touches as Lear dividing her kingdom by cutting up a birthday cake during a backyard barbecue or actors playing crucial scenes on a miniature golf course evoked widely disparate reactions. As Melanie Kirkpatrick in the *Wall Street Journal* suggested, "it should have been called *Lear on a Hot Tin Roof.*"

Two plays this season offered insight into the "Queen of the Harlem Renaissance," **Zora Neale Hurston** (2-4-90, American Place). Elizabeth Van Dyke played the black author whose writing about the South made her a creative force in the 1920s and 1930s. From her youth in Alabama to her success in Manhattan to her downfall (she was accused of molesting a ten-year-old boy, but the case never got to court) and final days working as a maid in Florida, Hurston's story was ripe for the theatre, and Laurence Holder's script managed to pack an awful lot into the two-person play. (Tim Johnson played fellow writers Richard Wright and Langston Hughes, as well as others in her life.)

An oddball offering by Peter Hedges called **Imagining Brad** (2-6-90, Circle) intrigued some aisle-sitters with its disturbing dark humor. After church one Sunday, Dana Sue Kaye (Sharon Erns-

ter), a talky Nashville bleached blonde with several bruises from a car accident, meets Valerie (Erin Cressida Wilson), who has just moved to Tennessee with her husband, Brad. While Dana Sue brags about her spouse—her high school sweetheart, who is still "the best looking man in Tennessee"—Valerie is secretive about Brad. But it turns out Dana Sue's bruises are from her abusive husband, while Brad is a blind, armless, legless, bedridden "bag of flesh" Valerie has to care for around the clock. Yet Dana Sue sees such a "freak" as an ideal husband and considers moving in with them when Valerie offers a sanctuary from her brutish husband. The evening opened with a curtain raiser, *The Valerie of Now*, that showed teenager Valerie (Melissa Joan Hart), having been sexually molested by her father, dealing with her upcoming birthday party and her first menstrual period. The double bill was directed by beginner Joe Mantello, who would stage better scripts in the near future.

Eric Bogosian's latest monologue, **Sex, Drugs, Rock & Roll** (2-8-90, Orpheum), was his "funniest and scariest yet" but also his most satisfying and well-sustained theatre piece. Notices along the lines of "spiky, stinging, caustic without being cauterizing" widened Bogosian's audience, and he repeated the solo turn 103 times. Twelve characters from divergent walks of life were featured, most memorably a strangely coherent panhandler in a subway station, a hungover boozer who describes a stag party that turned into a sex orgy and a violent run-in with Hell's Angels, a wheeler-dealer on the phone who balances several phony conversations at a time, a convict who philosophizes about God in a down-and-dirty manner, and an ex-addict rock star on a TV talk show explaining how he kicked the habit and now gives his money to Amazon Indians (all the time he is still romanticizing about drugs).

Richard Nelson, an American playwright who lived now in England, where most of his plays premiered, took aim at his native countrymen in **Some Americans Abroad** (2-11-90, Mitzi E. Newhouse). A group of American professors and their wives and students take a grand tour of theatre centers in England, reveling in their Anglophile superiority and disgusted by all the gauche Americans who insist on seeing theatre in Great Britain. Within the group, petty hostilities rage, and one professor finds out he is to be replaced once he returns home. Some critics saw the piece as a "witty and erudite" comedy of manners, others as mere carping. Alexandra Byrne's setting was as coy as the characters: pieces of furniture hung from above, descended for particular scenes, then, when finished, were hoisted up into the air again to dangle over the action. Box office was strong enough that, after eighty-one showings, Lincoln Center moved the play on May 2 upstairs to the larger Vivian Beaumont, where it stayed another sixty-two performances.

An off-off-Broadway entry that created some interest (and earned a seven-week run) because of the stars involved was Steve Tesich's futuristic fable **Square One** (2-22-90, Second Stage). In a totalitarian state of Orwell-like temperament, "Artist Third Class" Adam (Richard Thomas) is the singing host of the "Patriotic Variety Hour" on TV. He falls in love with Dianne (Dianne Wiest), a dippy freethinker who wishes to escape from her small apartment filled with elderly relatives. So they wed, but soon Dianne finds living in government-sponsored housing for artists as stifling as her former prison, and Adam's complacency as he struggles to become a Second Class entertainer leaves her cold. She rebels against the suffocating system and is taken away by the state, her husband afraid to save her. Notices for the script varied, but the performers and Jerry Zaks's cockeyed direction were applauded. Tony Walton highlighted his purposely sterile setting with oversized toys ironically grinning in the background, while Paul Gallo's evocative lighting created an oppressive world, especially at the end when it "delicately wraps Mr. Thomas in incriminating forlorn shadows."

Martin Sherman, another American author situated in England, saw his London hit **When She Danced** (2-19-90, Playwrights Horizons) play off Broadway for a month with Elizabeth Ashley in the role that Vanessa Redgrave had created in London. In 1923 the eccentric dancer Isadora Duncan (Ashley) is approaching retirement age and worries how she is going to finance her dream of opening a dance school in Italy. She lives in a Paris salon with her Russian poet-husband, Sergei Essenine (Jonathan Walker), a bunch of artistic hangers-on, and Miss Belzer (Marcia Jean Kurtz), an interpreter on hand because Isadora doesn't know a word of Russian. Isadora, Sergei, and friends are as flamboyant as Miss Belzer is quiet and untalented, yet the mousy lady later reveals her deep feelings about art. The plot centered on the bohemians trying to act bourgeois at a dinner party for stuffy people with money, a situation not unlike *You Can't Take It with You* (12-14-36). The lobster-champagne affair becomes a farcical Tower of Babel as international guests misinterpret what is said, Sergei announces (not for the first time) that he will commit suicide,

and the party dissolves into a food fight. Colorful performances often outshone a lightweight script but most reviews were favorable.

We, Part IV: Burner's Frolic (2-25-90, Theatre Four) was generally thought to be the best installment yet in Charles Fuller's post–Civil War saga. Burner (Adam Wade) is the leader of a group of black businessmen in 1876 who hope to have a greater voice in the politics of their Virginia city. When Burner runs for office, white supremacists burn his land. The black group (they call themselves the Frolic) then finds itself broken into various factions over what course of action should be taken next, especially when white politicians try to bribe their members into voting for their candidate.

For two months no play or musical opened on Broadway, a sorry demonstration of Broadway's dwindling numbers. When one did arrive, it was a short-lived revival of *Miss Margarida's Way* (7-31-77) on February 15 at the Helen Hayes. Playwright Roberto Athayde directed Estelle Parsons (who originated the role off Broadway) as the tyrannical teacher who bullies her eighth-grade students in a fascist manner. While Parsons's quicksilver performance again won plaudits, this time around critics found the play dated, obvious, and lacking bite. The comedy was withdrawn after eleven showings. It was nearly another month before anything else arrived on Broadway, and again it was a revival, but this time a hit with 149 packed performances. With its $2 million advance and film star Kathleen Turner heading the cast, Tennessee Williams's *Cat on a Hot Tin Roof* (3-24-55) opened on March 12 at the Eugene O'Neill. British director Howard Davies used Williams's original script (before Elia Kazan insisted on changes) with its less sentimental ending, and William Dudley provided a naturalistic set (complete with console television set) in place of Jo Mielziner's surreal original. While some critics thought Turner's Maggie was too tough, most agreed with Clive Barnes in the *New York Post* when he described her as "mocking yet fearful, sassily funny yet itchy with desires that go beyond sex." Although Big Daddy no longer appeared in the third act, Charles Durning's Tony Award–winning portrayal was lauded for its bluster, while Daniel Hugh Kelly was commended for his understated, seething Brick. Polly Holliday's fussy yet tragic Big Mama completed the stellar lineup.

Elizabeth Page's "illogical" comedy **Spare Parts** (3-12-90, Circle in the Square Downtown), one of Off Broadway's few commercial entries this season, folded in a month. Lois (Robin Groves) and Jax (Donna Haley), a lesbian couple, want to raise a child, so they arrange for Lois to have a fling with unwitting college student Henry (Stephen Hamilton). But Henry is smitten with Lois, so, along with their gay friend Perry (Reed Birney), they all settle down together as one big happy family.

A one-person show that was neither historical nor about great social issues was **A Mom's Life** (3-13-90, Public: Shiva), Kathryn Grody's free-wheeling monologue about raising children on the Upper West Side of Manhattan. The autobiographical piece was filled with humor and insight, illustrating how an adult reverts to childish behavior when so much of one's adult life is preoccupied with kids. The program ran six weeks; a decade later Grody brought it back to Off Broadway with an updated perspective.

Craig Lucas (and the Circle Rep) finally had a hit with his "charming and highly original fantasy comedy" **Prelude to a Kiss** (3-14-90, Circle). Peter (Alec Baldwin) and Rita (Mary-Louise Parker) get married after a six-week courtship filled with passion and mutual understanding. But an odd thing happens at their wedding reception: an uninvited Old Man (Barnard Hughes) goes up to the bride and gives her a kiss. From that point on Rita is different, easily forgetting things and acting morose and moody. Peter runs from her and seeks out the Old Man, who, it turns out, behaves like the vibrant and funny Rita he once knew. It seems the Old Man is terminally ill and his kiss has caused him and Rita, unknowingly, to exchange bodies. After some difficulty, Peter comes to love "Rita" again even though she is in the failing body of the Old Man. Such commitment reverses the strange spell, and Peter and the true Rita are reunited. The off-Broadway run sold out so the play (with Timothy Hutton now as Peter) transferred on May 1 to the Helen Hayes, where it played 440 performances.

Two revivals from the 1970s received contrasting receptions. Terrence McNally's *Bad Habits* (2-4-74), revived by the Manhattan Theatre Club on March 20 at the City Center, had not stood the test of time. What had once seemed shocking and satirical now appeared silly and oafish. Nathan Lane, Faith Prince, and Kate Nelligan led a formidable cast, to no avail. The next night Alec McCowen brought his recitation piece *St. Mark's Gospel* (9-7-78) to the Lamb's and once again amazed critics and audiences for three weeks.

Playwright-director Frank Galati adapted and staged John Steinbeck's novel **The Grapes of Wrath** (3-22-90, Cort), winning a Tony Award for each effort. Originating at Chicago's Steppenwolf Theatre, this earthy and captivating version was perfectly suited to the gritty kind of acting at which the company excelled. Lois Smith was the indomitable Ma Joad, Gary Sinise was her ex-con son, Tom, and Terry Kinney was the preacher, Casey, the conscience of the epic tale about destitute "Oakies" who seek a new life in California. Presented simply on a planked stage with the Joads' overflowing truck as the visual focal point, the play allowed the powerful story to speak for itself without gimmicks or artsy flourishes. Despite some glowing notices (and the two Tonys), the drama only lasted 188 performances on Broadway.

Peter Shaffer's plays always provided marvelous acting opportunities, but most critics felt his latest effort, the London hit **Lettice & Lovage** (3-25-90, Ethel Barrymore), was not much more than a vehicle for Maggie Smith. The eccentric and imaginative Lettice Douffet (Smith) works as a tour guide at Fustian House, a stately home run by the Preservation Trust, where she embellishes the mansion's dull history with anecdotes and tidbits of history that never happened. Regional supervisor Lotte Schoen (Margaret Tyzack), a stern and humorless woman, learns of Lettice's theatrics and sacks her. Unable to find work, Lettice sinks into an impoverished (though still imaginative) life. Lotte hears of her plight and visits Lettice, and the two very different women find an odd but comforting friendship together. Soon Lotte has come out of her shell and the two ladies are reenacting scenes from history and protesting ugly new architecture in budding London developments. (In the London version they actually plan to bomb certain buildings, but Shaffer revised the script for New York.) While there were many reservations about the script, Smith was considered a show in herself, rhapsodizing over the details of Elizabethan cuisine or dramatically revealing a bright red dress of martyrdom when she loses her job. Both she and Tyzack won Tony Awards, keeping the comedy afloat for 284 performances.

Aaron Sorkin, whose *A Few Good Men* was thriving on Broadway, had a one-week flop off Broadway with **Making Movies** (3-27-90, Promenade), yet another play this season about filmmakers. At a script conference, a film director (Michael Countryman), screenwriter (David Marshall Grant), and producer (Sharon Schlarth) argue over their upcoming film epic, putting ego before everything else but claiming to be fighting for their art. Later the threesome go on location to a farm outside Schenectady where they attempt to film 150 marines charging down a hill at sunset, only to have three cows wander onto the scene. With the sun gone and money for retakes out of the question, the filmmakers put their heads together to figure out aesthetic reasons for the cows being in the movie's climax.

Critics continued to complain about the dreadful acoustics in the Roundabout's Yegen Theatre. Otherwise its revival of Arthur Miller's *The Crucible* (1-22-53) on March 29 was commended for its succinct direction by Gerald Freedman and its potent performances by Randle Mell and Harriet Harris as the Proctors, Justine Bateman as the accusing Abigail, and Vicki Lewis as Mary Warren, the girl torn between the two factions.

William O. Douglas's very active life was examined in Scott Douglas's **Mountain** (4-5-90, Lucille Lortel) with Len Cariou as the controversial Supreme Court justice. As Douglas lies dying in 1980, he recalls events from his past eighty-one years. A youth stricken with polio, Douglas climbed the Cascades to build up strength. As an adult he rose to become chairman of the Securities and Exchange Commission, where he battled corrupt Wall Streeters. Appointed by FDR to the Supreme Court, he stayed there thirty-six years, fighting two impeachment attempts and making bold decisions regarding civil rights, economics, and nature conservation. Also recalled were his four marriages and many mountain-climbing expeditions (including Mount Everest). John C. Vennema and Heather Summerhayes played all the other people Douglas encountered, but it was Cariou's commanding performance that propelled the play. Critics found the evening "powerful [and] thought-provoking" even though the script "was to be valued more for the information it conveyed than for drama."

The Negro Ensemble's short season ended with Gus Edwards's **Lifetimes on the Streets** (4-8-90, Theatre Four), a self-described "theatrical collage" made up of monologues by various characters on the streets of Harlem accompanied by a solo saxophone player. A woman (Peggy Alston) drifts into a bittersweet romance with a painter, an old man (Douglas Turner Ward) complains about the cold and explains how a new ice age has come to Harlem, a subway panhandler (O. L. Duke) goes up and down the aisles, badgering audience members, and a well-dressed man (Charles Brown) tries to work up the courage to go into a porn movie theatre. The montage program struck some critics as very satisfying, and audiences checked it out for seven weeks.

Added to August Wilson's usual flair for poetic vernacular and incisive characterization was a disquieting sense of mystery in **The Piano Lesson** (4-16-90, Walter Kerr), his fourth play in a series covering African Americans throughout the century. Berniece (S. Epatha Merkerson), a widow raising her young daughter, Maretha (Apryl R. Foster), in Pittsburgh in 1936, is half owner of an antique piano handed down in her family for generations. Dealers have offered to buy the piano at a high price because of the unique carvings in the woodwork depicting family members and their rise from slavery. But Berniece sees the piano as her family heritage and refuses to part with it, even when her brother, Boy Willie (Charles S. Dutton), drives up from the South to claim his half ownership of the valuable piano. Boy Willie is a loudmouthed dreamer, overflowing with optimism. He arrives with a truckful of watermelons that he sells to the rich folks in Pittsburgh's upper-class neighborhoods. But that is not enough money for him to buy the farm back home where his ancestors once worked as slaves. He wants Berniece to sell the piano (he has a dealer willing to pay $1,000), and he even tries to physically move it against her wishes. But a strange and haunting force, the ghost of the family's slaveowner, enters the house and battles Boy Willie. He is only kept from destroying Boy Willie by Berniece's going to the piano and playing a hymn that frightens the spirit away. The play was rich with memorable supporting characters: Boy Willie's friend Lymon (Rocky Carroll), who courts Berniece; the uncles Doaker (Carl Gordon) and Wining Boy (Lou Myers), who are living (and singing) scrapbooks of the past; and Berniece's preacher fiancé, Avery (Tommy Hollis), whose dreams of starting his own church are as fervent as Boy Willie's. Lloyd Richard's sensitive direction, a superior cast (Dutton was especially applauded), and Wilson's lyrical script were all praised, the drama winning the Pulitzer Prize and the New York Drama Critics Circle Award. It stayed on the boards for 329 performances. (The Walter Kerr was the old Ritz Theatre renamed this season for the much-respected theatre critic.)

Václav Havel, a playwright imprisoned in 1985 for his writing but recently released and made president of his native Czechoslovakia, was celebrated with two one-act revivals under the umbrella title **By and for Havel** (4-17-90, John

Houseman). Havel's autobiographical *Audience*, which was called *The Interview* in its American premiere (11-20-83), featured Lou Brockway as a dissident writer forced to work in a brewery and Kevin O'Connor as the boss who tries to bribe him to spy on fellow workers. Samuel Beckett's *Catastrophe* (6-15-83), which the author had dedicated to Havel in 1982, showed O'Connor and Evelyn Tuths as inquisitors trying to turn a mute artist (Brockway) into a propaganda figure for a totalitarian state. Some commentators found fault with Vasek C. Simek's direction, but the performances were strong, so audiences gladly attended the political pieces for 256 performances. (Beckett had died the previous December, one week before Havel became president.)

Zora Neale Hurston's second appearance this season was **Spunk** (4-18-90, Public: Martinson), a dramatization of three of her short stories. George C. Wolfe wrote and directed the playlets, which were punctuated with songs by Chick Street Man and used the "story theatre" technique of having characters serve as their own narrators. In *Sweat*, Delia (Danitra Vance), a young woman who works as a laundress, learns to overcome past abuses by her estranged husband, Sykes (Reggie Montgomery), who stomps all over the white people's clothes that fill her apartment. *Story in Harlem Slang* depicted two egotistical men, Jelly (K. Todd Freeman) and Slang Talk Man (Kevin Jackson), who boast of their romantic conquests and fight over a working girl (Vance) to gain her affection and a free meal. *The Guilded Six Bits* concerned adoring husband Joe (Jackson), who is betrayed by his seemingly sweet wife, Missy May (Vance), but her guilt over her brief infidelity brings the couple back together again. With reviews calling it "sophisticated, satirical, seriously funny," the lyrical program ran 165 performances.

Broadway's only thriller this season, Rupert Holmes's **Accomplice** (4-26-90, Richard Rodgers), was like most such genre offerings of late: more of a spoof than a thriller and more of a flop than a hit. In a cliché-ridden English country house (designed with playfulness by David Jenkins with a convenient mill wheel inside), a wife and her lover plan and carry out the murder of her husband. But what we are watching is a West End play on its out-of-town tryout tour. In reality the husband is the production's playwright and director, and he plans the murder of his real wife (the thriller's leading lady) so that he can run off with the show's leading man. Similar twists followed, including a mystery character from the audience, until the reversals had the audience's heads spinning. To maintain the confusion, no characters were listed in the program, but Jason Alexander, Natalia Nogulich, Michael McKean, and Pamela Brüll played the different combinations of couples, hetero- and homosexual. (The mystery character turns out to be the playwright himself, and Holmes coyly took a curtain call with the cast.) Although it had been well received at California's Pasadena Playhouse, New York critics called it "a little too generic," "incomprehensible," and "increasingly convoluted." The thriller hung on for fifty-two performances. (The Richard Rodgers was the old 46th Street Theatre, the third Broadway house this season renamed for a prestigious theatre figure.)

The season's second *King Lear*, on April 2 at BAM's Majestic for five showings, came from the Russian Georgian Rustaveli Theatre Company and was performed in Georgian with simultaneous translation via headsets for audience members.

The Public and London's Royal Court joined forces for another Caryl Churchill work, this one a double bill called **Ice Cream With Hot Fudge** (5-3-90, Newman), which continued with themes explored in her earlier *Serious Money* (12-3-87). The curtain raiser, *Hot Fudge*, showed two conniving couples who have lucrative careers defrauding banks and pulling off real estate swindles. (The title "fudge" was an expression for lying.) The bulk of the evening consisted of *Ice Cream*, a dark comedy about two Anglophile Americans, Lance (James Rebhorn) and Vera (Jane Kaczmarek), who travel to England to find Lance's third cousins. What they discover is the low-class, rootless Phil (Robert Knepper) and his sister, Jaq (Julianne Moore). Phil gets in an argument, shoots his landlord, and then has his American relatives help bury the body. Later the couple visit America, where Phil is run over by a car, and Jaq sets off in Lance's car to see the country, spending all her money and pushing a college professor off a cliff before returning to Vera and demanding money to go back to England. Churchill's trademark "overlapping speeches, startling imagery, [and] breathtaking theatrical swiftness" were in evidence, but much of the press considered the program "as empty as a vacuous vacuum" and "a livid, nasty piece of work."

Kevin Kline, who had played Hamlet at the Public four years earlier, returned to the role and directed the Shakespeare Marathon's *Hamlet* on

May 8 at the Anspacher, winning enthusiastic applause for both tasks. Kline's modern-dress production emphasized language and characters over showy theatrical business, and his shining performance ("youthful yet not childlike, verging on real maturity but not quite there yet") was the centerpiece of a superior cast. Brian Murray (Claudius), Dana Ivey (Gertrude), Diane Venora (Ophelia), and, in particular, Josef Sommer (Polonius) were all cheered.

Two nights later Mikhail Bulgakov's 1926 satire **Zoya's Apartment** (5-10-90, Circle in the Square), which New Yorkers had only seen in a short run off-off Broadway in 1978, arrived on Broadway. Zoya Denisova Peltz (Linda Thorson) runs a Moscow brothel disguised as a dress shop and dreams of running off to Paris. When the police raid one of her "fashion shows," Zoya's apartment is smashed up, as well as her dreams of escape. Reviewers complained of Boris A. Morozov's stodgy direction as well as Nicholas Saunders and Frank Dwyer's awkward new English translation, but they admitted there might be a worthwhile play hidden somewhere. The "well-meaning botch" lingered for forty-five showings.

John Ford Noonan wrote and performed in his two-character comedy **Talking Things Over with Chekhov** (5-10-90, Actors' Playhouse), which amused if not enthralled audiences for two months. Jeremy (Noonan), a fledgling playwright who has imaginary conversations with his idol Anton Chekhov, is finally going to have one of his plays produced, and his girlfriend, Marlene (Diane Salinger), is slated to star in it. Once rehearsals start and Jeremy's script is torn apart by the powers that be, he despairs and hires someone to kill him. But the attempted hit does not succeed, nor does the play. The critics rip the script apart as they extol Marlene, declaring her much better than her feeble vehicle.

Actual critics could find little good to say ("objectionable, as opposed to merely tedious") about Ivan Menchell's sentimental comedy-drama **The Cemetery Club** (5-15-90, Brooks Atkinson), but after its seven-week run on Broadway it frequently popped up in community theatres. Three Jewish widows from Queens meet monthly to have tea and visit their husbands' graves in nearby Forest Hills Cemetery. Ida (Elizabeth Franz), who like the other women is only in her fifties, is tempted to forgo the monthly ritual and try to move ahead with her life, but Doris (Doris Belack), very solemn and stubborn, refuses to let go of the past. The live wire in the trio is Lucille (Eileen Heckart), who is enjoying spending her late husband's money and bragging about all the hot dates she has. Yet when Ida becomes involved with Sam (Lee Wallace), a gentle widower who is a butcher by profession, both Lucille and Doris do everything to discourage the budding romance. Following a fiery confrontation among the three women, Ida quietly dies in her sleep. The surviving widows are left to question their selfish behavior.

1990–1991

Looking at the numbers, it seemed to be a dismal season for New York theatre. Only twelve new plays opened on Broadway (nine of them American) and forty-four off Broadway (all but four native works). Astonishingly, only one non-musical revival was seen on the Street and a mere fifteen off. Attendance dropped an alarming 9 per cent on Broadway, much of the blame being put on the war in the Persian Gulf, which kept patrons home that winter watching coverage on CNN-TV.

But numbers rarely indicate quality, and there were some superior plays this season. American playwrights John Guare and Neil Simon were in top form with *Six Degrees of Separation* and *Lost in Yonkers*, each entry arguably the finest of their careers. On the other hand, established playwrights Arthur Kopit, Michael Weller, Sam Shepard, Jules Feiffer, Beth Henley, and William Gibson stumbled, and only up-and-coming Jon Robin Baitz and Richard Greenberg were able to fill the void.

Thirteen one-person plays this season underscored the suffocating economics of producing. Only three of these were on Broadway; even Off Broadway was responding to the need to keep production costs down. Particularly damaging to non-profit groups both on and off the Street was a proposed 56 percent cut in the New York State Council on the Arts budget. Protests by arts groups helped restore some of the cuts, but the need to economize did not disappear. Similar protests helped repeal the requirement that groups sign a pledge of decency in order to secure money from the National Endowment for the Arts. Still, optimism did not run high this season.

The Manhattan Theatre Club continued its tradition of presenting new British works in American premieres with Andrew Davies's **Prin** (6-6-90, City Center), a play similar to Simon Gray's *Butley* (10-31-72) in that the title character in each is a gay teacher whose love life and career are both shattered in the course of a day. Prin (Eileen Atkins) is "principal" of a small teachers' college in Britain, but she runs it as strictly and pompously as if it were a world-class university. Demanding, insensitive, and egocentric, Prin is feared but not respected. Her shy lover, Dibs (Amy Wright), wants to leave her for a science teacher, Dr. Boyle (John Curless), but cannot bring herself to confront the formidable Prin. When the college's board decides to merge with a local polytechnic, Prin is reduced from leader to mere faculty member, and Dibs quietly abandons Prin to her lofty but cold ideals. Reviewers disagreed about the script, but all took kindly to Atkins's arrogant yet funny characterization.

Jules Feiffer once again offered an intriguing but unsatisfying look at contemporary life with **Elliot Loves** (6-7-90, Promenade), which satirically examined the gap between the sexes. Elliot (Anthony Heald) has been dating Joanna (Christine Baranski), a twice-divorced real estate broker, for six weeks, so he feels it is time she meets his three closest friends from high school: fussy accountant Phil (David Pierce), slob entrepreneur Larry (Oliver Platt), and black yuppie Bobby (Bruce A. Young). Waiting for the elevator to take them up to Bobby's apartment, Joanna panics and ducks out. So Elliot spends the evening complaining about women to the three men, whose insights are as narrow and immature as his own. When Joanna finally appears, she is cool and bossy, which brings on a quarrel with Elliot and a separation. But the two lovers are soon on the phone once again trying to reconcile their many differences. Feiffer's quicksilver one-liners continued to sparkle (Elliot confides that "sex without guilt is garbage—it has no moral dimension"), but critics felt the play was all anti-climax after a potent opening monologue by Elliot about the battling sexes. Mike Nichols directed the "muddled" production, which only survived forty-four performances, losing a hefty $600,000, a new record for an off-Broadway non-musical.

Actor Charles Grodin (not seen on a New York stage in fifteen years) turned author and put his film experiences into **Price of Fame** (6-13-90, Yegen). In his dressing-room trailer on location for a cheap sci-fi movie, film actor Roger (Grodin) must fend off a parade of visitors who seem to show up to pick his bones and gloat at his downspiraling career. Karen (Lizbeth Mackay) comes from *Vanity Fair* to interview Roger, but it is soon clear she plans a hatchet job to settle an old score for her editor-boyfriend. She is interrupted by others: the movie's neurotic leading lady, Evelyn

(Jeannie Berlin); Roger's alienated son, Matt (Jace Alexander), who works as a gofer on the set; Mario (Joseph R. Sicari), an eccentric make-up man assigned to turn Roger into an outer space beast; and Cappy (Michael Ingram), an actor providing the creature's voice, who feels his efforts are not fully appreciated. By the final curtain a romance develops between Roger and Karen, giving him some hope for the future. The Roundabout Theatre mounting received tepid reviews all around.

The season's first hit came early when Lincoln Center featured John Guare's **Six Degrees of Separation** (6-14-90, Mitzi E. Newhouse) in its downstairs space for 155 performances, then on November 8 moved it upstairs to the Vivian Beaumont for an additional 485 showings. A sophisticated Manhattan couple, Flanders (John Cunningham) and Ouisa Kittredge (Stockard Channing), are entertaining a businessman (Sam Stoneburner) when a beaten and bloody African-American youth (James McDaniel) stumbles into their swank apartment, claiming to be a friend of their children away at college. He says his name is Paul, that he is the son of film star Sidney Poitier, and that he has been robbed of his money and college thesis. The Kittredges take him in for the night, and he charms them by cooking a creative dinner and revealing his considerable knowledge of art, literature, and the lives of their two Ivy League children. But in the wee hours of the morning Ouisa discovers Paul in bed with a male street hustler, so she and Flanders kick them both out of the apartment. When the Kittredges go to tell their friends of the episode, the couple finds out that Poitier has no son and that the same con man has worked his way into other homes, claiming to know their children as well. Soon Paul has befriended would-be actors Rick (Paul McCrane) and Elizabeth (Mari Nelson) from the Midwest, telling them he is Flanders's illegitimate son. He seduces Rick, takes him for all the money the two actors have saved, then disappears, which leads Rick to suicide. Elizabeth and Oiusa work with the cops to have Paul arrested, but he disappears into the complex legal and prison system, leaving Ouisa haunted by the memory of the boy who briefly brought so much life and pain into their smug and self-satisfied existence. (The title came from one of Ouisa's speeches to the audience, describing how all people in the world are somehow connected if you trace them from person to person six times.) Rave reviews for Guare's script were typified by Douglas Watt in the *New York Daily News*, who called it "a magic carpet ride . . . endlessly stimulating and funny." Jerry Zaks was cited for his piercing yet understated direction, while Channing's "luminous" performance was declared her finest yet. The tragicomedy won the New York Drama Critics Circle Award, and Zaks won a Tony.

Film and television stars continued to give the Shakespeare Marathon high visibility if not always viability. A. J. Antoon set *The Taming of the Shrew* in the Wild West at the outdoor Delacorte on June 22 with Morgan Freeman as a gunslinging Petruchio and Tracey Ullman as an Annie Oakley–like spitfire Kate. Audiences (and even most of the press) enjoyed the gimmicky production. On August 3 Denzel Washington essayed *Richard III* at the same theatre and was pronounced a low-key and subtle villain, perhaps lacking charm and humor but a powerful presence all the same. The color-blind cast also featured Mary Alice (Queen Margaret), Daniel Davis (Buckingham), Sharon Washington (Anne), Jeffrey Nordling (Hastings), and Nancy Palk (Elizabeth).

Terrell Anthony satirized that easiest of targets, television soap operas, in **Quiet on the Set** (8-15-90, Orpheum), a transfer from Off Off Broadway that only lasted forty-seven performances in a commercial mounting. Tamra Lydell (Beth Ehlers), an actress who left the daytime drama *Sunset* two years ago to make prestigious films, returns to the soap when her career falters. Joining the cast as well is Taylor (Robert Newman), Tamra's brother, whose career is also in flux. His ex-girlfriend Judith Petri (Kate Collins) is a regular on the series and is bitter about Taylor being on the set. Rounding out this quartet of TV actors is Bruce Mitchell (Trent Bushey), a narcissistic leading man whose energy is spent on remembering his lines and keeping his hairstyle in top form. Little happened on the TV soundstage aside from bickering and the usual headaches in filming an underrehearsed program, but Anthony had one playful (if unoriginal) idea: one actor (Matt Servitto) played the director, makeup man, wardrobe mistress, and other characters on the set, each a stereotypic but entertaining cameo.

The Roundabout returned to its usual practice of mounting revivals with a very broadly played but still delightful production of Moss Hart's backstager *Light Up the Sky* (11-18-48) on August 21 at the Yegen. Charles Keating was the narcissistic director, John Bolger the nervous playwright, Peggy Cass his overbearing mother, Bruce Weitz the practical producer, Betsy Joslyn his addlebrained wife, Linda Carlson the flamboyant star, and Bill McCutcheon a stagestruck Shriner.

Joseph Papp, who had refused money from the NEA the previous season on grounds of censorship, opened this season with a direct attack on Senator Jesse Helms, the ultraconservative who was behind the attack on the arts agency. **Indecent Materials** (8-27-90, Public: Shiva) took Helms's actual speeches and had them read by two actors (David Ring and Patricia Esperon) while Rebecca Hitchins did interpretive dance in the background. The playlet, compiled by Edward Hunt and Jeff Stoner, was sometimes funny (Helms boldly states, "I have pictures of male genitals placed on this table") but rarely theatrical. Accompanying the piece was *Report From the Holocaust*, a monologue (delivered by Ring) that Hunt and Stoner fashioned from activist Larry Kramer's book of the same title. The bitter plea for a strong response to the AIDS epidemic was more a political diatribe than a play, but most commentators felt it was an argument worth being heard.

One of Off Broadway's few commercial entries this season was Edwin Schloss's **Money Talks** (9-6-90, Promenade), a "dreadful" comedy that closed after five showings. A gaggle of Jewish widows on Manhattan's Upper East Side spend their empty lives buying and selling stocks and bonds, wooing or harassing their brokers, and trying to get their daughters married off. While the play had many incidents, there was little plot. But Helen Gallagher and Dolores Gray, two non-Jewish ladies known for their musical comedy roles, gave notable performances as two of the harpies, and John Braden was amusing as an oversexed Italian art dealer.

Decidedly mixed reviews greeted Broadway's first (and rather late) entry of the season, Bill Cain's melodrama **Stand-Up Tragedy** (10-4-90, Criterion), which closed after fourteen showings. Tom Griffin (Jack Coleman), a preppie Georgetown University graduate who teaches in a Catholic high school for Hispanics in Lower Manhattan, tries to rescue Lee Cortez (Marcus Chong), a troubled youth who shows promise, from his hostile environment. But Lee is killed by his jealous brother, who cannot stand to see the boy succeed. Two aspects of the production helped keep it lively: Chong played his mother and brother as well as Lee, and the story was punctuated with rap songs and dances reflecting Lee's world.

Husband-and-wife team James Whitmore and Audra Lindley performed a pair of two-character plays in repertory, starting with Tom Cole's **About Time** (10-9-90, John Houseman). In the course of one day—at breakfast, lunch, dinner, and a late-night snack in the kitchen of their retirement condominium—we view an elderly married couple as they reminisce, argue, and complain about everything from their seldom-seen children to sex. The two-hander was doggedly unsentimental, one critic noting it had "an edge of stylization reminiscent of Beckett's minimalism." Both performers were applauded more enthusiastically than the script, which was described as "inconsequential and somewhere between a play and a vehicle." The second two-hander, William Gibson's **Handy Dandy** (10-22-90, John Houseman), joined *About Time* in repertory for three weeks. Gibson had written the popular two-character piece *Two for the Seesaw* (1-16-58), but this effort was described as "swollen and pat and obvious." Molly Egan is an activist nun in her seventies; with three husbands and four abortions in her past, she is still trying to make a change in the world. When she is arrested for picketing a nuclear arms research laboratory, Molly is hauled before Judge Henry Pulaski, an elderly conservative who is widowed and estranged from his one son. Henry is both irritated and impressed by the feisty Molly, and, after she is brought into his court on subsequent arrests, they strike up a friendship built on their mutual respect for each other's beliefs. But Molly goes on a hunger strike over one of her causes and dies, leaving Henry to question the strength of his own ideals. The principals performed the drama in regional theatres before and after this New York engagement.

Two superb actors tackled difficult classical roles with success the next week. The Roundabout's *King Lear* on October 9 boasted a towering performance by Hal Holbrook as the suspicious monarch. Frank Rich in the *New York Times* was among those critics who commented on Holbrook's "bitter humor" that "eventually turns inward into self-mockery as he falls into despair." Much of the rest of Gerald Freedman's traditional staging was "lightweight" with uneven casting and "an odd sense of dislocation." Two nights later Philip Bosco played Harpagon, that King Lear of comedy, in the Circle in the Square revival of *The Miser* and found depth as well as humor in the Molière character. John Beaufort in the *Christian Science Monitor* observed, "This fine actor is not content merely to epitomize the comic boor . . . in the end, he makes the man's obsession pitiable instead of merely contemptible." Stephen Porter staged John Wood's translation with finesse, and there were masterful supporting performances by Carole Shelley as the matchmaker Frosine and John Christopher Jones

as the wily coachman/chef Jacques. *King Lear* and *The Miser* each ran three months.

A more obscure revival followed: Sophie Treadwell's *Machinal* (9-7-28) on October 15 at the Public's LuEsther. This highly expressionistic piece about a Young Woman (Jodie Markell) who murders her suffocating Husband (John Seitz) and then dies in the electric chair was directed by Michael Greif in a stark, staccato style on a black and white set with episodes whirling by as quickly as its furniture rolled on and off. Some critics found the piece surprisingly effective; others thought it claptrap. Still, the six-week engagement was the most talked-about attraction of the Public's season.

Perhaps the most affecting (and most successful) Australian play to reach New York in many years was David Stevens's **The Sum of Us** (10-16-90, Cherry Lane), "an old-fashioned play in the best sense" that ran 335 performances and was a favorite in regional theatres thereafter. Widower Dad (Richard Venture) lives in a Melbourne suburb with his gay son, Jeff (Tony Goldwyn), the two of them quarreling over petty things but caring for each other deeply. When Jeff brings handsome young gardener Greg (Neil Maffin) home from the local pub for a night of lovemaking, Dad is cordial and encouraging, which not only surprises Greg but puts him off, so he leaves. Dad is dating a divorcée, Joyce (Phyllis Somerville), and it looks like marriage is in the air until she learns of Jeff's homosexuality and backs away. Dad suffers a stroke soon after, and while wheeling him through a public garden one day, Jeff meets up with Greg again. This time Dad, though incapacitated and silent, actually helps bring the two men together. The comedy was filled with funny and moving monologues (even Dad breaks out of his comatose-like state to tell the audience his thoughts), which flowed out of each situation seamlessly.

Audiences were promised that **Jackie Mason: Brand New** (10-17-90, Neil Simon) would live up to its title: the comedian offered $50,000 to anyone who could find any jokes from his previous show in this one. Using the format of a television newscast, Mason revisited old topics even if the one-liners were new, but no one seemed to mind. Critics welcomed him back again, and audiences came 216 times.

The Circle Repertory Company opened its disappointing season with Vincent J. Cardinal's comedy-drama **The Colorado Catechism** (10-21-90, Circle), a two-character play that had originated in Los Angeles. Ty Wain (Kevin James O'Connor) is a painter whose life of drugs and booze has landed him in a Colorado rehab center. There he meets and befriends teacher Donna Sicard (Becky Ann Baker), who is at the center for the third time. If she fails to kick her habit after this stay, she will lose her child to foster care. Yet their friendship doesn't help either of them beat their addiction, so they part ways. Three years later Ty tries to paint a portrait of Donna from memory, realizing that he is in love with her. Critics saw the script as little more than "an acting exercise" that often lapsed into "coy strategies to stretch the length."

David Greenspan reset Chikamatsu Monzaemon's eighteenth-century Bunraku play *Gonza the Lancer* in the 1950s for the October 22 revival at the Public's Shiva. The tale of a samurai warrior (Koji Okamura) who is engaged to the young Osai (Mary Schultz) but seduced by her mother (also Schultz) was told in both traditionally Asian (some characters played by puppets) and experimentally modern (one actor urinates onstage) styles. The "hodgepodge of pseudo-avant-garde gimmickry" was mostly dismissed by the press, yet Papp later named Greenspan one of his associate producers at the Public.

The Manhattan Theatre Club opened its extended season with Beth Henley's **Abundance** (10-30-90, City Center), a twenty-five-year epic about the Old West viewed with a revisionist slant. Mail order brides Bess Johnson (Amanda Plummer) and Macon Hill (Tess Harper) wait for their husbands to pick them up so they can begin new lives in Wyoming Territory in the 1860s. While Bess romanticizes her situation, Macon ambitiously considers the great things she hopes to accomplish. Bess marries the brutish Jack Flan (Michael Rooker), and the two struggle unsuccessfully to make a go of it in the new land. On the other hand, Macon weds Will Curtis (Lanny Flaherty), a one-eyed widower, and they prosper, though Macon treats him with contempt. Jack burns down his own home while in a desperate rage, so the couple move in with Macon and Will, and soon the two women are planning to run away together. But Bess is captured by Indians, and Jack and Macon eventually fall in love. When Bess returns years later, the threesome are facing financial ruin, so Bess writes a highly embellished account of how she escaped from the Indian camp, and Professor Elmore Crome (Keith Reddin) books her on a lecture circuit, where she becomes a sensation. Many years later the women meet once again in St. Louis and quietly assess "the boundlessness of it all." Some aisle-sitters considered Henley's long tale "her most provocative play

in years," while most thought it more "like a sketch for a play . . . or for three plays."

Another work previously seen in various California theatres was Philip Ken Gotanda's **The Wash** (11-6-90, City Center), which the Manhattan Theatre Club presented for a two-week run. Although they have been married forty-two years, the Japanese-American couple Nobu (Sab Shimono) and Masi Matsumoto (Nobu McCarthy) separate because of long-term differences. While Masi considered herself a new woman free from the Asian ideas of marriage, she still visits Nobu weekly to collect and drop off his laundry and to see how he is faring. Their two grown daughters have opposing opinions on the separation. Marsha (Diane Takei) believes in the tradition of the family and hopes for a reconciliation between the parents. Judy (Jodi Long), who is estranged from Nobu since she married an African American, supports her mother and her newfound freedom. When Masi begins a relationship with widower Sadao (George Takei), Nobu is more frustrated and confused than ever, rejecting his girlfriend Kiyoko (Shizuko Hoshi) and sinking into despair when Masi asks for a divorce. In the final scene Masi arrives with clean shirts for the last time, leaving the dirty shirts on the floor. The "entertaining and modest and trustworthy" play won several plaudits from the press.

Also applauded by some critics as "both funny and touching" was Tom Mardirosian's **Subfertile** (11-7-90, Playwrights Horizons) in which the author played Tom, a man about to turn forty who discovers that his low sperm count is the reason he and his wife (Susan Knight) cannot have children. Tom pursues a series of embarrassing medical methods to raise his count, and even considers letting a friend impregnate his wife for him, before he accepts his infertile fate. Tom narrated the piece, which was set in the Museum of Natural History, where the dinosaurs strike him as symbols of his own future extinction.

The dynamic young Hispanic actor John Leguizamo scripted and performed his own one-man show, **Mambo Mouth** (11-8-90, American Place), in which he created a cross-section of the Latino community, portraying males and females on the street with incisive if often raunchy humor. While many of the characters bordered on stereotype, Leguizamo's vivacious performance kept audiences laughing for 114 performances.

Thanks to two stellar performances, William Nicholson's London hit **Shadowlands** (11-11-90, Brooks Atkinson) managed to overcome mixed reviews (from "a polemical soap opera" to "a well-crafted drama with strong emotional appeal") and survive on Broadway for 169 performances. C. S. Lewis (Nigel Hawthorne), an Oxford don and acclaimed author, corresponds with American poet Joy Davidman (Jane Alexander) for some time before they finally meet. When Joy leaves her womanizing husband, Lewis marries her so that she can stay in England. But it is not until Joy is dying of cancer that Lewis, who often wrote of love theoretically and philosophically, discovers its true transforming power. Hawthorne won a Tony Award for his performance in the fact-based piece.

British playwright David Storey followed up his earlier family drama *In Celebration* (10-30-84) with **The March on Russia** (11-12-90, Hudson Guild), another play set around a wedding anniversary. Tommy Pasmore (John Carpenter) and his wife (Bethel Leslie) are celebrating their sixtieth, so their three restless children return to their Yorkshire home to deal with a past filled with unresolved conflicts. Colin (Sean Griffin), a coldhearted professor who has retired and bought the family home, and Wendy (Carol Locatell), involved in politics and regretting never having a child, seek some answers from the reunion, but it is the straightforward Eileen (Susan Browning) who refuses to be haunted by what might have been and realizes she must get on with her own life. The fading Pasmores were symbolic of a deteriorating social structure in Britain, but neither the politics nor the characters won the approval of the press. The play was the first of a planned series of works presented by a new (but, unfortunately, short-lived) group called Chelsea Stage.

Spalding Gray's latest autobiographical monologue, **Monster in a Box** (11-14-90, Mitzi E. Newhouse), was more scattered than his previous dozen one-man shows (most of them off-off Broadway), but several critics still found it "wildly, unpredictably witty." Gray recounted his experiences making a movie in Hollywood, interviewing people who claim to have been taken aboard UFOs, traveling to Nicaragua and Russia, and playing the Stage Manager in the recent Lincoln Center revival of *Our Town*. The title referred to 1,900 manuscript pages of his novel that sit in a box and haunt him to complete it. The program ran fifty-nine times in the Newhouse, then another sixteen on dark nights upstairs in the Vivian Beaumont.

Two more one-man shows followed in quick succession. Eric Bogosian brought back his *Sex, Drugs, Rock & Roll* (2-8-90) to the Orpheum on November 16 for a month. The next night Wallace Shawn took on the issues of poverty and guilt in **The Fever** (11-17-90, Public: Shiva), which he wrote, performed twelve times, then revived for various short engagements in other venues. A rich and pampered American lies feverish in a Third World hotel and contemplates the unfairness in life, his own wealth, the dire poverty of those around him, and his guilt over not having the courage to do anything about it. Some commentators condemned the piece as self-indulgent and preachy; others thought it "mesmerizingly theatrical."

Michael Weller's latest effort, **Lake No Bottom** (11-29-90, Second Stage), got no further than a three-week run off-off Broadway. Rubin (Daniel Davis), a well-known critic, has retired to his impressive country estate on Lake No Bottom to write books. His wife, Petra (Marsha Mason), is bored in the boondocks, so she willingly revives a love affair with Will (Robert Knepper), a novelist she has known since he was a student of Rubin's. Will has become famous for writing a trashy best-seller and is on his way to lecture at a nearby college, but he is also happy to take up his old lover. Rubin knows his marriage is growing cold, so he encourages the affair, setting them up for a deadly confrontation. Playing the jealous husband, Rubin then demands satisfaction. Each armed with pistols, the two men hunt each other through the New England woods, taking potshots at each other. Will is wounded (though not very seriously), Petra is thrilled by the attention of the two men, and the marriage is resuscitated. Reviewers attacked the "artificial and rhetorical" drama and laughed at the lavish estate members of their profession were supposedly able to acquire in retirement.

The Public's third non-Shakespeare revival of the season was Bertolt Brecht's *The Caucasian Chalk Circle* (3-24-66) on December 2 at the Martinson. George C. Wolfe set the Chinese tale in Haiti, and a cast of black and Hispanic actors employed masks, puppets, and Caribbean song and dance to tell the story. More than one critic declared Thulani Davis's adaptation and Wolfe's production "uplifting and exhilarating." Wolfe was one of the three directors Papp named associate producers at the Public; Wolfe would be sole producer before the decade was half over.

Also at the Public, John Patrick Shanley's **The Big Funk** (12-10-90, Anspacher) was on view for a week. Short scenes, monologues, and occasional nudity were used to illustrate how a quintet of aimless young people search for satisfaction. Jill (Jeanne Tripplehorn) likes Gregory (Skip

Sudduth), and he returns the feeling by covering her with petroleum jelly. Austin (Jake Weber), an out-of-work actor who believes that kindness to strangers will make the world a better place, gives her a bubble bath, thereby cleansing both of their souls. Omar (Graham Beckel) makes his living throwing knives in a sideshow, but the modern condition has him distracted until his wife, Fifi (Jayne Haynes), announces that she is pregnant with twins and both find new hope in the news. Sometimes lyrical, sometimes annoying, *The Big Funk* was definitely one of Shanley's lesser works.

Another promising playwright, Harry Kondoleon, stumbled with his awkward fantasy **Love Diatribe** (12-8-90, Circle). After leaving her husband, Sandy (Amy Aquino) returns to her parents' home to live and drifts into a romance with Mike (Michael Rispoli), the boy next door. At a family dinner with Sandy's brother, Orin (Barry Sherman), who is a disgruntled librarian, Freida (Martha Gehman) arrives unannounced, claiming to be an exchange student (she soon admits she is lying), and falls for Orin. Freida puts a love potion in the tea, and everyone who drinks it falls unconscious. Freida then delivers a mystical "love diatribe," and everyone awakes with a better understanding of each other and the world.

Much more satisfying was **The American Plan** (12-16-90, City Center) by another up-and-coming playwright, Richard Greenberg. Lili Adler (Wendy Makkena), the daughter of upper-class German-Jewish refugees, vacations in the Catskills with her mother, Eva (Joan Copeland), in the summer of 1960 and falls for the attractive Wasp Nick Lockridge (D. W. Moffett). But Eva, a hardboiled cynic since escaping from Hitler's Germany, is suspicious of the ideal young man. She lets the romance develop before destroying it with the revelation that Nick is a penniless fortune hunter and is really in love with someone else. Ten years later, after Eva has died, Nick visits Lili in her Central Park West apartment and tries to explain his actions years ago. But Lili has turned as cynical as her mother, quoting from an old German song her mother used to sing to her that "happiness exists but it is for other people." The Manhattan Theatre Club production was well received, with critics calling it "lyrical," "absorbing," and "spellbinding," and the *Best Plays* editors named the play one of the year's ten best.

Perhaps the saddest casualty of the season was John Olive's **The Voice of the Prairie** (12-18-90, Hudson Guild), which the Chelsea Stage ran only two nights before going bankrupt and folding forever. Two stories are told concurrently in this rich picaresque folk tale set in the Midwest. In the 1890s an orphaned teenager, Davey (Kevin Greer), travels the countryside with Frankie (Wendy Barrie-Wilson), a blind girl running away from her abusive father. These scenes alternate with events in the 1920s when the grown David, a storyteller on primitive radio broadcasts, tells his audiences about his travels with Frankie. The grown-up Francis, now a schoolteacher and engaged to a feverishly passionate minister (Jack Cirillo), hears the broadcast, and she and David are reunited in a bittersweet confrontation. Three actors played all the roles in this epic comedy-drama filled with deft narrative, vivid characters, and arresting dialogue. Obviously, few saw it in New York, but the play would resurface occasionally in regional theatres and schools.

Karen Allen was commended for her portrayal of Georgie Elgin, the woman torn between her alcoholic husband (David Rasche) and his director (Paul McCrane) in Clifford Odets's *The Country Girl* (11-10-50), which the Roundabout revived on December 26. The "well-acted, solid" production also was endorsed, running seven weeks.

Tony Kushner, a playwright who would cause quite a stir later in the decade, made his debut with **A Bright Room Called Day** (1-7-91, Public: LuEsther). In 1932 Berlin, a group of artists and leftists watch their world fall apart as the democracy they love to criticize is replaced by Hitler's fascism. Taking a modern point of view (the drama begins in 1990), Kushner makes far-from-subtle political parallels with today and argues that commitment is the only way out of having history repeat itself. The two-week engagement met with a mixed press, summarized by one critic who called it "wild, uneven, pugnacious, ragged, committed, smart, dumb, satirical, and utterly serious."

The parade of one-man shows continued with James Prideaux's **Lyndon** (1-17-91, John Houseman) in which Laurence Luckinbill portrayed thirty-sixth president Lyndon Johnson, looking and soundly surprisingly like the famous Texan. The president is supposedly delivering this monologue from the Oval Office in 1968, right after he announced on national television that he would not run for a second term. Johnson went back to his boyhood in Texas and proceeded to chronicle his political career, omitting embarrassing reference to his suspicious gubernatorial victory and the tricky aspects of the Vietnam War era. Reviewers lauded Luckinbill, but few approved of the script, more than one pointing out the lopsided and laundered nature of the piece. The off-Broadway commercial entry was kept on the boards for six weeks.

The most unlikely entry of the Broadway season was David Hirson's verse drama **La Bête** (2-10-91, Eugene O'Neill), which carefully (and often successfully) aped Molière's social satires. Elomire (Michael Cumpsty) runs a famous acting troupe in 1654 France, but his patron, Count Conti (Dylan Baker), feels that Elomire's theatricals have gone stale of late and suggests that the company spice things up by bringing in the street comedian Valere (Tom McGowan, replacing Ron Silver, who left during tryouts). Valere is a pompous bore who loves to hear himself talk (his entrance speech runs over twenty minutes), and Elomire immediately dislikes him. But, afraid of offending the Count, he allows Valere to perform with the players, hoping that the crude comedian will humiliate himself. On the contrary, the troupe springs to life, the Count is thrilled, and Elomire quits in disgust. Hirson's rhymed couplets throughout recalled Richard Wilbur's witty translations of Molière (Elomire was an anagram for Molière), and the comedy was classically structured and maintained itself consistently. Richard Hudson's costumes were elaborately cockeyed, and his pristine white setting, a distorted château with a crystal chandelier hanging askew, was very deconstructionist. Some reviewers admired the ambitious project, though few could wholeheartedly endorse it. The comedy only lasted three weeks, losing more than its $2 million investment, a new record for a non-musical on Broadway.

Two new (to New York) Alan Ayckbourn comedies arrived in February, both minor works but delightful all the same. The Manhattan Theatre Club offered **Absent Friends** (2-12-91, City Center) for six weeks, and it received mixed notices. When the young fiancée of Colin (Peter Frechette) dies unexpectedly, his friends invite him to tea in order to cheer him up. But they are a tense group filled with marital discord, obsession with business, and unsatisfying infidelities. When Colin arrives, he is the most good-natured of the lot, speaking glowingly about his fiancée (which sets some of the others off into tears) and radiantly accepting life. His optimism at first grates on the others, but then they break down and all their neuroses come spilling out. Ayckbourn's second entry was **Taking Steps** (2-20-91, Circle in the Square), a farce that typified the playwright's obsession with clever plotting and unusual use of space. Three floors of a British country house

(formerly a brothel) are viewed on James Morgan's set, but they are all on the same level, the steps being flat spaces in which the actors mime their ascent or descent. Business tycoon Roland (Christopher Benjamin) is considering buying the large house but wants to spend a night in it to be sure. During that night his dissatisfied wife (Jane Summerhays), her brother (Jonathan Hogan) and his fiancée (Pippa Pearthree), and a timid solicitor (Spike McClure) all sneak in and out causing various complications. (The funniest moment occurred when the wife crawls into the solicitor's bed and he does not resist, fearful that she is the ghost of the long-gone brothel keeper.) The farce entertained audiences for ten weeks.

It took sixty years for Langston Hughes and Zora Neale Hurston's folk comedy **Mule Bone** (2-14-91, Ethel Barrymore) to be produced (the two authors quarreled and parted company before the script was polished), but to some it was worth the wait. George Houston Bass revised the fragmented manuscript, adding a prologue and epilogue, and Taj Mahal provided some songs that turned the stereotypic piece into a lively celebration of southern life. In a small Florida town, sometime guitarist Jim (Kenny Neal) and sometime dancer Dave (Eric Ware) are best friends, but both love the town flirt, Daisy (Akosua Busia). In an argument, Dave hits Jim on the head with a mule bone, so is brought before a hilarious kangaroo court led by Mayor Joe Clark (Samuel E. Wright). The town banishes Dave, but he and Jim make up and both drop Daisy, realizing their friendship is worth more than any woman. This simple plot was just an excuse to illustrate life in the all-black town with its good-natured rivalry between happy-go-lucky Baptists and uptight Methodists. Michael Schultz staged the large (thirty characters) and colorful production with citizens breaking into dance, children underfoot, and vibrant storytellers springing to life. The result was "more a brimming treasure chest than a conventional drama," but most critics recommended the show and cheered the sparkling cast, which also included veterans Frances Foster, Leonard Jackson, Theresa Merritt, and Arthur French. Actually a Lincoln Center production, it ran sixty-seven times in a Broadway house.

Neil Simon offered one of his finest works, **Lost in Yonkers** (2-21-91, Richard Rodgers), and was rewarded with a Pulitzer Prize and a Tony Award for his efforts. Eddie Kurnitz (Mark Blum) has gone into debt because of his late wife's medical bills and is being threatened by loan sharks.

So in 1942 he drops off his young sons, Arty (Danny Gerard) and Jay (Jamie Marsh), to live with his mother in Yonkers while he goes on the road as a traveling salesman. Grandma (Irene Worth) is a cold, nasty penny-pincher who runs a candy store and torments her grown but feeble-minded daughter, Bella (Mercedes Ruehl). The boys are terrified of the old lady and bond with the innocently daffy Bella to survive. Also stopping in on occasion is Grandma's slick son Louis (Kevin Spacey) who works for the mob and carries laundered money in his suitcase. The household erupts when Bella finds a boyfriend (a movie-house usher who is also slightly retarded) and stands up to her mother for the first time and walks out. The encounter nearly destroys the iron matriarch, but Bella returns to make peace and assure everyone (including the two boys, who are finally rescued by their father) that life is full of possibilities. Reviewers were ecstatic about Simon's script, Gene Saks's poignant direction, and the cast (Worth, Ruehl, and Spacey all won Tonys). The "unusually tough . . . but wonderfully theatrical" play ran 780 performances.

The usual hot or cold reactions greeted JoAnne Akalaitis's treatment of Shakespeare when *Henry IV, Parts 1 and 2* opened on February 26 and 27 at the Newman, the greetings made hotter or colder by recent news that Akalaitis had been named an associate producer at the Public. The campy revival seemed more a parody than a history drama. Courtiers ate hot dogs and drank beer during the coronation scene, Poins (Rene Rivera) carried a stolen television set around with him all the time, Falstaff's favorite tavern became a bordello with copulating couples and a man defecating in a bucket, William Duell performed Shallow in an Elmer Fudd voice, and Philip Glass composed a score that alternated between old Hollywood movie soundtracks and British music hall. The cast met with similarly mixed notices, though Louis Zorich (Falstaff), Thomas Gibson (Prince Hal), Jared Harris (Hotspur), and Thomas Bryggman (King Henry) certainly had their champions.

Steve Tesich put aside his usual quirky sense of humor and wrote a full-fledged melodrama with **The Speed of Darkness** (2-28-91, Belasco). Vietnam veterans Joe (Len Cariou) and Lou (Stephen Lang) were close friends in Southeast Asia, but twenty years later they could not be more different. Joe is a successful businessman in Sioux Falls, South Dakota, with a wife and family. Lou is a homeless refugee from his haunted past, wandering the country and following a touring version of the Vietnam Memorial. (He has tried to inscribe his name on the monument, claiming to be one of the victims of the war.) When the memorial comes to South Dakota, Lou looks up his old buddy Joe, and their reunion brings out past sins (the two of them once poured barrels of toxic waste into the water supply of a town) and new revelations (Joe's daughter is not really his). Lou kills himself, and Joe is left to face the consequences of his past. Reviews ranged from "gripping and aflame with passion" to "unsatisfactory [with] a prevailing earnestness which is no substitute for seriousness." The drama, which had originated at Chicago's Goodman Theatre, was part of the new Broadway Alliance in which both costs and tickets were reduced. But the play did not catch on and closed in a month.

British comic actress Tracey Ullman dropped her Western twang from the summer's *The Taming of the Shrew* and became the tacky California stage mother Florence Aadland in Brooke and Jay Presson Allen's one-person play **The Big Love** (3-3-91, Plymouth) based on a tell-all book by Aadland and Tedd Thomey. Florence was the mother of fifteen-year-old Bev Aadland, who was violently seduced by Erroll Flynn in 1958 and had a torrid affair with the aging star during his final days. Neither the story nor the character of the celebrity-hungry Florence was worth telling, but Ullman had many fans (including several critics), so the show hung on for forty-one performances.

Eileen Atkins followed her sterling performance in *Prin* with **A Room of One's Own** (3-4-91, Lamb's) in which she played Virginia Woolf commenting on the role of women in literature and society. The text came from a series of lectures Woolf gave (and subsequently collected into a book), so there was no dramatic action as such. But Atkins offered "a virtuosic feat of acting and a luminous portrait of the artist" that dazzled audiences and critics alike. The solo show was held over for ninety-eight performances.

Continuing to produce promising young playwrights, the Manhattan Theatre Club had its weakest entry of the season with Keith Reddin's **Life During Wartime** (3-5-91, City Center). Tommy (Bruce Norris), a naive young man who has learned how to sell home security systems from his boss, Heinrich (W. H. Macy), falls in love with his first customer, Gale (Leslie Lyles). She is a divorced mother with a teenage son, Howard (Matt McGrath), and despite the difference in their ages, Tommy plans to propose to her. He then finds out that the business he works for is a scam and that the homes with the new system are robbed soon after installation. Before he can warn her, Gale and Howard are murdered during a robbery, and Tommy confronts Heinrich, who scoffs at his gullibility. In the end, Gale's ghost appears to Tommy and brings him comfort. The melodrama was interspersed with appearances by the sixteenth-century religious leader John Calvin (James Rebhorn), whose discourses on original sin paralleled Tommy's plight.

The Roundabout's revival of the perennial Shaw favorite *Pygmalion* on March 6 was considered "most impressive" by some aisle-sitters, "somehow tamer than it should be" by others. They also disagreed about Anthony Heald's young, immature Henry Higgins and Madeleine Potter's anti-romantic Eliza Doolittle. But everyone was thrilled with Charles Keating's ribald Alfred Doolittle and gave a nod to John Conklin's impressionistic unit setting, which consisted of pre-Raphaelite paintings and other icons of society scattered about the open stage, and Natasha Katz's lighting, which brought them into focus at appropriate moments.

Veteran playwright Arthur Kopit returned to the non-musical theatre with **Road to Nirvana** (3-7-91, Circle), a sly but hateful parody of David Mamet's *Speed-the-Plow* (5-3-88) and the Hollywood merry-go-round. (In its previous regional productions, the play was called *Bone-the-Fish*.) Down-and-out movie producers Jerry (Peter Riegert) and Al (Jon Polito) have the opportunity of a lifetime fall into their laps: sexy, Madonna-like rock singer Nirvana (Amy Aquino) has written an autobiography (patterned after *Moby Dick*, no less) and will star in a film version for them. The catch is, just to read the script Jerry must humiliate himself by eating excrement and then agree to further debasements (slashing wrists and castration, for example) to keep Nirvana happy and the deal alive. In the end, with the help of Al's girlfriend, Lou (Saundra Santiago), the elusive Nirvana (she likes to wear a mask) strikes a deal with Jerry to make the movie. Although most commentators agreed that it was "one of the meanest plays ever written," some found the scatological jokes funny, and a few even decided it was "a modern morality play." For a month audiences got to decide for themselves.

Jon Robin Baitz somewhat fulfilled the promising things said about his *The Film Society* (7-7-88) with **The Substance of Fire** (3-17-91, Playwrights Horizons), a drama that many critics found "remarkably intelligent" and "written with both scrupulous investigative zeal and bottomless sympathy." Isaac Geldhart (Ron Rifkin), a refugee from Nazi Germany, overcomes his wife's death and founds a little publishing house that puts out important (but rarely profitable) books. His latest project is a many-volumed history of Nazi medical experiments, which his son Aaron (Jon Tenney) believes will destroy the family-owned company. Aaron wants to publish a lucrative but trashy contemporary novel (Isaac dismisses its author as a "slickohipster"), so he convinces his brother, Martin (Patrick Breen), and sister, Sarah (Sarah Jessica Parker), to support him in taking over the company. Reluctantly they agree, and Isaac is forced into premature retirement. Three years later the old man has become so eccentric that his children begin the process of having him declared incompetent. Fighting against the demons of the past and the injustice within his own family, Isaac still manages to convince social worker Marge (Maria Tucci) that he is indeed sane. Playwrights Horizons held the drama over for 120 performances.

The financially distressed Negro Ensemble Theatre could not manage a full season of works but did produce Carlyle Brown's **The Little Tommy Parker Celebrated Colored Minstrel Show** (3-17-91, Master), a poignant look at black actors in the 1890s. Five minstrel performers wait in their unheated train car outside Hannibal, Missouri, for their show time. They pass the time with stories, songs, and reminiscences until fellow actor Percy (Charles Weldon) rushes in, pursued by a white mob. The actors furiously apply burnt cork to their faces so that Percy cannot be identified, but he decides to face the crowd alone so that they will not punish his friends. Douglas Turner Ward played the old-timer Henry and directed the "observant new play" that some critics thought glorious.

James McLure expanded his one-act *Pvt. Wars* (6-7-79) into a full-length piece, which opened on March 31 at the Actors' Playhouse. Little was gained from the rewriting, and it closed before three weeks had passed. Jason Werner, Richard Werner, and Adrian Basil played the three Vietnam vets recuperating in an army hospital.

A second one-man show this season featuring a colorful southern politician was Larry L. King and Ben Z. Grant's **The Kingfish** (3-24-91, John Houseman) about the controversial Louisiana governor Huey P. Long. Unlike *Lyndon*, the play did not have a well-known actor connected to it, but critics praised John McConnell's boisterous performance, and the program ran five weeks.

Yet another comedy about artistic but dissatisfied young New Yorkers was Douglas Carter

Beane's **Advice From a Caterpillar** (4-3-91, Lucille Lortel). Missy (Ally Sheedy), an avant-garde video artist who abhors her bourgeois family background, is having an affair with Suit (Harley Venton), a married man, but he is far from her ideal. When she meets Brat (David Lansbury), a bisexual actor who is the lover of Missy's close friend Spatz (Dennis Christopher), an unusual triangle develops. The presence of movie starlet Sheedy and the very personable cast helped the sassy comedy run seven weeks.

Playwright William Luce and Julie Harris teamed up again for a one-woman play, **Lucifer's Child** (4-4-91, Music Box), this time about Baroness Karen Blixen, who wrote stories about Africa under the pen name Isak Dinesen. In her study in Denmark as she prepares to travel to New York in 1958, Blixen recounts how she first went to Africa, wed a baron who was unfaithful to her and left her with syphilis, had a romance with an English aristocrat who died in a plane crash, and struggled to make a go of her coffee plantation alone in the foreign land. (Much of this tale was familiar to audiences from the popular film *Out of Africa* five years earlier.) In the second act, a year later, she is back in Denmark dying of syphilis. Blixen tells lively stories about her New York stay, including her visit to Harlem and her befriending Marilyn Monroe, and comments on the lessons her difficult life has taught her. (The title came from Blixen's claim that she sold her soul to the devil in return for the gift of narrative.) Few aisle-sitters thought the script adequate, but all agreed that "Ms. Harris captivates an audience as few other actresses can." The program played on Broadway twenty-eight times as part of its nationwide tour.

I Hate Hamlet (4-8-91, Walter Kerr) brought recognition to playwright Paul Rudnick, who would pen similar "unapologetically silly" plays throughout the decade. Television actor Andrew Rally (Evan Handler) relocates to Manhattan to pursue a theatre career, renting an atmospheric apartment (that once belonged to John Barrymore) through the services of tacky real estate broker Deirdre McDavey (Jane Adams). Andrew's agent, veteran Lillian Troy (Celeste Holm), who actually knew Barrymore in her youth, gets her client the role of Hamlet in Central Park's outdoor theatre, but Andrew claims to "hate Hamlet" and fears making a fool of himself. Only when Barrymore's ghost (Nicol Williamson), dressed as the Danish prince, appears to Andrew and convinces him to tackle the role does the TV

actor agree. Barrymore also gives Andew tips on playing the part and on romancing his virginal girlfriend, Felicia (Caroline Aaron). As the opening approaches, Gary Lefkowitz (Adam Arkin), an L.A. wheeler-dealer, flies in from the coast and offers Andrew a TV deal worth millions. But Andrew perseveres, and although he gets less-than-enthusiastic notices for his Hamlet, he nonetheless takes the wisdom of Barrymore with him on future endeavors. Curiously, none of the major critics pointed out the play's many similarities to Woody Allen's *Play It Again, Sam* (2-12-69) with Barrymore standing in for Bogart. While some of the plotting was clumsy and most characters fell into stereotypes, Rudnick's talent for one-liners was unmistakable. (Gary defines Shakespeare as "algebra onstage," and Barrymore comments on method acting with "we must never confuse truth with asthma.") Williamson's behavior problems onstage made the news several times during the run, especially on May 2 when he hit Handler on the backside with a sword; Handler brought charges against Williamson to Equity and quit the show. The comedy ran two months, then became a popular staple in summer stock.

Transferring from Off Off Broadway (where it ran over three months), Graham Reid's Irish play **Remembrance** (4-16-91, Irish Arts Center) garnered some approving reviews ("a heart-breaking, heart-lifting comedy") and remained another month. In a cemetery in Northern Ireland, Theresa Donaghy (Aideen O'Kelly), a Catholic widow visiting the grave of her slain son, meets Bert Andrews (Henry J. Quinn), a Protestant widower who also has a son buried nearby, and the elderly couple begin an unlikely friendship and soon a romance. Their surviving children try (unsuccessfully) to break up the pair, but Bert and Theresa have moved beyond bitterness about the past.

Robert Patrick's tragicomedy *The Haunted Host* was first seen off-off Broadway in 1964 and became an underground classic, being one of the earliest gay plays. Updated and revived this season at La Mama E.T.C. off-off Broadway, it moved to the Actors' Playhouse on March 19 for a total run of 101 performances. Harvey Fierstein played Jay Astor, a guilt-ridden homosexual who hires a straight young man (Jason Workman), who looks like his dead lover, so that Jay can reenact his past and thereby absolve himself. A new one-act by Patrick, **Pouf Positive** (4-19-91, Actors' Playhouse), was added when the program transferred to Off Broadway. Fierstein played a

Greenwich Village playwright who, right before he dies, delivers an extended monologue about his life.

The Manhattan Theatre Club rarely sponsored African-American playwrights, but this season they offered Leslie Lee's historical drama **Black Eagles** (4-21-91, City Center), "a heart-felt and rousing salute" to the Tuskegee airmen, Negro fighters during World War II. In 1989 General Colin Powell honors the surviving pilots in Washington, and soon the old men's reminiscences turn into scenes in 1944 when the young flyers were performing daring missions in Italy. What little plot there was concerned the efforts of the flyers to pursue German planes instead of merely serving as protectors for white pilots. Their chance finally comes, and the eager airmen go to battle with a religious revival-like vigor.

The final one-person entry of the season was **Ivy Rowe** (4-21-91, Provincetown Playhouse), a folksy narrative by an Appalachian mountain woman (Barbara Bates Smith) who in 1974 recalls her up-and-down life in southwest Virginia over the previous six decades. Mark Hunter and Smith adapted Lee Smith's novel *Fair and Tender Ladies* for the stage, and it ran five weeks

Despite a set of glowing reviews ("a bracing testament to the power of theatre to transform those on both sides of the footlights"), Timberlake Wertenbaker's British hit **Our Country's Good** (4-29-91, Nederlander) could not find an audience on Broadway and closed after forty-eight performances. (It also was presented as part of the new Broadway Alliance.) Based on Thomas Keneally's novel *The Playmaker*, the drama was set in 1789 in the prison colony of New South Wales, where the Governor General, Captain Arthur Phillip (Richard Poe), believes that his brutal convicts will become more human if they participate in amateur theatricals. He orders Second Lieutenant Ralph Clark (Peter Frechette) to present George Farquhar's comedy *The Recruiting Officer* with the prisoners as the players. Other officers find the idea ridiculous and try to put off the performance by humiliating the actors at rehearsals and accusing the leading lady, Liz Morden (Cherry Jones), of stealing food so that she is hanged in punishment. Yet the governor's idea is a good one, the convicts finding dignity and a sense of worth when their imagination transports them from their disease-ridden lives to a loftier world. Wertenbaker told the story in a series of short scenes and brief monologues, the cast of twelve playing a wide range of characters both

CHERRY JONES (1956–) was born in Paris, Tennessee, and studied theatre at Carnegie-Mellon University before playing many roles at the American Repertory Theatre in Cambridge and the Arena Stage in Washington. Making her off-Broadway debut in the 1983 revival of *The Philanthropist*, she was featured in *He and She*, *The Ballad of Soapy Smith*, *I Am a Camera*, and *Claptrap*. Jones made her Broadway debut as one of the amateur hoofers in *Stepping Out* (1986) but did not appear on Broadway in a major role until *Our Country's Good* moved from Hartford to the Nederlander. The diminutive actress would prove to be one of the most versatile performers in the business.

male and female, from British officers to a lone Aboriginal who comments on the strange ways of these visitors from beyond. Mark Lamos directed the American cast (the production had originated at his Hartford Stage) on Christopher Barreca's dynamic set that suggested the bones of a huge sailing vessel. Several in the cast were exceptional, but it was Cherry Jones who enjoyed the most attention for her "standout performance, making clear how the rage life has poured into her can . . . give her surprising mortal force."

Sam (Stephen Collins), the central character in A. R. Gurney's **The Old Boy** (5-5-91, Playwrights Horizons), had more than a little in common with Andrew Makepeace Ladd III in the same author's *Love Letters* (8-22-89), both being Wasp politicians who have spent their lives playing by the rules even when it meant sacrificing others. Sam is running for the governorship when he accepts an invitation from his old New England prep school to come and dedicate a new building on campus. Some time back Perry (Matt McGrath), a fellow "old boy" and close friend of Sam's, came out of the closet and shocked former classmates by admitting his homosexuality. He has since died of AIDS, and Perry's wealthy mother, Harriet (Nan Martin), has donated a great deal of money, wanting the new building named after her son. Sam is expected to say a few politically safe words about Perry, but the prospect forces him to recall how his own homophobia may have contributed to Perry's troubled life. (Years earlier, when Perry told Sam the truth about his sexuality, Sam went into denial and arranged a disastrous marriage between one of his discarded girlfriends and Perry.) In his speech at the dedication ceremony, Sam breaks down, champions the rights of social outcasts such as Perry, and thereby threatens his bid for the governorship. While a few reviewers felt the script "was as powerful as anything this playwright has written," the play never caught on like so many other Gurney works.

Another play in which a dead character was examined in flashbacks was Keith Curran's **Walking the Dead** (5-12-91, Circle). Friends of the late performance artist Veronica Tass (Ashley Gardner) gather at a memorial service arranged by Veronica's lover Maya Deboats (Myra Taylor), to reconstruct the past as a living piece of art. We learn how Veronica thought she was a lesbian until she decided she was a man trapped inside a woman's body. She undergoes a sex change operation and becomes Homer. But when his mother, Dottie (Scotty Bloch), remarries and Homer is invited to go to the wedding, he dresses up in drag as Veronica so he won't confuse old family friends. Walking home from the reception, Homer is attacked by two rapists who kill him when they find out he is not a woman. Some reviewers found "many moments of wit, insight, and honest beauty," and there were compliments for Cotter Smith as Bobby Brax, a bitterly funny gay copywriter.

Critics were in agreement that Sam Shepard's newest play, **States of Shock** (5-16-91, American Place), was one of his weakest efforts, calling it "interminable" and "empty and adolescent." Shepard's eighty-minute tirade concerns a wild-eyed Colonel (John Malkovich) who enters a desolate family restaurant with a wheelchair-bound paraplegic vet named Stubbs (Steve Nelson) to toast the death of the Colonel's son. Berating the waitress and the two other customers, the Colonel rants about war and America until the silent Stubbs finds his voice, rages about the end of the world, reveals his grotesque war wounds, and claims to be the Colonel's son. The two men then verbally and physically attack each other in true Shepard fashion, leading to the Colonel's extended monologue about wars, fatherhood, and "various states of insanity and self-abuse." The drama played only nineteen times then disappeared.

A "top-notch" revival of Frank D. Gilroy's multiple award winner *The Subject Was Roses* (5-25-64) concluded the Roundabout season on May 15. Most critics thought the play was dated and thin but saluted Jack Hofsiss's sensitive direction and his reputable cast: John Mahoney's robust father, Dana Ivey as his quietly suffering wife, and Pat-

rick Dempsey as their son, Timmy, who returns from World War II to settle old family scores.

There was something very old-fashioned about Tom Dulack's **Breaking Legs** (5-19-91, Promenade), peopled with the harmless, lovable kind of gangsters seen in *Three Men on a Horse* (1-30-35) and other old comedies. College professor Terence O'Keefe (Nicolas Surovy) takes a sabbatical from teaching to peddle a murder play he's written. His former student Angie (Sue Giosa), who lusts after Terence, invites him to the Italian restaurant she manages for her father to try to get her family to back the play. Her family, it turns out, is deep into organized crime (something Terence realizes only after he observes a minor underworld figure calmly wiped out in the parking lot outside the restaurant) but excited about sponsoring a legit operation. Angie's father, Lou Graziano (Vincent Gardenia), and his associate Mike Francisco (Philip Bosco) don't want to read the script but do have some suggestions: a new title, some songs perhaps, a part for Mike's wife's fat niece, even an accordion player. Terence is torn between losing his backing and losing his integrity. But in the end Angie threatens to leave home if they don't produce the play exactly as written, so the Mafiosos have no choice but to agree. While most of the critics considered the play "limp," they also felt the "merry and modest piece of nonsense" was a delightful vehicle for the players. Bosco and Gardenia played off each other beautifully, Giosa was a delicious seductress, and Victor Argo as the deadpan thug Tino De Felice was quite funny. Audiences laughed for 401 performances before the comedy toured and later enjoyed many summer stock productions. (It was Gardenia's last New York appearance; he died while touring the show.)

Lynda Barry's sassy memory play **The Good Times Are Killing Me** (5-21-91, Second Stage) was welcomed by the press as "an evening full of talent and good spirits." Cartoonist Barry adapted her novel about growing up in an interracial neighborhood in the 1960s into a breezy stage piece with twelve-year-old Edna Arkins (Angela Goethals) narrating her tale in time with pop songs that defined the period. The pre-adolescent befriends Bonna Willis (Chandra Wilson), a black girl her age who moves in across the street, and the two of them partake of each other's culture: Edna joins Bonna's family at a spirited church service, then Bonna accompanies the Arkinses on a neurotic camping trip. The two grow closer as they find familiar targets to mock, but the friendship is strained as they age, and by the seventh grade they treat each other with careful coolness. Some of the writing may have been uneven, but the cast was always winning, and the play never stooped to preaching or sentimentalizing. Originally an off-off-Broadway entry, word of mouth encouraged the producers to move it to Off Broadway, where it stayed for 207 performances.

David Greenspan continued his love affair with anachronism by staging William Congreve's Restoration classic *The Way of the World* in modern dress for the May 21 mounting at the Public's Shiva. The gimmick could not hide the cast's lack of verbal dexterity, and critics found them wanting, except for Andre Braugher, whose Mirabell was effective (even though he was forced to sport a polka-dot tie and suspenders).

Near season's end, Gregory Mosher announced that he would step down as artistic director of Lincoln Center Theatre, and by the end of May André Bishop of Playwrights Horizons was named his successor. Although the oft-troubled organization had fared well under Mosher's leadership, a new era headed by Bishop (and continuing executive director Bernard Gersten) would prove the most fertile in Lincoln Center's forty-year history.

1991–1992

The death of Joseph Papp on October 31 seemed to cast a shadow over the season, both on and off Broadway. His passing not only raised questions about the future of the Public Theatre and the New York Shakespeare Festival, but it highlighted the precarious position of non-profit theatres. For example, the Negro Ensemble Theatre no longer offered an entire season, just a sole production when it could scrape up the money. Difficulties with the National Endowment for the Arts continued, threatening much-needed funds for many non-profit groups. The economically adventurous Broadway Alliance was tried again this season but came up only with one quick flop, *Crazy He Calls Me*.

Many saw a bright ray of optimism on Broadway with the creation of the National Actors Theatre, the realization of the longtime dream of actor Tony Randall to present a season of classics in a reasonably priced subscription series. Randall contributed a million dollars out of his pocket and raised several million more, secured the rarely used Belasco Theatre from the Shubert Or-

ganization at a discount, and launched a subscription campaign that brought in 28,000 members. By January the new company was off and running, offering the first of three classics and securing the support and admiration of the theatre community (though not always complimentary reviews). Also encouraging was the Roundabout Theatre's move from the acoustically handicapped Yegan to the Criterion Center, officially a Broadway house, according the company Tony Award status. While some carped about another non-profit theatre on Broadway competing with commercial ventures, the move would bring quality revivals to the Street, sorely needed after last season's lone non-musical entry.

By July 1 there were only two non-musical plays on Broadway, the holdovers *Lost in Yonkers* and Lincoln Center's *Six Degrees of Separation*. Attendance dropped on Broadway even though the number of non-musical entries (nine new American works, four foreign ones, and ten revivals) rose slightly. The numbers off Broadway fell somewhat (including only nine revivals), but much of the season's best work was still to be found there. Ticket prices on Broadway rose to $50 for star attractions, and there were plenty of stars. But what was really needed was a new Joe Papp.

The season began with a return engagement of John Leguizamo's one-man tour de force *Mambo Mouth* (11-8-90) on June 5 at the Orpheum, staying another seventy-seven performances. Harvey Fierstein revised and starred in his *Safe Sex* (4-5-87) on June 7 at the Actors Playhouse. The nine-performance Broadway flop stuck around for six weeks this time.

Gregory Mosher finished out his tenure at Lincoln Center with Elaine May's **Mr. Gogol and Mr. Preen** (6-9-91, Mitzi E. Newhouse), directing this "modest comedy" that seemed the antithesis of everything bold and exciting that he had previously tried to do there. Mr. Preen (W. H. Macy) is an uptight Wasp who, believe it or not, in this modern age goes door to door selling vacuum cleaners. He comes to the slovenly apartment of Mr. Gogol (Mike Nussbaum), a crafty old anarchist who takes a liking to the young man and does everything in his power, including stealing his glasses and his three-piece suit, to make him stay. The result was a substandard *The Odd Couple* with the two opposites constantly quarreling and Gogol's longtime girlfriend (Zohra Lampert) banging on the door and yelling words of affection in Yiddish. Preen finally escapes, Gogol lets the Woman in, she rejects him, Preen returns, and Gogol dies. Critical reaction was one of mild disapproval or disappointment, but audiences enjoyed the comedy for nearly seven weeks.

June was full of visitors from abroad. The Royal Dramatic Theatre of Sweden brought three classics to the Brooklyn Academy of Arts on June 10 as part of the New York International Festival of the Arts. Strindberg's *Miss Julie*, O'Neill's *Long Day's Journey Into Night* (11-7-56), and Ibsen's *A Doll's House*, all directed by Ingmar Bergman, were performed in Swedish for three performances each. As part of the same festival, the State Theatre of Lithuania offered a revival of Chekhov's *Uncle Vanya* on June 13 at the Joyce. Listening to an English translation on headsets, some critics declared it one of the most poignant Chekhov productions seen in New York in years. The same company received thumbs down for its new entry, Eimuntas Nekrosius's **The Square** (6-19-91, Joyce), an expressionistic political piece about the savage treatment of political prisoners under the Communists. Nekrosius directed both productions, which were each presented for seventeen showings.

Charles Busch moved from the Nazi-infiltrated 1940s of his *The Lady in Question* (7-25-89) to the Communist-infiltrated 1950s in his **Red Scare on Sunset** (6-21-91, Lucille Lortel), which moved up from Off Off Broadway and stayed 102 performances. Musical stage star Mary Dale (Busch) arrives in Hollywood to make a film version of her *Lady Godiva* show and learns of the "red scare" of Communism from comedienne Pat Pilford (Julie Halston). She naively helps Pat in her campaign to stamp out all the undercover Commies in the film industry, but her ire is really raised when she learns that subversives at a Method acting studio (it's a front for the local Communist Party) want to abolish the star system. Soon Mary's husband, her director, her houseboy, and even Pat are sucked into the encroaching menace, but Mary perseveres, goes to the Committee on Un-American Activities and names names, and battles successfully to keep a star's name above the title. Several critics thought the spoof was Busch's most sustained piece of writing yet, and as always, the stylishly camp performances were applauded.

The Shakespeare Marathon continued with an intelligent and gimmick-free *Othello* on June 21 at the outdoor Delacorte in Central Park. Raul Julia was a complex and involving Moor, Kathryn Meisle a solid Desdemona, and Mary Beth Hurt a fiery Emilia. As for Christopher Walken's Iago, audiences were sharply divided (he was audibly booed on some nights). Commentators called his eccentric and very American delivery of the text everything from "ominously playful" to "it echoes Jackie Mason." But Joe Dowling's production was highly recommended by the press as one of the best in the series.

Some complimentary notices ("a sunny salute to romance" and "artful and unfashionably heart-warming") greeted Wil Calhoun's **The Balcony Scene** (6-23-91, Circle), which used adjacent terraces on a Chicago high-rise as the setting for a modern love story. Alvin (Jonathan Hogan) wishes to escape from civilization's ever-increasing downward spiral, so he rarely leaves his apartment. But when Karen (Cynthia Nixon) moves in next door, they strike up a conversation on their adjoining balconies. Although she is under a lot of pressure from her job and her persistent ex-boyfriend, Karen is optimistic about life and overcomes her difficulties (and Alvin's neuroses) to find love.

What would become one of Terrence McNally's most often produced plays, **Lips Together, Teeth Apart** (6-25-91, City Center), ran 406 times in its Manhattan Theatre Club mounting before conquering regional theatres. At a chic beachhouse on Fire Island, two straight couples celebrate the Fourth of July surrounded by a gay community they feel are staring at them all the time. Sally (Swoozie Kurtz) has inherited the house from her gay brother who has died of AIDS. She and her husband, Sam (Nathan Lane), invite Sam's abrasive sister, Chloe (Christine Baranski), and her smug husband, John (Anthony Heald), for the holiday weekend, but the air is filled with foreboding and dissension. John is uneasy because he once had an affair with Sally, and Sam doesn't want to to have children and subject new human beings to this world. Chloe hides her frustration with her constant babble about Broadway musicals and her amateur theatricals, while Sally, who is pregnant, is in continual panic about having a miscarriage. We later learn that John is silently battling a fatal disease, all the time trying desperately to hold on to his superiority. The two couples' gnawing deterioration is symbolized by a gay neighbor who goes out to sea to swim and drowns, either willfully or by accident. (McNally's title, by the way, is not as provocative as it sounds; it is Sam's dentist's suggestion to him on how to sleep to avoid grinding his teeth.) The script received mixed notices, from "a comedy that hurts" to "full of miscalculations and contrivances," but everyone applauded John Tillinger's production, its vivacious cast, and John Lee Beatty's simple but evocative set showing an elegant deck with an outdoor shower and part of a swimming pool, all backed by a wall of sliding glass panels.

The rest of the summer was filled with revivals. Shaw's rarely done 1908 play *Getting Married*, not seen in New York since a brief off-Broadway mounting in 1959, was revived on June 26 at the Circle in the Square, albeit most commentators found it of limited interest. The comedy is mostly a discussion on marriage that arises when a young about-to-be-wed couple (Jane Fleiss and J. D. Cullum) have second thoughts as they face the many technicalities of marrying in the rigid Anglican Church. Stephen Porter directed a first-rate cast that featured Simon Jones as a dull husband who must pretend to beat his spouse (Madeleine Potter) in order for her to secure a divorce, Lee Richardson as an overly sensitive bishop, Elizabeth Franz as his practical, uncomplicated wife, and Walter Bobbie as a deadpan solicitor-turned-chaplain who delivers the most ghastly pronunciations about marriage.

After *Othello*, the Delacorte was given over to two guest productions from South America as part of a city-wide Festival Latino. Brazil's Teatro do Ornitorrinco (Duckbilled Platypus Theatre) brought its *A Midsummer Night's Dream* on July 30, performed in Portuguese and featuring clowns, acrobats, jugglers, stilt-walkers, fire-eaters, archers, and a Titania and her court who were partially or fully nude at times. Less provocative was Venezuela's Fundación Rajatabla mounting of *The Tempest* on August 27. Performed in Spanish, the revival was distinguished by its set, a gargantuan pre-Columbian head surrounded by fossilized palm trees. Both productions were pronounced more curiosities than satisfying Shakespearean revivals, but audiences, Latinos or otherwise, headed to the park in droves. Few rushed to see Thornton Wilder's *The Matchmaker* (12-5-55) after it opened on August 27 and critics declared it "slack and dim-witted." A miscast Dorothy Loudon as Dolly Levi headed the revival, the last Roundabout production in its downtown space at the Haft.

The bare-breasted fairies in *A Midsummer Night's Dream* could hardly compete with the nudity, sex acts, rape, and mutilation going on in Brad Fraser's **Unidentified Human Remains and the True Nature of Love** (9-19-91, Orpheum), a Canadian play that tested the limits of decency. Three young couples (hetero-, homo- and bisexual but all sexually frustrated) in Edmonton, Alberta, meet, chat, play video games, make love, tell ghost stories, take drugs, and abuse each other while a serial killer is stalking the community. Bernie (Clark Gregg), who often shows up at gatherings with blood on him and explaining that he's been in another barroom brawl, ends up being the mass murder. While waiting for that startling revelation, audiences were treated to various kinds of sexual foreplay and intercourse, masturbation, sadomasochism, and humiliation. Critics were neither titillated nor impressed, though there were enough spectators to keep the play on the boards for ten weeks.

One of the Goliaths that Joseph Papp had to battle in his early days of free Shakespeare in the park was Robert Moses, a powerful city planner whose life and career were the subject of Theodora Skipitares's **The Radiant City** (10-6-91, American Place). No one in this century did more (good and bad) in shaping New York City than Moses, so his story was an intriguing one. Skipitares also directed and designed the piece, using nine actors, several puppets, slides, film clips, and even sculpture to try to cover her complex and unwieldy topic. While it may not have been very satisfying as theatre, it was often fascinating.

Moses would not have been too thrilled with the picture of New York City created in Timothy Mason's **Babylon Gardens** (10-8-91, Circle), a drama that used the urban landscape as a parallel for a deteriorating marriage. Bill (Timothy Hutton), a nurse-anesthetist, and his wife, Jean (Mary-Louise Parker), are recovering from the death of their first child, which was stillborn, in different ways. He starts taking drugs and reaches out to the elderly patients at the hospital, listening to their stories of yesteryear and even befriending a homeless woman, Opal (Cynthia Martells). Jean, on the other hand, cuts herself off from people and spends her days by the East River painting urban landscapes. It is there she notices the young boy Hector (Hector M. Estrada) fishing and, over time, becomes fascinated with him. But when Jean tries to get to know him better, Hector uses her openness to break into her apartment to steal her VCR and sexually harass her. Jean survives but retreats further into her shell. In the end, Bill brings Opal to live in the empty room meant for their dead newborn. Some reviewers felt the piece was impressive and "worth taking seriously," but most rejected it as overwrought.

Circle in the Square revived Paul Osborn's fantasy *On Borrowed Time* (2-3-38) on October 9 with George C. Scott directing and playing the crusty

Gramps who chases Death (Nathan Lane) up a tree. Matthew Porac was his orphaned grandson Pud, Teresa Wright the scolding Granny, and Bette Henritze the dragon-like Aunt Demetria who comes to see that the boy is raised properly. Rave reviews for the cast and the old play helped the revival stay for ninety-nine performances.

The longest run of the season was James Sherman's "lovable bundle of laughs" **Beau Jest** (10-10-91, Lamb's), which received some appreciative notices and was kept on the boards for 1,069 performances because of strong word of mouth. Sarah Goldman (Laura Patinkin), a single woman in Chicago, is dating Chris Kringle (John Michael Higgins), a Wasp account executive, but she has told her parents that she is seeing a Jewish "heart and brain surgeon" named Dr. David Steinberg. The parents (Bernie Landis and Rosalyn Alexander) press to meet him, so, against Chris's arguments to the contrary, Sarah calls the Heaven Sent Escort Service for a Jewish date to join in her father's birthday dinner. When Bob Schroeder (Tom Hewitt) arrives, Sarah learns he is not Jewish but an "at liberty" actor of Polish descent. Yet six months touring with Herschel Bernardi in *Fiddler on the Roof* has taught Bob enough Hebrew to get through the dinner and thoroughly impress Sarah's folks. Also impressed is Sarah herself; as she is forced to repeat the charade on other occasions, she falls in love with Bob. The ruse is finally discovered, Sarah breaks off with Chris, and her parents tentatively accept Bob even though he is neither a doctor nor Jewish. Though very contrived at times, Sherman's dialogue was breezy ("my mother is determined to make me happy whether I like it or not"), and the characters were likable. The comedy, which originated in Chicago, became popular in community theatres.

Decidedly mixed reviews could only keep Jane Anderson's **The Baby Dance** (10-17-91, Lucille Lortel) alive for seven weeks, but some considered it a "riveting, heart-gripping drama." Rachel (Stephanie Zimbalist) and Richard (Joel Polis), an upper-class and trendy California couple, cannot have children, so Rachel seeks out a pregnant woman to agree to an adoption. She finds Wanda (Linda Purl) and her husband, Al (Richard Lineback), a poor Louisiana couple who cannot afford another mouth to feed. Rachel starts paying Wanda's doctor's bills, hoping to give the child the best prenatal care possible, but is appalled by Wanda and Al's white-trash lifestyle. She is further upset when Al tries to come on to her, yet she rises above it and maneuvers the tricky legal negotiations successfully. When the baby is born, it is declared brain damaged. Rachel wants to adopt it anyway, but Richard talks her out of it, and Wanda and Al are left with another unwanted child.

Almost as grim, Seth Zvi Rosenfeld's **Servy-n-Bernice 4Ever** (10-22-91, Provincetown Playhouse) told of Bernice (Lisa Gay Hamilton), an attractive African American who has left her roots in the projects of Manhattan. Bernice works as a model in Boston, but when she is beaten up by her ex-boyfriend she calls on her closest friend, Servy (Ron Eldard), whom she has known since childhood in Alphabet City. Servy, a white man always in trouble with the law, has recently been released from prison for robbery and breaks his parole to visit Bernice, bringing his black friend Scotty (Erik King) with him to Boston. While Bernice and Servy try to rekindle their youthful camaraderie, Scotty has a fling with Caria (Cynthia Nixon), Bernice's white roommate. Scotty opts to return to New York with Bernice, both of them willing to face their past and its consequences. Terry Kinney of the Steppenwolf Theatre directed in the taut "Chicago style," getting explosive performances from the quartet. Even so, the commercial entry only survived five weeks.

The Manhattan Theatre Club opened its twentieth season with John Patrick Shanley's autobiographical **Beggars in the House of Plenty** (10-23-91, City Center). Johnny (Loren Dean), the sensitive offspring of a violent Irish-American family, recalls his past forty years in this breathless (it only ran ninety minutes) memory play. Pop (Daniel von Bargen), a crude butcher from the Bronx, berates but still loves his wife, Noreen (Judith Ivey), a hopeful but ultimately ineffective mother. Johnny's elder siblings are Joey (Jon Tenney), a high school dropout who joins the navy and serves in Vietnam, and Sheila (Laura Linney), who marries just to get out of the house. Johnny is fascinated by fire and stares at lit matches as tempestuous scenes from the past crowd into his mind. The most harrowing one is the time Pop insisted Noreen dance with him to "Danny Boy" in the living room; when interrupted by Joey, Pop struck and killed his eldest son. Reviews ranged from "painfully funny" to "numbing."

Arguably Brian Friel's finest play, **Dancing at Lughnasa** (10-24-91, Plymouth) came to Broadway with most of its Irish cast, running 421 performances and winning both the Tony and New

York Drama Critics Circle awards. Standing on the side of the stage, the adult Michael (Gerard McSorley) narrates the play, recalling the summer of 1936 when he was a young boy being raised by his unmarried mother, Chris (Catherine Byrne), and her four spinster sisters in the small Irish village of Ballybeg. Kate (Rosaleen Linehan) is the eldest and most practical of the clan, humorlessly working as a schoolteacher to keep the impoverished family together. Maggie (Dearbhla Molloy), on the other hand, is the fun-loving sister who cooks for the family. Plain Agnes (Bríd Brennan) and simple-minded Rose (Bríd Ní Neachtain), who both work at home sewing gloves, complete the Mundy family circle. The girls are joined that summer by their brother, Jack (Donel Donnelly), just returned in poor health from twenty-five years of missionary work in a Ugandan leper colony; he is filled with mysticism and an awe of paganism that disturbs and intrigues the sisters. Also making an appearance, though a brief one, is Gerry Evans (Robert Gwilym), Michael's father, who woos Chris once again, dances off into the fields with her, then leaves to join the war in Spain. When Kate loses her job and the glove manufacturer no longer needs the sisters' services, the family's finances worsen. Rose and Agnes go off to England to earn money but instead die in poverty. The play's title refers to the harvest festival of Lughnasa, when all the young people frolic about with wild abandon. In the drama's most thrilling scene, Kate harshly reminds the women that they are now too old for such carryings-on. But when their faulty radio (nicknamed Marconi) breaks into an Irish jig, the sisters (including Kate) burst into a dancing frenzy that illustrates both their pent-up frustration and indomitable sense of life. The child Michael was never seen, but the sisters reacted to him as he saw them in his memory. Director Patrick Mason also opted for an unrealistic set with the walls of the house open to fields of rushes that designer Joe Vanek placed on a raked hill surrounding the cottage. The acting ensemble was superb (Brennan won a Tony, as did Mason), yet the lyrical drama played nearly as well with an American cast after most of the originals returned to Ireland.

The Roundabout took residence in its new Broadway home at the Criterion with Harold Pinter's *The Homecoming* (1-5-67) on October 27. Several commentators felt the menacing drama had not weathered the past twenty-five years well but saluted the cast, which featured Roy Dotrice, Lindsay Crouse, Danny Gerroll, and Jonathan Hogan.

All the lights on Broadway were dimmed on November 1 in honor of Joseph Papp who died the day before. They had also been dimmed the previous summer when Colleen Dewhurst died on August 22.

Shirley Lauro's dramatic montage **A Piece of My Heart** (11-3-91, Union Square), based on a non-fiction book by Keith Walker, followed the lives of five nurses and a country-western singer (Novella Nelson) who went to serve in Vietnam during the war. Drawn from factual oral reports, the play covered the women's initiation to the strange land, their nursing or entertaining the troops there, and their difficult adjustment to civilian life afterwards. The last glimpse of the six women is at the Vietnam Memorial in Washington, where each leaves behind a personal token of her experiences. While it was unsatisfying as a play, many were moved by images and moments in the powerful collage.

The Shakespeare Marathon's *Pericles*, on November 5 at the Public's Newman, was the first entry since JoAnne Akalaitis had been named artistic director of the Public in July. Although Michael Greif supposedly directed this rarely produced Shakespeare script, Akalaitis's controversial hand seemed to be everywhere. Greif staged each section of the episodic tale in a different style, sometimes cartoonish, other times somberly classical, even a sequence played as a black-and-white silent film comedy. Critics were sharply divided, though several thought Campbell Scott made an effective Pericles and received able support from Cordelia Gonzalez as the hero's wife, Thaisa, Don R. McManus as the narrator, Gower, Saundra McLain as the evil queen, Dionyza, and, in three small roles, Bryon Jennings. The same day, in the Public's Martinson Hall, Mabou Mines' production of Brecht's *In the Jungle of Cities* (12-20-60) began a three-week stay. The story of a Malaysian lumber merchant in 1912 Chicago was presented as an expressionistic grotesquerie with the cast wearing Halloween makeup and pounding Brecht's ideas into the audience's heads with theatrical sledgehammers. Anne Bogart directed the revival, deemed a "mess" by most aisle-sitters.

While George C. Scott was playing a bearded old curmudgeon at the Circle in the Square, Jason Robards tackled a New England version of the same character with Israel Horovitz's **Park Your Car in Harvard Yard** (11-7-91, Music Box). Jacob Brackish (Robards), the "oldest living man in

Gloucester, Massachusetts," taught English and music appreciation for decades at the local high school but now lives in his family home, which is cluttered with books and dust. When his doctor gives him only a few months to live, Jacob hires a housekeeper to care for him so that he can end his days at home rather than in a hospital. Widow Katherine Hogan (Judith Ivey) takes the job, we soon find out, because in high school Jacob flunked her, her blue-collar parents, and her late husband, keeping them (she believes) from going to college and bettering themselves. She now wishes to see the old man suffer. To the surprise of no one, the two bitter people soon soften and start to take a liking to each other. By the end of a year, Katherine is growing to appreciate music (she retakes an old test on identifying composers and gets a perfect score), and the two are close friends when Jacob quietly dies in his favorite chair. While all the notices praised the two players and Zoe Caldwell's unobtrusive direction, few critics endorsed the "vehicular excuse" of a play. As Howard Kissel in the *Daily News* noted, "you keep wishing the play was worth all the talent and energy that has been poured into it." Nevertheless, the two-character piece ran 122 performances and enjoyed some success in regional and community theatre.

Endesha Ida Mae Holland's autobiographical drama *From the Mississippi Delta* (11-18-87) returned on November 11 and played at the Circle in the Square Downtown for 218 performances. At the Public, George C. Wolfe put together a program called *Moving Beyond the Madness: A Festival of New Voices*, which opened at the Anspacher on December 1. A dozen author-performers presented works-in-progress over a two-week period. One of the workshop pieces, John Leguizamo's *Spic-o-Rama*, would develop into a major attraction the following season.

Caryl Churchill took a documentary approach in **Mad Forest** (12-4-91, Perry Street) to recreate the recent upheaval in Romania. The piece materialized out of a trip Churchill, director Mark Wing-Davey, and a group of London theatre students took to Bucharest to study the situation. The result was a cinematic collection of brief scenes and monologues capturing the plight of two Romanian families—one working class, the other intellectual upper-middle class—as they existed under the totalitarian regime of dictator Ceaucescu, how they reacted to his overthrow, and then their strained new life under non-Communist leadership. The segments ranged from gritty (the two families' bitterness toward

each other explodes at the wedding of two of their members) to fantastical (a vampire explains to a dog how he came looking for fresh blood from the revolution), all staged dynamically by Wing-Davey. Despite some enthusiastic reviews and sold-out houses, the drama closed after its scheduled fifty-four performances but returned the next season. The British play was produced by a new group, the New York Theatre Workshop, which would prove very potent later in the decade.

Since former Catskills comic Jackie Mason had conquered Broadway with lucrative success, it wasn't surprising to find **Catskills on Broadway** (12-5-91, Lunt-Fontanne) this season. The program offered four performers—Freddie Roman, Dick Capri, Marilyn Michaels, and Mal Z. Lawrence—who each, in turn, did his or her nightclub act on a nostalgic setting by Lawrence Miller that recalled the Borscht Belt resorts of old. Jokes (mostly Jewish ones), impersonations, and a few songs filled out the evening. New York's heavily Jewish audiences wholeheartedly embraced the quartet for 452 performances, and even the critics gave in and recommended the show, admitting, "No surprises but a lot of fun."

The most promising new playwright of the season was Scott McPherson, whose **Marvin's Room** (12-5-91, Playwrights Horizons) became a critical and popular hit. (It won an armful of off-Broadway awards and ran 214 performances.) Bessie (Laura Esterman) leads a life of seeming drudgery in Florida. Unmarried and overworked, she cares for her invalid father, Marvin (Adam Chapnick), who lies in bed all day, his senility and depression only relieved by Bessie using a small mirror to create beams of light that dance on the walls of his bedroom. Living with them is Bessie's partially crippled aunt Ruth (Alice Drummond), who is obsessed with television soap operas and controls the pain in her vertebrae by an electrode switch (which also makes the automatic garage door open and close). Yet Bessie does not see her situation as hopeless, even when her chronic weariness is diagnosed as leukemia. Searching for a family member with compatible bone marrow for a transplant, Bessie contacts her estranged sister, Lee (Lisa Emery), who lives in Ohio. The divorcée travels to Florida with her two sons: Hank (Mark Rosenthal), a troubled teen just released from an institution, and preteen Charlie (Karl Maschek). The reunion is an uneasy one, Lee feeling guilty about leaving Bessie with all the responsibility yet resenting how inferior Bessie makes her feel. But the sisters come to an understanding, and the two boys warm up to Bessie, Hank even agreeing to be tested for the transplant. When none of the family members' marrow is compatible, Bessie faces her uncertain future with continued hope, explaining, "I am so lucky to have loved so much." The superior drama subsequently received numerous productions regionally. However, less than a year after opening night McPherson died of AIDS.

The National Actors Theatre debuted with Arthur Miller's *The Crucible* (1-22-53) on December 10 at the Belasco and played to subscribers and interested parties for a month. While critics pointed out several flaws (uneven performances, a variety of accents from the cast, heavy-handed direction by Israeli Yossi Yzraely), they applauded the venture and endorsed the revival. The strong cast featured Martin Sheen and Maryann Plunkett as John and Elizabeth Proctor, Michael York as the ambivalent Rev. Hale, Madeleine Potter as the bewitching Abigail, and Jane Adams as the fearful Mary Warren. The revival also presented marvelous actors in smaller roles, such as Fritz Weaver as the imperious judge Danforth, Carol Woods as the Barbados conjurer Tituba, and Martha Scott as the saintly Rebecca Nurse.

A popular attraction for the holidays was Patrick Stewart's one-man performance of Charles Dickens's *A Christmas Carol*, which opened for a two-week run at the Eugene O'Neill on December 19. Television favorite Stewart, who had not been seen on Broadway since he was a member of the Royal Shakespeare Company twenty-one years before, adapted the novella into a two-hour program in which he played all the roles as well as the narrator. Critics were favorably impressed ("unexpectedly beautiful and thrilling"), and box office was brisk enough to bring him back in the future.

Plays about the AIDS epidemic continued, Joe Pintauro's **Raft of the Medusa** (12-19-91, Minetta Lane) taking the form of a support group session. Members of the group, all infected with the virus, represented a wide cross-section of victims: hetero-and homosexual; men and women; black, white, and Hispanic; rich and poor; liberal and conservative. As they express everything from bitterness to resignation, the group discover that one of them, Larry (Bruce McCarty), does not have the disease but is a reporter who is tape-recording the meeting for an article he is writing. Members attack Larry verbally, and Nairobi (Brenda Denmark), a homeless woman, stabs him with her used syringe, infecting Larry with the deadly virus. Larry panics, and the others are so appalled that Nairobi confesses that it was a clean needle and that she wouldn't wish AIDS on her worst enemy. The session ends with the group asking Larry what it is like to experience the only known "cure" for the disease. Critical opinion ranged from "the play unquestionably hits home and hits hard" to "too calculated," but it was later produced by activist groups across the county.

Large-cast plays such as Richard Nelson's historical extravaganza **Two Shakespearean Actors** (1-16-92, Cort) demanded ambitious (and subsidized) theatre companies to perform them. (This one was written for and first presented by the Royal Shakespeare Company.) Lincoln Center Theatre, now under the artistic direction of André Bishop, took the RSC's lead and produced the elaborate production in a Broadway house for twenty-nine performances, gathering some glowing notices ("a big, populated show in which life, art, and melodrama happily co-exist") but not risking an extended run. It was a bold move on Bishop's part and clearly reestablished Lincoln Center as a cultural organization to be reckoned with. Nelson's plot concerned the famous Astor Place Riot of 1849 in which two rival productions of *Macbeth* in New York led to bloodshed. British actor-manager William Charles Macready (Brian Bedford) plans to open his visiting production of the Scottish play at the Astor Place Opera House the same night that Edwin Forrest (Victor Garber), the American matinee idol, is performing the same play in the Broadway Theatre. American patriots boo Macready's performance, but the Brit perseveres, and the next night when he goes on the stage, a riot erupts outside the Astor Place, killing twenty-two people. Macready is forced to flee the theatre and, in Nelson's version, takes refuge in Forrest's dressing room, where the two men engage in a lively discussion of their art and their memories of great theatre moments of the past. Scenes from rehearsals and performances of both productions were viewed, as well as several subplots involving various actors in each man's company. Regardless of the script's shortcomings, the performers were splendid, including vivid characterizations by Zeljiko Ivanek, Judy Kuhn, Michael Butler, Frances Conroy, Eric Stoltz, and Tom Aldredge (as Washington Irving). Perhaps the primary force behind the lavish production was Jack O'Brien, who directed the tricky play with skill and imagination.

Up-and-coming playwright Donald Margulies offered his most intriguing play yet, **Sight Unseen** (1-20-92, City Center), which was favorably reviewed and ran 263 performances for the Man-

JACK [George] **O'BRIEN** (1939–) was born in Saginaw, Michigan, the son of a business representative, and educated at the University of Michigan. He taught at Hunter College before joining the Association of Producing Artists (APA), where he served as Ellis Rabb's assistant beginning in 1969. That same year he made his directing debut at the Old Globe Theatre in San Diego, a theatre he would manage from 1981 to 1991. At first, O'Brien was primarily known for his staging of large musicals and operas, such as the acclaimed *Porgy and Bess* for the Houston Grand Opera in 1976, but soon he enjoyed a reputation for directing classics and modern dramas, most notably at the Ahmanson Theatre in Los Angeles and the Acting Company at Juilliard. When his Old Globe production of *The Cocktail Hour* (1988) transferred to Manhattan, he started to be known more and more as a New York director.

hattan Theatre Club. Jonathan Waxman (Dennis Boutsikaris) has become a superstar in the world of art; his paintings are in great demand, and millionaires offer large sums of money "sight unseen" for works not yet created. Yet he feels disconnected to his early dreams of art and sees through the superficiality of the many interviews and openings. When in London for a retrospective of his work, Jonathan travels to the North England home of Patricia (Deborah Hedwall), his former lover, who has married a British archaeologist, Nick (Jon De Vries). Jonathan hopes to find a link to his past but instead comes up against a cold Patricia who is still angry at him for dumping her years ago when his career took a turn upward. Nick is jealous and dislikes Jonathan and his art because he is an admirer of Renaissance works. Patricia has an early painting of Jonathan's, a nude portrait of her done when they were students and lovers, and Jonathan recognizes in the work the passion he has long since lost. He wants to buy or borrow the portrait for his London show, but Patricia refuses. Yet Nick convinces her to part with it, glad to get the ghost of her former lover out of his house. In a flashback to seventeen years earlier, Jonathan begins the portrait as he and Patricia dream of a pure and uncompromising future together.

Aisle-sitters remarked that the Roundabout's revival of Friedrich Dürrenmatt's *The Visit* (5-5-58) on January 23 made a rather nasty play even nastier by putting much of the cast in masks and having them act as inhuman as possible. But Jane Alexander, as the world's richest woman out for revenge, and Harris Yulin, as her victim, were quite adept at playing the cartoonish leads. For their second offering, on January 26, the National Actors Theatre moved from American tragedy to French farce to show off the versatility of the company, but Feydeau's *A Little Hotel on the Side*, known to most theatregoers as *Hotel Paradiso* (4-11-57), only revealed an uneven troupe floundering at the Belasco. NAT's founder/director Tony Randall headed the cast, but, like much of the company, his broad performance only seemed to please matinee audiences. Lynn Redgrave, Paxton Whitehead, Maryann Plunkett, and Madeleine Potter were considered more successful, and movie star Rob Lowe either enthralled or irritated subscribers.

Perhaps the most embarrassing flop of the Broadway season was Abraham Tetenbaum's odd romance **Crazy He Calls Me** (1-27-92, Walter Kerr), which appalled critics, disgusted audiences, and departed after seven performances. Benny (Barry Miller), a virginal, mother-fixated lawyer, meets Yvette (Polly Draper), a lively, vaguely accented immigrant, in Brooklyn in 1938 and, despite her erratic behavior, marries her. It takes him two years to discover what the audience already knew: Yvette is crazy. So he sues her, claiming fraud (she had a record of mental illness), loses the case, and, in the end, goes off into the sunset with her. Neither character was likable or even bearable (Yvette's idea of breaking the ice on the first date was to perform oral sex on Benny), and no one onstage or in the house could figure out if this was a comedy or not. It was the third entry in the Broadway Alliance, an admirable program seriously damaged by the two-character play.

Commentators agreed that Athol Fugard's *Boesman and Lena* (6-22-70) had gained power and prestige over the past two decades, as witnessed by the Manhattan Theatre Club's first-class revival on January 29. Lynn Thigpen and Keith David played the two wandering "coloreds" and, under Fugard's direction, gave "chilling" performances.

Paula Vogel launched her controversial playwriting career with **The Baltimore Waltz** (2-11-92, Circle), an allegory that some critics thought "an immensely likable winning comedy-drama" but others dismissed as "a muddled concept of conceivably more therapeutic use to [the playwright] than value to her audience." Anna (Cherry Jones), an unwed teacher in Baltimore, has been diagnosed with ATD (Acquired Toilet Disease), a new strain of illness that kills elementary school teachers. Accompanied by her brother, Carl (Richard Thompson), Anna sets off for Europe, hoping to engage in unbridled sex and fine dining before she dies. In Paris, Amsterdam, and Berlin, Anna tackles various men (all played by Joe Mantello with outrageous foreign accents) while Carl goes into dark alleys and meets with spies and black-market types (also played by Mantello) in order to find a cure for his sister. The siblings eventually find themselves in Vienna, where a renowned quack (also Mantello) offers no hope for a cure. Back home, Anna shows slides of her trip, but they are all scenes from Baltimore, proving the two never left America. Only after Carl dies of AIDS do we realize that Anna made up the whole dizzying adventure, her way of keeping her brother entertained as he lay dying. The New York engagement was limited to thirty-nine showings, but the play enjoyed many regional productions.

With **Grandchild of Kings** (2-16-92, Theatre for the New City), director Harold Prince turned author when he dramatized parts of Sean O'Casey's multi-volume autobiography into a stage piece. Covering the years of O'Casey's growing up in Dublin, the script was episodic, with the older O'Casey (Chris O'Neill) commenting on the actions of his youthful counterpart (Patrick Fitzgerald). Few critics thought the subject provoking enough for a play, but everyone admired Prince's spirited production in which "every moment is alive with characters, with music and dancing, and with feelings that explode and vanish." Eugene Lee's environmental set, capturing the excitement and squalor of the streets of Dublin between 1880 and 1910, was also praised. The play, the first of three O'Casey works proposed by Prince, ran ninety-seven performances, but further installments never materialized.

Television favorite Joan Collins made sure she did not disappoint her fans when she made her Broadway debut in Noel Coward's *Private Lives* (1-27-31) on February 20 at the Broadhurst: she played Amanda as the cold, vulgar, and sexy bitch that America so loved her for. Simon Jones was her unfortunate co-star and Arvin Brown her even less fortunate director. Aisle-sitters took potshots, claiming Collins was better than Elizabeth Taylor was when she had essayed the role nine years earlier but noting that that wasn't saying much. Fans had thirty-seven chances to see Collins (as part of a cross-country tour), and they eagerly seized the opportunity.

Several commentators compared Howard Korder (some favorably, most not) to David Mamet when Korder's **Search and Destroy** (2-26-92, Circle in the Square) arrived on Broadway from California and the Yale Repertory Theatre. The modern fable was told in short, brusque scenes littered with gritty dialogue, and even the plot (a huckster trying to get a movie made) recalled Mamet's *Speed-the-Plow* (5-3-88). Martin Mirkheim (Griffin Dunne) owes close to a million dollars in back taxes but sees a simple solution to his problem: make a film out of a best-selling motivational book by cable TV evangelist Dr. Waxling (Stephen McHattie). Martin sets off on a cross-country journey of self-discovery in which he bullies and blackmails his way into the popular guru's presence, only to find Waxling as callous and mercenary as himself. (Waxling wants $500,000 for the film rights.) But Martin pushes on, resorting to extortion and even murder to make his film about a "higher truth."

On February 27 Lincoln Center picked up one of last season's critical hits, *Substance of Fire* (3-17-91) by Jon Robin Baitz, and gave it a home in the Mitzi E. Newhouse for 174 performances. Most of the original cast returned.

Heretofore, plays about AIDS had been written by and about whites. The first black play of note about the plague was Cheryl L. West's **Before It Hits Home** (3-10-92, Public: LuEsther). Wendal (James McDaniel), a bisexual jazz musician, is diagnosed HIV positive and suffers from indecision whether to tell his lover, Douglas (Keith Randolph Smith), a married man and a father, and his fiancée, Simone (Sharon Washington), who is pregnant with his child. Fleeing both lovers, Wendal returns to his home and confesses his condition to his parents. His mother is disgusted and cuts him off, taking Wendal's teenage son from another marriage with her. But Wendal's father overcomes his initial prejudice and cares for his ailing son until Wendal dies. The drama, first seen at Washington's Arena Stage, garnered some appreciative reviews, one calling it "relentlessly observant and ruthlessly forthright."

Yet another foreign company visiting New York this season was the National Puppet Theatre of Japan, which brought its Bunraku presentation of *The Love Suicides at Sonezaki* to the City Center on March 10 for a week. The classic puppet play, a *Romeo and Juliet*–like tragedy by Monzaemon Chikamatsu, was performed in Japanese.

The second "waltz" play of the season, a romantic love story with a much happier ending than *The Baltimore Waltz*, was Allan Knee's **Shmulnik's Waltz** (3-11-92, John Houseman), which had an appealing ethnic folk-tale quality to it. When a Jewish immigrant, Shmulnik (Steve Routman), arrives in Manhattan at the turn of the century, he can only find work as a peddler even though he is well educated. Jonathan (Rob Gomes), on the other hand, is quite rich but illiterate and tongue-tied. So he hires Shmulnik to write a series of love letters to his beloved Rachel (Wendy Kaplan), hoping to win her heart. Rachel is not very interested in the highly intelligent letters, but her bookish sister Feyla (Ilana Levine) is, falling in love with "Jonathan." All ends happily as Jonathan wins Rachel on his own and Feyla happily discovers Shmulnik is the author of the poetic missives. The comedy, which had originated at the off-off-Broadway Jewish Repertory Theatre, ran nine weeks off Broadway.

Some high-powered acting by its three stars kept Ariel Dorfman's political melodrama **Death and the Maiden** (3-17-92, Brooks Atkinson) on the boards for 159 performances. In an unnamed South American country coming out of a ruthless dictatorship, Gerardo Escobar (Richard Dreyfuss) is asked to lead an investigation into human rights crimes during the previous regime. Gerardo's wife, Paulina (Glenn Close), had been a prisoner under the dictator and was blindfolded and tortured by an unseen official. When Dr. Roberto Miranda (Gene Hackman) comes to the Escobars' home to stay a few days and aid Gerardo in his investigation, Paulina recognizes his voice as that of her tormentor. That night when he is asleep, Paulina ties Roberto up and, brandishing a gun, accuses him of the crimes against her. Gerardo is torn between believing the rational denials by Roberto or the fanatical accusations by his wife. After raising several moral questions, mostly dealing with how quickly humans resort to brutality, Roberto admits he is the official in question, explaining how he was coerced into joining the torturers and how his conscience has in turn tormented him ever since. Some notices called the play a "terrifying moral thriller," while others described it as an "earnest but curiously inert evening." But there was little disagreement about Mike Nichols's taut direction and the stars' performances. Actors Equity and some Hispanic groups protested the use of white actors in roles that were obviously Latin American. Regardless, Close won a Tony at season's end.

Stockard Channing was starred in another new work by John Guare, but **Four Baboons Adoring the Sun** (3-18-92, Vivian Beaumont) was not like *Six Degrees of Separation* (6-14-90) in form or quality. Philip (James Naughton) and Penny McKenzie (Channing) are newlyweds but have children from previous unhappy marriages. The couple bring the nine offspring with them to Sicily, where Philip is working at an archaeological dig. The new couple had a passionate affair before they divorced their partners but have unsuccessfully tried to keep this fact from their children. Wayne (Wil Horneff) and Halcy (Angela Goethals), the eldest from each family, have fallen in love and want permission from the parents to have sex together. Before the issue can be resolved, an earthquake separates the group, and Wayne, fleeing his disapproving parents, falls to his death while trying to escape. Philip returns to the States with the rest of the children, but Penny remains on the island, seeking understanding from the ancient artifacts that surround her. (The title referred to one of these artifacts.) The allegorical drama was narrated by Eros (Eugene Perry), who served as a Greek chorus; indeed, Guare's dialogue throughout had an inflated kind of rhetoric meant to recall classical tragedy. Critics were sharply divided about the odd piece, some claiming it had "ineluctable emotional power" but more thinking it a "pedantic pageant." Peter Hall directed with an operatic flourish, and Tony Walton provided a stunning Bronze Age set with smoke pouring out of an opening that served as everything from an altar to a volcano. After the Lincoln Center production ran its thirty-eight-performance subscription engagement, the script became an obscure artifact of its own.

Ibsen's difficult tragedy *The Master Builder,* opening on March 19, completed the National Actors Theatre's premiere season at the Belasco. The lifeless revival garnered few positive reviews, leaving critics and subscribers hoping for better things in the future from the company. Tony Randall directed the luckless cast that featured Earle Hyman as Solness, Lynn Redgrave as his wife, Alvine, and Madeleine Potter as Hilde Wangel.

In a sense, Neil Simon's future was behind him. He found only modest success with his **Jake's Women** (3-24-92, Neil Simon), a reflective comedy that had premiered in California but was greatly changed by the time it hit Broadway. Novelist Jake (Alan Alda) watches his second wife, Maggie (Helen Shaver), walk out of their marriage of eight years and then conjures up various women in his life to provide consolation or answers. His first wife, Julie (Kate Burton), died when she was young but in his imagination she is still there for him. Also entering in person or in Jake's mind are his daughter, Molly, played as a twelve-year old in the past by Genia Michaela and by Tracy Pollan in the present, his overbearing sister, Karen (Brenda Vaccaro), his highly opinionated analyst, Edith (Joyce Van Patten) and his new girlfriend, Sheila (Talia Balsam), who may well become wife number three. Jake recognizes that his relationship with these women is better in fantasy than in reality. As Jake admits, his life has been "like putting together a jigsaw puzzle that has no picture on it." Simon specialist Gene Saks directed the accomplished cast, which got better reviews than the script. Naysayers called it "thankless and dishonest," while Jack Kroll in *Time* spoke for those who thought "it's good for your heart." The comedy ran an unprofitable 245 performances, far fewer than Simon was used to.

A similarly reflective memory play followed close at hand. Herb Gardner's **Conversations With My Father** (3-29-92, Royale) moved from 1976 back in time to 1936 and then proceeded through the years as Charlie (Tony Shalhoub) recalled his vibrant immigrant father, Eddie (Judd Hirsch). Born Itzik Goldberg in Odessa, Eddie embraces America by changing not only his name but those of his wife, Gusta (Gordanna Rashovich), to Gloria and sons Charlie (David Krumholtz as a young boy) and Joey (Jason Briggs as a youth, Tony Gillan as an adult). Opening the Golden Door Tavern on Canal Street in New York's Lower East Side, Eddie survives mobster threats in the Depression, rumors of the mass murder of Jews in Europe in the 1940s, and anti-Semitism in his own neighborhood off and on over the decades. There are lighthearted memories as well, such as Eddie's turning the bar into the Flamingo Lounge during the booming 1950s. But in 1976 Eddie dies, and the bar, now called the Homeland Tavern, is sold even as memories of the colorful patriarch still haunt the place. The portrait was funny, sentimental, and lively, punctuated by Hirsch's Tony Award–winning performance and Daniel Sullivan's expert direction. The scenery by busy Tony Walton (it was his third Broadway credit this month) depicted Eddie's saloon over the years with a dreamy yet detailed sense of nostalgia. The comedy, which originated at the Seattle Repertory Theatre, ran 402 performances thanks to some laudatory reviews and Hirsch's popularity.

The Roundabout's *Hamlet* on April 2 at the Criterion was considered "punctilious and intelligent" though there were differing opinions about Stephen Lang's grubby, bohemian prince with twigs in his hair. He was given capable support by Kathleen Widdoes (Gertrude), Michael Cristofer (Claudius), Elizabeth McGovern (Ophelia), and James Cromwell (Polonius). The Public revived John Ford's *'Tis Pity She's a Whore* on April 19 at the Newman with two movie stars playing the incestuous brother and sister of the Jacobean tragedy. Val Kilmer and Jeanne Tripplehorn headed the production, which director JoAnne Akalaitis and her designer, John Conklin, set in the Fascist Italy of the 1930s. The setting was immaterial since the revival was done surrealistically, the result considered either "surprisingly engrossing" or ridiculous.

Jon Robin Baitz took his usual global frame of reference and made it more cynical (and satiric) in **The End of the Day** (4-7-92, Playwrights Horizons), another play this season about the triumph of corruption. Dr. Graydon Massey (Roger Rees), a British psychiatrist who has become a naturalized American, gives up his lucrative Malibu practice and wealthy wife to work in an inner-city Los Angeles clinic. But his ex-wife's Mafia-connected family come after Graydon and demand repayment for the thousands they paid to put him through medical school. Graydon goes to his aristocratic family in London to ask for the funds but soon discovers their money comes from underworld activities connected to the Mafia back in the States. So Graydon loses his sense of honor and embarks on a plan of blackmail, con games, cocaine, and even murder, ending up a big-time operator in Hollywood. Similarities with this season's earlier *Search and Destroy* did not go unnoticed, though Baitz's script was funnier, with both American and British families (played by the same actors) portrayed as screwball types. Nancy Marchand was particularly entertaining as Rosamund, Graydon's American supervisor at the clinic, and Jocelyn, his amoral British mom.

A star-studded revival of Tennessee Williams's *A Streetcar Named Desire* (12-3-47) on April 12 at the Ethel Barrymore was poorly received, most critics finding Jessica Lange's Blanche sexy but distant and Alec Baldwin's Stanley brutal but simple-minded. Gregory Mosher staged the slow-paced revival (it ran three hours), and Amy Madigan (Stella) and Timothy Carhart (Mitch) provided able support. Regardless of the critical knocks, the attraction did vigorous business for 137 performances.

New York saw August Wilson's latest effort, **Two Trains Running** (4-13-92, Walter Kerr), only after it had been produced (and polished) in six different regional theatres. On Broadway it was generally hailed as "the most comic of the Wilson saga so far" and his "most delicate and mature work." At a dingy coffee shop in Pittsburgh in 1969, the regulars talk about two significant events planned for the same day. A prominent local preacher, Prophet Samuel, has died, and his funeral is expected to draw quite a crowd. At the same time, the recent assassination of Malcolm X has spurred a protest rally in the black section of town. Yet the occupants of the restaurant are more concerned with their own day-to-day lives, in particular Memphis Lee (Al White), who owns the diner and is anticipating being bought out as the neighborhood is starting to be developed. Also gathered are Holloway (Roscoe Lee Browne), an elderly local sage who believes in the power of magic; Risa (Cynthia Martells), an embittered waitress who has slashed her legs with a razor to frighten off men; ex-con Sterling (Larry Fishburne), who returns to his old neighborhood dreaming of a fresh start; and Hambone (Sullivan Walker), a feeble-minded man who has spent his life ranting about a ham he was once promised for a job and never received. Little overt action occurs in the Chekhov-like drama, but Sterling and Risa drift into a relationship, Hambone dies in his sleep, Memphis gets a huge amount of money from the city for his place, and Sterling steals a ham to put in Hambone's casket. As usual, Lloyd Richards directed superbly and the ensemble cast shone, Fishburne winning a Tony Award. The play won the New York Drama Critics Circle Award and ran 160 performances.

Broadway's shortest run of the season (four performances) was Jill Shearer's **Shimada** (4-23-92, Broadhurst), a pale echo of the earlier *Death and the Maiden* set in Australia. After World War II, Eric Dawson (Ben Gazzara), an Aussie who suffered in a Japanese prison camp, began a bicycle factory with Clive Beaumont (Robert Joy), a fellow inmate and close friend. Years later, Clive has died and a Japanese investor, Toshio Uchiyama (Mako), is trying to buy out the failing company. Eric is convinced that Uchiyama is Shimada, a sadistic guard who tortured them in the jungle camp. (Just as Glenn Close did in the earlier drama, Eric identifies the former enemy when he hears his voice.) Flashbacks to the past (including some gruesome torture scenes) parallel the current "trade war" between Japan and Australia, but it is Clive's son, Mark (also played by Joy), who realizes that the past must be forgotten in order to make the world any better. Stars Ellen

Burstyn and Estelle Parsons were wasted in minor roles as Clive's widow and a union organizer at the factory. Although the production (which had originated in Australia) was heavily backed by a corporation in Japan and boasted the first simultaneous translation into Japanese in a Broadway house, most critics found the play "anti-Japanese" in its stereotypic portrayal of Uchiyama/Shimada. They also had little positive to say about the "overqualified and at times ludicrously overzealous cast" and dismissed the script as an "obnoxious piece of goods."

Alan Ayckbourn's plays had been getting more serious over the years, but none was as disturbing as **A Small Family Business** (4-27-92, Music Box), which still managed to be a comedy. Like this season's *Search and Destroy* and *The End of the Day*, it told of an upright innocent who succumbs to corruption in the world. When Jack McCracken (Brian Murray) becomes managing director of his wife's family furniture-manufacturing business, he hopes to run it efficiently and honestly. But Jack immediately learns that all the relatives are milking the company for expensive cars, erotic playthings, and vacations in exotic locales. His wife, Poppy (Jane Carr), not only defends her relatives but insists that Jack start helping himself as well because she is tired of missing out on the extras. When their daughter, Samantha (Amelia Campbell), is picked up for shoplifting by private investigator Benedict Hough (Anthony Heald), Jack is blackmailed into a graft scheme to keep Benedict from prosecuting "Sammy." This leads to connections with drugs, Benedict's blackmailing Jack, the family planning to bump off Benedict, and Jack's total immersion into a life of crime and degradation. The comedy ends with Jack ironically toasting the company and its forthright business ethics. The uncomfortable comedy received mixed notices and only ran forty-eight performances.

The American Place brought back Laurence Holder's bio-drama *Zora Neale Hurston* (2-4-90) on April 29 and kept it on the boards for sixty showings. Elizabeth Van Dyke played the "Queen of the Harlem Renaissance"; Joseph Edwards, all the people she encountered there.

Anna Deavere Smith, an African-American actress who had long been doing performance pieces inspired by the headlines, joined the list of actor-playwrights who would present a series of successful one-person plays during the decade. Smith's **Fires in the Mirror** (5-12-92, Public: Shiva) brought her wide attention and rave reviews, summarized by Frank Rich in the *New York Times* as "quite simply, the most compelling and sophisticated view of urban racial and class conflict . . . that one can hope to encounter." The subject of the piece was the 1991 Crown Heights riots ignited when a young African-American boy in Brooklyn was accidentally killed by an elderly Jewish driver; subsequently, a group of blacks attacked a Hasidic rabbinical student and killed him. Smith interviewed dozens of Jews and blacks in the neighborhood, then fashioned the material into an evening of thirty monologues for herself, playing both male and female, black and white characters. Her versatility as an actress was matched by her ability to create highly dramatic passages from documentary material. The program was repeated 109 times.

The Public's "suitably intense and somber production" of Lorca's *Blood Wedding* on May 14 featured an all-black cast and used Langston Hughes's poetic 1938 translation for the first time. Reviewers were more approving than enthusiastic, though Gloria Foster as the tragic matriarch of the drama was highly esteemed, as was Elizabeth Peña as the unfortunate Bride.

Very few critics approved of Richard Greenberg's **The Extra Man** (5-19-92, City Center), calling it "arch, smug, and inept," though the editors of the *Best Plays* chose it as one of the season's best. Likable but passive Keith (Boyd Gaines), a short-story writer going through a dry spell, decides (for reasons never made clear) to match up his friend Laura (Laila Robins), a bright and successful editor, with Jess (Adam Arkin), a lovesick film reviewer, even though Laura is happily married to Keith's close friend Daniel (John Slattery). Keith is successful, and the two embark on a passionate affair. But soon Laura suspects Keith's manipulation in the romance and starts to question the relationship's validity. The affair eventually ends, leaving the three members of the triangle heartbroken, but Keith is his usual sympathetic self ready to comfort all three of his friends.

The season ended with John Logan's historical courtroom drama **Hauptmann** (5-28-92, Cherry Lane) about the 1936 Lindbergh kidnapping trial. Bruno Richard Hauptmann (Denis O'Hare) was presented as a victim of a society threatened by foreigners. The German immigrant's dark and arrogant temperament was contrasted with the heroic, all-American Charles Lindbergh (Gunnar Branson). Using actual court transcripts, the drama made a case for the inconclusive nature of the evidence against Hauptmann and suggested that, guilty or not, he never received a fair trial. Despite masterful performances and a competent script, the commercial entry could only find an audience for twenty-two performances.

1992–1993

It was certainly an American season in New York, with all but one of the new entries on Broadway and all but five off Broadway written by native playwrights. (All the *Best Plays* selections were American—the first time since the 1958–1959 season.) To add to all the Americana blossoming in New York, the Democratic National Convention in July seemed to overflow Madison Square Garden and affect the theatre district as well. The Clinton ticket made a point of more acceptance of gays (at least in terms of the military) and sought to restore the integrity of the National Endowment for the Arts.

The total number of productions both on and off the Street remained about the same, though there were fewer revivals off Broadway (only five not counting foreign-language offerings) and more on Broadway (up to eleven), all of them by non-profit theatre companies. It seemed that commercial producers were keeping revivals at arm's length. Even more interesting (and alarming) was the number of one-person shows this season: three on Broadway, fourteen off, and countless others off-off. And these were not literary monologues like *Mark Twain Tonight!* or fictitious monodramas like *Shirley Valentine*. Many were written and performed by actors who wrote about and played themselves. Some were engaging; many others were not. But audiences did not seem to tire of these autobiographical confessionals, for several this season were long-run hits.

While Lincoln Center seemed to be comfortably settling into its new administration and the Roundabout was prospering with its new Broadway status, the Public Theatre was in turmoil. With so many critics and patrons unhappy with JoAnne Akalaitis's *auteur* productions, the board of directors swiftly dismissed her in March and made George C. Wolfe the new artistic director. Meanwhile both the Negro Ensemble Company and the Circle in the Square Uptown skirted bankruptcy. Money was tight on commercial Broadway as well. Non-musicals *Redwood Curtain* and *Angels in America* cost $1 million and $2.2 million, respectively, to open. The former lost its entire investment, and the latter would not break even until eight years later, when regional productions provided the necessary royalties. No wonder there were so many one-person shows.

Ironically, this American season started out with a British triumph: the Royal National Theatre's stunning revival of *Richard III* on June 9 at BAM for a two-week run as part of its international tour. Director Richard Eyre set the drama in a fascist Britain of the 1930s with Ian McKellen as a dry and humorless villain who was all the more chilling because of his passionless quest for power. Some of the familiar speeches were delivered into a microphone and echoed through an old-time public address system—a memorable touch. The next night, high praise also greeted the Roundabout Theatre's revival of Arthur Miller's *The Price* (2-7-68) at the Criterion. Critics applauded the still-potent script, John Tillinger's expert direction, and the superior cast: Hector Elizondo and Joe Spano as the at-odds brothers Victor and Walter, Debra Mooney as Victor's bitter wife, Esther, and Eli Wallach as the wizened old furniture dealer Gregory Solomon.

The season's first of many solo performances was Josh Kornbluth's **Red Diaper Baby** (6-12-92, Actors' Playhouse) about growing up the son of two very different Communists. His father was a fiery schoolteacher who kept getting fired because he saw education officials as capitalistic dictators. His mother was a librarian who gathered and nourished an odd collection of writers and artists. Kornbluth's parents divorced when he was six because his father decided that the family unit was the root of the world's evils. The show detailed Kornbluth's life with each parent and his own political maturity. The monodrama had run five weeks off-off Broadway before transferring for fifty-nine more showings off Broadway.

Peter Parnell had resurrected Goethe in *The Sorrows of Stephen* (11-20-79) and a whole gaggle of dead American authors in *Romance Language* (11-14-84), so one could pretty much guess what his **Flaubert's Latest** (6-21-92, Playwrights Horizons) was going to be about. Novelist Felix (Mark Nelson) rents a house in rural Connecticut in order to complete Gustave Flaubert's unfinished *Bouvard et Pecuchet* but runs into writer's block. His total preoccupation with the project frustrates Felix's longtime companion, Colin (Mitchell Anderson), a dancer who is HIV positive. When their actress friend Ursula (Mary Louise Wilson), who is playing Madame Arcati in a local production of *Blithe Spirit*, visits and utilizes her talents as a part-time medium, Flaubert (John Bedford Lloyd) and his mistress Louise Colet

(Jean DeBaer), a poet and radical feminist, are conjured up in the flesh. Like Colin and Felix, Flaubert and Louise are always quarreling, both couples threatened by infidelity and writer's neuroses. Colin is seduced by a local gardener, Jace (Gil Bellows), and Flaubert struggles with writing *Madame Bovary*. Although the nineteenth-century couple enjoy their weekend in the future (Flaubert loves the Cuisinart and Felix's word processor, while Louise adores shopping at the mall and seeing how far women have progressed), they find themselves in another quarrel in which Louise tries to shoot Flaubert but only succeeds in wounding Felix. The French couple return to their crinoline era, and when Felix overcomes his writer's block, the gay lovers gain a new appreciation of each other.

A one-person autobiographical show that was just as popular when actors other than the author performed it was David Drake's **The Night Larry Kramer Kissed Me** (6-22-92, Perry Street). Drake recalled his childhood, his discovery that he was a homosexual, and his active adult life as a gay man in Manhattan. Though much of the same material had been covered before and would be again, Drake approached his subject with humor rather than pathos. The monologue became a cult hit, running 337 performances with various actors taking over for Drake.

The Manhattan Theatre Club had a disappointing season, typified by Keith Reddin's unfocused comedy **The Innocents' Crusade** (6-23-92, City Center). As high school senior Bill (Stephen Mailer) and his parents (James Rebhorn and Debra Monk) make the rounds of various college admissions offices, Bill is inspired by the tale of the disastrous Children's Crusade of the Middle Ages and starts to gather his own innocents along the way, including heiress-on-the-run Laura (Welker White) and a homeless man (Tim Blake Nelson) who only speaks in an archaic form of Middle English. When Bill's father loses his patience, kicking out the hangers-on and calling his son a loser, Bill takes off on his own. A ghost, the spirit of the medieval leader of the Children's Crusade, appears to the parents to tell them that their son has left to go on a crusade of his own.

Al Pacino returned to Broadway in a new and an old play that were presented in repertory at Circle in the Square, another company languishing through an unsuccessful season. Ira Lewis's two-hander **Chinese Coffee** (6-24-92, Circle in the Square) is an extended duel of words between two friends, struggling writer Harry Levine (Pacino) and photographer Jacob Manheim (Charles

Cioffi). Harry bangs on Jacob's door in the middle of a freezing February night demanding money that he owes him. But he really has come to see what Jacob thinks of his new novel, the manuscript having been in Jacob's hands for months. At first Jacob says he hasn't gotten around to reading it, but in the high-pressure talkathon that follows it is revealed that the novel is a thinly disguised version of Jacob's life. Jacob eventually admits that he has read it and thinks that it is very commercial and likely to be a big seller, but the refuses to let Harry use his life for art. Tossing the pages all over the dirty apartment, Jacob seeks to destroy the manuscript, but Harry admits he has another copy at home and leaves his ranting friend unsatisfied. Reviewers applauded the vigorous performances even as they panned the tedious, overlong acting exercise of a play. Four days later, Pacino essayed the lustful King Herod in a revival of Oscar Wilde's 1896 poetic curiosity *Salome*, not seen on Broadway since 1923. Critics described Robert Allan Ackerman's revival as "an explosion of Biblical kitsch" that was "often campy, usually overwrought, and sometimes just plain goofy, but never less than intriguing." Television starlet Sheryl Lee played Salome as a "petulant Valley Girl," but her erotic Dance of the Seven Veils and animalistic *pas de deux* with John the Baptist's head did not disappoint thrill seekers. Tickets were in demand, but when Pacino had to move on to other projects, the repertory was forced to close on July 23, still in the red.

The New York Shakespeare Festival's thirtieth season in Central Park (and its first without Joseph Papp) opened on July 2 with Adrian Hall's mounting of *As You Like It* at the Delacorte. Differing opinions about the cast (most approved of Elizabeth McGovern's Rosalind) and staging all pointed to a competent if unexceptional summer offering. Eugene Lee's depiction of the Forest of Arden, complete with farm tractor, windmill, chicken coop (with live chickens), and, in an absurd touch, a Louis IV dining room set, amused or confused spectators. The second Delacorte offering, *The Comedy of Errors* on August 6, took on a carnival atmosphere in which physical acrobatics outshone verbal antics. (In fact, an acrobatic troupe called Antigravity was slipped into the proceedings.) Some commentators found it joyous, others hyperactive and annoying.

Teaming Tom Stoppard's one-acts *The Real Inspector Hound* (4-23-72) and *The Fifteen-Minute Hamlet* (10-3-79) on August 13 at the Roundabout proved to be a surprising delight. (The short

Hamlet was originally seen as part of Stoppard's *Dogg's Hamlet*.) Simon Jones and David Healy played the two drama critics watching (and being sucked into) a West End mystery play in *Hound*, and Jones essayed the moody Dane in the pint-sized tragedy that indeed lasted a quarter of an hour.

One of Off Broadway's few commercial entries this season was Kevin Heelan's **Distant Fires** (8-20-92, Circle in the Square Downtown), a drama that only survived fifty-four performances. On a construction site in Ocean City, Maryland, local racial tension is symbolized by five workers (three black and two white) who labor together while the flames of the previous night's race riot burn in the distance. The situation is made more sensitive when Beauty (Jordan Lage), a black worker filling in for the group's injured foreman, and Thomas (Ray Anthony Thomas), a white fellow worker, find out that they are both in line for the same important union job. Foos (Giancarlo Esposito), an old man whose chronic drinking has made his continuing with the company questionable, predicts (correctly) that Thomas will get the job because of favoritism by the all-white union board. The announcement of Thomas's victory leaves both candidates dismayed, aware that neither was judged by his true ability.

A second commercial entry, one that fared slightly better, was Horton Foote's **The Roads to Home** (9-17-92, Lamb's), an evening of three related one-acts with recurring characters, all of them ignoring the truth in their past and present. *A Nightingale*, set in Houston in 1924, found two friends, Mabel Votaugh (Jean Stapleton) and Vonnie Hayhurst (Rochelle Oliver), who came to the big city from the same Texas town many years ago, confronted with past scandals when Annie (Hallie Foote), an unstable girl from back home, arrives for a visit. Vonnie's husband, Eddie (William Alderson), is having an affair with another woman in *Dearest of Friends*, the second one-act, and Vonnie wants help in getting a divorce, but Mabel and her husband Jack (Emmett O'Sullivan-Moore), cannot bring themselves to get involved. The evening ended with *Spring Dance*, in which Annie, confined to a sanitarium, finds that even her fellow patients would rather ignore her than face up to the reality of their situation. Some appreciative reviews ("a loving, fierce portrait of a sweet-tempered, brutal culture") and Stapleton's name helped the trio program run eight weeks.

On the same night, the Ridiculous Theatrical Company had a modest hit with **Brother Truckers** (9-17-92, Charles Ludlam), a campy "comedy noir" by Georg Osterman that ran seventy-two times. Lyla Balskin (Everett Quinton) is the undisputed Queen of Trash (she owns the biggest trash-removal company on Long Island) and uses her power and drop-dead chic to get the man she loves, despite the fact that she's already married to Harry (Eureka), a cigar-chomping garbage-hauler who has "nothing in common with class" except "the last three letters of the word." Lyla's pursuit of a hunky garbage truck driver, Lech Fabrinski (Grant Neale), is threatened by her rival Billie Wilson (Osterman), a sluttish waitress whose red hair is big enough to house ravens. In true Joan Crawford style, Lyla gets her man plus the opportunity to wear the evening's best clothes. (In one scene costumer Elizabeth Fried put Lyla in a geometric-patterned outfit that matched her purse, stockings, gloves, and the decor of the diner where she was lunching.) Quinton, who also directed, was lauded for his outrageously dead-on performance, perhaps the finest of his career.

Two recent off-Broadway dramas returned for longer runs. Graham Reid's *Remembrance* (4-16-91) opened on September 30 at the John Houseman and, despite lackluster notices, stayed for 142 performances (nearly four times the run of the original engagement). Milo O'Shea and Frances Sternhagen played the elderly Irish couple who find romance despite their different religions. The Manhattan Theatre Club brought back the New York Theatre Workshop production of Caryl Churchill's documentary drama *Mad Forest* (12-4-91) the next night at the City Center, and it ran an additional seventy performances. That same night in Brooklyn, France's Théâtre du Soleil began its ten-hour, four-play cycle of Greek plays under the umbrella title **Les Atrides** (10-1-92, BAM). Presented in French (with simultaneous headphone English translation) over the next ten days were Euripides' *Iphigenia in Aulis* in repertory with his *The Eumenides* and Aeschylus' *Agamemnon* and *The Libation Bearers*. The company's celebrated founder Ariane Mnouchkine staged the extended tale of the House of Atreus using dance techniques from India, Kabuki theatrics, and Celtic jigs, all on a barren bullring of a setting. Several critics called the event "mesmerizing" and "electrifying theatre"; others denounced it as "theatre of pain" and "trendy Euro-trash."

Simon Gray explored familiar territory (a publisher in turmoil) in **The Holy Terror** (10-8-92, Promenade) but with little of his past success. Mark Melon (Daniel Gerroll) takes over a struggling but respectable publishing firm and makes

it lucrative by firing much of the staff and sucking the soul out of the organization. His ruthlessness turns on himself as he starts to lose his grip on reality, suffers a nervous breakdown, and is committed to an asylum. But once there, having lost his business, wife, and family, he starts to piece together his soul. Negative reviews along the line of "a two-hour aria of justifiable self-loathing" aided in closing the comedy-drama after fourteen showings.

The Destiny of Me (10-20-92, Lucille Lortel), Larry Kramer's sequel to his long-running autobiographical *The Normal Heart* (4-21-85), received better notices than the original drama, though this one only ran 175 performances. Critics declared the Circle Rep mounting a "blistering confessional drama" that had the anger of the first play but also a "biting humor that comes not from a joy of life but from trying to make the best of it." Gay activist Ned Weeks (Jonathan Hadary) loses his lover to AIDS and then finds himself infected with the disease. Hospitalized at the National Institute of Health, the very organization he has publicly criticized, Ned is confronted with Alexander (John Cameron Mitchell), his teenage self, who grew up in Washington, D.C., dreaming of becoming an actor. Alexander escapes from his unhappy home (his mother is obsessed with charitable work, while his father dismisses his "sissy" of a son) by catching all the touring shows from the second balcony of the National Theatre. Only Alexander's elder brother, Ben (Peter Frechette), seems to understand him. In the present, Ned rails against the hospital staff trying experimental drugs to cure him (in the play's most harrowing scene, he smashes packets of blood samples against the wall), but as he faces death he begins to resolve some of his bitterness over the past and, together with Alexander, promises to keep fighting to the end.

The longest run of the season was Wendy Wasserstein's **The Sisters Rosensweig** (10-22-92, Mitzi E. Newhouse), a comedy that combined two of the author's ongoing subjects: feminism and dealing with one's Jewish heritage in today's world. The three Rosensweig sisters were born and raised in a very ethnic Brooklyn neighborhood, but each has come far in the world. Sara (Jane Alexander), currently single, has been married several times and has become an international financier living in London and representing a major Hong Kong bank. Her sister Gorgeous Teitelbaum (Madeline Kahn) is a housewife in Newton, Massachusetts, who gives "very Jewish" advice on her popular radio show, where she is called Dr. Gorgeous. Pfeni (Frances McDormond), the youngest Rosensweig, is a renowned travel writer constantly circling the globe and covering the jet set as well as Third World countries. The three sisters, reunited in Sara's posh London town house to celebrate her fifty-fourth birthday, reminisce about old times and try to help each other face their current problems. Sara's highly intelligent daughter Tess (Julie Dretzin) wants to run off to Lithuania with political activist Tom Valiunus (Patrick Fitzgerald), while Pfeni finds herself falling in love again with Geoffrey Duncan (John Vickery), a theatre director who is bisexual. Gorgeous, in London as part of a tour for Jewish ladies from Newton, is hoping that her advice show will move to television because of the great debts her husband has run up. To complicate matters, Sara has met and is attracted to American Mervyn Kant (Robert Klein), a Jewish furrier who seems to represent everything that Sara hoped to leave behind in Brooklyn. None of the sisters' dilemmas is resolved over the weekend, but together they find the strength to accept their femininity and Jewishness and to persevere. Wasserstein's "funny, observant" script, the splendid cast (Kahn won a Tony), and Daniel Sullivan's skillful direction made the comedy a quick sellout in the small Lincoln Center space. After 149 showings it transferred (with Christine Estabrook taking over the role of Pfeni) on March 18 to the Ethel Barrymore, where it entertained theatregoers for 556 performances.

The drama that led to more heated discussions than any other this season was David Mamet's **Oleanna** (10-25-92, Orpheum), which critics (as well as audience members) argued about throughout its 513-performance run. Carol (Rebecca Pidgeon), a college student having difficulty in a particular course, goes to John (William H. Macy), her pedantic and somewhat distracted professor, in his office. She has trouble understanding his lectures and assignments, so after some rhetorical detours he kindly offers to give her private tutorials to help her catch up in the course. In their next meeting we learn that Carol, encouraged by a feminist group on campus, has filed charges of sexual harassment against John. Awkwardly maintaining his cool, John goes through what was said at their first meeting, trying to see where she might have misinterpreted his words. He also tries (unsuccessfully) to get her to drop the charges. The third meeting, after John has lost his bid for tenure, is full of bitterness and incrimination. John gets so furious with Carol that he throws her to the floor and calls

her names, becoming what she has falsely made him out to be. Is John a victim or an instigator? Does Carol really believe that she was harassed, or is she deliberately out to destroy? Was John's patronizing attitude to Carol a form of harassment? These and other questions were being asked in the press and in theatre lobbies across the country. (The two-character piece was very popular in regional theatres.) Initial notices varied in their appreciation of the script, but everyone felt it a highly provocative play worthy of discussion.

John Leguizamo gave another tour de force performance in his autobiographical **Spic-O-Rama** (10-27-92, Westside), but this time director Peter Askin helped in developing the script, and the writing was deeper and more involving than the previous *Mambo Mouth* (11-9-90). Leguizamo played all the members of the Gigante family, a mixed-up Latino bunch gathered for the wedding of one of the sons. Battling parents, troubled brothers, and other specimens (the play took the format of the nine-year-old son's science project) were all on view; they were portrayed at first with hysterical theatrics but soon with disturbing precision. Favorable reviews and Leguizamo's growing popularity kept the solo program on the boards for eighty-six performances.

The Roundabout assembled a vivacious cast for its November 5 revival of George Kelly's perennial favorite *The Show-Off* (2-5-24) directed by Brian Murray. Pat Carroll was a wry Mrs. Fisher, Sophie Hayden and Laura Esterman her daughters, and Boyd Gaines a hammy but enticing Aubrey Piper.

Audiences got to see Stacy Keach both live and on video if they happened to catch Rupert Holmes's short-lived thriller **Solitary Confinement** (11-8-92, Nederlander). Ruthless billionaire Richard Jannings (Keach) has had architect Leonard (Keach) design an impregnable tomb of an apartment atop the corporate headquarters of Jannings Industries in Albuquerque. Afraid that one of his enemies is trying to kill him, Richard has no personal contact with anyone and communicates with his staff via a huge television screen. We soon learn that Richard's head security guard, French cook, control room supervisor, bookkeeper, and female librarian (all played by Keach on film) have conspired together to knock him off. Even though the room is hermetically sealed, an intruder manages to get in through the dumbwaiter. It turns out to be Leonard. Or is it Leonard pretending to be Richard, whom he killed sometime back but has on video to fool the others? As poison gas fills the room, Richard (or is it Leonard?) must correctly answer the questions on a quiz show seen on the screen in order to stop the lethal flow. He does, but not a moment too soon. Since only one live actor was allowed onstage at a time (not counting the time the intruder was dressed in a suit of armor), the Richard-Leonard question went from confusing to uninteresting; any way you looked at it, it was Keach. A round of pans for the script (and much lamenting that Keach's return to Broadway after fifteen years was such a waste) encouraged the play to depart after three weeks.

A silly yet dark comedy that a few commentators found possessing "a shaggy sense of humor," Thomas Strelich's **Dog Logic** (11-8-92, American Place) managed to bring up such topics as television evangelism, cavemen, amoebas, dinosaurs, and survival of the fittest in its simple plot. Hertel Daggett (Darrell Larson), a loner who owns and operates a run-down pet cemetery left to him by his late father, finds the job spiritually (though rarely financially) fulfilling. But Dale (Joe Clancy), an ex-janitor who took a TV course in real estate, has his eye on the dried-out forty acres of California desert and wants to develop it into a shopping mall. Of course Hertel resists, so Dale puts pressure on him by getting Hertel's mother, Anita (Lois Smith), whom Hertel thought was dead, to come and convince him. Dale also enlists the help of Kaye (Karen Young), Hertel's ex-wife, a restless deputy sheriff who wants to relocate either to Vermont or Australia. Despite Hertel's impassioned speeches about primal man and survival in nature, the cemetery is lost.

Auspicious notices and a *Best Plays* citation made Catherine Butterfield's **Joined at the Head** (11-15-92, City Center) the most "striking accomplishment" of the Manhattan Theatre Club season. Maggie Mulroney (Ellen Parker), a celebrated novelist on a promotional tour, decides to visit her old flame Jim Burroughs (Kevin O'Rourke) while in the Boston area. Jim is married to Maggy (Butterfield), who is dying of cancer, so the reunion is not at all what Maggie expected. But the brainy, quick-witted novelist is immediately drawn to the simple, warm Maggy, and the three soon find themselves in a friendship that helps them deal with Maggy's fatal illness and their own conceptions of real life (as opposed to fiction). When Maggy dies, Maggie gives up her phony New York lifestyle and moves to Iowa to teach and write books that mean something to her. (The play's odd title is the name of the sarcastic book Maggie was promoting.)

The recent controversies with the National Endowment for the Arts were not too deep below the surface of Neal Bell's **On the Bum; or, The Next Train Through** (11-18-92, Playwrights Horizons), which concerned government and the arts in an earlier era. Eleanor Ames (Cynthia Nixon) left the Midwest to come to New York to be an actress, so she is less than thrilled when unemployment forces her in 1938 to take a job through the Federal Theatre Project in backwater Bumfort somewhere near her own roots. The job is a role in a historic pageant about a Great Flood that nearly destroyed the town fifty years before. While rehearsing in Bumfort, Eleanor falls in love with Frank (Campbell Scott), an unhappily married local who provides her with information about what really happened in the past (as opposed to what the rhymed-verse play says): local officials built a substandard dam and mistreated area laborers, and a disgruntled worker sabotaged the project. When a suspicious government official comes to Bumfort to make sure there is nothing subversive about the pageant, Eleanor realizes the horrors of government-funded art. But the pageant never gets put on, and Eleanor has to be content with Frank's love as her reward. The comedy-drama received some enthusiastic reviews, one commentator describing it as "a screwball comedy with dangerously high stakes."

What seemed like a grim theatrical prospect, Frank McGuinness's **Someone Who'll Watch Over Me** (11-23-92, Booth), turned into a moderate Broadway hit at 232 performances. Three very different men are imprisoned together by terrorists in Beirut: Irish journalist Edward (Stephen Rea), African-American psychiatrist Adam (James McDaniel), and gay British professor Michael (Alec McCowen), all chained to the wall with leg irons. To survive their ordeal they exchange verbal wordplay, make imaginary movies, engage in a fantasy tennis game, and throw a lavish (if unreal) party for themselves. Inherent international rivalries among them are soon overcome by their growing interdependency. When Adam is released, the glib Edward starts to crack but is rescued by Michael's urgings to laugh out loud for his Arab captors. Then Edward is released, and Michael is left rattling his chains as if in a musical dirge. The production, direct from London, received rave reviews for the distinguished cast and several complimentary ones for McGuinness's "play with a heart, a soul and a sense of humor."

The National Actors Theatre opened its second season on November 29 at the Lyceum with *The Seagull*, translated by David French and directed by Marshall W. Mason. While still strongly criticized, the Chekhov classic was deemed the best entry yet by the company. Most agreed that Tyne Daly was miserably miscast as Madame Arkadina and several felt the same about Laura Linney's Nina and movie heartthrob Ethan Hawke's Konstantin. But Jon Voight was an impressive Trigorin, and there was admirable work by supporting players, especially Maryann Plunkett (Masha), who was clearly becoming the most versatile and commanding member of the struggling company.

Philip Glass composed a score for JoAnne Akalaitis's revival of Georg Büchner's *Woyzeck* on December 6 at the Public's Newman, and to several commentators, it was the haphazard production's chief asset. Somewhere behind the film footage, dancing, anachronisms, and other paraphernalia, Jesse Borrego essayed the self-destructive Franz Woyzeck. No one had any trouble finding Patrick Stewart onstage when he brought back his one-man version of *A Christmas Carol* (1-12-91) on December 17 at the Broadhurst. The three-week engagement once again proved to be a popular holiday attraction. The hottest ticket at the Roundabout this season was its star-studded revival of Eugene O'Neill's *Anna Christie* (11-2-21) on January 14. Natasha Richardson was Anna, Rip Torn her father Kris, Liam Neeson the sailor Matt who falls in love with her, and Anne Meara the crusty old Marthy. Exemplary reviews for the cast, production, and even the creaky old melodrama itself filled the house and won the company a Tony for Best Revival.

Tepid reviews and modest attendance greeted Arthur Miller's latest play, **The Last Yankee** (1-21-93, City Center), so the Manhattan Theatre Club saw no reason to hold it over past its five-week engagement. In a waiting room of a state mental hospital, two men with wives there as patients strike up a conversation. Leroy Hamilton (John Heard), a middle-aged carpenter, is a frequent visitor, his wife, Patricia, having been hospitalized several times. John Frick (Tom Aldredge), an elderly businessman, is new to the game, this being his wife's first stay. The men realize they once did business together (John owns a lumber company) and, despite their differing political and social views, confide in each other. When we meet Patricia (Frances Conroy), she seems to be recovering beautifully, no longer relying on her medication and anxious to return home to her hus-

band and seven children. John's wife, Karen (Rose Gregorio), has befriended Patricia, and the two have had deep conversations about their husbands. But Karen seems to be slipping further into depression as the tension in her marriage becomes clear. The foursome try to work out some of their problems but without success. The final curtain comes down on Leroy strumming on his guitar as Patricia breaks into a tap dance. The play had originally been done as a one-act off-off Broadway at the Ensemble Studio Theatre (only the two men appeared in that play); general opinion concurred that the piece worked better in its original short version.

Three days later in its second space, the Manhattan Theatre Club offered Cindy Lou Johnson's **The Years** (1-24-93, City Center), a drama that slipped into farce but rarely into favor with the press. Andrea (Nancy Hower) is mugged on her wedding day by desperate Bartholomew (Paul McCrane), who needs money to start a new life. Andrea goes through with the ceremony, with black eye and bruises, but the memory stays with her. Thirteen years later at a cousin's wedding, she meets Bartholomew, now a successful businessman. Andrea recognizes him and tells him how she has been haunted by their first encounter. This revelation so distresses Bartholomew that he plunges into a hopeless depression. Johnson filled out her play with family episodes of suicide, infidelity, remarriage, and bad catering at weddings, all presented with strained seriousness but coming across awkwardly comic.

Maryann Plunkett was finally put center stage in the National Actors Theatre's revival of Shaw's *Saint Joan* on January 31 at the Lyceum, greatly pleasing subscribers and critics. Michael Langham directed the large but uneven cast, which included Remak Ramsay, John Neville, Nicholas Kepros, and Michael Struhlbarge (as the Dauphin). A warm critical response encouraged the company to hold the production over for eight weeks.

Steve Tesich dealt with some saintly characters of his own in **On the Open Road** (2-16-93, Martinson), a dark allegory that ran at the Public for a month. In an unnamed country deep in civil war, Al (Bryon Jennings) pulls a cart full of art treasures that he has salvaged from bombed-out museums and churches, hoping to use them to bribe his way across the border to freedom. Just as the wagon is getting too heavy for Al, he comes across Angel (Anthony LaPaglia), a brutish fellow tied up and waiting to be hanged. Al helps him escape, and in gratitude Angel pulls the cart for him. During their travels, Al tries to educate Angel about the finer points of civilization, and the two form a strong kinship. Arriving at the border, they are offered freedom only if the two will execute a subversive prisoner named Jesus Christ (Andy Taylor), who is being kept in the ruins of a nearby monastery. Jesus has been so badly beaten his words make no sense, but he still manages to play the cello with skill. Al and Angel cannot bring themselves to kill the poor man, so a Monk (Henry Stram) has all three men crucified side by side. Some reviewers were intrigued ("full of scathing wit . . . painfully funny"), but most found the play pretentious and "full of pseudo-poetry."

For anyone who missed last season's *Park Your Car in Harvard Yard* (11-7-91), the same plot was recycled for Garry Marshall and Lowell Ganz's tearful comedy **Wrong Turn at Lungfish** (2-21-93, Promenade). Cantankerous old Peter Ravenswaal (George C. Scott), a former college professor now blind and confined to a hospital bed, takes an instant dislike to Anita Merendino (Jami Gertz), a streetwise girl who comes to read to him. Not only does she mispronounce every other word she reads and drop malapropisms all over the place, but Anita seems proud of her uneducated, working-class existence. In reality, Anita and her brutish boyfriend, Dominic (TV favorite Tony Danza,) are determined to con Peter out of his fortune, but in good sitcom fashion, she and the professor become friends. Peter helps Anita dump Dominic just before the old man dies. Despite reviews calling it "sentimental" and "ridiculous," audiences were drawn to the stars for 145 showings.

Silent clown Bill Irwin teamed up with pantomimist David Shiner for **Fool Moon** (2-25-93, Richard Rodgers), a plotless, wordless evening of physical comedy (created by both actors) that charmed audiences for 207 performances. Critics had trouble categorizing Irwin's work but had no difficulty in recommending it.

Earlier this season Flaubert had come back from the dead at Playwrights Horizons. Six months later two more artists from the past came alive at the same off-Broadway theatre, though few commentators agreed that there was much life in Eric Overmyer's **The Heliotrope Bouquet by Scott Joplin & Louis Chauvin** (2-28-93, Playwrights Horizons). From his deathbed in 1906 Harlem, ragtime pioneer Joplin (Delroy Lindo) looks back on his short and traumatic life, recalling his youth wasted in brothels and opium dens,

and his friendship (and spotty collaboration with) Chauvin (Duane Boutté), a composer who specialized in the art of syncopation. (Both men died young, leaving the two-step drag of the title as a legacy of the short-lived collaboration.) As usual, Overmyer played with language creatively, and wonderful ragtime music filled out the drama, but still the result was unsatisfying.

Although most of the foreign-language productions this season were in Brooklyn, Broadway hosted Japan's Chijinkai Theatre Company's *Yabuhara Kengyo* (The Great Doctor Yabuhara) (3-4-93, City Center), previously seen in various international festivals. Hisashi Inoue's dark parable about a musician who is blind was performed in Japanese for three performances.

The first successful comedy about the AIDS epidemic was Paul Rudnick's **Jeffrey** (3-6-93, Minetta Lane), declared "wildly funny" and "just the sort of play Oscar Wilde might have written had he lived in the 90s" and running 365 performances. Jeffrey (John Michael Higgins) is a gay actor-waiter who lives a sexually active lifestyle in Greenwich Village until the threat of AIDS cramps his style. "Safe sex" leaves him cold, so he decides to become celibate, enjoying gay social activities (the Gay Pride parade, working out at his gym, a socialite's "Hoe-Down for AIDS" benefit) with his flamboyant friends Sterling (Edward Hibbert), a razor-tongued interior designer, and Sterling's new partner, Darius (Bryan Batt), a chorus boy in the Broadway company of *Cats*. But the lure of sex is still strong, especially when Jeffrey meets Steve (Tom Hewitt), the sort of man he has always dreamed about. Even though Steve is HIV positive, Jeffrey cannot resist and decides to celebrate life and love rather than hiding from both. Rudnick's gift for one-liners was unmistakable; one character scolds Jeffrey with "How dare you give up sex when there are children in Europe who can't get a date!" Christopher Ashley staged the multi-scened comedy fluidly, allowing the sometimes stereotypical characters to come alive with zest and knowing wit.

One of the few British entries this season was Hugh Whitemore's character study **The Best of Friends** (3-7-93, Westside), based on letters George Bernard Shaw wrote to two unlikely acquaintances. Between 1924 and his death in 1950, Shaw (Roy Dotrice) corresponds with the upper-class gentleman Sir Sydney Cockerell (Michael Allinson), curator of Cambridge's Fitzwilliam Museum, and Dame Laurentia McLachlan (Diana Douglas), a cloistered nun at Stanbrook Abbey.

The trio discuss religion and art, disagree with each other (Laurentia often reprimands Shaw for some of the agnostic ideas in his plays and essays), and challenge each other in a highly intelligent but affectionate way. While not for all tastes, the "valuable tribute to the art of friendship" entertained discerning audiences for five weeks. (With major stars in the cast, the play had done much better in London.)

Two commercial entries off Broadway vividly portrayed contemporary life, one in the city and the other in a small town, though both grew repetitive before long. Frank Pugliese's **Aven' U Boys** (3-8-93, John Houseman) explored the frustrations and subsequent violent behavior of three Italian-American thugs living in Bensonhurst. Mark Dunn's **The Second Annual Heart o' Texas Eczema Telethon** (3-16-93, Actors' Playhouse) revealed the doings in a small Texas town that holds a telethon on the local cable access television station. Pugliese's raw but powerful drama lasted six weeks; the Dunn satire ran ten weeks.

Both critics and audiences were more thrilled by the joyous sounds of *a cappella* singing group Ladysmith Black Mambazo, who served as the Greek chorus in Tug Yourgrau's **The Song of Jacob Zulu** (3-24-93, Plymouth), than by the drama itself, one commentator describing it as "well-meaning to a fault." A bomb explodes in a South African mall crowded with Christmas shoppers, killing and wounding both black and white patrons, and Jacob Zulu (K. Todd Freeman), a nineteen-year-old member of the African National Congress, is arrested. Jacob is an honest and sensitive son of a preacher, so his trial is filled with shocked relatives and outraged political types. Flashbacks show what drove Jacob to such an act of violence (the last straw was the death of his brother when an ambulance came too slowly to his black neighborhood), and the play raises plenty of questions but comes to no conclusion except that the end of apartheid does not mean the end of racial strife in South Africa. The production, which came from Chicago's Steppenwolf Theatre, found an audience (most of whom came to hear the popular singing troupe) for fifty-three performances.

Robert Sean Leonard's poignant performance as the young poet Eugene Marchbanks was one of the few redeeming aspects of the Roundabout's revival of Shaw's *Candida* on March 25. Aisle-sitters were in agreement that film star Mary Steenburgen was miscast and lost as the liberated Candida and that television actor Robert Foxworth was tiresome as her husband, James Morell.

An autobiographical one-person show that went beyond the usual carping and angst, African-American Charlayne Woodard's **Pretty Fire** (3-26-93, City Center) presented a childhood filled with love and wonder. In five monologues, covering her difficult birth to age eleven when she discovers prejudice in the world, Woodard spun tales about her family that were "layered with great humor and warmth." The title came from an episode when, as a little girl, she saw a burning cross set up by white supremacists and upset her family by describing it as "pretty fire."

In the dark and brooding redwood forests of Northern California, Vietnam veterans are known to wander and live in seclusion, the area reminding them of the lost world of Southeast Asia. This was the setting for Lanford Wilson's **Redwood Curtain** (3-30-93, Brooks Atkinson), a play that only ran five weeks but deserved more. Lyman (Jeff Daniels), a scruffy homeless vet, is being shadowed by Geri (Sung Yun Cho), a seventeen-year-old Amerasian from Vietnam who was adopted by a rich American couple. Geri is a musical prodigy—a renowned concert pianist—who is disenchanted with the international music world and wants to find her father. When visiting her energetic Aunt Geneva (Debra Monk), who lives among the redwoods, Geri seeks out Lyman, but the gruff, monosyllabic recluse will have nothing to do with her at first. Eventually Lyman confronts Geneva and Geri and admits he knows who her father was: the same Vietnam vet who adopted her and encouraged her music studies. Her father was never able to tell Geri or her adopted mother the truth, and his guilt over the fact let to his early death by alcoholism. Wilson's dialogue crackled with theatricality (Monk got the best lines and won a Tony for her performance), and Marshall W. Mason directed the drama as a hypnotic dance, the story shifting back and forth from John Lee Beatty's evocative woodland setting to civilization. Notices were decidedly mixed, calling the work a "stunningly thin . . . odd little play" or "an engrossing drama of substance—a real rarity on Broadway these days."

Joe Mantello would have quite a season, acting on Broadway and directing off, and receiving acclaim for both efforts. His direction of Jon Robin Baitz's **Three Hotels** (4-6-93, Circle) managed to keep a relatively static play (it consisted of three long monologues in three hotel rooms) engrossing, fueled by two dynamic performers. In a Tangier, Morocco, hotel suite, corporation executive Kenneth Hoyle (Ron Rifkin) explains how he started as a 1960s idealist and Peace Corps volunteer but was corrupted over the years and now sells defective baby formula to Third World countries. We then see his wife, Barbara (Christine Lahti), in her hotel suite in the Virgin Islands remembering the death of their son (he was murdered for his watch) and preparing to address corporate wives on how to handle the company's crisis (they have been exposed on TV's *60 Minutes*), encouraging them to stick with their husbands through this difficult time. Kenneth delivers the third monologue from his hotel room in Oaxaca, Mexico, some time later. Fired from the company and separated from his wife, Kenneth is haunted by the memory of his son and realizes that all of his personal life's disappointments are global ones as well. Some exemplary reviews for Baitz's script, the two actors, and Mantello's direction helped the thought-provoking drama run 231 performances.

Two nights later another trio of monologues, all performed by Leslie Ayvazian, opened at the Manhattan Theatre Club. Richard Greenberg's **Jenny Keeps Talking** (4-8-93, City Center) illustrates three members of the same family, each solo section continuing the same story. Jenny is a feisty left-wing journalist who, after working for fourteen years for one newspaper, is fired when new management takes over. She reluctantly moves into her grandmother's ramshackle cottage on an island off the coast of Maine to re-evaluate her life, getting romantically involved with a local handyman. Jenny's sister, Claudia, a failed opera singer, has suffered a series of emotional and business setbacks but plans to redeem her life by turning Grandma's cottage into a chic little breakfast-only restaurant. She is miffed that Jenny has moved into the place, and the two argue over the phone about that and other old grievances. The grandmother has the last monologue, telling the audience how she has saved her money to someday support her two luckless granddaughters. The three women are about to meet at the cottage and settle their differences as the curtain falls.

Television favorites Tony Randall and Jack Klugman reteamed for the National Actors Theatre's season closer, John Cecil Holm and George Abbott's farce *Three Men on a Horse* (1-30-35) on April 13 at the Lyceum. Although clearly far too old for their roles as timid poet Erwin Trowbridge and professional gambler Patsy, Randall and Klugman pleased audiences if not very many

critics. They got fine support from veterans Jerry Stiller and Joey Faye, but the old comedy did not age gracefully, at least not in this "shoddy production."

The Second Stage, an off-off-Broadway troupe usually dedicated to remounting neglected plays, offered an original comedy at the Public, but Tina Howe's **One Shoe Off** (4-15-93, Anspacher) immediately joined the ranks of forgotten works by respected playwrights. In upstate New York, Leonard (Jeffrey DeMunn) and Dinah (Mary Beth Hurt) live in a crumbling Greek Revival farmhouse which is slowly being devoured by the local vegetation. Like their house, the unhappy couple are being swallowed up by a world they cannot handle. Leonard insists he is an actor, but he hasn't been in a play in eleven years; Dinah says she is a costume designer, although she has trouble dressing herself. The two invite their new neighbors, Tate (Daniel Gerroll) and Clio (Jennifer Tilly), to dinner to get acquainted, only to discover the newcomers are just as dysfunctional as the hosts. Tate is a stressed-out editor of children's books who is reduced to reciting (incorrectly) nursery rhymes, while his starlet wife, Clio, suffers from nymphomania. When Leonard and Dinah's friend Parker Bliss (Brian Kerwin), a prominent film director, arrives unexpectedly, the dinner party becomes an absurdist free-for-all with old ties and new entanglements running riot. The party is a failure, and the guests depart, leaving Dinah and Leonard to rake up the leaves in their house. Critics agreed the comedy was "a major misstep" for Howe but applauded Heidi Landesman's delightful set with plant life overtaking everything.

Three Thornton Wilder one-acts, all first published in 1931, were put together by off-off-Broadway's Willow Cabin Theatre Company and opened on Broadway as **Wilder, Wilder, Wilder** (4-21-93, Circle in the Square). *The Long Christmas Dinner, Pullman Car Hiawatha,* and *The Happy Journey to Trenton and Camden* were still considered refreshingly potent by the press, and there were compliments for the simple and gimmick-free presentations as well.

Lynn Redgrave offered a memoir, some theatre history, and lively excerpts from the Bard's plays in her one-woman show **Shakespeare for My Father** (4-26-93, Helen Hayes), which ran a profitable 272 performances. While concentrating on the last thirty years in the life and career of Michael Redgrave, the program came off less a tribute to her dad than a celebration of theatre itself and a showcase for his daughter's own considerable talents. Cheers for Redgrave and her unique show were typified by John Simon's comment in *New York Magazine*, "*Shakespeare for My Father* tells us more about parents and children, actors and those who are acted upon, theatrical shenanigans and existential fracases—the whole untidy and unruly human condition—than just about anything around these, or most other, days."

While few commentators had anything encouraging to say about Paula Vogel's **And Baby Makes Seven** (4-27-93, Lucille Lortel), Cherry Jones was roundly praised, showing even more proficiency than she had in Vogel's earlier *The Baltimore Waltz* (2-11-92). Anna (Jones) lives in a New York loft with her lesbian lover, Ruth (Mary Mara), and their "straight" friend Peter (Peter Frechette), who has willingly impregnated Anna so the gay couple can have a child. But Anna and Ruth are pretty much children themselves, always play-acting and taking on the personalities of two very specific youngsters (one French and the other British) and their pretend pet dog. With a real baby on the way, the couple realize that they must let go of the imaginary children and dog. (They decide that the dog dies of rabies, while the kids are shipped off to their homelands.) But once the baby arrives, the trio find the household lacking in spirit, so the imaginary family members are resurrected.

New Yorkers had been hearing about Tony Kushner's two-part saga **Angels in America** for some time, the drama having been successfully produced in London and Los Angeles. So expectations were high for **Part I: Millennium Approaches** (5-4-93, Walter Kerr), which George C. Wolfe staged on Broadway with a cast of mostly unknowns. Few aisle-sitters were disappointed. Frank Rich in the *New York Times* led the critical applause for the "vast, miraculous play . . . that never loses its wicked sense of humor." Part I introduces three main stories set during the Reagan era that soon overlap and, by the end of the first half, converge. Prior Walter (Stephen Spinella) is HIV positive, which frightens off his longtime lover, Louis Ironson (Joe Mantello), a Jewish intellectual who works at the Manhattan Court of Appeals. Louis furtively tries to rationalize his leaving Prior while their mutual friend Belize (Jeffrey Wright), a black former drag queen but now a nurse, tries to reconcile the two lovers. In the second plot line, Joe Pitt (David Marshall Grant), a conservative Mormon lawyer who refuses to leave his mentally unstable wife, Harper (Marcia Gay Harden), even though he has ceased to love her, is hired by Roy Cohn (Ron Leibman),

the bombastic lawyer whose infamy dates back to helping Joe McCarthy persecute Reds in the 1950s. In the third story, Cohn is diagnosed with AIDS, but he belittles his doctor, claiming only homosexuals can get the disease. To the world, Roy Cohn is not gay, but he is a closet homosexual, and news of his condition makes him more vicious than ever, sneering at the ghost of Ethel Rosenberg (Kathleen Chalfant) and telling her what joy it gave him to have her electrocuted back in 1953. Joe is also a closet gay; after striking up a conversation with Louis in the men's room at the Court of Appeals and finding himself attracted to him, he decides to face the truth about himself. Late one night Joe calls his mother, Hannah (Chalfant), back in Salt Lake City and tells her he is a homosexual and is leaving his wife. Hannah, a tough and unsentimental Mormon, refuses to believe him but hops on a plane to New York to fix things up. Harper sinks deeper into a fantasy, helped by drug-induced hallucinations in which she has conversations with Mr. Lies (Wright), a spirit of truth in a frozen wasteland. Prior's physical condition worsens, and he tells Belize that he has visions of an angel coming into his room, causing him sexual and emotional confusion. Ethel is also appearing to Cohn, warning him that "History is about to crack wide open. Millennium approaches." Part I concludes with the startling image of an Angel (Ellen McLaughlin) breaking through the ceiling of Prior's bedroom, hovering above and announcing, "Greetings, Prophet; the Great Work begins: the Messenger has arrived." In addition to the many vivid characters, engrossing plot developments, and profusion of ideas, *Angels in America* took time for lively discussions on race, politics, and religion. Fantasy mixed with gritty reality, yet the play never seemed to lose control. (Kushner subtitled his work a "Gay Fantasia on National Themes.") The three-hour production demanded much of its audiences but repaid them many times over. The drama won the Pulitzer Prize and the Tony Award, as well as Tonys for Leibman, Spinella, and Wolfe. Part I ran into November, when it was joined by Part II in repertory (for a total of 367 performances).

At Lincoln Center, Synge's *Playboy of the Western World* was rewritten and transported by Mustapha Matura to 1950s Trinidad and called **Playboy of the West Indies** (5-9-93, Mitzi E. Newhouse). Set in a rum shop in a fishing village near the coast, the comedy maintained the original plot but had "a poetry all its own" as the locals got caught up with Ken (Victor Love), the dashing stranger who supposedly killed his father. Peggy (Lorraine Toussaint) is the shopgirl who falls in love with him, and the local widow in this version is the sensual voodoo lady Mama Benin (Michele Shay). Gerald Gutierrez staged the music-filled piece, Paul Tazewell provided the colorful Caribbean costumes, and John Lee Beatty designed the lush and inviting tropical setting. Several enthusiastic reviews and positive word of mouth encouraged the company to hold the comedy over for three months.

On May 11 Ibsen's monumental folk epic *Peer Gynt* was revived by the Royal Dramatic Theatre of Sweden, which stayed at BAM for five showings as part of its international tour. Ingmar Bergman directed, Borje Ahlstedt played Peer, Bibi Andersson was his mother, Ase, and Lena Endre was his true love, Solveig.

Some one-person shows had gotten so personal that critics were left in the odd position of reviewing a performer's life rather than his craft. A good example was Evan Handler's **Time on Fire** (5-15-93, McGinn/Cazale) in which the actor talked about his bout with leukemia. Sometimes his monologue was grimly comic (such as his adventures at Sloan-Kettering Hospital), but mostly it was a very private revelation of an extremely dark episode in his life. How does one evaluate a person's disease? The Second Stage production gave audiences three weeks to decide for themselves.

Aisle-sitters applauded José Rivera's writing as "poetically powerful" and having "the potential to tickle a bruised city audience awake," but his nightmare fantasy **Marisol** (5-20-93, Public: Martinson) was more intriguing than fulfilling. Marisol Perez (Cordelia Gonzalez) is a Latino copy editor who works in Manhattan but still lives in the decaying Bronx neighborhood where she grew up. One day she is told by her guardian angel (Danitra Vance) that she can no longer protect Marisol because angels are needed elsewhere. It seems that God, a senile old white man, is dying, and the universe will collapse if all the angels don't band together and revolt against the deity. Such doings in heaven cause the moon to forget to shine, food to turn to salt, and fire from the heavenly revolution to come raining down on earth. Marisol journeys through this apocalypse innocently, encountering all sorts of surreal oddballs, such as a wheelchair-bound burn victim searching for his skin and an ice cream vendor demanding his pay for when he worked as an extra on the film *Taxi Driver*. Before long, angels armed and dressed in leather motorcycle jackets are joining the city's homeless to wage war against the universe itself.

The final foreign-language production at BAM this season was Yukio Mishima's *Madame de Sade* on May 20 by the Royal Dramatic Theatre of Sweden, put on for three showings. (The 1965 drama had been seen off-off Broadway in 1988.) Again Ingmar Bergman directed the period piece about six women whose lives have been affected by the famous Marquis de Sade (who was never seen in the play). John Lahr in *The New Yorker* described the difficult piece as "a meditation on the metaphysics of desire" and was not alone in declaring it "a thrilling and educational encounter."

The season ended with A. R. Gurney's **Later Life** (5-23-93, Playwrights Horizons), one of his Wasp comedies that allowed a handful of actors to play a variety of fun roles. At a party on a terrace overlooking Boston harbor, Austin (Charles Kimbrough) shies away from the crowd, as he has always done throughout his dull life. Recently divorced, Austin has been invited by the hostess in an effort to match him up with Ruth (Maureen Anderman), an oft-divorced woman who is unpredictable and lively. But Austin and Ruth already know each other. In fact, thirty years ago they almost married, but Austin's reticent behavior let the romance dwindle out. Given a second chance, the two rekindle the old spark, though their wooing is interrupted by various guests (all played by Carole Shelley and Anthony Heald) who come out onto the terrace: a couple representing new money from the South, another pair of old Bostonian blood, a bitter lesbian, a computer nerd, an elderly pair arguing about their impending retirement in Florida, and others. Ruth realizes that Austin is still on the outside of life looking in, so she departs, leaving Austin alone to contemplate what might have been. Superior performances (Shelley was particularly cheered) under the direction of Don Scardino and applause for Gurney's "charmingly clever yet immeasurably touching" script encouraged the play to run three months.

1993–1994

American works continued to dominate Broadway and Off Broadway, at least in terms of numbers. Yet British revivals of *Medea, An Inspector Calls,* and *The Winter's Tale* and the new *The Madness of George III* were definitely highlights in a season that saw many bold and ambitious ven-

tures. Broadway offered eleven new non-musicals
and ten revivals; Off Broadway had thirty-three
new works and only five revivals. But these numbers were getting more and more difficult to determine. Fourteen one-person shows opened on
and off the Street, all written by the performers.
Were these indeed new plays? Were they plays at
all?

Such solo efforts were balanced by several big-
cast, big-budget plays like *Angels in America* and
The Kentucky Cycle, each taking two nights to perform. High price tags kept both from being financial hits. In fact, no Broadway entry had broken even by the end of the season. With fewer
star vehicles and more plays with very serious
subject matter, producing non-musicals this season took more bravery than brains. True, box-
office figures were up again, and attendance
climbed as well. But, as usual, big musical holdovers accounted for the high numbers. The rest
of the field had to contend with a shrinking audience for non-musicals. They also had to deal
with a severe winter, which tallied fifteen snow-
storms that hurt "walk-up" business and saw the
TKTS booth sales drop 25 percent some weeks.

For decades the theatre community had been
complaining about the formidable power of the
New York Times critic. That power was not broken
this season, but it was clearly dispersed. Frank
Rich, first-string reviewer at the *Times* since 1980
and commonly referred to as "the butcher of
Broadway" for his sometimes harsh notices,
stepped down in September to write for the op-
ed page. He was replaced by David Richards as
first-stringer, Ben Brantley as second-stringer, and
Vincent Canby and Mel Gussow filling in the
gaps. As a result, no one critic wielded the influence Rich had possessed, though a review from
the *Times* (by whomever) still carried the most
weight. For the rest of the decade, theatre criticism in New York was an open field with many
team players and no stars.

More than a little of Athol Fugard's *Blood Knot*
(3-1-64) showed up in his latest work, **Playland**
(6-8-93, City Center), also a duet for two men of
opposite race and temperament who are somehow joined together emotionally. On New Year's
Eve 1989, Martinus Zoeloe (Frankie R. Faison), a
black night watchman for a shabby amusement
park called Playland, is repainting one of the
rusted bumper cars before the park opens. Gideon le Rous (Kevin Spacey), a white army vet,
enters looking for help in getting his stalled car
going. The two have a leisurely but pointed conversation, finding common ground because both

suffer from guilt over past wartime activities
(each man has killed another in his time) and
similar feelings about the new South Africa. Fugard seemed very hopeful about his country in
this work, which was minor and rather static but
it proved quite satisfying as an acting showcase.
It was the always magnetic Spacey's largest and
most demanding role in Manhattan so far.

The Manhattan Theatre Club, by now Terrence McNally's unofficial home off Broadway, offered his episodic **A Perfect Ganesh** (6-27-93, City
Center), which was received well enough to run
124 performances. David Richards at the *New York
Times* felt the drama was "arguably, his most
probing drama to date," although Howard Kissel
in the *Daily News* was not alone in noting that
"the writing is too facile to involve us." Two
Connecticut matrons, Margaret Civil (Frances
Sternhagen) and Katharine Brynne (Zoe Caldwell), travel to India together to find answers in
their frustratingly sterile lives. Although they are
good friends, each holds a secret from the other.
The uptight Margaret, who shies away from the
filth and mass of humanity they encounter in
Asia, has a lump in her breast and hopes the mysticism of India will cure her. The more adventurous Katharine, who embraces a foreign world
that holds such promise, once rejected her homosexual son, who was later killed in a gay-
bashing incident. Their guardian angel-of-sorts
throughout their journey is the always-smiling
Ganesh (Dominic Cuskern), a Hindu god with
the head of an elephant who watches over travelers. All of the people the two women met in
Asia were played with rugged charm by Fisher
Stevens. As the two ladies travel, their differences

in temperament lead to arguments, then to revelation of their secrets. The women find no answers (and McNally, as usual, has no satisfactory ending), but near the end of their trip, as they gaze in wonder at the Taj Mahal, Margaret asks, "Do you think this is why we exist? To create this?" John Tillinger directed seamlessly, and the two stars captured the play's humor and the sadness beautifully.

The Public Theatre's Shakespeare Marathon continued with two "problem" plays at the Delacorte in Central Park. *Measure for Measure* on July 8 was set in a Caribbean kingdom with Kevin Kline as the Duke, and the dark moral questions of the play were put aside for playful mugging and lots of slapstick. Aisle-sitters enjoyed much of it (including the fine Isabella by Lisa Gay Hamilton and Andre Braugher's smoldering Angelo) but wondered if this was really Shakespeare's *Measure for Measure*. The second entry, *All's Well That Ends Well* on August 5, featured familiar TV face Michael Cumptsy as the strutting Parolles. Much of the rest of the cast was routine, but Richard Jones's staging was quite fascinating, having different scenes occur simultaneously on Stewart Laing's long and narrow set that created a gallery of playing spaces side by side.

Having been booted out of the Public Theatre, JoAnne Akalaitis resurfaced at Lincoln Center, where she directed its opener, a revival of Jane Bowles's elusive drama *In the Summer House* (12-29-53) on August 1 in the Vivian Beaumont. Long considered by some a neglected classic, the play shone at moments, and for once Akalaitis's quirky staging may have been appropriate for the odd piece. Dianne Wiest played Gertrude Eastman Cuevas, an over-the-top mother who despises her own daughter, Molly (Alina Arenal). The show-stopping characters, though, are another mother and daughter: cynical Mrs. Constable and unfortunate Vivian, well acted by Frances Conroy and Kali Rocha. Few reviewers tried to defend the script, but some found it worth reviving all the same.

The Roundabout Theatre opened its season with a revival of Peter Shaffer's double bill *White Liars & Black Comedy* (2-12-67) on September 1. Gerald Gutierrez staged *Black Comedy* with a wacky playfulness that reviewers unanimously applauded. Kudos were also handed to the ensemble cast, especially Peter MacNicol as the harried artist Brindsley, Brian Murray as the antiques dealer Harold, Nancy Marchand as the dotty neighbor Miss Furnival, and Keene Curtis as the stern Colonel Melkett. Shaffer revised his curtain raiser *White Lies* (and retitled it *White Liars*) for this revival, but critics still thought it gimmicky and unsatisfying.

The Royal National Theatre of Great Britain presented Alan Bennett's **The Madness of George III** (9-28-93, BAM) in Brooklyn for seventeen performances as part of its international tour, and New York critics thought the historical drama from London was "absolutely engrossing." Still smarting from losing the American colonies, King George (Nigel Hawthorne) starts to slip into insanity, allowing the Prince of Wales (Nick Sampson) and other anti-Royalists to try to take over the country. Subjected to renowned quacks whose cures are merely tortures-in-disguise, George takes on qualities of King Lear until a simple country doctor, Francis Willis (Clive Merrison), brings him back to reason and, consequently, to power. (It turns out the king suffered from a little-known kidney disease now known as porphyria.) The elaborate pageant took time for human touches, such as the tender relationship between George and his wife, Charlotte (Selina Cadell), who playfully called him "Mr. King." Nicholas Hytner directed the splendid cast.

One of the most charming (and successful) solo performances this season was Claudia Shear's **Blown Sideways Through Life** (9-29-93, New York Theatre Workshop). Claiming that her one-person show was her sixty-fifth job in Manhattan, Shear then proceeded to catalog and describe with candor and wit her previous sixty-four jobs, from answering the phone for a call-girl service to selling cosmetics at Bloomingdale's. After fifty-one showings off-off Broadway, the program transferred on January 7 to a commercial run at the Cherry Lane Off Broadway, staying for a very profitable 262 performances. Anne Jackson and Eli Wallach also told the story of their careers in a piece called **In Persons** (9-30-93, Kaufman) but their jobs were all in the theatre, so for most of the evening they recreated scenes from plays that they had done together. This intimate and personal program, which one critic described as "an anthology of dramatic memorabilia," was repeated fifty-three times.

Julie Harris faithfully continued to return to the stage even though no vehicle worthy of her talents had come her way in decades. Such was the case again with Timothy Mason's melodrama **The Fiery Furnace** (10-5-93, Circle), which was kept on the boards for eight weeks. Eunice (Harris), a tormented Wisconsin housewife, hopes to escape her overbearing husband, Gunnar, by trying to go off to Chicago with her daughter Faith

(Ashley Gardner) when she enters the University of Chicago in 1950. But Gunnar (who is never seen in the play) hears of the plot and threatens to stop the tuition money if his wife leaves. A few years later Eunice's other daughter, Charity (Susan Batten), married to Jerry (William Fichtner) and the mother of twin boys, sympathizes with Eunice's troubled marriage because her own is very unsteady. Jerry is hoping to buy a parcel of land from Gunnar to build a drive-in movie theatre, but the old man sells it to a rival businessman, so Jerry becomes even more abusive to his family. At a Thanksgiving dinner in 1956, Faith returns home with her left-wing boyfriend, Louis (Zach Grenier), whom she admits to her mother and sister she doesn't love. Nevertheless, Faith marries Louis, and the next time we see the family, New Year's Eve 1963, she is like the other women, caught in an unhappy marriage. Jerry has gotten so violent that, while Gunnar is upstairs dying, Eunice, Faith, and Louis help Charity escape with her boys. When Gunnar dies, Eunice is finally free.

The longest-running solo act of the season (458 performances) was Sherry Glaser's **Family Secrets** (10-6-93, Westside), an autobiographical look at her Jewish relatives. In the first section Glaser portrayed her parents with wicked affection, then moved on to their two daughters and a wily grandmother. Critics called her portrayals "clear-sighted, funny and compassionate."

That same night a unique comic playwright, Nicky Silver, made his debut off-off Broadway with **Pterodactyls** (10-6-93, Vineyard), a dark, absurdist comedy about a truly dysfunctional family. Grace (Kelly Bishop) and Arthur Duncan (Dennis Creaghan) are not thrilled when their daughter, Emma (Hope Davis), a hypochondriac who suffers from chronic memory loss, brings to their Main Line Philadelphia home the orphan Tommy McKorckle (Kent Lanier) as her husband to be. They are even less thrilled when their son, Todd (T. Scott Cunningham), returns to the homestead and announces he has AIDS. While the parents put Tommy to work as the family maid, Todd gathers the dinosaur bones he has dug up in the backyard and begins assembling the full skeleton in the living room. Before the wedding can take place, Tommy falls in love with Todd and contracts AIDS. Emma is so upset she shoots herself with the gun Todd gave her as a wedding present. Grace takes to the bottle, Arthur also starts to lose his memory, and Todd blames Tommy for his sister's death and has him kicked out of the house. By the end of the farce, Arthur is also

banished, Grace dies of drink, Todd succumbs to AIDS (but remains onstage because the ground is too hard to bury him), and the dinosaur skeleton is completed, a symbol of extinction for the Duncans and perhaps life as we know it. Though often crude and out of control, Silver's writing was considered "clever, sharp, witty—it's a play that takes aim at the main-streamed, moneyed, conventional American family and buries it under one satiric jibe after another." Audiences kept the comedy running eight weeks.

Playwrights Horizons, which had often housed the Young Playwrights Festival, produced **Sophistry** (10-11-93, Playwrights Horizons) by Jonathan Marc Sherman, one of the teens the festival had once promoted. At an elite liberal arts college in New England, a group of self-absorbed students are temporarily shaken from their life of drugs, alcohol, and romantic entanglements when Whitey McCoy (Austin Pendleton), a beloved philosophy professor, is accused of sexually harassing the troubled student Jack Kahn (Anthony Rapp). Although the students and the audience hear both Jack's and the professor's versions of what happened, the truth is never made clear. So the students return to their own lives, and the issue of harassment dwindles away. Though most critics remarked that the play was structurally weak and the plot unsatisfying, many praised Sherman's "superbly realistic dialogue and believable characters brought to vivid life." The cast also included film actors Ethan Hawke and Calista Flockhart.

Three Broadway flops followed in quick succession. A comedy about an autumnal romance, Richard Baer's **Mixed Emotions** (10-12-93, John Golden) opened under the aegis of the Broadway Theatre Alliance but, even at discounted prices, survived only for fifty-five performances. Christine Millman (Katherine Helmond) has buried her husband, Moe, and has decided to leave her Manhattan apartment and move down to Florida to live with another widow. As two moving men carry out her furniture, Herman Lewis (Harold Gould), a widower and friend of Christine and Moe for thirty years, shows up and tries to persuade her not to go. He wants to marry her and tries his best to seduce her despite the many interruptions by the movers. By the end of the first act she agrees to sleep with him and by the end of the second, with the apartment now empty, she agrees to wed him. Aisle-sitters were gently but firmly dismissive, one critic calling it "a threadbare sketch struggling vainly to be a boulevard comedy for the '90s."

A critical drubbing ("displays telltale signs of dramatic anemia") forced Jonathan Tolins's problematic drama **The Twilight of the Golds** (10-21-93, Booth) to call it a run after twenty-nine showings. Suzanne Gold-Stein (Jennifer Grey) is pregnant, and her Manhattan family is thrilled for her and her husband, Rob Stein (Michael Spound). But Rob is a geneticist who has developed a new prenatal test that allows doctors to detect a strain of probable homosexuality in the fetus. David (Raphael Sbarge), Suzanne's gay brother, dares the couple to test their own baby, asking his parents (Judith Scarpone and David Groh) whether they would have aborted him if they had known what he would grow up to be. The test proves positive, and the parents-to-be decide, over David's protests, to abort the fetus. But the abortion is botched, and there will be no more children for the Steins to worry about. (David works for an opera company; hence the title and heavy-handed parallels to Wagner's destiny-obsessed *Ring Cycle*.)

Lasting even fewer performances was Brian Friel's poetic but plotless **Wonderful Tennessee** (10-24-93, Plymouth), which received mixed notices and closed in a week. Terry (Donal McCann) has long dreamed about a certain mysterious island off the coast of Ireland near Ballybeg. Some rumors say a boy was sacrificed there, others that it is an island of spiritual rebirth. Terry announces he has bought the island, and on his birthday one August night, he invites his wife, sister, and sister-in-law and their husbands to take a boat to the island and see for themselves. While they wait on the moonlit dock for the ferryman (who never comes), they while away the time with reminiscences, stories, a song or two (the title is the name of a once-popular ditty), and eventually revelations about their frustrated lives. Much of the talk was splendid, but few commentators were held by the characters or the dead-end story. Patrick Mason, who staged Friel's hit *Dancing at Lughnasa* (10-24-91), directed the Irish cast from the Abbey Theatre, who were warmly endorsed.

The Manhattan Theatre Club's most successful entry of the season was John Patrick Shanley's abrasive comedy **Four Dogs and a Bone** (10-31-93, City Center), which transferred on December 9 to the Lucille Lortel for a commercial run and stayed for 271 performances. The dogs of the title are movie people, and the bone they all covet is fame. Producer Bradley (Tony Roberts) is making a film on location in New York, but it is running over budget and he is panicking. Starlet Brenda (Mary-Louise Parker) suggests the film switch its focus away from the character played by the middle-aged Collette (Polly Draper) and center on herself. He agrees if Brenda can get her stepbrother, a box-office name, to make a cameo appearance in the film. Collette, meanwhile, is working on the movie's naive young screenwriter, Victor (Loren Dean), encouraging him to build up her part and revitalize her shaky career. All the backstabbing soon comes out in the open, resulting in a catfight between the actresses. As the foursome battle it out in a makeup trailer, the film continues to go over budget. Reviews ranged from "the neatest, if kinda affectionate, evisceration of that ol' dream factory" to "pretty familiar stuff."

Mixed notices also greeted John J. Wooton's "remarkably straightforward . . . family drama" **Trophies** (11-1-93, Cherry Lane), which ran two months in a commercial venture off Broadway. David Stone (Marc West) returns home from college for the Easter break. (He is studying theatre at Carnegie-Mellon and hopes to be an actor someday.) For the sake of his mother (Janet Nell Catt), David tries not to get into an argument with his father (John Henry Cox), who scoffs at his son's sissy ambitions. Mr. Stone's idea of a true son is Bobby (Mark Irish), David's younger brother, who was a football star in high school before an accident left him brain damaged. Laura (Christen Tassin), the kid sister, also quarrels with the father all the time and finds any excuse to be out of the house. For David's visit, Bobby has struggled to learn a passage from *Hamlet*, which he insists on delivering despite the father's protests and the family's embarrassment. While Mrs. Stone tries to keep peace in the house and cut back on her Valium intake, tempers flare, scenes from the past are enacted or discussed, and all end up bruised but beginning to accept each other for what they are.

Lincoln Center offered a Festival of New American Plays in its downstairs space, beginning with Howard Korder's **The Lights** (11-3-93, Mitzi E. Newhouse). This nightmare vision of the Big City (which was a bit reminiscent of Georg Kaiser's expressionistic classic *From Morn to Midnight*) begins when Lillian (Kathleen Dennehy) steals an expensive watch from the store where she works. After she lies to cover the theft, Lillian and her co-worker Rose (Kristen Johnston) embark on an all-night journey into the city's darker recesses, where they are picked up by some businessmen in a bar. Consequently Lillian is later raped by one of the men in his apartment. Lillian's boyfriend, Frederic (Dan Flutterman), goes through a similar night of hell, trying to get money owed to him so he can pay off a loan shark (who later beats him up). Come morning, Lillian and Frederic are at the store and plan to go straight, but soon the lies continue (she tells the manager that Frederic stole the watch) and the nightmare begins again. The dark drama met with some encouraging reviews and a few off-Broadway awards but has not been heard of much since its six-week run.

The National Actors Theatre opened its third season with a new "artistic advisor," Michael Langham, who staged *Timon of Athens* on November 4 at the Lyceum in a jazzy version set in the roaring twenties and reverberating with the music of Duke Ellington. The whole venture sounded foolhardy, but the result was "a production that illuminates, surprises, and hushes every last cough from the front row to the second balcony." Brian Bedford played Timon, backed by strong performances from Michael Cumpsty (Alcibiades), John Franklin-Robbins (Apemantus), and Jack Ryland (Flavius). The revival earned rave reviews all around, the company's first unqualified critical success.

Two weeks was all that James Duff's comedy **A Quarrel of Sparrows** (11-9-93, Promenade) could last off Broadway, although it had been popular in some regional theatres. Paul Palmer (Michael Lichtenstein), an up-and-coming playwright who has just signed a deal to have a film made of his off-Broadway hit, is stopped by an angel on Fifth Avenue one day and told that he must repent and avoid the lure of commercialism. Paul's wife, Angela (Jan Hooks), who is to star in the film version, disapproves of Paul's "conversion," and soon the marriage is falling apart. Paul visits the Sag Harbor home of his elderly friends August (Henderson Forsythe) and Rosanna Ainsworth (Polly Holliday), hoping they will tell him what to do. But the delightfully grumpy August will not make decisions for the young man, so Paul is forced to reconcile his new religious fervor with the real world of show business.

Paula Vogel deconstructed Shakespeare's *Othello* with her **Desdemona—A Play About a Handkerchief** (11-11-93, Circle). This Desdemona (J. Smith-Cameron) is not the naive innocent of the Bard but a promiscuous tramp who has slept with her husband's entire Cyprus company except for Cassio. Shakespeare's other two female characters are also changed. Emilia (Fran Brill) aids her husband, Iago, in his plots, hoping that he will be killed and she will inherit everything. Bianca (Cherry Jones) is a sweet-natured whore who befriends Desdemona. (Because of Desdemona's nighttime sexual activities, Bianca thinks she is a fellow prostitute.) Desdemona tells her intimate secrets about Bianca's beloved Cassio, thereby destroying their relationship. As with the original, Desdemona dies at the jealous hands of Othello, ironically, for her nonexistent love affair with Cassio. Some critics found Vogel's feminist take rather droll and thought-provoking; others dismissed it as half-baked feminism.

The season's most ambitious venture (and disappointing run) was Robert Schenkkan's two-part epic **The Kentucky Cycle** (11-14-93, Royale), which had won the Pulitzer Prize in 1992 after regional productions in Seattle, Los Angeles, and Washington. Three families (two white and one black) who inhabit a section of eastern Kentucky woodland were traced from 1775 to 1975, the sins of the ancestors coming back to haunt later generations. The play also served as a history of the whole nation as everything from tribal Indian skirmishes, the opening of the West, the Civil War, coal miners' strikes and the emerging labor movement, recession and the closing of the mines, and finally the government's "war on poverty" served as the background for the extended tale. The large cast, headed by Stacy Keach, appeared as various characters in the nine plays, often as direct descendants of themselves, which made for some virtuoso acting. But the strength of the production was Schenkkan's solid, old-fashioned storytelling techniques that sustained interest over two three-hour evenings. He also used recurring motifs to unify the epic, none more memorable than the newborn girl wrapped in buckskin who is buried alive by a cruel father, only to be discovered many generations later remarkably well-perserved in the waterproof skin. Reviews were mostly positive (though rarely raves), but so expensive an undertaking could only survive thirty-four performances.

A fantasy that struck some critics as "a bewitching bedtime story for growns-ups" but others as "attenuated whimsy," Elizabeth Egloff's **The Swan** (11-15-93, Public: Martinson) had fun playing with the idea of the animal instincts in man. Dora Hand (Frances McDormand), a thrice-divorced nurse living on the Nebraska prairie, is the neglected mistress of Kevin (David Chandler), a married milkman. One day a swan (Peter Stormare) crashes through her window, and she nurses it back to health, naming it Bill and making it her pet. Soon the childlike creature is learning to talk, dress as a human, play checkers, and drink beer. His animal side appeals to Dora, creating an awkward triangle among Dora and the two men in her life. But Bill becomes too "animal" in his jealousy, and when Dora tries to flee to Florida with Kevin, Bill breaks through the glass again and flies off with Dora.

Any Given Day (11-16-93, Longacre), a prequel of sorts to Frank D. Gilroy's Pulitzer winner *The Subject Was Roses* (5-25-64), did not fare nearly as well, closing in a month. The Benti family household in the Bronx of 1941 is lorded over by oppressive Mrs. Benti (Sada Thompson), a widow and German immigrant (though she married an Italian) who reads the future in tea leaves and tries to run the lives of her three children: former radio singer Carmen (Andrea Marcovicci), trusting Nettie (Lisa Eichhorn), and sickly Eddie (Peter Frechette). Nettie is married to John Cleary (Victor Slezak), and they have a sixteen-year-old son, Timmy (Gabriel Olds). (The three Clearys, five years later, are the principals in *The Subject Was Roses*.) Also in the household are Carmen's fiancé, Gus Brower (Andrew Robinson), a manipulative entrepreneur who nobody believes really loves Carmen, and Willis (Justin Kirk), Carmen's illegitimate son, who was brain damaged at birth and, now eighteen, is a wheelchair-bound victim the family uses to attack each other. Little plot but plenty of incidents followed, such as Carmen and Gus arguing over what to do with Willis, and John having an affair with Carmen behind his wife's back. In the end, young Tim lies about his age and joins the army, and tubercular Eddie is whisked off to a sanitarium; the rest are fated to remain in the tormented household. Aisle-sitters were politely dismissive ("earnest, plodding drama"), so the production proved to be yet another failure for the Broadway Theatre Alliance.

The Manhattan Theatre Club, which had premiered Donald Margulies's short-lived *The Loman Family Picnic* (3-20-89), brought it back on November 18 in a splendid production that was kept on the boards for sixty-two performances. Lynn Meadow directed an expert cast that featured Peter Friedman as the beleaguered dad, Herbie, Christine Baranski as his nervous wife, Doris, and Jonathan Charles Kaplan and Harry Barandes as their sons, Mitchell and Stewie. Although the script had not changed, the play received much better reviews than it had only four years earlier.

Even though it was about comedy writers for early television, Neil Simon's autobiographical **Laughter on the 23rd Floor** (11-22-93, Richard Rodgers) was sometimes harsh, bitter even. Max Prince (Nathan Lane) is the king of comedy, yet he is a tormented man, popping pills and becoming abusive when on the bottle. (He gets to put his fist through a wall four times in the play.) His gaggle of writers compete with each other to come up with the best one-liners and to catch Prince's inconsistent attention. The slight plot concerns the pressure from the network executives to cut down the running time, trim the budget, and "dumb down" the material for middle America. Behind all these moves is the fear of McCarthyism and the terror of offending anyone. The narrator of the comedy is a shy new writer named Lucas (Stephen Mailer), who acts as Simon's alter ego throughout but seemed the only lifeless character onstage. While the story was far from gripping, the jokes, under Jerry Zaks's direction, flew fast and furious, and stalwart character actors such as Lewis J. Stadlen, John Slattery, Ron Orbach, Randy Graff, and Mark Linn-Baker as the writers kept the evening "screamingly funny." Mixed reviews notwithstanding, the comedy pleased many and ran 320 performances.

Critics were not as responsive to Tony Kushner's **Angels in America, Part II: Perestroika** (11-23-93, Walter Kerr) as they were to the first installment the previous season, but it gathered exemplary notices all the same, Jack Kroll in *Newsweek* calling it "the broadest, deepest and most searching American play of our time." Leftist Louis Ironson (Joe Mantello) and Mormon attorney Joe Pitt (David Marshall Grant) become lovers, Louis not knowing that Joe is in the employ of the hated lawyer Roy Cohn (Ron Leibman). Joe's mother, Hannah (Kathleen Chalfant), arrives in New York from Salt Lake City and tries to comfort Harper (Marcia Gay Harden), Joe's unstable wife. Hannah goes to work at the Mormon Visitors Center in Manhattan, where she meets Prior Walter (Stephen Spinella), Louis's former lover who has AIDS. Although the idea of homosexuality repels the uptight Hannah, she befriends Prior and stays with him when he has an attack and is rushed to the hospital. Cohn is also hospitalized for the same disease, though he is admitted as a kidney-failure victim to keep his gay lifestyle a secret. His nurse is Belize (Jeffrey Wright), a black, gay friend of Louis and Prior who hates everything Cohn stands for. Cohn bribes an official to get him a private stock of the AIDS-combatant drug AZT. Meanwhile, Prior explains to Belize how an Angel (Ellen McLaughlin) came to him at night and announced that Prior was a prophet, giving him a book and ordering him to prepare the world for the new millennium. Belize tells him it was all a dream, but Prior insists the Angel is real. Louis leaves Joe when he finds out that Joe works for Cohn and, realizing that he still loves Prior, goes to Prior asking for forgiveness. As the American Bar Association is voting to disbar Cohn, he struggles to live but, under the vindictive eyes of the ghost of Ethel Rosenberg (Chalfant), dies still furiously barking orders on the phone. Belize steals Cohn's stash of AZT to help Prior and other gay men he knows. Joe returns to Harper as Louis returns to Prior, both reunions filled with guilt and recriminations. The saga ends at Central Park's Bethesda Fountain (with its stone statue of an angel) four years later, with Hannah, Prior, Louis, and Belize commenting on the end of the Cold War and anticipating life in America as the century begins to wane. While longer and more disjointed than *Millennium Approaches*, the play was still highly engrossing. Once again Kushner and director George C. Wolfe created many indelible images, such as the diorama at the Mormon Visitors Center coming to life with characters replacing some of the mannequins on display, and several uses of split staging that allowed two scenes to unfold simultaneously. *Perestroika* won the Tony for Best Play, and Spinella won again for his performance, the only time an actor has won two Tonys for the same role. Wright also took home a Tony at season's end. The second part played in repertory with the first, chalking up an unprofitable 216 performances. *Angels in America* would soon receive many regional and college productions, eventually allowing its investors to break even.

On Lincoln Center's dark Sunday and Monday evenings, the upstairs space was given over to monologuist Spalding Gray, who continued his autobiographical meanderings with **Gray's Anatomy** (11-28-93, Vivian Beaumont). When Gray found out he had a serious disease that might result in blindness in his left eye, he consulted a series of doctors, quacks, and faith healers. They provided no help, but he came away from the experience with a wealth of new stories and characters to mimic. (Ultimately Gray had a minor operation and the condition was cured. But doing that in the first place would have made for a very short evening.) More critics were getting used to Gray, calling this program "hilarious, harrowing, and masterful."

As with last season's *Two Shakespearean Actors* (1-16-92), Lincoln Center was able to present a large-cast historical drama that would be impossible for a non-subsidized theatre company. This year's offering was an elegant and stately revival of Robert E. Sherwood's *Abe Lincoln in Illinois* (10-15-38) on November 29 at the Vivian Beaumont. While most critics decided the Pulitzer Prize winner had not weathered the years well, Sam Waterston made a masterful Lincoln and was ably assisted by Lizbeth Mackay as Mary Todd, David Aaron Baker as Abe's secretary William Herndon, and Peter Maloney, David Huddleston, Robert Westenberg, and J. R. Horne as various politicians. Gerald Gutierrez staged the pageant fluidly on John Lee Beatty's many simple but evocative sets with Jane Greenwood providing rich period costumes.

With several popular one-man shows about gays in evidence over the past few seasons, lesbian comedienne Kate Clinton offered her solo act **Out Is In** (12-1-93, Perry Street) and found an audience for nine weeks. But unlike most previous one-person plays, this was standard stand-up comedy rather than a more personal exploration of the same themes.

Audiences were asked to guess which scenes were real and which were the product of an author's imagination in Peter Parnell's **An Imaginary Life** (12-5-93, Playwrights Horizons). When Matt Abelman (Chip Zien), a divorced, middle-aged playwright, discovers a lump that may be cancerous, he reacts to the crisis by writing a play about his life, fluctuating between true past events and invented ones, neither very interesting. A few aisle-sitters considered the conceit "remarkably clever," but most thought it "frustrates rather than delights."

Similar to this season's *Trophies*, Tom Dudzick's **Greetings!** (12-13-93, John Houseman) also revolved around a man who returns home to his retarded brother and sets off family tension. Yet Dudzick's play was not a domestic drama but a comedy that slipped comfortably into fantasy. Andy Gorski (Gregg Edelman) has been raised in a very Catholic household in Pittsburgh, so it is with caution that he returns home with his Jewish atheist fiancée, Randi Stein (Toby Poser), for Christmas. His good-natured mother, Emily (Lenore Loveman), and narrow-minded father, Phil (Darren McGavin), react as expected, but in the middle of a family argument, Andy's feeble-minded brother, Mickey (Aaron Goodwin), who has previously uttered only "wow" and "oh boy," suddenly says, "Greetings!" Soon he is speaking in a complex philosophical manner about the diversity of religion and the need for universal understanding. It turns out a wise old sage of a long-gone era has borowed Mickey's body in order to pacify and enlighten the Gorski family. He soon has the family pulling together and accepting each other. Then Mickey returns back to "normal" as the Christmas tree lights up by itself during a power failure and holiday joy overflows the house. Despite several enthusiastic reviews ("a comic jewel of a play . . . stunning and touching"), the for-profit entry only lasted six weeks. The comedy did find later life in regional and community theatres.

Aisle-sitters took back everything good they had said about the National Actors Theatre during *Timon of Athens* and unanimously panned the company's *The Government Inspector* on January 6 at the Lyceum. Gogol's wicked comedy, usually called *The Inspector General* in this country, was staged by Michael Langham as a cartoon, but the result was a "deadly pedestrian account of a satire" with performances that were a "meaningless, tedious exercise." Oddly, seventy-three-year-old Tony Randall played the twenty-nine-year-old clerk Ivan Khelestakov in a subdued manner while such accomplished actors as Peter Michael Goetz, Lainie Kazan, David Patrick Kelly, Michael Lombard, and Herb Foster bristled broadly around him.

An old-fashioned kind of one-woman show was **Irene Worth's Portrait of Edith Wharton** (1-11-94, Public: Shiva) in which the star played the famous novelist, her words coming from Wharton's autobiography *Backward Glance* and other writings. Worth also enacted other people in Wharton's life, most memorably a wry characterization of Henry James. Intelligent and stimulating, the program ran six weeks.

Some critics found newcomer Eugene Lee's **East Texas Hot Links** (1-13-94, Public: Anspacher) "a sizzling drama" that "detonates as neatly as a time bomb." The Top o' the Hill Cafe in East Texas caters to a black clientele who feel safe and relaxed there after a hard day's labor. But in the summer of 1955 tensions run high as the Klan is once again active in the area and young black men are disappearing or found dead. Nevertheless Delmus (Monté Russell) wants to celebrate his new job and throws a party. When one of the group betrays the others and is discovered, the party ends in violence and murder. There were some compliments about the ruthless dialogue, but the electric performances by Ruben Santiago-Hudson, Loretta Devine, Earle Hyman, and others carried the drama.

Actor-director Austin Pendleton made his New York playwriting debut with **Booth** (1-22-94, York Theatre Company), a well-received off-off-Broadway entry about the complex love-hate relationship between a famous father and his son. Junius Brutus Booth (Frank Langella), the nineteenth-century tragedian, suffering from alcoholism and insanity, takes his shy son Edwin (Garret Dillahunt) on tour with him in the 1850s as a nursemaid and companion. After many battles, Edwin gradually comes into his own as a man and an actor after Junius dies in 1852.

Yet another play this season that mixed reality and fantasy was Philip Kan Gotanda's **Day Standing on Its Head** (1-25-94, City Center), brought out by the Manhattan Theatre Club. Harry Kitamura (Keone Young), an Asian-American law professor facing a mid-life crisis (his wife no longer loves him, and his students think he is irrelevant), begins researching a paper about eruptive activities on college campuses in the early 1970s. Soon Harry is conjuring up scenes from his own past when he himself was an active participant in such events. Characters (including family members, friends, and even a Japanese Peggy Lee), music, news headlines, and groups such as the Red Guard invade Harry's consciousness until he can no longer distinguish between what he is dreaming and what is real.

While critics could not agree about the stage-worthiness of Harold Pinter's *No Man's Land* (11-9-76), revived by the Roundabout on January 27, they were unanimous in their appreciation of Christopher Plummer as the loquacious poet Spooner and mostly favorable in their evaluation of Jason Robards as the subdued millionaire Hirst. Audiences had eight weeks to decide for themselves.

David Rabe returned to the same off-Broadway theatre where his hit *Hurlyburly* (6-21-84) opened ten years earlier for **Those the River Keeps** (1-31-94, Promenade), a prequel to the other work. Phil (Paul Guilfoyle), a former hitman for the mob, has gone straight, married a waitress named Susie (Annabella Sciorra), and moved to Hollywood, where he is trying to make it as an actor. But Phil is under a lot of pressure: his career has only led to bit parts, and Susie is anxious to have a child. When Sal (Jude Ciccolella), a former colleague from the old days, comes to Los Angeles to execute a contract, he wants Phil as his partner, but Phil refuses. Sal taunts Phil, mocks his new lifestyle, and teases Phil that he has become nothing but a "mook" (a nobody). Convinced he can get Phil to return to his real calling, Sal plans to murder Susie. But Phil finds out and, in a violent confrontation, kills Sal. Notices declared the melodrama overwritten, overlong, and overblown, so the commercial entry closed in a week.

Eric Bogosian had two modest hits this season, the first another monodrama (his fifth) about unsavory characters called **Pounding Nails in the Floor with My Forehead** (2-3-94, Minetta Lane), which he performed eighty-four times. Although he offered nothing very new, audiences enjoyed Bogosian's familiar panhandlers, druggies, sleazeballs, and other damaged males thrashing out at life. As Frank Scheck in the *Christian Science Monitor* noted, "Eric Bogosian may be maturing, but he is not getting any less angry."

An off-off-Broadway drama that won some awards and impressed critics as an "often gripping investigation of painful four-way family relationships," Sybille Pearson's **Unfinished Stories** (2-4-94, New York Theatre Workshop) boasted a skillful performance by Joseph Wiseman. Walter (Wiseman), a Jewish intellectual and patriarch of an upper-middle-class family, escaped out of Germany in 1933 but, now that he is old and dying, he is drawn more and more to the past. He is cared for by his daughter-in-law Gaby (E. Katherine Kerr), a librarian and activist who is always trying to get her son Daniel (Christopher Collet) to make something of himself. (Daniel had tried to make it as an actor but now drives a cab.) When Gaby's ex-husband, Yves (Laurence Luckinbill), an actor who has recently married a younger woman, returns from his honeymoon in Paris, two days of infighting and bitter insinuations follow. Daniel remains bitter toward Yves, who can only respond to moments of crisis by quoting lines from plays, and toward his mother for her pushy left-wing ways. Walter is disappointed in Yves (his acting career is nothing to brag about), and the two have never been close. Yet Walter pleads for forgiveness in the family, and when he dies the survivors take tentative steps toward making peace with each other.

Timberlake Wertenbaker, an American playwright living in Britain, took potshots at both countries in her **Three Birds Alighting on a Field** (2-8-94, City Center), a satire on London's art scene in the late 1980s. Three people connected to the art business find themselves catering to crass foreign patrons (mostly Americans) who are systematically destroying art and culture in the world. Jeremy Bertrand (Daniel Gerroll) is a smooth-talking gallery owner who has absolutely no morals. Boreman (Zach Grenier) is an artist who was in vogue ten years earlier but now is out of fashion and is promptly dropped by the gallery. Biddy Andreas (Harriet Walter) is the British wife of a Greek millionaire who has been sent to the gallery by her husband to broaden her mind and make her "more interesting" to him. The thin plot concerned how the three get entangled in deals and deceptions, all pointing to the death of culture in the modern age. While much of it was funny, Wertenbaker's comedy was too exaggerated and facile to make much of a point.

A double bill about Jewish women, Jenna Zark's **A Body of Water** (2-9-94, Circle) collected some encouraging notices, one critic writing, "This is a writer of warm promise whose dialogue is true, humor sharp, and characters honest." *White Days* concerned Sandy (Jodi Thelen), a contemporary Jewish wife who goes through an ancient Hebrew ritual called *mikveh*, a bath of purification and renewal. Her mother and husband scoff, but Sandy begins to understand her marriage and her own sexual identity as a result of the ritual cleansing. In *Shooting Souls*, Devi (Stephanie Roth), a devout married woman, goes through a similar awakening. As an attendant at the *mikveh*, Devi is very close to the Jewish community. But when she finds herself pregnant for the sixth time (much against her choice), she curses God and the Hebrew world she is trapped in. Yet in a series of scenes with her family and her Rabbi (Don T. Maseng) as they all prepare for Rosh Hashanah, Devi reaches a level of acceptance of her ritualistic life.

Still another one-woman show this season, Regina Taylor's **Escape From Paradise** (2-17-94, Circle), chronicled the adventures of an African-American magazine editor who, instead of going to work one day, jumps on a plane to Italy. While on her trip she recounts moments from her past, playing all of the roles, such as her grandmother, her transvestite brother, and an Italian man she had a one-night stand with. Her lively solo performance ran eighteen times in repertory with *A Body of Water*.

Playwright David Ives had been contributing funny one-acts to various off- and off-off-Broadway theatres for a couple of years, but when Primary Stages put together six of them under the umbrella title **All in the Timing** (2-17-94, John Houseman) the author and company found themselves with a hit. All six playlets utilized wacky wordplay and absurd situations to make points about language and relationships. In *Sure Thing*, Bill (Robert Stanton) tries to pick up Betty (Nancy Opel) in a Manhattan cafe. Every time Bill says the wrong thing, a bell rings and the scene backtracks, thus giving him another chance to create the perfect conversation. Three monkeys named Swift, Kafka, and Milton (Stanton, Opel, and Michael Countryman) are put in a room with typewriters in *Words, Words, Words*, scientists hoping that they will eventually write *Hamlet*. Don (Stanton) has invented *The Universal Language* and offers to teach it to tongue-tied Dawn (Wendy Lawless). But just as she gets the hang of the gibberish, he falls in love with her and admits all his linguistics are a fraud. (What made this piece particularly clever was the way the audience started to understand the silly language as well.) *The Philadelphia* is a duologue in which two friends (Stanton and Ted Neustadt) discuss states of mind named after major cities. *Philip Glass Buys a Loaf of Bread* parodies the surreal opera-theatre pieces of the avant-garde composer, and *Variations on the Death of Trotsky* shows the revolutionary (Countryman), with an axe buried in his head, having philosophical conversations with his wife (Opel) and killer (Neustadt). Glowing reviews ("theatre that aerobicizes the brain and tickles the heart") and strong word of mouth helped the comic program run 526 performances, followed by dozens of regional productions.

Very mixed reactions to Suzan-Lori Parks's **The America Play** (3-10-94, Public: Martinson), a treatise on the role of African Americans in this country's history, made for interesting discussion. In a desert, the Founding Father (Reggie Montgomery), a black man dressed as Abraham Lincoln, digs a monument called the Great Hole of History. He tells us about his life, in particular how he portrayed Lincoln at a theme park and was so convincing that patrons would pay a penny to enact a mock assassination of him. Having dug the Hole, the Father goes in it to die. His wife, Lucy (Gail Grate), and son, Brazil (Michael Potts), enter and mourn his death, then find the old man still alive. But Father refuses to leave his coffin, and the son struggles to get out of the Great Hole in order to put the story of his people in the history books.

The National Actors Theatre suffered another blow when its mounting of Clifford Odets's *The Flowering Peach* (12-28-54) on March 20 at the Lyceum was generally panned, both production and script thought to be lacking. Eli Wallach and Anne Jackson as Noah and his wife, Esther, fared better but, most agreed, had done finer work on most previous occasions.

Anna Deavere Smith found further success with her second one-woman documentary piece, **Twilight: Los Angeles, 1992** (3-23-94, Newman), which ran fourteen times at the Public, then transferred on April 17 to the Cort for nine weeks. The event this time was the riots in Southern California that resulted when a jury acquitted four police officers of beating African-American Rodney King, even though the crime was captured on video. Smith portrayed forty-seven different people connected to the event, including King himself, using words from personal and public interviews. Smith's text and versatile acting talents were both praised, Robert Brustein in *The New Republic* noting, "Smith is not only an objective ear but a characterizing voice, and just as she shapes her text through editing and selection, so she achieves her emphasis through gesture and intonation." George C. Wolfe directed, creating a montage of Los Angeles under fire with projections, sound effects, and scenic pieces moving in and out.

Also at the Public, the Shakespeare Marathon's *Richard II* at the Anspacher on March 31 missed the mark completely. Steven Berkoff turned the subtle drama about abdication into a noisy showcase for synthesizer music and actors posed like marionettes. Michael Stuhlbarg was miscast as the king, but admirable supporting performances by Andre Braugher as Bolinbroke and Carole Shelley as the Duchesses of York and Gloucester compensated somewhat.

Two popular stand-up comics of yesteryear returned to the stage with new solo shows. **Mort Sahl's America** (4-4-94, Theatre Four) proved that the satirist was still in top form, commenting on current events and hilariously analyzing them with the same fervor he had shown for decades. The next night, **Jackie Mason: Politically Incorrect** (4-5-94, John Golden) marked the comic's fourth Broadway visit. Familiar targets got new jokes as Mason railed against the contemporary fear of treading on toes. Sahl stayed for seventy-two performances, Mason for 347 showings.

After twenty years of critical and commercial misfires, Edward Albee was back in fine form with **Three Tall Women** (4-5-94, Promenade), which played at Off-Off-Broadway's Vineyard Theatre for a month, then transferred to Off Broadway, where it ran 582 performances, winning the New York Drama Critics Circle Award and the Pulitzer Prize. The press declared the Beckett-like play was "beautiful and enduring" and "a perfect illustration why theatre is an indispensable art." In an elegant bedroom, a ninety-two-year-old woman, simply called A (Myra Carter), lies in bed assisted by her middled-aged companion, B (Marian Seldes), and bothered by

C (Jordan Baker), a young female lawyer trying to get A to answer questions about her finances. But A is more interested in reminiscing about her pint-sized husband (she calls him her "penguin"), their oddly cold marriage filled with mutual infidelities, and her son, whom she hasn't seen in years. Recalling the son, A suffers a stroke as the act ends. In Act II a dummy takes A's place in bed and a more lucid, active A joins the other two women in a lively discussion about how they got to where they are. Clearly B and C are younger versions of A, and the two piece together her lonely life. A's son (Michael Rhodes) finally enters to be reconciled with his mother, but it is too late. The silent son weeps over the body of A while the three women join hands, A realizing that the happiest moment is when "the greatest woes subside, leaving breathing space, time to concentrate on the greatest woe of all—the blessed one—the end of it."

London's Almeida Theatre brought its acclaimed production of Euripides' *Medea* (in a new translation by Alistair Elliot) to the Longacre on April 7 for ten weeks, setting off crackling debates in the press and in the lobby. Admirers argued that Diana Rigg brought a "blazing intelligence and an elegant ferocity to the part" of Medea, while naysayers found her cold and distant. Jonathan Kent's production, played on Peter J. Davison's setting of rusted steel panels that collapsed as Medea's mental state fell apart, was bold but obvious to some, "exciting theatre" to others. All the same, Rigg won a Tony at season's end.

In Brooklyn, critics raved and audiences packed the one-week engagement of the Royal Shakespeare Company's *The Winter's Tale* that began on April 19 at BAM. Adrian Noble staged the play, which designer Anthony Ward populated with balloons as a visual motif. (Balloons were not only used for decoration at parties but as means of transportation and communication as well.) The fine cast included John Nettles as Leontes, Gemma Jones as Paulina, Julian Curry as Polixenes, Suzanne Burden as Hermione, and Mark Hadfield as Autolycus. Notices for the Roundabout's mounting of William Inge's *Picnic* (2-19-53) on April 21 were generally favorable, although some of the principals were disappointing. TV starlet Ashley Judd played the restless, small-town beauty Madge, and Kyle Chandler was Hal, the out-of-towner who sweeps her away. More satisfying were Polly Holliday as Madge's mother, Flo, Anne Pitoniak as the neighbor Helen, and Debra Monk as the sexually frustrated schoolteacher, Rosemary. Scott Ellis's uneven production was, surprisingly, the play's first Broadway revival.

To think that Arthur Miller made his Broadway debut fifty years ago and was still writing (this was his second new play in as many seasons) amazed some playgoers. But his new work, **Broken Glass** (4-24-94, Booth), did not fullfill its many dramatic possibilities. Happily, as notices admitted, the playwright had not lost his touch, one critic noting that the play had some of Miller's "most focused and rousing dramatic writing in more than a decade." Philip Gellberg (Ron Rifkin) is the token Jew in a very Wasp bank in Brooklyn in late 1938. One day his wife, Sylvia (Amy Irving), cannot move, paralyzed from the waist down. Dr. Hyman (David Dukes) finds that there is nothing physically the matter with Sylvia and suggests psychoanalysis to discover the cause of her infirmity. Interviewing the Gellbergs separately, as well as Sylvia's sister Harriet (Lauren Klein), Hyman learns of Philip's self-hatred as a Jew and the couple's cold and resentful marriage. Then a further cause is found: Sylvia's collapse followed the news of the *Krystallnacht* ("night of broken glass") in Germany in which Jewish stores, homes, and synagogues were torched by Nazis and the Holocaust began. Sylvia's feeling of helplessness over the emerging anti-Semitism in Europe has literally crippled her. The triangle of doctor-patient-husband gradually becomes more complex but then is partially resolved when Philip suffers a heart attack and Sylvia forgives him before he dies. A superb cast, under John Tillinger's astute direction, created some powerful moments in the talky play. *Broken Glass* managed to survive nine weeks, Miller's most sustained Broadway run for a new work in decades.

The season's most popular revival was the National Theatre of Great Britain's radically impressionistic version of J. B. Priestly's *An Inspector Calls* (10-21-47) on April 27 at the Royale. The quaint drawing room mystery-drama was reenvisioned by director Stephen Daltry and designers Ian MacNeil (set) and Rick Fisher (lights) as a dark, surreal nightmare. On a stage cluttered with wartime debris, an upper-class home sits precariously on stilts, surrounded by street urchins who play in the rain, splash in the puddles, and peer into the windows to spy on the wealthy. Eventually the house opens up to let the principal characters come forth and continue their fashionable dinner party amid the surrounding squalor. As Inspector Goole (Kenneth Cranham) exposes each family member's sinful past (all of them knew a certain young girl and were partially responsible for her suicide), the house literally tilts and shifts, finally toppling over with furniture, dishes, and silverware crashing onto the cobblestone pavement. While some commentators decried the mounting as "ludicrously overheated and pompous," most found it "exhilarating" and "one of the more astonishing spectacles on Broadway." Audiences were not so torn, keeping the revival on the boards for 454 performances (over four times the original's run). It took a superior cast to compete with such visuals, but Philip Bosco and Rosemary Harris as the parents, Gerald and Sybil Birling, were as impressive as the scenery. Jane Adams as their daughter, Sheila, was equally accomplished, winning a Tony Award for her performance. Tonys were also won by Daldry and Fisher, as well as by the play for Best Revival.

Although it won awards and popular success in London, Jim Cartwright's **The Rise and Fall of Little Voice** (5-1-94, Neil Simon) found few supporters in New York and closed in a week. In a depressed North England city, Little Voice (Hynden Walch), a shy waif who rarely leaves her room, lives with her mother, Mari (Rondi Reed), a loud, vulgar boozer who will sleep with any man for a laugh. As an escape from her dreary existence, Little Voice plays her late father's records and has learned to mimic the voices of Judy Garland, Edith Piaf, Shirley Bassey, and other great chanteuses. When Say Ray (George Innes), a small-time producer, hears Little Voice sing one night when he is frolicking with Mari, he senses a major attraction. Coerced by Say Ray, Little Voice agrees to perform at a local nightclub, where she is a big hit. But singing in public also gives her the courage to stand up to her mother and to refuse to cooperate with Say Ray's future plans, keeping her remarkable talent to herself and for herself.

For the past few seasons the Circle Rep had been on its last legs, financially and artistically. Lanford Wilson, one of the company's founders, and his new work **Moonshot and Cosmos** (5-3-94, Circle) did little to reverse the downward trend. In each of two one-act monologues, a character is interviewed by an unseen person. In *A Poster of the Cosmos*, Tom (John Dossett), a gay man who has lost his lover to AIDS, is questioned by an unsympathetic cop about the disturbance Tom created in the hospital. *The Moonshot Tape* concerns Diane (Judith Ivey), a famous writer returning to her Missouri hometown of Mountain Grove to visit her mother in a nursing home. Interviewed by the local newspaper about her career, Diane is very obliging at first but, as she drinks more and more, soon reveals past nightmares and family secrets (such as her being sexually molested by her stepfather).

Popular TV and nightclub comedienne Joan Rivers surprised audiences and critics with her performance in **Sally Marr . . . and Her Escorts** (5-5-94, Helen Hayes), which she co-wrote with Erin Sanders and Lonny Price (who also directed). But fans of Rivers could only keep the play alive for fifty performances. Sally Marr was the mother of innovative comic Lenny Bruce and a proficient Jewish stand-up comic herself. (Marr was a friend and mentor of Rivers during the early years of her career.) The play was comprised mostly of monologues by the feisty Marr to her errant husband, her self-destructive son, and others in her life as she struggles to make her way in show business. But what mattered was what Richards called Rivers's "exuberant, fearless and inexhaustible" performance. Also of interest were David Dangle's costumes for Sally, a series of outrageous, colorful duds that one critic described as "resembling an exploded salad bar."

The Manhattan Theatre Club finished out its season with what was perhaps its best offering, Diane Samuels's **Kindertransport** (5-17-94, City Center). The humorless Englishwoman Evelyn (Dana Ivey) has a strained relationship with her college-age daughter, Faith (Mary Mara), until one day Faith runs across papers and photos in the attic of their London suburban home that help explain her mother's cautious view of life. As a ten-year-old, Eva was evacuated from Germany to England in 1938 along with 10,000 other children. Flashbacks depict Eva (Alanna Ubach) bidding a tearful goodbye to her mother, Helga (Jane Kazmarek), arriving in England, and being put into the care of Lil (Patricia Kilgarriff), a Manchester housewife who becomes her second mother. By the time Eva is eighteen, she has lost her German accent and has become quite British (calling herself Evelyn), even to the point of rejecting Helga, who miraculously survives the war and comes to bring her back home. Evelyn's guilt and fear over her past become clear to Faith, allowing the pair to begin to break down the barriers that have separated them for so long. While some of the writing was clumsy (a character called the Ratcatcher, played by Michael Gaston, kept popping up as all the villains in the piece), there were also moments of undeniable power. Critics were also impressed by the cast, especially the young Ubach.

Eric Bogosian's second entry this season was not a monodrama even though he filled **SubUrbia** (5-22-94, Mitzi E. Newhouse) with the crude, funny, desperate kind of people who had populated his previous one-man shows. In a convenience-store parking lot in suburban Burnfield, aimless teens gather to drink beer, smoke grass, harass the Pakistani owner, Norman (Firdous E. Bamji), and waste time until they figure out what they want to do now that they have finished high school. One night, Pony (Zak Orth), a local who has gone on to become a semifamous rock singer, arrives in a limo with his press aide Erica (Babette Renee Props), to check out the old neighborhood. At first everybody seems friendly, telling jokes and recalling old times. But soon the impromptu reunion disintegrates into jealousy and violence. One of the guys hits on Erica (romantically and physically), another pulls a gun and threatens Norman, and a third goes into a coma from a drug overdose. Critics reacted in extreme terms, calling the play "a scathing study of rootless youth" or vehemently denouncing it as trash. But audiences were intrigued enough to keep it on the boards for 113 performances.

During the blizzards of February, deals and decisions that would change the look of the theatre district were being made in boardrooms and lawyers' offices. The long-talked-about 42nd Street Redevelopment Project finally lifted off the ground when the Walt Disney Company purchased the New Amsterdam Theatre and (with help from government loans) planned to renovate the ninety-one-year-old gem. Other corporations would soon follow, and the transformation would be a reality faster than most people had thought possible.

ACT FOUR, 1994–2000

A MODEST RENAISSANCE

1994–1995

Any season that boasted new works by such established American playwrights as Neil Simon, David Mamet, Horton Foote, A. R. Gurney, Christopher Durang, and Sam Shepard, as well as new-generation writers Richard Greenberg, Donald Margulies, and Paul Rudnick, ought to have been memorable, but with very few exceptions these authors came up with second-class scripts. It was a season more notable for British imports and revivals (both native and foreign) than new American works. The eleven original entries and ten revivals on Broadway mirrored the previous season, but Off Broadway saw a slight increase with thirty-six new works and eight revivals. Off Broadway also saw a rise in commercial productions, and more turned a profit than in many a season previously.

As a sign of the times, Neil Simon and his producer Emanuel Azenberg opted to open *London Suite* off Broadway at a price tag of $600,000 as opposed to the $1.5 million needed to do the same show on the Street. As Azenberg noted, "Off Broadway, 400 seats at $40 makes me a smash. On Broadway, 400 seats at $55 closes me down." The quick and expensive failure of *On the Waterfront* on Broadway supported Azenberg's thesis. The Broadway Alliance, after four years of failures, finally had a hit when *Love! Valour! Compassion!* transferred from Off Broadway to the Walter Kerr Theatre. But it really did not do what the Alliance was created for: to produce risky plays by developing artists. McNally was far from an untried talent, and his play had been a sellout at the Manhattan Theatre Club before moving. Later in the season the Alliance production of *My Thing of Love*, an entry closer to the original intent of the plan, quickly folded.

Several theatre companies on, off, and off-off Broadway were struggling desperately. The nearly bankrupt Circle in the Square uptown hired Josephine Abady to run things with founder Theodore Mann; they managed to present a full season of sorts (three revivals) but found themselves still deep in the red at the end of May. The Circle Repertory Company was also in trouble, its three founders quitting the board when new co-directors Austin Pendleton and Lynne Thigpen canceled a production. The Circle was also in need of a new home, a problem shared by the Ridiculous Theatrical Company and the Signature Theatre.

After only one year on the job, David Richards resigned as first-string drama critic for the *New York Times*. Vincent Canby moved up into his position but, like Richards, never wielded the solo power that Frank Rich had in the same position.

Although the Soviet Union collapsed in Russia, conservatism in Congress reigned in the States, continuing to cause trouble for the National Endowment for the Arts. Censorship was much talked about, but, looking at the New York theatre, one sensed a "dare me to be quiet" attitude on the part of playwrights. Paul Rudnick, for example, took on censorship, as well as art, money, and sex, in his **The Naked Truth** (6-16-94, WPA) but ended up with merely a collection of jokes, albeit many of them very funny. Alex Del Favio (Victor Slezak), a gay photographer currently in vogue, is asked to remove three particularly distasteful photographs from his one-man show. The request comes from Nan Bemiss (Mary Beth Peil), a chic but conservative member of the museum's board of directors and the wife of a Republican senator who is about to make a bid for the presidency. But Alex sees Nan as a repressed woman in need of liberation and counters her request with his own for her to pose naked for him. Nan's frustration with her husband, Pete (John Cunningham), who is having a fling with *Playboy*'s Miss August (Debra Messing), drives her to accept Alex's offer. At the opening of the exhibit, the nude photograph of Nan is prominently placed so that Pete, Miss August, and others are caught up in the embarrassment. To complicate matters, Nan and Pete's married daughter Sissy (J. Smith-Cameron) has discovered her lesbian identity and is paired with Cassandra Keefer (Valarie Pettiford), Alex's African-American ex-con assistant, who goes berserk whenever white girls speak in French. Yet everything ends happily (and sentimentally) when the characters learn to put love before politics. While there was no question about Rudnick's comic flair (when a spectator asks Alex how many of the AIDS-inflicted subjects in his exhibit are dead, he replies, "Not as many as in the Rembrandt show"), many critics agreed with Ben Brantley in the *New York Times*, who described the script as "an old-fashioned, ultimately toothless mainstream comedy, steadfastly intent on making people like it."

The season's first solo show was the unique **Ian McKellen: A Knight Out at the Lyceum** (6-21-94, Lyceum) which was performed five times as part of the Cultural Festival of Gay Games IV. The title was more than just a play on words; McKellen had recently been knighted in Great Britain despite the fact that he publicly "came out" and declared his homosexuality. Sir Ian portrayed characters in works by Tennessee Williams, Martin Sherman, Peter Shaffer, and others, as well as delivering his personal commentary on acting and gay rights.

The rest of the summer was filled with revivals. On June 23 at the Delacorte in Central Park, the Shakespeare Marathon pressed on with *The Merry Wives of Windsor*, which Daniel Sullivan set in Windsor, Idaho, during the Gold Rush. Critics disagreed on the concept (the Elizabethan Garter Inn became a Wild West saloon) and the performances, though most admired Brian Murray's Falstaff. Also in the multi-racial cast were Tonya Pinkins and Margaret Whitton as Mistresses Ford and Page, David Alan Grier as Master Ford, Andrea Martin as Mistress Quickly, and George Hall as Justice Shallow. There was critical agreement, however, that the Roundabout's *Hedda Gabler* on July 10 was "blatantly misguided" and "spectacularly muddleheaded." British director Sarah Pia Anderson reset the drama in 1940s America to no effect whatsoever. Film star Kelly McGillis was out of her league as Hedda, with Jeffrey DeMunn and Jim Able similarly lost as Tesman and Lovborg.

The Two Gentlemen of Verona on August 9 at the Delacorte also suffered a change of locale, though most aisle-sitters enjoyed this lesser work by Shakespeare. Designer Eugene Lee opened up the back wall of the outdoor theatre so that Central Park itself became the setting. He also put up a huge billboard with a nude woman advertising perfume and placed a small lake onstage so that the male characters could strip down and go skinny-dipping. Adrian Hall directed, bursts of Puccini's music filled the air, and the characters, clad in Calvin Klein fashions, chased each other and cross-dressed all night long. The two pairs of lovers were played by Malcolm Gets, Lisa Gay Hamilton, Joel De La Fuente, and Nance Williamson. The Roundabout revived a more recent work, Brian Friel's *Philadelphia, Here I Come!* (2-16-66), on September 8 and received more welcoming reviews this time. Joe Dowling staged the wistful play, which seemed to stand the test of time well, and there were delightful performances by Milo O'Shea as the father and Jim True and Robert Sean Leonard as the Public and Private versions of Gareth O'Donnell.

Boston had loved Jack Neary's romantic comedy **First Night** (9-11-94, Westside Upstairs), but audiences off Broadway could not keep the commercial entry on the boards beyond six weeks. On New Year's Eve, Danny Fleming (Daniel McDonald), a daydreaming manager of a video store, is anxious to close up shop when in walks Meredith O'Connor (Lanny Stephens), the girl he went to parochial school with seventeen years earlier. Meredith was his first love, but she walked out of his life when she decided to become a nun. Meredith has never stopped thinking about Danny and has left her vocation to search him down. By midnight the romance has reblossomed, and the ex-nun gets her man. One commentator declared it "a two-character fluff-ball that works tirelessly to earn our affections."

Off-off Broadway, the Signature Theatre Company dedicated its season to Horton Foote's works, offering four plays by the veteran playwright, starting with **Talking Pictures** (9-23-94, Signature). In 1929, Myra Tolliver (Hallie Foote), a divorcée with a teenage son, Pete (Eddie Kaye Thomas), barely manages to make ends meet in Harrison, Texas. She plays the piano for the silent flickers in the town's only movie theatre and teaches piano to the two daughters of the Jackson family, with whom she boards. Myra is courted by Willis (Seth Jones), a bricklayer whose wife abandoned him five years earlier, and eventually she accepts his offer of marriage. Then Myra is suddenly faced with obstacles on all sides: Pete yearns to go and live with his womanizing father, Gerard (Kenneth Cavett), Willis's wife shows up and wants to get back together, and the introduction of talkies in town will soon end Myra's livelihood. But Gerard remarries and puts Pete off as Willis promises that he will stick with Myra and together they will weather the hard times ahead. Notices were approving yet mild in their enthusiasm, just as the play itself was quietly engrossing rather than exciting.

Two unusual Shakespearean productions arrived in the fall. The Ridiculous Theatrical Company's take on *A Midsummer Night's Dream* on September 29 at the Charles Ludlam (an Off-off Broadway space named after the troupe's late founder) offered plenty of sex reversals, phallic swords, husky male fairies, "rude mechanicals" with hardware as costumes, and a Titania (Beth Dodye Bass) with giant papier-mâché breasts so that Oberon (Eureka) could put the accent on the first syllable of her name. Everett Quinton essayed Bottom (in a very large ass's head with a very long tongue) and staged the merry burlesque, which critics found "zany, tasteless, and preposterous" but also not all that far from the spirit of Shakespeare's original. The British troupe Cheek by Jowl presented an all-male *As You Like It* on October 4 at BAM, which Declan Donnellan staged with black and white costumes on a stark white set. Far from the campy cross-dressing of the Ridiculous production, these men attacked all the roles with serious energy and fervor. Notices commended the mounting, calling it "pure magic" and full of "wild and happy exuberance." The two-week engagement in Brooklyn was so well attended that the comedy returned on December 6 for another week. (Some playgoers may have been reminded of the all-male *As You Like It* that the National Theatre brought to New York in 1974, which was equally accomplished, if not more so.)

A. R. Gurney first found success with *The Dining Room* (2-24-82), in which six actors played a variety of Wasp characters in several dining rooms. His new work, **A Cheever Evening** (10-6-94, Playwrights Horizons), utilized six actors enacting Wasp characters in seventeen short stories by John Cheever. The vignettes ranged from comic to somber, each one revealing the disappointment and frustrations of its supposedly superior class. One family prides itself on its state-of-the-art bomb shelter, a woman considers poisoning her husband's dinner, two brothers fight over Grandma's furniture, a disruptive neighbor tears off his clothes and moons a dinner party next door, and everyone tries to adjust to a changing world where they are not so special. Don Scardino directed the agile cast (John Cunningham, Jack Gilpin, Julie Hagerty, Mary Beth

Peil, Robert Stanton, and Jennifer Van Dyck) who brought Cheever's characters to life, but several critics complained that the total effect was more interesting than involving. Nevertheless, the play held on for 103 performances.

The Public Theatre, originator of so many one-person dramas of late, opened its season with **Some People** (10-18-94, Shiva), a solo work written and performed by Danny Hoch in which he portrayed eleven diverse New Yorkers. Hoch's versatility with different accents (and even foreign tongues) was his forte; he played a disk jockey punctuating his Spanish spiel with American brand names, a Polish repairman forced to use pantomime because no one understands him, a street kid dreaming of going to college, a housewife addicted to local news and gossip, a Hispanic father grieving for his slain son, and other people who went far beyond stereotypes. Encouraging reviews for the young Jewish actor from Queens helped the show run forty-five times.

Second Stage's revival of Wendy Wasserstein's early comedy *Uncommon Women and Others* (11-17-77) opened on October 26 at the Lucille Lortel and found an audience for ten weeks, even though several reviews claimed the play had dated: not old enough to be a period piece, not recent enough to be relevant. Carole Rothman directed this incisive look at college coeds at a posh girl's school in the early 1970s.

Another play about women living together was R. T. Robinson's **The Cover of Life** (10-27-95, American Place), which was set in a small Louisiana town in 1943. The wives of the three Cliffert brothers (who are away at war) move in with their no-nonsense mother-in-law, Ola (Carlin Glynn) to help each other get through the duration. A local newspaper features the foursome, bringing them to the notice of Henry Luce in New York; he assigns journalist Kate Miller (Sara Botsford) to write a cover story for his *Life* magazine. Kate moves in with the women for a week and overcomes her Manhattan attitude of superiority when she grows to admire the three very different brides. Sybil (Kerrianne Spellman) is the most outgoing, full of jokes, sexual energy, and daring. Weetsie (Melinda Eades), on the other hand, is very religious and fearful. The youngest, Tood (Alice Haining), is starting to wonder if there is more to life than being a submissive wife. With Kate's help, Tood breaks away from her cold husband, but both women are powerless to help Sybil when she is beaten up by the chauvinistic local Tommy (David Schiliro). While commentators found the women's roles juicy as acting exercises, the play was too formulaic to be totally convincing.

The Manhattan Theatre Club had an extremely productive season premiering seven new American works, three of them enjoying long runs. The most successful was Terrence McNally's **Love! Valour! Compassion!** (11-1-94, City Center), which ran seventy-two times off Broadway, then transferred to the Walter Kerr on February 14 for another 249 performances. Gregory Mitchell (Stephen Bogardus), a famous Manhattan choreographer, opens up his 1915 vintage summer house on a lake in Dutchess County for three holiday weekends (Memorial Day, Fourth of July, and Labor Day), inviting some of his closest gay friends to relax with him. But each guest brings so much emotional baggage with him that the weekends becomes fraught with subtle as well as overt tension. Bobby Brahms (Justin Kirk), an attractive young man who is blind, has been Gregory's young lover for some time but is now drawn to Ramon Fornos (Randy Becker), a Puerto Rican dancer who loves to flaunt his sexual prowess. Perry Sellars (Stephen Spinella) and Arthur Pape (John Benjamin Hickey) have been together for fourteen years, but they also suffer moments of insecurity and infidelity. John Jeckyll (John Glover), a bitter Englishman, is Gregory's rehearsal pianist, although he is really a frustrated composer. John's twin brother, James (Glover), a gentle soul who is dying of AIDS, joins them as well. The most flamboyant of the group is Buzz Hauser (Nathan Lane), a costume designer who also has AIDS and covers his fears with incessant chatter about Broadway musicals. There is little action in the three acts but plenty of incidents and a lot of lively talk. (Buzz declares, "I was having a musical comedy nightmare. They were going to revive *The King and I* for Tommy Tune and Elaine Stritch. We've got to stop them!") While much of the play seemed a Chekhovian version of McNally's earlier *The Lisbon Traviata* (10-31-89), and Lane's Buzz was obviously a repeat of that work's opera fanatic, Mendy, the comedy-drama appealed to most critics, who pronounced it "a greatly affecting, tender, funny, painful play." Joe Mantello staged the piece on Loy Arcenas's dreamy set, a suggestion of trees and a lake with a doll-house version of the farmhouse onstage to set the locale. The play won both the Tony and the New York Drama Critics Circle Award, and a Tony went to Glover as well for his graceful performances as the two Jeckyll brothers.

Oliver Mayer's melodrama **Blade to the Heat** (11-3-94, Anspacher), about Hispanic boxers in the late 1950s, received a stunning production at the Public. Pedro Quinn (Kamar De Los Reyes) is a quiet loner, so when he wins a middleweight championship on a split decision, he flees the victory party to be with his friend Garnet (Carlton Wilborn), an aspiring lounge singer. Pedro is sexually attracted to Garnet, but the singer spurns him, and Pedro is labeled a pervert in the Latino community. Mantequilla Decima (Paul Calderon), the champ before Pedro, takes his defeat bitterly, especially when he also is called a deviant by ruthless fellow boxer Wilfred Vinal (Nelson Vasquez). Spurred on by his coach, Alacran (Jaime Tirelli), Mantequilla is rematched with Pedro in a bloody fight in which the near-dead Pedro delivers a fatal blow to Mantequilla, and Pedro is left sobbing as he holds his dead rival in his arms. Few critics found the play anything better than clichés and action-packed melodramatics, but George C. Wolfe's staging, with dynamic boxing matches underscored with a percussion soundtrack, was considered explosive and thrilling.

Actor-director Kenneth Branagh, known primarily for his classic stage and film productions in Britain, turned to playwriting with his 1987 drama **Public Enemy** (11-3-94, Irish Arts Center) which ran 133 performances off Broadway even though critics dismissed it as "artificial" and "disappointing." Tommy Black (Paul Ronan), an unemployed youth in Belfast in the mid-1980s, idolizes movie actor Jimmy Cagney. He wins a talent show by tap-dancing to "Yankee Doodle Dandy" and puts on a Cagney persona (and actual movie dialogue) in his daily life. (He even insists that his girlfriend buy a grapefruit so that he can smash it in her face, as in the famous scene in *Public Enemy*.) Tommy and his drinking pal Davey Boyd (Brian D'Arcy James) are being coerced to join a Protestant group battling the IRA, but Tommy is more intent on stealing a videotape of *Public Enemy* that he can't afford. With Davey, he holds up the local video store, carried away with his Cagney act, he kills the owner. The community gets up in arms and Tommy is gunned down in pure Cagney style.

Five new short comedies by Christopher Durang comprised the Manhattan Theatre Club's second offering of the season, **Durang Durang** (11-13-94, City Center). The most notable of the playlets were parodies of Tennessee Williams and Sam Shepard, both more silly than scathing. In *For Whom the Southern Belle Tolls*, Williams's *The Glass Menagerie* (3-31-45) was given a gender change: shy and sensitive Lawrence (Keith Reddin), who collects glass cocktail stirrers, temporarily crawls out of his shell when feminine caller Ginny (Patricia Randell), a rough but genial lesbian, comes to pay a call. *A Stye of the Eye* lampooned Shepard's *A Lie of the Mind* (12-5-85) and other works as battling brothers Jake (Marcus Giamatti) and Frankie become the same person, wife Beth (Reddin) is played by a man, and every empty scene is filled with "meaning." Favorable but not enthusiastic reviews greeted the comic evening, which could not survive beyond its announced five-week engagement.

By a wild coincidence, a real Shepard play opened the next night, and Williams's actual *Glass Menagerie* the night after. At the Public, Shepard's **Simpatico** (11-14-94, Newman) was considered a minor and flawed work, running three hours while having very little to say. Years ago Vinnie (Fred Ward) and his partner Carter (Ed Harris) pulled a horseracing swindle and brought down local commissioner Simms (James Gammon) in a blackmail deal. Carter ran off with Vinnie's wife and his Buick but has been sending hush money to Simms each month. Vinnie wants to make amends with the wronged Simms and get his wife back, so he informs Carter he is going to reveal the scam to the public. Carter panics as Vinnie goes to Simms to offer evidence of the past crime. Surprisingly, Simms wants nothing to do with it and is willing to let the past die. Vinnie feels vindicated, but Carter is now left full of guilt. Shepard directed the production, getting some electric performances from a cast that also included Marcia Gay Harden as Vinnie's erratic girlfriend and Beverly D'Angelo as Carter's boozing wife.

Julie Harris headlined the Roundabout's fiftieth-anniversary revival of *The Glass Menagerie* (3-31-45) on November 15, and her Amanda was generally applauded as expert and commanding but not one of her usual triumphs. (Several notices pointed out that Harris was not physically or vocally right for the part.) There was some hesitation in saluting the rest of the cast: Zeljko Ivanek was a biting, cold Tom; Calista Flockhart a too-pretty and superficial Laura; and Kevin Kilner a showy and surface Jim. Frank Galati staged the memory play on Loy Arcenas's realistic setting that featured the projected titles that Williams had originally provided but had rarely been used before.

The Circle in the Square, whose space lately had been booked by others, had not produced its own plays since 1992. The company resurfaced again on November 20 with a revival of Michael Cristofer's *The Shadow Box* (3-31-77). With so many plays about AIDS and death in recent years, this Pulitzer Prize winner struck many commentators as primitive and obvious. Nonetheless, they admired Jack Hofsiss's powerful staging and his superb cast, in particular Estelle Parsons as the crotchety and ribald old patient Felicity, Marlo Thomas as her demure daughter Agnes, Mary Alice as the housewife Maggie trying to deal with her husband's fatal illness, Jamey Sheridan as the gay author Brian dying of an unnamed disease, and Mercedes Ruehl as his promiscuous ex-wife, Beverly.

Two of England's finest actresses, Eileen Atkins and Vanessa Redgrave, graced Off Broadway in **Vita & Virginia** (11-21-94, Union Square), which Atkins adapted from the letters of Vita Sackville-West (Redgrave) and Virginia Woolf (Atkins). (Atkins had previously played Woolf in her one-woman show *A Room of One's Own*.) The performances were luminous and the words delicious, even if the result was far from a drama. But rave reviews for the two ladies ("verbal chamber music for two superb instruments") and their popularity filled the house for 129 showings.

Tom Stoppard provided two superior, critically acclaimed plays this season (the *Best Plays* editors cited both), but neither enjoyed anything more than a modest run. Because it dealt with spies, double agents, triple agents, and even three sets of identical twins, **Hapgood** (12-4-94, Mitzi E. Newhouse) was perhaps Stoppard's most intricately plotted puzzle of a play. Yet there was still room for involving personal relationships and brilliant talk about physics as it applied to human behavior. British spymaster Elizabeth Hapgood (Stockard Channing), nicknamed "Mother" by those working under her, managed to turn Soviet physicist Kerner (David Strathairn) into a double agent for the Free World, falling in love at the same time and having a child by him. After years of reliable service, Kerner suddenly becomes a security risk as documents show up in Moscow that were not "fed" to them through Kerner. Twin Russian agents pull a fast one on Hapgood during a pickup at a London bath house, so a British spy, Ridley (David Lansbury), is suspected as the traitor. To catch him in the act, Hapgood fakes the kidnapping of her teenage son, Joe (Yaniv Segal), and even portrays her own sluttish twin sister, Celia, to ensnare Ridley. As Hapgood has suspected, there were two Ridleys needed to pull off the heist; one is shot and the other captured. But Kerner's cover as a double agent is blown, so he departs, leaving Hapgood saddened by the political turn that their relationship has taken. As usual, Stoppard's dialogue sparkled. Speeches by Kerner were particularly dazzling; he explained, "A double agent is like a trick of the light: you get what you interrogate for." Jack O'Brien's hypnotic yet clear direction, Bob Crowley's clever use of moving projections in his scenery, and the skillful cast prompted critics who saw the original London production to declare the New York one superior. (Also, Stoppard had tinkered with the script since its initial showing in Britain.) Reviews were mostly favorable but not the "money" kind, yet Lincoln Center kept the play on in its downstairs space for 129 performances.

Shades of *The Man Who Came to Dinner* (10-16-39) were evident in Elizabeth L. Fuller's **Me and Jezebel** (12-7-94, Actors' Playhouse), which was supposedly based on a true story. Aging movie star Bette Davis (Louise DuArt) is brought by a mutual friend to dinner at a Connecticut household one night in 1985, and because of a hotel strike, the actress asks if she can stay a few days. The Fuller family, which consists of writer Elizabeth (played by Fuller herself), her unseen husband, John, and their young son, Christopher, eagerly agree. But soon Davis starts to take over (ordering meals, determining family outings, demanding improvements to the house), and the stay is prolonged into weeks. John threatens to move out if Davis doesn't, and little Christopher is picking up on Davis's mannerisms and language. (Elizabeth recounts how her four-year-old greeted his babysitter with "I hope you know how to play Candyland, for Chrissake!") Happily, after thirty-two agonizing days, the hotel strike ends and Davis waltzes out of their lives. The two-character play, originally a book and then a one-person performance piece, only lasted two weeks.

A second two-week failure followed when unanimous pans greeted Donald Margulies's **What's Wrong With This Picture?** (12-8-94, Brooks Atkinson), the much-admired playwright's Broadway debut. The play had been workshopped and seen off-off Broadway in 1990 and evidently had qualities that did not surface in the glitzy, broadly played Joe Mantello mounting that hammered for laughs and handled the fantasy element like an obvious sitcom. (Margulies continued to tinker with the script after the brief run.) A middle-class Brooklyn family is mourning the death of Shirley, wife and mother, who died after choking on Chinese food at a local restaurant. Her husband, Mort (Alan Rosenberg), is crushed by Shirley's death, feeling lost and afraid and pilling all his affection on his teenage son, Artie (David Moscow), to fill the gap. Mort's elderly parents (Florence Stanley and Jerry Stiller) are concerned about Mort but seem to be little help. Then suddenly the door opens and Shirley (Faith Prince) enters, covered with dirt from the cemetery and ready and willing to pick up where she left off when she was alive. Of course Shirley is not alive (her body is cold), but she knew she was needed at home, so home she came. Mort is thrilled, content to have the dead Shirley rather than no Shirley at all. But Artie realizes that they have to let go of Mom if father and son are ever to move on. So Shirley returns to the grave, and everyone is wiser for the experience.

That same night, another play featured a character returning from the dead. Charles Busch forsook the showy female roles he usually wrote/ played and took on more conventional theatrics in his farce **You Should Be So Lucky** (12-8-94, Westside Upstairs), which transferred from Primary Stages off-off Broadway for a run of twelve weeks off. Christopher (Busch), a timid gay electrologist in Manhattan's West Village, watches his business and love life falter until he befriends Mr. Rosenberg (Stephen Pearlman), a millionaire widower and client of his. Rosenberg wishes his overbearing daughter, Lenore (Julie Halston), were more like Christopher, so when Christopher accidentally electrocutes Rosenberg, no one is surprised to discover that his will leaves a $10 million fortune to Christopher. Of course, Lenore fights Christopher for the money (they even go on a sensational TV talk program called *The Wanda Wang Show* and battle in public), but Mr. Rosenberg returns as a ghost to help Christopher outwit the crafty Lenore. Busch proved to be a capable farceur even in trousers, and the "outlandish . . . and magical tale of transformation" won applause by the press.

Also off-off Broadway, Tony Kushner's **Slavs!** (12-12-94, New York Theatre Workshop), a ninety-minute coda to his epic *Angels in America*, intrigued audiences for eight weeks. In Russia, as the great Communist experiment is falling apart, the "world's oldest living Bolshevik" (Joseph Wiseman), peasant women in babushkas, fearful diplomats, a little girl dying of radiation poisoning (Mischa Barton), and two lesbian scientists (Marisa Tomei and Mary Schultz) are all spouting off about dialectical materialism, sometimes with farcical effect, other times in a very sobering manner. The plot (about the danger of nuclear reactors in Russia) was rather thin, but Lisa Peterson staged the collage of images in such an arresting manner that the result was eccentric but mesmerizing. As John Lahr in *The New Yorker* commented, "Even in a small work like *Slavs!*, [Kushner] is capable of cajoling us out of our received opinions through the power of his heart and his mind."

A sequel that many thought was better than the original was **A Tuna Christmas** (12-15-94, Booth), Ed Howard, Joe Sears, and Jaston Williams's Yuletide follow-up to their popular *Greater Tuna* (10-21-82). As the holidays approach, the town of Tuna, Texas (third smallest in the state), is being terrorized by a Christmas Phantom who is destroying lawn decorations entered in an annual display competition. Also at risk is the local production of *A Christmas Carol*, which won't go on unless someone pays the delinquent electric bill. Old favorites and new characters populated the stage (all twenty-two citizens again played by Sears and Jaston), yet this time the broad satire sometimes led to touching scenes of honesty (such as the put-upon Bertha Bumiller finding affection late in life). The comedy stayed on Broadway for twenty showings as part of its national tour.

Under the blunt but accurate title **Comedy Tonight** (12-18-94, Lunt-Fontanne), producer Alexander Cohen presented four comedians, each doing a solo act, for a one-week holiday engagement. Mort Sahl provided the political humor, Michael Davis juggled and did impressions of Richard Nixon, Dorothy Loudon talked about her career (with some songs thrown in), and Joy Behar did a routine about Jews and women. An additional holiday treat followed when Patrick Stewart brought back his one-man version of *A Christmas Carol* (12-19-91) on December 22 and for eighteen showings filled the large Richard Rodgers stage with his lively portrayal of all the Dickens characters.

The oddest entry at the Public this season was Christopher Walken's **Him** (1-5-95, LuEsther), which was labeled a "workshop," played weeks of previews, then "opened" for a mere thirteen performances. In limbo somewhere between life and death, Elvis Presley, identified as Him (Walken), parades around in a green velvet jumpsuit and cape and argues with Bro (Rob Campbell), his stillborn twin brother, who likes to fool people and show up places dressed as the famous singer even though everyone knows Elvis died in 1977. But Him tells us what really happened: Elvis plotted his own disappearance and escaped to a Morocco clinic where he was changed into a woman. He/she now works as a waitress at a truckstop somewhere in the Deep South. The seventy-five-minute play reached its most ludicrous moment when Walken donned female garb and debated whether "she" should tell the public the truth or let matters stay as they were. Unanimous pans described the venture as a "farrago of nonsense" and "garbage."

At the Anspacher, *The Merchant of Venice* on January 17 met with decidedly mixed press for the Public's production but a round of cheers for Ron Leibman's "harrowing, fierce, and complicated" Shylock. He was supported by Laila Robins as Portia, Jay Goede as Bassanio, and Bryon Jennings as Antonio. That same night off-off Broadway, the Ridiculous Theatrical Company presented its outlandish version of *Carmen*, adapted and directed by Everett Quinton. Carmen (Quinton) works in a condom factory, her lover Don José, here called Don Johnson (Lenys Sama), is a sailor with an Elvis dialect, and the opera's toreador becomes Torre Adore (Julia Dares), a lesbian from Tijuana. The cast did not sing, though Bizet's music was heard in the background at times. Mixed notices ranged from "a loose, loud, coarse burlesque" to "exuberant."

Again off-off Broadway, Bruce Jay Friedman returned to the stage after twenty-five years with his sarcastic allegory **Have You Spoken to Any Jews Lately?** (1-23-95, American Jewish Theatre). The "Anti-Semitic Hall of Fame" in the theatre lobby was a tipoff to the kind of show patrons were in for. In a resort town in the Northeast, Jack Horowitz (Larry Pine), a former screenwriter and assimilated Jew, sits indoors listening to the radio with a snowstorm raging outside, the phone lines down, and the roads closed. Soon he has entered the "Jewish Twilight Zone" where he and his friend Danny (Stephen Singer) notice that all the Jews they know, from the local plumber to a Hollywood agent, are disappearing. Every time either of them says anything remotely Jewish, Nazi sirens are heard in the distance. Jack and Danny set out to find out where the Jews are going, but soon they are herded into a boxcar as an American Holocaust begins. The "increasingly unpleasant little play" was unanimously panned, and Friedman returned to the world of magazine and short-story fiction.

The most acclaimed off-off-Broadway play of the season (though it hardly enjoyed a long run) was **The Young Man from Atlanta** (1-27-95, Kampo Cultural Center), part of the Signature Theatre's Horton Foote season. Will (Ralph Waite) and Lily Dale Kidder (Carlin Glynn) are in mourning for their only son, Bill, who drowned by deliberately walking into a lake even though he could not swim. Lily Dale has looked to religion for an answer and calls Bill's death an accident. Will, on the other hand, is a practical man of business and sees things as they are: Bill committed suicide. But Will's faith in his judgment is crumbling, especially when, after years of service, he loses his executive job in wholesale groceries and finds he cannot raise the money to start a business of his own. Soon Will suffers a heart attack and is forced to consider that his choices in life have been less than wise. The Young Man of the title is Randy, a friend and roommate of Bill who is never seen but haunts the Kidder household. Was Bill homosexual, and was Randy his lover? All they know is Bill gave Randy money and, to Will's surprise, so did Lily Dale because the Young Man was so comforting to her in her time of sorrow. Finally Will and Lily Dale are reconciled and resigned to the presence of the Young Man in their lives. Though patently old-fashioned in many ways (it was set in 1950, so none of the characters was even allowed to voice anything overt about Bill's sexuality), the drama was applauded by the press, one critic calling it "a simple, immensely satisfying play, crafted with elegance, alive with feeling." The engagement was limited to three weeks, but in the spring the drama won the Pulitzer Prize, so it returned the next season.

Actress Anne Meara made a notable playwriting debut with **After-Play** (1-31-95, City Center), a seriocomic character piece that was lauded as "astonishingly strong" and "unusually entertaining." After Manhattanites Marty (Merwin Goldsmith) and Terry Guteman (Rue McClanahan) have run into their old friends from Los Angeles, Renee (Barbara Barrie) and Phil Shredman (Larry Keith), at the theatre, the four go for a late-night dinner at a fashionably "in" restaurant. Throughout drinks, dinner, and dessert, the couples discuss the play (Mary and Terry were moved by it, Renee and Phil thought it manipulated the audience), and their disagreements put an edge on the other topics of conversation: their children, bumpy careers, even bumpier sex, and the specter of death itself. Near the end of the evening, two friends of the Gutemans, Emily (Rochelle Oliver) and Matt Paine (John C. Vennema), come over to the table, spill out their miseries about their son who has recently died of AIDS, then leave. The incident sobers the remaining couples, who find the strength to keep up their friendship. Following forty performances at the Manhattan The-

atre Club, the play transferred (with Meara now playing Terry) to a commercial run at Theatre Four, where it stayed for 400 performances.

Craig Lucas's new play, **Missing Persons** (2-1-95, Atlantic), was a misfire. Aisle-sitters were in agreement that the "smirkingly pretentious" comedy-fantasy had "not one rounded, unlopsided, believable human being in sight." Addie Peneck (Mary Beth Peil) is a literary critic who twenty years ago drove her husband (Jordan Lage) away by always criticizing his poetry. Now her son, Hat (Todd Weeks), has become a poet, and she seems to be doing the same thing to him. The action shifts from the past, when young Hat (Cameron Boyd) had to deal with his crazy parents, to the present, when Hat's divorced wife (Mary McCann) still inhabits the house and has fallen for a simpleton (John Cameron Mitchell) she picked up in the supermarket. The one memorable aspect of the production was David Gallo and Lauren Helpern's set, a cozy Philadelphia suburban home lined with seemingly endless shelves of books.

That same night, all the lights on Broadway were dimmed in memory of George Abbott, who had died on January 31 at the age of 107. He had made a career in writing or directing slambang melodramas, door-slamming farces, and fast-paced musical comedies, all of which were scarce on Broadway by the time he passed away.

The Roundabout found itself with an unexpected hit on February 2 when it offered a double bill called *The Molière Comedies*, which featured the period one-acters *The School for Husbands* and *The Imaginary Cuckold*, translated by Richard Wilbur and directed by Michael Langham. The nimble cast included Suzanne Bertish, Malcom Gets, Remak Ramsay, and Brian Bedford, who was particularly singled out for his two very different Sganarelles, a hilarious prig in the first play and a fearful cuckolded husband in the second. All sixty-one scheduled performances quickly sold out.

Cries of "sophomoric" and "unexpectedly, almost astonishingly clumsy" led the round of pans for Joyce Carol Oates's satiric comedy **The Truth Teller** (2-9-95, Circle). "Tiny" Culligan (John Seitz), a businessman who has made a fortune manufacturing fences, and his subservient wife, Nora (Kathleen Widdoes), live in an affluent Buffalo suburb surrounded by guard dogs and, of course, high fences. Also in the compound are Maggie (Barbara Gulan), their sexually repressed daughter, who drinks to forget her three failed marriages, and Biff (Craig Bockhorn), their ineffectual son and heir, who can only mimic his father's words. For Tiny and Nora's thirty-fifth anniversary their daughter Hedda (Lynn Hawley), the family black sheep who walked out years ago, returns with her Jewish boyfriend, Saul Schwartz (Andrew Polk), a good-natured teacher and "psycho-socio-linguist." The Culligans are narrow-minded Roman Catholics, so family members drop anti-Semitic epigrams at every opportunity. Hedda and Saul believe in absolute truth telling and force the Culligans to face the reality about themselves (just as characters do in all the Ibsen and Tennessee Williams dramas that their names are stolen from). The result is chaos, tears, and then freedom: Saul runs off with Maggie, Biff realizes he is a transsexual, Hedda makes plans to take over the family business, and Nora has a sweet reunion with her old flame Nelson "Nelly" Rockefeller (Richard Seff).

Nicky Silver again annoyed or thrilled critics with his new comedy **Raised in Captivity** (2-9-95, Vineyard), which ran off-off Broadway for a month. Sebastian Bliss (Peter Frechette) and his twin sister, Bernadette (Patricia Clarkson), are reunited after many years when they attend their mother's funeral. (She was killed by a malfunctioning shower head.) Bernadette cannot stop weeping for her departed mother, and her husband, Kip (Brian Kerwin), sees the old lady's death as a sign for him to give up dentistry and become an artist. While Kip paints the very-pregnant Bernadette, Sebastian informs his therapist, Dr. Hillary MacMahon (Leslie Ayvazian), that he no longer needs treatment because he is in love with a convicted murderer named Dylan Taylor Sinclair (Anthony Rapp) to whom he has been writing in prison. Hillary responds by stabbing her hand in frustration and following Sebastian home, where she falls in love with Kip. When Sebastian brings home Roger (Rapp), a male hustler, the punk cuts Sebastian in the throat with his knife. Sebastian doesn't die, but he does experience a vision of his dead mother telling him that her twins are the offspring of a rapist. Dylan writes back to Sebastian saying he is not interested in him, Kip runs off with Hillary, and Bernadette and Sebastian plan to raise the baby together.

Mayo Simon's **The Old Lady's Guide to Survival** (2-16-95, Lamb's) was worth sitting through to see June Havoc's performance, described by one critic as "tight, detailed, and rigorous—a model of the actor's craft." Netty (Havoc) is elderly but self-sufficient. Her neighbor Shprintzy (Shirl Bernheim), on the other hand, needs to be looked after more and more, especially since she has started to forget who she is. Netty is determined not to end up caretaker for Shprintzy, but as Netty's eyesight fails her she relents, and the two senior citizens become roommates.

Another performer who rose above her material was Elizabeth Marvel, who played the Diane Arbus–like photographer Suzie in Stuart Greenman's fanciful concoction **Silence, Cunning, Exile** (2-19-95, Public: Martinson). "Inspired" by the life of Arbus, the play starts and ends with Suzie's suicide at the age of forty-eight, the voices of the Apollo 15 astronauts heard as they lift off in 1971 while Suzie lies bleeding to death in her bathroom. Then, in a series of dreamlike flashbacks, Suzie's career as a cult artist in the 1950s and 1960s is examined, with particular emphasis placed on her obsession with photographing grotesque and pathetic people. Her husband Donald (Denis O'Hare), lover Frank (Tim Hopper), and colleague Isaac (Rocco Sisto) float in and out of her life as the production resembles a montage of photos set to pop songs of the era. While most commentators regarded the play as "a sophomoric exploitation," Marvel managed to make Suzie alive and intoxicating.

History and conjecture met in Mark St. Germain's "literate, funny, and captivating" **Camping With Henry & Tom** (2-20-95, Lucille Lortel), which gathered some highly complimentary reviews and an audience for eighty-eight performances. According to the history books, President Warren G. Harding (Ken Howard) went on a camping trip in Maryland in 1921 with Henry Ford (John Cunningham) and Thomas Edison (Robert Prosky). St. Germain has the three of them stranded in the woods for a few hours after Ford's Model T hits a deer and crashes into a tree. While the three wait to be rescued, Ford gets down to business. He has dug up enough dirt on Harding (a mistress and an illegitimate child) to try to blackmail him into supporting Ford for the presidency. Surprisingly, Harding knows he is a mediocrity in public office, is sick of the job (he was forced into it by his party), and is more than willing to be exposed and driven out of the White House. But Edison, a crusty philosopher at heart, realizes that what made Ford a leading captain of industry would make him a disastrous president. Edison threatens to talk about Ford's own indiscretions (several servant girls and stenographers he has impregnated and paid off) and even to run against Ford himself in a presidential election if he has to. Ford relents, the trio are found by the Secret Service, and history continues as written.

Few commentators favored Cheryl L. West's **Holiday Heart** (2-21-95, City Center), a "flat-footed spectacle" about an African-American family that wavered between sitcom and soap opera. Adolescent Niki Dean (Afi Clendon) lives on Chicago's South Side with her drug-dependent mother, Wanda (Maggie Rush), who is in a panic about growing older. Niki, in actuality, is being raised by Holiday Heart (Keith Randolph Smith), a too-good-to-be-true neighbor who is built like a football player but is a drag queen by profession. The churchgoing Holiday keeps Wanda off drugs and helps Niki to accept others (and herself) for what they are. But Wanda is smitten by drug dealer Silas Jericho (Ron Cephas Jones), who moves into the household and kicks Holiday out. Niki is left to deal with the world using what Holiday has taught her. The Manhattan Theatre Club production boasted strong performances all around, and the play was able to hold on for seven weeks.

Reactions to the Circle in the Square revival of Chekhov's *Uncle Vanya* on February 24 varied, some praising the "crisp British efficiency" of the revival, others declaring it a "stiff" and "lifeless, aimless production." (Although the Jean-Claude van Itallie translation was American, the director, Brian Murray, and some of the cast were British.) The same disagreements extended to the players, led by James Fox (Dr. Astrov), Amanda Donohue (Yelana), and Tom Courtenay (Vanya). The play was only performed twenty-nine times, another financial disaster for the floundering company.

New Yorkers were used to visits by the august RSC from Britain, but they were hardly prepared for the hilarity of another RSC, San Francisco's Reduced Shakespeare Company, that presented its **The Compleat Works of Wllm Shkspr (Abridged)** (2-26-95, Westside Downstairs) off Broadway after touring the States and Europe. The script by Jess Borgeson, Adam Long, and Daniel Singer managed to lampoon, paraphrase, discuss, or at least mention all thirty-seven plays in a rapid evening of clowning and high spirits. Christopher Duva, Peter Jacobson, and Jon Patrick Walker performed all the roles as they focused on the gender problems in *Romeo and Juliet*, pondered about *Hamlet's* ponderings, turned all the *Henry* history plays into a football match, presented *Titus Andronicus* as a television cooking show, and, as an encore, performed *Hamlet* back-

wards. Reviewers accepted the silliness in the spirit in which it was offered, and audiences happily partook of the fun for 140 performances. (The comedy was even more popular in London, running, off and on, for several years.)

Although not applauded nearly as much as his *All in the Timing* (2-17-94), David Ives's **Don Juan in Chicago** (3-3-95, Primary Stages) found some critical favor and an audience off-off Broadway for a month. In 1599 Seville, Don Juan (Simon Brooking), an alchemist who is still a virgin, makes a pact with Mephistopheles (Peter Bartlett) that he can live forever as long as he seduces a different woman every night. Juan's first conquest is easy: Donna Elvira (J. Smith-Cameron), a local lass who is desperately in love with him. But when Juan drops her to seek out another woman for the next night, Elvira makes her own contract with the devil to pursue Juan through the ages and trick him back into her bed. The centuries fly by, and in contemporary Chicago, Juan (now calling himself Don Johnson—the second character this season named after the popular TV actor) is weary of his endless romancing, declaring, "Another day, another Dolores." He has three candidates for that night's seduction: the young and beautiful Zoey (Dina Spybey), who is actually his illegitimate daughter; the worldly-wise Sandy (Nancy Opel), whom he slept with twenty years ago in Illyria, Illinois, and who is Zoey's mother; and Elvira in disguise. Juan falls in love with Elvira and finds fatherly affection for Zoey. Instead of damning him for his failure to secure a new lover, Mephistopheles is so moved by Juan's true love that he sends Juan and Elvira to heaven. The play may have worn out its premise long before the final curtain, but Ives's punning ("better latex than never," Juan comments about sex in the 1990s) and verbal acrobatics were still in evidence.

Under the umbrella title **Death Defying Acts** (3-6-95, Variety Arts), three new one-acts by David Mamet, Elaine May, and Woody Allen made their New York debut. Mamet's *An Interview* was the least impressive, a curtain raiser in which a sleazy lawyer (Paul Guilfoyle) argues with an attendant (Gerry Becker) at the pearly gates of heaven to let him in. May's *Hotline* was an extended monologue in which a desperate and suicidal hooker (Linda Lavin) calls a support group hotline and rants about the horrors of urban life to a novice counselor. The most satisfying, though nastiest, of the threesome was Allen's *Central Park West*, which explored the dark underside of upper class Manhattanites. When psychiatrist Phyllis

(Debra Monk) finds out her best friend, Carol (Lavin), has been cheating with her husband, Sam (Guilfoyle), she gets drunk, then invites Carol over to hurl insults at her. But Sam doesn't love either wife or mistress and plans to run off with a college coed, Juliet (Tari T. Signor), until she in turn rejects him. Allen's dialogue was more scatological and cruel than that usually found in his films, but it was also uncomfortably funny. Conflicting reviews (most preferred the Allen piece) did not stop audiences, who kept the triple bill on the boards for 407 performances.

The most acclaimed (and satisfying) revival of the Broadway season was Lincoln Center's sterling production of Ruth and Augustus Goetz's *The Heiress* (9-29-47) on March 9, which ran 341 performances at the Cort. Cherry Jones achieved wide recognition and star status with her scintillating performance as the shy spinster Catherine Sloper. Clive Barnes in the *New York Post* wrote: "Radiant in hope, tragic in despair, chilling in conviction, [she] resonates with passions that seem all the more vibrant for being suppressed and thwarted." Philip Bosco was her demanding father, Jon Tenney the opportunist who wooed her, and Frances Sternhagen her aunt who tries to save her. Designer John Lee Beatty's Washington Square town house allowed one to look through the walls just as Gerald Gutierrez's expert direction peered hauntingly into each of the characters. Jones, Sternhagen, and Gutierrez

GERALD [Andrew] GUTIERREZ (1952–), the son of a police detective and a flamenco dancer, was born in Brooklyn and educated at the State University of New York at Stony Brook and Juilliard. After graduation in 1972, he worked as an actor and director in various small theatres, most notably the St. Nicholas Theatre in Chicago. His Off-Broadway production of *A Life in the Theatre* (1977) brought him some recognition, and he made his Broadway directing debut with *The Curse of the Aching Heart* (1982). In the 1980s he directed productions at Playwrights Horizons and the Acting Company and taught directing at NYU. While his was never a familiar name to audiences, Gutierrez's productions of *Geniuses* (1982), *Isn't It Romantic* (1983), *Terra Nova* (1984), *Hyde in Hollywood* (1989), and last season's *Black Comedy* made him one of the most reliable and successful off-Broadway directors. Although he would later stage musicals and classical pieces, Gutierrez is best known for his insightful direction of realistic plays that have an edge of mystery to them.

each took home Tony Awards, and the committee named it the season's Best Revival.

Peter Brook was at his most enigmatic with **The Man Who** (3-13-95, BAM), Oliver Sacks's *The Man Who Mistook His Wife for a Hat* as adapted for the stage by Sacks, Brooks, Marie-Helene Estienne, and the cast. The program was a series of interrogations of patients by neurologists, the doctors hooking each subject up to electrodes and causing them to reveal memories and fears. Brook's staging was inventive (the same four actors played all the doctors and their subjects, while one musician played a variety of instruments to accompany each section) and Sacks's ideas were indeed intriguing but the piece was too austere and detached to captivate most theatregoers.

The Broadway revival of Brian Friel's *Translations* (4-7-81) on March 19 at the Plymouth boasted a strong cast (including Brian Dennehy, Donal Donnelly, Amanda Campbell, Rufus Sewell, and Michael Cumpsty), and the script was more highly thought of by the press than when it first appeared in New York. But few had much good to say about the "flat, mostly uninspired" production directed by Howard Davies. It folded in three weeks.

A week later a one-man show, previously a hit in Chicago and other cities, opened on Broadway with little fanfare and stayed for nearly three years. Rob Becker's **Defending the Caveman** (3-26-95, Helen Hayes) was not a play but an evening of stand-up comedy and wry observations about men and woman that was as truthful as it was entertaining. According to Becker, men are basically hunters and women gatherers; from that premise he covered the battle of the sexes over the eons. Unlike Jackie Mason or Lily Tomlin, who drew crowds with their comic personas, Becker was an unknown, but his ideas had wide appeal. Critics were mildly approving of Becker's act, but word of mouth kept it running 784 performances, the longest continuous run for a one-person show in Broadway history.

For many the most brilliant script of the season was Tom Stoppard's London hit **Arcadia** (3-30-95, Vivian Beaumont), although there was disagreement about its American mounting. Trevor Nunn directed both productions, but commentators suggested that this "play of wit, intellect, language, brio, and emotion" was not well served at Lincoln Center. (Several complained that the pace was too fast for the densely literate script.) In a room in the English country estate of the Coverly family, two stories are being enacted at

the same time. In 1809, the handsome tutor Septimus Hodge (Billy Crudup) teaches Thomasina
Coverly (Jennifer Dundas), a teenage prodigy in
the family, the mathematical intricacies of Fer-
mat's Last Theorem while he carries on a loveless
affair with the wife of a visiting poet, Ezra Chater
(Paul Giamatti). The jealous husband confronts
Septimus, but the clever tutor distracts Chater
with flattery about his poems. Lady Croom (Lisa
Banes), Thomasina's mother, is working with
landscape architect Richard Noakes (Peter Maloney), who is outfitting the estate in the latest
gothic-romantic style, complete with a hermitage. Lady Croom, who insists that Noakes find a
hermit to live in the hermitage, has her eye on
the attractive Lord Byron, Septimus's college
friend who is visiting. But after a tryst with both
Lady Croom and Chater's wife, Byron (never
seen in the play) takes off for the Continent. The
second story is set in the present day in the same
room, where two rival scholars, Bernard Nightingale (Victor Garber) and Hannah Jarvis (Blair
Brown), are going through the family records to
learn more about Byron and a mysterious hermit
who lived on the estate for some twenty years.
The estate's heir, Valentine Coverly (Robert Sean
Leonard), is a brilliant mathematics scholar who
is attracted to Hannah and helps her outwit the
pompous Nightingale, proving an article Nightingale published about Byron killing Chater in a
duel was not true. In the final scenes the past and
the present converge as we learn that Thomasina
died in a fire just as Septimus fell in love with
her, and Hannah finds the proof that it was Septimus who lived in the hermitage, mourning
Thomasina in seclusion until he died. Stoppard's
wit was at its Wildean best; when Noakes suggests they advertise in the papers for a hermit,
Lady Croom notes, "But surely a hermit who
takes a newspaper is not a hermit in whom one
can have complete confidence." Despite what
was said about the production, it featured some
marvelous performances and beautiful decor. The
intricate comedy won the New York Drama Critics Circle Award but only managed to run 173
performances. (In London it had run two years.)

Dan Butler's solo performance on coming out,
**The Only Thing Worse You Could Have Told
Me . . .** (4-2-95, Actors' Playhouse), portrayed a
world very different from that with which Ian
McKellen opened the season. In this "whirlwind
tour of the gay American landscape," ten homosexuals (ranging from the flip to the questioning to the self-hating) tell about "being gay," their
commentaries creating a complex mosaic of dif-

fering attitudes. The commercial venture became
popular enough to run 175 times.

Monologues were also featured in Jeffrey
Hatcher's **Three Viewings** (4-4-95, City Center),
a trio of one-person vignettes all set in a midwestern funeral parlor over a Christmas holiday
weekend. In *Tell-Tale*, undertaker Emil (Buck
Henry) finds himself preparing the body of a
woman whom he has loved from afar for many
years. *The Thief of Tears* showed Mac (Margaret
Whitton), an attractive drifter and small-time
thief, as she returns home for her grandmother's
funeral and tries to pry the diamond ring the old
lady had promised her as a child off the corpse's
finger. *Thirteen Things About Ed Carpolotti* concerned widowed Virginia (Penny Fuller), whose
speculator husband left her in debt to the mob
but she is saved by a mysterious benefactor.
Some critics decreed Hatcher a talent to reckon
with, and others thought the O. Henry-like playlets contrived, yet most agreed that the acting
was exceptional.

Two distinguished performances also highlighted **Having Our Say** (4-6-95, Booth), Emily
Mann's dramatization of the nonfiction book by
Sarah L. and A. Elizabeth Delany and Amy Hill
Hearth. Subtitled *The Delany Sisters' First 100 Years*,
the play is set in the Mt. Vernon, New York,
home of 103-year-old Sadie (Gloria Foster) and
101-year-old Bessie (Mary Alice), who regale the
audience with stories of their family and careers
while they prepare a birthday celebration in
memory of their father. Daughters of a minister
born in slavery and a biracial mother, the sisters
grew up during Reconstruction and lived to witness Jim Crow laws, two world wars, the Harlem
Renaissance, the difficult birth of civil rights, and
the women's movement. Professional ladies long
before it was common for African Americans (Sadie was a high school teacher, Bessie a dentist),
the women provide wisdom on many topics and
soon transcend race to become spokeswomen for
all Americans. Critical cheers for the two-person
cast (and the Delany sisters themselves, who
were still alive at the time) kept this intimate
piece on the boards for 308 performances.

For the first time in Neil Simon's long career,
a play of his debuted off Broadway rather than
on. **London Suite** (4-9-95, Union Square), Simon's
third anthology of one-acts set in a hotel, followed in the footsteps of his hit *Plaza Suite* (2-14-
68) and less popular *California Suite* (6-10-76). *Settling Accounts* pitted Brian (Jeffrey Jones), a
drunken Welsh author, against Billy (Paxton
Whitehead), his sneaky accountant, whom he has

caught at Heathrow trying to abscond to Buenos Aires with the writer's money. As Brian holds him at gunpoint in a room at a deluxe London hotel, Billy comes up with outrageous and hilarious explanations for his behavior. American widow Mrs. Semple (Carole Shelley) is encouraged by her daughter Lauren (Kate Burton) in *Going Home* to spend her last night in London with a wealthy and unwed Scotsman who has shown an interest in her. The farcical *The Man on the Floor* concerned a harried couple from New York, Mark (Jones) and Annie (Burton), who have lost their Wimbledon tickets and are being driven out of their suite because Kevin Costner is waiting to check in. The final one-acter, *Diana and Sidney*, was the most effective, offering the most involving characters of the evening. A follow-up to the British couple at the Oscars in *California Suite*, the comedy-drama reunited actress Diana (Shelley), now a popular favorite on an American TV mystery show, and her bisexual ex-husband, Sidney (Whitehead), who seeks out Diana to get money for his male lover dying of cancer. Mixed notices, applauding the performers more than Simon's script, did not help business, and the comedy only ran 169 performances.

Greek tragedy met an African-American *Godfather* in Keith Glover's blistering melodrama **Dancing on Moonlight** (4-11-95, Public: Anspacher). In 1934 Harlem, gamblers Eclipse (Badja Djola) and Dady Jerry (Terry Alexander) come to blows over a pair of loaded dice. Dady slashes Eclipse across the chest, then flees. Meanwhile, Dady's wife, who is in labor, is killed by Eclipse's girlfriend, Neptune (Anna Marie Horsford), and the newborn boy is given to Eclipse as ransom. But Eclipse raises the child as his own, and by 1959 he has grown to become Apollotis's (Kevin Jackson), a kingpin in the Harlem numbers racket. Apollotis's restlessness is heightened by new developments: Eclipse's plan to move from gambling to narcotics, Apollotis's association with a Black Muslim group that stirs his fervor for the civil rights movement, and the reappearance of Dady. The tale ended as foreshadowed with Apollotis finding out the horrible truth about his past. Notices ranged from "earnest but unpersuasive" to "crackles with energy and a genuine love of language."

Four actors, each dressed identically in gray suits, red sweater vests, and school ties, played all the characters in **Travels With My Aunt** (4-12-95, Minetta Lane), Giles Havergal's clever stage adaptation of Graham Greene's 1969 novel. Henry Pulling, a middle-aged ex-banker who is rather timid and spends his life raising dahlias in his garden, meets his flamboyant Aunt Augusta (Jim Dale) at his mother's funeral. Soon he is whisked off by the eccentric lady and finds himself on an international adventure involving smuggling and romance. Dale, Brian Murray, Martin Rayner, and Tom Beckett each played Henry at one point, then doubled as such characters as a South American beauty, CIA agent, Augusta's mysterious black consort, an American hippie, even a dog. The "oddly diverting" piece, previously seen in Glasgow, London, and New Haven, garnered mixed notices, but the quartet got raves, and audiences came 199 times.

David Mamet's second play in as many months was **The Cryptogram** (4-13-95, Westside), which (atypical of the author) featured a woman as its focal character. When Donnie (Felicity Huffman) receives a note from her husband, Robert, that he is leaving her, she takes comfort in her gay friend Del (Ed Begley, Jr.), while her young son, John (Shelton Dane), bears the brunt of her bitterness. When Donnie finds out Del helped Robert by lending his apartment for trysts with his lover, Donnie throws Del out of her life. Meanwhile, John cannot sleep and complains of hearing voices. He waits for his father to return and begs for his favorite blanket, which is packed away in a box upstairs. Feeling betrayed by all the men in her life, Donnie lashes out again at John, then gives him Robert's hunting knife to cut open the package; John slowly goes upstairs, knife in hand, to silence the voices forever. The eighty-minute, intermissionless drama was lauded by some aisle-sitters as a "radical, elliptical new work . . . not casually titled," dismissed as a hoax by others. Nevertheless, Donnie was one of Mamet's most intriguing creations. However, audiences were not overwhelmed, forcing the commercial entry to close after sixty-two performances.

Yet another play about a gay relationship destroyed by AIDS, Chay Yew's **A Language of Their Own** (4-20-95, Public: Shiva) was unique only in the fact that the lovers were Asian-Americans. Ming (B. D. Wong) is a totally assimilated "American-born Chinese" (jokingly called an "ABC") who sports a baseball cap and speaks in American slang. His lover, Oscar (Francis Jue), was born in China and is both envious and resentful of Ming's way of fitting in. When Oscar finds out he is HIV positive, he does not tell Ming but breaks off the relationship and forms an attachment with Daniel (Alec Mapa), a Filipino business student at Harvard. Although he still loves Oscar, Ming links up with Robert (David Drake), a handsome white waiter whose devotion to Oscar is like that of an eager puppy. Eventually Oscar dies of AIDS and Ming realizes why Oscar left him but is too grief-stricken to go to the funeral. The talky play explored the warm language of lovers, the characters often finishing each other's sentences. But most aisle-sitters found the talk "generic" and the players much better than the play.

Helen Mirren, whom most Americans knew from British television dramas, made her New York debut as the Russian wife Natalya obsessed with her son's tutor Aleksei (Alessandro Nivola) in Turgenev's *A Month in the Country* on April 25 at the Roundabout. Bryon Jennings was her husband Arkady, Ron Rifkin her long-languishing admirer Mikhailo, and F. Murray Abraham the late-blooming romantic Dr. Shpigelsky. Few commentators approved of Scott Ellis's production, and there was even disagreement about much of the cast (especially Abraham), but Mirren was warmly welcomed. Also notable was Santo Loquasto's spare set made out of pale wood and accented by white curtains that were rearranged into different configurations to denote various locales.

The infamous TV quiz show scandals of the 1950s served as the subject for Richard Greenberg's **Night and Her Stars** (4-26-95, American Place), which the Manhattan Theatre Club offered for thirty-nine performances. Herbert Stempel (Patrick Breen), a brilliant but nerdy Jewish intellectual, is the reigning champ on the quiz show *21*. Unfortunately, audiences are getting tired of him, so producer Dan Enright (Peter Frechette), who also serves as the play's narrator, brings in handsome Wasp Charles Van Doren (John Slattery), the son of renowned poet Mark Van Doren (Keith Charles). Stempel is paid to lose to the all-American Charles, who is supplied with answers and goes on to win week after week, becoming an idol of the airwaves. Only when a congressional probe looks into the matter does Charles break down and confess to the deception. A man of high principles who was corrupted by wealth and popularity, the humbled celebrity returns to his father for forgiveness. Even though it garnered few enthusiastic reviews, the editors of the *Best Plays* cited it, and much in the play was admirable. The script had moments of poetic poignancy (it was written in blank verse), and the performances were very telling. Unfortunately for Greenberg and his producers, they

were eclipsed by the popular film *Quiz Show* that told the same story and was released a few months before the play opened.

One Broadway revival that packed a wallop was Jean Cocteau's **Indiscretions (Les parents terribles)** (4-27-95, Ethel Barrymore) in a new translation by Jeremy Sams and a British production directed by Sean Mathias. The 1938 play, first seen by New Yorkers as *Intimate Relations* (11-1-62), features a sexually rampant (and confused) Parisian family in which father (Roger Rees) and son (Jude Law) are both having an affair with the same young woman (Cynthia Nixon) while the mother (Kathleen Turner) throws all her affections on the son as her spinsterish sister (Eileen Atkins) carries a torch for the husband. The outrageous play demanded outrageous performances, and its American-British cast rose to the occasion with gusto. Also exaggerated but delightful were Stephen Brimson Lewis's bold scenic designs, most memorably a white spiral staircase that climbed up and out of sight and left actors dangling in space as they struggled to make sense out of their lives. Laudatory reviews for the play and the stars (though some disapproved of Turner) kept business brisk for 221 performances.

Critics were less in agreement about the Circle in the Square's revival of Tennessee Williams's *The Rose Tattoo* (2-3-51) on April 30, although Mercedes Ruehl was considered a passionate and gutsy Serafina by several aisle-sitters. Robert Fall's production and the script itself came under some severe criticism, but audiences supported the play for nine weeks. Anthony LaPaglia was warm and funny as Alvaro, the truck driver who comes into Seraphina's life.

The season's unluckiest entry was a stage version of **On the Waterfront** (5-1-95, Brooks Atkinson), which went through changes of director and cast on its way to Broadway and then saw one of its supporting players suffer a heart attack onstage during a press preview. Budd Schulberg and Stan Silverman adapted Schulberg's acclaimed screenplay for the stage, and Eugene Lee designed a large and cluttered set filled with industrial artifacts that reminded one of his famous *Sweeney Todd* set. It all but dwarfed the cast, which included Ron Eldard as the "pigeon" Terry Malloy (the Marlon Brando role in the film), Penelope Ann Miller as his girl, Edie Doyle, and Kevin Conway as the union boss, Johnny Friendly. Adrian Hall directed stylishly, but it all added up to an "earnest, perfunctory, overproduced" play. Vilified by the critics, the expensive production folded in a week, losing close to $3 million (a new high for a nonmusical).

The parade of British productions on Broadway resumed with London's Almeida Theatre Company's *Hamlet* on May 2 at the Belasco. Rising young film favorite Ralph Fiennes essayed the prince and was esteemed for his rapid, intelligent performance. Director Jonathan Kent propelled the tragedy forward with speed and efficiency, though commentators could not agree whether this was a plus or a minus. The revival stayed for ninety-one showings, and Fiennes won the Tony, the first time an actor had taken home the prize for that most challenging of roles.

Broadway had a notorious reputation for looking askance at any play that proved a hit in rival cities such as Los Angeles or Washington. Such may have been the case again with Chicago's **My Thing of Love** (5-3-95, Martin Beck), which the Steppenwolf Theatre sent, along with its famous alumna Laurie Metcalf (then very popular on television), to Broadway, where the venture folded in two weeks. (This was another case where director and cast changes were made on the way to New York.) Alexandra Gersten's dark comedy about the perennial triangle (wife-husband-mistress) moved unsteadily from sitcom to Milleresque drama and back again with only flashes of success. At breakfast one morning, Elly (Metcalf), an unstable suburban housewife, confronts her husband, Jack (Tom Irwin), with her knowledge of his affair with another woman. He confesses and begs for forgiveness, which Elly tentatively offers. Then on the morning Elly is expecting a guidance counselor (Mark Blum) to discuss her troubled daughter, Jack's mistress, Kelly (Jane Fleiss), shows up, desperately afraid of losing Jack. The predictable complications that followed provided enough laughs and pathos until Jack finally dumps Kelly and returns to Elly. Unanimous pans for the script were balanced by praise for Metcalf.

Madeline Newell (Kristine Nielsen) and Peter Szczepanek (Albert Macklin) are perfect for each other in Constance Congdon's **Dog Opera** (5-10-95, Public: Martinson) except that he is gay and she is heterosexual. But the twosome, friends since high school in Queens and now in their thirties, stand by each other as she goes through a series of affairs with men who treat her badly and he avoids commitment with others by hiding behind brittle putdowns and escapist rhetoric. Weaving in and out of these scenes is Jackie

(Kevin Dewey), a gay hustler, thief, and poet who cynically comments to the audience on the status of love and sex in the city. All the romantic wanderings come to a halt when Peter is diagnosed HIV positive. Gerald Gutierrez, now greatly in demand, staged the many short scenes fluidly, but few critics found much to recommend in the script.

The Circle Rep's plague of intriguing but unfulfilling plays continued with Yugoslav Dunsan Kovacevic's **The Professional** (5-11-95, Circle). After the fall of Communism, Belgrade publisher Teya (Jonathan Hogan) is approached one day by Luke (Fritz Weaver), a former member of the secret police. Luke shows him thousands of manuscript pages that appear to be a book but are in reality the contents of the police file on Teya. In fact, Luke knows more about Teya than the publisher knows about himself. What seemed a fascinating beginning for a play then turned into a discussion about self-revelation and public knowledge versus privacy, teasing the audience into thinking some conclusions might be forthcoming. None were.

That same night, teasing of a different nature could be found in David Dillon's **Party** (5-11-95, Douglas Fairbanks). Kevin (David Pevsner), a gay New Yorker with not much else to do, invites six of his friends over to his place for a game of Truth or Dare. Challenging each other to reveal deep secrets or describe their darkest fantasies, the seven homosexuals (all stereotypes) systematically told tales and disrobed until the whole cast was naked. The gathering of homosexuals at a party where everyone engages in a dare may have recalled *The Boys in the Band* (4-15-68), but the two plays could not have been further apart in quality. Critics dismissed the evening of contrived voyeurism, but there were enough indiscriminating patrons to let it run for nearly a year.

A gritty melodrama by Marion McClinton called **Police Boys** (5-13-95, Playwrights Horizons) had plenty of action, plot, and characters but was also dismissed as being "shallow," "shapeless," and "meaningless." In an inner-city police station (set in "a future you can touch with your hand"), several cops are former members of a street gang of African-American roughs called the Police Boys. Sergeant Christopher "Comanche" Chileogus Cummings (Richard Brooks) co-founded the gang years ago but now finds more satisfaction is performing voodoo rituals in his office. He is at odds with Captain Jabali Abdyl LaRouche (Chuck Cooper), whose son is dying in a hospital, a victim of the same gang. Billy (Akili Prince), a gang member called The Royal Boy on the streets, is brought into the station and charged with raping and killing a white female jogger. It is clear Billy is guilty (audiences get to see a graphic flashback of the crime), but he is an old acquaintance of several of the cops, so Cummings wants to go easy on him. Sergeant Ruth "Babe Ruth" Milano (Nancy Giles), a lesbian officer second in command, also finds her loyalties are divided because her ex-lover Meredith Fellows (Judith Hawking) is the prosecuting attorney and is in the pay of a governor campaigning to wipe out gang violence. While Billy is in a holding cell, the various characters argue about his fate and leave the audience wondering who is the law and who is the criminal.

A Doll's House and *Othello* made up the touring Acting Company's repertory, which it brought to the TriBeCa Performing Arts Center on May 15 for a week. Zelda Fichandler directed the Ibsen drama, and Penny Mitropulos staged the Shakespearean tragedy.

The Manhattan Theatre Club closed its winning season with another hit, A. R. Gurney's comedy **Sylvia** (5-23-95, City Center). Greg (Charles Kimbrough) and Kate (Blythe Danner) have reached that time in their lives when they can do what they please since the children are grown and on their own. They move from the suburbs back to Manhattan, Kate pursues a new career as an English teacher in the public school system, and Greg starts to pull away from his stressful job as a financial trader. Then one day Greg brings home a stray dog called Sylvia. Soon his affection and devotion to the mutt start to threaten his marriage, in no small way because Sylvia is played by a scruffy but beautiful woman (Sarah Jessica Parker) who does not behave like a dog but rather like an adoring mistress. (No sexual attraction is implied; Sylvia simply worships Greg, calling him "my god!") As Greg becomes more and more obsessed with Sylvia, Kate makes an ultimatum: either the dog goes or she will. The confrontation forces the couple to re-evaluate their marriage. Greg agrees to give up Sylvia, but at the last minute Kate sees that the dog is no longer a rival and lets her stay. In an epilogue, Greg and Kate describe the many years of joy Sylvia gave them and share with the audience a picture (projected on a screen behind) of a happy mixed-breed poodle-lab. Critics agreed that it was one of Gurney's neatest little hat tricks of a play, "involving, beautiful, funny, touching, and profound." John Tillinger directed with just

the right amount of whimsy, and Parker was applauded for her sexy, innocent, "howlingly funny" performance. The comedy ran 283 performances and was later popular with regional theatres across the country.

Frederick Stroppel's **Fortune's Fools** (5-24-95, Cherry Lane) provided an example of that increasingly rare commodity: a cheerful comedy about heterosexual love. Chuck Galluccio (Danton Stone) and Gail Hildebrandt (Dorie Joiner) have asked their friends Jay Morrison (Tuc Watkins) and Bonnie Sparks (Marissa Chibas) to be part of their wedding party, hoping to play matchmaker for the two. But Jay and Bonnie are like fire and water and take an instant dislike to each other. Yet as the two are forced to be together during the wedding preparations, they start to soften. After the wedding, Chuck and Gail deal with the reality of married life while Jay and Bonnie struggle through an up-and-down courtship. Slight but enjoyable, the comedy met with divided notices and had a one-month commercial run.

The season ended in Brooklyn, where Ingmar Bergman's staging of *The Winter's Tale* arrived at BAM on May 31 for four showings. The Royal Dramatic Theatre of Sweden production took the form of a play-within-a-play, Shakespeare's tale being put on by the guests and staff at a nineteenth-century manor house in Sweden as part of a birthday celebration. Most aisle-sitters considered it a "masterfully direct, plain, and unfanciful" revival and strongly recommended it.

1995–1996

The New York theatre season was getting shorter. Although it still officially started on June 1 and ran to May 31, in reality a large percentage of shows on Broadway were being crowded into March and April as producers hoped to cash in on the awards season. On March 1, 1996, sixteen of Broadway's thirty-two houses were empty; by the end of April only four were dark. This annual blossoming of so much theatre in late spring was becoming an embarrassment of riches and made for some pretty sparse theatregoing during the earlier months.

Broadway saw eleven new non-musicals this season (only one not an American entry), and Off Broadway presented forty-eight (ten of them foreign works). Those numbers were close to the previous season's, but there were some noticeable changes. Off Broadway offered nine commercial plays (a substantial rise) but only seven revivals (a considerable drop). Broadway, on the other hand, ended up with a whopping seventeen non-musical revivals, only two of them foreign and many of them very accomplished.

Also encouraging, the redevelopment of 42nd Street, after many years of discussion and planning, actually began on December 11 when the old Victory Theatre (originally built as the Republic by Oscar Hammerstein I in 1900) reopened as the New Victory, a beautifully restored 499-seat house slated for family fare and guest engagements. Next door the old Lyric and Apollo were being rearranged into one new musical house, and across the street the Disney company had begun restoration of the beloved New Amsterdam. The block between Seventh and Eighth avenues, until recently the heart of midtown's prostitution and porno film business, was being revitalized into a theatre, shopping, and dining thoroughfare. Even better, other old theatres on the block were earmarked for restoration. Talk about an embarrassment of riches!

On the darker side, both the National Endowment for the Arts and the New York State Council on the Arts suffered further cuts, adversely affecting non-profit theatre in New York. The Circle Repertory Company and the Negro Ensemble Company were on their last legs, the Ridiculous Theatrical Company lost its home of twenty years, and Tony Randall's National Actors Theatre was down to half the number of subscribers it had started with when it opened in 1991. The numerous revivals outshone new works, and no new playwright of note made an appearance this season. At this rate the theatre district was on its way to becoming a classy museum of past glories. As *Best Plays* co-editor Jeffrey Sweet noted: "For many with fond memories of those [past] years, Broadway won't truly be Broadway again unless, as a matter of course, straight plays of substance once more premiere next door to productions of musicals and revivals."

Veteran playwright and librettist Arthur Laurents returned to the non-musical theatre with his caustic comedy **The Radical Mystique** (6-6-95, City Center) but met with little success. Near the end of the 1960s, two wealthy liberals plan to throw a chic benefit for the Black Panthers' Self-Defense Fund. Josie Gruenwald (Mary Beth Fisher) is married to a millionaire German-Jewish entrepreneur. Janice Catlett (Sharon Washington) is the daughter of an internationally recognized African-American opera star and married to a southern businessman who is very rich and very

white. The two women consider themselves the most open-minded members of a progressive society, so when an FBI agent, Merriwell (Jake Weber), urges them to cancel the benefit, they refuse on principle. But Merriwell has dug up dirt on both families (Josie's husband and son are gay, and Janice's teenage son has impregnated an older Jewish woman), so the two women flounder and soon find themselves as bigoted and narrow-minded as the rest of the world. Critics commended Laurents's "wit and moments of wisdom" but felt the comedy of manners was "too schematic" and "artificial" to be effective. Laurents directed the Manhattan Theatre Club production himself.

Two surrealistic plays that had had initial short runs returned and received slightly better reviews than previously. In Brooklyn, Ingmar Bergman and the Royal Dramatic Theatre of Sweden brought back their revival of Yukio Mishima's *Madame de Sade* (5-20-93) on June 7 for four performances at BAM. Lincoln Center revived James Lapine's *Twelve Dreams* (12-22-81) the next night at the Mitzi E. Newhouse. While a few critics welcomed the "strange and wonderful" play back, most still thought it "hollow, pretentious, and mendacious." Harry Groener, Mischa Barton, Kathleen Chalfant, Jan Rubes, and Donna Murphy headed the cast, Lapine directed, and the expressionistic drama lasted nine weeks this time around.

Following in the footsteps of Jackie Mason and others, **Buttons on Broadway** (6-8-95, Ambassador) brought seventy-six-year-old Red Buttons (who billed himself as the "oldest living burlesque comic") to the Street, where he charmed audiences with anecdotes, old jokes, memories, and a song or two for thirty-three performances. It was the first of over a dozen one-person shows seen on and off Broadway this season.

The Second Stage Theatre, an off-off-Broadway troupe that had specialized in revivals of neglected plays, was now operating as an off-Broadway company and switched to a season of four original works, starting with Lynn Nottage's **Crumbs From the Table of Joy** (6-20-95, Second Stage). In the late 1950s, African-American widower Godfrey Crump (Daryl Edwards) moves from rural Florida to Brooklyn with his two daughters, Ernestine (Kisha Howard) and Ermina (Nicole Leach), to make a new life for themselves. Soon Godfrey's sister-in-law Lily Ann Green (Ella Joyce), a radical civil rights activist from Harlem, moves in to help raise her nieces but only infuriates Godfrey (who is very religious) with her Communist ideas and sexually liberated ways. So Godfrey marries Gerte Schulte (Stephanie Roth), a quiet, somber immigrant who escaped wartime Germany, to keep his family together and drive Lily out. The plan succeeds, but when Ernestine graduates from high school, she refuses Godfrey's offer to work in his business and opts to join her Aunt Lily in Harlem and be part of the "revolution." The drama, traditionally plotted in the style of the post-war masters (one critic referred to it as "a glass menagerie in the sun"), never rose above soap opera melodramatics.

Eschewing feminine angst and preachiness, Karen Trott's solo piece **The Springhill Singing Disaster** (6-22-95, Playwrights Horizons) recounted how she and her guitar have been constant companions since fourth grade and told about their life together performing folk songs. Never sentimentalizing, Trott delighted audiences with stories of growing up in a wealthy Boston suburb as a teenager wearing black and singing protest songs while she hoped to catch the blues. Some songs were presented, but most were in a satirical style that parodied her past performance style. "Refreshingly unhip," the program did brisk business during its two-week engagement and returned the following season.

Two revivals followed, both castigated by the press. The Public Theatre's Shakespeare Marathon, now eight years running and slowly approaching the finish line, continued on June 22 at the outdoor Delacorte with *The Tempest*, which George C. Wolfe turned into a diatribe about colonialism and racism. Patrick Stewart was an angry Prospero, Yeagle F. Bougere was a bitter Caliban, and even Aunjanue Ellis's Ariel seemed more petulant than spiritual. The acting area was a circle of sand populated with actors on stilts, giant puppets, and an onstage band. Critics enjoyed some of the spectacle but lamented the lack of poetry and the "willful misreading of the play . . . into a circus." Yet audiences flocked to Central Park (mainly to see Stewart), so on November 1 Wolfe brought the fantasy to Broadway, where it played at the Broadhurst for two months. The Roundabout's mounting of Molnár and Wodehouse's *The Play's the Thing* (11-3-26) on July 9 was similarly dismissed as "miscast and lumpish," though commentators thought the old farce still worth producing.

The Circle Repertory Theatre continued to sink into obscurity with Steven Dietz's **Lonely Planet** (7-12-95, Circle), which the group only kept open for two weeks. A pair of gay friends

react to the AIDS epidemic in different ways: Jody (Mark Shannon), a middle-aged owner of a map store, hides in his shop, while his friend Carl (Denis O'Hare) goes out and comforts his dying friends, staying with them to the end, then bringing back a chair from each one's home to place in the map shop as a kind of memorial. As the store fills with chairs, Carl tries to convince Jody to go out and join the rest of the world and, especially, to get tested for the disease. Their arguments, which move into an absurdist duologue that reveals a deep friendship, result in Jody finally leaving the store to be tested. But when he returns, Carl is sitting silently in one of the chairs, having joined their many friends in death. Jody must now become caretaker for those still needing help. An obvious nod to *The Chairs* (at one point Jody is reading the Ionesco play), Dietz's script failed to take off and was generally disparaged in the press.

The summer's second Shakespeare offering in Central Park, *Troilus and Cressida* on August 4 at the Delacorte, was possibly more reviled by the critics than *The Tempest* had been. The "relentlessly trendy, deliberately effeminate travesty of a play" included many visual and auditory references to AIDS, television news reporting, and Bosnia, highlighted by plenty of group sex (both hetero- and homosexual). Mark Wing-Davey staged the "wholly unendurable" three-hour-long production.

With **The Food Chain** (8-24-95, Westside Upstairs), Nicky Silver continued to impress critics with his "poisonously funny" portrayal of characters deep in misery, several commentators citing the new work as his best yet. Amanda Dolor (Hope Davis), an anorexic poet whose husband of only three weeks has been missing for two, calls a crisis hotline where she talks with Bea (Phyllis Newman), a Jewish mother who is less interested in listening to Amanda than complaining about her embarrassing son and her dead husband who never gave her enough attention. Without warning, the lost husband, Ford (Rudolf Martin), walks in and Amanda hangs up on the talkative Bea. At the same time on the other side of town, Serge Stubin (Patrick Fabian), a self-absorbed gay model, anxiously awaits his new boyfriend, who is planing to move in. There is a knock at the door but, instead of the intended lover, Otto Woodnick (Tom McGowan), a three-hundred-pound obsessive who once had a one-night stand with Serge, enters and pleads, cajoles, and threatens Serge to take him back, all the time stuffing himself with junk food and taking calls from his concerned mother. Serge's ploys to be rid of Otto collapse, and he is further deflated when a phone call from his new friend informs him that he is not moving in after all. The next morning at Amanda and Ford's apartment, Serge is pounding on the door and demanding his lover, who, to Amanda's surprise, is Ford. While Ford says little, Serge begs him to come back to him. Otto enters looking for Serge and carrying a gun to kill Ford. Bea, who has hunted down Amanda's address, enters to scold her for hanging up on her. Bea turns out to be Otto's mother, and Amanda recognizes Otto as her old school friend. (Amanda was as fat as Otto back then.) After Serge insists he loves Ford, Otto attempts to shoot himself. But Bea grabs the gun, exclaiming, "Must ya put everything in your big fat greasy mouth?" Since Ford seems willing to go with either Serge or Amanda, and Amanda is sexually attracted to Serge, Bea suggests they make a trio of it as she drags Otto off to put him on a weight-reducing program. *The Food Chain* immediately found an audience and ran 332 times.

Avi Hoffman's solo piece **Too Jewish?** (9-7-95, Westside Downstairs) was less autobiographical than most one-person shows this season, preferring to look at Yiddish vaudeville and theatre as history. But the effect was still personal and intimate, and Hoffman's style was warm rather than in-your-face. Seen briefly off-off Broadway the previous winter, the program ran 189 times off Broadway.

Just as he had with his popular *Lend Me a Tenor* (3-2-89), Ken Ludwig fashioned an old-style farce about show business, set it in the past, and peopled it with broad types, this time calling it **Moon Over Buffalo** (10-1-95, Martin Beck). At Buffalo's Erlanger Theatre in 1953, a third-rate "Lunt and Fontanne" acting couple, George (Philip Bosco) and Charlotte Hay (Carol Burnett), are touring with a repertory of *Cyrano de Bergerac* and *Private Lives*. Of course everything is going wrong. Box-office receipts are pathetic, the second male lead has quit because he hasn't been paid in two weeks, and the company's ingenue, Eileen (Kate Miller), has informed George that she is pregnant with his child. When Charlotte finds out, she throws a fit, then plans to abandon George and run off with her agent, Richard Maynard (James Valentine). The Hays' daughter, Rosalind (Randy Graff), tries to patch things up while she is being wooed by her old boyfriend Paul (Dennis Ryan). Just after George goes off on a drunken binge, word arrives that Hollywood director Frank Capra is coming to the matinee because he wants

George and Charlotte to replace Ronald Colman and Greer Garson in a costume drama he is filming. By the time the staff finds George he is so drunk that he goes onstage performing the wrong role. Rosalind's nerdy fiancé Howard (Andy Taylor), a weatherman on television, wanders backstage, is mistaken for Capra, and is accidentally locked in a closet. The matinee is a disaster, but it turns out Capra never made it. Charlotte is crushed but forgives George, and the two are reunited; Howard drops Rosalind so she accepts Paul's affections. Then a phone call from Capra informs the company that his plane was delayed and that he'll be attending that night's performance. So once again everyone bursts into a flurry of anticipation, arguing which of the repertory plays they are supposed to be doing that night. While it was more contrived and less clever than *Lend Me a Tenor*, critics found enough in the "forlorn attempt at a farce" to recommend, especially Bosco's delightfully hammy George and Carol Burnett's desperately eager Charlotte. (It was her first Broadway role in thirty-one years.) Although rarely a sellout, the play found an audience for 308 performances.

Thousands had been attending *Tony 'n' Tina's Wedding* (2-6-88) over the years, so it was only a matter of time before another family event became an interactive environmental comedy piece. **Grandma Sylvia's Funeral** (10-4-95, SoHo Playhouse), written by Glenn Wein, Amy Lord Blumsack, and the cast, allowed patrons to become part of a Jewish funeral and mitzvah meal. Grandma died when hit by a garbage truck, and her body was mistakenly taken to a funeral parlor in Bensonhurst. While everyone waits for the hearse to deliver the coffin, spectators are greeted by bereaved family members outside the theatre. When "Grandma" arrives, all go inside to hear reminiscences and watch the family bicker, then everybody partakes of kosher food. Critics declared the evening "wacky and engaging," and audiences continued to participate for four years.

Two Tennessee Williams one-acters, *Suddenly Last Summer* and *Something Unspoken*, were paired together on October 10 at the Circle in the Square just as they had been originally under the umbrella title *Garden District* (1-7-58). Despite uneven acting and lackluster direction, the two works proved very playable. Elizabeth Ashley, as the rich and vindictive Mrs. Venable in *Suddenly Last Summer*, led the casts and was in top form. The next night off Broadway, J. B. Priestley's *Dangerous Corner* (10-27-32) was revived by the Atlantic Theatre Company and ran eleven weeks. David

Mamet directed the drawing room thriller in a style opposite that of the recent Broadway mounting of Priestley's *An Inspector Calls*: simple, quiet, mysterious and economic (spartan almost). The characters were stripped to their essentials, just as James Wolk's set, a series of latticework over a spare frame of a house, created a stark landscape for the drama.

Avery (Kelly Coffield), the high-principled heroine of Wendy MacLeod's **Sin** (10-11-95, Second Stage), cannot speak anything but the truth. As a traffic reporter flying over San Francisco in a helicopter in 1989, Avery tells it like it is. But on the ground she only upsets everyone by saying the truth even when it is cruel. She lost her husband, Michael (Bruce Norris), because she was too blunt about his alcoholism, and now she ruins every blind date she gets by saying the wrong (but truthful) thing. Avery is just as uncompromising with her overweight roommate, Helen (Camryn Manheim), and her brother, Gerard (Jeffrey Hutchinson), who lies in a hospital bed dying of AIDS. (He looks dreadful, and Avery, though she loves him, cannot say otherwise to his face.) Suddenly the earthquake of 1989 hits the city, and Avery tries to shelter Gerard from the falling debris in his room, but she fails. At the same time she loses Gerard, Helen turns against her, and Avery finds herself alone, "trapped . . . with my best self inside." Critics disfavored the odd drama, first produced at the Goodman Theatre in Chicago, and it shuttered after three weeks.

Tom Courtenay returned to New York in Stephen Mulrine's one-person play **Moscow Stations** (10-15-95, Union Square) and was welcomed with admiration though few aisle-sitters recommended his vehicle, described as "two hours of bemused philosophical inebriation." Ever since Venidikt Yerofeyev lost his job in the Russian bureaucracy, he has turned to vodka and train travel, bribing conductors with his tall tales to let him ride free. As he goes from Moscow to Petushki to see his dying son, announcements on the speaker system (over which angels also speak to him) interrupt Yerofeyev's narration. Yerofeyev sees himself as a metaphor for the lost and intoxicated Russian people. Based on a novel by Yerofeyev that was a cult classic in his homeland, the play could not interest Americans enough to keep Courtenay employed for more than a month.

Moonlight (10-17-95, Roundabout), Harold Pinter's first new full-length play in seventeen years, was characteristically oblique and intriguing though most critics were far less than approving.

Andy (Jason Robards), a retired British civil servant, lies dying in bed, attended to by his wife, Bel (Blythe Danner). In another bedroom in another place their two sons, Jake (Liev Schreiber) and Fred (Barry McEvoy), sit and reminisce about their father, joking about his difficult ways. They are more than content to be estranged from Andy, even when Bel pleads with them to come to his deathbed. Bridget (Melissa Chalsma), Andy and Bel's daughter who died young, is seen in a space above the bedrooms speaking fondly of the family and sending her love. Andy and Bel are visited by old friends Maria (Kathleen Widdoes) and Ralph (Paul Hecht), who, their chat suggests, were once lovers of Andy and Bel. But all the friendly talk cannot hide the fact that Andy is dying, and his final days remind the other characters of their own mortality. Karl Reisz directed his exceptional cast in a chilling and atmospheric manner (though Robards made no effort at a British accent). The Roundabout presented the work in its new off-Broadway space, the Laural Pels Theatre, located next to its Broadway house at the Criterion Center.

One of the most vivacious portrayals of the season was Mary Louise Wilson's "glitteringly played and envisaged" Diana Vreeland, fashion magazine publisher and dictator of style for five decades, in **Full Gallop** (10-18-95, City Center), which packed the Manhattan Theatre Club for its scheduled thirty-nine performances. Vreeland lounges in her Park Avenue apartment in 1971, having recently been fired from *Vogue* and now hoping to bankroll a new fashion magazine. The solo performance was filled with Vreeland's memories, dead-on observations of the rich and famous, and illustrations of the grande dame's zest for life. Wilson and Mark Hampton co-authored the solo piece, which would return the next season.

Another actor who turned to playwriting, Steve Martin made a notable Manhattan debut with his **Picasso at the Lapin Agile** (10-22-95, Promenade), which entertained thinking audiences for 249 performances. The local regulars at Paris's little Cafe Lapin in 1904 include Pablo Picasso (Tim Hopper) and Albert Einstein (Mark Nelson), both young and idealistic and on the eve of becoming famous. A battle of wits between the two and commentary from the bartender (Harry Groener), Picasso's mistress (Susan Floyd), an old codger (Carl Don), and others (including a young Elvis Presley) filled the intermissionless ninety minutes with lively and cerebral talk that, according to Vincent Canby in the *New York*

Times, managed to "mix the sublime with the ridiculous [so] that they can't be easily disentangled." The comedy, which had already enjoyed successful runs in Chicago and Los Angeles, was well reviewed and soon became popular in regional and college theatres.

Another cerebral off-Broadway hit was Nicholas Wright's **Mrs. Klein** (10-24-95, Lucille Lortel), which brought Uta Hagen back to the stage after a long absence. (The seventy-six-year-old actress was celebrating her fiftieth year on the professional stage.) The title character is the factual Melanie Klein (Hagen), a noted Berlin psychoanalyst who went to England in the 1930s to continue her famous study of children. In 1934, news comes to Mrs. Klein's London home that her son Hans has died in a mountain climbing accident. With Mrs. Klein in her grief are her daughter, Melitta (Laila Robins), also a psychoanalyst but of a rival school, and Paula Heimann (Amy Wright), a pupil of Mrs. Klein but coming into her own in the field. Melitta suggests that Hans's death was not an accident and, using her mother's system of analysis, demonstrates how both Hans and herself were scarred by their childhood. (Both siblings were intimidated by their famous mother and showered with experiments rather than love.) It is Melitta's conclusion that Hans committed suicide to kill that part of him that was like his mother. Mrs. Klein rejects her suggestion (as well as Melitta's opinion of the past) and orders her daughter out of her house. Then Paula turns from disciple to teacher as she starts to analyze Mrs. Klein, replacing Melitta, who is ringing the doorbell and trying once again to gain her mother's favor. The British drama met with conflicting opinions, but Hagen was welcomed back with raves. Clive Barnes in the *New York Post* described her performance as "magnificent, deep and superficial by turn, commandingly manipulative, superbly imperious." Despite the play's tricky tone (critics argued whether it was a comedy or a tragedy) and its difficult subject matter, audience reception prompted the ten-week limited engagement to run 280 performances.

A superb cast under the direction of Gerald Gutierrez helped Tom Donaghy's bleak drama **Northeast Local** (10-29-95, Mitzi E. Newhouse) run eighty-one performances at Lincoln Center even though reviews were less than enthusiastic. (The drama was forced to close three days before originally slated because of a fire in the Newhouse that destroyed the scenery.) When Gi (Mary Elizabeth Mastrantonio) meets Mickey (Anthony LaPaglia) in 1963, he is a steelworker who believes that American industry will never let the working man down. She has feminist leanings and feels the future of women is indeed bright. They marry and struggle through the next thirty years, during which both become disillusioned. The steel industry flounders, Gi's hopes for total equality for women are dampened, and both find themselves in 1993 bitter about the world and their marriage, which has sustained them for so long. Ultimately Gi leaves Mickey and moves in with her black neighbor Jesse (Terry Alexander). In addition to LaPaglia and Mastrantonio's splendid portrayals, Eileen Heckart was memorable in the supporting role of Mair, Gi's immigrant mother who never quite accepts the way things are in the New World. Several critics also commended Jane Greenwood's costumes, which told more about the passage of time than the script did.

That same night on Broadway, Bill Irwin and David Shiner brought back their popular *Fool Moon* (2-25-93) to the Ambassador, where the clowning continued for eighty more showings.

Yet another actor, Laurence (formerly Larry) Fishburne, took up playwriting (as well as directing), but his **Riff Raff** (11-1-95, Circle) met with decidedly pallid reviews, so it folded after only thirty-four showings despite the presence of its movie-star author in the cast. Two small-time criminals hide out on Halloween in a room in an abandoned apartment building on Manhattan's Lower East Side after a drug heist that went wrong. Mike "20/20" Leon (Fishburne) and his half brother, Billy "Torch" Murphy (Titus Welliver), have mistakenly killed the henchman of one of the area's most powerful drug dealers. Uncertain what to do next, Mike calls on his trusted colleague Tony "Tiger" Lee (Heavy D) to help them. Tony has the two relate the night's events in detail but offers no solutions to their dilemma. Instead the three take heroin and get into conversations and arguments over friendship, their lousy upbringing, and what brought them to crime as a living. Since the plot had nowhere to go, Mike had time to tell about his night of sexual ecstasy with a hot woman, and Tony recited a poem about a pimp who murdered his whore. Only ninety minutes long, the drama was "perhaps three times longer than its material can sustain." (More than one critic pointed out the play's similarity to Mamet's *American Buffalo,* but none thought it approached the earlier work in quality.)

An earnest if flawed "old-fashioned problem play" about religion, Diane Shaffer's **Sacrilege** (11-

2-95, Belasco) raised many questions and was filled with several thought-provoking ideas. Sister Grace (Ellen Burstyn) is a nun who works with the homeless and campaigns for women priests in the Roman Catholic Church. Her good friend Cardinal King (Herb Foster) respects her ideas but cautions her on offending the wrong people. Nevertheless Grace pursues her life's work, rescuing a street hustler, Ramon (Giancarlo Esposito), and helping him discover his religious vocation. When Grace's activities start to get national notoriety, the Vatican arranges a hearing and, forcing both Father Ramon and Cardinal King to testify against her, finds her guilty of anti-Church behavior. She is expelled from her order, and her colleagues are left to ponder the fate of Christian heroism in this modern day. Alexander Cohen returned to Broadway to produce the play, Don Scardino staged it with delicacy, and Burstyn shone as the fervent but accessible heroine. Some reviewers described the drama as "bracing and provocative," but more dismissed it as "a feminist screed," so it folded after twenty-one performances.

Another commanding star performance on Broadway followed with Terrence McNally's **Master Class** (11-5-95, John Golden). Zoe Caldwell played opera diva Maria Callas as she conducts one of her famous master classes in singing in 1971. The audience is a privileged group of spectators who watch Callas ask for water and a cushion, scold the pianist (David Loud), complain about the lighting, make snide comments about other opera singers, and demand passion and fervor from three aspiring opera singers (Karen Kay Cody, Audra McDonald, Jay Hunter Morris) who are her selected "victims." At two points during the class, when a student is performing, the voice of Callas singing is heard drowning out the student and transporting Callas to a past time. She reveals secrets in her heart (her ugly ducking childhood, an abortion, a failed marriage, how the press hurt her deeply) and intimate conversations with her lover Aristotle Onassis. Caldwell never sang a note, but her "extravagant, vulnerable, terrifying, human" performance convinced one that this was the greatest of all divas. While critical response to the script was guarded ("not so much a play, for it has no real shape or structure, as a dramatic portrait"), nothing but raves greeted Caldwell. She won the Tony Award, as did the play and McDonald as the student who stands up to Callas and delivers a piercing aria of her own. Audiences came to see Caldwell and her star replacements (Patti LuPone and Dixie

Carter) for 601 performances, a second hit in a row for McNally and the Broadway Alliance.

Once again American playwright Richard Nelson was not embraced in his native land when his **New England** (11-7-95, City Center), first produced successfully in Britain, played at the Manhattan Theatre Club. Just as Nelson had portrayed ugly Americans in England with his *Some Americans Abroad* (2-11-90), this time he revealed ugly Brits living in the States. After Harry Baker (Larry Bryggman), a depressed music teacher at a Connecticut community college, puts a gun to his head and blows his brains out in the first scene, British expatriates from all over the States come to grieve and comfort Harry's live-in lover, Alice (Penny Fuller). The gathering, which includes Harry's twin brother, Alfred (also Bryggman), serves as a sounding board for the foreign residents, all disdaining their crude adopted country and waxing nostalgic about an England that is long gone. The sexual misbehavior of the mourners, jumping in and out of bed with each other, implied that they were not any better than their despised neighbors. A few critics found the play's ambiguity intriguing (the editors of the *Best Plays* selected it as one of the ten best of the season), but most simply found its characters mildly repulsive and the evening dull.

Six performances of **Danny Gans on Broadway** (11-8-95, Neil Simon) was more than enough for New Yorkers. The Las Vegas impressionist, billed as "the Man of Many Voices," claimed to have over 200 difference voices in his repertory. What he didn't have was material acceptable outside of a casino lounge.

Several commentators found Christopher Kyle's comedy of manners **The Monogamist** (11-9-95, Playwrights Horizons) "smart, funny, articulate, and wisely touched with rue." Dennis Jensen (Arliss Howard), a no-longer-young poet who has recently wed his longtime lover Susan Barry (Lisa Emery), has published a collection of poems about the beauty and importance of monogamy in the 1990s. But his world falls apart when he catches Susan, who is a women's literature professor at Princeton, in bed with Tim Hapgood (Timothy Olyphant), one of her most amoral students. Dennis searches for what has gone wrong with modern mores but only ends up in bed with Sky Hickock (Chelsea Altman), a dippy coed whose politics are as confused as her syntax. Yet when Sky meets Tim, they hit it off and she leaves Dennis. Susan finds that she's pregnant, so she goes to the Princeton Women's Health Cooperative, where Sky is a counselor. Hearing from Sky that Dennis is free, Susan decides to keep the baby, and the married couple are reunited.

The National Actors Theatre joined forces with the Great Lakes Theatre Festival and the Acting Company for the NAT's season opener, Sheridan's *The School for Scandal* on November 19 at the Lyceum, but the result was an "amiable and typically soporific" production that was blasted by the critics for its uneven acting and direction. Simon Jones played Joseph Surface in a highly stylized British manner, while Kate Forbes's too-American Lady Teazle was compared to Ado Annie and Annie Oakley. Also in Gerald Freedman's production were founder Tony Randall (Sir Peter Teazle), Tom Hewitt (Charles Surface), Mary Lou Rosato (Lady Sneerwell), and Ted Sorel (Sir Oliver Surface).

The Broadway season's second play about religion, David Hare's **Racing Demon** (11-20-95, Vivian Beaumont), was also about a questioning individual who is destroyed by the conservative orthodoxy of the church. Rev. Lionel Espy (Josef Sommer) is a burnt-out clergyman whose poor South London parishioners need social-work assistance more than religious ceremonies. His cohort in this difficult job is Rev. Harry Henderson (Brian Murray), a tireless worker and a closet homosexual. Espy's bishop, the Rt. Rev. Charlie Allen (George N. Martin), sends the young curate Tony Ferris (Michael Cumpsty) to help in the parish, but Tony is a theatrical born-again zealot whose conservatism, as well as his fire-and-brimstone approach to the parishioners, greatly disturbs Lionel and Harry. Through Tony's machinations, the bishop exposes Harry's homosexuality and he is defrocked, while Lionel is removed from the parish. The drama received several exemplary reviews for the script ("a crackling jolt of dramatic indignation and moral complexity") and for Richard Eyre's elegant production; but a play about the Church of England had limited appeal to Americans, so Lincoln Center closed it after its six-week subscription engagement.

The Circle in the Square offered an "absolutely delectable production" of Philip Barry's comedy of manners *Holiday* (11-26-28) on December 3 that, encouraged by mostly favorable reviews, ran forty-nine performances (the longest run of the theatre's season). Tony Goldwyn played the adventurous Johnny Case, Kim Raver was his fiancée, Julia, and Laura Linney her sister Linda, who ultimately wins Johnny's heart.

The next night off-off Broadway, Doug Wright's **Quills** (11-27-95, New York Theatre Workshop) opened to conflicting notices calling it everything from a "cunningly structured and gorgeously written" work to a "thoroughly inept piece of writing, directing, and acting." The aged Marquis de Sade (Rocco Sisto), confined to a lunatic asylum outside of Paris, is visited by Renee (Lola Pashalinski), his harridan wife of fifty years, who comes not to comfort the old man but to gloat at his misfortune and to vent her anger at how his notoriety has destroyed her social life. She bribes Dr. Royer-Collard (Daniel Oreskes), the chief medical officer, to take away de Sade's writing instruments and to promise her that when her husband dies, he will "be left as carrion for the rodents and the worms." The doctor agrees, assuring Renee that the money will be used to make improvements at the asylum; once she leaves, he uses it to buy a château for his wife.

Critics were not so divided about Ron Nyswaner's **Oblivion Postponed** (12-7-95, Second Stage) which was termed "artificial and hokey." Jeffrey (John Glover), an ex-alcoholic, ex-junkie, and ex-poet, travels to Rome with David (David Aaron Baker), his ex-pupil and now his lover, because David is HIV positive and they hope "to get a glimpse of God" in the Eternal City. They meet an American couple, Kyle (James Rebhorn) and Patti (Mary Beth Hurt), who are still recuperating from the death of their son. Kyle is a homophobic alcoholic and Patti is a ditzy health nut, but when the two couples decide to have dinner on their last night in Rome they all hit it off very well, Jeffrey and Kyle talking about booze and Patti taking a maternal interest in David. After a long dinner broken up by many monologues, the couples part, supposedly changed by the experience. The only feature of the evening to score with critics was Scott Bradley's evocative terrace set rendered in rich Roman terracotta.

The Manhattan Theatre Club continued its very productive season with Athol Fugard's first play since the end of apartheid in his homeland, **Valley Song** (12-12-95, City Center), an intimate drama about the twilight years of two men and, implied, the end of an era in South Africa. Abraam "Buks" Jonkers (Fugard) is a wizened old "colored" who has farmed the semi-arid valley of the Karoo all his life. In addition to keeping his meager vegetable gardens alive, he is raising his granddaughter Veronica (Lisa Gay Hamilton), a sixteen-year-old beauty overflowing with life. As fond as she is of her grandfather, Veronica longs to go to Johannesburg and attempt a singing career. This worries Abraam, as does the news that a wealthy white man in the area, simply called the Author (also played by Fugard), has bought the land Buks has always farmed and may turn him out. Both men worship Veronica and are drawn together by their hopes of keeping her from leaving. But together they reach the wisdom to let the youthful girl free; they realize she is the future, they are the past. The press advocated the "poignantly beautiful new play" as well as the two actors.

The Negro Ensemble Company's only contribution this season was as presenter for **Dick Gregory Live** (12-14-95, Samuel Beckett), a vibrant and timely solo show. Stand-up comic and activist Gregory was still sharp and funny as he covered such topics as Bosnia, O. J. Simpson, hypocrisy in America, and even dietary advice. (Gregory was a firm believer in drinking lots of water each day, something he learned on his celebrated hunger strikes in the 1960s.) The African-American comic still had his loyal fans who came for seventy-eight performances.

While his *Picasso at the Lapin Agile* was still packing them in at the Promenade, Steve Martin saw four of his one-acts presented at the Public under the title **WASP and Other Plays** (12-17-95, Martinson), though they met with mixed notices and were only kept on the boards for three weeks. The title playlet, previously seen off-off Broadway, was the most notable, showing a wacky upper-class family in the 1950s whose arch-conservative and fundamentalist attitude to life is threatened by information provided by a space alien and the female voice of God.

A Broadway revival of Phillip Hayes Dean's *Paul Robeson* (1-19-78) on December 20 at the Longacre was limited to eleven performances. Avery Brooks portrayed the famous athlete-singer-activist (as he had in a 1988 revival), and Ernie Scott was his accompanist-friend Lawrence Brown.

Even the highly talented Olympia Dukakis came off looking ridiculous in Kevin Heelan's fantasy drama **The Hope Zone** (1-4-96, Circle), which pounded another nail in the Circle Rep's coffin. Various lowlifes have made their home in a ramshackle rooming house run by the Countess (Dukakis). Her cop lover Newton (Craig Bockhorn), her repellent daughter Maureen (Anne Scurlia), and a faith healer, Veeche (George Morfogen), all try to beat their drug and/or alcohol addictions along with the unstable Countess. In one scene Veeche teaches the Countess the value of sin and has her drink some of Maureen's blood in order to perform an incantation. The press unanimously slammed the "onslaught of over-blown, bloody theatrics, and self-conscious verbiage in a bogus, hyper-realistic environmental style." (This "environment" was created by replacing all the seats in the auditorium with an odd assortment of thrift shop chairs and littering the acting and seating areas with trash.)

Brian Friel's remarkably durable career continued with **Molly Sweeney** (1-7-96, Roundabout), a meditative little drama praised for its "dispassionate eloquence and psychological honesty." The play's three characters sit on the stage all evening, each telling the audience his or her part of the story in monologue form. Molly Sweeney (Catherine Byrne), blind from birth, has made something of herself by becoming a physiotherapist and finding love and friendship. Her husband, Frank (Alfred Molina in his stage debut), is an aggressive man who attacks noble causes like a shark. He brings Molly to Dr. Rice (Jason Robards), a brilliant eye surgeon whose life and reputation have been wasted by drink. Restoring Molly's eyesight will bring both Rice and Frank glory and self-recognition, while Molly fears such an operation and what seeing will do to her world. Yet she goes through with it, the surgery is a success, and Molly starts to see images. But Rice and Frank still find dissatisfaction in life, Molly cannot adapt to the changes and withdraws into herself, and the two men despair as Molly slips into catatonia. Physically stagnant (the three actors rarely left their chairs) but verbally exciting, the drama provided a unique showcase for the three expert actors. The play won the New York Drama Critics Circle Award for Best Foreign Play and ran out the season.

On Monday, January 8, a blizzard dropped twenty inches of snow on Manhattan. All theatres with Monday night performances were closed except the Eugene O'Neill, where a revival of *Grease* played to a full house.

Jonathan Marc Sherman, the only author to come out of the Young Playwrights Festival and make a writing career for himself, received some propitious notices for his light-hearted **Wonderful Time** (1-11-96, WPA) which ran a month off-off Broadway. Linus Worth (Josh Hamilton), a naive film student in California, is a hopeless romantic, dazzled and confused by women. When his girlfriend, Robin (Anne Giobbe), asks if he has been unfaithful, he honestly answers yes and is shocked when she walks out. Desperate for a date for his friend's wedding in Manhattan, Linus brings fellow student Betsy Flynn (Marin Hinkle), whom he barely knows, to New York City, where they do the town, throwing coins in the pool surrounding the Temple of Dendur and necking on top of the Empire State Building. Returning to California together, the couple vow to make their love the real thing, but Linus ends up staring at the Pacific Ocean just as confused as before.

Frank Langella and F. Murray Abraham each played tormented fathers in classic revivals in January. Strindberg's *The Father,* in a "blunt" new adaptation by Richard Nelson, opened on January 11 at the Roundabout and stayed for fifty-two performances. According to the critics, Langella had successfully graduated from dashing hero roles to tragic parts. Nancy Franklin in *The New Yorker* noted that he portrayed the Captain as "an impressive picture of sturdy middle-aged manhood which makes his descent into madness—inevitable though it is—all the more pathetic and terrifying." Clifford Williams directed the taut drama, and Gail Strickland played the Captain's vicious wife, Laura, who is leading him to insanity. The press was not as pleased with Abraham's *King Lear* on January 25 at the Anspacher, more than one commentator finding his king too matter-of-fact in the early scenes (though many said Abraham came into his own during the mad scenes). The Public production, directed by Adrian Hall, boasted a commendable supporting cast: Jared Harris (Edmund), Thomas Hill (Gloucester), Jeffrey Wright (Fool), Elizabeth Marvel (Regan), and Rob Campbell (Edgar) were most often cited in the reviews. The Manhattan Theatre Club revived *Blue Window* (6-12-84) on February 6 with a sparkling production by Joe Mantello. Some commentators who appreciated the early Craig Lucas work a dozen years ago stated that it was already dated; those who thought it aimless and amateurish then still thought so.

A very personal solo program that failed to catch on was **The Amazing Metrano** (2-15-96, Union Square), written by Art Metrano and Cynthia Lee and performed by Metrano. The self-subtitled "Accidental Comedy" told about actor Metrano who fell from a ladder and was partially paralyzed. The tale of how he slowly recovered the use of his legs (and his psychological equilibrium) was related in a rapid-fire, stand-up–comic style. The commercial entry folded inside of three weeks.

Possibly Jon Robin Baitz's finest play yet, **A Fair Country** (2-19-96, Mitzi E. Newhouse) garnered uneven notices yet thrived in Lincoln Center's downstairs space for five months. In a Mexican jungle in 1987, Gil Burgess (Matt McGrath), an archaeologist working alone on a dig, is surprised by the appearance of Patrice (Judith Ivey),

his long-estranged mother. Flashbacks follow, starting in 1977 when the family was stationed in Durban, South Africa, where Gil's father, Harry (Laurence Luckinbill), was a U.S. information officer. Patrice is on the edge of a nervous breakdown, Gil seems lost with his father gone much of the time, and his older brother, Alec (Dan Futterman), a radical journalism student visiting from Columbia University, is getting involved in the explosive politics of South Africa. Unknown to the others, Harry makes a deal with his superiors: they will post him to a safe, cultural affairs job in The Hague if Harry gives them the names of Alec's subversive friends in Durban. Harry refuses at first, but Patrice's erratic behavior and growing alcoholism convince him to comply. Two years later, with the family comfortably settled in The Hague, Alec returns from a visit to South Africa, where he has learned that all his friends are either dead or imprisoned. (Alec returns because he has received death threats and was then deported.) Harry admits his duplicity, Alec severs ties with the family, and Gil leaves with his brother. Back in the Mexican jungle, it is revealed that Alec has been murdered for writing an article on South Africa and that Harry has also died. Patrice has sought out Gil, hoping to put together the few remaining pieces of her life. Gil is not forgiving, but when threatened by a poacher who will kill anyone for some of the dig's valuable artifacts, mother and son are drawn together for survival (she scares off the poacher) and perhaps understanding. Baitz's plays had always dealt with global issues, but rarely had the characters come to life so vividly, transcending politics and principles. Daniel Sullivan directed the talented cast (Ivey was particularly applauded), and Tony Walton provided the scenery, which simply but pointedly evoked the story's many locations.

Most aisle-sitters lamented that William Inge's *Bus Stop* (3-2-55) had not aged well but nonetheless complimented the Circle in the Square's revival on February 22. Billy Crudup's naive, expansive Bo, Kelly Bishop's quietly tough Grace, and Larry Pine's soft-spoken Virgil gathered the best notices. Mary-Louise Parker proved a capable Cherie, under the direction of Josephine R. Abady, but the "likable if unpersuasive revival" did poor box-office business and was withdrawn after twenty-nine performances.

Nothing but scorn greeted Nilo Cruz's **Dancing on Her Knees** (2-29-96, LuEsther), "a repetitive parading of show-offy gestures and hyped-up, dislocated feelings" that the Public offered for three weeks. In Miami Beach, drag queen Francine (Luis Antonio Ramos) lights a candle on All Souls' Day hoping to bring his dead lover back to life but instead conjures up the ghost of Ramona (Franca Barchiesi) and Federico (Paul Calderon), a famous Latin dance team Francine idolized in his youth. Accompanying the dancers for their twenty-four-hour resurrection are two insensitive angels, Anuncio (Julio Monge) and Rosario Del Cielo (Marianne Filali). The angels mistakenly also bring to life the German widower Matthias (Henry Stram), who thinks Francine is his dead wife. When the dead characters refuse to return to heaven, chaos ensues until the message "you have to keep dancing to live" is hammered home. Renowned choreographer Graciela Daniele directed the production, but her staging was as disdained as the script.

A minor A. R. Gurney effort, **Overtime** (3-5-96, City Center) was a comic sequel to *The Merchant of Venice* set in the twentieth century and commenting on prejudice in modern times. Society leader Portia (Joan McMurtrey) throws a lavish party to celebrate her upcoming marriage to Bassanio (Jere Shea) and her victory over Shylock even though her accountant, Salerio (Robert Stanton), informs Portia that her financial state is very shaky. At the party, tempers flare up. Antonio (Rocco Sisto), who is gay and in love with Bassanio, has an argument with the groom-to-be. Gratiano (Michael Potts), an African American, and Nerissa (Marissa Chibas), a Hispanic, get fed up with being treated like minorities and leave the gathering to seek their own kind. Lorenzo (Willis Sparks) has second thoughts about Jessica (Jill Tasker), who is showing feminist tendencies. Soon Bassanio is punching Antonio, blaming his bad behavior on his Irish ancestry. Finally Shylock (Nicholas Kepros) shows up and suggests to Portia that they form a new society in which tolerance and understanding rule. Few critics were inclined to endorse the lightweight comedy ("it too soon outstays its laughs and wears out its welcome"), and it has rarely been heard of since its six-week engagement presented by the Manhattan Theatre Club.

Carlo Gozzi's commedia dell'arte classic *The Green Bird* inaugurated the New Victory on 42nd Street on March 7 with a series of fifteen matinees and evening shows for families. Director-designer Julie Taymor told the eighteenth-century tale with masks, puppets, bright costumes, music, magic, and even three singing apples that flew about the stage. Critics called the mounting a bit overextended at times but also decreed it "spectacular, charming, and smug."

By this time playgoers had probably stopped counting the number of plays and one-person programs about Irish author Brendan Behan. But some were still interested enough to let Michael L. Kavanaugh's solo piece **Bein' With Behan** (3-10-96, Irish Repertory Theatre) run seventy-eight times. The "two-hour pub monologue" featured Behan telling tales and reading from his stories, taking time from each to swig some Guinness for fortification.

Nearly as many plays had been written about Richard M. Nixon, but none with success. Russell Lees's **Nixon's Nixon** (3-12-96, MCC) also failed (the commercial offering only lasted five weeks) but was a notable attempt. In the Lincoln Sitting Room of the White House on the night before Nixon (Gerry Bamman) is to resign, Henry Kissinger (Steve Mellor) arrives to convince the president to bow out. He also suggests that Nixon order Gerald Ford to retain Kissinger as secretary of state so that he can complete "our work" in the international arena. But the paranoid Nixon is only interested in recalling old times, and soon he and Kissinger are acting out scenes from the past. These recreations soon turn surreal with Nixon playing Brezhnev and others while Kissinger portrays Kennedy, Mao, and even Nixon himself. The satire was more intriguing than satisfying, yet the performers were chillingly accurate in their impersonations of the two famous men.

Paranoia and surreal conversations were plentiful also in Richard Dresser's **Below the Belt** (3-15-96, John Houseman), which ran two months on the strength of Judd Hirsch's appearance in the cast. Dobbitt (Robert Sean Leonard), a "checker" for an international corporation, arrives in a remote foreign country where he is put up in a compound that resembles a prison bunkhouse. (Everything onstage was gray, from the set to the costumes to the props.) He is met by Hanrahan (Hirsch), an old cowpoke who has been there for years, and Merkin (Jude Ciccolella), their inept boss with monumental insecurities. The trio are supposed to check on the undisclosed product the company makes, but instead they engage in a three-way battle of words and one-upmanship as each jockeys for dominance. All the while, deadly little animals are surrounding the compound and planning to wipe out the men. The satire on corporate power had its moments of hilarity (the cast was top notch), but the comedy became tiresome long before it ended.

Television comedienne Andrea Martin gave her solo show the tongue-in-cheek title **Nude Nude Totally Nude** (3-15-96, Public: Anspacher), so her fans were laughing before they even entered the theatre. Martin recreated some of the routines and characters that she had developed as an improv comic in clubs and on TV, but she also talked about her personal life and her recent discovery of her Armenian roots. As enjoyable as it was, one longed to see this remarkable talent in a real play.

Stephen Sondheim made his non-musical Broadway debut with **Getting Away With Murder** (3-17-96, Broadhurst), a thriller he co-wrote with George Furth. Everyone has moved out of a crumbling old Manhattan apartment building to make way for the wrecking ball except the renowned Dr. Conrad Bering (Herb Foster), a psychoanalyst who is neurotically particular about whom he treats. He only has seven patients, and they are a bizarre cross-section of New Yorkers: Pamela Prideaux (Kandis Chappell), a snooty socialite; Martin Chisholm (John Rubinstein), an ambitious political aide; Dossie Lustig (Christine Ebersole), a sexy waitress; Gregory Reed (Terrence Mann), a power-hungry real estate mogul; Dan Gerard (Frank R. Faison), a bitter black cop; Nam-Jun Vuong (Jodi Long), a frustrated college teacher; and Vassili Laimorgos (Josh Mostel), a greasy antiques dealer. When the seven arrive for their group session, they discover Dr. Bering murdered in his office; but, instead of calling the police, the patients decide to solve the crime themselves to avoid scandal. (Each of them has a terrible past crime corresponding to the seven deadly sins.) At the first act's curtain, the audience learns that Martin murdered the doctor, so the second act was filled with his clever maneuvering (and killing off the others) to escape detection. By the last blackout, everyone is killed, the building explodes because of an electrical short, and all evidence of the crime is hidden. While the characters were all stereotypes, each less likable than the next, the plotting was intricately worked out, complete with flashbacks, repeated scenes, empty elevator shafts conveniently nearby, and even a guard at the front door to turn the whole building into a locked-room mystery. But the situations were as contrived as they were clever, and the sarcastic dialogue wore thin quickly. Between its tryout engagement in California and the New York opening, the play went through title, cast, and plot changes but to no avail. Unanimous pans ("utterly thrill-free and almost utterly laugh-free") shuttered the messy enterprise after seventeen performances.

Only Cherry Jones's poignant portrayal of spinsterish Hannah Jelkes was unanimously endorsed in the Roundabout's mounting of Tennessee Williams's *The Night of the Iguana* (12-28-61) on March 21. Aisle-sitters varied in their opinion of the play itself, and reactions to Robert Falls's production were just as divided; Canby described it as a "handsome, wildly uneven revival which . . . is risky to the point of wrongheadedness." William Peterson was the defrocked minister Shannon, and Marsha Mason played the man-hungry Maxine Faulk.

Just as *Too Jewish?* celebrated long-gone Yiddish show business in New York, Marga Gomez's one-person piece **A Line Around the Block** (3-22-96, Public; Anspacher) revealed a thriving Hispanic variety entertainment that few Anglos were aware of. Gomez, daughter of the late Cuban comic Willy Chevalier, saluted him as well as other Spanish-speaking performers of the 1960s. The history was personal, funny, and fascinating.

After Red Buttons, Dick Gregory, Danny Gans, Andrea Martin, and others, it was time for Jackie Mason, who had started the solo-comic-in-a-theatre trend, to return, and return he did in **Love Thy Neighbor** (3-24-96, Booth). Mason's fourth Broadway outing was set on a Lower East Side street (created with gentle mockery by designer Neil Peter Jampolis) where the sixty-one-year-old comic quipped about Starbucks coffee, Princess Di, the Internet, and, of course, Jews. He even had the Harlem Boys' Choir singing "Hava Nagila" on video. Audiences were far from tired of Mason; this time he stayed for 225 performances.

The sixth play in August Wilson's cycle about African Americans in the twentieth century, **Seven Guitars** (3-28-96, Walter Kerr) was perhaps his most musical yet. Jack Kroll in *Newsweek* described it as "a kind of jazz cantata for actors . . . a gritty, lyrical polyphony of voices that evokes the character and destiny of these men and women who can't help singing the blues." The title itself refers to the play's seven characters, all residents of Pittsburgh's Hill District in the late 1940s. In the backyard of a tenement, the friends of Floyd Barton gather after his funeral and mourn, joke, sing, and reminisce about the promising young blues singer who was on the brink of a notable career. The play then moves back to a week earlier and shows the events that led up to Floyd's untimely death. Having cut a record in Chicago, Floyd (Keith David) returns to Pittsburgh to convince his side men Canewell (Ruben Santiago-Hudson) and Red Carter (Tommy Hollis) to go back to the Windy City with him. He also tries to sweet talk his ex-lover Vera (Viola

Davis) into coming, but she is still angry at Floyd for running off to Chicago with another woman. Vera's friend Louise (Michele Shay) tells Vera not to trust Floyd or any man. Her proof is Ruby (Rosalyn Coleman), Louise's young niece from the South who got into man trouble (one of her lovers shot the other) and is now coming to Pittsburgh to have her baby. Ruby is a flighty girl, flirting with all the men, even the elderly Hedley (Roger Robinson), a mysterious and half-crazed man who raises chickens and dreams of building a plantation in Pittsburgh with money owed him from his father. (At the end of the first act, Hedley kills a rooster onstage and chants as he baptizes the yard with its blood.) Floyd cannot convince Canewell and Red Carter to go to Chicago, but he does soften Vera. Desperate for the money to get his guitar out of hock and to buy bus tickets to Illinois, Floyd takes part in a robbery in which his young partner is killed. Floyd escapes with the money and buries it in the yard, but when Hedley sees him dig it up he is convinced it is his inheritance, so he kills Floyd with a machete, thinking he is the mysterious man who has been cheating him all these years. As in the previous Wilson entries, Lloyd Richards directed and the cast was impeccable. (Santiago-Hudson won a Tony Award.) The drama won the New York Drama Critics Circle Award and ran 187 performances.

The Royal Shakespeare Company's *A Midsummer Night's Dream*, which opened on March 31 at the Lunt-Fontanne for an eight-week engagement, somewhat recalled Peter Brook's famous 1970 version (the new production opened with Hippolyta sitting on a trapeze) but quickly distinguished itself as a marvelous revival in its own right. Adrian Noble's staging was vivid with both tenderness and knockabout farce, and Anthony Ward's scenery and costumes were splashes of color, highlighted by a forest of dangling lightbulbs and umbrellas. The masterful cast included Alex Jennings (Theseus/Oberon), Lindsay Duncan (Hippolyta/Titania), Desmond Barrit (Bottom), and Barry Lynch (Philostrate/Puck).

The National Actors Theatre finally came up with a rousing good revival, Lawrence and Lee's *Inherit the Wind* (4-21-55) on April 4 at the Lyceum. But, like that troubled organization, the production was plagued with bad luck. George C. Scott headlined as the Clarence Darrow–like Drummond, but illness kept him from most previews; Tony Randall (who had appeared as the wry reporter E. K. Hornbeck in the original) took his place. After postponing the opening, Scott finally

managed to perform and got rave notices. ("You must catch this performance, or remain forever deprived of one of those rare moments when our theatre attained genius.") But before a month was out, Scott left town citing medical reasons. The newspapers were full of another reason: a lawsuit slapped on Scott by a former assistant for sexual harassment. Randall returned to the role, but a week later the show closed prematurely. John Tillinger directed the large cast that was filled with thrilling performances in addition to Scott's, most memorably Charles Durning as the belligerent Brady, Tom Aldredge as the pompous Rev. Brown, and Anthony Heald as Hornbeck. Randall vowed to reopen the popular attraction in the fall with Scott, but it never happened. In fact, Scott never returned to the stage again.

Trish Vradenburg's comedy-drama **The Apple Doesn't Fall . . .** (4-14-96, Lyceum) was Broadway's only one-night casualty this season, roundly panned as "ghastly" and "a play of excruciating awfulness." TV writer-producer Kate Griswald (Margaret Whitton) must tend to her aging mother, Selma (Florence Stanley), when the old lady develops both Alzheimer's and Parkinson's disease. Selma is particularly fragile since her husband, Jack (Lee Wallace), abandoned her for a younger woman, Lorna (Madeline Miller). But when Sam Gordon (Richard Cox), a handsome young doctor, gives Selma a miracle drug, both diseases go into remission, and mother and daughter set off on a joyous cross-country tour (skydiving over the Grand Canyon, white-water rafting down the Colorado, dancing the lambada in Los Angeles, testifying in Washington before a Senate committee on aging) and attending Jack's wedding in Miami. But alas, the trip was all a fantasy, and Selma dies without ever leaving New York. As pointed out by a few commentators, the play's plot, structure, and theme were all embarrassingly close to those of *The Baltimore Waltz* (2-11-92).

Billy Tipton was a respected jazzman who played with top bands for many years. Yet when he died, his obituary revealed that Billy was really a woman who had disguised herself most of her life in order to play in the all-male orchestras. This true story had the makings of a stimulating play, but Carson Kreitzer's **The Slow Drag** (4-17-96, American Place), loosely based on Billy's dilemma, was a preachy drama that flubbed the opportunity. The female "Johnny Christmas" (Peggy Shaw) goes into drag in order to perform, and she even makes an arrangement with torch singer June Wedding (Ann Crumb) to masquerade as Johnny's "wife." Paralleling Johnny's story is that of a close friend, Chester Kent (Vernel Bagneris), an African American who is so light-skinned that he passes for white. Filled with monologues, the drama rarely gave the three gifted players a chance to interact.

Critics were more interested in Nicol Williamson than his subject in **Jack** (4-24-96, Belasco), a one-man play subtitled "A Night on the Town with John Barrymore." While Jack boozes it up he recalls his colorful life, from his early stage successes to his movie career to his many marriages (which he wryly calls "bus accidents"). Williamson, who had already played Barrymore's ghost in *I Hate Hamlet* (4-8-91), was in top form and told some amusing stories, but commentators found the evening lacking and felt the respected actor was wasting his time. The play, co-written by Williamson and Leslie Megahey, only survived twelve performance. Ironically, a different one-person piece on Barrymore would become a big hit on Broadway the following season.

Four outstanding revivals followed in close succession. The team that brought last season's *The Heiress* (9-29-47) to Broadway pulled a second rabbit out of the hat with Edward Albee's obscure *A Delicate Balance* (9-22-66), which opened on April 21 at the Plymouth and was met with cheers of "flawless," "exquisite," and "has the impact of an entirely new work." Lincoln Center produced the rarely revived Pulitzer Prize winner, and director Gerald Guiterrez made the chilly living-room drama crackle with humor, mystery, and devastation. The superior cast consisted of George Grizzard and Rosemary Harris as the sophisticated but desperate Tobias and Agnes, Mary Beth Hurt as their shrill daughter Julia, John Carter and Elizabeth Wilson as their close friends Harry and Edna, and Elaine Stritch as the boozing Claire, all at the peak of their powers. Once again John Lee Beatty provided a setting filled with icy-cold elegance, and Jane Greenwood deftly costumed the upper-middle-class characters in a chic but telling wardrobe. The Tony voters named it Best Revival and also honored Gutierrez and Grizzard. The revival ran 186 times, slightly more than the original.

The producers of the Broadway revival of Sam Shepard's *Buried Child* (12-5-78) on April 30 at the Brooks Atkinson argued that the playwright had made so many substantial changes that the production should be viewed as a new work. (The Tony committee bought the argument and nominated it for Best Play.) This mounting, by Chicago's Steppenwolf Theatre Company and directed by Gary Sinese, marked Shepard's first Broadway production since *Operation Sidewinder* (3-12-70). The press declared the new version sharper and funnier than the original, but, in fact, the changes were minor and a thrilling production actually gave the illusion of a crisp new piece. Favorable reviews kept the drama on the boards for seventy-one performances. On the same night, the renowned Comédie Française brought the first of two classic revivals to BAM, Molière's *Don Juan* performed five times in French with English supertitles. Andrzej Seweryn essayed Juan; even more applauded, Roland Bertin played his sidekick, Sganarelle. The final Broadway entry of the season was Peter Hall's "gleaming production" of Oscar Wilde's complex comedy *An Ideal Husband* on May 1 at the Ethel Barrymore. Rave reviews for the British cast (particularly Martin Shaw as the cynical dandy Lord Goring), Hall's direction (strong on "clarity and simplicity"), and Carl Toms's elegant sets and costumes made the revival a popular attraction for 309 performances, the longest New York run on record for a Wilde play.

These outstanding revivals off and running, matter turned grim again. Critics denounced both script and production ("not only shallow and empty but also bizarrely pretentious and boring") when Richard Foreman directed Suzan-Lori Parks's odd bio-drama **Venus** (5-2-96, Public: Martinson), based on a figure from the footnotes of history. Sartje Baartman (Adina Porter), a young African woman with an oversized posterior, leaves her dreary life in the early 1880s to go to England and become a phenomenon and make lots of money. Instead she is exploited first by a freak-show manager (she is billed as Venus Hottentot) and then by a doctor who wants to study her for science but ends up lusting after her. Eventually the poor creature is forgotten and dies in obscurity. Foreman staged the piece with his usual puzzling images (it was yet another Foreman show where actors were attached to strings) that surprised or delighted few.

Just as John Barrymore recalled his past as he was on a bender in *Jack*, Ernest Hemingway regaled audiences about his stormy life while hitting the bottle in John deGroot's one-man play **Papa** (5-5-96, Douglas Fairbanks). Two years before his suicide in 1961, Hemingway (Len Cariou) is in Cuba being photographed for *Life* magazine, drinking and remembering as he flaunts (and mocks) his macho image, all the time railing against Faulkner and other "contenders" who are his competition. Critics thought Cariou gave a "valiantly gruff portrayal" of the famous author but declared his vehicle an "overloaded script which has no surprises." Nevertheless, the commercial entry ran for ten weeks.

The second offering by the visiting Comédie Française was Marivaux's romantic fairy tale *La Double Inconstance* (The Inconstant Lovers) on May 7 at BAM for five performances. The 1723 comedy (also performed in French with English supertitles) was even better received than *Don Juan*, critics admiring both the script (which was unfamiliar to them) and Jean-Pierre Miquel's piquant production.

Few aisle-sitters pretended to fully understand Caryl Churchill's nightmarish fantasy **The Skriker** (5-12-96, Public; Newman), yet many of them applauded it, one calling the odd piece "new and nutty . . . science fiction for the James Joyce set." Josie (Caroline Seymour), released from a London mental hospital (she had killed her newborn), has been haunted by the Skriker (Jayne Atkinson), a gremlin that changes form and language as it tries to bedevil humans by offering wishes. Josie wishes that the Skriker would leave her and instead haunt her friend Lily (Angie Phillips), who is pregnant and unmarried. But she regrets her action and tries to warn Lily of the various forms the Skriker takes: a little girl, a sick old woman in the hospital, a slick ex-boyfriend, a ranting street woman, and others. The Skriker is especially interested in Lily's new baby, but Lily sees through the various disguises and, in the end, agrees to go to the Underworld with the Skriker if it will leave Josie and the baby alone. Churchill played with language, creating a string of clichés, puns, and nursery rhyme–line repetition for the Skriker to utter as she changes her attack with each transformation. (The Skriker taunts Josie with "When I'm weak at the need, you'll be a last tiny totter of whiskey whistle to keep my spirits to keep me stronger linger longer gaga.") Mark Wing-Davey staged the surreal circus, Marina Draghici designed the outlandish costumes and masks (at one point when Josie speaks, money comes from her mouth, and once frogs jump out of Lily's mouth) as well as the scenery, which was filled with cockeyed images such as an urban skyline made out of milk cartons. While far from a popular attraction (the Public only kept the play on the boards for two weeks), it was much talked about for months afterward.

Steve Tesich, whose plays had often suffered at the hands of theatre critics, tried to get even with **Arts and Leisure** (5-19-96, Playwrights Horizons),

a caustic comedy about a self-absorbed aisle-sitter. Alex Chaney (Harris Yulin) judges life and people the same way he criticizes drama on the stage: by how the dramatic impact hits him. Several women in Alex's life (ex-wife, mother, daughter, an actress he has hurt, and a stand-up comedienne he criticized) all materialized in JoAnne Akalaitis's expressionistic production and bitterly gave him a bad review. So did the press.

On the other hand, some commentators found much to applaud in Stephen Bill's British comedy-drama **Curtains** (5-21-96, John Houseman), from the vivid performances to Scott Elliott's expert direction and the script itself. Ida (Kathleen Claypool) is celebrating her eighty-sixth birthday with a family gathering, including her daughter Susan (Lisa Emery), a prodigal who has been away for twenty-five years. Ida is in great pain and moves in and out of lucidity, so she has made Katherine (Laura Esterman), the daughter who has looked after her, promise to help her end her suffering. (Katherine has tried in the past to help Ida commit suicide but with no luck.) When the party is over and the family leaves, mother and daughter again attempt to end Ida's life, this time successfully getting her to swallow a full bottle of pills. Members of the family learn what Katherine has done and, rather than debate the morality of her actions, bring up old gripes and argue over past grievances. Meanwhile, in the other room, a doctor examines Ida's body to determine if she died of natural causes, his decision unknown as the play ends. The play originated off-off Broadway but switched to commercial off-Broadway status, running eight weeks.

That same night off-off Broadway, David Ives attempted another full-length play, **Ancient History** (5-21-96, Primary Stages), but once again it was much less satisfying than his short pieces. A married couple, Ruth (Vivienne Benesch) and Jack (Michael Rupert), consider themselves "tall, thin and funny," but they are also too clever for their own good. Their marriage flounders for various reasons (including the fact that he is Catholic and she is Jewish), but as Ruth notes, "the sad thing isn't that love comes to an end . . . the really sad thing about the world is that you get over it." The couple struggle to make the relationship work, hoping that their marriage won't be "ancient history" in a year's time. While Ives's dialogue remained acute (when Ruth declares "sex is not all there is to life," Jack argues, "well, it's partly all there is"), the two characters became "tedious," and as one critic bemoaned, "the play goes on forever."

Eric Overmyer's crime melodrama **Dark Rapture** (5-23-96, Second Stage) was dismissed by the press as a "meandering, toneless and derivative effort," but it did boast a zestful cast and clever direction by Scott Ellis. Julia (Marisa Tomei) is determined to be a movie producer, while her husband, Ray (Scott Glenn), hopes to write screenplays. When Julia is in Mexico making a pitch for a film, the couple's California house burns down in a brush fire. Before fleeing the fire, Ray grabs a cardboard box of Julia's containing $5 million and flees. He then takes on a new identity, letting the world think he died in the fire. But the money belongs to the mob (Julia was supposed to launder it for them), so Julia, a Cuban hitman, and other film-noir types chase Ray to Seattle, Key West, New Orleans, and other points, everyone stopping for plenty of sex and tequila along the way.

The last revival of the Circle in the Square's season was a modernization of Molière called **Tartuffe: Born Again** (5-30-96, Circle in the Square), which Freyda Thomas translated and adapted, placing the comedy in a Baton Rouge cable television station. Tartuffe (John Glover) is a deposed TV evangelist who dupes the wealthy station owner Orgon (David Schramm) and nearly compromises his wife, Elmire (Haviland Morris). Tartuffe's plans to take over the family fortune are thwarted, not by King Louis XIX as in the original, but by an FBI agent. The timeless classic gained nothing by the obvious and modern parallels (more than one commentator described it as a "cartoon"), but the acting was delightful (in addition to the leads, Alison Fraser was a wry Dorine and Jane Krakowski an astute Maryann), and the evening proved to be "slick and entertaining." Still, business did not justify running more than twenty-nine performances.

The season ended with a made-to-order triple bill in which three playwrights, Lanford Wilson, Joe Pintauro, and Terrence McNally, drew straws for a time of day and then provided one-acts for **By the Sea By the Sea By the Beautiful Sea** (5-30-96, City Center) for the Manhattan Theatre Club. All three plays take place on the same beach on the same day. In Pintauro's *Dawn*, Quentin (Timothy Carhart), his sister, Veronica (Lee Brock), and his wife, Pat (Mary Beth Fisher), come to the water's edge at first light to scatter Quentin and Veronica's mother's ashes to the waters. The moment brings on the expected memories and unresolved sibling strain between the two. Lighter in tone, Wilson's *Day* showed Ace (Carhart), a gardener who spends his lunch hour

in the sun, being flirted with by Macy (Brock), a yuppie who coyly asks Ace to spread suntan lotion on her back. When Ace's high-strung girlfriend "Bill" (Fisher) shows up and catches him rubbing Macy's back, a merry showdown ensues. McNally's *Dusk* concerns the very married and very self-confident Willy (Carhart), who is pursued by two women, Dana (Fisher) and Marsha (Brock). Without hesitation or guilt, Willy seduces them both, freeing everyone from their personal anxieties in the process. The press was not overwhelmed with the program ("the material looks frail and homesick"), and what was meant to be a clever gimmick for three writers ended up being a showcase for three enjoyable actors.

1996–1997

With high spirits Broadway celebrated the highest attendance in sixteen years. Income rose nearly 15 percent and at one point in April all but one of the district's thirty-five playhouses was occupied. But musicals accounted for most of these figures, and the Street actually declined in numbers of new plays (only five American and two British) and revivals (eleven). Off Broadway, the total of new works stayed about the same (if you counted the fourteen solo shows) and revivals rose slightly, offering fifteen productions.

More telling was the sad state of non-profit theatre companies off and off-off Broadway. After twenty-eight years the Circle Repertory closed, as did the seventeen-year-old Lamb's Theatre Company. The Circle in the Square declared bankruptcy in August, hired a new artistic staff in September, reopened in February with a unique subscription bargain, then saw its co-directors quit as the season ended. The Negro Ensemble Company existed on paper only, never officially declared dead but gone all the same. There was also something depressing about the *Best Plays* no longer citing its opinion of the ten best; instead the editors acknowledged the season's half dozen award-winning entries. (They had to bend the rules a little to come up with six titles, including *Old Wicked Songs* in the list because it had been nominated for the Pulitzer.)

Even some lackluster musicals did brisk business this season, but *Skylight* was the only nonmusical to break even by the end of May. The quality of play revivals on Broadway was admirable, but very few made any money. The flood of two-character works and solo performances off

Broadway did better, but most of them were non-profit ventures. Maybe the high spirits this season were misplaced. They certainly weren't with the producers of comedies and dramas.

The season started with a questionable commercial hit off Broadway, Ronnie Larsen's **Making Porn** (6-12-96, Actors' Playhouse), which concerned Jack Hawk (Rex Chandler), a straight man who becomes a gay porn film star. The titillating view of the homosexual pornography business had found audiences in several cities, and New York was no exception, providing audiences for 511 performances.

The Public Theatre's Shakespeare Marathon continued on June 18 at the outdoor Delacorte with *Henry V*, which critics judged to be "more adequate than memorable." Andre Braugher, an African-American actor currently gaining popularity on television, essayed the king with distinction and intelligence but rarely with fire.

An off-off-Broadway entry by the Jewish Repertory Theatre, Cynthia Ozick's **The Shawl** (6-20-96, Playhouse 91), was notable for Dianne Wiest's heart-wrenching portrayal of Rosa, a survivor of Auschwitz who, in the late 1970s, is haunted by the memory of her child killed by the SS decades before. (Rosa still clings to her little girl's shawl.) Her niece Stella (Wendy Markkena) convinces Rosa to go to a retirement home in Miami Beach, where a mysterious man, Garner Globalis (Boyd Gaines), enters both women's lives and tries to seduce them into the idea that the Holocaust never really happened. Bob Dishy shone as a retired buttonmaker who courts Rosa.

The Roundabout's Theatre's revival of Herb Gardner's *A Thousand Clowns* (4-5-62) generated some publicity when director Gene Saks (who staged the original), star Robert Klein, and leading lady Jane Adams were all dismissed because of "artistic differences" with the author. When the show finally opened on July 14, Gardner favorite Judd Hirsch played nonconformist Murray Burns and pleased audiences, if not critics, who found him too old and cranky for the role. The "uninspired" production (Scott Ellis was the last-minute director) played four weeks for subscribers, then quickly closed.

Playgoers who wanted to see another two-character comedy-drama about a grumpy oldster befriended by a guilt-ridden youngster had several opportunities this season, beginning with Tom Ziegler's **Grace & Glorie** (7-16-96, Laura Pels), which offered a female version of *Park Your Car in Harvard Yard* (11-7-91). Grace (Estelle Parsons) is a cantankerous, ninety-year-old mountain woman with cancer who leaves the hospital to die alone in her ramshackle cabin high in Virginia's Blue Ridge Mountains. Grace purposely left her pain medication behind, but hospice volunteer Glorie (Lucie Arnaz) comes to the cabin to check on the old woman and to bring her morphine drops. Glorie had been a high-powered Manhattan executive, but after the death of her twelve-year-old son, she and her husband gave up the urban world and moved to the mountains. The contrast between the high-strung urban Glorie and the feisty rural Grace results in an odd couple who move from belligerent opposites to close friends. Before long each is revealing personal secrets (Glorie was driving the car when her only son was killed in an accident; Grace admits she is afraid of dying and, leaving no offspring, that she will disappear without a trace), and by the final curtain Glorie needs Grace as much as Grace needs her. The contrived "sentimental crowd pleaser . . . with a steady drip of easy laughs and injections of topics like religious faith" met with lukewarm reviews, but word of mouth (especially about the two energetic stars) saw to it that the commercial offering ran 134 performances.

The highlight of the first annual Lincoln Center Festival of the International Arts was the Gate Theatre of Dublin's presentation of all of Samuel Beckett's stage works presented in various locales between July 29 and August 11. Rave reviews greeted the focal piece of the festival, *Waiting for Godot* (4-19-56) at the John Jay with Barry McGovern and Johnny Murphy as the two tramps. Walter Asmus staged the modern classic in a simple and direct manner that proved "lucid, straightforward and droll."

August brought four revivals. The WPA Theatre's mounting of Mart Crowley's *The Boys in the Band* (4-15-68) was so well received off-off Broadway that it transferred to the Lucille Lortel on August 6 and stayed for eighty-eight performances. Commentators differed on how relevant the landmark drama was after twenty-eight years, several noting that the characters were stereotypes and the construction a bit forced. Yet many admitted the early gay play was "still moving and enormously entertaining." Also on August 6, *Timon of Athens* in Central Park featured Michael Cumpsty as the title monarch, and critics approved of his performance, as many did of Brian Kulick's swift, broadly played production that found some comedy in the gory play. Also singled out were Henry Stram as Timon's steward Flavius and Geoffrey Owens as the greedy Lucius.

Reviewers disagreed about how well Tennessee Williams's *Summer and Smoke* (10-6-48) held up but concurred that Mary McDonnell as Alma Winemiller in the Roundabout revival on August 16 gave a "lovely, febrile performance, choking with lost hopes, yet still radiant." They were less enthused by Harry Hamlin's John Buchanan, Jr. David Warren's production was generally pronounced "shrill" and filled with "compromise and ineffectuality." To help the floundering Circle in the Square Uptown, Al Pacino directed and starred in Eugene O'Neill's one-acter *Hughie* (12-22-64) on August 22, and it quickly sold out all of its fifty-six showings. The movie star garnered his usual mixed notices, and few were impressed with his directorial debut. But the show became something of an event, especially with tickets so scarce.

John Marans's **Old Wicked Songs** (9-5-96, Promenade), a male variation of *Grace & Glorie*, got better notices ("a fascinating and intriguing journey") even though it used the same contrived plot. Professor Josef Mashkan (Hal Robinson), a cranky old vocal coach in 1986 Vienna, takes on an American pupil, Stephen Hoffman (Justin Kirk), who has been recommended to him. Stephen is a gifted pianist, but lately he suffers from an emotional block. To put passion and sensitivity back into his playing, he is told to take voice lessons with Josef, so he begrudgingly agrees to give it a try. The two do not hit it off at first (Josef is a penny-pinching eccentric who charges Stephen for the pastries he offers; Stephen is disdainful of Josef and the art of the "song"), but as they work together through a cycle of love songs by Schumann, Stephen rediscovers his passion for music. Just as Grace and Glorie opened up and revealed secrets, so do the teacher and pupil here: Stephen has denied his Jewish heritage, and Josef, originally thought to be a Nazi sympathizer, was actually an inmate at Dachau. The lessons come to an end, and the two bid each other a tearful good-bye by joining together in one final song. The two-hander, which had come from the Jewish Repertory Theatre off-off Broadway, ran 210 performances off Broadway, then enjoyed many subsequent productions in regional theatre.

David Beaird's West End play **900 Oneonta** (9-15-96, Circle) is worth noting only because it was the last offering by the Circle Rep. The dark comedy, about a dying Louisiana oil baron (Jon Cryer) and his emotionally disturbed family, closed in a week. By October the Circle was officially disbanded, and one of Off-Broadway's most revered homes for new American plays was gone forever.

David Hare put politics and social issues in the background for his character piece **Skylight** (9-19-96, Royale), a London hit that came to Broadway with its two principal actors. Tom Sergeant (Michael Gambon in his American stage debut), a rich restaurateur in London, and his wife, Alice, once took his employee Kyra Hollis (Lia Williams) into their home, where she befriended Alice and became Tom's mistress. When Alice discovered the affair, Kyra moved out and has made no contact with the family over the past three years. Edward (Christian Camargo), Tom and Alice's teenage son, goes looking for Kyra and one February day visits her in her chilly flat in a London slum. Edward says he has never understood why Kyra left their home so abruptly, but she does not want to tell him the truth. That night, Tom shows up at the flat, hoping to make amends and rekindle his affair with Kyra. Alice has recently died and, filled with guilt, Tom is looking to Kyra for forgiveness. Kyra has left the business world (she now teaches underprivileged kids) and despises Tom as an unfeeling corporate monster, even though she is still attracted to him. Tom accuses Kyra of living and working like a martyr to make up for the guilt she feels over having cheated on her friend Alice. Through a spaghetti dinner and a night of lovemaking, the couple thrash out their feelings and, by dawn, learn to accept each other's weaknesses. While most of the press approved of Hare's script ("luminously beautiful and wildly truthful"), it was Gambon's "tornado of a performance" that enthralled the critics. Williams measured up to Gambon, and their scenes were considered "major romantic chemistry" even though Gambon was far from a dashing lover and much older than she. The play won the New York Drama Critics Circle Award for Best Foreign Play and ran a profitable 116 performances.

Mary Louise Wilson's mesmerizing portrayal of Diana Vreeland in *Full Gallop* (10-18-95) returned on September 24 in a commercial offering at the Westside, and she continued to mesmerize for 392 performances. The next night the National Theatre of Greece offered six performances of Sophocles' *Elektra* in modern Greek (with English supertitles) at the City Center. Aisle-sitters thought Lydia Koniordou's revengeful Electra fiery and indignant but her staging too somber and lifeless. On October 2 a new group, the Valiant Theatre Company, revived Ionesco's *Rhinoceros* (1-9-61) at Theatre Four. The two holdouts in a town where everyone was turning into rhinos were played by Peter Jacobson as Berenger and

Zach Grenier as Jean (called John in this new adaptation by Theresa Rebeck).

Although it had been a major hit in Chicago, Vicki Quade and Maripat Donovan's interactive comedy **Late Nite Catechism** (10-3-96, St. Luke's Church) opened quietly and met with modestly approving reviews. But word of mouth soon established it as a hit, and the jolly program stayed on past the year 2000. The audience are members of an adult catechism class in a church basement run by Sister (Donovan), who explains doctrine, tells about the lives of the saints, answers questions from the class, and even reprimands her students with a swift smack of a ruler when they get out of line. Less cruel than Christopher Durang's *Sister Mary Ignatius Explains It All for You* (10-21-81), the satirical participation program was actually quite respectful of religion by the evening's end.

A week later Durang himself had a new work (his first in nine years) on the boards, **Sex and Longing** (10-10-96, Cort), presented by Lincoln Center in a Broadway house, but it folded after forty-five performances. Lulu Dubois (Sigourney Weaver), a sexual addict in Washington, meets the gay Justin (Jay Goede) at a clinic for sexual overachievers, and they become roommates. The clinic must not have worked, because Lulu still needs to experience an orgasm every fifteen minutes (Justin can hold off for up to three hours), so she goes out on the prowl, gets raped and slashed by a street pickup, and is saved by a minister (Peter Michael Goetz) who, in turn, takes advantage of her. When Lulu and Justin write a coffee-table book about their last 300 sexual experiences, the religious right attacks them, and a Senate hearing ensues in which Jesus (Eric Thal) testifies. The oversexed Senator Harry McCrea (Guy Boyd), who ran the hearing, becomes the next president, with his overbearing wife, Bridget (Dana Ivey), telling him what to do and say. Unanimous pans called it a "skit stretched to three acts" and sent condolences to Weaver and Ivey, both of whom were valiant in the face of an all-out disaster.

A thought-provoking play from London, Ronald Harwood's **Taking Sides** (10-17-96, Brooks Atkinson) offered intriguing ideas about politics and culture but, accurately based on historical characters, could not clearly resolve itself, leaving the audience to "take sides" during its two-month run. During Hitler's rise to power in Germany, many symphony conductors fled the country either from persecution or sympathy for the persecuted. But renowned maestro Wilhelm Furt-wängler (Daniel Massey) stayed and continued to conduct concerts. In 1946 the British and Americans in Berlin are trying to determine whether Wilhelm cooperated with the Nazis. His chief interrogator is Major Steve Arnold (Ed Harris), a scrappy American who browbeats Wilhelm and cannot understand when the old man argues that music and art have no politics. Wilhelm is acquitted, but the question hangs over him for the rest of his days. Some commentators regarded it as "a play which encourages thought and promotes moral judgments," while others called it "dull" and "deeply shallow." But Harris was a magnetic prosecutor, Massey a soft-spoken, enigmatic defendant; and their scenes together were quite a show.

Fit To Be Tied (10-20-96, Playwrights Horizons) might serve as an appropriate title for any Nicky Silver play, and this new effort was no exception. Arloc Simpson (T. Scott Cunningham) is rich but neurotic, obsessed with death ever since he read in a newspaper that a former male lover of his has died of pneumonia. Arloc has a blood test done but cannot bring himself to open the letter containing the results. Then he meets the love of his life, a young runaway named Boyd (Matt Keeslar) who plays an angel in the nativity scene in Radio City's Christmas Spectacular. Afraid to lose him, Arloc kidnaps the youth, binds and gags him, and puts him in the closet, where Nessa (Jean Smart), Arloc's hard-drinking, fast-talking mother, finds him. She has just run away from her uncaring second husband, Carl, and hopes to live with her son. Bribing Boyd to pretend to love Arloc, Nessa moves in with the two men, and they settle into a cozy threesome until Carl (Dick Latessa) comes looking for his wife. After much argument, namecalling, and guilt, Nessa returns to Carl, Boyd is free to go, and Arloc is ready to open the letter and deal with its contents. Not as well received as Silver's previous efforts, the comedy ran only three weeks (though Smart was roundly cheered for her "astonishing" performance).

Off-off Broadway, designer Tony Walton made an impressive forray into directing with Wilde's *The Importance of Being Earnest* on October 24 at the Irish Repertory Theatre, though some critics thought his lush Victorian costumes and sets were more effective than his staging. The revival did boast an estimable cast, featuring Nancy Marchand as Lady Bracknell and Eric Stoltz, Melissa Errico, Schuyler Grant, and Daniel Gerroll as the young lovers, and was popular enough to run two months.

Linda Lavin made a funny, terrifying Lillian Hellman in Peter Feibleman's **Cakewalk** (11-6-96, Variety Arts) about his long-term friendship with the famous authoress. Although over twenty years her junior, "Cuff" Feibleman (Michael Knight), a puppyish bisexual writer, meets and is bewitched by Hellman. For the next two decades the two fight, laugh, love, and destroy each other. Marshall W. Mason directed (with uncredited help from Mike Nichols) the lively two-hander, and Lavin "burn[ed] the stage up with a chilling fire" for nine weeks.

Two extended monologues, under the umbrella title **The Santaland Diaries** (11-7-96, Atlantic), ran just as long. Joe Mantello adapted and directed the pieces from stories by David Sedaris, both dealing with the Christmas season. In the opener, *Season's Greetings*, a housewife (Karen Valentine) is confronted by a visitor on her doorstep (her husband's illegitimate child), and the expected heart-wrenching theatrics follow. But it was the title monologue that was hailed as a "sardonic, merrily subversive tale" filled with "cynical, misanthropic wit." David (Timothy Olyphant) is out of work, so he gets a job as an elf in Santaland, the Christmas display surrounding Santa Claus at Macy's department store. David's caustic observations about drunk Santas, kids going wee-wee in the fake snow, and one elf trying to come on to the other elves made for delicious anecdotes. As the shopping crowds increase and the job gets more hectic, David turns bitter until one day a new Santa joins the staff; his sincere and loving attention to the children makes David realize there might be something to Christmas after all.

The Moscow Theatre Sovremennik brought two productions to Broadway in November as part of its international tour. The press was divided over Chekhov's *The Three Sisters* on November 7 at the Lunt-Fontanne: some cheered the respected ensemble company; others judged the production "a lifeless affair." The drama was presented with simultaneous Russian translation via headphones for five performances.

Carl Ritchie's sex comedy **Family Values** (11-8-96, Irish Arts), a Canadian play first presented off-off Broadway, switched to off-Broadway status and entertained audiences for three months. Ed (Joel Fabiani), a Manhattan podiatrist who left his wife, Barbara (Ellen Evans), for a younger woman, is having second thoughts. (He particularly misses the way Barbara used to rub his sore feet.) Ed is also concerned about his sissy son whom he suspects is homosexual and his daugh-

ter whom he wishes wasn't so actively heterosexual. The sitcom tale concludes with Ed returning to his wife for her to straighten everything out.

Playgoers who attended *Tony 'n' Tina's Wedding* (2-6-88) and *Grandma Sylvia's Funeral* (10-4-95) had a chance to partake of another familiar ritual with Jeanne Michaels and Phyllis Murphy's **Queen of Bingo** (11-10-96, Greenwich House). Patrons got to participate in a night of bingo at St. Joseph's Church in Battle Creek, Michigan, and hear siblings Babe (Nancy-Elizabeth Kammer) and Sis (Carmen Decker) gossip about Father Mac (Tracy Davis) and all the regulars. Although the show had been quite an attraction in Chicago, it only lasted a month in Manhattan even though a frozen turkey was the door prize each night.

That same night, Spalding Gray offered his latest solo piece, **It's a Slippery Slope** (11-10-96, Vivian Beaumont), which he performed in the Lincoln Center upstairs space on Sunday and Monday nights into the new year. Gray, who "turned self-absorption into a cottage industry," began by relating his experiences about learning to ski but soon was off explaining his guilt over the death of his father and his divorce, describing the look on the face of his newborn son, and moaning about the many diseases there are in the modern world. As usual Gray was chatty, sincere, and strictly for the initiated.

The Public compressed *Henry VI, Parts 1, 2, and 3* into two evenings of history and ran them in repertory in the Martinson starting on November 12. Of the many gimmicks director Karen Coonrad employed in telling the mammoth epic, having ten actors play all the roles in a stylized, timeless setting worked the best. A BBC documentary on the royal family and characters hoofing to "Tea for Two" were among the less successful ideas. Critical response was mixed, most feeling it was a relatively painless way to push the Shakespeare Marathon toward its long-delayed conclusion.

A family drama that garnered some laudatory reviews was Leslie Ayvazian's **Nine Armenians** (11-12-96, Manhattan Theatre Club) about three generations of Armenian Americans. Ani (Sevanne Martin) has always thought her vivacious, noisy clan was just a simpleminded group of relatives arguing over trivialities. But when she is twenty-one, Ani travels to her homeland and discovers not only poverty and despair but also a tragic side to her family heritage. It is her stoic, eccentric grandmother Non (Kathleen Chalfant) who teaches her how to live with both the suffering and joy in life. Chalfant stood out from the ensemble, as she often did. The sentimental play produced gentle sobs in the audience for seventy-two performances.

The acclaimed British duo of actress Fiona Shaw and director Deborah Warner brought their solo performance piece of T. S. Eliot's poem **The Wasteland** (11-14-96, Liberty) to New York in a unique venue: the empty stage of the derelict Liberty Theatre with bare lightbulbs hanging down and casting ominous shadows all over the musty old house. Shaw delivered the famous poem as an exciting collage of characters rather than a refined, highbrow reading, and critics extolled her performance even if most agreed the program was "a good gulp of theatre, if not of drama." Regardless, the old Liberty saw live theatre again sixty-seven times.

The Sovremennik's second offering was a "claustrophobic nightmare of tyranny" entitled **Into the Whirlwind** (11-15-96, Lunt-Fontanne), also with simultaneous Russian translation. Newspaper editor Eugenia Ginzburg (alternated by Marina Neyolova and Yelena Yakovleva) is arrested in 1937 for refusing to testify against a Trotskyite and sentenced to ten years' imprisonment by the Stalinist regime. A series of interrogations and tortures follow as both peasants and members of the intelligentsia find camaraderie together under the adverse conditions. Critics declared the large cast (thirty-four speaking characters plus extras) profoundly moving and much of the production powerful, if overly long and repetitious at times. The drama, based on Ginzburg's 1967 memoir, was performed three times.

Except for Frank Langella's delightfully hammy portrayal of the vain and aging actor Garry Essendine, the press had trouble approving the revival of Noel Coward's *Present Laughter* (10-29-46) on November 18 at the Walter Kerr. Director Scott Ellis turned the drawing room comedy's sly innuendo and sexual subtext into a rowdy, libidinous romp with lots of groping, some nudity, and plenty of overt lust. Young playwright Roland Maule (Tim Hopper) didn't just idolize Garry, in this mounting he was sexually aroused by him. Ben Brantley in the *New York Times* observed, "We feel closer to Joe Orton than Noel Coward." But audiences enjoyed Langella so much that word of mouth kept the comedy afloat for 175 (unprofitable) performances. The next night the Valiant Theatre revived Charles Fuller's military drama *A Soldier's Play* (11-20-81) at Theatre Four for three weeks.

The Public's first non-Shakespeare offering this season was its finest, David Henry Hwang's **Golden Child** (11-19-96, Newman), which ran three weeks before undergoing extensive revisions and reappearing on Broadway the next season. James Lapine directed the drama about a prosperous Chinese landowner (Stan Egi) who tries to introduce Western ideas into his very traditional home, resulting in both destruction (his first wife commits suicide) and hope (his favorite daughter—his golden child—has her feet unbound and faces the future with pride). Mixed notices were encouraging but cautious, suggesting a fine play was hidden somewhere in the long and overly episodic evening.

Was it coincidence or just a sign of the times that two one-person plays arrived this season both about comediennes from television's *Saturday Night Live* (Julia Sweeney and Gilda Radner) who had been stricken with cancer? Sweeney's **God Said "Ha!"** (11-19-96, Lyceum) recounted her brother's death from the disease as well as her own on-going battle with cervical cancer. Sweeney was an accomplished stand-up comic, but her tone was gentle, even as she lampooned family members, doctors, TV actors, and show business in general. Several critics were favorable ("extremely touching and extremely funny"), yet most concurred that it belonged in a small off-Broadway house. On Broadway it was shuttered after twenty-one performances.

There seemed to be no limit to who could do a solo show on stage. John DiResta, a New York City transit police officer and part-time stand-up comic, put together tales about his **Beat** (11-20-96, Kaufman) and subtitled the program "A Subway Cop's Comedy." The rotund DiResta found both humor and pathos in his subterranean job, and audiences were more than happy to listen to him for 155 performances.

Karen Trott brought back her cheery one-person show *The Springhill Singing Disaster* (6-22-95) to the 47th Street Theatre on November 20 and delighted audiences with stories and a few songs for a month. The next night, the Roundabout gathered a transatlantic cast for its revival of Anouilh's cynical tragicomedy *The Rehearsal* (9-23-63), which used a new translation by Jeremy Sams that was decreed too British and too humorless. Nicholas Martin directed an uneven cast that featured such American and British favorites as Roger Rees, Frances Conroy, David Threlfall, and Nicholas Kepros. But few commentators recommended the production, "in which what can go wrong does."

Some aisle-sitters thought playwright Robert O'Hara promising, based on his historical fantasy **Insurrection: Holding History** (12-11-96, Lu-Esther), which played at the Public for two weeks. Ron (Robert Barry Fleming), an African-American grad student at Columbia University in the 1990s, is researching the history of slavery in America when he is transported back in time by his great-great-grandfather TJ (Nathan Hinton), who was a member of the violent slave revolt of 1831 led by Nat Turner (Bruce Beatty). Ron discovers not only his cultural roots but also his sexual identity, having a love affair with a male slave. Alternately cartoonish and emotional, the play was considered "strained" but worthy of note.

Just as he had with last season's revival of *Buried Child* (12-5-78), Sam Shepard revised his *The Tooth of Crime* (3-7-73) and, now titled *Tooth of Crime (Second Dance)*, saw it produced on December 23 at the Lucille Lortel under the auspices of the Second Stage and the Signature Theatre Company. Again the changes were not major, but unlike *Buried Child*, few found the new version a rediscovered masterwork.

José Rivera's fairy-tale romance **Cloud Tectonics** (1-5-97, Playwrights Horizons) followed Celestina del Sol (Camilia Sanes), a pregnant woman searching for the father of her child, as she hitchhiked around Los Angeles during a torrential rainstorm. Picked up by Anibal de la Luna (John Ortiz), a baggage handler at the L.A. airport, the two find romance and the meaning of life together. While Tina Landau's staging was intriguing and Rivera's poetic construction offbeat at times (Celestina has been pregnant for two years, and another two years pass during the one night she and Aibal spend together), the play itself was declared "often undone by apocalyptic pretensions," and it was withdrawn after seventeen performances.

Charlayne Woodard followed up her solo piece *Pretty Fire* (3-26-93) with **Neat** (1-7-97, Manhattan Theatre Club), another autobiographical monologue about growing up black in the 1960s. Woodard reminisced about various family members, most memorably her Aunt Beneatha, called "Neat" by the relatives. When Neat was an infant, her mother, who could not read, mistakenly gave her camphor oil instead of cod-liver oil. They rushed the baby to the nearest hospital, but it was for whites only, and by the time they reached the "coloreds" facility, Neat was brain damaged. But the feeble-minded aunt provided some of Woodard's warmest memories, and au-

diences were quite taken with the program for a month.

Popular clown actor Bill Irwin directed, starred in, and adapted (with Mark O'Donnell) Molière's *Scapin* for the Roundabout's revival on January 9, which was expectedly physical and filled with anachronisms. (Bugs Bunny and other Warner Brothers cartoons seemed to be major influences on the show.) The "perfect blend of sweetness and anarchy" amused audiences for nearly eleven weeks. The same night, New Yorkers got a taste of what the International Shakespeare Globe Center in London was up to when it brought *The Two Gentlemen of Verona* to the New Victory Theatre for twenty-one performances. Mark Rylance, the new company's artistic director, played Proteus and was ably supported by Lennie James as Valentine and Stephanie Roth as Julia. The lively modern-dress production kept the house lights on so that the actors could interact directly with the audience, much as they would at their Globe-replica theatre back in England.

Nothing could have been further from David Ives's delightfully comic anthology *All in the Timing* (2-17-94) than his **The Red Address** (1-13-97, Second Stage), a grim melodrama about E. G. Triplett (Kevin Anderson), a straitlaced American businessman who has a guilty secret: to escape the pressure of work he, with the approval of his wife, Lady (Vady McClain), puts on a bright red dress and high heels and parades around the house. But a mysterious business rival (Jon DeVries) comes to town and proposes to take over Triplett's company and threatens to expose E. G.'s aberration. Soon Lady is brutally murdered and, when he seeks to find the killer, so is Triplett. While this sort of plot might have served for an irreverent Nicky Silver or Christopher Durang dark farce, *The Red Address* was done in dire earnestness. The critics lambasted the play, and Ives returned to writing comedies.

Irish playwright Sebastian Barry's autobiographical **The Steward of Christendom** (1-18-97, BAM) had its American premiere in Brooklyn. Thomas Dunne (Donal McCann) was Chief Superintendent of the Dublin Metropolitan Police, an organization devoted to the British until the Irish war of independence in the 1920s. Thought to be a traitor to the cause, Dunne was imprisoned for seven years. The play concerns the old and beaten Dunne, confined to a madman's cell as he recalls his past life, in particular the son he lost in World War I and never had a chance to love. The drama was part of Barry's cycle of plays about his ancestors (Dunne was Barry's great-grandfather), but most critics were more impressed with McCann's vibrant performance than the script.

The Broadway season's second *Three Sisters* (in a Lanford Wilson version that dropped the title's *The*) opened on January 22 at the Roundabout and was generally considered "superficial" and "offbeat," but most commentators found some worthwhile performances in the Scott Elliott mounting. The alluring Amy Irving was miscast as the dour Olga, Lili Taylor made a lightweight Irina, and Jeanne Tripplehorn was a modern, yuppie-like Masha. But David Strathairn's Vershinin, Billy Crudup's Solyony, Paul Giamatti's Andrei, and Jerry Stiller's Chebutykin were better received. Also in the all-star cast were Calista Flockhart (Natasha), David Marshall Grant (Kulygin), and Eric Stoltz (Tuzenbach).

Three solo pieces off Broadway followed. Donal Donnelly recreated his George Bernard Shaw portrait *My Astonishing Self* (1-18-78) on January 23 for the Irish Repertory Theatre and charmed audiences with his witty impersonation for seven weeks. At the Public, Roger Guenveur Smith wrote and performed **A Huey P. Newton Story** (2-5-97, LuEsther), a solo show about the life of the self-destructive founder of the Black Panther party in the 1960s. Shortly before his drug-related death, Newton is being interviewed and reveals himself to be an educated and disturbed prophet who regrets not dying as a martyr for the cause. Critics praised Smith's "emotionally compelling" play as well as his "illuminating" performance. Television comic Richard Kline's performance in Richard W. Krevolin's one-man drama **Boychik** (2-6-97, Theatre Four) was much more tender and revealing than expected from a sitcom actor. A middle-aged son mourned the passing of his strict Orthodox Jewish father and, going through the family safe deposit box, conjured up bittersweet memories of their many years of conflict and love. Reviews ranged from "schmaltz-lite" to "appealing in a low-key way," but Kline was applauded. The commercial entry could only survive forty-five performances.

After a long dry spell, David Rabe found some favor in the press when his drama **A Question of Mercy** (2-7-97, New York Theatre Workshop) played off-off Broadway for six weeks. Dr. Robert Chapman (Zach Grenier), a retired surgeon, is the play's narrator, telling how Thomas (Stephen Spinella) came to him one day and asked the doctor to help his lover, Anthony (Juan Carlos Hernandez), die. Anthony has been suffering from AIDS

and has made a rational decision to end his life. Chapman finds it difficult at first to go against his ethics (and the law), but after he meets Anthony he agrees and instructs the two men how to administer a series of barbiturate doses that will allow him to die somewhat painlessly. But in the end Anthony dies of natural causes, and the question of doctor-assisted suicide is left in the air. Although it was more clinical than personal, critics considered the play "gripping" and highly commended the cast.

Vanessa Redgrave was not the controversial figure she had been two decades earlier, but her *Antony and Cleopatra*, which she directed and starred in for the Public on February 18, was much discussed, adulated, and derided. Antony was a young African American (David Harewood), and the petulant youth Octavius Caesar was played by a woman, Carrie Preston. Ann Hould-Ward's costumes covered several periods, and John Arnone's set of scaffolds and catwalks defied any specific time or place. Television screens carried close-up views of the actors, Roman Catholic church music filled the air, and messengers announced the news over bullhorns. As for Redgrave's performance, many thought it "compelling," making the Egyptian queen an intelligent, magnetic force rather than merely a passionate woman. Her suicide scene, with Redgrave draped in a golden gown and long veil that stretched across the stage, was judged to be a "stunner." The revival in the Anspacher was limited to six weeks.

Bryan Goluboff's "bleakly pessimistic" **In-Betweens** (2-18-97, Cherry Lane) transferred from Off Off Broadway in a commercial run that only lasted a month. Ex-con Eddie (Tony Cucci) lives with his transvestite brother, Peanut (Andrew Miller), in a Bronx walk-up, the two existing in relative peace and quiet despite Eddie's volatile nature. When Ray (Mark Hutchinson), just released from prison, comes on the scene and asks for a place to sleep one night, Eddie agrees because he owes Ray big time. (In prison, Eddie killed a fellow inmate in a fight; Ray saw it but, despite torturous pressure, refused to testify against Eddie.) But Ray's stay is prolonged, and Eddie tries to get rid of him by matching him up with Lolli (Carolyn Baeumler), a local prostitute. A lot of sexual activity results, but still Ray doesn't move out. Eddie gets very protective of his brother and finally explodes in a jealous rage, revealing an incestuous, homoerotic relationship between Eddie and Peanut. The powerful performances were thought more highly of than the "overheated direction" and the "overwrought" script.

An African-American tour guide named La Wanda (Lisa Louise Langford) leading tourists through Stonewall Jackson's historic home in Virginia is so weary of her job and dead-end life that she asks a retired couple to take her back with them to their Ohio farm, where she will willingly be their slave. Such a politically incorrect premise is the play-within-a-play in Jonathan Reynolds's **Stonewall Jackson's House** (2-19-97, American Place), which was about a progressive theatre company considering a controversial script for its season. The company's black dramaturg (also played by Langford) finds it offensive, but the theatre's manager (Ron Farber) thinks it is just the play to stir up debate and throw light on important issues. Reynolds's script certainly did, with characters discussing the advantages and downside of a slave-based society, but it turned into a debate rather than a play. Notices were mixed ("soapbox oratory—of the very best kind"), but audiences were drawn to the "American play of ideas" for 128 performances.

Antony Sher, one of Britain's most acclaimed young actors, made his Broadway debut as the tormented artist Stanley Spencer in Pam Gems's bio-drama **Stanley** (2-20-97, Circle in the Square). Landscape painter Stanley has a devoted wife, Hilda (Deborah Findlay), but is obsessed with Patricia (Anna Chancellor), a sensuous but self-centered beauty who is also a lesbian. It is not until after Hilda dies that Stanley is aware of his deep love for his wife, reconciling his feelings with Hilda's ghost. The press was unsure about Gems's award-winning script ("overlong . . . and more interesting than likable"), but Sher was a marvel to behold, one critic noting he was "as vivid as the three-walled mural used as a backdrop to the drama." John Caird staged the drama using the awkward space as a giant canvas to be filled with bright images. (Stanley's murals were seen behind the audience as well as in progress onstage.) Because of demand for Sher back in England, the National Theatre engagement was limited to two months.

Lyle Kessler, who had found success with his gritty drama *Orphans* (5-7-85), had to settle for a one-week run for his **Robbers** (2-23-97, American Place). Ted (Michael Rapaport) takes a job in a Brooklyn canning factory, but unknown to his fellow laborers, he is being paid to spy and find out who is pilfering large quantities of goods. Vinnie (Paul Ben-Victor), the man who has most warmly embraced Ted and taken him into his family, and Cleo (Elizabeth Rodriguez), the woman Ted is falling in love with, turn out to be the guilty employees. Ted turns them in (even though he believes their motives were altruistic) and destroys a part of himself in the process. Marshall W. Mason directed the talented ensemble, but commentators called the script "contrived" and "nonsensical."

Although it won some regional awards and a few critics declared it "artful and haunting," Naomi Wallace's **One Flea Spare** (2-25-97, Public: Martinson) struck most critics as the ugliest play of the season. During the bubonic plague of 1665, Bunce (Bill Camp), a fugitive sailor with a gaping wound in his side that never heals, and Morse (Mischa Barton), a twelve-year-old orphan who still carries the stench of her decayed parents' bodies, take refuge in the wealthy London home of William (Jon De Vries) and Darcy Snelgrave (Dianne Wiest), whose house has been quarantined ever since their servants died of the disease. Darcy, greatly scarred from a fire years ago, is sexually frustrated because her husband has turned her out of his bed. She is attracted to Bunce, fingering his open wound and leveling class distinctions with erotic talk. They later copulate in front of a blindfolded William, which infuriates him because he is equally attracted to Bunce, shoving his walking stick down the sailor's mouth as his own way of bridging the social gap. Little Morse has her own talents, letting a guard (Paul Kandal) fondle her foot in return for fruits and sweets. When Darcy comes down with the plague, Morse obliges her by stabbing the lady in the breast; William succumbs to the disease as well, leaving the two commoners as lords of a brave new world. The "dark and numbing drama" kept tongues wagging at the Public for a month.

Perhaps John Patrick Shanley's most light-hearted effort, **Psychopathia Sexualis** (2-26-97, Manhattan Theatre Club) was welcomed by the press as a "salty boulevard comedy with a bittersweet theme." Arthur (Andrew McCarthy), a minor Manhattan artist, has become engaged to Lucille (Park Overall), a wealthy Texas socialite with a no-nonsense approach to life. The trouble is, as Arthur confesses to his best friend, Howard (Daniel Gerroll), he suffers from an odd fetish: he cannot make love unless he is wearing his father's old pair of argyle socks. Arthur's shrink, the narcissistic Dr. Block (Edward Herrmann), has stolen

Arthur's socks in his attempt to cure him, and Arthur panics. Howard goes to Block to retrieve the socks, but the bombastic doctor soon reduces him to a sniveling mass of neuroses. When Lucille hears about both the fetish and Block from Howard's wife, Ellie (Margaret Colin), the bride-to-be accepts Arthur's apology and then goes to the psychiatrist's office to demand the socks. Block's psychological games do not work on the commonsensical Lucille, so he tries to seduce her, only to be interrupted by Arthur and Howard, who steal back the socks and save the marriage. Daniel Sullivan directed the agile cast (Herrmann was a comic surprise), and audiences laughed for eight weeks.

The author of *Driving Miss Daisy* (4-15-87), as well as its director and star, returned to the Atlanta of the past and came up with **The Last Night of Ballyhoo** (2-27-97, Helen Hayes), Alfred Uhry's serious comedy about prejudice within a southern Jewish community. It is December 1939 and, while *Gone With The Wind* is opening in town and Hitler is invading Poland, the big talk among the local Jews is Ballyhoo, a festival ending with a formal dance at the exclusive Standard Club that is the Jewish social event of the season. Beulah "Boo" Levy (Dana Ivey), a widow and a German Jew whose family has successfully assimilated into southern culture, lives in the home of her brother, Adolph (Terry Beaver), but rules the roost as if it was her own. (Adolph calls her "the Jewish Tallulah Bankhead.") Boo's plain-Jane daughter, Lala (Jessica Hecht), hasn't been asked to the Ballyhoo dance, but Lala's beautiful cousin Sunny Freitag (Arija Bareikis), in town on her college break from Wellesley, is going to the dance with Joe Farkas (Paul Rudd), an Eastern European Jew from Brooklyn who is not quite up to Boo's high standards. Sunny and her family try to ignore the fact that they are Jewish; they celebrate none of the Hebrew holidays and have a Christmas tree in the living room. Joe, a more traditional Jew, is upset at the dance when he learns that his "kind" would never be admitted to the Standard Club if he hadn't come with Sunny. Joe leaves in disgust, but only a week later he and Sunny come to an understanding and resolve their different notions of their Jewish heritage. Lala, in the meantime, is asked to the dance by the well-connected, redheaded "Peachy" Weil (Stephen Largay), who, to the surprise of everyone and to the delight of Boo, proposes marriage. Some months later the whole family is gathered together at Adolph's house, Sunny leading the group in the Friday night ritual Shabat Shalom.

Ron Lagomarsino directed the superior cast, John Lee Beatty designed the period locales, and Jane Greenwood provided the stylish costumes. The "well-crafted, audience-pleasing play" won the Tony Award and the critics' approval; the public agreed for a year and a half.

A revival of *The Changeling* on March 1 at St. Clements came from Israel and was featured for two weeks by the Theatre for New Audiences. Robert Woodruff cut the Middleton-Rowley text, added some material from Webster's *The White Devil*, and opened the Jacobean drama with a long dance prologue featuring naked female inmates in a mental institution slapped into cages. Little of what followed was much better.

Deke Winters (Reed Birney), the pivotal character in Bruce Graham's **Minor Demons** (3-16-97, Century), had the same dilemma as Ted in the earlier *Robbers*: lie and save a friend, tell the truth and destroy him. After a lucrative law career defending mobsters in Philadelphia and getting criminals off the hook, Deke moves back to the small Pennsylvania town he grew up in and hopes to practice simple and honest law. But the first case that comes his way is defending Kenny Simmonds (Charlie Hofheimer), an unbalanced fifteen-year-old who has sexually assaulted and killed a thirteen-year-old girl. The chief of police who arrested Kenny is Vince DelGatto (Steve Ryan), Deke's oldest and closest friend. Although Kenny admitted the murder to the police, Vince did not read him his rights properly, so Deke can get Kenny off on a technicality. Yet if he does it will ruin Vince's career and let a murderer go free. But Deke is tired of lying, so he exposes the policeman's mistake, Vince is kicked off the force and leaves town, and Deke is left haunted by his decision. The commercial entry received a few commendations but only lasted a month.

Broadway's second one-person play this season was a hit: William Luce's "fiendishly entertaining" **Barrymore** (3-25-97, Music Box), in which Christopher Plummer portrayed John Barrymore. (To be accurate, there was a second character, an unseen stage manager played by Michael Mastro.) On an empty stage in 1942, Barrymore rehearses his lines for a proposed revival of *Richard III* that will never happen. (He died a month later.) But little rehearsing gets done as Barrymore keeps avoiding the work at hand and tells stories to the stage manager, Frank, about his upbringing in the famous Drew-Barrymore family, his spectacular triumphs (and disasters) on New York and London stages, his love-hate relationship with Hollywood, his chronic alcoholism and four tormented marriages, his deep friendship with Ned Sheldon, and his thoughts on acting and the theatre. Although the situation was as contrived as last season's *Jack* (4-24-96), it did not seem like it as Luce managed to balance anecdotes with true character monologues and found warmth and humor in the troubled Barrymore. Gene Saks's astute direction also helped. Yet it was Plummer's "artful and agile" performance that earned him another round of raves. He won the Tony Award, and the play enjoyed brisk business for 238 performances.

Horton Foote's Pulitzer winner *The Young Man From Atlanta* (1-27-95) finally made it to Broadway on March 27, but the mildly approving reviews were not strong enough to keep the drama at the Longacre any longer than eighty-eight performances. Robert Falls directed a first-rate cast led by Rip Torn and Shirley Knight as the parents slowly discovering the mystery of their dead son.

Critics spent more column space on David Gallo's scenery for **Bunny Bunny** (4-1-97, Lucille Lortel) than on Alan Zweibel's autobiographical play. Gallo provided panels of colorful cartoon cutouts that moved, reacted, and spoke on occasion, often garnering bigger laughs than the script. But Zweibel's play was a worthy one, about his fourteen-year friendship with Gilda Radner, presented as a series of comic sketches not unlike those the twosome wrote and performed for TV's *Saturday Night Live*. Alan (Bruno Kirby) and Gilda (Paula Cale) meet when they are auditioning for a television program and become close friends (and almost lovers), a friendship that withstood her rise to fame, unhappy marriage, and terminal case of ovarian cancer. The show started light and wacky but gradually turned to pathos without getting maudlin. Christopher Ashley staged the likable cast (and the performing scenery), which included Alan Tudyk playing twenty-five bit parts in the story, each one a comic gem.

The most awarded revival of the Broadway season was a British production of Ibsen's *A Doll's House* on April 2 at the Belasco that ran 150 times. The focal point of the revival was Janet McTeer's "revelatory" portrayal of Nora as a tall, gangly, hyperactive wife who blossoms into a giant stronghold of independence in the final scene. As directed by Anthony Page, her husband, Torvald (Owen Teale), was a lusty, compassionate man whose inability to see Nora as she really is was rather farfetched. There were some complaints about Frank McGuinness's very Irish-sounding adaptation (it surely did not help Irishman Teale

not to sound like a Hibernian tough at times), and some critics considered McTeer's very physical Nora overdone (she "flings herself about as if playing racketball with her own six-foot-plus body"). But the Tony committee was impressed enough to honor McTeer, Teale, and Page and to name it Best Revival.

The derelict Selwyn Theatre was dusted off (barely) and used for a revival of Eugene O'Neill's *The Hairy Ape* (3-9-22) on April 3. The Wooster Group, under the direction of Elizabeth LeCompte, deconstructed the expressionistic drama, turning it into a circus of lighting effects, amplified clanging and music, metal scaffolding, and a cast of six actors performing gymnastics while the dialogue was run together in a stream-of-consciousness manner. There were some compliments for Willem Dafoe's grimy, brutish Yank, and curious audiences came to the crumbling old theatre for forty-seven performances.

Craig Lucas's **God's Heart** (4-6-97, Mitzi E. Newhouse) was the first play to use the Internet as an intregal part of its plot and presentation, but the human aspects of the expressionistic drama sank the cybernetic venture. Three characters are each having a nightmare. Janet (Amy Brenneman), a doctor's wife and recently a mother, uses her laptop to explore a world of sexual excitement that she and her husband (John Benjamin Hickey) are lacking. But the Internet also brings her information about a grisly murder in her apartment building, and she goes off in search of details, ending up in a crack den filled with unsavory characters. Carlin (Ndehru Roberts), a black youth doing his homework in a park, is also in awe of technology, but in his dream he becomes a lookout for a drug deal that turns violent. Barbara (Julie Kavner), a documentary filmmaker, travels to a Manhattan computer clinic with her lover, Eleanor (Viola Davis), an African-American TV celebrity stricken with cancer; there the dying woman's brain is bombarded with information, turning her into some sort of computerized library. After Eleanor dies she reappears on one of the many video screens and displays her newfound knowledge by discussing chess, physics, baseball, and same-sex marriages in the Vatican. Each of the trio awakens at the end and makes a resolution: Janet to be a better mother, Carlin to study harder at school, and Barbara to embrace Eleanor's compassionate philosophy. Joe Mantello directed the hyperspeed drama, and some cast members were judged to be effective, but the play was roundly panned as "a muddled high-tech study in confusion," and it limped through its seven-week engagement at Lincoln Center.

After winning awards in London, Patrick Marber's play about obsessive gambling addicts, **Dealer's Choice** (4-8-97, Manhattan Theatre Club), enjoyed a superb mounting with John Tillinger directing a mixed British and American cast. Stephen (Dermot Crowley) runs a profitable London restaurant but lives for the weekly poker game held in the basement after hours. These are high-stakes games, with Stephen's waiters and other employees often losing their entire paychecks or more. Mugsy (Jamie Harris) hopes to earn enough at poker to open his own restaurant, which he plans to finance with Stephen's son, Carl (Sam Trammell). But Carl is so deep in debt that a loan shark, Ash (Bryon Jennings), has come to kill the boy if he doesn't pay up. Carl is afraid to go to his father once again for the money, so he brings Ash to the weekly game, telling him that a professional gambler like himself will clean up on the amateurs. Ash agrees, and the stakes rise as everyone drops out of the game except Ash and Stephen. At the game's climax, Ash tells him about Carl's debts and blames Stephen, calling him a worse addict than his hapless son. Sobered by the accusation, Stephen forgives Carl and tries to make amends.

Busy Lincoln Center used a Broadway house to premiere Wendy Wasserstein's **An American Daughter** (4-13-97, Cort), her most political play but still one with a comic and accurate eye on the role of women in contemporary America. Health care expert Dr. Lyssa Dent Hughes (Kate Nelligan) is nominated for the post of surgeon general by the president, so the press descends on her Georgetown home. Timber Tucker (Cotter Smith), a relentless TV reporter, uncovers an indiscretion in Lyssa's past (she once neglected a jury summons) and stirs up a scandal, portraying Lyssa as a privileged, upper-class snob who sees herself above the law. When Lyssa tries to address the issue, her remarks are misconstrued as a slur on American housewives. With her confirmation threatened, she must decide between fighting on and facing a brutal Senate hearing or giving up and becoming a scapegoat for the president's party. To save her children and aimless husband, Walter (Peter Riegert), from further media attention, Lyssa withdraws from the battle. The cautionary tale about American politics avoided preachiness by offering vibrant supporting characters who served as colorful spokespersons as well as friends for Lyssa to vent to: Senator Alan

Hughes (Hal Holbrook), Lyssa's father and a man torn between political and family loyalties; Charlotte "Chubby" Hughes (Penny Fuller), the senator's thin wife who treats feminism like a chic new dress; Quincy Quince (Bruce Norris), Lyssa's gay friend who is a bastion of conservatism; and Judith B. Kaufman (Lynn Thigpen), an outspoken black Jew desperately trying to conceive a child. Daniel Sullivan directed, getting superior performances from his cast, but the critics were guarded in their appreciation for Wasserstein's "most ambitious work to date." Word of mouth about the cast (Thigpen won a Tony Award) helped the comedy survive eleven weeks.

With his Circle Repertory Company gone, Lanford Wilson premiered his new work at the Second Stage, but **Sympathetic Magic** (4-16-97, Second Stage) was mostly dismissed as "frustrating." Two stories are being told, each one taking on philosophical and even extraterrestrial issues. Ian Anderson (David Bishins), an astronomer and popular college professor, and his colleague Mickey Picco (Jordan Mott) work together in a university observatory and discover a new galaxy that threatens the validity of the mathematical and astronomical status quo. Their boss, Carl Conklin White (Herb Foster), is nervous about the discovery, worrying how it will affect accepted scientific knowledge and, more important, college funding. (Yet he is willing to take credit for the discovery if it proves worthwhile.) Ian's live-in girlfriend, Barbara De Biers (Ellen Lancaster), a gifted sculptor on the cusp of a brilliant career, finds out that she is pregnant, and though neither she nor Ian wanted children, they agree to keep this second "new discovery." Added to the double plots are Barbara's mother, Liz Barnard (Tanya Berezin), an anthropologist studying West Coast urban gangs, her gay son, Don (Jeff McCarthy), who is an Episcopal minister of a poor parish, and Don's ex-lover Pauly Scott (David Pittu), a flamboyant choirmaster. Just as Carl plans to destroy evidence of Ian and Mickey's galactic discovery, Barbara changes her mind and decides to abort her baby. All the characters are left pondering the "dark matter" in the universe, which cannot be easily explained.

Irene Worth presented her own version of Prosper Merimée's famous tale of *Carmen*, which she performed as a solo piece, **The Gypsy and the Yellow Canary** (4-16-97, Public: Martinson). Don José, about to face execution, narrates the passionate story of his ill-fated love for the gypsy Carmen. Worth became all the characters in the tale, moving from Spanish soldier to seductive Carmen using the subtlest of gestures and vocal inflections.

One again there was a rush of Broadway revivals for the awards season. Brian Bedford made a "magnificently vain" Sir Harcourt Courtley in the Roundabout's April 16 revival of Boucicault's 1841 comedy *London Assurance*, but Joe Dowling's American cast had some trouble with the very British piece. The National Actors' Theatre had a hit with the first New York revival of D. L. Coburn's *The Gin Game* (10-6-77) on April 20 at the Lyceum, but credit was rightly given to its two stars, Julie Harris and Charles Durning, rather than the script. Charles Nelson Reilly directed the two-hander more as a farce than the dark comedy Hume Cronyn and Jessica Tandy had originated. The slight play entertained audiences for 144 performances, the longest run yet for the troubled company.

Lincoln Center's mounting of Lillian Hellman's *The Little Foxes* (2-15-39) on April 27 in the Vivian Beaumont was both extolled and dismissed by the press, both sides very fervent in their opinions. Stockard Channing played the manipulative Regina Giddons in a more subtle and intelligent manner than the obvious monster often portrayed on stage and screen. Her ruthless behavior grew out of desperation to succeed rather than cold-hearted maliciousness, and with each vindictive deed Regina performed she seemed to destroy herself more and more. Naysayers thought the performance lacked theatrics, others judged it one of the finest portrayals of the season. Jack O'Brien's production was filled with other assets as well: a sterling supporting cast (especially Brian Murray as a smiling, vicious Ben and Frances Conroy as an intelligent, self-aware Birdie), John Lee Beatty's two-story set ablaze with rich mahogany and stained glass, and Jane Greenwood's opulent but realistic costumes. Although as accomplished as the company's recent successes *The Heiress* and *A Delicate Balance*, this revival only played fifty-seven times. In the Roundabout's off-Broadway space, a revival of Arthur Miller's *All My Sons* (1-29-47) on May 4 was well received, even aisle-sitters who thought the play a bit dated applauding Barry Edelstein's production. John Cullum was a commanding Joe Keller, Linda Stephens his wife, Kate, and Michael Hayden their tormented son, Chris.

The most awarded new play of the season, winner of some off-Broadway honors, the New York Drama Critics Circle Award, and later the Pulitzer Prize, was Paula Vogel's **How I Learned to Drive** (5-6-97, Century), which moved into a commercial run after originating at Off-Off-Broadway's Vineyard Theatre. Li'l Bit (Mary-Louise Parker) narrates the memory play, using sarcasm and jokes while revealing the long-term sexual abuse she endured from her Uncle Peck (David Morse). While he teaches her to drive, Li'l Bit is drawn to Peck as a man who understands the world, and she is eager to learn from him. To Peck, Li'l Bit is not only youth and hope, but also a trusting soul to anchor his wavering despair and increasing alcoholism. The family surrounding them is a vulgar lot, sensing that something is not quite right about the twosome's relationship but preferring to make jokes about it. Not until the end of the play is it revealed by Li'l Bit that their sexual fumbling did not start with the driving lessons but when Li'l Bit was only eleven years old. Memories of their relationship, from Peck photographing Li'l as a pre-teen to petting in the car to finally engaging in intercourse, flood into her mind. Now, at thirty-five years old, she gets in her car and drives off into life with a compassionate understanding of those in her past. Reviewers were mostly enthusiastic, marveling at how Vogel managed to make Peck much more than a mere monster and at her ability to portray a complicated situation in a palatable manner. The encouraging notices, controversial subject matter, and strong word of mouth enabled the play to run 400 performances.

Although the press was quick to dismiss it, Renée Taylor and Joseph Bologna's stage sitcom **Bermuda Avenue Triangle** (5-11-97, Promenade) was an audience pleaser for 177 performances. Two elderly mothers, the Jewish Fannie (Taylor) and the Irish Catholic Tess (Nanette Fabray), have been set up together in a retirement village in Las Vegas by their affluent daughters. Except for visiting the casinos on occasion, life is pretty uneventful. But on one of their outings they are rescued from a mugger by Johnny (Bologna), an affable middle-aged gambler down on his luck. Having been wiped clean at the tables, he is invited to camp out in the living room of the ladies' condo. But soon he charms his way into both Fanny and Tess's beds (without the other knowing) and is taking each for her money as well. The two old girls look upon Johnny as a new lease on life (they even start to wear miniskirts from the local secondhand boutique), but the con man suddenly discovers a conscience and tells the ladies the truth.

The season's final solo turn was Guillermo Reyes's **Men on the Verge of a His-Panic Breakdown** (5-13-97, 47th Street), in which Felix A. Pire played a series of Latino immigrants in Miami's gay community. While the quality of writing in the sketches varied (most appreciated was one about a stressed-out teacher of English as a second language), Pire's vivacious performance never flagged. The one-person piece became a cult favorite, running 117 times.

In some ways Donald Margulies's **Collected Stories** (5-20-97, Manhattan Theatre Club) was another version of this season's *Grace Glorie* and *Old Wicked Songs* in that a grumpy oldster is visited and gradually befriended by a troubled youngster. But Margulies's two-character piece was not nearly as contrived and went beyond the tale of two opposites warming up to each other. Ruth Stein (Maria Tucci), an acclaimed short-story writer approaching late middle age, now teaches at a Manhattan university and holds private tutorials with select grad students in her messy Greenwich Village walk-up. Lisa Morrison (Debra Messing) is a bubbly young writer who comes as a student but soon is made Ruth's secretary and eventually her protégé. Over a period of six years Lisa becomes a well-known writer as Ruth's fortunes waver, but the two manage to keep adjusting to their ever-changing relationship. (The greatest strain on the friendship occurs when Lisa writes a book about Ruth's secret love affair with Delmore Schwartz, Lisa seeing it as an homage, Ruth as a betrayal.) In addition to some stimulating talk about writing and writers, the characters rose beyond stereotypes and grew richer over the years of their friendship. Reviews were mostly exemplary, Michael Feingold in the *Village Voice* praising how the play captured "changing styles in feminist thought, the tangled connections between creativity and ideology, the writer's odd place in our money-centered world, [and] the way we turn our friends into surrogate families." The play enthralled discerning audiences for eighty performances.

1997–1998

Once again box office on Broadway rose nearly 12 percent and attendance another 9 percent, but, also once again, non-musicals had little to do with it. The New Amsterdam Theatre and Ford Theatre Center, both musical houses, opened this season, so there were more seats to fill than in several decades past. Musicals provided most of the patrons while a handful of plays did nicely but hardly caused a ripple in the wave of prosperity on the Street. In reality, only five new American plays opened on Broadway this season, all commercial failures. The five foreign entries from England, Ireland, and France did better, and there were nine revivals, most of them quite noteworthy. Off Broadway, on the other hand, jumped up to thirty-four new American works and nineteen revivals (though many of those were foreign guests). Off Off Broadway provided more crossover productions than usual, and many of them were quite traditional in nature. The days when each of the three venues had a distinct character seemed to be gone.

No non-musical opened on Broadway this season until the end of October (and that was a revival from Russia). Yet nine plays opened on the Street between March 1 and the end of the season. It was still a puny number, but it showed how off-balance the season was. Top ticket price for a non-musical on Broadway was $60.00. (Off Broadway went as high as $47.50.) Yet top price to see *The Lion King* at the newly restored New Amsterdam or *Ragtime* at the spanking new Ford Center was $75.00 How could *Honour* or a revival of *A View From the Bridge* compete when patrons could see musical blockbusters for such a small price difference? One of the season's most satisfying plays, *Golden Child*, opened under the Broadway Alliance and kept its top ticket to $50.00 But this gentle play (which was generally well reviewed) could hardly get noticed and had to close before Tony night even though it had been nominated for Best Play. Producing non-musicals on Broadway appeared to be more suicidal than ever until one watched the one-man *Freak* and the three-person *Art* open late in the season and still earn back their investments by May 31.

The off-Broadway season began with an unlikely hit, Moisés Kaufman's **Gross Indecency: The Three Trials of Oscar Wilde** (6-5-97, Minetta Lane), which transferred from Off Off Broadway and ran nearly two years. Taking a documentary approach to the courtroom battles between Wilde (Michael Emerson) and the Marquess of Queensberry (Robert Blumenfeld) over the author's "gross indecency" with Lord Alfred Douglas (Bill Dawes), Kaufman used trial transcripts, newspaper accounts, personal letters, and interviews to create a reader's theatre program (actors sometimes read from books and papers) that rarely dramatized events but let the actual words carry the play. Reviews ranged from "at once compelling history and chilling human drama" to "annoying cuteness . . . annoying sentimentality."

Peter Hedges's cautionary comedy **Baby Anger** (6-8-97, Playwrights Horizons) preached more than it entertained and was withdrawn after a week. Larry (John Pankow) and Mary Kay Paterson (Kristen Johnson) are thrilled when their baby boy, Shawn, is cast as a little girl in a TV commercial that wins awards and bring them fame and fortune. But over the next ten years, as they exploit the ever-confused Shawn (Carl J. Matusovich), the parents become more and more like children as they promote their son and bask in his celebrity in order to forget their own failed dreams.

The Public Theatre's Shakespeare Marathon finally came to a close, not with a bang but with a whimpering production of *Henry VIII* on June 13 at the outdoor Delacorte in Central Park. The masque elements of the history play were downplayed on Riccardo Hernandez's simple set of arches, though Toni-Leslie James's costumes were lavish and, unusual for a Delacorte Shakespeare, in the correct historical period. Ruben Santiago-Hudson essayed the oft-married king, Jayne Atkinson was his first wife, Katharine, Marin Hinkle played his second spouse, Anne Boleyn, and Josef Sommer stole the show as the smiling, villainous Cardinal Wolsey. Mary Zimmerman staged the lackluster production that no critic seemed to feel strongly about either way.

Lightning did not strike twice for James Sherman, who tried to copy the success of his farce *Beau Jest* (10-10-91) with **Jest a Second!** (6-15-97, Playhouse 91), a "half-hearted new comedy" than ran a month for the Jewish Repertory Theatre and then disappeared. Just as a Jewish woman tried to hide her gentile boyfriend from her parents in *Beau Jest*, Joel (Michael Perreca) has kept his homosexuality and gay boyfriend, Randy (Jordan Leeds), from his Jewish parents. His brother-in-law Bob (Paul Urcioli), an actor who once toured in *La Cage Aux Folles*, dresses up in drag, and Joel tries to pass him off to the parents as his girlfriend. After several contrived shenanigans, Mom and Dad find out the truth and accept Joel for what he is, especially when it turns out Randy is really Dr. Rosen and their son has got himself a Jewish doctor.

Some gay spokesmen protested Paul Corrigan's "one-joke farce" **Queens Blvd.** (6-23-97, Players) during its one-month commercial run, claiming the comedy was a slur on homosexuals. (Most critics dismissed it as "an affectionate, albeit incompetent, blast from the past.") Gay couple Frank (Steve Hayes), a pastry chef reduced to working for Krispy Kreme Doughnuts, and librarian Jules (Russell Leib), who worships at a homemade shrine to Audrey Hepburn, need cash, so they let out their extra room to David (Tony Meindl), a handsome hunk who seems to be straight but (they hope) is secretly attracted to them. Jules and Frank perform a series of tests to find out how straight David really is, from having him pick out fabric swatches to their dressing up in drag to encourage him to "come out." But David remains unattainable, and the two learn to settle for each other.

Another off-off-Broadway entry that moved to Off Broadway and became a hit was Douglas Carter Beane's "delicious soufflé of a satire" **As Bees in Honey Drown** (6-24-97, Lucille Lortel), which was well received ("a delightful pointed comedy") and ran nearly a year. Struggling gay writer Evan Wyler (Bo Foxworth) captures modest attention when his first novel is published, but it is enough to catch the eye of Alexa Vere de Veer (J. Smith-Cameron), a madcap celebrity who dresses in black, knows all the right people, and lists record producer and international femme fatale as her occupation. Alexa wants Evan to write a screenplay based on her notorious life, and the two of them spend a whirlwind week of dining, shopping, and eventually making love. But on the day the couple are to fly to California to pitch the movie treatment, Alexa disappears, and Evan is left with thousands of dollars' debt on his credit card. When he seeks to find Alexa, Evan learns that she has pulled the same scam on several other "hot-young" up-and-coming artists. From her ex-boyfriend Mike (T. Scott Cunningham), Evan finds out she was actually Brenda Gelp, "po' white trash" from rural Pennsylvania, who invented herself and continues to reinvent herself every day. (Alexa believes "you're not the person you were born—who wonderful is?") Evan arranges for several of Alexa's victims to gather at the Four Seasons restaurant when she is to show up to con a young violinist, but the shrewd Alexa gets wind of the plan and confronts Evan, asking him to join her in her future endeavors. Realizing that he was in love with the idea of success more than with Alexa, he refuses and writes a book about their relationship that becomes popular enough to expose and end her theatrical exploits. The comedy was well plotted and filled with sparkling dialogue (Alexa tells Evan "you are, *sans* doubt, my favorite new writer and, if Cheever is dead, you are my favorite living writer"). Its centerpiece was Alexa herself, a sly, maddening, lovable Auntie Mame for the 1990s, and Smith-Cameron was superb in the role.

The Roundabout's off-Broadway mounting of Shaw's *Misalliance* on August 7 was more physical than thought-provoking, but the press judged it a merry romp all the same and applauded the fine ensemble. Brian Murray (Mr. Tarleton), Patricia Connolly (Mrs. Tarleton), Joanna Going (Hypathia), and Remak Ramsay (Lord Summerhays) led the cast, who, under David Warren's frantic staging, turned the talky comedy into "a frothy pleasure" for ten weeks.

David Ives returned to the one-act form for his anthology of six playlets called **Mere Mortals and Others** (8-13-97, John Houseman). The most memorable pieces in the program were *Foreplay or The Art of the Fugue*, in which a date at a miniature golf course is strung out to show years of frustrated wooing; *Time Flies*, which chronicled the wooing, mating, and death of two mayflies whose life span is twenty-four hours; and the title one-acter, in which three gruff construction workers on lunch break each reveal his secret lineage: one is the Lindbergh baby, another a lost Romanov, and the third the reincarnation of Marie Antoinette. Though not nearly as sparkling as *All in the Timing* (2-17-94), the comedy was popular enough to transfer from Off Off Broadway and run 166 times.

Plays were still being written in the *Big Chill* format, as witnessed by Christopher Kyle's **Plunge** (9-28-97, Playwrights Horizons), in which three old college friends clinging to the past and fearful of the future gather for a Labor Day weekend at a Connecticut country house belonging to one of the old gang. The reunion turns nasty when an old boyfriend arrives and challenges the yuppies to reveal their hostilities, thereby destroying old friendships and making their uncertain future even more uncertain. What Kyle lacked in plotting and character was somewhat balanced by his incisive dialogue, leading some critics to call the play "funny, spicy, and smart."

The producers of Erik Jackson's "extended comic drag sketch" **Tell-Tale** (10-15-97, Cherry Lane) unwisely moved it from Off Off Broadway for a commercial run off Broadway, where it folded in two weeks. Lenore Usher (Keith Levy, a drag queen known as Sherry Vine) is a mentally unstable illustrator of gory novels who lures a pizza delivery boy (Mario Diaz) into her lair, clubs him to death, slices his body into pieces, and hides them in a cabinet. Jackie Beat (Cora Tripetta), Lenore's housekeeper and secretary, is

out to rob her employer using a fraudulent insurance scheme but gets caught up in the mayhem while other victims (all played by Diaz) are dismembered. (At one point the severed limbs joined Lenore in a song-and-dance number.) Although trying to draw parallels to Edgar Allan Poe's works (there was even a pet raven named Poe), Jackson only succeeded in providing a showcase for Vine's oddball talents. Marc Happel designed the sequined gowns for the drag artist, which were dazzling, especially when set against Kevin Adams' clinically white scenic design.

Ronnie Larsen, who had found an audience for his *Making Porn* (6-12-96), returned to a similar subject for his **Ten Naked Men** (10-16-97, Actors' Playhouse), which was also poorly received in the press but ran four months on the strength of its title. The ten characters of the title were either male prostitutes or customers, all in the lurid world of present-day Hollywood.

Both Broadway and Off Broadway saw a considerable drop this season in the number of solo shows (only five), and most of these were uninvolving and unpopular. Anne Galjour's **Alligator Tales** (10-21-97, Manhattan Theatre Club) was no exception, critics calling it "bayou blarney" and "confusing and ponderous." Galjour played eight residents of a Louisiana community threatened by gators, hurricanes, flooding, and oil companies. Some of the townspeople were eccentric and amusingly odd (one man seems to be the local lightning rod), but few were very believable, and Galjour's "emphatic mannerisms" did not help. All the same, the one-person program was presented fifty-six times.

Later in the week another southern tale, Peter Zablotsky's **H. Finn, Esq.** (10-26-97, Kaufman), was roundly rejected by the critics, and the commercial entry shuttered within three weeks. Tom (Gary Lowery) is a con man (and supposedly the great-great-grandson of Twain's Tom Sawyer) who travels up the Mississippi with H. Finn (Michael Genet), his defense attorney, who is Huckleberry Finn's descendant. Their misadventures on the way to Hannibal, Missouri, parallel some of those in the famous novel, but the similarity ended there.

Tony Kushner's adaptation of Ansky's haunting drama *A Dybbuk; or, Between Two Worlds* opened on October 28 at the Public's Newman and was greeted with accolades of "passionate and illuminating." Kushner and co-author Joachim Neugroschel managed to highlight both the ghost tale and the love story, drawing conclusions about the future Holocaust along the way. Brian Kulick staged the fantasy, which featured Marin Hinkle as the possessed Leah, Michael Stuhlbarg as Khonen, who loves her, and Ron Leibman as the exorcist Rabbi Azriel. Moscow's Sovremennik Theatre Company's second visit in as many seasons brought "an affecting production" of Chekhov's *The Cherry Orchard* to the Martin Beck on October 30, one aisle-sitter finding it "more accessible than anything Russian since Stolichnaya vodka." The unfussy production concentrated on the actors, who were unanimously praised, even though they performed in Russian with an English translation for audiences via headset. The company stayed for two weeks this time around.

Two popular Canadian actors, Ted Dykstra and Richard Greenblatt, wrote and performed **Two Pianos Four Hands** (10-30-97, Promenade), a play with music that had been a hit in Toronto and repeated its success in Manhattan, running 231 times. Dressed in tuxedos and sitting at twin grand pianos, the two performers portrayed themselves (as children and adults) as well as family members, piano teachers, and others. From fidgety kids forced to practice to restless teenagers getting caught up in competitions to frustrated candidates for demanding music conservatories to adults playing in noisy piano bars or trying to earn a living teaching piano to untalented housewives, the two pianists' journey was funny, sentimental, and truthful. They also got to perform a wide range of selections (from Bach to Billy Joel) in telling their story.

The tragic *Challenger* explosion in 1986 that killed schoolteacher-astronaut Christa McAuliffe served as the inspiration for Jane Anderson's **Defying Gravity** (11-2-97, American Place), a play full of lofty ideas that rarely took flight. Impressionist Claude Monet (Jonathan Hadary) serves as the piece's narrator, reflecting on the beauty of space and questioning man's need to escape from his own planet. McAuliffe is called Teacher (Candy Buckley) as she wanders in and out of the play, commenting on the ideas Monet brings up. "When you're defying gravity, you're that much closer to God," she notes. Other characters—an older couple who travel to see the liftoff, a crew member, his girlfriend, and his chummy bartender—also weave in and out of the narrative, all affected by the explosion in different ways. Commentators thought the play "ambitious" and "adventurous" but inconclusive and ultimately unsatisfying.

Neil Simon returned to Broadway with his Chekhovian comedy **Proposals** (11-6-97, Broadhurst) but met with decidedly mixed reviews ("Simon's most sweetly personal play" to "the least creditable in the playwright's canon") and a run of only seventy-six performances, the shortest run of his career save *Fools* (4-6-81), which ran only forty times. In the late 1950s, television salesman Burt Hines (Dick Latessa) returns to his summer cottage on a lake in Pennsylvania's Pocono Mountains with his grown daughter, Josie (Suzanne Cryer), and their devoted housekeeper, Clamma (L. Scott Caldwell), an African American who has cared for them since before Bert's wife, Annie (Kelly Bishop), left them to marry a more ambitious businessman. Josie is engaged to Ken Norman (Reg Rogers), a suicidal law student from New York, but she has broken off the affair and is attracted to Ken's best friend, Ray Dolenz (Matt Letscher), a writer working as a golf instructor at a nearby resort. This triangle is complicated by the arrival of three outsiders: Vinnie Bavasi (Peter Rini), a malaproping Italian from Florida who has his eye on Josie, Clamma's estranged husband, Lewis (Mel Winkler), who wants to be forgiven and taken back, and Annie, who has come to see Burt when she hears of his ailing health. Josie, who has never forgiven her mother for leaving, has some strained moments with Annie, while it is clear that Burt still worships his ex-wife. Clamma is cool and dismissive to Lewis, but he persists all the same. Vinnie, it turns out, becomes more interested in the bubble-headed Sammii (Katie Finneran), Ray's fashion model girlfriend, and drops Josie just as Ray finally gets around to proposing to her. The gentle comedy was unique for Simon on several fronts. It was rural rather than urban and had a more leisurely attack than in his other works. Clamma and Lewis were Simon's first fully developed African-American characters, and their complex wooing scene was very satisfying. Finally, the play was practically plotless as Simon concentrated on relationships, few of which concluded with any definite resolution. Joe Mantello directed the skillful cast (Caldwell was particularly winning), and John Lee Beatty provided the lush and verdant setting, perhaps too overpowering for the plaintive character piece.

When someone in Gip Hoppe's **Jackie** (11-10-97, Belasco) told Jacqueline Kennedy (Margaret Colin) that "it's not what you do but how you look," the words rang true because this panorama subtitled "An American Life" was a visual wonder that did very little indeed. As much about America's obsession with celebrity as about the famous first lady, Hoppe told Jackie's story in a breezy, tongue-in-cheek way that was neither satirical nor reverent. The colorful pageant used puppets, cartoon cutouts, and a fashion parade of period clothes to create a gently mocking comic-book version of Jackie's life—from her youthful days riding ponies to the White House years to a later life with Aristotle Onassis. Hoppe directed the amiable cast, David Gallo provided the colorful sets, and Susan Santoian designed the splashy costumes. Some of their combined effects were delightful, such as Jackie riding on a cutout horse, gawkers at the auction of Jackie's possessions being literally herded off by a shepherd, and the press descending in the form of a huge vulture puppet. Reviews were neither encouraging ("an overextended goof") nor vindictive, but audiences were confused by the advertising (was this another attack on the Kennedys or an homage?) and could only keep the venture alive for 128 performances.

Philip Ken Gotanda continued to offer intriguing plays with Asian characters, his **Ballad of Yachiyo** (11-11-97, Public: Martinson) being no exception. In 1919, when many Japanese are living and working on the Hawaiian Islands, sixteen-year-old Yachiyo (Sala Iwamatsu) is taken out of the sugar-cane fields and sent by her poor family to another island to live with and serve Hiro Takamura (Francois Chau), a pottery artist, and his wife, Okusan (Emily Kuroda). Yachiyo's eyes are opened to the beauty (and cruelties) of the world as Okusan grooms her for Japanese society. At the same time Hiro, who does not love his wife and lives under the domination of his father, Hisao (Sab Shimono), finds inspiration in the youthful Yachiyo, and the two are drawn to each other. But the tale ends tragically with Hiro's art reaching perfection just as their love affair (and their lives) are cut short by the very society that Yachiyo has been groomed to enter. Critics differed in their opinion of the play (most decided "style overwhelmed the slender substance") but saluted Loy Arcenas's exotic scenery and Peter Maradudin's evocative lighting.

Better notices greeted Richard Greenberg's **Three Days of Rain** (11-12-97, Manhattan Theatre Club), which commentators called "a poignant, unsettling new play." When Ned (John Slattery), a famous architect, dies in 1995, his estranged son, Walker (also played by Slattery), and unstable daughter, Nan (Patricia Clarkson), return to the dusty Manhattan loft where the architect's firm first began. In his will, Ned has left his celebrated home not to either of his children but to Pip (Bradley Whitford), the son of his old partner

Theo. Pip joins the siblings in the loft as they discuss the past and try to figure out the cold and silent Ned and the charismatic Theo. In the second act, the time is 1960, when the loft is home to the new firm and the older generation are seen in their youth, sometimes answering the questions their children posed earlier. Ned and Theo (Whitford) work well together, but the team is nearly broken when Ned falls for Theo's girlfriend Lina (Clarkson), wooing her and, "after three days of rain," winning her heart. Greenberg's dramaturgy was quite skillful, planting and discovering clues to understanding the play's complex relationships, and the three actors were very adept at playing both generations.

Martin Sherman, an American playwright living in England, had to wait nearly ten years for his drama **A Madhouse in Goa** (11-17-97, McGinn-Cazale) to cross the Atlantic; but what had been an acclaimed London hit with Vanessa Redgrave was now a three-week stint at off-Broadway's Second Stage. On the Greek island of Corfu in 1966, David (Rick Stear), a gay artist vacationing on the islands to get over an unhappy love affair, meets and befriends Mrs. Honey (Judith Ivey), a faded American belle who journeys around the world staying at the same familiar haunts. When the hotel manager (Daniel Gerroll) asks her to give up her favorite bayside table to the visiting King of Greece, Mrs. Honey refuses, and a scene ensues. Soon David is drawn into a blackmail scheme that brings down both Mrs. Honey and himself. Twenty years later, on a different Greek isle, the novelist and stroke victim Daniel Hosani (Russ Thacker), whose most famous book was about the table incident on Corfu, is being wooed by a greasy film producer (Gerroll) to make a movie of the novel, but distorted it out of recognition. Daniel's guardian, Heather (Ivey), was a firsthand witness to the Corfu episode and wants the truth to be told, claiming both book and film are cases of art destroying life. The tension among the characters is paralleled by a volcano on the island that threatens to erupt, and before long the issues of AIDS, terrorism, and nuclear fallout are thrown in to make the hazy tale even murkier. Aisle-sitters found much to compliment in the play (Ivey's performance, the nightmarish quality of the production, and the shrewdly pathetic characters), but several admitted that it was flawed and uneven.

Judging by **The Old Neighborhood** (11-19-97, Booth), David Mamet was starting to mellow, for the trilogy of related one-acters was a quiet exploration of relationships with little of the blistering dialogue or crude characters often associated with this playwright. Bobby Gould (Peter Riegert), middle-aged, divorced, and searching for meaning in his disheveled life, returns to the Chicago neighborhood of his youth and has three encounters with people from the past. In *The Disappearance of the Jews*, Bobby and his old buddy Joey (Vincent Guastaferro) recall growing up as Jews in the 1950s and fantasize about a perfect Hebrew paradise so different from their unhappy families. In the second playlet, Bobby visits his sister *Jolly* (Patti LuPone), and they sit in her kitchen and dredge up old grievances, both comic and sobering, intermittently joined by Jolly's husband, Carl (Jack Willis). The final encounter is with *Deeny* (Rebecca Pidgeon), Bobby's estranged wife, who prattles on nonstop about everything from physics to gardening to sex, the odd encounter masking frustration on both sides. Reviews were mostly favorable for the script ("by turns angry, sorrowful, bitter, and poignant") and even more enthusiastic for the players, especially LuPone, who captured both the tough and vulnerable sides to the complex Jolly. But business was sluggish, and the drama struggled on for an unprofitable 197 performances in the small house.

Four notable revivals followed in close succession. Chekhov's early work *Ivanov*, in a new adaptation by David Hare, opened on November 20 at the Vivian Beaumont and did bustling business during its six-week Lincoln Center engagement because of the presence of Kevin Kline as the impoverished Russian landowner of the title. Gerald Gutierrez staged the melancholy comedy briskly, and the cast was top notch, but most critics felt the result was less than the sum of its parts. Kline took a "flip, offhand approach" to Ivanov that was considered either disappointing or brilliant. The talented supporting cast included Jayne Atkinson as Ivanov's sickly wife, Anna, Max Wright as the drunken councilman Lebedev, and Marian Seldes as the predatory matron Zinaida. Wendy Wasserstein made some slight revisions to Goodrich and Hackett's *The Diary of Anne Frank* (10-5-55), which opened at the Music Box on December 4. The new version emphasized Anne's darker side (her bitter battles with her mother and her blossoming sexuality) and added an epilogue recounting the fate of the Frank family and those who hid with them. Notices were mostly approving, though few thought movie starlet Natalie Portman (in her stage debut) was quite up to the title role. But the rest of the cast was laudable, especially Harris Yulin and Linda Lavin as the tempestuous Mr. and Mrs. Van Daan. Though rarely a sellout, the revival managed to run six months.

The National Actors Theatre had its biggest hit yet with Neil Simon's *The Sunshine Boys* (12-20-72) on December 8 at the Lyceum. The main attraction was Tony Randall and Jack Klugman, reunited as the bickering pair of aging vaudevillians attempting a comeback. Critics applauded the play, the cast, and John Tillinger's expert direction, calling the venture "fine, populist fare, modern boulevard comedy with all its pieces in place." While far from the ensemble kind of classic revival that the company was founded for, *The Sunshine Boys* instead was a good old-fashioned Broadway hit, running over six months. The next night the Roundabout *did* attempt one of those ambitious classics, but its mounting of Rostand's *Cyrano de Bergerac* in its off-Broadway space was disfavored by the press, only Frank Langella's "grizzled, world-weary and weathered Cyrano" getting any compliments. Langella edited and directed the swashbuckling melodrama (celebrating its one hundredth anniversary), cutting many characters, deleting an hour of the text, and presenting it with a small company on a nearly bare stage. The supporting cast was uneven and unmemorable, and the thrift-shop staging seemed to turn the elaborate period piece into "a concert reading."

Cherry Jones continued to prove herself "a primary source of warmth in the New York theatre today" with her magnetic performance in Tina Howe's **Pride's Crossing** (12-7-97, Mitzi E. Newhouse) in which she played a woman at various points in her long life, from an awkward child to a ninety-one-year-old eccentric. As Ben Brantley in the *New York Times* exclaimed, her "transformations are achieved without wigs or makeup, only changes of costume (usually in sight of the audience), carriage, and facial expression." Aged Mabel Tidings Bigelow has decided to throw a croquet party for the Fourth of July even though few of her friends are still alive and even fewer are able to play any sort of outdoor game. Her granddaughter Julia (Kandis Chappell) and great-granddaughter Minty (Julia McIlvaine) try to talk her out of the party but instead are caught up in Mabel's stories about the past, the action shifting back and forth through time. From her spoiled upbringing by a very conservative, chauvinistic family through her unhappy romances and problematic marriage to the drunkard Porter Bigelow

(Casey Biggs) to the day in 1928 when she swam the English Channel, Mabel's life was filled with a vigor for life and a passion for swimming. The final scene showed the youthful and determined Mabel leaping into a dive as she set off across the Channel. The raves for Jones were not repeated for the script, some aisle-sitters finding it "delightful and moving" but many judging it "merely competent." Nevertheless it won the New York Drama Critics Circle Award, and audiences were able to enjoy Jones's "fluid, finely graded portrait" 137 times.

Roger Rees made his New York directorial debut with Lynn Nottage's political drama **Mud, River, Stone** (12-14-97, Playwrights Horizons), which offered plenty of food for thought but little in the way of coherent drama. An African-American couple, investment banker Sarah Bradley (Paula Newsome) and her music critic husband, David (Michael Potts), travel to Southeast Africa to search for their roots but, more important, to impress their yuppie friends back in New York. When the pair strays off the beaten path, they find themselves in a deteriorating old hotel staffed by a belligerent bellhop, Joaquim (Makuda Steady), and a resident British drunk, Mr. Blake (Brian Murray), whose father built the establishment in the former days of European rule. They are joined by the Belgian explorer Neibert (John McAdams) and the native woman Ama Cyllah (Oni Faida Lampley). All of them are taken hostage by Joaquim, who demands grain for his starving tribesmen. What might have been a taut thriller instead became a long-winded discussion of politics and colonialism with a United Nations arbitrator (Mirjana Jokovic) showing up and taking part in the rhetoric. Like the new and struggling African nations, Joaquim does not know how to deal with power when he gets it, and the situation dissolves into philosophical musings and regret. Commentators found little to recommend except Neil Patel's crumbling hotel lobby set, and the drama was withdrawn after two weeks.

Anthony LaPaglia's "smoldering" performance as Eddie Carbone was the highlight of the Roundabout's mounting of Arthur Miller's *A View From the Bridge* (9-29-55) on December 14. Even those who thought Michael Mayer's staging was overwrought and much of the rest of the cast was uneven raved about LaPaglia. According to Alexis Greene in *InTheatre*, his "thick body feels barely contained, [and] the eyes with which Eddie sees the world flash now and again with a want or a hate so deep, it terrifies those around him—and frightens Eddie most of all." Allison Janney was

his wife, Beatrice; Brittany Murphy played their niece, Catherine; and, in an unusual bit of casting, youthful Stephen Spinella was the narrator/lawyer Alfieri. The Roundabout transferred the revival to the Neil Simon on April 15 for 158 performances; it won the Best Revival Tony, and LaPaglia walked off with a Tony of his own.

Jeff Baron's **Visiting Mr. Green** (12-17-97, Union Square) was so old-fashioned and predictable that audiences might have been watching a revival. In fact, the sentimental two-hander shared the same plot as *Park Your Car in Harvard Yard* (11-7-91), *Grace & Glorie* (7-16-96), *Old Wicked Songs* (9-5-96) and other 1990s plays. Octogenarian Mr. Green (Eli Wallach), a retired dry cleaner, was bumped by a car when crossing a Manhattan street, and the judge sentenced driver Ross Gardiner (David Alan Basche), a young American Express executive, to visit Mr. Green once a week for six months. But Mr. Green doesn't want Ross in his messy fourth-floor walk-up, especially when Ross brings groceries, tries to get him to eat better, and makes futile attempts to straighten up the apartment. Ross is not too crazy about the stubborn, cantankerous old widower either, but to the surprise of no one who has ever owned a television, the two eventually become friendly and start revealing personal secrets: Ross is gay, and Mr. Green hasn't spoken to his daughter since she married a goy many years ago. By the final scene, Mr. Green has gotten Ross and his father to deal with his homosexuality, and Ross has arranged a reunion between Mr. Green and his estranged daughter. While several critics dismissed the script as "lumpy TV-dinner porridge," everyone loved Wallach's crusty, adorable performance so much that the play ran nearly two years.

Ring Lardner and George S. Kaufman's Tin Pan Alley comedy *June Moon* (10-9-29), which had received welcome reviews off-off Broadway the previous season and was further polished at the McCarter Theatre in Princeton, arrived off Broadway on January 15 and garnered another set of valentine notices. Mark Nelson directed the "glittering and polished ensemble cast [that brought] steady snap and crackle to the bon mots." Just as many cheers hailed the old play itself, one critic writing, "It combines freewheeling antic comedy, romantic charm, and a plaintive echo of an innocent, long-ago era." The Drama Dept. production stayed at the Variety Arts for nearly nine weeks.

Like *Gross Indecency*, John Logan's **Never the Sinner** (1-24-98, John Houseman) also dramatized a famous trial, this time the 1924 Leopold and Loeb murder case, but the author was more interested in delving into the accused ones' psyches than in the documents in the case. Shifting back and forth in time, the drama chronicles the first meeting of Richard Loeb (Michael Solomon) and Nathan Leopold (Jason Bowcutt), how they planned a perfect murder of a Chicago student, and their arrest, interrogation, confession, and trial. Robert Hogan played their lawyer Clarence Darrow (his speech to the jury to "hate the sin but never the sinner" provided the play's title), and Glenn Pannell was prosecuting attorney Crowe. Aided by favorable reviews (Solomon and Bowcutt were unanimously applauded) and strong word of mouth, the drama moved from Off-Off-Broadway's American Jewish Theatre and ran 146 performances off Broadway.

The Acting Company's mounting of *Romeo and Juliet* on January 29 at the New Victory Theatre was mostly panned. Its ten performances, part of the troupe's national tour, would be eclipsed by a much more successful version of the tragedy later in the season.

There was something Noel Coward–ish about Richard Dresser's **Gun-Shy** (2-1-98, Playwrights Horizons), which explored a neurotic divorced couple and their new amours. (John Simon in *New York* called it "a *Private Lives* for our time.") Evie (Maryann Urbano) and Duncan (Jeffrey DeMunn) divorced after fourteen years of marriage and moved to opposite coasts but keep in touch with each other through acerbic phone calls, mostly dealing with their son, who is always getting into trouble at boarding school. Evie's new romance is the wimpy coffee distributor Carter (Christopher Innvar), and Duncan has taken up with the young, ever-dieting Caitlin (Jessalyn Gilsig), who claims not to have eaten a thing in seventy-one days. When both couples decide to act civilized and spend a weekend together outside of Boston, emotional fireworks explode, and Evie and Duncan find more comfort in each other than in their new lovers. Quicksilver performances, under the direction of Gloria Muzio, and high-flying dialogue (at one point Duncan declares, "Our divorce is in a shambles!") earned the comedy some salutatory notices.

The Brooklyn Academy of Music hosted eight visiting productions of world classics throughout the spring, beginning with the Moscow Art Theatre (celebrating its centennial) in a revival of Chekhov's *Three Sisters* on February 6. The renowned company presented "a shadowy, atmospheric production staged with unhurried grace and simplicity," and the cast (performing in Russian with simultaneous translations on headsets) was strongly endorsed.

Although the material was too random and disjointed to hold together as theatre, **My One Good Nerve: A Visit with Ruby Dee** (2-8-98, Sylvia & Danny Kaye Playhouse), taken from her book of the same name, allowed the seventy-four-year-old veteran to beguile and charm audiences for twenty-seven performances. Dee recollected growing up black and poor, meeting and loving Ossie Davis for fifty years, and partaking of various movements, from civil rights to women's rights, over the decades. Charles Nelson Reilly directed but failed to make the evening cohesive; yet Dee was a treasure, and reviewers welcomed her warmly.

Sam Shepard's run of unsatisfying new works continued with **Eyes for Consuela** (2-10-98, Manhattan Theatre Club), a supranatural fairy tale suggested by a short story by Octavio Paz. Henry (David Strathairn), a tormented husband who has left his wife in the snows of Michigan, awakes to find himself in tropical Mexico in a filthy motel run by the one-eyed Viejo (Jose Perez). Although he is warned about bandits in the jungle, Henry takes a stroll late at night and is assaulted by Amado (Daniel Faraldo), who bears a machete and threatens to cut out Henry's eyes and present them as a gift to his wife, Consuela. The attack takes on a surreal air as the two men talk about what sacrifices they would make for love, their conversation interrupted by the vision of Consuela herself (Tanya Gingerich) coming and going through the jungle. Eventually Amado admits that Consuela is dead and that the offering of Henry's eyes was to appease her ghost. Reviews were more disappointed than vilifying, and the "uneasy blend of American naturalism and south-of-the-border mysticism" was repeated sixty-four times.

John Leguizamo's most acclaimed one-person show yet was **Freak** (2-12-98, Cort), which he workshopped in San Francisco and Los Angeles and off-off Broadway before bringing it to Broadway. As in his previous monologue programs, Leguizamo addressed Hispanic culture and characters in the Latino community, but *Freak* was his most autobiographical work, conjuring up his alcoholic and abusive father, his budding-feminist mother, his pudgy, too-eager-to-please younger brother, and himself, discovering sex, friendship, and family devotion. Leguizamo even impersonated the Irish and Italian thugs in his neighborhood, a German prostitute his father bought for him, and his "triple threat" uncle who is Latino, gay, and deaf. While there was some argument over whether this was a play (the Tony committee raised many eyebrows when it nominated *Freak* for Best Play), the sight of Leguizamo ricocheting about the stage, playing dozens of characters, and finding "authentic human woe" in his outrageous stories was surely theatre. The well-received program ran a profitable six months.

Theatre for a New Audience offered *Richard II* and *Richard III* in repertory beginning on February 15 at St. Clements. Portuguese-born director Ron Daniels set the first history play in a glistening church and the second in a bombed-out version of the same building. Steven Skybell essayed Richard II and Christopher McCann his later successor; both were favorably reviewed, as was Pamela Payton-Wright as the prophetic Queen Margaret.

Although it was lighter fare than his admirers were used to, Jon Robin Baitz's **Mizlansky/Zilinsky or "Schmucks"** (2-17-98, Manhattan Theatre Club) met with some appreciative notices and ran ten weeks on the strength of Nathan Lane's vibrant, crass, and funny performance. Davis Milansky (Lane) is a has-been Hollywood producer who, in the early 1980s, has turned to offering phony tax shelters to make a buck. He has a naive but suspicious Arkansan investor, Horton De Vries (Larry Pine), interested in a series of biblical children's records that promise to be reverent and hip at the same time. To pull off his scheme, Milansky recruits has-been scriptwriter Alan Tolin (Mark Blum), ex-alcoholic TV actor Lionel Hart (Paul Sand), crooked lawyer Miles Brook (Lee Wilkof), and, most important, Milansky's former partner Sam Zilinsky (Lewis J. Stadlen), who is as low-key and sophisticated as Milansky is oily and erratic. The scam almost comes off, but Lionel has a twinge of conscience and various members of the con betray each other, so the deal falls through. Joe Mantello directed the vivacious cast, and Santo Loquasto designed the clever scenery that flowed effortlessly from a slick L.A. restaurant to Milansky's tacky home to Zilinsky's chic poolside terrace. The script had its flaws (stereotypic characters, a talky first act, a contrived resolution), yet it was a case of, as one commentator wrote, "a sharp production of a blunt play."

A new comedy by Nicky Silver, **The Maiden's Prayer** (2-22-98, Vineyard), premiered off-off Broadway and, meeting with mixed notices, failed to move on after its month-long engagement. Ad copywriter Paul (Geoffrey Nauffts) has loved his best friend, Taylor (Christopher C. Ful-ler), since they were young kids, but Taylor is marrying Cynthia (Joanna Going), so Paul engages in a series of one-night stands to smother his grief. Cynthia's sister, Libby (Patricia Clarkson), a recovering alcoholic, has also fallen for Taylor (who has a similar alcohol problem), so she tries to overcome her disappointment by becoming a prostitute. After Cynthia has a miscarriage, she decides she doesn't love Taylor and takes off, which makes Taylor start drinking again. By the final curtain, no one has gotten what they wanted except Andrew (Daniel Jenkins), one of Paul's pickups, who refuses to leave the apartment, claiming all he ever wanted out of life was a lover with cable TV. Several critics considered it a "frustratingly unrealized play" but enjoyed the cast, especially Clarkson.

Young and popular Irish playwright Martin McDonagh made his mark in New York with two productions this season, starting with **The Beauty Queen of Leenane** (2-26-98, Atlantic), which ran off Broadway for a month and was so well received that it transferred to the Walter Kerr on April 23 and stayed for a year. Maureen Folan (Marie Mullen), a homely spinster living in the bleak Galway area of Leenane, begrudgingly cares for her ailing mother, Mag (Anna Manahan), a demanding and crafty old witch who does everything in her power to keep Maureen from having any life of her own. When an invitation to a local farewell party is delivered by the village tough, Ray Dooley (Tom Murphy), Mag burns it in the stove before her daughter comes home. But Maureen hears about the party and goes, bringing home Pato (Brian F. O'Byrne), Ray's gentle but dense brother, for a night of lovemaking and to goad the old woman the next morning. Pato falls for Maureen (he calls her "the beauty queen of Leenane"), and when he leaves for England to complete a job, he writes to Maureen proposing marriage and a new life together in America. Ray delivers the letter and, weary of waiting for Maureen and hating the snipes of the old woman, leaves it with Mag, who burns it in the stove as well. But again Maureen discovers the existence of the letter and tortures her mother (she burns the old woman's hand on the stove) until she learns the contents. Then Maureen turns vindictive and, not wanting Mag to stand in the way of her marriage, murders her mother with a fireplace poker and claims the old lady fell on the rocks. Yet all her efforts are in vain since Pato leaves for America without her, and the audience is left questioning Maureen's sanity and wondering if the engagement itself was one of Maureen's delusions. McDonagh's gift for gripping storytelling, acid dialogue, vivid characters, and twisting the plot as easily as he led audiences in new directions were all noted and acclaimed by the press, who announced the playwright was "destined to be one of the theatrical luminaries of the twenty-first century." Critics were just as enthralled by Ireland's Druid Theatre Company, who (with New York's Atlantic Theatre) presented the "gothic dark comedy." Garry Hynes directed the superlative cast, and she was honored with a Tony Award, as were Mullen, Murphy, and Manahan.

An even bigger hit opened a week later when French playwright Yasmina Reza's comedy-drama **Art** (3-1-98, Royale), a major success in Paris and then London, arrived in New York with an American cast and stayed an even 600 performances. Christopher Hampton translated the three-character piece, which was short and a bit slight but engrossing all the same. When Serge (Victor Garber), a wealthy Parisian doctor, buys an expensive painting that is all white, his friend Marc (Alan Alda) is shocked that a man to whom he taught the aesthetics of wine, music, and art would "betray" him like that. Their mutual friend Yvan (Alfred Molina) tries to soothe ruffled feathers (Serge feels Marc's attack on his painting is a personal attack on himself), but Yvan has troubles of his own, being a no-talent nothing in a world that strives for cleverness. The trio start to unravel the delicate layers of their friendship until Serge, vowing that Marc means more to him than the painting, offers him a felt-tip pen and Marc vandalizes the canvas with a drawing of a skier sliding through the snow. The friendships are saved, they all manage to clean the painting up, and the threesome continue on with their fragile lives. Most critics agreed that Reza had written "a graceful, subtle and elegant meditation on male friendship and what it is that binds people together," but it was the charismatic performances that made the evening so effective. Molina was particularly brilliant as an ineffectual man lashing out to overcome his frustrating inferiority. The play won both the Tony and New York Drama Critics Circle awards.

An unlikely commercial hit off Broadway followed: Joe Calarco's take on *Romeo and Juliet* called **R & J** (3-3-98, John Houseman). In secret after school hours, four prep school boys (Sean Dugan, Danny Gurwin, Greg Shamie, and Daniel J. Shore) perform the famous love story dressed in their uniform shirts, ties, and V-neck sweaters, playing all the roles without a bit of camp or

mockery. Not only was Shakespeare's play presented in earnest, but the repressed Catholic-school boys became parallel characters and gave the evening a twofold fascination. Props were minimal (one long red cloth became a costume piece, a stream of blood, and even a substitute for a sword), but Calarco's inventive direction and the four players' quick and dead-on portrayals of the many characters filled the stage with intensity. The tight little production, which had originated off-off Broadway, was well reviewed and became a sleeper success, running ten months, the longest New York run of *Romeo and Juliet* on record.

Farceur Bill Irwin staged Feydeau's *A Flea in Her Ear* for the Roundabout on March 5 and met with conflicting notices. Some commentators though it a "delicious and stylish romp," while just as many considered the frantic production "labored silliness." But most agreed that Mark Linn-Baker was doubly funny as both the aristocratic husband Victor and his look-alike, the drunken hotel bellhop Dodo. Compliments were also forthcoming for Douglas Stein's elegant cream and maroon hotel setting filled with all the requisite doors.

There was something of 1960s angst in Tom Strelich's dark comedy **BAFO (Best and Final Offer)** (3-8-98, American Place), which vented against everything from military buildup to Microsoft. While the executives at a small aerospace company try to propose a new government contract that will sell, P. K. Peet (Sam Freed), a disgruntled employee recently let go because of downsizing, breaks into the conference room with a rifle and holds the group hostage. Peet uses the opportunity to rant to his captive audience about African killer bees, rap music, and the way African Americans keep changing their label every generation. The endless tirade eventually concludes with an obvious shootout that left the audience more numb than satisfied. Reviews berated the "repetitive and tiresome" play that was "old news, shrilly announced."

An off-off-Broadway entry took a while to catch on (but catch on it did), Warren Leight's domestic drama **Side Man** (3-11-98, Classic Stage Company) beautifully captured the life of itinerant musicians in the waning days of the big band era. The memory play is told by Clifford (Robert Sella), thirty-five years old in 1985 when he visits his parents, estranged from each other for many years, to say good-bye before leaving New York City. Flashbacks (poetically narrated by Clifford) reveal how Gene (Frank Wood), a jazz trumpet player in the 1950s when jazz was in its prime, meets, woos, and weds Terry (Edie Falco), an Italian Catholic girl from New England who has been dumped by her husband in Baltimore. The two begin a tortured love affair that stretches across the decades, with Gene off on the road neglecting his wife and newborn son while Terry grows bitter and alcoholic. The two eventually separate, but their lives are continually fueled by the love and hate they still have for each other. Gene's fellow musicians provided the play's atmosphere and an inside look into a lonely, dedicated profession. The drugged-out trombone player Jonesy (Kevin Geer) with only one eye, lisping trumpeter Ziggy (Michael Mastro), and Jewish trumpet player Al (Joseph Lyle Taylor) were colorful characters and a play in themselves as they descended from admired side men playing for Sinatra to warm-up acts in 1960s rock concerts. Michael Mayer delicately directed the tricky piece that drifted back and forth in time, allowing one telling scene, in which the side men listen to a favorite jazz recording, to go on at length without a word spoken but with thrilling effect. Critics called the play "haunting and beautiful" and a "sorrowing but trenchantly humorous family drama" and aroused enough interest for it to move to Broadway the next season.

Tyne Daly portrayed five very different but equally frustrated women in Paul Selig's **Mystery School** (3-11-98, Orensanz Center), which consisted of five tragicomic monologues. An eccentric talk-show hostess, a gossipy preacher, a schoolteacher delivering a flipped-out commencement address, an alcoholic lesbian, and an archaeologist's wife narrating a slide presentation for the local historical society were all looking for fulfillment of some kind, but none of the quintet was of much consequence. Yet the press considered Daly an "imposing and always interesting theatrical presence," and audiences agreed for fifty performances.

Although the Public's Shakespeare Marathon was finished, producer George C. Wolfe opted to stage *Macbeth* on March 15 at the Martinson. With movie stars Alec Baldwin and Angela Bassett playing the royal couple, the two-week engagement quickly sold out. Some critics rejected Baldwin's "working-class thane," but most concurred that Bassett was "electrifying" as his queen.

Michael Cristofer's **Amazing Grace** (3-16-98, Theatre Four) had won the American Theatre Critics Association Award after its premiere in Pittsburgh, but New Yorkers were not taken with the Blue Light Theatre mounting off-off Broadway. The drama, based on an actual event that happened in North Carolina in 1984, told the chilling tale of Selena Goddall (Marsha Mason), who quietly murdered eight people with rat poison. First she kills off her invalid mother (Bethel Leslie), then her husband (Stephen Bradbury); then Selena poisons a group of babies at a childcare center before she is caught and tried in court. Sentenced to die, Selena finds religion (and a lesbian lover) in jail before going off to the gas chamber. The drama sought to raise disturbing questions about capital punishment, justice, and mercy killing, but most reviews decreed it "formulaic" and "hackneyed." Only Mason, Leslie, and some other cast members were generally appreciated.

Like its title, Mark Ravenhill's **Shopping and Fucking** (3-17-98, New York Theatre Workshop) was hell-bent on shocking audiences (graphic fellatio, vomiting, and anal sex were included just to be sure), but it didn't take audiences long to figure out that there was little intriguing or erotic about the British play, and it closed after thirty performances. Despite the title (which the *Best Plays*, the *New York Times*, and some other publications refused to print in its entirety), the bleak comedy was really about selling. Lulu (Jennifer Dundas Lowe) and her gay flatmate, Robbie (Justin Theroux), agree to sell some drugs for a sleazy film producer/dealer, but Robbie gets high and gives all the stuff away free. Their friend Mark (Philip Seymour Hoffman), an ex–heroin addict, goes in search of love but settles for the fourteen-year-old "rent boy" Gary (Torquil Campbell), who insists, "I want to be owned." The foursome were all bitter, lost, disillusioned, and only occasionally interesting. (Most critics also felt they were poorly acted.)

The parade of pleasing revivals of American classics this season continued with Lincoln Center's "warm and accessible" mounting of Eugene O'Neill's *Ah, Wilderness!* (10-2-33) on March 18 at the Vivian Beaumont. Daniel Sullivan found both the "inherent comedy" and the "prickly conflicts under the surface," directing a talented ensemble that "never confuses honest respect for a classic text with stultifying reverence." Craig T. Nelson and Debra Monk played the Miller parents, Leslie Lyles was Aunt Lily, and Leo Burmester portrayed Uncle Sid, but the acting honors went to newcomer Sam Trammell's "delightfully intense" Richard. Great Britain's irreverent troupe Cheek by Jowl was the next visitor to BAM, bringing its

Much Ado About Nothing to Brooklyn on March 25. Donal Donnellan set the comedy in a very male-oriented Edwardian society and, unlike previous Jowl offerings, used actresses for the female roles. An unlikely revival opened the next night: Terrence Rattigan's post-war melodrama *The Deep Blue Sea* (11-5-52). The press differed in opinion on the quality of the play (from "highly provocative and thoroughly entertaining" to "dreary, garrulous drama") but thought Mark Lamos's production for the Roundabout was worthwhile. Blythe Danner played the central character of Hester Collyer, who leaves her barrister husband, William (Edward Herrmann), for a handsome young RAF flyer, Freddie Page (David Conrad).

Tim Blake Nelson's "seventy-five minutes of jumbled rhetoric" called **Anadarko** (4-1-98, MCC) was set in a filthy police station in the small Oklahoma town of the title. Ray (David Patrick Kelly) is a drifter thrown into a prison cell, where he is regularly beaten by a sadistic guard (J. R. Horne) until Jimmy (Myk Watford), a petty thief who is Native American, is tossed in the cell next to Ray. The two embark on a stilted philosophical duologue ("Are you a *good* person?") in between torture sessions delivered by the giant bully Bobby Boy (Paul Romero). The commercial offering of the "grim and ugly tale" folded inside of three weeks.

Rarely does an absurdist play become a hot ticket (unless propped up with movie stars), but the London hit revival of Ionesco's *The Chairs* (1-9-58), in a new translation by Martin Crimp, opened on April 1 at the John Golden and packed the house for its two-month engagement. Geraldine McEwan and Richard Briars recreated their award-winning performances as the old man and woman greeting a houseful of invisible guests and awaiting the arrival of the Orator (Mick Barnfather). Simon McBurney staged the dark farce elegantly in a stunning set by the Quay Brothers, a ramshackle structure with dozens of doors of various sizes. Despite some gimmicky deconstructionist bits (the Orator was dressed as a mime, and the set collapsed dramatically at the end of the show), the "utterly mesmerizing production" was a treat for the many who sought it out.

The next night David Henry Hwang's revised version of *Golden Child* (10-19-96) came to the Longacre, a much more coherent and powerful work than seen at the Public the previous season. In 1918 in southeast China, the successful businessman Eng Tieng-Bin (Randall Duk Kim, returning to the New York stage after years in California theatres) tries to Westernize his household, which includes his three wives and his favorite daughter, Eng Ahn (Julyana Soelistyo), whom he calls his "golden child." First Wife (Tsai Chin) is an opium addict who has survived her jealousy and hatred of the two younger wives, but she refuses to cooperate with Eng's newfangled ideas, especially his insistence on having little Ahn's feet unbound. Eng brings in an Anglican minister, Rev. Anthony Banes (John Horton), to teach the family about Christianity and to help the household become more modern. The two younger wives (Kim Miyori and Ming-Na Wen) pretend to go along with Eng's plan, but First Wife will not, and she commits suicide by eating opium, blessing her daughter Ahn as she dies. Framing this complex (and sometimes very humorous) tale is Eng's ancestor Andrew Kwong (also Kim), who lives in America in the 1990s and is told of his heritage by the aged old lady Ma (also Soelistyo). The play was more a comedy of manners than a tragedy as the East and West tried to assimilate into each other. It was also filled with indelible scenes and images: young Ahn's suffering as her bloodied and bruised feet are unbound, the pompous minister speaking (as the Chinese hear him) in ridiculous pidgin-English, and Eng playing a record of a European opera aria with the wives cringing at the inhuman sounds the soprano is making. Tony Straiges designed the elegant Eng home, Martin Pakledinaz provided the colorful Chinese garb, and James Lapine directed the exemplary cast. (Soelistyo was especially fascinating, shifting from the ancient Ma to the youthful Ahn.) Although several reviews were very supportive ("in many ways the best Broadway play of the year") and the script and production were nominated for three Tony Awards, audiences did not come, so *Golden Child* closed after sixty-nine performances.

Because the April 5 Broadway revival of Frederick Knott's thriller *Wait Until Dark* (2-2-66) marked movie director Quentin Tarantino's stage debut (he played the killer Harry Roat) and featured the increasingly popular Marisa Tomei (as the blind victim Suzy Hendrix), there was a lot of pre-opening press. But what followed were disparaging notices that questioned the durability of the script and roundly panned Tarantino's performance, which "displays a surprising lack of both menace and stage technique." Tomei came off looking somewhat better, and Stephen Lang was in fine form as Mike, a thug who was more than a stereotype. The revival's limited two-month run at the Brooks Atkinson did spotty business at the box office.

Most critics concurred that Martin McDonagh's **The Cripple of Inishmann** (4-7-98, Public: New-man) was an even finer play than his previously seen *The Beauty Queen of Leenane* (which was written first), but they also agreed that the American production was lacking. Jerry Zaks directed the tragicomic piece as a cumbersome farce, which made the play "look like a parody of bad Irish theatre." On the remote island of Inishmann off the west coast of Ireland, the orphan Cripple Billy (Ruaidhri Conroy) lives with his two "aunties" Kate (Elizabeth Franz) and Eileen (Roberta Maxwell), spinsters who run the local general store. The two ladies took in the deformed boy years ago and now dote on him as if he were indeed their own kin. Billy likes to read, stare at cows, and worship from afar Slippy Helen (Aisling O'Neill), a mean-spirited girl who breaks eggs on the head of her brother Bartley (Christopher Fitzgerald) in order to illustrate the friction between Ireland and England. The island residents' dull lives are only relieved by the less-than-fascinating pieces of gossip delivered by Johnnypateenmike (Donal Donnelly), a quarrelsome parasite who is trying to kill off his harridan of a mother (Eileen Brennan) by slipping her liquor, strictly against doctor's orders. But one day in 1934 truly exciting news arrives: filmmaker Robert Flaherty is making a documentary about life on the Aran Islands. Helen and Bartley manage to get fisherman Bob-bybobby (Michael Gaston) to take them over to the neighboring isle of Inishmore, where the filming is to take place. Billy bribes Bobbybobby to take him as well (though it is bad luck to put a cripple on a boat), telling the brutish widower that Billy is dying of TB (the same disease that killed Bobbybobby's wife). The film crew are interested in the freakish Billy and take him to Hollywood to play the role of a cripple in a movie, but he is a dismal failure; the studios find it is easier to get an actor to pretend to be crippled than to get a cripple to perform like an actor. To the delight of his "aunties," Billy returns to Inishmann, where he is beaten up by Bobbybobby when he discovers that Billy lied to him about the TB. Ironically, Billy does develop the disease and is about to drown himself in the sea until Helen begrudgingly gives him a kiss and agrees to be his girl for a while. One of the most telling scenes in the play was the viewing of the completed film *Man of Aran*, which the villagers looked at with boredom; it seems great documentary art is dull when one lives the documentary subject every day. Only Conroy was kept from the renowned London production, but the American cast was very capable, just misdirected to caricature the roles. Even Tony Walton's scenery was criticized for being too realistic and "clunky" for the tricky comedy-drama. The play closed after its scheduled six-week run but would be rediscovered by audiences in later and better productions.

The Royal National Theatre of Great Britain sent its acclaimed production of *Othello* to BAM on April 8, and it was esteemed by the press. Sam Mendes, the *en vogue* young director, staged the tragedy simply but effectively, setting it in the colonial British Empire between the wars and emphasizing the military world of Othello (David Harewood) and Iago (Simon Russell Beale). Superb acting, graceful scenery, and a potent musical score blended together in a "compelling" revival.

Although it was a hit in England, New York had no use for Peter Whelan's "bodice-ripping melodrama" **The Herbal Bed** (4-16-98, Eugene O'Neill), The critics disdained both the script and the production, and audiences were indifferent enough to let it close after only thirteen performances. Based on a slight but intriguing historical fact (Shakespeare's daughter Susanna Hall was accused of infidelity in 1613, but the charge was dropped), the drama was torrid with passion, both sexual and legal. Local drunk Jack Lane (Trent Dawson), who along with all the other men in Stratford worships Susanna (Laila Robins), sees her in the herb garden one night with a married man, Rafe Smith (Armand Schultz). Lane yells adultery and brings Susanna to task before the church court. He recants soon enough, but Susanna's husband, John (Tuck Milligan), a prominent physician, cannot risk his reputation being damaged, so he has his wife sue Lane for slander. The court proceedings that follow give everybody a chance to spout off on honesty, love, and truth, but the issue is never resolved. (It even turns out Dr. Hall himself saw something suspicious in the herbal bed.) Shakespeare never turns up in the play, to the disappointment of the characters and the audience. Uneven acting, under the direction of Michael Attenborough, did little to save the play, though Robins was considered the best of the lot.

Contradictory notices greeted Tom Donaghy's comedy-fantasy **From Above** (4-23-98, Playwrights Horizons), which was lauded for its "skillful, smart and funny . . . brilliant dialogue" or scolded for its "archly wacky, disjointed and utterly false-ringing dialogue." Widow Evvy (Patricia Kalember) still grieves for her late husband, Jimmy (who was thirty years her senior), a year after his death. But one day a young man (Neal Huff) in his twenties enters Evvy's kitchen, wringing wet from rescuing a kitten from a nearby lake, and claims to be Jimmy back from the dead. Evvy does not believe him but is attracted to the youth. When he reveals intimate details about Evvy that only Jimmy knew, she is stunned. Is he the late Jimmy or just an illusion "from above"? Actually, it turns out he is an employee from a nearby mental hospital who worked there with Jimmy and learned all about Evvy without ever meeting her. The young man leaves (with the kitten), and Evvy gets on with her life.

After four years in Washington as the head of the National Endowment for the Arts, Jane Alexander returned to the stage in Joanna Murphy-Smith's talky drama **Honour** (4-26-98, Belasco), an Australian play about an American marriage. Gus Spenser (Robert Foxworth) is a famous New York journalist who is smitten by a grad student, sexy young Claudia (Laura Linney), who comes to interview him for a book she is writing about contemporary geniuses. So Gus leaves his wife of thirty-two years, Honor (Alexander), and their daughter, Sophie (Enid Graham), who is close in age to Claudia. What follows is ninety minutes of everyone talking about what they are feeling and making speeches at each other with strained epigrams like "What is loyalty but resistance to change?" Eventually Honor, who was a poet before she gave it up to be a mother, starts to discover the woman she was before she married, and there is more talk about honor (or honour, as they insisted on spelling it). Gerald Gutierrez staged the long one-act at breakneck speed, which made the artificial dialogue seem even more exhausting. Generally castigated by the press, the drama could only survive on the Street for seven weeks.

The Broadway season ended as the off-Broadway season had begun, with a drama about Oscar Wilde. But David Hare's **The Judas Kiss** (4-29-98, Broadhurst) was a quiet, introspective drama about the private Wilde, while *Gross Indecency* was about the public man. In London's Cadogan Hotel in 1895, Wilde (Liam Neeson) has lost his slander suit against the Marquess of Queensberry, and it looks very much like he will be arrested for "gross indecency." His old friend and former lover Robbie Ross (Peter Capaldi)

urges him to flee to the Continent, while Bosie, Lord Alfred Douglas (Tom Hollander), wants Wilde to stay and fight it out. But Wilde is already a defeated man, succumbing to Bosie's wishes in everything, and he patiently awaits the arrival of the police. Two years later, after serving hard time in Reading Gaol, Wilde is reunited with Bosie in Naples, but the youth seems more interested in the handsome Italian fisherman Galileo (Daniel Serafini-Sauli) he has bedded the night before. Wilde continues to love Bosie, even in the youth's betrayal, because "love is not illusion," he sadly declares, "life is." The British drama met with a mixed press: some judged the play to be static and Neeson to be too detached and unemotional; others found it a rich and resonant piece and Neeson's performances subtle and affecting. But the British import overcame the uneven reviews (and a total shutout by the Tony committee) and ran a profitable three months on the marquee appeal of movie star Neeson.

Two one-person shows opened off Broadway on May 5. The Second Stage presented Sanbdra Tsing Loh's wry comedy **Bad Sex With Bud Kemp** (5-5-98, McGinn-Cazale) for a week, illustrating the horrors of the dating game in contemporary New York. In a series of sketches about various unsuccessful affairs, Loh introduced the audience to such lovers as Bud (who hums when he makes love), a Yale graduate architect who looks like Ralph Fiennes, an opera buff whose apartment is so clean it frightens her, a boxer from Weehawken, a Hispanic car valet, and a rugged Montana man who likes to make love in log cabins. But she ends up marrying Bud because "the thing about bad sex—with practice, it can get better." Anne Bogart's **Bob** (5-5-98, New York Theatre Workshop) was a solo piece celebrating avant-gardist Robert Wilson. Will Bond was the single performer who conjured up Wilson's life and background, creating with Bogart (who also directed) visual images, sounds, shadows, and, of course, the contorted physical poses that were so distinctively Wilson.

Off-off Broadway, the Signature Theatre offered a season dedicated to the work of Arthur Miller, including a new play, **Mr. Peters' Connections** (5-17-98, Signature), which brought Peter Falk back to the New York stage after twenty-seven years. The haunting memory play is set in an abandoned nightclub where Harry Peters (Falk), a retired Pan Am pilot, recalls past events as various characters, now all dead, come and go. A former mistress, the Marilyn Monroe–like blonde

Cathy Mae (Kris Carr), is among the remembered specters. Harry's wife, the very-much-alive Charlotte (Ann Jackson), enters looking for her husband, so the ghosts of the past all go quietly to their "warm oblivion," and Harry resignedly looks forward to joining them someday. The chamber piece was more atmospheric than riveting, and Falk was judged to "bring humor and a crusty warmth to the weathered Mr. Peters." Irish director Garry Hynes, represented by *The Beauty Queen of Leenane* this season, staged the reflective play, which was limited to forty-nine performances.

Alan Arkin and Elaine May, who both started in Chicago's Second City improv troupe three decades earlier, wrote, directed, and performed together in **Power Plays** (5-21-98, Promenade), a trio of one-acters that the Manhattan Theatre Club ran nearly eight months. May's *The Way of All Fish* pitted a high-powered Madison Avenue executive (May) against her mousy secretary (Jeannie Berlin, who is May's daughter), who, during an impromptu Chinese dinner in the office, reveals herself to be a scheming dreamer, quietly explaining how she will find fame by killing a rich celebrity. Arkin's *Virtual Reality* was an absurdist comedy about two men (Arkin and his son Anthony) in a warehouse who rehearse what they will do when a shipment of important materials come in, the two of them miming carrying, sorting, and checking off invisible items with exacting precision. May's *In and Out of the Light* was an old-fashioned farce about a lecherous dentist (Alan Arkin) who tries to seduce his big-breasted nurse (May). But he is interrupted, first by a panic-stricken psychologist (Berlin), who insists on an immediate root canal, and then by the dentist's son (Anthony Arkin), who decides this is the time to tell his father that he is gay. Critics pronounced the comedies "wild and dazzling" if not exceptional and applauded all four performers, especially May and the elder Arkin, whose comic rapport offered "a master class in timing and delivery."

Britain's other famous subsidized theatre, the Royal Shakespeare Company, brought its repertory of five classics to BAM on May 21 and gave New Yorkers varied examples of what it was up to back home. Matthew Warchus (who directed *Art*) radically cut the text of *Hamlet*, which did not please some aisle-sitters, but they all thought Alex Jennings's youthful, quicksilver prince a treat. The season's second *Henry VIII* featured Paul Jesson as the multi-wived monarch, Jane Lapotaire was Katharine, and Ian Hogg played Cardinal Wolsey. Edward Petherbridge directed and appeared in Beckett's *Krapp's Last Tape*, Adrian Noble staged *Cymbeline*, and the RSC rep was completed with *Everyman*, which featured Joseph Mydell as the title hero.

A considerable amount of praise ("uncluttered and gripping . . . taut and disturbing") for Craig Lucas's **The Dying Gaul** (5-31-98, Vineyard) was not enough to override a negative review in the *New York Times*, so the drama was not extended after its five-week engagement off-off Broadway. Robert (Tim Hopper), a struggling Hollywood writer, has penned a screenplay about the death of his lover Malcolm. Film producer Jeffrey (Tony Goldwyn) is interested enough in the script to offer a million dollars for it, but he wants one change: the victim in the film must be a female and the relationship a heterosexual one. Robert is hesitant, but the bisexual Jeffrey seduces him in more ways than one. Jeffrey's wife, Elaine (Linda Emond), knows of Jeffrey's indiscretions yet is taken with Robert herself. Using the pseudonym of Arckangell, Elaine breaks into a gay chatline on the Internet that Robert favors. Pretending to be a male, she gets Robert to open up and reveal intimate secrets about himself, then tries to tell him that Arckangell is the ghost of Malcolm communicating with him from the dead. Having reduced Robert to a trembling mass of insecurity, Elaine then reveals the truth to Robert and walks out on Jeffrey, breaking up her marriage and the men's affair. The movie is made with a woman as the dying lover, but it fails at the box office. *The Dying Gaul* would return the next season.

Just as the Drama Dept. had a critical and popular winner earlier with the old comedy *June Moon*, the Atlantic Theatre revived Kaufman and Hart's *Once in a Lifetime* (9-24-30) on May 31 and found similar success. How complicated New York theatre could be: one-man shows on Broadway, star vehicles off Broadway, and vintage Broadway comedies from the 1920s and 1930s playing off-off Broadway. The three venues could barely recognize each other.

1998–1999

Because musicals were scarce (and unimpressive) this season, plays seemed to dominate the theatre scene. It was not just an illusion. More plays (sixteen new works) opened on Broadway than in the previous season, and a good number of them stayed for noteworthy, if not always profitable, runs. Alas, many were foreign entries; but any season that offered sellout revivals of two classics by Eugene O'Neill and Arthur Miller (*The Iceman Cometh* and *Death of a Salesman*) as well as two never-before-seen works by O'Neill and Tennessee Williams (*Bread and Butter* and *Not About Nightingales*) sure felt American. Miller also had a new play, as did native playwrights Christopher Durang, John Guare, Terrence McNally, Beth Henley, Paul Rudnick, Paula Vogel, and A. R. Gurney (who offered two). But, with only one or two exceptions, they were secondhand goods. New works by established foreign playwrights Alan Ayckbourn, Harold Pinter, and David Hare (who had three) fared better. And up-and-coming Irish authors Martin McDonagh and Conor McPherson were also represented, the latter coming up with two. Good or bad, American or not, it was a playwrights' season.

Yet much of the excitement was for revivals, seven on the Street and twenty off. Some were star-driven (Nicole Kidman, Brian Dennehy, Judi Dench, Kevin Spacey, Uta Hagen, Diana Rigg, Matthew Broderick, Stockard Channing, Laurence Fishburne), while several held their own as accomplished productions of worthwhile scripts. But, once again, a good number of the best revivals were British.

Off Broadway was healthy, offering forty-three new American plays and a dozen foreign entries. Theatre companies such as the Manhattan Theatre Club and Playwrights Horizons had active and ambitious seasons. The quality of the new scripts varied, but the patrons kept returning, several shows surviving poor notices (such as *The Most Fabulous Story Ever Told*) or thriving on controversy (*Corpus Christi*).

According to a study released in September by the Theatre Development Fund and the League of American Theatres and Producers, the makeup of the Broadway audience was changing. Patrons were younger (over 20 percent were under 25 years old) and more multicultural (13 percent were African-American, Asian, or Hispanic). The audiences for non-musicals varied somewhat (only 6 percent were under twenty-five, and less than 2 percent were under eighteen), but the trend was unmistakable: theatre, even on Broadway, was no longer just for the tired businessman.

The season began with veteran playwright A. R. Gurney returning to his past in **Labor Day** (6-1-98, Manhattan Theatre Club), a sequel to his *The Cocktail Hour* (10-20-88). In the earlier work, young playwright John upset his parents by writing a play about them; in the new entry, late-middle-aged John (Josef Sommer) upsets his grown children by putting them all in his autobiographical script. John has survived both cancer and family conflicts, so he writes a warm and sentimental ending for his play. But hotshot director Dennis (Brooks Ashmanskas) doesn't like the ending (neither does the Seattle Rep nor Robert Redford, who wants to star in a film version) and arrives at John's Connecticut home for the Labor Day weekend, pushing for an denouement in which the hero leaves his wife and children and runs off with his African-American mistress. John's turmoil over whether he should change the play is paralleled by new family crises, none of which struck critics as very gripping. But John sticks to his guns, arguing that real life is more important than art. Joyce Van Patten, as John's feisty wife, Ellen, was commended, as was Jack O'Brien's direction (he had staged the earlier *The Cocktail Hour* as well). The "determinedly inconsequential" play ran two months, then faded away, failing to join the list of oft-produced Gurney works.

The first summer offering by the New York Shakespeare Festival at the outdoor Delacorte in Central Park was Thornton Wilder's expressionistic comedy *The Skin of Our Teeth* (11-18-42) on June 12, which met with mixed notices. Kristen Johnston was applauded for her sly and funny Sabina, and Frances Conroy was quite adept at playing Mrs. Antrobus, but few commentators thought John Goodman was up to the central role of Mr. Antrobus.

John C. Russell's "strange and strangely poignant comedy" **Stupid Kids** (6-13-98, WPA) pitted unpopular high schoolers Kimberly (Mandy Siegfried) and Neechee (Keith Nobbs) against in-crowd teenagers Jim (James Carpinello) and Judy (Shannon Burkett), the foursome getting to know each other one night after a party where they are arrested together. Jim, the new kid in town, wants to bed Judy, so Neechee and Kimberly help matters along, even though the two outsiders are gay and secretly lust after these popular classmates. Mostly episodic, the play reaches its climax when Neechee and Kimberly declare their same-sex attraction to Jim and Judy and the two preppies freak out, opting instead to have sex together in front of a motorcycle gang as part of an initiation for joining the in crowd. Michael Mayer staged the piece in a hyped-up and even surreal manner yet got honest and touching performances from the quartet of actors. The dark comedy ran a month, then reopened on August 25 at the Century, where it played for six weeks more. (Author Russell would have been considered a promising talent, but he had died of AIDS in 1994, giving the piece a tragic undertone.)

Playwrights Horizons provided the season's first of many solo turns, **Lillian** (6-15-98, New Theatre Wing), a one-woman show delivered by a man. David Cale wrote and performed the monologue about middle-aged housewife Lillian who, married to a dull husband, has a lengthy affair with Jimmy, a passionate man half her age. Critics complimented Cale's writing ("the sweet, wistful quality of a Noel Coward encounter") and his acting ("invests his narrative with the varied colors and shadings of a supple, melodious voice"), noting the program was "laced with racing wit and gentle melancholia."

Critics were mostly enthusiastic about the Roundabout's mounting of Shaw's *You Never Can Tell* on June 21, complimenting Nicholas Martin's smart-looking production even if some of the acting was overdone. Robert Sean Leonard, as the young dentist Valentine, continued to prove himself one of the theatre's finest leading men, and Katie Finneran held her own as Gloria, the liberated woman he pursues. The lovely production ran out the summer.

The Acting Company's commissioned anthology program, **Love's Fire** (6-22-98, Public: Newman), featured seven new short plays, each one based on a Shakespearean sonnet and penned by an acclaimed American playwright: Wendy Wasserstein, John Guare, Marsha Norman, William Finn, Ntozake Shange, Eric Bogosian, and Tony Kushner. While it had its high points, the evening was not nearly as satisfying as it promised to be. The most intriguing playlets were Guare's *The General of Hot Desire*, involving overzealous students reenacting the Bible while God keeps kvetching, Wasserstein's social satire *Waiting for Philip Glass*, in which a Hamptons hostess has an anxiety attack over her guest list, Bogosian's *Bitter Sauce*, with a bride-to-be confessing her frequent infidelities to her fiancé on the eve of their wedding, and Kushner's *Terminating, or Lass meine Schmertzen nicht verloren Sein, or Ambivalence*, which concerned a therapist, her neurotic patient, and their two demanding lovers. The program attracted audiences to the Public for four weeks.

Running much longer (190 performances) was Assif Mandvi's one-man panorama of Indian immigrants in New York called **Sakina's Restaurant** (6-24-98, American Place). Azgi arrives in Manhattan from India in search of the American dream, but his view is limited to the "Little Bombay" section of New York, where he works at a restaurant run by Hakim and his frustrated wife, Farrida. Their teenage daughter, Sakina, though engaged to Muslim med student Ali through a prearrangement, is also trying to embrace the American way of life, and Azgi finds in her a true soulmate. While the "narrative's slender thread lack[ed] a cohesive flow," critics applauded Mandvi's versatile portrayals and his "comic, grave, wistful, [and] angry" tone.

Broadway's first entry of the season was surely one of its high points. Warren Leight's memory play *Side Man* (3-11-98) transferred to the Roundabout on June 25, moving to the John Golden in November and staying over a year. Wendy Makkena now played the self-destructive mother, Terry, but the rest of the cast was the same from Off Broadway, all under Michael Mayer's telling direction. The play and Frank Wood (as the father, side man Gene) won Tony Awards at season's end.

Bob Crowley's magical set for Lincoln Center's *Twelfth Night* on July 16 was unanimously cheered, though nearly everything else about the revival was greeted with decidedly mixed opinions. Crowley turned the Vivian Beaumont stage into a shimmering water world with ponds deep enough to swim in, bridges that seemed to float over them, and hanging lanterns that punctuated the deep blue expanse like stars. Acclaimed British director Nicholas Hytner staged the comedy like an Arabian Nights fairy tale (Catherine Zuber's costumes ranged from Turkish harem wear to Victorian British Empire uniforms), but the American cast was drastically uneven. Brian Murray and Max Wright were generally applauded for their funny and yet touching Sir Toby Belch and Sir Andrew Aguecheek, and most approved of Philip Bosco's dry and low-key Malvolio. But the three movie stars recruited for the romantic leads were lacking: Helen Hunt was an efficient but "mannered" Viola, Paul Rudd made an exotic ("Hedy Lamarr with a goatee") but lifeless Orsino, and Kyra Sedgwick's gushing Olivia was "less a countess than a living Barbie doll." The popular revival ran fifty-three times; the final performance was broadcast live on PBS-TV, making it the most-viewed play of the season.

Twelfth Night was presented as part of the Lincoln Center Festival, a three-week program of dance, music, and theatre from around the world. The theatre entries were: Joshua Sobol's pastoral comedy **Village** (7-7-98) and Alexander Chervinsky's Holocaust drama **Adam Resurrected** (7-14-98), both offered by Israel's Gesher Theatre as part of the fiftieth anniversary of the founding of the state of Israel; Britain's Théâtre de Complicité's inventive dramatization of short stories by the Polish author Bruno Schulz called **The Street of Crocodiles** (7-16-98); and Spain's La Fura dels Baus's cockeyed (and rather violent) take on Goethe's masterwork retitled **F@ust: Version 3.0** (7-22-98).

While film stars pulled in audiences at Lincoln Center, a television favorite did likewise with **Jerry Seinfeld: I'm Telling You for the Last Time—Live on Broadway** (8-5-98, Broadhurst), which easily filled the house for its ten-performance run. The media-hyped event turned out to be less than an hour of stand-up comedy, but Seinfeld's many fans did not seem to be disappointed.

Uta Hagen found a role worthy of her talents in Donald Margulies's *Collected Stories* (5-20-97), which was revived on August 13 at the Lucille Lortel and ran six months. Hagen played the fictional author Ruth, and Lorca Simons was her young protégé Lisa. Like the summer's earlier *Twelfth Night*, the August 15 mounting of *Cymbeline* at the Delacorte boasted an intoxicating set that far outshone the performances. Designer Mark Wendland provided a circle of white sand, a green mound of grass surrounded by trees, and panels that formed geometric shapes and defined various locales in Italy and England. Director Andrei Serban took a minimalist approach to the text, reducing characters to obvious stereotypes, but trying to keep Shakespeare's convoluted plot clear.

Critics were at a lost as how to describe Alan Ayckbourn's **Communicating Doors** (8-20-98, Variety Arts), which had elements of bedroom farce, thriller, social comedy, and sci-fi fantasy. Some declared it "a clever and finally quite moving work," while others dismissed it as "half-baked" and "a negligible piece of West End fluff." In a plush hotel suite in London in 2014, call girl Poopay Dayseer (Mary-Louise Parker), who insists on being called a Specialist Sexual Consultant, is hired by the elderly Mr. Reece (Tom Beckett) not for sex but to witness and sign a confession. Reece and his assistant, Julian (Gerrit Graham), have committed several crimes over the years, not the least of which is murdering Reece's two wives. Poopay signs but then is pursued by the vengeful Julian, so she hides in a closet, which turns out to be a communicating door to another hotel room. But what Poopay enters is the same suite twenty years earlier, and she comes face to face with Reece's second wife, Ruella (Patricia Hodges). She convinces Ruella

that her life is in danger, and the two women plan to thwart Julian's murder attempt. But when Poopay passes through the same door, she finds herself back in 1974, so she tries to warn Reece's first wife, Jessica (Candy Buckley), about Julian and Reece. With the help of the hapless house detective, Harold (David McCallum), the three women outwit Julian and rewrite their own futures. No other play this season was so complicated, yet puzzle master Ayckbourn (this was his forty-ninth play) knew how to sustain his multi-layered plot, helped by an expert cast and Christopher Ashley's sharp direction. Audiences enjoyed the merry confusion for nearly five months.

Off Broadway, at the newly reopened Provincetown Playhouse (where Eugene O'Neill's early one-acts were first performed nearly ninety years before), a troupe called the Playwrights Theatre presented the New York premiere of O'Neill's first full-length play, **Bread and Butter** (8-21-98, Provincetown Playhouse), written when he was twenty-six, never produced in his lifetime, and not published until 1988, when it was found in the Library of Congress. John Brown (Kristoffer Polaha) has always done what his wealthy family (they made their fortune in the hardware business) told him to do. Slated to study law and marry the girl picked out for him, John suddenly breaks away and goes to New York to pursue his dream of being an artist. Of course the family and his fiancée drag him back home. Years later, unhappily married, drinking too much, frequenting his favorite whorehouse, and with all his artistic impulses dried up and dead, John ends his life with a gunshot. While the seeds of many of the great O'Neill works could be observed, the drama was overwritten (a great deal of repetition in the dialogue needed to be cut), overlong, and overstated. But the bare-bones production, directed by Stephen Kennedy Murphy, boasted an eager (if young and inexperienced) cast that brought this theatre history footnote to life.

Broadway's second one-man show in August, **Colin Quinn: An Irish Wake** (8-27-98, Helen Hayes), also boasted a television star, but Quinn could only find an audience for twenty-two showings. Set at the wake of local favorite Jackie Ryan in an Irish Catholic neighborhood in Brooklyn in 1976, the one-hour monologue sought to recreate the various characters gathered to say good-bye to the beloved rascal. Quinn's portrayals were more in the line of stand-up comedy, and the characters were "more vehicles for amusing anecdotes than fully imagined creations."

Quinn and Lou DiMaggio scripted the "dispassionate, mildly amusing" program.

The career of avant-gardist Robert Wilson had been surrealistically dramatized by Anne Bogart in *Bob* (5-5-98) with some success, but few commentators approved of her take on pop artist Andy Warhol in **Culture of Desire** (9-14-98, New York Theatre Workshop), calling it a "tepid satire" and a "boringly one-message work." Warhol (Kelly Maurer) is shot to death in the first scene, then travels through hell with fashion diva Diana Vreeland (Jefferson Mays in drag) as his Virgil-like guide. In Bogart's view (she directed as well as wrote the piece), hell is full of well-dressed people pushing shopping carts and carrying shopping bags, everyone surrounded by familiar Warhol memorabilia: Marilyn Monroe posters, Campbell's soup cans, and Brillo Pad boxes. The startling revelation that America is obsessed with consumerism gave off-off Broadway audiences something to think about for three weeks.

The season's most awarded play and widely acclaimed performance appeared quietly when Barbara Edson's **Wit** (9-17-98, MCC) opened off Broadway. But rave reviews and enthusiastic word of mouth encouraged the play to transfer on October 6 to the larger Union Square, where it stayed for a year and a half. Kathleen Chalfant had been "stealing the show" in supporting roles for years, but few were prepared for her "towering and heartbreaking performance" as Dr. Vivian Bearing, a recognized English literature scholar who faces ovarian cancer with a probing, thorough, and witty sense of discovery. Vivian narrates the action, chronicling her eight-month treatment with candor and wryness. "*The Faerie Queene* this is not," she announces. "It is not my intention to give away the plot, but I think I die in the end." Through a series of humiliating treatments and recollections of her past life, Vivian moves closer and closer to death and finally rises from her bed in bittersweet release when she departs this world. The details of the ordeal were clinical and honest (Vivian is bald throughout, endures graphic pelvic examinations onstage, and even appears naked in the most unerotic of circumstances) but were balanced by Vivian's love of literature (she is a John Donne expert and merrily discusses his works and style throughout). In addition to unanimous praise for Chalfant, Edson's script was equally admired, most critics agreeing with Donald Lyons of the *Wall Street Journal*, who called it "an original and urgent work of art." The play won the Pulitzer Prize at the end of the season, and a tour went out while the original production was still running in New York.

Off Off Broadway's Vineyard Theatre brought back Craig Lucas's *The Dying Gaul* (5-31-98) on September 18 for a five-week encore featuring the same cast that many had admired the previous season. Also off-off Broadway, the Signature Theatre Company dedicated its season to old and new works by John Guare. A revival of *Marco Polo Sings a Solo* (1-12-77) on September 27 opened the tribute, directed by Mel Shapiro, who had staged the original. Critics still found the science fiction fantasy "overgrown and overblown" but applauded Guare's "extravagantly undisciplined" inventiveness. More successful was a revival of Charles Ludlam's gothic spoof *The Mystery of Irma Vep* (10-2-84) on October 1 at the Westside, which entertained audiences for nine months. Everett Quinton (from the original mounting) and Stephen DeRosa played the many wacky characters, and they were well supported by William Ivey Long's outlandish costumes and John Lee Beatty's detailed sets.

Another pseudo-Victorian comedy followed, Evan Smith's **The Uneasy Chair** (10-4-98, Playwrights Horizons), which sought to present a Wildean view of nineteenth-century love and marriage in Britain. Prim and spinsterish Amelia Pickett (Dana Ivey) rents rooms in her very respected household to gentlemen, but she meets her match in Captain Josiah Wickett (Roger Rees), a meticulous man who sets out his demands for a quiet abode with exacting detail. Yet when Wickett tries to help his nephew John Darlington (Paul Fitzgerald) woo Pickett's niece Alexandrina Crosby (Haviland Morris) by writing a letter, the words are misconstrued by the women as a proposal by the Captain for Amelia's hand. The misunderstanding lands Pickett and Wickett in a farcical courtroom trial for breach of promise in which the same barrister (Michael Arkin) represents both sides of the argument. Pickett loses the case and, rather than pay the damages, agrees to marry Amelia. Smith often captured the upper-crust Victorian rhetoric (Amelia exclaims to the audience in one of the play's many asides, "I was on the verge of using profanity, or worse, slang!"), but several critics found the text talky and "overstuffed" and the production "tedious a lot of the time." Rees and Dana were roundly praised, though.

The press did not respond very favorably to Joe DiPietro's extended sitcom **Over the River and Through the Woods** (10-5-98, John Houseman), calling it "strained humor" and "unadulterated corn . . . as spiceless as ketchup," but audiences immediately warmed to the sentimental piece, and it ran into the millennium. When Nick Cristano (Jim Bracchitta), a Manhattan marketing executive, is offered a promotion that requires a move to Seattle, he tries to break the news gently to his four Italian-American grandparents in Hoboken. (His parents are in Florida, and the four senior citizens fawn over Nick during his weekly visits for dinner.) The fear of losing their Nicky to the West Coast prompts the grandparents into action, trying anything to keep him close by. They even play matchmakers and hope Nick will fall for the unmarried nurse whom they invite to dinner, Caitlin O'Hare (Marsha Dietlein). But Nick suffers an anxiety attack, and in the silly but heartfelt care of his doting grandparents, he realizes that family means more to him than a new job. Much of the comedy concerned the foursome's individual peccadilloes: Emma (Marie Lillo) sends a mass card for any occasion, Nunzio (Dick Latessa) uses cockeyed logic to win at Trivial Pursuit, Aida (Joan Copeland) believes food is the remedy for any crisis, and Frank (Val Avery) won't admit his sight is going, despite a series of fender benders. The play may have come from New Jersey's American Stage Company and the Berkshire Theatre Festival, but it was clearly heading to community theatre heaven.

Critics also dismissed **Duet! A Romantic Fable** (10-6-98, Actors' Playhouse), a "plainly—even proudly—lame" comedy by Gregory Jackson and Erin Quinn Purcell that still managed to run three months. Mike (Jackson), a nervous nerd and lounge singer, falls for the ravishing blonde Marcia (Purcell); she, in turn, is attracted to the geek because of his suave singing style. But during a romantic moonlit walk, Mike shows off by swallowing a dead frog. Marcia is repulsed but, after a ludicrous dream sequence in which she sees her dashing lover as a frog prince, realizes no one is perfect and resumes her romance with Mike. Like *Over the River and Through the Woods*, the play aped television comedy (in this case the outlandish humor of early *Saturday Night Live* programs), but the result was "knowingly sophomoric" rather than daring.

That same night a much more serious but just as shallow entry opened off-off Broadway, Edward Napier's domestic drama **'Til the Rapture Comes** (10-6-98, WPA), which boasted a strong performance by Pamela Payton-Wright as another in a long line of monster mothers. Althea Dale Walker was an army nurse during World War II and now, in the mid-1970s, still has night-

mares about her brother killed in battle and the many maimed soldiers she tended to at the VA hospital. After an overdose of Seconal, Althea is confined to her West Virginia home, where she torments her lawyer husband, Wilbur (Richard Poe), her two sons, Ian (Jace Blankfort) and Willy (Zach Shaffer), and her foul-mouthed housekeeper, Petunia (Cynthia Darrow). Teetering on the line between fantasy and insanity, Althea was a juicy character, and Payton-Wright made the most of it, even if the play went nowhere while everyone onstage made a lot of noise.

No one would have paid much attention to the Blue Light Theatre Company's **Oedipus** (10-11-98, CSC), Dare Clubb's take on Sophocles' drama, if Billy Crudup and Frances McDormand had not been in the cast. Instead the "four-hour long orgy of self-indulgence" was roundly panned, and there was more sympathy than praise for the two stars. In this retelling of the legend, Oedipus (Crudup) is still in Corinth, where he lusts after his adopted mother, Merope (McDormand), prompting the (unintentionally) funniest line of the season: "I can't marry you; I'm not your mother."

No other play in America made more news this season than Terrence McNally's **Corpus Christi** (10-13-98, City Center). When the Manhattan Theatre Club had announced the previous spring that it would produce the new play and word got out about its subject matter (Jesus Christ as a homosexual and his disciples as gay followers), Catholic groups protested and anonymous threats to burn down the theatre followed. In a panic, MTC canceled the production, which brought a wave of protests from artists and civil libertarians crying censorship. Embarrassed, the theatre company reinstated the play. Two hundred police were on hand opening night and patrons were required to go through metal detectors as they passed the protest signs of the two thousand members of the Catholic League for Religious and Civil Rights and other groups. Of course the seven-week engagement was sold out long before the play actually opened. But what the audience saw inside the theatre had to be the greatest disappointment of the season. McNally skimped on humor, wit, or insight and told his allegorical tale in a somber, stilted, and pretentious way that left critics numb (Ben Brantley in the *New York Times* pronounced it "as stimulating as a glass of chocolate milk") and arts activists with egg on their faces. Joshua (Anson Mount) grows up gay in Corpus Christi, Texas (McNally's hometown), lonely and not fitting in with the usual crowd.

So he leaves home and hitchhikes across the West with a blind truck driver (whom he cures), ending up at a gay wedding in Cana, where he works other miracles. Soon he has twelve disciples, ranging from a millionaire lawyer who gives away all to follow Joshua to an overendowed street hustler. Eventually Joshua is proclaimed the gay Messiah and the person to bring the AIDS epidemic to an end. But he returns to Texas, is betrayed by his lover Judas, is crucified by the locals, and dies (without a hint of a resurrection). One of the disciples turned to the audience at the end and admitted that "maybe other people have told His story better," and everyone enthusiastically agreed.

Radio and nightclub comic Rob Bartlett attempted to write a play, but **More to Love: A Big Fat Comedy** (10-15-98, Eugene O'Neill) was a ninety-minute stand-up routine disguised by scenery and two peripheral characters. As comic Rob (Bartlett) approaches his fortieth birthday, he despairs that his career has not taken off while some of his friends from the old days are well established. Ordered by his wife, Alice (Dana Reeve), to clean out the garage one Saturday morning, Rob addresses the audience while he works and awaits word from his agent, Maxine (Joyce Van Patten), about a possible spot on an HBO-TV special. Much of the evening was Rob doing one-liners about his Brooklyn upbringing, airplane travel, and his love of food, the two women making brief appearances to break up the act. (For some reason Alice did a bump-and-grind routine, singing about how Rob is "my extra chunky hunk o' burning love.") Reviews were mildly dismissive ("only occasionally rises beyond mediocrity"), and the Broadway entry closed after four performances.

Film actress Holly Hunter returned to the theatre with **Impossible Marriage** (10-15-98, Roundabout) by her favorite playwright, Beth Henley. (Hunter had appeared in seven Henley stage works at various locales.) But the reunion met with mixed notices, most commentators enjoying the delightful cast but finding Henley's comedy "sometimes insufferably precious and sometimes disarmingly charming." In a lush garden on the Kingsley estate outside Savannah, Georgia, the family prepares for the May wedding between sprightly young Pandora (Gretchen Cleevely) and the older Edvard Lunt (Christopher McCann), a European poet prone to melancholia. Pandora's mother, Kandall (Lois Smith), is not pleased with the match, and she enlists the help of her elder daughter, Floral (Hunter), to break off the mar-

riage without causing a scandal. Floral is married to the narcissistic Jonesy (Jon Tenney) and is very pregnant, but that does not stop the restless gal from rolling down hills in the mud when the spirit moves her. Sidney (Daniel London), Edvard's son by a previous marriage, arrives to announce that both he and his mother will commit suicide if Edvard remarries, thereby exposing a series of secrets and revelations: Floral and Joney have never consummated their marriage, and the father of her baby is the guilt-ridden Reverend Jonathan Larence (Alan Mandell), Kandall is seriously ill and is drawn to the mother-fixated Sidney; and Pandora loves Edvard only because he worships her and put her in one of his books. By the end of the weekend Sidney tries to shoot his father only to wound himself in the foot, Pandora and Edvard elope, and Floral and Larence decide to attempt another "impossible" relationship. The problematic script was helped by Stephen Wadworth's ethereal direction and Thomas Lynch's verdant garden which Martin Pakledinaz lit with magical effect, creating a fantasy atmosphere for these rather unlikely characters. The Roundabout was able to keep the comedy on the boards for ninety-five performances.

When Tracy Letts's squalid drama **Killer Joe** (10-18-98, Soho Playhouse) appeared briefly off-off Broadway in 1993, it was little noticed, but the play went on to engagements in Edinburgh and London, where it was popular. Returning to New York, the melodrama about white-trash Texans found a cult following off Broadway and ran out the season. The Smith family lives in a rusting trailer with nothing but beer in the refrigerator and Doritos in the cupboard. Beer-bellied Ansel (Marc A. Nelson) can't seem to hold on to his second wife, the slutty Sharla (Amanda Plummer), but he does have a yen for his teenage daughter, Dottie (Sarah Paulson). When brother Chris (Mike Shannon) gets in debt over a drug deal gone wrong, the family plans to kill off Ansel's first wife so that Dottie can inherit the $50,000 life insurance policy and pay everybody off. They hire Killer Joe Cooper (Scott Glenn), a cold-blooded cop without scruples and with a lusting for Dottie as well, but everything goes wrong and the piece ends in a bloodbath. Critics either fervently cheered or despised the violent and quirky drama, describing it as either a "stunning, uncomfortable, funny experience" or a "vicious and repellent little Tarantino-era play."

Mark R. Shapiro's **Retribution** (10-24-98, Lamb's) may have been the first thriller to use the Holocaust for its contrived plot twists. Concentration camp survivor Jud Kramer (Jack Laufer) is a prominent director in 1965 and is soon to stage a Broadway play about the Holocaust with his movie-star wife, Marianne (Jenna Stern), in the lead. But a mysterious man named Carl Walkowitz (Dennis Christopher), who claims to come from the same death camp as Jud, enters the Kramers' lives. Even though he is a limping, one-eyed oddity, he worms his way into the production and even manages to seduce Marianne. (She is supposedly drawn to him because he will help her understand her husband's past suffering.) Soon Walkowitz is sabotaging the production and, in a showdown onstage, reveals Jud's sordid past (he cooperated with the Nazis) and exacts his revenge. The press was nonplused, though several commentators felt the play traded on "emotional opportunism" by having Jud describe atrocities in the death camp for no other reason than to juice up the "plodding suspenser." The commercial entry only lasted twenty-nine performances.

Critics could not determine whether Michael J. Chepiga's **Getting and Spending** (10-25-98, Helen Hayes) was a comedy, a drama, or a sermon, but they did agree that "the plot is a jerrybuilt jumble of stock situations and lame contrivances." Successful Manhattan lawyer Richard O'Neill (David Rasche) is too honest and upright for his profession ("Injustice made me angry," he philosophizes), so he retires to a monastery in Kentucky. There he is sought out by the investment banker Victoria Phillips (Linda Purl), who has been indicted for insider trading and needs Richard to take her case. He refuses to listen to Victoria until she threatens to run bare-breasted through the monastery. After some initial spatting, the two fall in love, and he goes to court for her. In a moral twist, it turns out that Victoria is as noble as he is, raising lots of money for homeless people. The "dreary" and "inept" play struggled for a month on Broadway, then shuttered.

Aisle-sitters were equally at a loss as how to define the Australian **Wolf Lullaby** (10-28-98, Atlantic), Hilary Bell's examination of a child murderer, which seemed at times to be more a case study than a play. Nine-year-old Lizzie Gael (played by adult Kate Blumberg) lives in a small town in Tasmania with her hairdresser mother, Angela (Mary McCann), and usually absent father, Warren (Jordan Lage). Lizzie has shown signs of mischief, such as shoplifting for no reason, but when she leads the police to the dead body of a two-and-a-half-year-old child in an empty lot, suspicion falls on her. The blood on Lizzie's tennis shoes matches that of the dead boy, and Sergeant Ray Armstrong (Larry Bryggman), who leads the investigation, poses questions to the parents that no one (including the author) can easily answer. Was it the parents' fault? Or is Lizzie just, as Armstrong puts it, "a bad egg"? The play drew no firm conclusions, for Lizzie was portrayed as a complex and disarming figure unlike the tidy villainess in Maxwell Anderson's old chestnut *The Bad Seed* (12-8-54), which some critics compared it to.

Musical star Leslie Uggams turned to the dramatic stage with John Henry Redwood's **The Old Settler** (10-28-98, Primary Stages), and both star and author were warmly commended by the press. Elizabeth Borny (Uggams) is an "old settler," an old-fashioned term for a woman approaching middle age without a prospect for a husband. She lives with her sharp-tongued sister, Quilly (Lynda Gravatt), in Harlem in the early 1940s, and they take in boarders to help pay the rent. Young and naive Husband Witherspoon (Godfrey L. Simmons, Jr.) comes to New York from South Carolina to be reunited with his girlfriend, the sassy floozie Lou Bessie Preston (Rosalyn Coleman), and boards with Elizabeth and Quilly. It doesn't take Husband long to see that Lou Bessie has changed and has lost interest in a country boy. He goes to Elizabeth for comfort, and soon, much to Quilly's disapproval, he and the fifty-five-year-old "settler" have fallen in love. After dealing with Quilly's jealousy, Elizabeth accepts Husband's proposal of marriage, and the two plan to return to the South together. The drama was well written and old-fashioned, "but its sentiment is honest and never mawkish." The four-member cast was admired, but Uggams was the evening's chief surprise, giving an "incandescent performance . . . of restraint and dignity." The play, which had been seen previously in various regional theatres, ran three months.

The next night, Laurence Holder's biographical drama *Zora Neale Hurston* (2-4-90) was revived off Broadway at the American Place with Elizabeth Van Dyke as the title author and Joseph Edward playing all the men in her life. The revival ran a month and a half; Hurston would return as a character in another play later in the season. Five classic revivals, ranging from the ancient Greeks to Beckett, opened off Broadway within a month of each other. The Public offered Shakespeare's late romance *Pericles* on November 1 at the Martinson, and while some aisle-sitters found Brian Kulick's highly stylized production intriguing, most decreed the acting hopelessly floundering.

More interesting was Mark Wendland's steel-frame set that moved into different configurations to create the many lands that Pericles (Jay Goede) encountered on his travels.

Another off-off-Broadway play to resurface after a time was Kenneth Lonergan's **This Is Our Youth** (11-3-98, Second Stage), which had been seen briefly two years earlier but stayed for six months this time. Lonergan, a product of the first annual Young Playwrights Festival in 1983, recreated the aimless sons and daughters of wealthy Upper West Siders in 1982 who have everything but are still lacking. Post-adolescent Warren Straub (Mark Ruffalo), the son of a rich lingerie retailer with shady business deals on the side, is mentally and physically abused by his father, so he steals $15,000 from his dad's briefcase and leaves home. Warren finds sanctuary in the apartment of his best friend, Dennis Ziegler (Mark Rosenthal), an independent twenty-year-old who occasionally deals in drugs, and the two decide to engage in some big-time coke deals. While Dennis goes out to meet his contacts, Warren has a fumbling love scene with Jessica Goldman (Missy Yager), a fashion design student, as the two unsuccessfully try to find more than sex in their relationship. She leaves Warren, and Dennis returns to have a contrived fight over the value of their friendship, the two youths as dissatisfied and confused as before. The plotting in the "sad, revelatory play" was awkward, but critics complimented the acute performances and Mark Brokaw's steady direction.

Broadway's third one-person offering of the season was **Sandra Bernhard: I'm Still Here . . . Damn It!** (11-5-98, Booth), which brought the television and concert stand-up comedienne to the Street rather than Off Broadway, the venue for her popular *Without You I'm Nothing* (13-31-88). The mockingly sincere Bernhard covered such topics as celebrity, rock music (she even growled a few songs herself), and her live-in girlfriend. (Bernhard was an early icon of lesbian visibility.) Only fans came, but they were legion enough to keep Bernhard on the boards for two months.

A much different solo turn followed. Seventy-eight-year-old producer Alexander H. Cohen recalled his long and illustrious career in the theatre with **Star Billing** (11-9-98, Douglas Fairbanks), a chatty, personal journey that told more about the many stars he worked with over the years than about himself. But the anecdotes were delicious, the cast of characters (ranging from Marlene Dietrich to Jerry Lewis to Richard Burton) fascinating, and Cohen's unmistakable love for the

theatre heartwarming. As one commentator described the evening, "it was like being at a dinner party whose host is chef, charmer, and resident character all at once."

With the clamor over *Corpus Christi* quickly forgotten, the Manhattan Theatre Club offered a "cozy family comedy-drama," Shelagh Stephenson's **The Memory of Water** (11-10-98, City Center), for its subscribers. A Yorkshire family is reunited when the mother, Vi, dies, bringing her three daughters together for reminiscing, quarreling, the reopening of old wounds, and the revelation of not-so-startling secrets. The eldest, Mary (J. Smith-Cameron), is a wisecracking woman who is deeply troubled underneath. Teresa (Suzanne Bertish), who stayed home and cared for Vi, is frustrated with her small-town existence and spills all her emotions after a few drinks. The youngest sibling, Catherine (Seana Kofoed), is a reckless, spoiled girl who resents everyone. Also making occasional appearances is the ghost of Vi (Robin Moseley) herself, casting off acid remarks and putdowns. Much of the play was overly familiar and rather contrived, but the press enjoyed the American-British cast, especially Bertish and Smith-Cameron. John Tillinger directed with a sure hand, and James Noone designed the single set, the mother's surreal bedroom suggesting a dreamlike existence.

Canada's Stratford Festival brought two of its summer offerings to the City Center on November 12 and ran them in rep for two weeks. *Much Ado About Nothing* presented a much older Benedick (Brian Bedford) and Beatrice (Martha Henry) than usual, but Richard Monette's production gained a wistful and autumnal quality that was touchingly funny. Less impressive was a routine mounting of Molière's *The Miser* that featured William Hutt as Harpagon.

It took quite a while for Arthur Miller's 1991 drama **The Ride Down Mt. Morgan** (11-16-98, Newman) to reach New York (it had been produced in London and regionally), and critical reaction when it did arrive was so pallid it only stayed a month at the Public. Lyman (Patrick Stewart), a former poet and now a Manhattan insurance executive, became bored with his wife, Theo (Frances Conroy), so he took up a second life with Leah (Meg Gibson), a sexy younger woman in Elmira, driving back and forth between his two families (he has a child by each woman). This familiar farce plot, most recently seen in the British *Run for Your Wife* (3-7-89), was turned by Miller into an introspective drama about guilt and a search for fulfillment. When

Lyman's car goes over an embankment on Mt. Morgan and he is hospitalized, both "wives" come to his bedside, Theo discovering the existence of Leah for the first time. This results in a heated three-way discussion and some flashbacks that rarely were theatrical, although Theo does suffer a mild nervous breakdown by the end. Most critics declared the work "ponderous" and "ultimately tedious" and even found the fine cast at a loss. All the same, the production found itself on Broadway the next season.

The Classic Stage Company enlisted some film stars for its November 17 mounting of Beckett's *Waiting for Godot* (4-19-56), but the production was far from gimmicky or celebrity-crazed. John Turturro and Tony Shalhoub played the two tramps, Christopher Lloyd was Pozzo, and Richard Spore was a mesmerizing Lucky. The off-off-Broadway revival ran five weeks. Bill Irwin and David Shiner brought their unique theatre piece *Fool Moon* (2-25-93) back again to Broadway on November 22 and entertained old and new fans at the Brooks Atkinson for forty-nine performances.

Actor David Marshall Grant made a promising playwriting debut with his "compassionate yet utterly unsentimental" **Snakebit** (11-22-98, Grove Street Playhouse), which extended its off-off-Broadway run, then transferred on March 1 to the Century Center, where it ran an additional six months. When a trio of friends gather in a sleek Hollywood pad, all sorts of contrasting elements meet: hetero- and homosexual, lover and wife, New Yorker and Los Angelino, friend and enemy. California social worker Michael (Geoffrey Nauffts) is considering giving up on L.A. and returning to Connecticut when his best friend, Jonathan (David Alan Basche), a New York actor on the verge of a film breakthrough, arrives with his wife, Jenifer (Jodi Markell). Although Michael is gay, he once had an affair with Jenifer. Other issues complicating the situation include Jonathan and Jenifer's ailing daughter back in Manhattan, Michael's obsessive feeling for one of his young clients, and the appearance of a mysterious Young Man (Michael Weston) who seems to be intertwined in all their pasts. Several critics applauded both the play and the precise performances.

A British-American revival of Sophocles' *Electra* opened on December 3 at the Ethel Barrymore, was greeted with enthusiastic notices, and stayed through the end of March, one of the longest Broadway runs on record for a Greek tragedy. Frank McGuinness's new adaptation was considered "robust, straightforward and contemporary" by the press, and David Leveaux's stark production was also commended. Johan Engels's set was a junk heap of discarded machinery and industrial waste with a steady dripping of water, giving the play its relentless tempo. But it was the powerful cast that was the revival's main attraction. Zoe Wanamaker was a bitter, biting Electra, and though some felt her performance too actorish at times, it was theatrically enthralling. Claire Bloom gave a stately and elegant interpretation of Clytemnestra, and the mother-daughter scenes between her and Wanamaker crackled with excitement. They were given able support by Michael Cumpsty (Orestes), Marin Hinkle (Chrysothemis), Mijana Jokovic (Chorus), and Pat Carroll (Chorus of Mycenae). The production had been seen previously at London's intimate Donmar Warehouse and at New Jersey's McCarter Theatre.

The Public offered a "small treasure" with Diana Son's "entirely engaging new play" **Stop Kiss** (12-6-98, Shiva). Sara (Sandra Oh) leaves behind her suffocating parents and overprotective boyfriend Peter (Rick Holmes), in St. Louis and moves to New York, where she gets a job teaching at an elementary school in the Bronx. She soon meets Callie (Jessica Hecht), an aimless and restless woman who reports traffic conditions from a helicopter for a local news station. The two seem to have little in common, but before long Callie is neglecting her off-and-on boyfriend, George (Kevin Carroll), to spend more time with Sara. Late one night, walking home from a Greenwich Village bar, Callie and Sara find the courage to admit their feelings, and they kiss each other. A man sees them, taunts them, and, when provoked by Sara, beats them up; Sara ends up in a coma in the hospital. Her parents and Peter come to New York and plan to take her back to St. Louis to recuperate, but Callie vows to fight to keep Sara in her life. What made the straightforward tale theatrically interesting was the way Son told her story, cutting back and forth from scenes with the two of them before the attack to scenes afterward in the hospital, all culminating with that crucial moment when they kissed. Appreciative reviews helped the play run three months.

When Terrence McNally introduced homosexuality to the New Testament in *Corpus Christi*, outrage followed. When Paul Rudnick did the same for the Old Testament, the only reaction was unconcerned laughter. **The Most Fabulous Story Ever Told** (12-10-98, New York Theatre Workshop) was a comic take on the Garden of Eden story with Adam (Alan Tudyk) and Steve

(Juan Carlos Hernandez) as the first humans, discovering their gayness and enjoying unbridled sex until they are cast out of the Garden and have to learn to "go shopping" for themselves. The world's first two lesbians, Jane (Becky Ann Baker) and Mabel (Kathryn Meisle), join the two men, and together they weather the Flood and the news that heterosexuals are in the neighborhood and are flaunting their baby-making talents. By the second act, it is Christmas Eve in contemporary New York with the same actors as two couples dealing with gay life and AIDS near the end of the millennium. At their Christmas party, discussion of God and His True Identity turns sentimental, and the play loses some of its punch, even though Jane gives birth during a wedding ceremony with Mabel. (Rudnick continued to be better at dialogue and character types than plot.) But reviewers enjoyed the one-liners ("Oh look. It's a poinsettia . . . the gift that won't die!"), the likable cast, and Christopher Ashley's playful direction. Business was brisk during the month-long engagement, so the comedy reopened at the Minetta Lane on January 29 and ran three more months.

Off-Off-Broadway's Drama Dept. found few compliments with Frank Pugliese's **"Hope" Is the Thing with Feathers** (12-10-98, Greenwich House), a "turgid and static" new play that was only kept on the boards for two weeks. Six characters, given such generic names as Boy, Girl, Old Man, Old Woman, and so on, are literally up in the air about their lives. (Wendall K. Harrington's set was all sky with the actors perched on different levels.) A poor Bronx tough (Keith Nobbs) impregnates his cliché-spouting girlfriend (Paula Garces) and knowingly infects her with HIV. A dying doctor (Robert Hogan) and his protective wife (Maria Tucci) appeal to their daughter (Cynthia Nixon) in California to return east for a final visit, but she is all involved with her black anthropologist boyfriend (Avery Glymph), who's more interested in health food recipes than in her. The characters remained dangling, yet the play was declared hopelessly earthbound, though there was some applause for the cast (especially the always reliable Nixon).

The second production of the month to come from Britain's Donmar Warehouse was **The Blue Room** (12-13-98, Cort), David Hare's first of three Broadway entries this season. (All three were financial hits, none more so than this first outing.) New Yorkers had heard about this new contemporary version of Arthur Schnitzler's *La Ronde* from the raves that crossed the Atlantic. London critics had forgotten their British reserve and acclaimed movie actress Nicole Kidman the sexiest thing to hit the West End in years. While the critical response in Manhattan was not as effusive ("a chilly, empty experience"), Kidman's appeal was just as strong, and the limited three-month engagement quickly sold out. Two actors, Kidman and Iain Glen, played all ten copulating couples, giving broad, sketch-like portrayals as they ran through costume changes, undressing, fornicating, and dressing in quick succession. Kidman was considered a floundering stage actress, but she milked the eroticism of the piece effectively, so most spectators left satisfied. Stage actor Glen was not much better, though his nude cartwheel onstage kept him from disappearing into the blue scenery.

That same night, aisle-sitters remained unsure of *Bosoms and Neglect* (5-3-79), the second John Guare play revived by the Signature Theatre in its tribute season; most still thought it adventurous but severely flawed. All agreed that Mary Louise Wilson brought "an electric charge" to the role of the suffocating mother, Henny, but she was available for other work after thirteen performances.

Brian Murray's riveting performance as an aging gay actor was the focal point of (and only reason to recommend) Jim Luigs's **Spread Eagle** (12-15-98, WPA), which was based on the sad demise of British character actor George Rose. Toby Arundel (Murray) makes the talk-show rounds and maintains a witty and cultured demeanor, keeping his homosexuality a secret. But when he visits a fellow actor at his villa in Mexico, Toby falls for the attractive houseboy Javier (Matthew Saldivar), and the two engage in a curious mating game. Soon Toby has bought the house and moved the youth into the master bedroom with him, even going so far as to officially adopt him as well. But when Toby starts to give acting lessons to the new houseboy, Diego (Joe Quintero), Javier gets so jealous he murders Toby. Some of the scenes were potent and revealing, others melodramatic and forced. But Murray was the show, portraying the reticent Toby "with moving delicacy."

Even a quartet of fine actors could not save Laura Cahill's **Mercy** (12-15-98, Vineyard), yet another play this season about aimless youth. Sarah (Amelia Campbell), a documentary filmmaker in her twenties, lives on the Upper West Side and lusts after Bo (Matt Keeslar), who claims to be a "New Jersey cowboy." Her friend Isobel (Marianne Hagan) is panting over Stu (Adam Trese), a cynical medic (and Sarah's ex-boyfriend), whose idea of wit is to make fun of the suburbs. At a dinner party, the foursome fumble with sex and language, failing to communicate with either. None of the characters was as interesting as they kept telling each other they were, and critics thought all four performers more intriguing than their dreary roles.

Amy Freed's comedy **Freedomland** (12-16-98, Playwrights Horizons), about a dysfunctional family in upstate New York, was highly thought of in California, where it originated, but met with tepid notices in Manhattan and only stayed two weeks. New York artist Sigrid (Veanne Cox), whose forte is painting pictures of hobo clowns, visits her family home with art journalist Titus (Jeff Whitty) in tow. Her father, Noah (Dakin Matthews), is a former flower child who taught comparative religion in college for many years; now he is philosophical about his collection of power tools. Sigrid's sister, Polly (Carrie Preston), is a Greek-studies student and a fragile creature (she falls apart when Sigrid paints her as a clown) while their brother, Seth, hides his insecurity behind machismo posturing. Seth's pregnant girlfriend, Lori (Heather Goldenhersh), has run away from her abusive husband and is basing her future on *The Lord of the Rings*. This band of eccentrics engage in sometimes clever, often artificial, bantering for a few days before being drawn together in the warm memory of visiting the early theme park Freedomland in their youth. Notices considered the cast bright and engaging but judged the script was not "as deep as it seems to think it is."

London's Almeida Theatre Company brought Diana Rigg to BAM in two Racine tragedies on January 5, staging *Phèdre* and *Britannicus* in repertory for two and a half weeks. Rigg's *Phèdre* was widely praised, one critic describing her performance as "the wrenching cries of a soul rent by a shameful passion she's powerless to deny." Toby Stephens, as her stepson, Hippolytus, struck some aisle-sitters as too mannered, but most appreciated his petulant, spoiled Nero in *Britannicus*. Rigg played his manipulative mother, Agrippina, with relish, and Kevin McKidd was enthralling as the ousted title character. Both productions were staged simply but effectively by Jonathan Kent, and Maria Bjornson provided elegant sets and costumes for the repertory.

Also from England came new playwright Joe Penhall whose award-winning drama **Some Voices** (1-7-99, St. Clements) received an American production by the New Group for a month off Broadway. When Ray (Jamie Harris) is supposedly cured of his schizophrenia and released from a mental hospital, he moves in with his brother, Pete (Max Baker), in his dreary London flat. Refusing to take his pills or see his social worker, Ray embarks on a new life but then gets involved with a quarreling couple from Ireland. Dave (David Thornton) is an alcoholic brute who beats his girlfriend, Laura (Ana Reeder), so she is drawn to Ray's tenderness and even his odd behavior patterns. Added to this nervous triangle is Ives (Mitchell McGuire), another recently released hospital patient, who looks up Ray for a place to stay. With his restaurant business failing, Pete loses his patience with the lot of them, and the two brothers have a showdown that reduces both to desperate clinging children. Critics thought the play "well observed if ultimately predictable" but saluted Harris and Baker for their truthful portrayals.

A. R. Gurney took on a much more serious subject than usual for his **Far East** (1-10-99, Mitzi E. Newhouse), yet he still successfully captured the unflappable Wasp sense of duty even through pain and regret. On an American naval base in Japan in 1954, the rich Milwaukee youth "Sparky" Watts (Michael Hayden) is finishing out his tour of duty by having an affair with a Japanese waitress from the officers' club. His commanding officer, Captain James Anderson (Bill Smitrovich), sees the dalliance as a healthy extracurricular activity (after all, he himself kept a Filipino girl before he settled down and married), but the captain's wife, Julia (Lisa Emery), who knows Sparky's folks back home, confronts the youth about his responsibility to his family. Although Sparky claims he will marry his mistress (who never appears in the play), he soon finds himself attracted to the older and neglected Julia. In a subplot, Sparky's friend Bob Munger (Connor Trinneer) is being blackmailed by his male Japanese lover. When the navy finds out, Bob is court-martialed and discharged. By the final scene, Sparky has left his mistress, Julia has decided to stick with her husband, and the three sit silently together on a plane taking them back to the States, where they will bravely do right by family and class. Although the script met with mixed notices, the cast and Daniel Sullivan's engaging production were applauded, and audiences came to Lincoln Center for six months to see it.

Best-selling novelists Frank and Malachy McCourt fashioned episodes from their autobiographies *Angela's Ashes* and *A Monk Swimming* into the two-person memoir **A Couple of Bla-guards** (1-13-99, Triad). Shay Duffin and Mickey Kelly played the two brothers, plus an array of other characters, as they grew up in Ireland and eventually found themselves in Manhattan as struggling writers. Alternately farcical and senti-mental, the play was meanderingly scattershot, but the stories and the performers were enjoyable enough to keep audiences entertained for two months. In May the duo returned for an encore and stayed another four months.

A memoir of a different tone followed: Athol Fugard's **The Captain's Tiger** (1-19-99, City Cen-ter), which received disappointing notices ("a minor-key and ultimately rather uninvolving play") and only ran three weeks at the Manhattan Theatre Club. In 1952, a young Author (Fugard) works as a gofer on a cargo ship traveling from South Africa to Japan while he tries to write his first novel, a memoir of his mother, Betty, and her difficult life. The ghost of Betty (Felicity Jones) appears throughout, helping and question-ing the author until he finally gives up the novel, too haunted by her memory to put it in words.

For playgoers not satisfied with *Electra, Phèdre,* and *Britannicus,* more classic tragedy was availa-ble at the American Place, where Theatre for a New Audience presented *The Iphigenia Cycle* on January 24, an evening of Euripides' *Iphigenia at Aulis* and *Iphigenia in Tauris* combined in a trans-lation by Nicholas Rudall. But these obscure dra-mas were made all the more obscure by director JoAnne Akalaitis, who set them in a TV studio where a "tell-all" talk show is in progress. The "unilluminating, unmoving, and unentertaining" travesty pleased or irritated audiences for a month.

Off-Off-Broadway's Jewish Repertory Theatre's revival of Leonard Spigelgass's *A Majority of One* (2-16-59) on January 24 also ran a month, but the "shamelessly sentimental" comedy about the courtship of a Brooklyn Jewish widow (Phyllis Newman) and a Japanese businessman (Randall Duk Kim) still had life in it and played rather well.

Caryl Churchill remained as inventive as ever with her new work **Blue Heart** (1-30-99, BAM), an evening of one-acts that deconstructed tradi-tional playwriting with hilarious and then sober-ing results. In *Heart's Desire,* an English family awaits the return of a daughter who has been living in Australia. Their inane small talk while they wait is stopped, repeated with slight changes, then repeated again and again until the audience can fill in the missing phrases. Just when

the discussion gets most ludicrous, three terror-ists burst into the house and gun down the whole family. After a pause, they haltingly start their mundane dialogue again, but it is now strained and somber. *Blue Kettle* concerns a youth, Derek (Pearce Quigley), who approaches a series of women on the street, claiming to each one that he is the son she gave up for adoption years ago. The encounters are somewhat realistic at first, but soon the words "blue" and "kettle" are sub-stituted for other words and the banter takes on a Beckett-like absurdism. Eventually the title's words are the only ones spoken. By the last en-counter it is clear that Derek has a mother, but she is dying and he is desperately searching for a replacement.

Another British import, Harold Pinter's **Ashes to Ashes** (2-7-99, Gramercy), was also intriguing but much less satisfying. An English couple, Dev-lin (David Strathairn) and Rebecca (Lindsay Dun-can), discuss the wife's former lover for fifty minutes; he seems obsessed by the unknown man, she seems distant from the events she re-lates. This being Pinter territory, the lover and the details of the past may all be in Rebecca's imagination (or in Devlin's, for that matter). Au-diences were invited to stay for a discussion after the short piece and, the play being archly oblique, many of them did. Critical reaction was mixed, but Duncan was unanimously adulated for her "mysteriously incandescent" performance. The Roundabout kept the drama on the boards for seventy-eight performances.

Bad-boy playwright Nicky Silver had been called a variety of things by reviewers, but not until **The Eros Trilogy** (2-8-99, Vineyard) was his work described as "sentimental" and "pedes-trian." Over a period of twenty-five years, the uptight housewife Miriam (Betty Buckley in a rare non-musical role) writes letters to her gay son, Roger (T. Scott Cunningham), beginning when he is ten years old at summer camp. As with A. R. Gurney's *Love Letters* (8-22-89), the two sit at desks on opposite sides of the stage and read their letters aloud—she discussing her failed marriage, bouts with alcoholism, and the discov-ery of guilt-free sex; he telling about his sexual awakening, going to study acting at NYU, and his various failed love affairs. This routine set of epis-tles was preceded by two monologues that opened the evening: a gay youth (Zak Orth) ag-onizing over his obsession with an unknown man, and his mother (Buckley) bemoaning how crass the world has become (everyone spits on the sidewalk these days) and finding escape in the arms of her young lover. The playlets were not well received, but Buckley fans filled the small house for the three-week engagement.

The most awarded revival of the season was the fiftieth-anniversary mounting of Arthur Miller's *Death of a Salesman* (2-10-49) on February 10 at the Eugene O'Neill. Brian Dennehy found the gleam of hope as well as the despair in Willy Loman, and Elizabeth Franz made his wife, Linda, a strong, unbending woman. They were given firm support by Kevin Anderson (Biff), Ted Koch (Happy), and Howard Witt (Charley), all under Robert Falls's fine-tuned direction. (The production had originated and been polished at Chicago's Goodman Theatre.) Riding on enthusiastic reviews and a clutch of awards (Dennehy, Franz, and Falls all won Tonys, and the play was voted Best Revival), the drama ran 274 performances.

Also from Chicago came Jonathan Harvey's **Beautiful Thing** (2-14-99, Cherry Lane), a British play (that had inspired a popular movie) not yet produced in New York. In Southeast London, working-class teenager Jaime (Matt Stinton) has only one friend in the world, the outcast misfit Leah (Susan Bennett), who is obsessed by the memory of singer Mama Cass. When a neighboring teen, Ste (Daniel Eric Gold), escapes from his abusive father and is invited to live with Jaime and his single mother, Sandra (Kirsten Sahs), the two boys are attracted to each other, first as friends and then as lovers. Some aisle-sitters thought the play better than the film; others judged it less effective. Fans of the movie came for four months to see for themselves.

That same night, the Classic Stage Company featured two stars in its updated version of Molière's *The Misanthrope*. Roger Rees essayed the world-weary Alceste (now a screenwriter in Hollywood) and Uma Thurman his Célimène (here called Jennifer, an American film star) in Martin Crimp's adaptation set in the movie business. The conceit only partially worked (jokes about Steven Spielberg quickly grew thin), but Crimp's rhymed couplets were not without bite and playfulness. Rees was quite adept at the facetious style, though Thurman (in her stage debut) rarely could keep pace with him.

Many commentators were disappointed in Paula Vogel's "cartoon of a play" **The Mineola Twins** (2-18-99, Roundabout) but enjoyed Swoozie Kurtz's double performance and Joe Mantello's lively production. The comedy follows the lives of twin sisters from Mineola, Long Island, from the Eisenhower era to the Reagan years, watching them deal (in very different ways) with high school, losing their virginity, marriage, children, social changes, the Vietnam War, and the women's movement. Myrna is the typical "good" girl who won't sleep with her fiancé, Jim (Mo Gaffney in male drag), before the wedding. Myra is the perennial "bad" girl who willingly shacks up with Jim to relieve his sexual frustration. Myrna becomes an uptight, conservative housewife, has a nervous breakdown, and later hosts a right-wing radio show. Myra leaves Mineola behind for Greenwich Village, becomes an anti-war activist, and robs a bank, ending up a lesbian and a women's libber. The two sisters rarely communicate but face each other with defiance and affection when they meet during a demonstration at an abortion clinic at the end of the play. Vogel's sociopolitical points were clumsy, and the characters were stereotypic, but the comedy had some truly funny scenes, and Kurtz played the two sisters with high-flying abandon.

Perhaps the most powerful play on Broadway this season was Tennessee Williams's **Not About Nightingales** (2-25-99, Circle in the Square), a melodrama written in the 1930s but never produced. Vanessa Redgrave had found the lost manuscript and campaigned for a London production. The National Theatre mounting was a hit, and after a run in Houston by the co-producing Alley Theatre, it arrived in New York. Based on an incident that actually happened in a Pennsylvania prison, the drama is set in the South during the Depression. A vile warden, "Boss" Whalen (Corin Redgrave), tells the press that he runs a modern, progressive institution, but in truth the conditions at his prison are medieval with strict punishment for the slightest infractions. The dreaded Klondike is a room where steam is turned on prisoners until they are literally roasted alive. When the inmates stage a hunger strike to protest the living conditions, Whalen has a group of malcontents thrown into Klondike, but he goes too far this time; a riot breaks out, Whalen and some guards are butchered, and the outside police move in. Although it came close to agitprop, Williams created a cast of individual and vivid characters that were far from stereotypic. The playwright's spokesman is the would-be poet Jim Allison (Finbar Lynch), who kowtows to Whalen (the other inmates derisively call him Canary Jim) and helps feed his propaganda machine in order to secure an early parole. Jim discovers his conscience when he falls for Whalen's young secretary, Eva Crane (Sherri Parker Lee), and the two hope for a future together when Jim breaks out during the riot. Even the brutish Butch O'Fallon (James Black), Jim's enemy and the ringleader of the strike, is written with compassion and honesty as he imagines his sweetheart, Goldie (Sandra Searles Dickinson), while he sweats into unconsciousness in Klondike. Williams even presents a gay and a black character, both handled sympathetically but with unembellished candor. Critics may have varied on whether *Not About Nightingales* was a rediscovered masterpiece, but all agreed it was "an extraordinary work" and an "enthralling" play by any standards. They also unanimously extolled Trevor Nunn's "spectacular production," from the masterful American-British cast to Richard Hoover's Tony Award–winning set (all steel with a black-and-gray cinematic palette) to Chris Parry's highly dramatic lighting. Even with the enthusiastic reviews, the play was a hard sell on Broadway (it was three hours long and unrelenting in its oppressiveness) yet managed to run 125 performances.

Another early work by a famous playwright, Harold Pinter's *The Hothouse* (5-6-82), was revived on February 25 by the Atlantic Theatre Company. Written in 1960 but not produced until 1980 in England, this early effort seemed even less accomplished on second viewing, though the "deficient" production certainly did not help. Kathryn Grody revised her one-person show *A Mom's Life* (3-13-90) at the ArcLight on February 28, bringing audiences up to date on the seriocomic travails of being a mother in New York City. Emlyn Williams's *Night Must Fall* (9-28-36) received a stylish mounting on March 8 at the Lyceum; John Tillinger staged the play as an old black-and-white movie. Judy Parfitt essayed the demanding Mrs. Bramson, J. Smith-Cameron was her inquisitive niece Olivia, and both were well received. But the press was of differing opinions about Matthew Broderick's Dan. Some felt Broderick's boyish, charming persona heightened the role; others found him unconvincing as a murderer. The Broadway revival struggled, even moving into the smaller Helen Hayes to cut expenses, but was deep in the red when it closed on June 27.

Harlem writer Zora Neale Hurston, who had recently been rediscovered onstage and in print, showed up as the main character in Thulani Davis's factual melodrama **Everybody's Ruby** (3-9-99, Public: Anspacher). When Ruby McCollum (Viola Davis), a well-off African-American woman living in a small Florida town in the early 1950s, is arrested for murdering a white doctor, C.

Leroy Adams (Beau Gravitte), Pittsburgh newspaper reporter Hurston (Phylicia Rashad) goes down south to cover the trial and write a book about the case. But none of the whites in the town will speak to Hurston, and the black members of the community are afraid to. With the help of William Bradford Huie (Tuck Milligan), a hardboiled white reporter, Hurston uncovers the truth behind the story: Dr. Adams first raped Ruby, then they became lovers, encouraged by Ruby's husband, Sam (Bill Nunn), who hoped to profit from the arrangement. But when Ruby became pregnant by the doctor, Sam flew into a rage and killed Adams. Scenes from the trial, episodes about Hurston's investigation (and writer's block), and flashbacks to past events were all jumbled together in such a way that many critics and audience members were confused. But the cast was first-rate (Rashad was particularly applauded), and the documentary-like drama certainly had its share of "intrigue, sex, melodramatic suspense, and racial and gender politics" to keep its audience entertained.

The Roundabout's revival of James Goldman's *The Lion in Winter* (3-3-66) on March 11 met with mostly favorable notices, though only Stockard Channing as Queen Eleanor of Aquitaine was enthusiastically endorsed. Laurence Fishburne played King Henry II, and the busy Michael Mayer directed the uneven production, which was kept on the boards for eleven weeks.

On the other hand, Christopher Durang's new comedy, **Betty's Summer Vacation** (3-14-99, Playwrights Horizons), left after four weeks thanks to decidedly mixed notices. New Yorker Betty (Kellie Overbey) watches her vacation at her summer-share condo turn into a sitcom nightmare as guests and family descend on her out-of-town hideaway. Her friend Trudy (Julie Lund) is a nonstop talker; Keith (Nat DeWolf) arrives with a hatbox that Trudy believes contains a human head (she must have caught the current revival of *Night Must Fall*); Betty's mother, Mrs. Siezmagraff (Kristine Nielson), laughingly dismisses her daughter's claims of sexual abuse by her father and instead pursues the oversexed Mr. Vanislaw (Guy Boyd), who always wears a raincoat; and a stud named Buck (Troy Sostillio) insists on showing everyone photos of his genitalia. Before the weekend is out, everyone plays charades, Mom gets drunk, Keith seduces Mr. Vanislaw, Trudy gets raped, Mr. Vanislaw's penis is cut off and put in the refrigerator, Keith cuts off Mr. Vanislaw's head, and Buck loses a few appendages as well. Durang called for a laugh track throughout these activities; it was supposed to drive home the sitcom satire but only irritated an already benumbed audience. While Brantley found the comedy "relentlessly fierce, relentlessly funny," most commentators termed it a "tiresome screech of a play," which suffered from poor direction and a cast that mistook mugging for high style.

That same night there was also plenty of mugging at the American Place, where the Theatre for a New Audience's *Macbeth* opened for a three-week run. Bill Camp was a firm Macbeth and Elizabeth Marvel an accomplished Lady Macbeth, but much of the rest of the cast suffered from "lack of restraint, along with the noticeably uneven handling of the verse."

Of the three David Hare plays seen on Broadway this season, his solo piece **Via Dolorosa** (3-18-99, Booth) seemed the least likely to succeed. But favorable reviews ("Hare's unique talents and remoteness from the issues make this journey of heart and mind theatrically invigorating") and positive word of mouth helped fill the house for its profitable run of ninety-nine performances. Hare, who made no claims to being a performer ("normally I get Judi Dench to do this sort of thing"), talked about his various trips to Israel and his observations on life on the West Bank and a land where enemies are "bound up in each other's unhappiness." Part history, part travelogue, all of it pointed and personal, the monologue contained more fertile ideas than the usual Broadway entry.

Off Broadway, the Manhattan Theatre Club and New Haven's Long Wharf Theatre presented Chay Yew's **Red** (3-23-99, City Center), a drama about how Chairman Mao's Cultural Revolution destroyed a famous opera singer. Chinese-American author Sonja (Jodi Long) has written a handful of best-sellers in America but welcomes an invitation to travel to China, where she hopes to write a book about the performer Hua (Ric Young). An acclaimed star of the Shanghai Opera House, Hua would not stick to Mao's pronounced guidelines regarding art and was driven from his profession and later killed. Sonja's research takes the form of fantasy sequences in which she interviews the long-dead Hua as well as his pupil Ling (Liana Pai), who turned in his master to government officials and even helped murder him. Much of the tale that enfolded was of interest, but like the similar *Everybody's Ruby* earlier that month, the storytelling was confusing and "hamstrung by the tricky maneuvering between past and present."

Audiences familiar with *The Innocents* (2-1-50) were in for few surprises at **The Turn of the Screw** (3-24-99, Primary Stages), Jeffrey Hatcher's adaptation of the Henry James novel that used two actors and a very minimalist approach to tell the famous ghost story. Enid Graham played the governess Miss Giddens, narrating events rather than experiencing them, while Rocco Sisto played the other characters, from the suspicious housekeeper Mrs. Grose to the youth Miles to the ghost Peter Quint. Several aisle-sitters agreed it was "disappointingly unsubtle, unsuspenseful, and altogether ineffectual."

A major award-winner in London, Patrick Marber's provocative drama **Closer** (3-25-99, Music Box) offered a painfully uncompromising look at contemporary love and sex. Dan (Rupert Graves), an aspiring author who makes his living writing obituaries, meets the stripper Alice (Anna Friel) when she (purposely?) steps in front of the cab he is riding in. He goes with her to a London hospital (she only has a minor leg injury), and the unlikely pair fall into a dangerous, abrasive affair. Over a year later, Dan has finally been published and is being photographed for the dust jacket by Anna (Natasha Richardson). The sexual chemistry between the two is unmistakable, and soon Dan is betraying Alice. Larry (Ciaran Hinds), the Scottish dermatologist who treated Alice at the hospital, is drawn into this savage triangle when Dan, posing as a woman he calls Anna, strikes up a conversation with Larry in an Internet chat room. They agree to meet the next day at the aquarium, but the real Anna shows up and the quartet of romantic deception is complete. Over the next few years the foursome switch partners and explore each other's hearts, never arriving any closer to the truth. Marber's dialogue was simple, poetic, and shattering, leaving off embellishment and going straight for the jugular. Dan tells Alice he is leaving her for Anna "because she doesn't need me," and Anna, speaking of the emotional baggage each person carries, states that "the greatest myth men have about women is that we overpack." Raves for the script agreed with *New York Magazine*'s John Simon, who called it "sad, witty and wise . . . *Closer* does not merely hold your attention; it burrows into you." The play won the New York Drama Critics Circle Award, and the four British performers were also esteemed (newcomer Friel was the most admired). The mounting ran five months.

Perhaps the most welcomed off-Broadway one-person performance of the season was Lisa Kron's **2.5 Minute Ride** (3-28-99, Public: Shiva), which one critic described as "a model example of the autobiographical solo show at its unaffected best." Kron, a member of the cultist Five Lesbian Brothers comedy troupe, describes three trips she took: a family outing to the Ohio theme park Cedar Point, where her elderly father pops heart pills before going on the roller coasters; a jaunt to New York for her brother's very Orthodox Jewish wedding; and a journey to Auschwitz, where her grandparents died. Jumping back and forth from one narrative to another, the evening managed to be giddy, absurd, and compelling. The triple tale ran nearly four months.

Another award-winner from London, Conor McPherson's "beautiful and devious" drama **The Weir** (4-1-99, Walter Kerr) opened to mixed notices but surprisingly found an audience for 277 performances. In a small rural bar in present-day Ireland, Jack (Jim Norton), a crusty old bachelor, and Jim (Kieran Ahern), who does odd jobs in the village, are drinking on a windy, cold night and discussing local gossip with Brendan (Brendan Coyle), the young bartender and owner. Finbar (Dermot Crowley), a local businessman and self-proclaimed dandy, enters with Valerie (Michelle Fairley), a woman from Dublin who has bought the Nealson house nearby. Stories about the house (some believe it is on the "fairy road" to the sea, and consequently knocking is occasionally heard on the doors and windows) and other local ghost tales follow, including a ghastly one Jim tells about a child molester whose ghost asked to be buried in the grave of a young girl. Then Valerie relates why she has come to live in the secluded town: she has been separated from her husband since their young daughter drowned in a swimming-pool accident. Valerie relates how, a few weeks after the funeral, she got a desperate phone call from the child asking her mother to come and pick her up at her grandmother's house. Valerie is convinced the voice was real, and the local belief in ghosts makes her feel that she is not crazy to think the episode really happened. The storytelling was first-rate, and the superb cast turned the talky piece into a "haunting, insinuatingly spellbinding play."

Actress Ellen McLaughlin wrote five juicy roles for women in her debut play **Tongue of a Bird** (4-4-99, Martinson), and the Public came up with a quintet of superior actresses to play them, but the pretentious drama was not well reviewed. Pilot Maxine (Cherry Jones) specializes in finding lost hikers in the wilderness, so a desperate Dessa (Melissa Long) hires her to search for her preteen daughter, Charlotte, who has been missing in the

Adirondacks for a week. While Maxine flies through the air she is haunted by thoughts of Amelia Earhart and visions of her suicide-victim mother, Evie (Sharon Lawrence), her grandmother Zofia (Elizabeth Wilson), who raised her, and the lost Charlotte (Julia McIlvaine). The psuedo-poetic script was not helped by its shaky production, but the five performers were viewed with favor.

Although Joan Vail Thorne's **The Exact Center of the Universe** (4-7-99, WPA) only ran thirty-five performances, it was much better received and returned the next season in an extended run. Vada Love Powell (Frances Sternhagen) is the leading citizen in a small southern town who always gets her way. So she is quite rattled when her pampered son, Apple (Reed Birney), elopes with the Italian-Irish-Catholic Mary Ann (Tracy Thorne) while Mary Ann's twin sister, Mary Lou (Thorne), is having tea with Vada, pretending to be the prospective daughter-in-law. As the years pass and Apple and Mary Ann have a family, Vada's opinion of her son's wife does not change. She throws a fit when Mary Ann takes photographs of nude natives while on an anthropological expedition and dares to show them to her young children. But as Vada approaches death she softens and realizes that her son is no longer safely "in the exact center" of her heart. Adding color and pathos to the play are Vada's canasta-playing friends Enid (Bethel Leslie) and Marybell (Marge Redmond), who age with her, moving deeper into senility and reminding Vada of her own vulnerability. Most commentators agreed that the comedy-drama was a "charming, insightful reflection on age, change . . . and the limitations of love" and declared Sternhagen "an authentic theatre treasure."

A British import that was nearly as hard to get into as *The Blue Room* (but for very different reasons) was the London revival of O'Neill's *The Iceman Cometh* (10-9-46) which opened on April 8 at the Brooks Atkinson and packed the house for its three-month engagement. Word had already reached New York about Kevin Spacey's towering performance as Hickey, but critics were just as enthusiastic about Howard Davies's "exuberant, utterly transfixing" production that turned the long, talky drama (it ran nearly four and a half hours) into a lively dark comedy. The American-British cast included Tim Pigott-Smith, Robert Sean Leonard, Clarke Peters, Tony Danza, James Hazeldine, Paul Giamatti, and Jeff Weiss.

Also from London, two star vehicles for mature actresses followed, one a flop and the other a hit, though neither boasted very accomplished scripts. Pam Gems's "staggeringly inept" biodrama **Marlene** (4-11-99, Cort) sought to explore the offstage persona of film star Marlene Dietrich (Sian Phillips) but only wallowed in clichés. Waiting to go onstage in a 1969 concert, Marlene bullies her companion-maid-lover Vivian (Margaret Whitton) while a mute concentration-camp survivor named Mutti (Mary Diveney) cowers in the corner. The last third of the play was the concert, Phillips croaking out the familiar songs and garnering some applause for her tireless efforts. Roundly disdained, the entry lasted only twenty-five performances.

David Hare's **Amy's View** (4-15-99, Ethel Barrymore) boasted a bravado performance by Judi Dench (her first Broadway appearance in forty years), but most critics found her vehicle just as creaky as *Marlene*. West End actress Esme Allen (Dench) is of the old school, so she finds herself immediately at odds with Dominic Tyghe (Tate Donovan), a film journalist who disowns theatre and is sleeping with Esme's daughter, Amy (Samantha Bond). Because Amy gets pregnant, the two wed, but years do not mend the shaky marriage, nor soothe the troubled waters between Esme and Dominic, nor bridge the gap between mother and daughter. As Esme's fortunes dwindle, Dominic's rise (he becomes a hot-shot film director), and after Amy's death the two adversaries meet one more time, still with locked horns but both in grief. Esme's dithering mother, Evelyn (Anne Pitoniak), and dusty old suitor Frank Oddie (Ronald Pickup) filled out the soap-opera tale, but the play sagged considerably whenever Dench was out of sight. Raves for Dame Judi's Tony-winning performance and her ever-growing popularity (she had recently won an Oscar for playing Queen Elizabeth in *Shakespeare in Love*) allowed the three-month engagement to make a handsome profit.

Off Broadway's Second Stage Theatre moved into a brand-new performance space near Times Square on April 21 and returned to its policy of reviving American works by mounting Jason Miller's Pulitzer winner *That Championship Season* (5-2-72). Scott Ellis directed the "sturdy production," which featured James Gammon as the crusty old Coach and Michael O'Keefe, Ray Baker, Dylan Baker, and Dennis Boutsikaris as his former basketball players.

Amy Tan's best-selling novel **The Joy Luck Club** (4-22-99, St. Clements) may have been too sprawling for the stage, but Susan Kim's adaptation and the Pan Asian Repertory production, directed by Tisa Chang, had some powerful moments and an expert cast. When Chinese-born Suyuan (Jo Yang) dies, her American-Chinese daughter, Jing-Mei Woo (Scarlett Lam), takes her place in the neighborhood mahjong quartet and learns about her heritage (and secrets about her own mother's past) from the three elderly ladies (Ruth Zhang, Kati Kuroda, and Tina Chen). While the flashbacks to their roots in China were sometimes melodramatic, scenes in the 1980s were very potent, especially the ending, when Jing-Mei journeys to China with her father to meet long-lost relatives for the first time. After a one-month run, the play reopened on July 6 at Theatre Four for four weeks.

Although it was not nearly as popular as his *The Beauty Queen of Leenane* (2-26-98), Martin McDonagh's **The Lonesome West** (4-27-99, Lyceum), set in the same village, was still "a compellingly lurid comedy-drama." Two brothers, Coleman (Maeliosa Stafford) and Valene Connor (Brian F. O'Byrne), return to their house after their father's funeral and are comforted by Father Welsh (David Ganly), the local priest, who is filled with so many self-doubts that the two brothers end up comforting him. It doesn't take long for the siblings to reveal their true colors: a battling, scornful, and violent twosome who would kill for the flimsiest of reasons. In fact, Coleman murdered his father in a drunken rage, and Valene is blackmailing him, keeping his brother as a slave and getting endless satisfaction by tormenting him at every turn. After Coleman smashes up Valene's collection of plaster statues of the saints, Valene rushes out to kill Coleman, but the brother survives to continue brawling. Only when Father Welsh commits suicide and leaves a letter begging the brothers to live in peace with each other do the quarreling siblings call a truce, at least for the time being. While notices for the script were not propitious, critics agreed that the Druid Theatre production, Garry Hynes's detailed direction, and the vibrant performers were very accomplished. The play only managed to run fifty-six times.

Lincoln Center's very uneven revival of Jean Anouilh's *Ring Round the Moon* (11-23-50) at the Belasco on April 28 had so many wonderful things in it that aisle-sitters were able to recommend it in spite of itself. Director Gerald Gutierrez did not capture the whimsical nature of the comedy, but some of the performances created a magic of their own. Toby Stevenson was charming as the twin brothers Hugo and Frederic, Frances Conroy made a delightfully daffy lady's companion Capulat, and Fritz Weaver shone as the wealthy but frustrated businessman Messerschmann. Most surprising was Marian Seldes with her cynical but slightly zany portrayal of the demanding Madame Desmermortes. The comedy was only kept on the boards for thirty-eight performances.

The Signature Theatre closed its John Guare season with a new work by the quirky writer, **Lake Hollywood** (4-29-99, Signature), which met with disappointing notices but found an audience for nearly seven weeks. The first act is a somewhat absurd look at a kooky family in 1940 as they vacation at their summer home on New Hampshire's Scroon Lake. (The play's title refers to the same lake; one character has dreams of turning it into a resort for Hollywood stars.) Agnes (Kate Burton) celebrates the Feast of the Assumption by performing a ritual cleansing in the water; her sister, Flo (Amy Wright), is playing bridge out on the lawn while her husband, Randolph (Joshua Harto), is fighting off a brush fire that is threatening the area; and Randolph's mother, Mrs. Larry (Pamela Nyberg), orders everybody about in a thick German accent, even though she was born in Berlin, New Hampshire. By the end of the act Agnes agrees to marry her boyfriend, Andrew (Adam Grupper), the two optimistically looking to the future. By the second act, set years later, middle-aged Agnes (Betty Miller) and Andrew (Ralph Waite) live in Manhattan and are visited by their daughter, Hildegarde (Burton), and her nervous husband, George (Grupper), because Agnes is going into the hospital for exploratory surgery. The wacky playfulness of the first act turned into soap-opera theatrics with Hildegarde whining about how she was never loved and Agnes revealing that she has long been tormented by the fear that an unknown man who once attacked her will someday return. Once again, an exceptional cast was wasted on a "discombobulated piece of work."

Another best-selling work of fiction was brought to the off-Broadway stage this season: **The Cider House Rules, Part I: Here in St. Cloud's** (5-6-99, Atlantic), which Peter Parnell adapted from John Irving's Dickensian epic. The tale of the orphaned Homer Wells (Josh Hamilton) who, after several failed adoptions, becomes the pupil and protégé of abortion doctor Wilber Larch (Colm Meaney) was theatrical at times, but Part I seemed more a tease than a satisfying play. Both parts had been previously produced in Los Angeles and Seattle, but only the first was presented in New York. Mixed notices and poor attendance did not prompt the Atlantic Theatre Company to present Part II, as it had hoped to do.

Peter Ackerman's contemporary bedroom farce **Things You Shouldn't Say Past Midnight** (5-13-99, Promenade) met with mixed critical response, but audiences enjoyed it enough to keep laughing for 197 performances. Three Manhattan couples in three beds that pop through a wall are all in crisis because of a slip of the tongue during lovemaking. When Nancy (Erin Dilly) calls her boyfriend, Ben (Mark Kassen), a "hook-nosed Jew" during a moment of passion, their relationship immediately shifts into suspicion and questioning. To make a point about prejudice, Ben suggests that he might be bisexual, and the gulf between the two lovers widens. Nancy's friend Grace (Clea Lewis) has a different problem with her lover: Gene (Jeffrey Donovan), a hitman for the Mafia, wants to have intellectual talk as foreplay. The third couple, psychiatrist Mark (Andrew Benator) and his older lover, Mr. Abraham (Nicholas Kepros), gets drawn into the plot when Ben is sent to Mark for therapy. The merry confusion climaxed in a scene with each couple in their own bedroom but connected by a three-way phone conversation that threw off sparks and laughs.

Like Brian Friel's *Molly Sweeney* (1-7-96), Conor McPherson's **This Lime Tree Bower** (5-19-99, Primary Stages) was an Irish drama in which three characters told a story in alternating monologues. And like McPherson's *The Weir*, its strength was in his talent for narrative. Seventeen-year-old Joe (T. R. Knight) admires Damien, a new student at his school, and befriends him even though it means skipping classes, smoking behind the religion room at lunch, and patronizing a disco where the women are as tough as the bouncers. Joe's older brother, Frank (Thomas Lyons), works in the family fish-and-chips shop and pities his father, an alcoholic who never recovered from the death of his wife. Dad is deep in debt to the local bookie, Simple Simon McCurdie, and the family has to kowtow to the small-time racketeer. Ray (Drew McVety) is a burnt-out philosophy professor who sleeps with his students even as he is going with Joe and Frank's sister Carmel. Frank's disgust with the oily McCurdie prompts him to get hold of a gun and, in disguise, rob his bookie joint. Ray happens to be driving by and helps Frank get away after the holdup. When the police come to the fish-and-chips shop a few days later, Frank thinks he is discovered; but the cops are there to investigate the rape of a girl from the disco, and the accused Damien has named

Joe as the culprit. Joe is cleared by way of a blood test, Frank puts the stolen money away for Joe's college education, and Ray heads to Chicago, where he writes a philosophy book no one will read—but, as Ray says, "that was the point." Most reviews were favorable, if not "money" notices, and the drama ran two months.

Gritty realism in acting, scenery, dialogue, and issues pervaded Ayub Khan-Din's London play **East Is East** (5-25-99, Manhattan Theatre Club), a slice-of-life piece about an Anglo-Pakistani family in Britain in 1971. Although he emigrated to the West and married an Englishwoman, George Khan (Edward A. Hajj) wants his six children raised in the Muslim religion and respecting old-world traditions. But George is also a demanding tyrant who beats his wife and kids and makes them work long hours in the family fish-and-chips shop. When George arranges Pakistani wives for two of his sons and insists that a third be circumcised, members of the family revolt with seriocomic results. Scott Elliott directed with a firm hold on detail (Derek McClane's set was also a striking piece of naturalism), and much of the acting by the large cast was truthful and engrossing.

Goodnight Children Everywhere (5-26-99, Playwrights Horizons), another London play, though written by American Richard Nelson, was received with modest approval, some commentators calling it "sensitive," others judging it "underdeveloped." During World War II, when many British children were sent to Canada and the States for the duration, Peter (Chris Stafford) lived in Toronto with friends of his parents. Six years later he returns to his London home, but everything has changed for seventeen-year-old Peter. His parents died in the war, and the household now consists of his three older sisters, who fight over him for his affection. (One sister, unhappily married and pregnant, seduces the sexually confused Peter.) While the family struggles through the difficult post-war times, Peter comes of age and starts to understand his frustrated sisters and his own identity.

The final entry of the season was **Tennessee Williams Remembered** (5-30-99, ArcLight), not so much a recollection about the playwright as an autobiographical memoir by Anne Jackson and Eli Wallach in which they charted their careers and marriage in terms of the many Williams plays they had appeared in. For two weeks the couple engaged in reminiscences, anecdotes, readings from Williams's letters and poems, and scenes from the plays themselves.

When the season ended on May 31, there were thirteen plays on Broadway; five of them were revivals, all but one from this season. For those with long memories, the number was puny, but in light of recent history, thirteen concurrent entries on the Street was a veritable gold mine.

1999–2000

The oh-so-modest renaissance continued with Broadway seeing nineteen plays open this season, ten of them new. Even more encouraging, fourteen of the works were American. As expected, box-office receipts climbed even though attendance slid 2 percent, proving again that prices rose faster than inflation. While the average ticket price for all shows was figured at $53.02, many non-musicals on the Street were asking over $60.00 top. In fact, the price gap between musicals and plays was getting smaller, which only hurt non-musicals.

The numbers off Broadway remained strong; both attendance figures and number of productions (over ninety with only thirty-four of them revivals) were quite impressive. While few plays on Broadway had lengthy runs, over ten off-Broadway entries managed to run way past the 100 mark. Broadway boasted some superb revivals, but Off Broadway presented several new works of note. There was no shortage of exceptional acting in both venues, but, interestingly, there was just as much talk about the scripts themselves.

In many ways it was a playwright's season. Eugene O'Neill, Arthur Miller (twice), Tom Stoppard, Chekhov, Sam Shepard, Michael Frayn, and Noel Coward were all represented on the Street, and newer playwrights Richard Greenberg, Beth Henley, A. R. Gurney, Arthur Kopit, Anna Deavere Smith, Charles Busch, August Wilson, and Donald Margulies all provided Off Broadway with new works, though only the last three were able to come up with first-class goods. More important, new names appeared and offered very promising entries: David Lindsay-Abaire's *Fuddy Meers*, Becky Mode's *Fully Committed*, Claudia Shear's *Dirty Blonde*, Gregory Murphy's *The Countess*, and David Auburn's *Proof*. Whether these were the beginnings of notable careers or just superior initial efforts would not be known for several seasons into the new century.

Richard Greenberg's farce **Hurrah at Last** (6-3-99, Gramercy), which had premiered at California's South Coast Repertory and was presented by the Roundabout off Broadway for three months, was a disappointment for supporters of the usually intriguing playwright. The comedy about writer's angst was "so light it evaporates while you watch" and was described by one critic as "a Saturday morning cartoon as written by August Strindberg." Novelist Laurie (Peter Frechette) has found respect among the literary critics but little money. During a Christmas Eve gathering at the trendy loft apartment of his sister, Thea (Ileen Getz), Laurie bitterly complains and annoys everyone, from his noncommittal parents (Larry Keith and Dori Brenner) to his rich brother-in-law, Eamon (Kevin O'Rourke), to his best friend, Oliver (Paul Michael Valley), a successful playwright who will not disclose his salary but willingly exposes his genitals to Laurie as a sign of their friendship. When Laurie learns that Oliver is going to be paid handsomely for writing the film version of one of Laurie's novels, the writer's misery grows. By the second act he is hospitalized for some unnamed disease, and in a fantasy possibly brought on by medication, all of Laurie's family and acquaintances appear and bare their souls to the invalid, his mother even gloating at the prospect of outliving her own children. Laurie recovers and is last seen happily going off to pitch screenplay ideas to Hollywood producers. Frechette made an amusing hero, and Judith Blazer, as Oliver's Italian wife, Gia, lit up the stage even though she never spoke English and never understood what the other characters were talking about.

The Manhattan Theatre Club had trouble keeping **La Terrasse** (6-8-99, City Center) on the boards for its five-week engagement, both critics and audiences finding the absurdist farce "consistently flat-footed and desultory." Mark O'Donnell translated Jean-Claude Carrière's Paris success, and it was given a handsome production by director Mike Okrent and designers Santo Loquasto (set) and William Ivey Long (costumes), but the comedy failed to translate on any level. No sooner have Madeleine (Sarah Knowlton) and her beefy boyfriend, Etienne (Jeremy Davidson), broken off their relationship than a real estate agent (Annie Golden in the evening's merriest performance) shows up and is showing the high-rise apartment to prospective tenants who take over the place: the mysterious tramp Mr. Astruc (David Schramm), his associate Maurice (Bruce Norris), who instantly falls for Madeleine and throws himself off the titular terrace when she doesn't return his affections, and a half-blind old General (Tom Aldredge) whose wife (Margaret Hall) un-

successfully tries to push him off the same terrace. Maurice survived the fall, but the play could not survive the Atlantic crossing and left audiences baffled and annoyed.

That same day, Gregory Murphy's period drama **The Countess** (6-8-99, Samuel Beckett) moved from Off Off Broadway to Off Broadway, where it opened quietly but soon found an audience. Based on an 1853 scandal, the drama recounted a triangular love affair involving celebrities of the day. Stuffy art critic John Ruskin (James Riordan) vacations in Scotland with his put-upon wife, Effie (Jennifer Woodward), and his handsome young protégé, painter John Everett Millais (Jy Murphy), and soon his petty and demeaning ways send her into the arms of the promising pre-Raphaelite. The play dealt with small-mindedness and lack of communication, yet critics declared the script "wonderfully witty" and "tremendous fun." The commercial venture ran nine months, then reopened on April 24 at the Lamb's for an open-end run.

Theodore Bikel returned to the New York stage as a crusty, speechifying Holocaust survivor in Arje Shaw's **The Gathering** (6-10-99, Playhouse 91), and the seventy-four-year-old actor was considered to be in top form. The gathering in question is a Sabbath meal in 1985 where sculptor Gabriel (Bikel) gets into an argument with his son, Stuart (Robert Fass), a speechwriter for Ronald Reagan. The president plans to visit Germany and tour the Bitburg cemetery, where Nazi soldiers are buried. Father and son rage at each other with clichés ("I didn't survive the camps to forget and forgive!") and sarcastic humor ("I was a Communist; I raised a Republican. You figure it out!"). Gathered at the cemetery in Act II are Gabe and his sympathetic grandson, Michael (Adam Rose), protesting the presidential visit. There was even an amiable German soldier (Peter Hermann) on hand to add his bits of wisdom ("My grandfather hated Jews as you hate Germans; when does it stop?") and keep the discussion going until Gabe breaks down and reveals further horrors about his death-camp ordeal. Critics varied on their opinion of the script, calling it everything from "engaging potent theatre" to "superficial emotional wallowing," but the Jewish Repertory Theatre production and Bikel were popular enough to be held over into October.

The Second Stage revived Albert Innaurato's *Gemini* (3-13-77) on June 16, and while some commentators felt the comedy about "homosexual panic" had not dated well, most agreed that Mark Brokaw's production was "pungent" and "respectful." Brian Mysliwy played Frances, the college student who finds himself attracted to his girl-friend's Wasp brother, but Linda Hart, as the foul-mouthed, funny neighbor Bunny, stole the show with her "audacious, extravagantly heartfelt performance."

Youthful television stars Calista Flockhart and Ron Eldard and film hearttrob Paul Rudd turned Neil LaBute's trilogy of one-acts, **Bash** (6-24-99, Douglas Fairbanks), into a popular off-Broadway item for its one-month engagement. In *Medea Redux,* a working-class woman (Flockhart) sits alone at a table and and tells a tape recorder about an affair she had with an older man and how her unwanted pregnancy led her to perform a Medea-like act of murder. A Mormon businessman (Eldard) sits in a Las Vegas hotel room in *Iphigenia in Orem* and tells an unseen woman how he clawed his way to the top and revealed that he too killed his own child. *A Gaggle of Saints* concerned two Mormon college students (Flockhart and Rudd) going to New York City for a big social event, but he ends up participating in a deadly gay-bashing incident in Central Park. Joe Mantello directed the three celebrities with careful intensity, but the playlets were considered "gimmicky and pretentious" and "like staring into the souls of statistics."

A broadly played *The Taming of the Shrew* on July 1 was the first summer offering at Central Park's Delacorte. Few aisle-sitters could recommend the "relentless sideshow" that Mel Shapiro mounted, but the "Bard as reinterpreted by the Three Stooges" entertained audiences to July 11. Although it was set at a period Italian villa, Petruchio (Jay O. Sanders) arrived in a contemporary wrestling outfit and later changed into a gaucho costume. Allison Janney was a very physical Katherina who delivered the final speech with gusto. But little in the raucous production was approved of in the press except Max Wright as the wily Christopher Sly in the often-cut Induction sequence.

The first notable solo show of the season was also one of the most unique. Margaret Cho's **I'm the One That I Want** (7-8-99, Westbeth) was a "frank and brutally funny recounting" of her brief celebrity and crashing descent after being the first Asian to star in her own network sitcom. Selected as the lead in 1994 for *All-American Girl,* Cho found fame and horror as the producers tried to remake her, forced her to lose thirty pounds in two weeks, which sent her to the hospital with kidney failure, then abruptly canceled the show the minute it was clear that the ratings were dis-

appointing. The lesbian actress soon found herself deep into sex, alcohol, and depression. Yet Cho's stand-up delivery was far from whining as she told ribald stories, did canny impersonations of those closest to her, and viewed herself honestly: "Am I gay, am I straight? I'm just slutty. Where's my parade?" Complimentary reviews and a gay following allowed the monologue program to run out the summer.

A major portion of this year's Lincoln Center Festival was devoted to Irish playwright Brian Friel with two revivals of his plays and his translation of Chekhov's *Uncle Vanya* on July 6 at the La Guardia Drama Theatre. Friel's fluid version of the Russian classic was complimented, but the press was less sure about the Gate Theatre's mounting, some finding it as dry and stagnant as the three-foot high stalks of wheat that surrounded the action. Reviews were much more enthusiastic about the Abbey Theatre's production of Friel's *The Freedom of the City* (2-17-74) at the John Jay College Theatre, which Conall Morrison staged with vitality and power. Gerard Crossan, Sorcha Cusack, and Michael Colgan played the three innocents who are mistaken by the police for a gang of Irish terrorists and gunned down, and each gave a vital and unsentimental performance that stung with laughter. Concluding the Friel tribute was a revival of his very Chekhovian play *Aristocrats* (4-25-89) on July 20 at the La Guardia. Ban Barnes directed the Gate production, which boasted some splendid performances, in particular Frank McCusker as the bragging Eamon and Catherine Byrne, Donna Dent, and Alison McKenna as the three sisters in a decaying noble family.

Also part of the Lincoln Center Festival was the world premiere of Robert Wilson's **The Days Before: Death, Destruction & Detroit III** (7-7-99, New York State Theatre), a typical avant-garde piece that stimulated or bored audiences for four performances. Classified by the festival as a music-theatre program, there was more spoken text than usual for a Wilson offering, everything from excerpts from Umberto Eco's *The Island of the Day Before* to tone poems by Christopher Knowles chillingly delivered by Fiona Shaw. While a good number of commentators dismissed Wilson's effort as "self-indulgent claptrap," the experimental icon of the 1970s and 1980s seemed to be going strong and heading into the millennium as enigmatic as ever.

The summer's Hibernian flavor continued with the Irish Repertory Theatre's "diverting and often poignant" revival of Jerome Kilty's epistolary

Dear Liar (3-17-60) on July 22 with Donal Donnelly as George Bernard Shaw and Marian Seldes as Mrs. Patrick Campbell. Notices were approving if not enthusiastic, and the two-hander ran two months.

Cheryl L. West's domestic comedy-drama **Jar the Floor** (8-11-99, Second Stage) had been kicking around various regional theatres for years before appearing off Broadway for a month. Four generations of African-American mothers gather for the ninetieth birthday of MaDear (Irma P. Hall), and the evening is spent in jokes, outbursts of regret, accusations, and sarcastic bitterness. MaDear's middle-aged daughter, Lola (Lynn Thigpen), is belittled by her daughter, Maydee (Regina Taylor), who is in turn ridiculed by her teenage daughter, Vennie (Linda Powell), everyone blaming everyone else for not loving them and ending with even the semi-senile MaDear ranting about her cruel mother. Commentators mostly agreed that the script was "dismayingly overstuffed with conflict and contention," but all roundly applauded the dynamic cast and West's way with salty humor.

The first play of the Broadway season was also its sole thriller, John Pielmeier's **Voices in the Dark** (8-12-99, Longacre), which suffered the same fate as others in the genre of late: poor notices, better-than-average acting, and an unprofitable run (in this case, sixty-eight performances). Lil (Judith Ivey), a therapist who hosts a popular radio call-in show titled *Last Resort,* gets a threatening call on the air from an obviously psychotic male, but she is more concerned about getting away to her Adirondacks cabin, where she hopes to patch up her shaky marriage. Lil goes to the mountains, but the husband is delayed, and she finds herself getting further threats on her answering machine. Each character that enters the cabin, from Lil's producer to a local handyman, is eyed with suspicion, and before you know it a storm sets in, the lights and telephone are cut dead, and Lil is playing *Wait Until Dark* with her stalker. The plot echoed with clichés—a body found in the Jacuzzi, a retarded youth who drools over Lil's lingerie, a body that refuses to die, and a detective who may not really be a detective—and provided the audience with enough opportunity to gasp and scream at the expected surprises. The culprit turns out to be the drooling boy, whom Lil dispatches by electrocuting him in the hot tub conveniently situated in the living room. Ivey was declared better than her vehicle, and there was praise for the atmospheric setting by David Gallo and Lauren Hel-

pern, which had as many deer antlers as the infamous *Moose Murders* (2-22-83).

Self-centered businessman Ron (F. Murray Abraham) announced to his wife and children at the beginning of **It's My Party (And I'll Die If I Want To)** (8-19-99, ArcLight) that he had only 110 minutes to live, and he was as good as his word, although the "stillborn, unfunny play" couldn't end quickly enough, according to the critics. Australian Elizabeth Coleman's comedy had Ron's wife (Joyce Van Patten) and grown children (Andrea Gabriel, Adam Grupper, and Rene Augesen) revealing secrets to the old boy before he kicked off from some unexplained disease. Then an undertaker (John Cariani) arrived, Ron settled back on the couch and died, and the audience was left to argue what was worse: the play or its title. The "trite theatrical" stayed for a month.

The second offering at the outdoor Delacorte was a pleasing and faithful revival of Molière's *Tartuffe* on August 22. Mark Brokaw directed a winning cast on Ricardo Hernandez's glistening gold setting, and the Richard Wilbur translation was delivered with bouncy abandon but with little gimmickry. Dylan Baker was a slinky Tartuffe, but he was overshadowed by Charles Kimbrough's frantic and pious Orgon. Also admired were J. Smith-Cameron (Elmire), Mary Testa (Dorine), and Dana Ivey (Madame Pernelle).

Joan Vail Thorne's "delightful, old-fashioned" *The Exact Center of the Universe* (4-7-99) returned on September 8 and played at the Century until January. Frances Sternhagen received another round of valentines for her imposing portrayal of a small-town matriarch. No revival this season got more vitriolic reviews than the New York Theatre Workshop's mounting of Tennessee Williams's *A Streetcar Named Desire* (12-3-47) on September 12. Director Ivo van Hove deconstructed the American classic, turning the play into an absurdist circus with Stanley (Brice McKenzie) doing a Jimi Hendrix impersonation on an electric guitar, Stella (Jenny Bacon) outscreaming her husband, and Mitch (Christopher Evan Welch) trying to rape Blanche (Elizabeth Marvel) long before Stanley ever considers it. Everyone ends up getting naked, and several principals took a bath before the play was over. As one aisle-sitter noted, the story was "not only told from the point of view of . . . Stanley, it appears to have been directed by him as well."

No season in the 1990s would be complete without a new interactive theatre piece, so the producers of the still-running *Tony 'n' Tina's Wedding* (2-6-88) offered **Finnegan's Farewell** (9-22-

99, St. Luke's Church) on Wednesday evenings, an Irish version of the no-longer-running *Grandma Sylvia's Funeral* (10-4-95). When Paddy Finnegan dies, his bumpkin-headed family arrives at the wake and has to put up with the buxom Busty Quivers (Sharon Angela), a special favorite of Paddy's when he was still alive. Then everyone heads to Vinnie Black's Coliseum (the Edison Hotel) for corned beef and cabbage, family fistfights, bagpipers, and a cash bar. But a funeral could not compete with a wedding, and by November Paddy was buried for good.

It was left to Off Off Broadway to present the first satisfying new play of the season: Douglas Carter Beane's contemporary comedy of manners **The Country Club** (9-22-99, Greenwich House). Former debutante Soos (Cynthia Nixon) leaves California and returns to her Wasp roots in Wyomissing, Pennsylvania, where she was the popular class secretary back in high school. Arriving at the local country club, Soos is reunited with former school chums: Zip (Tom Everett Scott), her class president; her best pal, Pooker (Amy Holm); the cynical alcoholic Hutch (Frederick Weller); and others. In a series of holiday events held at the club during a year's time, the group is seen trying to hold their own in a changing world. When Hutch marries the Catholic, lower-class Chloe (Calie Thorne), they snub her, but Zip has a passionate fling with her on the Club Room floor. The play seemed to enjoy these clever, vacant people, and all ended happily. As with Beane's *As Bees in Honey Drown* (6-24-97), the dialogue sparkled. Pooker had the best of the bons mots, such as her observation "We all have our little stories. And no one brings them up. That's what is known as community spirit." Christopher Ashley directed the talented cast (Nixon was the most praised), and James M. Youmans designed the ultrachic white setting. Critics varied; some were disappointed and labeled the comedy "glibly formulaic," but many others found it "devilishly well observed and niftily constructed." The play was popular enough that its five-week run was extended into December.

The Signature Theatre Company gave its full season over to old and new works by avant-gardist Maria Irene Fornes, beginning with a double bill of two one-acts first performed off-off Broadway in the 1980s. **Mud** (9-26-99, Signature), written in 1983, concerns a love triangle among the illiterate, poverty-stricken Maer (Deirdre O'Connell), who desperately tries to educate herself by reading kindergarten books, her pig-farmer husband, Lloyd (Paul Lazar), who is only

interested in his erections, and the elderly Henry (John Seitz), who is educated and speaks fluently but also lusts after Mae. **Drowning,** first produced in 1986, is a ten-minute piece in which three men, wearing bizarre masks by Teresa Snider-Stein that seemed to resemble humanoid walruses, argue over a newspaper article, one of them falling in love with the photo of a woman. Fornes was called everything from "the truest poet of the American theatre" to an artist who "so dependably plumbed the depths of stultifying ineptitude." Some fans of the playwright's work complained about director Davis Esbjornson's naturalistic approach to the one-acts, preferring Fornes's own absurdist treatment when she initially staged them off-off Broadway. The subsequent Fornes entries by the Signature were of little interest and passed out of sight quietly, making it the least intriguing collection of works since the Signature started dedicating its seasons to one playwright.

Director Jerry Zaks returned to the non-musical theatre with the jokey comedy **Epic Proportions** (9-30-99, Helen Hayes) but stumbled badly, helped by a thin script by television writers Larry Coen and David Crane. On location in a remote desert, a movie company in the 1930s is making a biblical epic with thousands of extras on hand. Louise Goldman (Kristin Chenoweth) is the "assistant director in charge of atmosphere personnel," and she keeps up her spunky enthusiasm as she field-marshals the hoards into acting and reacting as needed for the big crowd scenes. Benny (Alan Tudyk) and Phil Bennett (Jeremy Davidson), two brothers serving as extras, both fall for Louise, but Benny wins her heart when Phil takes over for the director and becomes a movie mogul. The jokes came fast and furious ("Yesterday was the last day of Pompeii, and boy was I glad to see it go!"), but the comedy went nowhere, and the laughs dried up long before its hour and fifteen minutes were up. The reviews were mostly pans, yet critics enjoyed Chenoweth (her pep talks to the crowd were the play's only engaging moments), and the cast played their paper-thin characters with verve, especially Ruth Williamson as a sulky Egyptian queen. The small house remained mostly empty as the producers allowed the run to drag into January before calling it quits.

That same night, one of the season's many hit solo shows opened. Becky Mode's **Fully Committed** (9-30-99, Vineyard) revealed actor-clerk Sam Peliczowski (Mark Setlock) in the basement of an Upper East Side four-star restaurant answering the phone reservation lines and dealing with the chef and maître d' upstairs via an intercom. As customers plead, demand, and try to bribe their way into getting a prime-location table at the "in" eatery, Setlock played both Sam and his many callers, including his discouraging agent, a rival actor who is getting impressive auditions, and his dad in Ohio. Aisle-sitters praised Setlock's frantic, funny performance, Nicholas Martin's inspired direction, and Mode's "sassily written" script, which was deemed a "play rather than a strung together series of vignettes or anecdotes." The five-week engagement quickly filled up, so the comedy reopened on December 16 for a commercial run at Cherry Lane, playing far into the next season.

Another solo hit followed, Eve Ensler's **The Vagina Monologues** (10-3-99, Westside), though it had been seen in various venues since 1996. Ensler began the program explaining its genesis: how she interviewed dozens of women about their genitalia and fashioned their comments into a series of monologues. Some sequences were expectedly shocking (as the title hinted at), others reflective and moving. From testimonies of rape victims to comic recounting of sexual adventures to a graphic but poetic description of giving birth, Ensler managed to rise above cheap jokes or simpleminded politics and create "an indelible theatrical experience which is both a work of art and an incisive piece of cultural history, a poem and a polemic." Although Ensler was scheduled to perform the monologues for only two months, the show continued indefinitely with a series of three actresses (often celebrities) performing the script together.

Having had the opportunity to view three Brian Friel revivals at Lincoln Center the previous summer, theatregoers were offered a new play by the Irish playwright, **Give Me Your Answer, Do!** (10-5-99, Gramercy), which the Roundabout Theatre Company presented for three months. In a crumbling family manse not unlike that in *Aristocrats* (there were several other similarities with that very Chekhovian drama), middle-aged writer Tom Connolly (John Glover) and his alcoholic wife, Daisy (Kate Burton), await the decision of David Knight (Michael Emerson), an American purchasing agent for the University of Texas, who is upstairs going through Tom's papers and determining if the college will buy them. Since Tom has always been a respected but not a popular author and has suffered writer's block for some years, the Connollys are in need of the money as well as the recognition the purchase will bring.

With them is the hack writer Garret Fitzmaurice (Gwan Grainger), whose novels sell well but who is constantly reminded of his lack of talent by his sour wife, Grainne (Helen Carey). Daisy's mismatched parents are also on hand: her spry father, Jack Donovan (Joel Grey), and put-upon wife, Maggie (Lois Smith). During the course of the afternoon while they await Knight's decision (he is also considering buying Garret's papers), the three couples reveal the many demons in their lives, from Jack's secret kleptomania to the Connollys' institutionalized retarded daughter, Bridget (Woodwyn Koons). Notices were cautious in their assessment of the play ("a dirge that admits no leavening warmth") but applauded the superb cast as directed by Kyle Donnelly.

A one-man show that did not please ("plagued by contrivances, pat characterizations, and excess verbiage") nor run more than a month was Lee Blessing's **Chesapeake** (10-14-99, Second Stage), which featured comic actor Mark Linn-Baker as a bisexual performance artist who is battling a right-wing southern senator over government funding for the arts. By the second act the artist has been transformed into a Chesapeake Bay retriever who, being any man's best friend, manages to save the life of the obnoxious senator. Blessing's point was obscure, but Linn-Baker was clearly a first-rate performer "maintaining a delicate balance between humanness and doghood."

If a performance artist can play a dog, why not a middle-aged Australian male comic as a glitzy housewife? Barry Humphries had been portraying Dame Edna Everage (self-billed as "probably the most popular and gifted woman in the world today") for over thirty years in nightclubs, on television, and in theatres on three continents. He/she attacked Broadway with a program called **Dame Edna: The Royal Tour** (10-17-99, Booth) and won unanimous raves and crowded houses willing to be insulted and entertained by this vulgar, razor-sharp grande dame who breathed celebrity even as she mocked celebrity worship. Much of Humphries's act was working the crowd and bringing willing (and unwilling) patrons onstage to answer leading questions, eat dinner, and generally make fools of themselves. "I wouldn't pay to see you," she told her patrons. "I wouldn't even take a complimentary ticket to see you." Although the Dame was backed by two chorines (billed as "Ednaettes") and a pianist, the audiences (she called them "possums") were her costars, and they never failed to come through. After suggesting to one patron that the babysitter at home was probably an illegal immigrant, Edna quipped, "One of the advantages of a democracy is that you can have a slave class with a clear conscience." As John Lahr in *The New Yorker* noted, "Of course Dame Edna is a star; she is also a ferocious satire on stardom. It's a generous and gallant performance." Edna's possums agreed and kept the show on the boards for eight months. After receiving a special Tony Award at season's end, Humphries set off on a tour of North America.

A. R. Gurney added "a pleasant if minor addition" to his canon with **Ancestral Voices** (10-18-99, Mitzi E. Newhouse), a play meant to be read, just like his previous *Love Letters* (8-22-89), although it did not take the epistolary format of the earlier work. An upper-crust Buffalo family is shaken when the grandmother (Elizabeth Wilson) decides to leave the grandfather (Philip Bosco) to run off with his best friend. Grandson Eddie (David Aaron Baker) narrates the "chamber piece for voices" as he explains how this very unlikely event affected his parents (Edward Herrmann and Blythe Danner) and himself as he grows wise to the ways of adults and foresees the end of an era and his Wasp way of life. The "mild and only mildly touching play" was saved by its skillful cast, though they were quickly replaced by other well-known actors, who needed little preparation for the reading, which was only performed on Sunday and Monday evenings when the Newhouse was dark. More than one critic questioned charging $45 for a staged reading, but audiences filled the downstairs space through December, encouraging the producers to reopen the piece on February 3 and run to April 3.

The Atlantic Theatre Company devoted its season to co-founder David Mamet, opening with revivals of his two one-acts *Mr. Happiness* and *The Water Engine* (12-20-77) on October 20. Bob Balaban was "quietly mesmerizing" as the radio advice columnist in the first play, and Steven Goldstein played the unfortunate inventor in the second. Neither piece was highly recommended by the press, but the program gave Mamet devotees a chance to see these two early, seldom-performed plays.

A surprise hit off-off Broadway was the curiosity **Charlie Victor Romeo** (10-21-99, Collective: Unconscious Theatre), which was slated for three months but ran seven. The script, compiled by the company members, consisted of transcripts from the black box in aircraft known as the CVR (Cockpit Voice Recorder, or the slang term of the play's title). The cast played airline pilots and flight attendants, recreating verbatim the crises in the cockpit when equipment malfunctioned or a bird was sucked into an engine or other midair mishaps occurred. All the scenes were taken from actual crashes with casualties, so the documentary piece held a macabre fascination for certain audiences. The bare-bones production was generally commended, especially Jaime Mereness's sound effects, which provided the horrifying details of each catastrophe.

British playwright Shelagh Stephenson's **An Experiment With an Air Pump** (10-31-99, Manhattan Theatre Club) was compared (favorably or not) to Tom Stoppard's *Arcadia* (3-30-95) by all the critics, and the similarities were hard to miss. In an elegant house in Newcastle, two stories are being told. Near the end of the eighteenth century, scientist Joseph Fenwick (Daniel Gerroll) is unhappily married to Susannah (Linda Edmond) while people on the street are rioting for cheaper fish prices. Their daughters (Clea Lewis and Ana Reeder) put on a silly play to entertain two guests, the young scientist Thomas Armstrong (Jason Butler Harner) and Peter Mark Roget (Christopher Duva), the father of the thesaurus. In the same house 200 years later, a professor (Gerroll) muses over a set of bones discovered nearby while his wife, Ellen (Edmond), a geneticist, tries to decide whether to take a job that involves questionable "pre-embryonic" cell research. The two stories link up eventually—the bones are probably those of the hunchback Scottish maid Isobel (Seana Kofoed) whom Armstrong seduced in order to study her deformed body—with much discussion about science, the future, and the price of experimentation. (The play's title is that of a famous painting, which parallels Joseph's theory that life cannot exist in a vacuum.) Notices ranged from "a strenuously ambitious play but a rather dull and talky one" to "a remarkable new play" and "a heartbreaking tale."

Monologuist Spalding Gray took on the subject of fatherhood in **Morning, Noon and Night** (10-31-99, Vivian Beaumont), which performed on Sunday and Monday evenings when the Lincoln Center upstairs theatre was dark. The cutting-edge father of monodramas was clearly mellowing as he told cute stories about the cute things his three cute kids said. Gray seemed as surprised as the audience that his reflections on life had come to this, but patrons were willing to listen for the twenty scheduled performances.

Two off-Broadway hits opened the next week, making theatregoing off the Street as exciting as matters on the Street were dismal. David

Lindsay-Abaire's **Fuddy Meers** (11-2-99, City Center) was an absurdist comedy that touched on serious issues but left the question of reality up to the audience. Claire (J. Smith-Cameron) suffers from psychogenic amnesia, which causes her to wake up each morning with no memory of her past. Every day her husband, Richard (Robert Stanton), and teenage son, Kenny (Keith Nobbs), have to show her scrapbooks of her past to explain her dilemma, but by the next morning she is starting with a blank slate again. One day a Limping Man (Patrick Breen), who claims to be her brother, kidnaps Claire and takes her to the home of their mother, Gertie (Marylouise Burke), who has suffered a stroke and mispronounces her words. (The play's title is Gertie's attempt to say "funny mirrors.") Richard and Kenny discover Claire at her mother's, as do an incompetent cop (Lisa Gorlitsky) and the psychotic Millet (Mark McKinney), who has a foul-mouthed hand puppet named Hinky Binky. Claire may not remember her past, but everyone else has enough demons in theirs that they would like to hide. But revelations abound, a murder is attempted, and Claire learns to confront her mysterious past in order to save her family's future. Amidst all the farcical shenanigans, Lindsay-Abaire provided some pungent dialogue and stinging insight. (When Claire is shown an old photo of herself from before she lost her memory, she says, "Oh, yes. I look much happier now.") Ben Brantley in the *New York Times* led the critical praise, calling the comedy "dark, sweet and thoroughly engaging" with "top-notch performances that remind us just how cartoonish real people can be." The Manhattan Theatre Club engagement was extended to January 2, then the production transferred on February 10 to a commercial run at the Minetta Lane, where it stayed nine weeks.

Two nights later Donald Margulies's **Dinner With Friends** (11-4-99, Variety Arts) proved to be even more successful. "Wry, keenly observed, and as satisfyingly professional as they come," the bittersweet comedy showed how a four-way friendship dissolves when a marriage falls apart. Suburban couple Gabe (Matthew Arkin) and Karen (Lisa Emery) are international food writers who once introduced friend Beth (Julie White) to Tom (Kevin Kilner), the latter two marrying and all four bonding in a cozy friendship. But years later, when Tom leaves Beth for another woman, the breakup not only shatters the trust each of the quartet had for the other but threatens Gabe and Karen's marriage as well. It was a variation of a familiar plot, but critics agreed with John Simon

in *New York* that "Margulies is a master of observing what might seem old hat with fresh eyes, hearing it with fresh ears." As in the recent *Art* (3-1-98), the fragility of friendship proved to be more interesting than the delicate bonds of marriage. When Tom explains that his marriage was a lie, Gabe cannot help but point out that "Karen and I were a big part of that terrible life you had to get the hell away from." Daniel Sullivan directed the quartet with a masterful touch, and audiences responded for several months. In April the comedy-drama was awarded the Pulitzer Prize.

The box-office appeal of television and film star Woody Harrelson was not strong enough to allow the Roundabout's revival of N. Richard Nash's *The Rainmaker* (10-28-54) on November 11 at the Brooks Atkinson to run out its full engagement; it closed on January 23, a week earlier than originally announced. Harrelson's "slouching, squeaky-voiced, red-neck accented" Starbuck was not most people's idea of the dashing con man who steals the heart of spinster Lizzie (Jayne Atkinson). Director Scott Ellis went for the big emotions and effects (including an actual downpour onstage at the play's end), but the evening was considered "pallid" and "parched" by most commentators. The production had originated at the Williamstown Theatre Festival in Massachusetts, as had the Broadway revival of Arthur Miller's *The Price* (2-7-68) on November 15 at the Royale. Critics were much more welcoming this time, some classifying the work as secondary Miller but finding much to admire in the strong cast: Jeffrey DeMunn as the cop, Victor; Lizbeth Mackay as his frustrated wife, Esther; Harris Yulin as his prosperous brother, Walter; and Bob Dishy as the crusty old furniture dealer, Gregory Solomon. The "forthright and sensitive" revival managed to run nearly four months on Broadway.

The Public Theatre had a less-than-dazzling season, starting with Suzan-Lori Parks's **In the Blood** (11-18-99, Shiva), which was generally labeled as "provocative but messy" by the press. As with her previous works, Parks took on American icons of the past to make contemporary points. The icon this time was Hawthorne's *The Scarlet Letter* with a modern-day Hester (Charlayne Woodard) as the welfare mother of five struggling to make ends meet in a world filled with hypocrisy. Some of the five men who fathered her illegitimate offspring make an appearance, including a hypocritical preacher (Reggie Montgomery) and a burnt-out doctor (Bruce MacVittie), both content to let Hester bear the burden of their sins. In an effective touch, the children were played by the same adult actors who portrayed Hester's tormentors, and a scene in which the mother tells the kids a bedtime story as they huddle under a bridge was the most moving in the play. Woodard was roundly cheered, but a month's run was sufficient to handle interested patrons.

Marsha Norman's latest play, **Trudy Blue** (12-2-99, MCC), departed from the abrasive realism seen in her earlier works and opted for an expressionistic approach that few aisle-sitters took kindly to. The drama is told through the mind of novelist Ginger (Polly Draper), who may or may not have lung cancer. Her alter ego is Trudy (Sarah Knowlton), a character from Ginger's pulp romance novel who acts as adviser, rival, and friend. With an unsatisfying marriage and a daughter whom she does not get along with, Ginger and Trudy have a lot to talk about, little of it very engrossing. By the end of the play (when it is determined that Ginger is truly dying of cancer), she reconciles with her family and sends Trudy off on her own. The unsatisfying drama was not helped by the fact that its plot often resembled the recent hit *Wit* (9-17-98), which had originated at the same theatre. *Trudy Blue* had premiered at Louisville's Humana Festival in 1995, where it was deemed very promising; in New York it barely lasted into the new year.

Unintentional giggles were heard throughout Tina Landau's theatrical meditation on **Space** (12-5-99, Public: Martinson), a script reviewed as "stultifying, pretentious New Age drivel," though most commentators complimented Landau's creative direction. When therapist Dr. Allan Saunders (Tom Irwin) finds similar symptoms in a handful of patients who claim to have had contact with aliens, he consults Dr. Bernadette Jump Cannon (Amy Morton), a scientist who has been listening to the cosmos for signs of life. After a lot of fancy talk about the universe "(Oh, Dr. Saunders, how can we know what our minds can't yet even perceive?"), she expands Allan's mind and wins his heart. Unfortunately she dies, and their future reunion in the stars brings the mind-expanding play to a close. Projections, eerie sounds, beguiling background music, and other high-tech effects made the production more interesting than the play.

A talented cast shone in Bryan Goluboff's formulaic domestic comedy **Shyster** (12-6-99, Blue Heron Arts Center). When an East Side Jewish landlord dies, his disjointed family gathers to sit shiva: the hard-nosed widow, Ada (Phyllis New-

man), no-good son Harry (Fisher Stevens), and daughter Rebecca (Annabella Sciorra), fresh from a military installation on the Gaza Strip. Also on hand is the African-American Elly (Saundra McClain) and her talented son, Ellis (Charles Malik Whitfield), who live in the dead father's building rent free because the old man liked them. But the family is nearly bankrupt, and complications arise when Harry turns "shyster" and demands rent money from Ellis. By the final curtain, family members are reconciled with each other and a deal is struck with Ellis and Elly. The old-fashioned play found little favor, but all of the performers were applauded, especially Newman, who "wonderfully underplayed," and Fisher, who, as one reviewer noted, "embraces premature decrepitude with gusto . . . he is Jack Nicholson on Slimfast."

Another transfer from Louisville's Humana Festival, Arthur Kopit's **Y2K** (12-8-99, Lucille Lortel) was not, as the title implied, about the threat of computer glitches as the year 2000 approached (something on the mind of theatregoers and everyone else as the last month of 1999 arrived), but about the dangers of computer hackers and the power they have over the unsuspecting and innocent. Joseph Elliot (James Naughton), a reputable publisher at Random House, is interrogated by federal agents for dealing with kiddie porn on the Internet. Joseph is innocent, of course, but soon he and his attractive wife, Joanne (Patricia Kalember), an executive at Sotheby's auction house, are tossed out of their jobs and find their bank accounts depleted. The villain (and narrator of the thriller) is Costa Astrakhan (Erik Jensen), a brilliant but demented Harvard student who was thrown out of one of Joseph's writing classes for plagiarism. Not only is he out for revenge, but Costa tells the audience that he fell in love with Joanne after seeing her naked in her bedroom and has been having an affair with her. Soon it becomes clear that Costa's narration is wildly unreliable, and his real motivation for destroying the Elliots turns out to be "because I can." There were plenty of holes in the plot, though the cautionary tale was uncomfortably thrilling at times. The Manhattan Theatre Club production, directed by Bob Balaban, was slick and satisfying, but audiences were not interested enough to keep the play on the boards for more than six weeks.

Jonathan Tolins's **If Memory Serves** (12-12-99, Promenade), one of the few commercial entries off Broadway this season, only lasted two weeks despite a fiery, comic performance by Elizabeth

Ashley as an aging television star who strives for a comeback. Once a reigning celebrity on the tube, Diane Barrow is now reduced to making cut-rate workout videos. Her grown son, Russell (Sam Trammell), does stand-up comedy and tells stories of his physically and sexually abusive mother, getting laughs by relating how she hit him with her Emmy Award and climbed into his bed on occasion. Ironically, the stories are true, and when the word reaches the public, who are starved for juicy tales of celebrity incest and cruelty, Diane is in the limelight once again. The dark comedy rarely worked, "undone by the very standards it attempts to satirize: the shallowness of television morality." Leonard Foglia directed an able cast, Ashley and Trammell going far beyond the call of duty.

The same night in the same building, another satire failed: Daniel Goldfarb's **Adam Baum and the Jew Movie** (12-12-99, McGinn/Cazale), which was mildly dismissed by the press as a "pointed but unbalanced comedy." Sam Baum (Ron Leibman), a Goldwyn-like Hollywood mogul, wants to make a "Jew movie" and get it released before gentile rival producer Daryl F. Zanuck can release his *Gentleman's Agreement*. The script provided by "the best goyishe writer in Hollywood," Garfield Hampson, Jr. (Christopher Evan Welch), is too Jewish for Baum's taste, and they battle about how much ethnicitiy the public will accept. Thrown into the arguments is Sam's teenage son, Adam (Adam Lamberg), about to make his bar mitzvah and struggling with his own Jewishness. Much of the dialogue was amusing (Leibman got to deliver such invented Goldwynisms as "I just finished reading half your script all the way through"), and the Blue Light Theatre mounting was polished and professional. Some critics thought Leibman gave "a powerhouse performance, the portrait of a man at odds with himself," while others claimed he "can overact even when he has nothing to say or do."

A revival of Peter Shaffer's *Amadeus* (12-15-80) that was a hit in London opened on December 15 at the Music Box. Aisle-sitters disagreed about the play, the performances, and even the decor but generally declared it a "respectable but uninspired production." Peter Hall staged the period comedy-drama (as he had the original London and Broadway productions), and Shaffer rewrote the script a bit, making Salieri (David Suchet) less villainous and more subtle. Some commentators thought Suchet's performance "magisterial . . . imbued with melancholy wit and dignified pathos"; others claimed that "there isn't enough

voltage in the performance." Michael Sheen's Mozart was also perceived in various ways, from "intensely physical, intensely felt" to "a black hole." Audiences still liked the play enough to let it run an unprofitable 165 performances.

On December 16, the one hundredth anniversary of Noel Coward's birth, Broadway finally saw his 1960 play **Waiting in the Wings** (12-16-99, Walter Kerr), a gentle comedy about retired actresses that was given a boost by the return of Lauren Bacall to the New York stage. A flop in London at its premiere forty years earlier (Coward was considered too *passé* in the 1960s world of John Osborne and Harold Pinter) and overlong and plagued with difficulties when this revival tried out in Boston, the Michael Langham production arrived on Broadway trimmed and glistening, providing one of the finest acting ensembles seen in many a season. The Wings is a charity home for actresses no longer working on the stage, run by the efficient ex-military officer Sylvia Archibald (Dana Ivey) and the affectionate Perry Lascoe (Simon Jones). The residents include the optimistic Bonita Belgrave (Elizabeth Wilson), the sardonic Cora Clarke (Rosemary Murphy), the gloom-and-doom Irishwoman Deirdre O'Malley (Helena Carroll), the piano-playing, childlike Maudie Melrose (Patricia Connolly), the guilt-ridden Almina Claire (Bette Heinritze), the lovable pyromaniac Sarita Myrtle (Helen Stenborg), and the grande dame May Davenport (Rosemary Harris). When the American actress Lotta Bainbridge (Bacall) joins the household, trouble brews because she and May have not spoken to each since Lotta (supposedly) stole her husband thirty years earlier. There were various subplots rather than one throughline—a journalist (Crista Moore) comes snooping for a sob story, an aged admirer (Barnard Hughes) regularly visits an old idol, Lotta's estranged son (Anthony Cummings) makes an appearance, the ladies fight the board of directors to get a solarium put in, the old feud between May and Lotts is settled—and the play never approached anything close to gripping. But the characters and the players were such wonderful company that the evening sparkled. Notices were mixed, Brantley summing up the hesitant commentators with his label "an unsteady interpretation of a patchy play" and Simon leading the praise with "a minor gem in that bittersweet mode at which Coward excelled." Originally announced as a limited run, the production was held over and ran out the season. It was, sadly, co-producer Alexander Cohen's last Broadway venture.

The Public took a widespread drubbing for its "gaudy, frantic" *Hamlet* on December 19 at the Newman; director Andrei Serban turned the tragedy into a "travesty." Among the silliest moments: Osric (Francis Jue) flying in like Peter Pan; Laertes (Hamish Linklater) lusting after his sister, Ophelia (Lynn Collins); a king (Colm Feore) and queen (Diane Venora) who cannot stop groping each other; and Fortinbras played by two angels. Some critics argued that Liev Schreiber might have made a passable Hamlet if he hadn't been directed to vomit onstage a lot, wear a pig mask and a bloody apron at court, and follow other ludicrous instructions.

Neither could acclaimed actress Kathleen Chalfont save Sybille Pearson's **True History and Real Adventures** (12-19-99, Vineyard), a surreal treatise on Calamity Jane and the American West. Scottish immigrant Margaret Mackenzie (Angela Goethals) settles in Ontario, Canada, in 1893 and becomes obsessed with the mythic figure of sharpshooter Jane. So she and a gang of ragtag teens head south to the United States to seek out the aged Jane (Chalfont). The "illogical, implausible" plot was often interrupted for vaudeville-like reflections on the dying of the West, racism, and corporate monopolies. Michael Mayer directed but, like Chalfant and Goethals, was done in by the "well-meant but wayward script." After two weeks they were all free to pursue better things.

Instead of getting weary of the stand-up comic (it was his fifth Broadway show), both audiences and critics embraced **Jackie Mason: Much Ado About Everything** (12-30-99, John Golden), and he got even better reviews and did even better box office than in his previous engagements. President Clinton's affair with White House intern Monica Lewinsky provided fodder for much of the evening, but Mason also found time to comment on old and new singing idols, nouvelle cuisine, airline travel, African Americans, Hispanics, and, of course, Jews. Mason filled the house through July, when he set out on tour.

New Year's Eve, usually one of the hottest nights for theatregoing, was a financial dud for Broadway as all the theatres canceled their evening performances because of the millions of visitors descending on Times Square for the "millennium" festivities. The new year arrived, computers (and the world) did not die, and then it was business back to normal.

Two off-off-Broadway revivals of rarely seen plays proved to be flawed but more intriguing than many new entries this season. Mae West's infamous *Sex* (4-26-26) on January 6 at the Gershwin Hotel Living Room was obviously dated, but watching a play that scandalized New York, was closed by the police, and was the center of censorship legislation was more interesting than a mere bit of history trivia. Carolyn Baeumler played West's role, an ambitious prostitute who moves up in the world. The revival did well enough during its three-week run that it returned at the Players Theatre in June. The Pan Asian Rep revived John Patrick's Pulitzer Prize winner *Teahouse of the August Moon* (10-15-53) on January 9 with Ernest Abuba giving a wry and wise performance as the narrator, Sakini. Since this comedy was about the bumbling efforts of the American military to democratize a Japanese village after World War II, its presentation by an Asian troupe made the evening all the more engrossing.

Playwrights Horizons offered Kira Obolensky's offbeat **Lobster Alice** (1-9-00, Wilder) for less than two weeks, there being few to recommend it or wish to see it. The play's premise was not uninteresting: in 1946, Salvador Dali worked with Disney animators on a surreal short that was never completed. In Obolenshy's take on the situation, the reasons for the abortive film revolve around the inability that Dali (David Patrick Kelly) and straitlaced animator John Finch (Reg Rogers) have working together, though the Spanish artist has a lasting effect on the animator, who is also currently animating *Alice in Wonderland*. The Alice of the title refers to the Lewis Carroll creation as well as Alice Horowitz (Jessica Hecht), the studio secretary who hopes to be transformed by Dali but instead falls into a normal romance with Finch. This hardly riveting triangle was often interrupted by images or characters from Dali's and Carroll's works, rarely adding anything to the proceedings but some clever costumes by Ann Hould-Ward. Reviews ranged from mildly amused ("a whimsical riff") to highly annoyed ("a pitiful exhumation of moldering Surrealism").

Two radically different revivals opened on January 12. The Atlantic's Mamet season continued with the double bill that first brought him recognition: *Sexual Perversity in Chicago* and *Duck Variations* (9-29-75). The press found the one-acts "decently if not brilliantly produced" and disagreed whether these early works were better or inferior to Mamet's later and longer plays. Off-off-Broadway, the Mint Theatre Company encored its spring 1999 revival of Harley Granville-Barker's 1905 Edwardian problem play *The Voysey Inheritance* for ten weeks. When a prosperous banker admits to his son that large sums of money have been fraudulently used, the idealistic young man falls into the trap of continuing the deception until he is caught and redeems himself. The potency of the old drama impressed most of the critics; D. J. R. Bruchner in the *New York Times* declared, "Few theatrical works so shrewdly raise profound questions about the role of ordinary morality in the making of money . . . as this 95-year-old play . . . and none in English does it with such elegance and wit." Ironically, the rarely produced Granville-Barker would enjoy two acclaimed revivals this season.

Broadway's first new work of the new year, David Hirson's **Wrong Mountain** (1-13-00, Eugene O'Neill), concerned a self-centered poet, Henry Dennett (Ron Rifkin), who decries the modern theatre and makes a bet with the prosperous playwright Guy Halperin (Michael Winters) that in six months he can write a piece of trash and have it produced and praised. Henry does just that; the play wins an award and is produced by a regional theatre, where the sour writer eventually starts to believe the compliments paid him. To drive home the point, Henry is also suffering from a sickness, a form of tapeworm that is slowly devouring his insides. Hirson was remembered for his ambitious verse drama *La Bête* (2-10-91), in which verbiage ran rampant. Such was the case with his new offering as well. Although it was written in prose, "every line either sounds like a quotation (bad enough), is a quotation (worse), or is one character quoting another (worse yet)." Much of this dialogue was Henry spouting off about the inanity of the theatre and the stupidity of "the suburban know-nothings" who patronize it, such as calling a play "a macabre peep show for third-rate minds eager to have their sympathies titillated and their sense of humanity massaged by the dime-store imaginings of second-rate minds." The mostly negative notices slammed the script ("a shrill, simplistic, and rather muddled play") and David Jones's "disjointed" and "excessive" direction, which had the stage filled with oversized props as distorted Grieg music filled the air. *La Bête* had closed after twenty-four performances and became a cause célèbre of sorts. *Wrong Mountain* closed after twenty-eight showings, but few came to its defense.

American icon Mae West showed up a second time this season with **Dirty Blonde** (1-14-00, New York Theatre Workshop). Claudia Shear, who had gained some recognition for her solo show *Blown Sideways Through Life* (9-29-93), wrote a full-bodied play for herself and triumphed as actress

and playwright. Part of the play was a quirky biography of West (Shear) as she struggles through vaudeville, has a controversial career on Broadway, and then conquers Hollywood. The second plot was a contemporary story about aspiring actress Jo (Shear), who idolizes West (and cannot help but copy her mannerisms and inflections), and cinema devotee Charlie (Kevin Chamberlain), who once met West when he was a teenager. The two fans meet while visiting West's gravesite on her birthday and fall into a tentative romance. But when Jo learns that Charlie has a penchant for dressing up like West, the relationship is strained until both learn to accept their inner selves and not depend on the movie star's persona. The play ends with the two Wests (Shear and Chamberlain in drag) embracing and walking off into the sunset. Chamberlain and Bob Stillman played all the men in West's life, most memorably two queens teaching the young Mae about the art of exaggeration. James Lapine directed the tricky script, and Douglas Stein designed the inventive set, a pink box that became different locales as pieces popped in and out. Notices were mostly approving, from "a silly-sweet confection that will be enshrined in the annals of fluff" to "a wonderfully warm-blooded play" that shows that "being a caricature doesn't mean you can't be a character too." The three-week engagement was so popular the comedy-drama reopened on Broadway at the Helen Hayes on May 1 for a long run.

Theatre for a New Audience revived Shakespeare's infrequently produced *King John* on January 30 at the American Place with some success. While director Karen Coonrod could not solve many of the history drama's inherent difficulties, the mounting was deemed one of "admirable clarity" that "makes its central points (which, refreshingly, are also the play's) with gusto."

If avant-gardist Robert Wilson was still going strong this season, so was his colleague Richard Foreman, whose **Bad Boy Nietzsche** (2-8-00, St. Mark's Church) beguiled (and irritated) audiences for eleven weeks. Foreman and his Ontological Theatre explored the mind of the German philosopher of the title with his usual profusion of startling images, noises, and mystery. Foreman's work was always difficult to review; this piece was labeled everything from "mesmerizing" to a "happy surprise" to "rubbish." Someone who had kept track noted that this was Foreman's forty-seventh play.

A British troupe called Shared Experience brought an offbeat stage adaptation of Charlotte Brontë's **Jane Eyre** (2-8-00, BAM) to Brooklyn for six performances. Polly Teale's version presented the first Mrs. Rochester, Bertha (Harriette Ashcroft), as the alter ego of Jane (Penny Layden), the two of them together from childhood and side by side through the famous scenes with Mr. Rochester (Sean Murray) and others. The "psychodrama" and its versatile cast were both applauded.

The Roundabout's off-Broadway mounting of Shaw's *Arms and the Man* on February 10 at the Gramercy met with general disfavor in the press, most critics complaining about how actor-turned-director Roger Rees emphasized "the play's farcical aspects without being very funny." Henry Czerny (Bluntschli), Katie Finneran (Raina), and Paul Michael Valley (Sergius) led the cast, who were criticized for everything from their "strident" performances to their affected British accents (for a comedy that takes place in Bulgaria!).

A new Hispanic play at the Public, Nilo Cruz's **Two Sisters and a Piano** (2-15-00, Shiva), received a mixed critical reaction but boasted an "extraordinarily vibrant performance" by Daphne Rubin-Vega. In 1991 in Castro's Cuba, two sisters are released from prison and return to their empty family home in Havana, where the air is filled with memories and recriminations about the past. Maria Celia (Adriana Sevan) is a writer who offended the regime, and her pianist sister, Sofia (Rubin-Vega), was also imprisoned because she had signed the incriminating manifesto. While Maria Celia broods about the past and her absent husband, who is in exile in Europe, Sofia has a tender and romantic encounter with Victor Manuel (Gary Perez), a man who comes to tune the piano. He promises Sophia to return, but he never does, and the two sisters are left clutching each other in despair and understanding. Both script and production were criticized, but Rubin-Vega's performance was "alive with conflicting feelings—childish anger at the tedium of knitting (the sisters' lone source of income), desperate loneliness . . . pent-up anger at her sister . . . and bitter resentment for the years of life sacrificed to ideas she was too young to understand."

Off Broadway had better luck than Broadway with the thriller genre with Nancy Hasty's **The Director** (2-15-00, ArcLight), which the press called "funny, suspenseful, and entertaining" and a "thoroughly absorbing new experiment in terror." Young playwright Annie (Tasha Lawrence) finds the ideal director for her autobiographical drama: burnt out Grotowski-like artist Peter (John Shea), whose early, radical stage work was so impressive. But Peter has given up on the commercial theatre and now works as a janitor.

Tasha has convinced the temperamental director to take on her play, but she has her doubts once he starts rehearsals and is more interested in doing scenes from Strindberg and playing mind games with his put-upon cast. Soon Peter is controlling both playwright and actors in a deadly game of psychological suicide. While there was no body or bucket of blood, the climatic destruction of the director was gripping and penetrating. Plaudits for Evan Bergman's taut direction, the fine cast, and Hasty's ability to "reinvent and revitalize the [thriller] form" helped the little drama run past the summer.

Two very enjoyable revivals followed, both older plays that might be considered dated but were so well acted that they were warmly welcomed by the press and the public. Lincoln Center mounted a glowing revival of Arthur Laurents's *The Time of the Cuckoo* (10-15-52) on February 21 downstairs in the Mitzi E. Newhouse. Debra Monk gave a "riveting" performance as Leona, the spinster filled with "love-starvedness and suspicion, hopeful fantasizing and injured pride." Olek Krupa was Renato, the Italian glass merchant with whom she has a bittersweet fling; Tom Aldredge and Polly Holliday were the elder touristing couple, Adam Trese and Ana Reeder the younger pair; and Cigdem Onat played the worldly-wise Signora Fioria, who runs the Venice *pensione* where the Americans are staying. The skillful cast, Nicholas Martin's knowing direction, and James Noone's evocative setting were all saluted. The revival ran into May. On February 23, Off Broadway's Drama Dept. revived George Kelly's forgotten comedy *The Torch-Bearers* (8-29-22) at Greenwich House for two weeks, and again a glittering cast breathed life into an old work. Dylan Baker's direction of this tale about a group of Philadelphia socialites putting on an amateur theatrical for a worthy cause was faulted by several commentators, but the ladies on hand were delicious, Marian Seldes, Faith Prince, Joan Copeland, Claire Beckman, and Judith Blazer in particular. Audiences packed the small house for the "rickety but irresistible revival."

Charles Busch, described by one commentator as a "campy downtown playwright," offered his "most accessible yet" comedy with **The Tale of the Allergist's Wife** (2-29-00, City Center Stage II). Upper-class New Yorker Marjorie Taub (Linda Lavin), a failed novelist and frequent patron of the arts, is depressed because she feels all her cultural knowledge (Hermann Hesse is her favorite author) and savoir faire is a fraud. Marjorie's therapist has died, her retired allergist husband, Ira (Tony Roberts) doesn't understand her, and her continually constipated mother (Shirl Bernheim) is driving her crazy. (Marjorie is so overwrought that just before the play begins she has tried to commit suicide in a Disney Store.) Then into her life comes Lee Green (Michele Lee), a virtuoso of a woman who has done everything from sleep with Gunther Grass to introduce Lady Diana to land mines. Lee seems too good to be true; in fact, it seems that she is not only Marjorie's ideal companion but also probably a figment of her imagination. In either case, Lee puts a new spin on Marjorie's existence and even sparks up her marriage before Marjorie learns she doesn't need Lee to find purpose in her life. Busch abandoned the realm of parody for the first time in his career and created original, daffy characters of his own, Marjorie in particular, whom one critic described as "a Neil Simon heroine in Pinterland." Lavin's portrayal of the delightfully miserable woman was extolled by all the critics, Lahr calling her "Nancy Walker's natural heir . . . small but not demure, Lavin has backbone; even when she shuffles about the stage in her black slippers, she walks like a guardsman on parade." Praise for the rest of the cast, Lynn Meadow's brisk direction, and Busch's "nicely structured, intelligently funny, satirically relevant" comedy helped fill the theatre for the six-week engagement and encouraged the Manhattan Theatre Club to move the production to Broadway in the fall.

Another "downtown" playwright in the same vein as Busch, Nicky Silver fared less well with his dark farce **The Altruists** (3-6-00, Vineyard) about well-meaning, socially conscious New Yorkers who are less than kind when it comes to those closest to them. East Village resident Ronald (Joey Slotnick) is a gay man from the upper class who believes in civil rights for all and in saving both the whales and the rain forests. He purposely lives in a small apartment, thinking it will help others, and tries to rehabilitate the handsome young hustler, Lance (Eddie Cahill), he picked up the night before. Then Ronald's hyperactive sister, Sydney (Veanne Cox), enters in her usual shocking-pink garb, proclaiming that she has shot her boyfriend, Ethan, as he lay under the covers because he sold her Louis XIV armoire to finance some worthy cause. But soon Ethan (Sam Robards) enters unharmed, confusions abound as everyone sleeps with everyone else, and all the do-gooders are revealed to be the least tolerant of people. Few commentators felt the rapid comedy was able to maintain its stamina ("both exhilarating and exhausting"), but Cox was

unanimously lauded, reviews describing her as "one, long, skinny, exposed nerve" and noting that she turns "theatrical cardboard into fuel for a one-woman bonfire."

Also off-off Broadway, Michael Hollinger's farce **An Empty Plate in the Café du Grand Boeuf** (3-8-00, Primary Stages) pleased few critics, but it too had a delectable cast. Victor (George Wendt) sits in his favorite Parisian restaurant in 1961, depressed over the fact that his girlfriend, Miss Berger (Nance Williamson), has rejected his proposal of marriage because, among other reasons, a case of the mumps has left him sterile. Being a big Ernest Hemingway fan, Victor had popped the question to Miss Berger during a bullfight in Madrid, and now he plans to commit suicide just as Papa recently has. Victor decides to starve himself while sitting in his favorite eatery, much to the horror of the maître d' Claude (Jonathan Freeman), who describes in sensuous detail all the dishes that the chef, Gaston (Michael McCormick), is more than willing to prepare for him. Also on hand are Claude's wife, the waitress Mimi (Annie Golden), whom Gaston lusts after, and a waiter, Antoine (Matt Stinton), who has a stutter but compensates for it by playing "Lady of Spain" on the tuba whenever possible. John Rando directed the less-than-filling script, but the cast was more than satisfying, especially Freeman, who turned his descriptions of food into a gastronomic striptease.

The final months of the Broadway season saw a handful of superior revivals, beginning on March 9 with Sam Shepard's *True West* (12-23-80) at the Circle in the Square. Film actors John C. Reilly and Philip Seymour Hoffman alternated in playing the two brothers, switching roles after every two performances, which became even more interesting (and somewhat confusing) because in the script the two rivaling siblings exchange personalities. Mostly rave notices for the two performers and Matthew Warchus's precise direction made the "smashing" and "thrilling" revival a hot ticket, the first hit the Circle had seen in years. The limited engagement was extended but, when the original stars departed, the box office plummeted and the revival closed on July 29.

Few theatregoers got to see James Lapine's **The Moment When** (3-12-00, Playwrights Horizons), which postponed its opening and then quietly closed in less than a week, but some reviewers found it an "ambitious piece of writing" and felt both script and production deserved better. The title refers to those points in one's life when a decision or a twist of fate alters all subsequent events. Book-cover designer Steven (Mark Ruffalo) tries to pick up author Alice (Illeana Douglas) at a literary cocktail party in 1984 but is sidetracked by the appearance of editorial assistant Dana (Arija Bareikis), whom he seduces instead. Over the next fifteen years of Steven and Dana's marriage and divorce, the unexpected turns in life are explored, presenting the proposition that life would have been much different for all of them had Steven pursued Alice that night at the party. J. B. Priestley had explored the same premise decades earlier with his *Dangerous Corner* (10-27-32), and the crisscrossing of relationships reminded some aisle-sitters of the recent *Closer* (3-25-99). Michael Lindsay-Hogg directed the expert cast, which also featured Phyllis Newman as the pushy literary agent, Paula, and Kieran Culkin as Steven and Dana's philosophical son, Wilson.

The second Harley Granville-Barker revival of the season was the Theatre for a New Audience mounting of *Waste* at the American Place on March 12. This controversial drama, about a politician whose career is threatened when his mistress dies aborting their unborn child, was written in 1907 but not allowed a production in England until 1936. Once again, commentators marveled at the potency of Granville-Barker's writing and applauded the "handsomely designed, thoughtfully staged production." With such issues as a woman's right to abortion, the conflict between church and state, and the power of a sex scandal to bring down an administration, the play was considered by some to be "the most immediately topical play on a New York stage." Bartlett Sher staged the drama, and designer John Arnone provided the many locations through a series of doors and archways. Notices were mixed for the Atlantic Theatre Company's revival of *American Buffalo* (2-16-77) on March 16, the conclusion of its David Mamet season. (This production had originated in London, where it was an immediate sellout.) William H. Macy, considered the quintessential Mamet actor for his many roles in the writer's plays and films, played small-time thief Teach, but most critics found his portrayal "pallid" and lacking the menace that the role demanded. Low-key performances by Mark Webber and Philip Baker Hall as his cohorts in crime did not help, and many reviews labeled the revival "bland" and "hollow." But audiences thought otherwise and willingly came to see Macy for the play's two-and-a-half-month run.

On the other hand, both critics and theatregoers responded enthusiastically to the Broadway revival of Eugene O'Neill's *A Moon for the Misbegotten* (5-2-57) on March 19 at the Walter Kerr.

Cherry Jones triumphed as the crude, overpowering Josie Hogan, even though most commentators pointed out she was neither physically nor vocally ideal for the role. Film star Gabriel Byrne (in his New York stage debut) surprised and astonished as the guilt-ridden James Tyrone, and Roy Dotrice stole his scenes (and won a Tony Award) as Josie's crafty father, Phil. Daniel Sullivan directed the "heart-stopping" revival, which extended its limited run to July 2.

Unanimous raves greeted Eileen Heckart for her "meticulous, truthful and utterly unsentimental performance" as a woman descending into senility in Kenneth Lonergan's **The Waverly Gallery** (3-22-00, Promenade). Gladys Green (Heckart) was once a radical Party member, but now she sits in her Greenwich Village art gallery and rants about Koreans and blacks invading her neighborhood. Poor business and her difficulties in coping with everyday tasks are forcing Gladys to give up her gallery, and she is losing her reason as well. As she both torments and depends more and more on her family, Gladys's downfall is both tragic and annoying. Much of the play was a clinical documentary about the ravages Altzheimer's disease has on the victim and her loved ones, and the writing, while piercingly accurate, failed to make a play. But Heckart gave "a beautiful coherent portrayal of a woman sliding into incoherence." Scott Ellis directed a strong cast that included Maureen Anderman, Mark Blum, and Josh Hamilton. The drama ran two months, and although it was not a Broadway entry, the Tony committee gave Heckart a special award for her long and fruitful career.

The latest docudrama written and performed by Anna Deavere Smith, **House Arrest** (3-26-00, Public: Newman), failed to catch fire and was rejected by the press as "unfocused and discursive," so it was only kept on the boards for two weeks. Instead of recreating the reactions to one particular event as she had in the past, Smith this time took on the history of the U.S. presidency, interviewing hundreds of people about their views on the office. Quoting from politicians, historians, and the common folk on the street, the script was too diffuse to be effective and too removed to be engaging, even though a lot of attention was put on the recent Clinton sex scandal. When the piece had tried out in regional theatres in Los Angeles and Washington, it was performed by an ensemble of actors. But at the Public, Smith did a solo turn again, and even her quicksilver changes of character seemed less impressive.

Critics were even harsher with Jessica Goldberg's **The Hologram Theory** (3-27-00, Promenade), a "half-baked and annoying play" about youths who kill, the ghost of one of their victims who appears to his twin sister in a dream, and a journalist who beds down with one of the murderers to get a good story. The title referred to an interfering filmmaker's grand realization that, like a hologram, all the pieces of the world around us are connected into one whole. There were few compliments for the cast, all of whom were "at liberty" in two weeks.

Running just as long and only slightly more appreciated was Jean-Marie Besset's **What You Get and What You Expect** (3-28-00, New York Theatre Workshop), but this time the direction and cast were commended. The farcical plot centered on two rival architects, Phillipe Derrien (Stephen Caffrey) and Robert Lebret (Peter Jacobson), who are competing for a government commission to design a monument on the moon. Architects, government officials, wives, and secretaries all hop in and out of bed with each other as they jockey for political or artistic dominance. Christopher Ashley directed the Hal J. Witt translation of the French original, keeping the proceedings crisp and playful, and the cast also included Pamela Payton-Wright, T. Scott Cunningham, Kathryn Meisle, and Daniel Gerroll, all in first-rate form.

The British-born actor David Cale, who had worked for some years in New York and put together solo pieces in the past, wrote a two-hander called **Betwixt** (3-30-00, St. Clements) in which he and Cara Seymour portrayed several similarly displaced Brits through a series of monologues. From a cocky cockney who finds a new life on a soap opera to the sensuous receptionist at a phone sex service ("for royalty, press three"), the various characters were mostly caricatured stereotypes but were sensitively performed. Reviews ranged from "modestly entertaining" to "ineffably flat-footed."

Two revivals boasting movie stars opened on April 9. Patrick Stewart was reunited with most of the original company for Arthur Miller's *The Ride Down Mt. Morgan* (11-16-98) at the Ambassador for a sixteen-week engagement. Miller had supposedly revised the script, but few reviewers could detect any major changes, still gently criticizing the play and approving of the cast. Stewart's portrayal of bigamist Lyman Felt was more endorsed than extolled, but notices were enthusiastic for Frances Conroy's Wasp wife, Theo. The "stubbornly lifeless play" did get a bit of publicity halfway through the run when Stewart publicly denounced his producers and the Shubert

Organization from the stage after one performance, claiming that they did not care about the play and were not publicizing it properly. The producers countered with statistics showing that more money was spent on advertising the revival than just about any other Broadway non-musical and had Stewart brought before Actors' Equity on charges of unprofessional behavior. Despite all the brouhaha and Stewart's legion of fans, the Ambassador rarely played at capacity. Film ingenue Mira Sorvino returned to the stage and was saluted for her "delicate, quietly captivating performance" as Ersilia Drei, the suicidal nanny in Pirandello's *Naked* (11-8-26), at the Classic Stage Company off Broadway. Few aisle-sitters were impressed with Nicholas Wright's new translation or the clumsy production, but Sorvino was intoxicating as a woman whose only reality is what she reads in the newspapers about herself.

By April 10 all of Broadway's thirty-seven theatres had occupants, the first time the Street was fully booked in many seasons. Fourteen of the houses were featuring non-musicals (seven of them revivals), which was also impressive. Six days later the musical James Joyce's *The Dead* closed, and once again there was room on Broadway.

Two major off-Broadway disappointments followed. Beth Henley's **Family Week** (4-10-00, Century) received such a drubbing from the press ("the most flagrantly miserable play to be seen in some time") that it quickly closed. After her son is murdered and her marriage falls apart, Claire (Angelina Phillips) is sent to the expensive Pastures Recovery Center for treatment. The black comedy focused on the seven days that constitute "family week," in which Claire is visited by her bitter alcoholic sister, Rickey (Carol Kane), her guilty alcoholic mother, Lena (Rose Gregorio), and her bitter and guilty daughter, Kay (Julia Weldon). In a series of sessions with Claire's relatives, everyone gets to dredge up the past and hurl insults at each other. But Henley's gift for walking the fine line between farce and heartbreak was not in evidence, and the result was as irritating as it was monotonous. The same night, a program titled **Suite in Two Keys** (4-10-00, Lucille Lortel) featured two of Noel Coward's later one-acts: *A Song at Twilight* (2-28-74) and **Shadows of the Evening,** which was written in 1966 but had not been seen in New York before. In the first, Judith Ivey played the actress Carlotta Gray, who tries to blackmail aging author Sir Hugo Latymer (Paxton Whitehead) with letters from his dead male lover while Hugo's German wife, Hilde

(Haley Mills in her New York stage debut), continues to turn a blind eye. *Shadows of the Evening* concerned dying businessman George Hilgay (Whitehead), who had left his wife and children seven years earlier to live with Linsa Savignac (Ivey). She invites his betrayed wife, Anne (Mills), to join her, and together they hope to make George's final months more pleasant, although how such a thing is possible seems beyond the three of them. Despite the fine cast and the usually reliable John Tillinger as director, the evening was generally declared "bottom-drawer Coward," and the producers quickly withdrew it.

The most awarded new play of the Broadway season was Michael Frayn's three-character drama **Copenhagen** (4-11-00, Royale), which had been a hit in London and arrived here with Michael Blakemore directing an American cast. In 1941, German physicist Werner Heisenberg (Michael Cumpsty) traveled from his native Germany to Nazi-occupied Copenhagen to visit his colleague, mentor, and friend Niels Bohr (Philip Bosco), the renowned Danish scientist and father of atomic physics. History recorded their meeting but has never learned what happened at the fateful reunion of two brilliant scientists on opposite sides of a world war, both sides frantically trying to create an atom bomb. Frayn's play is a fictionalized account of what might have occurred, with Niels's wife, Margrethe (Blair Brown), joining the two for a philosophic and emotional triangle. Characters spoke to each other and to the audience, moving from present tense to the past within single speeches. The acting area, designed by Peter J. Davison, was a bright circular chamber that made the trio of actors look like they were being examined under a microscope. Blakemore even put audience members on the stage so that the characters were able at any point to turn to a spectator and reveal some new tidbit of narration or commentary. The talk, ranging from fond reminiscences to scientific debates to chilling insinuations, was intellectually potent, if often a bit contrived and artificial. Just as Heisenberg's Uncertainty Principle states that a particle being observed is changed by the very act of observation, the truth was bounced about the stage as each character tried to make sense of the many factors at work on them. Heisenberg proclaimed at one point, "I am a particle; I'm also a wave." But Frayn's treatment was so earnest and serious that, as Lahr noted, "you defensively want to tousle its well-kempt appearance and tell it to lighten up." Surprisingly, no major critic recalled that Tom Stoppard had used the same Heisenberg

principle to define changing human relationships in his thriller-comedy *Hapgood* (12-4-94) but did so with the kind of panache Lahr and others longed for in *Copenhagen*. Nevertheless, notices were highly complimentary, and the play won the Tony Award and New York Drama Critics Circle Award for best foreign play. (Brown and Blakemore also won Tonys.) Audiences responded to the "extraordinarily ambitious play" well enough to allow it to run far into the next season.

Another London hit opened the next night, Martin Sherman's one-woman drama **Rose** (4-12-00, Lyceum), although both the playwright and the star, Olympia Dukakis, were American. Jewish octogenarian Rose sits on a park bench in Miami Beach and recounts her life history: her youth in a Ukrainian shetl; falling in love with a one-eyed artist in Poland; losing her daughter and surviving the war years in the Warsaw ghetto; traveling to the new state of Israel, where she meets and marries a Jewish-American sailor; moving to Atlantic City and starting a family; running off with a young lover to a commune after her husband dies; and spending her old age in Florida. It was certainly a life filled with incidents, and Dukakis grabbed the opportunity and ran with it, but few critics found the narrative very fulfilling as a play. Sherman peppered the tale with gentle humor (Rose recalls that the one-eyed Pole "wasn't a bad artist. He wasn't exactly Chagall, but then who is? Jews aren't visual—look at what they wear") and some touching moments that audiences found palatable enough to allow it to run out its limited fifty-five-performance engagement.

Arguably the finest revival in this spring of revivals was London's Donmar Warehouse remounting of Tom Stoppard's *The Real Thing* (1-5-84) on April 17 at the Belasco. No stars were in evidence in the sterling British cast, but high praise was bestowed on all, particularly Stephen Dillane as the too-clever-by-half writer Henry, Sarah Woodward as his actress-wife Charlotte, and Jennifer Ehle as Annie, the activist-actress Henry falls in love with. Also lauded was director David Leveaux's "intentionally muted, intensely thoughtful production." The engagement was limited to nineteen weeks, but before it left it won Tony Awards for Dillane and Ehle and as Best Revival.

Lee Blessing's second off-off-Broadway entry this season was **Cobb** (4-17-00, Melting Pot), a multi-layered look at baseballer Ty Cobb. The famous hitter was portrayed by three actors (Michael Cullen, Matt Mabe, and Michael Sabatino) as he looks back over his life and finds his fame clouded by injustice and narrow-mindedness. From his days as a schoolyard bully to his later blindness from success, Cobb is haunted by the memory of Negro Leaguer Oscar Charleston (Clark Jackson), whose bitterness and dignity force Cobb to confront his own inadequacies. Some enthusiastic notices ("brilliantly constructed" and "triumphant") kept the little house crowded for seven weeks.

In a much more lavish production than originally seen, Julie Taymor's theatricalized pageant of Carlo Gozzi's *The Green Bird* (3-7-96) came to Broadway's Cort on April 18 and revealed once again that the magic of her musical *The Lion King* could be captured even on a smaller scale. The eighteenth-century fairy tale became a vivid display of masks, puppets, feathers, lights, music, and dance (though the play was technically a non-musical) that was meant to appeal to adults as much as children. Papier-mâché clothes that dissolve into silken rainments, levitating apples that sing, and a giant Bunraku-like bird that takes on a human form were among the treats presented for the audience. Mixed critical reaction greeted the unusual entry, and the revival only did modest business as it struggled for fifty-five performances.

The British invasion continued with London's Out of Joint and the Royal National production of Sebastian Barry's **Our Lady of Sligo** (4-20-00, Irish Rep), "a bleak portrait of Irish lives" that was distinguished by Sinead Cusack, who, as Brantley wrote, "floods the stage with a magnetic force of will, giving one of those performances that keeps replaying itself in your mind." Another in Barry's series of dramas about his ancestors, the drama revolves around Mai O'Hara (Cusack), a middle-aged victim of liver cancer who lies dying in a Dublin hospital in 1953 and is visited by her husband, engineer Jack (Jarlath Conroy), and her daughter, the out-of-work actress Joanie (Melinda Page Hamilton). Mai's morphine treatments put her into a delirium that also allows her to imagine visitors from the dead, her father (Tom Lacy) in particular. Alcoholism, infidelity, and other sins of the past are heaped onto the dying Mai, but she meets them with fierce determination and a mordant sense of humor. Critics were less enthused about the script than about Cusack, most finding Barry's colorful verbiage ("pierced up out of . . . slumbers like a gannet surfacing through the salty power of the river tide") a bit tedious after a while. But for ten weeks New

Yorkers had a chance to see one of the most "captivating" performances of the season.

The last new play of the Broadway season, Elaine May's urban comedy **Taller Than a Dwarf** (4-24-00, Longacre), was arguably the worst of the season, according to the critics, though audiences were willing to pay to see its stars Matthew Broderick and Parker Posey (in her Broadway debut) for fifty-six showings. Howard Miller (Broderick), a Queens resident who works for a market research firm in Manhattan, goes through midlife crisis, urban angst, and various other torments during one day in which he feels the modern-day world is ganging up on him. Something as simple as a broken shower handle escalates into a wild confrontation with the super (Michael McShane). Howard retreats to his bed and refuses to join the working world despite the pleas from his wife, Selma (Posey), and their stereotypic Jewish parents (Joyce Van Patten, Marcia Jean Kurtz, and Jerry Adler). When Howard finally emerges from his bed and plans on making millions in a law suit, he is proclaimed a champion of the common man and a hope for us all. Typical of the notices, Charles Isherwood wrote in *Variety* that "its dialogue is alternately aimless and inane, the jokes tired or crude, the slapstick strained and graceless." May's old friend and associate Alan Arkin was the unlucky director.

August Wilson scored another critical success with **Jitney** (4-25-00, Second Stage), a play he had written back in 1979 before he had found recognition as a playwright. Greatly revised by the author and beautifully directed by Marion McClinton, the drama concerned a group of African-American gypsy-cab drivers in Pittsburgh in 1977. Cabbies and various neighborhood hangers-on drift in and out of the decaying office of the cab company run by Becker (Paul Butler), who acts as boss and referee during the many confrontations that spring up. The interfering driver Turnbo (Stephen McKinley Henderson) makes trouble for co-worker and Vietnam vet Youngblood (Russell Hornsby) when he suggests to his girlfriend, Rena (Michole Briana White), that the restless hothead is cheating on her with her own sister. Cab driver Fielding (Anthony Chisholm) has taken to the bottle again, lamenting over the wife he hasn't seen in over twenty years, and Becker has to threaten to fire him if he doesn't shape up. But Becker is even more concerned about his son, Booster (Carl Lumbly), who is getting out of prison after serving a twenty-year sentence. (A promising science major in college, Booster shot his white girlfriend when she pretended not to know him when his father caught them in bed together.) News that the whole block is to be demolished for a city renewal project also hangs over the heads of all the characters, causing them to be more uncertain of their future than ever. Because each character was vividly written, the whole cast was able to shine, creating one of the best ensembles of the season. But the real star was Wilson, whose gift for rich and textured dialogue and detailed characterization was once again in evidence. Brantley commented with others on how the play's "varied musicality and stylish detail [allows] a complete urban symphony [to] emerge." The drama won the New York Drama Critics Circle Award for Best American Play and played to full houses for many months.

Yet another British import this season was Rebecca Prichard's "intense, lopsided" street drama **Yard Gal** (4-26-00, MCC), which the Royal Court Theatre brought to New York for a month. A gang of female toughs in Hackney, a London East End neighborhood, rules the streets, holding on to their turf (or yardies) and getting nicknamed yard gals. Two of the gang members, the Nigerian Boo (Sharon Duncan-Brewster) and the local native Marie (Amelia Lowdell), are the featured characters, but they often voice the comments and opinions of the other girls. Dealing with their pimp, the rivalries within the gang, the occasional smashed bottle in the face, unwanted pregnancy, and drug trafficking, the two girls have a close yet deadly bond between them. When Marie kills one of the yard gals, she frames Boo for the crime, and the two ex-friends face each other in the final scene, prison bars between them but still irrevocably linked together. While commentators questioned the violent and haphazard script, they admitted that the acting was vibrant and that Prichard had expertly captured the language of the streets. (The dialogue was filled with so many localisms and slang that the Playbill program provided a glossary of terms for the audience.)

Two of Broadway's most illustrious post-war producers died within days of each other in late April: Alexander Cohen, the venerable impresario active on the Street from 1941 to the current season, and David Merrick, the "abominable showman" who created controversy, news, and hit shows from 1954 to 1996. Their passing was perhaps the most telling symbol for the end of the century as well as the demise of an era now relegated to fading memories and history books.

Four more revivals followed, the least likely being a remounting of Philip Barry's *Hotel Universe* (4-14-30) on April 27 by the Blue Light Theatre Company at the McGinn/Cazale. This problematic piece, about wealthy and/or artistic expatriates vacationing in the South of France in 1929 as Europe is about to explode into a world war, had little of Barry's characteristic wit and playfulness, and the Darko Tresnjak production wallowed in the apocalyptic pretensions of the script. Cast, production, and play were equally derided, one commentator declaring it "painful to the eye and ear." The Roundabout offered the season's second *Uncle Vanya* on April 30 at the Brooks Atkinson with a cast of American and British actors that on paper looked impressive, but most aisle-sitters were disappointed in Michael Mayer's production, which alternated between slow, reflective scenes ("three hours of dead air") and high-flying histrionics ("a tantrum in a samovar"). The players included Derek Jacobi (Vanya), Roger Rees (Astrov), Laura Linney (Yelena), Brian Murray (Serebryakov), Amy Ryan (Sonya), and Ann Pitoniak (Marina). Despite the generally negative notices, business was healthy enough to hold over the limited engagement until July 2.

The Acting Company concluded its tour of fifty-two cities with a two-week stint at the St. Clements beginning with Sheridan's *The Rivals* on May 3 and continuing with *Macbeth* on May 11. The comedy of manners was considered the better of the two offerings, with the ever-busy Nicholas Martin directing the youthful cast.

Eric Bogosian returned to the solo-performance format for his **Wake Up and Smell the Coffee** (5-4-00, Jane Street), which ran its scheduled forty-five performances without the same level of curiosity he used to inspire. Although lighter in tone than some of his past diatribes, this series of monologues (some were delivered by characters, others were just the actor-author speaking) was familiar but incisive. America's obsession with money, the temptations of fame, and (a Bogosian standard) the mystifying power of drugs were all handled sharply and with sardonic humor, but the shock value of his earlier works was gone. As Nancy Franklin in *The New Yorker* noted, "Bogosian is still very good at what he does, and what he does is still worth doing, but in too much of this show the coffee he's serving tastes reheated."

The Royal Shakespeare Company brought three very different revivals to BAM and met with variable critical comments. The most unique offering was T. S. Eliot's rarely seen verse drama *The Family Reunion* (10-20-58) on May 10. While there was applause for Adrian Noble's acute direction and the expert cast headed by Margaret Tyzak as Amy, the dowager whose birthday precipitates the family gathering, few aisle-sitters could recommend the play, calling it "virtually meaningless and yet overwrought." Fredrich Schiller's just-as-rare history play *Don Carlos* on May 16 was considered a difficult but worthwhile script, but Gale Edwards's modern-dress production met with scant approval. On May 21, mixed opinions greeted the RSC's *A Midsummer Night's Dream*, a classic the company had triumphed with several times over the previous four decades. Michael Boyd staged the comedy as broad farce on a wooden set filled with trapdoors and potholes, and more than one critic noted that the whole cast behaved like the "rude mechanicals" Shakespeare had provided for the low humor.

Off Off Broadway saw a snob hit like few others when Wallace Shawn's **The Designated Mourner** (5-13-00, 21 South William Street) was presented in a space that allowed only thirty spectators to gather around and listen to a diatribe on the decline of culture in our society. When a renowned artist dies, three members of the cultural elite (Shawn, Larry Pine, and Deborah Eisenberg) gather and lament how bourgeois art has become. André Gregory directed Shawn's "snooty adaptation" of an Edward Gorey story (the play had been seen a few seasons earlier in a workshop production), and it ran for the privledged few for two months. A handful of critics found it provocative, but most thought it "so theatrically indulgent that it dares you to find it pretentious or precious."

John Guare revised his period pieces *Lydie Breeze* (2-25-82) and *Gardenia* (4-13-82), added some scenes from a 1984 work called *Women and Water*, and put them all together into a two-play cycle, which the New York Theatre Workshop presented twenty times beginning on May 15. Now called *Lydie Breeze, Part I: Bullfinch's Mythology* and *Lydie Breeze, Part II: The Sacredness of the Next Task*, the family chronicle again concerned the dreams and disillusionments of some nineteenth-century Americans hoping to create a utopia. Notices were polite ("a work easier to admire than enjoy") to the script (most preferred Part I) and complimentary to the cast, headed by Elizabeth Marvel as the former Civil War nurse Lydie.

A family affair of another sort was Daisy B.

Foote's domestic drama **When They Speak of Rita** (5-17-00, Primary Stages), directed by her father, Horton Foote, and featuring Hallie Foote, her sister, as the title character. Middle-aged Rita has a husband and children but is feeling unfulfilled, so she runs off with the virginal teenage friend of her son. After a few equally unsatisfying months, she returns home, is forgiven by her husband (but not her son), and returns to her former life, no one in the household quite understanding why she ran off in the first place. The "small old-fashioned play" gathered some appreciative reviews (it "gradually ascends to scenes of rare poignancy") during its extended run off-off Broadway.

The next night, critics raved about the powerful docudrama **The Laramie Project** (5-18-00, Union Square), calling it "enormously good-willed, very earnest and often deeply moving" and "a terrific piece of theatre, history, and life in the heartless heartlands." Moisés Kaufman and his company, Tectonic Theatre Project, went to Laramie, Wyoming, soon after the 1998 murder of gay college student Matthew Shepard and interviewed dozens of residents of the community who were shocked (along with the rest of the country) by the youth's torture and symbolic crucifixion. Commentaries by witnesses, family members, neighbors, media personalities, and ordinary locals were woven into a tapestry that did not attempt to dramatize the events (in fact, Shepard was not a character in the piece) but rather explored the sensibilities before, during, and after the investigation into the crime. Unlike Kaufman's bookish and distant documentary *Gross Indecency* (6-5-97), this collage was intimate, revealing, heartbreaking, and even funny at times. Eight actors vividly portrayed the many citizens, and Kaufman directed in a clear-minded and efficient manner.

While Broadway audiences were pondering quantum physics in *Copenhagen*, the Manhattan Theatre Club offered a similarly intricate journey into mathematics off Broadway with David Auburn's **Proof** (5-23-00, City Center). Robert (Larry Bryggman) is a brilliant mathematician who was driven to insanity and death by the realization that he could never surpass the intellectual peak he reached in his twenties. As a ghost, Robert appears in the imagination of his equally brilliant daughter Catherine (Mary-Louise Parker), who is slipping into the same kind of melancholia. Catherine's older sister, Claire (Johanna Day), from New York, comes on the scene to offer her a new life in Manhattan (or an all-paid visit to a mental hospital), while an awkward math teacher, Hal (Ben Shenkman), comes to study Robert's piles of notebooks and to pursue his longtime crush on Catherine. The math talk was often stimulating (and there was much ado about a missing math proof that proved as gripping as any thriller), but it was the funny, complex characters that made the play sparkle. Notices were enthusiastic for the script (several commentators preferred it to *Copenhagen*), the penetrating cast, and Daniel Sullivan's astute direction. Designer John Lee Beatty was in top form with his suggested back-porch setting that let one look into and through the house, revealing touches of autumn and neighboring structures all around. *Proof* made the move to Broadway the next season.

The season ended as it began, with an improbable farce about writer's angst: **Anonymous** (5-31-00, McGinn/Cazale) by Glen Merzer. Cloistered and reticent Harris Harbison (Chip Zien) has had three novels published, but each was a commercial bomb, and his financial situation is so dire he is living off peanut butter sandwiches. Harris's friend from his Yale days, Tim (David Arrow), spends time at the writer's apartment, gobbling down the poor writer's sandwiches and trying to escape from his wife and kids. Tim gets Harris a job as a copywriter at the ad agency where he works, despite the fact that Harris insulted his boss Ed Lustig (Kevin O'Rourke) at the interview, and tries to set Harris up with the oft-divorced neurotic Donna (Betsy Aidem). Also entering Harris's chaotic life are the Mafioso Roy (Peter Appel), who needs to have his action manuscript polished, and Michaela (Rosemary DeWitt), a young housewife and mother from "Missoura," who has read Harris's three books and, after writing him a score of fan letters, shows up unannounced. While it was all contrived nonsense, the play appealed to some critics ("a neat construction, a certain teasing ambiguity to all the characters, and a way of making the preposterous slightly plausible"), while others were annoyed at its facile tone and its "characters and dialogue straight from prime television's greatest hits."

As the season closed, Neil Simon's new comedy *Hotel Suite* was in previews. A Simon comedy set in a hotel room? It sounded like the 1960s all over again. But this new work had originated in regional theatre, was playing off Broadway rather than on, and (for the first time for Simon) was being presented by a non-profit theatre company for a limited run. Simon, the most financially successful American playwright of the twentieth century, no longer a commercial entity? It didn't sound like the 1960s after all.

EPILOGUE

When Gerald Bordman began this *Chronicle of Comedy and Drama*, he choose the 1869–1870 season because it was one in which the American theatre turned a corner and began a new era in ambitious and quality theatricals. It is too tempting not to look back to that post–Civil War season and see how New York theatre at the end of the twentieth century compared. Are we again on the brink of a new era or in the diminishing shadows of a declining one?

Wily producers such as Augustin Daly and Lester Wallack were the most influential figures on the Street in 1869. Not only did they produce plays and own playhouses, they also ran theatre companies, directed productions, and, in the case of Daly, wrote and/or adapted dozens of plays. One hundred and thirty years later the solo producer is an endangered species. Theatre companies, groups of producers, and even corporations present plays. Usually they are businessmen and women, rarely directors, never playwrights.

While the established stage stars (such as John Gilbert, Charlotte Crabtree, Edwin Booth, and Mrs. Gilbert) who dominated the Broadway stages in 1869 were American, most of the plays were foreign or American adaptations of European works. In many ways the *Chronicle of Comedy and Drama* began before there truly was an American theatre. The great American playwrights were still waiting in the wings or were yet to be born. Of the eighty different productions seen in that long-gone season, only six were original American scripts. British and French plays were the norm; American theatre was really European theatre with American actors. Yet how do we compare today? With many fewer productions, the ratio of American to foreign works is probably inaccurate, but the figure of fourteen native works on Broadway during the 1999–2000 season, as compared to the five British ones, is somewhat comforting to the patriotic playgoer. Off Broadway and Off Off Broadway are even more American, and musicals (which barely existed in 1869) are once again a homegrown product. But one still has to ask how American the American theatre really is.

The matter of revivals is also of interest. In that 1869–1870 season, only a quarter of the productions were new. Revivals of everything from classics like *Twelfth Night* and *The School for Scandal* to the more recent popular favorites such as *East Lynne* and *Uncle Tom's Cabin* dominated New York theatre. No one then seemed to be concerned that contemporary theatre meant old theatre. Yet today our many musical and non-musical revivals give us a sense of inferiority, as if we are falling behind because we cannot begin to complete with the glory years of the 1920s when over a hundred new plays opened in one season. Perhaps a bit disconcerting is the fact that many of the revivals today are of plays from not that long ago. Of the nine Broadway revivals seen in this last season, only two were more than twenty years old. Is the repertory shrinking, or is it simply safer to revive a two-decade-old hit rather than risk a production of an old classic or a new script?

Which brings us to the problem of finances. Comparing ticket prices and expenses now with those of 1869 is frustrating, even when adjustments are made for inflation. The $4 top asked 130 years ago may translate close to the $70 top for a non-musical on the Street in 2000. But $4 was an elitist price, and lower-priced seats were always available. By the end of the twentieth century all the prices were elitist. There was no such thing as "popular prices" on the Street in 1999–2000. Even previews were full-priced, and the range of price choices for the ticket buyer was practically nonexistent. Wallack boasted that his theatre took in $27,000 during the month of October 1869. The similar-sized Plymouth Theatre brought in $349,000 during one week in October 1999. Compare that to the inflationary rise of ticket prices over 130 years and it is clear something is wrong. Not only had the ticket prices become elitist by the end of the twentieth century, so had the expenses. To produce a Broadway play was no longer within the power of an ambitious individual. It used to be anyone could be a producer; now it seems no one can afford to become one.

One final comparison, and perhaps the most important, is the nature of the plays themselves. Theatregoing in 1869–1870 was considered a safe and predictable venture. Not only were most of the plays alike, three playwrights (T. W. Robertson, Tom Taylor, and Dion Boucicault) wrote one third of all the new works seen that season. The drawing room comedy or drama placed in a box set was the expected entertainment, and even the elaborate productions of Shakespeare seemed to all look alike. While the audience makeup was somewhat democratic, the subject matter of the plays was rather narrow-minded and homogeneous. This was before Ibsen, O'Neill, and Shaw, and audiences were not accustomed to finding anything remotely startling or disturbing in the theatre.

How democratic were the audiences and plays by 1999–2000? While many complained that the big-budget musicals with spectacular effects dominated Broadway, in reality much of the theatre in New York was pretty varied. On the Street, one-person shows ran alongside contemporary comedies and esoteric dramas. Off Broadway and Off Off Broadway were even more diverse, many works defying traditional classification and appealing to far-from-mainstream audiences. The quality of the products in all three venues was certainly debatable, but no one could call the group of entries safe and predictable. As Broadway has become a more and more risky venue for new work, the plays elsewhere seem to flaunt risk and welcome financial disaster. How else can one applaud the Public Theatre which offered little of value in 1999–2000 yet was still a symbol of diversity and experimentation in New York theatre?

Those observers continually predicting the end of the American theatre find little comfort in the dozens of stubborn little theatre companies throughout New York City. They live and breathe for a while, one in twenty will make a noticeable noise, then they fade away only to be replaced by several others. Yes, they are of questionable quality, and yes, they wear their diversity like a red badge of courage. Yet even as these alternative groups sneer at the big-time productions, they all secretly dream of hitting it big themselves and transferring to Broadway. Perhaps theatre at the end of the twentieth century has become as diverse and unmanageable as the country itself. Nothing seems to fit into neat categories in our society, and the arts are no exception. If theatre is undisciplined, unreliable, torn in too many directions, and suspicious of its own popularity, perhaps it is a truly American theatre after all.

TITLES INDEX

PEOPLE INDEX